# Organizational Behavior

**An Evidence-Based Approach**         Twelfth Edition

### Fred Luthans

*George Holmes Distinguished Professor
of Management, University of Nebraska*

McGraw-Hill
Irwin

**McGraw-Hill Irwin**

ORGANIZATIONAL BEHAVIOR: An Evidence-Based Approach

Published by McGraw-Hill/Irwin, a business unit of The McGraw-Hill Companies, Inc., 1221 Avenue of the Americas, New York, NY, 10020. Copyright © 2011, 2008, 2005, 2002, 1998, 1995, 1992, 1989, 1985, 1981, 1977, 1973 by The McGraw-Hill Companies, Inc. All rights reserved. No part of this publication may be reproduced or distributed in any form or by any means, or stored in a database or retrieval system, without the prior written consent of The McGraw-Hill Companies, Inc., including, but not limited to, in any network or other electronic storage or transmission, or broadcast for distance learning.

Some ancillaries, including electronic and print components, may not be available to customers outside the United States.

This book is printed on acid-free paper.

1 2 3 4 5 6 7 8 9 0 WDQ/WDQ 1 0 9 8 7 6 5 4 3 2 1 0

ISBN:   978-0-07-353035-2
MHID:   0-07-353035-2

Vice president and editor-in-chief: *Brent Gordon*
Publisher: *Paul Ducham*
Director of development: *Ann Torbert*
Managing development editor: *Laura Hurst Spell*
Editorial coordinator: *Jane Beck*
Vice president and director of marketing: *Robin J. Zwettler*
Associate marketing manager: *Jaime Halteman*
Vice president of editing, design and production: *Sesha Bolisetty*
Senior project manager: *Harvey Yep*
Senior production supervisor: *Debra R. Sylvester*
Design coordinator: *Joanne Mennemeier*
Media project manager: *Suresh Babu, Hurix Systems Pvt. Ltd.*
Cover design: *Joanne Mennemeier*
Cover image: *Digital Vision*
Typeface: *10.5/12 Times Roman*
Compositor: *Glyph International*
Printer: *Worldcolor*

**Library of Congress Cataloging-in-Publication Data**

Luthans, Fred.
    Organizational behavior : an evidence-based approach / Fred Luthans.—12th ed.
        p. cm.
    Includes index.
    ISBN-13: 978-0-07-353035-2 (alk. paper)
    ISBN-10: 0-07-353035-2 (alk. paper)
    1. Organizational behavior.   I. Title.
HD58.7.L88 2011
658.4—dc22

2009041522

For
Kay, Kristin, Brett, Kyle, and Paige

# About the Author

**Fred Luthans** is the George Holmes Distinguished Professor of Management at the University of Nebraska–Lincoln. He received his B.A., M.B.A., and Ph.D. from the University of Iowa where he received the distinguished alumni award in 2002, and did postdoctoral work at Columbia University. While serving as a Captain in the U.S. Army, he taught at the U.S. Military Academy at West Point. He has been at the University of Nebraska since 1967, his entire academic career, and won the distinguished teaching award in 1986, the excellence in graduate education award in 2000, and in 2008 the highest award in the system for outstanding research. In 2003, he received an honorary doctorate from DePaul University. A prolific writer, he has published a number of major books and about 200 articles in applied and academic journals. His book *Organizational Behavior Modification,* coauthored with Robert Kreitner, won the American Society of Personnel Administration award for outstanding contribution to human resource management, and another book entitled *Real Managers* is the result of a four-year research study that observed managers in their natural settings. *International Management,* coauthored with the late Richard Hodgetts and Jonathon Doh, also published by McGraw-Hill, is in its seventh edition. He also has two recent books, *The High Impact Leader* (with Bruce Avolio, McGraw-Hill, 2006) and *Psychological Capital* (with Carolyn Youssef and Bruce Avolio, Oxford, 2007). The co-editor-in-chief of the *Journal of World Business,* Professor Luthans is also the editor for *Organizational Dynamics* and *Journal of Leadership and Organizational Studies.* He has been very active in the Academy of Management over the years and was elected a fellow in 1981. He is a former president of the National Academy in 1986 and, in 1997, received the Academy's distinguished educator award. In 2000 he became an inaugural member of the Academy's Hall of Fame for being one of the "Top Five" all-time published authors in the prestigious Academy journals. Also active in the Decision Sciences Institute (DSI), he was elected a fellow in 1987. Professor Luthans has a very extensive research program at the University of Nebraska. Most recently, he has developed positive organizational behavior, or POB (outlined in 2002 articles in the *Academy of Management Executive* and *Journal of Organizational Behavior*), and is conducting research on positive psychological capital and, with close colleague Bruce Avolio, authentic leadership. He has been a visiting scholar at a number of universities in the United States and has lectured at universities and conducted workshops for managers in many countries around the world. In recent years, he has been actively involved in Germany, China, Thailand, Singapore, Russia, Albania, and Macedonia. In addition, he has been on the executive committee of the annual Pan Pacific Conference since its beginning in 1984 and in 1995 was elected a fellow. This international research and experience is reflected in his approach to the field of organizational behavior. In addition, he is an active consultant and trainer to both private- (such as Walmart and Ameritas Life Insurance, Inc.) and public-sector organizations. Since 1998 he has been a senior research scientist with the Gallup Organization. He is an avid golfer and University of Nebraska sports fan. He and Kay, his wife of 47 years, have four grown children and so far six adorable grandchildren.

# Preface

Here is the twelfth edition. As I indicated in the last edition, I am still in what positive psychologists call "flow." I am so engrossed and passionate about my field of organizational behavior that time just flies. As I have said before, I take considerable pride in the sustainability of this text. It took me four years to write the first edition, and then about a year to do each subsequent edition. Because of the rapidly expanding body of knowledge in organizational behavior, these revised editions through the years have become increasingly challenging. However, I am still—actually even more than ever—in flow in trying to keep this first mainline organizational behavior text totally up-to-date with the very latest and relevant theory building, basic and applied research, and best-practice applications. I decided with this edition to give special recognition of this scientific foundation by adding the subtitle—*An Evidence-Based Approach.*

As is now emphasized in the introductory chapter, the time has come to help narrow the theory/research—effective application/practice gap. This has been my mission from the beginning of this text and my now over 20-year editorship of the journal *Organizational Dynamics*. As "hard evidence" for this theory/research base for this text, I can say unequivocally that no other organizational behavior text has close to the number of footnote references. For example, whereas a few texts may have up to 40 or even 50 references for some chapters, the chapters of this text average more than twice that amount. This latest edition continues the tradition by incorporating recent breakthrough research to provide and add to the evidence on the theories and techniques presented throughout.

Before getting into the specific additions of this new edition, I would like to again point out the distinguishing features that no other organizational behavior textbook can claim:

1. I am convinced at this stage of development of the field of OB, we need a comprehensive theoretical framework to structure our introductory textbooks. Instead of a potpourri of chapters and topics, and maybe using an inductive (or should it be deductive?) sequencing, there is now the opportunity to have a sound conceptual framework to present our now credible (evidence-based) body of knowledge. I use the widely recognized, very comprehensive social cognitive theory to structure this text. I present the background and theory building of this framework in the introductory chapter and also provide a specific model (Figure 1.5) that fits in all 14 chapters. Importantly, the logic of this conceptual framework requires two chapters not found in other texts and the rearrangement and combination of several others. For example, in the organizational context part there is Chapter 4, "Reward Systems," and in the cognitive processes part, Chapter 7, "Positive Organizational Behavior and Psychological Capital," that no other text contains.

2. Besides having the only comprehensive theoretical framework for an introductory OB text, a second unique feature is one or more OB Principles at the end of each chapter. Importantly, these principles are derived from meta-analytic research findings. The reason for including meta-analytically derived principles is that the field of organizational behavior has matured to the point where there are not just isolated studies but a stream of research on a number of topics that now need to be systematically (quantitatively) summarized for students and practitioners. For example, Alex Stajkovic and I have completed a meta-analysis of the studies with which I have been most closely associated over the past 35 years, focusing on the positive effect that organizational behavior modification (O.B. Mod.) has on task performance. (This analysis is published

in the *Academy of Management Journal;* a follow-up research study conducted in the largest credit card processing company in the world is in a subsequent issue of *AMJ;* another meta-analysis of all behavioral management studies with emphasis on the different types of interventions was published in *Personnel Psychology;* and most recently nonfinancial rewards were found to be as impactful on unit performance outcomes and employee retention over time as were financial rewards, published in the *Journal of Applied Psychology* with Suzanne Peterson). In addition, Alex and I published in *Psychological Bulletin* a meta-analysis (114 studies, 21,616 subjects) that found a very strong positive relationship between self-efficacy and task-related performance. These provide end-of-chapter evidence-based OB Principles.

3. A third unique feature is an "Evidence-Based Consulting Practices" summary to open up each major part of the text. Specifically, in addition to my long academic appointment at the University of Nebraska, since 1998 I have been a senior research scientist with the Gallup Organization. Mostly known for the famous Gallup Poll, this world-class firm also has a widely known management consulting practice. About half of the "*Fortune* 50" are among Gallup's recent clients. With my input, Tim Hodges, executive director of Gallup University, drew from Gallup's tremendous survey research-base consisting of thousands of organizations and millions of people over the years. We provide Gallup's evidence-based practices relevant to each major part of the text.

4. The fourth unique feature reflects my continuing basic research program over the years. Chapter 7 contains my most recent work on what I have termed "Positive Organizational Behavior" and "Psychological Capital" (or PsyCap). To meet the inclusion criteria (positive; theory and research based; valid measures; open to development; and manage for performance improvement), for the first time the topics of optimism, hope, happiness/subjective well-being, resiliency, emotional intelligence, self-efficacy, and the overall core construct of psychological capital have been given chapter status. Because of my involvement in the emerging Positive Psychology movement through Gallup and my research on PsyCap and authentic leadership with colleagues in the University of Nebraska's Leadership Institute, I feel the time has come to incorporate this positive approach into the mainstream organizational behavior field.

Besides these truly significant four unique features, there are a number of specific revisions and additions to this edition. These include:

1. The new subtitle "An Evidence-Based Approach" reaffirms the importance of the research foundation to the text. A new major section has been added to Chapter 1 that explains why this evidence-based focus is so critical and what it entails.

2. Because communication, decision making, and perception continue to be important to organizational behavior, in this edition there is a new Chapter 8, "Communication and Decision Making" and perception is added to Chapter 5, "Personality, Perception, and Employee Attitudes."

3. To make room for the new chapter, the separate chapter on job design and goal setting is now incorporated into Chapter 6, "Motivational Needs, Processes, and Applications."

4. Besides updating the evidence-base and providing new real-world examples in each chapter, breakthroughs on important new topics such as the following are included:

   • Contextual impact of the recent financial crisis and stock market crash on organizational behavior

- Collins' "Good to Great" expectations
- Managing the global workforce
- Global mindset
- Diversity management skills
- Glass ceiling outside the United States
- Corporate social responsibility (CSR)
- Ethics of downsizing
- "Hollow" organization design
- Modular organization design
- Organization culture in an economic crisis
- Incentive/rewards analysis of the financial crisis
- Costs of obesity
- Neuroscience explanations
- Health-Relationships-Work (H-R-W) well-being model
- Intentional component of psychological capital (PsyCap)
- Background on PsyCap
- Performance impact and research summary of PsyCap
- PsyCap development model and research summary
- Evidence-based happiness
- Broaden and Build Theory of positivity
- Use of Facebook
- Gen X and Gen Y
- Stress from 24/7 technology and job loss threat
- Stress levels around the world
- Bullying problem
- "Slacker teammate" problem
- Followership
- Positive and authentic leadership research

Just as real-world management can no longer afford to evolve slowly, neither can the academic side of the field. With the uncertain, very turbulent environment most organizations face today, drastically new ideas, approaches, and techniques as represented above are needed both in the practice of management and in the way we study and apply the field of organizational behavior. This revision mirrors these needed changes.

**Social Cognitive Conceptual Framework.** The book contains 14 chapters in four major parts. Social cognitive theory explains organizational behavior in terms of both environmental, contextual events and internal cognitive factors, as well as the dynamics and outcomes of the organizational behavior itself. Thus, Part One provides the evidence-based and organizational context for the study and application of organizational behavior. The introductory chapter provides the environmental perspective, historical background, methodology, theoretical framework, and specific social cognitive model for the field of organizational behavior in general and specifically for this text. This is followed by an overall environmental context chapter:

**Chapter 2,** "Environmental Context: Globalization, Diversity, and Ethics (with major sections on globalization, diversity, and a major ending section on the impact of ethics on "bottom-line" outcomes).

After this broad environmental context is laid out in Chapter 2, there are two chapters for the organizational context of the social cognitive framework:

**Chapter 3,** "Organizational Context: Design and Culture" (with special emphasis given to the learning organization and horizontal, hollow, modular, network, and virtual designs; best-practice cultures; and a major section on the culture clashes from mergers and acquisitions) and

**Chapter 4,** "Organizational Context: Reward Systems" (a unique chapter with special emphasis given to money as a reward, effectiveness of pay, forms of "new pay," recognition systems, and benefits).

The second part of the text recognizes the well-known micro-oriented cognitive processes of the social cognitive framework plus unique topics such as the following:

**Chapter 5,** "Personality, Perception, and Employee Attitudes" (with unique major sections on the role of heredity and the brain and emphasis given to "Big Five" personality traits, the Myers-Briggs personality indicator, the perceptual process, and organizational citizenship behavior);

**Chapter 6,** "Motivational Needs, Processes, and Applications" (with major sections on extrinsic versus intrinsic motives, procedural justice, attribution theory, job design and goal setting); and

**Chapter 7,** the most unique chapter, not only for this text, but any other, on "Positive Organizational Behavior and Psychological Capital." In addition to the focus on the unique POB psychological states of efficacy, optimism, hope, resiliency, and overall psychological capital, there are also major sections on emotion, multiple intelligences, and general mental abilities.

Parts Three and Four are concerned with the dynamics and behavior management and leadership dimensions of organizational behavior in the social cognitive framework. Part Three contains, in addition to widely recognized topics, the following four chapters:

**Chapter 8,** "Communication and Decision Making" with particular emphasis given to nonverbal and interpersonal communication and behavioral dimensions, styles, and techniques of decision making.

**Chapter 9,** "Stress and Conflict" (with material on stress and conflict from advanced technology and globalization, burnout, and work-family initiatives);

**Chapter 10,** "Power and Politics" (with material on empowerment, trust, resource dependency, and the dynamics of power and politics in the new environment); and

**Chapter 11,** "Groups and Teams" (with material on the punctuated equilibrium model of groups, group/team effectiveness, role conflict and ambiguity, social loafing, cross-functional teams, virtual teams, and cultural/global issues with the use of teams).

The final Part Four gives an applied emphasis to the text. It focuses on *how* to manage and lead for high performance. These applied organizational behavior chapters include the following:

**Chapter 12,** "Behavioral Performance Management" (with material on the role of social cognition, critical analysis of reinforcement theory, pay for performance, social recognition, and the latest research on contingencies with type of organization and interventions for O.B. Mod. effectiveness).

**Chapter 13,** "Effective Leadership Processes" (with major sections on the historical studies, traditional and modern theories of leadership and the new "authentic leadership" being developed at the University of Nebraska's Leadership Institute, and leadership across cultures and the GLOBE project).

**Chapter 14,** "Great Leaders: An Evidence-Based Approach" (with major sections on leading in the new environment, leadership styles, including the new positive, authentic style, the activities and skills of leadership, and leadership development programs).

**Pedagogical Features.** Besides the many unique features already described, there are also several strong pedagogical features that have characterized the text over the years. To reflect and reinforce the applications orientation of the text, highlighted, currently relevant, boxed real-world OB in Action examples appear in each chapter. In this twelfth edition there are many new real-world examples drawn from *BusinessWeek* articles. In addition to these application boxes, the text also features experiential exercises at the end of each part. The exercises get participants involved in solving simulated problems or experiencing firsthand organizational behavior issues. Also there are end-of-chapter Internet exercises to get students involved in online relevant resources and vehicles for discussion and critique.

Besides the usual end-of-chapter short organizational behavior discussion cases, there is also at least one Real Case at the end of each chapter. These cases are drawn from recent real-world events (excerpted from current *BusinessWeek* articles) and are intended to enhance the relevancy and application of the theories and research results presented in the chapter. These end-of-chapter real cases serve as both examples and discussion vehicles. It is suggested that students read them even if they are not discussed directly in class. The intent is that they can serve as supplemental readings as well as discussion cases.

This edition also contains learning objectives at the start of each chapter. These objectives should help students better focus and prepare for what follows in the chapter. Finally, the chapters have the usual end-of-chapter summaries and review and discussion questions.

**Intended Audience.** Despite the four unique features and very extensive updating (having anywhere from 5–30 or more new references per chapter) throughout, the purpose and intended audience of the book remain the same. As in the earlier editions, this edition is aimed at those who wish to take a totally up-to-date, evidence-based approach to organizational behavior and management. It does not assume the reader's prior knowledge of either management or the behavioral sciences. Thus, the book can be used effectively in the first or only course in either four-year or two-year colleges. It is aimed primarily at the required organizational behavior course, at the undergraduate level or in the M.B.A. program. I would like to especially acknowledge and thank colleagues in countries around the world who have used previous editions of the book and point out that the continued international perspective and coverage should make this new edition relevant and attractive. Finally, the book should be helpful to practicing managers who want to understand and more effectively manage their most important assets—their human resources.

**Acknowledgments.** Every author owes a great deal to others, and I am no exception. First and foremost, I would like to acknowledge the help on this as well as many other writing projects over the years that I received from my deceased friend and colleague, Professor Richard M. Hodgetts of Florida International University. Next, I would like to acknowledge the total support and standards of excellence provided by my friend and longtime department chairman, Sang M. Lee and my former colleague now at the University of Washington, Bruce Avolio. Special thanks goes to Cathy Watson from the Management Department staff who has been very helpful to me over the years. I can never forget the education, encouragement, and scholarly values I received from Professors Henry H. Albers and the deceased Max S. Wortman when starting out in my academic career. Over the years, I have been very lucky to have been associated with excellent doctoral students. I would like to thank them all for teaching me as much as I have taught them. In particular, I would like to thank Don Baack, Steve Farner, and Suzanne Peterson who have helped on previous editions. I am also very grateful to those professors who used the previous editions of the book and gave me valuable feedback for making this revision. The reviewers for this edition are Charles B. Daniels, Old Dominion University; Laura Finnerty Paul, Skidmore College; and James Harbin, Texas A&M University–Texarkana. Finally, as always, I am deeply appreciative and dedicate *Organizational Behavior,* twelfth edition, to my wife and now grown children and their families, who have provided me with a loving, supportive relationship and climate needed to complete this and other projects over the years.

# Contents in Brief

# Contents

## Chapter 4
## Organizational Context: Reward Systems   88

## Experiential Exercises for Part One   118

## PART TWO
## COGNITIVE PROCESSES OF ORGANIZATIONAL BEHAVIOR   123

## Chapter 5
## Personality, Perception, and Employee Attitudes   125

## Chapter 6
## Motivational Needs, Processes, and Applications   156

## Chapter 7
## Positive Organizational Behavior and Psychological Capital   199

## Experiential Exercises for Part Two   240

## PART THREE
## DYNAMICS OF ORGANIZATIONAL BEHAVIOR   245

## Chapter 8
## Communication and Decision Making   247

## Chapter 11
## Groups and Teams   339

## Experiential Exercises for Part Three   365

## PART FOUR
## MANAGING AND LEADING FOR HIGH PERFORMANCE   373

## Chapter 12
## Behavioral Performance Management   378

# Environmental and Organizational Context

## EVIDENCE-BASED CONSULTING PRACTICES

A major component of the evidence-based theme of this text and the link to practice are these part openers from the world-famous Gallup Organization. Gallup draws from its internationally recognized survey science and cadre of internal and external researchers (e.g., the author of this text and a Nobel Prize winner in behavioral economics are Gallup Senior Scientists), publishes its findings in the top academic journals such as *Journal of Applied Psychology,* and provides this evidenced-based perspective and representative practices for each text part. Gallup is the recognized world leader in the measurement and analysis of human attitudes, opinions, and behavior, building on over three-quarters of a century of success. Gallup employs many of the world's leading scientists in management, economics, psychology, and sociology. Gallup performance management systems help organizations maximize employee productivity and increase customer engagement through measurement tools, management solutions, and strategic advisory services. Gallup's 2000 professionals deliver services on-site at client organizations, through the Web, at Gallup University's campuses, and in 40 offices around the world. Gallup has subsidiary operations in 20 countries, covering 75 percent of the world's GNP. Gallup clients include top-performing organizations such as Toyota, Marriott, Wal-Mart, Wells Fargo, and Best Buy.

    The details and depth of Gallup's consulting practices can be found in the best-selling books such as *First, Break All the Rules* (Simon & Schuster, 1999) *Now, Discover Your Strengths* (The Free Press, 2001), *How Full Is Your Bucket* (Gallup Press,

2004), and *Strength Finder 2.0* (Gallup Press, 2007), which recently passed the million copies sold mark. These books are all authored by Gallup scientists and practice leaders. All the part opening Gallup practices for this text are written by Tim Hodges, Executive Director of the Gallup University, with some input by former Gallup Senior Analyst Dr. Dennis Hatfield and this author. The following gives an introductory overview of the Gallup evidenced-based approach, and the other openers are more directly concerned with the theme of the respective part.

## AN INTRODUCTION TO THE GALLUP EVIDENCE-BASED APPROACH: THE GALLUP PATH

According to numerous think tanks, recent global competition caused corporate executives to pose one common, all-consuming question: What is the role of human nature in driving business outcomes?

As described in Coffman and Gonzalez-Molina's *Follow This Path*, the Gallup Organization sorted through unprecedented bits of economic information and data from customers and employees to develop The Gallup Path™ management theory, answering the question concerning the role of human nature in driving business outcomes.

The Gallup Path™ serves as Gallup's premier management consulting model. At the model's core is the theory that within every organization, every employee, at all levels, contributes to some degree to sales growth, profitability, and ultimately, share price. The path serves as the first management theory to track the connectedness of managers to employees, employees to customers, and customers to real financial outcomes.

The "steps" along The Gallup Path™ progress from (1) individual's identification of strengths to (2) finding the right fit to (3) great management to (4) engaged employees to (5) engaged customers to (6) sustainable business growth to (7) real profit increase to (8) stock increase.

Just as The Gallup Poll reports the will of global citizens, The Gallup Path™ reports the will of customers and employees around the world through Gallup's HumanSigma™ metrics.

## GALLUP'S GREAT PLACE TO WORK

One of Gallup's core practices involves the measurement and development of employee engagement, leading to the creation of "great places to work." As described in Buckingham and Coffman's *First, Break All the Rules,* Gallup consultants use the Q12® to provide a measure of the extent to which individuals are rightly placed and rightly managed, creating the great place to work. These Q12® questions are: (1) Do I know what is expected of me at work? (2) Do I have the materials and equipment I need to do my work right? (3) At work, do I have the opportunity to do what I do best every day? (4) In the last seven days have I received recognition or praise for good work? (5) Does my supervisor, or someone at work, seem to care about me as a person? (6) Is there someone at work who encourages my development? (7) At work, do my opinions seem to count? (8) Does the mission/purpose of my company make me feel like my work is important? (9) Are my coworkers committed to doing quality work? (10) Do I have a best friend at work? (11) In the last six months, have I talked with someone about my progress? (12) At work, have I had opportunities to learn and grow? (See Buckingham & Coffman, 1999, p. 28. These questions are the results of Gallup research, and as such they are proprietary. They cannot be reprinted or reproduced in any manner without the written consent of the Gallup Organization. Copyright © 1993–1998 The Gallup Organization, Washington, DC. All rights reserved).

A recent issue of the *Journal of Applied Psychology* published a meta-analysis of 7,939 business units in 36 companies examining the relationship between employee engagement and work-related outcomes of customer satisfaction, profit, productivity, turnover, and safety (Harter, Schmidt, & Hayes, 2002). Generalizable relationships of substantial practical value were found for all outcome measures, providing research evidence of the connection between an employee's level of engagement and the level of quality of his or her performance. Related published workplace studies (e.g., Schmidt & Rader, *Personnel Psychology,* 1999) have also illustrated the validity of the right fit and management of talent in predicting supervisory ratings of job performance, sales volumes, production records, and absenteeism.

## GALLUP'S APPROACH TO STRENGTHS-BASED DEVELOPMENT

For decades following World War II, the science of psychology focused almost completely on what is wrong with people. Bucking this trend of negativity, Gallup scientists analyzed more than 30 years of research on what is right about people. This in-depth study of over two million individuals led to the creation of the StrengthsFinder, Gallup's Web-based talent assessment tool and psychology's first taxonomy of strengths. For his leadership in the development of the StrengthsFinder and for his thought leadership that changed the entire field of psychology, in 2003 Gallup's former chairman and chief scientist, Dr. Donald O. Clifton, was officially named the "Father of Strengths Psychology" and "Grandfather of Positive Psychology" by the American Psychological Association.

The StrengthsFinder serves as the starting point for self-discovery in all of Gallup's strengths-based development programs. After an individual has completed the assessment, a list of developmental suggestions is customized to the individual's top five themes of talent—called Signature Themes. Over the past several years, StrengthsFinder has been used in the development of millions of individuals across hundreds of roles including manager, salesperson, teacher, student, leader, pastor, nurse, and many more. StrengthsFinder is available in more than a dozen languages. Role-specific strengths-based developmental information is available through the following Gallup books (each including a personal ID number allowing the reader to complete the StrengthsFinder): *Now, Discover Your Strengths* (Buckingham & Clifton, 2001); *StrengthsQuest* (Clifton & Anderson, 2002); *Discover Your Sales Strengths* (Smith & Rutigliano, 2003); *Living Your Strengths* (Winseman, Clifton, & Liesveld, 2003); and *StrengthsFinder 2.0* (Rath, 2007).

# EXAMPLES OF CLIENT SUCCESS: GALLUP'S EVIDENCED-BASED PRACTICES IN ACTION

An important aspect of Gallup's evidence-based approach is measuring the value of client engagements, known as Business Impact Analysis. The following examples of recent client success illustrate the impact of Gallup's research in action.

1. A national clothing retailer was experiencing declining business. The retailer brought Gallup in to create an integrated performance management system designed to provide each store manager with the tools to optimize employee and customer engagement. The client engagement consisted of several administrations of employee and customer engagement, followed by in-depth analysis, executive consulting, and manager training. Gallup's Business Impact Analysis uncovered a trend where employee and customer engagement significantly influenced each store's financial performance. In fact, the group of stores with top-level performance on employee and customer engagement metrics realized a significant net benefit to the organization of approximately $114.8 million in sales, $47.6 million in margins, and $34.7 million in operating profit when compared to the group of stores with lower employee and customer engagement metrics.

2. Gallup's extensive work in the health care sector has also led to valuable results for clients. For example, a relationship with one of the largest for-profit hospital networks created value for many years. Since the inception of an ongoing, systemwide program to improve employee engagement, more than 26,000 employees of this hospital network have moved from being "not engaged" (neither positive nor negative about their work environment) or "actively disengaged" (fundamentally disconnected from their work) to being engaged, or emotionally invested, in their jobs. According to the client's estimates, these engaged employees represent over $46 million in reduced absenteeism costs alone. Further, over a recent three-year period, systemwide employee engagement levels closely reflect steady, incremental increases in the client's stock price. Positive multimillion dollar relationships between employee engagement and reduced malpractice claims, earnings per admission, patient loyalty, and decreased nurse turnover have also been realized over the course of this successful client partnership.

3. One of the largest banks in North America entered into a partnership with Gallup to improve sales performance in three call centers. Gallup consultants studied the call center structure and business strategy, reviewed job performance criteria, and studied the best performers in each role to identify the talents that contributed to their success. Gallup developed and implemented hiring systems for customer service representatives and inbound sales representatives. Not only did employees hired through the Gallup system deliver a higher sales success rate, high-scoring new hires substantially outperformed their lower-scoring counterparts in revenues, sales, call handling time, and loan accuracy.

Many more examples of successful client partnerships, as well as actionable management insights and perspectives from Gallup experts, are available in the monthly online newsletter, the Gallup Management Journal (http://www.gallupjournal.com).

# Introduction to Organizational Behavior: An Evidence-Based Approach

**Learning Objectives**

- **Provide** an overview of the major challenges and the paradigm shift facing management now and in the future.
- **Outline** an evidence-based approach to organizational behavior.
- **Summarize** the Hawthorne studies as the starting point of the study of organizational behavior.
- **Explain** the methodology that is used to accumulate knowledge and facilitate understanding of organizational behavior.
- **Relate** the various theoretical frameworks that serve as a foundation for the study of organizational behavior.
- **Present** the social cognitive model of organizational behavior that serves as the conceptual framework for the text.

Every era laments about daunting challenges. However, even previous generations would probably agree that effectively managing today's organizations is very difficult. Ask anyone today—management professors, practitioners, or students—what the major challenges are in today's environment, and the answer will be fairly consistent: A turbulent economy and dangerous geopolitics preoccupy everyone's concerns. However, at the organization level, understanding global competition and diversity, and trying to solve ethical problems and dilemmas come to the fore. These are unquestionably major issues facing contempory organizations and are given major attention in this text. However, the basic premise and assumptions of the field of organizational behavior in general, and of this text in particular, are that managing the people—the human resources of an organization—have been, are, and will continue to be, *the* major challenge and critical competitive advantage.

Globalization, diversity, and ethics serve as very important environmental or contextual dimensions for organizational behavior. However, as Sam Walton, the founder of Wal-Mart and richest person in the world when he died, declared to this author over lunch a number of years ago when asked what the answer was to successful organizations—"People are the key!" The technology can be purchased and copied; it levels the playing field. The people, on the other hand, cannot be copied. Although it may be possible to clone human bodies, their ideas, personalities, motivation, and organization cultural values cannot be copied. The human resources of an organization and how they are managed represent the competitive advantage of today's and tomorrow's organizations. A recent study of over three hundred companies for over 20 years provides evidence for this statement. The researchers found that management of human resources through extensive training and techniques such as empowerment resulted in performance benefits, but operational initiatives such as total quality management or advanced manufacturing technology did not.[1]

At first employees were considered a cost, then human resources, and now are becoming widely recognized as "human capital"[2] (what you know—education, experience, skills). Recent research indicates that investing in this human capital results in desired performance outcomes such as increased productivity and customer satisfaction.[3] Even going beyond human capital are more recently recognized "social capital"[4] (who you know—networks, connections, friends) and "positive psychological capital"[5] (who you are—confidence, hope, optimism, resiliency) and (who you are in terms of confidence, hope, optimism, resiliency, and, more importantly, who you can become, i.e., one's possible authentic self). Although Chapter 7 will be specifically devoted to positive organizational behavior in general and psychological capital in particular, let it be simply noted here that there is growing research evidence that employees' psychological capital is positively related to their performance and desired attitudes.[6] As the ultimate "techie" Bill Gates astutely observed: "The inventory, the value of my company, walks out the door every evening."

Interestingly, whereas the technology dramatically changes, sometimes monthly or even weekly, the human side of enterprise has not changed and will not change that fast. As noted by well-known international management scholar Geert Hofstede, "Because management is always about people, its essence is dealing with human nature. Since human nature seems to have been extremely stable over recorded history, the essence of management has been and will be equally stable over time."[7] The nature of work and the workplace itself,[8] the traditional employment contract,[9] and the composition of the workforce[10] are all dramatically changing and given attention in this text. Yet, the overriding purpose of the first edition, now 38 years ago, of trying to better understand and effectively manage human behavior in organizations remains the essence of this twelfth edition.

This introductory chapter gives the perspective, background, methodology, and evidence-based approach to the field. After a brief discussion of the current environmental challenges and the paradigm shift facing management and why an evidence-based approach is needed, the historical background is touched on. Particular attention is given to the famous Hawthorne studies, which are generally recognized to be the beginning of the systematic study and understanding of organizational behavior. Next, an overview of the methodology used in the scientific study of organizational behavior is given. The chapter concludes by defining exactly what is involved in organizational behavior and by providing a conceptual model for the rest of the text.

# THE CHALLENGES FACING MANAGEMENT

The academic field of organizational behavior has been around for about a half century. However, as the accompanying OB in Action: Some Things Never Really Change clearly indicates, problems facing managers of human organizations have been around since the beginning of civilization. This case, with but a few word modifications, is taken from the Old (not New) Testament of the Bible (Exodus 18:13–27), recognized by the Jewish, Christian,

A powerful, charismatic leader is having problems. A well-known consultant is called in to help. The consultant notices that the leader tries to handle all problems and conflicts of his people himself. People queue up before his office; because he is overwhelmed, he cannot handle all the business. So the consultant has a private talk with the leader and tells him to structure his organization by delegating authority, empowering subordinates to handle the workload. These subordinates should be selected not only on their leadership abilities, but also on their character: They should be truthful, not driven by material gain. The new structure should resolve all daily issues at the lowest possible level; only the big and difficult issues should be brought before the leader. He should focus on strategy—on dealing with the higher authority, on establishing new approaches and teaching these to the people, on showing them the way to go and the work to be done. The case states that the leader listens to the consultant and carries out the reorganization, which is a success, and the consultant returns home.

and Islam religions. The case took place over 3,000 years ago, the charismatic leader was Moses (when he led his people from Egypt to Palestine), the well-known consultant was Jethro, Moses' father-in-law, and the higher authority was God. Embedded in the case are many topics covered in this text—for example, charismatic leadership, management of conflict, empowerment, management of change, and nonfinancial incentives.

Although the problems with human organizations and the solutions over the ages have not really changed that much, the emphasis and surrounding environmental context certainly have changed. For example, in the 1980s to the mid-1990s managers were preoccupied with restructuring their organizations to improve productivity and meet the competitive challenges in the international marketplace and quality expectations of customers. Although the resulting "lean and mean" organizations offered some short-run benefits in terms of lowered costs and improved productivity, instead of making significant changes to meet the changing environment, most organizations continued with more of the same. For example, one analysis of *Fortune* 500 firms between 1995 and 2005 found the most prominent initiatives were restructuring (downsizing), cost reduction programs, globalizing supply chains, creating shared services and Six Sigma (almost perfect) quality programs.[11] During this era, top management compensation was primarily tied to stock options (covered in Chapter 4) and thus the firm's stock price, which in turn led to high-risk mergers, acquisitions, and a highly regulated, winner-take-all environment.[12] For example, the head of nearly century-old investment house Merrill Lynch bet his firm—and ultimately lost—on the subprime financial market and outsized leverage and then took a whopping $160 million severance package on the way out the door.[13]

This type of behavior, and of course many other social, economic, and geopolitical factors, led to the financial crisis and stock market crash starting at the end of 2008. Although most of the focus has been on financial markets, government intervention through the so-called bailouts, and massive unemployment, the impact on those not laid off, the remaining employees, human resources of organizations, has been slighted. As an expert on the psychology of the corporate environment recently noted, "after years of downsizing, outsourcing, and a cavalier corporate attitude that treats employees as costs rather than assets, most of today's workers have concluded that the company no longer values them. So they, in turn, no longer feel engaged in their work or committed to the company."[14]

This turmoil has certainly left employees hurt and fearful, and feeling very vulnerable. There is also powerful evidence from the Gallup World Poll (a representative sample of the population of over 100 countries) that by far the single most dominant thought and primary driver of almost everyone, in every corner of the plant, is, "I want a good job."[15] As the head of Gallup, Jim Clifton, concluded on the basis of this evidence, "Work is crucial to every adult human because work holds within it the soul of the relationship of one citizen to one government and one country."[16] In other words, even though recent history has been tough not only on the economy but also on organizations and employees, the burning desire for a good job still prevails among all people.

In the tradition of an effective strategy of turning threats into opportunities, such an environment as the world has experienced in recent times may ironically be the ideal time to meet the challenges facing the management of human resources. As in the words of popular leadership author (*Good to Great*) Jim Collins, "A crisis is a terrible thing to waste."[17] The time has come to not only recognize and appreciate the importance of human resources, but also to use recent history as a catalyst for paradigmic change in the way we understand and manage human resources. This process starts with understanding what is meant by a paradigm shift, not just keeping up with incremental change, but a new way of thinking about and managing human resources in today's dramatically changed workplace.

# UNDERGOING A PARADIGM SHIFT

The term *paradigm* comes from the Greek *paradeigma,* which translates as "model, pattern, or example." First introduced years ago by the philosophy of science historian Thomas Kuhn,[18] the term *paradigm* is now used to mean a broad model, a framework, a way of thinking, or a scheme for understanding reality.[19] In the words of popular futurist Joel Barker, a paradigm simply establishes the rules (written or unwritten), defines the boundaries, and tells one how to behave within the boundaries to be successful.[20] The impact of globalization, diversity, and ethics given detailed attention in the next chapter, a turbulent, very problematic economy,[21] and a workforce described as a "blend of traditionally trained baby boomers, in-your-face Gen Xers, people with inadequate literacy skills from disadvantaged areas, and techies raised on computers,"[22] has led to a paradigm shift. For example, James Brian Quinn offers the "intelligent enterprise" as new paradigm. He believes that "the organization of enterprises and effective strategies will depend more on development and deployment of intellectual resources than on the management of physical assets."[23] These human and intellectual resources have moved into the new paradigm, and as indicated by the interview with Jim Collins in the accompanying OB in Action: Good to Great Expectations, with a new set of challenges and required ways of thinking. In other words, for today's and tomorrow's organizations and management, there are new rules with different boundaries requiring new and different behavior inside the boundaries for organizations and management to be successful. Paradigm shifts have invalidated advantages of certain firms (e.g., consider the well-known problems of almost all auto, financial, and retail firms in recent years) and created new opportunities for others (e.g., Google and Costco).

Those who study paradigm shifts, such as the shift that took place in the basic sciences from deterministic, mechanistic Cartesian-Newtonian to Einstein's relativity and quantum physics, note that "real controversy takes place, often involving substantial restructuring of the entire scientific community under conditions of great uncertainty."[24] Commonly called the "paradigm effect," a situation arises in which those in the existing paradigm may not even see the changes that are occurring, let alone reason and draw logical inferences and perceptions about the changes. This effect helps explain why there is considerable resistance to change and why it is very difficult to move from the old management paradigm to the new. There is discontinuous change in the shift to the new paradigm. As one observer of the needed new paradigm organization noted:

For Jim Collins, the Stanford Graduate School of Business lecturer-turned-management thinker, "the workplace" is a pleasant office suite set amid the Rocky Mountains in Boulder, Colo. Managing generational tension amounts to shepherding a team of smart, curious students who help him with the research projects that have led to blockbuster books like *Built to Last* and *Good to Great*. And dealing with difficult bosses means stepping outside to do some rock climbing in the mountain air if he gets frustrated with himself.

But the author of *Good to Great*, the world's bestselling guide to taking companies to the next level, still has plenty of insights for those of us stuck in gray-walled cubicles where the "scenic view" is often the parking lot of a drab corporate campus. Management Editor Jena McGregor asked Collins to translate some of his popular concepts to today's workplace. Here are edited excerpts of that conversation:

**One of the big concepts in your book is "first who," or that the most important thing is getting the right people "on the bus." But for cubicle dwellers who can't trade in their boss or their co-workers, what should they think about doing?**

The idea of a personal board of directors came to me when I was in my 20s. I drew a little conference table on a sheet of paper with seven chairs around it and wrote names on them of people I admired. I pasted it above my computer and would look up and in my mind poll the personal board when I was wrestling with tough questions. If I was really stuck, I might talk to some of them. It's sort of like a group of tribal elders that you create for yourself.

**How many of the leaders running the companies in *Good to Great* had any kind of work-life balance? Is it possible to run a great company and also have a great life?**

The bad news is, about half the CEOs didn't really seem to have a life. They defined a great life as building a great company. A lot of people who do extraordinary things are not balanced. I'm not even convinced that the idea makes sense [since] there's a certain neurotic obsession with doing exceptional things. But here's the good news: It was only about half. So I draw the conclusion that it's a choice.

**But haven't BlackBerrys and globalization made such choices nearly impossible?**

The imperative is to manage our time, not our work. This is why the whole question of balance and finishing our work is insane. There are only 24 hours in a day, so what difference does it really make if you work 10 hours or 14, given that there are a thousand potential hours of work? The real question is the incredible rigor of what goes into the hours you allocate.

As I look at the most effective people we've studied, a "stop-doing" list or not-to-do list is more important than a to-do list, because the to-do list is infinite. For every big, annual priority you put on the to-do list, you need a corresponding item on the stop-doing list. It's like an accounting balance.

You've got to admit, though, that technology has made it harder today. I don't think it's obviously harder today at all. Technology helps, not hurts, as long as you have the discipline to turn these things off. You don't report to your BlackBerry.

What we know about people who are really effective is that they think. The key is to build pockets of quietude into your schedule—times when you have an appointment with yourself and it's protected. I have on my calendar "white space" days. I set them six months in advance, and everyone around me can see them. It's not that I'm not working, but absolutely nothing can be scheduled on a white space day.

**You talk in *Good to Great* about leaders needing to confront brutal facts. But organizations loaded with bureaucracy are the exact places where truth doesn't rise to the top. What do the best managers do to break down that bureaucracy?**

How do you create a climate in which the truth is heard? The first thing is to increase your questions-to-statements ratio. Have someone track it and see if you can double it in the next year. The leaders in our studies asked lots of questions. They were Socratic. By asking questions, they got the brutal facts, as well as lots of insights and ideas.

**What can people who aren't in leadership positions do to better navigate bureaucracies?**

I think about how the leaders we studied handled this before they were in charge. If you look at [former Gillette CEO] Colman Mockler or Ken Iverson before he became CEO of Nucor, what did they do? They were focused on what they could control. That is Job One. But they were also really good at figuring out the three to four people in the organization who really mattered and became very good at presenting to them evidence and arguments that were persuasive.

If you produce exceptional work, your ability for influence is very high. Most people, even in bureaucracies, *(continued)*

(*continued*)

are hard-working, well-intentioned people trying to do good things. If you ever wake up and say the majority of people here aren't that, then for sure it's time to jump.

**You manage a team of student researchers. Any secrets you've discovered to managing Generation Y?**

I don't understand this generational tension thing other than that I think the tension is great. You should find a way to have young people in your face all the time. Wrestle with it. Revel in it. Learn from them. My view is, we ought to get those people into positions of leadership as fast as we can.

The depth of change required demands that those charged with charting a passage through hurricane-like seas do more than run up a new set of sails. What is involved equates to a quantum shift in, not just learning, but how we learn; not just doing things differently, but questioning whether we should be doing many of the things we currently believe in, at all; not just in drawing together more information but in questioning how we know what it is (we think) we know.[25]

This text on organizational behavior has the goal of helping today's and tomorrow's managers make the transition to the new paradigm. Some of the new paradigm characteristics include Chapter 2's coverage of globalization, diversity, and ethics; Chapter 3 on the organizational context of design and culture; and Chapter 4 on reward systems. The new paradigm sets the stage for the study, understanding, and application of the time-tested micro cognitive processes (Chapters 5–7), dynamics (Chapters 8–11), and the final part on managing and leading for high performance (Chapters 12–14). However, before getting directly into the rest of the text, we must know why management needs a new perspective to help meet the environmental challenges and the shift to the new paradigm. We must gain an appreciation of the historical background, methodology, and theoretical frameworks that serve as the basis of this text's perspective and model for organizational behavior.

## A NEW PERSPECTIVE FOR MANAGEMENT

How is management going to meet the environmental challenges and paradigm shift outlined above? Management is generally considered to have three major dimensions—technical, conceptual, and human. The technical dimension consists of the manager's functional expertise in accounting or engineering or marketing and increasingly in information technology. There seems little question that today's managers are competent in their functional specialization. Overall, however, although managers are certainly more aware and becoming competent in their functional/technical component, few today would question that, at least in the past, most practicing managers either slighted the conceptual and human dimensions of their jobs or made some overly simplistic assumptions.

Following the assumptions that pioneering management scholar Douglas McGregor labeled many years ago as Theory X, most managers thought, and many still think, that their employees were basically lazy, that they were interested only in money, and that if you could make them happy, they would be high performers. When such Theory X assumptions were accepted, the human problems facing management were relatively clear-cut and easy to solve. All management had to do was devise monetary incentive plans, ensure job security, and provide good working conditions; morale would then be high, and good performance would result. It was as simple as one, two, three. Human relations experts, industrial/

organizational psychologists, and industrial engineers supported this approach, and human resource managers implemented it.

Unfortunately, this approach no longer works with the current environmental demands under the new paradigm. Although good pay, job security, and working conditions are necessary, it is now evident that such a simplistic approach falls far short of providing a meaningful solution to the complex challenges facing today's human resource management. For example, a recent report in *The Economist* in reference to McGregor's Theories X and Y include that "companies are coming to realize that knowledge workers, who have been identified as the creators of future wealth, thrive only under Theory Y. Theory X is becoming extinct."[26]

The major fault with the traditional approach is that it overlooks and oversimplifies far too many aspects of the problem. Human behavior at work is much more complicated and diverse than is suggested by the economic-security–working-conditions approach. The new perspective assumes that employees are extremely complex and that there is a need for theoretical understanding backed by rigorous empirical research before applications can be made for managing people effectively. In the academic world, transition has now been completed. The traditional human relations approach no longer has a dominant role in business and applied psychology education. Few people would question that the organizational behavior approach, with its accompanying body of knowledge and applications, dominates the behavioral approach to management education now and will do so in the foreseeable future. Unfortunately, still only a minority of practicing managers and their organization cultures really buy into, fully implement, and then stick with this research-based organizational behavior approach to management practice.

Stanford professor Jeff Pfeffer has summarized the status of the organizational behavior approach to real-world management as a "one-eighth" situation.[27] By one-eighth he means that roughly half of today's managers really believe and buy into the importance of the human side of enterprise and that the people are truly the competitive advantage of their organizations. Taken a step further, however, only about half of those who believe really do something about it. Thus, he says that only about one-fourth are fully implementing the high performance work practices (HPWPs) that flow from organizational behavior theory and research—such as pay for performance, self-managed teams, 360 degree (multisource) feedback systems, behavioral management, and investing in psychological capital. Most organizations have tried one or a few of the approaches and techniques emphasized in the chapters of this text, but only about a fourth fully implement the whole approach. So now that we are down to one-fourth, where does the one-eighth come from? Well, Pfeffer estimates that only about one-half of the one-fourth who implement the approach stick with it over time. Thus, only about one-eighth ($\frac{1}{2} \times \frac{1}{2} \times \frac{1}{2} = \frac{1}{8}$) of today's organizations believe it, do it, and stick with it (the "3 Its"). The so-called one-eighth organizations have as their organizational cultural values the importance of human capital and the techniques in place to carry it out over time. Importantly, as Pfeffer well documents in his book *Human Equation,* these one-eighth organizations are world class, the best in the world—such as General Electric, Southwest Airlines, Google, Gallup, and SAS (the software development firm).

Today there is ample accumulated research findings and documented practices of the best firms to prove the value of the human factor. Pfeffer and Sutton felt compelled to try to explain why most managers today know this importance and how to implement the approach to improve organizational performance, but still are not doing it (i.e., *The Knowing-Doing Gap*).[28] They identify five sources that seem to prevent the majority of managers from effective implementation and sustainability: (1) hollow talk, (2) debilitating fear, (3) destructive internal competition, (4) poorly designed and complex measurement systems, and (5) mindless reliance on precedent. They are convinced that if these obstacles (i.e., resistance to change) can be overcome, then "Competitive advantage comes from being able to do something others don't do. When most companies are stuck talking about what should be done, those that get down to business and actually *do* will emerge as star performers."[29] This new perspective is now called evidence-based management or simply EBM and, as indicated by the subtitle, is the approach taken by this text.

# EVIDENCE-BASED MANAGEMENT

Although the academic study and research of management in general and organizational behavior in particular is thriving (e.g., membership in the academic professional association Academy of Management has doubled in the past 10 years), there is growing concern that the divide, the gap, between theory/research and practice seems to be widening. As noted in the introductory comments of a special issue of the *Academy of Management Journal,* devoted to the problem, "It is hardly news that many organizations do not implement practices that research has shown to be positively associated with employee productivity and firm financial performance," and this "gap between science and practice is so persistent and pervasive that some have despaired of its ever being narrowed."[30]

The problem largely comes from the fact that when it comes to people, everyone is an expert. However, management academics add to the gap by too often concentrating only on the creation of knowledge by rigorous scientific methods and pay too little attention on the translation and diffusion of research findings to practice.[31] Both management consultants and journalists (and popular book authors) also contribute to the problem. Too often consultants tend to conduct "in house" (not peer-reviewed scientific process) research and depend only on narrow personal or client experience, and the journalists tell interesting stories and make interpretations based on some facts, but also depend too much on limited anecdotes and personal experience.[32]

Obviously, the bridge to help close the theory/research-practice gap must be built from both sides, practice and academic. Traditionally, practitioners have neither had the time nor the desire to read and translate rigorous academic research and academics have not had the time, desire, nor talent to write (translate the research) for practitioners.[33] In other words, practitioners must take on more of a "Practitioner-Scientist" role and academics must assume a more "Scientist-Practitioner" role. This movement to not only recognize, but also do something about what Pfeffer and Sutton called the "Knowing-Doing Gap," is the recently emerging movement toward evidence-based management (EBM).

Drawing from how professions such as education and especially medicine have handled this similar gap problem, Denise Rousseau in her recent presidential speech to the Academy of Management called for the field to take an evidence-based approach. She defined evidence-based management or EBM as "translating principles based on best evidence into organizational practices. Through evidence-based management, practicing managers develop into experts who make organizational decisions informed by social science and organizational research—part of the zeitgeist moving professional decisions away from personal preference and unsystematic experience toward those based on the best available scientific evidence."[34] The historical roots for this EBM can be traced back to one of the founding fathers of social psychology, Kurt Lewin, who astutely observed many years ago that there is nothing so practical as a good theory and "No action without research, no research without action."[35] Following this sage advice, advocates of EBM stress the need to refocus management education based on valid theory and research, translated for effective practice.

As indicated, this text from the beginning and through subsequent editions has been known for and prided itself on the theory and research foundation for everything presented. Whereas other texts typically have no theoretical framework and relatively few research citations per chapter, this text has a theoretical model to tie all the chapters together (presented at the end of this chapter) and a great number (in some cases over two hundred) of research citations in each chapter. In other words, this text takes an EBM approach to contribute to the reader/student to become a Practitioner-Scientist. The starting point in this journey of closing the science-practice gap and becoming a Practitioner-Scientist is to have an understanding and appreciation of history and research methods.

# HISTORICAL BACKGROUND: THE HAWTHORNE STUDIES

Most of today's organizational behavior texts have dropped any reference to history. Yet, the position taken in this evidence-based approach is that history always has important lessons to teach, and as was recently brought out again, "It is an interesting phenomenon that that which is touted as fundamentally 'new management practice' is essentially the readapting of existing 'old management truths.'"[36] There is no question that the early practicing management pioneers, such as Henri Fayol, Henry Ford, Alfred P. Sloan, and even the scientific managers at the end of the nineteenth century such as Frederick W. Taylor, recognized the behavioral side of management. However, they did not emphasize the human dimension; they let it play only a minor role in comparison with the roles of hierarchical structure, specialization, and the management functions of planning and controlling. An example would be the well-known Nobel Prize–winning French engineer turned executive Henri Fayol.

About the time of World War I Fayol headed up what was at that time the largest coal-mining firm in Europe. Writing the generally considered first book about management, he emphasized that the purpose of the organization was to get the work done in specialized, machinelike functions. He did not emphasize that the organization is made up of people; it is not a machine. Yet, perhaps the most widely recognized management expert in modern times, Peter Drucker, stated, "The organization is, above all, social. It is people."[37] There were varied and complex reasons for the emergence of the importance of the organization as a social entity, but it is the famous Hawthorne studies that provide historical roots for the notion of a social organization made up of people and mark the generally recognized starting point for the academic field of organizational behavior.

## The Illumination Studies: A Serendipitous Discovery

In 1924, the studies started at the huge Hawthorne Works of the Western Electric Company outside of Chicago. The initial illumination studies attempted to examine the relationship between light intensity on the shop floor of manual work sites and employee productivity. A test group and a control group were used. The test group in an early phase showed no increase or decrease in output in proportion to the increase or decrease of illumination. The control group with unchanged illumination increased output by the same amount overall as the test group. Subsequent phases brought the level of light down to moonlight intensity; the workers could barely see what they were doing, but productivity increased. The results were baffling to the researchers. Obviously, some variables in the experiment were not being held constant or under control. Something besides the level of illumination was causing the change in productivity. This something, of course, was the complex human variable.

It is fortunate that the illumination experiments did not end up in the wastebasket. Those responsible for the Hawthorne studies had enough foresight and spirit of scientific inquiry to accept the challenge of looking beneath the surface of the apparent failure of the experiments. In a way, the results of the illumination experiments were a serendipitous discovery, which, in research, is an accidental discovery. The classic example of serendipity is the breakthrough for penicillin that occurred when Sir Alexander Fleming accidentally discovered green mold on the side of a test tube. That the green mold was not washed down the drain and that the results of the illumination experiments were not thrown into the trash can be credited to the researchers' not being blinded by the unusual or seemingly worthless results of their experimentation. The serendipitous results of the illumination experiments provided the impetus for the further study of human behavior in the workplace.

## Subsequent Phases of the Hawthorne Studies

The illumination studies were followed by a study in the relay room, where operators assembled relay switches. This phase of the study tried to test specific variables, such as length of workday, rest breaks, and method of payment. The results were basically the same as those of the illumination studies: each test period yielded higher productivity than the previous one. Even when the workers were subjected to the original conditions of the experiment, productivity increased. The conclusion was that the independent variables (rest pauses and so forth) were not by themselves causing the change in the dependent variable (output). As in the illumination experiments, something was still not being controlled that was causing the change in the dependent variable (output).

Still another phase was the bank wiring room study. As in the preceding relay room experiments, the bank wirers were placed in a separate test room. The researchers were reluctant to segregate the bank wiring group because they recognized that this would alter the realistic factory environment they were attempting to simulate. However, for practical reasons, the research team decided to use a separate room. Unlike the relay room experiments, the bank wiring room study involved no experimental changes once the study had started. Instead, an observer and an interviewer gathered objective data for study. Of particular interest was the fact that the department's regular supervisors were used in the bank wiring room. Just as in the department out on the factory floor, these supervisors' main function was to maintain order and control.

The results of the bank wiring room study were essentially opposite to those of the relay room experiments. In the bank wiring room there were not the continual increases in productivity that occurred in the relay room. Rather, output was actually restricted by the bank wirers. By scientific management analysis—for example, time and motion study—the industrial engineers had arrived at a standard of 7,312 terminal connections per day. This represented 2½ equipments (banks). The workers had a different brand of rationality. They decided that 2 equipments was a "proper" day's work. Thus, 2½ equipments represented the management norm for production, but 2 equipments was the informal group norm and the actual output. The researchers determined that the informal group norm of 2 equipments represented restriction of output rather than a lack of ability to produce at the company standard of 2½ equipments.

Of particular interest from a group dynamics standpoint were the social pressures used to gain compliance with the group norms. The incentive system dictated that the more a worker produced, the more money the worker would earn. Also, the best producers would be laid off last, and thus they could be more secure by producing more. Yet, in the face of this management rationale, almost all the workers restricted output.

Social ostracism, ridicule, and name-calling were the major sanctions used by the group to enforce this restriction. In some instances, actual physical pressure in the form of a game called "binging" was applied. In the game, a worker would be hit as hard as possible, with the privilege of returning one "bing," or hit. Forcing rate-busters to play the game became an effective sanction. These group pressures had a tremendous impact on all the workers. Social ostracism was more effective in gaining compliance with the informal group norm than money and security were in attaining the scientifically derived management norm.

## Implications of the Hawthorne Studies

Despite some obvious philosophical,[38] theoretical,[39] and methodological limitations by today's standards of research (which will be covered next), the Hawthorne studies did provide some interesting insights that contributed to a better understanding of human behavior in organizations.[40] For instance, one interesting aspect of the Hawthorne studies is the contrasting results obtained in the relay room and the bank wiring room. In the relay room, production continually increased throughout the test period, and the relay assemblers were very positive. The opposite was true in the bank wiring room; blatant restriction of output was practiced by disgruntled workers. Why the difference in these two phases of the studies?

One clue to the answer to this question may be traced to the results of a questionnaire administered to the subjects in the relay room. The original intent of the questions was to determine the health and habits of the workers. Their answers were generally inconclusive except that *all* the operators indicated they felt "better" in the relay test room. A follow-up questionnaire then asked about specific items in the test room situation. In discussions of the Hawthorne studies, the follow-up questionnaire results, in their entirety, usually are not mentioned. Most discussions cite the subjects' unanimous preference for working in the test room instead of the regular department. Often overlooked, however, are the workers' explanations for their choice. In order of preference, the workers gave the following reasons:

1. Small group
2. Type of supervision
3. Earnings
4. Novelty of the situation
5. Interest in the experiment
6. Attention received in the test room[41]

It is important to note that novelty, interest, and attention were relegated to the fourth, fifth, and sixth positions. These last three areas usually are associated with the famous "Hawthorne effect." Many social scientists imply that the increases in the relay room productivity can be attributed solely to the fact that the participants in the study were given special attention and that they were enjoying a novel, interesting experience. This is labeled the *Hawthorne effect* and is, of course, a real problem with all human experimental subjects. But to say that all the results of the relay room experiments were due to such an effect on the subjects seems to ignore the important impact of the small group, the type of supervision, and earnings. All these variables (that is, experimental design, group dynamics, styles of leadership and supervision, and rewards), and much more, separate the old human relations movement and an evidence-based approach to the field of organizational behavior. So do the refinement and fine-tuning of the research methodology used to accumulate meaningful evidence about organizational behavior.

# RESEARCH METHODOLOGY TO DETERMINE VALID EVIDENCE

An evidence-based approach to organizational behavior depends on rigorous research methodology. Accumulating valid evidence of why people behave the way they do is a very delicate and complex process. In fact, the problems are so great that many scholars, chiefly from the physical and engineering sciences, argue that there can be no precise science of behavior. They maintain that humans cannot be treated like chemical or physical elements; they cannot be effectively controlled or manipulated. For example, the critics state that, under easily controllable conditions, 2 parts hydrogen to 1 part oxygen will always result in water and that no analogous situation exists in human behavior. Human variables such as motives, bias, expectations, learning, perception, values, and even a Hawthorne effect on the part of both subject and investigator confound the controls that are attempted. For these reasons, behavioral scientists in general and organizational behavior researchers in particular are often on the defensive and must be very careful to comply with accepted methods of science.[42]

## The Overall Scientific Perspective

Behavioral scientists in general and organizational behavior researchers in particular strive to attain the following hallmarks of any science:

1. The overall purposes are understanding/explanation, prediction, and control.
2. The definitions are precise and operational.
3. The measures are reliable and valid.
4. The methods are systematic.
5. The results are cumulative.

Figure 1.1 summarizes the relationship between the practical behavioral problems and unanswered questions facing today's managers, research methodology, and the existing body of valid evidence. When a question arises or a problem evolves, the first place to turn for an answer is the existing body of valid evidence. It is possible that the question can be answered immediately or the problem solved without going any further. Unfortunately, the answer is not always found in the body of valid evidence and must be discovered through appropriate research methodology.

Although behavioral science in general compared to the physical and biological sciences is relatively young, and the field of organizational behavior is even younger—its

**FIGURE 1.1**
**Simple Relationships
Among Problems,
Methodology, and
Valid Evidence.**

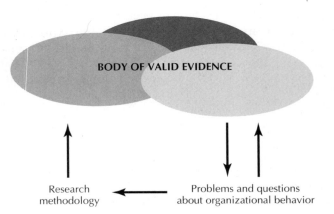

BODY OF VALID EVIDENCE

Research
methodology

Problems and questions
about organizational behavior

direct origins really go back only to the early 1970s—there is now enough accumulated valid evidence that organizational behavior principles can be provided for the effective management of human behavior in organizations. As explained in the preface, this is the only text that presents evidence-based principles of organizational behavior at the end of each chapter. Interestingly, it is the research technique of meta-analysis providing the quantitative synthesis and testing of all available studies that permits confidently stating these evidence-based principles. As Williams points out, meta-analysis "shows what works and the conditions under which management techniques may work better or worse in the 'real world.' Meta-analysis is based on the simple idea that if one study shows that a management technique doesn't work and another study shows that it does, an average of those results is probably the best estimate of how well that management practice works (or doesn't work)."[43]

Although there are now enough research studies in organizational behavior to have this evidence-based text, it is also recognized that many questions and problems in organizational behavior cannot yet be answered or solved directly by existing evidence or, as the accompanying OB in Action: Forget Going with Your Gut points out, certainly not just common sense. A working knowledge of research methodology becomes especially important to practitioner-scientists, both as knowledgeable and critical consumers of the rapidly expanding literature reporting the results of organizational behavior research and as practitioner-scientists who are capable of applying appropriate research methods to solve difficult problems in the workplace.

## Starting with Theory

Although theory is often devalued as being unrealistic and overly complicated by practitioners, as noted earlier Lewin may have been right when he declared there is nothing as practical as a good theory. As the editors of the *Journal of Applied Psychology* recently reminded, "Theory tells us *why* something occurs, not simply *what* occurs."[44] Yet students and practitioners of organizational behavior are usually "turned off" by all the theories that pervade the field. The reason for all the theories, of course, is the still relative newness of the field and the complexity and multidimensionality of the variables involved.[45] The purpose of any theory, including those found in organizational behavior, is to explain and predict the phenomenon in question; theories allow the researcher to deduce logical propositions or hypotheses that can be tested by acceptable research designs. However, as Don Hambrick points out, "A theory, by its very nature, is a simplification of reality. When we develop or test theories, we inevitably exclude an array of factors that might potentially affect the phenomena under examination."[46] Thus, theories are ever changing on the basis of the empirical results. In other words, theory and research go hand in hand in evidence-based management.

After pleading for more and stronger theory in organizational behavior, Sutton and Staw have pointed out that references, data, lists of variables or constructs, diagrams, and hypotheses are *not* theory. Instead, they note that

> theory is the answer to queries of *why*. Theory is about the connections among phenomena, a story about why acts, events, structure, and thoughts occur. Theory emphasizes the nature of causal relationships, identifying what comes first as well as the timing of such events. Strong theory, in our view, delves into the underlying processes so as to understand the systematic reasons for a particular occurrence or non-occurrence.[47]

Such theorizing is not easy. "Theorizing takes scientists on mental journeys between the world of observed events, such as falling apples, and the imagined world of hypothetical concepts, such as gravity. Bridging gaps between concrete experience and abstract

For the average patient, the fact that "evidence-based medicine" is now one of the hottest forces in health care might seem pretty absurd. After all, isn't all medicine based on hard facts? Actually, no. To make decisions, many physicians rely on clinical experience, conventional wisdom passed down through training, and sometimes, outdated research. The evidence-based medicine movement, which has been gaining traction in hospitals and among insurers in recent years, calls for better integration of the most current, most carefully designed research into everyday medicine.

The practice of business management could use a similar movement, argue Jeffrey Pfeffer, a professor of organizational behavior at Stanford University's Graduate School of Business, and Robert I. Sutton, a professor of management and engineering at Stanford. In their densely researched book, *Hard Facts, Dangerous Half-Truths & Total Nonsense: Profiting from Evidence-Based Management,* the authors fret that managers' fondness for casual benchmarking ("GE does it? We should too!"), past practices, and pet ideologies may hold serious harm for their organizations.

At a time when intuition is on the ascent, thanks in part to Malcolm Gladwell and his best-selling *Blink, Hard Facts* is a useful reminder that the gut is often trumped by the facts. The book's deconstruction of some of the most widely applied management truisms and fads is thought-provoking but will leave some managers, especially those in metrics-driven cultures, unsatisfied.

The authors are at their best when dispelling the copycat tactics managers use for evaluating and rewarding talent. Take forced ranking, for instance. Popularized by General Electric Co. under Jack Welch, the process requires managers to divide employees into the top 20%, middle 70%, and bottom 10% of performers, often culling the lowest group. Practiced by as many as one-third of companies today, the authors say the approach has many flaws. A 2004 survey of more than 200 human-resource managers found that even though more than half of them used forced ranking, they felt it resulted in lower productivity, skepticism, reduced collaboration, and impaired morale. Breaking up teams by automatically firing the bottom 10% of workers can even be dangerous: Citing a National Transportation Safety Board study, the authors note that 73% of commercial airline pilots' serious mistakes happen on crews' first day together.

Pfeffer and Sutton also make a persuasive case against paying widely divergent rewards to high and low performers, a popular practice in talent management today. Many studies show that tying pay to performance can drive good results when individuals are working solo. But the same can't be said for the collaborative, interconnected teams that now make up most companies. The authors cite a 2005 study that surveyed senior management groups at 67 publicly traded firms. Those with greater gaps between the best- and worst-paid executives also had weaker financial performance. Managers who implement wide pay differences in heavily team-based groups, argue Pfeffer and Sutton, forget that people get a lot of fulfillment from their social bonds at work, and creating such distinctions often diminishes trust.

concepts presents a challenge."[48] As Sumantra Ghoshal noted, "Our theories and ideas have done much to strengthen the management practices that we are all now so loudly condemning."[49] There is also the danger that theories can become self-fulfilling without empirical verification. As recently noted by Ferraro, Pfeffer, and Sutton, "Theories can 'win' in the marketplace for ideas, independent of their empirical validity, to the extent their assumptions and language become taken for granted and normatively valued, therefore creating conditions that make them come 'true'."[50] However, as Karl Weick, perhaps the most widely recognized theorist in organizational behavior, notes: a good theory explains, predicts, and delights.[51]

## The Use of Research Designs

Research design is at the very heart of scientific methodology and evidence-based management; it can be used to answer practical questions or to test theoretical propositions/hypotheses. The three designs most often used in organizational behavior research today are the experiment, the case, and the survey. All three have played important roles in the development of EBM. The experimental design is borrowed largely from psychology, where it is used extensively; the case and survey designs have traditionally played a bigger role in sociology. All three designs can be used effectively for researching organizational behavior.

A primary aim of any research design is to establish a cause-and-effect relationship. The experimental design offers the best possibility of accomplishing this goal. All other factors being equal, most organizational behavior researchers prefer this method of testing hypotheses. Simply defined, an experiment involves the manipulation of independent variables to measure their effect on, or the change in, dependent variables, while everything else is held constant or controlled. If possible, an experimental group and a control group are randomly assigned so that the participants are equivalent. The experimental group receives the input of the independent variables (the intervention), and the control group does not. Any measured change in the dependent variable in the experimental group can be attributed to the independent variable, assuming that no change has occurred in any other variable and that no change has occurred in the control group. The controls employed are the key to the successful use of the experimental design. If all intervening variables are held constant or equal, the researcher can conclude with a high degree of confidence that the independent variable caused the change in the dependent variable.

## The Validity of Studies

The value of any evidence is dependent on its validity. In particular, research results must have both *internal validity* and *external validity* in order to make a meaningful contribution to evidence-based management. A study has internal validity if there are no plausible alternative explanations of the reported results other than those reported. The threats to internal validity include uncontrolled intervening events that occur between the time the preexperiment measurement is taken and the time the postexperiment measurement is taken or does A cause B, or does B cause A, a problem with correlational studies.

The threats to internal validity can be overcome with careful design of the study. However, this is not always true of external validity, which is concerned with the generalizability of the results obtained. In order for a study to have external validity, the results must be applicable to a wide range of people and situations. Field studies tend to have better external validity than laboratory studies because at least the study takes place in a real setting. In general, the best strategy is to use a number of different designs or mixed methods (including qualitative research) to answer the same question. The weaknesses of the various designs can offset one another and the problem of common method variance (the results are due to the design, rather than the variables under study) can be overcome.

Normally, the research would start with a laboratory study to isolate and manipulate the variable or variables in question. This would be followed by an attempt to verify the findings in a field setting. This progression from the laboratory to the field may lead to the soundest conclusions. However, free observation in the real setting should probably precede laboratory investigations of organizational behavior problems or questions. Specifically, in recent years qualitative methods are being suggested as a starting point or supplement, if not an alternative, to quantitatively based and statistically analyzed methods of researching organizational behavior. Van Maanen explains that this qualitative approach "seeks to describe, decode, translate, and otherwise come to terms with the meaning, not the frequency, of certain more or less naturally occurring phenomena in the social world."[52] Multiple designs and multiple measures have the best chance for valid, meaningful research contributing to an evidence-based approach to organizational behavior.

**FIGURE 1.2**
The Relationship of
Organizational
Behavior to Other
Closely Related
Disciplines.

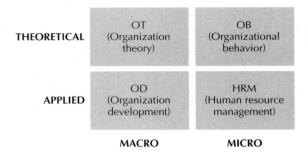

## DEFINING ORGANIZATIONAL BEHAVIOR

With a rich historical background such as the Hawthorne studies and using an accepted scientific methodology as briefly outlined above, the field of organizational behavior is now an accepted academic discipline. As with any other relatively new academic endeavor, however, there have been some rough spots and sidetracks along the way. Besides the healthy academic controversies over theoretical approach or research findings, perhaps the biggest problem that organizational behavior had to overcome was an identity crisis. Early on, the field of organizational behavior had to answer questions such as: Is it an attempt to replace all management with behavioral science concepts and techniques? How, if at all, does it differ from traditional applied or industrial psychology? Fortunately, these questions have now been answered to the satisfaction of most management academicians, behavioral scientists, and management practitioners.

Figure 1.2 shows in very general terms the relationships between and emphases of organizational behavior (OB) and the related disciplines of organization theory (OT), organization development (OD), and human resource management (HRM). As shown, OB tends to be more theoretically oriented and at the micro level of analysis. Specifically, OB draws from many theoretical frameworks of the behavioral sciences that are focused on understanding and explaining individual and group behavior in organizations. As with other sciences, OB accumulates evidence and tests theories by accepted scientific methods of research. In summary, *organizational behavior* can be defined as *the understanding, prediction, and management of human behavior in organizations.*

## THEORETICAL FOUNDATION FOR ORGANIZATIONAL BEHAVIOR

Although organizational behavior is extremely complex and includes many inputs and dimensions, the cognitive, behavioristic, and social cognitive theories can be used to develop an overall framework for an evidence-based approach. After the major theories are briefly summarized, the last section of the chapter presents a model that is used to conceptually link and structure the rest of the text.

### Cognitive Framework

The cognitive approach to human behavior has many sources of input. The micro-oriented chapters in the next part provide some of this background. For now, however, it can be said simply that the cognitive approach gives people much more "credit" than the other approaches. The cognitive approach emphasizes the positive and freewill aspects of human behavior and uses concepts such as expectancy, demand, and intention. *Cognition,* which is the basic unit of the cognitive framework, can be simply defined as the act of knowing an item of information. Under this framework, cognitions precede behavior and constitute input into the person's thinking, perception, problem solving, and information processing. Concepts such as cognitive maps can be used as pictures or visual aids in comprehending a person's "understanding of particular, and selective, elements of the thoughts (rather than thinking) of an individual, group or organization."[53]

The classic work of Edward Tolman can be used to represent the cognitive theoretical approach. Although Tolman believed behavior to be the appropriate unit of analysis, he felt that behavior is purposive, that it is directed toward a goal. In his laboratory experiments, he found that animals learned to expect that certain events would follow one another. For example, animals learned to behave as if they expected food when a certain cue appeared. Thus, Tolman believed that learning consists of the *expectancy* that a particular event will lead to a particular consequence. This cognitive concept of expectancy implies that the organism is thinking about, or is conscious or aware of, the goal. Thus, Tolman and others espousing the cognitive approach felt that behavior is best explained by these cognitions.

Contemporary psychologists carefully point out that a cognitive concept such as expectancy does not reflect a guess about what is going on in the mind; it is a term that describes behavior. In other words, the cognitive and behavioristic theories are not as opposite as they appear on the surface and sometimes are made out to be—for example, Tolman considered himself a behaviorist. Yet, despite some conceptual similarities, there has been a controversy throughout the years in the behavioral sciences on the relative contributions of the cognitive versus the behavioristic framework. As often happens in other academic fields, debate has gone back and forth through the years.[54]

Because of the recent advances from both theory development and research findings, there has been what some have termed a "cognitive explosion" in the field of psychology. For example, an analysis of articles published in the major psychology journals found by far the greatest emphasis is on the cognitive school over the behavioral school starting in the 1970s.[55] Applied to the field of organizational behavior, a cognitive approach has traditionally dominated units of analysis such as personality, perception, and attitudes (Chapter 5), motivation and goal setting (Chapter 6), and positive constructs such as psychological capital (Chapter 7). Recently, there has been renewed interest in the role that cognitions can play in organizational behavior in terms of advancement in both theory and research on social cognition. This social cognitive process can be a unifying theoretical framework for both cognition and behaviorism. However, before getting into the specifics of social cognitive theory, which serves as the conceptual framework for this text, it is necessary to have an understanding of the behavioristic approach as well.

## Behavioristic Framework

Chapter 12 discusses in detail the behavioristic theory in psychology and its application to organizational behavior. Its historical roots can be traced to the work of Ivan Pavlov and John B. Watson. These pioneering behaviorists stressed the importance of dealing with observable behaviors instead of the elusive mind that had preoccupied earlier psychologists. They used classical conditioning experiments to formulate the stimulus-response (S-R) explanation of human behavior. Both Pavlov and Watson felt that behavior could be best understood in terms of S-R. A stimulus elicits a response. They concentrated mainly on the impact of the stimulus and felt that learning occurred when the S-R connection was made.

Modern behaviorism marks its beginnings with the work of B. F. Skinner. Deceased for a number of years, Skinner is widely recognized for his contributions to psychology. For example, a recent study drawing from publication citations and a large survey of psychologists ranked Skinner as the most influential psychologist of the twentieth century.[56] He felt that the early behaviorists helped explain respondent behaviors (those behaviors elicited by stimuli) but not the more complex operant behaviors. In other words, the S-R approach helped explain physical reflexes; for example, when stuck by a pin (S), the person will flinch (R), or when tapped below the kneecap (S), the person will extend the lower leg (R). On the other hand, Skinner found through his operant conditioning experiments that the consequences of a response could better explain most behaviors than eliciting stimuli could. He emphasized the importance of the response-stimulus (R-S) relationship. The organism has to operate on the environment (thus the term *operant conditioning*) in order to receive the desirable consequence. The preceding stimulus does not cause the behavior in operant conditioning; it serves as a cue to emit the behavior. For Skinner and the behaviorists, behavior is a function of its contingent environmental consequences.

Both classical and operant conditioning and the important role of reinforcing consequences are given detailed attention in Chapter 12. For now, however, it is important to understand that the behavioristic approach is environmentally based. It posits that cognitive processes such as thinking, expectancies, and perception may exist but are not needed to predict and control or manage behavior. However, as in the case of the cognitive approach, which also includes behavioristic concepts, some modern behaviorists feel that cognitive variables can be behaviorized.[57] However, the social cognitive theory that has emerged in recent years incorporating both cognitive and behavioristic concepts and principles may be the most unifying and comprehensive foundation for an evidence-based approach to organizational behavior.

## Social Cognitive Framework

The cognitive approach has been accused of being mentalistic, and the behavioristic approach has been accused of being deterministic. Cognitive theorists argue that the S-R model, and to a lesser degree the R-S model, is much too mechanistic an explanation of human behavior. A strict S-R interpretation of behavior seems justifiably open to the criticism of being too mechanistic, but because of the scientific approach that has been meticulously employed by behaviorists, the operant model in particular has made a significant contribution to the study and meaning of human behavior[58] and in turn an evidence-based approach to organizational behavior. The same can be said of the cognitive approach. Much research has been done to verify its importance as an explanation of human behavior in general and organizational behavior in particular. Instead of polarization and unconstructive criticism between the two approaches, it now seems time to recognize that each can make an important contribution to the understanding, prediction, and control of organizational behavior. The social cognitive approach tries to integrate the contributions of both approaches and serves as the foundation for an evidence-based approach to organizational behavior.

About 30 years ago we (Davis and Luthans) proposed a social learning approach to organizational behavior,[59] and over 25 years ago we (Luthans and Kreitner) suggested a social learning approach to organizational behavior modification (O.B. Mod.).[60] Based on the work of Albert Bandura[61] and our own theory building and application to

**FIGURE 1.3**
A Social Learning
Approach to
Organizational
Behavior.

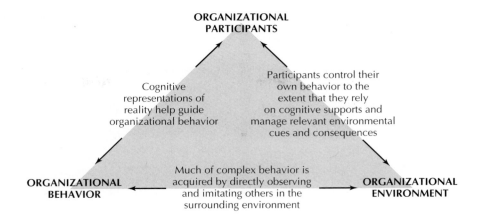

organizational behavior, social learning theory provided the conceptual framework for the 3rd to 8th editions of this text. Social learning takes the position that behavior can best be explained in terms of a continuous reciprocal interaction among cognitive, behavioral, and environmental determinants. The person and the environmental situation do not function as independent units but, in conjunction with the behavior itself, reciprocally interact to determine behavior. Bandura explains that "it is largely through their actions that people produce the environmental conditions that affect their behavior in a reciprocal fashion. The experiences generated by behavior also partly determine what a person becomes and can do, which, in turn, affects subsequent behavior."[62] The triangular model shown in Figure 1.3 takes this social learning work of Bandura and translates it into relevant units of analysis and variables in organizational behavior.

Bandura has taken his social learning and developed it into the more comprehensive social cognitive theory (SCT),[63] and we (Stajkovic and Luthans) in turn have translated this SCT into the theoretical foundation for organizational behavior.[64] SCT is much more comprehensive than the cognitive or behavioristic pproaches by themselves and its predecessor, social learning theory. Specifically, SCT recognizes the importance of behaviorism's contingent environmental consequences, but also includes cognitive processes of self-regulation. "The *social* part acknowledges the social origins of much of human thought and action (what individuals learn by being part of a society), whereas the *cognitive* portion recognizes the influential contribution of thought processes to human motivation, attitudes, and action."[65]

Similar to the social learning model in Figure 1.3, SCT explains organizational behavior in terms of the bidirectional, reciprocal causation among the organizational participants (e.g., unique personality characteristics such as conscientiousness), the organizational environment (e.g., the perceived consequences such as contingent recognition from the supervisor or pay for increased productivity), and the organizational behavior itself (e.g., previous successful or unsuccessful sales approaches with customers). In other words, like social learning, in an SCT theoretical framework, organizational participants are at the same time both products (as in the behaviorism approach) and producers (as in the cognitive approach) of their personality, respective environments, and behaviors. Bandura goes beyond social learning with SCT by explaining the nature of the bidirectional reciprocal influences through the five basic human capabilities summarized in Figure 1.4.

**FIGURE 1.4** **The Basic Human Capabilities According to Bandura's Social Cognitive Theory (SCT).**

Source: Alexander D. Stajkovic and Fred Luthans, "Social Cognitive Theory and Self-Efficacy: Going beyond Traditional Motivational and Behavioral Approaches," *Organizational Dynamics,* Spring 1998, p. 65.

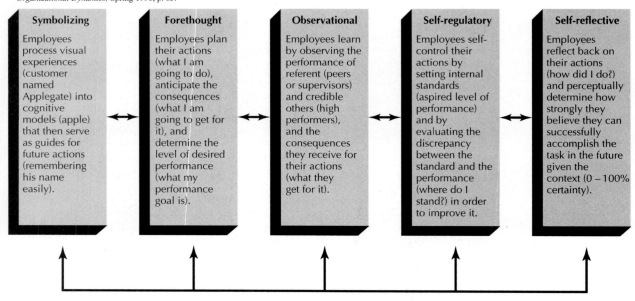

**FIGURE 1.5** **A Conceptual Model for the Study of Organizational Behavior: An Evidence-Based Approach.**

**Environmental Context**
    2. Globalization, Diversity, & Ethics
**Organizational Context**
    3. Design & Culture
    4. Reward System

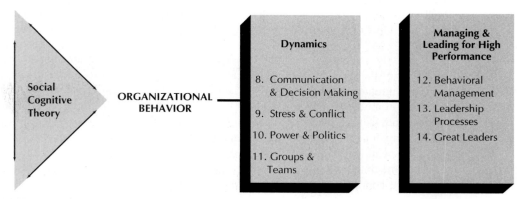

**Cognitive Processes**
    5. Personality, Perception, & Attitudes
    6. Motivational Processes and Application
    7. Positive Organizational Behavior and Psychological Capital

# THE CONCEPTUAL FRAMEWORK FOR THE TEXT

The conceptual model used to structure this text is shown in Figure 1.5. As indicated, social cognitive theory is the foundation and consists of the reciprocal interaction among the environmental and organizational context (Part One, Chapters 2–4); cognitive processes (Part Two, Chapters 5–7); and, importantly, the organizational behavior itself, which produces and is a product of the environmental/organizational context and the cognitive processes. At a more macro level are graphic depiction of the dynamics (not necessarily the outcomes) of organizational behavior (Part Three, Chapters 8–10). Finally, at an applied level is the graphic representation of the role that managing and leading for high performance (Part Four, Chapters 11–14) play in the conceptual framework for organizational behavior.

Obviously, this conceptual framework gives only a bare-bones sketch of organizational behavior rather than a full-blown explanation. Nevertheless, it can serve as a point of departure for how this text is organized. It helps explain why particular chapters are covered and how they relate to one another. As the chapters unfold, some of the fine points will become clearer and some of the seemingly simplistic, unsupported statements will begin to make more sense. Figure 1.5 serves merely as the welcoming mat to the study of the exciting, but still developing, field of organizational behavior.

## Summary

This chapter first gives a brief overview of the significant challenges currently facing management. Besides the new workplace, environmental changes such as globalization and recognition and management of diversity and ethics represent a paradigm shift. This shift is characterized by new rules, new boundaries, and, importantly, new thinking and behaviors that are essential for organizations and managers to be successful or even survive. This new paradigm facing management requires a new perspective and not only an appreciation of the human, behavioral side of management but also apply the greatly expanding research findings for more effective practice. After first identifying the existing knowing-doing gap, the evidence-based approach used by this text over the years and the new call for evidence-based management (EBM) is summarized.

The historical roots start this evidence-based approach to organizational behavior. The beginnings are usually attributed to the famous Hawthorne studies, which had several phases (illumination, relay, bank wiring studies) and often-overlooked implications for modern management. Whereas the Hawthorne studies are often unfairly dismissed because of methodological flaws, today's organizational behavior field is characterized by rigorous scientific methodology. Both theory development and research designs are given considerable attention. Specifically, the attempt is made to eliminate or minimize the threats to internal validity through carefully designed experiments. Field studies are used over laboratory studies whenever possible in order to have more external (generalizable) validity.

Because organizational behavior is a relatively new field, it must be precisely defined: the understanding, prediction, and management of human behavior in organizations. It is also important to see how OB (micro, theoretical) relates to other closely related disciplines such as organization theory or OT (macro, theoretical), organizational development or OD (macro, applied), and human resource management or HRM (micro, applied). Finally, it is important to provide a theoretical foundation to develop a specific model that can be used as a conceptual framework for this text. The cognitive, the behavioristic, and the more integrative social cognitive theories are used for such a foundation. The cognitive model gives the human being more "credit" and assumes that behavior is purposive and goal oriented.

Cognitive processes such as expectancy and perception help explain behavior. The behavioristic approach deals with observable behavior and the environmental contingencies of the behavior. Classical behaviorism explained behavior in terms of S-R, whereas more modern behaviorism gives increased emphasis to contingent consequences, or R-S. The social cognitive approach emphasizes that the person, the environment, and the behavior itself are in constant interaction with one another and reciprocally determine one another. This social cognitive approach incorporates both cognitive and behavioristic elements and is used as the theoretical foundation for the organizational behavior model used as the conceptual framework to structure this evidence-based text.

# Ending with Meta-Analytic Research Findings
## OB PRINCIPLE FOR EVIDENCE-BASED PRACTICE

Because a growing number of important concepts and techniques have a stream of research findings, meta-analysis can be conducted on them. The meta-analysis results provide the basis for organizational behavior (OB) principles for effective evidence-based practice.

### Meta-Analysis Results:

The end of each chapter will report the result of usually one but in some cases two or three representative meta-analyses. The stated principles, relevant to each chapter, are based on these meta-analytic findings. A results section will report the number of studies and participants and the meta-analytic average effect statistic $d$. Importantly, to make these meta-analytic results as user friendly as possible, the $d$ effect size is transformed using Grissom's (see source below) table to a percentage "probability of superior outcome of one treatment over another." Besides this percentage probability evidence to support the "OB Principle," this section will also briefly discuss any moderating contingencies that were found and give the full citation of the meta-analysis in a source line like that below from Grissom's conversion of $d$ to probability of success.

### Conclusion:

Each chapter's Ending with Meta-Analytic Research Findings is patterned after this presentation: statement of OB Principle for Evidence-Based Practice, Meta-Analysis Results, and Conclusion. The purpose of the conclusion is to tie the principle back to the chapter topic and make some final comments. The contribution of meta-analysis at this stage of development of the organizational behavior field is that it is able to draw overall, sound evidence-based conclusions (i.e., state principles) from a large number of studies (often over 100) and usually thousands of subjects. Instead of just choosing one study here or there to support (or not support) a statement, meta-analysis provides a quantitative summary of individual studies across an entire body of research evidence on a given concept (e.g., conscientiousness or self-efficacy) or technique (e.g., job characteristics model or organizational behavior modification). Many of the meta-analyses conducted to date on relevant topics in this text are included as being representative, but as research continues to accumulate, many more meta-analytically derived OB principles exist and will be forthcoming.

**Sources:** Robert J. Grissom, "Probability of the Superior Outcome of One Treatment over Another," *Journal of Applied Psychology,* Vol. 79, No. 2, 1994, pp. 314–316. For those wanting more information on meta-analysis, see: L. V. Hedges and I. Olkin, *Statistical Methods for Meta Analysis,* Academic Press,

San Diego, 1985 and J. E. Hunter and F. L. Schmidt, *Methods of Meta-Analysis,* Sage, Beverly Hills, Calif., 1995. For a critical analysis and limitations of meta-analysis, see: P. Bobko and E. F. Stone-Romero, "Meta-Analysis May Be Another Useful Tool, but It Is Not a Panacea," in G. R. Ferris (Ed.), *Research in Personnel and Human Resources Management,* Vol. 16, JAI Press, Stamford, Conn., 1998, 359–397. Finally, to gain insight into teaching organizational behavior through such a principles approach, see: Edwin A. Locke, "The Epistemological Side of Teaching Management: Teaching through Principles," *Academy of Management Learning and Education*, Vol. 1, No. 2, 2002, pp. 195–205.

## Questions for Discussion and Review

1. What are some of the major challenges facing today's and tomorrow's organizations and management? Briefly describe these developments.
2. What is a paradigm? How will the paradigm shift affect management? What are the implications of this paradigm shift for organizational behavior?
3. Why do you think there is a "knowing-doing" gap and how can evidence-based management help close it?
4. Why do you feel the Hawthorne studies made such an important historical contribution to the study of organizational behavior?
5. Why are theory development and rigorous scientific methodology important to the field of organizational behavior? What role does validity play in the design of research studies?
6. How does organizational behavior relate to, or differ from, organizational development? Organization theory? Human resource management?
7. In your own words, identify and summarize the various theoretical frameworks for understanding organizational behavior. How does the social cognitive approach differ from the cognitive approach? How does the social cognitive approach differ from the behavioristic approach?
8. Explain the model for organizational behavior that is used in this text.

## Internet Exercise: Nonjobs or Telecommuting

This chapter sets the tone for the new paradigm environment. One dimension of this environment has been the dramatic increase in the number of nonjob or "telecommuters," those that work from home or at least outside the organization. Inexpensive computers, the changing nature of jobs, and workers' demands for a more flexible schedule have all contributed to this trend. Go to **http://www.tjobs.com/** and look at the jobs that they offer specifically designed around telecommuting. In fact, Putnam Investments has a page dedicated to jobs available at home. Visit their site at **http://www.putnaminv.com/**. Then, click on "career opportunities." You may also want to visit the International Telework Association Council's (ITAC) site at **www.workingfromhome.com.** You will find many current articles on telecommuting at **http://www.harveynash.com/usa/**. Browse through these sites, and consider the following questions.

1. Would you consider a job that kept you at home for a significant part of the workweek? What would be the advantages of this? Disadvantages?
2. As a manager, consider the challenges of managing those who work at home or virtually out of the organization. What are your challenges? Consider, for example, how to monitor performance, motivate workers, and help them manage workplace problems.
3. Do you think the trend toward telecommuting will increase or decrease in the coming years? What impact will this have on some of the major topics in this text? Be as specific as you can by looking at the table of contents and Figure 1.5.

# Real Case:   *The Big Squeeze on Workers*

On his recent family vacation in Arizona, Peter Spina spent much of his time camped out under a palm tree while his kids splashed around in the Scottsdale Princess Hotel's luxurious pool. Spina wasn't lounging. He was working—hammering out deals on his cell phone in a mad dash to break new accounts at Vulcan Ventures Inc., where he's publisher of *The Sporting News*. Spina says the downturn has forced him to work even longer hours than he did during the boom—about 15% more. Ditto for his sales force. Whereas once he had lots of bonus money to throw around, he now tries to make up for the tough slog by bringing popsicles to the office on hot days. The added hustling is one reason his team has racked up revenue gains of 46% this year in an abysmal ad market. "They're working longer and harder," says Spina.

Much has been made of the recent upsurge in productivity. Although recessions usually bring slides in this efficiency measure, technology has made the economy more productive than ever before. But tell that to white-collar workers, and you're likely to hear that the gains have come on their backs. Rather than bring relief, layoff survivors say, the downturn has only socked it to them more. They complain about managing the orphaned workloads of downsized colleagues, scouring new avenues for business, and fighting for high-profile posts so if the ax falls, it won't hit them. "What we're discovering is that in this early stage of recovery, not only are companies making people work harder, but, believe me, some people want to," says J.P. Morgan Chase & Co. senior economist James E. Glassman. "They're trying to protect their job security."

That gripping desperation is easy for companies to use in their favor. Mike Hewitt, director of client services at consulting firm Aquent, says he and his staff have been bending over backwards to meet with clients who don't have any work for them so the company can get a jump on future business and be ready to roll when the rebound kicks in.

But it's not just fear that's motivating today's workplace. A number of other structural changes are also helping bosses to extract maximum productivity from their ranks. From the increased use of temps, to the reclassification of hourly workers into salaried employees ineligible for overtime pay, to the rise in variable pay that puts part of workers' paychecks at risk, companies are now able to get more out of less.

It's hard to say just how much more, given the state of statistical record-keeping. The Bureau of Labor Statistics says overall weekly hours worked have dropped—in part due to manufacturers slashing hours. But economists say it's impossible to draw an accurate picture from the BLS data. They note that the data is flawed because it often builds in an assumption that all levels of employees work 35 hours a week—managers and hourly staff alike. To which many economists reply: Come on. Morgan Stanley Dean Witter & Co. chief economist Stephen Roach, for example, believes the BLS numbers understate the number of hours worked, therefore overstating productivity.

Still, whatever the numbers say, there's no doubt that right now employees feel they have little choice but to accept the grueling loads. Despite some evidence of a rebound, the job market in many quarters is still weak. Job cuts are no longer a last resort in hard times but an ongoing tool for matching supply with demand.

This is one reason some economists predict a replay, at least initially, of the early-1990s jobless recovery. Rather than scoop up more permanent hires at the first whiff of demand, economists say CEOs are likely to be leery, especially with economic data so mixed. Many have bad memories of boom-time hiring binges in which they took on mediocre people just to fill slots and then wound up having to pay weeks of costly severance. Instead, economists say CEOs are likely to focus first on extracting even more from their existing ranks until demand reaches a breaking point. The big question now, asks Mary Hammershock, vice-president for human resources for Silicon Valley's Blue Martini Software, is "how much longer can you get people to do this when the upside has gone away?"

Already, companies are looking first to bring in contract workers that they can quickly tap and zap without paying any benefits or severance. In fact, the temps have been the fastest growing sector of employment. And they aren't accounted for as regular employees. This helps companies that use a lot of them, like Cisco Systems Inc., to drive up revenue per employee.

The growing use of the just-in-time workforce is not the only means by which companies are priming the productivity pump. Workers complain that many employers are taking advantage of outdated labor laws by misclassifying them as salaried-exempt so they can skirt overtime pay. Already, Wal-Mart Stores, Taco Bell,

Starbucks, and U-Haul, among others, have been slapped with class actions. In the case of General Dynamics Corp., this resulted in a $100 million award that is now on appeal. At Farmer's Insurance, employees got $90 million. Some employers are so worried about the issue that they are now doing wage-and-hour audits.

Another potential productivity enhancer: incentive pay, which enables bosses to motivate people to work harder during tough times to make up for lost wages. General Electric Co. will soon start factoring customer performance into employee pay, putting an even greater chunk of compensation at risk. Under this system, if a customer's business suffers, so does the GE employee's paycheck.

Yet even as they push existing employees, companies also have to think about what's down the road—the likely return of tight labor markets and a replay of the 1990s' battle for talent. Demographers and labor experts note that the recession merely masked the deep skills shortages lurking within the labor force. "It will be even worse than it was in 2000," predicts Texas Instruments Inc. Chairman, CEO, and President Tom Engibous.

Like many CEOs, Engibous faces the tough job of balancing the need to juice profits right now with the longer term goal of cultivating his choice employees. That's why he has launched a "re-recruiting initiative" at TI, asking workers what they need—days off, new assignments, a different boss—to keep them satisfied right now. For companies that squeeze too hard, it probably already is too late.

1. Do you agree or disagree with the feeling of many downsizing survivors that increased productivity "comes on their backs"? What does this mean and how does this have implications for managing these employees?
2. What impact can employing temporary, just-in-time workers have for employers? For existing full-time employees? For the temporary workers?
3. On balance, on the basis of this case, do you believe the challenges facing the management of human resources will be easier or more difficult in the near future? Why?

---

# Organizational Behavior Case: *How Is This Stuff Going to Help Me?*

Jane Arnold wants to be a manager. She enjoyed her accounting, finance, and marketing courses. Each of these provided her with some clear-cut answers. Now the professor in her organizational behavior course is telling her that there are really very few clear-cut answers when it comes to managing people. The professor has discussed some of the emerging challenges and the historical background and ways that behavioral science concepts play a big role in the course. Jane is very perplexed. She came to school to get answers on how to be an effective manager, but this course surely doesn't seem to be heading in that direction.

1. How would you relieve Jane's anxiety? How is a course in organizational behavior going to make her a better manager? What implications does an evidence-based approach have?
2. Why did the professor start off with a brief overview of emerging challenges?
3. How does a course in organizational behavior differ from courses in fields such as accounting, finance, or marketing?

---

# Organizational Behavior Case: *Too Nice to People*

John has just graduated from the College of Business Administration at State University and has joined his family's small business, which employs 25 semiskilled workers. During the first week on the job, his grandfather called him in and said: "John, I've had a chance to observe you working with our employees for the past two months and, although I hate to, I feel I must say something. You are just too nice to people. I know they taught you that human behavior stuff at the university, but it just doesn't work here. I remember when we discussed the Hawthorne studies when I was in school and everybody at the university seemed excited about them, but believe me, there is more to managing people than just being nice to them."

1. How would you react to your grandfather's comments if you were John?
2. Do you think John's grandfather understood and interpreted the Hawthorne studies correctly?
3. What phases of management do you think John's grandfather has gone through in this family business?

Do you think he understands the significance of recent trends in the environment and how the new paradigm will affect his business?

4. How would you explain to your grandfather the new perspective that is needed and how the study of an evidence-based approach to organizational behavior will help the business be successful in the new paradigm?

---

# Organizational Behavior Case: *Conceptual Model: Dream or Reality?*

Hank James has been section head for the accounting group at Yake Company for 14 years. His boss, Mary Stein, feels that Hank is about ready to be moved up to the corporate finance staff, but it is company policy to send people like Hank to the University Executive Development Program before such a promotion is made. Hank has enrolled in the program; one of the first parts deals with organizational behavior. Hank felt that after 14 years of managing people, this would be a snap. However, during the discussion on organizational behavior, the professor made some comments that really bothered Hank. The professor said:

Most managers know their functional specialty but do a lousy job of managing their people. One of the problems is that just because managers have a lot of experience with people, they think they are experts. The fact is that behavioral scientists are just beginning to understand human behavior. In addition, to effectively manage people, we also have to somehow be able to better predict and control organizational behavior. Some models are now developed and research is accumulating that we hope will help the manager better understand, predict, and manage organizational behavior.

Hank is upset by the fact that his professor apparently discounts the value of experience in managing people, and he cannot see how a conceptual framework that some professor dreamed up and some esoteric research can help him manage people better.

1. Do you think Hank is justified in his concerns after hearing the professor? What role can experience play in managing people?
2. What is the purpose of conceptual frameworks such as those presented in this chapter? How would you weigh the relative value of studying theories and research findings versus "school-of-hard-knocks" experience for the effective management of people?
3. Using the conceptual framework presented in the chapter, how would you explain to Hank that this could help him better manage people in his organization?

# Environmental Context: Globalization, Diversity, and Ethics

**Learning Objectives**

- **Discuss** the impact of globalization as an environmental context for organizational behavior.
- **Identify** what is meant by diversity and how it has become an important dynamic in the field of management and organizational behavior.
- **Examine** diversity in today's organizations and the individual and organizational approaches to effectively manage diversity.
- **Discuss** the meaning of ethics and the major factors of ethical behavior.
- **Describe** major areas of ethical concern, including "bottom-line" impact and some of the steps that can be taken to effectively address the major ethical concerns.

Today's environmental context for organizational behavior is markedly different from that of the past. As pointed out in the opening chapter, globalization, diversity, and ethics have forced management of all types of organizations to totally rethink their approach to both operations and human resources. Because of the paradigm shift, organizations are now more responsive to both their external and internal environments. This chapter examines globalization, diversity, and ethics as the environmental context for today's organizational behavior.

## GLOBALIZATION

Most scholars and practicing managers would agree that a, if not the, major environmental context impacting organizational behavior is globalization. The advances made in information technology and in air travel have truly made the world a smaller place. This has led to a borderless "flat" world described by Thomas Friedman.[1] The best-selling author and widely recognized commentator feels we have now entered the third phase of globalization. The first, from about 1492–1800, was characterized by countries globalizing. The second (1800–2000) was companies globalizing. And the third, since the turn of the new century, mainly fueled by information technology available to everyone in the world, groups and individuals. As Friedman declares, "In Globalization 1.0 there was a ticket agent. In Globalization 2.0 the e-ticket replaced the ticket agent. In Globalization 3.0 *you* are your own ticket agent."[2]

The implications of this globalization for organizational behavior are profound and direct.[3] As the head of Brunswick Corporation declared, "Financial resources are not the problem. We have the money, products, and position to be a dominant global player. What we lack are the human resources. We just don't have enough people with needed global leadership capabilities."[4] GE's Jack Welch, arguably the best-known corporate leader in modern times, stated before leaving GE: "The Jack Welch of the future cannot be like me. I spent my entire career in the United States. The next head of General Electric will be somebody who spent time in Bombay, in Hong Kong, in Buenos Aires. We have to send our best and brightest overseas and make sure they have the training that will allow them to be the global leaders who will make GE flourish in the future."[5] The accompanying OB in Action: Managing the Global Workforce indicates that the new globalization context has changed the way global, transnational leaders strategize, organize, and manage.

Although there is a trend toward similar clothes, entertainment, and material possessions, and even general recognition that English is the international business language, there are still important differences in the ways in which people think and behave around the world.[6] In other words, cultures around the world impact the organizational behavior of managers and employees quite differently. For example, a recent study found that cultural differences (by country, race/ethnicity, and religion) affected the attitudes and behaviors of managers toward profit and other related business concerns.[7]

In understanding and applying organizational behavior concepts in other countries around the world, one must be aware of the similarities and differences. For example, a research study conducted by Welsh, Luthans, and Sommer found that U.S.-based extrinsic rewards and behavioral management approaches significantly improved the productivity of workers in a Russian factory, but a participative technique did not.[8] A follow-up critique concluded:

> What this study shows is that there are both potential benefits and problems associated with transporting U.S.-based human resource management theories and techniques to other cultures. On the one hand, the findings confirmed that the use of valued extrinsic rewards and improved behavioral management techniques may have a considerable impact on productivity among Russian workers in ways that are similar to American workers. On the other hand, participation had a counterproductive effect on Russian workers' performance.[9]

Another example would be that in some countries managers prefer to use—and may be more effective with—an autocratic leadership style rather than the typical U.S. manager's leadership style. Germany is a visible example. Typical U.S. managers who are transferred to Germany may find their leadership style to be too participative. German subordinates may expect them to make more decisions and to consult with them less. Research on obedience to authority found that a higher percentage of Germans were obedient than were their U.S. counterparts.[10] Similarly, a U.S. manager in Japan who decides to set up a performance-based incentive system that gives a weekly bonus to the best worker in each work group may be making a mistake. Japanese workers do not like to be singled out for individual attention and go against the group's norms and values. Perhaps this impact of similarities and differences across cultures was best stated by the cofounder of Honda Motor, T. Fujisawa, when he stated: "Japanese and American management is 95 percent the same, and differs in all important aspects."[11]

The global context is now an accepted reality, but its impact on the study and application of organizational behavior will increase into the future. The problem is that the

The war for talent never ends. Middle managers in China? Good luck finding them, let alone keeping them. Assembly line workers in Central Europe? They're well-educated and hardworking: Trouble is, every company wants them. The cubicle warriors of Bangalore? They get the job done—if they stick around. For corporations, managing this widely scattered, talented, restive, multicultural workforce has never been harder. This Special Report, written to coincide with the 2008 World Economic Forum in Davos, Switzerland, brings readers to the front lines of the struggle. It delves into IBM's effort to reinvent the way it gets tasks done around the world, follows a Nokia manager as he recruits a workforce from scratch in Transylvania, meets a restless generation of IT workers in India, and hears from the corporate road warriors who never, ever stop traveling.

These and other stories make a simple but powerful point: The old way of managing across borders is fading fast. In the first half of the twentieth century, the globalization of business was based on the British colonial model. Headquarters, functions, and capital were in one place, with managers dispatched to run regional operations like colonies. In the second half of the 1900s, companies adopted the multinational model, replicating their home country operations in other places where they did business. Country units rarely dealt with other divisions in other markets.

Today, global corporations are transforming themselves into "transnationals," moving work to the places with the talent to handle the job and the time to do it at the right cost. The threat of a U.S. recession only makes such efforts at lowering expenses and grabbing the best talent even more urgent. William J. Amelio, the CEO of Lenovo, the world's third-largest computer maker, calls his global workforce strategy "worldsourcing." Lenovo has executive offices in five cities worldwide and organizes its workforce around hubs of expertise, such as hardware designers in Japan and marketers in India. "You operate as if there's just one time zone," Amelio says. "And you're always on."

If anything, companies are devising new strategies to reach global scale faster. To retain workers in China, for example, PepsiCo's snacks unit funneled nearly 300 extra people into its talent assessment program last year and promoted three times as many managers as it did in 2006. In mid-2007 storage equipment maker EMC started a global innovation network for research and development workers at six labs around the globe. EMC set up a wiki Web site for scientists and engineers to develop technologies and product concepts together.

Moving people across borders and ensuring that workers' visas and permits are compliant with local immigration rules are also vital to the tasks of globalization. Deloitte principal Robin I. Lissak has a client, a CEO of a large multinational, who was told he could quintuple his business in Dubai if he quickly moved 2,000 workers there from India. But like half of the companies in Deloitte's 2007 Global Mobility Survey, the CEO simply wasn't set up to do it. "You're not just moving people from the U.S. to the rest of the world anymore," says Lissak. "You're sending people from all continents to all continents." The companies that play this global, mobile game best will emerge the winners.

increasingly frequent intercultural encounters cannot be solved by just simple guidelines (e.g., when dealing with Spaniards, be aware that they tend to be late, or when the Japanese say "yes" they may mean "no"). Nardon and Steers recently summarized some of the reasons for the complexity of cross-cultural management:

1. People are influenced by multiple cultures—national, regional, organizational, functional, and professional.
2. Even though people are from the same country, they still have different beliefs, values, and behaviors.
3. Counterparts from other cultures are becoming savvy in how to deal with foreigners and thus may not be typical of their own culture.
4. Because of the complexity of culture, simplistic categorizations may initially be helpful, but turn out to be poor predictors of behavior.[12]

Because of this complexity and the fact that managers today often deal with several cultures at a time in their current role, they must have ready access to cross-cultural training tools,[13] but more importantly, develop learning skills that will on-the-spot compensate for cultural knowledge gaps.[14] In other words, today's organizational leaders must develop and use a "global mindset."

Although there are many meanings, a conference dedicated to global mindset derived the following comprehensive definition: "a set of individual attributes that enable an individual to influence individuals, groups, and organizations from diverse social/cultural/institutional systems."[15] Those with such a global mindset are able to view and evaluate a cultural event or interaction through a broad array of potential categories and quickly recognize nuances (e.g., nonverbals) that differentiate cultural groups. An example would be an encounter with a smiling business person from Thailand:

> To an outsider, such Thai smiles are not readily transparent. However, an outsider with a global mindset would have the wherewithal to develop strategies to such nuances, demonstrating a keen awareness and understanding of cultural differences, and know how to act accordingly. Once encoded into the individual's global mindset, this information could be readily accessed when dealing with different cultural groups in which nonverbal expressions carry greater weight when interpreting how people are thinking, feeling, and ultimately behaving. [16]

Such global mindset development is needed for effectively dealing with the complex cultural context facing the study and application of organizational behavior.

# DIVERSITY IN THE WORKPLACE

Similar to globalization, diversity and social issues have had a dramatic effect on the study and application of management and organizational behavior. In the past, diversity was treated primarily as a legal issue; that is, for well over 45 years it has been directly against the law to discriminate against anyone, on any basis. Now organizations are beginning to realize that diversity is not just something to deal with, but instead a reality to build on to make a stronger, more competitive enterprise. As noted in a recent report on needed strategic initiatives to succeed in the new global economy, "Diversity must be recognized and nurtured as the organization's greatest asset, and the ability to attract and work with diverse talent must be seen as a critical competitive advantage."[17] In other words, the contemporary environmental context of diversity is no longer simply a "tack on" or afterthought in the study of organizational behavior; it plays a central role in today's environmental context.

Although surveys indicate that a vast majority of organizations believe that workplace diversity is important and virtually all value diversity management skills and strategies to achieve diversity initiatives, they still are not sure of the meaning or domain of diversity.[18] The trend, however, is clear: "Diversity means much more than ethnicity, gender, or sexual orientation. New and evolving diverse populations include a full range of ages, as well as career and geographic experiences."[19] As the head of the huge Society of Human Resource Management (SHRM) diversity initiatives recently noted, "Organizational diversity initiatives should not simply focus on getting people of color and women in the door, but embracing an inclusive culture to maintain these employees."[20] SHRM has identified outcomes such as the following for effective diversity management:

1. Creating a work environment or culture that allows everyone to contribute all that they can to the organization.
2. Leveraging differences and similarities in the workforce for the strategic advantage of the organization; and
3. Enhancing the ability of people from different backgrounds to work effectively together.[21]

**FIGURE 2.1**
**Major Reasons for
Increasing Diversity.**

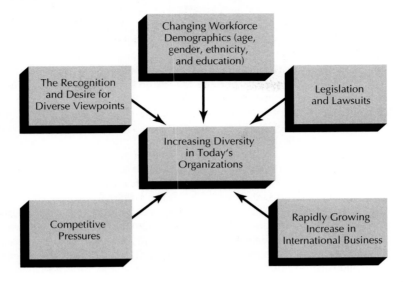

## Reasons for the Emergence of Diversity

As shown in Figure 2.1, a major reason for the emergence of diversity as an important reality is changing demographics. Older workers, women, minorities, and those with more education are now entering the workforce. The composition of today's and tomorrow's workforce is and will be much different from that of the past. For example, *USA Today* calculates a Diversity Index (based on population racial and ethnic probabilities) that shows now about 1 out of 2 people randomly selected in the United States are racially or ethnically different, up from 1 out of 3 in 1980. In addition, the U.S. Department of Labor estimates that the majority of new workers entering the workforce will be women or minorities. At the more micro level, assuming talent and ability are equally distributed throughout the population and that everyone has an equal opportunity, there should be diversity in every level of an organization. Unfortunately, such an assumption is not yet valid because diversity has not to date noticeably reached the top levels of most organizations. There is still only a handful of women who have broken through the "glass ceiling" of large corporations to become CEO, and only a small minority of *Fortune* 500 board directors or corporate officers are women.[22] In addition, the U.S. Bureau of Labor Statistics indicates that women on average continue to trail men in terms of pay for the same types of jobs.[23] However, prospects for the future may be better because women now make up more than half of all college students, about half of all medical and law students, account for over a third of MBA (Master of Business Administration) degree-holders, and now make up about half of middle managers.[24] Also, outside of business organizations, about a quarter of university presidents are women (including currently half of the Ivy League schools) and they are well-represented in senior management levels in health care and NGOs (nongovernmental organizations such as the United Way).[25]

As shown in the accompanying OB in Action: Cracks in a Particularly Thick Glass Ceiling, the glass ceiling may be worse in other countries, especially in Asia. Yet, U.S. women executives also are facing a particularly thick glass ceiling when it comes to receiving desirable foreign assignments and experience.[26] In the global economy, not being able to obtain such international experience may be a major obstacle (i.e., contribute to the glass ceiling) in reaching upper management.

South Koreans are a bit conflicted about career women. Gender wasn't much of an issue in the selection of a female astronaut to fly on the country's first space mission. But when women are seeking workaday corporate jobs, some South Korean men still resist change. Outer space is one thing, but a woman in the next cubicle is something else.

For years, most educated women in South Korea who wanted to work could follow but one career path, which began and ended with teaching. The situation started to change after the 1998 Asian financial crisis. Thousands of men lost their jobs or took salary cuts, and their wives had to pick up the slack by starting businesses in their homes or seeking part-time work. A couple of years later, the government banned gender discrimination in the workplace and required businesses with more than 500 employees to set up child care facilities. It also created a Gender Equality Ministry.

These days the government hires thousands of women (42 percent of its new employees last year), many for senior positions in the judiciary, international trade administration, and foreign service. Startups and foreign companies also employ (and promote) increasing numbers of Korean women.

## ONE OF THE GUYS

But at the top 400 companies, many of which are family-run conglomerates, it's hard for women to reach the upper ranks. *In all, about 8 percent of working women hold managerial positions. In the United States nearly 51 percent do.* "We have a long way to go," says Cho Jin Woo, director of the Gender Equality Ministry.

South Koreans are grappling with traditional attitudes about women, a hierarchical business culture, and the need to open up the workplace to compete globally. A senior manager at SK Holdings, which controls the giant mobile phone carrier SK Telecom, says he avoids hiring women because he believes they lack tenacity. When deadlines are tight, he says, "you need people prepared to put in long hours at the office." Park Myung Soon, a 39-year-old woman who is in charge of business development at the carrier, says, "Many men are preoccupied with the notion that women are a different species." To get ahead, Park says she had to achieve 120 percent of what her male colleagues did—as well as play basketball and drink with them after work. "Luckily, I like sports, and I like to drink," she says.

When Choi Dong Hee joined SK's research arm in 2005, she was the only woman there and had no major assignment until she created one. After conducting a year-long study, Choi, 30, proposed changing the company's policy to allow subscribers to use any wireless portal. Her managers ignored her. She persisted. Finally, they agreed to let her brief the division head, who agreed to let her make her case to the company chairman. Choi worked on the presentation for three weeks straight, sometimes alone in the office overnight (to her boss's horror). In the end, the company did adopt the open policy she advocated. Now her managers are quick to say that women's perspectives can help SK better serve its customers.

Sonia Kim, who is in charge of TV marketing at Samsung Electronics, says her male colleagues rarely argue with the boss, even if they think he's wrong. Kim, though, persuaded her manager to let her develop a promotional campaign rather than rely on an ad agency she thought had lost its creative edge. Kim also says some of the men used to overturn decisions made during the day while out drinking after hours. Since she and other women at Samsung complained, Kim says, the practice has mostly stopped.

Although challenges facing women in the workplace receive relatively more attention in the media, the problems facing people of color, an aging workforce, and others fighting for equal opportunities and inclusion remain significant. As indicated, legislation going as far back as the Civil Rights Act of 1964 prohibited discrimination in employment on any basis. The full effects of that landmark law and other more recent legislation, such as the following, are still being determined.

1. *Age Discrimination Act of 1978.* This law at first increased the mandatory retirement age from 65 to 70 and then was later amended to eliminate an upper age limit altogether.

2. *Pregnancy Discrimination Act of 1978.* This law gives full equal opportunity protection to pregnant employees.

3. *Americans with Disabilities Act of 1990.* This law prohibits discrimination against those essentially qualified individuals challenged by a disability and requires organizations to reasonably accommodate them.

4. *Civil Rights Act of 1991.* This law refined the 1964 act and the reinstated burden of proof falls on employers to eliminate discrimination and ensure equal opportunity in employment to employees. It also allows punitive and compensatory damages through jury trials.

5. *Family and Medical Leave Act of 1993.* This law allows employees to take up to 12 weeks of unpaid leave for family or medical reasons each year.

These laws, along with lawsuits and the threat of lawsuits, have put teeth into diversity. Individuals and groups that have found themselves excluded from organizations or managerial positions can bring and have brought lawsuits in an effort to overcome discriminatory barriers and ensure themselves equal opportunity in employment. For example, successful lawsuits with resulting multimillion dollar penalties have in recent years been brought against many well-known firms.

Still another reason for the emergence of the importance of diversity to organizations is the realization that diversity can help them meet the competitive pressures they currently face. Firms that aggressively try to hire and promote women and minorities are going to end up with a more talented and capable workforce than those that do not take such a proactive, affirmative action approach. For example, a large study by the American Management Association found that the more accurately the senior team of a company represents the demographics of its market, the more likely it is that the company will design products, market services, and create ad campaigns that score a hit.[27] Moreover, companies that gain a reputation for "celebrating diversity" are more likely to attract the best employees regardless of age, gender, or ethnicity. The most talented and qualified people will feel that opportunities are better with these firms than with others. In other words, diversity can provide an organization with competitive advantage.[28] For example, one study examined the relationships among racial diversity, business strategy, and firm performance in the banking industry.[29] It was found that racial diversity interacted with business strategy in determining company performance as measured in three different ways: productivity, return on equity, and market performance. This study concluded that the results demonstrated that diversity not only adds value but, in the proper context, also contributes to a firm's competitive advantage. Such research findings are not limited to U.S. firms. For example, a recent study found that the percentage of women on the boards of Spanish firms was positively related to their value.[30]

Stimulated by competitive pressures, organizations now recognize and strive to obtain diverse viewpoints in their decision-making processes and teams. Recent academic research points out the complex linkage between work group diversity and work group functioning,[31] but there is also growing practical evidence that diversity leads to innovation and often breakthrough competitive advantages. For example, women working for Reebok pointed out that there was no good shoe available for aerobics. The firm took this advice and began marketing aerobic shoes, which became very profitable and served as a breakthrough for Reebok in the very competitive athletic shoe industry. Another example occurred at the giant chemical firm DuPont, which used input from African American employees to develop and successfully market agricultural products for small farmers in the South.

A final major reason for the emerging challenge of diversity is that more and more organizations are entering the international arena. A natural by-product of going international is increased diversity, in this case cultural diversity. If domestic organizations have and promote diversity, then, as they expand globally, they will be accustomed to working with people who have different cultures, customs, social norms, and mores. For example, a multicultural team at DuPont is given credit for gaining the firm about $45 million in new business worldwide. Among other things, this diverse team recommended an array of new colors for countertops that was very appealing to overseas customers.

The international arena is not a threatening place for diverse firms, a fact that is particularly important because of the major role that international operations and sales will play in the growth, and even survival, of companies in the global economy. The percentage of overall revenues from international operations and sales continues to increase dramatically. The advantage of multinational companies that have and value cultural diversity becomes abundantly clear in this global environment discussed in the previous section.

## Developing the Multicultural Organization

The foundation and point of departure for creating and effectively managing diversity is the development of a truly multicultural organization.[32] A multicultural organization has been described as one that:

1. Reflects the contributions and interests of diverse cultural and social groups in its mission, operations, and product or service
2. Acts on a commitment to eradicate social oppression in all forms within the organization
3. Includes the members of diverse cultural and social groups as full participants, especially in decisions that shape the organization
4. Follows through on broader external social responsibilities, including support of other institutional efforts to eliminate all forms of social oppression[33]

Several stages have been identified in leading up to such a multicultural organization:[34]

1. *Exclusionary organization.* This type of organization is the furthest from a multicultural organization. It is devoted to maintaining the dominance of one group over all others on factors such as age, education, gender, or race. This organization is characterized by exclusionary hiring practices and other forms of discrimination. Even though such organizations are directly violating laws, they unfortunately still exist.

2. *Club organization.* This organization is characterized by the maintenance of privileges by those who traditionally have held power. These organizations may technically get around the laws by hiring and promoting women and minorities, but only those who are deemed to have the "right" credentials and perspectives. For example, a recent analysis noted that such organizations do not practice "overt discrimination of forty years ago but, rather, subtler forms that can arise from seemingly rational behavior and can operate at an institutional level" and end up hiring "people just like us."[35]

3. *Compliance organization.* This type of organization is committed to removing some of the discriminatory practices that are inherent in the exclusionary and club organizations. For example, women and minorities are hired and promoted to give the impression of openness and fair play. However, the strategy is more of meeting the letter of the laws, not the spirit. For example, only tokenism is carried out; the basic exclusionary or club culture of the organization remains entrenched. For instance, a research study found de facto segregation in a bank.[36] White and African American employees were assigned to supervisors of the same race in numbers that could not be attributed to mere statistical chance. Although the bank may not have done this deliberately, the fact remains that there was simply compliance going on, not the development of a true multicultural organization.

4. *Redefining organization.* This advanced stage organization is characterized by an examination of all activities for the purpose of evaluating their impact on all employees' opportunity to both participate in and contribute to their own and the firm's growth and success. Redefining the organization goes beyond being just proactively antiracist and antisexist. This approach questions the core cultural values of the organization as manifested in the mission, structure, technology, psychosocial dynamics, and products and

services. The redefining organization not only deals with but recognizes the value of a diverse workforce; it engages in visionary planning and problem solving to tap the strength of the diversity. This approach involves both developing and implementing policies and practices that distribute power among all diverse groups in the organization.

5. *Multicultural organization.* The true multicultural organization is characterized by core cultural values and an ongoing commitment to eliminate social oppression and promote dignity and respect for everyone throughout the organization. All members of diverse cultural and social groups are involved in the decisions that shape the mission, structure, technology, psychosocial dynamics, and products and services of the organization.

The true multicultural organization as defined is the stated ideal of an increasing number of organizations, although most are still in transition to this fifth stage. If carefully studied and objectively analyzed, most of today's organizations would still be best described by one of the other preceding forms discussed. A high-profile exception would be a generally recognized multicultural firm such as Microsoft. It has a Diversity Department and Diversity Advisory Council that is charged with upholding the vision of "maximizing the company's performance through understanding and valuing differences." As the Microsoft Diversity Director declared:

> We need to stress that all human cultures have common needs, a common sense of humanity. But there are differences, too. How in the world do you please a customer, for example, if you don't know what he or she values? That's what culture is all about, that's what differences are all about. Diversity assumes not only that people are different—we know that—but that their difference is value-added. If you know how to harness that difference, you'll be more competitive as a corporation than those firms that don't, whether in the domestic marketplace, and certainly in the global marketplace.[37]

Moving toward and building a truly multicultural organization, as Microsoft has done, is perhaps the most important, but there are also some individual- and organization-level steps and techniques that can be used to effectively manage diversity. Unfortunately, to date, most of these diversity programs have fallen short of their objectives. For example, one study by the New York–based research organization Catalyst asked African American women if diversity programs were effective in addressing subtle racism. A large majority (64 percent) said that they were not, and only 12 percent said that they had benefited from these programs to a great or very great extent.[38] The following sections provide some individual and organizational approaches that may help make managing diversity more effective.

## Individual Approaches to Managing Diversity

Individual approaches to managing diversity typically take two interdependent paths: learning and empathy. The first is based on acquiring real or simulated experience; the second is based on the ability to understand feelings and emotions.

### *Learning*

Many managers are often unprepared to deal with diversity; because of their inexperience they are unsure of how to respond. Even those who think they are knowledgeable may actually need, but not seek, diversity training. For example, one recent study revealed an interesting counterintuitive finding. Those with low competence in the diversity domain were unaware of their deficiency and therefore were not motivated to participate in diversity training, while those who were relatively competent expressed more interest in additional diversity training and the opportunity to attend a voluntary session.[39] In other words, those who may not think they need to learn about diversity must work especially hard to learn and experience as much as they can about developing appropriate behavior.

At the heart of this learning process is communication. Managers must openly communicate one-on-one, regardless of age, gender, ethnicity, sexual preference, religion, or those challenged with a disability, in order to determine how best to understand and interact with them. In this way managers can learn more about a diverse group's personal values and how the individuals like to be treated.

Managers can also begin to develop a personal style that works well with each member of a diverse group. For example, to their amazement, many managers have learned that people who are challenged with a disability do not want special treatment. They want to be treated like everyone else, asking only for equal opportunities in employment. Many managers are unaware of their biased treatment of these employees. For example, after a review of the research literature in this area, the following conclusion was drawn:

> It should be noted that several of these studies have found that the physically challenged workers were more intelligent, motivated, better qualified, and had higher educational levels than their nonphysically challenged counterparts. While these findings may help account for the superior performance of those physically challenged, they may also reflect hidden biases whereby a physically challenged person must be overqualified for a specific job. In addition, they may reflect hesitancy to promote physically challenged individuals: the physically challenged may stay in entry-level jobs whereas similarly qualified nonphysically challenged individuals would be rapidly promoted.[40]

In this learning process, managers can also encourage diverse employees to give them candid feedback regarding how they are being treated. In this way, when the manager does something that an employee does not feel is proper, the manager quickly learns this and can adjust his or her behavior. This form of feedback is particularly important in helping organizations gain insights to effectively manage diversity.

### Empathy

Closely linked to the individual learning strategy is empathy, the ability to put oneself in another's place and see things from that person's point of view. Empathy is particularly important in managing diversity because members of diverse groups often feel that only they can truly understand the challenges or problems they are facing. For example, many women are discriminated against or harassed at work because of their gender, and, despite surface efforts to discourage these problems, discrimination and a negative climate for women have become institutionalized through male-dominated management. Discrimination and harassment may become the way things are done. A recent meta-analysis of 62 studies of gender differences in harassment perceptions found that women perceive a broader range of social-sexual behaviors as harassing. In particular, women were most different from men on perceptions involving a hostile work environment, derogatory attitudes toward women, dating pressure, or physical sexual contact, but women and men were closer on their perceptions of sexual propositions or sexual coercion.[41] These problems have sometimes resulted in sex bias or sexual harassment suits against organizations, and in recent years, the courts have favorably ruled on these charges.[42]

Empathy is an important way to deal with more subtle problems because it helps the manager understand the diverse employee's point of view. For example, many women in business offices say that they are willing to get coffee for their male counterparts or bosses if they are on their way to the coffee room, but, importantly, they feel that they should be given similar treatment and have coffee brought to them on the same basis. Similarly, many managers try very hard to promote minorities into management positions and to give them work-related experiences that can help their careers. At the same time, however, these managers need to empathize with the fact that some minority members may be ambivalent or have mixed emotions about being promoted. They may like advancement in terms of pay and prestige, but at the same time they may be concerned about receiving special treatment, failing, or not living up to everyone's expectations. By learning how to empathize with these feelings and by offering encouragement, guidance, and after-the-fact backup support, the manager can play an important individual role in more effectively managing diversity.

## Organizational Approaches to Managing Diversity

Organizational approaches to managing diversity include a variety of techniques. Some of the most common involve testing, training, mentoring, and programs designed to help personnel effectively balance their work and family lives. The following sections examine each of these techniques.

### *Testing*

A problem that organizations have encountered with the use of tests for selection and evaluation is that they may be culturally biased. As a result, women and minorities may be able to do the job for which they are being tested even though their test scores indicate that they should be rejected as candidates. Most tests traditionally used in selection and evaluation are not suited or valid for a diverse workforce. As a result, in recent years a great deal of attention has been focused on developing tests that are indeed valid for selecting and evaluating diverse employees.[43]

One way to make tests more valid for diverse employees is to use job-specfic tests rather than general aptitude or knowledge tests. For example, a company hiring word processing personnel may give applicants a timed test designed to measure their speed and accuracy. The applicant's age, gender, and ethnic background are not screening criteria. This approach differs sharply from using traditional tests that commonly measure general knowledge or intelligence (as defined by the test). People from different cultures (foreign or domestic) often did poorly on the traditional tests because they were culturally biased toward individuals who had been raised in a white, middle-class neighborhood. Older applicants may also do poorly on such culturally biased tests. Job-specific tests help prevent diversity bias by focusing on the work to be done.

Besides being culturally unbiased, tests used in effectively managing diversity should be able to identify whether the applicant has the necessary skills for doing the job. The word processing example above is a good illustration because it measures the specific skills, not the subjective personal characteristics, required for the work. In some cases carefully conducted interviews or role playing can be used because this is the only effective way of identifying whether the person has the necessary skills. For example, a person applying for a customer service job would need to understand the relevant language of customers and be able to communicate well. The customer service job would also require someone who listens carefully, maintains his or her composure, and is able to solve problems quickly and efficiently. Carefully constructed and conducted interviews could be useful in helping identify whether the applicant speaks well, can communicate ideas, and has the necessary personal style for dealing effectively with customers. Role-playing exercises could be useful in helping identify the applicant's ability to focus on problems and solve them to the satisfaction of the customer. Also, the applicant could be given a case or exercise in a group setting to assess interpersonal skills. The point is that multiple measures and multiple trained raters would yield the most valid assessment of needed complex skills.

If pencil-and-paper or online tests are used, then to help ensure that they are not biased, scientific norming could be used. This is a process that ensures the tests are equivalent across cultures. As a result, all test questions have the same meaning regardless of the person's cultural background.

### Training

Surveys indicate that the majority of U.S. companies have diversity training and have moved into the mainstream from the traditional role of merely equal employment opportunity compliant.[44] A comprehensive research study found those firms that adopted diversity training tended to have the following profile: (1) large size, (2) positive top-management beliefs about diversity, (3) high strategic priority of diversity relative to other competing objectives, (4) presence of a diversity manager, and (5) existence of a large number of other diversity supportive policies.[45] There are two ways in which this training can play a key role in managing diversity. One way is by offering training to diverse groups. Members from a diverse group can be trained for an entry-level skill or how to more effectively do their existing or future job. The other approach is to provide training to managers and other employees who work with diverse employees. In recent years a number of approaches have been used in providing such diversity training.

Most diversity training programs get the participants directly involved. An example is provided by Florida International University's Center for Management Development (CMD). This center provides diversity training for employers in South Florida, a geographic area where Latinos and African Americans constitute a significant percentage of the population. One of CMD's programs involves putting trainees into groups based on ethnic origin. Then each group is asked to describe the others and to listen to the way its own group is described. The purpose of this exercise is to gain insights into the way one ethnic group is perceived by another ethnic group. Each group is also asked to describe the difficulties it has in working with other ethnic groups and to identify the reasons for these problems. At the end of the training, both managers and employees relate that they have a better understanding of their personal biases and the ways in which they can improve their interaction with members of the other groups.

Sometimes training games are used to help participants focus on cultural issues such as how to interact with personnel from other cultures. Here is an example:

> In Hispanic families, which one of the following values is probably most important?
> a.  Achievement
> b.  Money
> c.  Being on time
> d.  Respect for elders

The correct answer is "d." As participants play the game, they gain an understanding of the values and beliefs of other cultures and learn how better to interact with a diverse workforce.

In many cases these diversity-related games are used as supplements to other forms of training. For example, they are often employed as icebreakers to get diversity training sessions started or to maintain participant interest during a long program. Research has found that the major key to the success of diversity training is top-management support for diversity; also important are mandatory attendance for all managers, long-term evaluation of training results, managerial rewards for increasing diversity, and a broadly inclusionary definition of diversity in the organization.[46] However, it must be remembered that awareness training is valuable to shift perceptions, but may not lead to behavioral change.[47] Allstate and other firms learned that the training must be linked to business outcomes in order to produce actual behavioral change.[48]

A major problem of training in general, and diversity training in particular, is the transfer problem. Those going through the diversity training may see the value and gain some relevant knowledge, but then do not transfer this training back to the job. A major reason for this transfer problem is a lack of confidence or self-efficacy (i.e., the trainees do not believe that they can successfully carry out the diversity training objectives back on the job in their specific environment). A recent field experiment by Combs and Luthans was designed to increase trainees' diversity self-efficacy. The results were that the training intervention significantly increased the trainees' (N = 276 in 3 organizations) measured diversity self-efficacy. More importantly, there was a strong positive relationship between the trained participants diversity self-efficacy and the number and difficulty of their stated intentions for initiating diversity goals in their specific environments of insurance and manufacturing firms and a government agency.[49] Chapter 7 will get into the self-efficacy psychological state in detail, but it is these types of organizational behavior concepts that are needed to improve important application areas such as diversity training.

## *Mentoring*

A *mentor* is a trusted counselor, coach, or advisor who provides advice and assistance. In recent years, many organizations have begun assigning mentors to women and minorities. The purpose of the mentor program is to help support members of a diverse group in their jobs, socialize them in the cultural values of the organization, and pragmatically help their chances for development and advancement. There are a number of specific benefits that mentors can provide to those they assist, including the following:

1. Identify the skills, interests, and aspirations the person has
2. Provide instruction in specific skills and knowledge critical to successful job performance
3. Help in understanding the unwritten rules of the organization and how to avoid saying or doing the wrong things
4. Answer questions and provide important insights
5. Offer emotional support
6. Serve as a role model
7. Create an environment in which mistakes can be made without losing self-confidence[50]

A number of organizations now require their managers to serve as mentors, but besides the above types of benefits, there may also be a downside. One problem is that mentors may become overly protective and encase those they mentor into a "glass bubble" by shunting them into jobs with adequate pay and professional challenges, but eliminate all chance of further advancement.[51]

Some guidelines for establishing an effective mentoring program typically involves several steps. First, top-management support is secured for the program. Then mentors and their protégés are carefully chosen. The mentor, who provides the advice and guidance, is paired with an individual who is very likely to profit from the experience. Research on the networking strategies of minorities has implications for this step. It seems that highly successful, fast-track minorities are well connected to both minority and white informal circles, whereas their unsuccessful counterparts have very few, if any, network ties with other minorities.[52] In other words, this study would indicate that the effective mentor would be one who would be able to get the protégé involved in both the majority and the minority inner circles. Sometimes the advice has been to avoid association with other minorities, but this research would indicate the contrary.

The third step in an effective mentoring program would be to give both mentors and protégés an orientation. The mentors are taught how to conduct themselves, and the protégés are given guidance on the types of questions and issues that they should raise with their mentor so that they can gain the greatest value from the experience. Fourth, throughout the mentoring period, which typically lasts one year or less, mentor and protégé individually and together meet with the support staff of the program to see how well things are going. Fifth, and finally, at the end of the mentoring cycle, overall impressions and recommendations are solicited from both mentors and protégés regarding how the process can be improved in the future. This information is then used in helping the next round of mentors do a more effective job.

### *Work/Family Programs*

In the typical family today, both the mother and the father have jobs and work-family issues have recently received considerable attention in research and practice. Initially the needs of the dual-career family were met through alternative work schedules, which allow the parents flexibility in balancing their home and work demands. The most common alternative work schedule arrangements are flextime, the compressed workweek, job sharing, and telecommuting, but there are also some newer programs that help balance work and family.

Flextime allows employees greater autonomy by permitting them to choose their daily starting and ending times within a given time period called a bandwidth, as shown in Figure 2.2. For example, consider the case of two parents who are both employed at a company that has a bandwidth of 7 A.M. to 7 P.M. Everyone working for the firm must put in his or her eight hours during this time period. For example, the father may go to work at 7 A.M. and work until 3 P.M., at which time he leaves and picks up the children from school. The mother, meanwhile, drops the children at school at 8:45 A.M. and works from 9:30 A.M. to 5:30 P.M. Thus both parents are able to adjust their work and home schedules to fit within the bandwidth. Many companies are using this concept and similar ones to help their employees meet both organizational and personal demands. Recent U.S. Bureau of Labor Statistics data indicate that over a quarter of working women with children under 18 work flexible schedules.[53] Prominent examples are that about three-fourths of the workforce of both Hewlett-Packard and IBM use flexible work arrangements.

Another alternative work arrangement is the compressed workweek. This arrangement, which has been widely used in Europe, compresses the workweek into fewer days. For example, while the typical workweek is 40 hours spread over five days, a compressed workweek could be four 10-hour days. For those working a 35-hour week, the time could be compressed into three days of approximately 12 hours each. These arrangements give employees more time with their families, although their full impact on productivity, profitability, and employee satisfaction is still to be determined.

Job sharing is the splitting of a full-time position between two people, each of whom works part-time. This arrangement is more common in professional positions in banking, insurance, and teaching. A husband and wife, or any two people, could share the job 50-50 or in any other combination. For example, parents who want to return to work on a part-time basis only have found job sharing to be an attractive employment alternative.[54] Compared to decade ago, on average, working mothers increasingly indicate that part-time work over full-time or not working at all would be ideal for them.[55]

**FIGURE 2.2**
**A Flextime**
**Framework.**

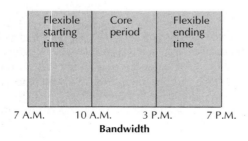

Still another alternative work schedule that is gaining in popularity is telecommuting. Currently about a third of organizations allow employees to work from home or off site on a regular basis.[56] For example, over 9,000 Hewlett-Packard employees work entirely from home. This entails receiving and sending work between home and the office and is currently being used to supplement the typical work arrangement. For instance, employees may come into the office on Monday and Tuesday, work out of their homes on Wednesday and Thursday via telecommuting, and come in again on Friday. By varying the on-site assignments of the personnel, companies are able to reduce the number of people who are in the building at any one time, thus cutting down on the amount of floor space and parking spots they need to rent. Increasingly employees have no office and work from home on a permanent basis.

Besides alternative work schedules, very innovative family-friendly programs are starting to emerge. When large numbers of women began entering the workforce a number of years ago, organizations were ill prepared for the resulting conflict that both women and men had between their work and family responsibilities. Research shows that conflict goes both ways with dysfunctional outcomes. Specifically, for both men and women, work-to-family conflict was found to be linked to job dissatisfaction, turnover intentions, and stress, while family-to-work conflict resulted in stress and absenteeism.[57] However, there is additional research evidence indicating that multiple roles provide benefits (e.g., practice at multitasking, relevant experience) for the managerial role at work and those who are committed to multiple roles (i.e., doing it all) may have higher life satisfaction, self-esteem, and self-acceptance.[58]

Today there are programs to help solve the reality of dual-career families and working parents. Table 2.1 provides a broad sampling of these work/family programs.[59] Of course,

**TABLE 2.1**
**Innovative Work/Family Programs**

| | |
|---|---|
| Child care or elder care benefits | These may include child care facilities at the work site and transportation of aging parents to a senior citizens center. |
| Adoption benefits | These include leave policies and reimbursement for legal fees, medical expenses, agency or placement fees, temporary foster care, and/or travel expenses. |
| Leave/time-off policies | These may include free time off for no reason or prior notice and paybacks for unused days off. |
| Convenience benefits | This refers to on-site services such as dry cleaning, ATM machines, postal services, and video rentals. |
| Life-cycle accounts | These are savings accounts designed to pay for specific life events, such as a college education. Often employers will match employee contributions. |
| Health promotion benefits | These include such things as fitness centers, health screenings, flu shots, and stress-management clinics. |
| Education assistance benefits | Examples include tutoring programs, tuition reimbursement, and scholarships. |
| Housing assistance | This refers to such items as relocation assistance, seminars, and preferred mortgage arrangements. |
| Group purchase programs | These include legal and financial planning assistance, discounts with local merchants, group auto and home owners insurance, and fleet arrangements for auto purchases. |
| Casual day program | This would be dress-down days to have everyone relaxed in an on-the-job family atmosphere. |

not all organizations are using these programs, but an increasing number are, and a few well-known firms such as the following have even more unique programs.[60]

1. PepsiCo has a "concierge service" (similar to hotels) that helps employees with errands or tasks that need to be done during the workday (e.g., getting an oil change, lining up a baby-sitter, or contracting for house repairs).
2. Eastman Kodak has a "humor room" where employees can read light, funny materials or engage in activities to take their minds off a stressful day.
3. Ben & Jerry's has a "Joy Gang" charged with creating happiness in the workplace. This group plans birthday and anniversary celebrations and creates other joyful events.

Research by Thomas and Ganster found work/family programs decrease family conflict, job dissatisfaction, and stress-related problems,[61] but it is difficult to empirically demonstrate the direct positive impact that these programs have on performance outcomes. However, one comprehensive research study did find a strong link between work/family programs and the use of high-commitment work systems containing employee involvement/participation and total quality initiatives.[62]

# ETHICS AND ETHICAL BEHAVIOR IN ORGANIZATIONS

Ethics involves moral issues and choices and deals with right and wrong behavior. Although ethics was given at least surface attention through the years, starting with the now infamous Enron debacle that ended in bankruptcy in 2001, soon followed by other high-profile cases such as high-ranking executives arrested and charged with "looting" their companies, public accounting firms being found guilty of obstruction, and celebrity entrepreneurs such as Martha Stewart sent to prison for illegal business practices, and then the financial crisis at the end of 2008 that revealed many questionable, if not illegal practices, ethics has taken center stage. In this post-Enron, corporate ethics meltdown era, the study of ethics becomes critical to business education in general and organizational behavior in particular.[63] As the dean of Northwestern's Kellogg School of Management declared, "We are facing new realities, and for that we need a new body of knowledge."[64]

For starters, it is now realized that not only individuals and groups but also a number of relevant factors from the cultural, organizational, and external environment determine ethical behavior. Cultural influences on ethical behavior come from family, friends, neighbors, education, religion, and the media. Organizational influences come from ethical codes, role models, policies and practices, and reward and punishment systems. The external forces having an impact on ethical behavior include political, legal, economic, and international developments. These factors often work interdependently in shaping the ethical behavior of individuals and groups in organizations. For example, minimum wage jobs may lock people into an economic existence that prevents them from bettering their lives. Is it ethical to pay people only a minimum wage? Or what about Nike initially denying charges of sweatshop labor conditions in its overseas factories, then trying to justify its low wages on the basis of different living standards? What about unsafe products or the tobacco chief executive officers denying the addictive properties of nicotine? Or consider the facts that many obese workers and those with certain types of appearance (e.g., tattoos/piercings, facial hair or manner of dress) report that they are discriminated against in the workplace.[65] Also, what about the research study that found applicants judged to be relatively less attractive were at a distinct disadvantage in decisions involving suitability for hiring and probable organizational progression?[66] Is it ethical to treat these workers differently, given that very limited legal protection is afforded to them and thus they have no recourse?

These questions help illustrate the problems and controversies in determining what ethical behavior is, and why good people sometimes do unethical things.[67] Moreover, as Rosabeth Kanter recently observed, the often cited Enron debacle resulted from a number of factors besides the unethical behavior of the leaders. She notes that there was also

> a tendency during boom years in the economy not to examine success too closely; managerial hubris—confidence turning into over-confidence when Enron turned from oil and gas leasing to other financial transactions; managers being egged on by Wall Street and the business press that wanted heroes in a growth story, which produced a tendency to hide any weakness or mistake, and assuming that one could make up for any mistakes later with growth. And at least one good theory was involved in the Enron case: innovation—which requires breaking some "rules" in the sense of departing from tradition.[68]

Besides these other factors leading to ethical problems in organizations, many people would argue that they are highly ethical in their own personal dealings. However, empirical evidence has found that such people are often viewed as unlikable by their peers in the organization.[69] Simply put, there is peer pressure on many people to be less ethical. Additionally, what one person or group finds unethical may be viewed differently by another individual or group.[70] For example, a study investigated attitudes toward unauthorized copying of software among both business executives and business faculty members. It was found that the faculty members did not view this to be as big an ethical problem as did the executives.[71]

These examples all help illustrate the elusiveness and contingent nature of determining guidelines for ethical behavior. Besides the obvious ethical concerns relating to the protection of the environment (the so-called green or sustainability issues),[72] the use of bribes, price fixing, "creative" accounting, and other illegal activities now legislated by the Sarbanes-Oxley (S-Ox) Act—and responding by drawing up and disseminating an ethical code which the vast majority of large firms now have—only in recent years has it been recognized that ethics needs theory-building and basic research in the study of organizational behavior.[73] In addition, with the arrival of the global economy, ethics has broadened out to become a major concern for international management.[74] Taking an organizational behavior perspective, Stajkovic and Luthans have proposed a social cognitive model (see Chapter 1) of ethics across cultures.[75] This model uses national cultures as the social foundation for institutional (ethics legislation), organizational (codes of ethics), and personal (values and self-regulatory mechanisms) factors that interact to influence the perception of ethical standards and actual ethical behavior across cultures.

## The Impact of Ethics on "Bottom-Line" Outcomes

Besides the morality issues surrounding ethics in the workplace,[76] there is increasing evidence that ethics programs and being ethical pays off for organizations. Although in the past the linkage between corporate social performance and bottom-line results has been vague or dependent on faith and anecdotal evidence, the cost of illegal, unethical practices is now clearly documented, and recent research studies find a statistically significant relationship. For example, one study compared 67 *Fortune* 500 firms that were convicted of acts such as antitrust violations, product liabilities, and acts of discrimination with 188 firms in the same time period that were not. The results indicated that the convicted firms had significantly lower returns on assets and returns on sales.[77]

Every summer for the past 10 years, Jack Stack has been going to Massachusetts Institute of Technology's Sloan School of Management to speak with young chief executives about the ideals and values of the engine manufacturing company he helped to make a management paragon. In the late 1980s, Stack's Springfield ReManufacturing Corp. emerged as a model for how management and labor could successfully work together in a culture of trust and ownership. Thousands of managers flocked to his company to hear his ideas while others gathered to hear him during his annual trek to MIT for its Birthing of Giants program for new CEOs.

But as the dot-com era took hold in the late 1990s, Stack saw a change in the attitudes of the business leaders who showed up at MIT. They seemed far more ambitious for themselves than for their companies. They were building organizations to flip, not to last. They were more interested in the value of their stockholdings than the profits of their companies. They told him his ideas for tapping into the enthusiasm, intelligence, and creativity of working people were antiquated. And they said he was out of touch.

Stack says that even he began to think of himself as a dinosaur. "So many young CEOs were mesmerized by getting a $1 million or $2 million pop, selling out, and then getting out of town," he says. "They forgot that business is all about values."

Suddenly, leaders like Stack—people who take concepts like ethics and fairness seriously—are back in vogue in a big way. In the post-Enron, post-bubble world, there's a yearning for corporate values that reach higher than the size of the chief executive's paycheck or even the latest stock price. Trust, integrity, and fairness do matter, and they are crucial to the bottom line. The corporate leaders and entrepreneurs who somehow forgot that are now paying the price in a downward market roiled by a loss of investor confidence. "The chasm that separates individuals and organizations is marked by frustration, mistrust, disappointment, and even rage," says Shoshana Zuboff, a Harvard Business School professor and co-author of a book called The Support Economy.

The realization that many companies played fast and loose with accounting rules and ethical standards in the 1990s is leading to a reevaluation of corporate goals and purpose. Zuboff and many other business observers are optimistic that the abuses now dominating the headlines may result in healthy changes in the post-Enron modern corporation. What's emerging is a new model of the ideal corporation.

Business leaders say corporations will likely become far more transparent—not only for investors, but also for employees, customers, and suppliers. The single-minded focus on "shareholder value," which measured performance on the sole basis of stock price, will diminish.

Instead, companies will elevate the interests of employees, customers, and their communities. Executive pay, which clearly soared out of control in the past two decades, is already undergoing a reassessment and will likely fall back in an effort to create a sense of fairness. And corporate cultures will change in a way that puts greater emphasis on integrity and trust.

In the anything-goes 1990s, too many companies allowed performance to be disconnected from meaningful corporate values. "A lot of companies simply looked at performance in assessing their leaders," says Larry Johnston, CEO of Albertson's Inc., the food retailer. "There have to be two dimensions to leadership: performance and values. You can't have one without the other."

This and other changes will be driven less by the threat of government intervention and more by the stigma of being branded an unethical enterprise. That's why the government's newfound zeal to indict individuals and even companies carries such power, regardless of how the cases are resolved. "Social sanctions may eclipse the law in imposing penalties for misconduct and mischief," says Richard T. Pascale, a management authority and author of Surfing the Edge of Chaos. "The corporation of the future has to think about this new development as an increasingly formidable factor to be reckoned with."

That's a change from the 1990s, when pressure from Wall Street and the dot-com mania led to much of the corporate excess. During those years, when Stack found his ideas decidedly out of favor, he stuck with the "open-book management" culture that had made him something of a celebrity years earlier. By sharing all of the company's financials with all employees and giving them an ownership stake in the company, Stack had built a level of mutual trust and respect unusual in business.

If there's one change that nearly everyone foresees today, it's a move to make the corporation far more transparent. That's obvious when it comes to investors, who are demanding truth in the numbers and clarity in disclosure. But it's also important for employees if they're to have a true sense of ownership in their company's affairs. At Stack's company, there are weekly huddles with workers and managers, prominent scorecards on factory walls charting work progress, and ongoing emphasis by managers on building a company and not just a product. Workers undergo training so they can understand the numbers on a balance sheet and an income statement.

Corporate cultures, which in many cases veered out of control in the 1990s by emphasizing profit at any cost, are also in for an overhaul. More than anything else, those beliefs and attitudes are set by the top execs. The values they espouse, the incentives they put in place, and their own behavior provide the cues for the rest of the organization.

Other studies have found a strong link between a company's ethical commitment and its market value added (MVA)[78] and the investment in social programs and the firm's financial outcomes.[79] The social programs involved community and employee relations, product characteristics, diversity, and especially an ethical organizational culture.[80] Some firms with widely recognized reputations for having an ethical culture include Ben & Jerry's (ice cream), Johnson & Johnson's (health care), Levi Strauss (clothing), and Newman's Own (food). For example, Johnson & Johnsons "credo," authored by the son of the founder, spells out the firm's first responsibility is to customers, second to employees, third to the community and environment, and then fourth to the shareholders. As a current VP at J&J explains, "When we operate according to these principles, the stockholders should realize a fair return. What that means is that the credo is not a brake on our success; it's the engine of our success."[81] In terms of research, one study focusing on the environment found a strong positive relationship between having preventative, proactive programs (e.g., pollution control and/or reduction of hazardous waste) and bottom-line profitability gains.[82]

This accumulating evidence on the value of ethical practices is leading to the development of theory, research, and measurement of corporate social responsibility (CSR) or performance (CSP).[83] Although there are various definitions of CSR, "most share the theme of engaging in economically sustainable business activities that go beyond legal requirements to protect the well-being of employees, communities, and the environment."[84] For example, besides the currently popular efforts on the part of companies to reduce carbon emissions to help sustain the planet, there are also less publicized CSR programs such as Burger King's perspective and policies with regard to animal rights (e.g., the use of cage-free chicken products). In practice there are newly created ethics officer positions, and control systems are being suggested to monitor ethical behaviors.[85] As the accompanying OB in Action: After Enron: The Ideal Corporation indicates, there are some ideal organizations, such as the Springfield ReManufacturing Corporation, that are based on trust, total transparency (i.e., the famous "open-book management" pioneered at ReManufacturing), and mutual respect leading to ethical organizational cultures. On the other hand, there are also simple guidelines for employees to follow in doing the authentic,[86] right thing in ethical gray areas. Here is an "ethics quick test" when employees are faced with such a dilemma:

1. Is the action legal?
2. Is it right?
3. Who will be affected?
4. Does it fit the company's values?
5. How would I feel afterwards?
6. How would it look in the newspaper?
7. Will it reflect poorly on the company?[87]

Besides the moral issues and ethics program's guidelines and organizational cultural climate, in the framework of this chapter on the environmental context for today's organizations, ethics also has an impact on the way employees are treated and how they perform their jobs. In other words, like globalization and diversity, ethics can affect the well-being of employees and their performance.

## Summary

This chapter examines the environmental context in terms of globalization, diversity, and ethics. The new "flat-world" international context in which organizational behavior operates has become an increasingly important environmental context. Few would question that there is now globalization and that cultural differences must be recognized in the study and understanding of organizational behavior.

Two other major environmental realities facing modern organizations are diversity and ethics. There are a number of reasons for the rise of diversity in organizations, including the increasing number of women, minorities, and older employees in the workforce and legislative rulings that now require organizations to ensure equal opportunity to women, minorities, older employees, and those challenged by a disability. There are individual and organizational approaches to managing diversity. Approaches at the individual level include learning and empathy; at the organizational level, testing, training, mentoring, and the use of alternative work schedules and work/family programs can be implemented.

Ethics is involved with moral issues and choices and deals with right and wrong behavior. A number of cultural (family, friends, neighbors, education, religion, and the media), organizational (ethical codes, role models, policies and practices, and reward and punishment systems), and external forces (political, legal, economic, and international developments) help determine ethical behavior. These influences, acting interdependently, serve to help identify and shape ethical behavior in today's organizations. There is increasing evidence of the positive impact that ethical behavior and corporate social responsibility programs have on "bottom-line" performance.

# Ending with Meta-Analytic Research Findings
## OB PRINCIPLE FOR EVIDENCE-BASED PRACTICE

Women and men currently differ in their perceptions of ethical business practices.

### Meta-Analysis Results:

[66 samples; 20,000 participants; $d = .22$] *On average, there is a **56 percent probability** that women will perceive higher ethical standards than men in evaluating business practices.* Results of a moderator analysis revealed that gender differences are smaller for samples of nonstudents than students. Moreover, gender differences in ethical perceptions also decline with age and work experience. Those who are older or who have considerable work experience display smaller gender differences in ethical perceptions.

### Conclusion:

As women have become established in the workforce, not only is the workplace more diverse, but also ethical perceptions are changing. In particular, the ethical climate has emerged as an important managerial and societal concern. How this ethical climate is perceived by organizational participants, both male and female, can become important to decision making and business practices. A growing body of evidence suggests that gender plays a role in perceptions of ethical climate. As the chapter points out, diverse input from society at large is affecting the cultural values of today's organizations. Thus, through early socialization, stereotypes associated with social role norms or actual organizational experiences, men and women may develop or bring diverse interests, traits, and values into the workplace. This learning and development may lead to differences in ethical perceptions regarding issues such as pay equity, bribery, and sexual harassment. However, over time as more men and women work together and assimilate into both the changing norms and cultures of both the overall society and organizations concerning working women, the current differences in ethical perceptions will undoubtedly decrease.

**Source:** Adapted from George R. Franke, Deborah F. Crown, and Deborah F. Spake, "Gender Differences in Ethical Perceptions of Business Practices," *Journal of Applied Psychology,* Vol. 82, No., 1, 1997, pp. 920–934.

# OB PRINCIPLE FOR EVIDENCE-BASED PRACTICE

Employee integrity tests can predict unethical and deviant workplace behaviors and performance.

## Meta-Analysis Results:

[305 studies; 349,623 participants; $d = .84$ for overt tests; $d = .43$ for personality tests; and $d = .75$ when tests are related to performance] *On average, there is a **72 percent probability** that job applicants who score well on overt integrity tests will participate in less unethical and/or deviant behaviors than those who score poorly. Moreover, on average, there is a **62 percent probability** that job applicants who score well on personality-based integrity tests will participate in less unethical and/or deviant behaviors than those who score poorly.* Finally, not only does the use of integrity tests help predict unethical and/or deviant behavior, but they can also help organizations predict better performers. *On average, there is a **70 percent probability** that employees who score well on integrity tests will outperform those who score poorly.* Further analysis indicates the measurement method is a moderator. That is, measures of deviant behavior can be divided into external and self-report (admission) criteria. External criteria involve actual records of rule-breaking incidents, disciplinary actions, dismissals for theft, etc. Self-report criteria include all admissions of theft, past illegal activities, and counterproductive behaviors. Interestingly, the validity of self-report measures was higher than that for external criteria—perhaps because not all thieves are caught or illegal activities detected.

## Conclusion:

Because unethical and deviant behavior not only can impact the well-being of employees, but also can have a detrimental effect on individual and organizational performance, the study of ethics has been receiving increased attention in organizational behavior. One way for organizations to screen out potentially unethical individuals is to give job applicants some form of overt or personality-based integrity/honesty test. These tests are commonly used to predict employee participation in illegal activity (e.g., theft), unethical behavior, excessive absences, drug abuse, or workplace violence. Over the past decade, the evidence for integrity test predictive validities has been strong. Overt integrity tests are designed to directly assess attitudes regarding dishonest behaviors. Examples are asking test takers questions such as the following: "Should a person be fired if caught stealing $5?" Personality-based integrity tests are designed to predict deviant behaviors at work by using personality measures such as reliability, conscientiousness, adjustment, trustworthiness, and sociability. The meta-analysis of research studies of both overt and personality integrity tests can help organizations reduce unethical and/or deviant employee behavior as well as help them predict better performers.

**Source:** Adapted from Deniz S. Ones, Chockalingman Viswesvaran, and Frank L. Schmidt, "Comprehensive Meta-Analysis of Integrity Test Validities: Findings and Implications for Personnel Selection and Theories of Job Performance," *Journal of Applied Psychology Monograph,* Vol., 78, No., 4, 1993, pp. 679–703.

| | |
|---|---|
| **Questions for Discussion and Review** | 1. What is meant by and what are some examples of globalization? |
| | 2. What are some of the major reasons why diversity has become such an important dimension of today's organizations? |
| | 3. How can diversity be effectively managed? Offer suggestions at both the individual and organizational levels. |
| | 4. What is meant by ethics, and what types of factors influence ethical behavior? |
| | 5. What is meant by corporate social responsibility? How can and does it affect the "bottom-line" of today's organizations? |

| | |
|---|---|
| **Internet Exercise: Ethical Issues in the Workplace** | Ethical issues are very much at the forefront of organizational behavior in today's environment. One controversial issue concerns monitoring employees. Technology has now made it easy and inexpensive for employers to closely monitor the behaviors of employees. Visit the Web site **http://www.legalethics.com** for information on ethics and laws relevant to the current workplace. It may be helpful for you to test your knowledge and understanding of the ethical climate by going to **httl://www.mhhe.com/business/ management/buildyourmanagementskills/ethics/exercise.html.** Then, going from these, search to see if you can come up with other perspectives on employee monitoring as an ethical issue. |

1. Do you believe employers should be allowed to electronically monitor workers? Would you like to be monitored in this fashion?
2. Summarize the different perspectives that you found on the Internet. Be specific as to where you found this information.
3. Discuss other ethical issues that surfaced when looking at the suggested Web sites or others that you found.

# Organizational Behavior Case: *How Far-Reaching Are Globalization and Technology?*

Bob is the owner and operator of a medium-sized grocery store that has been in his family for more than 30 years. Currently his business is flourishing, primarily because it has an established customer base in a busy part of town. Also, Bob is a good manager. He considers himself to be highly knowledgeable about his business, having continuously adapted to the changing times. For example, he recently expanded his business by putting in a full-service deli. His philosophy is that by continuously providing customers with new products and services, he will always have a satisfied customer base to rely on.

At a management seminar he attended last year, the hot topic was globalization and the impact of technology on going global. He has also been bombarded by the many television ads and mailers regarding the opportunities available in international markets. For the most part, Bob doesn't think that globalization is an issue with his business, as he doesn't even intend to expand outside the city. Furthermore, he feels that the Internet has no applications in his branch of the retail industry and would simply be a waste of time.

1. Is Bob correct in his assessment of how globalization will impact his business?
2. Can you think of any global applications that Bob could profit from?
3. How could Bob's business be negatively impacted by both technology and globalization if he does not keep on top of these developments?

# Organizational Behavior Case: *I Want Out*

When the Budder Mining Equipment company decided to set up a branch office in Peru, top management felt that there were two basic avenues the company could travel. One was to export its machinery and have an agent in that country be responsible for the selling. The other was to set up an on-site operation and be directly responsible for the sales effort. After giving the matter a great deal of thought, management decided to assign one of their own people to this overseas market. The person who was chosen, Frank Knight, had expressed an interest in the assignment, but had no experience in South America. He was selected because of his selling skills and was given a week to clear out his desk and be on location.

When Frank arrived, he was met at the airport by Pablo Gutierrez, the local who was hired to run the office and break Frank in. Pablo had rented an apartment and car for Frank and taken care of all the chores associated with getting him settled. Frank was very impressed. Thanks to Pablo, he could devote all his efforts to the business challenges that lay ahead.

After about six months, the vice president for marketing received a call from Frank. In a tired voice Frank indicated that even though sales were okay, he couldn't take it anymore. He wanted to come home. If nothing could be worked out within the next three months, Frank made it clear that he would resign. When his boss pressed him regarding the problems he was having, here is what Frank reported:

> Doing business over here is a nightmare. Everyone comes to work late and leaves early. They also take a two-hour rest period during the afternoon. All the offices close down during this afternoon break. So even if I wanted to conduct some business during this period, there would be no customers around anyway. Also, no one works very hard, and they seem to assume no responsibility whatsoever. There seems to be no support for the work ethic among the people. Even Pablo, who looked like he was going to turn out great, has proved to be as lazy as the rest of them. Sales are 5 percent over forecasted but a good 30 percent lower than they could be if everyone here would just work a little harder. If I stay here any longer, I'm afraid I'll start becoming like these people. I want out, while I still can.

1. In Frank's view, how important is the work ethic? How is this view causing him problems?
2. Why do the people not work as hard as Frank does? What is the problem?
3. What mistake is Frank making that is undoubtedly causing him problems in managing the branch office?

# Real Case: *Not Treating Everyone the Same*

As recently as the 1980s, managers in some of the most productive organizations in the country used to pride themselves on treating all their employees equally. This typically meant holding the line on rules and regulations so that everyone conformed to the same set of guidelines. Moreover, when people were evaluated, they were typically assessed on the basis of their performance in the workplace. In recent years there has been a dramatic change in management's thinking. Instead of treating everyone the same, some organizations are now trying to meet the specific needs of employees. What is done for one individual employee may not be done for another. Additionally, instead of evaluating all employees on how well they work in the workplace, attention is being focused on how much "value added" people contribute, regardless of how many hours they are physically at the workplace. This new philosophy is also spilling over into the way alternative work arrangements are being handled.

An example is Aetna Life & Casualty, where workers are given the option of reducing their workweek or compressing the time into fewer days. Under this arrangement, a parent who wants to spend more time at home with the children can opt to cut working hours from 40 down to 30 per week or put in four 10-hour days and have a long weekend with the kids. In either case, these personal decisions do not negatively affect the employee's opportunities for promotion. Why is the company so willing to accommodate the personal desires of the workers? One of the main reasons is that

Aetna was losing hundreds of talented people every year and felt that the cost to the company was too great. Something had to be done to keep these people on the payroll. As a result, today approximately 2,000 of Aetna's 44,000 employees work part-time, share a job, work at home, or are on a compressed workweek arrangement. The company estimates that it saves approximately $1 million annually by not having to train new workers. Moreover, the company reported that in one recent year 88 percent of those employees who took family leave returned to work. An added benefit of this program is the fact that Aetna's reputation as a good place to work has been strengthened. The Families and Work Institute recently named Aetna one of the top four "family-friendly" companies.

Duke Power & Light is another good example of how companies are changing their approach to managing employees. Realizing that child care is a growing need among many employees, because in most households both parents now work, the company joined forces with other employers to build a child care center. The firm has also changed its work schedule assignments. In the past, many employees reported that they hated working swing shifts: days one week, evenings the next, and then nights. So the firm created 22 work schedules and now lets employees bid on them annually, based on seniority. Some of these shifts are the traditional five-day week of eight-hour days. Others, however, are compressed work-week alternatives, including four 10-hour days and three 12-hour days. At the same time, the company has been turning more authority over to the personnel and has driven up its employee-to-manager ratio from 12 to 1 to 20 to 1. As a result, the company now has an attrition rate that is over three times lower than the industry average, and most of this attrition is a result of people's transferring to other jobs in the utility. As one manager put it, "We needed to recognize that people have lives." On the basis of results, it is obvious that the new arrangement is a win-win situation for both the workers and the firm.

1. How is the new management philosophy described in this case different from that of the old, traditional philosophy? Identify and describe the differences.
2. In what way are alternative work schedules proving helpful to managing diversity?
3. Do you think these new programs are likely to continue or will they taper off? Why?

# Organizational Behavior Case: *Changing with the Times*

Jerry is director of marketing for a large toy company. Presently, his team of executives consists entirely of white males. The company says it is committed to diversity and equal opportunity. In a private conversation with Robert, the company president, about the makeup of top-level management in the marketing department, Jerry admitted that he tends to promote people who are like him.

Jerry stated, "It just seems like when a promotion opportunity exists in our department, the perfect person for the job happens to be a white male. Am I supposed to actively seek women and minorities, even if I don't feel that they are the best person for the job? After all, we aren't violating the law, are we?"

Robert responded, "So far the performance in your department has been good, and as far as I know, we are not violating any discrimination laws. Your management team seems to work well together, and we don't want to do anything to upset that, especially considering the big marketing plans we have for this coming fiscal year."

The big marketing plans Robert is referring to have to do with capturing a sizable share of the overseas market. The company thinks that a large niche exists in various countries around the world—and who better to fill that niche than an organization that has proved it can make top-quality toys at a competitive price? Now the marketing team has the task of determining which countries to target, which existing toys will sell, and which new toys need to be developed.

1. Do Jerry and Robert understand what "management of diversity" means? How would you advise them?
2. Considering the marketing plans, how could they benefit from a more diverse management team? Be specific.

# Real Case: *The Ethics of Downsizing*

Downsizing refers to a company's decision to reduce its workforce for reasons other than poor performance, criminal conduct, or unethical behavior on the part of those being let go. The word is a euphemism meant to soften the blow as much for the company as it is for the soon-to-be eliminated. There is nothing wrong with making a difficult task easier to bear. In fact, there are good ethical reasons for doing so, as we'll soon see. Still, there is no getting around the fact that downsizing is a type of layoff, with all that this implies. The ethical manager will keep in mind what is really going on when he or she is charged with letting good people go.

## WHY DOWNSIZING IS AN ETHICAL ISSUE

Anytime we're faced with a decision that can affect the rights or well-being of others, we're looking at an ethical issue. No matter how strong the justifications for reducing the workforce are or seem to be, laying off loyal and productive employees is an upsetting experience for all concerned, and those on the receiving end face not just financial but psychological injury.

How so? For many of us, the workplace isn't just a place for work; it's where we develop and maintain some of the most important relationships we have. During the week, we spend more time with coworkers than with our families, and for better or worse, work is how many of us define ourselves and give meaning to our lives. Getting laid off compromises all of these things, so managers should think of downsizing as a deep and painful trauma for those being let go, and not as a mere setback or reversal of fortune.

Yes, downsizing has legal implications, and it is understandable that companies want to minimize their liability when they downsize. Yes, there are economic matters to consider, which makes downsizing a management issue, too. But at its core, downsizing is an ethical issue, and the good manager is concerned not just with protecting the company's financial and legal interests but also with honoring the dignity and integrity of the human beings who work on the front lines and who are the lifeblood of the organization.

## DOING IT THE RIGHT WAY

### 1. Do It in Person.

This seems the obvious thing to do, but I'm surprised by the number of reports I've heard about employees who were downsized on the phone or by e-mail. Managers who use this method claim it makes the whole thing easier to deal with. Yes, but for whom? Certainly not for the employee being let go. As uncomfortable as it is to end someone's employment, the right thing to do is to have a private conversation with him or her in person. The ethical principle of respect for others requires nothing less.

### 2. Do It Privately.

Respecting others means honoring their wishes and values, and it is reasonable to assume that most people would prefer to have troubling news delivered in private. This means in your office, with the door closed. I've heard of managers who broke the bad news at the employee's cubicle within earshot of everyone in the vicinity. Again, one would think that this would be a matter of common sense and common decency, but apparently neither is all that common.

### 3. Give the Person Your Full Attention.

Interrupting the conversation to take phone calls, check your BlackBerry, or engage in other distractions isn't just rude, it tells the other person that the matter at hand isn't all that important to you. That's yet another violation of the principle of respect. The impulse to turn your attention to less troubling matters is understandable, but along with the privileges of being a manager come responsibilities, and downsizing with integrity is one of the most important obligations you have.

### 4. Be Honest, but Not Brutally So.

Must you always tell the truth, the whole truth, and nothing but the truth? Yes, if you're giving sworn testimony in a court of law, but beyond the courtroom the duty to tell the truth is constrained by the duty to minimize harm. In practical terms, this means being forthright with the employee but also choosing with the care the words, tone of voice, and demeanor you use. Compassion—literally, "suffering with" someone—honors the dignity of your employee and speaks to the better part of your nature.

We can't always make things better, but we shouldn't make things worse.

## 5. Don't Rush.

A shock takes time to absorb. Imagine that your physician says you have a serious illness. Wouldn't you expect him or her to allow the news sink in, rather than to summarily dismiss you and call for the next patient? Being let go isn't as serious as getting a diagnosis of cancer or heart disease, but it is still a major, life-changing event. You owe your employee the space to absorb the information, and you may have to explain more than once what is happening and why. You would demand nothing less if it were happening to you, and you would be right to do so.

1. Do you agree that downsizing is an ethical issue?
2. Do you agree with the five guidelines for downsizing ethically? Would you add any others?
3. What if you do not agree with the reason for the downsizing? Ethically, how would you respond? Would you be willing to resign?

# Organizational Context: Design and Culture

**Learning Objectives**

- **Explain** the organizational theory foundation for design and culture.
- **Present** contemporary horizontal, hollow, modular, network, and virtual designs of organizations.
- **Define** organizational culture and its characteristics.
- **Relate** how an organizational culture is created.
- **Describe** how an organizational culture is maintained.
- **Explain** some ways of changing organizational culture.

This chapter moves from the external environments to the organizational context for organizational behavior. Specifically, this chapter is concerned with organization design and culture. Organization structure represents the skeletal framework for organizational behavior. As the discussion of the conceptual framework in Chapter 1 points out, the organization design and culture are dominant environmental factors that interact with the personal cognitions and the behavior. The first part of the chapter presents the organization from the viewpoint of theory and design. As Chapter 2 points out, globalization has had a dramatic impact on organization structures. Theories, designs, and networks have emerged to meet the contemporary situation. For example, well-known companies, such as General Electric, have eliminated vertical structures and adopted horizontal designs. The new environment has forever changed organization design and interorganizational relationships.

The modern approach to organization theory and design consists of very flexible networks and recognizes the interaction of technology and people. For example, one organization theorist has noted: "Organization structure is more than boxes on a chart; it is a pattern of interactions and coordination that links the technology, tasks, and human components of the organization to ensure that the organization accomplishes its purposes."[1] There is also a renewed recognition for the role that structure (or lack of structure) plays in innovation, change, and learning in today's and future organizations.

The remainder of the chapter is concerned with the cultural context that the organization provides for organizational behavior. After first defining what is meant by organizational culture, the discussion turns to the different types, how they are changing, and how they can be changed to meet the challenges of the new external environment and organization designs.

# THE ORGANIZATIONAL THEORY FOUNDATION

Some organization theorists argue that the classical hierarchical, bureaucratic theory of organizations was mistranslated and really was not meant to be an ideal type of structure. Instead, the hierarchical bureaucracy from the beginning emphasized the need to adapt to environmental change. However, until the late 1970s organizations were largely self-contained and a vertical chain of command with high degrees of control (i.e., a bureaucratic structure) sufficed. After a brief overview of the historical roots, the more recent theories that expand upon and are more sophisticated than the classic bureaucratic theory are summarized. These serve as a point of departure and foundation for the contemporary organization designs.

## Historical Roots

The real break with classical thinking on organizational structure is generally recognized to be the work of Chester Barnard. In his significant book *The Functions of the Executive,* he defined a *formal organization* as a system of consciously coordinated activities of two or more persons.[2] It is interesting to note that in this often-cited definition, the words *system* and *persons* are given major emphasis. People, not boxes on an organization chart, make up a formal organization. Barnard was critical of the existing classical organization theory because it was too descriptive and superficial. He was especially dissatisfied with the classical bureaucratic view that authority should come from the top down. Barnard, using a more analytical approach, took an opposite viewpoint. He maintained that authority really should come from the bottom up, rather than the top-down bureaucratic approach.

Besides authority, Barnard stressed the cooperative aspects of organizations. This concern reflects the importance that he attached to the human element in organization structure and analysis. It was Barnard's contention that the existence of a cooperative system is contingent on the human participants' ability to communicate and their willingness to serve and strive toward a common purpose. Under such a premise, the human being plays the most important role in the creation and perpetuation of formal organizations.

## Modern Theoretical Foundation

From this auspicious historical beginning from Barnard, modern organization theory has evolved in several directions. The first major development in organization theory was to view the organization as a system made up of interacting parts. The open-systems concept especially, which stresses the input of the external environment, has had a tremendous impact on modern organization theory. This development was followed by an analysis of organizations in terms of their ability to process information in order to reduce the uncertainty in managerial decision making. The next development in organization theory is the contingency approach. The premise of the contingency approach is that there is no single best way to organize. The organizational design must be fitted to the existing environmental conditions.

One of the modern theoretical approaches is a natural selection—or ecological—view of organizations. This organizational ecology theory challenges the contingency approach. Whereas the contingency approach suggests that organizations change through internal transformation and adaptation, the ecological approach says that it is more a process of the "survival of the fittest"; there is a process of organizational selection and replacement.

Finally are information processing and organizational learning. These most recent approaches to organization theory are based largely on systems theory and emphasize the importance of generative over adaptive learning in fast-changing external environments such as is covered in Chapter 2 on globalization. All these organization theories serve as a foundation for the remaining discussion of the organizational context for organizational behavior. The learning organization represents contemporary organization theory and is compatible with and is relevant to the new paradigm environment facing today's organizations.

## What Is Meant by a Learning Organization?

The organization portrayed as a learning system is certainly not new.[3] In fact, at the turn of the last century Frederick W. Taylor's learnings on scientific management were said to be transferable to workers to make the organization more efficient. However, the beginning of today's use of the term *learning organization* is usually attributed to the seminal work of Chris Argyris and his colleagues, who made the distinction between first-order, or "single-loop," and second-order, or dentero or "double-loop," learning.[4] The differences between these two types of learning applied to organizations can be summarized as follows:

1. Single-loop learning involves improving the organization's capacity to achieve known objectives. It is associated with routine and behavioral learning. Under single-loop, the organization is learning without significant change in its basic assumptions.

2. Double-loop learning reevaluates the nature of the organization's objectives and the values and beliefs surrounding them. This type of learning involves changing the organization's culture. Importantly, double-loop consists of the organization's learning how to learn.[5]

The other theorist most closely associated with learning organizations, Peter Senge and his colleagues, then proceeded to portray this type of organization from a systems theory perspective and made the important distinction between adaptive and generative learning.[6] The simpler adaptive learning is only the first stage of the learning organization, adapting to environmental changes. In recent years, many banks, insurance firms, and old-line manufacturing companies made many adaptive changes such as implementing total quality management (or TQM), benchmarking (comparing with best practices), Six Sigma (a goal of virtually no defects in any process) programs, and customer service initiatives. However, despite the popularity and general success of these efforts to adapt to changing customer expectations for quality and service, organizations have still struggled with their basic assumptions, cultural values, and structure. They have not gone beyond mere adaptive learning.[7] The more important generative learning was needed.

Generative learning involves creativity and innovation, going beyond just adapting to change to being ahead of and anticipating change.[8] The generative process leads to a total reframing of an organization's experiences and learning from that process. For example, the largest car dealer, AutoNation, totally reframed and showed generative learning from the nightmare customers typically experience in trying to buy a used auto. This firm anticipated customer needs by proactively addressing key issues such as a no-haggling sales process, providing a warranty on used cars, and being able to buy from any one of hundreds of car lots.

With the theoretical foundation largely provided by Argyris (double-loop learning) and Senge (generative learning), we conducted a comprehensive review to identify the major characteristics of learning organizations.[9] Figure 3.1 shows the three major dimensions or characteristics of learning organizations that emerged out of the considerable literature. The presence of tension—Senge calls it "creative tension"—serves as a catalyst or motivational need to learn. As shown in Figure 3.1, this tension stems from the gap between the organization's vision (which is hopefully always being adjusted upward) and reality and suggests the learning organization's continually questioning and challenging the status quo. The systems characteristic of learning organizations recognizes the shared vision of employees throughout the whole organization and the openness to new ideas and the

**FIGURE 3.1**
**Characteristics
of Learning
Organizations.**

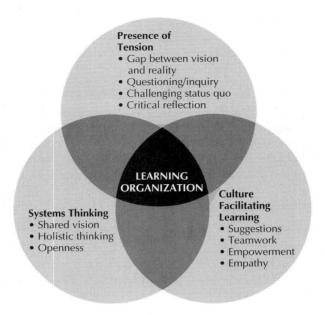

external environment. The third major characteristic shown in Figure 3.1 is an organizational culture conducive to learning. The culture of the organization places a high value on the process of learning and goes beyond mere lip service by setting mechanisms in place for suggestions, teams, empowerment, and, most subtly but importantly, empathy. This empathy is reflected by the genuine concern for and interest in employee suggestions and innovations that can be operationalized through reward systems.

## Organizational Behavior in the Learning Organization

Taken to a more individual employee, organizational behavior level, the adaptive learning organization would be associated with employees' reacting to environmental changes with routine, standard responses that often result in only short-run solutions. In contrast, generative learning, with its emphasis on continuous experimentation and feedback, would directly affect the way personnel go about defining and solving problems. Employees in generative learning organizations are taught how to examine the effect of their decisions and to change their behaviors as needed. A good example occurred at Children's Hospital and Clinic of Minnesota. They learned to institute a new policy of "blameless reporting" that replaced threatening terms such as "errors" and "investigations" with less emotional terms such as "accidents" and "analysis." As described by Garvin, Edmondson, and Gino, "The result was that people started to collaborate throughout the organization to talk about and change behaviors, policies, and systems that put patients at risk. Over time, these learning activities yielded measurable reductions in preventable deaths and illnesses at the institution."[10]

Learning organizations are also characterized by human-oriented cultural values such as these: (1) everyone can be a source of useful ideas, so personnel should be given access to any information that can be of value to them; (2) the people closest to the problem usually have the best ideas regarding how to solve it, so empowerment should be promoted throughout the structure; (3) learning flows up and down, so managers as well as employees can benefit from it; (4) new ideas are important and should be encouraged and rewarded; and (5) mistakes should be viewed as learning opportunities.[11] The last point of learning from failures is an especially important cultural value for people in the learning organization.

## Learning Organizations in Action

There are a number of ways that the learning organization can be operationalized into the actual practice of management. For example, managers must be receptive to new ideas and overcome the desire to closely control operations. Many organizations tend to do things the way they have done them in the past. Learning organizations break this mold and teach their people to look at things differently. For example, several years ago British Petroleum (BP) was bogged down in their bureaucratic structure and control procedures, accumulated a huge debt, and had some of the highest costs in the industry. Then a new CEO took over, sold off the firm's unrelated business, and implemented a corporate strategy mostly based on speed and rapid learning. BP was redesigned as follows:

> Functional and divisional walls that inhibited cooperation, resource sharing, and internal debate were leveled to promote forward thinking, the learning of new managerial competencies, and the adoption of risk taking behaviors. Most importantly, a rejuvenated senior management team began cultivating a new culture that emphasized knowledge sharing, open communications, team-building, and breakthrough thinking throughout the firm.[12]

By the turn of the century, BP had a learning-driven culture in place, the old bureaucratic boundaries were down, everyone in the firm shared knowledge with everyone else, and BP became the lowest-cost producer in the oil industry.

As was done at BP, the move toward a learning organization entails breaking out of the highly controlled, layered hierarchy that is characteristic of bureaucratic structures. The accompanying OB in Action: Breaking Out of the Box gives a number of real-world managers' examples of problems with bureaucracies and how to think outside the box and bust out of them. In other words, the beginning point in establishing a learning organization is to recognize that bureaucracies have too often become an end to themselves instead of supporting the vision and goals that require adapting to the changing environment and learning how to do that.

Besides breaking out of bureaucracies, another way to operationalize the learning process in organizations is to develop systemic thinking among managers. This involves the ability to see connections among issues, events, and data as a whole rather than a series of unconnected parts. Learning organizations teach their people to identify the source of conflict they may have with other personnel, units, and departments and to negotiate and make astute trade-offs both skillfully and quickly. Managers must also learn, especially, how to encourage their people to redirect their energies toward the substance of disagreements rather than toward personality clashes or political infighting. For example, in most successful firms today, interfunctional teams, increasingly at a distance (virtually), work on projects, thus removing the artificial barriers between functional areas and between line and staff. For example, at Mars Drinks, the top management team is structured globally, with both regional general managers and functional heads. Even the president is not only on this team, but also multiple other teams depending on, in his words, "what the issue of the day is and whether I have particular expertise in those areas."[13] A research study confirms the important impact that team learning can have on organizational learning.[14]

Another practice of learning organizations is to develop creativity among personnel. Creativity is the ability to formulate unique approaches to problem solving and decision making. In generative learning organizations, creativity is most widely acknowledged as a requisite skill and ability. Two critical dimensions of creativity, which promote and help

Anyone who has worked in the corporate world, held a government job—or lived in Europe—knows well how bureaucracy can drive even those of sound mind to distraction. All too often it stifles good ideas, slows progress, and frustrates employees.

A recent survey ranked "Negotiating a Stultifying Bureaucracy" third among most pressing workplace problems. "You can't even get a light bulb changed without putting in a work order," says Wayde Alford, a cost estimator at a major defense contractor near Jacksonville, Florida. Alford says he cuts through red tape by cozying up to colleagues and requesting favors. Otherwise, a task as simple as changing that bulb can take two months to accomplish. Maybe it's not that bad in your organization. But just in case, here's a sampling of other suggestions for bureaucracy-busting:

**Bill Fox, managing partner, VanguardComm, New Brunswick, New Jersey.** It's been said that successful corporate survivors are "system beaters." Just like in judo, where you use your opponent's momentum against them, in bureaucracies if you learn the system you can use it against the bureaucrats. For example, very often bureaucratic requirements are more about form than substance. So as long as you fill out the proper paperwork, dot the i's, and cross the t's, you can get what you want approved; your request complied with the bureaucrats' system and that's their primary concern.

**Arthur "Buck" Nimz, certified Defense Dept. enterprise architect and principal research specialist, MS2, Lockheed Martin, Moorestown, New Jersey.** Foster an environment of innovation that reaches out beyond your org chart and tries to capture the intellectual diversity of others in your company who have different perspectives on the business and the market. Legendary GE CEO Jack Welch called this "boundaryless thinking," which is a mindset that transcends bureaucracy and creates a behavioral culture of innovation.

**Marshall Potts, managing director, Jasper International, Nottingham, England.** Bureaucracies don't tolerate deviation from set ways of doing things. In an increasingly competitive world, this inflexibility is a major stumbling block. One way leaders could address this is to find someone to explain to their organization's senior team what sustains the bureaucracy, what it costs them, what the competition is doing differently, and finally, the impact of resisting change.

**John Sheeran, Bateau Bay, Australia.** Keep a very low hierarchy and give all levels of staff a vested interest in the success of the company . . . Also, keep the family of staff involved.

**Chris Bylander, CEO, International American Group, St. Louis and Stockholm.** We delegate responsibility whenever possible. Employees, no matter what rank, come to understand "bureaucracy" as something else—namely corporate governance—when they voluntarily interact with it on a get-the-job-done basis.

**Daniel S. Mulhall, educational consultant, Laurel, Maryland.** The challenge is to control and manage bureaucracy so that it serves the corporate body, not controls it. Bureaucracy itself should be reviewed and evaluated on a regular basis so that harmful pieces are rejected and helpful pieces kept and reinforced.

**George Peterson, vice-president for international relations, SolBridge International School of Business, Daejeon, South Korea.** Work to eliminate bureaucracy: Make a nonbureaucratic environment part of the corporate policy statement; have an efficient process to get input from employees on bureaucracy problem areas; eliminate the problems identified.

**Brian Behler, Lomita, California.** Transparency with regular communication is the only solution. There are huge differences in the amount of bureaucracy at various companies today. A supervisor who doesn't engage and communicate will lose his best and brightest to a more nimble company.

**Cecil Sunder, Level 3 Communications, Broomfield, Colorado.** Map processes and executives will soon realize where the bottlenecks are. Because of SarbOx and other mandates it is a necessary evil to have some kind of bureaucracy, but it should not stagnate the work.

unleash creativity, are personal flexibility and a willingness to take risks. As a result, many learning organizations now teach their people how to review their current work habits and change behaviors that limit their thinking. Whereas typical organizations focus on new ways to use old thinking, learning organizations focus on getting employees to break their operating habits and think "outside the box" (see the OB in Action: Breaking Out of the Box). Creativity also includes the willingness to accept failure. A

**TABLE 3.1**   Senge's Summary of Traditional versus Learning Organizations

Source: Adapted from Peter M. Senge, "Transforming the Practice of Management," *Human Resource Development Quarterly,* Spring 1993, p. 9.

| Function | Traditional Organizations | Learning Organizations |
|---|---|---|
| Determination of overall direction | Vision is provided by top management. | There is a shared vision that can emerge from many places, but top management is responsible for ensuring that this vision exists and is nurtured. |
| Formulation and implementation of ideas | Top management decides what is to be done, and the rest of the organization acts on these ideas. | Formulation and implementation of ideas take place at all levels of the organization. |
| Nature of organizational thinking | Each person is responsible for his or her own job responsibilities, and the focus is on developing individual competence. | Personnel understand their own jobs as well as the way in which their own work interrelates with and influences that of other personnel. |
| Conflict resolution | Conflicts are resolved through the use of power and hierarchical influence. | Conflicts are resolved through the use of collaborative learning and the integration of diverse viewpoints of personnel throughout the organization. |
| Leadership and motivation | The role of the leader is to establish the organization's vision, provide rewards and punishments as appropriate, and maintain overall control of employee activities. | The role of the leader is to build a shared vision, empower the personnel, inspire commitment, and encourage effective decision making throughout the enterprise through the use of empowerment and charismatic leadership. |

well-known story at IBM tells of the worried manager going to a meeting with his boss after his project had failed. Getting right to the point, the trembling manager blurted out, "I suppose you're going to have to fire me." But his boss quickly replied, "Why would I do that, we've just invested $6 million in your education." In other words, learning organizations such as IBM treat failure as a learning opportunity, and also the way it is treated creates a climate for future creativity. Managers encourage risk-taking, creative behavior by providing a supportive environment. A cultural value or slogan such as "ready, fire, aim" depicts such an environment.

Well-known learning organization theorist and consultant Peter Senge summarizes the differences between learning organizations and traditional organizations in Table 3.1. These differences help illustrate why learning organizations are gaining in importance and why an increasing number of enterprises are now working to develop a generative learning environment. They realize the benefits that can result. There is also empirical research evidence suggesting a positive association between the learning organization concept and firms' financial performance.[15] The classical organization theories are still depended upon in today's organizations, but organizational learning goes a necessary step further to the understanding of effective organizations in the new paradigm environment.

# MODERN ORGANIZATION DESIGNS

Along with organization theorists, many practicing managers are becoming disenchanted with traditional ways of designing their organizations. Up until a decade or so ago, most managers attempted only timid modifications of classical bureaucratic structures[16] and balked at daring experimentation and innovation. However, with changing environmental demands, managers overcame this resistance to making drastic organizational changes. They realized that the simple solutions offered by the classical theories were no longer adequate in the new paradigm environment.[17] In particular, the needs for flexibility, adaptability to change, creativity, innovation, knowledge, as well as the ability to overcome environmental uncertainty, are among the biggest challenges facing a growing number of organizations. The response was first to move away from the self-contained, control-oriented, vertical hierarchical bureaucratic structures to horizontal designs (and thinking).

## Horizontal Organizations

Horizontal designs are at the other end of the continuum from the traditional vertical, hierarchical structures. In a comprehensive analysis of the recent evolution of organizational design, Anand and Daft noted that "the horizontal organization advocates the dispensing of internal boundaries that are an impediment to effective business performance. If the traditional structure can be likened to a pyramid, the metaphor that best applies to the horizontal organization is a pizza—flat, but packed with all the necessary ingredients."[18] The modern environment covered in the last chapter has stimulated the change to horizontal designs that better facilitate cooperation, teamwork, and a customer rather than a functional orientation. Frank Ostroff, a McKinsey & Company consultant, along with colleague Douglas Smith, is given credit for developing some of the following guiding principles that define horizontal organization design.[19]

1. *Organization revolves around the process, not the task.*   Instead of creating a structure around the traditional functions, the organization is built around its three to five core processes. Each process has an "owner" and specific performance goals.
2. *The hierarchy is flattened.*   To reduce levels of supervision, fragmented tasks are combined, work that fails to add value is eliminated, and activities within each process are cut to the minimum.
3. *Teams are used to manage everything.*   Self-managed teams are the building blocks of the organization. The teams have a common purpose and are held accountable for measuring performance goals.
4. *Customers drive performance.*   Customer satisfaction, not profits or stock appreciation, is the primary driver and measure of performance.
5. *Team performance is rewarded.*   The reward systems are geared toward team results, not just individual performance. Employees are rewarded for multiple skill development rather than just specialized expertise.
6. *Supplier and customer contact is maximized.*   Employees are brought into direct, regular contact with suppliers and customers. Where relevant, supplier and customer representatives may be brought in as full working members of in-house teams.
7. *All employees need to be fully informed and trained.*   Employees should be provided all data, not just sanitized information on a "need to know" basis. However, they also need to be trained how to analyze and use the data to make effective decisions.

Today, this horizontal structure is used by a number of organizations. For example, most large firms today (e.g., the auto firms, Xerox, Lexmark Printers, Eastman Kodak) use it for new product development. Another example would be AT&T units doing budgets based not on functions but on processes, such as the maintenance of a worldwide telecommunications network. Importantly, AT&T is also rewarding its people based on customer evaluations of the teams performing these processes. General Electric has also scrapped the vertical structure that was in place in its lighting business and replaced the design with a horizontal structure characterized by over 100 different processes and programs. In particular, to cut out bureaucracy and solve organizational problems that cut across functions and levels, GE implemented its famous "Work Out" (as in get the work out and work out any problems to get it done) described as follows:

> Large groups of employees and managers—from different organizational levels and functions—come together to address issues that they identify or that senior management has raised as concerns. In small teams, people challenge prevailing assumptions about "the way we have always done things" and come up with recommendations for dramatic improvements in organizational processes.[20]

The Government Electronics group at Motorola has redesigned its supply-chain management organization so that it is now a process structure geared toward serving external customers. These horizontal designs are more relevant to today's environmental needs for flexibility, speed, and cooperation. However, there may also be potential problems such as feelings of neglect and "turf battles" for those individuals and departments not included in the horizontal process flow and the advantages of technical expertise gained under the functional specializations may be diluted or sacrificed. A book on *The Horizontal Organization* suggests guiding principles such as the following to make horizontal designs as effective as possible.

1. Make teams, not individuals, the cornerstone of the organizational design and performance.
2. Decrease hierarchy by eliminating non-value-added work and by giving team members the authority to make decisions directly related to their activities within the process flow.
3. Emphasize multiple competencies and train people to handle issues and work in cross-functional areas.
4. Measure for end-of-process performance objectives, as well as customer satisfaction, employee satisfaction, and financial contribution.
5. Build a corporate culture of openness, cooperation, and collaboration, a culture that focuses on continuous performance improvement and values employee empowerment, responsibility, and well-being.[21]

## Contemporary Designs: Hollow and Modular

Around the turn of the new century, especially with the advent of advanced information technology (i.e., the Internet and mobile/cell phones) and globalization (especially the emerging economies of China and India with their low-cost, skilled workforce), new organization designs emerged. Whereas the horizontal designs broke down the former bureaucratic hierarchical and functional specialization boundaries within an organization, the twenty-first century designs have extended and broken the boundaries of the organization itself. Specifically, in order to compete in the global economy, far-thinking management recognized and then embraced the fact that they needed to outsource selected tasks, functions, and processes. For example, much of manufacturing on all levels and industries was outsourced to China and other developing countries, while information processing and customer service was outsourced to India and a few other countries. This movement of entire processes outside the organization left what has been termed the "Hollow Organization" design[22] and when just parts of the product or service are outsourced, it's called the "Modular Organization" design.[23]

Initially, organizations involved in labor intensive manufacturing of toys, apparel, shoes (e.g., Nike and Reebok) moved to hollow designs that outsourced the entire process of making of their products and left them to focus on product design and marketing. Then in recent years manufacturing of all kinds has moved outside the United States and also financial, accounting, and even medical service processes have left hollow organizations. Anand and Daft summarized the advantages of this design in terms of cost savings, tapping into best sources of specialization and technology, supplier competition and technology, and flexibility, but also the disadvantages of loss of in-house skills and innovation, reduced control over supply and quality, and even the threat of being entirely supplanted by suppliers.[24] With an economic downturn such as the United States has experienced in recent times and rising wages abroad, there could be a movement toward what could be called "onshoring," bringing outsourced jobs back to the United States. For example, DESA Heating Products had outsourced hundreds of jobs to China but is now bringing those jobs back to its Kentucky factory based on quality and transportation costs and service.[25]

As indicated, the modular designs are also based on outsourcing, but instead of the entire process being taken offshore, as in hollow designs (e.g., manufacturing, logistics, or customer service), the modular design consists of "decomposable product chunks provided by internal and external subcontractors."[26] For example, Bombardier's business jet design consists of a dozen chunks provided by both internal (cockpit, center, and fuselage) and external subcontractors from around the world (e.g., Australia, Taiwan, Japan, Austria, and Canada) as well as the United States (e.g., General Electric for the engine and the avionics from Rockwell Collins). Industries that commonly use modular designs include auto, bicycle, consumer electronics, appliances, power tools, and computing products and software.

Anand and Daft summarize the advantages of modular designs in terms of cost, speed of response to market changes, and innovation through recombination of modules in different ways.[27] This flexibility advantage, however, is counterbalanced by problems with interfacing the modules and laggards in the supply chain affecting the whole system. An example of these advantages and disadvantages would be the auto firms Nissan and DaimlerChrysler. Nissan's modular design is known for being very efficient because parts such as the frame, dashboard, and seats are made by subcontractors and then shipped to the Nissan plant for assembly. DaimlerChrysler, also using a modular design in producing its two-seater Smart Car, had trouble because the various subcontracted parts failed to properly snap into place. The resulting extensive debugging was very costly to DaimlerChrysler and embarrassingly delayed the launch of its hyped-up innovative car.

## Network Designs

The commonality found in the horizontal, hollow, and modular organization designs is that they all provide an alternative to the traditional bureaucratic model in terms of both perspective and actual structure. All three of these contemporary designs are sometimes subsumed under the single term "Network Designs" because of the boundaryless conditions created by advanced information technology and globalization. As Rosalie Tung observed:

> The advent of the Internet (one of the world's biggest networks), quantum advances in other means and modes of telecommunications, and continued globalization of the world economy have changed all that—it is now possible to form networks that link phenomenal numbers of people, organizations, and systems in disparate corners of the world at an alarming rate and speed. For example, some popular Web sites receive as many as 5 million hits a day, thus making instantaneous access to information and exchange of ideas among peoples from different geographic locations possible. In a similar vein, people from far corners of the world now regularly work together in virtual teams on various types of projects.[28]

Network organizations have been discussed in the academic literature for a number of years. For example, organization theorists Miles and Snow identified what they call the *dynamic network.*[29] This involves a unique combination of strategy, structure, and management processes. They more recently have described the network organization as follows:

"Delayered, highly flexible, and controlled by market mechanisms rather than administrative procedures, firms with this new structure arrayed themselves on an industry value chain according to their core competencies, obtaining complementary resources through strategic alliances and outsourcing."[30] There is also research showing the impact that structure and information technology can have on network behavior and outcomes.[31]

With the advent of teams, outsourcing and, especially, alliances (two or more firms building a close collaborative relationship), network designs are being increasingly used by practicing organizations. Tapscott and Caston note that such networked organizations are "based on cooperative, multidisciplinary teams and businesses networked together across the enterprise. Rather than a rigid structure, it is a modular organizational architecture in which business teams operate as a network of what we call client and server functions."[32] Table 3.2 compares the various dimensions and characteristics of the traditional, hierarchical organization with the network organization. Although the network design cannot readily be drawn, as can the classical hierarchical and horizontal structures, Figure 3.2 is an attempt to at least show the concept.

Miles and colleagues identified three types of radical redesign of organizations:[33]

1. *Greenfield redesign.* As the term implies, this means starting from just a piece of green field or from a clean slate, breaking completely from the classical structure and establishing a totally different design. Examples include such highly successful firms as Google and Southwest Airlines. For example, when Southwest Airlines started under the unique leadership of Herb Kelleher, the firm made a complete break from the traditional airline industry. The now retired Kelleher was described as having enormous intellectual capabilities, a love for people, a playful spirit, and a commanding personality; he once arm-wrestled an opponent in an advertising slogan dispute rather than going to court.[34] Southwest created an organization that "flies in the face of bureaucracy: it stays lean, thinks small, keeps it simple—and more."[35] The successor to Kelleher, Jim Parker, noted the cross-functional nature of jobs at Southwest is more perceptual than real: "People should not be doing other people's job but they need to understand all of those other jobs; they need to understand how their job fits into the overall performance of the vision and how the other jobs do as well."[36]

**TABLE 3.2**    **Tapscott and Caston Summary of Traditional Hierarchical versus the Network Organizations**

Source: Don Tapscott and Art Caston, *Paradigm Shift*, McGraw-Hill, New York, 1993, p. 11. Used with permission of McGraw-Hill.

| Dimension/Characteristic | Traditional Organization | Network Organization |
|---|---|---|
| Structure | Hierarchical | Networked |
| Scope | Internal/closed | External/open |
| Resource focus | Capital | Human, information |
| State | Static, stable | Dynamic, changing |
| Personnel focus | Managers | Professionals |
| Key drivers | Reward and punishment | Commitment |
| Direction | Management commands | Self-management |
| Basis of action | Control | Empowerment to act |
| Individual motivation | Satisfy superiors | Achieve team goals |
| Learning | Specific skills | Broader competencies |
| Basis for compensation | Position in hierarchy | Accomplishment, competence level |
| Relationships | Competitive (my turf) | Cooperative (our challenge) |
| Employee attitude | Detachment (it's a job) | Identification (it's my company) |
| Dominant requirements | Sound management | Leadership |

**FIGURE 3.2**
**Miles and Snow Summary of Hierarchical versus Network Organizations**

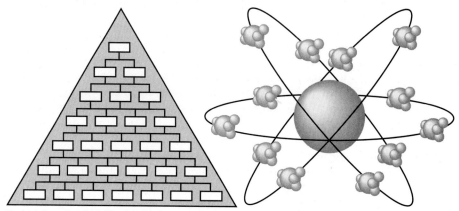

Rather than the old inflexible hierarchical pyramid, network organizations demand a flexible, spherical structure that can rotate competent, self-managing teams and other resources around a common knowledge base. Such teams, capable of quick action on the firm's behalf both externally and internally, provide a distinct competitive advantage.

2. *Rediscovery redesign.* This is a more usual type of redesign, whereby established companies such as General Electric return to a previously successful design by eliminating unproductive structural additions and modifications. For example, several U.S. electronics firms such as Texas Instruments have reverted to some highly formalized, bureaucratic procedures in their product development process.[37]

3. *Network design.* Firms such as Harley-Davidson are not just redesigning in the "Greenfield" sense or rediscovering and extending their past. Instead, they are undergoing efforts to disaggregate and partner. In the network approach, the firm concentrates on where it can add the greatest value in the supply chain, and it outsources to upstream and/or downstream partners who can do a better job. This network of the firm and its upstream and downstream partners can be optimally effective and flexible. Another network approach is to require internal units of the firm to interact at market prices—buy and sell to each other at prices equal to those that can be obtained by outsourcing partners. This "insourcing" approach to the internal network organization can be found in global firms such as the well-known Swiss conglomerate Asea Brown Boveri (ABB). In addition, globalization challenges these multinational corporations to make sure they account for cultural differences (see OB in Action: One Size Doesn't Fit All).

## The Virtual Organization

Besides the more specific horizontal, hollow, and modular contemporary designs, another more all-encompassing design besides the network organization is the so-called virtual organization. This term *virtual organization* has emerged not so much because it describes something distinct from network organizations but because the term itself represents the new environment and the partnering, alliances, and outsourcing arrangements found in an increasing number of global companies. Anand and Daft note that "collaboration or joint ventures with competitors usually takes the form of a virtual organization—a company outside a company created to specifically respond to an exceptional market opportunity that is often temporary."[38] Interestingly, the word *virtual* as used here comes not from the popular *virtual reality* but from *virtual memory,* which has been used to describe a way of making a computer's memory capacity appear to be greater than it really is but does require a strong information technology platform.

There are some things in the world that seem to be the same regardless of geographic location. Whether a pilot is flying into Kennedy International in New York or Heathrow in the U.K., one would assume the procedures for taking off and landing to be identical. The truth is, however, cultural differences may violate such assumptions. For example, most countries of the world have indeed agreed that English should be the universal language when pilots from anywhere are talking to air traffic controllers. On the other hand, French unions have encouraged their pilots to continue talking in French when landing at Charles de Gaulle airport. These culturally generated differences are not restricted to the airline industry.

Many multinational companies are finding that it is extremely difficult to take a product that sells well in the home country and achieve equal success in a foreign market. The customs, culture, and behaviors of people in these markets are often quite different from those in the home country. For example, when Office Depot and Office Max entered the Japanese market, they were convinced that their wide variety of products, convenient store layout, and low prices would help them attain a significant market share. They were wrong. One of their major Japanese competitors realized something that the big American multinationals did not—small business firms account for a significant percentage of the office supply market, and these firms were anxious to get the same big discounts on their purchases as did large firms. So the Japanese company created a catalogue business that was geared specifically to small firms. In these companies clerks did much of the purchasing of business equipment, and they were happy to be able to look through a catalog and place orders from their desk rather than traveling to the store.

Although chagrined by their efforts to compete effectively with their smaller Japanese rival, Office Depot and Office Max believed that they would be able to capture a large percentage of the remaining market—the walk-in customer. Again, they were foiled by their Japanese competitors. Unlike American customers, Japanese buyers do not mind shopping at small stores where the merchandise is crammed together. As a result, Office Depot and Office Max built large stores with wide aisles and ended up paying twice as much as their smaller competitors for rent and personnel salaries and were eventually forced to admit defeat. Their experience is not unique.

When Bob's Big Boy, the Michigan-based restaurant minichain, opened a series of units in Thailand, management was surprised to learn that local customers really did not care for the firm's hamburgers. Local customers would rather buy a sweet satay, noodle bowl, or grilled squid from a street vendor at one-fifth the cost. In fact, the owner of the Thai franchise system did not start making money until he began closely studying the potential customers who were walking past his restaurants. He then realized that these potential customers fell into two broad categories: European tourists and young Thai people. This resulted in his changing the menu of his restaurants. For German customers he began offering specialties such as spatzle, beef, and chocolate cake. For local Thais there were country-style specialties such as fried rice and pork omelets. The owner also added sugar and chile powder to Big Boy's burgers to better match Thai taste buds. Commenting on his eventual success, the adaptable owner recently noted, "We thought we were bringing American food to the masses. But now we're bringing Thai and European food to the tourists. It's strange, but you know what? It's working." And the reason is that the owner realizes market offerings have to be tailored to local demand. One size does not fit all.

Different from traditional mergers and acquisitions, the partners in the virtual organization share costs, skills, and access to international markets. Each partner contributes to the virtual organization what it is best at—its core capabilities. Briefly summarized, here are some of the key attributes of the virtual organization:

1. *Technology.* Informational networks will help far-flung companies and entrepreneurs link up and work together from start to finish. The partnerships will be based on electronic contracts to keep the lawyers away and speed the linkups.

2. *Opportunism.* Partnerships will be less permanent, less formal, and more opportunistic. Companies will band together to meet all specific market opportunities and, more often than not, fall apart once the need evaporates.

3. *No borders.* This new organizational model redefines the traditional boundaries of the company. More cooperation among competitors, suppliers, and customers makes it harder to determine where one company ends and another begins.

4. *Trust.* These relationships make companies far more reliant on each other and require far more trust than ever before. They share a sense of "codestiny," meaning that the fate of each partner is dependent on the other.

5. *Excellence.* Because each partner brings its "core competence" to the effort, it may be possible to create a "best-of-everything" organization. Every function and process could be world class—something that no single company could achieve.[39]

Importantly, virtual organizations can help competitiveness in the global economy. The alliances and partnerships with other organizations can extend worldwide, the spatial and temporal interdependence easily transcend boundaries, and the flexibility allows easy reassignment and reallocation to take quick advantage of shifting opportunities in global markets.[40] To avoid disintegration and attain effective needed focus, the lead virtual organization must have a shared vision, a strong brand, and, most important, a high-trust culture.[41] For instance, competitors P&G and Clorox recently collaborated in forming a new generation of plastic wrap called GLAD Press'n Seal in order to effectively compete with market leader Saran.

Other examples of firms that have formed virtual collaborations include Harley-Davidson and ABB—and also, on a smaller scale, firms such as Clark Equipment, a manufacturer of forklifts and other industrial equipment; Semco, a Brazilian firm producing pumps, valves, and other industrial products; Sweden's Skandia Insurance Group (with 91,000 partners worldwide); and the Australian firm Technical and Computer Graphics (TCG). In the information technology industry, Sun Microsystems views itself as an intellectual holding company that designs computers and does all other functions (product ordering, manufacturing, distribution, marketing, and customer service) through contractual arrangements with partners located throughout the world, and Intel uses virtual teams with members from Ireland, Israel, England, France, and Asia working on a wide variety of projects. As with the network organization, it is not really possible to show a virtual organization, but Figure 3.3

**FIGURE 3.3**
**Miles and Snow's Example of a Virtual Organization: Technical and Computer Graphics (TCG), an Australian-Based Multinational Firm.**

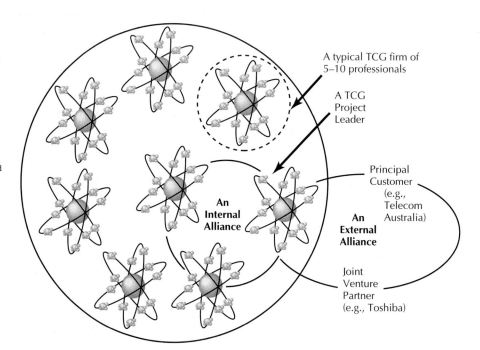

A typical TCG firm of 5–10 professionals

A TCG Project Leader

An Internal Alliance

An External Alliance

Principal Customer (e.g., Telecom Australia)

Joint Venture Partner (e.g., Toshiba)

depicts graphically how TCG would look as a virtual organization. Because networks and virtual organizations both represent such radically different ways to structure firms, there are many challenges ahead, especially on the human side of these contemporary structural forms.

# THE ORGANIZATIONAL CULTURE CONTEXT

Going from Chapter 2's discussion of the globalization context to more of a micro cultural impact on organizational behavior is organizational culture. The remainder of the chapter defines organizational culture and examines the types and ways to change and manage organizational culture.

## Definition and Characteristics

When people join an organization, they bring with them the values and beliefs they have been taught. Quite often, however, these values and beliefs are insufficient for helping the individual succeed in the organization. The person needs to learn how the particular enterprise does things. A good example is the U.S. Marine Corps. During boot camp, drill instructors teach recruits the "Marine way." The training attempts to psychologically strip down the new recruits and then restructure their way of thinking and their values. They are taught to think and act like Marines. Anyone who has been in the Marines or knows someone who has will verify that the Corps generally accomplishes its objective. In a less-dramatic way, today's organizations do the same thing. For example, UPS is known for having a militarylike corporate culture. However, as an outside observer who embedded himself (i.e., riding "shotgun" next to drivers and aiding with deliveries during the Christmas rush) noted: "Although the job is highly regimented, it includes enough independence for workers to be energized by the daily challenge of getting all the packages out and importantly, when there were problems, drivers, not technology, were the best at solving them."[42] The same is true in more complex organizations where a key challenge is to instill and sustain a corporatewide culture that encourages knowledge sharing. As the partner in charge of Ernst & Young's knowledge-based business solution practice notes, "If you're going to have a rich knowledge-sharing culture, that can't just be a veneer on top of the business operation. You have to have people who can make sense out of it and apply it."[43]

Edgar Schein, who is probably most closely associated with the study of organizational culture, defines it as

> a pattern of basic assumptions—invented, discovered, or developed by a given group as it learns to cope with its problems of external adaptation and internal integration—that has worked well enough to be considered valuable and, therefore, to be taught to new members as the correct way to perceive, think, and feel in relation to those problems.[44]

More recently, Joanne Martin emphasizes the differing perspectives of cultures in organizations. She notes:

> As individuals come into contact with organizations, they come into contact with dress norms, stories people tell about what goes on, the organization's formal rules and procedures, its formal codes of behavior, rituals, tasks, pay systems, jargon, and jokes only understood by insiders, and so on. These elements are some of the manifestations of organizational culture.[45]

However, she adds that there is another perspective of culture as well:

> When cultural members interpret the meanings of these manifestations, their perceptions, memories, beliefs, experiences, and values will vary, so interpretations will differ—even of

the same phenomenon. The patterns or configurations of these interpretations, and the ways they are enacted, constitute culture.[46]

In other words, organizational culture is quite complex. Although there are a number of problems and disagreements associated with the conceptualization of organizational culture, most definitions, including the preceding, recognize the importance of shared norms and values that guide organizational participants' behavior. In fact, there is research evidence that not only are these cultural values taught to newcomers, but newcomers seek out and want to learn about their organization's culture.[47]

Organizational culture has a number of important characteristics. Some of the most readily agreed upon are the following:

1. *Observed behavioral regularities.* When organizational participants interact with one another, they use common language, terminology, and rituals related to deference and demeanor.

2. *Norms.* Standards of behavior exist, including guidelines on how much work to do, which in many organizations come down to "Do not do too much; do not do too little."

3. *Dominant values.* There are major values that the organization advocates and expects the participants to share. Typical examples are high product quality, low absenteeism, and high efficiency.

4. *Philosophy.* There are policies that set forth the organization's beliefs about how employees and/or customers are to be treated.

5. *Rules.* There are strict guidelines related to getting along in the organization. Newcomers must learn those "ropes" in order to be accepted as full-fledged members of the group.

6. *Organizational climate.* This is an overall "feeling" that is conveyed by the physical layout, the way participants interact, and the way members of the organization conduct themselves with customers or other outsiders.

Each of these characteristics has controversies surrounding it and varying degrees of research support. For example, there is controversy in the academic literature over the similarities and differences between organizational culture and organizational climate.[48] However, there is empirical support for some of the characteristics, such as the important role that physical layout plays in organizational culture. Here is a real-world illustration:

> Nike Inc. serves as an excellent example of a company that successfully revealed its corporate culture through corporate design. Set on 74 sprawling acres amid the pine groves of Beaverton, Oregon, the Nike World campus exudes the energy, youth and vitality that have become synonymous with Nike's products. The campus is almost a monument to Nike's corporate values: the production of quality goods and, of course, fitness. Included in the seven-building campus is an athletic club with a track, weight rooms, aerobic studios, tennis, racquetball and squash courts, and a basketball court.[49]

The six characteristics of culture are not intended to be all-inclusive. For example, a study examined why companies were rated as most and least admired. Statistical analysis was conducted that compared the findings from a subjective opinion survey of reputation with what one might expect perceptions to be if they are based solely on financial performance. The financial measures that correlated most closely with the opinion of a firm's "reputation" over a decade ago were, in order, 10-year annual return to shareholders, profits as a percent of assets, total profits, and stock market value.[50] As the head of Coca-Cola, one of the most admired companies for many years, declared at that time: "I get paid to make the owners of Coca-Cola Co. increasingly wealthy with each passing day.

Everything else is just fluff."[51] Obviously, bottom-line financial performance remains important, but a more recent analysis of *Fortune*'s admired companies found the most highly correlated attribute of those that scored in the top three of their industry was the "attraction and retention of top talent," and a major way these top firms do this is to take their culture and values seriously.[52] For example, currently admired firms such as the software firm SAS, Southwest Airlines, and Google attract and retain their best people because they give a lot of attention and care to their legendary cultures and values. As a recent analysis of how Toyota's culture led it to become the top automaker concluded, the curiosity and spirit of Toyota people, as much as anything, has determined its success.[53] In his final days, the former CEO of KPMG recognized the importance of a compassionate culture and urged his staff to "get the most out of each moment and day—for the firm's benefit and the individual's."[54] These cultures and values also drive business results and make them successful.[55]

## Uniformity of Culture

A common misconception is that an organization has a uniform culture. However, at least as anthropology uses the concept, it is probably more accurate to treat organizations "as if" they had a uniform culture. "All organizations 'have' culture in the sense that they are embedded in specific societal cultures and are part of them."[56] According to this view, an organizational culture is a common perception held by the organization's members. Everyone in the organization would have to share this perception. However, all may not do so to the same degree. As a result, there can be a dominant culture as well as subcultures throughout a typical organization.

A *dominant culture* is a set of core values shared by a majority of the organization's members. For example, most employees at Southwest Airlines seem to subscribe to such values as hard work, company loyalty, and the need for customer service. Southwest employees take to heart cultural values such as: irreverence is okay; it's okay to be yourself; have fun at work; take the competition seriously, but not yourself; and do whatever it takes for the customer.[57] Table 3.3 summarizes the FUNdamentals that are the core of the Southwest cultural values that are taught to the 25,000 associates who go through its corporate University for People every year. Those who work for Disney are: in the show, not on the job; wearing costumes, not uniforms; on stage or backstage, not at positions or workstations; cast members, not employees. When Disney cast members are presented with the riddle: "Ford makes cars, Sony makes TVs, Microsoft makes software, what does Disney make?"—all respond, "Disney makes people happy!"[58] These values create a dominant culture in these organizations that helps guide the day-to-day behavior of employees. There is also evidence that these dominant cultures can have a positive impact on desirable outcomes such as successfully conducting mergers and acquisitions (e.g., when Dow AgroSciences purchased Cargil Hybris Seeds),[59] supporting product-innovation processes,[60] and helping firms cope with rapid economic and technological change.[61]

Important, but often overlooked, are the subcultures in an organization. A *subculture* is a set of values shared by a minority, usually a small minority, of the organization's members. Subcultures typically are a result of problems or experiences that are shared by members of a department or unit. For example, even though GE has one of the most dominant overall corporate cultures of being boundaryless between the highly diversified divisions (e.g., ranging from power generation to media, plastics, financial services, aircraft engines, locomotives, medical equipment, and lighting and appliances), each also has a distinctive subculture. GE Capital has a distinctive culture compared to the high-tech manufacturing cultures of aircraft engines and gas turbines.[62]

**TABLE 3.3**
**Southwest Airlines'**
**Core Cultural Values**

Source: Adapted from Anne
Bruce, "Southwest: Back to the
FUNdamentals," *HR Focus,*
March 1997, p. 11.

| | |
|---|---|
| Hire for attitudes, Train for skill. | The company deliberately looks for applicants with a positive attitude who will promote fun in the workplace and have the desire to "color outside the lines." |
| Do it Better, Faster, Cheaper. | Cost control is a personal responsibility for employees at Southwest and is incorporated into all training programs. |
| Deliver positively outrageous customer service (POS) to both internal and external customers! | The Southwest philosophy? Put your employees first and they will take care of the customers. |
| Walk a mile in someone else's shoes. | For example, a pilot works with ramp agents for a full day; a reservationist works in the University for People; a customer service agent helps the skycaps. And President Herb Kelleher frequently passes out peanuts and serves drinks on flights. He even helps the baggage handlers load and unload on holidays. |
| Take accountability and ownership. | A great value is placed on taking initiative, thinking for yourself, even if that means going against something in the policy manual. For instance, employees have been known to take stranded passengers back to their own homes in emergencies. |
| Celebrate and let your hair down. | Chili cook-offs, lavish Halloween productions, and Christmas parties in July are all tools for motivating people. When people have fun on the job, their productivity and performance improve. |
| Celebrate your mistakes as well as your triumphs. | Turning failures into personal growth is part of celebrating mistakes, a philosophy that encourages trying new ideas without the fear of repercussions. |
| Keep the corporate culture alive and well. | Members of the culture committee visit regularly at stations all across the country, infusing the corporate culture, reiterating the company's history, and motivating employees to maintain the spirit that made the airline great. |

Subcultures can weaken and undermine an organization if they are in conflict with the dominant culture and/or the overall objectives. Successful firms, however, find that this is not always the case.[63] Most subcultures are formed to help the members of a particular group deal with the specific day-to-day problems with which they are confronted. The members may also support many, if not all, of the core values of the dominant culture. In the case of GE, the success of the company is their "social architecture," which pulls the subcultures all together. As former president Jack Welch stated, "GE is greater than the sum of its parts because of the intellectual capacity that is generated in the businesses and the sharing that goes on of that learning and the rapid action on that learning."[64]

## CREATING AND MAINTAINING A CULTURE

Some organizational cultures may be the direct, or at least indirect, result of actions taken by the founders. However, this is not always the case. Sometimes founders create weak cultures, and if the organization is to survive, a new top manager must be installed who will sow the seeds for the necessary strong culture. Thomas Watson, Sr. of IBM is a good example.

When he took over the CTR Corporation, it was a small firm manufacturing computing, tabulating, and recording equipment. Through his dominant personality and the changes he made at the firm, Watson created a culture that propelled IBM to be one of the biggest and best companies in the world. However, IBM's problems in the early 1990s when the computer market shifted from mainframes to PCs also were largely attributed to its outdated culture. After Watson and his son, the leaders of IBM made some minor changes and modifications that had little impact and eventually left the company in bad shape. However, in recent years IBM, under the leadership of Louis Gerstner, launched into a bold new strategy that changed IBM from top to bottom. Mr. Gerstner became convinced that "all the cost-cutting in the world will be unable to save IBM unless it upends the way it does business."[65] This cultural change at IBM led to an outstanding turnaround that included getting out of the sale of computers. IBM is an example of an organization wherein a culture must be changed because the environment changes and the previous core cultural values are not in step with those needed for survival. The following sections take a close look at how organizational cultures get started, maintained, and changed.

## How Organizational Cultures Start

Although organizational cultures can develop in a number of different ways, the process usually involves some version of the following steps:

1. A single person (founder) has an idea for a new enterprise.
2. The founder brings in one or more other key people and creates a core group that shares a common vision with the founder. That is, all in this core group believe that the idea is a good one, is workable, is worth running some risks for, and is worth the investment of time, money, and energy that will be required.
3. The founding core group begins to act in concert to create an organization by raising funds, obtaining patents, incorporating, locating space, building, and so on.
4. At this point, others are brought into the organization, and a common history begins to be built.[66]

Most of today's successful corporate giants in all industries basically followed these steps. Two well-known representative examples are McDonald's and Wal-Mart.

- *McDonald's.* Ray Kroc worked for many years as a salesperson for a food supplier (Lily Tulip Cup). He learned how retail food operations were conducted. He also had an entrepreneurial streak and began a sideline business with a partner. They sold multimixers, machines that were capable of mixing up to six frozen shakes at a time. One day Kroc received a large order for multimixers from the McDonald brothers. The order intrigued Kroc, and he decided to look in on the operation the next time he was in their area. When he did, Kroc became convinced that the McDonald's fast-food concept would sweep the nation. He bought the rights to franchise McDonald's units and eventually bought out the brothers. At the same time, he built the franchise on four basic concepts: quality, cleanliness, service, and price. In order to ensure that each unit offers the customer the best product at the best price, franchisees are required to attend McDonald University, where they are taught how to manage their business. Here they learn the McDonald cultural values and the proper way to run the franchise. This training ensures that franchisees all over the world are operating their units in the same way. Kroc died many years ago, but the culture he left behind is still very much alive in McDonald's franchises across the globe. In fact, new employees receive videotaped messages from the late Mr. Kroc. Some of the more interesting of his pronouncements that reflect and carry on his values are his thoughts on cleanliness: "If you've got time to lean, you've got time to clean." About the competition he says: "If they are drowning to death, I would put a hose in their mouth." And on expanding he declares: "When you're green, you grow; when you're ripe, you rot." So even though he has not been involved in the business for many years, his legacy lives on. Even his office at corporate headquarters is preserved as a museum, his reading glasses untouched in their leather case on the desk.

- *Wal-Mart.* Sam Walton, founder of Wal-Mart Stores, Inc., opened his first Wal-Mart store in 1962. Focusing on the sale of discounted name-brand merchandise in small-town markets, he began to set up more and more stores in the Sun Belt. At the same time, he began developing effective inventory control systems and marketing techniques. Today, Wal-Mart has not only become the largest retailer but also one of the biggest firms in the world. Although Sam died many years ago, his legacy and cultural values continue. For example, Walton himself stressed, and the current management staff continues to emphasize, the importance of encouraging associates to develop new ideas that will increase their store's efficiency. If a policy does not seem to be working, the company quickly changes it. Executives continually encourage associates to challenge the current system and look for ways to improve it. Those who do these things are rewarded; those who do not perform up to expectations are encouraged to do better. Today, Walton's founding values continue to permeate the organization. To make sure the cultural values get out to all associates, the company has a communication network worthy of the Pentagon. It includes everything from a satellite system to a private air force of numerous planes. Everyone is taught this culture and is expected to operate according to the core cultural values of hard work, efficiency, and customer service.

Although the preceding stories of cultural development are well known, in recent years these and other well-known companies founded by charismatic leaders have had varied success. The same is true of the dot-com firms. Some, like Jeff Bezos's founding and cultural development of Amazon.com, are in some ways similar to and in some ways different from the stories of Ray Kroc at McDonald's or Sam Walton at Wal-Mart. They are similar in that both started from scratch with very innovative, "out of the box" ideas to build an empire and change the way business is done. They are different in terms of speed and style. Other corporate culture stories today are not necessarily about the founders, but about those who took their company to the next level. For example, John Chambers, the CEO of Cisco, is largely credited for taking this well-known high-tech firm from a market capitalization of $9 billion when he took over in 1995 to being the highest-valued corporation in the world five years later and then repositioning the firm when the economy began to slump.[67] The culture of Cisco is largely attributed to his old-school values such as trust, hard work, and customer focus, but as the subsequent economic downturn and the rapid decline in the stock values of Cisco brought out, being at the right place at the right time in terms of the technology environment also had had a lot to do with Cisco's initial success. After the bubble had burst for Cisco and the other high-tech and especially dot-com firms, those who had the strong, but flexible, cultures were the ones that survived the extreme roller-coaster ride of the economy in recent years. Chambers indicated such desirable organizational cultural values when he declared, "I have no love of technology for technology's sake. Only solutions for customers."[68]

## Maintaining Cultures through Steps of Socialization

Once an organizational culture is started and begins to develop, there are a number of practices that can help solidify the acceptance of core values and ensure that the culture maintains itself. These practices can be described in terms of several socialization steps. Figure 3.4 illustrates what Richard Pascale has identified as the sequence of these steps.[69]

**FIGURE 3.4**
**Pascale's Steps of Organizational Culture Socialization.**

*Source:* Richard Pascale, "The Paradox of Corporate Culture: Reconciling Ourselves to Socialization." Copyright © by the Regents of the University of California. Reprinted from the *California Management Review,* Vol. 27, No. 2, Winter 1985, p. 38. By permission of the Regents.

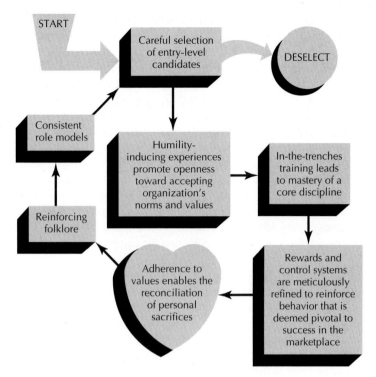

### Selection of Entry-Level Personnel

The first step is the careful selection of entry-level candidates. Using standardized procedures and seeking specific traits that tie to effective performance, trained recruiters interview candidates and attempt to screen out those whose personal styles and values do not make a "fit" with the organization's culture. There is research indicating that newcomers' and their supervisors' perceptions of organization culture fit are related to organizational commitment and intention to leave the organization.[70] There is also accumulating evidence that those who have a realistic preview (called realistic job preview, or RJP) of the culture will turn out better.[71] An example of effective selection for cultural fit is North Shore Bank, a community bank in Wisconsin. One approach that they have implemented in order to maximize the "fit" as well as productivity is through recruitment and selection in neighborhoods closest to its branches. This helps customers and employees alike identify with the unique differences between their local bank and their large national bank competitors.

### Placement on the Job

The second step occurs on the job itself, after the person with a fit is hired. New personnel are subjected to a carefully orchestrated series of different experiences whose purpose is to cause them to question the organization's norms and values and to decide whether or not they can accept them. For example, many organizations with strong cultures make it a point to give newly hired personnel more work than they can handle. Sometimes these assignments are beneath the individual's abilities. At Procter & Gamble, for example, new personnel may be required to color in a sales territory map. The experience is designed to convey the message, "Although you're smart in some ways, you're in kindergarten as far as what you know about this organization." The objective is also to teach the new entrant into the culture the importance of humility. These experiences are designed to make newly hired personnel vulnerable and to cause them to move emotionally closer to their colleagues, thus intensifying group cohesiveness. Campus fraternities and the military have practiced this approach for years.

### Job Mastery

Once the initial "cultural shock" is over, the next step is mastery of one's job. This is typically done via extensive and carefully reinforced field experience. For example, Japanese firms typically put new employees through a training program for several years. As personnel move along their career path, their performance is evaluated, and additional responsibilities are assigned on the basis of progress. Quite often companies establish a step-by-step approach to this career plan, which helps reduce efforts by the personnel to use political power or to take shortcuts in order to get ahead at a faster pace. Highly successful "Coca-Cola slowly steeps its new employees in the company culture—in this case, an understanding of the trademark's image. The people system then ensures that only Coke managers who have been thoroughly socialized into worrying about the company as a whole get to make decisions affecting the company."[72]

### Measuring and Rewarding Performance

The next step of the socialization process consists of meticulous attention to measuring operational results and to rewarding individual performance. These systems are comprehensive and consistent, and they focus on those aspects of the business that are most crucial to competitive success and to corporate values. For example, at Procter & Gamble there are three factors that are considered most important: building volume, building profit, and making changes that increase effectiveness or add satisfaction to the job. Operational measures are used to track these three factors, and performance appraisals are tied to milestones. Promotions and merit pay are determined by success in each of these critical areas. Motorola personnel are taught to adhere to the core cultural values through careful monitoring of team performance and through continual training programs. Typically, in companies with a strong culture, those who violate cultural norms, such as overzealousness against the competition or harsh handling of a subordinate, are sent to the "penalty box." This typically involves a lateral move to a less-desirous location. For example, a branch manager in Chicago might be given a nebulous staff position at headquarters in Newark. This individual is now off-track, which can slow his or her career progress.

### Adherence to Important Values

The next step involves careful adherence to the firm's most important values. Identification with these values helps employees reconcile personal sacrifices brought about by their membership in the organization. They learn to accept these values and to trust the organization not to do anything that would hurt them. As Pascale observes: "Placing one's self 'at the mercy' of an organization imposes real costs. There are long hours of work, missed weekends, bosses one has to endure, criticism that seems unfair, job assignments and rotations that are inconvenient or undesirable."[73] However, the organization attempts to overcome these costs by connecting the sacrifices to higher human values such as serving society with better products and/or services. Today's firms in the global economy must give special attention to cultural differences around the globe, but maintain the core values. For example, when Wal-Mart Stores entered the German market a few years ago, it took along the "cheer"—Give me a W! Give me an A!, etc. Who's Number One? The customer!—which went over as well with the German associates as it did with their counterparts in the United States. However, the cultural value of greeting any customer within a 10-foot radius did not. German employees and shoppers were not comfortable with this Wal-Mart custom, and it was dropped from the German stores.

### *Reinforcing the Stories and Folklore*

The next step involves reinforcing organizational folklore. This entails keeping alive stories that validate the organization's culture and way of doing things. The folklore helps explain why the organization does things a particular way. One of the most common forms of folklore is stories with morals the enterprise wants to reinforce. For example, Leonard Riggio, the CEO of Barnes & Noble, often tells stories about his childhood experiences in Brooklyn and in particular his father's stint as a boxer. These often-told stories have been a great help to communicate a populist culture that needed to shed its elitist past. Also, Bill Hewlett of Hewlett-Packard is known for the often-told story of him using a bolt cutter to remove a lock that he encountered on the supply room. He left a note behind instructing that the door never be locked again to forever communicate the important cultural value of trust at H-P. 3M is probably the best known firm to use stories and sagas to emphasize cultural values. The famous Post-it Notes legacy is a great example.

> The idea originated with Art Fry, a 3M employee who used bits of paper to mark hymns when he sang in his church choir. But these markers kept falling out of the hymnals. He decided that he needed an adhesive-backed paper that would stick as long as necessary but could be removed easily, and soon found what he wanted in a 3M laboratory. Fry saw the market potential of his invention, but others did not. Market survey results were negative; major office supply distributors were skeptical. Undeterred, because he had heard stories about other 3M employees that conveyed the importance of perseverance, Fry began giving samples to 3M executives and their secretaries. Once they actually used the little notepads, they were hooked. Having sold 3M on the project, Fry used the same approach with the secretaries of other companies' executives throughout the United States.[74]

The rest is history. Post-it Notes became a huge financial success for 3M, and retelling the story reinforces cultural values of innovation that can come from anywhere, perseverance, and championing of your good ideas.

### *Recognition and Promotion*

The final step is the recognition and promotion of individuals who have done their jobs well and who can serve as role models to new people in the organization. By pointing out these people as winners, the organization encourages others to follow their example. Role models in strong-culture firms are regarded as the most powerful ongoing training program of all. Morgan Stanley, the financial services firm, chooses role models on the basis of energy, aggressiveness, and team play. Procter & Gamble looks for people who exhibit extraordinary consistency in such areas as tough-mindedness, motivational skills, energy, and the ability to get things done through others. There is considerable research evidence that recognition can serve as a powerful reinforcer,[75] and thus those exhibiting cultural values that are given either formal recognition or even one-on-one social attention/recognition from relevant others can build and sustain the organizational culture.[76]

## Changing Organizational Culture

Sometimes an organization determines that its culture has to be changed. For example, the current environmental context has undergone drastic change and either the organization must adapt to these new conditions or it may not survive. In fact, as Chapters 1 and 2 pointed out, it is no longer sufficient just to react to change. Today, as was pointed out in the earlier discussion in this chapter about organizational learning, organizations must have a culture that learns and anticipates change. New product development, advanced information technology and the economy are changing so rapidly that any examples would be soon out-of-date. However, if the appropriate organization culture is in place, then such rapid change can be welcomed and accommodated with as little disruption and as few problems as possible. One example of an organization culture literally built around change is Steelcase's corporate development center, shaped like a pyramid with an open atrium containing a huge swinging pendulum to remind employees that the world is always changing. Another example of keeping up with the changing workplace is Zenith, who uses its intranet as a kind of virtual water cooler. As the head of the marketing group notes, "Every day we say who is having a birthday, a service anniversary, or if we've had an incredible sales day."[77]

Even though some firms have had a culture in place to anticipate change, moving to a new culture or changing old cultures can be quite difficult: a case can even be made that it really can't be done successfully. Predictable obstacles include entrenched skills, staffs, relationships, roles, and structures that work together to reinforce traditional cultural patterns. For example, the head of Bell Canada, which is trying to undergo a significant cultural change (from its 122-year-old monopolist mentality to a highly competitive environment), started with implementing formal quality and cost cutting programs, but realized very quickly that "We needed to get to the front lines of the organization, and my view is that it's very hard to do that through formal programs."[78] Another example would be the traditional tough, macho culture found on offshore oil rigs. It was very difficult to change the traditional cultural values of displaying masculine strength and daring to a caring, helping environment. This shift was difficult but over a long period of time these "rough necks" came to "appreciate that to improve safety and performance in a potentially deadly environment, they had to be open to new information that challenged their assumptions, and they had to acknowledge when they were wrong."[79] The result of this cultural change on the oil rigs dramatically decreased the accident rate by 84 percent and productivity, efficiency, and reliability all increased beyond the industry benchmarks.[80] In addition to the importance of frontline workers in cultural change, powerful stakeholders such as unions, management, or even customers may support the existing culture and impede the change. The problems are compounded by the cultural clash that is the rule rather than the exception in mergers and acquisitions (M&As), emerging relationship enterprises, and the recent economic crisis.

### The Case of Mergers and Acquisitions

Although M&As were thought to have peaked over a decade ago, they have again become very common because the wide divergence in stock-market values between firms, globalization, and the recent financial/economic crisis have left a climate for both friendly buyouts and hostile takeovers. Besides the financial implications of M&As, the often slighted or even ignored organizational culture implications can be dramatic. As one veteran of a number of M&As concluded about the cultural side of mergers: (1) you can't do too much, and (2) too little will be done. In the heat of the deal, he says, "people issues, as real as they are, become obscured."[81] The clash between the two cultures in a merger or acquisition can be focused into three major areas:

1. *Structure.* These factors from the two cultures include the size, age, and history of the two firms; the industry in which the partners come from and now reside; the geographic locations; and whether products and/or services are involved.

2. *Politics.* Where does the power and managerial decision making really reside? Corporate cultures range from autocratic extremes to total employee empowerment, and how this plays out among the partners will be important to cultural compatibility.

3. *Emotions.* The personal feelings, the "cultural contract" that individuals have bought into to guide their day-to-day thoughts, habits, attitudes, commitment, and patterns of

daily behavior. These emotions will be a major input into the clash or compatibility of the two cultures.[82]

The potential (high probability) cultural clash from M&As will be greatly compounded when the partners are from different countries.[83] With globalization now a reality (see Chapter 2), cross-border alliances are commonplace. Announcements of megamergers such as DaimlerChrysler, British Petroleum-Amoco, and Deutsche Bank-Bankers Trust reach the headlines, but the cultural clash aftermath seldom, if at all, is discussed. The highly visible DaimlerChrysler merger problems with advertising and U.S.-government-sponsored research aimed at fuel efficiency and cleaner cars is given attention, but the cultural issues are not given as much attention. Yet, the day-to-day cultural clashes at all levels are the reality. As auto industry analysts have pointed out, Daimler-Benz had a conservative, slow-moving corporate culture while Chrysler at the time of the merger had a fast, lean, informal, and daring corporate culture. For example, the Mercedes-Benz plant in Vance, Alabama, represents the merger in microcosm. The German "wunderkind" plant manager deliberately selected German, U.S., and Canadian managers (some with Japanese auto firm experience) for his team. They clashed not just over the operations system, but also on more subtle but explosive cultural issues such as image and decorum. This type of cultural conflict is greatly trying to be worked out, but guidelines and help are still needed for meeting the challenge of managing the cultural change on both sides.

### The Case of Emerging Relationship Enterprises

Today's networked global environment is going beyond formal M&As with what are being called "relationship enterprises."[84] Somewhat like network and virtual organization designs discussed earlier in the chapter, these relationship enterprises consist of a global network of independent companies that act as a single company with a common mission. Examples include the following:

- The aerospace industry at the turn of the century is controlled by two networks— Boeing (based in the United States) and Airbus (France). Importantly, each of these relationship enterprises consists of more than 100 partners around the world.

- In the telecommunications industry, the Global One joint venture, led by Sprint, Deutsche Telekom, and France Telecom, serves 65 countries and functions as one relationship enterprise to serve the global telecom needs of many corporations.

- In the airline industry, United, Lufthansa, SAS, Varig, Thai Airways, and others have formed into a relationship enterprise called Star Alliance. They provide the international traveler with seamless service anywhere on the planet and share systems, marketing, in-country operations, schedules, and frequent flier miles—everything except crews.

In the near future such relationship enterprises will become common in more traditional industries such as chemicals, textiles, and food, as well as new frontier industries such as biotech and memory. The reason that this loose network of alliances is the trend over more formal M&As has to do with legal terms (by law some countries do not allow majority purchase of their firms by foreigners), but mainly with political nationalism and organizational cultural values. Pride and pragmatic needs are driving this new form of global alliance, but the perspective and management of the organizational cultures in this new relationship is a challenge. Issues such as trust, communication, and negotiation skills become very relevant and important to success. The organizations and managers in the global relations "must learn to communicate across the cultural divide; each must understand that the other perceives and interacts in a fundamentally different way."[85] Importantly, three-fourths of companies believe their alliances failed because of an incompatibility of country and corporate cultures.[86]

### Impact of Organizational Culture in an Economic Crisis

Besides M&As and the new organizational designs having an impact on organizational cultural change, the recent economic crisis has also stimulated both scholars and practitioners to reexamine the role that culture played and the lessons to be learned to effectively change the culture. For example, the mortgage companies (e.g., Countrywide Financial) and investment banks (e.g., Lehman Brothers) that collapsed at the end of 2008 were known to have very strong corporate cultures. However, as one analysis pointed out, "they were cultures characterized by rampant individualism, little attention or oversight from supervisors, and huge rewards for successful performance. Those values generated tremendous pressure to maximize individual performance and payouts, often by taking outsized risks and hiding failures. That same pressure often caused players to push the environment as to acceptable ethical behavior."[87]

By contrast, at least at this writing, Goldman Sachs was one of the few that escaped the purge in investment banking. They are known for having a team-oriented culture (as opposed to "rampant individualism") and according to Steven Kerr, a former organizational behavior professor who then became chief learning officer at GE and then Goldman Sachs, the managers had several meetings a day and "making any decision required checks with many people, and before we made a decision to invest, many eyes had seen the proposal."[88] In other words, lessons from the recent economic crisis are that first, the organizational culture can affect not only the ethical, "right thing to do," but also survival in the long-term. Second, organizations need to continually challenge and change their cultural values. For example, Goldman managers regularly review their cultural values by asking questions such as: "Which are we most or least faithful to?" and "Which need refreshing or reaffirming?"[89] Such a culture of continual questioning seems to be an effective starting point in cultural change, but there is also a need to go beyond such specific guidelines and focus on a more comprehensive approach that will be able to adapt to changing conditions.

### Guidelines for Change

Despite the complexity, significant barriers, and resistance to change, organizational cultures can be managed and changed over time.[90] This attempt to change culture can take many different forms. Simple guidelines such as the following can be helpful:[91]

1. Assess the current culture.
2. Set realistic goals that impact the bottom line.
3. Recruit outside personnel with industry experience, so that they are able to interact well with the organizational personnel.
4. Make changes from the top down, so that a consistent message is delivered from all management team members.
5. Include employees in the culture change process, especially when making changes in rules and processes.
6. Take out all trappings that remind the personnel of the previous culture.
7. Expect to have some problems and find people who would rather move than change with the culture and, if possible, take these losses early.
8. Move quickly and decisively to build momentum and to defuse resistance to the new culture.
9. Stay the course by being persistent.

Also, organizations attempting to change their culture must be careful not to abandon their roots and blindly abandon their core, but distinctive, competencies and core values. For example, it is generally recognized that the reason "New Coke" failed was that it broke away from the tried-but-true Coca-Cola traditional culture; and the reason Google so far has remained at or near the top in all categories, from profits, to growth, to best places to work, is because it has remained true to its core cultural values and all Googlers buy into them. As was recently observed:

> Talk to more than a dozen Googlers at various levels and departments, and one powerful theme emerges: Whether they're designing search for the blind or preparing meals for their colleagues, these people feel that their work can change the world. That sense is nonexistent at most companies, or at best intermittent, inevitably becoming subsumed in the day-to-day quagmire of PowerPoints, org charts, and budgetary realities.[92]

Where Coca-Cola is an example of a firm with a long history and strong corporate culture, and Google is a new age company with a very powerful corporate culture, IBM, discussed earlier under creating and maintaining a corporate culture, is a good example of a firm that has successfully undergone cultural changes.

## Summary

Organization theory is presented from a historical perspective and the learning organization. The learning organization draws on systems theory and emphasizes the importance of not only adaptive learning but also generative learning, leading to creativity, innovation, and staying ahead of change.

Modern organization designs are a marked departure from the classical bureaucratic model. The horizontal, hollow, modular, network, and virtual organization designs have emerged to better meet the needs for flexibility and change in the new environment.

The second half of this chapter on the organization context is concerned with organizational culture. It is a pattern of basic assumptions that are taught to new personnel as the correct way to perceive, think, and act on a day-to-day basis. Some of the important characteristics of organizational culture are observed behavioral regularities, norms, dominant values, philosophy, rules, and organizational climate. Although everyone in an organization will share the organization's culture, not all may do so to the same degree. There can be a dominant culture, but also a number of subcultures. A dominant culture is a set of core values that are shared by a majority of the organization's members. A subculture is a set of values shared by a small percentage of the organization's members.

A culture typically is created by a founder or top-level manager who forms a core group that shares a common vision. This group acts in concert to create the cultural values, norms, and climate necessary to carry on this vision. In maintaining this culture, enterprises typically carry out several steps such as the following: careful selection of entry-level candidates; on-the-job experiences to familiarize the personnel with the organization's culture; mastery of one's job; meticulous attention to measuring operational results and to rewarding individual performance; careful adherence to the organization's most important values; a reinforcing of organizational stories and folklore; and, finally, recognition and promotion of individuals who have done their jobs well and who can serve as role models to new personnel in the organization.

In some cases organizations find that they must change their culture in order to remain competitive and even survive in their environment. The cultural change process at IBM demonstrates how this may be successfully accomplished.

# Ending with Meta-Analytic Research Findings
## OB PRINCIPLE FOR EVIDENCE-BASED PRACTICE

Organizational configurations affect organizational performance.

### Meta-Analysis Results:

[33 studies; 40 organizations; $d = .55$] *On average, there is a* **65 percent probability** *that an identified organizational configuration will better predict performance of included organizations than if no configuration is identified and utilized.* Moderator analyses revealed that organizations' configurations contributed more to the explanation of performance to the extent that studies used broad definitions of configuration, single-industry samples, and longitudinal designs.

### Conclusion:

Organizational configurations are groups of firms sharing a common profile of organizational structural characteristics. The Miles and Snow typology describes four such configurations—defender, prospector, analyzer, and reactor. Each of these examines the relationship between strategy and structure. At the heart of configuration research is the relationship that firms have with their environments. Specifically, organizations that exist in environments where goals are attainable, resources are acquirable, internal processes are growing and thriving, and stakeholders are satisfied will be more effective than those that do not have such a configuration.

**Source:** Adapted from David J. Ketchen Jr., James G. Combs, Craig J. Russell, Chris Shook, Michelle A. Dean, Janet Runge, Franz T. Lohrke, Stefanie E. Naumann, Dawn Ebe Haptonstahl, Robert Baker, Brenden A. Beckstein, Charles Handler, Heather Honig, and Stephen Lamoureux, "Organizational Configuration and Performance: A Meta-Analysis," *Academy of Management Journal,* Vol. 40, No. 1, 1997, pp. 223–240.

| Questions for Discussion and Review | |
|---|---|
| | 1. What was Chester Barnard's contribution to organization theory? |

**Questions for Discussion and Review**

1. What was Chester Barnard's contribution to organization theory?
2. How does a learning organization differ from a traditional organization?
3. Briefly define the horizontal, hollow, modular, network, and virtual organization designs. How do these differ from the classical design? How do they better meet the challenges of the new environment?
4. What is meant by the term *organizational culture*? Define it and give some examples of its characteristics.
5. How does a dominant culture differ from a subculture? In your answer be sure to define both terms.
6. How do organizational cultures develop? What four steps commonly occur?
7. How do organizations go about maintaining their cultures? What steps are involved? Describe them.

**Internet Exercise: The Structure and Culture of Organizations**

As this chapter has discussed, there are dramatic differences in both the design and culture of organizations. In part, the culture of an organization is determined by the structure. Some organizations tend to be hierarchical and rigid, whereas others are horizontal and flexible. Visit some corporate Web sites that describe various structural design components and corporate values. To get an idea of corporate culture preferences, go to **http://www.mhhe.com/business/management/management_tutor_series/corp CulturePrefScale/index.html.** Then going from there, choose a specific firm such as Toyota or Google or search under "organization design" and/or "organization culture" to see where it leads you. Try to determine what the company's structure and culture may be.

1. Compare structure and culture of two or more firms in the same industry. Which would you prefer to work for?
2. What other issues do the structure and culture have for other topics of organizational behavior (motivation, reward systems, etc.)?

---

# Real Case: *Web-Based Organizations*

There is hope, and the promise of at least partial liberation from the tyranny of time constraints. Why? Because the long-term interests of individuals and smart companies are aligned. To compete, successful corporations will have to make it easier and less time-consuming for their employees to collaborate. They will learn how to live with fewer time-sapping meetings and unnecessary feedback loops—or find themselves outrun by more nimble competitors. The eventual result: less frustration for knowledge workers.

Moves in this direction are already under way as savvy companies analyze their internal social networks and identify bottlenecks. Intel Corp., for example, sees an opportunity in creating technology that lowers the time cost of teamwork. And others, such as Eli Lilly & Co., are providing more corporate support for both internal and external networks. "It's a new mental model for how you run a company," says McKinsey's Bryan. "The winners will be those who can handle more complexity."

At the same time we may see a rise in new forms of Web-based organizations where people can contribute without having their time eaten up by existing hierarchy. Blogs, collaborative online databases (called *wikis*) and open-source software development all use the Net to handle much of the coordination among people rather than relying on top-down command and control. Such a shift to a digital spine could eventually lessen bureaucratic time burdens on over-worked professionals, especially those in such high-cost industries as health care.

Even high pay can't compensate for unrelenting time pressure. Top managers have to realize that encouraging networks and collaboration demands as much attention and resources as supervising and measuring performance in traditional ways. Most companies have built up large human-resources departments, but few have a department of collaboration. "Most managers don't manage social networks effectively," says Babson's Davenport.

At Intel, the drive to reduce the time spent sharing knowledge and collaborating is an outgrowth of efforts to better coordinate far-flung operations that stretch from Israel to India. One idea being pursued by Luke Koons, director for information and knowledge management, is "dynamic profiling"—technologies that automatically summarize areas on which a researcher or a manager is focusing, based on the subjects of their e-mails and Web searches. Such a regularly updated profile could make it less time-consuming to locate potential collaborators and resources, an especially daunting prospect in a large, innovation-minded company such as Intel. Equally important, dynamic profiling doesn't force individuals to spend hours manually updating their profiles as their focus changes.

1. How can the organization structure facilitate speed, collaboration, and teamwork? Contrast traditional bureaucratic organizations with the examples in this case.
2. What is meant by a Web-based organization? How does this fit into the various organization theories discussed in the first part of the chapter?
3. Are there any downside risks inherent in the way the firms are organized in this case? What do you think the future will be for organization designs?

# Organizational Behavior Case: *The Outdated Structure*

Jake Harvey has a position on the corporate planning staff of a large company in a high-technology industry. Although he has spent most of his time on long-range, strategic planning for the company, he has been appointed to a task force to reorganize the company. The president and board of directors are concerned that they are losing their competitive position in the industry because of an outdated organization structure. Being a planning expert, Jake convinced the task force that they should proceed by first determining exactly what type of structure they have now, then determining what type of environment the company faces now and in the future, and then designing the organization structure accordingly. In the first phase they discovered that the organization is currently structured along classic bureaucratic lines. In the second phase they found that they are competing in a highly dynamic, rapidly growing, and uncertain environment that requires a great deal of flexibility and response to change.

1. What type or types of organization design do you feel this task force should recommend in the third and final phase of the approach to their assignment?
2. Do you think Jake was correct in his suggestion of how the task force should proceed? What types of problems might develop as by-products of the recommendation you made in question 1?

# Organizational Behavior Case: *Keeping Things the Same*

Metropolitan Hospital was built two years ago and currently has a workforce of 235 people. The hospital is small, but because it is new, it is extremely efficient. The board has voted to increase its capacity from 60 to 190 beds. By this time next year, the hospital will be over three times as large as it is now in terms of both beds and personnel.

The administrator, Clara Hawkins, feels that the major problem with this proposed increase is that the hospital will lose its efficiency. "I want to hire people who are just like our current team of personnel—hardworking, dedicated, talented, and able to interact well with patients. If we triple the number of employees, I don't see how it will be possible to maintain our quality patient care. We are going to lose our family atmosphere. We will be inundated with mediocrity, and we'll end up being like every other institution in the local area—large and uncaring!"

The chairman of the board is also concerned about the effect of hiring such a large number of employees. However, he believes that Clara is overreacting. "It can't be that hard to find people who are like our current staff. There must be a lot of people out there who are just as good. What you need to do is develop a plan of action that will allow you to carefully screen those who will fit into your current organizational culture and those who will not. It's not going to be as difficult as you believe. Trust me. Everything will work out just fine."

As a result of the chairman's comments, Clara has decided that the most effective way of dealing with the situation is to develop a plan of action. She intends to meet with her administrative group and determine the best way of screening incoming candidates and then helping those who are hired to become socialized in terms of the hospital's culture. Clara has called a meeting for the day after tomorrow. At that time she intends to discuss her ideas, get suggestions from her people, and then formulate a plan of action. "We've come too far to lose it all now," she told her administrative staff assistant. "If we keep our wits about us, I think we can continue to keep Metropolitan as the showcase hospital in this region."

1. What can Clara and her staff do to select the type of entry-level candidates they want? Explain.
2. How can Clara ensure that those who are hired come to accept the core cultural values of the hospital? What steps would you recommend?
3. Could Clara use this same approach if another 200 people were hired a few years from now?

# Organizational Behavior Case: *Out with the Old, In with the New*

The Anderson Corporation was started in 1962 as a small consumer products company. During the first 20 years the company's R&D staff developed a series of new products that proved to be very popular in the marketplace. Things went so well that the company had to add a second production shift just to keep up with the demand. During this time period the firm expanded its plant on three separate occasions. During an interview with a national magazine, the firm's founder, Paul Anderson, said, "We don't sell our products. We allocate them." This comment was in reference to the fact that the firm had only 24 salespeople and was able to garner annual revenues in excess of $62 million.

Three years ago Anderson suffered its first financial setback. The company had a net operating loss of $1.2 million. Two years ago the loss was $2.8 million, and last year it was $4.7 million. The accountant estimates that this year the firm will lose approximately $10 million.

Alarmed by this information, Citizen's Bank, the company's largest creditor, insisted that the firm make some changes and start turning things around. In response to this request, Paul Anderson agreed to step aside. The board of directors replaced him with Mary Hartmann, head of the marketing division of one of the country's largest consumer products firms.

After making an analysis of the situation, Mary has come to the conclusion that there are a number of changes that must be made if the firm is to be turned around. The three most important are as follows:

1. More attention must be given to the marketing side of the business. The most vital factor for success in the sale of the consumer goods produced by Anderson is an effective sales force.

2. There must be an improvement in product quality. Currently, 2 percent of Anderson's output is defective, as against 0.5 percent for the average firm in the industry. In the past the demand for Anderson's output was so great that quality control was not an important factor. Now it is proving to be a very costly area.

3. There must be a reduction in the number of people in the operation. Anderson can get by with two-thirds of its current production personnel and only half of its administrative staff.

Mary has not shared these ideas with the board of directors, but she intends to do so. For the moment she is considering the steps that will have to be taken in making these changes and the effect that all of this might have on the employees and the overall operation.

1. What is wrong with the old organizational culture? What needs to be done to change it?

2. Why might it be difficult for Mary to change the existing culture?

3. What specific steps does Mary need to take in changing the culture? Identify and describe at least two.

# Chapter **Four**

# Organizational Context: Reward Systems

## Learning Objectives

- **Discuss** the theoretical background on money as a reward.
- **Present** research evidence on the effectiveness of pay.
- **Describe** some of the traditional methods of administering pay.
- **Relate** some forms of "new" pay and their value in helping attract and retain talented employees.
- **Explain** how recognition is used as an organizational reward.
- **Discuss** the role of benefits as organizational rewards.

Although reward systems are not necessarily found in the first part of organizational behavior textbooks, it is placed here for two very important reasons. First, in the social cognitive theory presented in Chapter 1 as the conceptual framework for this text, the environment variable in the triadic reciprocal interaction model (along with the personal/cognitive and organizational behavior itself) consists of both the external and organizational contexts. The last chapter covered the structural design and culture of the organization, and especially in a social cognitive approach, the reward system covers the remaining major contextual variable for organizational behavior. Specifically, in social cognitive theory, reward consequences or contingencies play an important role in organizational behavior. For example, Bandura has noted that human behavior cannot be fully understood without considering the regulatory influence of rewards,[1] and basic research has found that reward systems have a significant impact on employees' perception of organizational support and leadership.[2] Although behavioral management is not covered until the last part of the book (Chapter 12), it can be said now that the organization may have the latest technology, well-designed structures, and a visionary strategic plan, but unless the people at all levels are rewarded, all these other things may become hollow and not be carried out for performance improvement. One way to put this importance of organizational rewards as simply as possible is to remember: you get what you reward![3]

The second major reason for putting organizational reward systems up front is to emphasize the emerging importance of human capital introduced in Chapter 1. Because intellectual/human capital is now recognized as being central to competitive advantage in the new paradigm environment, attention must be given to rewarding this capital to sustain/retain it and leverage it.[4] Since humans represent such a significant cost to organizations, as the accompanying OB in Action: Now It's Getting Personal indicates, more attention is being given to analyzing the return on this human capital. The importance of reward systems is now recognized as being a vital dimension of the organizational environment, and that is why it is

Imagine that your company's human resources department does away with standard salaries, one-size-fits-all benefits, and the usual raft of yawn-inducing seminars. Instead, HR execs huddle over computer programs that slice and dice data on you and your cube-mates—controlling for age, tenure, educational background, commute time, residential Zip Code, even the age and condition of the office you work in. The aim is to predict your behavior, ascertaining exactly how to cut costs without sabotaging morale—as well as which incentives would spike your productivity the most. Could they pay you 20% less but give you a three-month sabbatical every two years, cementing your allegiance and jolting your output? If they dumped your 401(k) match, would you bolt from your job or barely notice? Does your boss's managerial touch inspire you or undermine your ability to produce? And what if, instead of parking you in a lecture in some stuffy hotel ballroom, you got a customized seminar that unleashed your ability to lock in 20% more in annual sales?

This may seem the stuff of corporate sci-fi—but it's actually here. A growing vanguard of HR heads are quickly embracing a new discipline, human capital management, that attempts to capture new gains from workers just as Six Sigma squeezed new efficiencies from factories. Some of the most groundbreaking work is coming from Mercer Human Resource Consulting, which is pioneering its new statistical modeling technology with clients including Quest Diagnostics, FleetBoston Financial, and First Tennessee. These kinds of analyses are helping a lengthening list of blue chips figure out exactly what kind of a return on investment they are getting from the millions of dollars they spend on their workforces. "This is the new thinking in new HR," says Kurt Fischer, vice-president of HR at Corning Inc. "Here's what we're spending. What are we getting for it?"

Caught in the profits crunch, companies crippled by anemic growth are desperate to energize earnings. Labor costs, which account for an average 60% of sales, represent a huge opportunity. Instead of placing precise bets on what compensation mix or management approach would work best, companies have usually thrown "everything at the wall, ratcheting things up slowly every year and hoping some of it works," says Dave Kieffer, head of Mercer's human capital group. When companies make cuts, just as much guesswork—and potential for backlash—comes into play. With the new technologies, companies can now accurately measure the ROI on their people.

The growing interest in the new human capital metrics stems from a rejection in some quarters of benchmarking—the practice, promoted by many big consulting firms and management gurus, of aping the best-performing companies such as General Electric Co. and Microsoft Corp. The result has been a cascade of CEOs copying everything Jack Welch and Bill Gates did—with many of them failing. Some developed a mania for rank-and-yank performance reviews, without ascertaining if tenure actually enhanced productivity. Others adopted flexible, just-in-time workforces that they could switch off and on like a spigot, without assessing the drag on productivity part-timers could cause.

The perils of this kind of blind benchmarking were evident at one major hospital chain, where the CFO bragged that his aggressive use of part-timers was saving the company $5 million a year. Each time the CFO found a rival with a lower ratio of full-timers, he would ax more at his own hospitals—to the point where one facility was being run by a staff of 80% part-timers. Not surprisingly, those employees were often clueless about local hospital practices and wound up wasting the time of the full-time staff. What Mercer's analysis showed was that the use of so many part-timers was actually costing the company $25 million in reduced productivity—3% of annual revenues. By hiking the ratio of full-timers back up to 63%, the chain regained 18% in overall productivity within two months.

This points to one big difference between the new human capital management and old-era HR: Instead of looking outside to others for cookie-cutter answers, the new thinking argues that it's better to look at the company's internal labor market. One blue-chip beverage maker assumed its longest-tenured drivers were the most productive. After a time-series analysis—controlling for factors such as older drivers getting their pick of the best routes—the company realized that once its drivers hit the nine-year mark, productivity plummeted even as their pay rose. In this case the company reassigned the drivers to less physically taxing jobs. The new human capital initiatives can provide valuable insights. After studying its ranks, First Tennessee realized that bank customers reacted far more favorably to experienced employees than it did to new hires. That meant that no matter how many college grads the bank hired nor how many experienced pros it brought in, it could not beat the tens of millions more in annual sales it could reap merely by increasing retention of current workers by at least one year.

In another such analysis, a blue-chip technology company learned that its pay structure was penalizing the highest performers and rewarding the weakest; lackluster employees were clustered in a cash-cow unit, while superstars were toiling in a still-profitless upstart division. "Most companies are just cutting without this kind of analysis," says Kieffer. That's not likely to last, as more and more businesses realize how much they're spending on something about which they know so little.

included here to conclude the introductory environmental context for the study and application of organizational behavior.

Certainly the tendency with most people, and often in actual organizational practice, is to equate organizational reward systems only with money. Obviously, money is the dominant reward and will be given first and foremost attention in this chapter. The theory, research, and analysis of all the ways money can be administered by today's organizations is given detailed attention. However, this is followed by the potentially powerful, and importantly much less costly, recognition rewards system.[5] Finally, the costly, but often not effective, use of benefits is presented.

# PAY: THE DOMINANT ORGANIZATIONAL REWARD

Organizations provide rewards to their personnel in order to try to motivate their performance and encourage their loyalty and retention. Organizational rewards take a number of different forms including money (salary, bonuses, incentive pay), recognition, and benefits. This first part examines money as the most dominant reward system in today's organizations.

## The Theoretical Background on Money as a Reward

Money has long been viewed as a reward and, at least for some people, it is more important than anything else their organization can give them. Some surveys of employees rank money at the top of their list of motivators[6] and others rank it lower. It seems to vary widely with the individual and the industry. However, as the well-known scholar and consultant Manfred Kets de Vries recently declared, "It's easy to say money isn't everything as long as we have enough of it. Unfortunately, though, the typical scenario is that the more money we have, the more we want."[7] Also, commenting on money, Steven Kerr, the well-known organizational behavior scholar and executive at both GE and Goldman Sachs referenced in the last chapter, noted that "Nobody refuses it, nobody returns it, and people who have more than they could ever use do dreadful things to get more."[8] By the same token, a large majority (82 percent) of employees in the United States and worldwide (76 percent) recently indicated they would take a pay cut to pursue their dream job.[9]

### *Money Can Explain Behavior*

Money provides a rich basis for studying behavior at work because it offers explanations for why people act as they do.[10] For example, Mitchell and Mickel have noted that money is a prime factor in the foundation of commerce, that is, people organize and start businesses to make money.[11] Money is also associated with four of the important symbolic attributes for which humans strive: achievement and recognition, status and respect, freedom and control, and power.[12] In fact, in most of the management literature dealing with money, researchers have focused on money as pay and the ways in which pay affects motivation, job attitudes, and retention. In particular, money helps people attain both physical (clothing, automobiles, houses) and psychological (status, self-esteem, a feeling of achievement) objectives. As well-known moneymaker Donald Trump has said, "Money was never a big motivation for me, except as a way to keep score. The real excitement is playing the game."[13] As a result of this perspective, money has been of interest to organizational behavior theorists and researchers who have studied the linkages between pay and performance by seeking answers to questions such as: How much of a motivator is money? How long lasting is its effects? What are some of the most useful strategies to employ in using money as a motivator?[14]

Money has also played an integral role in helping develop theories of organizational behavior. For example, if employees are interested in money, how much effort will they expend in order to earn it, and how much is "enough"? It is like the philosopher Arthur Schopenhauer once said, "Wealth is like seawater, the more we drink the thirstier we become."[15] Moreover, if people work very hard but do not receive the rewards they expect, how much of a dampening effect will this have on their future efforts? Answers to these types of questions have helped develop some of the most useful theories of motivation, which will be covered in Chapter 6.

### An Agency Theory Explanation

Another important perspective on money as a reward is provided by agency theory, a widely recognized finance and economics approach to understanding behavior by individuals and groups both inside and outside the corporation. Specifically, *agency theory* is concerned with the diverse interests and goals that are held by a corporation's stakeholders (stockholders, managers, employees) and the methods by which the enterprise's reward system is used to align these interests and goals. The theory draws its name from the fact that the people who are in control of large corporations are seldom the owners; rather, in almost every case, they are agents who are responsible for representing the interests of the owners.

Agency theory seeks to explain how managers differ from owners in using pay and other forms of compensation to effectively run the organization. For example, the owners of a corporation might be very interested in increasing their own personal wealth, and so they would minimize costs and work to increase the stock value of the enterprise. In contrast, their agents, the managers, might be more interested in expending corporate resources on activities that do not directly contribute to owner wealth. Agency theory also examines the role of risk and how owners and managers may vary in their approach to risk taking. For example, owners may be risk aversive and prefer conservative courses of action that minimize their chances of loss. Managers may be greater risk takers who are willing to accept losses in return for the increased opportunity for greater profits and market share; when their decisions are incorrect, the impact may be less than it would be on the owners and thus not greatly diminish their willingness to take risks.[16] Finally, agency theory examines the differences in time horizons between owners and managers. Owners may have longer time horizons because their goal is to maximize their value over time. Managers may have much shorter time horizons because their job tenure may require good short-term results, in addition to the fact that their bonuses or merit pay may be tied closely to how well they (or the corporation) performed in the last four quarters.

This last point about managers trying to look good in the short run is given as one of the major reasons for the recent economic crisis. For example, Cascio and Cappelli conclude in their analysis, referred to in the last chapter, by noting that even one of the founding fathers of agency theory recognized that "Where questionable ethics intersect with company and individual incentives, managers may end up cheating on practices such as budgeting because it makes their lives easier." They go on to note that "every scandal has involved executives pushing the financial and accounting envelope to the point of breaking to inflate profits, cover losses and make their own performances better."[17] There are also other analyses critical of agency theory predictions such as the spectacular rise and sudden fall of Nortel (the large multinational Canada-headquartered telecommunications company) that illustrates "excesses of actors within, and contradictions of the system of corporate governance implied by the agency model."[18] Despite these limitations, there is still considerable evidence that agency theory provides useful insights into pay as a reward.[19] This becomes increasingly clear when research on the effectiveness of pay is examined.

## Research on the Effectiveness of Pay

Despite the tendency in recent years to downgrade the importance of pay as an organizational reward, there is ample evidence that money can be positively reinforcing for most people[20] and, if the pay system is designed properly to fit the strategies,[21] can have a positive impact on individual, team, and organizational performance.[22] For example, many organizations use pay to motivate not just their upper-level executives but everyone throughout the organization. For example, recently in the oil industry where personnel are extremely well paid, the CEO of Exxon Mobil was compensated $16.7 million,[23] new petroleum engineering graduates earned about $80,000, and experienced "roughnecks" out on the offshore rigs earned around $100,000.[24] Moreover, these rewards may not always have to be immediately forthcoming. Many individuals will work extremely hard for rewards that may not be available for another 5 or 10 years. As Kerr has noted:

> Such attractive rewards as large salaries, profit sharing, deferred compensation, stock grants and options, executive life and liability insurance, estate planning and financial counseling, invitations to meetings in attractive locations, and permission to fly first class or use the company plane, are typically made available only to those who reach the higher organizational levels. Do such reward practices achieve the desired results? In general, yes. Residents and interns work impossible hours to become M.D.s, junior lawyers and accountants do likewise to become partners, assistant professors publish so they won't perish, and Ph.D. students perform many chores that are too depressing to recount here to obtain their doctorates.[25]

Additionally, not only is money a motivator, but, as was said in the introductory comments, the more some people get, the more they seem to want. The idea here is that once money satisfies basic needs, people can use it to get ahead, a goal that is always just out of their reach, so they strive for more. Conversely, there is evidence that shows that if an organization reduces its pay, morale may suffer. So pay may need to continue to escalate. One researcher, for example, interviewed more than 330 businesspeople and found that employee morale can be hurt by pay cuts because the employees view this is an "insult" that impacts on their self-worth and value to the organization.[26] There is recent basic research indicating that reward systems have a strong influence on employee trust in the workplace.[27] In other words, employee morale and other psychological variables such as trust are very fragile, and when employees feel they are not being compensated fairly, this can impact on their performance and hurt the bottom line. Even in the midst of the recent financial crisis, a large sample of firms indicated they were taking deliberate measures to reward their people with special bonuses and stock awards to boost their morale and confidence.[28]

There is also considerable evidence showing that money means different things to different people.[29] Moreover, sometimes these "individual differences" end up affecting group efforts. For example, one study examined pay and performance information among baseball players.[30] With statistical methods used to control for such things as total team payroll, team talent, and market size,[31] the data were analyzed from 1,644 players on 29 teams over a nine-year period. It was found that, all other things being equal, the greater the pay spread on a team, the more poorly the players performed. These findings led to the conclusion that pay distributions have significant negative effects on player performance.

Perhaps a better gauge of the effect of pay on performance of baseball teams may be total payroll. This reflects the overall salaries of the players; and if pay is indeed a motivator, would not a well-paid group outperform their less-well-paid counterparts? Again in application to baseball, for example, the New York Yankees have had the highest payroll in recent years, and their performance in these years has been very good. Compensation expert Edward Lawler echoes these sentiments, noting that there is a strong relationship between the total payroll of teams and how many games they win. "In a world of free agency, it takes a high payroll to attract and retain top talent. Thus, teams with the highest payrolls usually end up in the World Series."[32] Additionally, Lawler has argued that the rewarding of team performance is more important than the size of the pay differences among the individual players.

The question of pay ranges and their impact on productivity is one that merits more consideration as organizations seek to determine the effectiveness of pay on performance. A case in point is the huge pay package most CEOs of large firms receive, but the performance of their firms certainly did not justify the millions of dollars of compensation. The result of such disparities is that a growing number of corporate shareholders are demanding that the chief executive officer pay be tied to a multiple of the lowest worker's pay, thus controlling the range between the lowest and highest paid person in the organization.[33] A public poll indicated that a vast majority (87 percent) believe that executives "had gotten rich at the expense of ordinary workers."[34]

Although money was probably overemphasized in classical management theory and motivation techniques, the pendulum now may have swung too far in the opposite direction. Money remains a very important but admittedly complex potential motivator. In terms of Maslow's well-known hierarchy of needs covered in Chapter 6, money is often equated only with the most basic requirements of employees. It is viewed in the material sense of buying food, clothing, and shelter. Yet, as indicated in the earlier comments, money has a symbolic as well as an economic, material meaning. It can provide power and status and can be a means to measure achievement. In the latter sense, as Chapter 12 will discuss in detail, a recent meta-analysis of 72 studies found money to be a very effective positive reinforcement intervention strategy to improve performance.[35]

Beyond Maslow, more sophisticated analyses of the role of money are presented in cognitive terms. For example, a number of years ago some organizational psychologists concluded, based on their laboratory studies, that the use of extrinsic rewards such as money decreased the intrinsic motivation of subjects to perform a task.[36] Extrinsic and intrinsic motivation will be given specific attention in Chapter 6, but for now it is sufficient to know that the intrinsic motivation was usually measured in the laboratory by time spent on a task following the removal of the reward. However, through the years, there have been many criticisms of these studies, and a meta-analysis of 96 experimental studies concluded that "overall, reward does not decrease intrinsic motivation."[37] Although these studies used other rewards besides money, and the controversy still continues between the behavioral and cognitive schools of thought as outlined in Chapter 1, it is becoming clear that the real key in assessing the use of monetary rewards is not necessarily whether they satisfy inner needs but rather how they are administered.

In order for money to be effective in the organizational reward system, the system must be as objective and fair as possible[38] and be administered contingently on the employee's exhibiting critical performance behaviors.[39] This has been made particularly clear by Kerr, who notes that an effective pay system for rewarding people has to address three considerations. First, the organization must ask itself what outcomes it is seeking. Examples include higher profits, increased sales, and greater market share. Second, the enterprise must be able to measure these results. Third, the organization must tie its rewards to these outcomes. The problem for many of today's organizations is that they do still not know what they want to achieve or are unable to measure the results.[40]

## Traditional Methods of Administering Pay

Traditionally, organizations have used two methods of administering pay: base pay and merit pay. These methods are then sometimes supplemented by pay-for-performance plans and "new pay" programs that extend, and in some cases radically revise, the traditional approaches.

### Base Pay Approach

Base wages and salary is the amount of money that an individual is paid on an hourly, weekly, monthly, or annual basis. For example, a person working on a part-time basis may earn $12.00 an hour. This is the hourly wage for that position. Most managers are paid on an annual salary basis, and the sum is broken down into weekly, biweekly, or monthly amounts. As another example, a new college graduate may be offered $36,000, which comes to just over $692 a week before taxes and other deductions.

Base pay is often determined by market conditions. For example, graduating engineers may be paid $55,000 annually whereas engineering managers with 10 years of experience earn $110,000. If base pay is not in line with the market rate, organizations may find that they are unable to hire and retain many of their personnel. At the same time, one of the major problems with base pay forms of compensation is that they tend to be most competitive at the entry level and are often less competitive thereafter. So an engineering manager who is making $105,000 may be $5,000 off the market when compared to what other engineering managers within the same region and similar job requirements are making, but the individual may also find that firms paying higher salaries prefer to develop their own management talent internally and do not hire from outside. In any event, most organizations have some form of merit pay system that is used to give annual salary increases, thus raising the base pay and preventing personnel from getting too far out of step with the market.

### Merit Pay Approach

Merit pay is typically tied to some predetermined criteria. For example, a company may give all of its employees a cost-of-living allowance and then allocate additional funds for those who are judged "meritorious." The amount of merit pay can take one of two forms: a flat sum, such as $3,000, or a percentage of the base salary, such as 6 percent. In some cases companies use a combination of the two, such as giving everyone who qualifies for merit pay an additional 6 percent up to a maximum amount of $5,000. This approach ensures that those who are making lower salaries get larger percentage increases, whereas those earning higher salaries get a flat merit raise. For example, under the combination merit pay just described, a lower-level manager with a base salary of $50,000 will get an additional $3,000 (6 percent of $50,000), whereas a top-level manager with a base salary of $150,000 will get $5,000.

The intent of merit pay is to reward and thus motivate and retain the star performers. One seasoned compensation expert describes the process as follows:

> Differentiation is the name of the game now when it comes to rewards. By differentiating, companies are increasingly willing to pay more money to employees who are accomplishing the most for the organization—at all levels in their companies. We believe that in any organization there are three kinds of employees: the middle group, which is the largest and gets the job done; those that truly make a difference; and some small percentage at the bottom that are not getting the job done for a variety of reasons. Make sure you take care of those that make a difference. Make sure you take care of the middle group—pay them fairly. The bottom group is the group you should constantly keep trading so, hopefully, you can hire more stars.[41]

Unfortunately, merit pay also has a number of major shortcomings. One of the problems is that the criteria for determining merit are often nebulous because the organization does not clearly spell out the conditions for earning this pay. An example is a firm that decides to give merit to its best employees as described above. Unless the criteria for "best" are objectively spelled out, most of those who do not get merit money will feel left out because they believe they are among the best. A second, and related, problem is that it can often be difficult to quantify merit pay criteria. In particular, the work output of some people, production-line and salespeople being good examples, is easily measured, but the work output of others, such as accountants, engineers, and other staff specialists, office personnel, and managers/supervisors, may be quite difficult to objectively measure. Recent Web-enabled employee software may help the measurement of performance. For example, British Airways installed software that ensures a customer service rep's time in the break room or on personal calls doesn't count, but customer complaint resolutions and sales revenue are measured for merit pay.[42]

A second major problem is that merit pay can end up being "catch-up" pay. For example, everyone may be given a 2 percent across-the-board raise and then those whose pay is extremely low are given merit to get them closer to market value. This approach is common in enterprises that suffer salary compression brought on by the need to pay higher salaries to hire new personnel at the lower levels. Over time, the salary range between new hires and those who have been with the organization for, say, five years may be totally eliminated. So unless the longer-tenured employees are given more money, there is the likelihood that they will look for jobs at companies that are willing to pay them more based on their job experience.

In a way, merit pay is supposed to be a form of "pay for performance." Individuals who do superior work are given increases greater than the rest of their colleagues. However, because of the problems of linking merit pay directly with performance, many organizations have created specific pay-for-performance plans.

## Pay for Performance

There are two basic types of "pay-for-performance" plans: individual incentive plans and group incentive plans. Individual incentive plans have been around for many years. They were particularly popular during the height of the scientific management movement over a hundred years ago in the form of piece rate incentive plans. For example, in those early days a person loading iron ingots in a steel mill could earn as much as 7 cents per long ton (2,200 pounds) under an incentive plan. As a result, a highly skilled loader could make 50 percent more money per day than an individual who was being paid a basic day rate.[43] So individuals who were willing to work hard and had the necessary stamina could opt for incentive pay that was determined by the amount of iron ore they were able to load each day.

### *Individual Incentive Pay Plans*

Like the piece rate incentive plan of the pioneering scientific managers, today's individual incentive plans also pay people based on output or even quality. For example, at Woolverton Inn's hotels, housekeepers are given a 40-item checklist for each room. Those who meet 95 percent of the criteria over six months of random checks receive an extra week's salary. Most salespeople work under an individual incentive pay plan earning, for example, 10 percent commission on all sales. At Lincoln Electric in Cleveland, Ohio, there is an individual incentive plan in effect that, over the years, has helped some factory workers earn more than $100,000 annually.[44]

Pay for some jobs is based entirely on individual incentives. However, because of the risk factor, in the very turbulent economy of recent years many companies have instituted a combination payment plan in which the individual receives a guaranteed amount of money, regardless of how the person performs. So a salesperson might be paid 10 percent of all sales with a minimum guarantee of $2,000 per month. Another popular approach is to give the person a combination salary/incentive such as $26,000 plus 5 percent of all sales. A third approach is to give the person a "drawing account" against which the individual can take money and then repay it out of commissions. An example would be a salesperson who is paid a flat 10 percent of all sales and can draw against a $25,000 account. If the first couple of months of the year are slow ones, the individual will draw on the account, and then as sales pick up the person will repay the draw from the 10 percent commissions received.

### The Use of Bonuses

Another common form of individual incentive pay is bonuses. The signing bonus is one of the biggest incentives for athletes and upper-level managers. For example, Conseco Inc., an insurance company, paid Gary Wendt, a former executive at General Electric, a $45 million bonus for agreeing to join the company for at least five years as its chairman and chief executive officer. Additionally, Conseco also paid Wendt a multimillon dollar bonus at the end of his second year based on the firm's performance, and a minimum bonus of $2.8 million was to be paid at the end of the fifth year.[45] Although this bonus package is extremely large, successful managers and individuals who can generate large accounts for a firm can also expect sizable bonuses. For example, the PaineWebber Group recruited a top-producing brokerage team from one of its competitors by offering the group a signing bonus of $5.25 million and an additional $2 million if they bring more customers to PaineWebber.[46] In the roller-coaster economy, most companies are moving to bonus pay based on performance rather than fixed pay increases. A survey of a wide array of firms found that 10.8 percent use bonuses compared to only 3.8 percent ten years before,[47] but *The Wall Street Journal* report at the end of 2008 indicated that pay raises of any kind were likely to sink in the coming years.[48]

### The Use of Stock Options

Another form of individual incentive pay is the stock-option plan. This plan is typically used with senior-level managers and gives them the opportunity to buy company stock in the future at a predetermined fixed price. The basic idea behind the plan is that if the executives are successful in their efforts to increase organizational performance, the value of the company's stock will also rise.[49] During the boom period several years ago, many firms depended greatly on stock options to lure in and keep top talented managers and entrepreneurs. However, if these lucrative options were not exercised, when the economy had a meltdown, these stock values in many cases were halved or less. For example, Oracle's stock was off 57 percent from its high when CEO Lawrence J. Ellison exercised his option and lost more than $2 billion, but he still made $706 million, more than the economy of Grenada and one of the biggest single year payoffs in history.[50] More recently, there are reports of increasing numbers of firms trying to counteract unprofitable stock options held by top managers by exchanging the options for cash and/or issuing new options with a better chance of becoming profitable. The organizations doing this feel it is necessary to keep and motivate top talent, but of course the stockholders (and general public) object because nobody makes good their losses when stocks decline.[51]

### Potential Limitations

Although bonuses and stock options remain popular forms of individual pay, there are potential problems yet to be overcome. A general problem inherent in these pay plans may have led to the excesses and ethical breakdowns experienced by too many firms in recent years. For example, as an editor for the *Financial Times* observed, "If we treat managers as financially self-interested automatons who must be lured by the carrot of stock options and beaten with the stick of corporate governance, that attitude will become self-fulfilling."[52] There is recent research evidence supporting such observations. A study found that the heads (CEOs) of corporations holding stock options leads to high levels of investment outlays and brings about extreme corporate performance (big gains and big losses). The results thus indicate that stock options prompt CEOs to take high-variance risks (not simply larger risks), but importantly it was also found that option-loaded CEOs deliver more big losses than big gains.[53]

In addition to these underlying problems, another obstacle is that reward systems such as pay for performance are practical only when performance can be easily and objectively measured. In the case of sales, commissions can work well. In more subjective areas such as most staff support jobs and general supervision, they are of limited, if any, value. A second problem is that individual incentive rewards may encourage only a narrow range of behaviors. For example, a salesperson seeking to increase his or her commission may spend less time listening to the needs of the customer and more time trying to convince the individual to buy the product or service, regardless of how well it meets the buyer's needs. Also, there may be considerable differences along customer and industry lines with salespeople operating under the same incentive plan. For example, the *New York Times* sales force had considerable heterogeneity among clients that resulted in substantial earnings inequity and failure to pay for performance. When the plan was restructured and customized for each area, the sales force perceived the new plan as fairer and more motivational.[54]

Finally, especially in light of the ethical issues brought out in the recent economic crisis, the pay for performance, unfortunately, does not add the qualifier, pay for performance with *integrity*. As explained by a recent analysis of executive compensation:

> The omission—evident from compensation committee reports in top companies' proxy statements—is striking. Corporations, after all, face unceasing pressures to make the numbers by bending the rules, and an integrity miss can have catastrophic consequences, including indictments, fines, dismissals, and collapse of market capitalization. Furthermore, performance with integrity creates the fundamental trust—inside and outside the company— on which corporate power is based. A board should explicitly base a defined portion of the CEO's cash compensation and equity grants on his or her success in handling the foundational task of fusing high performance with high integrity at all levels of the company.[55]

Bonuses are also proving unpopular in some situations such as educational compensation. Delegates to the National Education Association convention, for example, recently rejected the idea of linking job performance to bonuses. One reason is that the association believes that a bonus system will discourage people from teaching lower-ability students or those who have trouble on standardized tests, as bonuses would be tied to how well students perform on these tests.[56] Finally, individual incentive plans may pit employees against one another that may promote healthy competition, or it may erode trust and teamwork.[57] One way around this potential problem is to use group incentive plans.

### Group Incentive Pay Plans

As Chapter 11 will discuss in detail, there has been a growing trend toward the use of teams. There is increasing evidence that teams and teamwork can lead to higher productivity, better quality, and higher satisfaction than do individuals working on their own.[58] As a result, group incentive pay plans have become increasingly popular.[59] One of the most common forms of group pay is *gain-sharing plans*.[60] These plans are designed to share with the group or team the net gains from productivity improvements. The logic behind these plans is that if everyone works to reduce cost and increase productivity, the organization will become more efficient and have more money to reward its personnel.

The first step in putting a gain-sharing plan into effect is to determine the costs associated with producing the current output. For example, if a computer manufacturer finds that it costs $30 million to produce 240,000 printers, the cost per printer is $125, and these data will be used as the base for determining productivity improvements. Costs and output are then monitored, while both the workers and the managers are encouraged to generate cost-saving ideas and put more effort into producing more with better quality. Then, at some predetermined point, such as six months, costs and output are measured and productivity savings are determined. For example, if the firm now finds that it costs $14 million to produce 125,000 printers, the cost per unit is $112. There has been a savings of $13 per printer or $1,625,000. These gain-sharing savings are then passed on to the employees, say, on a 75:25 basis.

A number of organizations use gain-sharing in one form or another. At Owens Corning, for example, the company has instituted a gain-sharing plan designed to reduce costs and increase productivity in the production of fiberglass. Savings in the manufacturing cost per pound are then shared with the employees. In another example, Weyerhaeuser, the giant forest and paper products company, employs what it calls "goalsharing" in its container board packaging and recycling plants. The company's objective is to enlist the workforce in a major performance improvement initiative designed to achieve world-class performance by reducing waste and controllable costs and increasing plant safety and product quality. Although the research evidence to date is somewhat mixed and complex, there is definitive evidence that gain-sharing plans can have a significant impact on employee suggestions for improvement.[61]

Another common group incentive plan is *profit sharing.* Although these plans can take a number of different forms, typically some portion of the company's profits is paid into a profit-sharing pool, and this is then distributed to all employees. Sometimes this is given to them immediately or at year-end. Some plans defer the profit share, put it into an escrow account, and invest it for the employee until retirement. To date, research on the impact of profit sharing on performance via improved employee attitudes has been mixed. However, one study of engineering employees did find that favorable perceptions of profit sharing served to increase their organizational commitment (loyalty).[62]

A third type of group incentive plan is the *employee stock ownership plan* or *ESOP.* Under an ESOP the employees gradually gain a major stake in the ownership of the firm. The process typically involves the company taking out a loan to buy a portion of its own stock in the open market. Over time, profits are then used to pay off this loan. Meanwhile the employees, based on seniority and/or performance, are given shares of the stock, a key component of their retirement plan. As a result, they eventually become owners of the company. However, because new accounting rules require more oversight, many companies such as Kodak, Aetna, and Time Warner are reducing the number of employees who are eligible to receive ownership in their firm as part of the incentives package.[63] Also, when the media company Tribune recently filed for bankruptcy, it exposed the risks to employees who had bought into the ESOP, especially retirees and those who were promised deferred compensation.[64]

### Potential Limitations

As noted earlier, group incentives plans are becoming increasingly popular. However, they may have a number of shortcomings. One is that they often distribute rewards equally, even though everyone in the group may not be contributing to the same degree. So all of a team or defined group may get a gain-sharing bonus of $2,700, regardless of how much each did to help bring about the productivity increases and/or reduced costs. A second shortcoming is that these rewards may be realized decades later as in the case of an employee's profit sharing or ESOP that is placed in a retirement account. So their motivational effect on day-to-day performance may, at best, be minimal. A third shortcoming is that if group rewards are distributed regularly, such as quarterly or annually, employees may regard the payments as part of their base salary and come to expect them every year. If the group or firm fails to earn them, as has been the case in recent years, motivation and productivity may suffer because the employees feel they are not being paid a fair compensation.

Realizing that base pay, merit pay, and both individual and group forms of incentive pay all have limitations, organizations are now beginning to rethink their approach to pay as an organizational reward and formulate new approaches that address some of the challenges they are facing in today's environment.[65] For example, especially labor-intensive firms such as Marriott Hotels, which annually pays billions to their people, have undergone an examination of their reward systems to align with associates' needs, improve attraction and retention, enhance productivity, and in general increase the return invested in people.[66] The result has been the emergence of what are sometimes called "new pay" techniques.

## New Pay Techniques

As noted earlier in this section, the standard base-pay technique provides for minimum compensation for a particular job. It does not reward above-average performance nor penalize below-average performance. Pay-for-performance plans correct this problem. In fact, in many cases, such as those in which pay is tied directly (i.e., contingently) to measured performance, pay-for-performance plans not only reward high performance but also punish low performance. Sometimes, of course, these plans are unfair in the sense that some jobs may be easy to do or carry very high incentives, thus allowing employees to easily earn high rates of pay, whereas in other cases the reverse is true. Similarly, in a group incentive arrangement in which all members are highly productive, the personnel will maximize their earnings, but in groups where some individuals are poor performers, everyone in the group ends up being punished.

Despite the downside to some of these pay-for-performance plans and the fact that they have been around for many years, they have become quite popular and can be considered new pay techniques. Examples include especially the group or team incentives such as gain-sharing, profit sharing, employee stock-ownership plans, and stock-option plans. Although recently the extremely high incentive pay packages are under attack by unions, shareholders, and the general public (e.g., there have been resolutions banning stock options for senior executives at firms such as American Express and AOL Time Warner), surveys have found that a large majority of *Fortune* 1000 firms are using them.[67] Additionally, as organizations undergo continual changes brought about by technology, globalization, legislation, and the economic crisis, many enterprises are rethinking and redesigning their pay plans to reflect the demands of the new environment. For example, attention has been given to the role that reward systems play in both knowledge management[68] and globalization.[69] What is emerging are the so-called new pay approaches. The following is a brief summary of some of these.[70]

1. *Commissions beyond sales to customers.* As with all of these new pay plans, the commissions paid to sales personnel are aligned with the organization's strategy and core competencies. As a result, besides sales volume, the commission is determined by customer satisfaction and sales team outcomes such as meeting revenue or profit goals.

2. *Rewarding leadership effectiveness.* This pay approach is based on factors beyond just the financial success of the organization. It also includes an employee-satisfaction measure to recognize a manager's people-management skills. For example, at Nationwide Insurance, management bonuses are tied to their people's satisfaction scores.

3. *Rewarding new goals.* In addition to being based on the traditional profit, sales, and productivity goals, rewards under this approach are aimed at all relevant employees (top to bottom) contributing to goals such as customer satisfaction, cycle time, or quality measures.

4. *Pay for knowledge workers in teams.* With the increasing use of teams, pay is being linked to the performance of knowledge workers or professional employees who are organized into virtual, product development, interfunctional, or self-managed teams. In some cases, part of this pay is initially given to individuals who have taken additional training, the assumption being that their performance will increase in the future as a result of their newly acquired knowledge or skills.[71]

5. *Skill pay.* This approach recognizes the need for flexibility and change by paying employees based on their demonstrated skills rather than the job they perform. Although it is currently used with procedural production or service skills, the challenge is to apply this concept to the more varied, abstract skills needed in new paradigm organizations (e.g., design of information systems, cross-cultural communication skills).

6. *Competency pay.* This approach goes beyond skill pay by rewarding the more abstract knowledge or competencies of employees, such as those related to technology, the international business context, customer service, or social skills.

7. *Broadbanding.* This approach has more to do with the design of the pay plan than do the others. Formally defined as a compensation strategy, broadbanding "is the practice of collapsing the traditional large number of salary levels into a small number of salary grades with broad pay ranges."[72] So, for example, rather than having three levels of supervisors whose salary ranges are $25,000 to $40,000, $35,000 to $55,000, and $50,000 to $80,000, the company will have one supervisory salary grade that extends from $25,000 to $80,000. This allows a manager to give a salary increase to a supervisor without having to first get approval from higher management because the supervisor's salary puts the individual in the next highest salary level. Broadbanding sends a strong message that the organization is serious about change and flexibility, not only in the structural and operational processes but also in its reward system. Simply put, with broadbanding the organization puts its money where its mouth is.

These new pay techniques are certainly needed to meet new paradigm challenges. If organizations expect customer satisfaction, leadership, satisfied employees, quality, teamwork, knowledge sharing, skill development, new competencies (e.g., technical, cross-cultural, and social), and employee growth without promotions, then they must reward these as suggested by the new pay techniques. Once again, you get what you reward.

# RECOGNITION AS AN ORGANIZATIONAL REWARD

Pay is an unquestionably important form of reward. However, it is not the only way in which organizations can reward their people. In addition to money, forms of recognition to identify and reward outstanding performance can be a vital, but too often overlooked, part of the organizational reward system. When people are asked what motivates them, money is always prominently featured on their list. However, both formal organizational recognition and social recognition used systematically by supervisors and managers is very important to their people and their day-to-day behaviors and performance effectiveness. For example, there is considerable research evidence that social recognition (in formal acknowledgment, attention, praise, approval, or genuine appreciation for work well done) has a significant impact on performance at all levels and types of organizations.[73]

## Recognition versus Money

There are a number of reasons why recognition may be as important as, or even more important than, money as a reward for today's employees. One of the most obvious is that enterprises typically have pay systems that are designed to review performance and give incentive payments only once or twice a year. So if someone does an outstanding good job in July, the manager may be unable to give the person a financial reward until after the annual performance review in December. Nonfinancial rewards, on the other hand, such as genuine social recognition, can be given at any time. It is these more frequent nonfinancial rewards that have a big impact on employee productivity and quality service behaviors.

Recognition rewards can take many different forms, can be given in small or large amounts, and in many instances are controllable by the manager. For example, in addition to social recognition and formal awards, a manager can give an employee increased responsibility. The human resource manager for Orient-Express Hotels, Inc. notes, "I'm a big believer in empowerment. I always tell employees, 'I'm the HR expert; you're the expert at what you do.' I put the power in their hands and say 'I trust you.' That pays off."[74] The employee may find this form of recognition motivational, and the result is greater productivity and quality service to customers. As a follow-up, the manager can then give this employee even greater responsibility. Unlike many financial forms of reward, there is no limit to the number of people who can receive this type of reward or how often it is given. One expert on rewards puts it this way:

> You can, if you choose, make all your employees . . . eligible for nonfinancial rewards. You can also make these rewards visible if you like, and performance-contingent, and you needn't wait for high level sign-offs and anniversary dates, because nonfinancial rewards don't derive from the budget or the boss, and are seldom mentioned in employment contracts and collective bargaining agreements. Furthermore . . . if you inadvertently give someone more freedom or challenge than he can handle, you can take it back. Therefore, organizations can be bold and innovative in their use of nonmonetary rewards because they don't have to live with their mistakes.[75]

Research shows that there are many types of recognition that can lead to enhanced performance and loyalty.[76] One of these that is receiving increased attention is recognition of the fact that many employees have work and family responsibilities and when the organization helps them deal with these obligations, loyalty increases. This finding is particularly important in light of findings such as a survey that found 25 percent of the most sought after employees (highly educated, high-income professionals) reported they would change jobs for a 10 percent increase in salary and 50 percent would move for a 20 percent raise.[77]

These data are not an isolated example. Another survey of the attitudes and experiences of a large number of employees in business, government, and nonprofit organizations around the United States revealed the following: (1) only 30 percent feel an obligation to stay with their current employer; (2) individuals who are highly committed to their organization tend to do the best work; (3) workers who are discontent with their jobs are least likely to be productive; (4) employees in large organizations (100 or more people) tend to be less satisfied than their peers in small enterprises; (5) lower-level employees are less satisfied than those in higher-level positions; and (6) the things that the respondents would like their companies to focus on more include being fair to employees, caring about them, and exhibiting trust in them.[78]

Recognizing creativity is becoming increasingly necessary for competitive advantage. One recent estimate is that professionals (e.g., software developers and other knowledge workers) whose primary responsibilities include innovating, designing, and problem solving (i.e., the creative class), make up an increasing percentage of the U.S. workforce. To get peak performance from its creative workforce, the widely respected and successful software company SAS rewards excellence with challenges, values the work over the tools, and minimizes hassles.[79]

Although research on the complexities of the relationship of satisfaction and commitment with outcomes will be given attention in Chapter 5, it is interesting to note here that groups such as the National Association for Employee Recognition have concluded that practicing human resource professionals and managers still seem to underestimate how useful recognition can be in motivating employees to achieve goals. Moreover, recognition as a reward does not have to be sophisticated or time consuming. In fact, many firms that are now working to improve their recognition systems all use fairly basic and easy-to-implement programs. Steps such as the following need to be set up to effectively manage a formal and informal recognition program:[80]

1. When introducing new recognition procedures and programs, take advantage of all communication tools including Intranet and other knowledge-sharing networks—let everyone know what is going on.

2. Educate the managers so that they use recognition as part of the total compensation package.

3. Make recognition part of the performance management process, so that everyone begins to use it.

4. Have site-specific recognition ceremonies that are featured in the company's communication outlets such as the weekly newsletter and the bimonthly magazine.

5. Publicize the best practices of employees, so that everyone knows some of the things they can do in order to earn recognition.

6. Let everyone know the steps that the best managers are taking to use recognition effectively.

7. Continually review the recognition process in order to introduce new procedures and programs and scrap those that are not working well.

8. Solicit recognition ideas from both employees and managers, as they are the ones who are most likely to know what works well—and what does not.

## Examples of Effective Formal Recognition Systems

Chapter 12 on behavioral performance management focuses on social recognition as an effective contingent reinforcer that supervisors/managers can use as a style in interpersonal relations. Research has clearly demonstrated that this improves employee performance.[81] In this chapter on the role rewards play in the organizational context, formal recognition programs implemented by organizations are the primary focus, along with money and benefits (covered next). Formal recognition is a vital part of the reward system that makes up the environmental component of the social cognitive framework for understanding and effectively managing organizational behavior (see Chapter 1).

Today there are a wide number of formal recognition systems that are being effectively used by organizations nationwide. Many of these are the result of continual modification, as organizations have altered and refined their reward systems to meet the changing needs of their workforce. However, all effective programs seem to have two things in common. First, they are designed to reward effective employee performance behavior and enhance employees' satisfaction and commitment. In other words, effective recognition systems lead to improved employee performance and retention. Second, they are designed to meet the specific and changing needs of the employees. Simply put, a recognition system that worked in the past or in one enterprise may have little value in another. This is why many firms have gone through a trial-and-error approach before they have settled into a unique system that works best today for their employees. Thus, recognition programs often vary widely from company to company—and many of them are highly creative. For example, one expert on implementing recognition systems offers the following creative, but practical, suggestions:[82]

1. Select a pad of Post-it Notes in a color that nobody uses and make it your "praising pad." Acknowledge your employees for work well done by writing your kudos on your praising pad.
2. Hire a caterer to bring in lunch once a week. Besides showing your respect and appreciation, this encourages mingling and the sharing of information, knowledge, ideas, and innovative solutions.
3. To get a team motivated during an important project, have them design a simple logo for the assignment. This will give the team not only a sense of camaraderie and cohesion, but also group identification and focus.

These tidbits represent useful suggestions, but many companies have gone much further by designing formal recognition systems that align their overall objectives (increased productivity, reduced cost, better-quality products and customer service, and even higher profitability) and employee performance behaviors. For example, at Dierbergs Family Market, a supermarket chain in Missouri, the firm has created what it calls the "Extra Step" program. This formal recognition program is designed to reward employees who are proactive in meeting customer needs. The objective of the program is twofold: make the company a place where employees love to work and keep customers coming back. In achieving this, the company rewards workers who go out of their way to do things for customers. For example, in one case, a customer left some of her purchases at one of the stores during a snowstorm. The store manager did not want any of the employees going out in the inclement weather, so he called a cab and paid the driver to deliver the packages she had left behind. In another case, an employee on his way to work recognized a good customer trying to change a flat tire. He went over, introduced himself as working for Dierbergs, and changed the tire for the customer.

These "extra steps" are rewarded by Dierbergs in a number of ways, including gift certificates, movie passes, and even lunch with the chief executive officer. They also help the company achieve its objectives of increased revenues through word-of-mouth advertising (the best form, at no cost) and repeat business, customer satisfaction, and employee productivity and retention. Customer feedback has been overwhelmingly complimentary, and the firm's turnover rate has rapidly declined, in an industry where labor turnover is extremely high. For its efforts, Dierbergs was given an Award for Best Business Practices for Motivating and Retaining Employees.

Dierbergs is not alone. A growing number of firms are finding that well-structured and implemented employee recognition reward systems yield very positive cost-benefit results. In particular, formal recognition systems have become important in the hotel and restaurant industry, where annual turnover rates of 100 percent are typical. Firms that have implemented recognition systems have experienced dramatic improvement in retention of their best employees. For example, at the Hotel Sofitel Minneapolis the director of human resources has reported that thanks to the organization's recognition system, annual turnover has declined significantly. One of the most successful plans in its system is called the Sofitel Service Champions. This program is inexpensive to monitor and all employees participate. It works this way: When employees do something noteworthy, they are given a little slip of paper by a customer or a manager. This resembles a French franc (that goes with the Hotel's French theme), and when an employee gets three of these francs, he or she receives a $35 gift certificate that can be redeemed at one of the hotel's restaurants. Seven francs can be exchanged for dinner at one of the restaurants or a $35 gift certificate redeemable at any area store or restaurant. Ten francs entitles the person to a day off with pay or a $50 gift certificate that can be used in any store or restaurant in the area.

Another successful component in the Sofitel recognition system is the Team Member of the Month program. These members are chosen from one of the department teams within the hotel (e.g., housekeeping, receiving, room service, accounting, front office, etc). Each department director fills out a nomination form with the name of the team member who is believed to have done something outstanding that month. If chosen, the employee receives a $50 check, a special luncheon honoring the recipient in the employee cafeteria, a picture taken with the general manager and the direct report manager, which is placed in a display case, and a specially designated parking spot. If a person is nominated but does not win, the individual still remains eligible for the next three months. All monthly winners and nominees are tracked throughout the year and are eligible for the Team Member of the Year Award. This winner is given either $500 or a trip to one of the other Sofitel Hotels in North America.

A key success factor in such public recognition plans is that it is viewed as being fair, and those not recognized agree that recipients are deserving. At Sofitel the recognition programs are continually changed based on input from the employees. One of the additions to the recognition system at Sofitel is a recognition program called Department Appreciation Days. Each month, one department is chosen to be recognized by another. The recognition is typically something small and inexpensive, such as a jar of cookies, and has proven to be very popular with the personnel and departments and has led to constructive, friendly competition to win this award.

Other organizations use similar approaches to recognizing and praising their people. (See the accompanying OB in Action: Some Easy Ways to Recognize Employees.) For example, at the Fremont Hotel & Casino in Las Vegas, a large portion of the human resource budget is set aside for recognition programs. One of these is called "Personality with a Hustle" and is designed to encourage employees to do everything they can to proactively help customers stay and play at the Fremont. Personnel who do so can end up being nominated as employee of the month. Winners are given $100, dinner for two at any of the company's restaurants, two tickets to a show, a special parking spot, and an Employee of the Month jacket. They are also eligible to win the Employee of the Year Award, which entitles them to an extra week's vacation, an all-expense-paid trip to Hawaii with $250 spending money, and a dinner for two with the company's chief executive officer.

In addition to these representative types of recognition systems, there are many other innovative, fun recognition awards in today's firms. At First Chicago, for example, there are Felix and Oscar awards (based on the characters in *The Odd Couple*) given to employees with the neatest and messiest work areas. At Chevron USA in San Francisco, an employee who is recognized for an outstanding accomplishment is immediately brought to a large treasure chest and is allowed to choose an item from the box: a coffee mug, pen-and-pencil set, gift certificate, or movie tickets. At Goodmeasure, a management consulting firm in Cambridge, Massachusetts, a person who does something outstanding is given an "Atta Person" award. At Mary Kay Cosmetics, pink Cadillacs, mink coats, and diamond rings are given to their leading sellers. At Hewlett-Packard, marketers send pistachio nuts to salespeople who excel or who close an important sale. Salespeople at Octocom Systems in Chelmsford, Massachusetts, receive a place setting of china each month for meeting their quota. In a different, and for the long run perhaps questionable, approach, at Microage Computer in Tempe, Arizona, employees who come to work late are fined, and this money is passed out to people who arrive on time. The Commander of the Tactical Air Command of the U.S. Air Force rewards individuals whose suggestions are implemented with bronze, silver, and gold buttons to wear on their uniforms.[83]

Employees never seem to tire of recognition. In psychological terms, they do not seem to become satiated, or filled up with recognition as they do, say, with food or even money. For some, in fact, the more recognition they get, the more they want. Fortunately, it is not difficult to recognize people, and there are many ways in which it can be done. Some of the easiest and representative ways are the following:

1. Practice giving concentrated, focused recognition by calling deserving employees into your office and thanking them for doing an outstanding job. During this interaction, focus is only on the detailed recognition and nothing else, so that the effect is not diluted by the discussion of other matters.

2. Buy a trophy and give it to the most deserving employee in the unit or department. Inscribe the individual's name on the trophy, but leave room for additional names. To help ensure fairness and acceptance, at the end of a month, have this recipient choose the next member of the unit to be recognized and explain why this individual was chosen.

3. Recognize an employee who is located in another locale and does not get a chance to visit the home office very often. Deal with this "out of sight, out of mind" problem by faxing, e-mailing, or leaving a voice mail for the person that says "thank you for a job well done."

4. Write a note that recognizes an individual's contributions during the last pay period and attach this note to the person's paycheck.

5. When you get a raise or a promotion, acknowledge the role that was played by your support staff by taking all of them out to lunch. In sports, a smart quarterback who receives all the attention for a win will always recognize especially his line in front of him and may even take these "unsung heroes" out for dinner or buy them something.

6. Take a picture of someone who is being congratulated by his or her manager. Give a copy of the photo to the employee and put another copy in a prominent location for everyone to see.

7. Have a senior manager come by and attend one of your team meetings during which you recognize people for their accomplishments.

8. Invite your work team or department to your house on a Saturday evening to celebrate their completion of a project or attainment of a particularly important work milestone.

9. Recognize the outstanding skill or expertise of an individual by assigning the person an employee to mentor, thus demonstrating both your trust and your respect.

10. The next time you hear a positive remark made about someone, repeat it to that person as soon as possible.

11. Stay alert to the types of praise and recognition that employees seem to like the best and use these as often as possible.

12. Catch people doing things right—and let them know!

In some cases, recognition awards are delivered on the spot for a job well done. For example, at Kimley-Horn, a big engineering firm in North Carolina, at any time, for any reason, without permission, any employee can award a $55 recognition check ($50 plus $5 for tax payment) paid by the company to any other employee. As the HR director notes, "Any employee who does something exceptional receives recognition from peers within minutes."[84] In a recent year, 6,174 such awards ($339,570) were made with very little oversight and virtually no abuses. In another example, at Tricon, a spin-off of PepsiCo that has become the world's largest restaurant company in units and second behind McDonald's in sales, the chief executive officer gave a Pizza Hut general manager a foam cheesehead for achieving a crew turnover rate of 56 percent in an industry where 200 percent is the norm. Commenting on the event, the CEO noted, "I wondered why anyone would be moved by getting a cheesehead, but I've seen people cry. People love recognition."[85] Yet, as pointed out at the beginning of this section, this powerful reward is still being underutilized, as seen by the results of a survey in which 96 percent of the respondents said that they had an unfulfilled need to be recognized for their work contributions.[86] As the now deceased head of the Gallup Organization Don Clifton used to say, "I've never met an employee who was suffering from too much recognition." A more visible and much more costly form of organizational reward system involves the benefits that are provided to employees.

# BENEFITS AS ORGANIZATIONAL REWARDS

Every permanent employee receives benefits, even though they often seem to be unaware and not know the usually high monetary value of these benefits. For example, a recent survey indicated that 50 percent of Americans spend more time filing their taxes and doing their holiday shopping than they do reviewing and trying to understand their benefit choices. As one benefits expert noted, "Employees can be overwhelmed with the variety of health care and retirement choices offered to them."[87] Even though employees may not be aware, the fact is that benefits constitute a large percentage of most company's expenses. In recent years these costs have been escalating. For example, over the past decade premiums for health coverage alone have increased well over 75 percent and the employees normally pay only a small portion of that cost.[88] Benefit costs to employers range between 30 to 35 percent of wages and salaries. So a company that is paying an employee $70,000 annually is spending an additional $22,000 in benefits including life and health insurance, a pension plan, mandated government benefits such as Social Security, vacation time, and so forth.

Although some managers and small business owners question the high cost of benefits, many believe that it is money well spent because it is a vital part of the organization's reward system and helps attract, maintain, and retain outstanding employees. This reasoning is known as *efficiency wage theory* and holds that firms can save money and become more productive if they pay higher wages and better benefits because they are able to hire and leverage the best talent. This theory is particularly useful in explaining the importance of offering benefits that appeal to and are needed by today's employees to make them satisfied, stress free, and productive. For example, in recent years, with so many women in the workforce, a growing number of companies have been helping their people deal with family-related challenges by providing on-site day care, dual parental maternity leave, and flexible work hours so individuals who have young children or elderly relatives who need their assistance can deal with these issues.

In general, the benefits portion of the organizational reward system can be categorized in a number of different ways. The following examines both the traditional and newly emerging benefits used in today's organizational reward system.

## Traditionally Offered Benefits

Commonly offered benefits are of two types: those that must be offered because they are required by law and those that most organizations typically have given to their personnel. When benefits are used as part of the organizational reward system, these are standard offerings and, for the most part, differ very little from one organization to another.

### Federal Government–Mandated Benefits

One traditional government-mandated benefit is Social Security. The initial purpose of Social Security, officially known as the Old Age Survivors and Disability Insurance Program, was to provide limited income to retired people to supplement such things as their personal savings, private pensions, and part-time work earnings. Both employees and employers are required to pay a Social Security tax. Additionally, both employees and their employer pay Medicare taxes. In turn, this federal government–mandated program pays both a retirement benefit and Medicare benefits, although payments will vary depending on a number of factors such as the age at which the person elects to start receiving payments.

Another mandated benefit is workers' compensation. This is insurance that covers individuals who suffer a job-related illness or accident. Employers pay the cost of this insurance.

Other mandated programs that are offered to employees do not specify a particular benefit, but they do require the employer to take specific types of actions. For example, the Family and Medical Leave Act of 1993 covered in Chapter 2 requires all organizations with 50 or more employees to grant any worker who has been employed there for at least one year an *unpaid* leave of up to 12 weeks for childbirth, the adoption of a child, to care for a family member with a serious health problem, or because of a personal health problem. During this period, all of the employee's existing health benefits must remain intact, and the individual must be allowed to return to the same or an equivalent job after the leave.

Another mandated program is the Employee Retirement Income Security Act of 1974, which requires that if an employer sets up a pension fund for employees and deducts contributions to that fund, the company must follow certain guidelines. These guidelines restrict the firm's freedom to take money out of the fund and provides formulas for employee vesting (when the employee has a right to the employer's contributions to the fund) and portability (the employee's ability to transfer funds to a different retirement account). A third mandated program is the result of the Pregnancy Discrimination Act of 1978, which protects a woman from being fired because she is pregnant. A fourth program is a result of the Economic Recovery Act of 1981, which allows employees to make tax-deductible contributions to a pension, savings, or an individual retirement account (IRA). All of these programs provide government-mandated benefits to employees.

### *Life, Disability, and Health Insurance*

Another major category of traditional benefits consists of insurance coverage. Virtually all large (but less than half of those with 10 or fewer employees) companies offer health insurance to their employees and pay a major portion of the premiums for this coverage. However, about three-quarters (and growing) of U.S. employers do require employee participants to share the health costs via deductibles, coinsurance, copayments, and other means.[89] Life insurance is often based on the individual's annual salary so that the premium provides protection, for example, for two times the person's yearly salary. Additionally, employers often make disability insurance available for a minimum premium fee.

In recent years, even though health coverage costs are rapidly escalating, they have become an expected benefit. Thus, firms are trying to manage for cost containment through copayment and preferred providers in order to compete for top employees and retain the best. In fact, many employers are expanding coverage to encompass a variety of health care including prescription drugs, vision care products, mental health services, and dental care. Over half of employees are enrolled in preferred provider organization (PPO) plans and less than half have the option to join a health maintenance organization (HMO) that offers medical and health services on a prepaid basis. This HMO approach has seemed to run its course and now an increasing number of firms are implementing what are sometimes called "disease management programs." As explained:

> Disease management programs are a sophisticated version of old-style preventative medicine. Rather than rationing services through managed care, employers throw lots of early medical attention at chronically ill workers, who absorb about 60 percent of all health dollars.[90]

Another example would be the growing recognition by companies of the costs of obesity (now estimated by the Centers for Disease Control and Prevention to affect one of three adults). Having overweight employees not only affects a firm's health care costs, but also lost productivity due to absenteeism. One report estimated that obesity costs a company with a thousand employees an extra $395,000 per year and, for private employers in general, obesity-related costs stemming from medical expenditures and work loss amount to $45 billion annually.[91] An increasing number of firms are trying to combat this increasing problem through preventative programs. For example, VSM Abrasives, a sandpaper manufacturer in Missouri, offers cash and time-off incentives for employees who maintain or lose weight and have saved 10–15 percent on annual insurance claims.[92]

### Pension Benefits

In addition to the pension benefits that are provided by Social Security, most organizations today have also established private pension plans. Contributions are generally made by both the employer and employee, and there are a variety of plans available. Two of the most popular are individual retirement accounts (IRAs) and 401(k) plans that allow employees to save money on a tax-deferred basis by entering into salary-deferral agreements with the employer. These built-up funds are then available to the employee in retirement and typically provide far more money than the monthly Social Security checks from the federal government. Many of these plans are invested in stock and when the market goes up these pension plans do very well, but of course when the stock values go down, as they did at the end of 2008, the pensions of many people take a big hit.

### Time-Off Benefit

Another common benefit, often taken for granted by many, is paid time off. In the accompanying OB in Action: You Can't Make More Time, Randy Pausch, the college professor who gave the famous "last lectures" while he was dying of cancer, passionately points out that time is indeed a precious gift. Increasingly, this message of the importance of more free time is being taken to heart by employers as an effective benefit for their employees. For example, retailer Eddie Bauer focuses on making sure its benefit programs give time back to employees, help employees save time, and equate the saving of time with money. One such benefit at Eddie Bauer was to have employees save time by having services on the corporate campus such as dry cleaning and film developing pick-up and delivery, an ATM machine, a gym, will preparation, and flu shots. This firm believes that employee time saving results in productivity and retention. An innovative way to meet corporate social responsibility objectives would be to give employees paid time off to do charitable and volunteer work in the community. There is evidence that such a benefit helps in recruiting and retaining top talent.[93]

The more traditional time benefit is vacation time. In most organizations employees are entitled to at least one week of vacation with pay after being with the firm for one year, and by the end of five years, most are given at least two weeks and, in some cases, as many as four. Moreover, some firms will pay, say, 1.5 times the person's weekly salary for every week of vacation that the individual forgoes, and some employers allow people to accumulate vacation time and, at some point, pay them for any unused time.

Another form of time off is paid religious holidays. Still another is paid sick leave. In many organizations individuals are given a predetermined number of sick days per year, such as six, whereas in others there is no limit. Finally, many firms give paid personal leave such as a day to attend the funeral of a friend or relative or for simply any personal reasons.

## Newer Types of Benefits

In recent years, a number of newer types of benefits have emerged and are gaining in popularity. One example of these is wellness programs, and another, mentioned earlier in this section, is assistance with family-related responsibilities. These, in addition to others, are emerging as an important part of today's organizational reward system.

## Randy Pausch's Heartfelt Views on Using Time to the Fullest

Randy Pausch was truly passionate about the benefits of time management. He was asked to write this not long before his death on July 25, 2008 at age 47, and he was excited to have the opportunity. In fact, it led to one of the last e-mails I got from him, which was full of exclamation points and closed with the word "AWESOME!" In the end, he didn't have the energy to finish it. Thus, his friends have put the following together using the phrases he used many times.

So you've decided to take the time to read this article. Every moment of our lives requires this kind of decision, which is the fundamental time-management question: Should I do X, or should I do Y?

All his life, Randy Pausch knew time was a gift. He was always logical about time, sometimes to the point of exasperating his friends with comments about the size of their in-boxes. But his reverence for hours, minutes—even seconds—served him well.

He would stand before a room full of students and tell them time was their most precious commodity. They all knew they had finite money, but they lived as if they had infinite time. "You can always make more money later," Randy would say. "But you can't make more time." Time, like money, he explained, must be explicitly managed.

He had all sorts of practical advice for work. Stand while on the phone. (You'll be more eager to finish up.) Avoid copying five people on an e-mail when you want something done. (Each will assume that one of the other four is going to step up to the plate.) Minimize interruptions. (Turn off the "new e-mail" pop-up alert or shut down e-mail during your good working hours.)

Other tips were reminders of the big picture. Do the "ugliest" thing first—everything else will come more easily after that. Make time for the important things, not just for critical things; it is all too easy to spend time fighting fires rather than doing the necessary deep thinking. And recognize that the best reason to save time in your work is to increase time with your family.

### SO LITTLE OF IT LEFT

Toward the end of his life, Randy became something of a poster boy for the limits of time. Last September he gave a "last lecture" at Carnegie Mellon. He talked about the joys of life and how much he appreciated it, even with so little of his own left. It was a talk for his students and colleagues, but because it was recorded, he hoped it could be a message to his three kids, too.

Footage of the talk unexpectedly spread online, and he heard from thousands of people. (As a result, another lecture of his, on time management, was widely watched online, too.) Many wanted to know if his views on time changed as he got closer to the end of his life. But there were no great epiphanies. "Everything now is more so," he told people.

He lived longer than doctors predicted, and he mapped out that "extra" time with fervor. He went on a few romantic trips with his wife, Jai. He made a point of doing memorable activities with his children, such as swimming with dolphins and visiting Disney World. He was trying to give his kids—ages 2, 3, and 6—vivid memories of their time together.

Even before the last stages of his illness, people asked him how to best prioritize their time. His answer was simple: "If I don't do X, will it matter? And if I have to pick either X or Y, which one is more important? At the end of my life, which of these things will I be glad I did?" Time is all we have. And, like Randy, we may find one day we have less than we think.

Note: Randy Pausch's time-management lecture is viewable at www.thelastlecture.com.

### Wellness Programs

Wellness programs, which will also be discussed in Chapter 9 on coping with stress, are a special type of benefit program that focuses on keeping employees from becoming physically and/or mentally ill. There is considerable evidence that employees who exercise regularly and maintain or lose excess weight are less likely to take sick days and thus reduce health insurance premiums and lost productive time. As a result, more and more firms are now encouraging their people to work out regularly by installing a gymnasium or workout center on the premises or offering to finance at least part of the cost of joining a local health club. Another wellness practice is to encourage employees to exercise by giving them a financial payment such as $1 for every mile they jog during the year. So a person who jogs three miles a day at the company gym will earn $15 a week. As indicated earlier in the chapter, some also encourage their people to keep their weight under control, and individuals who are too heavy are paid to lose the extra weight. For example, a firm may pay $10 for every pound an employee loses. Of course, once the individual has reached the weight recommended by the doctor, this weight must stay off. If the person gains it back, the individual may have to pay the firm $10 for every pound above the doctor's recommended limit. Many firms find that these are small sums to pay when contrasted with the cost of having someone, for example, out of work six days a year due to poor health. In fact, in order to encourage everyone to stay healthy, some organizations pay people for unused sick days. So those who are in good health have an incentive to maintain this status. Finally, a growing number of large firms have on-site health care services that primarily focus on prevention rather than treatment.[94]

### Life Cycle Benefits

Another popular group of new benefits comes under the heading of what collectively are being called "life cycle" benefits. These are based on a person's stage of life and include such things as child care and elder care.

Child care benefits are extremely popular and many of the "best places to work" such as the software development firm SAS have on-site day care. Employees can drop off their child at the day care center, come by and have lunch with the child, and then pick up the youngster after work and drive home together. In a few instances, firms have even installed TV cameras so employees can view and keep track of their child throughout the day in the center. One of the primary benefits of this program is the elimination of day care costs, which can run well over $100 a week, as well as spending quality time with the child before, during, and after work, or, in the case of the TV-monitored systems, during the workday.

Elder care takes a number of different forms. One of the most common is referral services, which can be used by an employee who has a disabled parent or one who needs constant care. Another form is long-term health care insurance, which provides for nursing homes or at-home care.

Another popular benefit is employee assistance programs (EAPs for short), which were originally designed to assist employees who had problems with alcohol. In recent times, EAPs deal with drug abuse and now have generally expanded into marital problems and financial planning. The purpose of these programs is to provide help to employees in dealing with personal problems that can negatively impact their lives and their job performance. The use of EAPs should be kept confidential so that employees are not hesitant to use the services for fear of career repercussions.

### Other Benefits

In recent years a number of other benefits have begun to appear, many of them offered by especially innovative companies. One is concierge services that help employees choose gifts for presents, get tickets to concerts, schedule home or auto repairs, and so forth. Another is the use of tuition assistance to help employees obtain a college education or advanced degree. A third is the use of noninsured benefit programs that help low-wage and part-time workers purchase medicines and medical assistance at a discount. Still another example is prepaid legal plans that offer a variety of services such as legal advice, wills and estate planning, and investment counseling. Finally, some firms just come up with relatively small, but still effective benefits for their employees. For example, at the accounting firm KPMG, employees received a hot summer surprise: six pints of gourmet ice cream, toppings, and a scooper; the L.A. law firm DLA Piper recently whisked 400 employees and their families off to Disneyland for the day; in Dallas the PR firm Weber Shandwick encourages employees to use their expense account to pay for cab rides after drinking alcohol; and Safeco, Microsoft, and IBM offer employees work-from-home opportunities and subsidies for alternative transportation.[95]

### Flexible, Cafeteria-Style Benefits

Every organization has its own way of providing/administering the benefit package, but in recent years a growing number have begun offering flexible, cafeteria-style benefit plans. Just like most firms today[96] offer their employees flexible times for arriving and departing work (see Chapter 2), they also offer plans that allow employees self-control and choice over the benefits received. Employees are allowed to put together their own package by choosing those benefits that best meet their personal needs. Under this arrangement, the organization will establish a budgeted amount that it is willing to spend per employee, and the individual is then allowed to decide how to spend this money. For example, some employees may want more life insurance because they have a young family, whereas others may prefer to spend more on health insurance coverage because they have a spouse with a debilitating illness.

There is evidence that these cafeteria-style programs can lead to increased satisfaction and reduced turnover.[97] However, organizations have also found that these plans can be somewhat expensive to administer because there are many different types of benefit packages, and someone has to keep track of what each person has chosen. Additionally, employees are usually allowed to make changes in their package on an annual basis, further complicating the problem of administering the benefits and the accompanying tax implications.[98] Finally, even though employees seem to like cafeteria-style benefit plans, there is no assurance that they always make rational decisions.[99] For example, young employees with families may opt to deal only with more immediate concerns such as better hospital coverage for their spouse and children and completely ignore the benefits of contributing to a retirement program for their future.

In summary, benefits are clearly an important component of the organizational reward system. Unfortunately, because they are so common and everyone gets them, their value as a reward often goes unnoticed. Benefits are too often taken for granted and are considered to be an entitlement and thus become a hollow reward for employee performance and retention.

---

## Summary

This chapter examines reward systems as an important part of the organizational context for organizational behavior. For most organizations, pay dominates the organizational reward system. There is considerable evidence that pay is vital not only for hiring and retaining talented employees, but also if properly administered for its positive impact on desirable outcomes such as productivity, quality, and customer service. In particular, pay provides employees with the opportunity to meet both lower-level maintenance and upper-level growth and achievement needs. The challenge for managers is to administer rewards properly. In particular, this means setting up pay systems that allow employees to know the outcomes that are to be rewarded, that measure these outcomes as fairly and objectively as possible, and that tie monetary incentives directly to the results.

Pay administration takes several forms. Traditional methods include base salary and merit pay. Both of these, however, are often insufficient for retaining talented people. Organizations have to offer incentives for desirable outcomes. As a result, pay-for-performance systems are in place in many firms. These include both individual and group incentive plans. Common examples of individual incentives include commissions based directly on sales or work output, bonuses, and stock options. Group incentives include gain sharing, profit sharing, and employee stock ownership plans.

In recent years many organizations have realized that they must develop new pay approaches. One example is the use of commissions that go beyond sales to outcomes such as customer service. Others include skill pay that is based on employees' demonstrating completion of training and competency in particular job-related skills, competency pay that is based on rewarding people for abstract knowledge or competencies related to things such as technology or leadership, and broadbanding in which salary levels are collapsed into a small number of salary grades with broad pay ranges.

Another important but often overlooked component of organizational reward systems is recognition. In contrast to money, recognition is easier to control for an individual supervisor or manager and can be easily altered to meet the individual employee needs. Social recognition is provided by managers/supervisors contingent on performing desirable behaviors and is given more detailed attention in Chapter 12 on behavioral performance management. As part of the organizational reward system discussed in this chapter, formal recognition systems can innovatively provide awards for desirable outcomes, and many actual examples are provided.

Benefits are the third major component of organizational reward systems. Some of these benefits are mandated by the federal government (e.g., Social Security and workers' compensation). However, numerous other benefits are received by today's permanent employees (not by temps, and this is a major problem for them). Examples include paid vacations, days off for religious holidays, personal leave, life and health insurance, and pensions. In addition there are benefits that have emerged in recent years that are proving quite popular. Examples include wellness programs, child care benefits, employee assistance programs (EAPs), tuition assistance, prepaid legal expenses, and a host of other perks. In recent years the value of benefits as part of the reward system has increased, but so has the cost. The challenge for today's management is to make sure there is a favorable cost-benefit ratio and go beyond what is required by law to contribute to desired outcomes such as retention and performance.

# Ending with Meta-Analytic Research Findings

## OB PRINCIPLE FOR EVIDENCED-BASED PRACTICE

The systematic administration of pay-for-performance reward systems can increase employee performance.

### Meta-Analysis Results:

[19 studies; 2,818 participants; (1) $d = 1.36$ for pay incentive in manufacturing firms; (2) $d = 1.82$ for pay incentive combined with performance feedback and social recognition in manufacturing settings; (3) $d = .42$ for pay incentive in service organizations; (4) $d = .89$ for pay incentive combined with performance feedback in service organizations (there were no studies with this combination in manufacturing); and (5) $d = .27$ for pay incentive combined with performance feedback and social recognition in service organizations] *On average, there is a:*

1. **83 percent probability** that a systematically administered pay-for-performance reward system to employees in manufacturing settings will increase their performance more than those who do not receive this approach;

2. **90 percent probability** that a systematically administered pay combined with social recognition and feedback-for-performance reward system to employees in manufacturing settings will increase their performance more than those who do not receive this approach;

3. **62 percent probability** that a systematically administered pay-for-performance reward system to employees in service organizations will increase their performance more than those who do not receive this approach;

4. **74 percent probability** that a systematically administered pay combined with feedback-for-performance reward system to employees in service organizations will increase their performance more than those who do not receive this approach; and

5. **58 percent probability** that a systematically administered pay combined with social recognition and feedback-for-performance reward system to employees in service organizations will increase their performance more than those who do not receive this approach.

As the preceding probability statements reflect, moderator analyses revealed that the impact of the systematically administered pay (and its combinations with social recognition and feedback) varied depending on the type of organization. As indicated, the pay-for-performance reward system had a bigger impact in manufacturing than in service organizations.

## Conclusion:

As discussed in this chapter, although there are a variety of techniques in organizational reward systems, pay is the one that comes to the forefront in any discussion or analysis. There is an automatic assumption that pay has a positive effect on employee performance. Despite this assumption and the popularity of money as a reward, managers are still searching for answers of effective ways to increase the incentive effects of money. Pay for performance or incentive pay is one answer because it supposedly links pay directly to performance results. It motivates employees because it gives something extra—compensation above and beyond basic wages or salaries. However, just as there have been problems with pay in general, as the chapter points out, there have also been mixed results with pay for performance. One way to improve pay for performance is to systematically administer the plan so that employees can clearly see the contingent (i.e., the if-then) relationship between their behaviors, the resulting performance, and what they are paid. One way to systematically administer such a pay-for-performance plan is through the behavioral management steps that will be given attention in Chapter 12. Such a systematic application of pay for performance, as was shown in the meta-analysis reported here, can have a positive impact on employee performance.

**Source:** Alexander D. Stajkovic and Fred Luthans, "A Meta-Analysis of the Effects of Organizational Behavior Modification on Task Performance," *Academy of Management Journal,* Vol. 40, No. 5, 1997, pp. 1122–1149.

**Questions for Discussion and Review**

1. In what way does agency theory provide understanding for pay as an important component of the organizational reward system?

2. Is pay an effective organizational reward? Does the fact that the chief executive officer makes 20 times as much as the lowest-paid member of the company have any effect on the value of pay as a determinant of organizational performance?

3. "The team with the highest payroll usually ends up in the World Series." How does this statement relate to the importance of pay as a reward?

4. Why have many organizations begun to supplement their traditional pay systems with "pay-for-performance" plans? Of these plans, what about individual versus group incentives?

5. How can the so-called new pay techniques help solve some of the major challenges facing today's organizations? Give some specific examples.

6. Why have more and more firms begun developing recognition programs as part of their organizational reward system? Why not just give people more money?

7. What role do benefits play in the organizational reward system? How can these costly benefits contribute more to desirable organizational outcomes?

**Internet Exercise: Rewards in the Workplace**

Visit Web sites such as **http://www.adcentive.com** and **http://www .corporaterewards.com/index.cfm?track_id=1314.** Here you will find various ideas on how to use and implement various reward and incentive systems. Find various tips and programs currently being used by organizations. Also, search under "pay for performance" to see other developments of this type of reward system.

1. From information you gained from the Web sites, how do you think these suggestions could influence work behavior? Which ones do you think will work better than others? Why?

2. Using a search engine to go to specific companies, what other types of reward systems can you find? Give the specifics and critique their value to improving performance in the workplace.

---

# Real Case: *CEOs Get Fewer Perks*

New SEC rules requiring companies to disclose perks that cost more than $10,000 lead to a decline in swanky extras

It may still be good to be king, but increasingly the job is coming with fewer perks. In its third annual study of fringe benefits for chief executives, compensation research firm Equilar found that the median values of seven of the nine major CEO perquisites that it tracks—from personal aircraft use to country club memberships—were down or remained flat from 2006 to 2001. The prevalence of such swanky extras fell too, with most categories showing lower rates of occurrence this year.

The decline is an expected result of SEC rules that went into effect last year. The new rules stipulate that companies disclose perks that cost more than $10,000, far lower than the previous $50,000 threshold. With a brighter spotlight on lavish extras that could prove embarrassing to a company, more boards have been ending or reducing CEO benefits. "For many shareholders, the presence of excessive perquisites has become an acid test on governance," says David Wise, a senior consultant in the compensation practice at management consulting firm Hay Group.

In addition, more disclosure may explain some of the increases that remain, such as the prevalence of corporate housing benefits, says Equilar research manager Alexander Cwirko-Godycki, which may not have been disclosed separately in the past. Some companies, especially after the SEC sent letters to companies last fall asking for more detail on compensation decisions, are choosing to disclose more than what's required. Others may be disclosing more because, due to the timing of their fiscal calendar, this was the first year they were required to file under the new regulations.

## Beefed-Up Security at Dell

Still, the study, which examines perks for CEOs of the 95 largest public companies by revenue, did show two increases that ran counter to the overall trend. Tax payments on perks and benefits—extra cash to make up for taxes assessed for the imputed income of fringe benefits for CEOs—actually rose in value this year by 43.6%, from a median of $23,951 in 2006 to $34,396 in 2007. [These payments are separate from the tax "gross-ups," as they're often called, that some CEOs receive for their severance packages.] That's surprising," says Cwirko-Godycki, especially given how much attention has been paid to this issue. "Perks have always been a controversial issue; paying the taxes on top of the perks has been even more so."

Meanwhile, the median value of personal and home security benefits for CEOs also increased by 14.4%, from $25,609 to $29,291. But Cwirko-Godycki is quick to point out that the value would have actually fallen this year had it not been for one significant outlier: Michael Dell, who received $1,034,750 in security benefits. [The amount was similar to what Dell earned as chairman the year before, but he was included in Equilar's study only after returning as CEO in early 2007.] In a statement to *BusinessWeek,* a spokesman for Round Rock, Texas–based Dell (DELL) says the company does not consider the security payments a perk, but a *business-related* expense mandated by the board. The company also says the amount of security Michael Dell receives is determined

with consideration that he is a recognizable industry leader and public figure worldwide.

Most perks, however, declined in value or prevalence. The median value of club memberships dropped most significantly, falling 64% from $11,070 in 2006 to $3,996 in 2007. Financial planning fees were down 9.2%, from $17,156 to $15,575. And personal use of aircraft, the perk that most "seems to get under shareholders' skin," says Hay Group's Wise, also fell. In 2007, the median outlay for CEOs flying on corporate jets was $109,743, down 9.8% from $121,676 in 2006.

1. Make a case both for and against executive perks. Do you agree that such perks should be cut? Why?
2. Do you think paying the taxes on top of the perks is ethical?
3. Would you turn down the perks if you ever become a CEO?

# Real Case:   *Rewarding Teamwork in the Plains*

In the past, most reward systems have been geared to the individual employee. However, with the emergence of teams in most of today's organizations, systems are being revamped to reward teamwork. A good example is Behlen Manufacturing Company in Columbus, Nebraska. The 1,100 mostly production employees are organized into 32 teams. Some of these teams have only a handful of members, whereas others have as many as 60. Although each individual receives a relatively low base-pay component, the rest of the compensation is variable and is determined in a number of different ways, including how one's team is performing.

The centerpiece of the manufacturing company's variable-reward plan is gain sharing, an increasingly popular form of compensation whereby all members share a usually fixed percentage of the documented savings or performance gain accomplished by the team. Behlen employees can earn monthly gain sharing of up to $1 an hour when their teams meet productivity goals. The CEO explained this team reward system as follows: "If you're in a group that makes stock tanks, for example, from the start of the process to the end of the process, over all shifts, all month long, if the team achieves certain levels of productivity, each of its members is rewarded anywhere from 0 cents to $1 an hour for every hour worked

in that area." Documentation of the gains is based on actual pounds of products, so that everyone on the team knows exactly how well their team is doing.

Another part of the company's variable-reward system involves profit sharing. Employees receive 20 percent of the profits. In recent years this has resulted in everyone's getting a profit-sharing bonus equivalent to three weeks' salary. Still another part of the reward package is the employee stock ownership plan. Each employee receives company stock equal in value to 2 percent of his or her base salary each year. Senior managers in the company participate in the same reward system as the workers, receiving the same proportional benefits. However, in the case of managers, performance is calculated on the gross margin of their business unit before selling and administrative costs are deducted.

How well has this company in the middle of the Great Plains performed with this organizational reward system? In each of the eight years this pay plan has been in place, performance has exceeded top management's expectations. In addition to the $5 million the firm saved because of safety, quality, and efficiency ideas that were submitted through the teams, the company has exceeded its profit goals each year. In fact, in the most recent reported year profits were $1 million greater than expectations. The CEO explained it this way, "As people focused in on their gain-sharing opportunities—and they've understood their profit-sharing opportunities—we're seeing positive productivity improvements in every corner of the plant."

1. Explain the organizational reward system this firm uses.

2. Although this reward system has obviously been very effective, what more can be done? What specific recommendations would you make?

3. What if the agricultural economy goes bad and the sales of this agribusiness company greatly decreases? What will be the impact on the reward system this company uses, and what would you now recommend?

---

# Real Case: *Different Strokes for Different Folks*

Organizations are finding that the best reward system entails a combination of money, recognition, and benefits. Money is important, of course, but if a person earns $50 in incentive pay every month, after a while this monetary reward may begin to lose some of its power. So financial rewards have to be altered and different ones offered. The same is true for recognition awards; although people never suffer from too much recognition, organizations have to be sure awards are fair, and highly creative organizations often ensure that change is built into the recognition system. The important thing that many firms have found is that what is truly rewarding for one person may not have the same impact for another. In short, there are individual differences when it comes to reward systems, and there have to be different strokes for different folks. Here are some representative innovative monetary and recognition rewards that have been offered by a variety of different enterprises.

- At Busch Gardens in Tampa, the company gives a Pat on the Back Award to employees who do an outstanding job and also has a copy of the notice of the award put in the employee's file.
- At Metro Motors in Montclair, California, the name of the Employee of the Month is put up on an electronic billboard over the dealership.
- At Colin Service Systems, a janitorial service in White Plains, New York, coworkers vote for the employees that they feel should be given awards as the Most Helpful Employee and the Nicest Employee, and executives make the presentations.
- At the Amway Corporation, on days when some workloads are light, the department's employees help

out in other departments, and after accumulating eight hours of such work, employees get a personal thank-you note from the manager of programs and services.
- At South Carolina Federal financial services in Columbia, the president and other top managers serve employees lunch or dinner as a reward for a job well done.
- At the Gunneson Group International, a total-quality consulting firm in Landing, New Jersey, when an employee refers business that results in a sale, the individual receives a cash award of 1 to 5 percent of the gross sale, depending on the value of the new business to the company.
- At QuadGraphics printing company in Pewaukee, Wisconsin, employees are paid $30 to attend a seminar devoted to quitting smoking, and the company gives $200 to anyone who quits for a year.
- At the Taylor Corporation, a printing company in North Mankato, Minnesota, in lieu of year-end bonuses, employees are allowed to make selections from a merchandise catalog.

1. Why are more and more companies complementing their monetary incentives with recognition awards in their organizational reward system?

2. How would you rate each of the examples? What are some strengths and weaknesses of each?

3. If you work for a human resource management consulting firm and are given the assignment to head up a project team to develop reward systems that would be appealing to today's employees, what would you recommend?

# Organizational Behavior Case: *Huge Benefits, Little Understanding or Use*

The Velma Company designs and manufactures high-tech communications equipment. The firm is a world-class supplier, and its three largest customers are *Fortune* 50 firms. Velma also has major clients in China and the European Union. Over the last five years the company's sales have tripled, and the biggest challenge it faces is hiring and retaining state-of-the-art people. In particular, there are two groups that are critical to the company's success. One is the design people who are responsible for developing new products that are more efficient and price competitive than those currently on the market. The other is the manufacturing people who build the equipment.

In an effort to attract and keep outstanding design people, Velma has a very attractive benefit package. All of their health insurance premiums and medical expenses are covered (no copay or deductibles). The company contributes 10 percent of their annual income toward a retirement program, and these funds are vested within 24 months. So a new design person who is earning $75,000 annually will have $7,500 put into a retirement fund by the company, and the individual can make additional personal contributions. Each year all designers are given 100 shares of stock (the current sales price is $22) and an option to buy another 100 shares (the current stock price is $25 and this option is good for 10 years or as long as the person works for the firm, whichever comes first).

The manufacturing people are on a pay-for-performance plan. Each individual is paid $7 for each unit he or she produces, and the average worker can turn out three units an hour. There is weekend work for anyone who wants it, but the rate per unit does not change. In addition, the company gives all of the manufacturing people free health insurance and covers all medical expenses.

Another benefit is that everyone in the company is eligible for five personal days a year, and the company will pay for any unused days. Velma also has a large day care facility that is free for all employees, and there is a state-of-the-art wellness center located on the premises.

Last year the company's turnover was 9 percent, and the firm would like to reduce it by 50 percent this year.

One proposed strategy is to strengthen the benefits package even more and make it so attractive that no one will want to, or could afford to, leave. Some top managers privately are concerned that the firm is already doing way too much for these employees and are troubled by the fact that exit interviews with designers who left in the last year indicated that many of them were unaware of the benefits they were receiving. For example, most of the designers who have gone elsewhere reported that they were attracted to the stock offered them, yet they did not exercise the options to buy additional shares of Velma stock because they were not sure what the financial benefits were to them. The manufacturing people who left reported that $7 per unit was acceptable, although a higher rate would have resulted in their remaining with the firm. The manufacturing people also liked the stock that the company gave them, but were somewhat confused about the options they held.

Both groups—designers and manufacturing personnel—seemed pleased with the contribution that the company made to their retirement program, but most of them did not put any additional personal contributions into their retirement fund. When asked why, the majority of them were unaware that this could be done on a before-tax basis, thus temporarily shielding the contributions from taxes and making it easier to build a nest egg for the future. Finally, all of those who left said that they liked the child care benefit, although most of them did not have young children so they did not use it, and they thought the wellness center was also a good idea but they were so busy working that they admitted to never using the facilities.

1. Which benefits did the employees who were leaving seem to best understand and like?

2. Which benefits did they find confusing or of little value?

3. Based on your answers and other relevant considerations, what recommendations would you make to Velma's management regarding how they can do a better job of using the benefits package in their organizational reward system?

# Experiential Exercises for Part One

## EXERCISE:

Synthesis of Student and Instructor Needs*

### Goals:

1. To "break the ice" in using experiential exercises
2. To initiate open communication between students and the instructor regarding mutual learning goals and needs
3. To stimulate the students to clarify their learning goals and instructional needs and to commit themselves to these
4. To serve as the first exercise in the "experiential" approach to management education

### Implementation:

1. The class is divided into groups of four to six students each.
2. Each group openly discusses what members would like from the course and drafts a set of learning objectives and instructional aims. The group also makes up a list of learning/course objectives that they feel the instructor wants to pursue. (About 20 minutes.)
3. After each group has "caucused," a group spokesperson is appointed to meet with the instructor in an open dialogue in front of the class about course objectives.
4. The instructor meets with each group representative at the front of the classroom to initiate an open dialogue about the semester of learning. (About 30 minutes.) Several activities are carried out:
   a. Open discussion of the learning objectives of both the students and the instructor
   b. Recognition of the constraints faced by each party in accommodating these goals
   c. Identification of areas of goal agreement and disagreement, and feasible compromises
   d. Drafting a set of guidelines for cooperation between the parties, designed to better bring about mutual goal attainment

## EXERCISE:

Work-Related Organizational Behavior: Implications for the Course*

### Goals:

1. To identify course topic areas from the participant's own work experience
2. To introduce experiential learning

***Sources:** (1) "Synthesis of Student and Instructor Needs" was suggested by Professor Philip Van Auken and is used with his permission. (2) "Work-Related Organizational Behavior: Implications for the Course" is from "Getting Acquainted Triads," in J. William Pfeiffer and John E. Jones (Eds.), *A Handbook of Structured Experiences,* Vol. 1, University Associates, San Diego, Calif., 1969, and "Defining Organizational Behavior," in James B. Lau, *Behavior in Organizations,* Irwin, Burr Ridge, Ill., 1975.

## Implementation:

Task 1: Each class member does the following:

1. Describes an experience in a past work situation that illustrates something about organizational behavior. (Some students have had only part-time work experience or summer jobs, but even the humblest job is relevant here.)
2. Explains what it illustrates about organizational behavior. (Time: five minutes for individuals to think about and jot down notes covering these two points.)

Task 2: The class forms into triads and each triad does the following:

1. Member A tells his or her experience to member B. Member B listens carefully, paraphrases the story back to A, and tells what it illustrates about organizational behavior. Member B must do this to A's satisfaction that B has understood fully what A was trying to communicate. Member C is the observer and remains silent during the process.
2. Member B tells his or her story to C, and A is the observer.
3. Member C tells his or her story to A, and B is the observer. (Each member has about five minutes to tell his or her story and have it paraphrased back by the listener. The instructor will call out the time at the end of each five-minute interval for equal apportionment of "airtime" among participants. Total time: 15 minutes.)

Task 3: Each triad selects one of its members to relate his or her incident to the class. The instructor briefly analyzes for the class how the related story fits in with some topic to be studied in the course, such as perception, motivation, communication, conflict, or leadership. The topic areas are listed in the table of contents of this book.

## EXERCISE:

Organizations*

## Goals:

1. To identify some of the important organizations in your life
2. To determine relevant, specific characteristics of organizations
3. To describe some of the important functions of management in organizations

## Implementation:

Read the Overview and Procedure sections. Complete the Profile of Organizations form, which follows these sections.

## Overview:

Undoubtedly, you have had recent experiences with numerous organizations. Ten to 15 minutes of reflective thinking should result in a fairly large list of organizations. Don't be misled by thinking that only large organizations, such as your college or Microsoft, are relevant for consideration. How about the clinic, with the doctors, nurses, and secretary/bookkeeper? Or the corner garage or service station? The local bar, McDonald's, and the

*Source: Reprinted with permission from Fremont E. Kast and James E. Rosenzweig, "Our Organizational Society," in *Experiential Exercises and Cases in Management*, McGraw-Hill, New York, 1976, pp. 13–15.

neighborhood theater are all organizations. You should have no difficulty listing several organizations with which you have had recent contact.

The second part of the exercise, however, is tougher. Describe several of the key characteristics of the organizations that you have listed. One of the major issues in studying and describing organizations is deciding *what* characteristics or factors are important. Some of the more common characteristics considered in the analysis of organizations are:

1. Size (small to very large)
2. Degree of formality (informal to highly structured)
3. Degree of complexity (simple to complex)
4. Nature of goals (what the organization is trying to accomplish)
5. Major activities (what tasks are performed)
6. Types of people involved (age, skills, educational background, etc.)
7. Location of activities (number of units and their geographic location)

You should be able to develop a list of characteristics that you think are relevant for each of your organizations.

Now to the third, final, and most difficult task. Think about what is involved in the management of these organizations. For example, what kinds of functions do their managers perform? How does one learn the skills necessary to be an effective manager? Would you want to be a manager in any of these organizations?

In effect, in this exercise you are being asked to think specifically about organizations you have been associated with recently, develop your own conceptual model for looking at their characteristics, and think more specifically about the managerial functions in each of these organizations. You probably already know a great deal more about organizations and their management than you think. This exercise should be useful in getting your thoughts together.

## Procedure:

*Step 1.* Prior to class, list up to 10 organizations (for example, work, living group, club) in which you have been involved or with which you have had recent contact.

*Step 2.* Enter five organizations from your list on the form on the next page (use extra sheets as needed).

1. List the organization.
2. Briefly outline the characteristics that you consider most significant.
3. Describe the managerial functions in each of these organizations.

*Step 3.* During the class period, meet in groups of five or six to discuss your list of organizations, the characteristics you consider important, and your descriptions of their management. Look for significant similarities and differences across organizations.

*Step 4.* Basing your selections on this group discussion, develop a list entitled "What we would like to know about organizations and their management." Be prepared to write this list on the chalkboard or on big sheets of paper and to share your list with other groups in the class.

**Profile of
Organizations**

| Organization | Key Characteristics | Managerial Functions |
|---|---|---|
| 1. _____ | _____ <br> _____ <br> _____ <br> _____ | _____ <br> _____ <br> _____ <br> _____ |
| 2. _____ | _____ <br> _____ <br> _____ <br> _____ | _____ <br> _____ <br> _____ <br> _____ |
| 3. _____ | _____ <br> _____ <br> _____ <br> _____ | _____ <br> _____ <br> _____ <br> _____ |
| 4. _____ | _____ <br> _____ <br> _____ <br> _____ | _____ <br> _____ <br> _____ <br> _____ |
| 5. _____ | _____ <br> _____ <br> _____ <br> _____ | _____ <br> _____ <br> _____ <br> _____ |

# Part **Two**

# Cognitive Processes of Organizational Behavior

# EVIDENCE-BASED CONSULTING PRACTICES

## GALLUP'S ANSWER FOR AN EMOTIONAL ECONOMY: HUMANSIGMA™

This second major part of the text is concerned with the micro, individual level of analysis of organizational behavior. Recent workplace research by The Gallup Organization has led to the management metric known as HumanSigma™ (for example, see the book by this title by Gallup principals John Fleming and Jim Asplund published by Gallup Press). This is a measure of "the human difference" and is made up of two complementary economic factors, known as employee and customer engagement. Together, these factors assess an organization's success in managing the Emotional Economy and driving financial performance. HumanSigma™ is a reliable indication of how organizations manage and leverage employee and customer engagement and productivity. It is a new way of thinking about how human differences interact. At the same time, it is a process, or sequence, of activities to leverage this human difference. Finally, it is a metric that indicates how well companies are progressing in the deployment of their human difference. Because there is significantly more HumanSigma variance within companies than between companies in the same industry, it is most effectively measured and managed at the work group level, one employee and one customer at a time. Successful management of these metrics requires the active involvement of local managers and associates. The Gallup Path™, the sequence of linkages between human performance and financial metrics including revenue, earnings, and stock value, further explains the components of HumanSigma™ management.

## WHAT IS EMPLOYEE ENGAGEMENT?

A recent issue of the *Journal of Applied Psychology* included an article summarizing a meta-analysis of Gallup research that illustrated the meaningful relationship between employee engagement and important workplace measures such as productivity, retention, customer ratings, and safety. Engaged employees are those who are emotionally invested in their jobs. Employee engagement is measured by Gallup's 12 questions, known as the $Q^{12®}$. These powerful questions measure dimensions that can be influenced at the local level by leaders, managers, and employees. Organizations that have implemented performance management systems designed to increase employee engagement have realized many of the workplace performance improvements outlined above.

## WHAT IS CUSTOMER ENGAGEMENT?

Customer engagement goes beyond customer satisfaction and loyalty to a deeper, emotional attachment to the organization's brands or services. For organizations to succeed in today's emotional economy, they must understand, develop, and sustain engaged customers. Gallup's extensive research led to 11 questions, known as the $CE^{11®}$, that measure customer engagement and powerfully link to financial performance. As with employee engagement, these items measure dimensions able to be influenced at the local level. Successful performance management programs have produced customers with increased emotional attachment to products, services, and brands, resulting in improved financial performance for the organization.

## WHY DOES HUMANSIGMA™ MATTER?

HumanSigma takes performance management beyond total quality management gurus Deming and Juran's Six Sigma to optimize human performance by reducing variability in the extent to which both employees' and customers' emotional needs are met. Recent estimates indicate that at least 10 percent of the U.S. gross domestic product (GDP) is wasted by organizations due to unmanaged variation of the human aspects of performance. HumanSigma research has shown that, in general, the top 10 percent of organizations' business units generate earnings up to seven times higher than the bottom 10 percent. Further, variation of HumanSigma across time determines the variation of earnings growth and sustained potential. Thus, it's not enough just to measure HumanSigma; managers and employees need to take responsibility for effective HumanSigma management to realize meaningful increases in earnings. Increasing research evidence suggests that managing HumanSigma™ can generate more earnings than most of the management initiatives currently being pursued. It seems that the future success of organizations will be realized by leveraging human potential within the emotional economy.

# Chapter **Five**

# Personality, Perception, and Employee Attitudes

## Learning Objectives

- **Define** the overall meaning of personality.
- **Identify** the "Big Five" personality traits and the Myers-Briggs types.
- **Describe** the perceptual process and its major dimensions.
- **Examine** the sources and outcomes of the major employee attitudes of job satisfaction, organizational commitment, and organizational citizenship behaviors.

This chapter discusses the cognitive, personal variables of personality, perception, and employee attitudes. These major psychological constructs are very popular ways to describe and analyze what goes into organizational behavior. Yet, like the other cognitively oriented processes, personality, perception, and employee attitudes are quite complex. The aim of this chapter is to facilitate a better understanding of such complexities of today's employees. Such an analysis of personality and attitudes is vital to the study of organizational behavior.

The first section of the chapter defines and clarifies the concept of personality. The next section is devoted to personality development and the socialization process. This foundation of understanding of the complex personality and how it is developed is followed by the two major applications to organizational behavior. Specifically, attention is given to the "Big Five" personality traits that have been found to best relate to performance in organizations and the Myers-Briggs Type Indicator (MBTI) based on Carl Jung's personality theory, which has been a very popular personal development and career assessment tool. The remaining sections of the chapter then focus on two more important cognitive processes, perception and attitudes. After examining the perceptual process and dimensions, a detailed analysis is first made of the dispositions of positive and negative affectivity, the two most widely recognized attitudes to organizational behavior, job satisfaction and organizational commitment, and finally the more recent relevant construct of prosocial/organizational citizenship behaviors.

## THE MEANING OF PERSONALITY

Through the years there has not been universal agreement on the exact meaning of personality. Much of the controversy can be attributed to the fact that people in general and those in the behavioral sciences define "personality" from different perspectives. Most people tend to equate personality with social success (i.e., having a "good or popular personality," or having "a lot of personality") and to describe personality by a single dominant characteristic (i.e., strong, weak, or polite). When it is realized that thousands of words can be used to describe personality this way, the definitional problem becomes staggering. Psychologists, on the other hand, take a different perspective. For example, the descriptive-adjective approach commonly used by most people plays only a small part. However, scholars also cannot agree on a definition of personality because they operate from different theoretical bases.

Some of the historically important definitions come from trait theory (observable patterns of behavior that last over time), Freud's psychoanalytic or psychodynamic theory (the unconscious determinants of behavior), and Carl Rogers and Abraham Maslow's humanistic theory (self-actualization and the drive to realize one's potential). More recently, and the position taken in this chapter, is a more integrative theoretical approach drawing from all the historical theories, but more importantly, the self-concept including nature (heredity and physiological/biological dimensions) and nurture (environmental, developmental dimensions), dispositional traits, the social cognitive interactions between the person and the environment, and the socialization process.

In this text *personality* will mean how people affect others and how they understand and view themselves, as well as their pattern of inner and outer measurable traits and the person-situation interaction. How people affect others depends primarily on their external appearance (height, weight, facial features, color, and other physical aspects) and traits. For example, in terms of external appearance, a very tall worker will have an impact on other people different from that of a very short worker. There is also evidence from meta-analysis that there are gender differences in certain personality characteristics.[1] However, of more importance to the physiological/biological approach in the study of personality than the external appearance is the role of heredity and the brain.

# THE ROLE OF HEREDITY AND THE BRAIN

Although heredity's role in personality was traditionally downplayed, studies of twins in recent years have led to renewed interest. Identical twins share the same genetic endowment, but if they are raised apart (say, through separate adoptions), then the similarities and differences can provide insight into the relative contribution of heredity versus environment or nature versus nurture. That is, identical twins (who have the same genetic endowment) raised together (i.e., they have similar environment and developmental experiences) can be compared to the identical twins raised apart (same genetic endowment but different environment). If the identical twins raised together have the same traits, and this sameness is also found in those raised apart, then the conclusion can be drawn that heredity and not environment plays the largest role. However, if those raised together have similar traits, but those raised apart have significantly different traits, then the importance of the environment must be considered.

Although twin studies in general are open to criticism of political influence and lack of scientific controls,[2] most behavioral scientists now agree that genes play a role not only in physical characteristics and the brain, but also in personality. For example, a report by the American Psychological Association concludes, "Studies over the past 20 years on twins and adopted children have firmly established that there is a genetic component to just about every human trait and behavior, including personality, general intelligence and behavior disorders."[3] However, the search for identifying genes that affect the potential for certain diseases[4] or personality is very complex and may explain very little. For example, a summary analysis concluded:

> Many genes are responsible for various aspects of people's temperament, and those genes appear to interact with each other in complicated ways that influence several traits at once— and then likely only in very subtle ways, with any one gene likely accounting for only 1 or 2 percent of the variance in a trait.[5]

In other words, it appears that hundreds of genes do at least slightly influence the personality traits, but so does the environment. The debate should not be nature *or* nurture, but nature *and* nurture that contributes to one's personality.[6] However, the genes also affect brain functions that in turn affect how people interact with their environment and thus their personalities.

The brain, which some call the last frontier because we still know relatively little about it, may hold more answers for personality than does heredity. Both evolutionary psychologists (those that suggest humans evolve and retain not only physically over the ages, but also psychologically) and neuropsychologists (those that explain psychological characteristics primarily through the brain) have traditionally not played a mainstream role in the study and understanding of personality. In recent years, however, they are gaining increasing attention because of rapid advances in their respective fields of study. Evolutionary psychologists are suggesting that humans may be "hardwired" from distant previous generations. As was noted in a *Harvard Business Review* article:

> Although human beings today inhabit a thoroughly modern world of space exploration and virtual realities, they do so with the ingrained mentality of Stone Age hunter-gatherers . . . an instinct to fight furiously when threatened, for instance, and a drive to trade information and share secrets. Human beings are, in other words, hardwired. You can take the person out of the Stone Age, but you can't take the Stone Age out of the person.[7]

There is also a recent position being taken on what is called social evolution. This suggests that humanity is evolving along the lines of social phenomena such as trust, collaboration, and competition. This social evolutionary process is explained as follows:

> People who are related collaborate on the basis of nepotism. It takes outrageous profit or provocation for someone to do down a relative with whom they share a lot of genes. Trust, though, allows the unrelated to collaborate, by keeping score of who does what when, and punishing cheats. . . . The human mind, however, seems to have evolved the trick of being able to identify a large number of individuals and to keep score of relations with them . . ."[8]

Very few animals (bats being one of the exceptions) have been able to evolve to this type of collaboration and competition.

As to neuropsychology, recent breakthroughs in brain-scanning technology, called functional magnetic resonance imaging (fMRI), allow measurement of brain activity by mapping specific regions that are linked to specialized roles. Although brain dominance theory has been around a long time and has probably been too oversimplified (e.g., the right-side creative brain and the left-side analytical or management brain), there is now general agreement that

> The frontal lobes are the part of the brain that anticipates events and weighs the consequences of behavior, while deeper brain regions, including the seahorse-shaped hippocampus and the nearby amygdala, are associated with such things as memory, mood and motivation.[9]

Besides the left and right regions, fMRIs are also able to detect that the amygdala part of the brain has to do with the emotion of the individual. Although there is a very complicated interaction between emotions and thinking, personality and/or behavior,[10] there is enough evidence for some to conclude the following implications for the workplace:

> Recent discoveries in neuroscience reveal that talent and better-quality performance involve not just the frontal lobes—the decision-making brain circuitry that houses intellect—but also the amygdala . . . In tough economic times, talent and emotional engagement are the only natural competitive advantages.[11]

*The Wall Street Journal* even reported a study that indicated those with brain damage impairing their ability to experience emotion made better financial decisions than normal players in a simple investment game.[12] It seems that the emotional brain damaged (but normal IQ) participants were more willing to take risks that yielded high payoffs and less likely to react emotionally to losses. They finished the game with significantly more money than the other players. There is also work being done on linking areas of the brain to specific organizational behaviors (e.g., the nucleus accumbens part of the brain responds to money much the way it reacts to sex or cocaine; money is valued for itself and not just for what it can purchase). Other examples include neuroscientific explanations for why employees resist change (i.e., change taps fear receptors in the brain and taxes the brain's cognitive capacity to learn new ways of doing things[13]) and beginning research evidence that leaders with high levels of psychological capital (i.e., confidence, hope, optimism, and resiliency, covered in Chapter 7) have different brain activity on a vision task exercise than do those with low psychological capital.[14]

Although not without criticism,[15] there is little question that major inroads are being made in the role that genetics and the brain play both in organizational behavior in general, and personality in particular. However, at present the field of psychology as a whole and organizational behavior itself is still dominated by the developmental, "soft" or nurture side, which is also making significant advances in understanding and application. For example, five personality traits (the so-called Big Five) have emerged from research as being especially related to job performance.[16] These specific traits will be given detailed attention after the more theoretical foundation components of personality of self-esteem, person-situation interaction, and socialization are discussed.

## Self-Esteem

People's attempts to understand themselves are called the *self-concept* in personality theory. The self is a unique product of many interacting parts and may be thought of as the personality viewed from within. This self is particularly relevant to the widely recognized self-esteem and the emerging self-variables of multiple intelligences, emotion, optimism, and, especially, efficacy, which are all relevant to the field of organizational behavior. These and other newly emerging self-variables and positive psychological capacities are given specific attention in Chapter 7.

The more established, recognized *self-esteem* has to do with people's self-perceived competence and self-image. Applied to the analysis of personality, the research results have been mixed, and there is growing controversy about the assumed value of self-esteem. For example, one study found that people with high self-esteem handle failure better than those with low self-esteem.[17] However, an earlier study found that those with high self-esteem tended to become egotistical when faced with pressure situations[18] and may result in aggressive and even violent behavior when threatened.[19] After reviewing the research literature, Kreitner and Kinicki conclude, "High self esteem *can* be a good thing, but only if like many other human characteristics—such as creativity, intelligence, and persistence—it is nurtured and channeled in constructive and ethical ways. Otherwise, it can become antisocial and destructive."[20]

Self-esteem has obvious implications for organizational behavior. Although it is considered a global concept, there are attempts to specifically apply it to the organization domain. Called organization-based self-esteem (OBSE), it is defined as the "self-perceived value that individuals have of themselves as organization members acting within an organization context."[21] Those who score high on OBSE view themselves positively, and a meta-analysis found a significant positive relationship with performance and satisfaction on the job.[22]

Also, both early[23] and the more recent studies indicate that self-esteem plays at least an important moderating role in areas such as emotional and behavioral responses and stress of organizational members.[24] As has been noted, "Both research and everyday experience confirm that employees with high self-esteem feel unique, competent, secure, empowered, and connected to the people around them."[25] By the same token, as the author of the book, *Self-Esteem at Work,* notes: "If your self-esteem is low and you aren't confident in your thinking ability, you are likely to fear decision making, lack negotiation and interpersonal skills and be reluctant or unable to change."[26] One study found that leaders can overcome such self-esteem problems of their people by practicing procedural fairness and rewarding for a job well done.[27]

As will be noted in Chapter 7, self-esteem is more of a global, relatively fixed trait, whereas other self-variables, such as self-efficacy, are more situation and context specific. There seems little doubt that self-esteem plays an important role in one's personality, but, as pointed out earlier, the exact nature and impact are still to be determined. For now, the person-situation interaction and socialization are presented to serve as an important part of the social cognitive foundation for the rest of this chapter and for the more specific, positive self-concepts in Chapter 7.

## Person-Situation Interaction

The dimensions of enduring traits and the self-concept add to the understanding of the human personality. The person-situation interaction dimension of personality provides further understanding. Each situation, of course, is different. The differences may seem to be very small on the surface, but when filtered by the person's cognitive mediating processes such as perception (covered next), they can lead to quite large subjective differences and diverse behavioral outcomes. In particular, this dimension suggests that people are not static, acting the same in all situations, but instead are ever changing and flexible. For example, employees can change depending on the particular situation they are in interaction with. For instance, it should be understood that even everyday work experience can change people. Especially today, with organizations transforming and facing a turbulent environment, those that can find, develop, and retain people who can fit into this dynamically changing situation will be most successful.[28] Specifically, there is evidence that the employee's personality will influence interpersonal behavior[29] and the perception and the outcomes of organizational support.[30] The next section dealing with the socialization process is especially relevant to today's important person-organization interaction.

## The Socialization Process

Study of, and research on, the development of personality has traditionally been an important area for understanding human behavior. Modern developmental psychology does not get into the argument of heredity versus environment or of maturation (changes that result from heredity and physical development) versus learning. The human being consists of both physiological *and* psychological interacting parts. Therefore, heredity, the brain, environment, maturation, and learning *all* contribute to the human personality.

At least historically, the study of personality attempted to identify specific physiological and psychological stages that occur in the development of the human personality. This "stage" approach was theoretical in nature. There are many well-known stage theories of personality development. However, as with most aspects of personality, there is little agreement about the exact stages. In fact, a growing number of today's psychologists contend that there are *no* identifiable stages. Their argument is that personality development consists of a continuous process and the sequence is based largely on the learning opportunities available and the socialization process.

There is increasing recognition given to the role of other relevant persons, groups, and, especially, organizations that greatly influence an individual's personality. This continuous impact from the social environment is commonly called the *socialization process*. It is especially relevant to organizational behavior because the process is not confined to early childhood; rather, it takes place throughout one's life. In particular, evidence is accumulating that socialization may be one of the best explanations for why employees behave the way they do in today's organizations.[31] As Edgar Schein notes: "It is high time that some of our managerial knowledge and skill be focused on those forces in the organization environment which derive from the fact that organizations are social systems which do socialize their new members. If we do not learn to analyze and control the forces of organizational socialization, we are abdicating one of our primary managerial responsibilities."[32] A study found that the socialization tactics that organizations employ can have a positive, long-run impact on the adjustment of newcomers (i.e., lower role conflict and ambiguity, less stress, and higher job satisfaction and commitment)[33] and related recent research has found that social processes facilitate job search behavior[34] and advancement in management from entry level to upper management.[35]

Socialization starts with the initial contact between a mother and her new infant. After infancy, other members of the immediate family (father, brothers, and sisters), close relatives and family friends, and then the social group (peers, school friends, and members of the work group) play influential roles. As the accompanying OB in Action: Using Information Technologies to Nurture Relationships indicates, the way these socialization processes are being done is changing, but the impact is still dramatic. However, of particular interest to the study of organizational behavior is Schein's idea that the organization itself also contributes to socialization.[36] He points out that the process includes the learning of those values, norms, and behavior patterns that, from the organization's and the work group's points of view, are necessary for any new organization member.

Specific techniques of socializing new employees would include the use of mentors or role models, orientation and training programs, reward systems, and career planning. Specific steps that can lead to successful organizational socialization would include the following:

1. Provide a challenging first job
2. Provide relevant training
3. Provide timely and consistent feedback
4. Select a good first supervisor to be in charge of socialization
5. Design a relaxed orientation program
6. Place new recruits in work groups with high morale[37]

Such deliberate socialization strategies have tremendous potential impact on socialization. Evidence shows that those new employees attending a socialization training program are indeed more socialized than those who do not[38] and have better person-organization fit.[39]

In summary, personality is very diverse and complex. It incorporates almost everything covered in this text, and more. As defined, personality is the whole person and is concerned with external appearance and traits, self, and situational interactions. Probably the best statement on personality was made many years ago by Kluckhohn and Murray, who said that, to some extent, a person's personality is like all other people's, like some other people's, and like no other people's.[40]

Just as businesses are shifting from Industrial Age hierarchies to collaborative networks, so, too, is the American family undergoing a parallel social revolution. Parents and children are no longer on the same schedule—unlike the way things were a generation ago. With many educated mothers and fathers working longer hours, they are linked to their kids by a web of cell phones and e-mails.

At the same time, kids are taking the initiative to pursue more activities and are using information technologies to nurture their own electronic networks of relationships, from friends at school to cousins in distant cities. "The catalyst for change has been the same in the work hemisphere and family time," says Julie Morgenstern, a time management consultant and founder of Task Masters in New York. "It's technology."

The networked economy is leading to far different standards and expectations of what it means to be a parent and a child. It's not simply enough for the young to get an education. Instead, the goal is to raise children to be creative and adaptable, able both to compete successfully and to collaborate with their Chinese and Indian peers. "We have an economy [whose] functioning depends for the first time on the enhancement of human capability," says Richard Florida, professor of public policy at George Mason University in Fairfax, Va. Adds Luke Koons, director of information and knowledge management at Intel Corp.: "Fourteen-year-olds are truly collaborating and thinking together. There's a lot we can learn to apply to a corporate setting."

So how can the typical overworked white-collar American—bombarded by e-mails, beset with late-night meetings, and confronted with unexpected business trips—simultaneously manage at warp speed and cope with the new challenges at home? Gradually, a new body of shared rules-of-thumb is emerging, passed along at playgrounds and in offices. Among them: Transform technology from an oppressor into a liberator. "I love tech," says Margaret M. Foran, senior vice-president and associate general counsel at Pfizer Inc., who uses her BlackBerry and her cell phone to mix work and family time. "I can go to the soccer games at 3 P.M. I can go to the play, the book sale, the science demonstration, and the doctor appointments." Others have mastered the art of interweaving work obligations and home life in a way that was not possible before, answering an e-mail from work one minute and helping with homework the next. And the younger members of the family—already far more sophisticated at multitasking and networking than their parents—are getting a chance to see what approaches work and what falls flat.

"My daughter, now working, knows how important it is to use her time well," says Carrie J. Hightman, president of SBC Illinois, who is married to a regional administrator for Pitney Bowes Inc. "She has seen me do it. Now she's doing it."

Historically, the organization of the family has mirrored, to some degree, the organization of the workplace. Take the classic middle-class family of the 1950s and '60s, the "Golden Age" economy of strong productivity growth and lush gains in real wages. With a secure corporate job, Dad could afford to work not much more than 40 hours a week, and Mom could stay at home to raise the children. The family of that era did many things together. The classic example is eating dinner every evening at the kitchen table. The kids also tagged along when Mom and Dad visited friends. In essence, a family acted like a single unit, with a hierarchy that mirrored the top-down management of factories or large industrial organizations of the day, such as General Motors Corp.

Fast-forward to the 2000s. Today, both Mom and Dad are more likely to have careers. The combined workweek of a husband and wife in their prime working years with children is 68 hours, up from 59 hours in 1979, according to calculations by the Economic Policy Institute. The better educated the couple, the more hours they put in. At the same time, their jobs have changed. The rote work is either being done by computers or is in the process of being outsourced to Asia. Instead, what's left are the more complicated and creative tasks that can't be easily reduced to a set of instructions.

At home, standards for a healthy, emotionally rich family life are a lot higher than they used to be. Schedules during "leisure hours" are crammed with music lessons and play dates for the kids, exercise classes for Mom, and occasional tee times for Dad. Parents are aware that colleges and universities look more favorably on high school students with a demonstrated ability to do many things well, not unlike the skills they will need in the workplace. Says Ann Swidler, a sociologist at the University of California at Berkeley: "It's the complex management of a life with a wealth of choices."

To achieve these goals, families are learning to turn technology to their advantage. Yes, BlackBerrys, cell phones, e-mail, and other high-tech gear erode traditional boundaries between the office cubicle and the kitchen table, or even the bedroom. But many time-pressed workers now realize that technology creates greater possibilities for busy families to stay in touch and, at the same time, increase family times.

**TABLE 5.1**
The "Big Five"
Personality Traits

| Core Traits | Descriptive Characteristics of High Scorers |
|---|---|
| Conscientiousness | Dependable, hardworking, organized, self-disciplined, persistent, responsible |
| Emotional stability | Calm, secure, happy, unworried |
| Agreeableness | Cooperative, warm, caring, good-natured, courteous, trusting |
| Extraversion | Sociable, outgoing, talkative, assertive, gregarious |
| Openness to experience | Curious, intellectual, creative, cultured, artistically sensitive, flexible, imaginative |

## The "Big Five" Personality Traits

Although personality traits, long-term predispositions for behavior, have been generally downplayed and even totally discounted, in recent years there is now considerable support for a five-factor trait-based theory of personality. Many years ago no less than 18,000 words were found to describe personality. Even after combining words with similar meanings, there still remained 171 personality traits.[41] Obviously, such a huge number of personality traits is practically unusable, so further reduction analysis found five core personality traits. Called the Five-Factor Model (FFM),[42] or in the field of organizational behavior and human resource management, the "Big Five," these traits have held up as accounting for personality in many analyses over the years[43] and even across cultures.[44]

Table 5.1 identifies the Big Five and their major characteristics. Importantly, not only is there now considerable agreement on what are the core personality trait predispositions, but there is also accumulated research that these five best predict performance in the workplace.[45] The Big Five have also been extended through meta-analytic studies to also demonstrate a positive relationship with performance motivation[46] (goal setting, expectancy, and self-efficacy, all given detailed attention in later chapters) and job satisfaction.[47] Although the five traits are largely independent factors of a personality, like primary colors, they can be mixed in countless proportions and with other characteristics to yield a unique personality whole. However, also like colors, one may dominate in describing an individual's personality.

The real value of the Big Five to organizational behavior is that it does bring back the importance of predispositional traits,[48] and these traits have been clearly shown to relate to job performance. Importantly, it should also be noted that these five traits are quite stable. Although there is not total agreement, most personality theorists would tend to agree that after about 30 years of age, the individual's personality profile will change little over time.[49] This does not intend to imply that one or two of the Big Five provide an ideal personality profile for employees over their whole career, because different traits are needed for different jobs. The key is still to find the right fit.[50] The following sections examine the research to date on the relationships of the various Big Five traits to dimensions of performance in organizations.

### *The Positive Impact of Conscientiousness*

There is general agreement that conscientiousness has the strongest positive correlation (about .3) with job performance. From this level of correlation (1.0 would be perfect), it should be noted that less than 10 percent (the correlation squared, or $R^2$) of the performance in the studies is accounted for by conscientiousness. Yet, it should also be noted that this is still significant and conscientious employees may provide a major competitive advantage. As a meta-analysis concluded, "individuals who are dependable, persistent, goal directed, and organized tend to be higher performers on virtually any job; viewed negatively, those who are careless, irresponsible, low achievement striving and impulsive tend to be lower performers on virtually any job."[51]

Put in relation to other organizational behavior areas as a personality trait per se, conscientious employees set higher goals for themselves, have higher performance expectations, and respond well to job enrichment (take on more responsibility, covered in Chapter 6) and empowerment strategies of human resource management. As would be expected, research indicates that those who are conscientious are less likely to be absent from work,[52] and a study found in international human resource management that conscientiousness of expatriates related positively to the rating of their foreign assignment performance.[53] Yet, there are also recent studies with nonsupporting and mixed results pointing to the complexity of this personality trait. For example, in a recent study conscientiousness was found not to be influential in determining managerial performance and in another study of Middle Eastern expatriate managers, conscientiousness was related to home-country ratings of the expats' performance, but not the host-country ratings of the same expats.[54] In addition, studies had indicated that the individual's ability moderates the relationship between conscientiousness and performance (positive for high ability but zero or even negative for low ability), but a more recent study found no such moderator.[55] Another study found the relationship of conscientiousness to job performance was strong when job satisfaction was low, but was relatively weak when satisfaction was high.[56]

Applied to peer evaluations, as hypothesized, a study found the raters' conscientiousness was negatively related with the level of the rating. In other words, conscientious raters did not give inflated evaluations, but those with low conscientiousness did.[57] Such multiplicative relationships with variables such as culture, ability, and job satisfaction indicate, like other psychological variables, that conscientiousness is complex and is certainly not the only answer for job performance. This has led to a recent research stream that supports the hypothesized interactive effects between conscientiousness and extraversion[58] and agreeableness[59] on performance and the interaction of conscientiousness and openness to experience and creative behavior.[60] The same is true of research on the mediating and moderating effects of conscientiousness when influenced by various organizational behavior dynamics.[61] In other words, without getting to the depth of these analyses, it can simply be said that there is considerable complexity involved with the impact of the personality trait of conscientiousness on various work-related variables. However, this is one area of personality where there is enough research evidence to conclude that conscientiousness should be given attention in understanding the impact that personality traits can have on job performance, job satisfaction, and work motivation, and pragmatically for personnel selection for most jobs.

### The Impact of the Other Traits

Although conscientiousness has been found to have the strongest consistent relationship with performance and thus has received the most research attention, the remaining four traits also have some interesting findings. For example, a large study including participants from several European countries, many occupational groups, and multiple methods of measuring performance found both conscientiousness and emotional stability related to all the measures and occupations.[62] Yet, the absenteeism study found that conscientiousness had a desirable inverse relationship: but, undesirably, the higher the extraversion trait the more absent the employee tended to be.[63]

The other traits have a more selective but still logical impact. For example, those with high extraversion tend to be associated with management and sales success; those with high emotional stability tend to be more effective in stressful situations; those with high agreeableness tend to handle customer relations and conflict more effectively; and those open to experience tend to have job training proficiency and make better decisions in a training problem solving simulation.[64] Another study found that those with a strategic management style were most characterized by conscientiousness and openness to experience, while those with a strong interpersonal management style were most characterized by extraversion and openness.[65] Interestingly, with groups rather than individuals becoming more important in today's workplace, the Big Five may also be predictive of team performance. A study found that the higher the average scores of team members on the traits of conscientiousness, agreeableness, extraversion, and emotional stability, the better their teams performed.[66] In other words, depending on the situation, all the Big Five traits should be given attention in the study and application of organizational behavior.

## Myers-Briggs Type Indicator (MBTI)

Whereas the Big Five has recently emerged from considerable basic research and has generally been demonstrated to significantly relate to job performance, the MBTI is based on a very old theory, has mixed at best research support,[67] but is widely used and very popular in real-world career counseling, team building, conflict management, and analyzing management styles.[68] The theory goes back to pioneering Swiss psychiatrist Carl Jung in the 1920s. He felt people could be typed into extraverts and introverts and that they had two basic mental processes—perception and judgment. He then further divided perception into sensing and intuiting and judgment into thinking and feeling. This yields four personality dimensions or traits: (1) introversion/extraversion, (2) perceiving/judging, (3) sensing/intuition, and (4) thinking/feeling. He felt that although people had all four of these dimensions in common, they differ in the combination of their preferences of each. Importantly, he made the point that one's preferences were not necessarily better than another's, only different.

About 20 years after Jung developed his theoretical types, in the 1940s the mother-daughter team of Katharine Briggs and Isabel Briggs-Myers developed about a 100-item personality test asking participants how they usually feel or act in particular situations in order to measure the preferences on the four pairs of traits yielding 16 distinct types. Called the Myers-Briggs Type Indicator or simply MBTI, the questions relate to how people prefer to focus their energies (extraversion vs. introversion); give attention and collect information (sensing vs. intuiting); process and evaluate information and make decisions (thinking vs. feeling); and orient themselves to the outside world (judging vs. perceiving). Table 5.2 summarizes the characteristics of the four major dimensions, which in combination yield the 16 types. For example, the ESTJ is extraverted, sensing, thinking, and judging. Because this type likes to interact with others (E); sees the world realistically (S); makes decisions objectively and decisively (T); and likes structure, schedules, and order (J), this would be a manager type. The MBTI *Atlas* indicates that most managers studied were indeed ESTJs.

As Jung emphasized when formulating his theory, there are no good or bad types. This is a major reason the MBTI is such a psychologically nonthreatening, commonly used (millions take it every year) personality inventory. Although the MBTI has shown to have reliability and validity as a measure of identifying Jung's personality types[69] and predicting occupational choice (e.g., those high on intuition tend to prefer careers in advertising, the arts, and teaching), there still is not enough research support to base selection decisions or predict job performance.[70] Yet, the use of MBTI by numerous firms such as AT&T, Exxon, and Honeywell for their management development programs and Hewlett-Packard for team building seems justified. It can be an effective point of departure for discussion of similarities and differences and useful for personal development. However, like any psychological measure, the MBTI can also be misused. As one comprehensive analysis concluded, "Some inappropriate uses include labeling one another, providing a convenient excuse that they simply can't work with someone else, and avoiding responsibility for their

**TABLE 5.2**
**The Jung Theory Dimensions and the Myers-Briggs Type Indicators**

| Where do you get your energy? | |
| --- | --- |
| **Extraversion (E)** | **Introversion (I)** |
| Outgoing | Quiet |
| Interacting | Concentrating |
| Speaks, then thinks | Thinks, then speaks |
| Gregarious | Reflective |

| What do you pay attention to and collect information on? | |
| --- | --- |
| **Sensing (S)** | **Intuiting (N)** |
| Practical | General |
| Details | Possibilities |
| Concrete | Theoretical |
| Specific | Abstract |

| How do you evaluate and make decisions? | |
| --- | --- |
| **Thinking (T)** | **Feeling (F)** |
| Analytical | Subjective |
| Head | Heart |
| Rules | Circumstance |
| Justice | Mercy |

| How do you orient yourself to the outside world? | |
| --- | --- |
| **Judging (J)** | **Perceiving (P)** |
| Structured | Flexible |
| Time oriented | Open ended |
| Decisive | Exploring |
| Organized | Spontaneous |

own personal development with respect to working with others and becoming more flexible. One's type is not an excuse for inappropriate behavior."[71]

# THE PERCEPTION PROCESS

Besides personality covered so far, another important cognitive, personal construct is one's perceptual process. The key to understanding perception is to recognize that it is a unique *interpretation* of the situation, not an exact recording of it. In short, perception is a very complex cognitive process that yields a unique picture of the world, a picture that may be quite different from reality. Applied to organizational behavior, an employee's perception can be thought of as a filter. Because perception is largely learned, and no one has the same learnings and experience, then every employee has a unique filter, and the same situations/stimuli may produce very different reactions and behaviors. Some analyses of employee behavior place a lot of weight on this filter:

> Your filter tells you which stimuli to notice and which to ignore; which to love and which to hate. It creates your innate motivations—are you competitive, altruistic, or ego driven? . . . It creates in you all of your distinct patterns of thought, feeling, and behavior. . . . Your filter, more than your race, sex, age, or nationality, is you.[72]

Recognition of the difference between this filtered, perceptual world and the real world is vital to the understanding of organizational behavior. A specific example would be the universal assumption made by managers that associates always want promotions, when, in fact, many really feel psychologically *forced* to accept a promotion.[73] Managers seldom attempt to find out, and sometimes associates themselves do not know, whether the promotion should be offered. In other words, the perceptual world of the manager is quite different from the perceptual world of the associate, and both may be very different from reality. One of the biggest problems that new organizational leaders must overcome are the sometimes faulty or negative perceptions of them. If this is the case, what can be done about it? The best answer seems to be that a better understanding of the concepts involved should be developed. Direct applications and techniques should logically follow complete understanding. The place to start is to clearly understand the difference between sensation and perception and have a working knowledge of the major cognitive subprocesses of perception.

## Sensation versus Perception

There is usually a great deal of misunderstanding about the relationship between sensation and perception. Behavioral scientists generally agree that people's "reality" (the world around them) depends on their senses. However, the raw sensory input is not enough. They must also process these sensory data and make sense out of them in order to understand the world around them. Thus, the starting point in the study of perception should clarify the relationship between perception and sensation.

The physical senses are considered to be vision, hearing, touch, smell, and taste. There are many other so-called sixth senses. However, none of these sixth senses, such as intuition, are fully accepted by psychologists. The five senses are constantly bombarded by numerous stimuli that are both outside and inside the body. Examples of outside stimuli include light waves, sound waves, mechanical energy of pressure, and chemical energy from objects that one can smell and taste. Inside stimuli include energy generated by muscles, food passing through the digestive system, and glands secreting behavior-influencing hormones. These examples indicate that sensation deals chiefly with very elementary behavior that is determined largely by physiological functioning. Importantly, however, researchers now know that ears, eyes, fingers, and the nose are only way stations, transmitting signals that are then processed by the central nervous system. As one molecular biologist declares, "The nose doesn't smell—the brain does."[74] In this way, the human being uses the senses to experience color, brightness, shape, loudness, pitch, heat, odor, and taste.

Perception is more complex and much broader than sensation. The perceptual process or filter can be defined as a complicated interaction of selection, organization, and interpretation. Although perception depends largely on the senses for raw data, the cognitive process filters, modifies, or completely changes these data. A simple illustration may be seen by looking at one side of a stationary object, such as a statue or a tree. By slowly turning the eyes to the other side of the object, the person probably *senses* that the object is moving. Yet the person *perceives* the object as stationary. The perceptual process overcomes the sensual process, and the person "sees" the object as stationary. In other words, the perceptual process adds to, and subtracts from, the "real" sensory world. The following are some organizational examples that point out the difference between sensation and perception:

1. The division manager purchases a program that she thinks is best, not the program that the software engineer says is best.

2. An associate's answer to a question is based on what he heard the boss say, not on what the boss actually said.

3. The same team member may be viewed by one colleague as a very hard worker and by another as a slacker.

4. The same product may be viewed by the design team to be of high quality and by a customer to be of low quality.

**FIGURE 5.1**   **The Subprocesses of Perception**

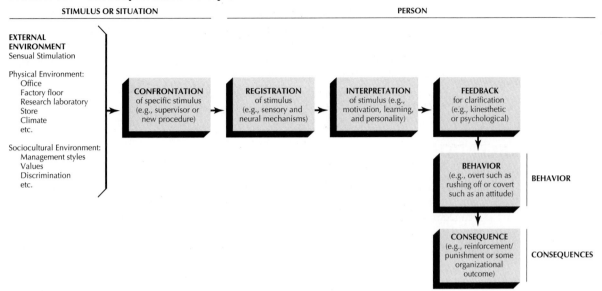

## Subprocesses of Perception

The existence of several subprocesses gives evidence of the complexity and the interactive nature of perception. Figure 5.1 shows how these subprocesses relate to one another. The first important subprocess is the *stimulus* or *situation* that is present. Perception begins when a person is confronted with a stimulus or a situation. This confrontation may be with the immediate sensual stimulation or with the total physical and sociocultural environment. An example is the employee who is confronted with his or her supervisor or with the total formal organizational environment. Either one or both may initiate the employee's perceptual process. In other words, this represents the stimulus situation interacting with the person.

In addition to the situation-person interaction, there are the internal cognitive processes of *registration, interpretation,* and *feedback.* During the registration phenomenon, the physiological (sensory and neural) mechanisms are affected; the physiological ability to hear and see will affect perception. Interpretation is the most significant cognitive aspect of perception. The other psychological processes will affect the interpretation of a situation. For example, in an organization, employees' interpretations of a situation are largely dependent on their learning and motivation and their personality. An example would be the kinesthetic feedback (sensory impressions from muscles) that helps manufacturing workers perceive the speed of materials moving by them in the production process. An example of psychological feedback that may influence an employee's perception is the supervisor's raised eyebrow or a change in voice inflection. Research has shown that both facial expressions and the specific situation will influence perceptions of certain emotions, such as fear, anger, or pain.[75] The behavioral termination of perception is the reaction or behavior, either overt or covert, which is necessary if perception is to be considered a behavioral event and thus an important part of organizational behavior. As a result of perception, an employee may move rapidly or slowly (overt behavior) or make a self-evaluation (covert behavior).

As shown in Figure 5.1, all these perceptual subprocesses are compatible with the social cognitive conceptual framework presented in Chapter 1. The stimulus or environmental situation is the first part; registration, interpretation, and feedback occur within the cognitive processes of the person; then there is the resulting behavior itself; and the environmental consequences of this behavior make up the final part. The subprocesses of registration, interpretation, and feedback are internal cognitive processes that are unobservable, but the situation, behavior, and environmental consequences indicate that perception is indeed related to behavior. Recent summaries of research using the meta-analysis technique have found empirical support for the relationship between cognitive variables such as perception and behaviors.[76]

# SOCIAL PERCEPTION

Although the senses and subprocess provide understanding of the overall perceptual process, most relevant to the study of organizational behavior is social perception, which is directly concerned with how one individual perceives other individuals: how we get to know others.

## Characteristics of Perceiver and Perceived

A summary of classic research findings on some specific characteristics of the perceiver and the perceived reveals a profile of the perceiver as follows:

1. Knowing oneself makes it easier to see others accurately.
2. One's own characteristics affect the characteristics one is likely to see in others.
3. People who accept themselves are more likely to be able to see favorable aspects of other people.
4. Accuracy in perceiving others is not a single skill.[77]

These four characteristics greatly influence how a person perceives others in the environmental situation. Interestingly, this classic profile is very similar to our very new approach that we call an "authentic leader."[78] Covered in detail in the leadership chapter at the end of the book, for now it can be simply said that authentic leaders are those who know themselves (are self-aware and true to themselves) and true to others. In other words, the recognition and understanding of basic perceptual profiles of social perception can contribute to complex processes such as authentic leadership.

There are also certain characteristics of the person being perceived that influence social perception. Research has shown that:

1. The status of the person perceived will greatly influence others' perception of the person.
2. The person being perceived is usually placed into categories to simplify the viewer's perceptual activities. Two common categories are status and role.
3. The visible traits of the person perceived will greatly influence others' perception of the person.[79]

These characteristics of the perceiver and the perceived suggest the complexity of social perception. Organizational participants must realize that their perceptions of another person are greatly influenced by their own characteristics and the characteristics of the other person. For example, if a manager has high self-esteem and the other person is pleasant and comes from the home office, then the manager will likely perceive this other person in a positive, favorable manner. On the other hand, if the manager has low self-esteem and the other person is an arrogant salesperson, the manager will likely perceive this other person in a negative, unfavorable manner. Such attributions that people make of others play a vital role in their social perceptions and resulting behavior.

Participants in formal organizations are constantly perceiving one another. Managers are perceiving workers, workers are perceiving managers, line personnel are perceiving staff personnel, staff personnel are perceiving the line personnel, frontline employees are perceiving customers, customers are perceiving frontline employees, and on and on. There are numerous complex factors that enter into such social perception, but most important are the problems associated with stereotyping and the halo effect.

## Stereotyping

The term *stereotype* refers to the tendency to perceive another person (hence social perception) as belonging to a *single* class or category. The word itself is derived from the typographer's word for a printing plate made from previously composed type. In 1922, Walter Lippmann applied the word to perception. Since then, *stereotyping* has become a frequently used term to describe perceptual errors. In particular, it is employed in analyzing prejudice. Not commonly acknowledged is the fact that stereotyping may attribute favorable or unfavorable traits to the person being perceived. Most often a person is put into a stereotype because the perceiver knows only the overall category to which the person belongs. However, because each individual is unique, the real traits of the person will generally be quite different from those the stereotype would suggest.

Stereotyping greatly influences social perception in today's organizations. Common stereotyped groups include managers, supervisors, knowledge workers, union members, young people, old people, minorities, women, white- and blue-collar workers, and all the various functional and staff specialists, for example, accountants, salespeople, computer programmers, and engineers. There may be a general consensus about the traits possessed by the members of these categories. Yet in reality there is often a discrepancy between the agreed-upon traits of each category and the actual traits of the members. In other words, not all engineers carry laptop computers and are coldly rational, nor are all human resource managers do-gooders who are trying to keep workers happy. On the contrary, there are individual differences and a great deal of variability among members of these and all other groups. In spite of this, other organization members commonly make blanket perceptions and behave accordingly. For example, one analysis noted that a major problem General Motors has is the institutionalized set of managerial beliefs about its customers, workers, foreign competitors, and the government. These perceptions cause the GM leadership to blame their problems on the famous stereotyped "them" instead of recognizing the need for fundamental corporate culture change.[80] There is also research indicating that long exposure to negative stereotypes may result in the members having an inferiority anxiety or lowered expectations.[81] There are numerous other research studies[82] and common, everyday examples that point out stereotyping and its problems that occur in organizational life.

## The Halo Effect

The *halo effect* in social perception is very similar to stereotyping. Whereas in stereotyping the person is perceived according to a single category, under the halo effect the person is perceived on the basis of one trait. Halo is often discussed in performance appraisal when a rater makes an error in judging a person's total personality and/or performance on the basis of a single positive trait such as intelligence, appearance, dependability, or cooperativeness. Whatever the single trait is, it may override all other traits in forming the perception of the person. For example, a person's physical appearance or dress may override all other characteristics in making a selection decision or in appraising the person's performance. The opposite is sometimes called the "horns effect" where an individual is downgraded because of a single negative characteristic or incident.[83]

The halo effect problem has been given considerable attention in research on performance appraisal. For example, a comprehensive review of the performance appraisal literature found that halo effect was the dependent variable in over a third of the studies and was found to be a major problem affecting appraisal accuracy.[84] The current thinking on the halo effect can be summarized from the extensive research literature as follows:

1. It is a common rater error.
2. It has both true and illusory components.
3. It has led to inflated correlations among rating dimensions and is due to the influence of a general evaluation and specific judgments.
4. It has negative consequences and should be avoided or removed.[85]

Like all the other aspects of the psychological process of perception discussed in this chapter, the halo effect has important implications for the study and eventual understanding of organizational behavior. Unfortunately, even though the halo effect is one of the longest recognized and most pervasive problems associated with applications such as performance appraisal in the field of organizational behavior, a critical analysis of the considerable research concludes that we still do not know much about the impact of the halo effect[86] and attempts at solving the problem have not yet been very successful.[87] In other words, overcoming perceptual problems such as stereotyping and the halo effect remains an important challenge for effective human resource management.

# WORK-RELATED ATTITUDES: PA/NA

Besides the traditional recognition given to personality and perception in the cognitive domain, in the field of organizational behavior more recent and directly relevant is the attention given to affective (feelings) dispositions as antecedents of important work-related attitudes such as job satisfaction and to lesser extent organizational commitment and organizational citizenship. In particular, the dispositions of positive affectivity (PA) and negative affectivity (NA) have been found to be important antecedents to attitudes about one's job. As explained by George,[88] NA reflects a personality disposition to experience negative emotional states; those with high NA tend to feel nervous, tense, anxious, worried, upset, and distressed. Accordingly, those with high NA are more likely to experience negative affective states—they are more likely to have a negative attitude toward themselves, others, and the world around them. There is accumulating research supporting this biasing effect of NA.[89] For example, one study found that employees high in negative affectivity more often perceived themselves as victims and thus open themselves up to be more likely targets of coworkers' aggressive actions.[90] Another study found NA moderated the link between favorable performance appraisal feedback and job attitudes.[91]

Those with high PA have the opposite disposition and tend to have an overall sense of well-being, to see themselves as pleasurably and effectively engaged, and to experience positive attitudes. Whether PA is the bipolar opposite and independent of NA is still the subject of debate and interpretation of research results.[92] People do not necessarily move between opposite mood states, but can be both happy and unhappy. However, most of the time there are swings in mood, that is, NA to PA or PA to NA. Research finds that PAs tend to perform better,[93] are less absent from work,[94] and are more satisfied,[95] whereas NAs may experience more stress.[96] There is even evidence that teams with a positive affective tone (i.e., the average PA of members is high) are more effective than teams with a negative affective tone.[97] In other words, one's mood or affective disposition may become a self-fulfilling prophecy as far as organization outcomes are concerned.

Similar to the Big Five personality traits, the PA/NA attitudes have reached such a level of development that increasing research attention is being given to refining the concepts. In recent years studies focus on how affectivity is determined (e.g., through the congruence between employee preferences and organizational human resources practices[98] or the impact of self-, internally generated information on NA[99]) and on multiple levels of analysis.[100] Besides the interest in the dispositions of PA/NA, over the years there is major attention given to job satisfaction and organizational commitment.

# EMPLOYEE ATTITUDES

Specific employee attitudes relating to job satisfaction and organizational commitment are of major interest to the field of organizational behavior and the practice of human resource management. Whereas the above discussion of positive and negative affectivity are considered to be antecedents of work attitudes, more directly job satisfaction focuses on employees' attitudes toward their job and organizational commitment focuses on their attitudes toward the overall organization. The more traditionally recognized job satisfaction is first discussed. Next is the discussion of the widely recognized attitude of organizational commitment. Finally, the more recent prosocial or organizational citizenship behaviors are presented to end this chapter.

## What Is Meant by Job Satisfaction?

Locke gives a comprehensive definition of job satisfaction as involving cognitive, affective, and evaluative reactions or attitudes and states it is "a pleasurable or positive emotional state resulting from the appraisal of one's job or job experience."[101] Job satisfaction is a result of employees' perception of how well their job provides those things that are viewed as important. It is generally recognized in the organizational behavior field that job satisfaction is the most important and frequently studied employee attitude.

Although theoretical analyses have criticized job satisfaction as being too narrow conceptually,[102] there are three generally accepted dimensions to job satisfaction. First, job satisfaction is an emotional response to a job situation. As such, it cannot be seen; it can only be inferred. Second, job satisfaction is often determined by how well outcomes meet or exceed expectations. For example, if organizational participants feel that they are working much harder than others in the department but are receiving fewer rewards, they will probably have a negative attitude toward their work, boss, and/or coworkers. They will be dissatisfied. On the other hand, if they feel they are being treated very well and are being paid equitably, they are likely to have a positive attitude toward the job. They will be job-satisfied. Third, job satisfaction represents several related attitudes. Through the years five job dimensions have been identified to represent the most important characteristics of a job about which employees have affective responses. These are:

1. *The work itself.*   The extent to which the job provides the individual with interesting tasks, opportunities for learning, and the chance to accept responsibility
2. *Pay.*   The amount of financial remuneration that is received and the degree to which this is viewed as equitable vis-á-vis that of others in the organization
3. *Promotion opportunities.*   The chances for advancement in the organization
4. *Supervision.*   The abilities of the supervisor to provide technical assistance and behavioral support
5. *Coworkers.*   The degree to which fellow workers are technically proficient and socially supportive[103]

These five dimensions were formulated many years ago and have been widely used to measure job satisfaction over the years, and a meta-analysis confirmed their construct validity.[104]

## Influences on Job Satisfaction

There are a number of factors that influence job satisfaction. For example, one study even found that if college students' majors coincided with their jobs, this relationship predicted subsequent job satisfaction.[105] However, the main influences can be summarized along the above five dimensions.

### The Work Itself

The content of the work itself is a major source of satisfaction. For example, research related to the job characteristics approach to job design, covered in the next chapter, shows that feedback from the job itself and autonomy are two of the major job-related motivational factors. Research has found that such job characteristics and job complexity mediate the relationship between personality and job satisfaction,[106] and if the creative requirements of employees' jobs are met, then they tend to be satisfied.[107] At a more pragmatic level, some of the most important ingredients of a satisfying job uncovered by surveys over the years include interesting and challenging work, and one survey found that career development (not necessarily promotion) was most important to both younger and older employees.[108] Also in line with Chapter 2 on diversity and ethics, a study found work satisfaction is associated with equal opportunities and family-friendly and anti-harassment practices.[109] Firms on the annual *Fortune* list of "100 Best Companies to Work For," such as VSP, the nation's largest provider of eye care benefits, which is known for innovative human resources practices, have sustained high levels of employee satisfaction with work.[110]

### Pay

Chapter 4 gave detailed attention to both pay and benefits. Wages and salaries are recognized to be a significant but cognitively complex[111] and multidimensional factor in job satisfaction.[112] Money not only helps people attain their basic needs but is also instrumental in providing upper-level need satisfaction. Employees often see pay as a reflection of how management views their contribution to the organization. Fringe benefits are also important, but they are not as influential. One reason undoubtedly is that most employees do not even know how much they are receiving in benefits. Moreover, most tend to undervalue these benefits because they do not realize their significant monetary value.[113] However, research indicates that if employees are allowed some flexibility in choosing the type of benefits they prefer within a total package, called a flexible or cafeteria benefits plan, there is a significant increase in both benefits satisfaction and overall job satisfaction.[114]

### Promotions

Promotional opportunities seem to have a varying effect on job satisfaction. This is because promotions take a number of different forms and have a variety of accompanying rewards. For example, individuals who are promoted on the basis of seniority often experience job satisfaction but not as much as those who are promoted on the basis of performance. Additionally, a promotion with a 10 percent salary raise is typically not as satisfying as one with a 20 percent salary raise. These differences help explain why executive promotions may be more satisfying than promotions that occur at the lower levels of organizations. Also, in recent years with the flattening of organizations and accompanying empowerment strategies, promotion in the traditional sense of climbing the hierarchical corporate ladder of success is no longer available as it once was. Employees operating in the new paradigm, as outlined in Part One of this text, know that not only are traditional promotions not available, but as was pointed out earlier, they may not even be desired. A positive work environment and opportunities to grow intellectually and broaden their skill base has for many become more important than promotion opportunities.[115]

### Supervision

Supervision is another moderately important source of job satisfaction. Chapter 14 discusses the impact of leadership skills. For now, however, it can be said that there seem to be two dimensions of supervisory style that affect job satisfaction. One is employee-centeredness, which is measured by the degree to which a supervisor takes a personal interest and cares about the employee. It commonly is manifested in ways such as checking to see how well the employee is doing, providing advice and assistance to the individual, and communicating with the associate on a personal as well as an official level. American employees generally complain that their supervisors don't do a very good job on these dimensions. There is considerable empirical evidence that one of the major reasons employees give for quitting a company is that their supervisor does not care about them.[116]

The other dimension is participation or influence, as illustrated by managers who allow their people to participate in decisions that affect their own jobs. In most cases, this approach leads to higher job satisfaction. For example, a meta-analysis concluded that participation does have a positive effect on job satisfaction. A participative climate created by the supervisor seems to have a more substantial effect on workers' satisfaction than does participation in a specific decision.[117]

### Work Group

The nature of the work group or team will have an effect on job satisfaction. Friendly, cooperative coworkers or team members are a modest source of job satisfaction to individual employees. The work group, especially a "tight" team, serves as a source of support, comfort, advice, and assistance to the individual members. Research indicates that groups requiring considerable interdependence among the members to get the job done will have higher satisfaction.[118] A "good" work group or effective team makes the job more enjoyable. However, this factor is not essential to job satisfaction. On the other hand, if the reverse conditions exist—the people are difficult to get along with—this factor may have a negative effect on job satisfaction. Also, cross-cultural research finds that if members are resistant to teams in general and self-managed teams in particular, they will be less satisfied than if they welcome being part of teams.[119]

### Working Conditions

Working conditions have a modest effect on job satisfaction. If the working conditions are good (clean, attractive surroundings, for instance), the personnel will find it easier to carry out their jobs. If the working conditions are poor (hot, noisy surroundings, for example), personnel will find it more difficult to get things done. In other words, the effect of working conditions on job satisfaction is similar to that of the work group. If things are good, there may or may not be a job satisfaction problem; if things are poor, there very likely will be.

Most people do not give working conditions a great deal of thought unless they are extremely bad. Additionally, when there are complaints about working conditions, these sometimes are really nothing more than manifestations of other problems. For example, a manager may complain that his office has not been properly cleaned by the night crew, but his anger is actually a result of a meeting he had with the boss earlier in the day in which he was given a poor performance evaluation. However, in recent years, because of the increased diversity of the workforce, working conditions have taken on new importance. Chapter 2 discussed ways in which today's organizations are trying to make conditions more supportive and more nondiscriminatory/nonthreatening. There is also evidence of a positive relationship between job satisfaction and life satisfaction,[120] and that the direction of causality is that people who are satisfied with their lives tend to find more satisfaction in their work.[121]

## Outcomes of Job Satisfaction

To society as a whole as well as from an individual employee's standpoint, job satisfaction in and of itself is a desirable outcome. However, from a pragmatic managerial and organizational effectiveness perspective, it is important to know how, if at all, satisfaction relates to desired outcome variables. For instance, if job satisfaction is high, will the employees perform better and the organization be more effective? If job satisfaction is low, will there be performance problems and ineffectiveness? This question has been asked by both researchers and practitioners through the years. There are no simple answers, and the results range from weak to strong. In examining the outcomes of job satisfaction, it is important to break down the analysis into a series of specific outcomes. The following sections examine the most important of these.

### *Satisfaction and Performance*

Do satisfied employees perform better than their less-satisfied counterparts? This "satisfaction-performance controversy" has raged over the years. Although most people assume a positive relationship, the research to date has been mixed. About 25 years ago, the studies assessed by a meta-analysis indicated a weak (.17 best-estimate correlation) relationship between satisfaction and performance.[122] However, conceptual, methodological, empirical, and practical analyses have questioned and argued against these weak results.[123] So, more recently a sophisticated meta-analysis conducted by Tim Judge and his colleagues on 312 samples with a combined $N$ of 54,417 found the mean true correlation to be .30.[124] This latest analysis thus shows a much stronger relationship between employee job satisfaction and performance, but still not greater than the Big Five personality trait of conscientiousness discussed earlier in this chapter nor as great as the meta-analytic findings of other psychological constructs such as the relationship between self-efficacy (covered in Chapter 7) and performance (.38).[125]

Perhaps the best conclusion about satisfaction and performance is that there is definitely a positive relationship, but probably not as great as conventional wisdom assumed concerning happy workers as productive workers. Although there is recent supporting research evidence on the causal direction (that correlational studies do not permit), showing satisfaction influences performance rather than vice versa,[126] the relationship may even be more complex than others in organizational behavior. For example, there seem to be many possible moderating variables, the most important of which are rewards. If people receive rewards they feel are equitable, they will be satisfied, and this is likely to result in greater performance effort.[127] Also, research evidence indicates that satisfaction may not necessarily lead to individual performance improvement but does lead to departmental[128] and organizational-level improvement.[129] A meta-analysis of such business units (7,939 in 36 companies) found that when satisfaction is defined and measured by employee engagement, there is a significant relationship with performance outcomes of productivity, customer satisfaction, and even profit.[130] In total, job satisfaction should not be considered the endpoint in human performance, but there is accumulating evidence that it should, along with the other dimensions discussed throughout this text, play an important role in the study and application of organizational behavior.

### Satisfaction and Turnover

Does high employee job satisfaction result in low turnover? Research has uncovered a moderately inverse relationship between satisfaction and turnover.[131] High job satisfaction will not, in and of itself, keep turnover low, but it does seem to help. On the other hand, if there is considerable job dissatisfaction, there is likely to be high turnover. Obviously, other variables enter into an employee's decision to quit besides job satisfaction. For example, age, tenure in the organization, and commitment to the organization (covered in the next major section), may play a role. Some people cannot see themselves working anywhere else, so they remain regardless of how dissatisfied they feel. Another factor is the general economy. When things in the economy are going well and there is little unemployment, typically there will be an increase in turnover because people will begin looking for better opportunities with other organizations. Even if they are satisfied, many people are willing to leave if the opportunities elsewhere promise to be better. On the other hand, if jobs are tough to get and downsizing, mergers, and acquisitions are occurring, as in recent years, dissatisfied employees will voluntarily stay where they are. Research findings verify that unemployment rates do directly affect turnover.[132] On an overall basis, however, it is accurate to say that job satisfaction is important in employee turnover. Although absolutely no turnover is not necessarily beneficial to the organization, a low turnover rate is usually desirable because of the considerable training costs and the drawbacks of inexperience, plus the loss of the tacit knowledge that those who leave take with them.

### Satisfaction and Absenteeism

Research has only demonstrated a weak negative relationship between satisfaction and absenteeism.[133] As with turnover, many other variables enter into the decision to stay home besides satisfaction with the job. For example, there are moderating variables such as the degree to which people feel that their jobs are important. For example, research among state government employees has found that those who believed that their work was important had lower absenteeism than did those who did not feel this way. Additionally, it is important to remember that although high job satisfaction will not necessarily result in low absenteeism, low job satisfaction is more likely to bring about absenteeism.[134]

### Other Effects and Ways to Enhance Satisfaction

In addition to those noted above, there are a number of other effects brought about by high job satisfaction. Research reports that highly satisfied employees tend to have better physical health, learn new job-related tasks more quickly, have fewer on-the-job accidents, and file fewer grievances. Also on the positive side, it has been found that there is a strong negative relationship between job satisfaction and perceived stress.[135] In other words, by building satisfaction, stress may be reduced.

Overall, there is no question that employee satisfaction in jobs is in and of itself desirable. It cannot only reduce stress, but as the preceding discussion points out, may also help improve performance, turnover, and absenteeism. Based on the current body of knowledge, the following evidence-based guidelines may help enhance job satisfaction.[136]

1. *Make jobs more fun.*   World-class companies such as Southwest Airlines have a fun culture for their employees. Southwest management makes it clear that irreverence is okay; it's okay to be yourself; and take the competition seriously, but not yourself.[137] Having a fun culture may not make jobs themselves more satisfying, but it does break up boredom and lessen the chances of dissatisfaction.

2. *Have fair pay, benefits, and promotion opportunities.*   These are obvious ways that organizations typically try to keep their employees satisfied. Recent national surveys

indicate that employees rank benefits and pay as very important to their job satisfaction.[138] As Chapter 4 pointed out, an important way to make benefits more effective would be to provide a flexible, so-called cafeteria approach. This allows employees to choose their own distribution of benefits within the budgeted amount available. This way there would be no discrepancies between what they want, because it's their choice.

3. *Match people with jobs that fit their interests and skills.* Getting the right fit is one of the most important, but overlooked, ways to have satisfied employees. This, of course, assumes that the organization knows what those interests and skills are. Effective human resource management firms such as Disney, Southwest Airlines, Google, and Microsoft put considerable effort into finding out interests and skills of potential new hires, as well as existing employees, in order to make the match or fit with the right job.

4. *Design jobs to make them exciting and satisfying.* Instead of finding people to fit the job as in point 3, this approach suggests designing jobs to fit the people. Most people do not find boring, repetitive work very satisfying. For example, the Canadian aerospace firm Nordavionics was losing too many of their talented engineers. They found that they could increase job satisfaction and reduce turnover by being more sensitive to and providing their engineers with more challenging work and professional growth. Unfortunately, too many jobs today are boring and should be changed or eliminated as much as possible. Chapter 6 is concerned with designing jobs to help motivate and satisfy today's employees. Examples include providing more responsibility and building in more variety, significance, identity, autonomy, and feedback.

In summary, most organizational behavior scholars as well as practicing managers would argue that job satisfaction is important to an organization. Some critics have argued, however, that this is pure conjecture because there is so much we do not know about the positive effects of satisfaction. On the other hand, when job satisfaction is low, there seem to be negative effects on the organization that have been well documented. So if only from the standpoint of viewing job satisfaction as a minimum requirement or point of departure, it is of value to the employees' well-being and the organization's overall health and effectiveness and is deserving of study and application in the field of organizational behavior.

## Organizational Commitment

Although job satisfaction has received the most attention of all work-related attitudes, organizational commitment has become increasingly recognized in the organizational behavior literature. Whereas satisfaction is mainly concerned with the employee's attitude toward the job and commitment is at the level of the organization, a strong relationship between job satisfaction and organizational commitment has been found over the years.[139] Yet, there are always many employees who are satisfied with their jobs, but dislike, say, the highly bureaucratic organization they work for, or the software engineer may be dissatisfied with her current job, but be very committed to the overall visionary high-tech firm.

On balance, research studies and the field of organizational behavior in general treat satisfaction and commitment as different attitudes. In light of the new environment that includes downsizing, telecommuting, mergers and acquisitions, globalization, and diversity, organizational commitment has resurfaced as a very important topic of study and concern. Although some expert observers feel that *organizational* commitment is a dead issue because of the new environment and should be replaced by career commitment,[140] others such as the following see organizational commitment as the major challenge in modern times:

> Today's workplace is enveloped by the fear of downsizing, loss of job security, overwhelming change in technology and the stress of having to do more with less . . . managers [need to] establish the type of caring, spirited workplace that will ignite employee commitment.[141]

After first defining commitment and its dimensions, what research has found to date about its outcomes is then summarized.

## The Meaning of Organizational Commitment

As with other topics in organizational behavior, a wide variety of definitions and measures of organizational commitment exist.[142] As an attitude, organizational commitment is most often defined as (1) a strong desire to remain a member of a particular organization; (2) a willingness to exert high levels of effort on behalf of the organization; and (3) a definite belief in, and acceptance of, the values and goals of the organization.[143] In other words, this is an attitude reflecting employees' loyalty to their organization and is an ongoing process through which organizational participants express their concern for the organization and its continued success and well-being. Using this definition, it is commonly measured by the Organizational Commitment Questionnaire shown in Figure 5.2.

The organizational commitment attitude is determined by a number of personal (age, tenure in the organization, career adaptability, and dispositions such as positive or negative affectivity, or internal or external control attributions) and organizational (the job design, values, support, procedual fairness, and the leadership style of one's supervisor) variables.[144] Even nonorganizational factors, such as the availability of alternatives after making the initial choice to join an organization, will affect subsequent commitment.[145]

Also, because of the new environment where many organizations are not demonstrating evidence of commitment to their employees, recent research has found that an employee's

**FIGURE 5.2**
**Organizational Commitment Questionnaire (OCQ)**

Source: R. T. Mowday, R. M. Steers, and L. W. Porter, "The Measure of Organizational Commitment," *Journal of Vocational Behavior,* Vol. 14, 1979, p. 288. Used with permission

Listed below are a series of statements that represent possible feelings that individuals might have about the company or organization for which they work. With respect to your own feelings about the particular organization for which you are now working, please indicate the degree of your agreement or disagreement with each statement by checking one of the seven alternatives below each statement.*

1. I am willing to put in a great deal of effort beyond what is normally expected in order to help this organization be successful.
2. I talk up this organization to my friends as a great organization to work for.
3. I feel very little loyalty to this organization. (R)
4. I would accept almost any type of job assignment in order to keep working for this organization.
5. I find that my values and the organization's values are very similar.
6. I am proud to tell others that I am a part of this organization.
7. I could just as well be working for a different organization as long as the type of work was similar. (R)
8. This organization really inspires the very best in me in the way of job performance.
9. It would take very little change in my present circumstances to cause me to leave this organization. (R)
10. I am extremely glad that I chose this organization to work for over others I was considering at the time I joined.
11. There's not too much to be gained by sticking with this organization indefinitely. (R)
12. Often, I find it difficult to agree with this organization's policies on important matters relating to its employees. (R)
13. I really care about the fate of this organization.
14. For me this is the best of all possible organizations for which to work.
15. Deciding to work for this organization was a definite mistake on my part. (R)

*Responses to each item are measured on a 7-point scale with scale point anchors labeled (1) strongly disagree; (2) moderately disagree; (3) slightly disagree; (4) neither disagree nor agree; (5) slightly agree; (6) moderately agree; (7) strongly agree. An "R" denotes a negatively phrased and reverse-scored item.

career commitment is a moderator between the perceptions of company policies and practices and organizational commitment.[146] For example, even though employees perceive supervisory support, they would also need to have a commitment to their careers, say, in engineering or marketing, in order to have high organizational commitment.

Because of this multidimensional nature of organizational commitment, there is growing support for the three-component model proposed by Meyer and Allen.[147] The three dimensions are as follows:

1. *Affective commitment* involves the employee's emotional attachment to, identification with, and involvement in the organization.
2. *Continuance commitment* involves commitment based on the costs that the employee associates with leaving the organization. This may be because of the loss of senority for promotion or benefits.
3. *Normative commitment* involves employees' feelings of obligation to stay with the organization because they should; it is the right thing to do.

There is considerable research support for this three-component conceptualization of organizational commitment.[148] It also generally holds up across cultures.[149]

## The Outcomes of Organizational Commitment

As is the case with job satisfaction, there are mixed outcomes of organizational commitment. Both early[150] and more recent research summaries[151] do show support of a positive relationship between organizational commitment and desirable outcomes such as high performance, low turnover, and low absenteeism. There is also evidence that employee commitment relates to other desirable outcomes, such as the perception of a warm, supportive organizational climate[152] and being a good team member willing to help.[153] Yet, as with satisfaction, there are some studies that do not show strong relationships between commitment and outcome variables[154] and others where there are moderating effects between organizational commitment and performance. For example, one study found a stronger relationship between organizational commitment and performance for those with low financial needs than for those with high ones,[155] and another study found that the more tenure the employees had on the job and with the employing organization, the less impact their commitment had on performance.[156] Also, a study found that commitment to supervisors was more strongly related to performance than was commitment to organizations.[157] These and a number of other studies indicate the complexity of an attitude such as commitment.[158] On balance, however, most researchers would agree that the organizational commitment attitude as defined here may be a better predictor of desirable outcome variables than is job satisfaction[159] and thus deserves management's attention.

## Guidelines to Enhance Organizational Commitment

As the opening discussion of commitment indicated, management faces a paradoxical situation: "On the one hand today's focus on teamwork, empowerment, and flatter organizations puts a premium on just the sort of self-motivation that one expects to get from committed employees; on the other hand, environmental forces are acting to diminish the foundations of employee commitment."[160] Dessler suggests the following specific guidelines to implement a management system that should help solve the current dilemma and enhance employees' organizational commitment:

1. *Commit to people-first values.*  Put it in writing, hire the right-kind managers, and walk the talk.

2. *Clarify and communicate your mission.*    Clarify the mission and ideology; make it charismatic; use value-based hiring practices; stress values-based orientation and training; build the tradition.

3. *Guarantee organizational justice.*    Have a comprehensive grievance procedure; provide for extensive two-way communications.

4. *Create a sense of community.*    Build value-based homogeneity; share and share alike; emphasize barnraising, cross-utilization, and teamwork; get together.

5. *Support employee development.*    Commit to actualizing; provide first-year job challenge; enrich and empower; promote from within; provide developmental activities; provide employee security without guarantees.[161]

## Organizational Citizenship Behaviors (OCBs)

An appropriate concluding section for this chapter covering personality, perception, and attitudes are the prosocial/organizational citizenship behaviors, simply known as OCBs. This now very popular construct in organizational behavior was first introduced over 25 years ago with a cognitively based theoretical foundation. Organ defines OCB as "individual behavior that is discretionary, not directly or explicitly recognized by the formal reward system, and that in the aggregate promotes the effective functioning of the organization."[162]

The personality foundation for these OCBs reflects the employee's predispositional traits to be cooperative, helpful, caring, and conscientious. The attitudinal foundation indicates that employees engage in OCBs in order to reciprocate the actions of their organizations. Motivational dimensions,[163] job satisfaction,[164] and organizational commitment[165] clearly relate to OCBs. More important to OCBs, however, is that employees must perceive that they are being treated fairly, that the procedures and outcomes are fair. A number of studies have found a strong relationship between justice and OCBs.[166] It seems that procedural justice affects employees by influencing their perceived organizational support, which in turn prompts them to reciprocate with OCBs, going beyond the formal job requirements.[167]

Besides being extra-role or going beyond "the call of duty," other major dimensions are that OCBs are discretionary or voluntary in nature and that they are not necessarily recognized by the the formal reward system of the organization.[168] OCBs can take many forms, but the major ones could be summarized as: (1) altruism (e.g., helping out when a coworker is not feeling well), (2) conscientiousness (e.g., staying late to finish a project), (3) civic virtue (e.g., volunteering for a community program to represent the firm), (4) sportsmanship (e.g., sharing failure of a team project that would have been successful by following the member's advice), and (5) courtesy (e.g., being understanding and empathetic even when provoked).[169] Research also examines antecedents such as job attitudes that account for loyalty OCBs, personality that accounts for service delivery OCBs, effects of nationality on the role of OCBs,[170] the amount of control people have over their job relates to OCBs,[171] customer knowledge and personality that jointly predict participation in OCBs,[172] and relationship quality and relationship context as antecedents of person- and task-focused interpersonal citizenship behaviors.[173]

Obviously, all these different types of OCBs are valuable to organizations and, although they frequently go undetected by the reward system, there is evidence that individuals who exhibit OCBs do perform better and receive higher performance evaluations.[174] Also, OCBs do relate to group and organization performance and effectiveness.[175] However, as with job satisfaction and organizational commitment, there is still some criticism of the conceptualization and research on OCBs,[176] and more research is certainly warranted. For example, one study found that OCBs do influence organizational outcomes rather than the other way around[177] and another study has begun to analyze the influence of gender on the performance of OCBs.[178] Also, although the research has focused on the positive impact of OCBs, a recent study found that at least too much of the individual initiative portion of OCB is related to higher levels of employee role overload, job stress, and work-family conflict.[179] Yet, as a summary statement, today's managers would be very wise in trying to enhance not only job satisfaction and organizational commitment, but also prosocial, organizational citizenship behaviors of their employees.

## Summary

Personality, perception, and attitudes represent important micro, cognitively oriented variables in the study of organizational behavior. Personality represents the "whole person" concept. It includes perception, learning, motivation, and more. According to this definition, people's external appearance and traits, their inner awareness of self, and the person-situation interaction make up their personalities. Although the nature versus nurture debate continues, the findings of twin studies point out the importance that heredity may play in personality, and recent breakthroughs in neuropsychology indicate the importance of the brain in personality have led most psychologists to recognize nature *and* nurture. However, the nurture side still dominates. Self-esteem, the person-situation interaction, and the socialization process of personality development are all very relevant to the understanding and application of organizational behavior.

Besides the recent advances in the genetic and brain input into personality, the study of relatively fixed dispositions have recognized importance in the form of the "Big Five" personality traits. Conscientiousness, emotional stability, agreeableness, extraversion, and openness to experience have been found to significantly relate to job performance, especially conscientiousness. In addition, the Myers-Briggs Type Indicator (MBTI) remains a popular tool for personal and career development. Whereas the Big Five is based on research, the MBTI is based on the historically important Carl Jung theory of personality types and mental processes. Both the Big Five and MBTI if carefully interpreted and used can make a contribution to the understanding and application of organizational behavior.

Whereas personality is an important cognitive construct to help explain organizational behavior, perception is an important cognitive process. Through this complex perceptual process or filter, persons make interpretations of the stimulus or situation facing them. The social context that this process takes place is particularly important to the study of organizational behavior. Particularly relevant problems in this social perception are stereotyping (the tendency to perceive another person as belonging to a single class or category) and the halo effect (the tendency to perceive a person on the basis of one trait).

The remainder of the chapter is concerned with cognitively based attitudes. Personality traits, perceptions, and dispositions such as positive affectivity (PA) and negative affectivity (NA), are important antecedents to attitudes about one's job. However, traditionally the most important attitude studied in organizational behavior and given concern in the real world is job satisfaction. This attitude is defined as a pleasurable or positive emotional state resulting from the appraisal of one's job or job experience. A number of factors influence job satisfaction. Some of the major ones are the work itself, pay, promotions, supervision, the work group, and working conditions. There are a number of outcomes of job satisfaction. For example, although the relationship with performance was thought to be relatively weak, more recent research is showing a much stronger relationship. Low job satisfaction tends to lead to both turnover and absenteeism, whereas high job satisfaction often results in fewer on-the-job accidents and work grievances, less time needed to learn new job-related tasks, and less stress. There are also specific guidelines to enhance employee satisfaction such as making jobs fun, ensuring fairness, getting the right fit, and designing jobs to make them more exciting and satisfying.

Closely related to job satisfaction is the organizational commitment attitude. It traditionally refers to the employees' loyalty to the organization and is determined by a number of personal, organizational, and nonorganizational variables. Now commitment is generally conceived as having three components: affective (emotional attachment), continuance (costs of leaving), and normative (obligation to stay). Like job satisfaction, the organizational commitment attitude is very complex and has mixed results, but in general, it is thought to have a somewhat stronger relationship with organizational outcomes such as performance, absenteeism, and turnover. Like satisfaction, organizational commitment can be enhanced.

The concluding section draws from personality, perception, and attitudes. The extra-role, prosocial/organizational citizenship behaviors (OCBs) involve predispositional traits to be cooperative and conscientious and reflect through attitudes fair treatment from the organization. OCBs can take a number of forms such as altruism, conscientiousness, civic virtue, sportsmanship, and courtesy. Although there is still some criticism of the conceptualization and research on OCBs, there is growing evidence that OCBs positively relate to individual, group, and organizational performance.

# Ending with Meta-Analytic Research Findings

## OB PRINCIPLE:

Conscientious employees are effective performers.

### Meta-Analysis Results:

[117 studies; 19,721 participants; $d = .26$] *On average, there is a **57 percent probability** that conscientious employees will turn out to be better performers than those who do not have the conscientious personality trait.* Out of all the "Big Five" personality dimensions tested, only conscientiousness showed consistent relations with all job performance criteria across occupational groups.

### Conclusion:

Personality measures are widely used in employee analysis and selection because they contribute to the learning and understanding of today's employees. Though many personality traits have been investigated over the years, the Big Five personality dimensions (conscientiousness, extroversion, agreeableness, openness to experience, and emotional stability) have emerged as the most important because of their relationship with performance. However, consistent with what was discussed in this chapter, conscientiousness is the single strongest Big Five predictor of work performance. Conscientious people can be characterized as dependable, hardworking, responsible, persevering, and achievement oriented—all desirable qualities of effective, high-performing employees.

**Source:** Adapted from Murray R. Barrick and Michael K. Mount, "The Big Five Personality Dimensions and Job Performance: A Meta-Analysis," *Personnel Psychology,* Vol. 44, 1991, pp. 1—26.

## OB PRINCIPLE:

Employees who are satisfied with their jobs participate more in prosocial, organizational citizenship behaviors (OCBs).

## Meta-Analysis Results:

[28 studies; 6,746 participants; $d = .47$] *On average, there is a **63 percent probability** that employees who are satisfied in their jobs will participate in more prosocial, organizational citizenship behaviors (OCBs) than those who are not satisfied.* Self—versus other—ratings of organizational citizenship behaviors was a notable moderator of the relationship. Self-reports of citizenship behaviors tend to be inflated. Overall, the evidence provides support that measures of OCBs will be better related to job satisfaction than would in-role performance, with the exception that this applies mainly to nonmanagerial, nonprofessional employees.

## Conclusion:

Individuals who contribute to organizational effectiveness by doing things that are above and beyond their primary task or role are assets to their organizations. Examples of organization citizenship behaviors or OCBs are volunteering for extra job activities, helping coworkers, and making positive comments about the company. As this chapter has discussed, OCBs are of value to the organization because, although they are not viewed as a traditional measure of performance, they can still impact on an organization's performance by supporting ongoing task activities and influencing performance evaluations. Employees who exhibit citizenship behaviors such as helping others or making innovative suggestions receive higher performance ratings. Moreover, other attitudinal variables discussed in this chapter such as job satisfaction and organizational commitment predict and may lead to OCBs.

**Source:** Adapted from Dennis W. Organ and Katherine Ryan, "A Meta-Analytic Review of Attitudinal and Dispositional Predictors of Organizational Citizenship Behavior," *Personnel Psychology,* Vol. 48, 1995, pp. 775—802.

## Questions for Discussion and Review

1. Critically analyze the statement that "the various psychological processes can be thought of as pieces of a jigsaw puzzle and personality as the completed puzzle picture."
2. What is the comprehensive definition of *personality*? Give brief examples of each of the major elements.
3. What side would you prefer to argue in the nature versus nurture debate? What would be the major points each side would make? How would you resolve the controversy?
4. What are the "Big Five" personality traits? Which one seems to have the biggest impact on performance? How would knowledge of the Big Five help you in your job as a manager?
5. What are the four major dimensions of the Myers-Briggs Type Indicator (MBTI) that yield the 16 types? How can the MBTI be used effectively?
6. In understanding the process of perception, do you agree with the observation that people are human information processors? Why?
7. How does sensation differ from perception?
8. What does stereotyping mean? Why is it considered to be a perceptual problem?
9. What is meant by the halo effect? Summarize the current thinking on this halo effect.
10. What is negative affectivity (NA)? What would be an example of an employee with high NA? What is PA? Provide an example.
11. What is meant by the term *job satisfaction*? What are some of the major factors that influence job satisfaction?

12. What are some of the important outcomes of job satisfaction?

13. What is organizational commitment? What three components have emerged to help better explain the complexities of commitment? Why may an understanding of organizational commitment be especially important in the years ahead?

14. What are organization citizenship behaviors (OCBs)? How do they come about and what are some examples?

## Internet Exercise: Assessing Your Personality

This chapter was concerned with how personality traits may affect performance in the workplace. To understand this better, many organizations are using outside resources to assess employee personalities in an effort to get them into jobs that fit their characteristics. One such organization can be found at **http://www.personality-tests-personality-profiles.com/home.htm.** This site discusses the services that they provide, and provides some sample personality questions. Another interesting Web site is **http://www.queendom.com/alltests.html.** They have many different types of assessment tools that you can take online. Many of them are related to the workplace. Still another possibility is **http://www.hartmancommunications.com.** Browse through these sites and take some of the tests. Then consider the following questions:

1. Did you learn anything that you didn't already know about yourself? If so, what? How do you think your personality will affect your work performance?

2. Is there anything you would like to change about yourself in order to improve yourself? If so, what? If not, what type of job would seem to be most suited to your personality?

3. See if you can locate still other Web sites that assess personality. How, if at all, do these personality assessments match up with what you have covered in this chapter on personality and attitudes?

---

# Real Case: *It's All a Matter of Personality*

Largely because of downsizing, the survivors are working harder and longer hours every year—and although some get burned out and stressed, others seem to thrive on it. At Apple Computer, for example, development teams are well known for wearing T-shirts that proclaim, "90 Hours a Week and Loving It!" And high-tech firms are now coaxing double and triple time out of their employees, a practice that is spreading to other sectors of the economy. One of the best examples is provided by the increasing number of telecommuters who work at home. By giving employees PCs, cellular phones, pagers, and other devices, the company can stay in contact. However, many of these telecommuters are now finding that they are on call 24 hours a day. One of the new rules of survival in an increasing number of workplaces appears to be: If you don't have the personality to work round-the-clock, don't bother applying for a job here.

Of course, for some people work is extremely enjoyable, and they do not mind the new demands. Take the case of entrepreneur Wayne Huizenga, a self-made billionaire. Huizenga started out with a partner in the garbage collection business, confident that his firm could outperform the small mom-and-pop garbage companies and get their business. He was supremely confident of his own ability; it was not long before his plan started to come true. Wall Street did not think much of his ideas, however, and when he issued his first stock offering in 1971 it was to raise a mere $5 million. By the time Huizenga left in 1984, the market value of the firm's stock was $3 billion.

Huizenga's next move was to Blockbuster Entertainment. He was convinced that the movie rental business was a wave of the future. Again he was right. For a mere $18.5 million, he and his partners were able to buy the company—and soon thereafter sales took off, rising from $43 million annually to over $2 billion. By the time he sold out to Viacom in 1994, he had put another billion dollars in his pocket.

The same can be said for Steve Wynn of Mirage Resorts. Wynn's company was listed as one of *Fortune's*

10 most admired firms in America. Why? Part of it is a reflection of Wynn's own personality. He is eternally optimistic and wants his people to be the same. Wynn's strategy is to keep everybody happy. If anyone is not, Wynn's employees are to fix it. As he tells his people, "If you see a hotel guest with the tiniest frown on her face, don't ask a supervisor, take care of it. Erase the charge, send the dinner back, don't charge for the room." In addition, Wynn sponsors elaborate parties to honor staffers who have kept the most customers happy. At one recent party for a Vietnamese woman who was being honored as employee of the year, Wynn brought in George and Barbara Bush to congratulate the lady. It cost a lot of money for the party, but, as Wynn puts it, "It's an investment."

1. Why do employees at firms such as Apple Computer work so hard and put in such long hours?
2. How would you describe Wayne Huizenga in terms of the self-concept, specifically self-esteem?
3. Why is job satisfaction and organizational commitment so high at Mirage Resorts? How does Steve Wynn manage to keep his employees so happy?

# Organizational Behavior Case: *Same Accident, Different Perceptions*

According to the police report, on July 9 at 1:27 P.M., bus number 3763 was involved in a minor noninjury accident. Upon arriving at the scene of the accident, police were unable to locate the driver of the bus. Because the bus was barely drivable, the passengers were transferred to a backup bus, and the damaged bus was returned to the city bus garage for repair.

The newly hired general manager, Aaron Moore, has been going over the police report and two additional reports. One of the additional reports was submitted by Jennifer Tye, the transportation director for the City Transit Authority (CTA), and the other came directly from the driver in the accident, Michael Meyer. According to Tye, although Mike has been an above-average driver for almost eight years, his performance has taken a drastic nosedive during the past 15 months. Always one to join the other drivers for an afterwork drink or two, Mike recently has been suspected of drinking on the job. Furthermore, according to Tye's report, Mike was seen having a beer in a tavern located less than two blocks from the CTA terminal at around 3 P.M. on the day of the accident. Tye's report concludes by citing two sections of the CTA Transportation Agreement. Section 18a specifically forbids the drinking of alcoholic beverages by any CTA employee while on duty. Section 26f prohibits drivers from leaving their buses unattended for any reason. Violation of either of the two sections results in automatic dismissal of the employee involved. Tye recommends immediate dismissal.

According to the driver, Michael Meyer, however, the facts are quite different. Mike claims that in attempting to miss a bicycle rider he swerved and struck a tree, causing minor damage to the bus. Mike had been talking with the dispatcher when he was forced to drop his phone receiver in order to miss the bicycle. Because the receiver broke open on impact, Mike was forced to walk four blocks to the nearest phone to report the accident. As soon as he reported the accident to the company, Mike also called the union to tell them about it. Mike reports that when he returned to the scene of the accident, his bus was gone. Uncertain of what to do and a little frightened, he decided to return to the CTA terminal. Because it was over a five-mile walk and because his shift had already ended at 3 P.M., Mike stopped in for a quick beer just before getting back to the terminal.

1. Why are the two reports submitted by Jennifer and Mike so different? Did Jennifer and Mike have different perceptions of the same incident?
2. What additional information would you need if you were in Aaron Moore's position? How can he clarify his own perception of the incident?
3. Given the information presented above, how would you recommend resolving this problem?

# Organizational Behavior Case: *Ken Leaves the Company*

Good people—valuable employees—quit their jobs every day. Usually, they leave for better positions elsewhere. Take Ken, an experienced underwriter in a northeastern insurance company, who scribbled the following remarks on his exit interview questionnaire:

> This job isn't right for me. I like to have more input on decisions that affect me—more of a chance to show what I can do. I don't get enough feedback to tell if I'm doing a good job or not, and the company keeps people in the dark about where it's headed. Basically, I feel like an interchangeable part most of the time.

In answer to the question about whether the company could have done anything to keep him, Ken replied simply, "Probably not."

Why do so many promising employees leave their jobs? And why do so many others stay on but perform at minimal levels for lack of better alternatives? One of the main reasons—Ken's reason—can be all but invisible, because it's so common in so many organizations: a systemwide failure to keep good people.

Corporations should be concerned about employees like Ken. By investing in human capital, they may actually help reduce turnover, protect training investments, increase productivity, improve quality, and reap the benefits of innovative thinking and teamwork.

Human resource professionals and managers can contribute to corporate success by encouraging employees' empowerment, security, identity, "connectedness," and competence. How? By recognizing the essential components of keeping their best people and by understanding what enhances and diminishes those components.

Ken doubts that his company will ever change, but other organizations are taking positive steps to focus on and enhance employee retention. As a result, they're reducing turnover, improving quality, increasing productivity, and protecting their training investments.

1. Do you think that Ken's self-esteem had anything to do with his leaving the firm?

2. What do you think were Ken's satisfaction with and commitment to the job and firm he is leaving? How does this relate to the research on the determinants and outcomes of satisfaction and commitment?

3. What lesson can this company learn from the case of Ken? What can and should it now do?

# Chapter **Six**

# Motivational Needs, Processes, and Applications

## Learning Objectives

- **Define** the motivation process.
- **Identify** the primary and secondary needs.
- **Discuss** the major theories of work motivation.
- **Present** the motivational application of job design.
- **Describe** the motivational application of goal setting.

Motivation is a basic psychological process. Few would deny that it is the most important focus in the micro approach to organizational behavior. In fact, a data-based comprehensive analysis concluded that "America's competitiveness problems appear to be largely motivational in nature."[1] Many people equate the causes of behavior with motivation; however, as evidenced in this book, the causes of organizational behavior are much broader and more complex than can be explained by motivation alone.

Along with many other psychological constructs, motivation is presented here as a very important process in understanding behavior. Motivation interacts with and acts in conjunction with other mediating processes and the environment. It must also be remembered that, like the other cognitive processes, motivation cannot be seen. All that can be seen is behavior. Motivation is a hypothetical construct that is used to help explain behavior; it should not be equated with behavior. In fact, while recognizing the "central role of motivation," many of today's organizational behavior theorists "think it is important for the field to reemphasize behavior."[2]

This chapter first presents motivation as a basic psychological process. The more applied aspects of motivation on job design and goal setting are covered in the last part of the chapter. The first section of this chapter clarifies the meaning of motivation by defining the relationship among its various parts. The need–drive–incentive cycle is defined and analyzed. The next section is devoted to an overview of the various types of needs, or motives: both primary and secondary. The next section of the chapter presents both the historical and more complex contemporary theories of work motivation. Finally, the two major motivation applications of job design and goal setting are given attention.

**FIGURE 6.1**
**The Basic Motivation Process**

NEEDS ⟶ DRIVES ⟶ INCENTIVES

# THE BASIC MOTIVATION PROCESS

Today, virtually all people—practitioners and scholars—have their own definitions of motivation. Usually one or more of the following words are included: *desires, wants, wishes, aims, goals, needs, drives, motives,* and *incentives.* Technically, the term *motivation* can be traced to the Latin word *movere,* which means "to move." This meaning is evident in the following comprehensive definition: *motivation* is a process that starts with a physiological or psychological deficiency or need that activates a behavior or a drive that is aimed at a goal or incentive. Thus, the key to understanding the process of motivation lies in the meaning of, and relationships among, needs, drives, and incentives.

Figure 6.1 graphically depicts the motivation process. Needs set up drives aimed at goals or incentives; this is what the basic process of motivation is all about. In a systems sense, motivation consists of these three interacting and interdependent elements:

1. *Needs.* Needs are created whenever there is a physiological or psychological imbalance. For example, a need exists when cells in the body are deprived of food and water or when the personality is deprived of other people who serve as friends or companions. Although psychological needs may be based on a deficiency, sometimes they are not. For example, an individual with a strong need to get ahead may have a history of consistent success.

2. *Drives.* With a few exceptions,[3] drives, or motives (the two terms are often used interchangeably), are set up to alleviate needs. A physiological drive can be simply defined as a deficiency with direction. Physiological and psychological drives are action oriented and provide an energizing thrust toward reaching an incentive. They are at the very heart of the motivational process. The examples of the needs for food and water are translated into the hunger and thirst drives, and the need for friends becomes a drive for affiliation.

3. *Incentives.* At the end of the motivation cycle is the incentive, defined as anything that will alleviate a need and reduce a drive. Thus, attaining an incentive will tend to restore physiological or psychological balance and will reduce or cut off the drive. Eating food, drinking water, and obtaining friends will tend to restore the balance and reduce the corresponding drives. Food, water, and friends are the incentives in these examples.

These basic dimensions of the motivation process serve as a point of departure for the rest of the chapter. After discussion of primary and secondary motives, the work-motivation theories and applications that are more directly related to the study and application of organizational behavior and human resource management are examined.

## Primary Motives

Psychologists do not totally agree on how to classify the various human motives, but they would acknowledge that some motives are unlearned and physiologically based. Such motives are variously called *physiological, biological, unlearned,* or *primary.* The last term is used here because it is more comprehensive than the others. However, the use of the term *primary* does not imply that these motives always take precedence over the learned secondary motives. Although the precedence of primary motives is implied in some motivation theories, there are many situations in which the secondary motives predominate over primary motives. Common examples are celibacy among priests and fasting for a religious, social, or political cause. In both cases, learned secondary motives are stronger than unlearned primary motives.

Two criteria must be met in order for a motive to be included in the *primary* classification: It must be *unlearned,* and it must be *physiologically based*. Thus defined, the most commonly recognized primary motives include hunger, thirst, sleep, avoidance of pain, sex, and maternal concern. Although these very basic physiological requirements have been equated with primary needs over the years, just like personality traits discussed in the last chapter, in recent years recognition is given to the role that the brain may play in people's motives.[4] The "hard-wiring" of emotional needs would meet the primary criteria of being unlearned and physiologically based. Neuropsychologists are just beginning to do research on the role the brain plays in motivation, but potential applications to the workplace are already being recognized. For example, Coffman and Gonzalez-Molina note: "What many organizations don't see—and what many don't want to understand—is that employee performance and its subsequent impact on customer engagement revolve around a motivating force that is determined in the brain and defines the specific talents and the emotional mechanisms everyone brings to their work."[5] However, even though the brain pathways will be developed in different ways and people develop different appetites for the various physiological motives because people have the same basic physiological makeup, they will all have essentially the same primary needs, but not the learned secondary needs.

## Secondary Motives

Whereas the primary needs are vital for even survival, the secondary drives are unquestionably the most important to the study of organizational behavior. As a human society develops economically and becomes more complex, the primary drives give way to the learned secondary drives in motivating behavior. With some glaring exceptions that have yet to be eradicated, the motives of hunger and thirst are not dominant among people living in the economically developed world. This situation is obviously subject to change; for example, the "population bomb," nuclear war, the greenhouse effect and even dire economic times as indicated in the accompanying OB in Action: Managing Amid Economic Uncertainty, may alter certain human needs. In addition, further breakthroughs in neuropsychology may receive more deserved attention.[6] But for now, the learned secondary motives dominate the study and application of the field of organizational behavior.

Secondary motives are closely tied to the learning concepts that are discussed in Chapter 12. In particular, the learning principle of reinforcement is conceptually and practically related to motivation. The relationship is obvious when reinforcement is divided into primary and secondary categories and is portrayed as incentives. Some discussions, however, regard reinforcement as simply a consequence serving to increase the *motivation* to perform the behavior again,[7] and they are treated separately in this text. Once again, however, it should be emphasized that although the various behavioral concepts can be separated for study and analysis, in reality, concepts like reinforcement and motivation do not operate as separate entities in producing human behavior. The interactive effects are always present.

A motive must be learned in order to be included in the *secondary* classification. Numerous important human motives meet this criterion. Some of the more important ones are power, achievement, and affiliation, or, as they are commonly referred to, *n Pow, n Ach,* and *n Aff*. In addition, especially in reference to organizational behavior, security and status are important secondary motives. Table 6.1 gives examples of each of these important secondary needs.

During the Internet bust a few years ago, I had lunch with a corporate HR leader. His company, a telecommunications giant, was in trouble. Every week, more layoffs were announced. People who could find better jobs were leaving in droves.

I asked the HR fellow: "How are you dealing with employee morale?" "Oh, we don't think about morale," he chuckled. "We focus on Engagement with the Mission." I was astounded by his reply, and I could all but hear the capitalized "E" and "M" in the phrase. Lots of HR people talk about engagement, and they also talk about missions. These are good things to talk about when half the workforce isn't in fear of losing jobs at any moment. How does one get engaged with the organization's lofty mission when one is preoccupied with job security, the threat of missing a mortgage payment, or worse?

"Isn't it tough to rally the troops around the mission when business conditions are so challenging?" I asked. I had just met a marketing director from this man's company the night before at a networking event. "Yes, I took a job working for XYZ," she told me, mentioning her employer by name with a shudder. "Don't judge me for working there. I had to take the job. Any port in a storm."

## Hollow Ring

That's how my lunchmate's company brand was being publicly trashed by its own new management hires. Yet he clung to the notion that Engagement with the Mission would prevail. "We just have to keep talking about it, to keep the Mission uppermost in employees' minds," he said.

My lunch partner was wrong in thinking that the most important issue then was Mission instead of morale, and the same holds true now. When employees are distracted by zooming foreclosure rates, the cost of fuel, the threat of job loss, and other real life concerns, our corporate mission is the last thing they want to hear about. We're foolish if we don't respond to our teams' fears directly.

Like any issue that can suck time and mental energy away from our work, employees' economic concerns are an elephant in the room. Job One is to address those concerns forthrightly, and often. We can't guarantee our employees a job for life, or even for the next 12 months. What we can and must do is level with them, with as much detail as possible, about what's happening in our firms and what the future appears to hold. We need to talk about orders in the pipeline, the state of our customers' business, the state of our competitors. We need to address the impact of the financial industry's woes on our own business. If senior-leadership teams aren't convening this week to craft an internal communications strategy dealing with these top-of-mind and scary issues, they're deluding themselves.

## When Basic Needs Are Threatened

People won't stick to their knitting when their own and their families' stability and future are at risk. They can't. They shouldn't. Maslow's famous pyramid shows us why. Next year's new product launch is fun and exciting to think about when one's housing, health care, nourishment, and other basic needs are well in hand. When a person is worried about his ability to take care of basic needs, his attention to lesser matters—the new product launch being one example—goes out the window. Who can blame him?

Frequent and relevant employee communication is the name of the game during challenging economic times. And outbound communication is just half the battle. The other half is responding.

For instance, employers who have been slow to accommodate employees' telecommuting requests should delay no more. All employers should be stretching their views of what constitutes a day's work right now, because fuel prices have increased employees' household expenses dramatically. If people can accomplish their work from home one day a week, this is the time to let them do it. If you've looked at the flextime and flexplace concepts all summer without acting, there's no more time for delay.

Now is the time to listen to employees, and now is the time to act.

## The Whole Truth

Nothing that we can invent to stimulate and reward employees—not a trip to Hawaii, not free flu shots, not even the promise of a hefty year-end bonus—can allay the fears of personal disruption or catastrophe that preoccupy our teams. No fun promotion, slogan, or contest that we dream up at a staff meeting will turn our teams' attention away from their instinctive fears for their own economic stability—nothing except plain, unvarnished truth.

Now's the time to open the kimono and share the company's plans for the next 12 or 18 months; now's the time to talk frankly about hard choices that must be made, about the leadership team's battle plan and the associated risks and opportunities. "Just keep working, and we'll let you know if anything changes" will not cut it, not if we want people focused on their work instead of their plummeting home value and mutual funds.

If ever there were a time to lose the corporate happy talk and be honest with employees, it's now.

Employers who speak to what's real for their employees—the stock market, the firm's fortunes, and the cost of getting through the day—will earn the privilege of talking about Engagement and Missions months down the road. Those who insist on sticking to the party line may look back and see their efforts to avoid tough conversations as an exercise in rearranging deck chairs on the Titanic.

**TABLE 6.1** **Examples of Key Secondary Needs**

Source: Adapted from Gary Yukl, *Skills for Managers and Leaders,* Prentice Hall, Upper Saddle River, N.J., 1990, p 41. The examples of need for status were not covered by Yukl.

| | |
|---|---|
| *Need for Achievement* <br>• Doing better than competitors <br>• Attaining or surpassing a difficult goal <br>• Solving a complex problem <br>• Carrying out a challenging assignment successfully <br>• Developing a better way to do something | *Need for Security* <br>• Having a secure job <br>• Being protected against loss of income or economic disaster <br>• Having protection against illness and disability <br>• Being protected against physical harm or hazardous conditions <br>• Avoiding tasks or decisions with a risk of failure and blame |
| *Need for Power* <br>• Influencing people to change their attitudes or behavior <br>• Controlling people and activities <br>• Being in a position of authority over others <br>• Gaining control over information and resources <br>• Defeating an opponent or enemy | *Need for Status* <br>• Having the right car and wearing the right clothes <br>• Working for the right company in the right job <br>• Having a degree from the right university <br>• Living in the right neighborhood and belonging to the country club <br>• Having executive privileges |
| *Need for Affiliation* <br>• Being liked by many people <br>• Being accepted as part of a group or team <br>• Working with people who are friendly and cooperative <br>• Maintaining harmonious relationships and avoiding conflicts <br>• Participating in pleasant social activities | |

## Intrinsic versus Extrinsic Motives

Motives can be thought of as being generated not only by the primary and learned secondary needs, but also by two separate but interrelated sets of sources. One method to characterize these two sources is to label them as being either *intrinsic* or *extrinsic* motives. Extrinsic motives are tangible and visible to others. They are distributed by other people (or agents). In the workplace, extrinsic motivators include pay, benefits, and promotions. Chapter 4 covered these commonly recognized extrinsic motivators and, especially in tough economic times, low- or no-cost extrinsic alternatives include food (from doughnuts to gourmet meals), games (e.g., one CPA firm holds a "mini-Olympics" with games such as who can pack a suitcase to take to an audit assignment the fastest for a prize), or bring in someone to do manicures or at-desk massages.[8] Extrinsic motives also include the drive to avoid punishment, such as termination or being transferred. In each situation, an external individual distributes these items. Further, extrinsic rewards are usually contingency based. That is, the extrinsic motivator is contingent on improved performance or performance that is superior to others in the same workplace. Extrinsic motivators are necessary to attract people into the organization and to keep them on the job. They are also often used to inspire workers to achieve at higher levels or to reach new goals, as additional payoffs are contingent on improved performance.[9] They do not, however, explain every motivated effort made by an individual employee. There is growing research evidence on how to enhance intrinsic motivation (e.g., providing the individual with a choice).[10] Another study found that when intrinsic motivation accompanies other types, for example, prosocial motivation, there will be a more positive impact on desired outcomes such as persistence, performance, and productivity.[11]

Intrinsic motives are internally generated. In other words, they are motivators that the person associates with the task or job itself. Intrinsic rewards include feelings of responsibility, achievement, accomplishment, that something was learned from an experience, feelings of being challenged or competitive, or that something was an engaging task or goal. Performing meaningful work has long been associated with intrinsic motivation.[12] As Manz and Neck noted, "Even if a task makes us feel more competent and more self-controlling, we still might have a difficult time naturally enjoying and being motivated by it if we do not believe in its worthiness. Most of us yearn for purpose and meaning."[13]

It is important to remember that these two types of motivators are not completely distinct from one another. Many motivators have both intrinsic and extrinsic components. For example, a person who wins a sales contest receives the prize, which is the extrinsic motivator. At the same time, however, "winning" in a competitive situation may be the more powerful, yet internalized, motive.

To further complicate any explanation of intrinsic and extrinsic motivation, *cognitive evaluation theory* suggests a more intricate relationship. This theory proposes that a task may be intrinsically motivating, but that when an extrinsic motivator becomes associated with that task, the actual level of motivation may decrease.[14] Consider the world of motion pictures, where an actor often strives for many years to simply be included in a film. The intrinsic motive of acting is enough to inspire the starving artist. Once, however, the same actor becomes a star, the extrinsic motivators of money and perks would, according to cognitive evaluation theory, cause the individual to put less effort into each performance. In other words, according to this theory, extrinsic motivators may actually undermine intrinsic motivation. This may seem like a confusing outcome, but there is some research that supports this theoretical position.[15] However, as the meta-analytically based principle at the end of the chapter notes, there is considerable research evidence that extrinsic rewards may not detract from intrinsic motivation, and at least for interesting, challenging tasks, extrinsic rewards may even increase the level of intrinsic motivation (see the end of the chapter OB Principle).[16]

The seemingly contradictory findings make more sense when the concept of negative extrinsic motives is included. That is, threats, deadlines, directives, pressures, and imposed goals are likely to be key factors that diminish intrinsic motivation. For example, consider the difference between writing a book for fun versus writing a book that must be completed by a certain deadline in order to receive payment.[17] There are also a series of criticisms of the cognitive evaluation theory, including that it was built on studies largely using students as subjects rather than workers in the workplace setting and that actual decrements in intrinsic motivation were relatively small when extrinsic rewards were introduced.[18] Chapter 7 will extend this discussion into social cognitive variables such as self-efficacy, and Chapter 12 will use an extended reinforcement theory–based approach to behavioral performance management.

## WORK-MOTIVATION THEORIES

So far, motivation has been presented as a basic psychological process consisting of primary, general, and secondary motives; drives such as the *n Pow, n Aff,* and *n Ach* motives; and intrinsic and extrinsic motivators. In order to understand organizational behavior, these basic motives must be recognized and studied. However, these serve as only background and foundation for the more directly relevant work-motivation theories.

Figure 6.2 graphically summarizes the various theoretical streams for work motivation. In particular, the figure shows three historical streams. The content theories go as far back as the turn of the twentieth century, when pioneering scientific managers such as Frederick W. Taylor, Frank Gilbreth, and Henry L. Gantt proposed sophisticated wage incentive models to motivate workers. Next came the human relations movement, and then the content

**FIGURE 6.2** The Theoretical Development of Work Motivation

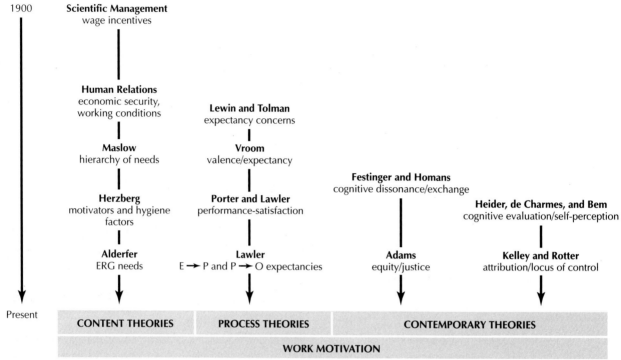

theories of Maslow, Herzberg, and Alderfer. Following the content movement were the process theories. Based mainly on the cognitive concept of expectancy, the process theories are most closely associated with the work of pioneering social psychologists Kurt Lewin and Edward Tolman and then organizational behavior scholars Victor Vroom, Lyman Porter, and Ed Lawler. Finally, with roots in social psychology, equity and its derivative procedural/organizational justice, and attribution theories have received attention in work motivation.

Figure 6.2 purposely shows that at present there is a lack of integration or synthesis of the various theories. In addition to the need for integration, a comprehensive assessment of the status of work-motivation theory also noted the need for contingency models and group/social processes.[19] At present the content and process theories have become established explanations for work motivation, and there is continued research interest in equity and organizational justice theories, but no agreed-upon overall theory exists. Moreover, unlike most of the other constructs in organizational behavior, reviews conclude that there has been relatively little new theory-building and research in work motivation in recent years.[20] As Steers concluded, "over the past decade little will be found focusing on genuine theoretical development in this area."[21] The rest of the chapter gives an overview of the widely recognized historical and contemporary theories of work motivation.

## Maslow's Hierarchy of Needs: An Important Historical Contribution

Although the first part of the chapter mentions the most important primary and secondary needs of humans, it does not relate them to a theoretical framework. Abraham Maslow, in a classic paper, outlined the elements of an overall theory of motivation.[22] Drawing chiefly

**FIGURE 6.3**
**Maslow's Hierarchy of Needs**

from humanistic psychology and his clinical experience, he thought that a person's motivational needs could be arranged in a hierarchical manner. In essence, he believed that once a given level of need is satisfied, it no longer serves to motivate. The next higher level of need has to be activated in order to motivate the individual.

Maslow identified five levels in his need hierarchy (see Figure 6.3). They are, in brief, the following:

1. *Physiological needs.* The most basic level in the hierarchy, the physiological needs, generally corresponds to the unlearned primary needs discussed earlier. The needs of hunger, thirst, sleep, and sex are some examples. According to the theory, once these basic needs are satisfied, they no longer motivate. For example, a starving person will strive to obtain a carrot that is within reach. However, after eating his or her fill of carrots, the person will not strive to obtain another one and will be motivated only by the next higher level of needs.

2. *Safety needs.* This second level of needs is roughly equivalent to the security need. Maslow stressed emotional as well as physical safety. The whole organism may become a safety-seeking mechanism. Yet, as is true of the physiological needs, once these safety needs are satisfied, they no longer motivate.

3. *Love needs.* This third, or intermediate, level of needs loosely corresponds to the affection and affiliation needs. Like Freud, Maslow seems guilty of poor choice of wording to identify his levels. His use of the word *love* has many misleading connotations, such as sex, which is actually a physiological need. Perhaps a more appropriate word describing this level would be *belongingness* or *social needs.*

4. *Esteem needs.* The esteem level represents the higher needs of humans. The needs for power, achievement, and status can be considered part of this level. Maslow carefully pointed out that the esteem level contains both self-esteem and esteem from others.

5. *Needs for self-actualization.* Maslow's major contribution, he portrays this level as the culmination of all the lower, intermediate, and higher needs of humans. People who have become self-actualized are self-fulfilled and have realized all their potential. Self-actualization is closely related to the self-concepts discussed in Chapter 7. In effect, self-actualization is the person's motivation to transform perception of self into reality.

Maslow did not intend that his needs hierarchy be directly applied to work motivation. In fact, he did not delve into the motivating aspects of humans in organizations until about 20 years after he originally proposed his theory. Despite this lack of intent on Maslow's part, others, such as Douglas McGregor in his widely read book *The Human Side of*

**FIGURE 6.4**
**A Hierarchy of Work Motivation**

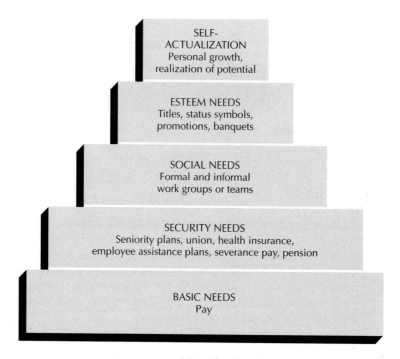

SELF-ACTUALIZATION
Personal growth, realization of potential

ESTEEM NEEDS
Titles, status symbols, promotions, banquets

SOCIAL NEEDS
Formal and informal work groups or teams

SECURITY NEEDS
Seniority plans, union, health insurance, employee assistance plans, severance pay, pension

BASIC NEEDS
Pay

*Enterprise,* popularized the Maslow theory in management literature. The needs hierarchy has tremendous intuitive appeal and is widely associated with work motivation.

In a very rough manner, Maslow's needs hierarchy theory can be converted into the content model of work motivation shown in Figure 6.4. If Maslow's estimates are applied to an organization example, the lower-level needs of personnel would be generally satisfied, but only a minority of the social and esteem needs, and a small percent of the self-actualization needs, would be met.

On the surface, the content model shown in Figure 6.4 and the estimated percentages given by Maslow seem logical and still largely applicable to the motivation of employees in today's organizations. Maslow's needs hierarchy has often been uncritically accepted by writers of management textbooks and by practitioners. Unfortunately, the limited research that has been conducted lends little empirical support to the theory. About a decade after publishing his original paper, Maslow did attempt to clarify his position by saying that gratifying the self-actualizing need of growth-motivated individuals can actually increase rather than decrease this need. He also hedged on some of his other original ideas, for example, that higher needs may emerge after lower needs that have been unfulfilled or suppressed for a long period are satisfied. He stressed that human behavior is multidetermined and multimotivated.

Research findings indicate that Maslow's is certainly not the final answer in work motivation. Yet the theory does make a significant contribution in terms of making management aware of the diverse needs of employees at work. As one comprehensive analysis concluded, "Indeed, the general ideas behind Maslow's theory seem to be supported, such as the distinction between deficiency needs and growth needs."[23] However, the number and names of the levels are not so important, nor, as the studies show, is the hierarchical concept. What is important is the fact that employees in the workplace have diverse motives, some of which are "high level." There is also empirical and experiential evidence supporting the importance of Maslow's various needs (e.g., Gallup survey research clearly indicates that Maslow's third level social needs are the single most important contribution to satisfaction with life[24] and a lot of, if not most, high-achieving people feel unfulfilled because they have not reached self-actualization[25]).

In other words, such needs as social and self-actualization are important to the content of work motivation. The exact nature of these needs and how they relate to motivation are not clear. At the same time, what does become clear from contemporary research is that layoffs and terminations (i.e., downsizing) can reduce employees to have concerns about basic-level needs such as security. Organizations that endeavor to reduce fears and other strong emotional responses during these moments through severance pay programs and outplacement services may be able to lessen the impact of individual terminations and layoffs, especially for those who remain with the company.[26]

In recent years there has been a resurgence of interest in humanistic psychology[27] and as will be discussed in the next chapter, positive psychology, of which Maslow was one of the pioneers. Throughout the years there have been attempts to revitalize and make his hierarchy of needs more directly applicable to work motivation. In particular, Herzberg's two-factor theory covered next is based on Maslow's concept, and a number of others use Maslow for constructing various hierarchies or pyramids. One example is Aon Consulting's Performance Pyramid that starts with safety and security and moves up through rewards, affiliation, growth, and work and life harmony.[28] There is little question that Maslow's theory has stood the test of time and still makes a contribution to the study and application to work motivation.

## Herzberg's Two-Factor Theory of Motivation

Another historically important contribution to work motivation is the content theory of Frederick Herzberg. Unlike Maslow, Herzberg many years ago conducted a widely reported motivational study on about 200 accountants and engineers employed by firms in and around Pittsburgh, Pennsylvania. He used the critical incident method of obtaining data for analysis. The professional subjects in the study were essentially asked two questions: (1) When did you feel particularly good about your job—what turned you on; and (2) When did you feel exceptionally bad about your job—what turned you off?

Responses obtained from this critical incident method were interesting and fairly consistent. Reported good feelings were generally associated with job experiences and job content. An example was the accounting supervisor who felt good about being given the job of installing new computer equipment. He took pride in his work and was gratified to know that the new equipment made a big difference in the overall functioning of his department. Reported bad feelings, on the other hand, were generally associated with the surrounding or peripheral aspects of the job—the job context. An example of these feelings was related by an engineer whose first job was routine record keeping and managing the office when the boss was gone. It turned out that his boss was always too busy to train him and became annoyed when he tried to ask questions. The engineer said that he was frustrated in this job context and that he felt like a flunky in a dead-end job.

Tabulating these reported good and bad feelings, Herzberg concluded that job satisfiers are related to job content and that job dissatisfiers are allied to job context. Herzberg labeled the satisfiers *motivators,* and he called the dissatisfiers *hygiene factors.* The term *hygiene* refers (as it does in the health field) to factors that are preventive; in Herzberg's theory the hygiene factors are those that prevent dissatisfaction. Taken together, the motivators and the hygiene factors have become known as Herzberg's *two-factor theory of motivation.*

### *Relation to Maslow's Need Hierarchy*

Herzberg's theory is closely related to Maslow's need hierarchy. The hygiene factors are preventive and environmental in nature (see Table 6.2), and they are roughly equivalent to

**TABLE 6.2**
Herzberg's Two-
Factor Theory

| Hygiene Factors | Motivators |
| --- | --- |
| Company policy and administration | Achievement |
| Supervision, technical | Recognition |
| Salary | Work itself |
| Interpersonal relations, supervisor | Responsibility |
| Working conditions | Advancement |

Maslow's lower-level needs. These hygiene factors prevent dissatisfaction, but they do not lead to satisfaction. In effect, they bring motivation up to a theoretical zero level and are a necessary "floor" to prevent dissatisfaction, and they serve as a platform or takeoff point for motivation. By themselves, the hygiene factors do not motivate. Only the motivators, Herzberg asserted, motivate employees on the job. They are roughly equivalent to Maslow's higher-level needs. According to Herzberg's theory, an individual must have a job with a challenging content in order to be truly motivated.

### Contribution to Work Motivation

Herzberg's two-factor theory provided a new light on the content of work motivation. Up to this point, management had generally concentrated on the hygiene factors. When faced with a morale problem, the typical solution was higher pay, more fringe benefits, and better working conditions. However, as has been pointed out, this simplistic solution did not really work. Management are often perplexed because they are paying high wages and salaries, have an excellent fringe-benefit package, and provide great working conditions, but their employees are still not motivated. Herzberg's theory offered an explanation for this problem. By concentrating only on the hygiene factors, management were not really motivating their personnel.

There are probably very few workers or associates who do not feel that they deserve the raise they receive. On the other hand, there are many dissatisfied associates and managers who feel they do not get a large enough raise. This simple observation points out that the hygiene factors seem to be important in preventing dissatisfaction but do not lead to satisfaction. Herzberg would be the first to say that the hygiene factors are absolutely necessary to maintain the human resources of an organization. However, as in the Maslow sense, once "the belly is full" of hygiene factors, which is the case in most modern organizations, dangling any more in front of employees will not really motivate them. According to Herzberg's theory, only a challenging job that has the opportunities for achievement, recognition, responsibility, advancement, and growth will motivate personnel.

### Critical Analysis of Herzberg's Theory

Herzberg's two-factor theory remains important in a historical sense and a popular textbook explanation of work motivation and it still makes intuitive sense to practitioners. However, it also is true that from an academic perspective, Herzberg's theory oversimplifies the complexities of work motivation. When researchers deviate from the critical incident methodology used by Herzberg, they do not get the two factors. Further, there is always a question regarding the samples used by Herzberg: Would he have obtained the results from low-complexity jobs such as truck drivers and third-shift factory workers or waitstaff personnel? Presumably both the hygiene factors and satisfiers could be substantially different when comparing these groups. Factors that affect research results include the age of the sample and other variables that are not held constant or under control. In international settings, older workers in an Israeli kibbutz preferred jobs that had better physical conditions and convenience. Also, Caribbean hotel workers reported being more interested in wages, working conditions, and appreciation for their work as key motivators.[29] These findings suggest that sample and setting may affect preferences for motivators and hygiene factors.

Finally, there seem to be job factors such as pay that lead to both satisfaction and dissatisfaction. For example, pay can be dissatisfying if not high enough, but, as pointed out in Chapter 4, also satisfying as a form of achievement and recognition. These findings indicate that a strict interpretation of the two-factor theory is not warranted by the evidence.

In spite of the obvious limitations, few would question that Herzberg has contributed substantially to the study of work motivation. He extended Maslow's needs hierarchy concept and made it more applicable to work motivation. Herzberg also drew attention to the importance of job content factors in work motivation, which previously had been badly neglected and often totally overlooked. However, even the context can be made to better fit the jobholder. For example, many Internet businesses never have employees directly interact with customers so their dress, appearance, and work space can be highly informal and designed according to personal choice.[30]

The job design technique of job enrichment is also one of Herzberg's contributions. Job enrichment is covered in the last part of the chapter. Overall, Herzberg added much to the better understanding of job content factors and satisfaction, but, like his predecessors, he fell short of a comprehensive theory of work motivation. His model describes only some of the content of work motivation; it does not adequately describe the complex motivation process of organizational participants that will now be given attention in the more complex theories of work motivation.

## The Porter-Lawler Expectancy Theory of Work Motivation

Comments in Chapter 5 on job satisfaction refer to the controversy over the relationship between satisfaction and performance that has existed since the beginnings of the human relations movement. The Maslow and Herzberg content theories implicitly assume that satisfaction leads to improved performance and that dissatisfaction detracts from performance. In particular, the Herzberg model is really a theory of job satisfaction, but still it does not adequately deal with the relationship between satisfaction and performance. It was not until Porter and Lawler that the relationship between satisfaction and performance was dealt with directly by a motivation theory. They start with the premise that motivation (effort or force) does not equal satisfaction or performance. Motivation, satisfaction, and performance are all separate variables and relate in ways different from what was traditionally assumed.

Figure 6.5 depicts the multivariable model used to explain the complex relationships that exist among motivation, performance, and satisfaction. As shown, boxes 1, 2, and 3 are basically drawn from earlier cognitive concepts from pioneering social psychologists such as Kurt Lewin and Edward Tolman and from the recognized seminal work motivation theory of Victor Vroom.[31] It is important to note, however, that Porter and Lawler point out that effort (force or motivation) does not lead directly to performance. It is moderated by abilities and traits and by role perceptions. More important in the Porter-Lawler model is what happens after the performance. The rewards that follow and how these are perceived will determine satisfaction. In other words, the Porter-Lawler model suggests—and this is a significant turn of events from conventional wisdom—that performance leads to satisfaction.

The model has had research support over the years. For example, a field study found that effort level and direction of effort are important in explaining individual performance in an organization.[32] Also, a comprehensive review of research verifies the importance of rewards in the relationship between performance and satisfaction. Specifically, it was

**FIGURE 6.5** **The Porter-Lawler Motivation Model**

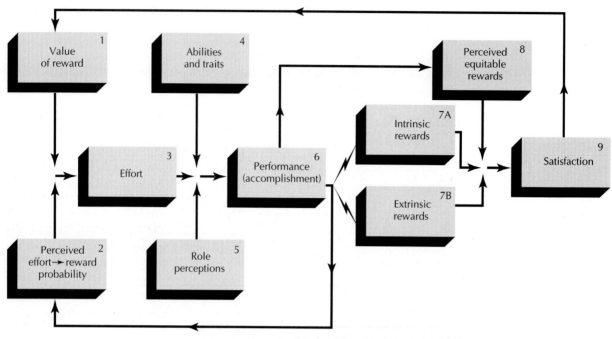

concluded that performance and satisfaction will be more strongly related when rewards are made contingent on performance than when they are not.[33]

### Implications for Practice

Although the Porter-Lawler model attempts to be more applications oriented than the earlier expectancy theories, it is still quite complex and has proved to be a difficult way to bridge the gap to actual human resource management practice. To Porter and Lawler's credit, they were very conscientious of putting their theory and research into practice. They recommended that practicing managers go beyond traditional attitude measurement and attempt to measure variables such as the values of possible rewards, the perceptions of effort-reward probabilities, and role perceptions. These variables, of course, can help managers better understand what goes into employee effort and performance. Giving attention to the consequences of performance, Porter and Lawler also recommended that organizations critically reevaluate their current reward policies. They stressed that management should make a concentrated effort to measure how closely levels of satisfaction are related to levels of performance, and in a practitioner-oriented article emphasized that the accuracy of role perceptions may be the missing link in improving employee performance.[34] The inference here is that employees need to better focus their efforts on high-impact behaviors and activities that result in higher performance. However, both studies[35] and comprehensive analyses[36] continue to point out the complex impact that the cognitive process has in relation to rewards and other outcomes in organizations.

### Contributions to Work Motivation

The Porter and Lawler model has definitely made a significant contribution to the better understanding of work motivation and the relationship between performance and satisfaction, but has not had much impact on the actual practice of human resource management. Yet this expectancy theory provides certain guidelines that can be followed by human resource management. For example, on the front end (the relationship between motivation and performance), it has been suggested that the following barriers must be overcome:

1. Doubts about ability, skill, or knowledge
2. The physical or practical possibility of the job
3. The interdependence of the job with other people or activities
4. Ambiguity surrounding the job requirements[37]

To overcome these barriers, it is helpful to understand the role other psychological variables such as self-efficacy (covered in the next chapter) play in effort-performance relationships. A series of successes combined with positive feedback build the employee's sense of self-efficacy, which can, in turn, lead to a heightened sense that "I can do this." Greater effort may often be the result.[38] In addition to psychological constructs such as self-efficacy, there are also pragmatic considerations such as that the opportunity must be present to actually perform. For example, there are many second-string players in pro sports that have stepped in for an injured starter to take the team to the championship. The back-up probably had sufficient valance (pay plus the bonus check paid to the winners), instrumentality or effort-performance calculations (ability combined with self-efficacy), and expectancy or performance-reward calculations (the belief that goal achievement would result in additional pay and recognition), yet still could not succeed until he was allowed to play due to the injury of the first-string player.

In addition, on the back end (the relationship between performance and satisfaction), guidelines such as the following have been suggested:

1. Determine what rewards each employee values
2. Define desired performance
3. Make desired performance attainable
4. Link valued rewards to performance[39]

The last point was given attention in Chapter 4 on the importance of pay for performance. At the same time, managers should be advised that an employee in a way calculates expectancies regarding future employment possibilities when seeking to leave an organization, and more importantly, often sees a connection between performance and reward that invites less effort in a group or team situation. The reduced value is based on the belief that the person's own efforts are not sufficient to raise group performance levels, and that group incentives are less valuable than individualized rewards.

Also brought out in Chapter 4, managers may also take advantage of this process motivational approach by considering the use of nonfinancial rewards for performance. Many times workers may be inspired by being given first choice in selecting weeks for vacation, being allowed to choose when they will go to lunch (ahead of lower performers), being awarded certificates or "employee of the month" parking spaces or, as the accompanying OB in Action: Nice Work If You Can Get It describes, new rewards such as sabbaticals. Recognition as a valence can be a powerful reward within the expectancy theory framework and was discussed in Chapter 4 and is given further detailed attention in Chapter 12.

## Equity Theory of Work Motivation

Equity theory has been around just as long as the expectancy theories of work motivation. However, equity has received relatively more recent attention in the organizational behavior field. As Figure 6.2 indicates, its roots can be traced back to cognitive dissonance theory and exchange theory. As a theory of work motivation, credit for equity theory is usually given to social psychologist J. Stacy Adams. Simply put, the theory argues that a major

Last winter, Intel Corp. paid Melanie Stagnitti to research and develop her tan. Fleeing the soggy dreariness of Hillsboro, Ore., the compensation and benefits manager and her stay-at-home husband, John, packed up their 5-year-old son and 3½-year-old daughter in their Ford Explorer and, towing a trailer full of camping gear, sauntered down to Mexico's sun-drenched Baja peninsula.

For eight weeks, Stagnitti was utterly unplugged. She had no access to e-mail, voicemail, the Internet, or, for much of the time, electricity. Today she's logging 50-hour workweeks again. But all that time lounging in a hammock helped make up for the long days. "The best part," she says, "was seeing the kids outside every day, playing in the water and being free."

These days many companies view employees as profit sponges, particularly sitting-bull seniors who have received pay raises year after year. Paternalism is out; lean and mean is in. But across the economy, a stubborn minority of employers is treating workers like tenured professors, lavishing paid sabbaticals on them. Such generosity actually helps the bottom line, managers insist. Giving employees a periodic respite is an antidote to the world of networked, always-on careers that lead to information overload. Sabbaticals reduce turnover and retain wisdom otherwise lost when veteran employees burn out. A recent study in the *Journal of Education for Business* found that the benefits of sabbaticals outweigh the costs when a good understanding between employer and employee regarding expectations is involved. The study also found that employees return more committed and more energized. In fact, sabbaticals are so alluring that companies report that it's almost impossible for competitors to poach anyone within a few years of his bonus vacation. The absences also give managers a chance to see how well others perform while filling in for their on-leave colleagues.

The number of companies offering paid sabbaticals is small but steady. An annual survey by the Society for Human Resource Management finds that 5% of corporate respondents offer the perk. Another 18% offer unpaid sabbaticals, which are increasingly being used as an alternative to layoffs when demand slackens. But there is some flux. Cracking the whip, Steve Jobs nixed Apple Computer Inc.'s program after returning as chief executive in 1997.

On the other hand, relative newcomers such as women's clothing designer Eileen Fisher Inc,. have initiated sabbaticals, while McDonald's Corp., where the perk dates back more than 40 years, is expanding the benefit in 2006 to every five years. "What it's all about today is, how do you differentiate yourself as a company?" says Richard Floersch, McDonald's chief human resources officer. "This gives us bragging rights."

Many HR managers argue that since sabbaticals encourage people to stick around, companies don't have to spend as much on recruitment and training. Assigning temporary fill-ins can be a plus, too. While Intel's Stagnitti was in Mexico, her supervisor tested someone else in her job. When she came back, that employee ended up staying on, and Stagnitti was promoted to a new job in HR. In addition, the generation just entering the workforce ranks time off as a top priority in survey after survey. Thus, offering sabbaticals should help attract young talent, says Hewitt consultant Raymond Baumruk.

input into job performance and satisfaction is the degree of equity (or inequity) that people perceive in their work situation. In other words, it is another cognitively based motivation theory, and Adams depicts how this motivation occurs.

Inequity occurs when a person perceives that the ratio of his or her outcomes to inputs and the ratio of a relevant other's outcomes to inputs are unequal. Schematically, this is represented as follows:

$$\frac{\text{person's outcomes}}{\text{person's inputs}} < \frac{\text{other's outcomes}}{\text{other'sinputs}}$$

$$\frac{\text{person's outcomes}}{\text{person's inputs}} > \frac{\text{other's outcomes}}{\text{other's inputs}}$$

Equity occurs when

$$\frac{\text{person's outcomes}}{\text{person's inputs}} = \frac{\text{other's outcomes}}{\text{other's inputs}}$$

Both the inputs and the outputs of the person and the other are based on the person's perceptions. Age, sex, education, social status, organizational position, qualifications, and how hard the person works are examples of perceived input variables. Outcomes consist primarily of rewards such as pay, status, promotion, and intrinsic interest in the job. In essence, the ratio is based on the person's *perception* of what the person is giving (inputs) and receiving (outcomes) versus the ratio of what the relevant other is giving and receiving. This cognition may or may not be the same as someone else's observation of the ratios or the same as the actual reality. There is also recent recognition that the cultural context may affect the entire equity process.[40]

### Equity as an Explanation of Work Motivation

If the person's perceived ratio is not equal to the other's, he or she will strive to restore the ratio to equity. This "striving" to restore equity is used as the explanation of work motivation. The strength of this motivation is in direct proportion to the perceived inequity that exists. Adams suggests that such motivation may be expressed in several forms. To restore equity, the person may alter the inputs or outcomes, cognitively distort the inputs or outcomes, leave the field, act on the other, or change the other.

It is important to note that inequity does not come about only when the person feels cheated. For example, Adams has studied the impact that perceived overpayment has on equity. His findings suggest that workers prefer equitable payment to overpayment. Workers on a piece-rate incentive system who feel overpaid will reduce their productivity in order to restore equity. More common, however, is the case of people who feel underpaid (outcome) or overworked (input) in relation to others in the workplace. In the latter case, there would be motivation to restore equity in a way that may be dysfunctional from an organizational standpoint. For example, the owner of an appliance store in Oakland, California, allowed his employees to set their own wages. Interestingly, none of the employees took an increase in pay, and one service technician actually settled on lower pay because he did not want to work as hard as the others.

### Research Support for Equity in the Workplace

To date, research that has specifically tested the validity of Adams's equity theory has been fairly supportive. A comprehensive review found considerable laboratory research support for the "equity norm" (people review the inputs and outcomes of themselves and others, and if inequity is perceived, they strive to restore equity) but only limited support from more relevant field studies.[41] One line of field research on equity theory used baseball players. In the first study, players who played out their option year, and thus felt they were inequitably paid, performed as the theory would predict.[42] Their performance decreased in three of four categories (not batting average) during the option year, and when they were signed to a new contract, the performance was restored. However, a second study using the same type of sample, only larger, found the opposite of what equity theory would predict.[43] Mainly, performance improved during the option year. The reason, of course, was that the players wanted to look especially good, even though they felt they were inequitably paid, in order to be in a stronger bargaining position for a new contract. In other words, individuals faced with undercompensation may choose to decrease performance, but only to the extent that doing so will not affect the potential to achieve future rewards.[44] In any event, there are no easy answers nor is there 100 percent predictive power when applying a cognitive process theory such as equity.

Despite some seeming inconsistencies, more recent studies using sophisticated statistical techniques to estimate pay equity among ballplayers[45] and focusing more sharply on subsequent performance and other outcomes are more in line with equity theory predictions.

For example, one study found a significant relationship between losing final-offer salary arbitration and postarbitration performance decline. The ballplayers who were losers in arbitration were also significantly more likely to change teams or leave major league baseball.[46] In another study of baseball and basketball players, it was found that the underrewarded players behaved less cooperatively.[47] This type of equity theory development and research goes beyond expectancy theory as a cognitive explanation of work motivation and serves as a point of departure for more specialized areas of current interest such as organizational justice.

## The Relationship between Equity Theory and Organizational Justice

Recent theory development specifies that equity theory can be extended into what is now commonly known as organizational justice.[48] Although procedural justice has received the most attention, there is now research evidence that in addition there is conceptual and measurement independence (i.e., construct validity) for distributive, interpersonal, and informational justice dimensions as well.[49] Equity theory serves as the foundation for the common thread of perceived fairness among these dimensions of justice. For example, equity theory explains conditions under which decision outcomes (pay levels, pay raises, promotions) are perceived as being fair or unfair. Persons engaged in this type of thinking examine the results as opposed to how those results were achieved. Equity theory supports a perception of *distributive justice,* which is an individual's cognitive evaluation regarding whether or not the amounts and allocations of rewards in a social setting are fair. In simple terms, distributive justice is one's belief that everyone should "get what they deserve." Culturally, the Judeo-Christian ethic is based, in part, on the notion that divine rewards accrue to those who lead good lives and behave appropriately, even while here are on earth. This reflects the distributive justice and equity perspectives. Importantly, meta-analytic results have demonstrated that employee perceptions of distributive justice are related to desirable outcomes such as job satisfaction, organizational commitment, organizational citizenship behavior, turnover, and performance.[50]

*Procedural justice* is concerned with the fairness of the procedure used to make a decision. For example, a pay raise may be based on a sales representative selling more units of, for example, automobiles or houses. Some coworkers may consider this procedure to be unfair, believing management should instead base pay raises on dollar volume. This conclusion may be reached because selling 10 houses or cars for a low amount of money each contributes very little to company profits and they are, at the same time, easier to sell. Selling high-priced cars or houses may take much longer to finalize, but the profits garnered for the company are also higher. In this case it is not the outcome in dispute, which is the amount of the pay received. Instead, it is the perceived justice (fairness) of the procedure used to reach the outcome. Like distributive justice, employee perceptions of procedural justice have been shown through meta-analysis to be related to all the desirable organizational outcomes.[51] Indeed, in another meta-analysis, procedural justice was found to be a better predictor of job performance than was distributive justice[52] and procedural justice seems to be particularly important to successfully implementing organizational changes.[53]

Procedural justice can raise issues of equality as opposed to equity. *Equality* means that in a promotion situation, males and females and all races would have equal opportunities to be selected, and that the criteria used would not discriminate. *Equity* would mean that the actual choice was fair, and that the criteria were correctly applied and therefore the most-qualified individual was promoted.

Unlike the traditional content and process theories of work motivation, research continues to refine and extend equity theory in general and procedural justice in particular. For example, in support of equity theory, a recent study found that managers who perceive effort-reward fairness perform better and are more satisfied than those who feel underre-warded and unfairly treated.[54] Another study used social exchange theory to differentiate *interactional justice* from procedural justice. Whereas procedural justice is the exchange between the employee and the employing organization, interactional justice is between individuals (e.g., the employee and the supervisor). The research supported the exchange theory predictions.[55] There is also some evidence that such interactional justice may not be as predictive as other justice perceptions. For example, a recent study found that manager trustworthiness was more predictive of organizational citizenship behaviors (covered in the last chapter) than was interactional justice.[56] Other recent studies focusing on procedural justice have found importance in being allowed the opportunity to voice an opinion on per-ceptions of fairness[57] and in the effects of group membership and status (i.e., one's social standing) on perceptions of fairness.[58] In particular, it was found in this latter study that procedural injustice was not perceived by all who observed it (in this case judges and attor-neys did not perceive bias against female attorneys). Finally, a recent study moved to the level of overall justice climate (procedural, informational, and interpersonal) and found it related to various work outcomes (commitment, satisfaction, and citizenship behaviors).[59]

In total, with equity theory serving as the foundation, the various dimensions of organi-zational justice play an important role in many dynamics and outcomes of organizational behavior. Organizational justice can help explain why employees retaliate against both inequitable outcomes and inappropriate processes. For example, retaliation in the form of theft, sabotage, forged time cards, and even violence toward the boss or owner can be explained using the principles of organizational justice.[60] On a positive note, besides all the findings summarized above, a recent study found that there is a trickle-down effect from organizational justice. Employees' perceptions of fairness not only positively affect their attitudes and performance, but also influence their fair treatment behaviors toward cus-tomers, which in turn cause the customers to react positively to both the employee and the organization.[61] In other words, organizational justice pays off not only for employees, but also for customers and the bottom line.

## Attribution Theory

Another contemporary theory of work motivation is attribution theory. *Attribution* refers simply to how people explain the cause of another's or their own behavior. Like equity the-ory, it is the cognitive process by which people draw conclusions about the factors that influence, or make sense of, one another's behavior.[62] There are two general types of attri-butions that people make: *dispositional attributions,* which ascribe a person's behavior to internal factors such as personality traits, motivation, or ability, and *situational attribu-tions,* which attribute a person's behavior to external factors such as equipment or social influence from others.[63] In recent years, attribution theories have been playing an increas-ingly important role in organizational behavior and human resource management.[64] An examination of the various theories, types, and errors of attribution can contribute to an understanding as work motivation and organizational behavior in general.

### An Overview of the Theory

Attribution theory is concerned with the relationship between personal social perception (covered in the last chapter) and interpersonal behavior. There are a number of attribution theories, but they share the following assumptions:

1. We seek to make sense of our world.
2. We often attribute people's actions either to internal or external causes.
3. We do so in fairly logical ways.[65]

Well-known social psychologist Harold Kelley stressed that attribution theory is concerned mainly with the cognitive processes by which an individual interprets behavior as being caused by (or attributed to) certain parts of the relevant environment. It is concerned with the "why" questions of work motivation and organizational behavior. Because most causes, attributes, and "whys" are not directly observable, the theory says that people must depend on cognitions, particularly perception. The attribution theorist assumes that humans are rational and are motivated to identify and understand the causal structure of their relevant environment. It is this search for attributes that characterizes attribution theory and helps explain work motivation.

As shown earlier in Figure 6.2, attribution theory has its roots in all the pioneering cognitive theorists' work (for example, that of Lewin and Festinger), in de Charmes's ideas on cognitive evaluation, and in Bem's notion of "self-perception," the theory's initiator is generally recognized to be Fritz Heider. Heider believed that both internal forces (personal attributes such as ability, effort, and fatigue) and external forces (environmental attributes such as rules and the weather) combine additively to determine behavior. He stressed that it is the *perceived,* not the actual, determinants that are important to behavior (see the discussion of perception in Chapter 5). People will behave differently if they perceive internal attributes than they will if they perceive external attributes. It is this concept of differential ascriptions that has very important implications for motivation and organizational behavior in general.

### Locus of Control Attributions

Using *locus of control,* work behavior may be explained by whether employees perceive their outcomes as controlled internally or externally. Employees who perceive internal control feel that they personally can influence their outcomes through their own ability, skills, or effort. Employees who perceive external control feel that their outcomes are beyond their own control; they feel that external forces such as luck or task difficulty control their outcomes. This perceived locus of control may have a differential impact on their motivation to perform. For example, classic studies by well-known social psychologist Julian Rotter found that skill versus chance environments differentially affect behavior. In addition, a number of studies have been conducted over the years to test the attribution theory-locus-of-control model in work settings. One study found that internally controlled employees are generally more satisfied with their jobs, are more likely to be in managerial positions, and are more satisfied with a participatory management style than employees who perceive external control.[66] Other studies have found that internally controlled managers are better performers,[67] are more considerate of subordinates,[68] tend not to burn out,[69] follow a more strategic style of executive action,[70] have improved attitudes over a long period of time following promotions,[71] and present the most positive impression in a recruiting interview.[72] In addition, the attribution process has been shown to play a role in coalition formation in the political process of organizations. In particular, coalition members made stronger internal attributions, such as ability and desire, and nonmembers made stronger external attributions, such as luck.[73]

The implication of these studies and many others is that internally controlled managers are somehow better than externally controlled managers. However, such generalizations are not yet warranted because there is some contradictory evidence. For example, one study concluded that the ideal manager may have an external orientation because the results indicated that externally controlled managers were perceived as initiating more structure and consideration than internally controlled managers.[74] In addition to the implications for managerial behavior and performance, attribution theory has been shown to have relevance in explaining goal-setting behavior,[75] group performance,[76] leadership behavior,[77] poor employee performance,[78] and employee interpretations of human resource practices that affect their satisfaction and commitment.[79] However, like other constructs in organizational behavior, attribution is now undergoing considerable refinement in the research literature. For example, studies have found that (1) attributions about poor performance are mediated by how responsible the employee is judged to be and how much sympathy the evaluator feels,[80] and (2) leaders providing feedback to poor performers is significantly affected by the performance attributions that are made.[81] A review article concludes that locus of control is related to the performance and satisfaction of organization members and may moderate the relationship between motivation and incentives.[82]

In addition, attributions are related to *organizational symbolism,* which in effect says that in order to understand organizations, one must recognize their symbolic nature.[83] Much of organization is based on attributions rather than physical or observed realities under this view.[84] For example, research has found that symbols are a salient source of information used by people in forming their impressions of psychological climate.[85]

### Other Attributions

Attribution theory obviously contributes a great deal to the better understanding of work motivation and organizational behavior. However, other dimensions besides the internal and external locus of control also need to be accounted for and studied. Bernard Weiner, for example, suggested that a stability (fixed or variable) dimension must also be recognized.[86] Experienced employees will probably have a stable internal attribution about their abilities but an unstable internal attribution concerning effort. By the same token, these employees may have a stable external attribution about task difficulty but an unstable external attribution about luck.

Besides the stability dimension, Kelley suggests that dimensions such as consensus (do others act this way in this situation?), consistency (does this person act this way in this situation at other times?), and distinctiveness (does this person act differently in other situations?) will affect the type of attributions that are made.[87] Figure 6.6 shows how this type of information affects the attributes that are made in evaluating employee behavior. To keep these dimensions straight, it can be remembered that consensus relates to other *people,* distinctiveness relates to other *tasks,* and consistency relates to *time.*[88] As shown in Figure 6.6, if there is high consensus, low consistency, and high distinctiveness, then attribution to external or situational/environmental causes will probably be made. The external attribution may be that the task is too difficult or that outside pressures from home or coworkers are hindering performance. However, if there is low consensus, high consistency, and low distinctiveness, then attributions to internal or personal causes for the behavior will probably be made. The supervisor making an internal attribution may conclude that the associate just doesn't have the ability, or is not giving the necessary effort, or does not have the motivation to perform well. There is some research evidence from field settings to directly support predictions from the Kelley model.[89]

In addition to Kelley, other well-known theorists, such as Weiner, use attribution theory to help explain achievement motivation and to predict subsequent changes in performance and how people feel about themselves.[90] Some research findings from Weiner's work include the following:

1. Bad-luck attributions (external) take the sting out of a negative outcome, but good-luck attributions (external) reduce the joy associated with success.

2. When individuals attribute their success to internal rather than external factors, they have higher expectations for future success, report a greater desire for achievement, and set higher performance goals.[91]

**FIGURE 6.6**
Kelley's Model of
Attribution

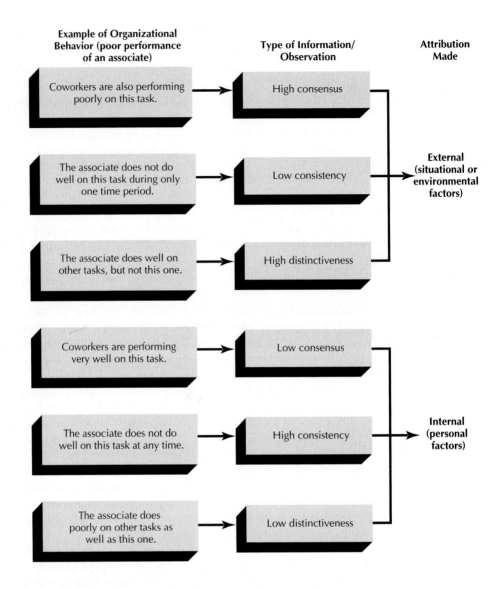

### Attribution Errors

Social psychologists recognize two potent biases when people make attributions. The first is called the *fundamental attribution error.* Research has found that people tend to ignore powerful situational forces when explaining others' behavior.[92] People tend to attribute *others'* behavior to personal factors (for example, intelligence, ability, motivation, attitudes, or personality), even when it is very clear that the situation or circumstances caused the person to behave the way he or she did.

Another attribution bias that has emerged from the research is that people tend to present themselves favorably. This *self-serving bias* has been found in study after study; people readily accept credit when told they have succeeded (attributing the success to their ability and effort), yet often attribute failure to such external, situational factors as bad luck or the problem's inherent "impossibility.[93] For example, in explaining their victories, athletes commonly credit themselves, but they are more likely to attribute losses to something else—bad breaks, poor officiating, or the other team's superior effort.[94]

When something goes wrong in the workplace, there is a tendency for the manager to blame the problem on the inability or poor attitude of associates, but the situation is blamed as far as he or she personally is concerned. The reverse is true of associates. They blame the situation for their difficulties but make a personal attribution in terms of their manager. By the same token, if something goes well, the manager makes personal attributions for him- or herself and situational attributions for associates, and the associates make personal attributions for themselves but situational attributions for the manager. In other words, it is typical to have conflicting attributional biases among managers and associates in organizations.[95] As a way of creating more productive relationships, theorists and researchers suggest that efforts must be made to reduce divergent perceptions and perspectives among the parties through increased interpersonal interaction, open communication channels and workshops, and team-building sessions devoted to reducing attributional errors.[96] Although Martinko, in his book on *Attribution Theory,* demonstrates the validity and potential of attributional perspectives within an organizational context, theoretical, information processing, and situational factors all affect the attribution models of organizational behavior.[97] Despite this complexity, attribution theory does seem to have considerable potential for application and relevance, instead of being a purely academic exercise in theory building.

## Other Work Motivation Theories: Control and Agency

In addition to the micro-oriented expectancy and equity motivation theories coming out of cognitive psychology, there are other, more broad-based theories that have emerged in organizational behavior. Representatives of such theories are control theory and agency theory.

One version of *control theory,* like the other theories discussed so far, is essentially a cognitive phenomenon relating to the degree that individuals perceive they are in control of their own lives, or are in control of their jobs. Recent studies have shown that those who believe they have such personal control tolerate unpleasant events and experience less stress on the job than those who do not perceive such control.[98] There is also some evidence that perceived control will affect job satisfaction and absenteeism.[99] Another version of control theory, which also has implications for organizational behavior, relates to the more traditional management function of control. Traditional guidelines for effective management have included controlling both the inputs and outputs of organizations, but research has also analyzed strategically controlling human resources as well.[100] Especially relevant to today's workplace environment is that a sense of control seems very helpful when increasing job demands are placed on the employee. Thus, persons who are given more work, but also the control to complete that work, may not feel as negatively about their new assignments. On the other hand, more peripheral aspects of work control, such as when they start or stop a task or arrange the work flow, seem less related to work motivation.[101]

Similar to control theory's being taken from the traditional management literature, agency theory as applied to organizational behavior comes from the financial economics literature. As given attention in Chapter 4, an agency relationship involves one or more individuals (the principal) engaging another person or persons (the agent) to perform some service on their behalf.[102] The key to *agency theory* is the assumption that the interests of principals and agents diverge or may be in conflict with one another. The implications for organizational behavior involve how the principals (owners, board members, or top management) can limit divergence from their interests or objectives by establishing appropriate rewards or incentives for the agents (subordinates, middle management, or operating employees) for appropriate outcomes. Although there was initial research evidence supporting an agency theory interpretation of areas in organizational behavior such as pay for performance,[103] compensation contracts,[104] foreign subsidiary compensation strategies,[105] and variable pay compensation strategies,[106] however, a recent meta-analysis of empirical ownership-performance studies found little overall support for agency theory.[107] Yet, agency theory is often used to explain some of the excesses and ethical meltdowns that have occurred in organizations in recent years. For example, Don Hambrick recently observed the following:

> Today's top executives, in America at least, are exceedingly obsessed with shareholder value, in ways that their predecessors were not. This obsession is due to the new "rules of the game" that the executives themselves face—rules that agency theorists applaud, even if they didn't literally engineer them.[108]

Like the other cognitive-based theories, agency theory helps us better understand the motivation of managers in today's organizations. However, because of the complexities involved, as was also noted in the other work motivation theories, agency theory obviously is not the final answer. One primary criticism of agency theory that has emerged is that, agency theory strongly emphasizes the roles that various forms of extrinsic motives play in shaping behaviors. Conversely, intrinsic motives, which may be quite powerful, are not accounted for in agency models. When combined with notions of control or the lack of control in a setting, the bias generated by an extrinsic-motive model may confuse any study or theoretical development.[109] Yet, as one argument for employee ownership noted, firms indicated that 75 percent experienced increases in sales, profits, and stock price when employees became owners and another study indicated that companies with employee stock ownership plans had total shareholder returns about 7 percent greater than firms where employees did not have an opportunity for ownership.[110]

Recently, agency theory has been expanded to the macro level. It has been used to explain financing decisions in franchising operations[111] and to study the various forms of control that limit the decision-making authority of professional service organizations.[112] In the latter study, community control, bureaucratic control, and client control combined with the degree of self-control exhibited by the professional service agent to reduce decision-making autonomy. Thus, agency theory is also related to control theory and, for the future, theory development and research can contribute to the better understanding of work motivation.

# MOTIVATIONAL APPLICATION THROUGH JOB DESIGN

Besides gaining an understanding of motivational needs and theoretical processes, the study of organizational behavior also focuses on motivational techniques of job design and goal setting. Job design may be defined as the methods that management uses to develop the content of a job, including all relevant tasks, as well as the processes by which jobs are constructed and revised. In light of the new environment, job design is an increasingly important application technique. Most importantly, the nature of work is changing because of advanced information technology and globalization. Consequently, two new developments have emerged. The first is a blurring of the distinction between on-work and off-work time. A person carrying a cell phone and/or PDA (personal digital assistant) and a home office containing a fax machine and Internet access is "at work" even when not in the office and is "on-call" practically every moment of the day. This includes drive time and time spent in airports or while flying across the world. The second development, which is tied to the first, is the rising number of telecommuting jobs or teleworking, in which the employee performs substantial amounts of work at home. An increasing number of organizations provide employees with advanced information technology for home use. These recent trends create new challenges for job design models, which are already based on an extensive and growing theoretical and research base and are being widely applied to the actual practice of management. A summary of the major job design applications follows.

## Job Rotation

The simplest form of job design involves moving employees from one relatively simple job to another after short time periods (one hour, half-days, every day). For example, at McDonald's, an employee may cook French fries one day, fry hamburgers the next, wait on the front counter during the next shift, and draw soft drinks the next. This form of job rotation has several advantages. First, the odds of injury are reduced, as each worker must refocus on a new task throughout the workday. Further, the incidence of repetitive strain injuries (e.g., carpal tunnel syndrome) may also be reduced. Second, as employees learn sets of tasks, they are more flexible and able to cover for someone who is absent or who quits. Third, supervisors who are promoted from the ranks know more about how the entire operation works. A manager promoted from the ranks at McDonald's after only six months on the job has probably been exposed to every production task performed at the unit. The primary disadvantage of job rotation is that each individual task eventually becomes as boring as the rest of the simple tasks. In other words, over the long term there is no substantial difference between cooking French fries and frying hamburgers. Consequently, job satisfaction and/or performance may decline. Rotation does, however, have some research evidence showing a positive impact,[113] especially for cross-training and developing employees for broadened responsibilities.[114] In any event, it is a better alternative to job design than doing nothing.

## Job Enlargement

This job design process involves increasing the number of tasks each employee performs. A sales clerk who waits on customers, finalizes the sale, helps with credit applications, arranges merchandise, and reorders stock has an enlarged job, when compared to a checkout clerk or a shelf stocker at Wal-Mart. Workers in enlarged jobs are able to use more skills in performing their tasks. Many times, however, enlargement reduces the efficiency with which tasks are completed, thereby slowing work down. Imagine being waited on individually at Wal-Mart. The company's competitive advantage for low labor costs compared to a full-service department store would be quickly and dramatically reduced. However, enlargement does not necessarily result in improved employee satisfaction and commitment. For example, one of the major by-products of recent downsizing is enlarged jobs assigned to the members of the organization who remain. The survivors with anxiety of "I'm next" and greatly enlarged jobs are less, rather than more, satisfied and committed to the organization.

## Job Enrichment

Job enrichment represents an extension of the earlier, more simplified job rotation and job enlargement techniques of job design. Because it is a direct outgrowth of Herzberg's two-factor theory of motivation (covered earlier in the chapter), the assumption is that in order to motivate personnel, the job must be designed to provide opportunities for achievement, recognition, responsibility, advancement, and growth. The technique entails "enriching" the job so that these factors are included. In particular, *job enrichment* is concerned with designing jobs that include a greater variety of work content; require a higher level of knowledge and skill; give workers more autonomy and responsibility in terms of planning, directing, and controlling their own performance; and provide the opportunity for personal growth and a meaningful work experience. As opposed to job rotation and job enlargement, which horizontally loads the job, job enrichment *vertically* loads the job; there are not necessarily more tasks to perform, but more responsibility and accountability. For example, instead of having workers do a mundane, specialized task, then passing off to another worker doing another minute part of the task, and eventually having an inspector at the end, under job enrichment, the worker would be given a complete module of work to do (job enlargement) and, importantly, would inspect his or her own work (responsibility) and put a personal identifier on it (accountability).

As with the other application techniques discussed in this text, job enrichment is not a panacea for all job design problems facing modern management. After noting that there are documented cases where this approach to job design did not work, Miner concluded that the biggest problem is that traditional job enrichment has little to say about when and why the failures can be expected to occur.[115] Some of the explanations that have been suggested include that job enrichment is difficult to truly implement, that many employees simply prefer an old familiar job to an enriched job, and that employees in general and unions in particular are resistant to the change. Some employees have expressed preferences for higher pay rather than enriched jobs, and others enjoy their current patterns of on-the-job socialization and friendships more than they do increased responsibility and autonomy. Essentially, job enrichment in some situations may inhibit a person's social life at work.

Despite some potential limitations, job enrichment is still a viable approach, and research provides continuing evidence that it has mostly beneficial results (more employee satisfaction and customer service, less employee overload, and fewer employee errors).[116] There is even a study that found employees were more creative when they worked in an enriching context of complex, challenging jobs and a supportive, noncontrolling supervisory climate.[117] However, management must still use job enrichment selectively and give proper recognition to the complex human and situational variables.[118] The job characteristics models of job enrichment are a step in this direction.

## The Job Characteristics Approach to Task Design

To meet some of the limitations of the relatively simple Herzberg approach to job enrichment (which he prefers to call *orthodox job enrichment,* or OJE), a group of researchers began to concentrate on the relationship between certain job characteristics, or the job scope, and employee motivation. Richard Hackman and Greg Oldham developed the most widely recognized model of job characteristics,[119] shown in Figure 6.7. This model recognizes that certain job characteristics contribute to certain psychological states and that the strength of employees' need for growth has an important moderating effect. The core job characteristics can be summarized briefly as follows:

**FIGURE 6.7**
**The Hackman-Oldham job Characteristics Model of Work Motivation**

1. *Skill variety* refers to the extent to which the job requires the employee to draw from a number of different skills and abilities as well as on a range of knowledge.
2. *Task identity* refers to whether the job has an identifiable beginning and end. How complete a module of work does the employee perform?
3. *Task significance* involves the importance of the task. It involves both internal significance—how important is the task to the organization?—and external significance—how proud are employees to tell relatives, friends, and neighbors what they do and where they work?
4. *Autonomy* refers to job independence. How much freedom and control do employees have, for example, to schedule their own work, make decisions, or determine the means to accomplish objectives?
5. *Feedback* refers to objective information about progress and performance and can come from the job itself or from supervisors or an information system.

The critical psychological states can be summarized as follows:

1. *Meaningfulness.*    This cognitive state involves the degree to which employees perceive their work as making a valued contribution, as being important and worthwhile.
2. *Responsibility.*    This state is concerned with the extent to which employees feel a sense of being personally responsible or accountable for the work being done.
3. *Knowledge of results.*    Coming directly from the feedback, this psychological state involves the degree to which employees understand how they are performing in the job.

In essence, this model says that certain job characteristics lead to critical psychological states. That is, skill variety, task identity, and task significance lead to experienced meaningfulness; autonomy leads to the feeling of responsibility; and feedback leads to knowledge of results. The more these three psychological states are present, the more employees will feel good about themselves when they perform well. Hackman states: "The model postulates that internal rewards are obtained by an individual when he *learns* (knowledge of results) that he *personally* (experienced responsibility) has performed well on a task that he *cares* about (experienced meaningfulness)."[120] Hackman then points out that these internal rewards are reinforcing to employees, causing them to perform well. If they don't perform well, they will try harder in order to get the internal rewards that good performance brings. He concludes: "The net result is a self-perpetuating cycle of positive work motivation powered by self-generated rewards. This cycle is predicted to continue until one or more of the three psychological states is no longer present, or until the individual no longer values the internal rewards that derive from good performance."[121] Not only did Hackman and Oldham provide original research supporting the existence of these relationships, but subsequent research has found strong support for the linkages between the core job dimensions and the critical psychological states, and between these states and the predicted outcomes.[122] (Also see the OB Principle at the end of this chapter).

An example of an enriched job, according to the Hackman-Oldham characteristics model, would be that of a surgeon. Surgeons must draw on a wide variety of skills and abilities; usually surgeons can readily identify the task because they handle patients from beginning to end (that is, they play a role in the diagnosis, perform the operation, and are responsible for postoperative care and follow-up); the job has life-and-death significance; there is a great deal of autonomy, as surgeons have the final word on all decisions concerning patients; and there is clear, direct feedback during the operation itself (real-time monitoring of the vital signs and the "scalpel"-"scalpel" type of feedback communication) and afterwards, because, of course, the patient's recovery and subsequent health determine the success of the operation. According to this explanation, these job characteristics determine the surgeon's considerable motivation—not the needs developed while growing up or his or her valences, instrumentalities, and expectancies as postulated by the process theories discussed earlier.

At the other extreme would be most traditional blue-collar and white-collar jobs. All five job characteristics would be relatively minimal or nonexistent in the perceptions of many such jobholders and thus can help explain the motivation problem with these low-level jobs. In other words, the job design, not just the person holding the job, helps explain the motivation to perform under this approach.

## Practical Guidelines for Redesigning Jobs

Specific guidelines such as those found in Figure 6.8 are offered to redesign jobs. Such easily implementable guidelines make the job design area popular and practical for more effective high performance management. An actual example would be the application that was made in a large department store.[123] In a training session format, the sales employees' jobs were redesigned in the following manner:

1. *Skill variety.* The salespeople were asked to try to think of and use
   a. Different selling approaches
   b. New merchandise displays
   c. Better ways of recording sales and keeping records
2. *Task identity.* The salespeople were asked to
   a. Keep a personal record of daily sales volume in dollars
   b. Keep a record of number of sales/customers
   c. Mark off an individual display area that they considered their own and keep it complete and orderly
3. *Task significance.* The salespeople were reminded that
   a. Selling a product is the basic overall objective of the store
   b. The appearance of the display area is important to selling
   c. They are "the store" to customers; they were told that courtesy and pleasantness help build the store's reputation and set the stage for future sales

**FIGURE 6.8**

**Specific Guidelines for Redesigning Jobs for the More-Effective Practice of Human Resource Management**

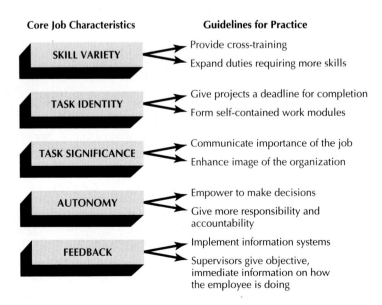

| Core Job Characteristics | Guidelines for Practice |
|---|---|
| SKILL VARIETY | Provide cross-training / Expand duties requiring more skills |
| TASK IDENTITY | Give projects a deadline for completion / Form self-contained work modules |
| TASK SIGNIFICANCE | Communicate importance of the job / Enhance image of the organization |
| AUTONOMY | Empower to make decisions / Give more responsibility and accountability |
| FEEDBACK | Implement information systems / Supervisors give objective, immediate information on how the employee is doing |

4. *Autonomy.*   The salespeople were
   a. Encouraged to develop and use their own unique approach and sales pitch
   b. Allowed freedom to select their own break and lunch times
   c. Encouraged to make suggestions for changes in all phases of the policy and operations

5. *Feedback from the job itself.*   Salespeople were
   a. Encouraged to keep personal records of their own sales volume
   b. Encouraged to keep a sales/customer ratio
   c. Reminded that establishing a good rapport with customers is also a success; they were told that if the potential customer leaves with a good feeling about the store and its employees, the salesperson has been successful

6. *Feedback from agents.*   Salespeople were encouraged to
   a. Observe and help each other with techniques of selling
   b. Seek out information from their boss and relevant departments on all phases of their jobs
   c. Invite customer reactions and thoughts concerning merchandise, service, and so forth

Both the salespeople's functional (conversing with customers, showing merchandise, handling returns, and so forth) and dysfunctional (socializing with coworkers or visitors, idly standing around, being gone for no legitimate reason) performance behaviors moved in the desired directions, and a subanalysis also indicated they were more satisfied. A control group of salespeople, with everything else the same except that they did not have their jobs redesigned, showed no change in their performance behaviors. Thus, this study provided evidence that the job characteristics approach can be practically applied with desirable performance and satisfaction results.[124] Many well-known companies have actually implemented job design changes in accordance with the job characteristics model. For example, in terms of building in autonomy in jobs, well-known firms in the hospitality (e.g., Disney, Ritz Carlton) and retail industries allow their frontline employees to "make it right" for the "guest"/customer at any cost. For instance, at the very successful Container Stores, every salesperson has a key to the till in order to make *any* decision the customer needs.

# MOTIVATIONAL APPLICATION THROUGH GOAL SETTING

As indicated, the other major motivational application technique besides job design is goal setting. Goal achievement is a factor that influences the success levels of individual employees, departments and business units, and the overall organization. A goal is a performance target that an individual or group seeks to accomplish at work. Goal setting is the process of motivating employees by establishing effective and meaningful performance targets. It is often given as an example of how the field of organizational behavior should progress from a sound theoretical foundation to sophisticated research to the actual application of more effective management practice.

## Theoretical Understanding of Goal Setting

Although a paper by Locke is usually considered to be the seminal work on a theory of goal setting,[125] he suggests that it really goes back to scientific management at the turn of the century. Locke credits its first proponent, Frederick W. Taylor, with being the "father of employee motivation theory,"[126] and he says that Taylor's use "of tasks was a forerunner of modern-day goal setting."[127]

Although Locke argues that the expectancy theories of work motivation discussed earlier originally ignored goal setting and were nothing more than "cognitive hedonism,"[128] his theoretical formulation for goal setting is very similar. He basically accepts the purposefulness of behavior, which comes out of Tolman's pioneering cognitive theorizing, and the importance of values, or valence, and consequences. Thus, as in the expectancy theories of work motivation, *values and value judgments,* which are defined as the things the individual acts on to gain and/or to keep, are important cognitive determinants of behavior. Emotions or desires are the ways the person experiences these values. In addition to values, *intentions* or *goals* play an important role as cognitive determinants of behavior. It is here, of course, where Locke's theory of goal setting goes beyond expectancy theories of work motivation, because people strive to attain goals in order to satisfy their emotions and desires. Goals provide a directional nature to people's behavior and guide their thoughts and actions to one outcome rather than another. The individual then responds and performs according to these intentions or goals, even if the goals are not attained. Consequences, feedback, or reinforcement are the result of these responses.

## Research Evidence on the Impact of Goal Setting

Locke's theory has generated considerable research. In particular, a series of laboratory studies by Locke and his colleagues and a series of field studies by Locke's frequent coauthor Gary Latham and other colleagues have been carried out to test the linkage between goal setting and performance.[129] Over the past 15 years, numerous studies have been conducted to refine and extend goal-setting theory and practice. Recently, Locke and Latham summarized the 35-year work on goal setting and task motivation and performance as follows:

> With goal-setting theory, specific difficult goals have been shown to increase performance on well over 100 different tasks involving more than 40,000 participants in at least eight countries working in laboratory, simulation, and field settings. . . . The effects are applicable not only to the individual but to groups, organizational units, and entire organizations.[130]

Specifically, Locke and Latham relate goals to performance and satisfaction in the model shown in Figure 6.9. The following sections give more detail on this model and a

**FIGURE 6.9**
**Model for Relating Goals to Performance and Satisfaction**

*Source:* Adapted from Edwin A. Locke and Gary P. Latham, "Building a Practically Useful Theory of Goal Setting and Task Motivation," *American Psychologist,* Vol. 57, No. 9, 2002, p. 714.

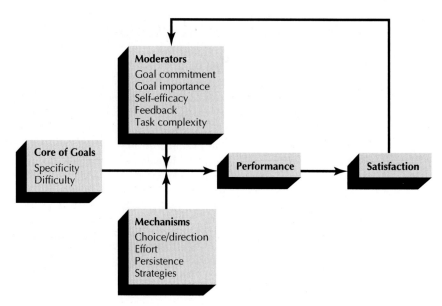

Goal setting is widely recognized as a technique to improve performance. However, there are a number of problems associated with the indiscriminate use of ambitious goals. Steven Kerr, a noted organizational behavior researcher and former chief learning officer at both General Electric and Goldman Sachs, has noted that many organizations fail to effectively use what he calls "stretch goals." The goals are set very high, but the needed support to accomplish them is often missing. For example, top management may ask their people to increase output by 25% but fail to provide them with the knowledge, tools, and means to reach such ambitious goals. As a result, the only way that people can meet these new and demanding challenges is by working longer—often on their own time. In fact, notes Kerr, everywhere in America people are working evenings and weekends in order to meet the goals that the organization has set for them.

This is not necessary, however, if the enterprise carefully examines what needs to be done and how it has to occur. Kerr recommends three rules that can help organizations create stretch goals and reach them without exhausting and burning out their human resources.

These include (1) do not set goals that overly stress people; (2) if goals require people to stretch, do not punish them if they fail; and (3) if they are being asked to do things that they have never done before, give them whatever tools and help are available.

How should goals be set? Kerr believes that easy goals are too simple and do not improve performance and that difficult goals may be so difficult that people cannot attain them—so they give up. Stretch goals force them to go beyond what they are accustomed to doing, and thus improve performance, but, importantly, they are also attainable. At the same time, the organization has to be willing to reward the personnel for attaining the stretch goals. How can this be done? One way is with money. Financial rewards are very direct and encourage individuals to continue their efforts. However, if management decide that they will give back to those involved one-third of the performance gain (i.e., gainsharing), they must stick to this and not back down when big gains are realized. If organizations follow these simple suggestions of using stretch goals and pay for performance, they can increase their productivity and employees can be challenged and rewarded for their efforts.

summary of the extensive research that makes goal-setting theory and application a prototype evidence-based approach for the field of organizational behavior.

### The Importance of Specific Goals

Specific goals have been found to be more effective than vague or general goals, such as "do your best," as well as no goals at all. Specific goals result in higher levels of performance. For instance, salespeople should have goals in dollar amounts or units of volume, production departments should have targeted and defined goals in terms of numbers, percentages, and dates, and all other departments should incorporate measurable objectives or specific metrics and dates rather than things such as "try as hard as you can" or "try to do better than last year."

### The Importance of Difficult and Challenging Goals

Besides clearly stated goals, performance targets should also be challenging rather than easy or routine. At the same time, goals should be reachable and not so difficult that pursuing them becomes frustrating. The accompanying OB in Action: Using Stretch Goals gives some practical guidelines.

Recent research indicates some moderators of the relationship between goal difficulty and subsequent performance. Two forms of feedback can enhance goal achievement: (1) process feedback and (2) outcome feedback. Process feedback is related to information as to how the individual or unit is proceeding in attempting to reach the goal, whereas outcome feedback is information related to and stated in terms of the actual goal itself.[131] Other researchers have investigated the role that competition plays in moderating the goal difficulty–performance relationship, but results have been mixed. One study revealed that the lack of competition combined with difficult goals led to higher performance, whereas another found no effects related to competition.[132]

In still another research stream, perceived goal difficulty had negative effects on self-reports of job performance. In other words, an employee who thought a job was highly difficult reported performing at a lower level. However, goal difficulty, when combined with goal clarity, led to increased reports of effort, which in turn led to more positive self-reports of performance in the same study.[133]

### Goal Acceptance, Participation, and Commitment

Specific goals are most likely to affect performance when employees accept and are committed to them. This ownership and acceptance of goals are best accomplished through a participative process.[134] Self-commitment can be given to assigned goals as well as to personal or self-set goals, especially when goals are equivocal. Commitment tends to run higher when goals are specific as opposed to general or broad. Monetary incentives can also increase commitment to goals if the goals are perceived as being achievable.[135] Some of the mixed results and complexity on the moderating role of goal commitment may be due to measurement problems that recent research may help solve for the future.[136]

### Self-efficacy and Goals

As will be given detailed attention in Chapter 7, self-efficacy is the perception or belief of the individual that he or she can successfully accomplish a specific task, and it is associated with goal commitment.[137] People exhibiting higher levels of self-efficacy tend to set more challenging personal goals and are more likely to achieve them, and commitment to self-set personal goals is normally also higher than commitment to goals set by others (imposed goals).[138] Self-efficacy is also related to imposed goals. Some individuals may reject imposed goals, but if they have self-efficacy still maintain high personal goals. Further, if the imposed goal is impossible, personal goals and self-efficacy may be reduced, along with performance.[139]

### Objective and Timely Feedback

Studies have also found objective and timely feedback is preferable to no feedback and, as noted earlier, can be related to the process used to achieve a goal or the content (degree of achievement) of the goal. It is probably fair to say that feedback is a necessary but not sufficient condition for successful application of goal setting.[140] In one research study it was found that daily feedback had positive influences on both productivity and employee satisfaction,[141] and in another study feedback on progress toward individual and team goals greatly affected the decisions being made.[142] "Just in time" information gathered through technology found in today's "expert systems" can also be effectively used to provide timely feedback.[143]

### Other Moderators in Goal Setting

Although the application guidelines from goal-setting theory and research are probably as direct as any in the entire field of organizational behavior, there are still some other moderating variables. Besides commitment, importance, self-efficacy, and feedback shown in Figure 6.9 and discussed above, it should be noted that task complexity[144] (also noted in the Locke and Latham model as indicated in Figure 6.9) and others are found in the literature, and there are some contradictory findings. For example, a study by Latham and Saari revealed that a supportive management style had an important moderating effect, and that, contrary to results in previous studies, specific goals did not lead to better performance than a generalized goal such as "do your best."[145] However, other studies have found a significant relationship between *goal levels* and performance.[146] Leader style may also affect goal commitment. Recent research revealed that an interaction between leader-member exchange and goal commitment accounted for a significant amount of variance in the performance level of a sales force.[147] Another analysis indicated that there are also some unexplored areas, such as the distinction between quantity and quality goals,[148] that may limit and make the application of goal setting more complex.

### *A Word of Caution Regarding Goal Setting*

In the words of Ambrose and Kulik, who conducted a comprehensive review of goal-setting research, there are boundary conditions that surround the relationships between goal setting and performance that should be carefully noted for effective application.[149] First, one study noted that goals can narrow an individual's focus to perform only behaviors directly associated with goal attainment, at the cost of other desirable behaviors. This type of tunnel vision was revealed in a study in which students were given a specific goal of correcting the grammar on a recruiting brochure. They did so at the expense of improving the content of the brochure. Those with a more general goal (e.g., make it better) worked on both the content and the grammar.[150] Furthermore, difficult goals increase the level of risk managers and employees are willing to take, and this increase may be counterproductive.[151] Also, a study found that goals inhibited subjects from helping others who were requesting assistance, which has implications for teamwork.[152] Other studies have found that difficult goals may lead to stress, put a perceptual ceiling on performance, cause the employees to ignore nongoal areas, and encourage short-range thinking, dishonesty, or cheating.[153] However, Locke and Latham do provide specific guidelines of how these potential pitfalls can be overcome by better communication, rewards, and setting examples.[154]

Recently, the argument has been made for the value of learning goals versus performance outcome goals. Setting very ambitious "stretch goals" to increase the numbers without providing the means to attain these goals may lead to not only stress and burnout, but also unethical behavior. As Seijts and Latham point out, "in situations where primarily the acquisition of knowledge and skills rather than an increase in effort and persistence is required, a specific challenging learning rather than an outcome goal should be set."[155] On balance, however, there has been very impressive evidence for the positive impact of setting specific, difficult goals that are accepted and of providing feedback on progress toward goals.

## Other Performance Management Application Techniques Associated with Goal Setting

Much of the discussion so far has been directly concerned with goal-setting theory, research findings, and application for performance improvement of an individual manager or work unit. Besides goal setting per se, because of its demonstrated relationship to performance, a related approach recently given attention is *goal orientation,* originally conceptualized by Carol Dweck through her research on children. She found a dispositional personality dimension related to pursuing goals in achievement situations that could be characterized as (1) *learning goal orientation* (those who want to develop competence by mastering challenging situations) and (2) *performance goal orientation* (those who want to demonstrate and validate competence by seeking favorable judgments).[156] Although conventional wisdom would indicate the superiority of performance goal orientation, considerable recent research in the field of organizational behavior over the past decade indicates otherwise.[157] A recent summary of this research concluded that a learning goal orientation has a positive impact on work-related behaviors and performance.[158] This learning goal orientation is especially relevant to effective performance in today's environment that requires proactive, problem-solving responses to setbacks, creativity and openness to new ideas, and adaptation to new and changing situations.[159]

More recently Dweck has evolved the learning goal orientation into what she calls a "growth mindset" (people who have the belief that their basic qualities can be developed through their efforts) and the performance goal orientation into a "fixed mindset" (those who believe their qualities are set and have an urgency to prove themselves over and over).[160] She uses infamous celebrity CEOs known for having a devastating effect on their firms such as "Chainsaw" Al Dunlop of Scott Paper and Sunbeam, Jerry Levin and Steve Case of AOL Time Warner, and Ken Lay and Jeff Skilling of Enron as examples of those having a fixed mindset. By contrast, those who led their firms to dramatically successful turnarounds such as Jack Welch, when he was at the pinnacle of General Electric, Lou Gerstner at IBM, and Anne Mulcahy at Xerox are good representatives of having a growth mindset. In concluding, Dweck observed,

> Jack, Lou and Anne—all believing in growth, all brimming with passion. And all believing that leadership is about growth and passion, not about brilliance. The fixed-mindset leaders were, in the end, full of bitterness, but the growth-minded leaders were full of gratitude. They called their workers the real heroes.[161]

Besides goal orientation or mindset, there are also other performance management techniques related to goal setting. One is *benchmarking,* which is a form of goal setting, though it is meant to be more inclusive and is often portrayed as part of total quality management. *Benchmarking* is the process of comparing work and service methods against the best practices and outcomes for the purpose of identifying changes stated as specific goals that will result in higher-quality output. Importantly, benchmarking incorporates the use of goal setting to set targets that are pursued, identified, and then used as the basis for future action. The benchmarking process involves looking both inside and outside the organization for ways of improving performance.

With benchmarking, the idea is to enable the organization to learn from others and then to formulate specific change goals based on procedures and work assignments that have been observed in world-class organizations. Companies that have effectively used benchmarking include IBM and Magnavox. IBM benchmarked its efforts in comparison to Xerox, Motorola, 3M, Hewlett-Packard, and some Japanese firms that used just-in-time inventory controls. Magnavox benchmarked a series of HR practices, which they turned into 14 training measures that are now commonly called metrics, again with strong evidence of success.

A *stretch target* or goal, discussed in the earlier OB in Action, is another currently popular technique associated with goal setting. *Stretch targets* may be defined as objectives or goals that force organizations to significantly alter their processes in ways that involve a whole new paradigm of operations.[162] In a manner similar to benchmarking, stretch targets seek to integrate and align the internal operation and culture with external best practices. Examples of stretch targets include enhancing motivation, performance, and creative decision making through specific numbers, percentages, and dates.

One area of application associated with goal setting with international implications is that of *goal source.* Questions remain as to how to implement goal-setting programs across cultures. During a goal-setting program, subordinates often receive information from a supervisor or leader. If that leader (the goal source) is distrusted, the message may be rejected. If the leader or goal source is trusted, goal acceptance and commitment and performance may be higher. One study conducted in England confirmed that English workers, who were more likely to trust a shop steward than a supervisor due to several key historical and cultural reasons, did indeed accept goals and perform at higher rates when the steward helped deliver the goals.[163] This goal source impact applied in a cross-cultural environment would suggest that, depending on cultural dimensions such as power distance, home country nationals involved in the goal-setting process may have more of an impact on home country employees than would expatriates or those from another country home office.

## Impact on the Psychological Contract

Goal setting can be used to create psychological contracts with employees. In any exchange situation at work, there are both formal and informal expectations regarding what is given and what should be received in return. Imposing new goals may violate existing views of what is present in the psychological contract, creating either resistance to the program or a renegotiation of the rewards to be received. Note that any linkage between goals and performance has a psychological contract implied in the relationship. Organizations that routinely demand higher performances yet fail to respond with rewards to their people can expect increasingly negative responses and reactions.[164]

A number of other instances of contract violations may inhibit the success rates of goal setting. These violations include restructuring, downsizing, increased reliance on temporary workers, and globalization. Goal setting in part constructs a social role at work that is intertwined with other elements of a psychological contract.[165] Consequently, successful applications of goal-setting programs must account for how resulting processes will affect existing psychological contracts of employees.[166]

---

## Summary

Motivation is probably more closely associated with the micro perspective of organizational behavior than is any other topic. A comprehensive understanding of motivation includes the need–drive–incentive sequence, or cycle. The basic process involves needs, which set drives in motion to accomplish incentives (anything that alleviates a need and reduces a drive). The drives, or motives, may be classified into *primary* and *secondary* categories. The primary motives are unlearned and physiologically based. Common primary motives are hunger, thirst, sleep, avoidance of pain, sex, and maternal concern. Secondary motives are learned and are most relevant to the study of organizational behavior. The needs for power, achievement, affiliation, security, and status are major motivating forces in the behavior of organizational participants.

Besides the various needs, motivation can also be broken down into its source—extrinsic and intrinsic. Extrinsic motives are the visible consequences external to the individual (e.g., money), usually contingently administered by others, to motivate the individual. Intrinsic motives are internal to the individual, and are self-induced to learn, achieve, or in some way better oneself.

When the theories are specifically focused on work motivation, there are both historically important and contemporary approaches. The older Maslow and Herzberg models attempt to identify specific content factors in the employee (in the case of Maslow) or in the job environment (in the case of Herzberg) that are motivating. Although such a content approach has surface logic, is easy to understand, and can be readily translated into practice, the research evidence points out some definite limitations. There is very little research support for these models' theoretical basis and predictability. The trade-off for simplicity sacrifices true understanding of the complexity of work motivation. On the positive side, however, these historically important models have given emphasis to important content factors that were largely ignored by the human relationists. In addition, the Herzberg model is useful as an explanation for job satisfaction and as a point of departure for practical application to enrich jobs.

The contemporary process theories provide a much sounder theoretical explanation of the complexity of work motivation. The expectancy model of Porter and Lawler help explain the important cognitive variables and how they relate to one another in the process of work motivation. The Porter-Lawler model also gives specific attention to the important relationship between performance and satisfaction. Porter and Lawler propose that performance leads to satisfaction, instead of the human relations assumption of the reverse. The research literature is generally supportive of such expectancy models, but conceptual and methodological problems remain. Unlike the older content models, these expectancy models are relatively complex and difficult to translate into actual practice.

Another contemporary approach to explaining work motivation is equity theory. This theory is based on perceived input–outcome ratios of oneself compared to relevant other(s). Like the expectancy models, equity theory can lead to increased understanding of the complex cognitive process of work motivation but also has the same limitation for prediction and control in the practice of human resource management. More recently, this equity theory has been applied to the analysis of organizational justice in the workplace. Other relevent cognitive understanding of motivation comes from attribution theory (i.e., internal versus external locus of control and stability, consensus, consistency, and distinctiveness attributions). Finally, control and agency theories, coming from other disciplines, are briefly discussed as representative of other approaches receiving research attention in organizational behavior.

The last part of the chapter deals with two of the most important application areas of work motivation: job design and goal setting. Although the concern for designing jobs goes back to the scientific management movement at the turn of the twentieth century, the recent concern for human resource management as a competitive advantage has led to renewed interest in, and research on, job design. The older and simpler job enlargement and rotation approaches have given way to first a job enrichment approach and then a job characteristics approach that relates to psychological or motivational states leading to improved employee satisfaction and performance. Characteristics such as skill variety, task identity, task significance, autonomy, and feedback have been found by research to be related to employee satisfaction and quality of work. The other major application technique for work motivation of goal setting has become a showcase for evidence-based management.

Basing his approach on a cognitive perspective, Locke has a well-developed goal-setting theory of motivation. This theory emphasizes the important relationship between goals and performance. Laboratory and field studies have verified this relationship. In particular, the most effective performance seems to result when specific, difficult goals are accepted and when feedback on progress and results is provided. An alternative theoretical perspective is goal orientation (fixed and growth mindsets), and an extension and systematic application of the goal-setting approach are benchmarking and stretch targets. The chapter concludes with the impact that goal setting may have on the psychological contract. To be successful, the human resources must also benefit and receive a return (reward) in order to not breach the psychological contract.

# Ending with Meta-Analytic Research Findings
## OB PRINCIPLE FOR EVIDENCE-BASED PRACTICE

On interesting, challenging tasks, providing extrinsic rewards can increase the level of intrinsic motivation.

## Meta-Analysis Results:

[13 studies; 729 participants; $d = .34$] *On average, there is a **60 percent probability** that administering extrinsic rewards such as money to employees performing interesting, challenging tasks will increase their level of intrinsic motivation more than those who do not receive extrinsic rewards.* However, a moderator analysis revealed that in some cases extrinsic rewards can actually decrease employees' intrinsic motivation by shifting the employee's focus away from wanting to perform well on a task because it is intrinsically interesting or challenging, to the desire for an external reward. Moreover, it is suggested that the extrinsic-intrinsic relationship depends on how intrinsic motivation is measured.

## Conclusion:

Although it is important that employees be genuinely interested and motivated to perform well, it is equally important that organizations reward people for their performance. However, the effects of combining extrinsic and intrinsic motivational techniques can be complex. Increasing levels of intrinsic motivation involves either increasing employees' level of competence that they can perform tasks, enhancing their perceptions of control over their behavior, or providing challenges in the work environment. Although in many cases providing extrinsic rewards adds to intrinsic motivation, organizations must be careful that the extrinsic rewards do not interfere with key cognitive processes. For example, employees who receive money for a job well done may attribute their performance to their motive for money rather than to a genuine interest or need for achievement. The result may be a decrease in intrinsic motivation on future tasks. This is perhaps one reason why organizations are turning to alternatives to money to spark motivation. As this chapter indicates, work motivation is a complex process and there are no easy answers, but there is a probability that extrinsic rewards can increase intrinsic motivation on at least interesting and challenging tasks.

**Source:** Adapted from Uco J. Wiersma, "The Effects of Extrinsic Rewards in Intrinsic Motivation: A Meta-Analysis," *Journal of Occupational and Organizational Psychology,* Vol. 65, 1992, pp. 101–114.

# OB PRINCIPLE FOR EVIDENCE-BASED PRACTICE

The more that employees perceive their work to be designed according to the characteristics in the job characteristics model (JCM), the more motivated and satisfied they will be.

## Meta-Analysis Results:

[72 studies; over 18,000 participants; $d = 1.6$] *On average, there is an **87 percent probability** that for employees who perceive the characteristics found in the job characteristics model (JCM) to be high, the higher their internal work motivation and overall job satisfaction will be compared to those who do not perceive these job characteristics.* Further analysis indicated that the critical psychological states of the JCM played a mediating role between job characteristics and outcomes.

## Conclusion:

The well-researched job characteristics model posits that the five core job dimensions (task identity, task significance, skill variety, feedback, and autonomy) designed into a job influence the critical psychological states of experienced meaningfulness, knowledge of results, and experienced responsibility, which in turn will affect work outcomes. The five job characteristics are measured by the perceptions of the jobholder and are combined into a single index called a motivating potential score (MPS). This MPS reflects the overall potential the job has to influence the employee's motivation and satisfaction. Overall, the job characteristics model represents a way to predict employee motivation and satisfaction and hopefully organizational outcomes such as quality of work and absenteeism/turnover.

**Source:** Adapted from Yitzhak Fried and Gerald R. Ferris, "The Validity of the Job Characteristics Model: A Review and Meta-Analysis," *Personnel Psychology*, Vol. 40, 1987, pp. 287–322.

# OB PRINCIPLE FOR EVIDENCE-BASED PRACTICE

Difficult, specific task goals will lead to a higher level of performance than routine, general goals such as "do your best."

## Meta-Analysis Results:

[Over 50 studies; over 5,800 participants; *d* range = .44 to .58] *On average, there is a **62 to 66 percent probability** that difficult and specific goals (if accepted) will lead to higher levels of task performance than easy or general "do-your-best" goals.* The setting (laboratory versus field) was found to be a moderator of the relationship, with lab studies in general having stronger findings.

## Conclusion:

Like job design (i.e., the JCM), goal setting has considerable research backup, but unlike the JCM, is a very commonly used motivational technique for enhancing human performance in today's organizations. Goals help clarify the sense of purpose and mission that is essential to success in the workplace. As the listed principle indicates, goal difficulty and goal specificity have been found to be strongly related to task performance across a wide variety of tasks and settings. This is because specific and challenging goals serve to focus employees' attention on exactly what is to be accomplished and to bring out their best performance. Moreover, as this chapter points out, goals must be specific and measurable so that employees know exactly what the goal is and can track their progress toward goal achievement. Goal setting as an indicator of performance represents one of the strongest and most consistent OB principles today. In addition, there are not many areas of the field of organizational behavior in which goal setting cannot play a role. For example, goal setting is widely recognized in areas such as cognitive motivation theories, self-efficacy, feedback-seeking behavior, job design, and behavioral management. In many ways, goal setting can be used as a prototype of how theory, research, and application should be done in organizational behavior.

**Source:** Adapted from Anthony J. Mento, Robert P. Steel, and Ronald J. Karren, "A Meta-Analytic Study of the Effects of Goal Setting on Task Performance: 1966–1984," *Organizational Behavior and Human Decision Processes*, Vol. 39, 1987, pp. 52–83.

| | |
|---|---|
| Questions for Discussion and Review | 1. Briefly define the basic motivation process and the two types of needs. What are some examples of each type of need? |
| | 2. What is the difference between an intrinsic and an extrinsic motive? Can both operate at the same time? If so, how? |
| | 3. In your own words, briefly explain Maslow's theory of motivation. Relate it to work motivation and Herzberg's model. |

4. What is the major criticism of Herzberg's two-factor theory of motivation? Do you think it makes a contribution to the better understanding of motivation in the workplace? Defend your answer.

5. In your own words, briefly explain the Porter-Lawler model of motivation. How do performance and satisfaction relate to each other?

6. Briefly give an example of an inequity that a manager of a small business might experience. How would the manager strive to attain equity in the situation you describe?

7. How does equity theory relate to procedural justice? Why is this so important to today's employees?

8. What is attribution theory? How can locus of control be applied to workers and managers?

9. What two major attribution errors or biases have surfaced? Give an example of each.

10. Briefly describe control theory and agency theory. What implications can these two theories have for work motivation?

11. What are the core job characteristics in the Hackman-Oldham model? How do you calculate the motivating potential of a job? How would a professor's job and a janitor's job measure up on these characteristics? Be specific in your answer.

12. In your own words, describe the theory behind goal setting. What has the research generally found in testing goal setting?

13. How does goal setting relate to goal orientation, benchmarking, stretch targets, and psychological contracts?

## Internet Exercises: What Types of Jobs Motivate You?

Now that you have a foundation for understanding human motivation from the chapter, it is very useful to understand what motivates you. Go to the Web site **http://company.monster.com/** and spend some time analyzing the jobs that they offer in your area of interest, and then answer the following questions.

1. Select one of the jobs listed. What motivational theories explain why or why not you would be a good, motivated employee in this job?

2. Would this job provide you motivation in each of Maslow's levels? How? How, if at all, would this job relate to Herzberg's two factors?

3. Using this job as a reference point, as best as you can trace through each step (the boxes in Figure 6.5) in the Porter and Lawler expectancy model of motivation.

## Internet Exercise: What Is the Motivation Potential of Jobs at Southwest Airlines?

Many companies have employment opportunities listed on their Web site. Go to **http://www.southwest.com/careers/** and look at the job openings at Southwest Airlines. Using the Hackman and Oldham job design model with identity, significance, skill variety, autonomy, and feedback, analyze the jobs listed according to each characteristic.

1. From a job design standpoint, which job would seem to have the most motivation potential? The least?

2. Of the jobs that you consider poorly designed, discuss some ways that they might be improved.

3. Compare these jobs to other companies that post jobs on their Web sites. Now go to company Web sites in manufacturing and the public sector in your local area that provide job openings and/or descriptions. Do you think some industries tend to have more motivating potential jobs than others?

# Real Case: *At UPS Managers Learn to Empathize with Their Employees*

At United Parcel Service Inc., rules are religion. Without them, UPS could never move millions of packages to their destinations on time each day. But a few years ago, Mark J. Colvard, a UPS manager in San Ramon, Calif., had to decide whether to buck the system. A driver needed time off to help an ailing family member, but under company rules he wasn't eligible. If Colvard went by the book, the driver would probably take the days anyway and be fired. If Colvard gave him the time off, he would catch flak from his other drivers. Colvard wound up giving the driver two weeks, took some heat—and kept a valuable employee.

Six months earlier, Colvard admits, he would have gone the other way. What changed his approach? A month he spent living among migrant farmers in McAllen, Tex., as part of a unusual UPS management training experience called the Community Internship Program (CIP). After building housing for the poor, collecting clothing for the Salvation Army, and working in a drug rehab center, Colvard said he was able to empathize with employees facing crises back home. And that, he says, has made him a better manager. "My goal was to make the numbers, and in some cases that meant not looking at the individual but looking at the bottom line," says Colvard. "After that one-month stay, I immediately started reaching out to people in a different way."

CIP began in 1968 as the brainchild of UPS founder James Casey, who wanted to open up the eyes of UPS's predominantly white managers to the poverty and inequality exploding into violence in many cities. By now, nearly 1,200 current and former middle managers have moved through the program. And it has evolved into an integral part of the UPS culture, teaching managers the crucial skill of flexibility at a company that is trying to fit a diverse base of employees into its rigid rules-based culture, which prescribes everything from how delivery people should carry their keys to how many steps they should take per second. UPS needs rules, but it also needs managers capable of bending them when necessary. "We've got 330,000 U.S. employees," says Don B. Wofford, the CIP coordinator and a graduate of the program. "There are all kinds of personalities and all kinds of diversity. We need managers who can manage those individuals."

In New York this summer, eight managers visited the emergency room at Bellevue Hospital, tutored inmates at Sing Sing in interviewing skills, and provided meals to the homeless. The experience took them far outside their comfort zones in ways large and small—whether it was using public transportation for the first time in years or an initial encounter with violent crime such as the triple homicide that took place a few steps from the Henry Street Settlement, the community center where they lived. "A lot of rising stars going off to this program have gotten sure of themselves. That leads them to be quick with solutions," says Jeffrey A. Sonnenfeld, an associate dean at Yale University's School of Management who has studied UPS. After CIP, "instead of reacting, they would listen. They learn incredible skills of empathy."

Managers who have been through the UPS program say it made them more likely to search for unconventional solutions. Patti Hobbs, a division manager in Louisville who spent a month on New York's Lower East Side, remembers being impressed by the creative ideas of uneducated addicts for steering teens away from drugs. Realizing that the best solutions sometimes come from those closest to the problem, she immediately started brainstorming with the entire staff instead of just senior managers. Says Hobbs: "You start to think there's no one person, regardless of position, who has all the answers. The answers come from us all."

One month living among the poor won't change the world. But it might help UPS managers see their employees as more than just a cog in a very efficient machine.

1. UPS through CIP (Community Internship Program) is trying to inject a new dimension into its corporate culture. What does this cultural change intend to look like and how can it affect the motivation of both managers and operating employees?

2. What motives can the CIP appeal to for the participating managers? What motivation theories could be used to explain the impact that the CIP may have on the participating managers?

3. UPS is known to pay their operating employees very high wages. Is this enough to motivate them? What from the case would support your answer?

# Real Case: *Making It a Nice Place to Work*

There are a number of ways in which organizations are trying to apply techniques to improve performance. For example, redesigning traditional, bureaucratic organizations and specialized jobs has emerged as a way to enhance employee satisfaction and performance. This can be done by restructuring the organization so that it is a more enjoyable, pleasant place in which to work. This is actually being accomplished in a number of different ways in the real world.

At Inhale Therapeutic Systems, a small start-up company in northern California that focuses on novel drug-delivery technology, everyone, including the president of the company, sits in large cubicles (they call them "bullpens") with four other people of various ranks and functions. There are no walls or barriers between any of them. This arrangement forces people to talk to each other, while limiting the amount of time they spend gossiping, and reduces the need to write memos and use e-mail—as, in most cases, the people to whom these messages would be directed are sitting in the same bullpen. Every nine months the company reshuffles everyone and assigns new bullpen partners. This arrangement has seemed to promote teamwork and reduce office politics.

At West Bend Mutual Insurance Company top management decided to make the workplace as comfortable as possible for people. Management put money where their mouth was by purchasing equipment that allows those in certain workstations to adjust the temperature, fresh air, and noise levels. Researchers from Rensselaer Polytechnic Institute have studied the impact of these changes and concluded that those who are allowed to control their own climate are at least 3 percent more productive than those who are not. The company management believe that these productivity increases are even higher, probably more in the range of 5 to 10 percent. In addition, the novel workstations have become an asset in recruiting and retaining workers.

Other companies are approaching the motivation challenge by asking: What else can we do to make the organization an enjoyable place to work? At Sun Microsystems, some members of top management are asking an even more radical question. Noting that many of their employees are never in the office because they are out in the field with clients or working from home, they ask: Why should we heat, cool, and clean offices when so few people ever use them? This has led management to consider reducing office space; if personnel who never come to the office need to get together for occasional meetings or face-to-face interactions, they can rent space at hotels or conference centers. Although this may not be the route Sun eventually takes, it does show that the old way of having everyone in their office from 9 to 5 may become a thing of the past.

An interesting issue that is beginning to emerge concerns "too much of a good thing." Is it possible that the new work arrangements such as those at Inhale Therapeutic Systems or West Bend Insurance will result in facilitating so much interaction that people become overstimulated or distracted? Moreover, the changes that are being made today may soon be outmoded by changes in tomorrow's technology, resulting in the need to reorganize the workplace again. On the positive side, however, some work design experts note:

> The good news . . . is that those involved in forging the new workplace realize there is no ideal, no cookie-cutter workplace template they can plop on top of organizations. And it's a rare alternative-office space that doesn't get adapted as trial runs reveal elements that don't work or could work better. "One thing we've realized is that not only must we assess what's possible but how far and how fast it can move." That would seem to signal an end to the age of the corporate "edifice complex" and a new era of workspaces that work.

1. How does redesign of jobs lead to improved performance and job satisfaction? In your answer include a discussion of Figure 6.2.

2. How do the examples in this case relate to the job characteristics model as discussed in this chapter?

3. Are we likely to see more workplace redesign in the future? Why or why not?

# Organizational Behavior Case: *What Do They Want?*

Pat Riverer is vice president of manufacturing and operations of a medium-size pharmaceutical firm in the Midwest. Pat has a Ph.D. in chemistry but has not been directly involved in research and new-product development for 20 years. From the "school of hard knocks" when it comes to managing operations, Pat runs a "tight ship." The company does not have a turnover problem, but it is obvious to Pat and other key management personnel that the hourly people are putting in only their eight hours a day. They are not working anywhere near their full potential. Pat is very upset with the situation because, with rising costs, the only way that the company can continue to prosper is to increase the productivity of its hourly people.

Pat called the human resources manager, Carmen Lopez, and laid it on the line: "What is it with our people, anyway? Your wage surveys show that we pay near the top in this region, our conditions are tremendous, and our fringes choke a horse. Yet these people still are not motivated. What in the world do they want?" Carmen replied: "I have told you and the president time after time that money, conditions, and benefits are not enough. Employees also need other things to motivate them. Also, I have been conducting some random confidential interviews with some of our hourly people, and they tell me that they are very discouraged because, no matter how hard they work, they get the same pay and opportunities for advancement as their coworkers who are just scraping by." Pat then replied: "Okay, you are the motivation expert; what do we do about it? We *have* to increase their performance."

1. Explain the "motivation problem" in this organization in terms of the content models of Maslow and Herzberg. What are the "other things" that the human resources manager is referring to in speaking of things besides money, conditions, and fringe benefits that are needed to motivate employees?

2. Explain the motivation of the employees in this company in terms of one or more of the process models. On the basis of the responses during the confidential interviews, what would you guess are some of the expectancies, valences, and inequities of the employees in this company? How about Pat?

3. How would you respond to Pat's last question and statement if you were the human resources manager in this company?

# Organizational Behavior Case: *Tom, Dick, and Harry*

You are in charge of a small department and have three subordinates—Tom, Dick, and Harry. The key to the success of your department is to keep these employees as motivated as possible. Here is a brief summary profile on each of these subordinates.

*Tom* is the type of employee who is hard to figure out. His absenteeism record is much higher than average. He greatly enjoys his family (a wife and three small children) and thinks they should be central to his life. The best way to describe Tom is to say that he is kind of a throwback to the hippie generation and believes deeply in the values of that culture. As a result, the things that the company can offer him really inspire him very little. He feels that the job is simply a means of financing his family's basic needs and little else. Overall, Tom does an adequate job and is very conscientious, but all attempts to get him to do more have failed. He has charm and is friendly, but he is just not "gung-ho" for the company. He is pretty much allowed to "do his own thing" as long as he meets the minimal standards of performance.

*Dick* is in many respects opposite from Tom. Like Tom, he is a likable guy, but unlike Tom, Dick responds well to the company's rules and compensation schemes and has a high degree of personal loyalty to the company. The problem with Dick is that he will not do very much independently. He does well with what is assigned to him, but he is not very creative or even dependable when he is on his own. He also is a relatively shy person who is not very assertive when dealing with people outside the department. This hurts his performance to some degree because he cannot immediately sell himself or the department to other departments in the company or to top management.

*Harry,* on the other hand, is a very assertive person. He will work for money and would readily change jobs for more money. He really works hard for the company but expects the company also to work for him. In his present job, he feels no qualms about working a 60-hour week, if the money is there. Even though he has a family and is supporting his elderly father, he once quit a job cold when his employer didn't give him a raise on the premise that he was already making too much. He is quite a driver. A manager at his last place of employ-ment indicated that, although Harry did do an excellent job for the company, his personality was so intense that they were glad to get rid of him. His former boss noted that Harry just seemed to be pushing all the time. If it wasn't for more money, it was for better fringe benefits; he never seemed satisfied.

1. Can you explain Tom's, Dick's, and Harry's motivations by one or more of the work-motivation models discussed in this chapter?
2. How, if at all, would equity theory apply to the analysis of the motivations of Tom, Dick, and Harry?

# Organizational Behavior Case: *The Rubber Chicken Award*

Kelly Sellers is really fed up with his department's performance. He knows that his people have a very boring job, and the way the technological process is set up leaves little latitude for what he has learned about vertically loading the job through job enrichment. Yet he is convinced that there must be some way to make it more interesting to do a dull job. "At least I want to find out for my people and improve their performance," he thinks.

The employees in Kelly's department are involved in the assembly of small hair dryer motors. There are 25 to 30 steps in the assembly process, depending on the motor that is being assembled. The process is very simple, and currently each worker completes only one or two steps of the operation. Each employee has his or her own assigned workstation and stays at that particular place for the entire day. Kelly has decided to try a couple of things to improve performance. First, he has decided to organize the department into work teams.

The members of each team would be able to move the workstations around as they desired. He has decided to allow each team to divide the tasks up as they see fit. Next, Kelly has decided to post each team's performance on a daily basis and to reward the team with the highest performance by giving them a "rubber chicken" award that they can display at their workbenches. The production manager, after checking with engineering, has reluctantly agreed to Kelly's proposal on a trial basis.

1. Do you think Kelly's approach to job redesign will work? Rate the core job dimensions from the Hackman-Oldham model of Kelly's employees before and after he redesigned their jobs. What could he do to improve these dimensions even more?
2. What will happen if this experiment does not work out and the production manager forces Kelly to return to the former task design?

# Organizational Behavior Case: *Specific Goals for Human Service*

Jackie Jordan is the regional manager of a state human services agency that provides job training and rehabilitation programs for the hearing impaired. Her duties include supervising counselors as well as developing special programs. One of the difficulties that Jackie has had was with a project supervisor, Kathleen O'Shean.

Kathleen is the coordinator of a three-year federal grant for a special project for the hearing impaired. Kathleen has direct responsibility for the funds and the goals of the project. The federal agency that made the grant made continuance of the three-year grant conditional on some "demonstrated progress" toward fulfilling the purpose of the grant. Jackie's problem with Kathleen was directly related to this proviso. She repeatedly requested that Kathleen develop some concrete goals for the grant project. Jackie wanted these goals written in a specific, observable, and measurable fashion. Kathleen continually gave Jackie very vague, nonmeasurable platitudes. Jackie, in turn, kept requesting greater clarification, but Kathleen's response was that the work that was being done was meaningful enough and took all her time. To take away from the work itself by writing these specific goals would only defeat the purpose of the grant. Jackie finally gave up and didn't push the issue further. One year later the grant was not renewed by the federal government because the program lacked "demonstrated progress."

1. Do you think Jackie was right in requesting more specific goals from Kathleen? Why or why not?

2. Do you think the federal government would have been satisfied with the goal-setting approach that Jackie was pushing as a way to demonstrate progress?

3. Would you have handled the situation differently if you were Jackie? How?

# Chapter Seven

# Positive Organizational Behavior and Psychological Capital

## Learning Objectives

- **Frame** the chapter in terms of the positive psychology movement.
- **Discuss** the theory, research, and application of self-efficacy/confidence, optimism, hope, and resiliency as best POB criteria-meeting psychological resources and when in combination represent psychological capital (PsyCap).
- **Feature** the theory, research, and development of psychological capital or PsyCap.
- **Present** the theory, research, and application of happiness/subjective well-being (SWB) as another positive construct.
- **Present** emotions, intelligence, and combined emotional intelligence (EI) as other positive constructs.

Just as the overall field of organizational behavior has become more comprehensive (as reflected in the social cognitive theoretical framework for this text, given detailed attention in Chapter 1), there are a few important variables that have more recently emerged to help in both the better understanding and the effective application of organizational behavior. This new positive organizational behavior approach draws from the positive psychology movement. The term *positive organizational behavior,* or simply *POB,* was coined and defined by this author (Luthans) as "the study and application of positive oriented human resource strengths and psychological capacities that can be measured, developed, and effectively managed for performance improvement in today's workplace."[1] Besides being positive[2] and a psychological resource capacity, to be included as a POB construct, the following operational criteria must be met:[3]

1. *Based on theory and research.* This criterion separates POB from the atheoretical, no research back-up popular, positive, self-help literature such as Steven Covey's *Seven Habits* or the best-seller *Who Moved My Cheese?* by Spencer Johnson. Like the positive psychology movement in general and the University of Michigan group's positive organizational scholarship (known as POS),[4] POB is based on constantly building theoretical grounding and continuing basic and applied research findings.

2. *Valid measures.* Related to the above criterion of needing a grounding in theory and research and to further differentiate from the popular self-development literature, to be included in POB, the construct must have reliable and valid measures.

3. *"Statelike" and thus open to development.* This criterion is especially critical to POB because it differentiates the approach from much of positive psychology. This criterion says that in order to be included in POB the construct must be statelike (situationally based, open to learning, change, and development) as opposed to traitlike (dispositional, relatively fixed across situations and time). Although on a continuum rather than dichotomous, the statelike criterion says that the psychological capacity can be developed and trained, whereas most of the positive psychology variables like virtue and character are more traitlike and thus relatively fixed.[5] The same is true of most of the mainstream organizational behavior constructs that come out of traitlike personality and motivation theories.

4. *Managed for performance improvement.* This criterion again separates POB from positive psychology. POB is concerned with the workplace and how the positive psychological resource capacity can be applied to improve human performance, that of both leaders/managers and human resources in general.

The positive psychological capacities that have been determined to best meet these four criteria and that will be covered in this chapter are efficacy, optimism, hope, and resiliency. When combined, these four positive psychological resources have been demonstrated theoretically[6] and empirically[7] to be a higher-order core factor that Luthans and colleagues term as psychological capital or PsyCap.[8] In addition, there are a number of other potential positive constructs that to varying degrees meet the above POB criteria[9] and the two featured in this chapter are happiness/subjective well-being (SWB) and emotional intelligence.

All texts to date give only very brief mention, if at all, to positive organizational behavior and psychological capital. However, there is now enough theory and research evidence on the linkage to desirable employee attitudes and effective performance in the workplace that they deserve special attention along with the established psychological constructs of personality, attitudes, and motivation. This chapter is framed in the positive psychology movement and then gives the theoretical background, research, and development of first efficacy, optimism, hope, and resiliency and then overall psychological capital. The balance of the chapter is devoted to the more widely recognized positive capacities of happiness (SWB) and emotional intelligence.

## POSITIVE PSYCHOLOGY

Mainly under the leadership of well-known psychologist Martin Seligman, the positive psychology movement emerged from a reaction to the almost exclusive preoccupation that psychology had given to the negative, pathological aspects of human functioning and behaving.[10] Seligman and a few others[11] became concerned several years ago that not enough attention was being given to the strengths and other positive features of people that make life worth living. Never claiming that they discovered the value of positivity, which has a very long and rich history, they simply wanted psychology to shift at least some of the emphasis away from just the worst things in life toward more of a balance to the study and understanding of some of the best things in life. The aim of *positive psychology* is to use scientific methodology to discover and promote the factors that allow individuals, groups, organizations, and communities to thrive. It is concerned with optimal human functioning instead of pathological human functioning.

In identifying the domain, Seligman and Csikszentmihalyi summarize the three levels of positive psychology as follows:[12]

1. *Valued subjective experiences.* Well-being, contentment, and satisfaction (in the past); hope and optimism (for the future); and flow and happiness (in the present).
2. *Positive individual traits.* The capacity for love and vocation, courage, interpersonal skill, aesthetic sensibility, perseverance, forgiveness, originality, future mindedness, spirituality, high talent, and wisdom.
3. *Civic virtues and the institutions that move individuals toward better citizenship.* Responsibility, nurturance, altruism, civility, moderation, tolerance, and work ethic.

These very "positive" goals have obvious implications not only for therapy, well-being, education, family life, social relations, and society at large, but, importantly, also for organizational life and behavior. In fact, there is considerable research evidence[13] that there is a significant (almost .3 average correlations in meta-analysis of numerous studies) correlation (also some causal evidence) between health (both physical and mental), relationships (both intimate and social) and work (both performance and satisfaction) or what could be called simply H-R-W well-being.[14] In other words, analogous to Bandura's triangular social cognitive model depicted in Chapter 1, the H-R-W model shown in Figure 7.1 indicates that there is an interactive, reciprocal determination between one's health, relationships, and work (i.e., individuals' health affects their relationships and their relationships affect their health, their health affects their work and their work affects their health, and so forth).

Importantly, evidence has now grown to the point where research positive psychologists such as Sonja Lyubomirsky confidently conclude that one's happiness (or level of positivity or H-R-W well-being) is determined as follows:[15]

1. About half can be attributed to a genetic, dispositional "hard-wiring" (but not immutable) set point. This seems like a lot, but as Lyubomirsky points out, "appreciate the fact that 50 percent is a long way from 100 percent, and that leaves ample room for improvement."[16]
2. Surprisingly, only about 10 percent seems to be the result of life's circumstances. As Lyubomirsky notes, "Although you may find it hard to believe, whether you drive to work in a Lexus hybrid or a battered truck, whether you're young or old, or have had

**FIGURE 7.1**
**The H-R-W Model (The Interaction of Health, Relationship, and Work)**

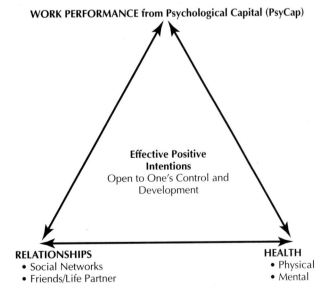

WORK PERFORMANCE from Psychological Capital (PsyCap)

**Effective Positive Intentions**
Open to One's Control and Development

**RELATIONSHIPS**
• Social Networks
• Friends/Life Partner

**HEALTH**
• Physical
• Mental

wrinkle-removing plastic surgery, whether you live in the frigid Midwest or the balmy West Coast, your chances of being happy and becoming happier are pretty much the same."[17]

3. Most importantly, the remaining 40 percent of one's happiness, positivity, or H-R-W well-being is determined by intentional activity. Knowing that such a large portion is under one's own control "is to appreciate the promise of the great impact that you can make on your own life through intentional strategies that you can implement to remake yourself as a happier person."[18]

It is from this relatively large 40 percent intentional component that positive organizational behavior in general and psychological capital in particular can have input and make an impact. Remembering the POB criterion of being *statelike* and open to development, the criteria-meeting POB positive psychological resources of efficacy, hope, optimism, and resiliency (and when combined into the core construct of psychological capital) can intentionally be used by one's self or by leading human resources to directly impact work performance, and, in turn, relationships and health. Using this work done in positive psychology as the foundation and point of departure, the theory, research, and development of the four major POB constructs and overall PsyCap are now examined in depth.

# SELF-EFFICACY/CONFIDENCE

The first and most theoretically developed and researched POB construct is self-efficacy. It may also be most relevant, at least for this particular text on organizational behavior, because as was presented in Chapter 1, social cognitive theory serves both as the conceptual framework for this text and the theory from which self-efficacy is derived. Largely due to the work of well-known psychologist Albert Bandura over the past three decades, self-efficacy has a widely acclaimed theoretical foundation,[19] an extensive body of knowledge gathered through basic research,[20] and proven effectiveness in a number of application areas, including the workplace.[21] Unmatched by any of the constructs covered in this text, to date nine large-scale meta-analyses consistently demonstrate that efficacy beliefs contribute significantly to the level of motivation and performance.[22] In POB, we tend to use the term *self-efficacy* interchangeably with confidence. We do this to recognize the rich theoretical and research foundation associated with self-efficacy, but also the more common and simplistic term of *confidence* more often used with application in business and sports.[23] In this more academic discussion, the term *efficacy* will tend to be used. After the meaning, process, and impact are provided, the sources and development of efficacy are given attention, and, finally, its application to human performance in organizations.

## The Theoretical Background and Meaning of Efficacy

Chapter 1 summarized Bandura's social cognitive theory (SCT). SCT incorporates both social/environmental and cognitive elements and the behaviors themselves. SCT explains psychological functioning in terms of environmental events; internal personal factors in the form of cognitive, affective, and biological variables; and behavioral patterns. These three (environment, personal cognitions, and behavior) operate as interacting determinants that influence one another bidirectionally. Embedded within SCT, along with the human's capabilities of symbolizing, forethought, and observational learning, is a self-theory including both self-regulation and self-reflection. It is the capability for self-reflection—people reflect back on their actions/experience with a specific event/task to then cognitively process how strongly they believe they can successfully accomplish this event/task in the future—that serves as the theoretical basis for self-efficacy.[24]

Bandura strongly emphasizes that this self-efficacy is the most pervading and important of the psychological mechanisms of self-influence. He declares, "Unless people believe that they can produce desired effects and forestall undesired ones by their actions, they have little incentive to act. Whatever other factors may operate as motivators, they are rooted in the core belief that one has the power to produce desired results."[25]

The formal definition of self-efficacy that is usually used is Bandura's early statement of personal judgment or belief of "how well one can execute courses of action required to deal with prospective situations."[26] A somewhat broader, more workable definition for positive organizational behavior is provided by Stajkovic and Luthans: "*Self-efficacy* refers to an individual's conviction (or confidence) about his or her abilities to mobilize the motivation, cognitive resources, and courses of action needed to successfully execute a specific task within a given context."[27] Notice that this definition deals with efficacy on a specific task and context. To further clarify the exact meaning of self-efficacy as it is used here in meeting the criteria of positive organizational behavior, specific versus general efficacy needs to be clarified. Earlier the differentiation between the various POB constructs was briefly discussed, but the difference between self-efficacy and closely related established organizational behavior constructs such as self-esteem, expectancy motivation, and attribution/locus of control also needs to be addressed.

### Specific versus General Self-Efficacy

Specific self-efficacy follows Bandura's conceptualization and is widely recognized by almost all efficacy scholars and the psychology field as a whole.[28] In recent years, however, general self-efficacy has been used as another dimension of self-efficacy by a few efficacy researchers.[29] They suggest that in addition to specific self-efficacy, there is a generalized efficacy that reflects people's belief in successfully accomplishing tasks across a wide variety of achievement situations. It should be recognized that this generalized efficacy is quite different from Bandura's portrayal of self-efficacy. In particular, the accepted task-specific version of self-efficacy is *statelike,* and thus meets this important criterion for POB. Specific self-efficacy is highly variable depending on the specific task and is cognitively processed by the individual before any effort is expended.

Bandura argues that self-efficacy represents a task-and situation-specific cognition.[30] On the other hand, general efficacy is conceptually the opposite; it is *traitlike.* That is, general efficacy is relatively stable over time and across situations; in this regard it is like a personality trait.[31] Bandura contends with his years of theory building and basic research that "an efficacy belief is not a decontextualized trait."[32] However, Bandura and others point out that even though self-efficacy is not traitlike, this does not mean that specific self-efficacy evaluations never generalize.[33] Instead, although not necessarily stable across situations, efficacy judgments on one task may generalize to others depending on the situation, the task, and the person.

In summary, as presented here as a POB construct, self-efficacy is statelike and therefore is aimed at specific tasks and open to training and development. For example, a systems analyst may have high self-efficacy on solving a particular programming problem, but low self-efficacy on writing up a report for the CIO (chief information officer) on how the problem was solved. Importantly for POB, this low efficacy can be raised through training and development, and the enhanced efficacy will result in improved performance.

### How Self-Efficacy Differs from Established Organizational Behavior Concepts

At first glance self-efficacy appears very similar and is often confused with widely recognized organizational behavior concepts, in particular, self-esteem (Chapter 5) and expectancy motivation (Chapter 6). The same confusion also often surfaces with the well-known construct of attribution/locus of control (covered in Chapter 6). A brief summary of the major differences will help clarify the exact meaning of self-efficacy.[34]

1. *Self-efficacy vs. self-esteem.* Following from the preceding discussion of specific versus general self-efficacy, there is no question that general self-efficacy is very similar to self-esteem, but the widely accepted specific self-efficacy as used here is quite different. The first difference is that self-esteem is a global construct of one's evaluation and belief of overall worthiness, whereas self-efficacy is one's belief about a task-and context-specific capability. Second, self-esteem is stable and traitlike, whereas self-efficacy is changing over time as new information and task experiences are gained and developed and is statelike. Finally, self-esteem is aimed at any aspect of one's current self, whereas self-efficacy is a current assessment of one's future success at a task. [35] An example of the differences would be the salesperson who has high self-efficacy of selling a luxury item to low-income customers, but low self-esteem because he knows his career has been based on selling unneeded items to his customers and this takes away from their ability to buy some of the basic necessities for their families.

2. *Self-efficacy vs. expectancy concepts.* Chapter 6 briefly discussed under expectancy theories of motivation the effort-performance (sometimes called E1) and behavior-outcome (sometimes referred to as E2) expectancy relationships. Although E1 and self-efficacy would both say that effort leads to performance, self-efficacy involves much more. Self-efficacy beliefs also involve perceptions of ability, skill, knowledge, experience with the specific task, complexity of the task, and more. In addition, self-efficacy has psychomotor reactions such as emotions, stress, and physical fatigue. With the E2 (behavior-outcome expectancy) there are even more pronounced differences. The process is different—efficacy is a judgment of one's ability to successfully execute a certain behavior pattern (i.e., "I believe I can successfully execute this task"), whereas the outcome expectancy is a judgment of the probable consequence such behavior will produce (i.e., "I believe that what I do will (or will not) lead to desired outcomes"). In other words, the individual's self-efficacy evaluation will usually come before any behavior outcome expectancies are even considered.[36]

3. *Self-efficacy vs. attribution/locus of control.* The third close, but different, construct that is often confused with self-efficacy comes from attribution theory, specifically locus of control. Those who make internal attributions about their behavior and its consequences (success or failure) believe they are in control of their own fate (e.g., "It is my effort or ability that makes the difference") and assume personal responsibility for the consequences of their behavior. Externals, on the other hand, make attributions to the circumstances ("The task was too hard") or to luck and do not take personal responsibility for the consequences of their behavior. Bandura has argued that locus of control attributions are causal beliefs about action-outcome contingencies, whereas self-efficacy is an individual's belief about his or her abilities and cognitive resources that can be marshaled together to successfully execute a specific task.[37]

Although the differences outlined above may seem quite technical, they must be pointed out to make sure that self-efficacy is indeed a valid, independent construct and help clarify its exact meaning.

## The Process and Impact of Self-Efficacy

The self-efficacy process affects human functioning not only directly, but has an indirect impact on other determinants as well. Directly, the self-efficacy process starts before individuals select their choices and initiate their effort. First, people tend to weigh, evaluate, and integrate information about their perceived capabilities.[38] Importantly, this initial stage of the process has little to do with individuals' abilities or resources per se, but rather how they perceive or believe they can use these abilities and resources to accomplish the given task in this context. This evaluation/perception then leads to the expectations of personal efficacy which, in turn, determines:[39]

1. The decision to perform the specific task in this context
2. The amount of effort that will be expended to accomplish the task
3. The level of persistence that will be forthcoming despite problems, disconfirming evidence, and adversity

In other words, from the preceding it can be seen that self-efficacy can directly affect:

1. *Choice behaviors* (e.g., decisions will be made based on how efficacious the person feels toward the options in, say, work assignments or even a career field)
2. *Motivational effort* (e.g., people will try harder and give more effort on tasks where they have high self-efficacy than those where the efficacy judgment is low)
3. *Perseverance* (e.g., those with high self-efficacy will bounce back, be resilient when meeting problems or even failure, whereas those with low self-efficacy tend to give up when obstacles appear)

In addition, there is research evidence that self-efficacy can also directly affect:[40]

4. *Facilitative thought patterns* (e.g., efficacy judgments influence self-talks such as those with high self-efficacy might say to themselves, "I know I can figure out how to solve this problem," whereas those with low self-efficacy might say to themselves, "I knew I couldn't do this, I don't have this kind of ability")
5. *Vulnerability to stress* (e.g., those with low self-efficacy tend to experience stress and burnout because they expect failure, whereas those with high self-efficacy enter into potential stressful situations with confidence and assurance and thus are able to resist stressful reactions)

These examples of the direct impact of efficacy on human functioning are right in line with high-performing individuals. Perhaps the best *profile of a high performer* on a given task would be the highly efficacious individual who really gets into the task (welcomes it and looks at it as a challenge); gives whatever effort it takes to successfully accomplish the task; perseveres when meeting obstacles, frustrations, or setbacks; has positive self-thoughts and talks; and is resistant to stress and burnout.

As if this high-performance profile is not enough, Bandura emphasizes that efficacy also plays a vital role in other important human performance determinants such as goal aspirations, the incentives in outcome expectations, and the perceived opportunities of a given project.[41] What level of goal is selected, how much effort is expended to reach the selected goal, and how one reacts/perseveres when problems are encountered in progressing toward the goal all seem to be greatly affected by self-efficacy.[42] So do the outcome incentives people anticipate. Those with high self-efficacy expect to succeed and gain favorable, positive outcome incentives, whereas those with low self-efficacy expect to fail and conjure up negative outcome disincentives (i.e., "I won't get anything out of this anyway"). Especially relevant to strategy formulation, entrepreneurial start-ups, and struggling transitionary economies in developing countries,[43] Bandura comments on the perceptions of opportunities as follows:

> People of high efficacy focus on the opportunities worth pursuing, and view obstacles as surmountable. Through ingenuity and perseverance they figure out ways of exercising some control even in environments of limited opportunities and many constraints. Those beset with

self-doubts dwell on impediments which they view as obstacles over which they can exert little control, and easily convince themselves of the futility of effort. They achieve limited success even in environments that provide many opportunities.[44]

Whether direct or indirect through other processes, high efficacy is strongly related and very predictive of high performance. The extensive research solidly supports this conclusion. Not only does Bandura's seminal book on self-efficacy cite hundreds and hundreds of studies, but, as the introductory comments indicated, there are no less than nine meta-analyses (including ours reported in the section at the end of the chapter, Ending with Meta-Analytic Research Findings[45]) that consistently find a positive relationship between self-efficacy and performance in different spheres of functioning under laboratory and naturalistic conditions.[46]

## Sources of Efficacy

Because Bandura has provided such a comprehensive, rich theoretical understanding, backed by years of research, there is common agreement on the principal sources of self-efficacy. Shown in Figure 7.2, it must be remembered from social cognitive theory that these four sources of efficacy only provide the raw data. The individual must select out, cognitively process, and self-reflect in order to integrate and use this information to make self-efficacy perceptual judgments and form beliefs. For example, the major input into self-efficacy of performance attainments, Bandura notes, "may vary depending on their interpretive biases, the difficulty of the task, how hard they worked at it, how much help they received, the conditions under which they performed, their emotional and physical state at the time, their rate of improvement over time, and selective biases in how they monitor and recall their attainments."[47] In other words, successful performance does not automatically raise the level of efficacy. Rather, the efficacy depends on how the individual interprets and cognitively processes the success.

In order of importance, the following briefly summarizes the major sources of information for self-efficacy:

**FIGURE 7.2**
**The Major Sources of Information for Self-Efficacy**

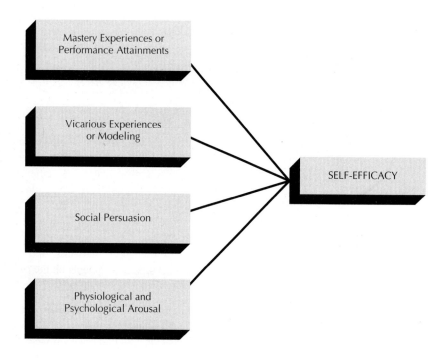

1. *Mastery experiences or performance attainments.* This is potentially the most powerful for forming efficacy beliefs because it is direct information about success. However, once again, it should be emphasized that performance accomplishments do not directly equate with self-efficacy. Both situational (e.g., the complexity of the task) and cognitive processing (e.g., the perception of one's ability) concerning the performance will affect the efficacy judgment and belief. Bandura also points out that mastery experiences gained through perseverant effort and ability to learn form a strong and resilient sense of efficacy, but efficacy built from successes that came easily will not be characterized by much perseverance when difficulties arise and will change more quickly.[48]

2. *Vicarious experiences or modeling.* Just as individuals do not need to directly experience reinforced personal behaviors in order to learn (they can vicariously learn by observing and modeling relevant others who are reinforced), the same is true of acquiring efficacy. As stated by Bandura, "If people see others like themselves succeed by sustained effort, they come to believe that they, too, have the capacity to succeed. Conversely, observing the failure of others instills doubts about one's own ability to master similar activities."[49] It is important to emphasize that the more similar the model (e.g., demographics such as age, sex, physical characteristics, and education, as well as status and experience) and the more relevant the task being performed, the more effect there will be on the observer's efficacy processing. This vicarious source of information is particularly important for those with little direct experience (e.g., a new assignment) and as a practical strategy to enhance people's efficacy through training and development.

3. *Social persuasion.* Not as powerful a source of information as the previous two, and sometimes oversimplified as a "can-do" approach, people's belief in their efficacy can be strengthened by respected, competent others persuading them that they "have what it takes" and providing positive feedback on progress being made on this particular task. On the other side of the coin, there is no question of the powerful impact that unkind words and negative feedback (e.g., "you can't do that") have in disabling and deflating one's confidence. Too often, a small negative comment or even nonverbal gesture can have a big impact on one's emotions and efficacy. Unfortunately, giving people positive feedback and pointing out their strengths for successfully accomplishing a task does not seem to be processed by most people with as much impact as the negative. However, by being genuine, providing objective information, and then taking follow-up actions to actually set up the individual for success and not failure, social persuasion can be selected and processed for building efficacy. Such social persuasion becomes more useful to fill in gaps when people begin to struggle or doubt themselves while pursuing a task than it is in trying to build one's efficacy for a new task.

4. *Physiological and psychological arousal.* People often rely on how they feel, physically and emotionally, in order to assess their capabilities. More than the other sources of information, if these are negative (e.g., the person is very tired and/or not physically well or is particularly anxious/depressed and/or feels under a lot of pressure) this will generally greatly detract from efficacy. On the other hand, if these physical and mental states are well off, they don't necessarily process as contributing much to the individual's efficacy. On balance, however, if the individual is in excellent physical and mental condition, this can serve as a good point of departure to build efficacy in other ways and may even in and of itself arouse a person's efficacy on a physically and/or psychologically demanding task.

Importantly for organizational behavior and human resource management, each of these sources of efficacy are highly malleable and changeable. As discussed earlier, specific self-efficacy is a state, not a trait. In other words, self-efficacy can definitely be enhanced

**TABLE 7.1** **Implications of Self-Efficacy for Effective Training**

*Source:* Adapted from Robert F. Mager, "No Self-Efficacy, No Performance," *Training,* April 1992, pp. 34–36.

| Sources of Efficacy: | Key for Successful Training and Transfer to the Job | Training Recommendations |
| --- | --- | --- |
| **1. Mastery experience and performance attainment** | Trainees must learn they are the cause of their performance. | 1. Plenty of practice so mastery (as defined by the training objectives) is reached. 2. Break learning into series of obtainable endpoints to help-self-confirmation of skills. 3. Provide feedback on progress (not shortfalls) and contributions |
| **2. Vicarious experience and modeling** | Model(s) used should have similar demographic attributes, and the training being done should be similar to what the trainees will be doing back on the job. | 1. Carefully select models used in the training to have similar characteristics as the trainees. 2. Set up training so that trainees perceive performance is due to the capability of the model and not other factors. 3. Models should take a task-diagnostic perspective (i.e., focus on task and if mistake is made, interpret as way to learn rather than personal inadequacy). |
| **3. Social persuasion** | All comments have impact, so feedback must be phrased positively to build trainee confidence. | 1. Set trainees up for success so feedback comments can be very positive. 2. Trainers must be careful and sensitive to keep positive things that are said and done in the presence of the trainee. |
| **4. Physical and psychological arousal** | Make sure trainees experiencing physical or psychological symptoms interpret them as the nature of the training task and not some personal inadequacy (i.e., lack of ability). | 1. Trainees must understand that the need to exert considerable physical (or psychological) effort does not mean a lack of personal capability. 2. Getting trainees physically and psychologically fit may help arouse motivation to learn and be successful. |

through training and development targeted at these four sources. For example, as shown in Table 7.1, training expert Robert Mager has pinpointed specific training implications for each of the sources of self-efficacy. In fact, developing self-efficacy in trainees may be a solution to the long-standing problem of transferring training to the job. As Mager notes,

> People need a strong sense of efficacy before they will *try* to apply what they have learned and before they will try to learn new things. Belief in their ability to perform makes them less vulnerable to on-the-job conditions that aren't always supportive. It helps them to survive rejection. It helps them to persevere in the face of obstacles and setbacks.[50]

Self-efficacy not only has these important implications for training, but also for many other areas of today's workplace as well.

## Implications for Efficacy in the Workplace and POB

Self-efficacy theory was first used over 30 years ago as a clinical framework "for analyzing changes achieved in fearful and avoidant behavior."[51] Psychotherapeutic treatments such as desensitization, symbolic modeling, and firsthand mastery experiences were clearly found to change behavior of clients through the common pathway of perceived self-efficacy. However, the scope of efficacy quickly broadened beyond this domain of clinical behavior change to be successfully applied in areas such as: (1) the promotion of health and recovery from physical setbacks, (2) the control of eating, (3) resistance to addictive substances, (4) educational achievement, (5) athletic performance, and, importantly, (6) for the study and application of organizational behavior and performance in work settings.[52]

Whereas the POB constructs discussed next have to date relatively few research studies in the workplace, efficacy has a very well-established body of knowledge as to its applicability and positive impact on work-related performance. Specifically, our (Stajkovic and Luthans) meta-analysis included 114 studies and 21,616 subjects.[53] The results indicated a highly significant, .38 weighted average correlation between self-efficacy and work-related performance. When converted to the effect size estimate commonly used in meta-analysis, the transformed value represents a 28 percent increase in performance due to self-efficacy.[54] By comparison, these results for self-efficacy in the workplace represent a greater average gain in performance than the results from the meta-analyses of other popular organizational behavior interventions such as goal setting (10.39%),[55] feedback (13.6%),[56] or organizational behavior modification (17%),[57] and also seems to be a better predictor of work-related performance than the personality traits (e.g., the "Big Five") or relevant attitudes (e.g., job satisfaction or organizational commitment) commonly used in organizational behavior research.[58] Also, a subanalysis of recent research on PsyCap indicated that the efficacy component by itself was significantly related to work performance and job satisfaction across different samples.[59]

Although the workplace is given considerable attention in Bandura's widely recognized book, *Self-Efficacy,*[60] more recently he provided a focused review of the growing research literature of the direct and indirect impact that self-efficacy has on work-related personal and organizational effectiveness.[61] This research review of the impact of self-efficacy includes a wide range of organizational behavior topics such as career choice and development, new employee training, work design/job enrichment, supportive communication, teams (i.e., collective efficacy), innovation, entrepreneurship, leadership, and stress. He then devotes considerable attention to the strategies and principles for developing and strengthening beliefs of personal efficacy in the workplace.

From this considerable body of theory and research on self-efficacy, the following sections offer some practical implications and specific guidelines for the more effective practice of managing human performance in today's and future organizations.

### *Selection of Human Resources*

In hiring for a particular job, making an assignment to a specific project, or promoting someone into an identifiable area of responsibility, assessing the person's present magnitude and strength of self-efficacy could be valuable input into the selection decision. *Magnitude* measures the level of task difficulty that a person believes he or she is capable of executing, and *strength* indicates whether the magnitude is strong and likely to produce perseverance when difficulties are encountered.[62]

**FIGURE 7.3**
**An Example of a Self-Efficacy Scale Developed for an Auto Sales Position**

| Number of Car Sales per month | Yes or No | Strength of Certainty (0–100%) |
|---|---|---|
| I believe I can sell 2 | | |
| I believe I can sell 4 | | |
| I believe I can sell 6 | | |
| I believe I can sell 8 | | |
| I believe I can sell 10 | | |
| I believe I can sell 12 | | |
| I believe I can sell 14 | | |
| I believe I can sell 16 | | |
| Totals | | |

Although most applicable to specific tasks within a job assignment or promotion, self-efficacy scales could be set up for each of the major tasks or for the overall domain of a given job. This scale would include, in ascending order, items that represent the increasing levels of difficulty. The respondent would check for each item yes or no (magnitude) and then next to it 0–100 percent probability of attainment (i.e., strength). Figure 7.3 shows such a scale. The efficacy scores are derived by getting a total of the probability strengths for each item with a yes. This so-called Composite I method of scoring has been shown to be a valid measure of self-efficacy and more reliable than other measures.[63]

If regular questionnaire item scales are developed, they should be tailor-made for each specific selection purpose. Bandura advises that the content of such scales "must represent beliefs about personal abilities to produce specified levels of performance, and must not include other characteristics."[64] Of course, people should not be selected only on the basis of their present self-efficacy assessment, but because it has been found to be such a good predictor of performance, self-efficacy could make a significant contribution to the selection process. This assessment could also be used as a training and development needs analysis.

### Training and Development

As discussed previously (see Table 7.1), because self-efficacy is a state (rather than a stable trait) and the sources have been identified (see Figure 7.2 and accompanying discussion), efficacy training and development can have considerable impact for employee performance management. Training can be set up around each (and in combination) of the sources of efficacy listed in Table 7.1.

Bandura recently categorized his approach to training and development into three areas.[65] First is what he calls *guided mastery,* which includes instructive modeling to acquire a skill or competency, guided skill perfection, and then transferring the training back to the job to ensure self-directed success. Second is for the more complex—but increasingly common for all levels in the modern workplace—ways to enhance efficacy for decision making and problem solving. He calls this *cognitive mastery modeling* to learn thinking skills and how to apply them by observing the decision rules and reasoning strategies successful models use as they arrive at solutions to problems and make effective decisions. For example, one study taught managers how to generate ideas to improve the quality of organizational functioning and customer service by providing them guidelines and practice in innovative problem solving.[66] Finally, he suggests the *development of self-regulatory competencies* (i.e., self-motivation or self-management).

The development of this increasingly important self-management involves a variety of interlinked self-referent processes such as self-monitoring, self-efficacy appraisal, personal goal setting, and use of self-motivating incentives.[67] A meta-analysis (117 studies) evaluating the effects of behavioral modeling training (BMT) found:[68]

1. The largest effects of BMT were on learning outcomes, but BMT also had an impact on job behavior and results outcomes.
2. Although the BMT effects on knowledge decayed over time, the effects on skills and job behavior remained stable or even increased.
3. The greatest impact of BMT was when:
   a. both negative and positive models were presented;
   b. practice included trainee-generated scenarios;
   c. trainers were instructed to set goals;
   d. trainees' supervisors were also trained; and
   e. rewards and sanctions were instituted in the trainees' work environment.

Whether using the more pragmatic training aimed at enhancing the four sources discussed earlier (Table 7.1 summarizes) or these more sophisticated approaches suggested by Bandura and others, there is proven effectiveness of this training and development of self-efficacy,[69] and the potential for the future seems unlimited. For example, our research has found that training managers and employees in manufacturing, insurance, and the public sector using Bandura's sources was able to significantly increase their efficacy beliefs of successfully coping with diversity initiatives.[70] As part of a larger PsyCap study including efficacy (and the other positive capacities covered next), we were able to raise the level of efficacy as part of PsyCap in an experimental, control group study design,[71] and also we have demonstrated the dollar utility impact on participants' performance improvement.[72]

### *Other Applications*

Besides selection and training/development, self-efficacy also has implications for stress management (Chapter 9), self-managed teams (Chapter 11), job design and goal setting (Chapter 6), and leadership (Chapters 13 and 14). One applications approach backed by research has been to enhance self-efficacy to better cope with stress[73] and facilitate productive teamwork[74] and collective efficacy[75] of self-managed teams. Another approach would be to use job designs that provide more responsibility, challenge, and empowered personal control over the work to enhance the jobholder's perception of self-efficacy.[76] In setting goals, goal difficulty and commitment will be affected by self-efficacy. By the same token, goal progress and attainment will in turn affect self-efficacy.[77] In addition to these more established applications, a more recent study has shown that efficacy can be applied to the creative process in organizations. It was found that creative self-efficacy (employees' beliefs that they can be creative in their work roles) predicted creative performance beyond the predictive effects of job self-efficacy.[78]

Perhaps at least potentially the most significant but still largely overlooked implication for application lies in leadership efficacy.[79] Although the importance of a leader's confidence has been recognized in the leadership literature over the years,[80] to date there have been very few attempts to measure and research the proposition drawn from self-efficacy theory and research presented here,[81] that leadership efficacy will have a strong positive impact on followers (e.g., the leader can serve as a model to enhance followers' self-efficacy) and performance outcomes. As part of the POB theoretical foundation and the positive, authentic, approach to leadership, we do include confidence/efficacy,[82] and this will be given attention in the leadership chapters. In addition, self-efficacy has implications for most of the remaining chapters in both Part Three, Dynamics of Organizational Behavior, and Part Four, Managing and Leading for High Performance.

# OPTIMISM

Optimism is a major construct in positive psychology and has long been recognized by both psychologists and people in general. The positive impact of optimism on physical and psychological health and the attendant characteristics of perseverance, achievement, and motivation leading to academic, athletic, political, and occupational success are well documented. By the same token, pessimism is known to lead to passivity, failure, social estrangement, and, in its extreme, depression and mortality.

Not as well known, except for the psychological researchers in the area, is that optimism also can have drawbacks, dysfunctions, and costs. Well people tend to be optimistic about their future health and therefore often neglect needed nutritional and physical maintenance, or in an organization optimistic managers may become distracted from making the necessary action plans to attain goals or contingency plans for clearly impending problems. For example, one expert on the financial crisis at the end of 2008 observed:

> The recent recklessness of residential and commercial real-estate lending was in plain view, and a vocal minority wrote about it. But the financial and business communities dismissed all the warnings, insisting that any damage—should it ever arrive—would be contained to the subprime section. The folly was obvious. Even if decision makers had deemed the grim forecasts to be of low probability, the potential outcomes were so dire that they demanded contingency plans.[83]

The problem of unbridled optimism, especially in retrospect when things go wrong, does seem to be a bigger problem than the downside of the other positive constructs (e.g., overconfidence or false hope). However, optimism is receiving growing attention in psychology, but except for the general knowledge carryover, the field of organizational behavior has to date largely neglected optimism as an important concept and application in improving employee performance.

In defining optimism, contemporary positive psychologists go far beyond the old adage of the "power of positive thinking" popularized by widely read and heard writers a number of years ago, such as Norman Vincent Peale and Dale Carnegie, in recent times Tony Robbins and Steven Covey, and political leaders such as Franklin Roosevelt, Ronald Reagan, and Barack Obama. Psychology treats optimism as a cognitive characteristic in terms of a generalized positive outcome expectancy (see Chapter 6) and/or a positive causal attribution. Optimism is also often used in relation to other positive constructs such as hope (covered next) and emotional intelligence. Emotional intelligence expert Daniel Goleman, for instance, devotes considerable attention to the role of optimism in his discussions of emotional intelligence and even at one point refers to optimism as an emotionally intelligent attitude.[84] However, as positive psychologist Christopher Peterson points out in a comprehensive analysis, "Optimism is not simply cold cognition, and if we forget the emotional flavor that pervades optimism, we can make little sense of the fact that optimism is both motivated and motivating."[85]

## The Dimensions of Optimism

Most psychologists treat optimism as human nature and/or an individual difference. Unfortunately, like other psychological and organizational behavior concepts, there are still many unresolved issues surrounding optimism.

### *Optimism as Human Nature*

Both the early philosophers (Sophocles, Nietzsche) and psychologists/psychiatrists (Freud, Allport, Erikson, Menninger) were generally negative about optimism. They felt that optimism was largely an illusion and that a more accurate perception of the hard facts of reality was more conducive to healthy psychological functioning. However, starting in the 1960s and 1970s, cognitive psychologists began to demonstrate that many people tend to have a more positive bias of themselves than cold reality, and that psychologically healthy people in particular have this positive bias. This positivity has gone all the way to being portrayed by some anthropologists, evolutionary psychologists, and neuropsychologists as inherent in the makeup of people—part of their basic human nature.[86]

### *Optimism as an Individual Difference*

More in tune with mainstream modern psychology is to treat optimism (as with other psychological constructs) as an individual difference; people have varying degrees of optimism. Treating optimism as an individual difference focuses on cognitively determined expectations and causal attributions. Most closely associated with the expectancy theoretical perspective are Carver and Scheier who simply state, "optimists are people who expect good things to happen to them; pessimists are people who expect bad things to happen to them."[87] Seligman, on the other hand, is associated with the attributional approach. He uses the term *explanatory style* to depict how an individual habitually attributes the causes of failure, misfortune, or bad events.[88] This explanatory style is an outgrowth of Seligman's earlier work on *learned helplessness* (also covered in Chapter 9 on stress and conflict). He had found that dogs and then humans, when continually experiencing uncontrollable, punishing, aversive events, eventually learn to be helpless. This helplessness generalized to the point that even when the animals or humans could subsequently control and escape the aversive conditions, they still acted in a helpless manner. Importantly, however, not all the subjects learned to be helpless. About a third resisted; they persevered and refused to give in and be helpless. Seligman extended this work on learned helplessness into generalized causal attributions or explanatory styles of optimism and pessimism.

Here are the causal attributions or explanatory style pessimists and optimists tend to habitually use in interpreting personal bad events:[89]

1. *Pessimists* make *internal* (their own fault), *stable* (will last a long time), and *global* (will undermine everything they do) attributions.
2. *Optimists* make *external* (not their fault), *unstable* (temporary setback), and *specific* (problem only in this situation) attributions.

Research continues on explanatory style, and it has been found that the internality attribution does not hold up as well as the stability or globality.[90] Overall, however, no matter how optimism is measured, it has been shown to be significantly linked with desirable characteristics such as happiness, perseverance, achievement, and health.[91] Again, under positive psychology, the emphasis shifted in both theory building and research from what can go wrong with people (e.g., learned helplessness, pessimism, and depression) to what can go right for people (e.g., optimism, health, and success).[92]

### *Some Unresolved Optimism Issues*

Even though there is considerably more research and definitive conclusions on optimism than, say, emotional intelligence, there is still much room for conceptual refinement and further research. Peterson identifies and summarizes three of the more important optimism issues as follows:[93]

1. *Little vs. big optimism.*  The magnitude and level of optimism may function quite differently. Little optimism involves specific expectations about positive outcomes (e.g., I will finish my assignment by 5 o'clock so I can watch the ball game tonight), whereas big

optimism refers to more generic, larger expectations of positive outcomes (e.g., our firm can become the leader in the industry). Although there may be some relationship between little and big, there is also the distinct possibility of someone being a little optimist, but a big pessimist, or vice versa. There seems little question that the strategies, mechanisms, and pathways linking optimism to outcomes may differ (e.g., time management versus visionary leadership).

2. *Optimism vs. pessimism.* Although the assumption is often made that optimism and pessimism are mutually exclusive, they may not be. Some people expect both good outcomes (optimism) *and* bad outcomes (pessimism) to be plentiful. Interestingly, explanatory style derived from attributions about bad events are usually independent of explanatory style based on attributions about good events. In other words, attributions about bad events are identified as optimistic or pessimistic, but attributions about good events are not. It would seem that attributions about good events would be as, if not more, important to understanding optimism.

3. *Learning and sustaining optimism.* Although optimism is sometimes portrayed as a stable personality trait (e.g., Scheier and Carver's dispositional optimism),[94] Seligman has led the way in popularizing *learned optimism*. This says that anyone, including pessimists, can learn the skills to be an optimist.[95] Of course, it is critical that this developable, state-like nature of optimism be included in POB. The social learning process of modeling (i.e., observing positive events and outcomes in one's relevant, valued environment) can contribute to the learning of optimism. By the same token, as Chapter 9 on stress will indicate, reducing and coping with bad events and stress can also help sustain optimism.

Overall, the past, present, and future of optimism as an exciting psychological construct for the better understanding and application of human functioning in general and for organizational behavior in particular seems very "optimistic."

## Optimism in the Workplace

As discussed, there is no question that optimism is both motivated and motivating; has the desirable characteristics of perseverance, achievement, and health; makes external, unstable, and specific attributions of personal bad events; and is linked with positive outcomes such as occupational success. Obviously by extrapolating this profile, optimism could be a very positive force in the workplace. For example, optimists may be motivated to work harder; be more satisfied and have high morale; have high levels of aspiration and set stretch goals; persevere in the face of obstacles and difficulties; make attributions of personal failures and setbacks as temporary, not as personal inadequacy, and view them as a one-time unique circumstance; and tend to feel good and invigorated both physically and mentally. The accompanying OB in Action: "Half-Empty" or "Half-Full" gives some real-world scenarios of such optimistic people in the workplace. There are some jobs and career fields where optimism would be especially valuable (e.g., sales, advertising, public relations, product design, customer service, and in the health and social services fields).

### *The Downside of Optimism*

Despite the overwhelming anecdotal evidence of the positive power of optimism in the workplace, it must be remembered that the academic literature does warn that in certain cases optimism can lead to meaningless or dysfunctional outcomes. For example, Peterson notes that optimistically driven behavior may be aimed at pointless pursuits (e.g., finish in the top five of the company golf league) or unrealistic goals (e.g., striving to attain an unattainable sales goal that results in stress, exhaustion, and high blood pressure).[96] Moreover, "realistic optimism" would result in more effective leadership than "false optimism."[97]

Although to date there are not many research studies of the role of optimism in the workplace, it is nevertheless happening day to day in the way in which organizational participants interpret and react to events. Some people view the "glass" (everyday and important events) as half-full (optimists) and some as half-empty (pessimists). Here are some actual examples.

1. Take the case of two executives who were passed over for promotion because of negative evaluations from their boss.

   A. The "half-empty" exec reacted to the snub in a rage. He had fantasies of killing his boss, complained to anyone who would listen of his unfair treatment, and went on a drinking binge. He felt like his life was over. He avoided his boss and looked down when passing him in the hall. In an interview, however, he admitted "Even though I was angry and felt cheated, deep down I feared that he was right, that I was sort of worthless, that I had failed, and there was nothing I could do to change that."

   B. The "half-full" exec who did not get the promotion was also stunned and upset. But instead of going into a rage, he reasoned to himself, "I can't say I was surprised, really. He and I have such different ideas, and we've argued a lot." Instead of sulking, he openly discussed the setback with his wife to determine what went wrong and what he could do to correct it. He realized that maybe he was not giving his all at work and resolved to talk to the boss. Here is how it went: "I had some discussions with him and things went very well. I guess he was troubled about what he had done, and I was troubled about not working up to potential. Since then, things have been better for both of us."

2. Another "half-full" case is Anne Busquet of American Express. She was relieved of her duties as head of the Optima Card division when it was discovered that some of her employees had hidden millions of dollars in bad debt. Although not involved, she was held accountable and was devastated by the setback. However, instead of quitting, she was still confident in her abilities and took a lower position trying to save the company's failing merchandising service division. She made a self-examination of what went wrong in the Optima Card division and concluded that maybe she was too strict and critical of her people. She reasoned that this style may have led her people to fear her to the point where they hid the losses. She resolved to soften her style and become more open, patient, and a better listener. Using this approach to manage the troubled merchandising service division, she saw it reach profitability within two years.

3. Perhaps the greatest "half-full" case is Arthur Blank, the founder of Home Depot. In 1978, after personality clashes with his boss at the hardware chain Handy Dan's, he was fired. Instead of getting angry, he got even. He believed in his abilities and vision for this type of retailing. He did not give up after the setback at Handy Dan's. When an investor approached him, he jumped at the chance to put his talents to work and founded Home Depot. The rest is history.

The half-full optimists interpret bad events in terms of Seligman's explanatory style, and, as the preceding three examples indicate, this can result in future positive outcomes. Whereas the half-empty pessimists tend to give up and go into a downward spiral after problems or failures, the half-fulls view setbacks as a lesson to be learned for future success.

---

There are also certain jobs in which at least mild pessimism would be beneficial (e.g., some technical jobs such as safety engineering or jobs in financial control and accounting).

### Seligman's Met Life Studies

For studies of optimism in the workplace, Seligman again leads the way with his pioneering work at Metropolitan Life Insurance. After conferring with the president of this huge company, he was able to test the obvious hypothesis that optimism and its attendant motivation and perseverance were the keys to sales success. A shortened version of his theory-based Attributional Style Questionnaire (ASQ) was administered to 200 experienced Met Life sales agents. This open-ended version of the ASQ was designed to determine the habitual explanatory style by asking the respondents to interpret six good and six bad vignettes in terms of personalization, permanence, and pervasiveness. Importantly, this test has been found to be very difficult to fake optimism; the right answers vary from test to test, and it does contain "lie scales" to identify those not telling the truth. Results were that agents who scored in the most optimistic half of the ASQ had sold 37 percent more insurance on average in their first two years than agents who scored in the pessimistic half. Agents who scored in the top 10 percent sold 88 percent more than the most pessimistic 10 percent.[98]

Despite the impressive findings from the initial study, Seligman was still not sure of the direction of causality from the correlational results (i.e., if the optimism caused the high performance or if high performers became optimistic). He next conducted a pilot study on 104 new hires that took both the standard insurance industry selection test and the ASQ. Interestingly, he found that new insurance agents are more optimistic than any other group tested (e.g., car salespeople, commodity traders, West Point plebes, managers of Arby's restaurants, baseball stars, or world-class swimmers). Optimistic scorers were much less likely to quit (a big problem in the insurance industry where about half turn over the first year) and did as well as the industry test in predicting performance.

He next launched a full-blown study involving 15,000 applicants to Met Life taking both the industry test and the ASQ. One thousand were hired and, importantly, 129 more (called the "Special Force") that had scored in the top half of those taking the ASQ but had failed the industry test were also hired. In the first year the optimists (those who scored in the top half of the ASQ) outsold the pessimists by only 8 percent, but in the second year by 31 percent. The "Special Force" (those who had flunked the industry test and would not have been hired except for scoring as optimists on the ASQ) outsold the hired pessimists in the regular force by 21 percent the first year and 57 percent the second. They sold about the same as the optimists in the regular force. Met Life, on the basis of Seligman's studies, then adopted the ASQ as an important part of their selection process of new agents.[99]

### Other Research and Application in the Workplace

With the exception of the comprehensive Met Life study, to date there has been relatively little research to directly test the impact of optimism in the workplace. An older study did examine competent managers and found that they attribute their failures to a correctable mistake, and then they persevere (i.e., an optimistic explanatory style).[100] As with the other positive resources, optimism has also been part of recent studies in POB. For example, one POB study found optimism was related to employee performance, job satisfaction and work happiness.[101] This optimism-performance relationship was also found with workers in Chinese factories.[102]

Other work on optimism has been applied to leadership. For example, there has been recognition given in leadership theory to the importance of optimism,[103] and a field study found the measured optimism of military cadets had a significant relationship with their military science professors' rating of leadership potential.[104] Another study of business leaders found that on average they were more optimistic than a sample of nonleaders, that those most effective in initiating change were less pessimistic, and that the more optimistic the leader, the more optimistic the followers.[105] There also have been a few publicized applications of deliberate attempts to use optimism in human resource management (HRM) such as in the selection process. One example is the highly successful Men's Wearhouse discount retailer, where an HRM executive stated:

> We don't look for people with specific levels of education and experience. We look for one criterion for hiring: optimism. We look for passion, excitement, energy. We want people who enjoy life.[106]

Besides selection, another example is American Express Financial Advisors that reportedly uses optimism training with their associates.[107]

# HOPE

In the positive psychology movement, optimism has received relatively more attention than hope, but in POB hope is a more central concept.[108] Most people think of hope in terms of "hope for the best," a bit of sunny, optimistic advice offered by friends, relatives, and counselors in times of trouble. In positive psychology, however, hope has taken on a specific meaning. Previously in clinical psychology, hope was largely portrayed as a unidimensional construct involving an overall perception that one can attain his or her goals.[109] However, recently deceased positive psychologist C. Rick Snyder provided the now most widely recognized bidimensional definition of hope that we use in POB. Through extensive theory and research, he and colleagues precisely defined hope as: "A positive motivational state that is based on an interactively derived sense of successful (a) agency (goal-directed energy), and (b) pathways (planning to meet goals)."[110] More simply, this meaning of hope consists of both the "willpower" (agency) and the "waypower" (pathways). Importantly, considerable research over the past several years indicates it has a very positive impact on academic achievement, athletic accomplishment, emotional health, the ability to cope with illness and other hardships.[111] Although not yet part of the mainstream organizational behavior literature, hope does make a good fit with the POB criteria.

Even though hope draws from each of the positive psychology constructs, there are some conceptually important differences. From the perspective of emotional intelligence, Goleman states that "having hope means that one will not give in to overwhelming anxiety, a defeatist attitude, or depression in the face of difficult challenges or setbacks."[112] In relation to optimism, Seligman states, "Whether or not we have hope depends on two dimensions of our explanatory style: pervasiveness and performance. Finding temporary and specific causes for misfortune is the art of hope."[113] Perhaps conceptually the term closest in meaning to *hope* is *self-efficacy* (covered in the last sections). However, Snyder[114] and others[115] demonstrated that efficacy (as well as other POB constructs) and hope are conceptually and psychometrically (measurement) distinct (i.e., hope has construct validity).

Over the past decade, Snyder and his colleagues developed a brief self-report "State Hope Scale" with items such as "I energetically pursue my goals" and "There are lots of ways around any problem"[116] and conducted a number of studies using this scale. This research finds a positive link between hope scores and work-related goal expectancies, perceived control, self-esteem, positive emotions, coping, and achievement.[117] Although the considerable research base showing the positive impact of hope deals with academic, athletic, and mental and physical health, the carryover implications for the workplace seem quite clear. For example, there is research evidence that those with hope in stressful professions such as human services perform better[118] and survive with the most satisfaction, are less emotionally exhausted, and are most likely to stay.[119] There is also direct work-related research beginning to emerge. For example, Snyder and colleagues, in an ongoing survey of U.S. firms, have found that those with higher-hope human resources are more profitable, have higher retention rates, and have greater levels of employee satisfaction and commitment.[120] Moreover, a field study we recently conducted found that managers with higher hope levels had correspondingly higher performing work units, better retention rates, and more satisfied employees.[121] More recent POB studies have found employees' level of hope related to their job satisfaction, organizational commitment, work happiness, and performance [122] and also, like optimism, there was a significant relationship between Chinese factory workers' hope and their performance.[123] Moreover, a recent comprehensive study focused on hope across different types of jobs and industries found more hopeful sales employees, mortgage brokers, and management executives had higher job performance, and the management executives also produced more and better quality solutions to a work-related problem.[124] Hope also seems to have a positive impact on the entrepreneurial process. We found that higher-hope entrepreneurs express greater satisfaction with business ownership and consider themselves relatively better compensated than their lower-hope peers.[125]

These initial studies indicate that hope may have as powerful of a positive impact in the workplace as it has demonstrated outside the workplace. In human resource management, hope may play an important role in selection, especially for certain types of jobs and because it is learned and statelike (can change) rather than a stable trait, it can be enhanced by training and development to improve on-the-job performance and retention of valuable employees.[126]

# RESILIENCY

Unlike the other criteria-meeting POB psychological resources, resiliency is reactive rather then proactive in nature. In positive psychology, resiliency is defined as "a class of phenomena characterized by patterns of positive adaptation in the context of significant adversity or risk."[127] As a component of positive organizational behavior, resiliency is viewed "as the capacity to rebound or bounce back from adversity, conflict, failure or even positive events, progress and increased responsibility."[128] This "bouncing back" capacity involves flexibility, adjustment, adaptability, and continuous responsiveness to change and uncertainty that can otherwise represent a source of psychological strain and challenge one's well-being over the long term. Traditionally in clinical psychology, resiliency was portrayed as an exceptional capability that only a select few possess. More recent theory and research now conclude that resiliency comes "from the everyday magic of ordinary, normative human resources."[129] Moreover, resiliency is not just an outcome that people strive to achieve, nor is it only a valuable input that enhances their chances of success. It is a lifelong journey, an elaborate process in which competence is developed over time as people interact with their environment most often characterized by continuous change and uncertainty.[130]

Although the research on resiliency and adaptation originally focused on at-risk children and adolescents (a negative perspective), recent studies have emphasized the positive aspects of resiliency.[131] Moreover, resiliency is increasingly being viewed not only as a desirable characteristic of humans in general, but also as an essential attribute of today's employees,[132] managers,[133] organizations,[134] and even countries,[135] especially in light of recent troubling and tragic events related to economic and geopolitical problems both in the United States and abroad. Important in meeting the criteria of positive organizational behavior, resiliency has been shown to be statelike, that is, it is trainable and developable.[136] This statelike conceptualization opens the door for proactive efforts to create and develop resilient individuals and organizations.[137] Several instruments have been developed to measure resilience, for example the "Ego-Resiliency Scale (ER89)" includes items such as "I quickly get over and recover from being startled" and "I enjoy dealing with new and unusual situations."[138]

Based on the established research of positive psychologist Ann Masten and her colleagues, resiliency has been found to be influenced and developed by three types of factors: assets, risks, and adaptational processes.[139] Resiliency can be developed through enhancing the *assets* that a person possesses, through education, training, and nurturing social relationships, and in general by improving the quality of resources available for the person to draw upon. *Risk factors* can be managed through appropriate physical and psychological health care. *Adaptational processes* can be enhanced through developing other positive psychological capacities such as self-efficacy, hope, and optimism, as well as through teaching people how to use effective coping, stress management, problem solving, and goal-setting strategies and practical techniques. In fact, resiliency may be more adversely impacted by the process that links risk conditions with specific dysfunctional outcomes than by the presence, number or frequency of risk factors, or lack of necessary assets.[140]

The overall profile of resilient people is that they are characterized by "a staunch acceptance of reality; a deep belief, often buttressed by strongly held values, that life is meaningful; and an uncanny ability to improvise."[141] As today's employees face the risks and uncertainties associated with economic turbulence, global sourcing, technological change, downsizing, work-life balance, extensive customer-service orientation, stress, and burnout, resiliency is becoming an indispensable factor that can turn such threats into opportunities for growth, development, and sustainable adaptability to change.[142]

Resiliency is also a positive strength from which not only individual managers and employees can benefit, but also overall organizations can no longer afford to be without.[143] Turbulence and instability have become the norm in today's business environment, and only organizations that can rejuvenate their adaptational systems and bounce back to swiftly respond to their ever-changing environments are likely to improve or even survive. A strong and stable organizational mission, vision, and set of values create a sense of community, direction, and purpose, enhancing a resilient corporate culture.[144] Strategic planning, teamwork, decentralization, employee involvement, and open communication channels can be used to build a resilient organization that aligns organizational, unit, and individual goals and objectives, and builds trust, commitment, and effective organizational learning and adaptational systems.[145] Counter to conventional wisdom, organizational rules and regulations that seemingly introduce rigidity and hinder creativity may actually help as effective structuring tools that foster an organization's resilience in times of turbulence.[146]

Whether at the individual or organizational level, this resiliency dimension of positive organizational behavior may have the most potential impact on development and sustainable performance in the current difficult times. Although theory-building and research on resiliency within the domain of positive organizational behavior is just getting started, the results to date are very encouraging.[147]

# PSYCHOLOGICAL CAPITAL (PSYCAP)

Using positive psychology and POB in general, and the four criteria-meeting psychological resources of efficacy, optimism, hope, and resiliency, in particular, as the foundation and point of departure, as indicated in the introductory comments, Luthans and colleagues have theoretically[148] and empirically[149] demonstrated a higher-order core construct called psychological capital or PsyCap. This PsyCap goes beyond economic (what you have, physical and financial assets), social (who you know, network of friends), and human capital (knowledge, skills, abilities, experience), and is defined as:

> An individual's positive psychological state of development that is characterized by: (1) having confidence (self-efficacy) to take on and put in the necessary effort to succeed at challenging tasks; (2) making a positive attribution (optimism) about succeeding now and in the future; (3) persevering toward goals and, when necessary, redirecting paths to goals (hope) in order to succeed; and (4) when beset by problems and adversity, sustaining and bouncing back and even beyond (resiliency) to attain success.[150]

## Background and Research on PsyCap

Each of the four psychological constructs or resources that currently make up PsyCap are commonly found in the positive psychology literature, but, perhaps with the exception of efficacy, have received relatively little, if any, attention in the organization behavior field. Luthans and colleagues' intent in the 2004 published articles[151] was to label these four resources that best met the established criteria (theory, research, valid measurement, state-like, and performance impact) when combined as "psychological capital" because to their knowledge the term had not been used before. We subsequently found that Csikszentmihalyi had mentioned the term a couple of times in a book[152] that was not yet published when the first PsyCap articles were written and then came out a bit later in the journals. Also, a recent Google search found the term in an economics article on wages in 1997. As noted by Luthans and colleagues, "Our aim in labeling this as a type of 'capital' was also related to the idea that there is considerable attention in workplace research being given to economic, social, human and even intellectual capital, but to our knowledge the positive resources we associate with psychological capital had not yet received interest or inquiry. In using the term PsyCap, we suggested that there was a common conceptual thread running through the four components characterized as "a positive appraisal of circumstances and probability for success based on motivated effort and perseverance."[153]

We firmly believed from the beginning and reiterated in a recent point/counterpoint article[154] that the most important "Point" we would like to make about positive organizational behavior in general and PsyCap in particular was the important role that research (i.e., an evidenced-based approach) must play. We noted at the outset that the value of positivity has been recognized through the years in psychology and even more so in the field of organizational behavior, but in this new focus on POB and now PsyCap we wanted to make sure we were not associated with the nonresearched positive, Pollyannaish approach too often found in the popular leadership and management literature. Thus, our first major research project was to validate a measure called the PsyCap Questionnaire or PCQ, and provide beginning empirical evidence that PsyCap was a second-order core construct accounting for more variance in employee performance and satisfaction than each of the four individual positive constructs that make it up.[155] Also, in this comprehensive basic research study we found that PsyCap was relatively less stable over time than were recognized personality traits, but not as unstable as positive emotions, thus providing empirical evidence for PsyCap meeting the state-like criterion.[156]

After the background and theory-building presented in our book (Luthans, Youssef, and Avolio, *Psychological Capital,* Oxford, 2007) and the first major research project outlined above, we (especially along with James Avey) have a stream of research to refine and expand PsyCap. The following is representative of the evidence-based facets of PsyCap to date.

1. PsyCap was found to be positively related to desired organizational citizenship behaviors (covered in Chapter 6) and negatively to undesired organization cynicism, intentions to quit, and counterproductive workplace behaviors. Importantly, PsyCap predicted unique variance in these attitudes and behaviors over and above their demographics (age, education, experience, etc.), core self-evaluation traits, personality traits, and person-organization and person-job fit.[157]

2. To determine if PsyCap held across cultures, an early preliminary study found that a sample of workers in Chinese factories (metallurgical products and shoe manufacturers) partially tested PsyCap related to their performance.[158] A recent follow-up study with different samples of Chinese factory workers using the full PsyCap model and PCQ measure replicated these findings.[159] Such evidence becomes very important to developing

countries such as China who need to leverage their still largely untapped wealth (in this case psychological capital) of their human (not just natural) resources for sustained growth and competitive advantage in the global economy.

3. Besides these studies relating PsyCap directly to attitudinal and performance outcomes, recent research indicates that PsyCap may also have implications for combating stress (there is a negative relationship);[160] help facilitate positive organizational change (PsyCap is related to positive emotions that are in turn related to their attitudes and behaviors[161] relevant to organization change); mediate the relationship between supportive organizational climate and employee performance;[162] and be related to both employee creativity[163] and employee well-being over time.[164]

4. Finally, PsyCap is also playing a role in our research on authentic leadership (covered in Chapter 13).[165] For example, one recent study found that a leader's level of PsyCap impacted followers' perceived trust and evaluations of leader effectiveness[166] and another found a positive relationship between a leaders' level of PsyCap and followers' level of PsyCap and performance.[167] Other such research is at various stages and PsyCap also has an input into the theory building of positive leadership in general.[168]

## PsyCap Development

Besides theory/research, valid measurement, and performance impact, a key distinguishing feature is that PsyCap is statelike and open to development. As indicated, the first major research project provided empirical evidence of this statelike nature of PsyCap,[169] and subsequent experimental research has indicated that PsyCap can indeed be developed in short (2 or 3 hours) training interventions.[170] Importantly, since these were experimental designs, the randomly assigned control groups, who had the same characteristics but received a group dynamics training intervention instead of the PsyCap intervention, did not increase their level of PsyCap. In other words, armed with this evidence, we can be more confident that PsyCap can be developed in a short training intervention. There is also preliminary experimental evidence that such PsyCap training causes performance to improve.[171]

The PsyCap intervention (PCI) model is drawn from the positive (and clinical) psychology field for each of the four components and is shown in Figure 7.4 and a brief verbal summary description in Figure 7.5. As indicated, this training intervention has been conducted in one- to three-hour highly interactive, large and small face-to-face sessions and even online (downloading exercises, use of movie clips, etc.). Using widely recognized human resource management utility analysis techniques,[172] on both publicly available corporate data and actual results from our studies, has yielded impressive results.[173] For example, one such analysis indicated a 270 percent return on investment in developing the PsyCap of a sample of high-tech engineers (the dollar return minus the cost of the PsyCap training divided by the cost of the PsyCap training).[174]

The results of the research on PsyCap so far seems to indicate a bright future for its role not only in positive organizational behavior, but also as an effective evidenced-based approach to leadership and employee development and performance management. Research to meet the call for longitudinal studies[175] has recently provided needed further evidence of the statelike nature of PsyCap and its causal impact on objective performance.[176] There is also just completed group-level research indicating that a work team's "collective PsyCap" is related to their citizenship behavior and performance.[177] Finally, there is a need to recognize other positive constructs besides those reviewed so far. Two of the more established are happiness/subjective well-being and emotional intelligence to which the rest of this chapter is devoted.

**FIGURE 7.4**
**Psychological Capital Intervention (PCI)**

*Source:* Adapted from F. Luthans, J. B. Avey, B. V. Avolio, S. M. Norman, and G. J. Combs, "Psychological Capital Development: Toward a Micro-Intervention," *Journal of Organizational Behavior*, Vol. 27, 2006, pp. 387–393.

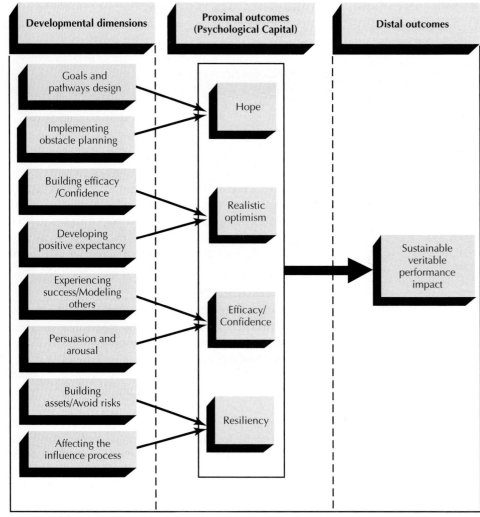

*Note:* The PCI is intended to affect each state as well as the overall level of PsyCap for performance impact.

## OTHER POSITIVE CONSTRUCTS

Although self-efficacy/confidence, optimism, hope, and resiliency have been determined to best meet the criteria established for inclusion in POB and PsyCap, as indicated, there are a number of other positive capacities that have potential for also being included.[178] Examples would include constructs such as wisdom, gratitude, forgiveness, courage, and even spirituality. However, the two positive constructs that have received the most attention over the years that are especially applicable to the workplace, would be happiness/subjective well-being (SWB) and emotional intelligence (EI).

### Happiness or Subjective Well-Being (SWB)

Both with the general public and academic psychology, the importance of happiness has been widely recognized. However, similar to the distinction that positive psychology makes with the common usage of the term *hope,* positive psychological theory and research prefers to use the more precise and operationally defined term *subjective well-being,* or

**FIGURE 7.5**  **Summary Descriptions of the Psychological Capital Intervention (PCI) Model**

*Source:* Adapted from F. Luthans, J. B. Avey, B. J. Avolio, S. M. Norman, and G. Combs "Psychological Capital Development: Toward a Micro-intervention," *Journal of Organizational Behavior,* Vol. 27, 2006, pp. 387–393.

### Hope Development

Hope was shown to be impacted and influenced by goals, pathways, and agency. Specifically, participants practiced generating work-related goals that were personally valuable and reasonably challenging and that included a clear beginning and end point. These goal characteristics generated sustained motivation, thus using goal components to increase agency. In addition, participants practiced generating multiple pathways to their work-related goals, and they identified obstacles that they should plan to encounter. After completing the exercise individually, each participant received feedback from the group on additional or alternative pathways that could be utilized and obstacles that could be expected. This practice increased each participant's pathway-generating skill and ability to identify and plan for obstacles, thus reducing the negative impact of obstacles on agency.

### Optimism Development

Building efficacy in pathway generation and obstacle planning provided a foundation for the development of generally positive expectations. When participants were confident that they could identify and plan to overcome obstacles, their expectations of achieving their goals increased. Negative expectations that goals would not be accomplished were challenged as individuals began to see pathways to success and options on how to overcome obstacles. Group feedback increased positive expectations as individuals saw other group members also expect and plan for success. As participants' expectations of success increased, optimism both individually and within the group increased.

### Efficacy Development

Participants practiced setting up stepwise techniques to accomplish goals. Then they explained each subgoal (each step) to the group, and they answered questions about how each was to be accomplished. Task mastery for designing and pursuing goals was thus attained. Vicarious learning took place as each participant saw peers work toward their goals and heard success stories about how goals were attained. This stage included emotional arousal, which was influenced by positive expectations of achieving goals as well as the social persuasion by the facilitator and group members by validating schedules and timelines, goals would be accomplished.

### Resiliency Development

Resiliency was increased by building awareness of personal assets in the form of talents, skills, and social networks. Participants were asked what resources they could leverage to accomplish a given goal. After creating the list of resources, the facilitator and peer group members identified additional resources participants did not include on their list. Participants were then encouraged to leverage these resources as necessary. Similar to planning for obstacles, participants were encouraged to identify in advance obstacles that could impede their progress. Whereas in the hope exercise the focus was on making plans to overcome these obstacles, in this exercise, the focus was on making plans to avoid the obstacles or to prevent them from becoming legitimate concerns. Finally, the influence process was impacted by each participant becoming aware of his or her initial thoughts and feelings when faced with adversity (i.e., confidence or despair, etc.) and choosing to focus on resilient thoughts based on their assessment of their resources and options to overcome adversity.

---

simply *SWB*, instead of happiness. As Seligman and Csikszentmihalyi recently noted: "In practice, subjective well-being is a more scientific-sounding term for what people usually mean by happiness."[179] Sometimes the terms are used interchangeably, but SWB is usually considered broader and is defined as people's affective (moods and emotions) and cognitive evaluations of their lives.[180] Under this psychological meaning, it is not necessarily what in reality happens to people that determines their happiness or subjective well-being; but instead how they emotionally interpret and cognitively process what happens to them is the key. Like hope, SWB has not been in the mainstream of the organizational behavior literature, and although it does not meet the POB criteria quite as directly as self-efficacy, optimism, hope, and resiliency, it is included here as part of POB and there have been some work-related studies in the SWB research literature.

## The Background on SWB

Positive psychologist Ed Diener's work over the past three decades is most closely associated with SWB.[181] As an important part of the positive psychology movement, SWB's popularity and importance reflect societal trends valuing the good life and what makes people happy. Almost everyone seems to rate happiness over money (e.g., in a survey of 7,204 college students in 42 countries, only 6 percent rated money more important than happiness).[182] Academically, Diener and his research group made a break from simple feelings of happiness and just the demographic characteristics that correlate with it. Most recently, the interest is more on the processes that underlie life satisfaction. Specifically, there has been a shift away from *who* is happy (i.e., the demographics) to *when* and *why* people are happy and on *what* the processes are that influence SWB.[183] Specifically, in their recent book Diener and Biswas-Diener provide the following evidence- based conclusions:[184]

1. Happiness is a process, not a place. "Happiness is an ongoing process that requires a way of experienced life and the world that includes positive attitudes, meaning, and spirituality. Being truly rich is as much about the attitudes within us as the circumstances surrounding us."[185]

2. There is actually an optimal level of happiness. Those "too happy" may perform less well at school and work, and even be less healthy (e.g., may ignore symptoms or required regiments).

3. Though not linear, happiness is clearly related to health and longevity, relationships, and effectiveness at work.

As to the last point on happiness leading to a longer life, a now famous study on the order of nuns who entered convents as young adults between 1931 and 1943 is very interesting and revealing about the power of happiness.[186] The researchers analyzed the autobiographies of the entering nuns as to their level of positivity and happiness. Since these nuns had almost identical food, activities, and circumstances (i.e., the environment was basically held constant or under control over their lifetime), the researchers could draw conclusions about the impact the nuns' level of happiness/positivity had on their length of life. Amazingly, the most happy nuns (the top 25% in the ratings) lived on average ten years longer than the least (25%) happy nuns. To put these results in perspective, smoking a pack of cigarettes a day is estimated on average to take three plus years off of one's life, regular exercise accounts for three to five extra years, statin drug therapy used to lower cholesterol levels 2.5 to 3.5 years, and even regular church attendance may add two to three additional years,[187] but being happy and positive may on average have three times as much impact on longevity.

Besides the relationship with health/longevity and relationships (e.g., Diener and Biswas-Diener note that "many studies show that happy people are more blessed with good families, friends, and supportive relationships"[188]) of interest here is the impact that SWB has on work outcomes.

### SWB in Work

Although not included in organizational behavior or HRM textbooks, SWB researchers do give attention to work and the workplace as one of its domains, and there are a growing number of studies. In particular, SWB has demonstrated a direct correlation to job satisfaction (covered in Chapter 5). A meta-analysis of 34 studies found an average correlation of .44 between job satisfaction and life satisfaction.[189] To determine whether job satisfaction leads to SWB or vice versa (i.e., the correlation studies do not yield the direction of causality), Judge and colleagues used sophisticated statistical designs. It was found that SWB was a significant predictor of job satisfaction five years later, but not vice versa.[190] Thus, it appears that people who are satisfied with their lives tend to find more satisfaction in their work.[191]

There is accumulating research evidence that happiness or SWB leads to desired outcomes beyond just job satisfaction in the workplace. Not only have happy employees been found to be more effective and productive,[192] but after a search of the research literature it was also concluded that "on average, happy workers make more money, receive more promotions and better supervisor ratings, and are better citizens at work."[193] An increasing number of organizations are recognizing and using this value of happiness with their employees and customers. Organizations such as Toyota, the American Red Cross, Sprint Nextel, and David's Bridal have launched training programs for their employees based on happiness principles. For example, at David's, the largest chain of bridal stores, salespeople have been taught techniques such as focusing on things that bring them joy when dealing with stressed-out, anxious brides-to-be. Also, increasingly market research in general is focusing on how products and services can appeal to customers' happiness.

Similar to PsyCap, happiness (SWB) is open to change and development. Although there is definitely a set point (i.e., approximately the 50 percent "hard-wiring" noted at the beginning of the chapter), the role of intentional control and effective developmental guidelines are becoming recognized. As Lyubomirsky points out, "intentional, effortful activities have a powerful effect on how happy we are, over and above the effects of our set points and the circumstances in which we find ourselves."[194] She then prescribes the following guidelines and specific activities for developing and sustaining happiness:[195]

1. Practicing gratitude and positive thinking (expressing gratitude, cultivating optimism, and avoiding overthinking and social comparison);
2. Investing in social connections (practicing acts of kindness and nurturing social relationships);
3. Managing stress, hardship, and trauma (developing strategies for coping, learning to forgive);
4. Living in the present (increasing flow experiences, savoring life's joys);
5. Committing to your goals;
6. Taking care of your body and soul (practicing religion and spirituality, meditation, physical exercise, and acting like a happy person).

Although these are all very general, Lyubomirsky provides details on how to do each, and importantly, supporting research evidence that they work. For example, on the last point of "acting like a happy person," citing published research[196] she notes, "Remarkably, pretending that you're happy—smiling, engaged, mimicking energy and enthusiasm—not only can earn you some of the benefits of happiness (returned smiles, strengthened friendships, successes at work and school) but can actually make you happier."[197] The future of the role that happiness may play in the workplace seems very bright.

## Emotional Intelligence (EI)

Emotional intelligence (EI) predates the emergence of POB and is more widely known in popular management circles. However, EI has to date not been featured as a major part of POB because it has not yet met the criteria of POB.[198] In particular, the major shortcoming in meeting the POB criteria has been the limited research support for a valid measure of EI and its relationship with performance outcomes. However, this is beginning to change somewhat[199] and is why it is included here. This concluding section of the chapter first examines its two conceptual components: emotion and intelligence. After these two important psychological constructs are examined separately, the synergy created by combining them into emotional intelligence becomes a potentially powerful positively oriented construct for the understanding and application approach to the study and application of organizational behavior.

### The Role of Emotion

Over the years, emotion has been a major variable in psychology, and, compared to the other POB constructs, has received relatively more attention in the organizational behavior field.[200] Similar to other psychological constructs, the exact definition and meaning of *emotion* are not totally agreed upon. However, most psychologists would agree that the best one word to describe emotion would be how a person *feels* about something. These emotional feelings are directed at someone or something, are not as broad as the meanings of the term *affect* (as used in the discussion of positive and negative affect in Chapter 5 on personality), and are more intense and specific than the definitions of the term *mood*. The specific differences between emotion, affect, and mood are summarized as follows:

> Emotions are reactions to an object, not a trait. They're object specific. You show your emotions when you're "happy about something, angry at someone, afraid of something." Moods, on the other hand, aren't directed at an object. Emotions can turn into moods when you lose focus on the contextual object. So when a work colleague criticizes you for the way you spoke to a client, you might become angry at him [emotion]. But later in the day, you might find yourself just generally dispirited. This affective state describes a mood.[201]

### Emotional Processing

How do emotional reactions come about, and what are the inputs into emotional processing? A very simple, layperson's explanation of the process is that emotional feelings are in contrast with rational thinking. Put into popular terms, emotions come from the "heart" whereas rational thinking comes from the "head." For example, a young manager given a choice between two assignments may undergo the following cognitive processing: "my 'head' tells me to get involved with Project A because it has the best chance of succeeding and helping my career, but my 'heart' says that Project B will be more fun, I like the people better, and I can take more pride in any results we achieve." Obviously, such emotions often win out over rational thinking in what people decide, do, or how they behave.

Traditionally in psychology, both personality traits (e.g., extraversion/neuroticism or conscientiousness) and mood states (either positive or negative) have separate influences or emotional processing. More recently, however, to represent the more realistic complexity involved, it is suggested that: (1) mood states interact with individual differences in emotion-relevant personality traits to influence emotional processing, and/or (2) personality traits predispose individuals to certain mood states, which then influence emotional processing.[202] In other words, for (1) above, someone in a positive mood may have to have (or will be enhanced by) a personality trait such as conscientiousness in order to experience emotional happiness. For (2) above, the individual may have to have the personality trait such as extraversion in order to get into a positive mood state. This positive mood in turn will lead the person to experience emotional happiness. These moderation and meditation models of emotional processing help resolve some of the inconsistencies that have been found in the research using the separate influences of moods and personality traits for emotions.[203]

### Types of Emotions

Like the meaning of emotion, there is also not total agreement on the primary types of emotions. Table 7.2 summarizes the primary emotions and their descriptors most often

**TABLE 7.2**
**Types of Emotions**

*Source:* Adapted from H. M. Weiss and R. Cropanzano, "Affective Events Theory," in B. M. Staw and L. L. Cummings (Eds.), *Research in Organizational Behavior,* Vol. 18, JAI Press, Greenwich, Conn., 1996, pp. 20–22 and Daniel Goleman, *Emotional Intelligence,* Bantam Books, New York, 1995, pp. 289–290.

| Positive Primary Emotions: | Other Descriptors |
|---|---|
| Love/affection | Acceptance, adoration, longing, devotion, infatuation |
| Happiness/joy | Cheerfulness, contentment, bliss, delight, amusement, enjoyment, enthrallment, thrill, euphoria, zest |
| Surprise | Amazement, wonder, astonishment, shock |
| **Negative Primary Emotions:** | **Other Descriptors** |
| Fear | Anxiety, alarm, apprehension, concern, qualm, dread, fright, terror |
| Sadness | Grief, disappointment, sorrow, gloom, despair, suffering, dejection |
| Anger | Outrage, exasperation, wrath, indignation, hostility, irritability |
| Disgust | Contempt, disdain, abhorrence, revulsion, distaste |
| Shame | Guilt, remorse, regret, embarrassment, humiliation |

mentioned in the psychology literature. Importantly, each of these emotions are very common in the workplace. For example:

- Juan has grown to *love* his paramedic emergency team as they solve one life-threatening crisis after another.
- Mary feels *happy* when her boss comments in front of the sales team that she just landed the biggest contract of the quarter.
- Jami is *surprised* to hear that the firm's stock price dropped two and one-half points today.
- George *fears* the new technological process that he believes may replace him.
- Trent feels *sad* for Alison because she does more than her share of the work, but gets no recognition from the supervisor.
- Lane is *angry* because he was passed over for promotion for the second time.
- Mark is *disgusted* with the favoritism shown to his colleague Steve when the regional sales manager assigns territories.
- Kent has a sense of *shame* for claiming expense reimbursement for a trip he did not take.

As shown by the preceding representative examples, the whole range of emotions are found in the workplace. In addition, it is probably not an exaggeration to state that most personal and many managerial/organizational decisions are based on emotional processes rather than rational thought processes. For example, career decisions are often based on emotions of happiness and affection or even fear, rather than on what is rationally best for one's career.[204] In fact, management decisions are often driven by negative emotions such as fear or anger rather than marginal costs, return on investment, or other criteria that the traditional rational economic/finance models would suggest.[205] By the same token, there is important basic research coming from the positive psychology movement that the capacity to experience positive emotions may be a fundamental human strength central to the study of human flourishing,[206] and positive emotions can also be applied to upward spirals in today's organizations.[207] For example, one of the most recognized breakthroughs in positive psychology that has particular relevance and understanding for POB and PsyCap is Barbara Fredrickson's "Broaden and Build" theory.[208] Supported by considerable research evidence,[209] this theory says that experiencing positive emotions broadens (i.e., opens people's hearts and minds) and builds (i.e., allows people to develop new skills, relationships, knowledge and to become more effective overall).

### *Emotional Categories and Continuum*

Besides identifying the different types of emotions, as shown in Table 7.2, they can be put into positive and negative categories. Whether a person feels a positive or negative emotion in the workplace has a lot to do with goal congruence (positive) or goal incongruence (negative).[210] For example, if salespeople meet or exceed their quota, they feel happy, are relieved, and like their customers, but if they fall short they may feel sad, disgusted, guilty, anxious and may blame or be angry with their boss and/or customers.

Emotions can also be conceptualized along a continuum. One classic emotional continuum is the following:[211]

Happiness—Surprise—Fear—Sadness—Anger—Disgust

Table 7.2 is arranged in the same order except with the positive extreme of love/affection on the front end and the negative extreme of shame on the back end.

The key is that the closer the primary emotions are related to one another, the more difficult it is for others to distinguish between them when expressed. For example, almost everyone can readily distinguish the facial expressions of positive versus negative categories of emotion, but may not readily interpret the differences within categories (e.g., between happiness and surprise or anger and disgust). Yet, based on the concept of *emotional labor*[212] which refers to service personnel required to express false, not natural expression, positive emotions such as smiling, most seasoned customers can easily pick up the difference. For example most "Frequent Flyers" can tell the difference between a genuine, natural smile and "Have a nice day!" and a forced, false smile and insincere happy comment from an angry or disgusted reservationist or flight attendant. The nonverbal facial cues and tone of voice are usually a loud and clear indication of what real emotions are being expressed. Recent organizational communication research indicates that positive emotions, not just negative emotions, need to be displayed in prevailing socially acceptable ways, and the appropriate display of negative emotions typically means masking those emotions,[213] that is, experience emotional labor.

Emotional labor not only has dysfunctional consequences for the employees doing it (e.g., stress and burnout),[214] but also detracts from effective customer service. World-class customer service firms such as Southwest Airlines recognize this by hiring only those with very positive personalities. As Herb Kelleher, the founder of Southwest, declared: "We want people who can do things well with laughter and grace."[215] By putting humor and happiness at the top of its hiring criteria, Southwest knows, and the academic literature would support,[216] that its people will tend to express positive, genuine emotions (not emotional labor) in all their encounters with customers and coworkers.

Most academics and practicing managers would agree with the systematic assessment that emotions permeate all of organizational life,[217] but the reason emotions are singled out for special attention in this chapter is the popularity of emotional intelligence and its potential relevance to the study and application to positive organizational behavior. Emotionally intelligent people not only can read the expressed emotions of other people, but also have the maturity to hold their *felt emotions* in check and not *display* undesirable, immature negative emotions such as anger or disgust. This distinction between felt and displayed emotions,[218] as well as the rest of the above discussion on the meaning, cognitive processing, and types/categories/continuum of emotions, when combined with the next section on intelligence, serve as the foundation and point of departure for the role that emotional intelligence may be able to play in positive organizational behavior.

# The Role of Intelligence

Intelligence has played a major role in psychology but a very minor role in organizational behavior. About a hundred years ago, Alfred Binet created a written test to measure the "intelligence quotient" or IQ of grade school children in Paris. Eventually the U.S. Army used the test with recruits in World War I, and then it was widely used in schools and businesses. IQ was assumed to be fixed at birth and went largely unchallenged as a predictor of school, job, and life success. However, just as in personality (covered in Chapter 5), in recent years there has been a renewed nurture versus nature debate on intelligence and the recognition of multiple intelligences.

## *Nature versus Nurture Intelligence*

Again, similar to personality (see Chapter 5), recent breakthroughs in genetic and neuroscience research seem to provide added support for the nature (biological) argument of intelligence. For example, one study suggested that a variation in the gene for IGF2R, a receptor for a human growth factor, was associated with extremely high SAT scores, and other studies have shown that IQ scores are correlated with the amount of gray matter in certain brain regions.[219] These types of findings receive a lot of popular press coverage, but often ignored are other facts such as the identified gene accounted for only about 2 percent of the variance in the SAT scores and that a follow-up study failed to even replicate the initial findings.[220]

On the nurture, developmental side of intelligence, there are also some recent interesting findings of support. For example, there is some theory and research suggesting that a "stereotype threat" may help explain the difference in average IQ scores between groups generalized on the basis of race, gender, age, and other social distinctions.[221] One study, for instance, found that television commercials that depict stereotypical female behavior impair women's performance on math tests and reduce their interest in pursuing quantitative careers.[222] Also, cross-cultural research is clearly indicating that how intelligence is conceptualized and measured depends on learned cultural values and ways of thinking. For example, it has been found that people in Western cultures view intelligence as a means for individuals to devise categories and to engage in rational debate, while those in Eastern cultures see it as a way for members of a community to recognize contradiction and complexity.[223] Moreover, "Many psychologists believe that the idea that a test can be completely absent of cultural bias—a recurrent hope of test developers in the twentieth century—is contradicted by the weight of the evidence."[224]

## *Recognition of Multiple Intelligences*

The impetus for an expanded and positive perspective of intelligence in psychology and education is mostly attributed to Howard Gardner. Over 25 years ago he published his breakthrough book, *Frames of Mind: The Theory of Multiple Intelligences*.[225] Binet's IQ basically measured two relatively narrow dimensions: mathematical/logical and verbal/linguistic. As shown in Table 7.3, Gardner recognized these two plus five others. In developing these seven multiple intelligences or MIs, he found that intelligence was not entirely genetic and fixed at birth, but instead it could be nurtured and grown.

To be considered an intelligence under Gardner's well-known multiple approach, the following three criteria must be met: (1) measurable, (2) valued by the person's culture, and (3) a strength that the person defaulted to when challenged to be creative or solve a problem. Gardner is careful to point out that his identified intelligences are: (1) a new kind of construct and should not be confused with a domain or discipline; (2) a capacity with component processes and should not be equated with a learning style, cognitive style, or working style; and (3) based wholly on empirical evidence that could be revised or added to on

**TABLE 7.3** **Gardner's Multiple Intelligences**

*Source:* Adapted from Lou Russell, *The Accelerated Learning Fieldbook,* Jossey-Bass/Pfeiffer, San Francisco, 1999, pp. 60–70. For the original work see: Howard Gardner, *Frames of Mind: The Theory of Multiple Intelligences,* Basic Books, New York, 1983 and Howard Gardner, "Are There Additional Intelligences? The Case for Naturalist, Spiritual and Existential Intelligences," Unpublished White Paper, 1996. It should be noted that emotional intelligence is not necessarily recognized as an MI by Gardner.

| Original Intelligences: | Characteristics | Famous Examples |
|---|---|---|
| 1. Logical/mathematical | Processes analytically, calculates, quantifies | Scientist Albert Einstein |
| 2. Verbal/linguistic | Thoughts through words, uses words to nurture | Consultant Tom Peters |
| 3. Interpersonal | Understands others, processes through interaction, empathizes, humor | Entertainer Oprah Winfrey |
| 4. Intrapersonal | Thinks in quiet, likes to be alone, goal oriented, independent, perseveres | Business Tycoon Howard Hughes |
| 5. Visual/spatial | Uses mental models, thinks three dimensionally, pictures how to get places or solve problems | Architect Frank Lloyd Wright |
| 6. Musical | Sensitivity to pitch, melody, rhythm, found in both performers and listeners | Composer Wolfgang Mozart |
| 7. Bodily/kinesthetic | Physical movement, involves whole body, processes by jumping or dancing | Basketball Player Michael Jordan |
| "New" Intelligences: | Characteristics | Famous Examples |
| 8. Naturalist | Needs to be with/survive in nature, strength in categorization in nature or urban world | Singer John Denver |
| 9. Existential | Not religion per se, knows why he or she is here, personal mission | Civil Rights Leader Martin Luther King |
| 10. Emotional | Emotionally mature, recognizes own anger, reacts to emotions of self and others | Pacifist Leader Mohandas Gandhi |

the basis of new empirical findings.[226] Importantly, the MIs are equal in importance and most people are strong in three or four but, because they are not fixed, there is always room for improvement in the others.

This expanded view of intelligence has had a dramatic impact on psychology, and many educators have used MI as a new paradigm for schools and classrooms.[227] However, there have to date only been a very few applications of MI in the business world, mainly in training workshops such as at 3M, Coseco Insurance, and Northeast Utilities Service. MI has only recently been acknowledged in the organizational behavior literature. However, with the recent addition of emotional intelligence or EI to Gardner's original seven (see Table 7.3), the recognition and theoretical foundation provided by Gardner's work becomes relevant and necessary to the understanding and application of EI in the workplace.

### Intelligence as Cognitive Mental Ability

Although the field of organizational behavior and human resource management has generally ignored multiple intelligences, there has been recognition and attention given over the years to the narrower concept of cognitive mental abilities. Applied to the workplace, *ability* refers to the aptitudes and learned capabilities needed to successfully accomplish a task. Both physical (e.g., manual dexterity, hand-eye coordination and body strength, stamina, and flexibility) and mental, intellectual, or cognitive abilities are recognized for jobs. However, with some obvious exceptions of jobs requiring considerable

**TABLE 7.4**  **Cognitive Abilities Related to Job Performance**

*Source:* Adapted from M. D. Dunnette, "Aptitudes, Abilities, and Skills," in M. D. Dunnette (Ed.), *Handbook of Industrial and Organizational Psychology,* Rand McNally, Skokie Ill., 1976, pp. 478–483.

| Mental Ability: | Characteristics of Ability | Examples of Job Task |
|---|---|---|
| Verbal comprehension | Comprehend what is read or heard, understand what words mean and the relationships to one another | Supervisors following organization policy on sexual harassment |
| Numerical | Make fast and accurate arithmetic computations | Auto salespeople calculating the sales tax and their commission |
| Spatial visualization | Perceive spatial patterns, imagine how an object would look if position in space were changed | A builder describing a change to a customer |
| Perceptual speed | Quickly identify visual similarities and differences, carry out tasks needing visual perception | A quality control engineer noting a product defect |
| Memory | Rote memory, retain and recall past incidents/experiences | A knowledge manager drawing from past experiences in the firm to advise a newly formed project team |
| Inductive reasoning | Identify logical sequence from specific to general | A scientist in the research department drawing from several independent studies to design an innovative product |

physical activity (e.g., in construction, manufacturing, repair services, sports or health clubs), the vast majority of jobs in today's workplace are concerned more with cognitive abilities.

Although some unique tasks require specific mental abilities (e.g., accounting tasks require numerical mental ability), most jobs, including those of an accountant or interior designer, require general mental ability (GMA). Over the years, psychologists have proposed numerous mental abilities, but those most widely recognized as underlying effective performance in jobs are summarized in Table 7.4

Importantly, there is considerable research evidence that GMA tests are a good personnel selection and job training program predictor of overall job performance. Specifically, Schmidt and Hunter summarized 85 years of research and based on meta-analytic findings concluded that the highest validities for predicting job performance were: (1) GMA plus a work sample test; (2) GMA plus an integrity test; and (3) GMA plus a structured interview.[228] An additional advantage of (2) and (3) is that they can be highly predicative for both entry-level selection and selection of experienced employees. One further refinement is that GMA predictive validity is higher for more-complex jobs and lower for less-complex jobs.

## Emotional Intelligence

As a point of departure for the important role that emotions have played in psychology over the years and Gardner's recognition of multiple intelligences has been the recent academic interest and popular appeal of emotional intelligence. Although its roots are usually considered to go back many years to what was called social intelligence,[229] at the beginning of the '90s psychologists Peter Salovey and John Mayer are usually given credit for having the first comprehensive theory and definition of emotional intelligence. Taking off

**TABLE 7.5** Goleman's Dimensions of Emotional Intelligence in the Workplace

*Source:* Adapted from Daniel Goleman, *Emotional Intelligence,* Bantam Books, New York, 1995, pp. 43–44, and Daniel Goleman, *Working with Emotional Intelligence,* Bantam Books, New York, 1998, p. 318.

| EI Dimensions: | Characteristics | Workplace Example |
|---|---|---|
| Self-awareness | Self-understanding; knowledge of true feelings at the moment | John recognizes that he is angry so he will wait to cool down and gather more information before making an important personnel decision. |
| Self-management | Handle one's emotions to facilitate rather than hinder the task at hand; shake off negative emotions and get back on constructive track for problem solution | Amber holds back her impulse to become visibly upset and raise her voice at the customer's unfair complaint and tries to get more facts of what happened. |
| Self-motivation | Stay the course toward desired goal; overcome negative emotional impulses and delay gratification to attain the desired outcome | Pat persisted to successful project completion in spite of the many frustrations from the lack of resources and top management support. |
| Empathy | Understand and be sensitive to the feelings of others; being able to sense what others feel and want | Because the head of the team knew her members were mentally if not physically exhausted, she took everyone bowling during an afternoon break and bought refreshments. |
| Social skills | The ability to read social situations; smooth in interacting with others and forming networks; able to guide others' emotions and the way they act | Jeremy could tell from the nonverbal cues from his staff members that they were not buying into the new policy being presented, so after the meeting he visited with each of them to explain how they will all benefit. |

from a foundation in the theory of emotion and multiple intelligence, Salovey and Mayer defined emotional intelligence as "the subset of social intelligence that involves the ability to monitor one's own and others' feelings and emotions, to discriminate among them, and to use this information to guide one's thinking and actions."[230] However, it was the publication of the 1995 best-selling book *Emotional Intelligence* by psychologist/journalist Daniel Goleman that greatly popularized the construct. He defines *emotional intelligence* or EI as

> The capacity for recognizing our own feelings and those of others, for motivating ourselves, and for managing emotions well in ourselves and in our relationships.[231]

Table 7.5 summarizes the major EI dimensions that Goleman has determined to have the most relevant and biggest impact on understanding behavior in the workplace.

As previously indicated, the major problem of EI not being considered to be a major construct of POB is that two streams have seemed to develop for EI. One is a very popular, applications-only approach stimulated and largely taken from Goleman's best-selling book. Unfortunately, this applications approach has been judged to have questionable theory, research, and carefully developed measures applied to it[232] as is being done more in the other stream in EI by theory- and research-oriented social psychologists such as Salovey and Mayer,[233] and more recently in the organizational behavior field.[234] As Mayer observed, "If you're going to take the term 'emotional intelligence' seriously as an intelligence, it's got to be about how one reasons about emotions and also about how emotions help reasoning, and most of the field does not do that."[235] However, even though the quality of theory, research, and measures to date is mixed, since Goleman did base his popular book on some theory and research and progress seems being made to refine the construct and its measures,[236] and its application in the field of organizational behavior (e.g., a recent study found that employees' EI was related to performance and satisfaction[237]), it is included here in the discussion of other positive constructs.

Importantly, Goleman, like Howard Gardner's recognition of multiple intelligences before him, makes a clear distinction between IQ and EI. The EI (or sometimes called EQ as a takeoff from IQ) literature carefully points out that the two constructs are certainly not the same but also not necessarily opposite from one another. As one summary of the analysis of IQ and EQ notes,

> Some people are blessed with a lot of both, some with little of either. What researchers have been trying to understand is how they complement each other; how one's ability to handle stress for instance, affects the ability to concentrate and put intelligence to use.[238]

Similar to the influence that neural activity and the brain play in IQ, Goleman also believes the brain pathways may help process EI. However, whereas IQ mostly is associated with the more recent (on the thousands-of-years-old evolutionary chain) neocortex (the thinking brain) located near the top of the brain, EI draws from the very early (in the evolution of the brain) inner subcortex more associated with emotional impulses. Importantly, however, unlike IQ, which has traditionally been considered largely inherited and fixed, Goleman also recognizes the role that personality and behavioral theories play in EI. Goleman provides a very comprehensive explanatory foundation for EI that includes the brain, but also suggests that learning seems to play an important role in EI. He states in his original book that

> Our genetic heritage endows each of us with a series of emotional set points that determines our temperament. But the brain circuitry involved is extraordinarily malleable; temperament is not destiny. The emotional lessons we learn as children at home and at school shape the emotional circuits, making us more adept—or inept—at the basics of emotional intelligence.[239]

In the second book, *Working with Emotional Intelligence,* he goes much further on the role of learning and the development of EI in maturing adults:

> Our level of emotional intelligence is not fixed genetically, nor does it develop only in early childhood. Unlike IQ, which changes little after our teen years, emotional intelligence seems to be largely learned, and it continues to develop as we go through life and learn from our experiences—our competence in it can keep growing. . . . There is an old-fashioned word for this growth in emotional intelligence: maturity.[240]

These seeming contradictions between the roles of genetic endowment, the brain, personality traits (that are pretty well set, see Chapter 5), and learning/development have drawn some criticism of Goleman's approach to EI.[241] However, there is recent research evidence that EI competencies can be developed in students working toward their masters of business administration.[242] Goleman also cites "studies that have tracked people's level of emotional intelligence through the years show that people get better and better in these capabilities as they grow more adept at handling their empathy and social adroitness."[243] In total, even though there remains some controversy and potential problems with the concept and operationalization of EI, it has such intuitive appeal and growing evidence for successful application to the workplace that it deserves further attention and research in the future of POB.

**Summary**

This chapter presents the recent focus on positive organizational behavior (POB) and psychological capital (PsyCap). It is based on the recent positive psychology movement—looking for strengths and what is right with people instead of concentrating on dysfunctions and what is wrong with people. Besides the positivity, specific criteria must be met to be included in POB: (1) based on theory and research, (2) valid measures, (3) statelike and open to development, and (4) managed for performance improvement. The psychological capacities (or capital) that to date best meet these POB criteria and are covered in this chapter are efficacy, optimism, hope, resiliency, and, when combined, form the core construct of psychological capital or PsyCap. The other positive constructs covered include happiness/SWB, emotions, intelligence, and emotional intelligence (EI).

Relatively most of the attention in the chapter is devoted to the theory, research, and application of the positive resource self-efficacy or confidence and overall psychological capital (PsyCap). Having the best fit with the POB criteria, social cognitive theory posits that environmental, behavioral, and personal cognitive dimensions are in interaction, and the self-reflective human capacity serves as the major theoretical underpinning of self-efficacy. Defined as the belief one has in his or her abilities to mobilize the motivation, cognitive resources, and courses of action necessary to successfully execute a specific task within a given context, self-efficacy is a state, not a trait. Through this theory building and extensive research of Bandura, four major sources of information to cognitively determine self-efficacy have been identified. These are, in order of importance, mastery experiences or performance attainments, vicarious experience or modeling, social persuasion, and physiological or psychological (emotional) arousal. Each of these can be used in training and development to enhance self-efficacy.

Self-efficacy started off as a clinical technique to change client behavior, but soon was successfully applied to many other health, educational, and athletic pursuits. Unlike the other POB constructs, there is also a considerable research-derived body of knowledge on the strong positive relationship between self-efficacy and work-related performance. The Stajkovic and Luthans meta-analysis (114 studies, 21,616 subjects) found a highly significant .38 weighted average correlation that transforms to an impressive 28 percent gain in performance (higher than the results of meta-analyses of other popular organizational behavior constructs and techniques). With such substantial theory and research backup, there are important implications for effective practical applications of self-efficacy. Besides training and development to enhance self-efficacy and thus help the transfer of training to the job and increase performance, the measurement of self-efficacy could be used in the selection process. Self-efficacy can also be used to make job design, goal setting, teams, and stress management more effective.

Besides efficacy/confidence, the other positive capacities that have been determined to best meet the POB criteria are optimism, hope, and resiliency. Although optimism has been around for a long time and is associated with many positive things in life, its use in a psychological and POB capacity applicable to the workplace is relatively recent. Both motivated and motivating, optimism has some evidence not only of being part of human nature, but also more support for contributing to individual differences. The pioneering work of Seligman treats optimism in terms of cognitively determined expectancies and causal attributions (i.e., explanatory style). Specifically, pessimists make internal, stable, and global attributions of bad events, whereas optimists make external, unstable, and specific attributions. Although there can be some dysfunctional consequences such as stress from pursuing unattainable goals and there are some cases where a mild pessimist may be needed in organizations (e.g., safety engineer or accountant), in general, realistic optimism is very beneficial in life and in the workplace. Research is just starting, but evidence from

Seligman's widely recognized extensive work with sales agents at Metropolitan Life and more recent studies in POB indicate the very positive impact that optimism can have on human performance in organizations.

Besides optimism, the closely related but conceptually and empirically distinct construct of hope also meets the POB criteria. As used in psychology and its potential applicability to organizational behavior, hope is more than the sunny advice of "hope for the best." Although both Goleman and Seligman talk about hope in relation to EI and optimism respectively, the work of Snyder on hope is most recognized in positive psychology. He defines hope not only in terms of the person's determination that goals can be achieved, but also as the beliefs that successful plans can be formulated, pathways identified, and self-motivation exhibited in order to attain the goals. In simple terms, this meaning of hope includes both the willpower (agency) and the "waypower" (the alternate pathways). There has been such strong evidence of the relationship between hope and academic, athletic, and mental/physical health positive outcomes that the carryover to the workplace is also being demonstrated by initial research in POB and seems very promising for the future.

The fourth major recognized positive capacity in POB is resiliency. Considerably different from the other POB variables, resiliency tends to be more reactive than proactive. Also with roots in clinical psychology, especially focused on at-risk children and adolescents, it has been characterized by positive adaptation to significant adversity or risk. In POB it is presented as the positive capacity to rebound or bounce back from adverse or even very good events. In recent years, such a resilient capacity is very relevant and desirable at the employee, manager, and organizational levels. Although studies in POB are just beginning, there appears to be unlimited potential for developing and managing resiliency as the environment becomes ever more uncertain and turbulent.

When the four resources are combined into PsyCap, there is both theory and research evidence that it is a higher-order, core construct. A valid measure of PsyCap (the PCQ) has been developed and there is growing evidence that it is related to not only performance and job satisfaction, but to other desirable outcomes such as combating stress, facilitating positive organizational change, mediating the relationship between supportive organizational climate and employee performance, and both employee creativity and well-being. There is initial evidence that PsyCap is also related to effective leadership. Finally, being statelike, beginning research is demonstrating that PsyCap can be developed in relatively short training interventions with causal impact on performance and yields a very high return on the investment in PsyCap development.

Because of meeting the established criteria, the lion's share of attention in this chapter has been devoted to the four positive resource states of efficacy, optimism, hope, resiliency and overall PsyCap. Obviously, there are other positive constructs that have been and will be important to POB. The other positive constructs covered in this chapter are happiness or what some academics prefer to call subjective well-being or SWB and then emotions, intelligence, and when combined, emotional intelligence (EI). In particular, there have been considerable work-related studies in the SWB research literature. For example, the work of Diener is very relevant to POB. As with the other positive constructs in this chapter, he is concerned with the underlying processes that influence life satisfaction, satisfaction with important domains (including work satisfaction). In particular, Diener and Biswas-Diener point out that happiness is a process (not a place), has an optimal (not linear) level, and is related to health and longevity (the famous nun's study results), relationships and work. Like PsyCap, there is evidence that happiness is related to desired outcomes in the workplace (and in life) and can be developed.

Emotional intelligence or simply EI is first discussed in terms of its major components of emotion (feelings) and intelligence. Intelligence in particular has played a relatively minor role in organizational behavior. In particular, the multiple intelligences, and specifically emotional intelligence, have only recently received attention. Broadly popularized by Goleman, EI is the capacity for understanding and managing one's own and others' emotions. Although there is still some controversy surrounding EI, the popularity, intuitive appeal, and growing supportive research on EI cannot be denied. There is increasing evidence that the characteristics of EI (e.g., self-awareness, self-motivation, empathy, and social skills) may be better than traditional IQ in predicting future life success, and in the future with continued theory-building and research may become a more accepted evidence-based positive construct in POB.

## Ending with Meta-Analytic Research Findings
## OB PRINCIPLE FOR EVIDENCED-BASED PRACTICE

The higher employees' self-efficacy on a specific task, the better they will perform.

### Meta-Analysis Results:

[114 studies; 21,616 participants; *d* = .82] *On average, there is a **72 percent probability** that employees with high self-efficacy on a specific task will have better performance than those with low self-efficacy.* The moderators found in the meta-analysis were task complexity and the setting for the study. Specifically, it was found that the more complex the task, the less, but still highly significant, impact self-efficacy will have on performance. Also, self-efficacy had a bigger impact in the studies conducted in laboratory settings than those in the field.

### Conclusion:

Although the POB constructs are becoming increasingly popular and important in the study and application of organizational behavior, to date, only self-efficacy has enough research to conduct a meta-analysis applicable to the workplace. There seems little question that self-efficacy has become one of the very best predictors of human performance. In today's work environment characterized by uncertainty, change, and complex undertakings, organizations will be challenged to do their part in increasing employees' beliefs in their personal competence so that organizational performance goals can be realized. In addition to self-efficacy, each of the other major POB constructs of optimism, hope, resiliency, and when combined into psychological capital (PsyCap), show considerable promise for the understanding and effective application of organizational behavior.

**Source:** Adapted from Alexander D. Stajkovic and Fred Luthans, "The Relationship between Self-Efficacy and Work-Related Performance: A Meta-Analysis," *Psychological Bulletin,* Vol. 124, No. 2, 1998, pp. 240–261.

| Questions for Discussion and Review | |
|---|---|
| | 1. How does positive psychology differ from regular psychology? |
| | 2. What are the four criteria for positive organizational behavior? How do the various POB constructs measure up to these criteria? |
| | 3. What is self-efficacy? Why is it important to make the distinction that self-efficacy is a state rather than a trait? What implications does this have for the workplace? |

4. Defend or argue against the statement that the characteristics of a highly efficacious employee may be "the best profile of a high performer." Describe this profile and give an example of this in the workplace.

5. What are the four widely recognized sources of self-efficacy? How could each be used to enhance employee efficacy to increase performance?

6. How does optimism in positive psychology go beyond the old "power of positive thinking"? Give an example of where "little optimism" may be different from "big optimism." Besides sales, give an example of where optimism may be very beneficial to work performance.

7. In positive psychology, how does the concept of hope go beyond "sunny advice"? Why may hope be particularly relevant to entrepreneurship and international human resource management?

8. Why is resiliency so important in recent times? Give a real example.

9. What is psychological capital (PsyCap)? Briefly summarize the research to date on PsyCap and why might this provide competitive advantage to an organization?

10. What is subjective well-being (SWB)? What were some of the defining characteristics about happiness and how can it be developed and attained?

11. What is an emotion? How do emotions differ from moods? Identify some primary emotions, and give examples of how they may be expressed in the workplace.

12. What are Gardner's original seven intelligences? Which two are the most closely associated with traditional IQ? What are the three "new" intelligences? Which of the 10 do you feel are most relevant and important to an effective manager?

13. Very simply, what is emotional intelligence (EI)? What are the major dimensions of EI that are particularly relevant to the workplace? Why do you think EI may be more important than IQ for an effective manager?

14. Of the POB constructs that are covered in the chapter, which one do you think has the most potential for impacting employee performance? Why?

## Internet Exercise: What Is Your IQ and EQ?

A good way to understand the value and the power of positive organizational behavior variables is to first understand yourself. By first understanding yourself, you can better understand others. For example, to compare and contrast your IQ with your EQ, there are a few such tests on the Web. Remembering that these are not scientifically valid and that you should only take them as interesting information and not too seriously, go to **http://www.queendom.com** for some cognitive exercises including an IQ test. To assess your happiness, visit **http://www.authentichappiness.com.** Also visit **http://www.positivepsychology.org** for a comprehensive site on positive psychology and **http://www.bus.umich.edu/Positive** for background and updates on positive organizational scholarship and **http://www.gli.unl.edu** for updates on positive organizational behavior.

1. Did the results of your IQ test surprise you? Considering that EQ can be learned, are there any areas you should try to improve on?

2. How do you think your close coworkers and/or friends would respond to these tests? Does that help you understand their behaviors better?

3. Do you agree that EQ (EI) may be more important than IQ and may be applicable to effective interpersonal relations and performance in the workplace? Why?

4. What impact does authentic happiness and/or positive organizational scholarship and behavior have on applications to the workplace?

# Real Case: *High Tech—High Fear*

Both the popular and academic press proclaim how wonderful advanced technology is for today's organizations. For example, B2B (business to business) processes can dramatically cut a firm's costs. The other side, the dark side of this high-tech revolution, however, is seldom mentioned. Although young employees who grew up with computers in their schools and homes may be adaptable and open to IT changes in the workplace, and certainly some middle-age and older employees at all levels welcome and are excited by the IT challenges, a significant number of today's employees of all ages are not only resistant, but downright terrified.

With the dramatic changes brought on by the new technological environment, today's employees have been thrust into a whole range of emotional reactions, from surprise to fear to anger to even shame. Competent, secure employees who were very optimistic and efficacious about their job duties in the old economy have become pessimistic and questioning of their abilities and cognitive resources necessary to be successful in this new high-tech environment.

Here is a recent list of human problems associated with the advent of advanced technology in today's organizations:

1. Feelings of being overwhelmed, intimidated, and ashamed of not being able to keep up with job demands.
2. Some employees' belief that they are actually being enslaved, not empowered, by new technology.
3. Fears of appearing inept, unintelligent, or resistant to change.
4. A diminished ability to solve problems, fostering a sense of hopelessness and worry.

5. Loss of respect by the boss, peers, and subordinates.
6. Physiological disturbances brought on by longer hours, time pressures, and even hormone shifts brought on by being physically isolated.
7. Mood swings, depression, exhaustion, and attention deficits.

Obviously, these feelings, beliefs, fears, and physical/mental dysfunctions are taking their toll on the people affected, but there also may be an impact on quality, productivity, and retention.

1. What are the trade-offs in today's organizations between the positives and negatives of advanced technology? Does it really matter if some of the older employees are having a hard time adjusting; aren't they on their way out anyway and they can be replaced by the technology? On balance, what do you feel about the impact of technology?
2. In the "dark side" of IT presented in this case, there are many implications for self-efficacy, optimism, hope, resiliency, and psychological capital. Describe a specific example of each of these POB constructs.
3. In general, how can the understanding of the POB constructs help overcome the list of problems presented in the case? How can the manager of a unit consisting of mostly older, computer anxious, if not illiterate, employees who were very effective under the old system use positive resources to make a more successful transition to a new, technologically sophisticated operating system?

# Organizational Behavior Case: *People Problems at HEI*

After graduating with honors with a management major from State University, Ashley James accepted an entry-level position in the Human Resources Department of Hospital Equipment Inc. (HEI), a medium-sized manufacturer of hospital beds and metal furniture (bedstands, tables, cabinets, etc.). This hospital room product line has been a "cash cow" for HEI since the founding of the

firm 35 years ago by James Robinson, Sr. In recent years, however, HEI's market share has become eroded by some of the big office furniture firms, both in the United States and abroad, who are starting to diversify into the health institution market.

Mr. Robinson has been easing into retirement the last couple of years. His only child, Rob, was made CEO three months ago. Rob came up through product engineering for two years and then headed up operations for the past four years. Rob had been a three-sport star athlete and student body president in high school. He then went on to State University where he graduated near the top of his class in mechanical engineering.

In his new leadership role at HEI, Rob's vision is to take the firm from being a low-tech bed and metal furniture manufacturer that is going downhill to become a high-tech medical equipment manufacturer. Rob is convinced that even though this would be a dramatic change for HEI, there is enough of a foundation and culture in place to at least start a new division focused initially on operating room equipment.

Rob's marketing manager had commissioned a study with a marketing research firm that concluded operating room equipment supply was not keeping up with demand and was way behind the rest of the health care supply industry in terms of innovative technology for patient comfort and care. The marketing manager, armed with this information, enthusiastically supported Rob's vision for the future of HEI.

The finance and operations people are another story. The finance manager is very pessimistic. HEI is already under a cash flow strain because of decreasing revenues from their existing product line and, although they currently have very little long-term debt, with Robinson Senior retiring, his contacts and long-term friends in the local lending community were gone. Only the big corporate banks with decision makers in other cities are left. The new head of operations, who has been very close to Robinson Senior over the years and had basically run the show for Rob the past four years, is also very pessimistic. In a recent executive committee meeting where Rob had asked for input on his vision for HEI, this operations head angrily blurted out, "I know we have to do something! But medical equipment? I have absolutely no hope that our engineers or operating people have the capacity to move in this direction. As you know, almost all of our people have been with us at least 15 to 20 years. They are too set in their ways, and the only way we could start a new medical equipment division would be from scratch, and I certainly don't see the funding for that!"

After weighing his senior management team's advice, consulting with his dad, doing some research on his own, and tapping his network of friends in and outside the industry, Rob decided to go ahead with the planning of a new medical equipment division. He also decided that this new division would have to be run by present people and he would seek no outside funding. At this point, he called in the young Ashley James from the HR department and gave her the following assignment:

> Ashley, I know you haven't been around here very long, but I think you can handle the challenge that I am going to give you. As you probably know by now, HEI is having some difficulties, and I have decided we need to move in a new direction with a medical equipment division. As I see it, we have some real people problems to overcome before this will be a success. Having worked in operations the past several years, I am convinced we have enough raw talent in both engineering and at the operating level to make the transition and pull this off successfully. But I need your help. Did you come across anything in your program at State U. that had to do with getting people to be more positive, more optimistic, and confident? I really think this is the problem, starting with management and going right down the line. I want you to take a week to think about this, talk to everyone involved, do some research, and come back with a specific proposal of what HR can do to help me out on this. The very survival of HEI may depend on what you come up with.

1. On the basis of the limited information in this case, how would you assess the efficacy, optimism, hope, resiliency, and overall psychological capital of Rob? Of the operations manager? Give some specifics to back your assessment. What implications do these assessments have for the future of HEI?

2. What's your reaction to the finance manager's pessimism? What about the market manager's optimism? What implications does this have for Rob and the company?

3. Do you agree with Rob's decision? Would you like to work for him? Why or why not?

4. If you were Ashley, what specific proposal would you make to Rob? How would you implement such a proposal?

# Experiential Exercises for Part Two

## EXERCISE:

Self-Perception and Development of the Self-Concept*

### Goals:

1. To enable the students to consider their own self-concepts and to compare this with how they feel they are perceived by others.
2. To explore how the self-concept in personality is formed largely on the basis of feedback received from others (the reality that we "mirror ourselves in others").
3. To stimulate student thinking about how management of human resources may involve perception and personality.

### Implementation:

1. The students take out a sheet of paper and fold it in half from top to bottom.
2. The students write "How I See Myself" and "How I Think Others See Me."
3. The students write down 5 one-word descriptions (adjectives) under each designation that, in their opinion, best describe how they perceive themselves and how others perceive them.
4. The students then share their two lists with their classmates (in dyads, triads, or the whole class) and discuss briefly. Each person may communicate what he or she is most proud of.
5. The instructor may participate in the exercise by sharing his or her list of adjectives.

*The exercise "Self-Perception and Development of the Self-Concept" was suggested by Philip Van Auken and is used with his permission.

## EXERCISE:

Job Design Survey*

### Goals:

1. To experience firsthand the job characteristics approach to job design, in this case through the Hackman-Oldham Job Diagnostic Survey (JDS).
2. To get personal feedback on the motivating potential of your present or past job and to identify and compare its critical characteristics.

### Implementation:

1. Please describe your present job (or a job you have held in the past) as objectively as you can. Circle the number that best reflects the job.

**\*Source:** The "Job Design Survey" is drawn from J. R. Hackman and G. R. Oldham, "Development of the Job Diagnostic Survey," *Journal of Applied Psychology,* Vol. 60, 1975, pp. 159–170.

*a.* How much *variety* is there in your job? That is, to what extent does the job require you to do many things at work, using a variety of your skills and talents?

1- - - - - - - - -2- - - - - - - - -3- - - - - - - - -4- - - - - - - - -5- - - - - - - - -6- - - - - - - -7

| Very little; the job requires me to do the same routine things over and over again. | Moderate variety. | Very much; the job requires me to do many different things, using a number of different skills and talents. |
|---|---|---|

*b.* To what extent does your job involve doing a "*whole*" and *identifiable piece of work*? That is, is the job a complete piece of work that has an obvious beginning and end, or is it only a small part of the overall piece of work, which is finished by other people or by machines?

1- - - - - - - - -2- - - - - - - - -3- - - - - - - - -4- - - - - - - - -5- - - - - - - - -6- - - - - - - -7

| My job is only a tiny part of the overall piece of work; the results of my activities cannot be seen in the final product or service. | My job is a moderate-sized "chunk" of the overall piece of work; my own contribution can be seen in the final outcome. | My job involves doing the whole piece of work, from start to finish; the results of my activities are easily seen in the final product or service. |
|---|---|---|

*c.* In general, *how significant or important* is your job? That is, are the results of your work likely to significantly affect the lives or well-being of other people?

1- - - - - - - - -2- - - - - - - - -3- - - - - - - - -4- - - - - - - - -5- - - - - - - - -6- - - - - - - -7

| Not very significant; the outcomes of my work are not likely to have important effects on other people. | Moderately significant. | Highly significant; the outcomes of my work can affect other people in very important ways. |
|---|---|---|

*d.* How much *autonomy* is there in your job? That is, to what extent does your job permit you to decide *on your own* how to go about doing the work?

1- - - - - - - - -2- - - - - - - - -3- - - - - - - - -4- - - - - - - - -5- - - - - - - - -6- - - - - - - -7

| Very little; the job gives me almost no personal "say" about how and when the work is done. | Moderate autonomy; many things are standardized and not under my control, but I can make some decisions. | Very much; the job gives me almost complete responsibility for deciding how and when the work is done. |
|---|---|---|

*e.* To what extent does doing the *job itself* provide you with information about your work performance? That is, does the actual *work itself* provide clues about how well you are doing—aside from any feedback coworkers or supervisors may provide?

1- - - - - - - - -2- - - - - - - - -3- - - - - - - - -4- - - - - - - - -5- - - - - - - - -6- - - - - - - -7

| Very little; the job itself is set up so that I could work here forever without finding out how well I am doing. | Moderately; sometimes doing the job provides feedback to me; sometimes it does not. | Very much; the job is set up so that I get almost constant feedback as I work about how well I am doing. |
|---|---|---|

2. The five questions above measure your perceived skill variety, task identity, task significance, autonomy, and feedback in your job. The complete JDS uses several questions to

measure these dimensions. But to get some idea of the motivating potential, use your scores (1 to 7) for each job dimension and calculate as follows:

$$\text{MPS} = \frac{\text{skill variety} + \text{task identity} + \text{task significance}}{3} + \text{autonomy} + \text{feedback}$$

Next, plot your job design profile and mps score on the following graphs. These show the national averages for all jobs. Analyze how you compare and suggest ways to redesign your job.

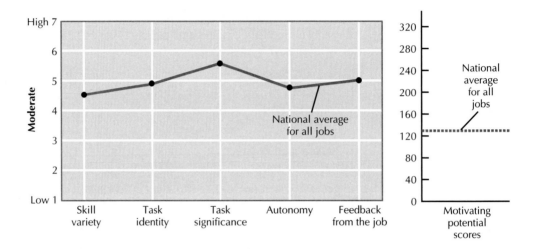

## EXERCISE:

Motivation Questionnaire*

## Goals:

1. To experience firsthand the concepts of one of the work-motivation theories—in this case, the popular Maslow hierarchy of needs.
2. To get personal feedback on your opinions of the use of motivational techniques in human resource management.

## Implementation:

The following questions for the Motivation Questionnaire on the next page have seven possible responses:

1. Please mark one of the seven responses by circling the number that corresponds to the response that fits your opinion. For example, if you "strongly agree," circle the number "+3."
2. Complete every item. You have about 10 minutes to do so.

*The "Motivation Questionnaire" is reprinted from "Motivation: A Feedback Exercise," in John E. Jones and J. William Pfeiffer (Eds.), *The Annual Handbook for Group Facilitators,* University Associates, San Diego, Calif., 1973, pp. 43–45, and is used with permission.

| | Strongly Agree | Agree | Slightly Agree | Don't Know | Slightly Disagree | Disagree | Strongly Disagree |
|---|---|---|---|---|---|---|---|
| | +3 | +2 | +1 | 0 | −1 | −2 | −3 |
| 1. Special wage increases should be given to employees who do their jobs very well. | +3 | +2 | +1 | 0 | −1 | −2 | −3 |
| 2. Better job descriptions would be helpful so that employees will know exactly what is expected of them. | +3 | +2 | +1 | 0 | −1 | −2 | −3 |
| 3. Employees need to be reminded that their jobs are dependent on the company's ability to compete effectively. | +3 | +2 | +1 | 0 | −1 | −2 | −3 |
| 4. Supervisors should give a good deal of attention to the physical working conditions of their employees. | +3 | +2 | +1 | 0 | −1 | −2 | −3 |
| 5. Supervisors ought to work hard to develop a friendly working atmosphere among their people. | +3 | +2 | +1 | 0 | −1 | −2 | −3 |
| 6. Individual recognition for above-standard performance means a lot to employees. | +3 | +2 | +1 | 0 | −1 | −2 | −3 |
| 7. Indifferent supervision can often bruise feelings. | +3 | +2 | +1 | 0 | −1 | −2 | −3 |
| 8. Employees want to feel that their real skills and capacities are put to use on their jobs. | +3 | +2 | +1 | 0 | −1 | −2 | −3 |
| 9. The company retirement benefits and stock programs are important factors in keeping employees on their jobs. | +3 | +2 | +1 | 0 | −1 | −2 | −3 |
| 10. Almost every job can be made more stimulating and challenging. | +3 | +2 | +1 | 0 | −1 | −2 | −3 |
| 11. Many employees want to give their best in everything they do. | +3 | +2 | +1 | 0 | −1 | −2 | −3 |
| 12. Management could show more interest in the employees by sponsoring social events after hours. | +3 | +2 | +1 | 0 | −1 | −2 | −3 |
| 13. Pride in one's work is actually an important reward. | +3 | +2 | +1 | 0 | −1 | −2 | −3 |
| 14. Employees want to be able to think of themselves as "the best" at their own jobs. | +3 | +2 | +1 | 0 | −1 | −2 | −3 |
| 15. The quality of the relationships in the informal work group is quite important. | +3 | +2 | +1 | 0 | −1 | −2 | −3 |
| 16. Individual incentive bonuses would improve the performance of employees. | +3 | +2 | +1 | 0 | −1 | −2 | −3 |
| 17. Visibility with upper management is important to employees. | +3 | +2 | +1 | 0 | −1 | −2 | −3 |
| 18. Employees generally like to schedule their own work and to make job-related decisions with a minimum of supervision. | +3 | +2 | +1 | 0 | −1 | −2 | −3 |
| 19. Job security is important to employees. | +3 | +2 | +1 | 0 | −1 | −2 | −3 |
| 20. Having good equipment to work with is important to employees. | +3 | +2 | +1 | 0 | −1 | −2 | −3 |

## Scoring:

1. Transfer the numbers you circled in the questionnaire to the appropriate places in the following chart.

| Statement No. | Score | Statement No. | Score |
|---|---|---|---|
| 10 | ———— | 2 | ———— |
| 11 | ———— | 3 | ———— |
| 13 | ———— | 9 | ———— |
| 18 | ———— | 19 | ———— |
| Total | ———— | Total | ———— |
| (Self-actualization needs) | | (Safety needs) | |
| 6 | ———— | 1 | ———— |
| 8 | ———— | 4 | ———— |
| 14 | ———— | 16 | ———— |
| 17 | ———— | 20 | ———— |
| Total | ———— | Total | ———— |
| (Esteem needs) | | (Basic needs) | |
| 5 | ———— | | |
| 7 | ———— | | |
| 12 | ———— | | |
| 15 | ———— | | |
| Total | ———— | | |
| (Belongingness needs) | | | |

2. Record your total scores in the following chart by marking an *X* in each row below the number of your total score for that area of needs motivation.

| | −12 | −10 | −8 | −6 | −4 | −2 | 0 | +2 | +4 | +6 | +8 | +10 | +12 |
|---|---|---|---|---|---|---|---|---|---|---|---|---|---|
| Self-actualization | | | | | | | | | | | | | |
| Esteem | | | | | | | | | | | | | |
| Belongingness | | | | | | | | | | | | | |
| Safety | | | | | | | | | | | | | |
| Basic | | | | | | | | | | | | | |

Low   use      High   use

By examining the chart, you can see the relative strength you attach to each of the needs in Maslow's hierarchy. There are no right answers here, but most work-motivation theorists imply that most people are concerned mainly with the upper-level needs (that is, belongingness, esteem, and self-actualization).

# Part Three

# Dynamics of Organizational Behavior

## Evidence-Based Consulting Practices

### GALLUP'S APPROACH TO THE DYNAMICS OF ORGANIZATIONAL BEHAVIOR: THE USE OF TALENT OF TEAM

For Gallup, the first issue for the dynamics of organizational behavior is that the team be led by an individual who has the right talent for the role. Certain individuals have this knack, or talent, to put people together so that the whole is greater than the sum of the parts. There is an essential leadership talent issue at the center of a truly successful team practice.

The best teams are created when the unique talents of each individual are brought together for the desired outcome. Teams are not always more productive than individuals working separately. In Gallup's approach, the best teams are paradoxically related to the right way to handle individuals. To have a great team, each member of the team needs to have a self-awareness of their own best contribution to the team and an assurance that others know that their primary contributions are related to these talents. In this way, each member is attentive to his or her best contribution to and for the team. It is also true that team members do not labor under inappropriate expectations derived from the leader, teammates, or self. Put another way, people expect the best from me and the best for me, and in this way one is best positioned to respond in a successful manner.

Gallup has found that great team leaders encourage employees to spend most of their time building their top talents into strengths by adding knowledge, skills, and experience. The remainder of their time is spent managing their weaknesses through building complimentary partnerships with other team members, developing support systems, or using their strengths to make their weaknesses irrelevant. Great team leaders pay attention to the difference in the talents that individuals bring to the table. Some people love to get things started. These same people frequently are bored with things long before they are finished. Their joy in life is "making things happen." Often these individuals are less interested in "permission" than "action." Often seen as "fire starters," they can be used well by moving them from team to team, timing their arrival at the point where the "analytical types" have things well in hand and are about to pass over into the paralysis of reanalyzing the analysis. Let the high-focus, detail people do cleanup operations. Such organizational behavior dynamics are talent based and create the greatest positive effect when people are encouraged to utilize their impact, rather than ignoring or actually seeking to thwart such inclinations.

Great team leaders will ask questions such as: "What are the talents of each of the members of my team? What experience, skills, and knowledge could I provide my team members to help them develop their themes of talent into strengths? Are my team's performance problems caused by a lack of skills and knowledge, which can be developed through training and experience? Are the performance problems caused by a lack of talent, in which case training will have a minimal impact? Is my team missing any talents that could make it more balanced? Likewise, when they follow the strengths-based approach, team members will start to ask themselves questions such as: "How does this role draw out my greatest talents? What can I do to further develop my talents into strengths? How can working from my areas of greatest strength impact my performance and the performance of our team? Who on my team has a talent that would make them a great complementary partner for me?"

In summary, Gallup's position is that great teams are those where individuals are set up for success according to their strengths.

# Chapter **Eight**

# Communication and Decision Making

### Learning Objectives

- **Relate** the perspective, historical background, and meaning of the communication process in organizations.
- **Identify** the dimensions of nonverbal communication.
- **Discuss** the specific dimensions of interpersonal and interactive communication processes.
- **Describe** the decision-making process and behavioral decision making.
- **Present** the styles and techniques of decision making.
- **Explore** the creative process.

Communication and decision making are frequently discussed dynamics in organizational behavior, but they are seldom clearly understood. Both are basic prerequisites for the attainment of organizational strategies and effective human resource management, but they remain big problems facing modern management. Both are extremely broad topics and of course are not restricted to the organizational behavior field. Both take up a lot of an active human being's life, and even higher proportions of a typical manager's time. The comprehensive study reported in Chapter 14, that directly observed a wide cross section of what were called "Real Managers" in their day-to-day behaviors, found that they devote about a third of their activities to routine communication—exchanging and processing routine information and over 10 percent in decision making.[1] More important, however, is the finding that the communication activity made the biggest relative contribution to effective managers and decision making accounts for a smaller but still critical input. Figure 8.1 summarizes these findings. In other words, there seems little doubt that communication and decision making play an important role in managerial and organizational effectiveness.

First, the background of the role of communication in management and organizational behavior is briefly discussed. This discussion is followed by a precise definition of communication and presentation of nonverbal communication. Next, the heart of the chapter is concerned with interpersonal and interactive communication. An interpersonal process, as opposed to a linear information flow perspective of communication, is taken throughout. The balance of the chapter is concerned with the decision-making process with particular attention given to behaviorally oriented styles and techniques.

**FIGURE 8.1**
**Activities of Real Managers' Effectiveness**

*Source:* Fred Luthans, Richard M. Hodgetts, and Stuart A. Rosenkrantz, *Real Managers,* Ballinger, Cambridge, Mass., 1988, p. 68. (Used with permission.)

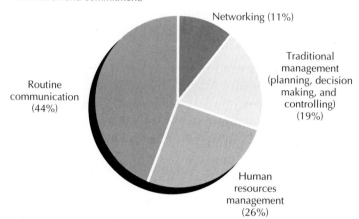

**LUTHANS ET AL. STUDY OF REAL MANAGERS' EFFECTIVENESS**
($N = 178$, drawn from participant observation data related to combined effectiveness measure of unit performance and subordinate satisfaction and commitment)

Networking (11%)

Traditional management (planning, decision making, and controlling) (19%)

Human resources management (26%)

Routine communication (44%)

# BACKGROUND OF THE ROLE OF COMMUNICATION

Early discussions of management gave very little emphasis to communication. Although communication was implicit in the managerial function of command and the structural principle of hierarchy, the early theorists never fully developed or integrated it into management theory. At the same time, they did generally recognize the role of informal communication in relation to the problem of supplementing the formal, hierarchical channels. But the pioneering theorist Chester Barnard, in his classic *Functions of the Executive,* was the first to develop the idea of the central, important role communication plays in the organization.

Since the original contributions by Barnard before WWII, the dynamics of communication have been one of the central concerns of organizational behavior and management theorists and especially practitioners. There has been a deluge of books and articles that deal specifically with interpersonal and organizational communication. Unfortunately, practically all this vast literature gives only a surface treatment of the subject and is seldom an evidence-based approach. For example, there have been complaints about an uncritical acceptance of the effectiveness of open communication, when a contingency perspective would be more in line with the evidence.[2]

One exception was the "Real Managers Study," reported in Chapter 14 and mentioned in the introductory comments of this chapter. One part of this study combined direct observation of managers in their natural setting with self-report measures to try to determine how they communicated.[3] The model shown in Figure 8.2 gives the results. The first dimension of the managerial communication model represents a continuum ranging from the humanistic interactor (who frequently interacts both up and down the organization system and exhibits human-oriented activities) to the mechanistic isolate (who communicates very little, except on a formal basis). The other dimension describes a continuum from the informal developer (who communicates spontaneously in all directions and exhibits activities related to developing his or her people) to the formal controller (who uses formally scheduled communication interaction and exhibits monitoring/controlling activities).[4] This empirically derived model describes two major dimensions of managerial communication. It provides a framework for *how* managers communicate on a day-to-day basis and can be

**FIGURE 8.2**
**Managerial Communication Model: How Managers Communicate**

*Source:* Fred Luthans and Janet K. Larsen, "How Managers Really Communicate," *Human Relations,* Vol. 39, No. 2, 1986, p. 175.

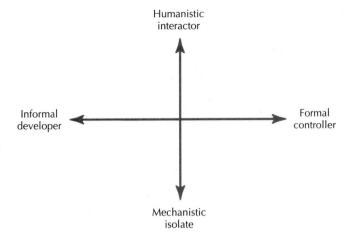

used as a point of departure for formally defining communication and the interpersonal processes of communication in today's organizations.

## The Definition of Communication

The term *communication* is freely used by everyone in modern society, including members of the general public, organizational behavior scholars, and management practitioners. In addition, the term is employed to explain a multitude of sins both in the society as a whole and in work organizations. Despite this widespread usage, very few members of the general public—and not a great many more management people—can precisely define the term. Part of the problem is that communication experts have not agreed on a definition themselves.

Most definitions of *communication* used in organizational behavior literature stress the use of symbols to transfer the meaning of information. For example, one analysis stresses that communication is the understanding not of the visible but of the invisible and hidden. These hidden and symbolic elements embedded in the culture give meaning to the visible communication process.[5] Of equal, if not more, importance, however, is the fact that communication is a personal process that involves the exchange of behaviors and information. Today, of course, this personal process is not just face-to-face, but is increasingly carried out electronically through Facebook, MySpace, blogs, wikis, texting, mobile phones, and e-mail.[6] Although associated with emerging Web 2.0 technologies, the still personal aspects have been noted in no uncertain terms by most organizational behavior scholars. For example, Ivancevich and Matteson noted that "communication among people does not depend on technology but rather on forces in people and their surroundings. It is a process that occurs within people."[7] This personal perspective of communication has been made particularly clear by Nickerson, who has found that many people tend to assume that the other person has the same knowledge that they do, and they communicate on this basis.[8] The result is often communication breakdown.

In addition to being a personal process, communication has other implications. A communication expert emphasizes the *behavioral* implications of communication by pointing out that "the only means by which one person can influence another is by the behaviors he performs—that is, the communicative exchanges between people provide the sole method by which influence or effects can be achieved."[9] In other words, the behaviors that occur in an organization are vital to the communication process. This personal and behavioral exchange view of communication takes many forms.

**FIGURE 8.3**
**The Continuum of Communication in Organizational Behavior**

The continuum in Figure 8.3 can be used to identify the major categories of communication that are especially relevant to the study of organizational behavior. On the one extreme is the increasingly important electronic (i.e., Internet) communication media and information technology, and on the other extreme is relatively simple nonverbal communication. The middle ground is occupied by interpersonal approaches (both electronically mediated and face-to-face), which represent the personal perspective taken in this chapter. The growing importance of the role that electronic media and information technology[10] plays in communication is certainly recognized by organizational behavior research and application. For example, the accompanying OB in Action: Go Ahead, Use Facebook points out the importance of social networking via the Internet to today's especially younger employees. There is also considerable research interest in areas such as virtual teams.[11] However, more directly relevant to the personal perspective taken here are the areas of nonverbal and interpersonal communication.

# NONVERBAL COMMUNICATION

The opposite end of the continuum from the tangible, often sophisticated electronic media and information technology is nonverbal communication. Although verbal communication has long been recognized as being important, nonverbal communication is particularly relevant to the study of organizational behavior. Sometimes called the "silent language," *nonverbal communication* can be defined as "nonword human responses (such as gestures, facial expressions) *and* the perceived characteristics of the environment through which the human verbal and nonverbal messages are transmitted."[12] Thus, whether a person says something or, equally important, does *not* say anything, communication still can take place.

## Body Language and Paralanguage

There are many forms of nonverbal communication. Probably the most widely recognized is body language. Body movements convey meanings and messages. This form of communication includes facial expressions and what people do with their eyes, feet, hands, and posture. For example, good salespeople, advertisers, and even poker players capitalize on their knowledge of people's eyes. As explained by Preston:

> when an individual is excited or aroused, the pupils of the eyes will dilate. When haggling over a price, the buyer will unconsciously signal an alert seller that a particular price is acceptable. . . . Some colors or shapes cause more excitement than others, and the reaction registers in the shopper's eyes. With this research information, marketing people redesign their products to better appeal to buyers in a competitive environment. Good poker players watch the eyes of their fellow players as new cards are dealt. The pupil dilation very often will show if the card being dealt improves the player's hand.[13]

Besides the obvious meanings attached to things such as a firm handshake or touching the other person when making an important point, at least one communication expert believes that what the person does with the lower limbs is the key to body language. He explains:

> That is where the tension and anxiety show. The person may claim to be relaxed, yet the legs are crossed tightly, and one foot thrusts so rigidly in the air that it appears to be on the verge

## Unilever Tries Bridging the Tech Divide

Wendy Wilkes was giving a presentation about Unilever's information technology to 30 new hires—most of them barely out of school—and they were not happy. They didn't like the company-issued mobile phones and laptops (or lack thereof). The employee Web site was so 1990s it didn't have interactive features, such as Facebook. And they couldn't download iTunes or instant-messaging software to communicate with people outside the company.

Wilkes can certainly identify with their gripes. The 27-year-old manager also joined the maker of such consumer staples as Lipton, Slim-Fast, and Vaseline right out of college. In school, she was accustomed to using her Hotmail account from any computer. But from her desktop at work she had access to corporate e-mail only. Not to mention that instant messaging—the foundation of her social life in college—was forbidden with anyone outside the company. "It was the amount of lockdown that surprised me the most," she says.

For anyone born after 1985, entering the workforce is a technological shock. Raised on MySpace.com and Wikipedia, these workers can't comprehend why they should have to wait 18 months for a company to build corporate software when they can download what they need instantly. "Technology is an important thing in my personal and work life, and I think the two of them should be connected," says Amy Johannigman, a 22-year-old college senior who worked at a company one summer where the use of social-networking sites was discouraged, camera phones verboten, and the interns were told to limit personal e-mails.

## REVOLT IN THE RANKS

Corporate policy isn't stopping Johannigman's contemporaries. Sure, there are official policies against using gear the tech department hasn't sanctioned, but the sheer number of workers who are flouting the rules makes enforcement nearly impossible. Consulting firm Forrester Research even coined a term for workers ignoring corporate policy and taking technology into their own hands: Technology Populism.

At Unilever, half of the desktop software and services used by employees comes from outside the company, and a lot of it shouldn't be there—Skype and iTunes, to name just a couple. "We can't stop them," says Chris Turner, Unilever's chief technology officer. "They're not accepting no as an answer."

Neither did Wilkes. She joined Unilever with a degree in information management and soon became a member of the marketing department's support team, where she experienced Unilever's rigid rules firsthand. So Wilkes put together some ideas about how employees could be more productive using consumer technology and sent her thoughts to Turner.

About six months ago, Turner offered Wilkes a new job, basically, in her words, to "get involved in trying to make a difference." Now Wilkes is one of 13 so-called consumerization architects whose job is to spread the use of popular—and in many cases free—technology. For example, Wilkes is looking into letting employees install Webcams so they can confer by videoconference and cut down on travel time.

Unilever is still testing how to give employees more digital freedom. It may move users outside the corporate firewall and allow them to connect via their own computers, provided they're using certain security technologies. Anecdotal evidence suggests that the savings could be millions of dollars. "We see this as a real opportunity to start altering the cost model to deliver IT," says Turner.

Turner's ideas are unpopular with some people in his own department. But, as he points out, the social and economic forces are overwhelming.

---

of breaking off. *Insight:* People concentrate on hiding their tension from the waist up. Their real state is revealed in their legs and feet.[14]

Even a person's clothing can become important in body language. In addition to dressing for success, physical appearance in general seems important. From her research with clients, one consultant concluded that physical attractiveness is "the single most important quality in determining your success at every stage in your life. People who are attractive are judged to be nicer people, more intelligent, more capable, more desirable mates and better employees."[15]

Besides the truly silent dimensions of nonverbal communication such as body language, time (for example, being late or early), or space (for example, how close one gets during a conversation or seating arrangements in a committee meeting), there are also *ways* in which people verbalize what are an important dimension of nonverbal communication. Sometimes called *paralanguage,* these include things such as voice quality, tone, volume, speech rate, pitch, nonfluencies (saying "ah," "um," or "uh"), laughing, and yawning. For example, tone of voice (genuine or fake) is important in customer service. Also, *who* says a word (for example, whether the boss or a coworker asks for "volunteers") and in what *environmental context* it is said (for example, in the boss's office or out on the golf course) make a difference.

### Improving Nonverbal Effectiveness

The study of those with high emotional intelligence, or EI (discussed in Chapter 7), reveals that one of the key characteristics of these successful, effective people is their ability to read the nonverbal cues and react accordingly in a social situation.[16] Although EI is developed over time, as with other forms of communication, there are specific guidelines that can be used to increase the accuracy of interpreting others' nonverbal behavior. Here are some specific suggestions to improve nonverbal communication:

1. *Look at what is happening in the situation.* When nonverbal behavior is an emotional response, it reflects what is going on at the moment and can be used to better understand the person's nonverbal behavior.
2. *Consider the discrepancies between the nonverbal behavior and the verbal statements.* If there is a mismatch, then this should be a signal for closer examination of what is going on. Sometimes the nonverbal signals are more accurate than the verbal ones.
3. *Watch for subtleties in the nonverbal behavior.* For example, the difference between a real smile and a fake one can usually be detected.[17]

Cultural differences must also be recognized in nonverbal communication. For example, in the first of the author's numerous trips to Albania starting almost 20 years ago to assist this small Eastern European country in the transformation to a market economy,[18] the audience responded to talks on the importance of human resource management by shaking their heads from side to side. I interpreted this as: "Oh, wow, they don't agree with me. I have a problem here." However, at the end of my talk, the Albanians enthusiastically cheered and gave one of the warmest and most heartfelt receptions I have ever received. Later, when I expressed my puzzlement to some of them, saying that they didn't seem to be agreeing with me during the talk, I learned that in Albania shaking the head from side to side means "yes, I agree" and shaking it up and down means "no, I don't agree." This one nonverbal gesture, with a completely opposite meaning in this culture, had a huge impact on my reading the other person—especially when they then became inconsistent because they *sometimes* remembered that Americans had a different meaning for the direction of head shakes.

The following are a few guidelines affecting communication in various cultures: expect more physical closeness in Latin America; the use of "thumbs up" is fine almost anywhere except Australia; and take your hands out of your pockets when meeting a Japanese person. The accompanying OB in Action: Nonverbal and Verbal Communication gives some further guidelines for both nonverbal and verbal communication in European cultures. Overall, nonverbal dimensions are extremely important to interpersonal communication and must be given as much recognition as the mounting attention given to electronic media and information technology.

## INTERPERSONAL COMMUNICATION

As was shown in the continuum in Figure 8.3, interpersonal communication represents the middle ground between electronic media and information technology on the one extreme and nonverbal communication on the other. At the heart of the study of organizational behavior is interpersonal communication.

One of the best ways of coping with different cultures and customs is to be careful in the use of both verbal and nonverbal communication. This means saying and doing the right things and, perhaps even more important, not saying or doing the wrong things. Here are some guidelines that U.S. managers are finding useful in treading their way through the intercultural maze of foreign countries:

1. In Europe, act as if you are calling on a rich old aunt. Dress well, do not chew gum, do not smoke without first seeking permission, do not use first names unless invited to do so by the other party, be punctual to meetings, and, if you are unsure of the proper dress, err on the side of conservatism.

2. When in France, speak English to your hosts. They know how to speak English and typically are appalled at the performance of foreigners trying to communicate in their tongue. Stick to the language you know best. Also, be on time for all engagements. The French are sticklers for promptness.

3. Remember that Germans differ from the French in a number of ways. One of these is that they are even bigger sticklers for promptness. Also, remember that gentlemen walk and sit to the left of all women and men of senior business rank. Do not get on the wrong side.

4. In Britain, social events are not used for discussing business. This is left at the office. Also, remember that the British religiously keep engagement calendars, so if you are inviting some people to lunch or dinner, send your invitation well in advance or you are likely to find that date already filled in your prospective guest's calendar. If you are attending a formal dinner, it is common to toast Her Majesty's health after the main course. This is the signal that you may now smoke. Do not light up prior to this time. Also, remember that although promptness is valued, if you are invited to dinner at 8 P.M., you may show up five or ten minutes late, but it is not good manners to show up early.

5. In Italy, it is common to shake hands with everyone. However, do not expect them to remember your name. No one does on the first introduction. Also, get in the habit of calling people by their title. For example, university graduates often prefer to be addressed as such, and there are different titles depending on the individual's field of study.

6. In Spain, punctuality is taken seriously only when attending a bullfight. Most offices and shops close for siesta from 1:30 P.M. to 4:30 P.M., and restaurants do not usually reopen until after 9 P.M. or get into full swing before 11 P.M. An early dinner in Spain often ends around midnight; a late dinner goes into the wee hours of the morning. If you are invited to dinner and are unaccustomed to late hours, take an afternoon nap. You are going to need it if you hope to last through dessert.

In interpersonal communication, the major emphasis is on transferring information from one person to another. Communication is looked on as a basic method of effecting behavioral change, and it incorporates the psychological processes (perception, learning, and motivation) on the one hand and language on the other. However, it must be noted that the explosion of advanced information technology is also having an impact on this human interaction process. For example, in a University of Southern California commencement address by Disney's Michael Eisner, he noted:

> As any drama coach can tell you, when accompanied by varied intonation and facial expressions, identical words can come across completely differently. If a person says "you dope" with a smile over the dinner table, it can be endearing. But, in the hard, cold cathode-ray light of e-mail, the same two words stand there starkly and accusingly. I'm afraid that spell check does not check for anger, emotion, inflection or subtext.

As an academic analysis noted: "Human communication has always been central to organizational action. Today, the introduction of various sophisticated electronic communication technologies and the demand for faster and better forms of interaction are visibly influencing the nature of [interpersonal] communication."[19] Thus, listening sensitivity and nonverbal communications are also closely associated with interpersonal communication. For example, Bill Marriott, Jr., of the highly successful hotel chain, spent nearly half his time listening and talking to frontline employees. It is important to note that he listened and then talked to his people.

## Importance of How to Talk to Others

In interpersonal communication, knowing *how* to talk to others can be very useful. One communication expert noted that when communicating with the boss, it is important to understand his or her preferred communication style. Here are some examples:[20]

1. *The Director.* This person has a short attention span, processes information very quickly, and is interested only in the bottom line. So it is best to present this type of manager with a bulleted list of conclusions and forget all of the background information.

2. *The Free Spirit.* This manager is a creative, big-picture type of person who likes to consider alternative approaches to doing things, but is not very good on follow-through. In communicating with this type of manager it is important to be patient and to be prepared for changes in direction. The manager often likes to assimilate what he or she is being told and to consider several alternatives before making a decision.

3. *The Humanist.* This manager likes everyone to be happy and is very concerned with the feelings of others. So any suggestions or recommendations that are given to him or her will be passed around the entire department for full consensus before any action is taken. In dealing with this type of manager, patience and tact are very important.

4. *The Historian.* This manager likes to know the whole picture and thrives on details. This individual wants to be given a thorough analysis and background information, especially if it is presented in linear fashion. This type of manager does not jump from subject to subject, but instead remains focused on the topic under consideration until it has been exhaustively reviewed and a decision is made.

In addition to these hints on how to talk with one's boss is the whole upward communication process, which is generally inhibited in traditional hierarchically structured organizations.

## The Importance of Feedback

The often posed philosophical question—Is there a noise in the forest if a tree crashes to the ground but no one is there to hear it?—demonstrates some of the important aspects of interpersonal communication. From a communications perspective, the answer is no. There are sound waves but no noise because no one perceives it. There must be both a sender and a receiver in order for interpersonal communication to take place. The sender is obviously important to communication, but so is the neglected receiver who gives feedback to the sender and becomes an important component of the upward process.

The importance of feedback cannot be overemphasized because effective interpersonal communication is highly dependent on it. Proper follow-up and feedback require establishing an informal and formal mechanism by which the sender can check on how the message was actually interpreted. There is even research evidence that a graphical feedback format has a more positive impact on performance than does a strictly tabular, numerical feedback format.[21]

In general, feedback makes communication a two-way process and is a big problem with much of e-mail that turns out to be only one-way. As electronic communication becomes more interactive, such problems can be overcome. There is continuing research evidence that feedback not only improves communication but also, in turn, leads to more effective manager and organizational performance.[22] For example, when businesses have secret salaries so that no one knows what anyone else is earning, or family-owned enterprises do not tell the employees how well the company is doing, many people believe that they are being paid less than they should.[23] On the other hand, when information is shared, even though this means giving up some control, the results are often well worth the effort.[24]

**TABLE 8.1**
Luthans and
Martinko's
Characteristics of
Feedback for Effective
and Ineffective
Interpersonal
Communication in
Human Resource
Management

| Effective Feedback | Ineffective Feedback |
|---|---|
| 1. Intended to help the employee | 1. Intended to belittle the employee |
| 2. Specific | 2. General |
| 3. Descriptive | 3. Evaluative |
| 4. Useful | 4. Inappropriate |
| 5. Timely | 5. Untimely |
| 6. Considers employee readiness for feedback | 6. Makes the employee defensive |
| 7. Clear | 7. Not understandable |
| 8. Valid | 8. Inaccurate |

Table 8.1 summarizes some characteristics of effective and ineffective feedback for employee performance. The following list explains these characteristics in more detail:

1. *Intention.*   Effective feedback is directed toward improving job performance and making the employee a more valuable asset. It is not a personal attack and should not compromise the individual's feeling of self-worth or image. Rather, effective feedback is directed toward aspects of the job.

2. *Specificity.*   Effective feedback is designed to provide recipients with specific information so that they know what must be done to correct the situation. Ineffective feedback is general and leaves questions in the recipients' minds. For example, telling an employee that he or she is doing a poor job is too general and will leave the recipient frustrated in seeking ways to correct the problem.

3. *Description.*   Effective feedback can also be characterized as descriptive rather than evaluative. It tells the employee what he or she has done in objective terms, rather than presenting a value judgment.

4. *Usefulness.*   Effective feedback is information that an employee can use to improve performance. It serves no purpose to berate employees for their lack of skill if they do not have the ability or training to perform properly. Thus, the guideline is that if it is not something the employee can correct, it is not worth mentioning.

5. *Timeliness.*   There are also considerations in timing feedback properly. As a rule, the more immediate the feedback, the better. This way the employee has a better chance of knowing what the supervisor is talking about and can take corrective action.

6. *Readiness.*   In order for feedback to be effective, employees must be ready to receive it. When feedback is imposed or forced on employees, it is much less effective.

7. *Clarity.*   Effective feedback must be clearly understood by the recipient. A good way of checking this is to ask the recipient to restate the major points of the discussion. Also, supervisors can observe facial expressions as indicators of understanding and acceptance.

8. *Validity.*   In order for feedback to be effective, it must be reliable and valid. Of course, when the information is incorrect, the employee will feel that the supervisor is unnecessarily biased or the employee may take corrective action that is inappropriate and only compounds the problem.

In recent years, multisource 360-degree feedback has received increasing attention as a process to communicate to a target manager about strengths and weaknesses. The multiple sources include peers (coworkers), managers, direct reports, and sometimes even customers (thus the term 360 degrees). This 360-degree feedback approach draws its conceptual roots from several different areas. One is the traditional organizational development technique of using surveys to assess employees' perceptions. These surveys measure items such as satisfaction with management, supervisors, pay, work procedures, or formal policies of the organization. The survey information is then fed back to those that generated it, with the goal of developing an action plan to improve the organization.

Another area in which 360-degree feedback has strong conceptual roots is the performance appraisal literature. Today's environment has forced organizations to provide much more information than the traditional performance review, thus spawning such creative efforts as 360-degree feedback.[25] It is now recognized that managers can improve their performance through increased multisource information.[26] Social cognitive theory (see Chapter 1), in particular the dimension of self-awareness, can also be used as an explanation.[27] Specifically, social cognitive theory posits that humans have the ability to assess their own capabilities and skills, and they often evaluate themselves quite differently than others do. Therefore, the 360-degree feedback provides managers with an external source of information designed to increase their self-awareness.[28] This enhanced self-awareness may improve managerial effectiveness by providing individuals with another source of outside information regarding what others expect of him or her. A recent study found that self-awareness from 360-degree feedback (closing the discrepancy between self and others' ratings) can be improved through combining the feedback with systematic coaching.[29]

## Other Important Variables in Interpersonal Communication

Besides feedback, other variables, such as trust, expectations, values, status, and compatibility, greatly influence the interpersonal aspects of communication. If the subordinate does not trust the boss, there will be ineffective communication.[30] The same is true of the other variables mentioned. People perceive only what they expect to perceive; the unexpected may not be perceived at all. The growing generation gap can play havoc with interpersonal communication. For example, here are some guidelines to communicate better with Generation X (those born between 1965 and 1980) and Generation Y (those born between 1981 and 1994):[31]

1. In terms of technology, for Gen X keep it up-to-date and motivating (music at work, BlackBerrys, and fast computers) and Gen Y (learn from them).
2. In terms of collaboration, for Gen X limit face-to-face meetings and offer alternatives such as conference calls, video, and Web conferencing and for Gen Y try to leverage social networks to encourage team collaboration and knowledge sharing.
3. In terms of the work ethic, for Gen X trust them and offer flexibility to telecommute and for Gen Y accept their expectations of new rules (e.g., productivity not hours at their desk).
4. In terms of socializing, for Gen X invite but do not push them to participate and for Gen Y appeal to their career goals to attend a networking event.

Giving attention to, and doing something about, these interpersonal variables such as trust and recognizing age differences can spell the difference between effective and ineffective communication.

# INTERACTIVE COMMUNICATION IN ORGANIZATIONS

Although closely related, interpersonal communication discussed above is more at the micro, individual level, whereas interactive communication is more at the macro, organizational level. The classical hierarchical organizational structure discussed in

Chapter 3 gave formal recognition only to vertical communication. Nevertheless, most of the classical theorists saw the need to supplement the vertical with some form of horizontal system. Horizontal communication is required to make a coordinated, cross-functional effort in achieving organizational goals. The horizontal requirement becomes more apparent as the organization becomes larger, more complex, and more subject to the flattening and networking of structures, covered in Chapter 3. Well-known companies such as General Electric, DuPont, Motorola, and Xerox have moved to such a horizontal model of organization. These and other modern network and team designs, formally incorporate horizontal flows into the structure. However, as is the case with vertical (downward and upward) flows in the organization structure, the real key to horizontal communication is still found in people and behaviors. Because of the dynamic, interpersonal aspects of communication, the *interactive* form seems more appropriate than just the *horizontal* form. The horizontal flows of information (even in a horizontal structure) are only part of the communication process that takes place across an organization.

## The Extent and Implications of Interactive Communication

Most management experts today stress the important but often overlooked role that inter-active communication plays in today's organizations. In most cases the vertical communication process still overshadows the horizontal. For example, the study of "Real Managers" reported at the beginning of the chapter found that approximately 100 interactions per week reportedly occurred between managers and their employees (both to them and from them). "While there was far more communication downward (between managers and their employees) than upward (between managers and top managers above them in the organization), there were no specific differences determined by initiation of interaction."[32] The horizontal communication in this study was mainly represented by the networking activity (socializing/politicking and interacting with outsiders) that was shown to be related to successful managers (those promoted relatively fast) more than any other activity.[33] Other studies have also found a relationship, although complex, between communication activities and leadership.[34]

Just as in other aspects of organizational communication, there are many behavioral implications contained in the interactive process.[35] Communication with peers, that is, with persons of relatively equal status on the same level of an organization, provides needed social support for an individual. People can more comfortably turn to a peer for social support than they can to those above or below them. The result can be good or bad for the organization. If the support is couched in terms of task coordination to achieve overall goals, interactive communication can be good for the organization. On the other hand, "if there are no problems of task coordination left to a group of peers, the content of their communication can take forms which are irrelevant to or destructive of organizational functioning."[36] In addition, interactive communication among peers may be at the sacrifice of vertical communication. Persons at each level, giving social support to one another, may freely communicate among themselves but fail to communicate upward or downward. In fact, in the study of "Real Managers," Figure 8.1 showed that networking had the least-relative relationship with effective managers (those with satisfied and committed employees and high-performing units), but routine communication activities (exchanging and processing information) had the highest.[37]

## The Purposes and Methods of Interactive Communication

Just as there are several purposes of vertical communication in an organization, there are also various reasons for the need for interactive communication. Basing his inquiry on several research studies, a communications scholar has summarized four of the most important purposes of interactive communication:

1. *Task coordination.* The department heads may meet monthly to discuss how each department is contributing to the system's goals.
2. *Problem solving.* The members of a department may assemble to discuss how they will handle a threatened budget cut; they may employ brainstorming techniques.
3. *Information sharing.* The members of one department may meet with the members of another department to give them some new data.
4. *Conflict resolution.* The members of one department may meet to discuss a conflict inherent in the department or between departments.[38]

The examples for each of the major purposes of interactive communication traditionally have been departmental or interdepartmental meetings, but in recent years they include teams and videoconferencing. Such meetings and teams that exist in most organizations have been the major methods of interactive communication. In addition, most organizations' procedures require written reports to be distributed across departments and to teams. The quantity, quality, and human implications discussed in relation to the vertical communication process are also inherent in interactive communication.

### The Role of the Informal Organization

Because of the failure of the classical structures to meet the needs of interactive communication, not only have new organizational forms emerged, but the informal organization and groups have also been used to fill the void. Informal contacts with others on the same level are a primary means of interactive communication. The informal system of communication can be used to spread false rumors and destructive information, or it can effectively supplement the formal channels of communication. For example, communication experts recognize that the hallways of an organization encourage creative, open-ended interactions because of two reasons: (1) the hallway takes away some of the sense of hierarchy, making the participants seem more equal and (2) the hallway invites multiple perspectives—anyone who wanders by can join in, adding their ideas to the mix.[39] In today's digital world, with increasing numbers of employees at all levels having less face-to-face interaction in "hallways," the same advantages apply to those who now commonly interact on chat rooms, blogs, PDAs, and e-mail. Face-to-face or electronically, the informal system can quickly disseminate pertinent information that assists the formal systems to attain goals. However, whether the informal system has negative or positive functions for the organization depends largely on the goals of the person doing the communicating. As in any communication system, the entire informal system has a highly personal orientation, and, as has been pointed out earlier, personal goals may or may not be compatible with organizational goals. The degree of compatibility that does exist will have a major impact on the effect that the grapevine or rumor mill has on organizational goal attainment.

Some organizational theorists are critical of the grapevine because its speed makes control of false rumors and information difficult to manage. By the same token, however, this speed factor may work to the advantage of the organization. Because the informal system is so personally based and directed, it tends to be much faster than the formal downward system of information flow. Important relevant information that requires quick responsive action by lower-level personnel may be more effectively handled by the informal system than by the formal system. Thus, the informal system is a major way that interactive communication is accomplished. The formal horizontal and upward systems are often either inadequate or completely ineffective. The informal system is generally relied on to coordinate the units horizontally on a given level.

# THE DECISION-MAKING PROCESS

Both communication and decision making are important dynamic, personal processes relevant to the social cognitive framework for this text (see Chapter 1) and the study of organizational behavior. After defining decision making, particular attention is given to behavioral (as opposed to economic or financial) decision making and then the styles and techniques of decision making most relevant to organizational behavior understanding and application.

*Decision making* is almost universally defined as choosing between alternatives. It is closely related to all the traditional management functions. For example, when a manager plans, organizes, and controls, he or she is making decisions. The classical theorists, however, did not generally present decision making this way. Pioneering management theorists such as Fayol and Urwick were concerned with the decision-making process only to the extent that it affects delegation and authority, whereas the father of scientific management, Frederick W. Taylor, alluded to the scientific method only as an ideal approach to making decisions. Like most other aspects of modern organization theory, the beginning of a meaningful analysis of the decision-making process can be traced to Chester Barnard. In *The Functions of the Executive,* Barnard gave a comprehensive analytical treatment of decision making and noted: "The processes of decision . . . are largely techniques for narrowing choice."[40]

Most discussions of the decision-making process break it down into a series of steps. For the most part, the logic can be traced to the ideas developed by Herbert A. Simon, the well-known Nobel Prize–winning organization and decision theorist, who conceptualized three major phases in the decision-making process:

1. *Intelligence activity.* Borrowing from the military meaning of "intelligence," Simon described this initial phase as consisting of searching the environment for conditions calling for decision making.
2. *Design activity.* During the second phase, inventing, developing, and analyzing possible courses of action take place.
3. *Choice activity.* The third and final phase is the actual choice—selecting a particular course of action from among those available.[41]

Closely related to these phases, but with a more empirical basis (that is, tracing actual decisions in organizations), are the stages of decision making of Mintzberg and his colleagues:

1. *The identification phase,* during which *recognition* of a problem or opportunity arises and a *diagnosis* is made. It was found that severe, immediate problems did not receive a very systematic, extensive diagnosis but that mild problems did.
2. *The development phase,* during which there may be a *search* for existing standard procedures or solutions already in place or the *design* of a new, tailor-made solution. It was found that the design process was a groping, trial-and-error process in which the decision makers had only a vague idea of the ideal solution.
3. *The selection phase,* during which the choice of a solution is made. There are three ways of making this selection: by the *judgment* of the decision maker, on the basis of experience or intuition rather than logical analysis; by *analysis* of the alternatives on a logical, systematic basis; and by *bargaining* when the selection involves a group of decision makers and all the political maneuvering that this entails. Once the decision is formally accepted, an *authorization* is made.[42]

Figure 8.4 summarizes these phases of decision making based on Mintzberg's research.

Whether they are expressed in Simon's or Mintzberg's phases, there seem to be identifiable, preliminary steps leading to the choice activity in decision making. Also, it should be

**FIGURE 8.4**
Mintzberg's
Empirically Based
Phases of Decision
Making in
Organizations

again emphasized, like communication, decision making is a dynamic, personal process, and there are many feedback loops in each of the phases. "Feedback loops can be caused by problems of timing, politics, disagreement among managers, inability to identify an appropriate alternative or to implement the solution, turnover of managers, or the sudden appearance of a new alternative."[43] The essential point is that decision making is a dynamic, personal process. This process has both strategic[44] and behavioral implications for organizations. Empirical evidence indicates that the decision process that involves making the right strategic choices does lead to successful decisions,[45] but there are still many problems of making the wrong decisions.[46] For example, casual observation and detailed analysis indicate many very wrong decisions were made in Katrina, Iraq, and the meltdown in the financial industry at the end of 2008.[47] To go beyond the recent dominance of the role that electronic media and information technology play in the analysis and practice of effective decision making, most relevant to the study and application of organizational behavior is what has become known as behavioral decision making.

## BEHAVIORAL DECISION MAKING

Why does a decision maker choose one alternative over another? Recently put another way, how do managers make the right decisions and learn from the wrong ones?[48] The answer to this question has been a concern of organizational behavior theorists as far back as March and Simon's classic book, *Organizations,* in 1958. Subsequently, however, the field became more interested in such topics as motivation and goal setting, and emphasis on decision making waned. The field of behavioral decision making was mainly developed outside the mainstream of organizational behavior theory and research by cognitive psychologists and decision theorists in economics and information science. Recently, however, there has been a resurgence of interest in behavioral decision making, and it has moved back into the mainstream of the field of organizational behavior.[49]

Whereas classical decision theory operated under the assumption of rationality and certainty, the new behavioral decision theory does not. Behavioral decision-making theorists argue that individuals have cognitive limitations and, because of the complexity of organizations and the world in general, they must act in situations where uncertainty prevails and in which information is often ambiguous and incomplete.[50] Sometimes this risk and uncertainty leads organizational decision makers to make questionable, if not unethical, decisions. Because of this real-world uncertainty and ambiguity, a number of models of decision making have emerged over the years. The foundation and point of departure for developing and analyzing the various models of behavioral decision making remain the degree and meaning of rationality.

### Decision Rationality

The most often used definition of *rationality* in decision making is that it is a means to an end. If appropriate means are chosen to reach desired ends, the decision is said to be rational. However, there are many complications to this simple test of rationality. To begin with, it is very difficult to separate means from ends because an apparent end may be only a means for some future end. This idea is commonly referred to as the *means-ends chain* or *hierarchy*. Simon pointed out that "the means-end hierarchy is seldom an integrated, completely connected chain. Often the connection between organization activities and ultimate objectives is obscure, or these ultimate objectives are incompletely formulated, or there are internal conflicts and contradictions among the ultimate objectives, or among the means selected to attain them."[51]

Besides the complications associated with the means-ends chain, it may even be that the concept is obsolete. Decision making relevant to the national economy supports this position. Decision makers who seek to make seemingly rational adjustments in the economic system may in fact produce undesirable, or at least unanticipated, end results. Simon also warned that a simple means-ends analysis may have inaccurate conclusions.

One way to clarify means-ends rationality is to attach appropriate qualifying adverbs to the various types of rationality. Thus, *objective* rationality can be applied to decisions that maximize given values in a given situation. *Subjective* rationality might be used if the decision maximizes attainment relative to knowledge of the given subject. *Conscious* rationality might be applied to decisions in which adjustment of means to ends is a conscious process. A decision is *deliberately* rational to the degree that the adjustment of means to ends has been deliberately sought by the individual or the organization; a decision is *organizationally* rational to the extent that it is aimed at the organization's goals; and a decision is *personally* rational if it is directed toward the individual's goals.[52]

At the opposite extreme from the classical economic rationality model, in which the decision maker is completely rational, is the social model drawn from psychology. Sigmund Freud viewed humans as bundles of feelings, emotions, and instincts, with their behavior being guided largely by their unconscious desires. Obviously, if this were the complete description, people would not be capable of making effective decisions.

Although almost all contemporary psychologists would take issue with the Freudian description of humans,[53] they would agree that psychological influences have a significant impact on decision-making behavior.[54] Furthermore, social pressures and influences may cause managers to make irrational decisions. The well-known conformity experiment conducted by Solomon Asch demonstrates human irrationality.[55] His study used several groups of seven to nine subjects each. They were told that their task was to compare the lengths of lines. All except one of the "subjects" in each group had prearranged with the experimenter to give clearly wrong answers on 12 of the 18 line-judgment trials. About 37 percent of the 123 naive subjects yielded to the group pressures and gave incorrect answers to the 12 test situations. In other words, more than one-third of the experimental subjects conformed to a decision they knew was wrong.

If more than one-third of Asch's subjects conformed under "right and wrong," "black and white" conditions of comparing the lengths of lines, a logical conclusion would be that the real, "gray" world is full of irrational conformists. It takes little imagination to equate Asch's lines with the alternatives of a management decision. There seems to be little doubt of the importance of social influences in decision-making behavior. In addition, there are many other psychological dynamics. For example, there seems to be a tendency on the part of many decision makers to stick with a bad decision alternative, even when it is unlikely that things can be turned around. Staw and Ross have identified four major reasons why this phenomenon, called *escalation of commitment,* might happen:[56]

1. *Project characteristics.*   This is probably the primary reason for escalation decisions. Task or project characteristics such as delayed return on investment or obvious temporary problems may lead the decision maker to stick with or increase the commitment to a wrong course of action.

2. *Psychological determinants.* Once the decision goes bad, the manager may have infor-mation-processing errors (use biased factors or take more risks than are justified). Also, because the decision maker is now ego-involved, negative information is ignored and defensive shields are set up.

3. *Social forces.* There may be considerable peer pressure put on decision makers and/or they may need to save face, so they continue or escalate their commitment to a wrong course of action.

4. *Organizational determinants.* Not only may the project or task characteristics lend themselves to the escalation of bad decisions—so may a breakdown in communication, dysfunctional politics, and resistance to change.

Recent research supports escalation of commitment as an interactive, complementary rela-tionship between predictors of *sunk costs* (e.g., because of the amount of time and money previously spent, decision makers become psychologically "stuck" to continue) and *project completion* (e.g., deciding to continue to spend time and money will increase the probabil-ity of successful completion).[57]

Certainly, the completely irrational person depicted by Freud is too extreme to be use-ful. However, escalation of commitment and other human dynamics covered throughout this text point out that there is little question of the important role that human complexity can and does play in management decision making.[58] Some management behavior is irra-tional but still very realistic. For example, the author and a colleague conducted two stud-ies that showed that subjects in both laboratory and field settings who did not have much computer experience were more influenced in their decision activities by information pre-sented by the computer than they were by information presented by noncomputer reporting procedures.[59] On the other hand, for those subjects with considerable computer experience, the reverse was true. In other words, decision makers are influenced in their choice activi-ties even by the type of format in which information is presented to them. Managers with-out much computer experience may still be intimidated by information technology and place more value on it than is justified, while those with considerable IT experience may be highly skeptical and may underrate its importance.

## Decision-Making Styles

Besides the attention given to decision rationality, another approach to behavioral decision making focuses on the styles that managers use in choosing among alternatives. For instance, one decision-style typology using well-known managers as representative exam-ples identified the following: (1) *Charismatics* (enthusiastic, captivating, talkative, domi-nant): Virgin Atlantic's Richard Branson or Southwest Airlines' founder Herb Kelleher; (2) *Thinkers* (cerebral, intelligent, logical, academic): Dell Computer's Michael Dell or Microsoft's Bill Gates; (3) *Skeptics* (demanding, disruptive, disagreeable, rebellious): Steve Case of AOL-Time Warner or Tom Siebel of the software developer Siebel Systems; (4) *Followers* (responsible, cautious, brand-driven, bargain-conscious): Peter Coors of Coors Brewery or former Hewlett-Packard head Carly Fiorina; and (5) *Controllers* (logical, unemotional, sensible, detail oriented, accurate, analytical): Ford's former CEO Jacques Nasser or Martha Stewart, Omnimedia).[60] These and other styles reflect a number of psy-chological dimensions including how decision makers perceive what is happening around them and how they process information.[61]

A simple $2 \times 2$ behavioral decision-making style matrix can be categorized into two dimensions: value orientation and tolerance for ambiguity. The value orientation focuses on the decision maker's concern for task and technical matters as opposed to people and social concerns. The tolerance for ambiguity orientation measures how much the decision maker

**FIGURE 8.5**
**Decision-Making Styles**

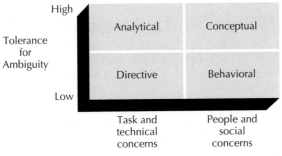

needs structure and control (a desire for low ambiguity) as opposed to being able to thrive in uncertain situations (a desire for high ambiguity). These two orientations with their low and high dimensions are portrayed in the matrix shown in Figure 8.5, with four styles of decision making: directive, analytical, conceptual, and behavioral.

### Directive Style

Decision makers with a directive style have a low tolerance for ambiguity and are oriented toward task and the technical concerns. These decision makers tend to be efficient, logical, pragmatic, and systematic in their approach to problem solving. Directive decision makers also like to focus on facts and get things done quickly. They also are action oriented, tend to have a very short-run focus, like to exercise power, want to be in control, and, in general, display an autocratic leadership style.

### Analytical Style

Analytical decision makers have a high tolerance for ambiguity and a strong task and technical orientation. These types like to analyze situations; in fact, they often tend to overanalyze things. They evaluate more information and alternatives than do directive decision makers. They also take a long time to make decisions, but they do respond well to new or uncertain situations. They also tend to have an autocratic leadership style.

### Conceptual Style

Decision makers with a conceptual style have a high tolerance for ambiguity and strong people and social concerns. They take a broad perspective in solving problems and like to consider many options and future possibilities. These decision makers discuss things with as many people as possible in order to gather a great deal of information and then rely on intuition in making their decisions. Conceptual decision makers are also willing to take risks and tend to be good at discovering creative solutions to problems. At the same time, however, they can foster an idealistic and indecisive approach to decision making.

### Behavioral Style

The behavioral style decision maker is characterized by a low tolerance for ambiguity and strong people and social concerns. These decision makers tend to work well with others and like situations in which opinions are openly exchanged. They tend to be receptive to suggestions, are supportive and warm, and prefer verbal to written information. They also tend to avoid conflict and be overly concerned with keeping everyone happy. As a result, these decision makers often have a difficult time saying no to people, and they do not like making tough decisions, especially when it will result in someone being upset with the outcome.

### Style Implications

Research reveals that decision makers tend to have more than one dominant style.[62] Typically managers rely on two or three decision styles, and these will vary by occupation, job level, and culture. These styles can be used to note the strong and weak points of decision makers. For example, analytical decision makers make fast decisions, but they also tend to be autocratic in their approach to doing things. Similarly, conceptual decision makers are innovative and willing to take risks, but they are often indecisive. These styles also help explain why different managers will arrive at different decisions after evaluating the same information. Overall, the analysis of decision-making styles is useful in providing insights regarding how and why managers make decisions, as well as offering practical guidelines regarding how to deal with various decision-making styles.

## PARTICIPATIVE DECISION-MAKING TECHNIQUES

Most of the behaviorally oriented techniques, at least traditionally, have revolved around participation. Used as a decision-making technique, participation involves individuals or groups in the process.[63] It can be formal or informal, and it entails intellectual and emotional as well as physical involvement. The actual amount of participation in making decisions ranges from one extreme of no participation, wherein the manager makes the decision and asks for no help or ideas from anyone, to the other extreme of full participation, where everyone connected with, or affected by, the decision is completely involved. In practice, the degree of participation will be determined by factors such as the experience of the person or group and the nature of the task. The more experience and the more open and unstructured the task, the more participation there will tend to be.[64]

In today's organizations there is an awakened interest in participation. Participative techniques have been talked about ever since the early human relations movement, and now, because of competitive pressures, the elimination of old hierarchical superior-subordinate relationships and the emergence of teams, horizontal structures, and boundary-spanning information technologies, organizations, teams, and individual managers are effectively using them.[65] For example, through the use of information technology, a Dallas-based engineer with Raytheon was faced with a technical decision. After searching for related problems in their online project library, he e-mails a colleague in the firm's West Coast office who is trying to answer the same question—and they participate with each other to solve the problem.[66]

Participation techniques are being applied informally on an individual or a team basis or formally on a program basis. Individual participation techniques are those in which an employee somehow affects the decision making of a manager. Group participation utilizes consultative and democratic techniques. In consultative participation, managers ask for and receive involvement from their employees, but the managers maintain the right to make the decision. In the democratic form, there is total participation, and the group, not the individual head, makes the final decision by consensus or majority vote.

There are many positive and negative attributes of participative decision making. Balancing these attributes in evaluating the effectiveness of participative decision making is difficult because of moderating factors such as leadership style or personality of the parties involved;[67] situational, environmental, and contextual factors;[68] and ideology.[69] Also, even though there is general research support,[70] the different forms of participative techniques can have markedly different outcomes. For example, informal participation was found to have a positive effect on employee productivity and satisfaction; representative participation had a positive impact on satisfaction, but not on productivity; and short-term participation was ineffective by both criteria.[71]

One problem is the tendency toward pseudoparticipation. Many managers ask for participation, but whenever subordinates take them up on it by making a suggestion or trying to make some input into a decision, they are put down or never receive any feedback. In some cases managers try to get their people involved in the task but not in the decision-making process. This can lead to a boomerang effect regarding employee satisfaction. If managers claim to want participation from their people but never let them become intellectually and emotionally involved and never use their suggestions, the results may be negative. Also, participation can be very time consuming, and it has the same general disadvantages of committees such as pinpointing responsibility. From a behavioral standpoint, however, the advantages of participative decision making far outweigh the disadvantages. Most of the benefits are touched on throughout this text. Perhaps the biggest advantage is that the participative approach to decision making recognizes that each person can make a meaningful contribution to the attainment of organizational objectives.

# CREATIVITY AND GROUP DECISION MAKING

Despite the increasing impact of advanced information technology on decision making, there is still a critical need for behaviorally oriented decision-making techniques. Unfortunately, generally only the participative behavioral techniques discussed so far have been available to managers, and there have been only a few scattered attempts to develop new techniques for helping make more creative and problem-solving types of decisions. Yet as knowledge management recognizes, it is these creative decisions that are still a major challenge facing today's management.

## The Process of Creativity

A key challenge facing organizations in today's highly competitive environment is to be more creative and innovative.[72] This is particularly true given the fact that many firms continue to downsize in an effort to become more efficient, but such a dramatic change on employees has been found to have a negative effect on the company's creativity.[73] Ironically, as the accompanying OB in Action box indicates, some firms have used creativity to eliminate the need to downsize at all.

Noted creativity researcher Teresa Amabile proposes that creativity is a function of three major components: expertise, creative-thinking skills, and motivation.[74] Expertise consists of knowledge: technical, procedural, and intellectual. Creative-thinking skills determine how flexibly and imaginatively people can deal with problems and make effective decisions. Motivation is the inner passion to solve the problem at hand, and this often results in decisions that are far more creative than expected. Her most recent research also indicates that this creative process is generally better off when given plenty of time, for example, AT&T's legendary Bell Labs, operating under its corporate philosophy that big ideas take time, produced world-changing innovations such as the transistor and the laser beam.[75]

Very simply, creativity results in people looking at things differently.[76] Research shows that, in contrast to the average person, creative people seem better able to do things such as abstracting, imaging, synthesizing, recognizing patterns, and empathizing.[77] They also seem to be good intuitive decision makers,[78] know how to take advantage of good ideas,[79] and are able to break old paradigms or ways of thinking and make decisions that sometimes seem to fly in the face of rationality. For example,

> former Chrysler president Robert Lutz was out for a drive several years ago, wondering how he could revive the flagging automotive company, when he got an idea for a new high-priced sports car. Lutz's subconscious, visceral feeling defied what everyone told him about what

Over the last decade, millions of workers have been laid off. One of the major reasons for these layoffs has been downsizing. Unfortunately, growing research evidence questions whether layoffs due to downsizing really do produce long-run benefits for an organization. After all, the personnel can be let go only once, and even if the enterprise has some short-run cost savings from this one-time act, the long-run cost is being found to be greater than the short-term gain. In addition, the more indirect costs of loss of experience/knowledge and commitment of those remaining is much greater. Most organizations now agree with this argument and have begun looking for creative ways to eliminate the need for downsizing.

At Lincoln Electric, the Cleveland-based manufacturer of arc-welding products, for example, the company expanded internationally and suffered severe financial losses as a result. Rather than laying off anyone, however, the firm redeployed people from manufacturing operations into the sales department. Result: In their first year these new salespeople generated $10 million in revenue. Commenting on its creative approach to dealing with business setbacks, Lincoln's director of corporate relations said, "Our people are too valuable. The loss of one person costs us $100,000 to replace them. We don't do business that way." As a result, the company pulled out of its tailspin, returning a bonus to all employees and top management that has now averaged between 52 and 56 percent of salary for 65 straight years!

Rhino Products of Burlington, Vermont, is another example of a firm that has used creative decision making to deal with an economic downturn. When this specialty dessert maker realized that it could not keep its workforce intact, the management turned to Ben & Jerry's Ice Cream, a firm located nearby, and asked them if they would hire some of the Rhino personnel. For the next two years these workers learned new skills and gained a better understanding of customer needs and best practices, while still being able to keep their Rhino benefits and seniority. Then, as things improved for Rhino, they were brought back. Today Rhino is going strong and is introducing new products as well as increasing the size of its workforce.

Other firms are using similar types of creative approaches to prevent downsizing decisions from negatively affecting the personnel. Some of these include: (1) finding personnel who are interested in reduced hours, part-time work, job sharing, leaves of absence, or sabbaticals to work in the community; (2) networking with local employers regarding temporary or permanent redeployment; (3) using attrition effectively by examining whether a job needs to be filled or can be eliminated; (4) developing multistep, voluntary early retirement packages; and (5) cross training so trained people are ready to step into new job openings within the firm. Commenting on the use of these creative approaches, one expert in the field has recently noted that:

> Since all downsizing alternatives are grounded in a knowledge of each employee and his or her skills, a company must start with comprehensive employee assessment tools. A skills database that helps match people with business needs is the basis of effective redeployments. A tuned-in employer community—wider than just the downsizing firm—can retrain and reabsorb workers who have been downsized, thereby keeping downsizing to a minimum and addressing personnel shortages.

Drawing on these types of strategies, companies are finding that downsizing can be done efficiently and with minimum negative effects on the personnel. It is all a matter of learning how to use creative decision making.

U.S. car buyers were looking for in the 1990s, yet he pushed ahead with this strong sense of being right. The result—the Dodge Viper—became a massive hit.[80]

Such intuitive decision makers draw from their *tacit knowledge*. This type of knowledge is not readily explainable, is acquired through observation and experience, and seems to be in the unconscious.[81] Often, this tacit knowledge is important to effective decisions that rationality would discount.

How can today's decision makers increase their own creativity and generate more interesting and profitable solutions to difficult problems?[82] A number of useful ideas have been offered by both successful professional managers and creativity researchers.[83] Michael Eisner, CEO and chairman of the Walt Disney Company, has long contended creativity is not a "bolt out of the blue," but rather the result of careful thought and examination. In fact, early in his career one of his bosses wanted to have him fired because every time the boss suggested a new idea, Eisner would ask the manager if he could "think about it and get back to you." The boss was convinced that creativity was based on rapid responses, whereas Eisner believes that creativity is typically a result of careful, deliberate thought, an idea that is often echoed by many successful managers.[84] In fact, Eisner has often said, in contrast to stereotypical views of the creative process, that creativity is a disciplined process. In a recent interview, he explained his thinking this way:

> Discipline is good for the creative process, and time limits are good. An infinite amount of time to do a project does not always make it creatively better. The image of an artist being temperamental and acting like a 16-month-old child is usually false. It's a cliché that we've helped perpetuate in the movie business. Artists are always depicted as crazies. But in reality, insane artists are rare. In fact, some of the most creative people I've ever met—Steven Spielberg, George Lucas, I. M. Pei, Frank Stella, and Frank Gehry, just to name a few—are the most organized, mature individuals you'll ever meet. Not many creative people have the urge to cut off an ear.[85]

Creative ideas from both individuals and groups are scarce. One of the problems may be that students educated in business schools know how to crunch numbers, read a balance sheet, and develop a Web page, but they have no knowledge of the creative process or how to develop creative solutions to problems. For example, General Foods held a competition in which student teams from prestigious business schools were given the charge to develop a new marketing plan that would stem the plunging sales of Sugar-Free Kool-Aid. Although they used quantitative analysis and the right terminology, they offered very few original ideas that the company could or would be able to use. The marketing manager concluded, "There were a couple of ideas that were of interest, but nothing we haven't looked at before."[86] A starting point for getting around this problem would be to understand the meaning and dimensions of creativity.

## Psychological Definition and Analysis of Creativity

A simple, but generally recognized, psychological definition of *creativity* is that it involves combining responses or ideas of individuals or groups in novel ways.[87] Creative thinking reaches out beyond what is now known into what could be. It draws on observation, experience, knowledge, and the indefinable ability each person has to arrange common elements into new patterns. For instance, how would you respond to the problem of coming up with as many uses for a newspaper as possible? Compare your solution with the following proposal from a 10-year-old boy:

> You can read it, write on it, lay it down and paint a picture on it. . . . You could put it in your door for decoration, put it in the garbage can, put it on a chair if the chair is messy. If you have a puppy, you put newspaper in its box or put it in your backyard for the dog to play with. When you build something and you don't want anyone to see it, put newspaper around it. Put newspaper on the floor if you have no mattress, use it to pick up something hot, use it to stop bleeding, or to catch the drips from drying clothes. You can use a newspaper for curtains, put it in your shoe to cover what is hurting your foot, make a kite out of it, shade a light that is too bright. You can wrap fish in it, wipe windows, or wrap money in it. . . . You put washed shoes in newspaper, wipe eyeglasses with it, put it under a dripping sink, put a plant on it, make a paper bowl out of it, use it for a hat if it is raining, tie it on your feet for slippers. You can put it on the sand if you have no towel, use it for bases in baseball, make paper airplanes with it, use it as a dustpan when you sweep, ball it up for the cat to play with, wrap your hands in it if it is cold.[88]

Obviously, this boy describing the uses of a newspaper was very creative, but what caused his creativity?

Psychologists point out that it is much easier to provide examples of creativity than it is to identify causes. However, two widely recognized dimensions have been identified that can help explain the creative process:

1. *Divergent thinking.* This refers to a person's ability to generate novel, but still appropriate, responses to questions and problems. This is in contrast to convergent thinking, which leads to responses that are based mainly on knowledge and rational logic. In the preceding newspaper problem, convergent thinking would answer, "you read it," but divergent thinking would say, "make a kite out of it." The latter—divergent thinking—is considered more creative.

2. *Cognitive complexity.* This refers to a person's use of and preference for elaborate, intricate, and complex stimuli and thinking patterns. Creative people tend to have such cognitive complexity and display a wide range of interests, are independent, and are interested in philosophical or abstract problems. It is important to note, however, that creative people are not necessarily more intelligent (if intelligence is defined by standard tests of intelligence or grades in school, which tend to focus more on convergent thinking skills).[89]

## Creativity Techniques for Management Decision Making

There are some techniques that managers can use to help them make more creative decisions. For example, a national survey of highly creative top managers found that they use techniques such as guided imagery, self-hypnosis, journal keeping, and lateral styles of thinking.[90] Not only does encouraging creativity help the organization; it may also help the employees. On the basis of interviews in several major Japanese companies, it was found that employee creativity is managed through deliberate structural means, not to effect direct economic outcomes to the organization, but to develop the employees' motivation, job satisfaction, and teamwork.[91] In other words, even though the Japanese are not known for their creative breakthroughs in product development or technology, they effectively structure their organizations to allow their people to creatively apply their ideas. A specific example of an organization structuring for creativity would be Toyota. This Japanese firm's designers think and work with sets of design alternatives rather than pursuing one alternative over and over. Toyota engineers gradually narrow the design sets until they come to a final solution. Analysis of the results of this seemingly slow and inefficient system concludes that the "set-based concurrent engineering" used by Toyota has made them quite effective auto developers.[92]

Other world-class auto manufacturers use similar creative approaches. A recent one is called *empathic design,* which relies heavily on visual information.[93] This creative technique is particularly useful when creating new products because it sidesteps the built-in problem associated with customer feedback. Most customers, when asked what new products they would like, typically respond in terms of the company's current products and suggest that they be made smaller or lighter or less expensive. Customers are notoriously poor in providing useful ideas for new products because their thinking is too closely linked to current products and their everyday uses.[94] Empathic design focuses on observing how people respond to products and services and drawing creative conclusions from the results. For example, when Nissan developed the Infinity J-30, it tested more than 90 samples of leather before selecting three that U.S. car buyers preferred. When Harley-Davidson builds a motorcyle it adjusts the motor so that it is pleasing to the customer's ears, that is, it sounds like a Harley (and it has sued competitors that have tried to imitate this sound).

By watching how people respond in the empathic approach, companies can generate more creative and consumer-pleasing offerings. This can be done in a number of ways. One is by taking pictures of people using the products. For example, when the Thermos Company had pictures taken of people using their charcoal grills, they saw that their units were much easier to use by men than by women, although women were often the ones doing the cooking. They then proceeded to redesign their grills so that they were equally appealing to women.

Envirosell, an international marketing research group, takes millions of photos every year of shoppers in retail stores to help answer the question: Who shops here and what do they like? Among other things, the research group has found that shoppers want wide aisles (they do not like to be bumped), good lighting (they like to see the merchandise clearly), and good signage (they want to know where things are located). Retail companies pay Envirosell large annual fees to provide them with marketing information regarding how to improve their sales. Where does Envirosell get these ideas? From analyzing the pictures of shoppers in their stores.[95] Instead of asking people questions about their shopping habits, the empathic design approach relies on observation to generate creative ideas and solutions. Table 8.2 provides some contrasts between the traditional method of asking customers questions and actually observing their behavior. Other creative approaches to decision making involve groups.

## Group Decision Making

Creativity in decision making can apply to individuals or groups. Because individual decision making has largely given way to group decision making in today's organizations, an understanding of group dynamics and teams, as discussed in Chapter 11, becomes relevant to decision making. For example, that chapter's discussion of groupthink problems and phenomena such as the risky shift (that a group may make more risky decisions than individual members on their own) helps one better understand the complexity of group decision making.[96] In fact, a number of social decision schemes have emerged from social psychology research in recent years.[97]

**TABLE 8.2**
**Inquiry versus Innovative Observation**

*Source:* Adapted from Dorothy Leonard and Jeffrey F. Rayport, "Spark Innovation through Empathic Design," *Harvard Business Review,* November–December 1997, p. 111.

| Traditional Inquiry | Innovative Observation |
|---|---|
| People are often unreliable when it comes to explaining the types of goods and services they would be interested in purchasing. | Observers can rely on how people act in drawing conclusions regarding what types of products and services they would be willing to buy in the future. |
| People often give answers that they feel are acceptable to the questioner. | People give nonverbal clues through body language and spontaneous, unsolicited comments. |
| People are often unable to recall how they felt about a particular product or service that they received. | Observers can see how well people like a product or service on the basis of their reactions. |
| The questions that are asked can bias the responses. | There are no questions asked; all data are based on open-ended observation. |
| Peoples' routines are often interrupted by someone stopping them to ask questions. | People continue doing whatever they are doing, oblivious to the fact that they are being observed. |
| When comparing two similar products, respondents often have difficulty explaining why they like one better than the other. | By giving people an opportunity to use two similar products, observers can determine which is better liked or easier to use by simply watching how they behave. |

These schemes or rules can predict the final outcome of group decision making on the basis of the individual members' initial positions. These have been summarized as follows:[98]

1. *The majority-wins scheme.* In this commonly used scheme, the group arrives at the decision that was initially supported by the majority. This scheme appears to guide decision making most often when there is no objectively correct decision. An example would be a decision about what car model to build when the popularity of various models has not been tested in the "court" of public opinion.

2. *The truth-wins scheme.* In this scheme, as more information is provided and opinions are discussed, the group comes to recognize that one approach is objectively correct. For example, a group deciding whether to use test scores in selecting employees would profit from information about whether these scores actually predict job performance.

3. *The two-thirds majority scheme.* This scheme is frequently adopted by juries, who tend to convict defendants when two-thirds of the jury initially favors conviction.

4. *The first-shift rule.* In this scheme, the group tends to adopt the decision that reflects the first shift in opinion expressed by any group member. If a car-manufacturing group is equally divided on whether or not to produce a convertible, it may opt to do so after one group member initially opposed to the idea changes her mind. If a jury is deadlocked, the members may eventually follow the lead of the first juror to change position.

Besides the listed schemes, there are also other phenomena, such as the status quo tendency (when individuals or groups are faced with decisions, they resist change and will tend to stick with existing goals or plans), that affect group decision making. Suggestions such as the following can be used to help reduce and combat the status quo tendency and thus make more effective group decisions:[99]

- When things are going well, decision makers should still be vigilant in examining alternatives.
- It can help to have separate groups monitor the environment, develop new technologies, and generate new ideas.
- To reduce the tendency to neglect gathering negative long-term information, managers should solicit worst-case scenarios as well as forecasts that include long-term costs.
- Build checkpoints and limits into any plan.
- When limits are reached, it may be necessary to have an outside, independent, or separate review of the current plan.
- Judge people on the way they make decisions and not only on outcomes, especially when the outcomes may not be under their control.
- Shifting emphasis to the quality of the decision process should reduce the need of the decision maker to appear consistent or successful when things are not going well.
- Organizations can establish goals, incentives, and support systems that encourage experimenting and taking risks.

Although just simple guidelines, proactively following them can make group decisions more effective by helping overcome the many problems that still plague most groups.

## Summary

At every level of modern society, communication is a problem. One of the problems when applied to organizations has been the failure to recognize that communication involves more than just linear information flows; it is a dynamic, interpersonal process that involves behavior exchanges. Various electronic media, information technology, and nonverbal approaches are also important to communication in today's organizations. The explosion of electronic media and information technology is having a huge impact on communication in organizations; e-mail alone has revolutionized the way people communicate, let alone social networking, "groupware," and "chat rooms" on the Internet. Yet, communication is still a dynamic, interpersonal and interactive process.

Besides communication, this chapter was also devoted to the process and techniques of decision making. Decision making is defined as choosing between two or more alternatives. However, viewed as a process, the actual choice activity is preceded by gathering information and developing alternatives. Most relevant to the study of organizational behavior is behavioral decision making, which includes the completely economic rationality model on one extreme, and the irrationally based social model on the other extreme. Each of these models gives insights into decision-making rationality. Understanding human dynamics, such as irrational conformity or escalation of commitment, gives more credibility to the social model of decision making. However, the various management decision styles have emerged as having the biggest practical impact on behavioral decision-making theory and practice. The techniques for decision making are currently being dominated by information technology, but it is the creative, problem-solving management decisions that may be crucial for organizational success. Understanding the strengths and weaknesses of participative techniques and the creative individual and group decision-making process and techniques can lead to more-effective decision making now and for the future.

---

# Ending with Meta-Analytic Research Findings
## OB PRINCIPLE FOR EVIDENCE-BASED PRACTICE

Communicating feedback about performance to employees can improve their subsequent performance.

### Meta-Analysis Results:

[131 studies; 12,652 participants; $d = .41$] *On average, there is a **61 percent probability** that providing feedback (even negative) to employees about their performance will lead to better subsequent performance than those who do not receive performance feedback.* Cases in which providing feedback was not as effective can be explained by various cognitive processes. Specifically, when feedback is targeted at the task itself, it produces the strongest results. However, if feedback becomes more personal in nature, individuals may not respond as positively due to the self-evaluative mechanisms it activates.

### Conclusion:

Feedback is one form of interpersonal communication that can be used to effectively manage behavior and improve performance. In fact, feedback may be more valued by some employees than money. This is because people have a strong need to know how they are doing. If managers communicate performance standards to their employees and provide feedback about the progress being made, then there will be a positive impact on performance. If employees are doing well compared to the performance standard, they are likely to maintain current efforts or set new performance goals. In contrast, if they are currently not performing well, feedback can provide employees with the necessary information to reevaluate current strategies and try new ones. Similar to other forms of communication, feedback is most effective when it is positive, immediate, clear, and to the point.

**Source:** Adapted from Avraham N. Kluger and Angelo DeNisi, "The Effects of Feedback Interventions on Performance: A Historical Review, a Meta-Analysis, and a Preliminary Feedback Intervention Theory," *Psychological Bulletin,* Vol. 119, No. 2, 1996, pp. 254–284.

# OB PRINCIPLE FOR EVIDENCE-BASED PRACTICE

Using decision techniques such as devil's advocacy and dialectical inquiry can lead to better problem-solving decisions.

## Meta-Analysis Results:

[432 participants; $d = .22$] *On average, there is a **56 percent probability** that those who use the devil's advocacy and/or dialectical inquiry approach to solve problems will make higher-quality decisions than those who do not use these techniques.*

## Conclusion:

As this chapter points out, there are many different processes and techniques associated with decision making. Some are highly rational whereas others are irrationally based. Recently, behavioral decision-making techniques aimed at making creative, problem-solving decisions have gained increased attention. The devil's advocacy (DA) and dialectical inquiry (DI) approaches are two of the most commonly studied techniques for helping individuals to make more effective decisions. DA is a decision-making method in which an individual or group is assigned a role of critic who is supposed to criticize the proposed solution to problems. DI on the other hand, is a method whereby alternative solutions are generated that are purposely opposite to the proposed solution. Both approaches help to improve decision making because they force decision makers to identify and criticize assumptions of decisions. This increases the likelihood that the "best" decision will be made.

**Source:** Adapted from C. R. Schwenk, "Effects of Devil's Advocacy and Dialectical Inquiry on Decision Making: A Meta-Analysis," *Organizational Behavior and Human Decision Performance,* Vol. 47, 1990, pp. 161–176.

Questions for Discussion and Review

1. Why is feedback so important to communication? What are some guidelines for the effective use of feedback? How can 360-degree feedback help?
2. What are the major purposes and methods of interactive communication?
3. What are the three steps in Simon's decision-making process? Relate these steps to an actual decision.
4. Identify and describe the four major management decision-making styles. What are some strengths and weaknesses of these styles?
5. What is the difference between divergent and convergent thinking, and what is their relationship to the process of creativity?

Internet Exercise: Communication in the Workplace

Visit the Web site **http://www.employer-employee.com/comm101.htm** and/or **http://www. meguffey.com** where you will find current articles about various communication topics such as how to get a raise or how to get your idea across. Read a few of the articles, and see if you can develop some insights into the topics discussed in the chapter, and specifically address these questions:

1. How is advanced information technology affecting interpersonal communication in organizations?

2. Suppose you are employed in an entry-level management position in a large bank. What specific considerations (contingencies) would you identify of sending an e-mail versus talking in person to someone else in the bank?

3. From your reading, what advice would you give to the training department to help improve communication effectiveness in your organization?

**Internet Exercise: Decision Making in Organizations**

Although decisions are made in organizations every day, it is oftentimes either the large decisions, such as laying off many workers, or bad decisions, such as evidenced in the corporate scandals involving Enron, Arthur Andersen, or WorldCom, that receive all the attention. Using your search engine, come up with several organizations that have recently had a decision with negative or positive outcomes in the national news. Then, take these decisions, and consider the following:

1. What were the reasons behind the poor decisions? Which framework did the poor decisions fall under (rational or social)? Were the poor decisions the result of using an incorrect decision-making model? Analyze the same issues for the good decisions that you found.

2. Could the decisions be improved by using one of the group decision-making techniques discussed in your text? Don't forget to consider the downside to this, such as increased time to make the decision.

3. Did you find any specific organizations that had a pattern of wrong decisions? If so, discuss the possible reasons for this.

---

# Real Case: *Online Communication to Share Knowledge*

At the heart of Buckman Laboratory's knowledge-sharing system is an online discussion forum called K'Netix. It has 54 discussion groups that focus on Buckman's main products—chemicals for papermaking, leather-tanning, and water treatment. A salesperson might survey colleagues around the world for the inside skinny on a particular client, say, or get ideas on how to solve a customer problem. Typically, employees post 50 to 100 messages a day. That has helped the company amass an easily searchable database of in-house expertise and past lessons learned that now contains more than 15,000 documents—all accessible by employees or customers via a Web browser. Before the online system was in place, "you would always be reinventing the wheel," says Cheryl Lamb, manager of Buckman's Knowledge Center.

Robert Buckman began experimenting with what he dubbed "knowledge sharing" in the mid-1980s, when he took charge of the company his father, Stanley, founded in 1945 and led until his death in 1978. Buckman's old way of distributing technical information—hiring PhDs and putting them on airplanes, Robert Buckman says— was getting too expensive as the company expanded globally. So Buckman began stationing people overseas. Today, 86 percent of its 1,300 employees work outside the home office.

With its staff scattered so far and wide, the company needed a way to keep people in touch. But getting the right information to the right people—fast—is easier said than done. For starters, in 1985, Robert Buckman told senior managers in Memphis to swap examples of innovative ideas through the company's e-mail system. But soon, the system became a network for chit-chat and gossip, and little else. "I realized the managers weren't going to share," he says. "They had information, but feared giving it up," because they felt they wouldn't get credit for their ideas.

So the CEO decided to adopt a more revolutionary strategy: empower the field staff to communicate with each other, rather than routing all information through managers in Memphis. He wanted his employees to share not just written reports but also the knowledge inside their heads gleaned from years of working in paper mills, tanneries, and treatment plants. "That's the real gold inside companies," he says. To pull that off, he set up a new computer system that linked the senior managers in Memphis plus Buckman 1,300 employees around the world.

Once again, Buckman's efforts met resistance. Many managers resented having to yield their control over the flow of information—and refused to participate. "They didn't want to open their cabinets to people," says Dean Didato, vice president for leather chemicals. So the CEO decided to get tough. First, he ordered marketing manager Alison Tucker to start compiling weekly statistics detailing each employee's use of the knowledge-sharing network.

Finally, Robert Buckman set up a system to promote those who shared information—and to punish those who did not. The clincher: A few years ago, he took the system's 150 most frequent users to a Scottsdale, Arizona,

resort for a week. Only then, he recalls, did the holdouts start getting the message.

1. Obviously, the "Information Age" has arrived. What impact do you think it has on interpersonal communication? What are some of the positives and the negatives?

2. Specifically cite examples from the case where the human dimension is dysfunctional for advanced communication technologies. How can these problems be overcome?

3. With such communication systems in place, what impact does interactive communication now play? Is this good or bad for organizational outcomes?

# Organizational Behavior Case: *Doing My Own Thing*

Rita Lowe has worked for the same boss for 11 years. Over coffee one day, her friend Sara asked her, "What is it like to work for old Charlie?" Rita replied, "Oh, I guess it's okay. He pretty much leaves me alone. I more or less do my own thing." Then Sara said, "Well, you've been at that same job for 11 years. How are you doing in it? Does it look like you will ever be promoted? If you don't mind me saying so, I can't for the life of me see that what you do has anything to do with the operation." Rita replied, "Well, first of all, I really don't have any idea of how I am doing. Charlie never tells me, but I've always taken the attitude that no news is good news. As for what I do and how it contributes to the operation around here, Charlie mumbled something

when I started the job about being important to the operation, but that was it. We really don't communicate very well."

1. Analyze Rita's last statement: "We really don't communicate very well." What is the status of manager-subordinate communication in this work relationship?

2. It was said in this chapter that communication is a dynamic, personal process. Does the situation described verify this contention? Be specific in your answer.

3. Are there any implications in this situation for inter-active communication? How could feedback be used more effectively?

# Organizational Behavior Case: *Bad Brakes*

Michelle Adams is the maintenance supervisor of a large taxicab company. She had been very concerned because the cabdrivers were not reporting potential mechanical problems. Several months ago she implemented a preventive maintenance program. This program depended on the drivers' filling out a detailed report in writing or into the office computer system when they suspected any problem. But this was not happening. On a number of occasions a cab left the garage with major problems that the previous driver

was aware of but had not reported. Calling out the field repair teams to fix the breakdowns not only was costing the company much time and trouble but also was very unsafe in some cases and created a high degree of customer ill will. The drivers themselves suffered from a loss of fares and tips, and in some cases their lives were endangered by these mechanical failures. After many oral and written threats and admonishments, Michelle decided to try a new approach. She would respond directly to each report of a potential mechanical problem sent in by a driver with a return memo indicating what the maintenance crew had found wrong with the cab and what had been done to take care of the problem. In addition, the personal memo thanked the driver for reporting the problem and encouraged reporting any further problems with the cabs. In less than a month the number of field repair calls had

decreased by half, and the number of turned-in potential problem reports had tripled.

1. In communication terms, how do you explain the success of Michelle's follow-up memos to the drivers?
2. Explain and give examples of the interactive communication process in this company.

---

# Real Case: *Putting a Human Face on Rational Decisions*

For more than two decades, behavioral economists such as Richard Thaler, Andrei Shleifer, Nobel Prize–winner Daniel Kahneman, and the late Amos Tversky have been pointing out all the ways in which people diverge from the hyperrational behavior that is assumed by conventional economics. They procrastinate on saving for retirement. They shop for hours to save pennies, then make snap decisions on big-ticket items. They run up huge credit-card debts even when they have ample savings to pay them off.

Behavioral economics says real people act like this because most of us lack the farsightedness or the willpower to do what the textbooks say we should. Makes sense, right? But even though it does a better job of describing reality, behavioral economics isn't part of the average economist's toolbox. One reason: Its psychological insights were never put into a formal language that economists could understand and work with. "The math was too complicated," says Colin F. Camerer, a business economist at the California Institute of Technology.

Now, behavioral economics is getting the mathematical rigor it needs to enter the mainstream of economics, where it can influence forecasting and policy decisions. That's thanks in large part to the formulations of Matthew Rabin, a 36-year-old economist at the University of California at Berkeley. Rabin, who wears tie-dyed T-shirts every day and does some of his best work at the counter of a San Francisco coffee shop, is considered a mathematical wizard by his colleagues. Rabin won a $500,000 John D. & Catherine T. MacArthur Foundation "genius" fellowship in recognition of his work on formalizing behavioral economics.

A bedrock assumption of standard economics is that people attempt to maximize their well-being, using all available information and always acting with their long-term self-interest in mind. From this starting point, economists build models of all economic activity, from how people respond to price changes to what careers

they pursue. In general, the assumption works pretty well. But not always. Rabin's goal is to improve the predictiveness of conventional economic models by plugging into them more realistic formulas for how people actually behave.

Take, for example, the exploding field of behavioral finance. Thaler, author of *The Winner's Curse: Paradoxes and Anomalies of Economic Life*, uses behavioral theories to explain what economists call the "equity premium puzzle": the odd fact that the long-term returns on equities are much higher than those on bonds—even more than their higher volatility would seemingly call for. Thaler says the answer to the puzzle is that people hate losses much more than they enjoy gains. So investors demand higher returns from stocks to compensate for their dread of losses. Likewise, sports fans who would not pay more than $200 for a Super Bowl ticket wouldn't sell one they own—i.e., "lose" it—for less than $400.

Rabin has made big contributions in the study of fairness. Imagine there's a drought. The more others conserve water, the more water a self-interested person could use without causing the reservoir to run dry. In fact, though, people are fair; they tend to conserve more when they see others conserving. That's what Rabin built into his formal model. Says Rabin: "People reciprocate public-spiritedness in others rather than counteract it." His model also takes into account that perceptions of unfairness breed retaliation, even when the cost of retaliating is very high.

Rabin's work on self-control problems such as procrastination is catching on most quickly. Cornell University economist Ted O'Donoghue and Rabin demonstrate that there's a good reason why many people put off the chore of financial planning—it takes a lot of work, and there's an insignificant cost of delaying the work until tomorrow. The difficulty comes from the fact that the same is true every day—and those small daily losses eventually add up to a tremendous sum. Rabin should know: He admits to having his own "severe procrastination problem." Rabin adds that people procrastinate longer on the most important things because the up-front effort is usually greatest.

O'Donoghue and Rabin recommend policies to fight procrastination, such as automatic enrollment in employee retirement plans, transaction deadlines, and on-the-job seminars on retirement planning. Economists once assumed such measures were unnecessary. But Thaler, who offers similar recommendations, says the steps "are designed to take into account people's humanness."

1. What is the "equity premium puzzle"? Can you give a personal example?
2. Why do you suppose that "work on self-control problems such as procrastination is catching on most quickly"? Can you provide an example and explanation of why people do this?
3. Why do you think it has taken so long for the "human face" to be widely recognized in decision-making analysis and practice?

---

# Organizational Behavior Case: *Harry Smart—Or Is He?*

Harry Smart, a very bright and ambitious young executive, was born and raised in Boston and graduated from a small New England college. He met his future wife, Barbra, who was also from Boston, in college. They were married the day after they both graduated cum laude. Harry then went on to Harvard, where he received an MBA, and Barbra earned a law degree from Harvard. Harry is now in his seventh year with Brand Corporation, which is located in Boston, and Barbra has a position in a Boston law firm.

As part of an expansion program, the board of directors of Brand has decided to build a new branch plant. The president personally selected Harry to be the manager of the new plant and informed him that a job well done would guarantee him a vice presidency in the corporation. Harry was appointed chairperson, with final decision-making privileges, of an ad hoc committee to determine the location of the new plant. At the initial meeting, Harry explained the ideal requirements for the new plant. The members of the committee were experts in transportation, marketing, distribution, labor economics, and public relations. He gave them one month to come up with three choice locations for the new plant.

A month passed and the committee reconvened. After weighing all the variables, the experts recommended the following cities in order of preference: Kansas City, Los Angeles, and New York. Harry could easily see that the committee members had put a great deal of time and effort into their report and recommendations. A spokesperson for the group emphasized that there was a definite consensus that Kansas City was the best location for the new plant. Harry thanked them for their fine job and told them he would like to study the report in more depth before he made his final decision.

After dinner that evening he asked his wife, "Honey, how would you like to move to Kansas City?" Her answer was quick and sharp. "Heavens, no!" she said, "I've lived in the East all my life, and I'm not about to move out into the hinterlands. I've heard the biggest attraction in Kansas City is the stockyards. That kind of life is not for me." Harry weakly protested, "But, honey, my committee strongly recommends Kansas City as the best location for my plant. Their second choice was Los Angeles and the third was New York. What am I going to do?" His wife thought a moment and then replied, "Well, I would consider relocating to or commuting from New York, but if you insist on Kansas City, you'll have to go by yourself!"

The next day Harry called his committee together and said, "You should all be commended for doing an excellent job on this report. However, after detailed study, I am convinced that New York will meet the needs of our plant better than Kansas City or Los Angeles. Therefore, the decision will be to locate the new plant in New York. Thank you all once again for a job well done."

1. Did Harry make a rational decision?
2. What model of behavioral decision making does this case support?
3. What decision techniques that were discussed in the chapter could be used by the committee to select the new plant site?

# Chapter **Nine**

# Stress and Conflict

## Learning Objectives

- **Define** the meaning of stress.
- **Identify** the extraorganizational, organizational, and group stressors.
- **Examine** individual dispositions of stress.
- **Describe** intraindividual and interactive conflict.
- **Discuss** the effects of stress and conflict.
- **Present** strategies for coping/managing stress and negotiation skills for conflict resolution.

Traditionally, the field of organizational behavior has treated stress and conflict separately. Even though they are conceptually similar, and individuals, groups, and organizations in interaction are more associated with conflict, at the individual (intraindividual) level, they can be treated together. Therefore, this chapter combines stress and conflict. Conceptually, going from micro to macro, the discussion starts off with the meaning of stress and then examines the causes of stress. This is followed by both the intraindividual and the interactive levels of conflict. Next, the effects of stress and conflict are examined, and the final part presents the ways of coping/managing stress and conflict with particular emphasis given to effective negotiation skills for resolving conflict.

## THE EMERGENCE OF STRESS

A leading expert on stress, cardiologist Robert Eliot gives the following prescription for dealing with stress: "Rule No. 1 is, don't sweat the small stuff. Rule No. 2 is, it's all small stuff. And if you can't fight and you can't flee, flow." What is happening in today's organizations, however, is that the "small stuff" is getting to employees, and they are not going with the "flow." Stress has become a major buzzword and legitimate concern of the times.

### Contemporary Environment Demands

There is considerable evidence that most managers and employees report feeling work-related stress,[1] and the recent environment is making things worse. For example, globalization and strategic alliances have led to a dramatic increase in executive travel stress[2] and relocation,[3] then there is 24/7 technology (i.e., BlackBerrys, laptops, and cell phones) keeping people constantly leashed to their job, and of course the specter of massive job losses in the wake of the worst economic crisis since the Great Depression. For example, on stress scales, people rank losing their job the eighth most stressful life experience, behind the death of a spouse (No. 1), or going to jail (No. 4), but ahead of the death of a close friend (No. 17), foreclosure on a mortgage or loan (No. 21) or in-law troubles (No. 24).[4] Besides these external pressures, much of the stress comes from within. As one expert

277

notes, "Too much stress from heavy demands, poorly defined priorities, and little on-the-job flexibility can add to health issues. By leaving stress unaddressed, employers invite an increase in unscheduled time off, absence rates, and health care costs."[5]

Increased work hours resulting from 24/7 technology and competitive pressures are also taking a toll on today's employees. Recent surveys indicate that a vast majority of employees work frequently after regular hours and reported their employer does not allow them to balance their work and personal life.[6] A growing number meet the definition of a "workaholic"—a compulsive need to work at the expense of everything else in one's life.[7] The estimated costs of such workaholism, in terms of lost productivity, increased health care costs, and potential legal ramifications (disabilities and wage-and-hour claims) is $150 billion a year, and the warning signs of such problems have been identified as follows:[8]

- Sending e-mails from home in the evenings or later;
- Being the last one in the office;
- Having difficulty delegating;
- Exhibiting excessive perfectionism;
- Skipping lunch;
- Looking tired; and
- Having an attitude consistent with depression or exhaustion.

This stressful workplace is highly variable around the world, with some countries better and some worse than the United States. For example, a recent Gallup world poll found about half of those in the United States described themselves as "thriving" compared to 83 percent in Denmark and only 2 percent in Cambodia.[9] In the competitive global economy workplace stress is common in the major economic powers, but may take different forms. For example, a recent cross-cultural study comparing U.S. and Chinese employees found the Americans reported significantly more lack of job control, direct interpersonal conflict, anger, frustration, feeling overwhelmed, and stomach problems, but their Chinese counterparts had relatively more stress from job evaluations, work mistakes, indirect conflict, employment conditions, and lack of training.[10] Even the French are feeling the pressure. At the big automaker Renault outside of Paris, in a recent five-month period three of its engineers killed themselves. "In the suicide notes and conversations with their families before taking their lives, the three men voiced anxiety about unreasonable workloads, high pressure management tactics, exhaustion, and humiliating criticism in front of colleagues during performance reviews."[11] In other words, there seems to be a worldwide stress epidemic and seems to be getting worse.

## What Stress Is, and Is Not

Stress is usually thought of in negative terms. It is thought to be caused by something bad (for example, a college student is placed on scholastic probation, a loved one is seriously ill, or the boss gives a formal reprimand for poor performance). This is a form of distress. But there is also a positive, pleasant side of stress caused by good things (for example, a college student makes the dean's list; an attractive, respected acquaintance asks for a date; an employee is offered a job promotion at another location). This is a form of *eu*stress. This latter term was coined by the pioneers of stress research from the Greek *eu,* which means "good." Applied to the workplace, a large study by researchers at Cornell University of 1,800 managers identified examples of "bad" stress as office politics, red tape, and a stalled career and "good" stress as challenges that come with increased job responsibility, time pressure, and high-quality assignments.[12] A recent meta-analysis found that *hindrance stressors* (organizational politics, red tape, role ambiguity, and in general those demands unnecessarily thwarting personal growth and goal attainment) had a negative effect on motivation and performance. On the other hand, so-called *challenge stressors* (high workload, time pressure, high responsibility, and in general those demands that are viewed as obstacles to be overcome in order to learn and achieve) were found to have a positive effect on motivation and performance.[13]

Another interesting delineation involves two types of energy—"tense energy," which is a stress-driven state characterized by a constant sense of pressure and anxiety, and "calm energy," which is a stress-free "flow" state characterized by low muscle tension, an alert presence of mind, peaceful body feelings, increased creative intelligence, physical vitality, and a deep sense of well-being.[14] On-the-job stress may enhance such energy levels. For example, a recent survey found over two-thirds of U.S. and international employees reported being either neutral or energized. Based on this evidence, one stress expert observed, "The number of employees who indicated a level of comfort and even positive energy in response to work-related stress confirms that challenging work helps employees remain focused and interested throughout their daily routines and more eager to contribute."[15]

In other words, a completely stress-free workplace is not the ideal. Stress can be viewed in a number of different ways and has been described as the most imprecise word in the scientific dictionary. The word *stress* has also been compared with the word *sin:* "Both are short, emotionally charged words used to refer to something that otherwise would take many words to say."[16] Although there are numerous definitions and much debate about the meaning of job stress,[17] Ivancevich and Matteson define stress simply as "the interaction of the individual with the environment," but then they go on to give a more detailed working definition, as follows: "an adaptive response, mediated by individual differences and/or psychological processes, that is a consequence of any external (environmental) action, situation, or event that places excessive psychological and/or physical demands on a person."[18] Note the three critical components of this definition: (1) it refers to a reaction to a situation or event, not the situation or event itself; (2) it emphasizes that stress can be impacted by individual differences; and (3) it highlights the phrase "excessive psychological and/or physical demands," because only special or unusual situations (as opposed to minor life adjustments) can really be said to produce stress.[19]

In another definition, Beehr and Newman define *job stress* as "a condition arising from the interaction of people and their jobs and characterized by changes within people that force them to deviate from their normal functioning."[20] Taking these two definitions and simplifying them for the purpose of this chapter, *stress* is defined as an adaptive response to an external situation that results in physical, psychological, and/or behavioral deviations for organizational participants.

It is also important to point out what stress is *not:*

1. *Stress is not simply anxiety.* Anxiety operates solely in the emotional and psychological sphere, whereas stress operates there and also in the physiological sphere. Thus, stress may be accompanied by anxiety, but the two should not be equated.

2. *Stress is not simply nervous tension.* Like anxiety, nervous tension may result from stress, but the two are not the same. Unconscious people have exhibited stress, and some people may keep it "bottled up" and not reveal it through nervous tension.

3. *Stress is not necessarily something damaging, bad, or to be avoided.* Eustress is not damaging or bad and is something people should seek out rather than avoid. The key, of course, is how the person handles the stress. Stress is inevitable; distress may be prevented or can be effectively controlled.[21]

## What about Burnout?

As far as the increasingly popular term "burnout" is concerned, some stress researchers contend that burnout is a type of stress[22] and others treat it as having a number of components.[23] One stress and trauma support coordinator makes the distinction between stress and burnout as follows, "Stress is normal and often quite healthy. However, when the ability to cope with stress begins to let us down, then we may be on the road to burnout."[24] John Izzo, a former HR professional in the occupational development area, suggests that burnout may be the consequence of "losing a sense of the basic purpose and fulfillment of your work." He goes on to say that "Getting more balance or getting more personal time will help you with stress—but it will often not help you with burnout."[25] Research in this area shows that burnout is not necessarily the result of individual problems such as character or behavior flaws in which organizations can simply change people or get rid of them. In fact, Christina Maslach, a well-known stress researcher, says the opposite is probably true. She concludes that "as a result of extensive study, it is believed that burnout is not a problem of the people themselves but of the social environment in which people work."[26] She believes that burnout creates a sense of isolation and a feeling of lost control, causing the burned-out employee to relate differently to others and to their work.[27] Burnout is also most closely associated with the so-called helping professions such as nursing, education, and social work. So, even though technically burnout may be somewhat different from stress, the two terms will be treated the same here and used interchangeably.

Finally, conceptually similar to stress is conflict. Although there is some overlap in analyzing the causes and effects and managing stress and conflict, they are both covered in this chapter. The major difference, except for intraindividual conflict, is that conflict in the field of organizational behavior is more associated with disagreement or opposition at the interpersonal or intergroup level. After examining stressors, these levels of conflict are given attention.

# THE CAUSES OF STRESS

The antecedents of stress, or the so-called stressors, affecting today's employees are summarized in Figure 9.1. As shown, these causes come from both outside and inside the organization, from the groups that employees are influenced by and from employees themselves.

**FIGURE 9.1**
**Categories of Stressors Affecting Occupational Stress**

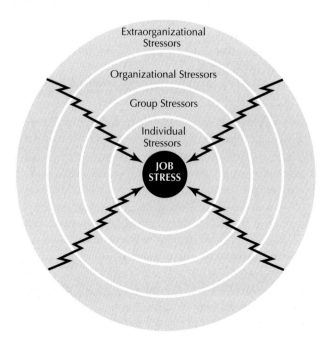

Extraorganizational Stressors

Organizational Stressors

Group Stressors

Individual Stressors

**JOB STRESS**

## Extraorganizational Stressors

Although most analyses of job stress ignore the importance of outside forces and events, it is becoming increasingly clear that these have a tremendous impact. Taking an open-systems perspective of an organization (that is, the organization is greatly affected by the external environment), it is clear that job stress is not limited just to things that happen inside the organization, during working hours. In fact, one research study found that stressors outside the workplace were related to negative affect and feelings on the job.[28] Extraorganizational stressors include things such as societal/technological change, globalization, the family, relocation, economic and financial conditions, race and gender, and residential or community conditions.

The phenomenal rate of change and economic turbulence, which is given detailed attention in the introductory chapters, has had a great effect on people's lifestyles, and this of course is carried over into their jobs. Although medical science has increased the life spans of people and has eradicated or reduced the threat of many diseases, the pace of modern living has increased stress and decreased personal *wellness*. The concept of wellness has been defined as "a harmonious and productive balance of physical, mental, and social well-being brought about by the acceptance of one's personal responsibility for developing and adhering to a health promotion program."[29] Because people tend to get caught up in the rush-rush, mobile, urbanized, crowded, on-the-go lifestyle of today, their anxiety[30] and wellness in general has deteriorated; the potential for stress on the job has increased. There is considerable evidence that "Balancing concern for one's health with effortful striving is essential to sustained, long-term achievement. Conversely, the failure to attend to one's health places an executive at risk of failure, and in the extreme, of death."[31]

It is generally recognized that a person's family has a big impact on one's stress level. A family situation—either a brief crisis, such as a squabble or the illness of a family member, or long-term strained relations with parents, spouse, or children—can act as a significant stressor for employees. Also, recent trends have made it increasingly difficult for employees to adequately balance the responsibilities of their jobs and their families. As employees are working longer hours and bringing more work home at night,[32] more and more pressure is being placed on work-family relationships[33] and more emphasis on the coordination of work and vacation schedules, and the search for elder and child care options has become prominent and very stressful.[34]

Relocating the family because of a transfer or a promotion can also lead to stress. For example, under globalization, expatriate managers (those with an assignment outside their home country) may undergo cultural shock and then when repatriated (relocated to the home country) may experience isolation; both are significant stressors.[35] For most people in recent years, their financial situation has also proved to be a stressor. Many people have been forced to take a second job ("moonlight"), or the spouse has had to enter the workforce in order to make ends meet. This situation reduces time for recreational and family activities. The overall effect on employees is more stress on their primary jobs.

Life's changes may be slow (getting older) or sudden (the death of a spouse). These sudden changes have been portrayed in novels and movies as having a dramatic effect on people, and medical researchers have verified that especially sudden life changes do in fact have a very stressful impact on people.[36] They found a definite relationship between the degree of life changes and the subsequent health of the person. The more change, the poorer the subsequent health. These life changes can also directly influence job performance. One psychologist, Faye Crosby, reports that divorce greatly interferes with work. She says, "During the first three months after a spouse walks out, the other spouse—male or female—usually is incapable of focusing on work."[37]

Sociological-demographic variables such as race and gender can also become stressors. As the workforce becomes increasingly diverse (see Chapter 2), potential stress-related issues include differences in beliefs and values, differences in opportunities for rewards or promotions, and perceptions by minority employees of either discrimination or lack of fit between themselves and the organization.[38] Researchers have noted over the years that minorities may have more stressors than whites.[39] Although a review of up-to-date evidence concludes that women experience more stress than men,[40] an earlier meta-analysis performed on 15 studies found no significant sex differences in experienced and perceived work stress.[41] There continues to be evidence that women perceive more job demands than men in both the male-dominated and female-dominated occupations.[42] Also, people in the middle and upper classes may have particular or common stressors. The same is true of the local community or region that one comes from. For example, one researcher identified the condition of housing, convenience of services and shopping, neighborliness, and degree of noise and air pollution as likely stressors.[43] With globalization adding to the cultural diversity of recent times, there is also recent research evidence suggesting that identical conflict episodes are perceived differently across cultures (in this case the United States and Japan).[44] Thus, not only must race and gender be considered in analyzing extraorganizational stressors, but also the country culture and economic system.[45]

## Organizational Stressors

Besides the potential stressors that occur outside the organization, there are also those associated with the organization itself. Although the organization is made up of groups of individuals, there are also more macrolevel dimensions, unique to the organization, that contain potential stressors.[46] Figure 9.2 shows that these macrolevel stressors can be categorized into administrative policies and strategies, organizational structure and design, organizational processes, and working conditions. Some specific examples of more specific job stressors especially related to performance includes role ambiguity, conflict and overload, job insecurity, work-family conflict, environmental uncertainty, and situational constraints. A recent meta-analysis found each of these to be negatively related to job performance.[47]

As organizations dramatically change to meet the environmental challenges outlined in the introductory chapters (globalization, economic turbulence, and diversity), there are more and more accompanying stressors for individual employees in their jobs. As recently described, organizations today must be fast, agile, and responsive; they must quickly respond to an ever-changing environment, constantly reinventing themselves.[48] For example, a study by Deloitte and Touche found that 84 percent of U.S. companies were undergoing at least one major change intervention in their business strategy in order to compete in today's environment. Programs such as reengineering, restructuring, and downsizing have become commonplace as the result of intense pressures to outperform the competition. Downsizing, in particular, has taken and continues to take its toll on employees.[49] The actual loss of jobs, or even the mere threat of being laid off, can be extremely stressful for employees. Additionally, the "survivors" of downsizing "often experience tremendous pressure from the fear of future cuts, the loss of friends and colleagues, and an increase in workload."[50] In other words, downsizing often translates to longer hours and more stress for the surviors.[51] Research indicates that such chronic occupational demands can lead to stress.[52]

## Group Stressors

Chapter 10 indicates the tremendous influence that the group has on behavior. The group or team can also be a potential source of stress. Here is how one member recently described her team's typical meeting:

**FIGURE 9.2**
**Macrolevel**
**Organizational**
**Stressors**

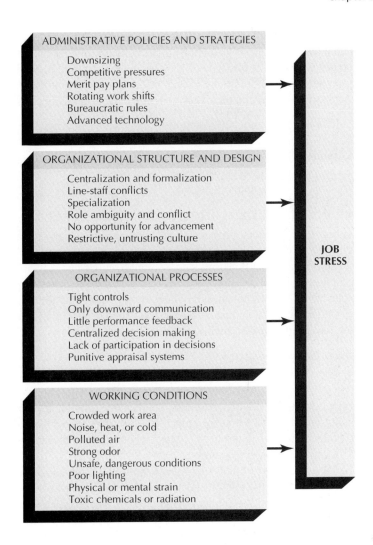

The people are loyal and competent but very slow to make proactive changes. They also have a hard time with conflict so that issues go unaddressed for years. When I sit in staff meetings, we may be talking about a budget issue or a marketing topic but the real underlying issue seems to be two warring managers or an old conflict being rehashed.[53]

Unfortunately, sometimes these interpersonal conflicts in a group end up in a "bullying" problem. This is only a recently recognized problem. Different from sexual harassment or incivility, bullying is defined as "repeated, health-harming mistreatment that could involve verbal abuse, threatening, humiliating, or offensive behavior or actions; or work interference."[54] Obviously, bullying leads to tremendous stress for a victim and even those who witness this problem. More generally, group stressors can be categorized into two areas:

1. *Lack of group cohesiveness.* Since the historically famous Hawthorne studies, discussed in Chapter 1, it has become very clear that cohesiveness, or "togetherness," is very important to employees, especially at the lower levels of organizations. If an employee is denied the opportunity for this cohesiveness because of the task design, because the supervisor does things to prohibit or limit it, or because the other members of the group shut the person out, the resulting lack of cohesiveness can be very stress producing.

2. *Lack of social support.* Employees are greatly affected by the support of one or more members of a cohesive group. By sharing their problems and joys with others, they are much better off. If this type of social support is lacking for an individual, the situation can be very stressful. There is even research evidence indicating that the lack of social support is so stressful that it accounts for some health care costs.[55]

In addition to the group per se, group-level dynamics may become stressors. For example, one study found that organizational politics was a potential source of stress in the work environment[56] and another study found social stressors such as conflicts with coworkers and supervisors and social dislikes or ill will of all kinds, over time, can lead to depressive symptoms for the employees involved.[57]

## Individual Stressors: The Role of Dispositions

In a sense, the stressors discussed so far (extraorganizational, organizational, and group) all eventually get down to the individual level. There is also more research and agreement on possible situational dimensions and individual dispositions that may affect stress outcomes. For example, individual dispositions such as Type A personality patterns, personal control, learned helplessness, and psychological hardiness may all affect the level of stress someone experiences. In addition, the intraindividual level of conflict stemming from frustration, goals, and roles, covered next under conflict, definitely has implications as individual stressors.

### *Type A Characteristics*

The discussion of personality in Chapter 5 points out the complexity of, and individual differences in, personality dispositions and traits. Personality traits such as authoritarianism, rigidity, extroversion, supportiveness, spontaneity, emotionality, tolerance for ambiguity, anxiety, and the need for achievement have been uncovered by research as being particularly relevant to individual stress.[58] Most attention over the years, however, has centered on the so-called Type A personality.

Although heart researchers have been working on the use of personality types and the resulting behavior patterns in order to predict heart attacks since the 1950s, in the late 1960s Friedman and Rosenman popularized the use of Type A and opposing Type B personalities in the study of stress. These types were portrayed as relatively stable characteristics, and initially Friedman and Rosenman's extensive studies found the Type A profile correlated highly with experienced stress and dangerous physical consequences.[59] In more recent years, however, there is increasing evidence that Type As face no higher risk of heart disease than anyone else.

Table 9.1 gives the reader a chance to see whether he or she tends to be a Type A or a Type B personality. A majority of Americans are Type A, and an even higher percentage of managers are Type A; one study found that 60 percent of the managers sampled were clearly Type A and that only 12 percent were Type B.[60]

Friedman and Rosenman define the Type A personality as "an action-emotion complex that can be observed in any person who is aggressively involved in a chronic, incessant struggle to achieve more and more in less and less time, and if required to do so, against the opposing efforts of other things or other persons."[61] Table 9.2 briefly summarizes the Type A and Type B profiles. Obviously Type A employees (managers, salespersons, staff specialists, secretaries, or rank-and-file operating employees) experience considerable stress. They are the ones who:

1. Work long, hard hours under constant deadline pressures and conditions for overload.
2. Often take work home at night or on weekends and are unable to relax.
3. Constantly compete with themselves, setting high standards of productivity that they seem driven to maintain.

**TABLE 9.1**
**Type A and Type B Self-Test**

*Source:* Adapted from R. W. Bortner, "A Short Rating Scale as a Potential Measure of Pattern A Behavior," *Journal of Chronic Diseases,* Vol. 22, 1966, pp. 87–91.

To determine your Type A or Type B profile, circle the number on the continuum (the verbal descriptions represent endpoints) that best represents your behavior for each dimension.

| | | |
|---|---|---|
| Am casual about appointments | 1 2 3 4 5 6 7 8 | Am never late |
| Am not competitive | 1 2 3 4 5 6 7 8 | Am very competitive |
| Never feel rushed, even under pressure | 1 2 3 4 5 6 7 8 | Always feel rushed |
| Take things one at a time | 1 2 3 4 5 6 7 8 | Try to do many things at once; think about what I am going to do next |
| Do things slowly | 1 2 3 4 5 6 7 8 | Do things fast (eating, walking, etc.) |
| Express feelings | 1 2 3 4 5 6 7 8 | "Sit" on feelings |
| Have many interests | 1 2 3 4 5 6 7 8 | Have few interests outside work |

Total your score: _____ Multiply it by 3: _____. The interpretation of your score is as follows:

| Number of points | Type of personality |
|---|---|
| Less than 90 | B |
| 90 to 99 | B+ |
| 100 to 105 | A− |
| 106 to 119 | A |
| 120 or more | A+ |

4. Tend to become frustrated by the work situation, to be irritated with the work efforts of others, and to be misunderstood by supervisors.[62]

Here is how one obviously Type A manager recently described her activities:

> 350 e-mails a day in my inbox. BlackBerry, cell phone, and laptop constantly in tow. Check my Outlook calendar and see that I'm double- or triple-booked in meetings every hour, plus a 7 A.M. global conference call. Being told by management that we cannot hire additional head count because of a hiring freeze, despite the hefty increase in responsibility for my team.[63]

By contrast, as shown in Table 9.2, Type B personalities are very laid back, are patient, and take a very relaxed, low-key approach to life and their job.

**TABLE 9.2**
**Profiles of Type A and Type B Personalities**

| Type A Profile | Type B Profile |
|---|---|
| Is always moving | Is not concerned about time |
| Walks rapidly | Is patient |
| Eats rapidly | Doesn't brag |
| Talks rapidly | Plays for fun, not to win |
| Is impatient | Relaxes without guilt |
| Does two things at once | Has no pressing deadlines |
| Can't cope with leisure time | Is mild-mannered |
| Is obsessed with numbers | It never in a hurry |
| Measures success by quantity | |
| Is aggressive | |
| Is competitive | |
| Constantly feels under time pressure | |

It is now accepted that Type As per se do not predict heart problems, and in fact Type As may release and better cope with their stress than do Type Bs. The more recent studies indicate that it is not so much the impatience that is closely associated with Type As that leads to heart problems, but rather anger and hostility.[64] A leading medical researcher noted that the term "Type A" probably has outlived its usefulness. He stated: "Being a workaholic, being in a hurry, interrupting people, are not necessarily bad for your heart. What is bad is if you have high levels of hostility and anger, and you don't bother to hide it when dealing with other people."[65] This conclusion was supported by an organizational psychiatrist who, after extensive study of the causes of stress in Japanese, German, and American workers, concluded that "how workers handle their own aggression is the key factor in determining whether they will experience the kind of stress that can lead to heart attacks, high blood pressure and other health problems."[66] However, before the relationship of Type A to severe physical outcomes is completely dismissed, it should be noted that anger, hostility, and aggression sometimes go along with a Type A personality.

Besides the debate surrounding the impact of Type A personality on health is the question of the performance and success of Type As versus Type Bs. It is pretty clear that Type As perform better[67] and are typically on a "fast track" to the top. They are more successful than Type Bs. However, at the *very* top they do not tend to be as successful as Type Bs, who are not overly ambitious, are more patient, and take a broader view of things.[68] The key may be to shift from Type A to Type B behavior, but, of course, most Type As are unable and *unwilling* to make the shift and/or to cope with their Type A characteristics.

### *Personal Control*

Besides Type A personality patterns, another important disposition is an individual's perception of control. As mentioned in Chapter 5's discussion on job satisfaction, people's feelings about their ability to control a situation are important in determining their level of stress. In particular, if employees feel that they have little control over the work environment and over their own job, they will experience stress.[69] Studies have shown that if employees are given a sense of control over their work environment, such as being given a chance to be involved in the decision-making process that affects them, this will reduce their work stress.[70] A large study by Cornell University medical researchers found that those workers who experience a loss of control, especially in relatively low-level jobs, have triple the risk of developing high blood pressure. The researchers concluded that lack of control turns stress into physical problems. They also found that if a high-stress job included latitude to control the situation, there was no increase in blood pressure.[71] A study in a hospital setting also found that employee perceptions of the amount of control they experience at work relate to stress, which in turn affects physiological outcomes such as blood pressure as well as psychological outcomes such as job satisfaction.[72] A recent study also found that job control has an impact on stress and strain if the employee perceives organizational justice.[73] In other words, it may not be job control per se, but the employee's perception of fairness that has the resulting impact on stress.

### *Learned Helplessness*

The feeling of loss of control goes back to some of the classic research on learned helplessness conducted by Seligman.[74] Chapter 7 introduced this concept in relation to optimism. In conducting experiments on dogs who could not escape shock, Seligman found that they eventually accepted it and did not even try to escape. Later, when the dogs could learn to escape easily, they did not—they had learned to be helpless. Other studies found that people, too, can learn to be helpless,[75] which helps explain why some employees just seem to have given up and seem to accept stressors in their work environment, even when a change for the better is possible.

More recently, Seligman and his colleagues have concentrated on people's attributions for their lack of control. Specifically, they suggest that people are most apt to experience helplessness when they perceive the causes of the lack of control:

1. To be related to something about their own personal characteristics (as opposed to outside, environmental forces)
2. As stable and enduring (rather than just temporary)
3. To be global and universal (cutting across many situations, rather than in just one sphere of life)[76]

Further study and research on the sense of control in general and learned helplessness in particular will provide much insight into stress and how to cope with it.

### Psychological Hardiness

Everyone has observed individual differences of people faced with stressors. Some people seem to go to pieces at the slightest provocation, whereas others seem unflappable in the face of extremely stressful situations. Those able to cope successfully with extreme stressors seem to have a "hardiness" disposition.

Kobasa and her colleagues studied executives under considerable stress who were both measurably hardy and nonhardy. She found that the hardy executives had a lower rate of stress-related illness and were characterized as having commitment (they became very involved in what they were doing); welcoming challenge (they believed that change rather than stability was normal); and feeling in control (they felt they could influence the events around them).[77] She suggests that the predisposition of psychological hardiness helps those with it to resist stress by providing buffers between themselves and stressors.

Such buffering drawn from hardiness may be an important quality as organizations now and in the future demand more and more from their employees at all levels. As has been noted:

> Why does the job seem so demanding? It isn't just long hours or clumsy direction from above, though there's plenty of that. All sorts of pressure, from the stress of participatory management techniques to the hyperkinesia of two-career marriages to the dismay of finding your workload increasing as you near 50, just when you thought you could adopt a more dignified pace, are working together to squeeze the oomph from heretofore steely-eyed achievers.[78]

Kobasa's research would say that those with hardiness will be able to survive and even thrive in such an environment, but those who do not possess hardiness may suffer the harmful outcomes of stress and conflict. As concluded by the closely related "toughness" researchers in positive psychology, "once an individual becomes tough and thereby experiences the sustained energy (with minimal tension) necessary for successful coping, that person is likely to experience a greater variety of situations as challenging rather than threatening."[79] Also from the positive organizational behavior literature, in Chapter 7 it was mentioned that Avey, Luthans, and Jensen recently found that there was a significant negative relationship between employees' psychological capital and their reported levels of stress.[80] In other words, employees may be able to draw from their positive psychological resources (i.e., efficacy, hope, optimism, resiliency, and overall psychological capital) in order to combat the stressors that they face at work.

**FIGURE 9.3**
**Level of Conflict in Organizational Behavior**

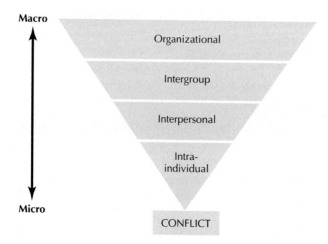

# INTRAINDIVIDUAL CONFLICT

Although stress and conflict are treated differently, they are combined in this one chapter mainly because of the conceptual similarity between individual dispositional stressors and intraindividual conflict. After presenting the intraindividual forms of conflict in terms of frustration, goals, and roles, some more macro interactive conflict models are briefly reviewed as shown in Figure 9.3.

## Conflict Due to Frustration

Frustration occurs when a motivated drive is blocked before a person reaches a desired goal. Figure 9.4 illustrates what happens. The barrier may be either overt (outward, or physical) or covert (inward, or mental-sociopsychological). The frustration model can be useful in the analysis of not only behavior in general but also specific aspects of on-the-job behavior. Theft of company property and even violence on the job may be a form of an aggressive outcome to job frustration. For example, a summary article on violence in the workplace noted that even though on-the-job killings have dropped over the last 15 years, this is because of fewer homicides in places like taxis and convenience stores. Workplace homicides by "associates"—current and former coworkers, customers, and clients—are

**FIGURE 9.4**
**A Model of Frustration**

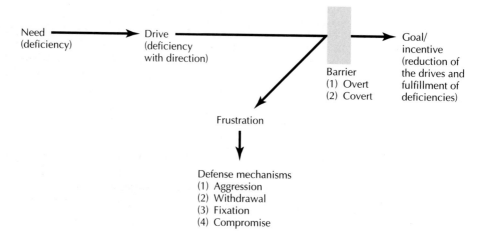

actually on the upswing since 1997.[81] In addition, employee crimes, as a form of displaced aggression (e.g., fictitious sales transactions, illegal kickbacks, and theft of office equipment and retail items meant for sales to customers), is also on the rise.[82]

There is increasing concern and research on aggression and violence in the workplace. Although self-reported incidences of workplace aggression are a reaction to frustration, there is research evidence that individual differences (e.g., trait anger, attribution style, negative affectivity, attitudes toward revenge, self-control, and previous exposure to aggressive cultures) account for this aggression,[83] but so do situational factors such as interactional justice and/or abusive supervision.[84] Another study also found personality variables such as stress reaction and control correlated with workplace aggression, and the incidence of aggression depended on the perception of being victimized by others.[85] The form of aggression may depend on the perception of organizational justice (i.e., the judged fairness),[86] and there is a recent study that violent crime rates in the community of the workplace predicted the amount of reported aggression at that workplace.[87] Implementing a violence-prevention policy and providing training to supervisors and employees in workplace-violence awareness seems to decrease the incidence rate for employee-on-employee violence.[88]

In addition to aggression and violence, the withdrawal reaction to frustration may be a major explanation for the "motivational problem" of employees. They may be apathetic or have "retired on the job" because they are frustrated, not because they have no motivation. Many employees' motives have been blocked by dead-end jobs, high degrees of job specialization, or supervisors who put up barriers. Similar to aggression there is research evidence that both perceived organizational support[89] and personality variables[90] affect what manner and what type of withdrawal behaviors employees exhibit. The fixation reaction to frustration may be used to explain irrational bureaucratic behavior. (The rules become the ends in themselves, and the frustrated employee pathetically adapts to the barriers.) Compromise can help explain midcareer changes (frustrated employees go around the barriers) or "living outside the job" (frustrated employees cannot achieve motivated goals on the job, so they seek fulfillment outside the job). These reactions to frustration often cost organizations a great deal because of the dysfunctions associated with aggression, withdrawal, and fixation. In the case of compromise, the employee's motivation is forced outside the organization. Although the discussion so far indicates the dysfunctional nature of frustration, such negativity should not be automatically assumed.

In some cases frustration may actually result in a positive impact on individual performance and organizational goals. An example is the worker or manager who has high needs for competence and achievement and/or who has high self-efficacy (see Chapter 7's discussion) in being able to do a job well. A person of this type who is frustrated on the job may react in a traditional defensive manner, but the frustration may result in improved performance. The person may try harder to overcome the barrier or may overcompensate, or the new direction or goal sought may be more compatible with the organization's goals. In addition, one research study found stress and strain levels were lower for participants with high self-efficacy than for those with lower self-efficacy.[91]

Once again, it should be remembered that defense mechanisms per se are not bad for the individual. They play an important role in the psychological adjustment process and are unhealthy only when they dominate the individual's personality. Also, those who have successfully overcome frustration in the past by learning that it is possible to surmount barriers or find substitute goals are more tolerant of frustration than those who have never experienced it, or than those who have experienced excesses in frustration. There is also evidence that "venting" (an emotional reaction of expressing one's negative feelings to others) has an adverse affect on performance and amplified the negativity.[92] However, in general, a major goal of management should be to eliminate the barriers (imagined, real, or potential) that are or will be frustrating to employees. This goal may be accomplished through job redesign efforts (see Chapter 6) that are more compatible with employee motivation or leadership skills that get the frustrating barriers out of people's way.

## Goal Conflict

Another common source of conflict for an individual is a goal that has both positive and negative features, or two or more competing goals. Whereas in frustration motives are blocked before the goal is reached, in goal conflict two or more motives block one another. For ease of analysis, three separate types of goal conflict are generally identified:

1. *Approach-approach* conflict, where the individual is motivated to approach two or more positive but mutually exclusive goals.

2. *Approach-avoidance* conflict, where the individual is motivated to approach a goal and at the same time is motivated to avoid it. The single goal contains both positive and negative characteristics for the individual.

3. *Avoidance-avoidance* conflict, where the individual is motivated to avoid two or more negative but mutually exclusive goals.

To varying degrees, each of these forms of goal conflict exists in the modern organization, but approach-avoidance is most relevant to the analysis of conflict.

Approach-avoidance conflict results from organizational goals having both positive and negative aspects for organizational participants. Basic research in psychology suggests that the positive aspects of a given organizational goal are stronger and more salient at a distance (in time and/or space) than the negative aspects. On the other hand, as a person gets nearer to the goal, the negative aspects become more pronounced, and at some point the individual may hesitate or fail to progress any further at the point where approach equals avoidance. For example, managers engaged in long-range planning typically are very confident of a goal (a strategic plan) they have developed for the future. Yet, as the time gets near to commit resources and implement the plan, the negative consequences seem to appear much greater than they did in the developing stage. Managers in such a situation may reach the point where approach equals avoidance. The result is a great deal of internal conflict and stress, which may cause indecision, physical reactions, or even depression.

Such approach-avoidance conflict and its aftermath are very common among decision makers and people in responsible positions in today's organizations described in the introductory comments. As noted in a cover story of *Fortune,* "To the survivors, the revolution feels something like this: scary, guilty, painful, liberating, disorienting, exhilarating, empowering, frustrating, fulfilling, confusing, challenging."[93] In other words, as these terms indicate, many managers in recent years have been experiencing very mixed feelings, or approach-avoidance reactions. The accompanying OB in Action: Dealing with Conflicting Goals gives some real-world examples.

## Role Conflict and Ambiguity

Closely related to the concept of norms (the "oughts" of behavior), *role* is defined as a position that has expectations evolving from established norms. People living in contemporary society assume a succession of roles throughout life. A typical sequence of social roles would be that of child, son or daughter, teenager, college student, boyfriend or girlfriend, spouse, parent, and grandparent. Each of these roles has recognized expectations that are acted out like a role in a play.

Besides progressing through a succession of roles such as those just mentioned, the adult in modern society fills numerous other roles at the same time. It is not uncommon for

How can managers deal with conflicting goals? One way is by recognizing that conflict exists in every organization and cannot be avoided. For example, many management experts argue that in order to bring about change, top executives have to be out front rallying the personnel and showing that they support the change. On the other hand, these same experts point out that change has to have a broad cadre of leaders at the middle and lower levels who are willing to carry the banner of change. So what is a leader to do: Get out front or encourage the personnel to assume this responsibility? The two approaches seem to be in conflict.

Or consider the independence versus interdependence conflict. Organizations demand that their managers act independently and assume personal initiative and responsibility for their units. However, when a manager initiates an action that steps on another unit's toes, the first manager often is called on the carpet and encouraged to "be more of a team player."

Another conflict is that of revenue growth versus cost containment. If managers spend all their time trying to grow the business, they face the criticism of not controlling their costs. If they put the primary focus on keeping expenses under control, they are asked why they are not increasing their revenue base.

What can managers do to deal with these conflicts? One way is to realize that conflict often forms into a central dilemma: empowerment versus alignment. Successful managers explore both approaches and balance their emphasis accordingly. For example, at General Motors there long has been a conflict between achieving low cost per unit through economies of scale (large-size enterprise) and responding to customer demands by reducing time to market. At IBM there has been an ongoing conflict between growing the business (raising revenues) and increasing profit (lowering costs). At Mercedes there has been a continual clash between factions in the firm who want to design and build quality cars (engineering emphasis) and those who argue that many people are unwilling to pay a premium for the car because they neither want nor appreciate such innovation (marketing emphasis). The successful manager often is the one who best can balance the conflicting demands while not losing sight of the organization's overall objectives. Through effective conflict management, the efforts of all concerned can be directed toward common goals that hopefully will be beneficial to both the people involved and the overall organization.

the adult middle-class male to be simultaneously playing the roles of husband, father, provider, son (to elderly parents), worker or manager, student (in a night program), coach of a Little League baseball team, church member, member of a social club, bridge partner, poker club member, officer of a community group, and weekend golfer. Women, of course, also have numerous, often conflicting, roles.[94] Although all the roles that men and women bring into the organization are relevant to their behavior, in the study of organizational behavior the organizational role is the most important. Roles such as software developer, clerk, team leader, salesperson, engineer, systems analyst, department head, vice president, and chairperson of the board often carry conflicting demands and expectations. There is recent research evidence that such conflict can have a negative impact on well-being[95] and performance and may be affected by cultural differences.[96] For example, in a study of CEOs in international joint ventures, it was found that role conflict was lower when the foreign partner was dominant in the venture, but higher when the local parent was dominant. Role conflict was inversely related to cultural distance.[97]

There are three major types of role conflict. One type is the conflict between *the person and the role*. There may be conflict between the person's personality and the expectations of the role. For example, a production worker and member of the union is appointed to head up a new production team. This new team leader may not really believe in keeping close control over the workers, and it goes against this individual's personality to be hard-nosed, but that is what the head of production expects. A second type is *intrarole* conflict created by contradictory expectations about how a given role should be played. Should the new team leader be autocratic or democratic in dealing with the team members? Finally, *interrole* conflict results from the differing requirements of two or more roles that must be played at the same time. Work roles and nonwork roles are often in such conflict. For example, a successful executive working for a computer company said that she often worked from 7:30 A.M. to 11:30 P.M. Her long hours led to the breakup of a relationship. When she got word that her mother was seriously ill, she remembered: "I had about five minutes to be upset before the phone started ringing again. You get so far into it, you don't even realize your life has gotten away from you completely."[98]

The production team leader and the fast-climbing executive obviously represent the extreme cases of organizational role conflict. Yet to varying degrees, depending on the individual and the situation, people in every other position in the modern organization also experience one or all three types of role conflict. Staff engineers are not sure of their real authority. The clerk in the front office does not know whether to respond to a union-organizing drive. The examples are endless. The question is not whether role conflict and ambiguity exist—they do, and they seem inevitable.[99] Rather, the key becomes a matter of determining how role conflict can be resolved or managed.[100]

# INTERACTIVE CONFLICT

Besides the intraindividual aspects of conflict that are closely related to stress, the interactive aspects of conflict are also an important dynamic of organizational behavior. This section is specifically concerned with analyzing the interactive conflict that can result at the interpersonal and intergroup levels in today's organizations.

## Interpersonal Conflict

Those who have interpersonal conflict most often attribute the cause to a personality problem or defect in the other party. For example, as discussed in Chapter 6, research from attribution theory on the so-called fundamental attribution error suggests that people attribute others' behavior to personal factors such as intelligence, ability, motivation, attitudes, or personality. Whetten and Cameron, however, go beyond this surface explanation and propose that there are four major sources of interpersonal conflict.[101] These can be summarized as follows:

1. *Personal differences.*  Everyone has a unique background because of his or her upbringing, cultural and family traditions, and socialization processes. Because no one has the same family background, education, and values, the differences can be a major source of conflict. Disagreements stemming from the differences "often become highly emotional and take on moral overtones. A disagreement about who is factually correct easily turns into a bitter argument over who is morally right."[102]

2. *Information deficiency.*  This source of conflict results from communication breakdown in the organization. It may be that the two people in conflict are using different information or that one or both have misinformation. Unlike personal differences, this source of conflict is not emotionally charged and once corrected, there is little resentment.

3. *Role incompatibility.*  This type of interpersonal conflict draws from both intraindividual role conflict (discussed in the previous section) and intergroup conflict (discussed in the next section). Specifically, in today's horizontal organizations, managers have functions and tasks that are highly interdependent. However, the individual roles of these managers may be incompatible. For example, the production manager and the sales manager have interdependent functions: one supports the other. However, a major role of the production manager is to cut costs, and one way to do this is to keep inventories low. The sales manager, on the other hand, has a dominant role of increasing revenues through increased sales. The sales manager may make delivery promises to customers

that are incompatible with the low inventory levels maintained by production. The resulting conflict from role incompatibility may have to be resolved by higher-level management or systems development through advanced information technology.

4. *Environmental stress.*   These types of conflict can be amplified by a stressful environment. In environments characterized by scarce or shrinking resources, downsizing, competitive pressures, or high degrees of uncertainty, conflict of all kinds will be more probable. "For example, when a major pet-food manufacturing facility announced that one-third of its managers would have to support a new third shift, the feared disruption of personal and family routines prompted many managers to think about sending out their résumés. In addition, the uncertainty of who was going to be required to work at night was so great that even routine management work was disrupted by posturing and infighting."[103]

In addition to identifying some of the major sources of interpersonal conflict as in the preceding, it is useful to analyze the dynamics of individuals interacting with one another. One way to analyze their confronting others is through the response categories of (1) forcing (assertive, uncooperative); (2) accommodating (unassertive, cooperative); (3) avoiding (uncooperative, unassertive); (4) compromising (between assertiveness and cooperativeness); and (5) collaborating (cooperative, assertive).[104] Like role conflict, there is research indicating the complexity of interindividual and intragroup conflict,[105] and it is not always bad. For example, one study found the following profile of high-performing teams: (1) low but increasing levels of process conflict; (2) low levels of relationship conflict, with a rise near project deadlines; and (3) moderate levels of task conflict at the midpoint of group interaction.[106]

## Intergroup Behavior and Conflict

In addition to interpersonal (which includes intragroup) conflict, social psychologists have been concerned about intergroup conflict for a number of years. Intergroup behavior is even specifically identified as follows: "Intergroup behavior occurs whenever individuals belonging to one group interact, collectively or individually, with another group or its members in terms of their reference group identification."[107]

Several antecedent conditions have been identified for explaining intergroup conflict. These can be summarized as follows:[108]

1. *Competition for resources.*   Most organizations today have very limited resources. Groups within the organization vie for budget funds, space, supplies, personnel, and support services.

2. *Task interdependence.*   If two groups in the organization depend on one another in a mutual way or even a one-way direction (as in a sequential technological process), there tends to be more conflict than if groups are independent of one another. The more diverse the objectives, priorities, and personnel of the interdependent groups (for example, research and operations), the more conflict there tends to be.

3. *Jurisdictional ambiguity.*   This may involve "turf" problems or overlapping responsibilities. For example, conflict might occur when one group attempts to assume more control or take credit for desirable activities, or give up its part and any responsibility for undesirable activities.

4. *Status struggles.*   This conflict occurs when one group attempts to improve its status and another group views this as a threat to its place in the status hierarchy. One group may also feel it is being inequitably treated in comparison with another group of equal status in terms of rewards, job assignments, working conditions, privileges, or status symbols.

Human resources departments justifiably often feel they are treated inequitably in relation to marketing, finance, and operations departments.

Groups in conflict behave differently from smoothly cooperating groups. Here is a real-world example:

A division of Litton Industries needed to integrate West and East Coast operations in order to provide customers a full spectrum of services. The West Coast group had been running call centers for 30-some years, were hard working, but resistant to change. The East Coast operation was cobbled together through recent acquisitions and specialized in enterprise-wide process consulting. This East Coast group was freewheeling, risk-taking and could care less about Litton culture and tradition. The resulting conflict left virtually no communication or unified sense of direction between the two groups. Covert sabotage was routinely waged by both sides to dilute one another's effectiveness.[109]

There is recent research evidence that such groups in conflict change both internally and in their intergroup perceptions. For example, one study of 70 top management teams found internally that the degree of trust moderated the relationship between task conflict (the perception of disagreements about decisions made by the group) and relationship conflict (an emotional perception of interpersonal incompatibility).[110] Another study found that low intragroup cohesiveness and negative relationships across groups were significantly related to higher perceptions of intergroup conflict.[111] Overall, most experts today emphasize the importance of making a cost-benefit analysis of the conflict situation at any level and then setting up dispute resolution systems[112] and, most recently, setting up systems through advanced information technology that eliminate conflict inherent in traditional (i.e., hierarchical and functional specializations) organization designs.

# THE EFFECTS OF STRESS AND INTRAINDIVIDUAL CONFLICT

As has been pointed out, stress and conflict are not automatically bad for individual employees or their organizational performance. In fact, it is generally recognized that low levels of stress and conflict can even enhance job performance. For example, one study found that mild stress, such as getting a new supervisor or being involuntarily transferred, may have the positive result of an increased search for information in the job.[113] This may lead employees to new and better ways of doing their jobs. Also, mild stress may get employees' "juices" flowing and lead to increased activity, change, and overall better performance. People in certain jobs, such as in sales or creative fields (for example, newspaper journalists and television announcers who work under time pressures), would seem to benefit from a mild level of stress. People in other jobs, such as police officers or physicians, may not benefit from constant mild stress.

Research is also emerging that indicates that the level of difficulty, the nature of the task being performed, personal dispositions (such as Type A, personal control and learned helplessness, and psychological hardiness, and psychological capital, discussed in previous sections), other psychological dispositions (such as negative affectivity[114]), and neuroticism[115] may affect the relationship between stress and performance. However, it is still safe to conclude that:

1. The performance of many tasks is in fact strongly affected by stress.
2. Performance usually drops off sharply when stress rises to very high levels.[116]

It is the dysfunctional effects of high levels of stress and conflict that should be and are a major concern for contemporary society in general and for effective human resource management in particular. The problems due to high levels of stress and conflict can be exhibited physically, psychologically, or behaviorally by the individual.

## Physical Problems Due to Stress and Conflict

Most of the attention and basic research over the years have been devoted to the impact that stress has on physical health. Specific physical health concerns that have been linked to stress include the following: (1) immune system problems, where there is a lessened ability to fight off illness and infection; (2) cardiovascular system problems, such as high blood pressure and heart disease; (3) musculoskeletal system problems, such as tension headaches and back pain; and (4) gastrointestinal system problems, such as diarrhea and constipation.[117] For example, heart attacks are a way of life (or death in this case) on stress-packed Wall Street. For the 5,000 people who work at the stock exchange, the heart attack death rate is 60 percent higher than the national rate for men between 18 and 65, and it was one of the first employers to install a defibrillator (used to restart the heart by electric shock).[118] The situation on Wall Street has even worsened in recent years because of the threat of terrorism, the corporate scandals, and the extreme volatility of the market.

Obviously, serious physical ailments from stress have a drastic effect on the individual; not always so obvious, but just as serious, are the effects that physical problems such as heart disease can have on the organization. Ivancevich and Matteson have provided the following worksheet for computing the costs of replacing employees lost to heart disease in a company employing 4,000 people.[119]

| | |
|---|---:|
| 1. Number of employees | 4,000 |
| 2. Men in age range 45 to 65 (0.25 × line 1) | 1,000 |
| 3. Estimated deaths due to heart disease per year (0.006 × line 2) | 6 |
| 4. Estimated premature retirement due to heart problems per year (0.003 × line 2) | 3 |
| 5. Company's annual personnel losses due to heart disorders (sum of lines 3 and 4) | 9 |
| 6. Annual replacement cost: the average cost of hiring and training replacements for experienced employees (line 5 × $50,000) | $450,000 |
| 7. Number of employees who will eventually die of heart disease if present rate continues (0.5 × line 1) | 2,000 |

These figures are just estimates, but they dramatically illustrate how heart disease alone can affect costs and sheer numbers of employees in a typical organization. Obviously, not all heart disease can be directly linked to stress; environmental conditions and the person's general state of health, heredity, and medical history also certainly contribute. However, there seems to be enough evidence that stress can and does contribute to this dreaded disease and to other physical problems as well.

## Psychological Problems Due to Stress and Conflict

Although considerable attention has been given to the relationship between stress and physical health, especially within the medical community, not as much has been given to the impact of stress on mental health. Yet, at least indirectly if not directly, the psychological problems resulting from stress may be just as important, if not more important, to day-to-day job performance as the physical problems.

High levels of stress may be accompanied by anger, anxiety, depression, nervousness, irritability, tension, and boredom. One study found that stress had the strongest impact on aggressive actions, such as sabotage, interpersonal aggression, hostility, and complaints.[120]

These types of psychological problems from stress, in turn, are especially relevant to poor job performance, lowered self-esteem,[121] resentment of supervision, inability to concentrate and make decisions, and job dissatisfaction.[122] These outcomes of stress can have a direct cost effect on the organization. For example, the National Centers for Disease Control reported that psychological stress is the source of numerous job-related insurance claims.[123] Court cases have also brought stress-related problems stemming from employment under the employer's workers' compensation insurance.[124] Experts are predicting that if the number of stress-related workers' compensation claims continues to grow at current rates, these claims will lead all other claims,[125] in an era when health care benefits for psychological problems have plummeted.[126]

Of even greater significance, the outcomes of stress can have a subtle, but very real, effect on the styles and effectiveness of managers in key positions. For example, managers who are under constant stress may become very moody, and their subordinates soon learn not to disturb them, even with important information, because they will just "bite your head off." Such managers may also realize, at times, that they are acting this way; they may feel that they are not living up to the expectations of their important position and suffer a loss of self-esteem. In this state they may also procrastinate and continue to put things off and not make needed decisions. And, finally, they may resent their boss for trying to get them back on track and begin to hate the job in general. Coworkers, subordinates, and bosses may become very disgusted with such a manager and explain the behavior away as being the result of a "rotten personality," when in fact the problems are the result of stress and conflict. If the manager had a heart attack, everyone would feel sorry and say that he or she was under too much stress, but a manager's moodiness, low self-esteem, inability to make a decision, and dissatisfaction with the boss and the job cause people to get angry and say that the manager is "no darned good" or "can't get along with anyone." Both a heart attack and a psychological problem may have the same cause (too much stress and conflict), and although people may react to them differently, the negative effect on performance is the same in the case of a psychological problem, or perhaps even worse.

## Behavioral Problems Due to Stress and Conflict

As has been the case with other topics covered in this text, the *behavioral* unit of analysis may be most helpful—in this case, in analyzing the effects of job stress and conflict. Direct behaviors that may accompany high levels of stress include undereating or overeating, sleeplessness, increased smoking and drinking, and drug abuse. When it is realized that 6 percent of the population are alcoholics, that another estimated 10 percent are problem drinkers, and that several billion doses of amphetamines and barbiturates are consumed annually,[127] the potential problems for employee behavior caused by alcohol and drug abuse become dramatically clear. For example, one company had such a problem with on-the-job drinking that it bought a breath-alcohol meter to test its employees. The president of the union in this firm stated: "There were a couple of people who came to work drunk every day."[128] Although the meter has not been used yet, one worker was overheard to say, "I guess I'll have to stop going to the bar at lunchtime."[129] Besides being dangerous, as in this company, which used a lot of dangerous equipment, these problems may be manifested in tardiness, absenteeism, and turnover.

There is research evidence over the years indicating a relationship between stress and especially absenteeism and turnover.[130] For example, workers may experience stress and react by getting drunk and staying home from work the next day with a hangover. They then feel bad about this drinking. They may feel that they are letting everyone down "the morning after" and eventually quit or are fired from the job. In the meantime the absenteeism rate

One of the major causes of stress for managers comes from time pressures. No matter how fast some managers work and how much time they put in, they are still unable to get all their work done. One of the most effective ways of dealing with this problem is the use of time management techniques. Today many organizations from Chase Manhattan to Exxon to Xerox are training their managers in how to get more done in less time. Some of the most helpful guidelines for effective time management are the following:

1. Make out a "to-do" list that identifies everything that must be done during the day. This helps keep track of work progress.

2. Delegate as much minor work as possible to subordinates.

3. Determine when you do the best work—morning or afternoon—and schedule the most difficult assignments for this time period.

4. Set time aside during the day, preferably at least one hour, when visitors or other interruptions are not permitted.

5. Have the secretary screen all incoming calls in order to turn away those that are minor or do not require your personal attention.

6. Eat lunch in the office one or two days a week in order to save time and give yourself the opportunity to catch up on paperwork.

7. Discourage drop-in visitors by turning your desk so that you do not have eye contact with the door or hallway.

8. Read standing up. The average person reads faster and more accurately when in a slightly uncomfortable position.

9. Make telephone calls between 4:30 and 5:00 P.M. People tend to keep these conversations brief so that they can go home.

10. Do not feel guilty about those things that have not been accomplished today. Put them on the top of the "to-do" list for tomorrow.

climbs, and subsequently the turnover rate increases, both of which are very costly to the organization in terms of filling in for absent workers and replacing those who have left. Staying away from a job that is causing stress or quitting the job is a "flight" reaction to the situation. Actually, this may be a healthier reaction than a "fight" reaction, in which the person may stay on the stress-producing job and become angry and/or aggressive.

Like the psychological problems resulting from stress and conflict, the behavioral problems are often not attributed to stress by coworkers or supervisors and generate little sympathy. But, also like the psychological and the physical symptoms of stress, the behavioral problems can be controlled, more effectively managed, and even prevented by the individual and the organization. These coping strategies are discussed next.

## COPING STRATEGIES FOR STRESS AND CONFLICT

Much of the discussion so far in this chapter and, at least indirectly, a lot of the material in previous and subsequent chapters (for example, discussions of job design, goal setting, organizational behavior modification, group dynamics, political strategies, leadership styles, organization processes and design, control techniques, management of change, and organization development techniques) suggest ways to manage and cope more effectively with stress and conflict. There are even overall theories being developed on coping with stress,[131] basic research on the role that personality[132] and trust[133] can play in coping with stress and conflict in organizations, and practical guidelines for converting stress into success.[134] The accompanying OB in Action: Taking Time to Manage Time suggests some simple techniques, such as time management, that can be used to cope with stress, and there are many lists of steps to take in order to avoid stress and burnout found in the practitioner literature.[135]

Interactive behavior at both the interpersonal and intergroup levels resulting in conflict rather than stress per se has its own solutions for coping and managing. For example, a win-win strategy of conflict resolution or types of strategies such as avoidance, defusion, containment, or confrontation[136] are well known in conflict management and there is emerging basic research indicating how conflict management can influence the success of global virtual teams in today's organizations.[137] There continue to be many practitioner-oriented books[138] on resolving conflict in the workplace, but the more academic, research-based approach has concentrated on negotiation skills. After a summary of both the individual and organizational coping strategies for stress, the negotiation skills of conflict resolution conclude the chapter.

## Individual Coping Strategies

Today, self-help remedies, do-it-yourself approaches, weight-loss clinics and diets, health foods, and physical exercise are being given much attention in the mass media. People are actually taking responsibility, or know they *should* be taking responsibility, for their own wellness. Individual coping strategies for dealing with stress make sense. In other words, as described in the accompanying OB in Action: Making it Work by Not Doing it All, most people don't have to be convinced of the value of taking charge and actually making a change in their lives. Today, this coping responsibility goes beyond physical well-being to also include psychological well-being, spiritual vitality, and ethics.[139]

Some specific techniques that individuals can use to eliminate or more effectively manage inevitable, prolonged stress are the following:

1. *Exercise.*   Today, it is not whether you win or lose, but whether you get some good exercise that counts. People of all ages are walking, jogging, swimming, riding bicycles, or playing softball, tennis, or racquetball in order to get some exercise to combat stress. Although this seems to make a great deal of sense and many laypeople and physicians swear by it, there still is no conclusive evidence that exercise will always reduce the chances of heart disease or stroke. But there seems little doubt that it can help people better cope with stress, even if only as a result of the side effects, such as relaxation, enhanced self-esteem, and simply getting one's mind off work for a while, and thus perform better in their daily tasks in the workplace.[140]

2. *Relaxation.*   Whether a person simply takes it easy once in a while or uses specific relaxation techniques such as biofeedback or meditation, the intent is to eliminate the immediately stressful situation or manage a prolonged stressful situation more effectively. Taking it easy may mean curling up with a good book in front of a fireplace or watching something "light" (not a violent program or a sports program) on television. There is even some recent research evidence that those who do expressive writing about stressful events in their lives experience health benefits.[141] Meditation involves muscle and mental relaxation; the person slowly repeats a peaceful phrase or word or concentrates on a mental picture in a quiet location. There is growing research evidence that such meditation can have a desirable physical[142] and mental[143] impact on people. Lyubomirsky notes, "An avalanche of studies have shown that meditation has multiple positive effects on a person's happiness and positive emotions, on physiology, stress, cognitive abilities, and physical health, as well as other harder-to-assess attributes, like 'self-actualization' and moral maturity."[144] However, whether it can have a practical impact on job stress is yet to be determined. Nevertheless, a number of firms are using it. For example, a stockbroker who regularly uses meditation stated: "It's widely known that this industry has a lot of stress. So where a lot of people drink alcohol, we meditate. It's not that we don't feel stress. It just doesn't hit us as much."

When Sophie Vandebroek was appointed head of Xerox Corp.'s Canadian research and development operations several years ago, she didn't move to its headquarters in Mississauga, Ontario. Instead, for a year and a half she would get in her car Monday morning at her Penfield (N.Y.) home, drive the 2 hours and 42 minutes it took to get there, and work until 11:00 at night. After a quesadilla dinner and a night's rest at the nearby Holiday Inn, she would work until 4 on Tuesday afternoon, then head home. Wednesdays were spent in Xerox research facilities in Webster, N.Y., near her home. Thursday and Friday was another round trip to Mississauga.

This was no one-time exercise in extreme commuting for Vandebroek, who has lived in the same home for the past 14 years. She has traveled by plane to jobs in Stamford and Hartford, Conn. When she was pregnant with her second child, she worked seven hours away, living in an apartment during the week while her toddler daughter, Elena, was home with her husband, Bart, an engineer.

But Vandebroek would be the first to disabuse anyone of the idea that she's a kind of superwoman. To some degree, she's simply done what she had to do. Ten years ago her husband died of a severe asthma attack while they were camping in the Adirondack Mountains, leaving Vandebroek to raise their three children an ocean away from family in Europe. Since then, she's made her life work not by trying to do it all, but by focusing on what's most important.

An ability to prioritize is part of why Vandebroek, 44, is such a successful executive. On Jan.1 the 14-year Xerox veteran became chief technology officer, overseeing its 600 researchers and engineers and directing the $760 million plus the copier maker spends each year on R&D. "Sophie is one in a million on a level of skill, knowledge, and intellect," says Bernard S. Meyerson, CTO for IBM Systems and Technology Group and a friend of Vandebroek's since the early 1990s, when they worked together in IBM's Thomas J. Watson Research Center. "But she maintains her modesty."

These days, the commute is a relaxing 12 minutes from her door to Xerox' Webster campus, but Vandebroek's latest job will be a big challenge.

Optimism seems a prerequisite for a job where taking the wrong path can easily cost millions. So is a lot of hard work. Vandebroek's typical workday, when she's in Webster, starts at 6:40 A.M., making breakfast for Elena, 17, Arno, 15, and Jonas, 13. At 7:15 they're on the school bus, and she's working out on her rowing machine while listening to the BBC news on satellite radio. At the office, the day is usually packed with meetings, many with participants piped in from one of the four other research centers she oversees around the world. On a January day, Vandebroek, dressed in a stylish pants suit with a silk scarf and high-heeled suede boots, rushed from one meeting to the next, often stepping aside to clear the e-mail from her BlackBerry or sip from her ever-present 1-liter bottle of lime seltzer. She tries to be home by 6:30 to dine with her kids. Then she spends most nights reading printouts of e-mails she couldn't get to earlier in the day.

A master of efficiency, Vandebroek had to teach herself not to be all business at work. In her early days as a manager she was so focused on getting the job done that she assumed everyone would buy her arguments on logic alone. An executive coach assigned to her as part of Xerox' talent-development program advised her to open up, talk about herself. Vandebroek laughs remembering the surprise of her staff when she opened a Monday morning meeting with a discussion of her weekend ski trip. Soon she was coordinating Thursday evening team outings for chicken wings and beer. The only rule: No talk about work. "It's about the human fabric of the organization," she says, "taking the time to listen to [employees'] concerns."

Still, for years many at Xerox didn't even know she was a widow. After her husband's death, Vandebroek plowed herself into work. In speeches, she often quotes a Chinese proverb that has guided her: "In crisis there is opportunity." Beyond the good that her focus on work has done for her career, Vandebroek sees ways in which her family has grown stronger since the tragedy. They are a close bunch, and she describes her children as "compassionate," a rare trait in any teenager.

3. *Behavioral self-control.* Chapter 12 gives specific attention to behavior management. By deliberately managing the antecedents and the consequences of their own behavior, people can achieve self-control. For example, sales managers who have a steady stream of customer complaints all day could change the antecedent by having an assistant screen all complaints and allow only exceptions to reach them. They could also manage the consequences by rewarding themselves with an extra break when they remain calm and collected after interacting with a particularly angry customer. Besides managing

their own behavior to reduce stress, people can also become more aware of their limits and of "red flags" that signal trouble ahead. They can avoid people or situations that they know will put them under stress. In other words, this strategy involves individuals' controlling the situation instead of letting the situation control them.

4. *Cognitive therapy.* Besides behavioral self-control techniques, a number of clinical psychologists have entered the stress field with cognitive therapy techniques. Techniques such as Ellis's rational emotive model and cognitive behavior modification have been used as an individual strategy for reducing job stress. Building self-efficacy (confidence, see Chapter 7) through Bandura's social cognitive theory has also been used.[145] Research has shown that those of low self-efficacy are stressed both emotionally and physiologically, but those with high self-efficacy are unfazed by heavy workloads.[146] Thus, the goal is to gain or enhance one's sense of efficacy over stressful situations, as an individual coping strategy for stress reduction, through successful performance experience, vicarious experience, social persuasion, and/or controlling physiological and emotional states.[147]

5. *Networking.* One clear finding that has come out of social psychology research over the years is that people need and will benefit from social support.[148] Applied as a strategy to reduce job stress, this would entail forming close associations with trusted empathetic coworkers and colleagues who are good listeners and confidence builders. These friends are there when needed and provide support to get the person through stressful situations. Today, such alliances, especially if deliberately sought out and developed, are called *networks* and now *social capital*.[149] Although the specific relationship between social support and stress reduction appears complicated,[150] there is some research evidence that a networking strategy may be able to help people cope better with job stress[151] and be more effective[152] and successful managers.[153]

## Organizational Coping Strategies

Organizational coping strategies are designed by management to eliminate or control organizational-level stressors in order to prevent or reduce job stress for individual employees. Earlier in the chapter, the organizational stressors were categorized in terms of overall policies and strategies, structure and design processes/functions, and working conditions (see Figure 9.2). A major challenge facing the management of conflict at this organization level is to answer questions such as: "How do you ensure that relevant information gets transferred between two parts of an organization that have different cultures? How do you encourage people from units competing for scare corporate resources to work together?"[154] It logically follows that each of these areas would be the focus of attention in developing organizational coping strategies. In other words, each of the specific stressors would be worked on in order to eliminate or reduce job stress. For example, in the policy area, attention would be given to making performance reviews and pay plans as equitable and as fair as possible. In the structural area, steps would be taken to back away from high degrees of formalization and specialization. The same would be done in the areas of physical conditions (for example, safety hazards would be removed, and lighting, noise, and temperature would be improved) and processes/functions (for example, communication and information sharing would be improved, and ambiguous or conflicting goals would be clarified or resolved). With increased globalization, the coping strategies to manage the stress of expatriates has received increased attention. For example, one study found that the effectiveness of problem-focused coping strategies of expatriate adjustment is moderated by cultural distance and position level but not by time on the assignment.[155]

Today, firms such as Hewlett-Packard and the large software firm SAS realize they are putting tremendous pressure on employees in competitive battles and are giving considerable effort to de-stressing the organization. For example, H-P requires employees to have personal/leisure goals (e.g., weight loss, exercise, take time off for the family) as well as job goals. If employees fall short of their personal/leisure goals, supervisors are held responsible. When a milestone is reached, for example, leaving at 2:00 P.M. to take a daughter in-line skating, coworkers are encouraged to applaud with the same gusto as landing a big sales order. At SAS they not only have all the usual benefits but also nutrition counseling, youth day camps, and medical facilities on-site. The firm's 4,000 employees bring 700 children to the day care facility and will soon enroll them in SAS kindergarten.

The Association for Fitness in Business estimates that thousands of companies today offer stress-coping programs ranging from counseling services, lunchtime stress-management seminars, and wellness publications to elaborate company-run fitness centers where employees can sweat out the tension. There is evidence that these stress management programs are increasing and are being evaluated more rigorously.[156] Some are getting quite creative. For example, Pixar (the movie maker) created Pixar University (PU), an in-house operation with free classes for employees in data programming, tai chi, gesture drawing, improvisational acting, and juggling.

In general, most firms today are trying to reduce stress and conflict through work-family initiatives. These involve both reorganization initiatives (e.g., restructuring of jobs and job duties, telecommuting, part-time work and job sharing, and flexible scheduling) and work and life benefit policies and programs (e.g., on-site child care and/or elder care, paid family and medical leave, release time for personal/family events, and limits on frequency and distance of business travel).

Employee assistance programs (EAPs) have also become a very valuable organizational response to help employees cope with stress. EAPs are currently implemented in over half of U.S. organizations with 50 or more employees and have been found to consistently reduce absenteeism, health care costs, and disciplinary action.[157] EAPs typically provide employees with services such as confidential counseling and/or follow-up on issues of personal or work-related concerns. They also provide family workshops and consultations (related to marriage, single parenting, working parents), stress management workshops, relaxation seminars, and other kinds of support. Often, the mere presence of mind that EAPs provide—knowing that there is support available—can help ease some of the stress that employees face in today's environment.[158]

Besides work-family programs and EAPs, because of the stress resulting from downsizing in recent years, growing concern is also being given to both those who are let go and those who survive. For example, theoretical models[159] are being created and basic research[160] is being done on coping with job loss. One stream of research has examined the role that procedural justice (perceptions of fairness) plays on those affected by downsizing. In three studies (of those already laid off, survivors of a firm that had downsized, and those scheduled to be laid off), it was found that fair procedural justice had a positive impact.[161] A summary of these studies noted:

> All three studies showed that the negative effects of layoffs can be blunted by the way company managers deal with the downsizing. Employees were more hostile when they thought procedures leading to the layoffs were not handled fairly, with sufficient notice and fair treatment of employees during downsizing. When procedures were seen as fair, employees still supported and trusted their firms even after the layoffs had occurred.[162]

Organizations experiencing downsizing need to be sure that those let go are as positive as possible so that there are not negative repercussions (e.g., in the community or even with customers). However, of even more concern are those suffering from what was described earlier as "survivor syndrome." As one survivor from a downsized firm describes this modern-day malady: "Just when we begin to think our jobs are safe, they change the rules on us. We don't know who's in charge, who we can trust or what we're supposed to be doing. The more unsettling it gets around here, the less productive we are."[163] The key issue is not only whether these survivors are stressed-out, but also whether stress is affecting their performance.

Some guidelines to help downsized organizations combat the problems of survivor syndrome include the following:[164]

1. *Be proactive.* Before Compaq Computer in Houston laid off 2,000 employees, the corporate human resources department developed a comprehensive communication campaign and trained all managers not only in how to outplace people but also in how to help survivors.

2. *Acknowledge survivors' emotions.* The state of Oregon, which had cut back 1,000 employees, held workshops for survivors that allowed them to vent their frustrations and develop skills that would allow them to think of change as an opportunity for growth.

3. *Communicate after the downsizing.* After laying off 20 percent of its workforce, Patagonia Inc., an outdoor apparel manufacturer in California, implemented a monthly (then twice-monthly) open forum during which employees can meet with the CEO during work hours to have their questions answered and hear about the firm's progress. In the jobholders' meetings at Pitney Bowes Inc., management gives an employee $50 for the toughest question asked.

4. *Clarify new roles.* Not only is there a need for communication of the big picture; it also is important to explain how each employee's job has changed, if at all, and relate how each individual contributes to the new big picture in the downsized organization.

# NEGOTIATION SKILLS: GOING BEYOND CONFLICT MANAGEMENT

In recent years negotiation has moved from the industrial relations field to the forefront of necessary managerial skills. As Neale and Bazerman noted: "Everyone negotiates. In its various forms, negotiation is a common mechanism for resolving differences and allocating resources." They then define negotiation as "a decision-making process among interdependent parties who do not share identical preferences. It is through negotiation that the parties decide what each will give and take in their relationship."[165]

Although some organizational behavior scholars note that there are similarities between negotiation strategies and conflict management,[166] negotiation can go beyond just resolving conflict and become a managerial skill for personal and organizational success. For example, a manager can successfully negotiate a salary raise or a good price for supplies. After note is taken of some of the biases or errors that negotiators commonly make and the traditional negotiation techniques that have been used, the remainder of the chapter is devoted to the newly emerging skills needed for effective negotiation for conflict resolution and successful careers.

## Traditional Negotiation Approaches

When negotiating, people in general and managers in particular tend to have certain biases and make certain errors, which prevents them from negotiating rationally and getting the most they can out of a situation. To compound the problem, there is recent research indicating that negotiators tend to repeat their mistakes.[167] The research on these common mistakes can be summarized as follows:

1. Negotiators tend to be overly affected by the frame, or form of presentation, of information in a negotiation.
2. Negotiators tend to nonrationally escalate commitment to a previously selected course of action when it is no longer the most reasonable alternative.
3. Negotiators tend to assume that their gain must come at the expense of the other party and thereby miss opportunities for mutually beneficial trade-offs between the parties.
4. Negotiator judgments tend to be anchored on irrelevant information, such as an initial offer.
5. Negotiators tend to rely on readily available information.
6. Negotiators tend to fail to consider information that is available by focusing on the opponent's perspective.
7. Negotiators tend to be overconfident concerning the likelihood of attaining outcomes that favor the individual(s) involved.[168]

Besides these common bias problems, negotiators traditionally have taken either a distributive or a positional bargaining approach. *Distributive bargaining* assumes a "fixed pie" and focuses on how to get the biggest share, or "slice of the pie." With teams so popular in today's organizations, there is growing research on the effectiveness of teams in distributive bargaining. One study found that teams, more than individuals, developed mutually beneficial trade-offs among issues in the negotiation and discovered compatible interests. However, the common belief that teams have a relative advantage over individual opponents in negotiations was not supported by actual outcomes.[169] The conflict management strategies of compromising, forcing, accommodating, and avoiding, mentioned earlier, all tend to be associated with a distributive negotiation strategy. As noted by Whetten and Cameron:

> Compromise occurs when both parties make sacrifices in order to find a common ground. Compromisers are generally more interested in finding an expedient solution. . . . Forcing and accommodating demand that one party give up its position in order for the conflict to be resolved. When parties to a conflict avoid resolution, they do so because they assume that the costs of resolving the conflict are so high that they are better off not even attempting resolution.[170]

Closely related to distributed bargaining is the commonly used *positional bargaining* approach. This approach to negotiation involves successively taking, and then giving up, a sequence of positions. In its simplest form, this is what happens when one haggles in an open market. However, positional bargaining also happens in international diplomacy. Fisher and Ury note that such positional bargaining can serve a useful purpose: "It tells the other side what you want; it provides an anchor in an uncertain and pressured situation; and it can eventually produce the terms of an acceptable agreement."[171]

Both distributed and positional bargaining have simplistic strategies such as "tough person," or "hard"; "easy touch," or "soft"; or even "split the difference." Characteristics of the "hard" strategy include the following: the goal is victory, distrust others, dig in to your position, make threats, try to win a contest of will, and apply pressure. By contrast, the "soft" strategy includes these characteristics: the goal is agreement, trust others, change your position easily, make offers, try to avoid a contest of will, and yield to pressure.[172] The hard bargainer typically dominates and has intuitive appeal. However, both research[173] and everyday practice are beginning to reveal that more effective negotiation approaches than these traditional strategies are possible.

## Contemporary Negotiation Skills

There are now recognized alternative approaches to traditionally recognized distributed and positional bargaining and the hard versus soft strategies in negotiation. Whetten and Cameron suggest an integrative approach that takes an "expanding the pie" perspective that uses problem-solving techniques to find win-win outcomes.[174] Based on a collaborating (rather than a compromising, forcing, accommodating, or avoiding) strategy, the integrative approach requires the effective negotiator to use skills such as (1) establishing superordinate goals; (2) separating the people from the problem; (3) focusing on interests, not on positions; (4) inventing options for mutual gain; and (5) using objective criteria.[175]

Recent practical guidelines for effective negotiations have grouped the techniques into degrees of risk to the user as follows:

1. Low-risk negotiation techniques
   a. Flattery—subtle flattery usually works best, but the standards may differ by age, sex, and cultural factors.
   b. Addressing the easy point first—this helps build trust and momentum for the tougher issues.
   c. Silence—this can be effective in gaining concessions, but one must be careful not to provoke anger or frustration in opponents.
   d. Inflated opening position—this may elicit a counteroffer that shows the opponent's position or may shift the point of compromise.
   e. "Oh, poor me"—this may lead to sympathy but could also bring out the killer instinct in opponents.
2. High-risk negotiation techniques
   a. Unexpected temper losses—erupting in anger can break an impasse and get one's point across, but it can also be viewed as immature or manipulative and lead opponents to harden their position.
   b. High-balling—this is used to gain trust by appearing to give in to the opponent's position, but when overturned by a higher authority, concessions are gained based on the trust.
   c. Boulwarism ("take it or leave it")—named after a former vice president of GE who would make only one offer in labor negotiations, this is a highly aggressive strategy that may also produce anger and frustration in opponents.
   d. Waiting until the last moment—after using stall tactics and knowing that a deadline is near, a reasonable but favorable offer is made, leaving the opponent with little choice but to accept.[176]

Besides these low- and high-risk strategies, there are also a number of other negotiation techniques, such as a two-person team using "good cop–bad cop" (one is tough, followed by one who is kind), and various psychological ploys, such as insisting that meetings be held on one's home turf, scheduling meetings at inconvenient times, or interrupting meetings with phone calls or side meetings.[177] There are even guidelines of if, when, and how to use alcohol in negotiations. As the president of Saber Enterprises notes, when the Japanese come over to negotiate, it is assumed that you go out to dinner and have several drinks and toast with sake.[178] Because of globalization and the resulting increase of negotiations between parties of different countries, there is emerging research on the dynamics and strategies of negotiations across cultures.[179]

In addition to the preceding guidelines for effective negotiation skills, there is an alternative to positional bargaining and soft versus hard strategies that has been developed by the Harvard Negotiation Project. This alternative to traditional negotiation is called the *principled negotiation,* or *negotiation on the merits,* approach. There are four basic elements in this alternative approach to negotiation. Very simply, they are:

1. *People.*     Separate the people from the problem.
2. *Interests.*  Focus on interests, not positions.
3. *Options.*    Generate a variety of possibilities before deciding what to do.
4. *Criteria.*   Insist that the result be based on some objective standard.[180]

The principled skills go beyond hard versus soft and change the game to negotiation on the basis of merits. For example, in soft bargaining the participants are friends, in hard bargaining they are adversaries, but in the principled approach they are problem solvers; in soft bargaining the approach is to trust others, in hard bargaining there is distrust of others, but in the principled approach the negotiator proceeds independent of trust; and in the soft approach negotiators make offers, in the hard approach they make threats, but in the principled approach they explore common interests.[181] These principled negotiation skills can result in a wise agreement. As noted by Fisher and Ury:

> The method permits you to reach a gradual consensus on a joint decision *efficiently* without all the transactional costs of digging in to positions only to have to dig yourself out of them. And separating the people from the problem allows you to deal directly and empathetically with the other negotiator as a human being, thus making possible an *amicable* agreement.[182]

Along with social, emotional, behavioral, leadership, team, and communication skills, these negotiation skills are becoming increasingly recognized as important to management of not only conflict but also effective management in general.

---

## Summary

This chapter examines both stress and conflict. Although not always bad for the person (for example, the father of stress studies, Hans Selye, feels that complete freedom from stress is death) or the organization (low levels of stress may lead to performance improvement), stress is still one of the most important and serious problems facing the field of organizational behavior. Stress can be comprehensively defined as an adaptive response to an external situation that results in physical, psychological, and/or behavioral deviations for organizational participants. The causes of stress can be categorized into extraorganizational, organizational, and group stressors, as well as individual stressors and dispositions. In combination or singly, they represent a tremendous amount of potential stress impinging on today's jobholder—at every level and in every type of organization.

In addition to stress, the dynamics of interactive behavior at interpersonal and group levels, and the resulting conflict, play an increasingly important role in the analysis and study of organizational behavior. Conflict and stress are conceptually and practically similar, especially at the individual level. Conflict at the intraindividual level involves frustration, goal conflict, and role conflict and ambiguity. Frustration occurs when goal-directed behavior is blocked. Goal conflict can come about from approach-approach, approach-avoidance, or avoidance-avoidance situations. Role conflict and ambiguity result from a clash in the expectations of the various roles possessed by an individual and can take the forms of role conflict, intrarole conflict, or interrole conflict.

Interpersonal conflict is first examined in terms of its sources (personal differences, information deficiency, role incompatibility, and environmental stress). Then the analysis of interpersonal conflict is made through the response categories of forcing, accommodating, avoiding, compromising, and collaborating. Intergroup conflict has also become important. The antecedents to intergroup conflict are identified as competition for resources, task interdependence, jurisdictional ambiguity, and status struggles.

The effects of stress and intraindividual conflict can create physical problems (heart disease, ulcers, arthritis), psychological problems (mood changes, lowered self-esteem, resentment of supervision, inability to make decisions, and job dissatisfaction), and/or behavioral problems (tardiness, absenteeism, turnover, and accidents). A number of individual and organizational strategies have been developed to cope with these stress-induced problems. Exercise, relaxation, behavioral self-control techniques, cognitive therapy techniques, and networking are some potentially useful coping strategies that individuals can apply to help combat existing stress. Taking a more proactive approach, management of organizations tries to eliminate stressors, reduce work-family conflict, and implement employee assistance programs (EAPs). A special concern for organizations today is to deal with the stress resulting from downsizing that affects both those laid off and the survivors. To manage this stress, downsizing organizations must fully communicate and display fair procedural justice for those let go. To counter survivor syndrome, downsized organizations can follow such guidelines as being proactive, acknowledging survivors' emotions, communicating after the cuts, and clarifying new roles. In any case, whether on an individual or an organizational level, steps need to be taken to prevent or reduce the increasing job stress facing today's employees.

The last part of the chapter is concerned with negotiation skills. Going beyond industrial relations and conflict management, negotiation skills are becoming increasingly recognized as important to effective management and personal success. Traditionally, negotiators have depended on distributed and positional bargaining. Relying on simplistic hard or soft strategies, this traditional approach is now being challenged by more effective alternative negotiation skills. Practical low-risk strategies include flattery, addressing the easy points first, silence, inflated opening position, and "oh, poor me." High-risk strategies include unexpected temper losses, high-balling, Boulwarism, and waiting until the last moment. In addition, alternatives to traditional distributed and positional bargaining are the integrative approach, which uses a problem-solving, collaborative strategy, and the principled, or negotiation on the merits, approach, which emphasizes people, interests, options, and criteria. These negotiation skills go beyond hard versus soft strategies and change the game, leading to a win-win, wise agreement.

## Ending with Meta-Analytic Research Findings
## OB PRINCIPLE FOR EVIDENCED-BASED PRACTICE

Employees who work abnormally long hours per week will experience more health problems.

### Meta-Analysis Results:

[21 studies; 37,623 participants; $d = .26$] *On average, there is a **57 percent probability** that employees who work over 48 hours per week will experience more health problems than those who work fewer hours.* Further analysis also points out that longer working hours are often associated with poor lifestyle behaviors such as heavy smoking, inadequate diet, and lack of exercise, which further leads to health problems.

### Conclusion:

Due to increasing workloads, job insecurity, and pressures to perform, many individuals are working longer hours. As a result, there is much concern that stress and fatigue levels are on the rise, which leads to negative organizational outcomes such as absenteeism, decreased performance, and escalating medical expenses. Employees who become distressed mentally and physically due to working long hours experience work overload. Overload combined with prolonged exposure to other workplace stressors may result in health problems such as work-related injuries, accidents, and cardiovascular disease, along with mental disorders such as depression and anxiety. However, as this chapter on stress shows, individuals and organizations can buffer the ill effects of stress by enhancing coping strategies. Exercising regularly, eating a healthy diet, and taking time to relax are some ways individuals can reduce stress. Organizations, too, can help by establishing a supportive climate, having well-designed jobs, and reducing role conflict and role ambiguity.

**Source:** Adapted from Kate Sparks, Cary Cooper, Yitzhak Fried, and Arie Shirom, "The Effects of Hours of Work on Health: A Meta-Analytic Review," *Journal of Occupational and Organizational Psychology,* Vol. 70, 1997, pp. 391–408.

# OB PRINCIPLE: FOR EVIDENCE-BASED PRACTICE

Type A personalities experience greater heart rate reactivity than Type Bs.

## Meta-Analysis Results:

[78 studies; 3,008 participants; $d = .22$] *On average, there is a* **56 percent probability** *that Type A personalities will experience greater heart rate reactivity (heart rate and blood pressure) than Type Bs.* Moderator analyses indicated that Type As showed especially greater cardiovascular reactivity in situations characterized as having positive or negative feedback and verbal harassment or criticism. Importantly, this study does not indicate that Type As necessarily have more heart attacks, just greater heart reactivity.

## Conclusion:

Cardiovascular disease is the leading cause of death among adults in Western industrialized countries. The role that stress and personality/behavior types such as A and B have with heart problems has received much attention. Because Type A behavior has the most obvious link with cardiovascular disease, identifying Type A characteristics and impact has been closely studied. As this chapter indicates, Type A personalities are hurried and competitive whereas Type Bs are more relaxed and related. Type A behavior would seem to be desired by organizations, and research has revealed that most managers are in fact Type As, except at the very top where Type Bs dominate, and in general perform better. However as this chapter on conflict and stress indicates, Type As may not necessarily need to change their personalities, which is likely an impossibility, but will need to learn to better cope with stressful situations that lead to emotional reactions such as anger in order to prevent physical problems such as heart disease. The key problem is anger, not just hyperactivity.

**Source:** Adapted from Scott A. Lyness, "Predictors of Differences between Type A and B Individuals in Heart Rate and Blood Pressure Reactivity," *Psychological Bulletin,* Vol. 114, No 2, 1988, pp. 266–295.

Questions for Discussion and Review

1. How is stress defined? Is it always bad for the individual? Explain.
2. What are the general categories of stressors that can affect job stress? Give some examples of each.
3. What are some of the dispositions that may influence an individual's reaction to stress? Give an example of each.

4. What is frustration? What are some of its manifestations? How can the frustration model be used to analyze organizational behavior?

5. Explain approach-avoidance conflict. Give a realistic organizational example of where it may occur.

6. What are some of the major sources of interpersonal conflict? Which do you think is most relevant in today's organizations?

7. How do groups or teams in conflict behave? What are some antecedent conditions of intergroup conflict?

8. Job stress can have physiological, psychological, and behavioral effects. Give an example of each and cite some research findings on the relationship between job stress and these outcomes.

9. Coping strategies for job stress exist for both the individual and the organizational levels. Summarize and evaluate these various strategies for preventing and/or more effectively managing stress.

10. A modern-day malady is survivor syndrome. What does this refer to, and how can organizations help combat it?

11. Compare and contrast the traditional versus the new negotiation skills. Why do you think the new skills lead to better agreements?

**Internet Exercise: Managing Stress in Organizations**

Visit the Web sites **http://www.mhhe.com/business/management/buildyour managementskills/typesStress/exercise.html, http://www.stress.org,** and **http://www.stresstips.com.** These sites provide information on the negative effects of stress in the workplace. They also have useful tips on how to manage stress in your personal life. While browsing through, consider the following:

1. What events in the workplace do you think cause the most stress? Does this match up with what is contained on the Web sites? Give some specific examples.

2. What things can an organization do to help manage stress? Which approach do you feel would be most effective? Are there any problems or a downside to any of these?

---

# Real Case:  *When Workers Just Can't Cope*

Until Congress passed the Americans with Disabilities Act (ADA) in 1990, most companies decided how to handle such problems on a case-by-case basis, often depending on such factors as just how challenged the employee was and how sympathetically the supervisor responded. And even the ADA didn't help employers much with deciding how far to go to accommodate people challenged with a disability. The law requires employers to make all "reasonable" accommodations for people with disabilities, including mental ones. But given how subjective and personal psychiatric issues can be, employers have struggled to develop clear policies about what to do in such cases.

In the past few years, the courts have begun to delineate how companies must act. The good news for employers is that the guidelines are surprisingly sympathetic to the dilemmas they face when someone shows signs of mental illness. If a worker becomes depressed or suicidal, the employer must try to find a way to help, by, for example, granting a short leave of absence or changing his or her work schedule. But companies don't have to lower work standards, tolerate misconduct, or give someone a make-work job—steps some employers have taken out of fear of a lawsuit, experts say. A key U.S. Supreme Court case further clarified the law by specifying that an employee suffering from mental illness isn't disabled if medication allows the person to function like anyone else. "Most courts are taking a narrow view of who is covered under the ADA," says Peggy Mastroianni, an associate legal counsel for the Equal Employment Opportunity Commission (EEOC).

Any signposts are welcome, because mental illness has posed one of the most difficult challenges to employers—and the courts—since the ADA took effect in mid-1992. Each year, clinical depression alone causes a loss of some 200 million working days in the United States, according to a report released by the International Labor Organization. Psychiatric claims filed with the EEOC doubled in a recent five-year period. This made them the single largest type of ADA claim.

A Supreme Court decision went even further. The case involved two sisters who didn't qualify to be pilots at United Airlines Inc. because of poor vision. The Court ruled that the sisters couldn't sue for discrimination under the ADA because their disability was correctable (with glasses or contacts). Since then, lower courts have applied the ruling to say that employers can consider the mitigating effects of interventions such as medication. In other words, if an antidepressant drug enables a depressed person to function normally, he or she isn't considered disabled and can't claim discrimination.

The new guidelines should help employers avoid being pushed into unreasonable actions. It's now clear that companies don't need to lower their standards to help a troubled employee, says K. Tia Burke, a Philadelphia management attorney who had one client company that did just that. Nor do employers have to invent light-duty jobs, as other clients have done, says Burke. "Many employers are so loath to get involved in these cases that they bend over backwards and provide more than what is reasonable," she says.

1. What responsibility do you think an employer has when an employee has mental illness? Do you agree with the current legal climate described in the case?

2. How can an employer manage to accommodate those with mental illness?

3. Can anything be learned from the study and management of stress and conflict that can be effectively applied to mental illness in the workplace?

# Real Case: *Round-the-Clock Stress*

Many employees feel that on-the-job stress is difficult to control, but at least when they get home they can relax. However, as the nature of work changes, the home is no longer the sanctuary it once was. With advanced information technology and customer demands for 24-hour service, an increasing number of employees are on call at all times or working the "graveyard" shift that used to exist only for factory workers. For example, today there are numerous Wal-Mart stores, Walgreens drugstores, and supermarkets that never close. And consider the Heartland Golf Park in Deer Park, Long Island. A golfer who wants a late evening tee-off time can get one up to 3:00 A.M. The strategy has proven so popular that within 90 days of the time it was introduced, the wait time at midnight had grown to two and a half hours. Avid golfers do not mind, however, as the course is well lit and they can play as if it were high noon.

All around the country, businesses are realizing that there is a great deal of profit that can be added to the bottom line if they remain open outside of "normal" hours. One research firm estimates that this strategy can add 5 percent to overall profits, a hefty sum given that more and more businesses are finding their profit margins being narrowed by the competition.

In some cases, the decision to expand working hours has been a result of customer needs. Kinko's Inc. moved to a 24-hour schedule when people literally started banging on their doors after regular business hours and asking them to let them come in for desperately needed photocopies. As a news article recently put it, "The company's . . . stores are magnets for ambassadors of the night: everyone from dreamers pursuing secret schemes and second careers to executives putting the final touches on tomorrow's presentation." In Chicago, Kinko's set up an office in the lobby of the Stouffer Renaissance Hotel, a favorite spot of international executives. Customers from different time zones had been coming down at odd hours to ask the hotel to fax materials abroad and to help them with their desktop publishing. The hotel was not equipped to provide these services, so it asked Kinko's to help out. The guests are delighted with the new service, and the hotel is happy to be able to accommodate them thanks to their profitable arrangement with Kinko's.

Banks have also begun to offer 24-hour service. In addition to their ATM machines, which can be found just about everywhere, some banks now offer round-the-clock service: customers can call in and find out within 10 minutes whether they qualify for a new-car loan. A growing number of banks also offer after-hours customer services ranging from safe deposit boxes to $1,000 credit lines to overdraft protection. All the customer has to do is call in at any hour and provide the necessary information.

Some critics are concerned that this development will result in increasing costs to business and added stress to employees. After all, when people work late at night or put in a 15-hour day, they are likely not only to make far more mistakes than if they were on a 9-to-5 schedule but also to become fatigued and burned out. Nevertheless, at the present time approximately two-thirds of all U.S. workers, around 75 million people, do not work traditional 9-to-5 hours—and the number is

definitely growing. Additionally, organizations that are engaged in international business, such as brokerage firms, are finding that their operations in Europe and Asia require them to keep odd hours. A U.S.-based broker must be up or on call in the wee hours of the morning because Europe's stock exchanges are doing business. By the time the broker wraps up trading on the Pacific Stock Exchange in the early evening (Eastern Standard Time), there are only a few hours before the Asian stock exchanges open. Simply put, in an increasing number of businesses, it is possible to work round-the-clock—and, of course, to pick up the stress that goes along with this lifestyle.

1. How would a Type A personality feel if his or her organization suddenly announced that everyone was to be on call 24 hours a day because the company was moving to round-the-clock customer service?

2. How would psychological hardiness help people deal with these emerging round-the-clock operations?

3. What are some ways employees and their organizations could cope with the stress caused by these new round-the-clock developments?

# Organizational Behavior Case: *Sorry, No Seats Are Left; Have a Nice Flight*

Jim Miller has been a ticket agent for Friendly Airlines for the past three years. This job is really getting to be a hassle. In order to try to reduce the mounting losses that Friendly has suffered in recent months, management have decided to do two things: (1) overbook their flights so that every seat possible will be filled and (2) increase their service to their customers and live up to their name. Jim, of course, is at the point of application of this new policy. When checking in passengers, he is supposed to be very courteous and friendly, and he has been instructed to end every transaction with the statement, "Have a nice flight." The problem, of course, is that sometimes there are more passengers holding confirmed reservations checking in than there are seats on the plane. Rightfully, these people become extremely upset with Jim and sometimes scream at

him and even threaten him. During these confrontations Jim becomes "unglued." He breaks into a sweat, and his face turns bright red. The company guidelines on what to do in these situations are very vague. When Jim called his supervisor for advice, he was simply told to try to book passengers on another flight, but be friendly.

1. Is Jim headed for trouble? What would be some physical, psychological, and behavioral outcomes of this type of job stress?

2. What could the company do to help reduce the stress in Jim's job?

3. What individual coping strategies could Jim try in this situation?

# Organizational Behavior Case: *A Gnawing Stomachache*

Sandy Celeste was 40 years old when her divorce became final. She was forced to go to work to support her two children. Sandy got married right after graduating from college and had never really held a full-time job outside the home. Nevertheless, because of her enthusiasm, education, and maturity, she impressed the human resources manager at Devon's Department Store and was immediately hired. The position involves supervising three departments of men's and women's clothing. Sandy's training consisted of approximately two months at another store in the Devon chain. She spent this training period both selling merchandise and learning the supervisor's responsibilities. On the first day of her supervisory job, Sandy learned that, because of size constraints at the store, six clothing departments are all located in the same area. In addition to Sandy, there are two other supervisors in the other departments. These three supervisors share the service of 28 full- and part-time salespeople. Because the various departments are so jammed together, all the salespeople are expected to know each department's merchandise. Devon's merchandising philosophy is that it will not finish one department or storewide sale without starting another. Both the clerks and the supervisors, who work on a commission and salary basis, are kept busy marking and remarking the merchandise as one sale stops and another starts. To make matters worse, Devon's expects the employees to re-mark each item just prior to closing time the night after a big sale. The pressure is intense, and customers are often neglected and irritated. However, all the salespeople realize that when the customer suffers, so do their commissions. As a supervisor, Sandy is expected to enforce the company's policy rigidly. Soon after taking the position as supervisor, Sandy began to experience severe headaches and a gnawing stomachache. She would like to quit her job, but realistically she can't because the pay is good and she needs to support her children.

1. To what do you attribute Sandy's health problems? What are some possible extraorganizational, organizational, group, and individual stressors?

2. Is there anything that this company could do to alleviate stress for its supervisors? What individual coping strategies could Sandy try?

# Organizational Behavior Case: *Drinking Up the Paycheck*

James Emery is the father of four children. He was raised in a hardworking immigrant family. His needs for achievement and power were developed while he was growing up. Now he finds himself in a low-paying, dead-end assembly line job with a large manufacturing firm. It is all he can do to get through the day, so he has started daydreaming on the job. On payday he often goes to the tavern across the street and generally spends a lot of money. The next day he is not only hungover but also very depressed because he knows that his wife cannot make ends meet and his children often go without the essentials.

Now he cannot take it any longer. At first he thought of going to his boss for some help and advice, but he really does not understand himself well enough, and he certainly does not know or trust his boss enough to discuss his problems openly with him. Instead, he went to his union steward and told him about his financial problems and how much he hated his job. The steward told James exactly what he wanted to hear. "This darn company is the source of all your problems. The working conditions are not suited for a slave, let alone us. The pay also stinks. We are all going to have to stick together when our present contract runs out and get what we deserve—better working conditions and more money."

1. Explain James's behavior in terms of the frustration model.

2. Cite a specific example of role conflict in this case.

3. What type of conflict resolution strategy is the union steward suggesting? Do you think the real problems facing James are working conditions and pay? Why or why not?

4. What, if anything, can be done to help the James Emerys of the world? Keep your answer related to human resources management

# Chapter **Ten**

# Power and Politics

## Learning Objectives

- **Define** power and its relationship to authority and influence.
- **Identify** the various classifications of power.
- **Discuss** the contingency approach to power.
- **Describe** the empowerment of employees.
- **Relate** the political implications of power.
- **Present** some political strategies for power acquisition in modern organizations.

Over the years, groups, informal organization, interactive behavior, conflict, and stress have received considerable attention as important dynamics of organizational behavior; power and politics, however, have not. As Rosabeth Kanter observed a number of years ago, "Power is America's last dirty word. It is easier to talk about money—and much easier to talk about sex—than it is to talk about power."[1] Yet it is becoming clear, and anyone who has spent any time in a formal organization can readily verify, that organizations are highly political, and power is the name of the game. For example, a major problem for most firms today is not necessarily formulating effective strategies, but implementing and executing them.[2] A recent large survey of executives identified "trying to execute a strategy that conflicts with the existing power structure" as a major obstacle to strategy execution.[3] However, from a political perspective of power, this same survey suggests that "an ability to form coalitions and gain the support of influential people in the organization will help immensely with the execution of formulated plans."[4]

Power and politics must be brought out from behind closed doors and recognized as an important dynamic in organizational behavior. For example, the dynamics of power—how to use it and how to abuse it—were discovered by Joseph O'Donnell, who was abruptly fired from his high-level executive position with JWT Group Inc. when he proposed stripping the CEO and chairman Don Johnston of his day-to-day operating duties. In other cases, however, such a grab for power has worked. One thing is certain, power takes many forms and there are many suggestions on the effective use of power in all types of situations. As Wesley Clark, a leader in many different venues (e.g., he was a career Army officer, a commander in Vietnam, NATO commander during the Kosovo campaign, one-time presidential candidate, and now chairman of an investment bank) recently observed:

> I have seen many kinds of power: the power of threats and of praise, of shock and surprise, and of a shared vision. Sometimes threatening works, but it usually brings with it adverse consequences—like resentment and a desire to get even in some way. People don't like to be reminded that they are inferior in power or status. And so, in business, it is important to motivate through the power of shared goals, shared objectives, and shared standards.[5]

The first part of the chapter defines what is meant by power and describes how power is related to authority and influence. The next part concentrates on the various classifications of power. Particular attention is given to the classic French and Raven identified sources of power. After an examination of some of the research results on power types, attention is given to some contingency approaches (for example, the influenceability of the target and an overall contingency model of power). Next, the popular approach of empowering employees is presented. The last part is concerned with organizational politics. Particular attention is given to a political perspective of power in today's organizations and to specific political strategies used in the acquisition of power.

# THE MEANING OF POWER

Although the concepts in the field of organizational behavior seldom have universally agreed-upon definitions, *power* may have even more diverse definitions than most. Almost every author who writes about power defines it differently. Going way back, for example, the famous pioneering sociologist Max Weber defined power as "the probability that one actor within a social relationship will be in a position to carry out his own will despite resistance."[6] More recently, a search of the literature on power found it referred to as the ability to get things done despite the will and resistance of others or the ability to "win" political fights and outmaneuver the opposition. The power theorists stress the positive sum of power, suggesting it is the raw ability to mobilize resources to accomplish some end without reference to any organized opposition.[7] Pfeffer, the organizational behavior theorist perhaps most closely associated with the study of power, simply defined power as a potential force and in more detail "as the potential ability to influence behavior, to change the course of events, to overcome resistance, and to get people to do things that they would not otherwise do."[8]

Usually definitions of power are intertwined with the concepts of authority and influence. For example, the preceding definition uses the word *influence* in describing power, the pioneering management theorist Chester Barnard defined power in terms of "informal authority," and many organizational sociologists define authority as "legitimate power."[9] These distinctions among concepts need to be cleared up in order to better understand power.

## The Distinctions among Power, Authority, and Influence

In Chapter 6 the power motive is defined as the need to manipulate others and have superiority over them. Extrapolating from this definition of the need for power, *power* itself can be defined as the ability to get an individual or group to do something—to get the person or group to change in some way. The individual who possesses power has the ability to manipulate or change others. Such a definition of power distinguishes it from authority and influence.

One of the primary sources of definitional controversy revolves around the question: Is power the *observed influence* over others, or is it merely the *potential to influence*? An argument can be made that those individuals who have the most power are the least likely to need to demonstrate outward evidence that they hold it. Their mere presence is enough to change the behaviors of others without lifting a finger or saying a word. This makes the study of power much more difficult, but at the same time conceptually should not be ignored.[10] An employee who takes the back stairs to avoid confronting an intimidating coworker is being influenced without the coworker even knowing of the power held over the frightened coworker.

Authority legitimatizes and is a source of power. Authority is the right to manipulate or change others. Power need not be legitimate. In addition, the distinction must be made between top-down classical, bureaucratic authority and Barnard's concept of bottom-up authority based on acceptance. In particular, Barnard defined *authority* as "the character of a communication (order) in a formal organization by virtue of which it is accepted by a contributor to or 'member' of the organization as governing the action he contributes."[11]

Such an acceptance theory of authority is easily differentiated from power. Grimes notes: "What legitimizes authority is the promotion or pursuit of collective goals that are associated with group consensus. The polar opposite, power, is the pursuit of individual or particularistic goals associated with group compliance."[12]

Influence is usually conceived of as being broader in scope than power. It involves the ability to alter other people in general ways, such as by changing their satisfaction and performance. Influence is more closely associated with leadership than power is, but both obviously are involved in the leadership process. Thus, authority is different from power because of its legitimacy and acceptance, and influence is broader than power, but it is so conceptually close that the two terms can be used interchangeably.

The preceding discussion points out that an operational definition of power is lacking, and this vagueness is a major reason power has traditionally received relatively little attention in the study of organizational behavior. Yet, especially when it is linked to the emerging concern for the informal organization and organizational politics, the study of power can greatly enhance the understanding of the ways in which organizations function and the dynamics of organizational behavior. As one observer of the dynamics of the informal power network of organizations keenly noted:

> Anyone who has ever worked knows that the org chart, no matter how meticulously rendered, doesn't come close to describing the facts of office life. All those lines and boxes don't tell you, for example, that smokers tend to have the best information, since they bond with people from every level and department when they head outside for a puff. The org chart doesn't tell you that people go to Janice, a long-time middle manager, rather than their bosses to get projects through. It doesn't tell you that the Canadian and Japanese sales forces don't interact because the two points of contact can't stand each other.[13]

## The Classifications of Power

Most discussions of power often begin and sometimes even end with a review of the widely recognized five categories of the sources of social power identified many years ago by social psychologists John French and Bertram Raven.[14] Describing and analyzing these five classic types of power (reward, coercive, legitimate, referent, and expert) serve as a necessary foundation and point of departure for the entire chapter. Most of the examples and applications to organizational behavior derive from the following five types of power.

### Reward Power

This source of power is based on a person's ability to control resources and reward others. In addition, the target of this power must value these rewards. In an organizational context, managers have many potential rewards, such as pay increases, promotions, valuable information, favorable work assignments, more responsibility, new equipment, praise, feedback, and recognition available to them. In operant learning terms (covered in Chapter 12), this means that the manager has the power to administer positive reinforcers. In expectancy motivation terms (covered in Chapter 6), this means that the person has the power to provide positive valences and that the other person perceives this ability.

To understand this source of power more completely, one must remember that the recipient holds the key. If managers offer their people what they think are rewards (for example, a promotion with increased responsibility), but the people do not value them (for example, they are insecure or have family obligations that are more important to them than a promotion), then managers do not really have reward power. By the same token, managers may not think they are giving rewards to their people (they calmly listen to chronic complainers), but if they perceive this to be rewarding (the managers are giving them attention by intently listening to their complaining), the managers nevertheless have reward power. Also, managers may not really have the rewards to dispense (they may say that they have considerable influence with top management to get their people promoted, but actually they don't), but as long as their people think they have it, they do indeed have reward power.

### Coercive Power

This source of power depends on fear. The person with coercive power has the ability to inflict punishment or aversive consequences on another person or, at least, to make threats that the other person believes will result in punishment or undesirable outcomes. This form of power has contributed greatly to the negative connotation that power has for most people. In an organizational context, managers frequently have coercive power in that they can fire or demote people who work for them, or dock their pay, although the legal climate and unions have stripped away some of this power. A manager can also directly or indirectly threaten an employee with these punishing consequences. In operant learning terms, this means that the person has the power to administer punishment or negatively reinforce (terminate punishing consequences, which is a form of negative control). In expectancy motivation terms, this means that power comes from the expectation on the part of the other person that they will be punished for not conforming to the powerful person's desires. For example, there is fear of punishment when the rules, directives, or policies of the organization are not carefully followed. It is probably this fear that gets most people to arrive at work on time and to look busy when the boss walks through the area. In other words, much of organizational behavior may be explained in terms of coercive power rather than reward power.

### Legitimate Power

This power source, identified by French and Raven, stems from the internalized values of the other persons that give the legitimate right to the agent to influence them. The others feel they have the obligation to accept this power. It is almost identical to what is usually called authority and is closely aligned with both reward and coercive power because the person with legitimacy is also in a position to reward and punish. However, legitimate power is unlike reward and coercive power in that it does not depend on the relationships with others but rather on the position or role that the person holds. For example, people obtain legitimacy because of their titles (captain or executive vice president) or position (oldest in the family or officer of a corporation) rather than their personalities or how they affect others. A recent study found that CEOs are perceived to have more power when they also chair the board.[15]

Legitimate power comes from three major sources. First, the prevailing cultural values of a society, organization, or group determine what is legitimate. For example, in some societies, the older people become, the more legitimate power they possess. The same may be true for a certain physical attribute, gender, or job. In an organizational context, managers generally have legitimate power because employees believe in the value of private property laws and in the hierarchy where higher positions have been designated to have power over lower positions. The same holds true for certain functional positions in an organization. An example of the latter would be engineers who have legitimacy in the operations or information systems areas of a company, whereas accountants have legitimacy in financial matters. The prevailing values within a group also determine legitimacy. For example, in a street gang the toughest member may attain legitimacy, whereas in a work group the union steward may have legitimacy.

Second, people can obtain legitimate power from the accepted social structure. In some societies there is an accepted ruling class. But an organization or a family may also have an accepted social structure that gives legitimate power. For example, when blue-collar workers accept employment from a company, they are in effect accepting the hierarchical structure and granting legitimate power to their supervisors.

A third source of legitimate power can come from being designated as the agent or representative of a powerful person or group. Elected officials, a chairperson of a committee, and members of the board of directors of a corporation or a union or management committee would be examples of this form of legitimate power.

Each of these forms of legitimate power creates an obligation to accept and be influenced. But, in actual practice, there are often problems, confusion, or disagreement about the range or scope of this power. Consider the following:

> An executive can rightfully expect a supervisor to work hard and diligently; may he also influence the supervisor to spy on rivals, spend weekends away from home, join an encounter group? A coach can rightfully expect [her] players to execute specific plays; may [she] also direct their life styles outside the sport? A combat officer can rightfully expect his men to attack on order; may he also direct them to execute civilians whom he claims are spies? A doctor can rightfully order a nurse to attend a patient or observe an autopsy; may he [or she] order [him or] her to assist in an abortion against [his or] her own will?[16]

These gray areas point to the real concern that many people in contemporary society have regarding the erosion of traditional legitimacy. These uncertainties also point to the complex nature of power.

### Referent Power

This type of power comes from the desire on the part of the other persons to identify with the agent wielding power. They want to identify with the powerful person, regardless of the outcomes. The others grant the person power because he or she is attractive and has desirable resources or personal characteristics.

Advertisers take advantage of this type of power when they use celebrities, such as movie stars or sports figures, to provide testimonial advertising. The buying public identifies with (finds attractive) certain famous people and grants them power to tell them what product to buy. For example, a review of research has found that arguments, especially emotional ones, are more influential when they come from beautiful people.[17]

Timing is an interesting aspect of the testimonial advertising type of referent power. Only professional athletes who are in season (for example, baseball players in the summer and early fall, football players in the fall and early winter, and basketball players in the winter and early spring) are used in the advertisements, because then they are very visible, they are in the forefront of the public's awareness, and consequently they have referent power. Out of season the athlete is forgotten and has little referent power. Exceptions, of course, are the handful of superstars (for example, Shaquille O'Neal, Michael Jordan, Wayne Gretzky, and Tiger Woods) who transcend seasons and have referent power all year long and even after they have long ago retired.

In an organizational setting, referent power is much different from the other types of power discussed so far. For example, managers with referent power must be attractive to their people so that they will want to identify with them, regardless of whether the managers later have the ability to reward or punish or whether they have legitimacy. In other words, the manager who depends on referent power must be personally attractive to subordinates.

### *Expert Power*

The last source of power identified by French and Raven is based on the extent to which others attribute knowledge and expertise to the power holder. Experts are perceived to have knowledge or understanding only in certain well-defined areas. All the sources of power depend on an individual's perceptions, but expert power may be even more dependent on this than the others. In particular, the target must perceive the agent to be credible, trustworthy, and relevant before expert power is granted.

Credibility comes from having the right credentials; that is, the person must really know what he or she is talking about and be able to show tangible evidence of this knowledge. There is basic research indicating the significant positive impact that credibility has on perceived power[18] and there is much evidence from everyday experience. For example, if a highly successful football coach gives an aspiring young player some advice on how to do a new block, he will be closely listened to—he will be granted expert power. The coach has expert power in this case because he is so knowledgeable about football. His evidence for this credibility is the fact that he is a former star player and has coached championship teams. If this coach tried to give advice on how to play basketball or how to manage a corporation, he would have questionable credibility and thus would have little or no expert power. For avid sports fans or players, however, a coach might have general referent power (that is, he is very attractive to them), and they would be influenced by what he has to say on any subject—basketball or corporate management. For example, successful coaches such as basketball's Pat Riley and Rick Pitino have written best-selling books aimed at effective business management.

In organizations, staff specialists have expert power in their functional areas but not outside them. For example, engineers are granted expert power in technical matters but not in personnel or public relations problems. The same holds true for other staff experts, such as computer experts or accountants. For example, the computer person in a small office may be the only one who really understands the newest software and how to use it, and this knowledge gives him or her considerable power.

As already implied, however, expert power is highly selective, and, besides credibility, the agent must also have trustworthiness and relevance. By trustworthiness, it is meant that the person seeking expert power must have a reputation for being honest and straightforward. In the case of political figures, scandals could undermine their expert power in the eyes of the voting public. The same could be said of recent years of the world of business. As noted by one devil's advocate for the blind belief in the value of trust in our business leaders:

> As September 11 and the collapse of Enron have reminded us, we have long operated under the illusion that we live and work over safety nets, not realizing—or even questioning—how flimsy those nets really are. Such high levels of trust have made us less vigilant and thus less able to protect ourselves.[19]

The same could be said of course of the more recent fallout of the financial crisis. Wall Street bankers have lost a lot of expert power for the foreseeable future. In addition to credibility and trustworthiness, a person must have relevance and usefulness to have expert power. Going back to the earlier example, if the football coach gave advice on world affairs, it would be neither relevant nor useful, and therefore the coach would not have expert power in this domain.

It is evident that expertise is the most tenuous type of power, but managers and especially staff specialists, who seldom have the other sources of power available to them, often have to depend on their expertise as their only source of power. As organizations become increasingly technologically complex and specialized, the expert power of the organization members at all levels may become more and more important. This is formally recognized by some companies that deliberately include lower-level staff members with expert power in top-level decision making. For example, Andy Grove, the former CEO of Intel, has stated: "In general, the faster the change in the know-how on which a business depends, the greater the divergence between knowledge and position power is likely to be. Since our business depends on what it knows to survive, we mix 'knowledge-power people' with 'position-power people' daily, so that together they make the decisions that will affect us for years to come."[20]

It must also be remembered that French and Raven did recognize that there may be other sources of power. For instance, some organizational sociologists recognize the source of power of task interdependence (where two or more organizational participants must depend on one another). An example would be an executive who has legitimate power over a supervisor, but because the executive must depend on the supervisor to get the job done correctly and on time, the supervisor also has power over the executive. There is research evidence that those in such an interdependent relationship with their boss receive better pay raises[21] and even that such interdependence can enhance the quality of the professor-student relationship.[22]

Closely related to interdependence is the use of information as a source of power. A person who controls the flow of information and/or interprets data before it is presented to others has such information power. Information power is distinguished from expert power because the individual merely needs to be in the "right place" to affect the flow and/or distribution of information, rather than having some form of expertise over the generation or interpretation of the information.[23]

Besides recognizing that there may be additional sources of power, French and Raven also point out that the sources are interrelated (for example, the use of coercive power by managers may reduce their referent power, and there is research evidence that high coercive and reward power may lead to reduced expert power),[24] and the same person may exercise different types of power under different circumstances and at different times.

Research indicates that French and Raven's five bases of power may be summed to develop a measure of global power.[25] This more global measure was found to be internally consistent and significantly related to each of the five individual power bases. It also accounted for additional variance in studies of the relationship between power and other variables such as resistance, compliance, and control. Additional research has found the role that procedural justice may play in the bases of power. One study indicates that although the bases of power are related to effective work reactions, they are also mediated by perceptions of procedure justice.[26] This means employees are inclined to form evaluative perceptions regarding the fairness of actions exhibited by power holders and respond accordingly. Specifically, when the actions seem fair or justifiable, employees respond more favorably to the power influences being used by their supervisors. These findings and the previous discussion of the impact of the situation and time lead to the contingency models of power in organizations.

## Contingency Approaches to Power

As in other areas of organizational behavior and management, contingency approaches to power have emerged. For example, Pfeffer simply says that power comes from being in the "right" place. He describes the right place or position in the organization as one where the manager has:

1. Control over resources such as budgets, physical facilities, and positions that can be used to cultivate allies and supporters

2. Control over or extensive access to information—about the organization's activities, about the preferences and judgments of others, about what is going on, and about who is doing it
3. Formal authority[27]

There is some research support[28] for such insightful observations, and there are also research findings that lead to contingency conclusions such as the following:

1. The greater the professional orientation of group members, the greater relative strength referent power has in influencing them.
2. The less effort and interest high-ranking participants are willing to allocate to a task, the more likely lower-ranking participants are to obtain power relevant to this task.[29]

Besides these overall contingency observations, there is increasing recognition of the moderating impact of the control of strategic contingencies such as organizational interdependence and the extent to which a department controls critical operations of other departments[30] or the role of influence behaviors in the perception of power.[31] Also, the characteristics of influence targets (that is, their influenceability) have an important moderating impact on the types of power that can be successfully used. An examination of these characteristics of the target and an overall contingency model are presented next.

### Influenceability of the Targets of Power

Most discussions of power imply a unilateral process of influence from the agent to the target. It is becoming increasingly clear, however, that power involves a reciprocal relationship between the agent and the target, which is in accordance with the overall social cognitive perspective taken in this text. The power relationship can be better understood by examining some of the characteristics of the target. The following characteristics have been identified as being especially important to the influenceability of targets:[32]

1. *Dependency.*    The greater the targets' dependency on their relationship to agents (for example, when a target cannot escape a relationship, perceives no alternatives, or values the agent's rewards as unique), the more targets are influenced.
2. *Uncertainty.*    Experiments have shown that the more uncertain people are about the appropriateness or correctness of a behavior, the more likely they are to be influenced to change that behavior.
3. *Personality.*    There have been a number of research studies showing the relationship between personality characteristics and influenceability. Some of these findings are obvious (for example, people who cannot tolerate ambiguity or who are highly anxious are more susceptible to influence, and those with high needs for affiliation are more susceptible to group influence), but some are not (for example, both positive and negative relationships have been found between self-esteem and influenceability).
4. *Intelligence.*    There is no simple relationship between intelligence and influenceability. For example, highly intelligent people may be more willing to listen, but, because they also tend to be held in high esteem, they also may be more resistant to influence.
5. *Gender.*    Although traditionally it was generally thought that women were more likely to conform to influence attempts than men because of the way they were raised, there is now evidence that this is changing.[33] As women's and society's views of the role of women are changing, there is less of a distinction of influenceability by gender.
6. *Age.*    Social psychologists have generally concluded that susceptibility to influence increases in young children up to about the age of eight or nine and then decreases with age until adolescence, when it levels off.

In recent years many American firms doing business internationally have found, to their chagrin, that their overseas hosts have been using the agenda to gain power over visiting dignitaries. Here is a story related by a business lawyer who recently returned from Japan.

"I went to Japan to negotiate a licensing agreement with a large company there. We had been in contact with these people for three months and during that time had hammered out a rough agreement regarding the specific terms of the contract. The president of the firm thought that it would be a good idea if I, the corporate attorney, went to Tokyo and negotiated some of the final points of the agreement before we signed. I arrived in Japan on a Sunday with the intention of leaving late Friday evening. When I got off the plane, my hosts were waiting for me. I was whisked through customs and comfortably ensconced in a plush limousine within 30 minutes.

"The next day began with my host asking me for my return air ticket so his secretary could take care of confirming the flight. I was delighted to comply. We then spent the next four days doing all sorts of things—sightseeing, playing golf, fishing, dining at some of the finest restaurants in the city. You name it, we did it. By Thursday I was getting worried. We had not yet gotten around to talking about the licensing agreement. Then on Friday morning we had a big meeting. Most of the time was spent discussing the changes my hosts would like to see made in the agreement. Before I had a chance to talk, it was time for lunch. We finished eating around 4 P.M. This left me only four hours before I had to leave for the airport. During this time I worked to get them to understand the changes we wanted made in the agreement. Before I knew it, it was time to head for the airport. Halfway there my host pulled out a new contract. 'Here are the changes we talked about,' he said. 'I have already signed for my company. All you have to do is sign for yours.' Not wanting to come home empty-handed, I signed. It turned out that the contract was much more favorable to them than to us. In the process, I learned a lesson. Time is an important source of power. When you know the other person's agenda, you have an idea of what the individual's game plan must be and can work it to your advantage. Since this time, I have all my reservations and confirmations handled stateside. When my host asks me how long I will be staying, I have a stock answer, 'As long as it takes.'

7. *Culture.* Obviously, the cultural values of a society have a tremendous impact on the influenceability of its people. For example, some cultures, such as Western cultures, emphasize individuality, dissent, and diversity, which would tend to decrease influenceability, whereas others, such as many in Asia, emphasize cohesiveness, agreement, and uniformity, which would tend to promote influenceability. As the accompanying OB in Action: Taking as Long as It Takes indicates, controlling the agenda and time in foreign cultures may be used to gain power and influenceability.

These individual differences in targets greatly complicate the effective use of power and point up the need for contingency models.

### An Overall Contingency Model for Power

Many other contingency variables in the power relationship besides the target could be inferred from the discussion of the various types of power, for example, credibility and surveillance. All these variables can be tied together and related to one another in an overall contingency model.

The classic work on influence process, by noted social psychologist Herbert Kelman,[34] can be used to structure an overall contingency model of power. The model in Figure 10.1 incorporates the French and Raven sources of power with Kelman's sources of power, which in turn support three major processes of power.

According to the model, the target will *comply* in order to gain a favorable reaction or avoid a punishing one from the agent. This is the process that most supervisors in work organizations must rely on. But in order for compliance to work, supervisors must be able to reward and punish (that is, have control over the means to their people's ends) and keep an eye on them (that is, have surveillance over them).

**FIGURE 10.1**
**An Overall Contingency Model of Power Based on the French-Raven and Kelman Theories**

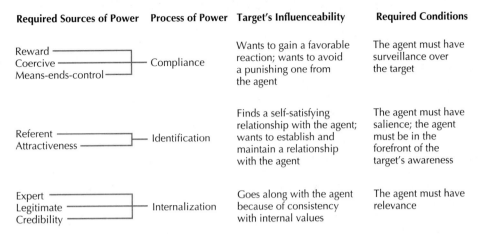

| Required Sources of Power | Process of Power | Target's Influenceability | Required Conditions |
|---|---|---|---|
| Reward<br>Coercive<br>Means-ends-control | Compliance | Wants to gain a favorable reaction; wants to avoid a punishing one from the agent | The agent must have surveillance over the target |
| Referent<br>Attractiveness | Identification | Finds a self-satisfying relationship with the agent; wants to establish and maintain a relationship with the agent | The agent must have salience; the agent must be in the forefront of the target's awareness |
| Expert<br>Legitimate<br>Credibility | Internalization | Goes along with the agent because of consistency with internal values | The agent must have relevance |

People will *identify* not in order to obtain a favorable reaction from the agent, as in compliance, but because it is self-satisfying to do so.[35] But in order for the identification process to work, the agent must have referent power—be very attractive to the target—and be salient (prominent). For example, a research study by Kelman found that students were initially greatly influenced by a speech given by a very handsome star athlete; that is, they identified with him. However, when the students were checked several months after the speech, they were not influenced. The handsome athlete was no longer salient; that is, he was no longer in the forefront of their awareness, and his previous words at the later time had no influence. As discussed earlier, except for the handful of superstars, athletes are soon forgotten and have no power over even their most avid fans. Once they have graduated or are out of season, they lose their salience and, thus, their power.

Finally, people will *internalize* because of compatibility with their own value structure. But, as Figure 10.1 shows, in order for people to internalize, the agent must have expert or legitimate power (credibility) and, in addition, be relevant. Obviously, this process of power is most effective. Kelman, for example, found that internalized power had a lasting impact on the subjects in his studies.

Researchers have had problems constructing ways to measure compliance, identification, and internalization.[36] However, this model of power does have considerable relevance as to how and under what conditions supervisors and managers influence their people. Many must depend on compliance because they are not attractive or do not possess referent power for identification to work. Or they lack credibility or do not have expert or legitimate power for internalization to occur. Kelman's research showed that internalization had the longest-lasting impact and, as shown in the model, does not need surveillance or salience. In other words, what is generally considered to be leadership (covered in the last two chapters) is more associated with getting people not just to comply but also to identify with the leader and, even better, to internalize what the leader is trying to accomplish in the influence attempt. This internalization would be especially desirable in today's highly autonomous, flat organizations with cultures of openness, empowerment, and trust.

### The Two Faces of Power

Besides the sources and situational, or contingency, nature of power, there are also different types of power that can be identified. Well-known social psychologist David McClelland did, as Chapter 6 points out, considerable work on the impact of the motivational need for power (what he called *n Pow*). His studies indicated that there are two major types of power, one negative and one positive.

As the introductory comments point out, over the years power has often had a negative connotation. The commonly used term "power-hungry" reflects this negative feeling about power. According to McClelland, power

> is associated with heavy drinking, gambling, having more aggressive impulses, and collecting "prestige supplies" like a convertible. . . . People with this personalized power concern are more apt to speed, have accidents, and get into physical fights. If . . . possessed by political officeholders, especially in the sphere of international relations, the consequences would be ominous.[37]

McClelland felt that this negative use of power is associated with *personal power.* People with this "face" of power are primarily looking out for themselves and how they can get ahead; they are very "I" oriented, as in "I should look good if this project is completed so I can get a raise and promotion out of it." McClelland felt that this personal power is primitive and does indeed have negative consequences.

The contrasting "other face" of power identified by McClelland is *social power.* It is characterized by a "concern for group goals, for finding those goals that will move people, for helping the group to formulate them, for taking some initiative in providing members of the group with the means of achieving such goals, and for giving group members the feeling of strength and competence they need to work hard for such goals."[38] In other words, social power types are very "we" oriented, as in "We are going to have the best unit in the company, and we will all reap the rewards." Under this definition of social power, the manager may often be in a precarious position of walking a fine line between an exhibition of personal dominance and the more socializing use of power. McClelland accumulated some empirical evidence that social power managers are quite effective. In some ways this role power may play in organizational effectiveness is in opposition to the more humanistic positions, which emphasize the importance of democratic values and participative decision making. There is also more recent empirical evidence that would counter McClelland's view. One study found that those with a high need for power may suppress the flow of information, especially information that contradicts their preferred course of action, and thus have a negative impact on effective managerial decision making.[39]

The negative use of power can also show up in situations such as sexual harassment. Unwelcome conduct of a sexual nature takes place when someone uses coercive power to threaten another with negative consequences if they do not submit to sexual advances. This is known as quid pro quo harassment. A hostile work environment (sexual jokes, leering, posters) is another inappropriate use of one's power over another. In all such inappropriate circumstances, harassment is based on power being used to intimidate another, especially those in a subordinate formal position. However, regardless of some of the controversy surrounding power, it is clear that power is inevitable in today's organizations. How the dynamics of power are used and what type of power is used can vitally affect human performance and organizational goals.

# THE SPECIAL CASE OF EMPOWERMENT

Closely related to social power is the popular technique of employee empowerment. Empowerment may be defined as "recognizing and releasing into the organization the power that people have in their wealth of useful knowledge and internal motivation."[40] Empowerment is the authority to make decisions within one's area of responsibility without first having to get approval from someone else. For example, the head of a large Indian outsourcer, HCL Technologies, says he wants to "destroy the office of CEO" in order to remind employees that they are empowered to make the decisions and should not look to him for answers.[41] Although this type of empowerment is similar to traditional delegated authority, there are two characteristics that make it unique. One is that employees are encouraged to use their own initiative, and, as they say at Cummins Engine, "Just do it." The second is that empowered employees are given not only the authority but also the resources, so they are able to make decisions and have the power to get them implemented.

Empowerment programs can transform a stagnant organization into a vital one by creating a "shared purpose among employees, encouraging greater collaboration, and, most importantly, delivering enhanced value to customers."[42] To do so, the organization must overcome certain obstacles, such as becoming impatient, assuming employees have all the needed skills without first checking to make sure they are qualified, and creating confusion through contradictory rewards and the model's behaviors. This means there must be a linkage of the power with self-reliance, managerial authority, and expecting individual contributor commitment.[43] In order for this to occur, empowerment must become embedded in an organization's cultural values operationalized through participation, innovation, access to information, and accountability.

## The Complexity of Empowerment

Empowerment assumes that employees are willing to accept responsibility and improve their daily work processes and relationships. A recent survey revealed that almost all U.S. workers do feel personally responsible and want to improve quality and performance. Many companies are now discovering that empowerment training can be extremely useful in showing employees how to participate more actively and make things happen. There is also empirical research evidence that where participation is part of an empowerment program, manufacturing performance improves,[44] and managers perceive that they are indeed empowered.[45]

A good example comes from the chemical division of Georgia-Pacific, where a quality and environmental assurance supervisor and a plant operator who had received empowerment training began participating through sharing ideas for more effectively preparing test samples of a certain chemical. Once they finalized their ideas, they used their empowerment status to produce a demonstration video. After seeing the video, management asked the two employees to share the tape with quality assurance supervisors in other plants. In turn, the supervisor and operator encouraged these other employees to provide feedback on the video and to share their own ideas. As a result, a more efficient system of preparing test samples was developed companywide.

At the same time, care must be given to the effects on other managers. For example, many middle managers find themselves in a dilemma of dealing with two cultures when empowerment strategies are enacted. The first tells them to "relinquish control" whereas another demands that they "maintain control." These contrasting values create role conflicts that must be resolved in order for the program to succeed.[46] Empowerment and participation have been found to work best when they open new avenues for action among all members of the organization and strengthen their resolve to go along with the new ideas.[47] Some critics argue that power and empowerment are only evoked when there is consonance between the "poetic" and the "rhetoric" of an organization, which means that a person's interpretative framework must account for every aspect of the program. Because there is a conflict between relinquishing and maintaining control, and the two demands must be resolved for the employee to feel empowered, care must be taken not to neutralize empowerment and render it impotent.[48]

### *Innovation Implications*

Empowerment encourages innovation because employees have the authority to try out new ideas and make decisions that result in new ways of doing things. For example, in one major consumer goods company, two engineers used their empowered status to design and test a new household product. After spending over $25,000 on the project, they realized that the product did not perform up to expectations. The design was faulty and performance was poor. The next day the president of the company sent for both of them. When they entered the executive office, they found they were guests of honor at a party. The president quickly explained that he appreciated all their efforts and even though they were not successful, he was sure they would be in the future. By encouraging their innovative efforts through empowerment, the president helped ensure that these two employees would continue to bring new ideas to the market. This climate for innovation is greatly facilitated by empowering employees.

### Access to Information

When employees are given access to information as a vital part of their empowerment, their willingness to cooperate is enhanced. At firms such as General Mills, self-managed work teams are given any information they need to do their jobs and improve productivity. This includes information as far ranging as profit and loss statements, manufacturing processes, and purchasing procedures. In addition, if employees desire additional training, even if the training is peripheral to their main jobs, it is provided. As a result of this accessibility to information, work teams are able to manage and control operations more effectively than under the old hierarchical bureaucratic and secretive, only on a need-to-know basis, information. With "open-book" cultural values and Intranet technology, empowered employees have all the organization's information (and knowledge) available to do their jobs as effectively as possible.

### Accountability and Responsibility

Although employees are empowered to make decisions they believe will benefit the organization, they must also be held accountable and responsible for results. This accountability is not intended to punish mistakes or to generate immediate, short-term results. Instead, the intent is to ensure that the associates are giving their best efforts, working toward agreed-upon goals, and behaving responsibly toward each other. When these behaviors are exhibited, management is able to continue empowering employees to proceed at their own pace and in their own ways. Empowering employees should raise the level of trust in the organization. Empowered employees feel that "we are in this thing together" and are almost compelled to act responsibly.[49] Trust is a must in today's open, empowered organizations that are in very competitive markets.

## Putting Empowerment into Action

There are a number of ways that managers can implement empowerment. Two common approaches are: (1) *kaizen* and "just do it" principles (JDIT), and (2) trust building. The goal is to tie empowerment with an action-driven results approach. This approach is found at Cummins Engine. The company provides a five-day training program in which *kaizen* (a Japanese term that means "continuous improvement") is combined with JDIT. The principles or operational guidelines used include: (1) discard conventional, fixed ideas about doing work; (2) think about how to do it rather than why it cannot be done; (3) start by questioning current practices; (4) begin to make improvements immediately, even if only 50 percent of them can be completed; and (5) correct mistakes immediately.[50]

The first day of the Cummins empowerment training program begins with a discussion about what *kaizen* and JDIT principles mean. Participants learn about the need for teamwork and the use of group problem solving. The second day is spent applying these ideas to a work area where improvement is needed. Cross-functional JDIT teams of three to five people are sent to the work floor to observe, document, and evaluate work practices. The third day is used to implement ideas that were identified and evaluated on the work floor. The next day is spent evaluating the improvements that have been initiated and making any final changes so that the new way of doing the work is more efficient than the previous method. The final day of the program is devoted to making presentations of the results to an audience of managers, explaining the changes that were made, and showing the results that were obtained.

Trust building is also vital. Violations of trust between employers and employees (sometimes called "organizational infidelity") means the terms of the psychological contract that has been built have been ignored or have been broken. Once this occurs, perceptions of rewards and contributions are reevaluated, usually resulting in reduced effort and lower commitment to the company.[51]

"Optimal trust" occurs when managers and employees reach an agreement where trust is counterbalanced with distrust, as there is always at least a degree of suspicion in organizational relationships. Reaching optimal levels of trust involves finding the point where distrust is low enough to not be disruptive and trust is strong enough to move forward with confidence.[52] Distrust is a major disruption to any change, including empowerment. Even at the highest levels of the organization, distrust can negatively affect operations. Unless trust is restored, the effects linger for a long time.[53]

Trust building matches the principles of empowerment. Professional and collaborative relationships can be built across functional and hierarchical lines when trust is present. This grants the ability to disseminate ideas and information quickly throughout the organization. A shared mind-set develops that encourages people to continually challenge old processes and take prudent risks in creating something new. This fosters the ability to form quality ad hoc teams that share knowledge and tackle problems.[54]

At the extreme, some organizations encourage silliness and fun to build trust. Matt Weinstein and Luke Barber are management consultants who help companies build better environments for empowerment using such unusual tactics as bringing champagne to work to celebrate an employee's greatest failure, to get rid of the negative stigma. They have set up dance-in-the-hallway sessions, candy prizes, and dress-up days, where workers showed up in Elvis costumes, biker togs, and nun outfits to release stress. When work is fun, employees feel more relaxed and truly empowered.[55]

Although empowerment implementation programs widely vary, they are all based on careful evaluations of the benefits and drawbacks of the process and the degree to which the organization's members are prepared to accept the ideas. The accompanying OB in Action: Empowerment and Trust indicates that today's employees seem ready for, and even demand, a high degree of empowerment and trust. However, some organizations have found that high degrees of empowerment work extremely well whereas others have discovered that the organization operates most efficiently with less empowerment. To account for these differences, Bowen and Lawler have suggested that organizations first identify at which of four levels of empowerment they should operate: (1) very little involvement, as reflected by traditional production-line firms; (2) moderate involvement, as reflected by organizations that employ suggestion programs and quality circles; (3) fairly substantial involvement, as reflected in organizations where jobs are designed so that employees can employ a variety of skills and have a great deal of autonomy in carrying out those jobs; and (4) high involvement, as reflected by organizations in which personnel share information and work together to solve problems and complete tasks.[56]

In general, empowerment can be viewed as the sharing of social power in an organization. Individual employees share goals and combine efforts to reach those goals. This fosters creativity and a stronger stake in the organization's outcomes and future.

If an organization wants to tap the full potential of their human resources and maintain their loyalty, how should people be managed? There are many answers to this question. For example, some researchers have noted that an ideal leader does things such as: develops and empowers people, shares authority, and encourages constructive challenge. Others, such as the well-known leadership guru Warren Bennis, contend that leaders have to build trust, and this is a two-way street. Managers have to believe in their employees and employees have to feel that the boss will never let them down.

Some insight into the question of how people should be managed may be found in a recent large interview study involving several hundred firms. Employees responded that their productivity and tenure with their employer was determined by how well they are treated by their boss. Forty percent of those who said they had poor bosses also reported that they would be willing to leave their company and take a job elsewhere if the opportunity arose. In contrast, of those who said their bosses were excellent, only 11 percent said they would be willing to leave.

The lesson from these findings is clear. Being a tough manager may have worked well a decade ago when corporate America was being "lean and mean." However, that era is now over. As one analyst put it, "The American workplace has evolved to a kinder, gentler state." Additionally, recent survey data show that most workers rate having a caring boss as more important than either money or fringe benefits.

In particular, employees report that they have strong loyalty to companies that help them develop their skills, provide them mentors, and adjust work schedules to meet their personal needs. Consider the case of Mary Morse, a software engineer at Autodesk, a computer-aided design company in San Rafael, California. Her first manager guided her through a six-month internship, accommodating her college schedule, and providing time off during finals week. Her next boss asked her how much she wanted as a starting salary and paid her $5,000 above this amount. Then this boss's supervisor approached Mary and asked if she could be her mentor. When Mary agreed, the supervisor had her write out a list of short-term and long-term objectives and then began working with her to ensure that these goals were met. Mary's third boss spent time talking to her about her career ambitions, and when she indicated that she wanted to move from designing and writing computer code to becoming a software engineer, he recommended classes and gave her the time off to attend them. So when Mary was wooed by a competitive firm that, among other things, offered her options for 7,000 shares of stock at less than $1 a share, she turned them down. Looking back at her decision and the options that became worth over $1 million, Mary still feels she made the right decision to stay with her current employer. She is not alone.

Recent research shows that people with poor bosses are four times more likely to leave their companies than are those with caring bosses. And that is why so many firms are now getting on the bandwagon. For example, Macy's West, a division of Federated Department Stores in San Francisco, began a program of assigning mentors to new managers and telling all managers that up to 35 percent of their compensation would now be linked to how well they retained the people under them. And at the International Paper plant in Moss Point, Mississippi, there are morning training sessions on positive reinforcement that are designed to change the way many supervisors manage by making these individuals friendlier and more approachable. The reason for these developments was best summed up by one of Mary Morse's managers at Autodesk, who said, "Job satisfaction and being challenged means as much to me as the money part of it—just so long as I feel rewarded." Simply put, a kind, caring approach can go a long way in motivating people.

## POLITICAL IMPLICATIONS OF POWER

Power and politics are very closely related concepts. A popular view of organizational politics is how one can pragmatically get ahead in an organization. Alvin Toffler, the noted author of *Future Shock, The Third Wave,* and *Powershift,* observed that "companies are always engaged in internal political struggles, power struggles, infighting, and so on. That's normal life."[57] There is even the view that there may be an inverse relationship between power and politics. For example, a recent publication aimed at practicing human resources (HR) managers noted that in this era of competing for limited resources, HR managers who lack power must use more politics. "Those who lack political skills will gain a reputation for folding under pressure and having no convictions."[58] Such political skills largely deal with the acquisition of power. In this latter view, power and politics become especially closely intertwined.[59] A recognition of the political realities of power acquisition in today's organizations and an examination of some specific political strategies for acquiring power are of particular interest for understanding the dynamics of organizational behavior.

## A Political Perspective of Power in Organizations

The classical organization theorists portrayed organizations as highly rational structures in which authority meticulously followed the chain of command and in which managers had legitimatized power. The discussion in the next chapter on informal managerial roles and organization portrays another, more realistic view of organizations. It is in this more realistic view of organizations that the importance of the political aspects of power and strategic advantage comes to the forefront.[60] As Pfeffer notes: "Organizations, particularly large ones, are like governments in that they are fundamentally political entities. To understand them, one needs to understand organizational politics, just as to understand governments, one needs to understand governmental politics."[61]

The political perspective of organizations departs from the rational, idealistic model. For example, Walter Nord dispels some of the dreams of ideal, rationally structured, and humanistic organizations by pointing out some of the stark realities of political power. He suggests four postulates of power in organizations that help focus on the political realities:

1. Organizations are composed of coalitions that compete with one another for resources, energy, and influence.
2. Various coalitions will seek to protect their interests and positions of influence.
3. The unequal distribution of power itself has dehumanizing effects.
4. The exercise of power within organizations is one very crucial aspect of the exercise of power within the larger social system.[62]

In other words, the political power game is changing, but is still very real in today's organizations.[63] Researchers on organizational politics conclude that

> politics in organizations is simply a fact of life. Personal experience, hunches, and anecdotal evidence for years have supported a general belief that behavior in and of organizations is often political in nature. More recently, some conceptual and empirical research has added further support to these notions.[64]

Even though the organizational politics has and will continue to flourish, its nature and how it is expressed changes over time. For example, younger workers often disdain the "Boomer" form of politics as "so last century." However, as an expert on organizational politics warns the young generation:

> By shunning the conventions of office politics, they risk burning bridges. So because you never know how long you'll be at a firm, I'd still advise sticking to the same old directives. They're the same today as they were two decades ago.[65]

Like other aspects of organizational behavior dynamics, politics is not a simple process. Besides the age of the participants, politics can vary from organization to organization and even from one subunit of an organization to another. A comprehensive definition drawing from the literature is that "organizational politics consists of intentional acts of influence undertaken by individuals or groups to enhance or protect their self-interest when conflicting courses of action are possible."[66] There is also a more recent view that different forms of power in organizations are connected to specific learning processes that help explain why some political insights become institutionalized and others do not.[67] The political behavior of organizational participants tends to be traditionally viewed as opportunistic for the purpose of maximizing self-interest,[68] but a counterargument is that organizational politics is actually the cornerstone of organizational democracy. As one theoretical analysis noted:

> politics is central to the development of real organizational democracy. It provides practical advice on how to work with a constructive political "mindset" and highlights how such behavior underpins, rather than undermines, the process of redistributing organizational influence.[69]

Thus, like other dynamics of today's organizations, the nature of politics is quite complex and still being studied for better understanding.

Research on organizational politics has identified several areas that are particularly relevant to the degree to which organizations are political rather than rational. These areas can be summarized as follows:[70]

1. *Resources.* There is a direct relationship between the amount of politics and how critical and scarce the resources are. Also, politics will be encouraged when there is an infusion of new, "unclaimed" resources.
2. *Decisions.* Ambiguous decisions, decisions on which there is lack of agreement, and uncertain, long-range strategic decisions lead to more politics than routine decisions.
3. *Goals.* The more ambiguous and complex the goals become, the more politics there will be.
4. *Technology and external environment.* In general, the more complex the internal technology of the organization, the more politics there will be. The same is true of organizations operating in turbulent external environments.
5. *Change.* A reorganization or a planned organization development (OD) effort or even an unplanned change brought about by external forces will encourage political maneuvering.

The preceding implies that some organizations and subunits within the organization will be more political than others. By the same token, however, it is clear that most of today's organizations meet these requirements for being highly political. That is, they have limited resources; make ambiguous, uncertain decisions; have unclear yet complex goals; have increasingly complex technology; and are undergoing drastic change. This existing situation facing organizations makes them more political, and the power game becomes increasingly important. Miles states: "In short, conditions that *threaten* the status of the powerful or *encourage* the efforts of those wishing to increase their power base will stimulate the intensity of organizational politics and increase the proportion of decision-making behaviors that can be classified as political as opposed to rational."[71] For example, with the political situation of today's high-tech, radically innovative firms, it has been suggested that medieval structures of palace favorites, liege lordship, and fiefdoms may be more relevant than the more familiar rational structures.[72] Recent theory-building does recognize the reality of territoriality in organizations. "Organization members can and do become territorial over physical space, ideas, roles, relationships, and other potential possessions in organizations."[73] As the accompanying OB in Action: You Are Where You Sit indicates, even where one sits at the table of a meeting indicates power and political maneuvering. The next section presents such practical political strategies for power acquisition in today's organizations.

## How to Decode the Psychology of the Morning Meeting

The client was a senior female executive at a major global company. She was hardworking, bright, and well-liked, but she had one big frustration: People often ignored her ideas at meetings.

After watching the woman interact with colleagues, executive consultant Constance Dierickx offered several suggestions. One of the most important: "I told her to stop sitting against the wall and sit around the table instead." Within six months, coworkers were commenting that she had more "executive presence and spoke with greater conviction," says Dierickx.

The moral of the story: Where you sit influences where you stand. If you take away their Brooks Brothers suits, Manolo Blahnik shoes, and BlackBerrys, managers are little more than naked apes—social mammals with primal methods of expressing group power hierarchies. Over the past few years, psychologists and consultants have begun to decode the secret meaning of office behavior and to understand one of the business world's deepest mysteries: Why do people tend to sit in the same place at routine meetings?

Blame it on the boss. The person with the most power determines how everybody else positions themselves around the typical rectangular or oblong office table. As a rule, leaders like to sit at the end of the table facing the exit so no one can sneak up on them.

From there on, things get quite complicated, according to Sharon Livingston, a clinical psychologist and founder of the Livingston Group, a marketing consultancy. Livingston has met with more than 40,000 people in her career at dozens of large companies and has found that people fit into one of seven personality types based on where they sit, which she explains using the nomenclature borrowed from Snow White's seven dwarves. Those sitting opposite the person leading the meeting tend to be Grumpy or Doc, or a combination of the two, says Livingston. Grumpy is openly argumentative and may be hard to control. Doc is the person who faces off against the leader to show off his or her intelligence.

The person who sits on the leader's right is Happy—a yes-man. In her Web-based questionnaire that quickly determines one's dwarf personality, 59% of the 20,000 people who have taken the test fall in the Happy category. "We've been trained in American society to be helpful and support the leader," says Livingston.

## KEEPING MUM

With an understanding of the psychology of office seating, managers can move people around to improve their chances of influencing them. Managers should, for instance, place potential foes on their right. Suspected brownnosers may offer more frank opinions if they are on the opposite sides of a table.

On the other hand, there's something to be said for ignoring the issue entirely. Some experts, such as leadership consultant Patrick Lencioni, believe that if too many people are worried about where they're sitting it signals a dysfunctional group. "If there's a strong insecurity, people are more aware of all the trappings like, What am I wearing? Where do I sit? When a team is functional and has a high amount of trust, you worry less about those details."

**The Boss** Leaders usually position themselves at the head of a table with their backs to a wall or corner. They like to face the door so they can see newcomers a few seconds ahead of everyone else.

**Left-Hand Manager** A complex position. This person's proximity to power signals support but he or she is likely to be a "yes, but" character. This player agrees in broad principle, then slips in an opposing view.

**Right-Hand Manager** The person who sits to the right of the boss tends to say yes to nearly everything the leader suggests. This manager tends to be focused on the boss instead of materials and others in the room.

**The Middleman** People who sit in the middle of long tables can easily maintain eye contact with most of the others at the table. They are often extroverts and may mediate between those at either side.

**The Sideliner** The person who sits at the corner of the table is often trying to hide in the crowd. He frequently leans back in his chair. He waits to hear others' views before expressing his own.

**The Opponent** Someone who sits directly opposite the leader is typically argumentative, often sitting with arms crossed. This type frequently asks rhetorical questions or finds other ways to announce his or her expertise.

**The Outsider** This person sits away from the group sitting at the table. This can signal that she maintains a "bigger-picture" perspective. Or perhaps she was just too late to get a seat.

## Specific Political Strategies for Power Acquisition

Once it is understood and accepted that contemporary organizations are in reality largely political systems, some very specific strategies can be identified to help organization members more effectively acquire power. For example, one research study found that a supervisor-focused political strategy resulted in higher levels of career success, whereas a job-focused political strategy resulted in lower levels of success.[74] Another taxonomy of political strategies included the following:[75]

1. *Information strategy*—targets political decision makers by providing information through lobbying or supplying position papers or technical reports
2. *Financial incentive strategy*—targets political decision makers by providing financial incentives such as honoraria for speaking or paid travel
3. *Constituency building strategy*[76]—targets political decision makers indirectly through constituent support such as grassroots mobilization of employees, suppliers, customers, or public relations/press conferences

Over the years, various political strategies for gaining power in organizations have been suggested.[77] Table 10.1 gives a representative summary of these strategies. Research is also being done on political tactics. For example, Yukl and Falbe derived eight political, or influence, tactics that are commonly found in today's organizations. These tactics are identified in Table 10.2. Yukl and his colleagues found that the consultation and rational persuasion tactics were used most frequently[78] and along with inspirational appeal were most effective.[79] Some modern organization theorists take more analytical approaches than most of the strategies suggested in Table 10.1 and Table 10.2, and they depend more on concepts such as uncertainty in their political strategies for power. For example, Pfeffer's strategies include managing uncertainty, controlling resources, and building alliances.[80] Others take a more pragmatic approach, such as the analysis that suggests that successful political behavior involves keeping people happy, cultivating contacts, and wheeling and dealing.[81] Law Professor Theresa Beiner coined the term "reindeer games" (from the song "Rudolf

| | |
|---|---|
| **TABLE 10.1**<br>**Political Strategies**<br>**for Attaining Power**<br>**in Organizations** | Taking counsel<br>Maintaining maneuverability<br>Promoting limited communication<br>Exhibiting confidence<br>Controlling access to information and persons<br>Making activities central and nonsubstitutable<br>Creating a sponsor-protégé relationship<br>Stimulating competition among ambitious subordinates<br>Seek out and befriend the most influential individual in a situation<br>Neutralizing potential opposition<br>Making strategic replacements<br>Committing the uncommitted<br>Forming a winning coalition<br>Developing expertise<br>Building personal stature<br>Employing trade-offs<br>Interact with others with the goal of building a positive relationship<br>Using research data to support one's own point of view<br>Restricting communication about real intentions<br>Withdrawing from petty disputes |

**TABLE 10.2**
**Political Tactics Derived from Research**

*Source:* Adapted from Gary Yukl and Cecilia M. Falbe, "Influence Tactics and Objectives in Upward, Downward, and Lateral Influence Attempts," *Journal of Applied Psychology,* Vol. 75, 1990, p. 133. Used with permission.

| Tactics | Description |
|---|---|
| Pressure tactics | Using demands, threats, or intimidation to convince you to comply with a request or to support a proposal. |
| Upward appeals | Persuading you that the request is approved by higher management, or appealing to higher management for assistance in gaining your compliance with the request. |
| Exchange tactics | Making explicit or implicit promises that you will receive rewards or tangible benefits if you comply with a request or support a proposal, or reminding you of a prior favor to be reciprocated. |
| Coalition tactics | Seeking the aid of others to persuade you to do something, or using the support of others as an argument for you to agree also. |
| Ingratiating tactics | Seeking to get you in a good mood or to think favorably of the influence agent before asking you to do something. |
| Rational persuasion | Using logical arguments and factual evidence to persuade you that a proposal or request is viable and likely to result in the attainment of task objectives. |
| Inspirational appeals | Making an emotional request or proposal that arouses enthusiasm by appealing to your values and ideals or by increasing your confidence that you can do it. |
| Consultation tactics | Seeking your participation in making a decision or planning how to implement a proposed policy, strategy, or change. |

the Red-Nosed Reindeer") to describe, like in the song, social activities that provide some, but not all, employees with opportunities to interact with other organization members, which helps build an individual's power base. For example, a boss who invites three male subordinates to play a round of golf and does not include a female subordinate is engaged in a reindeer game that could be considered discriminatory in terms of gaining access to the inner circle of power and influence.[82]

One of the more comprehensive and relevant lists of strategies for modern managers comes from DuBrin.[83] A closer look at a sampling of his and other suggested strategies provides important insights into power and politics in modern organizations.

### Maintain Alliances with Powerful People

As has already been pointed out, the formation of coalitions (alliances) is critical to the acquisition of power in an organization. An obvious coalition would be with members of other important departments or with members of upper-level management. Not so obvious but equally important would be the formation of an alliance with the boss's secretary or staff assistant, that is, someone who is close to the powerful person. An ethnographic study of a city bus company found that a series of dyadic alliances went beyond the formal system and played an important role in getting the work done both within and between departments.[84] For example, alliances between supervisors and certain drivers got the buses out on the worst winter snow days and kept them running during summer vacation periods when drivers were sparse.

### Embrace or Demolish

Machiavellian principles can be applied as strategies in the power game in modern organizations. One management writer has applied these principles to modern corporate life. For example, for corporate takeovers, he draws on Machiavelli to give the following advice:

> The guiding principle is that senior managers in taken-over firms should either be warmly welcomed and encouraged or sacked; because if they are sacked they are powerless, whereas if they are simply downgraded they will remain united and resentful and determined to get their own back.[85]

### Divide and Rule

This widely known political and military strategy can also apply to the acquisition of power in a modern organization. The assumption, sometimes unwarranted, is that those who are divided will not form coalitions themselves. For example, in a business firm the head of finance may generate conflict between marketing and operations in hopes of getting a bigger share of the limited budget from the president of the company.

### Manipulate Classified Information

The observational studies of managerial work have clearly demonstrated the importance of obtaining and disseminating information.[86] The politically astute organization member carefully controls this information in order to gain power. For example, the CIO (chief information officer) may reveal some new pricing information to the design engineer before an important meeting. Now the CIO has gained some power because the engineer owes the CIO a favor. In the Information Age, the amount of information being generated is growing rapidly; how it is managed can provide power. Specifically, knowledge managers such as this CIO can become powerful in today's firms.

### Make a Quick Showing

This strategy involves looking good on some project or task right away in order to get the right people's attention. Once this positive attention is gained, power is acquired to do other, usually more difficult and long-range, projects. For example, an important but often overlooked strategy of a manager trying to get acceptance of a knowledge management program is to show some quick, objective improvements in the quality of a product, service, or process.

### Collect and Use IOUs

This strategy says that the power seeker should do other people favors but should make it clear that they owe something in return and will be expected to pay up when asked. The "Godfather" in the famous book and movie of that name and Tony Soprano of the recent HBO TV series very effectively used this strategy to gain power.

### Avoid Decisive Engagement (Fabianism)

This is a strategy of going slow and easy—an evolutionary rather than a revolutionary approach to change. By not "ruffling feathers," the power seeker can slowly but surely become entrenched and gain the cooperation and trust of others.

### Attacking and Blaming Others

A political tactic some people try is to make others "look bad" in order to make themselves "look good." Blaming and attacking deflects responsibility onto others. It is unethical and unacceptable, but is also a common practice in many organizations.

### Progress One Step at a Time (Camel's Head in the Tent)

This strategy involves taking one step at a time instead of trying to push a whole major project or reorganization attempt. One small change can be a foothold that the power seeker can use as a basis to get other, more major things accomplished.

### *Wait for a Crisis (Things Must Get Worse Before They Get Better)*

This strategy uses the reverse of "no news is good news"; that is, bad news gets attention. For example, many deans in large universities can get the attention of central administration and the board of regents or trustees only when their college is in trouble, for instance, if their accreditation is threatened. Only under these crisis conditions can they get the necessary funding to move their college ahead.

### *Take Counsel with Caution*

This suggested political strategy is concerned more with how to keep power than with how to acquire it. Contrary to the traditional prescriptions concerning participative management and empowerment of employees, this suggests that at least some managers should avoid "opening up the gates" to their people in terms of shared decision making. The idea here is that allowing subordinates to participate and to have this expectation may erode the power of the manager.

### *Be Aware of Resource Dependence*

The most powerful subunits and individuals are those that contribute valuable resources. Controlling the resources other persons or departments need creates considerable bargaining power.

All of these political tactics are part of the games and turf wars that take place in today's organizations. On one level they are inevitable and cannot be prevented. On another, however, they are counterproductive and dysfunctional. They can impede participation and empowerment programs and cause people to waste time and resources. Consequently, many managers believe they must take steps to stop the game playing and turf wars through trust-building and goal-sharing programs.[87] These efforts are especially warranted in a situation in which an organization is undergoing a crisis. Effective crisis management must, at some level, include social-political and technological-structural interventions, mainly aimed at disruptive dysfunctional political agendas of individuals, groups, and/or departments in order to resolve the crisis.[88] Some knowledgeable observers have even suggested that managers would benefit from reading Shakespeare in order to understand the intrigues and intricacies of political tactics used in today's organizations.[89]

## A Final Word on Power and Politics

Obviously, the strategies discussed are only representative, not exhaustive, of the many possible politically based strategies for acquiring power in organizations. Compared to many of the other topics covered in the text, there is relatively less research backup for these ideas on power and, especially, politics.[90] There is also a call for a better framework and guidelines to evaluate the ethics of power and politics in today's organizations. This ethical concern goes beyond the notions of success or effectiveness. For example, of the 10 most unethical activities one study identified, three are directly political: (1) making arrangements with vendors for the purposes of personal gain; (2) allowing differences in pay based on friendships; and (3) hiring, training, and promoting personal favorites rather than those who are most qualified.[91]

To help overcome the negative impact that organizational politics can have on the ethics of an organization, the following guidelines can be used:

1. Keep lines of communication open.
2. Role-model ethical and nonpolitical behaviors.
3. Be wary of game players acting only in their own self-interests.
4. Protect individual privacy interests.
5. Always use the value judgment "Is this fair?"[92]

As one analysis pointed out: "When it comes to the ethics of organizational politics, respect for justice and human rights should prevail for its own sake."[93] There is recent research evidence of the role that the perceptions of organizational politics play in fairness and justice.[94]

Besides the possible ethical implications of power and politics carried to the extreme, there are, as previously mentioned, dysfunctional effects such as morale being weakened, victors and victims being created, and energy and time spent on planning attacks and counterattacks instead of concentrating on getting the job done.[95] There is also evidence that politics may play a large role in both base-pay and incentive-pay decisions,[96] and in one company the power struggles and political gamesmanship were the death knell of a gainsharing plan (see Chapter 4).[97] There is some empirical evidence that those managers who are observed to engage in more political activity are relatively more successful in terms of promotions but are relatively less effective in terms of subordinate satisfaction and commitment and the performance of their unit.[98] There is research evidence that this finding of the importance of political maneuvering in getting ahead in the organization, but detracting from effective performance of the unit, may hold across cultures (at least in Russia).[99]

The dynamics of power continue to evolve. In particular, information technology and the Internet/Intranet provide information access that was not previously available. Organizations with fewer boundaries and wider, even global, access to intellectual capital have political systems and processes that are altered considerably.[100] Also, the ups and recently the extreme downs of the economy in both the United States and the rest of the world have dramatically changed traditional power bases and processes. In the current social environment, many employees are as interested in jobs with meaning as they are with scoring political points and gaining power. As indicated earlier, this seems especially true of today's younger generation who seem more interested in economic control than in control over people or in status and climbing the corporate ladder.[101] In other words, today's organizational participants' passion for the good life and meaning may be replacing their ruthless search for power.[102]

One thing about power and politics, however, remains certain: modern, complex organizations tend to create a climate that promotes power seeking and political maneuvering. And, in today's environment, these political activities extend beyond the traditional boundaries of an organization. For example, Microsoft learned, the hard way, that ingratiation political tactics may have been much more successful than simply trying to bully government regulators when antitrust law violations were being investigated. Other important firms such as Google are learning from Microsoft's mistakes; it makes sense to investigate and carefully implement the best political approach when seeking to deal with outside agencies and individuals who could alter or harm a firm's inside operations and growth.[103] Power and politics are a fact of modern organizational life, and it is hoped that more future research will help managers better understand their dynamics, meaning, and successful application.

## Summary

This chapter examines one of the most important and realistic dynamics of organizational behavior—power and politics. *Power* and *politics* have a number of different meanings. Power can be distinguished from authority and influence, but most definitions subsume all three concepts. Most of the attention given to power over the years has centered on the French and Raven classic categories of social power types: reward, coercive, legitimate, referent, and expert. More recently, some contingency models for power have been developed that take into consideration the influenceability of the targets of power (that is, their dependency, uncertainty, personality, intelligence, gender, age, and culture). Overall contingency models are also beginning to emerge. Closely related to the contingency models of the French and Raven power types is the view of power by McClelland. He suggests that there are two faces of power: negative personal power and positive social power. Finally, the special case of empowerment is given attention. This popular approach goes beyond merely delegating authority to make decisions to include participation, innovation, access to information, and accountability/responsibility.

Politics is very closely related to power. This chapter gives particular attention to a political perspective of power in modern organizations, in terms of resources, decisions, goals, technology, external environment, and change, and to strategies for the acquisition of power. Some specific political strategies are to maintain alliances with powerful people, embrace or demolish, divide and rule, manipulate classified information, make a quick showing, collect and use IOUs, avoid decisive engagement, attacking and blaming others, progress one step at a time, wait for a crisis, take counsel with caution, and be aware of resource dependence. Above all, it should be remembered that, although there may be some changes on the importance and how to attain and use it, both power and politics represent the realities of modern organizational life. The study of these important dynamics can significantly improve the understanding of organizational behavior.

# Ending with Meta-Analytic Research Findings
## OB PRINCIPLE FOR EVIDENCED-BASED PRACTICE

Individualistic cultural values result in less conformity in the power and politics of organizations.

### Meta-Analysis Results:

[133 studies; 4,627 participants; $d = .41$]. *On average, there is a **61 percent probability** that strong individualistic cultural values will result in lower levels of conformity in the power and politics of organizations than when individualistic cultural values are weak (i.e., collectivist cultural values dominate).* Moderator analyses revealed that within just the United States, the larger the size of the majority and the greater the proportion of female respondents, the stronger the conformity. Interestingly, levels of conformity have declined in the United States since the 1950s when the infamous "organization man" and the "man in the gray flannel suit" dominated the power and politics of large corporations.

### Conclusion:

As discussed in this chapter, there are many dynamic complexities involved in organizational power and politics. One such dimension is conformity. The power to gain acceptance and cooperation through conforming to group and/or organizational norms can make a functional contribution to organizational effectiveness. However, conformity can also be mind numbing and dysfunctional in terms of stifling innovation or going along with unethical decisions. Powerful, politically astute managers must be able to read and make a fit with the prevailing cultural values in order to use or minimize conformity. Participants may feel a certain pressure to conform even at the expense of their better judgment or ethical standards. Although the pressure to conform appears to have declined in the United States over the decades, it still seems to be a product of cultural values. Certain societies do not tolerate dissidence and stress collective thought and action. Others foster values of independence and freedom of ideas. From a power and politics perspective, conformity can be either a strength or a weakness for the effectiveness of organizations. Conformity can contribute to the power of a manager, and a political strategy is to attain conformity to desired standards and ways of behaving.

**Source:** Adapted from Rod Bond and Peter B. Smith, "Culture and Conformity: A Meta-Analysis of Studies Using Asch's (1952b, 1956) Line Judgement Task," *Psychological Bulletin,* Vol. 119, No. 1, 1993, pp. 111–137.

## Questions for Discussion and Review

1. How would you define *power* in your own words? How does power differ from authority? From influence?
2. Identify, briefly summarize, and give some realistic examples of each of the French and Raven power types.
3. Using the Kelman contingency model of power and influence, who would you use to advertise products in the fall, winter, spring, and summer? Explain your choices.
4. Describe employee empowerment, giving specific attention to its operationalization and implications for effective outcomes. How, if at all, is empowerment related to traditional delegation? To social power?
5. In the chapter it is stated: "The political power game is very real in today's organizations." Explain this statement in terms of the discussion in the chapter and any firsthand experience you have had to verify it.
6. Identify three or four of the political strategies that are discussed in the chapter. Explain how these might actually help someone acquire power in today's organization.

## Internet Exercise: The Uses and Abuses of Power

For background on sources of power, see **http://www.mhhe.com/business/ management/management_tutor_series/sourcesOfPower/index.html.** With the classic French and Raven five sources of power discussed in this chapter as the framework, how can some jobs effectively use one or more of these five types to be more or less effective? For example, an airline captain may be much more effective by having high levels of legitimate and expert power. A different type or style of manager, such as a new product design team leader, may be more effective by having high levels of referent power, but be ineffective with use of legitimate power. You might look under some of the job listings for managers at such sites as **http://www.monster.com** or America's Job Bank at **http://www.ajb.dni.us/** to get some examples of specific jobs to analyze in terms of power.

1. For each of the five types of power, list a specific job listing found on the Web that would benefit from its use.
2. Consider managers (supervisors) that you have worked for in the past. What type of power did they have? Was it effective?
3. If you could be strong in one power category, which type would it be? Does this depend on the organization you work for? Why or why not?

# Real Case: *Fighting Back*

One of the areas in which organizations are finding power to be an extremely important consideration in today's knowledge management is the protection of intellectual property, specifically patent protection. When a firm secures a patent, it gains knowledge power over the marketplace. However, if this patent cannot be defended against violators, it has little value. A good example of a patent protection battle is that of Fusion Systems, a small, high-tech American firm, and Mitsubishi, the giant Japanese conglomerate.

Several years ago, Fusion developed a core technology that allowed it to manufacture high-intensity ultraviolet lamps powered by 500 to 6,000 watts of microwave energy. The company obtained patents in the United States, Europe, and Japan. One of its first big orders came from the Adolph Coors Company for lamp systems to dry the printed decoration on beer cans. Other customers included Hitachi, IBM, 3M, Motorola, Sumitomo, Toshiba, NEC, and Mitsubishi. The last purchased Fusion's lamp system and immediately sent it to the research and development lab to be reverse engineered. Once Mitsubishi had stripped down the product, it began filing patent applications that copied and surrounded Fusion's high-intensity microwave lamp technology. Fusion was unaware of what was going on until it began investigating and found that Mitsubishi had filed nearly 300 patent applications directly related to its own lamp technology. When Fusion tried to settle the matter through direct negotiations, the firm was unsuccessful. In addition, Mitsubishi hired the Stanford Research Institute to study the matter and the Institute concluded that the Japanese company's position was solid. However, the chairman of the applied physics department at Columbia University, who was hired by Fusion, disagreed and—after reviewing the patent materials from both companies—concluded that Mitsubishi had relied heavily on technology developed at Fusion and that Mitsubishi's lamp represented no significant additional breakthrough.

Mitsubishi then offered Fusion a deal: Mitsubishi would not sue Fusion for patent infringement if Fusion would pay Mitsubishi a royalty for the privilege of using "its" patents in Japan. Mitsubishi would then get a royalty-free, worldwide cross-license of all of Fusion's technology. Fusion responded by going to the Office of the U.S. Trade Representative and getting help. The company also found a sympathetic ear from the Senate Finance Committee and the House Republican Task Force on Technology Transfer, as well as from the secretary of commerce and the American ambassador to Japan. As the dispute was dragged through the courts, Mitsubishi began to give ground in the face of political pressure. At the same time, Fusion continued to develop innovations in its core field of expertise and remains the leader in both Japanese and worldwide markets. The company believes that as long as it maintains the exclusive rights to this technology, competitors will not be able to erode its market power.

1. What type of power does a patent provide to a company? Is this the same kind of power that people within a firm attempt to gain?
2. What types of political strategies has Mitsubishi used to try to gain power over Fusion? Using the material in Table 10.1, identify and describe three.
3. How has Fusion managed to retaliate successfully? Using the material in Table 10.2, identify and describe three tactics it has employed.

# Organizational Behavior Case: *Throwing Away a Golden Opportunity*

Roger Allen was a man on the move. Everyone in the firm felt that someday he would be company president. To listen to his boss, Harry Walden, it was only a matter of time before Roger would be at the helm.

The current president of the firm was a marketing person. She had worked her way up from field salesperson to president by selling both the product and her competency to customers and the company alike. In a manner of speaking, the marketing department was the "well-oiled" road to the top. Roger was the number-one salesperson and, according to the grapevine, was due to get Harry Walden's job when the latter retired in two years. However, Roger was not sure that he wanted to be vice president of marketing. Another slot was opening up in international sales. Roger knew nothing about selling to Europe, but this was the firm's first venture outside the United States, and he thought he might like to give it a try. He talked to Harry about it, but the vice president tried to discourage him. In fact, Harry seemed to think that Roger was crazy to consider the job at all. "Rog," he said, "that's no place for you. Things are soft and cozy back here. You don't have to prove yourself to anyone. You're number one around here. Just sit tight and you'll be president. Don't go out and make some end runs. Just keep barreling up the middle for four yards on each carry, and you'll score the big touchdown." Roger was not convinced. He thought perhaps it would be wise to discuss the matter with the president herself. This he did. The president was very interested in Roger's ideas about international marketing. "If you really think you'd like to head up this office for us, I'll recommend you for the job."

After thinking the matter over carefully, Roger decided that he would much rather go to Europe and try to help establish a foothold over there than sit back and wait for the stateside opening. He told his decision to Harry. "Harry, I've talked to the president, and she tells me that this new opening in international sales is really going to get a big push from the company. It's where the action is. I realize that I could sit back and take it easy for the next couple of years, but I think I'd rather have the international job." Harry again told Roger that he was making a mistake. "You're throwing away a golden opportunity. However, if you want it, I'll support you."

A week later, when the company selected someone else from sales to head the international division, Roger was crushed. The president explained the situation to him in this way: "I thought you wanted the job and I pushed for you. However, the other members of the selection committee voted against me. I can tell you that you certainly didn't sell Harry very strongly on your idea. He led the committee to believe that you were really undecided about the entire matter. In fact, I felt rather foolish telling them how excited you were about the whole thing, only to have Harry say he'd talked to you since that time and you weren't that sure at all. When Harry got done, the committee figured you had changed your mind after talking to me, and they went on to discuss other likely candidates."

1. Who had power in this organization? What type of power did Harry Walden have?
2. Do you think Roger played company politics well? If so, why didn't he get the international sales job?
3. At this point, what would you do if you were Roger? What political strategies could be used?

# Chapter **Eleven**

# Groups and Teams

## Learning Objectives

- **Describe** the basic nature of groups: the dynamics of group formation and the various types of groups.
- **Discuss** the implications that research on groups has for the practice of evidence-based management.
- **Explain** the important dynamics of informal groups and organizations.
- **Analyze** the impact of groupthink.
- **Present** the team concept and its practice.

This chapter approaches organizational behavior dynamics from the perspective of the group—both informal and formal—and the popular team concept and practice. The first section examines the way groups are formed, the various types of groups, some of the dynamics and functions of groups, and the findings of research on groups. The next section explores the dynamics of informal roles and organization. This discussion is followed by an analysis of the impact of groupthink. The balance of the chapter is devoted specifically to teams. The distinction is made between work groups and teams, and specific attention is devoted to self-managed and cross-functional teams. The way to make these teams more effective through training and evaluation is discussed.

## THE NATURE OF GROUPS

The group is widely recognized as an important sociological and social psychological unit of analysis in the study of organizational behavior.[1] Studying groups is especially valuable when the dynamics are analyzed. Group dynamics are the interactions and forces among group members in social situations. When the concept is applied to the study of organizational behavior, the focus is on the dynamics of members of both formal or informal work groups and, now, teams in the organization.

The use of work groups and teams is soaring. Although they were first used in corporate giants such as Toyota, Motorola, General Mills, and General Electric, surveys now indicate that virtually all organizations use groups and teams to varying degrees. Yet, as with many other areas of organizational behavior, the study and application of groups and teams are receiving increased research attention to make them more effective.

A recent review of this group/team literature concluded that "considerable theoretical and empirical progress has been made on this topic, with an underlying focus on understanding and modeling anticipated benefits, in terms of both motivation/satisfaction and performance."[2] However, despite this progress, there are still many challenges remaining in understanding and effectively using groups and teams in today's and future organizations. For example, today's economic and social environment surrounding groups is rapidly changing. In the social environment, Generation Xers and now what are called the "Echo Generation" (the offspring of the now aging "Baby Boomers") may be difficult to manage in groups because they have low needs for group affiliation, high needs for individual achievement, and "doing their own thing." The solution may be found in the careful construction of rewards and performance measures in order to obtain cooperation and collaboration.[3] After first providing the basic foundation for understanding all aspects of groups, the remainder of the chapter will focus on teams in today's workplace.

## The Meaning of a Group and Group Dynamics

Instead of quickly moving to teams per se, the discussion begins with groups and their dynamics, an understanding of which is basic to the field of organizational behavior. The term *group* can be defined in a number of different ways, depending on the perspective that is taken. A comprehensive definition would say that if a group exists in an organization, its members:

1. Are motivated to join
2. Perceive the group as a unified unit of interacting people
3. Contribute in various amounts to the group processes (that is, some people contribute more time or energy to the group than do others)
4. Reach agreements and have disagreements through various forms of interaction[4]

Just as there is no one definition of the term *group,* there is no universal agreement on what is meant by *group dynamics.* Although Kurt Lewin, widely recognized as the father of group dynamics, popularized the term in the 1930s, through the years different connotations have been attached to it. One normative view is that group dynamics describes *how* a group *should* be organized and conducted. Democratic leadership, member participation, and overall cooperation are stressed. Another view of group dynamics is that it consists of a set of *techniques.* Here, role playing, brainstorming, focus groups, leaderless groups, group therapy, sensitivity training, team building, transactional analysis, and the Johari window are traditionally equated with group dynamics, as are the more modern self-managed and virtual teams. An example of a recent group technique is called "creative abrasion," which is the search for a clash of ideas rather than "personal abrasion," or the clash of people. The goal here is to develop greater creativity from the group.[5] A third view is the closest to Lewin's original conception. Group dynamics are viewed from the perspective of the internal nature of groups, how they form, their structure and processes, and how they function and affect individual members, other groups, and the organization. The following sections are devoted to this third view of group dynamics and set the stage for the discussion of work teams.

## The Dynamics of Group Formation

Why do individuals form into groups? Before discussion of some very practical reasons, it would be beneficial to examine briefly some of the classic social psychology theories of group formation, or why people affiliate with one another. The most basic theory explaining affiliation is *propinquity.* This interesting word means simply that individuals affiliate with one another because of spatial or geographical proximity. The theory would predict that students sitting next to one another in class, for example, are more likely to form into a group than are students sitting at opposite ends of the room. In an organization, employees who work in the same area of the plant or office or managers with offices close to one another would more probably form into groups than would those who are not physically located together. There is some research evidence to support the propinquity theory, and on the surface it has a great deal of merit for explaining group formation. The drawback is that it is not analytical and does not begin to explain some of the complexities of group formation and the modern development of globalization and electronic, online networking and telecommunicating (i.e., virtual teams that are linked in cyberspace rather than physical proximity). These recent developments give new meaning to spatial or geographic proximity. Some theoretical and practical reasons for group formation need to be further explored.

### *Theories of Group Formation*

A more comprehensive theory of group formation than mere propinquity comes from the classic theory of George Homans based on activities, interactions, and sentiments.[6] These three elements are directly related to one another. The more activities persons share, the more numerous will be their interactions and the stronger will be their sentiments (how much the other persons are liked or disliked); the more interactions among persons, the more will be their shared activities and sentiments; and the more sentiments persons have for one another, the more will be their shared activities and interactions. This theory lends a great deal to the understanding of group formation and process. The major element is *interaction.* Persons in a group interact with one another not just in the physical propinquity sense or increasingly electronically, but also to accomplish many group goals through cooperation and problem solving.

There are many other theories that attempt to explain group formation. Most often they are only partial theories, but they are generally additive in nature. One of the more comprehensive is Theodore Newcomb's classic *balance theory* of group formation.[7] The theory states that persons are attracted to one another on the basis of similar attitudes toward commonly relevant objects and goals. Figure 11.1 shows this balance theory. Individual X will interact and form a relationship/group with individual Y because of common attitudes and values (Z). Once this relationship is formed, the participants strive to maintain a symmetrical balance between the attraction and the common attitudes. If an imbalance occurs, an attempt is made to restore the balance. If the balance cannot be restored, the relationship dissolves. Both propinquity and interaction play a role in balance theory.

Still another theoretical approach to group formation from social psychology is *exchange theory.*[8] Similar to its functioning as a work-motivation theory, discussed in

**FIGURE 11.1**
**A Balance Theory of Group Formation**

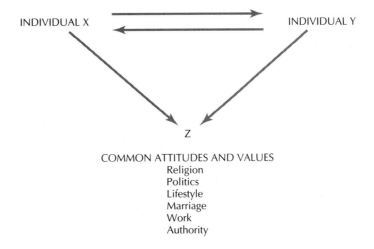

INDIVIDUAL X                    INDIVIDUAL Y

Z

COMMON ATTITUDES AND VALUES
Religion
Politics
Lifestyle
Marriage
Work
Authority

Chapter 6, exchange theory of groups is based on reward-cost outcomes of interaction. A minimum positive level (rewards greater than costs) of an outcome must exist in order for attraction or affiliation to take place. Rewards from interactions gratify needs, whereas costs incur anxiety, frustration, embarrassment, or fatigue. Propinquity, interaction, and common attitudes all have roles in exchange theory.

Besides these classic social psychology explanations for group formation, there are also some generally recognized identifiable stages of group development.[9] These well-known stages can be briefly summarized as follows:

1. *Forming.* This initial stage is marked by uncertainty and even confusion. Group members are not sure about the purpose, structure, task, or leadership of the group.

2. *Storming.* This stage of development, as indicated by the term, is characterized by conflict and confrontation. (In the usually emotionally charged atmosphere, there may be considerable disagreement and conflict among the members about roles and duties.)

3. *Norming.* Finally, in this stage the members begin to settle into cooperation and collaboration. They have a "we" feeling with high cohesion, group identity, and camaraderie.

4. *Performing.* This is the stage where the group is fully functioning and devoted to effectively accomplishing the tasks agreed on in the norming stage.

5. *Adjourning.* This represents the end of the group, which in ongoing, permanent groups will never be reached. However, for project teams or task forces with a specific objective, once the objective is accomplished, the group will disband or have a new composition, and the stages will start over again.

### Practicalities of Group Formation

Besides the conceptual explanations for group formation and development, there are some very practical reasons for joining and/or forming a group. For instance, employees in an organization may form a group for economic, security, or social reasons. Economically, workers may form a group to work on a project that is paid for on a group-incentive plan such as gainsharing (covered in Chapter 4),[10] or they may form a union to demand higher wages. For security, joining a group provides the individual with a united front in combating indiscriminant, unilateral treatment. For example, one study found that minority employees' obtaining membership in a network group proved to be useful in retaining them.[11] However, the most important practical reason individuals join or form groups is that groups tend to satisfy the very intense social needs of most people. Workers, in particular, generally have a very strong desire for affiliation. This need is met by belonging to a group or becoming a member of a team. Research going as far back as the Hawthorne studies revealed that the affiliation motive has a major impact on human behavior in organizations, and social identity and effectiveness as an important group process in organizations has been verified over the years.[12]

An alternative model that has more recently been proposed as an explanation for group formation processes is called the *punctuated equilibrium model.*[13] According to this approach, groups form in a first phase in which a target or mission is set and then are not altered very easily, due to a process called inertia, or systematic resistance to change. At some midpoint, the second phase begins. This phase commences when group members suddenly recognize that if they don't change tactics, the group's goal or mission will not be accomplished. This "midlife crisis" in the group's existence is exemplified by changes made in tactics followed by bursts of activity and energy designed to complete the task. The name of the model is derived from the equilibrium that exists in the first half of the group's life and the punctuated efforts and behavioral modifications in the second phase. Although there is just preliminary research on the punctuated equilibrium model, it has considerable intuitive appeal based on the common experiences most people have had in working on group projects.

Models of the dynamics of group formation and functioning should progress further when issues such as demographic diversity and globalization are incorporated. One analysis noted that "fault lines" within groups may form around individual member characteristics and lead to subgroup conflicts among members.[14] Diversity is the primary source of differences in member characteristics leading to such conflict. Another study found that at first greater demographic heterogeneity led to group norms emphasizing lower cooperation. However, over time, if team norms among those more demographically different from their work group changed more, then the norms became more cooperative as a function of contact with other members.[15] On the international front, another study notes that group efficacy (see Chapter 7 on efficacy, conceptually close to what is termed "collective efficacy" or "group potency") or the group's belief in its ability to perform effectively, as well as actual performance, may be impacted by intercultural variables such as collectivism and task uncertainty.[16] Further, there may be a relationship between personal self-efficacy and collective efficacy. For example, one study by Bandura and his colleagues revealed that socioeconomic status enhanced perceived personal self-efficacy, which in turn contributed substantially to a sense of collective efficacy to effect social change through unified action.[17]

## Types of Groups

There are numerous types of groups. The theories of group formation that were just discussed are based partly on the attraction between two persons—the simple dyad group. Of course, in the real world groups are usually much more complex than the dyad. There are small and large groups, primary and secondary groups, coalitions, membership and reference groups, in- and out-groups, and formal and informal groups. Each type has different characteristics and different effects on its members.

### *Primary Groups*

Often the terms *small group* and *primary group* are used interchangeably. Technically, there is a difference. A small group has to meet only the criterion of small size. Usually no attempt is made to assign precise numbers, but the accepted criterion is that the group must be small enough for fairly constant interaction and communication to occur face-to-face or, in recent times, electronically. In addition to being small, a primary group must have a feeling of comradeship, loyalty, and a common sense of values among its members. Thus, all primary groups are small groups, but not all small groups are primary groups.

Two examples of a primary group are the family and the peer group. Initially, the primary group was limited to a socializing group, but then a broader conception was given impetus by the results of the Hawthorne studies (see Chapter 1). Work groups definitely have primary group qualities. Research findings point out the tremendous impact that the primary group has on individual behavior, regardless of context or environmental conditions. An increasing number of companies have begun to use the power of primary groups by organizing employees into *self-managed teams.* Importantly, these teams are natural work groups with all the dynamics described so far. The team members work together to perform a function or produce a product or service. Because they are self-managing, they also perform functions such as planning, organizing, and controlling the work. For example, at 3M self-managed teams are empowered to take corrective actions to resolve day-to-day problems; they also have direct access to information that allows them to plan, control, and improve their operations. Importantly, however, such self-managed teams do not necessarily always make consensus decisions. As one executive recently observed:

> My feeling is that you try to make a decision by consensus, you water it down to the lowest level. Virtually none of our decisions are consensus—even choosing where to go for dinner, because I can't get everyone to agree. The bar is: Can you live with it?[18]

The last part of the chapter discusses this team concept and practice in detail.

### Coalitions

Although recent research indicates that the social structure will affect the increasingly popular strategic alliance formation patterns between organizations,[19] at a more micro level, coalitions of individuals and groups within organizations have long been recognized as an important dimension of group dynamics. Although the concept of coalition is used in different ways by different theorists, a comprehensive review of the coalition literature suggests that the following characteristics of a coalition be included:[20]

1. Interacting group of individuals
2. Deliberately constructed by the members for a specific purpose
3. Independent of the formal organization's structure
4. Lacking a formal internal structure
5. Mutual perception of membership
6. Issue-oriented to advance the purposes of the members
7. External forms
8. Concerted member action, act as a group

Although the preceding have common characteristics with other types of groups, coalitions are separate, usually very powerful, and often effective entities in organizations. For example, a study found that employees in a large organization formed into coalitions to overcome petty conflicts and ineffective management in order to get the job done.[21]

### Other Types of Groups

Besides primary groups and coalitions, there are also other classifications of groups that are important to the study of organizational behavior. Two important distinctions are between membership and reference groups and between in-groups and out-groups. These differences can be summarized by noting that membership groups are those to which the individual actually belongs. An example would be membership in a craft union. Reference groups are those to which an individual would like to belong—those he or she identifies with. An example would be a prestigious social group. In-groups are those who have or share the dominant values, and out-groups are those on the outside looking in. All these types of groups have relevance to the study of organizational behavior, but the formal and informal types are most directly applicable.

There are many formally designated work groups, such as committees, in the modern organization. The functional departmental committees (finance, marketing, operations, and human resources) and now cross-functional teams are examples, as are standing committees such as the public affairs committee, grievance committee, executive committee, and even the board of directors.[22] In today's mergers and acquisitions environment and global economy, a new type of committee or team has emerged. Called "factional" groups or teams, these have members that come from a limited number (usually just two) of entities such as merger integration teams, bilateral task forces, and joint venture teams.[23] When these formal committees meet, they are often frustrating to the members. In fact, one survey found only 42 percent felt that the meetings were productive.[24] To get around some of these problems, in recent years the perspective and function of such groups have shifted to teams that have now become the most important type of group in today's organizations.

Informal groups form for political, friendship, or common interest reasons. For political purposes, the informal group may form to attempt to get its share of rewards and/or limited resources. Friendship groups may form on the job and carry on outside the workplace. Common interests in sports or ways to get back at management can also bind members into an informal group. The dynamics of these informal groups are examined in more detail in an upcoming section.

## Implications from Research on Group and Team Dynamics

Starting with the Hawthorne studies discussed in Chapter 1, significant research has been abundant on groups and teams that indirectly contribute to the better understanding of organizational behavior.[25] In general, it can be concluded from research over the years that groups have a positive impact on both individual employee effectiveness (help learn about the organization and one's self, gain new skills, obtain rewards not available to individuals, and fulfill important social needs) and organizational effectiveness (strength in numbers of ideas and skills, improved decision making and control, and facilitating change as well as organizational stability).[26]

In addition to the somewhat general conclusions, there are also more specific research findings from social psychology that seem to have particular relevance to organizational behavior. For example, a meta-analysis of a number of studies over the years found that group cohesiveness has a highly significant positive effect on performance.[27] However, of even more importance to group performance may be leadership. For example, a highly cohesive group that is given positive leadership may have the highest possible productivity. On the other side of the coin, a highly cohesive group that is given poor leadership may have the lowest possible productivity.[28] A highly cohesive group is analogous to a time bomb in the hands of management. The direction in which the highly cohesive group goes, breaking production records or severely restricting output, depends on how it is led. The low-cohesive group is much safer in the hands of management. Leadership will not have a serious negative or positive impact on this group. However, the implication is that if management wishes to maximize productivity, it must build a cohesive group and give it proper leadership and, importantly, over time this highly cohesive group may become self-managing.

Recent work by widely recognized groups expert Richard Hackman supports this important role that leadership plays in group performance. In Hackman's book summarizing his extensive research, he notes: "work teams can, and sometimes do, perform much better than traditionally designed units. But they also can, and sometimes do, perform much worse."[29] He concludes that there is no magical solution for group effectiveness, but the leader can create the conditions that promote group effectiveness. Specifically, these conditions (induction) the leader can control include (1) setting a compelling direction for the group's work; (2) designing and enabling group structure; (3) ensuring that the group operates within a supportive context; and (4) providing expert coaching.[30] Other recent research studies also support the impact that leadership can have in work-group performance.[31]

In other words, Hackman's and others' theory-building and field research findings indicate there are some interesting insights and points of departure for organizational behavior analysis that can come out of classic social psychology theories and research. The same is true for the historically important Hawthorne studies, where both the relay room operatives and the bank wirers were highly cohesive work groups. As is brought out in Chapter 1, a possible explanation of why one highly cohesive work group (the relay room

**TABLE 11.1**
**Factors That Increase and Decrease Group Cohesiveness**

*Source:* Adapted from Andrew D. Szilagyi, Jr., and Marc J. Wallace, Jr., *Organizational Behavior and Performance,* 5th ed., Scott, Foresman/Little, Brown, Glenview, Ill., 1990, pp. 282–283.

| Factors That Increase Group Cohesiveness | Factors That Decrease Group Cohesiveness |
|---|---|
| Agreement on group goals | Disagreement on goals |
| Frequency of interaction | Large group size |
| Personal attractiveness | Unpleasant experiences |
| Intergroup competition | Intragroup competition |
| Favorable evaluation | Domination by one or more members |

workers) produced at a very high level and the other highly cohesive group (the bank wirers) produced at a very low rate is the type of supervision (or leadership) that was applied. In other words, both leadership and group dynamics factors, such as cohesiveness, can have an important impact on group performance in organizations. Table 11.1 briefly summarizes some of the major factors that can increase and decrease group cohesiveness. In addition to the leadership implications, there are some recent research findings regarding the effects of time on group cohesion. In one study, a longer time together gave group members the opportunity to engage in meaningful interactions. Importantly, for today's environment for groups, surface-level diversity issues (age, gender, race differences) were found to weaken over time, whereas deep-level diversity differences (attitudes and values) became stronger.[32]

## Group/Team Effectiveness

Besides the basic research coming out of social psychology, a more applied focus on the impact that groups/teams have on employee behavior, especially the contribution to satisfaction and performance, has also received attention. The following is an overall summary of the way to use groups to enhance satisfaction and performance:[33]

1. Organizing work around intact groups
2. Having groups charged with selection, training, and rewarding of members
3. Using groups to enforce strong norms for behavior, with group involvement in off-the-job as well as on-the-job behavior
4. Distributing resources on a group rather than an individual basis
5. Allowing and perhaps even promoting intergroup rivalry so as to build within-group solidarity

A review of the research literature determined three factors that seem to play the major role in determining group effectiveness: (1) task interdependence (how closely group members work together); (2) outcome interdependence (whether and how group performance is rewarded); and (3) potency (members' belief that the group can be effective).[34]

To assess group or team effectiveness first requires careful specification of criteria. Effective groups are characterized as being dependable, making reliable connections between the parts, and targeting the direction and goals of the organization. This is accomplished when members "buy in," achieve coordination, have the desired impact, and exhibit the kind of vitality that sustains the organization over time as the environment shifts or changes.[35] Factors that affect the success level of any given group include the type of task being performed and the composition of the group itself. Teams with self-leadership have been found to have varying levels of success, depending on whether the group's task is primarily conceptual or primarily behavioral in nature.[36] The composition of the group has been found to be optimal when there is a mix of member types. Groups with only one type, such as task "shapers" (those who define group tasks) are less successful than those with shapers, coordinators, completer-finishers, and team players.[37] Another recent study on group composition found that members who had higher cognitive ability, achievement, and openness had superior performance.[38]

Well-known leadership guru Warren Bennis argues that effective groups have shared dreams and manage conflict by abandoning individual egos in the pursuit of a dream. They also are protected from the "suits," or corporate leaders, have real or invented enemies, see themselves as underdogs who are winning, and pay a personal price to succeed.[39] Their leaders provide direction, meaning, trust, and hope and display a bias toward action, risk taking, and urgency. Others suggest that "hot groups," those that accomplish breakthrough performance, are ones in which members see distinction and importance in their work, that the tasks captivate members, and that the tasks take priority over interpersonal relationships. Building hot groups requires less micromanaging, more informal (as opposed to formal) feedback, and role modeling of successful hot group behaviors by experienced members working with other new groups. Leadership in this approach is less intrusive and emphasizes group rather than individual rewards, and, as a result, groups can "turn on a dime" and get things done more quickly.[40]

Some aspects of effectiveness may be influenced by how groups form. When they are established, social comparisons and competition exist between members. These may have an impact on the organizational citizenship behaviors (see Chapter 5) exhibited by group members. Citizenship behaviors include altruism, conscientiousness (or being a "good soldier"), courtesy, sportsmanship, and civic virtue, which are also involved in looking out for the welfare of the group and the organization. Perceptions of fairness[41] and group norms,[42] in group practices may impact such citizenship behaviors, which in turn help maintain the group's performance levels.

Group effectiveness may also be influenced by the conditions of adaptation to nonroutine events. Previous group literature suggested three behaviors as keys to adapting to unusual circumstances or events: (1) information collection and transfer, (2) task prioritization, and (3) task distribution. In one study of airline crews using flight simulations, it was found that the timing of key adaptive group behaviors was more strongly associated with performance than the behaviors themselves.[43] In other words, information must be collected at the right time, prioritized properly, and tasks divided in a frame that allows for successful adaptation to unusual events.

# THE DYNAMICS OF INFORMAL GROUPS

Besides the formally designated groups and teams, as indicated, informal groups in the workplace also play a significant role in the dynamics of organizational behavior. The major difference between formal and informal groups is that the formal group has officially prescribed goals and relationships, whereas the informal one does not. Despite this distinction, it is a mistake to think of formal and informal groups as two distinctly separate entities. The two types of groups coexist and are inseparable. Every formal organization has informal groups, and every informal organization eventually evolves some semblance of formal groups.

## Norms and Roles in Informal Groups

With the exception of a single social act such as extending a hand on meeting or responding to an e-mail or text message, the smallest units of analysis in group dynamics are norms and roles. Many behavioral scientists make a point of distinguishing between the two units, but conceptually they are very similar. *Norms* are the "oughts" of behavior. They are prescriptions for acceptable behavior determined by the group. Norms will be strongly enforced by work groups if they:

1. Aid in group survival and provision of benefits
2. Simplify or make predictable the behavior expected of group members
3. Help the group avoid embarrassing interpersonal problems
4. Express the central values or goals of the group and clarify what is distinctive about the group's identity[44]

A role consists of a pattern of norms; the use of the term in organizations is directly related to its theatrical use. A role is a position that can be acted out by an individual. The content of a given role is prescribed by the prevailing norms. Probably *role* can best be defined as a position that has expectations evolving from established norms. Some informal roles found in work groups include the following:

1. The *boundary spanner* who acts as a facilitator and bridge between units or groups which would not otherwise interact.
2. The *buffer* who protects and filters negative or disappointing news or information that might cause group members to be upset and cause morale to suffer.
3. The *lobbyist* who promotes and tells others how successful and important the group is to outsiders.
4. The *negotiator* who is empowered by the group to act on its behalf to get resources and make deals.
5. The *spokesperson* who is the voice of the group.[45]

These informal roles wield considerable power in organizations and are recognized by effective managers. As indicated in the accompanying OB in Action: The Office Chart That Really Counts, an increasing number of firms and their managers are determining informal networks to assist them.[46]

## The Informal Organization

Like the formal organization, the informal organization has both functions and dysfunctions. In contrast to formal organization analysis, the dysfunctional aspects of informal organization have received more attention than the functional ones. For example, conflicting objectives, restriction of output, conformity, blocking of ambition, inertia, and resistance to change are frequently mentioned dysfunctions of the informal organization. More recently, however, organizational analysis has begun to recognize the functional aspects as well. For example, the following list suggests some practical benefits that can be derived from the informal organization:[47]

1. Makes for a more effective total system
2. Lightens the workload on management
3. Fills in gaps in a manager's abilities
4. Provides a safety valve for employee emotions
5. Improves communication

Because of the inevitability and power of the informal organization, the functions should be exploited in the attainment of objectives rather than futilely combated by management. As one analysis of leadership points out: "Informal social networks exert an immense influence which sometimes overrides the formal hierarchy. . . . Leadership goes beyond a person's formal position into realms of informal, hidden, or unauthorized influence."[48]

Two years ago, Ken Loughridge, an information technology manager living in Cheshire, England, uprooted his family and moved to the other side of the world. His company, engineering and environmental consulting firm MWH Global, was reorganizing its various information technology offices into a single global division, establishing its main service center on New Zealand's more cost-effective shores and promoting Loughridge to manage the company's worldwide network, system, and desktop needs. "By and large, the staff I'd adopted were strangers," he says.

To help adjust to his new surroundings, Loughridge took a map with him. A map of his organization, that is. A few months before, MWH had surveyed its IT employees, asking them which colleagues they consulted most frequently, who they turned to for expertise, and who either boosted or drained their energy levels. Their answers were analyzed in a software program and then plotted as a web of interconnecting nodes and lines representing people and relationships. Looking a little like an airline's hub-and-spoke route maps, the web offered Loughridge a map—a corporate X-ray, in a sense—to how work really got done among his charges. It helped him visualize the invisible, informal connections between people that are missing on a traditional organizational chart.

Loughridge used the map to identify well-connected technical experts he should immediately visit face-to-face. And six months into the job, when a key manager in the Asia region left the company, he referred back to it, reaching out to the departed managers' closest contacts to help minimize the fallout. "It's as if you took the top off an ant hill and could see where there's a hive of activity," he says of the map. "It really helped me understand who the players were."

While not brand-new—independent consultants and researchers at IBM have been mapping informal networks for a number of years—the use of social network analysis as a management tool is accelerating. Given the current emphasis on managing talent, companies are hungry for ways to find and nurture their organizations' most in-the-know employees. And as innovation becomes more critical to corporate survival, the tool lets managers survey the informal interactions between different groups of employees that lead to exciting new ideas. Such a bird's-eye view also exposes the glaring gaps where groups aren't interacting but should be. "Making the collaboration visible makes it much easier to talk about," says Kate Ehrlich, a researcher at IBM who studies collaboration.

While knowledge sharing is one of the most common reasons that companies employ the practice, managers are finding other useful applications. Last year, Solvay, a Belgian pharmaceutical and chemical company, began using maps to help with leadership transitions, or "baton passing," as Philippe Drouillon, a knowledge management project specialist, calls it. "You have a map that you can provide to successors and say: 'These are the interactions I have with the people that you should know,'" he says.

For all of the benefits, charting informal networks can be disruptive. "Leaders feel pretty threatened by this," says Katzenbach principal Zia Khan, speaking of people who hold high perches on the organization chart but are more isolated on the informal map. When using social network analysis, suggests University of Virginia's Rob Cross, it's important to communicate to employees that more connections aren't necessarily better: It's O.K. for some people, such as those who spend a lot of time with customers or have expertise in niche areas, to show up on the periphery of the web. Maps can also highlight which employees might be too connected and therefore a potential bottleneck.

Confidentiality is also a touchy issue. A map that reveals who is well-connected and who is not can be destructive if it is shared too widely. "I know who I named, but when I look at the map, I might see [that person] didn't name me back," says Tracy Cox, director of enterprise integration at aerospace and defense contractor Raytheon Co. Now, says Cox, who does network analyses for the company's seven businesses, that hypothetical employee "knows that he is not valuable to his boss. And not only does he know it, but 50 of his closest friends know it, too."

Instead, the maps Cox shares with the groups that he works with are carefully coded; employees are described only by generic characteristics such as job titles. Cox provides a separate list of the group's most connected people to everyone. Individuals can ask to see their portion of the maps and are offered one-on-one coaching to interpret them, but their supervisors aren't allowed to see them.

# THE DYSFUNCTIONS OF GROUPS AND TEAMS

So far, the discussion has been mostly about the positive impact and the functional aspects of groups and teams. However, there are a number of recognized dysfunctions that should also be recognized. Of particular interest in work groups and teams are norm violation and role ambiguity/conflict, groupthink, risky shift, and social loafing.

## Norm Violation and Role Ambiguity/Conflict

Group norms that are violated can result in antisocial behaviors. At the extreme, these include sexual harassment and theft. Others include lying, spreading rumors, withholding effort, and absenteeism. One study found group members who are chronically exposed to antisocial behaviors are more likely to engage in them, and dissatisfaction with coworkers may also rise, especially when those coworkers exhibit more antisocial activities than the person in question.[49]

There may also be gaps between the prescribed role as dictated by norms and the individual's reaction to the role. *Role ambiguity* occurs when the individual employee is unclear about the dictates of a given situation, or, in more common terms, "doesn't know what he's supposed to be doing." Unclear job descriptions, incomplete orders given by a manager, and inexperience all contribute to role ambiguity. Such ambiguity can affect the person's ability to function effectively in a group or team. Also, *role conflict* occurs when the employee or team member is: (1) asked to perform conflicting tasks or (2) required to perform a task that conflicts with his or her own personal values. In group settings, the odds of role conflicts increase, especially when the group engages in unethical or antisocial behaviors and when the members of the group stress one set of norms while the leader and rules of the formal organization emphasize others.

## The Groupthink, Conformity Problem

A dysfunction of highly cohesive groups and teams that has received a lot of attention has been called *groupthink* by well-known social psychologist Irving Janis. He defines it as "a deterioration of mental efficiency, reality testing, and moral judgment that results from in group pressures."[50] Essentially, groupthink results from the pressures on individual members to conform and reach consensus. Groups and teams that are suffering from groupthink are so bent on reaching consensus that there is no realistic appraisal of alternative courses of action in a decision, and deviant, minority, or unpopular views are suppressed.

Janis has concluded that a number of historic fiascos by government policy-making groups (for example, Britain's do-nothing policy toward Hitler prior to World War II, the unpreparedness of U.S. forces at Pearl Harbor, the Bay of Pigs invasion of Cuba, and the escalation of the Vietnam war) can be attributed to groupthink. The Watergate affair during the Nixon administration, the Iran-Contra affair during the Reagan administration, the Whitewater affair in the Clinton administration, and the Iraq War in the Bush administration are also examples. Although retrospective analysis questions the groupthink conclusion of the now over a decade ago space shuttle *Challenger* disaster,[51] and attention has shifted to analyzing what went wrong with the *Columbia* tragic disintegration when it began reentering the Earth on February 1, 2003, through the years the decision process by which NASA launched *Challenger* on its fateful mission has been analyzed in terms of the characteristics of groupthink. For example, conformity pressures were in evidence when NASA officials complained to the contractors about delays. Other symptoms of groupthink shown in Table 11.2, for example, illusions of invulnerability and unanimity and mindguarding by management's treatment and exclusion of input by the engineers, have commonly been used in analyzing the *Challenger* launch decisions.

**TABLE 11.2**
**Symptoms of Groupthink**

*Source:* Adapted from Irving L. Janis, *Groupthink,* 2nd ed., Houghton Mifflin, Boston, 1982, pp. 174–175.

1. There is the *illusion of invulnerability.* There is excessive optimism and risk taking.
2. There are *rationalizations* by the members of the group to discount warnings.
3. There is an unquestioned belief in the group's *inherent mortality.* The group ignores questionable ethical or moral issues or stances.
4. Those who oppose the group are *stereotyped* as evil, weak, or stupid.
5. There is *direct pressure* on any member who questions the stereotypes. Loyal members don't question the direction in which the group seems to be heading.
6. There is *self-censorship* of any deviation from the apparent group consensus.
7. There is the *illusion of unanimity.* Silence is interpreted as consent.
8. There are *self-appointed mindguards* who protect the group from adverse information

Although historically notorious news events can be used to dramatically point out the pitfalls of groupthink, it may also occur in committees and work groups in business firms or hospitals or any other type of organization. Initially, there was at least some partial support of the groupthink model when applied to areas such as leader behavior and decision making[52] and has been used to analyze the ethical problems in recent years at firms such as WorldCom.[53] However, recently there have been criticisms of the groupthink model coming from the organizational behavior literature. First of all, there has been very little research conducted to test the propositions of groupthink, most notably because it is so difficult to incorporate all of the items mentioned as the indicators of the phenomenon into one study. Further, some of the results provide only very limited evidence for the model, and the continued uncritical acceptance of groupthink may be an example of groupthink itself.[54] At this point, some organizational behavior theorists/researchers are calling for either elimination of the groupthink model, reformulation of how it works, or revitalization of the approach used.[55] One such approach would be to integrate the assumptions into the general group decision-making and problem-solving literature to see if they would provide support for conformity/groupthink. These analyses suggest that the popularity of the groupthink model may come from its intuitive appeal rather than research support. Under an evidence-based approach as outlined in Chapter 1, studies should be used to replicate the research in order to confirm previous findings, and these studies should be cumulative over time. Without this type of research rigor, unconditional acceptance of any model or theory may exist, even when empirical findings are sketchy at best.

## Risky Shift Phenomenon

Even before excessive risk taking was brought out by groupthink, the so-called risky shift phenomenon of groups was recognized. Research going back many years has shown that, contrary to popular belief, a group may make more risky decisions than the individual members would on their own.[56] This conclusion, of course, must be tempered by the values attached to the outcomes, but most of the research over the years finds that group discussion enhances the initial tendency of individual members in a given direction.[57] Called group-induced attitude polarization, this means that, for example, if an employee has a prounion (or antiunion) attitude before group discussion, the group discussion results in an even more extreme attitude in the same direction.

## Dysfunctions in Perspective

Such symptoms as risky shift, polarization, and the others found in groupthink should make groups take notice and be very careful of the dysfunctions of groups.[58] To help overcome the potentially disastrous effects, free expression of minority and unpopular viewpoints should be encouraged and legitimized. Companies such as General Electric,

Bausch & Lomb, Apple Computer, Johnson & Johnson, and United Parcel Service are known for not only tolerating, but formally encouraging, conflict and debate during group/team work and committee meetings. The head of a consulting team recently described their group meetings as follows:

> Remember that this is not Pleasantville. We're not all sitting around a table agreeing on things. That's not the way it works. I was with my own core group of consultants this Saturday, in my office, discussing some contentious issues we had to deal with as a firm. In the end, we assigned a subteam to handle the issue—and I'm not on it. That tells me that it's working; that's what's supposed to happen.[59]

Although many studies show that successful companies advocate such open conflict and healthy debate among group members, other studies point to the value of consensus. This apparent contradiction may be resolved by recognizing the following:

> Consensus may be preferred for smaller, non-diversified, privately held firms competing in the same industry while larger firms dealing with complex issues of diversification may benefit from the dissent raised in open discussions. Larger firms in uncertain environments need dissent while smaller firms in more simple and stable markets can rely on consensus.[60]

## Social Loafing

Another more recently recognized dysfunction associated with groups and teams is called social loafing. This problem occurs when members reduce their effort and performance levels when acting as part of a group. Primary causes include lack of performance feedback within the group, tasks that are not intrinsically motivating, situations in which the performances of others will cover for the reduced effort given by some members, and the "sucker effect" of not wanting to do more than the perception of effort being given by others. An example of a "slacker teammate" problem was described by another team member as follows:

> My teammate is very good in front of customers, but otherwise he does little to no work. I pick up the slack, because our team results are what I'm evaluated on. And when I've spoken to my teammate about the problem, he says "I'm the front man, and you're the back-end guy." I am tired of doing literally all the work on our customer projects and being seen as my slacker teammate's first mate. I am pretty certain that my boss will not want to hear from me about my team problem, because he [my boss] believes that working through team issues is part of our responsibility.[61]

There is a cultural component inherent in such social loafing. Research has found that cultures dominated by individual, self-interest values, such as the above example, are more likely to have groups that experience loafing. On the other hand, more collectivist cultures, which are dominated by a "we feeling" and group goals, lead to a stronger focus on the collective good and therefore may endure less loafing by group members.[62]

Social loafing is more likely to appear in large teams, where individual contributions are more difficult to identify. To reduce the impact of members shirking their duties and to ensure that they are fully contributing members of the team, it has been suggested to keep teams smaller in size, specialize tasks so that individual member contributions are identifiable, measure individual performance, and select only motivated employees when building teams.[63]

# WORK TEAMS

The discussion so far on group and team dynamics serves as the background and foundation for a specific focus on work teams. Work teams have become so popular in today's organizations that they deserve special attention. The term *team,* of course, is not new to organizations, and teamwork has been stressed throughout the years. For example, the well-known quality guru Joseph Juran first took his "Team Approach to Problem Solving" to the Japanese in the 1950s and then in the 1980s to the United States. Today, teams are becoming increasingly popular. Estimates of the prevalence and type of teams among *Fortune* 1000 companies are as follows:

1. Almost all use project teams (diverse managerial/professional employees working on projects for a defined, but typically extended, period of time).
2. A large majority use parallel teams (employees working on problem-solving or quality teams in parallel to the regular organizational structure).
3. A majority use permanent work teams (self-contained work units responsible for manufacturing products or providing services).[64]

After first defining what is meant by a team and critically analyzing self-managed teams found in today's organizations, the chapter covers ways to develop self-managed teams and make them more effective.

## The Nature of a Team

Although the term *team* is frequently used for any group, especially to get individuals to work together and to motivate them, some team experts make a distinction between teams and traditional work groups. For example, the authors of a book on the use of teams for creating high-performance organizations note that the difference between a work group and a team relates to performance results. They note:

> A working group's performance is a function of what its members do as individuals. A team's performance includes both individual results and what we call "collective work-products." A collective work-product is what two or more members must work on together . . . [it] reflects the joint, real contribution of team members.[65]

They go on to note these specific differences between work groups and teams:

1. The work group has a strong, clearly focused leader; the team has shared leadership roles.
2. The work group has individual accountability; the team has individual and mutual accountability.
3. The work group's purpose is the same as the organization's; the team has a specific purpose.
4. The work group has individual work-products; the team has collective work-products.
5. The work group runs efficient meetings; the team encourages open-ended, active problem-solving meetings.
6. The work group measures effectiveness indirectly (for example, financial performance of the overall business); the team measures performance directly by assessing collective work-products.
7. The work group discusses, decides, and delegates; the team discusses, decides, and does real work.[66]

The point is that teams do go beyond traditional formal work groups by having a collective, synergistic (the whole is greater than the sum of its parts) effect.

The use of teams to produce products started in well-known, quality-conscious corporate giants, such as Toyota in Japan and Motorola and General Electric in the United States, and has quickly spread. Companies as different as Xerox (office equipment), Monsanto (chemicals), Hewlett-Packard (computers), and Johnsonville Sausage use self-managed, sometimes called autonomous, teams. As with other early popular management approaches, such as MBO (management by objectives) or TQM (total quality management), after the initial excitement,

Over the last five years, cross-functional teams have become increasingly popular—and for good reason. Research shows that by combining the abilities and skills of individuals, all of whom can contribute different inputs to the team, it is possible to reduce the time needed to get things done while simultaneously driving up productivity and profit.

Hewlett-Packard is a good example of the use of effective teams. Although the firm has many innovative practices, its distribution organization was second rate. On average, it took 26 days for an H-P product to reach the customer, and employees had to shuttle information through a tangle of 70 computer systems. This is when the firm decided to reorganize the distribution process and reduce delivery time. Two H-P managers who assumed responsibility for the project assembled a team of 35 people from H-P and two other firms and then began examining the work flow. First, they looked at the way things were being done currently and began noting ways of eliminating work steps and shortening the process. Next, the team completed a two-week training and orientation program to familiarize team members with the current process. Then the team redesigned the entire work process and got everyone on the cross-functional team to buy in. Finally, they implemented the process and then made changes to correct errors remaining in the system. In the process, they were allowed to empower the workforce and managed to get delivery time down to eight days. This enabled the firm to cut its inventories by nearly 20 percent while increasing service levels to customers.

Another good example of cross-functional teams is provided by the emergency-trauma team at Massachusetts General Hospital. On an average day, about 200 patients show up at the emergency room, and about one-third of them end up in the trauma center. At the center there is a group of doctors, nurses, and technicians who come together and work as a "seamless" team. Each person begins a task—checking out a wound, running an IV, hooking up a machine. Then someone takes the lead and decides the strategy for treatment. Usually this is a doctor, but the direction can come from an intern or a nurse who is well versed in the applicable field. As an attending physician puts it, "Nobody bosses everybody around. If someone has a thought that's useful, we are open to suggestions." The job is intense, but it is also rewarding, and the personnel enjoy a high degree of professionalism and an environment in which they are able to use their abilities to deal with situations that require rapid and skilled decisions if lives are to be saved.

A third example is the U.S. Navy SEALs (the acronym refers to the commandos' all-terrain expertise: sea, air, land). These individuals are put through months of rigorous physical training in which each is taught how to use his skills to contribute to the team effort. Commenting on those who fail to measure up to the rigorous demands, one SEAL officer notes, "If you are the sort of person who sucks all the energy out of the group without giving anything back, then you are going to go away." The result of this effort is a high-performance team that is able to fulfill a host of different functions from teaching Namibian game wardens how to track down poachers to training Singaporean army regulars to combat potential terrorists.

In each case, the contribution of each team member greatly influences the success of the group effort. And by submerging their own identities in the group's activities, each individual is able to achieve both personal and group goals.

it has now become clear that although self-managed teams are important, they are not *the* answer. Similar to these other high-profile approaches and high-performance work practices (HPWPs) such as 360-degree feedback systems, there have been back-and-forth applications and enthusiasm for the use of teams. For example, for over a decade, Steelcase tried three different times to establish effective work teams in its dozen main North American plants before finally succeeding.[67] Now at Steelcase and most other organizations, increasing attention is being given to the dynamics of groups/teams (already discussed) and the emergence of cross-functional, virtual, and self-managed teams.

## Cross-Functional Teams

As part of the movement toward horizontal designs (see Chapter 3) and the recognition of dysfunctional bureaucratic functional autonomy, the focus has shifted to the use of cross-functional teams. These teams are made up of individuals from various departments or functional specialities. For example, the U.S. Navy discovered that it was able to improve productivity by establishing cross-functional teams to manage and improve the core processes that affect both external customers and mission performance. At Massachusetts General, one of the nation's most prominent hospitals, doctors on the emergency-trauma team have created a "seamless" approach between the various functions for treating critical patients who are brought in with life-threatening gunshot and knife wounds. The accompanying OB in Action: Greater Productivity through Cross-Functional Teams provides details on these and other examples.

The key to ensuring successful performance of cross-functional teams is found in two sets of criteria: one inside the team and one in the organization at large. To improve coordination with cross-functional teams, organizations can carry out five steps. These include: (1) choosing the membership carefully, (2) clearly establishing the purpose of the team, (3) ensuring that everyone understands how the group will function, (4) conducting intensive team building up front so that everyone learns how to interact effectively, and (5) achieving noticeable results so that morale remains high and the members can see the impact of their efforts.[68] There is also research evidence that overall functional breadth and cross-training of team members enhances information sharing, team interaction, and team performance.[69]

## Virtual Teams

With the advent of advanced information technology, increasing globalization, and the need for speed, the requirement that groups be made up of members in face-to-face interaction is no longer necessary. Members can now communicate at a distance through electronic means, such as e-mail, texting, chat rooms, blogs, phone and video conferencing, satellite transmissions, and websites. Members performing knowledge-based tasks in remote locations can become members of so-called virtual teams. Also, those performing in telecommuting jobs often bear responsibilities to serve on virtual teams. Virtual teams are increasingly evident in global, partnered operations and even everyday activities. Recent research projects that over the next several years almost three-fourths of the U.S. population will spend 10 times longer per day interacting virtually.[70]

Virtual teams have reached the point where they can become operationally defined and have theory-building[71] and growing research supporting improved applications. A comprehensive definition would be that "virtual teams are groups of people who work interdependently with shared purpose across space, time, and organization boundaries using technology to communicate and collaborate."[72] Although most closely associated with technical or operations teams, virtual teams can now be found throughout an organization. For example, IBM has a top management virtual team that has responsibility for driving the overall mission and strategy throughout the firm. This IBM virtual team has 28 members from all divisions and is available "on-demand" for any purpose.

From research, a key to effective virtual teams has been the importance of choosing the appropriate communication media to fit the requirements of the task and the message.[73] For example, for complex tasks like determining strategy, the medium for effective virtual teams should be *synchronous technologies,* which allow members to interact at the same time, or in real time. Audio and videoconferencing are examples of synchronous technologies, whereas asynchronous technologies, such as e-mail, chat rooms, blogs, group calendars, bulletin boards, and Web pages may be used when delayed interaction is acceptable for low-task complexity. The low cost of e-mail makes it an excellent candidate for collecting data, generating ideas, and sometimes for negotiating technical and interpersonal conflicts.[74] Virtual teams can be effective because they are flexible and are driven by information and skills rather than time and location.[75] However, caution must also be paid when assembling a virtual group. Internet chat rooms, for example, may create more work and result in poorer decisions than face-to-face meetings and telephone conferences unless there is adequate training and some experience with the technology.[76] In total, there is little question that virtual teams will continue to rapidly escalate in usage, but the challenges to make them effective must be met with more research and skillful application.

## Self-Managed Teams

Teams are being set up or are evolving into being self-managed as part of the empowerment movement (see Chapter 10) and the more egalitarian cultural values in an increasing number of organizations. A self-managed work team can be defined as "a group of employees who are responsible for managing and performing technical tasks that result in a product or service being delivered to an internal or external customer."[77] For example, at Hewlett-Packard and Harley-Davidson, self-managed teams are empowered to hire, organize, and purchase equipment without managements direct approval. The results from these teams have reportedly been very positive.[78]

Although there has been considerable such testimonial evidence of the value of self-managed teams, supporting research and documented experience have also emerged. To date, both the research and the practice literature has been quite favorable to self-managed teams. For example, recent studies of the empowerment of self-managed teams found increased job satisfaction, customer service, and team organizational commitment[79] and the facilitation of emergent leadership.[80] Also, a comprehensive meta-analysis covering 70 studies concluded that self-managed teams had a positive impact on productivity and specific attitudes related to the team, but not on general attitudes, absenteeism, or turnover.[81] This finding on the impact on productivity is impressive, and more recent studies also find a more favorable impact on attitudes as well,[82] but there are still practical problems to overcome. For example, an in-depth interview survey of 4,500 teams at 500 organizations uncovered a host of individual and organizational factors behind self-managed team ineffectiveness.[83] Individual problems included the following:

1. Team members aren't willing to give up past practices or set aside power and position.
2. Not all team members have the ability, knowledge, or skill to contribute to the group. Team functioning slows because some members shoulder more responsibility than others.
3. As team members, workers often face conflicts or challenges to their own personal beliefs. What works for the group often does not work for the individual.[84]

Organizational-level problems uncovered by this survey included compensation and reward systems that still focused solely on individual performance; thus there was little incentive for teams to perform well.[85] A survey of 300 large companies found that only 9 percent of them were pleased with their team-based compensation.[86] One of the major problems resulting in such dissatisfaction is that with the proliferation of short-term, virtual, and cross-functional teams, members are not able to go through the gradual process of gaining confidence in one another's competence, honesty, and dependability. In other words, there is too often a lack of trust, which research indicates leads to dissatisfaction with team-based pay.[87] The next and final section explores how to make all types of teams more effective.

## How to Make Teams More Effective

The effectiveness of teams may be measured based on the extent to which the team achieves its objectives and performs on behalf of the overall organization. Previous research has, at times, failed to note the ways in which teams are embedded in overall organizations.[88] Consequently, studies of team effectiveness may not have revealed a complete picture of the nature of team success.

For teams to be more effective, they must overcome some of the problems and dysfunctions that groups in general encounter (see this summary above). Long-standing models of team effectiveness include creating the right environment where support, commitment, goals, reward systems, communication systems, and physical space are all in sync to allow the team to work in a productive atmosphere.[89] Tasks should be designed to be interdependent, team size should be kept as small as possible, and members should be selected based on both being motivated and competent. Further, team cohesion should be built by either establishing homogenous groups or overcoming potential problems associated with diversity, by encouraging interaction and contact, and by making the group seem somewhat "exclusive," so that the members are happy to be included.[90] Also, team success naturally tends to build greater cohesion, as does the presence of external competition and challenges. In particular, there is now enough research evidence and practical experience to indicate the following ways to enhance team effectiveness: (1) team building, (2) collaboration, (3) leadership, and (4) understanding of cultural issues in global situations.

### *Team Building*

Team building begins with the understanding that work groups require time and training before they develop into productive and cohesive units. There seems to be a learning curve in building an effective team.[91] Exceptions to this learning curve would be: a study of professional basketball teams found that over a very long time period there was actually a negative correlation (an inverse relationship) of earlier performance with later performance,[92] and the analysis of hijacked United Flight 93 on September 11th that crashed into the Pennsylvania field also suggests that a long development process is not always needed. Although an FBI report suggested that a terrorist ordered the jet to be crashed because of the heroic passenger uprising,[93] at least one recent analysis indicates the passengers and crew formed an effective team on the spot to bring the plane down and thus solve a very serious, complex problem. The key was that conventional wisdom about the need for a learning curve was violated in these brief fateful moments when "the passengers and crew responded in a way once thought possible only for a well-formed team—one that had matured through several developmental stages. Yet no passenger had prior experience with hijacking, and crew training had focused on compliance, not response."[94] Traditionally, however, at least in normal work teams, effective ones do seem to develop over time.

At first, some employees may be unwilling to join or buy into the group. Only when they see success and team member satisfaction will this feeling change. Once established, some form of accountability must be present. Managers should expect to see some uncertainty in the team, which may last for up to two years, and during that time there may even be a dip in productivity. As the team matures, members learn the basics of team work, understand their roles more clearly, make more effective group decisions, and pursue group goals.[95]

Effective team building establishes a sense of ownership[96] and partnership[97] and allows members to see the team as a unit and as an attractive work arrangement.[98] Team building succeeds when individuals share collective intelligence[99] and experience a sense of empowerment[100] and engagement.[101] Team building involves rapid learning, which takes place when there is a free-flowing generation of ideas.[102] When there is educational diversity among the team members, there is research evidence this will positively influence the range and depth of information use, but may detract from the integration of the information available to the team.[103] Quality team-building programs must fit with the corporate culture, have well-designed goals, allow members to translate skills to the workplace, often take place in a separate environment, and may even move employees outside of a comfort zone, but not so much that they cannot learn. Programs such as rope climbing and even cooking classes may help members of some teams bond and learn to work together.[104]

**TABLE 11.3**
**Training Guidelines for Developing Effective Self-Managed Teams**

*Source:* Adapted from Paul E. Brauchle and David W. Wright, "Training Work Teams," *Training and Development*, March 1993, pp. 65–68.

| Steps of Training | Summary |
|---|---|
| 1. Establish credibility. | The trainers must first establish their knowledge and believability. |
| 2. Allow ventilation. | The trainees must have their anxieties and unresolved issues cleared before starting. |
| 3. Provide an orientation. | The trainers should give specific verbal directions and provide clear expectations and models of behavior. |
| 4. Invest in the process. | Early on, have the team identify its problems and concerns. |
| 5. Set group goals. | The trainees create, through consensus, their own mission statement and then set goals and specific activities and behaviors to accomplish these goals. |
| 6. Facilitate the group process. | The trainees are taught about how groups function and are given techniques, such as nominal grouping and paired comparison. |
| 7. Establish intragroup procedures. | This involves setting up a meeting format that might include reporting minutes, making announcements, discussing problems and issues, proposing solutions, taking action, and making new assignments. |
| 8. Establish intergroup processes. | Although the team is self-managed, leaders must be selected in order to interact with others, such as supervisors, managers, and other teams. |
| 9. Change the role of the trainers. | As the team becomes more experienced and empowered, the trainers take on a more passive role. |
| 10. End the trainers' involvement. | At this point, the team is on its own and is self-managing. |

An example of an effective team training approach would be the 10-step model shown in Table 11.3. GE, in its Electrical Distribution and Control Division, has successfully used this training model. According to the trainers, the trained GE teams "are made up of dedicated people who enjoy working together, who maintain high standards, and who demonstrate high productivity and commitment to excellence."[105]

Besides going through the steps of training, teams also must be monitored and evaluated on a continuous basis. Five key areas that should be monitored and measured include: (1) the team's mission, (2) goal achievements, (3) feelings of empowerment, (4) communications, and (5) roles and norms that are positive.[106]

Team-building processes can take place in levels as high as corporate boards. To do so, members should be emotionally intelligent (see Chapter 7), rather than just have raw intelligence (i.e., IQ), and feel they are part of a real team with clear, stable boundaries requiring interdependent tasks.[107] Members must learn to do what they promise, even when it means a personal sacrifice may be involved.[108] Boards that function as effective teams can create a major competitive advantage for the firm[109] and ethical corporate governance.[110]

### *Collaboration*

Effective group leaders do not act alone. They assemble a group of highly talented people and figure out how to get the most creative efforts out of everyone by effectively organizing their collaborative efforts.[111] Perhaps one of the best examples of the power of collaboration is the computer "open-source" operating system Linux and the also free Web browser Firefox.[112] These effective (and competitive) products were developed by essentially a voluntary, self-organizing community of thousands of programmers and companies. As the authors of a recent *Harvard Business Review* article aptly titled "Collaboration Rules" noted, "Most leaders would sell their grandmothers for workforces that collaborate as efficiently, frictionlessly, and creatively as the self-styled Linux 'hackers.'"[113] As in the development of "freeware," the process of collaboration involves learning how to improve interpersonal interactions in group settings while committing to a common agenda. Various developmental milestones may indicate that these collaborative skills are being learned and effectively applied.[114]

### Group Leadership

Whether the assigned head of the team or the emergent leader in self-managed teams, there are two key ways in which leaders may affect performance of groups: (1) how they select members and (2) the tactics they use to affect those members.[115] Tactics that help create a more team-oriented climate include eliminating or reducing special offices for the group heads, major differences in perks and privileges, and a decline in the use of designated leader titles.[116] There is also recent research coming out of the procedural justice literature indicating that team members are more satisfied with their leader[117] and have lower absenteeism and better performance[118] when they feel they are being treated fairly. At the same time, leaders need to continue to be clear and decisive even as they work with different people, different teams, and different environments.

As described by widely recognized team researchers Richard Hackman and Ruth Wageman, "Team leaders engage in many different kinds of behaviors intended to foster team effectiveness, including structuring the team and establishing its purposes, arranging for the resources a team needs for its work and removing organizational roadblocks that impede the work, helping individual members strengthen their personal contributions to the team, and working with the team as a whole to help members use their collective resources well in pursuing team purposes."[119] Effective leaders know both how to teach[120] and how to share the glory by acknowledging group success,[121] but perhaps most importantly, how to gain the trust of their team members.[122] Finally, as a follow-on to the importance of positivity discussed in detail in Chapter 7, recent research finds that when team leaders exhibit positivity, their members tended to be more positive (i.e., a contagion effect) and also exhibited better coordination.[123]

### Cultural/Global Issues

Although today's times make global teams operating in a multicultural environment inevitable, there is recent evidence that they are experiencing problems. One study of 70 global business teams found only 18 percent considered their performance "highly successful," and the remaining 82 percent fell short of their intended goals; one-third rated their performance as largely unsuccessful.[124] This result is also verified by research findings that employees in global teams that resist the concept of teams will have low job satisfaction and resulting problems.[125] Importantly, certain cultural values lead to resistance to teams.[126] For example, in one study of managers from Mexico, the great majority of leaders indicated they believed there would be significant problems if their companies adopted self-directed work teams.[127] Clearly such cultural obstacles must be overcome to build effective teams. As revealed in a study of a German-Japanese joint venture, national culture remains a key factor in explaining patterns of relationships exhibited in teams.[128] For example, although workplace teams can borrow from and use successful sports teams as a model in the United States,[129] in other cultures such as Asia or Europe, making the language of sports the dominant model or metaphor in one analysis "may be confusing, demotivating, and counterproductive."[130]

To improve global teams, research indicates that creating a "hybrid" team culture can be linked to improved performance.[131] In this study, a U-shaped relationship existed between team heterogeneity and team effectiveness, where homogenous and highly heterogeneous teams outperformed moderately heterogeneous groups in the long run. Therefore, as noted in the preceding leadership discussion, selection of group members seems to play an important role in the effectiveness of the group. In addition to careful selection, some pragmatic guidelines would include: (1) adapting to each culture (e.g., team pay should be used cautiously in individualistic cultures, but may be readily accepted in collectivist cultures); (2) changing implementation of teams for each culture (e.g., in the United States members should be involved in the selection, reward systems, and task assignments; but in Argentina, China, or Mexico such participation may not be needed or wanted); and (3) respecting local laws (e.g., in Finland, labor laws do not allow the use of team pay).[132] Also, once again shared perceptions of procedural justice in cross-cultural alliance teams seems critical to success.[133] Such shared justice perceptions is especially critical when there is a wide cultural distance between the partners in the alliance.

In general, to help overcome some of the problems associated with more individualistic cultures, it is advisable to allow groups to form voluntarily or for members to join voluntarily. Those who volunteer are more likely to be cooperative and experience greater satisfaction, motivation, and fewer disciplinary problems. Further, group goal-setting processes may also serve to increase motivation and satisfaction when they build group or collective efficacy.[134]

As the review of the above four major processes indicates, there is a great deal left to be learned about how to build more effective teams. At the same time, the use of teams to accomplish tasks continues to grow. This makes the study of teams and performance remain as an important area for more organizational behavior research and effective application.

---

## Summary

Groups and teams represent an important dynamic in the study and application of organizational behavior. Group formation, types, and processes; the dynamics of informal roles and organization; and the dysfunctions of work groups and teams are all of particular relevance to the study of organizational behavior. Group formation is explained theoretically in classic social psychology by propinquity; as a relationship among activities, interactions, and sentiments; as a symmetrical balance between attraction and common attitudes; and as a reward–cost exchange. Participants in an organization also form into groups for very practical economic, security, and social reasons. Many different types of groups are found in today's organizations. Conceptually, there are primary groups, coalitions, and others such as membership and reference groups. Groups have been researched over the years, and findings from classic social psychology studies and increasingly from organizational behavior scholars have implications for organizational behavior.

The last half of the chapter discusses and analyzes the dynamics of informal groups and work teams. Informal norms and roles and the informal organization are very relevant to and often represent the real organization. Informal structure coexists with every formal structure. Traditionally, only the dysfunctional aspects of informal organization have been emphasized. More recently, the functional aspects have also been recognized.

The dynamics of the dysfunctions of groups and teams were examined in terms of norm violation resulting in antisocial behaviors, role ambiguity/conflict, group think conformity, the risky shift phenomenon, and social loafing. The remainder of the chapter focused on work teams per se. Initially, most publicity was given to quality circles, but now self-managed teams are in the spotlight. Self-managed teams have become an established form of doing work to meet the high-tech, quality challenges facing all modern organizations. To date, self-managed teams have a quite successful track record. In addition to self-managed teams, cross-functional and virtual teams are examples of more recent team forms that have also achieved success. Global teams in a multicultural environment have experienced some problems, but helpful solutions are forthcoming. Whether global or domestic, building effective teams requires long-standing principles regarding the creation of the proper environment in which support, commitment, rewards, communication, physical space, group size, membership, and cohesion are emphasized. Then, team effectiveness may be enhanced using team-building programs, collaboration, and effective leadership and by accounting for functional, demographic, or cultural diversity and global issues when teams are formed.

## Ending with Meta-Analytic Research Findings

## OB PRINCIPLE FOR EVIDENCED-BASED PRACTICE

Highly cohesive groups and teams are good performers.

### Meta-Analysis Results:

[16 studies; 372 groups; $d = .92$] *On average, there is a **74 percent probability** that highly cohesive groups and teams will have better performance than when cohesiveness is low. This relationship was found to be particularly straightforward, as no moderator variables were found.*

### Conclusion:

Theoretically, cohesive groups or teams should be motivated to advance group objectives and to fully participate in group activities. Thus, of particular interest is the relationship between group and team cohesiveness and performance. Group cohesion enables a group or team to exercise effective control over its members in relationship to its behavioral norms and needed teamwork. Less-cohesive groups, on the other hand, have greater difficulty exercising control over their members and enforcing standards of behavior. Moreover, as this chapter points out, one liability of cohesive groups is the tendency to develop groupthink, a dysfunctional process. Because cohesive groups tend to identify strongly with the group, the group members may prefer concurrency in decisions at the expense of critically evaluating other's suggestions for the best interest of the group. Nevertheless, group cohesion typically enhances members' satisfaction and improves organizational performance due to the strong motivation to maintain good, close relationships with other members.

**Source:** Adapted from Charles R. Evans and Kenneth L. Dion, "Group Cohesion and Performance: A Meta-Analysis," *Small Group Research,* Vol. 22, No. 2, 1991, pp. 175–186.

## Questions for Discussion and Review

1. Briefly discuss the major theoretical explanations for group formation. Which explanation do you think is most relevant to the study of organizational behavior? Defend your choice.
2. What are some functions of the informal organization? What are some dysfunctions?
3. What are some of the major symptoms of groupthink? Can you give an example from your own experience where groupthink may have occurred?

4. What is social loafing? How can it be overcome?

5. How, if at all, do teams as used in today's organizations differ from traditional work groups?

6. What are two ways to make and maintain self-managed teams' effectiveness?

7. Describe a cross-functional team and a virtual team. Why are these types of teams growing in popularity?

8. How should team effectiveness be measured?

**Internet Exercise: Work Environment in Team-Based Organizations**

Many organizations are recognizing the value of teamwork. In fact, many companies have promoted their team environment on their Web page. Go to **http://www.IBM.com** and look at their description of the organization under employment opportunities. Notice the emphasis that they put on group and team dynamics. Now pull up the Web sites of some firms in your local area and see if and how they emphasize the use of teams. Using these examples of teams in action as background and a point of departure, answer the following questions. (This would be an especially good exercise to use groups to discuss and arrive at answers.)

1. In these team environments, it takes longer to get tasks done. Is this an important consideration in determining whether or not a team approach is effective? Why or why not?

2. Besides time, what are some other important dynamics? Give two specific strengths and two weaknesses of teams in the workplace.

3. Does the type of organization and its work/projects make a difference on how and when to use teams? Use IBM vs. the others you found as examples in your answer.

---

# Real Case: *There Are Teams, and There Are Teams*

One of the most difficult challenges for multinational managers is that of understanding how to manage groups and teams across cultures. What works in the home country often has no value in other cultures. For example, in the late 1990s, while the Japanese economy continued to stagger, a number of U.S.-based multinational firms entered the Japanese market to take advantage of the weak competition. Large U.S. retailers set up super stores in Japan with a wide variety of offerings and low prices. However, Japanese customers found these stores to be too big and impersonal for many types of goods and preferred to shop at smaller, locally owned stores. As a professor of marketing at a Japanese business school put it, "Retailing is such a local business, it's not that easy to succeed."

The same challenges of appealing to Japanese customers also hold true for managing Japanese employees. What works in the United States often has little value in Japan. For example, in the United States it is common for firms to have work groups compete against each other and to reward the winning teams. In Japan's collectivist

cultural values, openly competing with others is frowned on. Those who win feel embarrassed and those who lose feel a sense of shame and loss of face. A good example is provided by an American manager who was in charge of a major department in a Japan-based, multinational bank. The manager, in an effort to increase the profits of his department, came up with a fairly simple idea. It involved combining two different futures contracts to create an arbitrage position (i.e., the simultaneous purchase and sale of the same securities and foreign exchange in different markets to then profit from unequal prices). A number of the bank's non-Japanese competitors were making money with this type of strategy, and the manager felt that his bank could do the same. Unfortunately, this is not what happened. When he presented this idea to the senior-level management group, the Japanese managers convinced the rest of their colleagues to veto it. Their reasoning was grounded in an understanding of Japanese culture. Because two different futures would have to be traded by two different departments, one group would make money on the trade and the other would lose. So even though the overall bank would profit from the two transactions, the Japanese managers realized that the group that lost money would be embarrassed in front of its peers and lose face.

This same situation applies when Japanese firms compete against each other for a local market. There is great social pressure for each of the competing firms to retain their relative position. Thus Sony would not attempt to dislodge Mitsubishi and become the largest competitor in a particular industry. Only when Japanese firms go international do they compete strongly for market share—and this is against local competitors in the foreign market and not each other.

Performance appraisal is another good example. If an American employee does not do a good job, the person may be replaced. However, this seldom happens in Japan. So when American and Japanese firms create a joint venture and assign teams to the undertaking, the Japanese do not use the same type of individual performance requirements. The Americans want results, but the Japanese are often more interested in everyone in the team being cooperative and helpful. Harmony is more important than productivity, and seldom is any direct action taken against poorly performing individual employees. However, the peers/teammates may subtly get the low performer straigtened out in an informal setting such as over drinks or on a fishing trip.

Another difference between American and Japanese teams is that U.S. managers try very hard to let their people know what is to be done, when it is to be completed, and how progress or performance will be determined. For example, the boss might say, "I want your team to take a look at our major competitors and tell me three products that they are likely to bring to market over the next six months." The Japanese manager will be much more indirect and vague. The Japanese exec might say something like, "What product changes do you think we can expect from the competition in the future?" As a result of these directives, the American team will generate a fairly short, well-focused report that contains a great deal of specific information. The Japanese team will submit a very long, detailed report that covers all aspects of the competition and provides a wealth of information on a host of products that may be introduced into the marketplace over the next year.

1. Based on the information in the case and your reading of the chapter, what would you recommend to be included in the following assignments you are given as a member of a large multinational corporation training department?
   a. How would you make the teams of the Japanese subsidiary more effective?
   b. How would you make the cross-functional team that is working on new product development for both the U.S. and Japanese markets as effective as possible?

2. How do you personally react to the statement in the case that "the Japanese are more interested in everyone in the team being cooperative and helpful. Harmony is more important than productivity"?

3. How do you explain that the Japanese have been using teams way before the United States, but they have had economic problems for a much longer period than has the United States? How would you explain to the CEO of your company that you recommend the use of teams in light of the prolonged Japanese competitive problems?

---

# Organizational Behavior Case: *The Schoolboy Rookie*

Kent Sikes is a junior at State University. He has taken a summer job in the biggest factory in his hometown. He was told to report to the warehouse supervisor the first day at work. The supervisor assigned him to a small group of workers who were responsible for loading and unloading the boxcars that supplied the materials and carried away the finished goods of the factory.

After two weeks on the job, Kent was amazed at how little the workers in his crew had accomplished. It seemed that they were forever standing around and talking or, in some cases, even going off to hide when there was work to be done. Kent often found himself alone unloading a boxcar while the other members of the crew were off messing around someplace else. When Kent complained to his coworkers, they made it very plain that if he did not like it, he could quit, but if he complained to the supervisor, he would be sorry. Although Kent has been deliberately excluded from any of the crew's activities, such as taking breaks together or having a Friday afternoon beer after work at the tavern across the street, yesterday he went up to one of the older members of the crew and said, "What gives with you guys, anyway? I am just trying to do my job. The money is good, and I just don't give a hang about this place. I will be leaving to go back to school in a few weeks, and I wish I could have gotten to know you all better, but frankly I am sure glad I'm not like you guys." The older worker replied, "Son, if you'd been here as long as I have, you would be just like us."

1. Using some of the theories, explain the possible reasons for the group formation of this work crew. What types of groups exist in this case?
2. What role does the supervisor play in the performance of this group?
3. What are the major informal roles of the crew members and Kent? What status position does Kent have with the group? Why?
4. Why hasn't Kent been accepted by the group? Do you agree with the older worker's last statement in the case? Why or why not?

# Organizational Behavior Case: *The Blue-Ribbon Committee*

Mayor Sam Small is nearing completion of his first term in office. He feels his record has been pretty good, except for the controversial issue of housing. He has been able to avoid doing anything about housing so far and feels very strongly that this issue must not come to a head before the next election. The voters are too evenly divided on the issue, and he would lose a substantial number of votes no matter what stand he took. Yet with pressure increasing from both sides, he has to do something. After much distress and vacillation, he has finally come upon what he thinks is an ideal solution to his dilemma. He has appointed a committee to study the problem and make some recommendations. To make sure that the committee's work will not be completed before the election comes up, it was important to pick the right people. Specifically, Sam has selected his "blue-ribbon" committee from a wide cross section of the community so that, in Sam's words, "all concerned parties will be represented." He has made the committee very large, and the members range from PhDs in urban planning to real estate agents to local ward committeepersons to minority group leaders. He has taken particular care in selecting people who have widely divergent, outspoken public views on the housing issue.

1. Do you think Sam's strategy of using this group to delay taking a stand on the housing issue until after the election will work? Why or why not?
2. What are some of the important dynamics of this group? Do you think the group will arrive at a good solution to the housing problems facing this city?
3. Do you think they will suffer from groupthink?
4. What types of informal roles is Sam exhibiting? Do you think he is an effective manager? Do you think he is an effective politician? Is there a difference?

# Experiential Exercises for Part Three

## EXERCISE:

Groups and Conflict Resolution*

## Goals:

1. To compare individual versus group problem solving and decision making
2. To analyze the dynamics of groups
3. To demonstrate conflict and ways of resolving it

## Implementation:

1. Divide any number of people into small groups of four or five.
2. Take about 15 minutes for individual responses and 30 minutes for group consensus.
3. Each individual and group should have a work sheet. Pencils, a flip chart (newsprint or blackboard), marker pens, or chalk may also be helpful to the groups.

## Process:

1. Each individual has 15 minutes to read the story and answer the 11 questions about the story. Each person may refer to the story as often as needed but may not confer with anyone else. Each person should circle "T" if the answer is clearly true, "F" if the answer is clearly false, and "?" if it isn't clear from the story whether the answer is true or false.
2. After 15 minutes each small group makes the same decisions using group consensus. Allow 30 minutes for group consensus. No one should change his or her answers on the individual questions. The ground rules for group decisions are as follows:
   a. Group decisions should be made by consensus. It is illegal to vote, trade, average, flip a coin, etc.
   b. No individual group member should give in only to reach agreement.
   c. No individual should argue for his or her own decision. Instead, each person should approach the task using logic and reason.
   d. Every group member should be aware that disagreements may be resolved by facts. Conflict can lead to understanding and creativity if it does not make group members feel threatened or defensive.

## Scoring:

1. After 30 minutes of group work, the exercise leader should announce the correct answers. Scoring is based on the number of correct answers out of a possible total of 11. Individuals are to score their own individual answers, and someone should score the group decision answers.
   The exercise leader should then call for:
   a. The group-decision score in each group.
   b. The average individual score in each group.
   c. The highest individual score in each group.

**\*Source:** Alan Filley, *Interpersonal Conflict Resolution,* Scott, Foresman, Glenview, Ill., 1975, pp. 139–142, as adapted from William H. Haney, *Communication and Organizational Behavior,* Irwin, Burr Ridge, Ill., 1967, pp. 319–324.

2. Responses should be posted on the tally sheet. Note should be taken of those groups in which the group score was (1) higher than the average individual score or (2) higher than the best individual score. Groups should discuss the way in which individual members resolved disagreements and the effect of the ground rules on such behavior. They may consider the obstacles experienced in arriving at consensus agreements and the possible reasons for the difference between individual and group decisions.

## The Story:

A businessman had just turned off the lights in the store when a man appeared and demanded money. The owner opened a cash register. The contents of the cash register were scooped up, and the man sped away. A member of the police force was notified promptly.

## Statements about the Story:

| | | |
|---|---|---|
| 1. A man appeared after the owner had turned off his store lights. | | T F ? |
| 2. The robber was a man. | | T F ? |
| 3. A man did not demand money. | | T F ? |
| 4. The man who opened the cash register was the owner. | | T F ? |
| 5. The store owner scooped up the contents of the cash register and ran away. | | T F ? |
| 6. Someone opened a cash register. | | T F ? |
| 7. After the man who demanded the money scooped up the contents of the cash register, he ran away. | | T F ? |
| 8. Although the cash register contained money, the story does *not* state *how much.* | | T F ? |
| 9. The robber demanded money of the owner. | | T F ? |
| 10. The story concerns a series of events in which only three persons are referred to: the owner of the store, a man who demanded money, and a member of the police force. | | T F ? |
| 11. The following events in the story are true: someone demanded money, a cash register was opened, its contents were scooped up, and a man dashed out of the store. | | T F ? |

## TALLY SHEET

| Group Number | Group Score | Average Individual Score | Best Individual Score | Group Score Better than Average Indiv.? | Group Score Better than Best Indiv.? |
|---|---|---|---|---|---|
| | | | | | |

# EXERCISE:

NASA Moon Survival Task*

## Goals:

The challenge in decision making is to obtain the best information within limits of time and other resources. This is often very difficult because information does not exist in pure form. It is always filtered through people who may or may not get along with each other and who might not even care about a good decision. This exercise is a means to help you look at the process of gathering information, working out group procedures, analyzing different contributions, and handling conflict and motivation. The exercise is intended to help you examine the strengths and weaknesses of individual decision making versus group decision making.

## Instructions:

You are a member of a space crew originally scheduled to rendezvous with another ship on the lighted surface of the moon. Because of mechanical difficulties, however, your ship was forced to land at a spot some 200 miles from the rendezvous point. During landing, much of the equipment aboard was damaged, and because survival depends on reaching the main ship, the most critical items available must be chosen for the 200-mile trip.

## Implementation:

1. On the next page are listed the 15 items left intact and undamaged after the landing. Your task is to rank them in terms of their importance to your crew in reaching the rendezvous point.

2. In the first column (step 1) place the number 1 by the most important item, the number 2 by the second most important, and so on, through number 15, the least important. You have 15 minutes to complete this phase of the exercise.

3. After the individual rankings are completed, participants should be formed into groups having from four to seven members.

4. Each group should then rank the 15 items as a team. This group ranking should be a consensus after a discussion of the issues, not just the average of each individual ranking. Although it is unlikely that everyone will agree exactly on the group ranking, an effort should be made to reach at the least a decision that everyone can live with. It is important to treat differences of opinion as a means of gathering more information and clarifying issues and as an incentive to force the group to seek better alternatives.

5. The group ranking should be listed in the second column (step 2).

6. The third phase of the exercise consists of the instructor's providing the expert's rankings, which should be entered in the third column (step 3).

## Scoring:

1. Each participant should compute the difference between the individual ranking (step 1) and the expert's ranking (step 3), and between the group ranking (step 2) and the expert's ranking (step 3).

2. Then add the two "difference" columns—the smaller the score, the closer the ranking is to the view of the experts.

*Source: This exercise was developed by Jay Hall, Teleometrics International, and was adapted by J. B. Ritchie and Paul Thompson, *Organization and People,* 2nd ed., West, St. Paul, Minn., 1980, pp. 238–239. Also see James B. Lau and A. B. Shani, *Behavior in Organizations,* 4th ed., Irwin, Burr Ridge, Ill., 1988, pp. 94–99.

## NASA TALLY SHEET

| Items | Step 1 Your individual ranking | Step 2 The team's ranking | Step 3 Survival expert's ranking | Step 4 Difference between Steps 1 and 3 | Step 5 Difference between Steps 2 and 3 |
|---|---|---|---|---|---|
| Box of matches | | | | | |
| Food concentrate | | | | | |
| 50 feet of nylon rope | | | | | |
| Parachute silk | | | | | |
| Portable heating unit | | | | | |
| Two .45-caliber pistols | | | | | |
| One case dehy-drated Pet milk | | | | | |
| Two 100-lb. tanks of oxygen | | | | | |
| Stellar map (of the moon's constellation) | | | | | |
| Life raft | | | | | |
| Magnetic compass | | | | | |
| 5 gallons of water | | | | | |
| Signal flares | | | | | |
| First-aid kit con-taining injection needles | | | | | |
| Solar-powered FM receiver-transmitter | | | | | |
| **TOTAL** (The lower the score, the better) | | | | **Your score** | **Team score** |

# EXERCISE:

TGIF (Thank God It's Friday!)*

## Goals:

This exercise provides an opportunity to experience and explore several facets of group dynamics. Although the activity itself is recreational in nature, it reflects many of the same challenges faced by managerial groups and contemporary empowered and self-managed teams. That is, the exercise calls on decision-making and interpersonal behavior skills necessary to effectively manage a collaborative work effort.

*Source: Professor Steven M. Sommer, Pepperdine University, developed the exercise around the two anonymous activity sheets. Used with permission.

## Implementation:

The activity itself involves the spelling out of a list of common or well-known phrases and items. Each quotation includes a number, and that number is the clue to solving the puzzle. For example, the sample puzzle is presented as "7 D. of the W."

The number 7 is part of the phrase and provides the clue that the saying is "7 days of the week." Another common item is "12 E. in a D." which stands for "12 eggs in a dozen."

## ACTIVITY SHEET A

*Instructions:* Each equation below contains the initials of words that will make it correct. Finish the missing words. For example:

    7 - D. of the W.                           Would be *7 days of the week.*

1. 26 - L. of the A.
2. 7 - W. of the A. W.
3. 1001 - A. N.
4. 54 - C. in a D. (with the J.)
5. 12 - S. of the Z.
6. 9 - P. in the S. S.
7. 13 - S. of the A. F.
8. 88 - P. K.
9. 18 - H. on a G. C.
10. 32 - D. F. at which W. F.
11. 90 - D. in a R. A.
12. 200 - D. for P. G. in M.
13. 8 - S. on a S. S.
14. 3 - B. M. (S. H. T. R.)
15. 4 - Q. in a G.
16. 24 - H. in a D.
17. 1 - W. on a U.
18. 5 - D. in a Z. C.
19. 57 - H. V.
20. 11 - P. on a F. T.
21. 1000 - W. that a P. is W.
22. 29 - D. in F. in a L. Y.
23. 64 - S. on a C. B.
24. 40 - D. and N. of the G. F.

## Procedure:

1. (Five minutes). Students should break up into groups of four or five.
2. Do not read the discussion questions before doing the task.
3. (Twenty to thirty minutes). The groups solve as many items on one of the following activity sheets (A or B) as possible.
4. (Five minutes). The instructor reads off the answers to the list. Groups may propose alternative solutions.
5. (Fifteen minutes). In a class forum, the groups discuss and compare their experiences by responding to the discussion questions.
6. As a follow-up activity, use the alternate list. The follow-up may be used to show effective group development, effective teamwork (after discussing problems that may have surfaced with the first list), or the power of groups over individuals (have students complete the list on their own, then as a group).

## ACTIVITY SHEET B

| | | | |
|---|---|---|---|
| 1. EZ / iiiiiii | 2. T O U C H | 3. Moth cry cry cry | 4. Black / coat |
| 5. Time Time | 6. L A N D | 7. Hurry ↑ | 8. Me Quit |
| 9. Le vel | 10. Knee / light | 11. Man / Board | 12. He's/Himself |
| 13. R\|e\|a\|d\|i\|n\|g | 14. AGES | 15. R ROAD A D | 16. O / M.A. B.A. PH.D |
| 17. WEAR / LONG | 18. DICE DICE | 19. ECNALG | 20. CYCLE CYCLE CYCLE |
| 21. CHAIR | 22. T O W N | 23. ii   ii o    o | 24. Stand / I |

## Discussion Questions:

1. How did the group try to solve the list? Did you plan out your approach? Did you explore answers as a group, divide parts among individuals? Or did each member try to solve the entire list individually and then pool answers? Did people take on different roles? Recorder? Encourager? Idea generator? Spy?

2. How important was it for the group to solve all 24 puzzles? Did the team initially set a goal to finish the list? How challenging was this exercise? What happened as you approached completion? Did commitment go up? As the last few unsolved items became frustrating, did the group start to lose its desire?

3. Describe the climate or personality of the group. Was everyone in agreement about how hard to work? How many to finish? Did members begin to react differently to the frustrations of getting the list completed? Did some argue to finish? Did others tell the team to quit?

4. Did some members try to dominate the process? The suggested solutions? How well did you get along in doing the exercise? Was there conflict? Did members fight fair in debating different answers? Was each discovery of a correct answer a source of excitement and pride? Or was it a sense of relief, a step closer to getting it over with?

5. Did the group develop any rules to regulate behavior? Was there a process of group development in which members discussed the assignment before beginning to tackle it? What changes in behaviors or expectations occurred as time progressed and the group became more or less focused on the activity? Did a form of self-discipline emerge to keep the team focused, to prevent being embarrassed in relation to other groups?

6. To what extent did public evaluation of performance become important? Did you begin to monitor how well other groups were doing? Did your group try to spy on their answers? Did you negotiate any trades?

# EXERCISE:

Power and Politics*

## Goals:

1. To gain some insights into your own power needs and political orientation
2. To examine some of the reasons people strive for power and what political strategies can be used to attain it

## Implementation:

Answer each of the following questions with "mostly agree" or "mostly disagree," even if it is difficult for you to decide which alternative best describes your opinion.

|  | Mostly Agree | Mostly Disagree |
|---|---|---|
| 1. Only a fool would correct a boss's mistakes. | _____ | _____ |
| 2. If you have certain confidential information, release it to your advantage. | _____ | _____ |
| 3. I would be careful not to hire a subordinate with more formal education than myself. | _____ | _____ |
| 4. If you do a favor, remember to cash in on it. | _____ | _____ |
| 5. Given the opportunity, I would cultivate friendships with powerful people. | _____ | _____ |
| 6. I like the idea of saying nice things about a rival in order to get that person transferred from my department. | _____ | _____ |
| 7. Why not take credit for someone else's work? They would do the same to you. | _____ | _____ |
| 8. Given the chance, I would offer to help my boss build some shelves for his or her den. | _____ | _____ |
| 9. I laugh heartily at my boss's jokes, even when they are not funny. | _____ | _____ |
| 10. I would be sure to attend a company picnic even if I had the chance to do something I enjoyed more that day. | _____ | _____ |

**\*Source:** Reprinted with permission from Andrew J. DuBrin, *Human Relations,* Reston, Reston, Va., 1978, pp. 122–123.

# Managing and Leading for High Performance

## EVIDENCE-BASED CONSULTING PRACTICES

### GALLUP'S APPROACH TO MANAGING FOR HIGH PERFORMANCE

Because this last part of the text is concerned with both managing and leading for high performance, and this is Gallup's major practice with clients, we will first look at the managing part and then at the leading part.

Managing for high performance starts with measurement. When the match of talent is right, people will do more of, and get better at, the things we measure. But what sort of things? In Gallup's practice, we seek to work in a context defined by outcomes. Because of this, it is imperative that all employees know their customers—both internal or external. From this relationship, right expectations can be created in ways that allow for measurement of quantity and quality of the person's performance. Once the "what" question is answered, objective, mutually agreed-upon measures can be developed. At Gallup, we believe "if you have a job that cannot be measured, you probably have a nonjob!"

Notice that the measurement is not about compliance to process. Except where issues such as safety are concerned, the idea is to allow room for initiative, creativity, individualization, and improvement of the systems and processes to the employee. We focus on the performance.

We have found that focusing on quantity alone can be counterproductive. Consequently, we always include quality assessment. It is the customer who determines quality. Of course, some issues are expected to manifest themselves in most any work environment—timelines, accuracy, responsiveness, and the like. Frequently, we find that other items such as "personal touch" may be included. When people get to see how much they are producing, and how well their efforts are being received, they have both a benchmark and a reason to see "how much better they can get."

At Gallup, we recommend reward systems that respond to the fact that people are differently motivated. Some choose to compete against themselves, for instance, whereas others choose to compete "in the wider arena." In addition to articulating systems in this way, we also pay attention to how people like to receive their recognition. Public recognition for winning against others can be largely counterproductive when given to a person who dislikes comparison to others and who is a "private person."

It is important to measure the right things, because you will get more of what you measure. Some issues, such as safety, can be tricky. Measuring "reduction of reported incidents" can get you exactly that: fewer reports! Likewise, in call centers certain companies have learned the hard way that rewarding short "duration of call" can be very harmful to customer service, creating only an appearance of high performance.

Intrinsic motivation is actually a presupposition of Gallup's approach to measurement and recognition. Because Gallup believes in matching a "right fit" for a person's talent for the desired outcomes, Gallup seeks to situate persons in roles that are "natural" to them. In this way, employees have the inner satisfaction of doing what they do well. They get good measures in their work, usually from the very start, and because their talent is a "fit," they have the requisite ability to keep growing and improving in their role. As this continues, rapid improvement becomes a "base" of motivation, which underwrites the measurement and recognition systems.

Obviously, Gallup does not support the notion that promotion should be used as a reward. Neither should people be rewarded for tenure. High performance is the key issue; measurement of outcomes and individually appropriate recognition are the means.

# GALLUP'S APPROACH TO LEADERSHIP FOR EFFECTIVE PERFORMANCE

Gallup's approach to leadership is not so much focused on the achievement of a goal, but rather it is the continuation of a journey. This journey includes improvement of performance and growth of the organization. However, in Gallup's point of view, these are managed outcomes that accompany the leadership process. At the center, leadership is more about the business of creating hope, possibility, and future. There is no "arrival" here, though various milestones are obtained along the way. Leadership at its best not only transforms individuals and organizations toward their highest aspirations, but it also creates moments of vision and comprehension that allow people to transcend to new, as yet unattained, levels of experience and performance.

In Gallup's research, leadership has been shown to be the "main driver" of employee retention and loyalty. In a rapidly changing, high-turnover environment, leadership has emerged as a "higher level" construct that influences employees through future, vision, values, and creation of culture constructed around these, and with behaviors that demonstrate regard, respect, and value for employees.

## LEADERS AS TALENT

Gallup's approach to leadership is largely based on the study of human talent. Although it may appear a "trait approach" at first glance, talent is not rooted in personality or "style." A talent, for Gallup, is a measurable, stable constellation of thought, feeling, and behavior. Talent is, in Gallup's methodology, the "soil" in which various skills and competencies can be "planted." It is the talents of the individual that create the basis for which "skills" will thrive, which will "do ok," and which will "languish." Talent, in its dominant or "signature" dimension, is much more about what people will do, rather than what they might do or might be managed or coerced to do. Possessing a methodology that allows us to measure talent in a reliable way, Gallup focuses on those talents that demonstrably distinguish top-performing or successful leaders from the "average."

## LEADERS VERSUS MANAGERS

A necessary first step is to distinguish leadership from management. Gallup has found that managers and supervisors exert their greatest and most significant influence in what could be called the "first synapse," the relationship between themselves and the individuals they manage. Leaders, on the other hand, exert their influence "over a distance." Although the literature recognizes indirect leadership (the influence of a focal leader on individuals not directly reporting to him or her), Gallup views this "leadership at a distance" not as an "indirect function" of leaders, but as *the principal activity of leaders*.

Who are leaders? For Gallup, leaders are individuals who successfully bring a constituency (more than an immediate group) to a commonly shared "destination" that initially "inhabited the future." Though all human beings may have such a capacity in some measure, and use it on some localized scale, it is also true that for certain individuals these capacities are so manifest that they can and frequently do exercise them over considerable range or distance. Those who "can do" are leaders. To be sure, other variables, such as the situation, Zeitgeist, context, and followers, do matter. That is why true leaders need the talent to navigate these challenges, and that is why Gallup measures not only the talents of the leader but also various related measures within the leader's constituency.

Gallup has developed methodologies related to the measurement of management and leadership. These methodologies allow leaders to have measured information of their own talent and critical, leverageable points within their constituency. In all this, Gallup feels, it is critical to keep managerial issues separated and clarified for managerial functioning and to deal with leadership in a similar way. Happily, these methods and measures have critical "intersections" between issues and functions and between managers and leaders, allowing for full organizational use of the information for effective outcomes.

## THE LEADER-SITUATION FIT

Gallup would agree with the contingency theories that there must be a "fit" between the leader and the situation. It is also important for a leader to use his or her talent in a manner that is "fitting" for the situation. Self-awareness is a significant ingredient in leadership success, as are the talents that serve to modulate the effective use of other talents. Gallup's studies would suggest that the ability to "modulate" one's talent for a wide range of situations is what typifies a successful leader. When the talents of an individual are the right "fit" for the role and used in a manner "fitting" to a role and the situation, Gallup refers to it as leadership "strengths." Hence, the measurement of talent has a predictive value for job placement, development, and succession planning.

## GALLUP'S IDENTIFIED DEMANDS OF LEADERSHIP

The process of leadership, in Gallup's assessment, proceeds on the leader's response to seven demands. (See Barry Conchie, *Gallup Management Journal,* 2004.) The first demand is that the leader *know one's self.* The process of continual development in the area of self-awareness is, in Gallup's research, of great importance. To know one's strengths and nonstrengths and act accordingly is to use oneself optimally and to limit the vulnerabilities caused by "blind spots" and "denial." Knowledge of strengths grounds the leader's self in authentic, ethical presence to others.

Leaders also need to *make sense of experience,* for themselves and others. A central reason is the reduction of fear in the organization. Anxiety can distract and dissipate human energy, drawing it away from productive engagement. Leaders reduce fear by having parsimonious explanations of "realities" that could otherwise be problematic. It is not necessary that the leader always have all the answers, but people need to know that their leaders are "aware and attentive" to the things that matter.

Leaders need to *mentor and be mentored.* Particularly in today's world of rapid change, leaders themselves continue their own growth when they make themselves available to the development of others. A best way to be focused on current and future issues is to be intimately acquainted with the fears and dreams of the rising stars of one's origination. Additionally, leaders also need others who can challenge their own trajectory. These mentoring relationships support the continued growth of leaders.

Successful leaders build their constituency strategically and continually. For leaders, every day is recruiting day. There are no leaders who do not have followers, and following is a choice. Leaders win loyalty through personal trust and to the vision and values they espouse. Leaders' behavioral congruency with words is required in this process. Leaders understand that "friends may come and go, but enemies tend to accumulate."

Leaders *harness the values* of the people in the organization. As the future is best expressed as an "embodiment" of organizational purpose or mission, leaders bring to the surface, to "resonance," this aspect of the human experience. Leaders lift up and clarify the shared human reason and passion for the endeavor. This gives meaning, purpose, and direction to the people. Leadership taps into heartfelt motivations and helps to enhance employee engagement.

Leaders work the effervescence of *vision*. For leaders, in Gallup's view, visioning is an ongoing process. Emerging from the values and purpose of the organization is an expression of a desirable, mutually shared image of a possible, shared future. As the organization proceeds, the vision reshapes as the continuity of values finds increasingly fresh and expansive expressions of possibility. Although specific goals support the pursuit of vision and should be achieved, vision always remains at the horizon of possibility. It is the work of leaders to make this be so.

Leaders challenge their people with *audacious goals*. Successful leaders use challenging, stretch goals to tell their people that they believe in them. This is a critically important message. Far-reaching goals that feel detached from the organization's mission and vision may be perceived as the leaders' "ego trip." But when leaders successfully create a continuity of values, vision, policy, action, and challenge, remarkable things can be achieved; future direction and hope can be created; and organizational effectiveness can be enhanced.

# Chapter **Twelve**

# Behavioral Performance Management

## Learning Objectives

- **Define** the theoretical processes of learning: behavioristic, cognitive, and social/social cognitive.
- **Discuss** the principle of reinforcement, with special attention given to the law of effect, positive and negative reinforcers, and punishment.
- **Analyze** organizational reward systems, emphasizing both monetary and nonfinancial rewards.
- **Present** the steps and results of behavioral performance management, or organizational behavior modification (O.B. Mod.).

In a sense, this whole text on organizational behavior is concerned with the *what* and *how* of managing and leading people for high performance in today's organizations. Certainly many of the chapters (e.g., Chapter 4 on reward systems, Chapter 6 on motivation, Chapter 7 on positive organizational behavior, and all of the chapters in Part Three) are directly, or at least indirectly, concerned with how to manage oneself and human resources more effectively. The same could be said of popular techniques that have strong consulting advocates such as the late Edwards Deming's "Total Quality Management," Steven Covey's "The Seven Habits of Highly Effective People," or Peter Senge's "Learning Organizations." As was pointed out in the Chapter 1 discussion of the evidenced-based approach taken by this text, purely academic approaches may not be directly applied enough, and the popular writers' techniques tend to be "quick fixes" and "fads" without research backup that come with a splash and then, unfortunately, go. In contrast, this last part of the text again takes an evidenced-based (theoretical foundation, research supported and sustainable, effective application techniques) approach to managing and leading for high performance. In particular, this chapter on behavioral management meets the evidence-based criteria. As one behavioral management advocate strongly points out:

> Behavior Performance Management is not a good idea to be tried for a while and then cast aside for some other good idea. It is a science that explains how people behave. It cannot go away anymore than gravity can go away. In a changing world, the science of behavior must remain the bedrock, the starting place for every decision we make, every new technology we apply, and every initiative we employ in our efforts to bring out the best in people.[1]

The purpose of this chapter is to provide an overview of learning theory and evidence-based principles and guidelines that serve as a foundation and point of departure for presenting the behavioral management approach. The first section summarizes the widely recognized theories of learning: behavioristic, cognitive, and social/social cognitive. Next, the principles of reinforcement and punishment are given attention, followed by a discussion of both monetary and nonfinancial rewards. The last part of the chapter is devoted specifically to behavioral management. Both the steps of organizational behavior modification, or O.B. Mod., and the results of its basic research and application are given attention.

# LEARNING THEORY BACKGROUND

Although learning theory has not been as popular in organizational behavior as motivation or personality theories, both scholars and practitioners would agree on its importance to both the understanding and the effective development and management of human resources. In fact, practically all organizational behavior is either directly or indirectly affected by learning. For example, a worker's skill, a manager's attitude, a staff assistant's motivation, a salesperson's optimism and confidence, and an accountant's mode of dress are all learned. With the application of learning processes and principles, employees' behavior can be analyzed and managed to improve their performance.[2]

The most basic purpose of any theory is to better understand and explain the phenomenon in question. When theories become perfected, they have universal application and should enable prediction and control. Thus, a perfected theory of learning would have to be able to explain all aspects of learning (how, when, and why), have universal application (for example, to children, college students, managers, and workers), and predict and control learning situations. To date, no such theory of learning exists. Although there is general agreement on some principles of learning—such as reinforcement—that permit prediction and control, there is still a degree of controversy surrounding the theoretical understanding of learning in general and some of the principles in particular. This does not mean that no attempts have been made to develop a theory of learning. In fact, the opposite is true. The most widely recognized theoretical approaches incorporate the behavioristic and cognitive approaches and the emerging social cognitive theory that Chapter 1 indicated serves as the conceptual framework for this text. An understanding of these learning theories is important to the study of organizational behavior in general and behavioral performance management in particular.

## Behavioristic Theories

The most traditional and researched theory of learning comes out of the behaviorist school of thought in psychology (see Chapter 1). Most of the principles of learning and organizational reward systems, covered in Chapter 4, and the behavioral performance management approach discussed in this chapter are based on behavioristic theories, or behaviorism.[3]

The classical behaviorists, such as the Russian pioneer Ivan Pavlov and the American John B. Watson, attributed learning to the association or connection between stimulus and response (S-R). The operant behaviorists, in particular the well-known American psychologist B. F. Skinner, give more attention to the role that consequences play in learning, or the response-stimulus (R-S) connection.[4] The emphasis on the connection (S-R or R-S) has led some to label these *connectionist theories* of learning. The *S-R* deals with classical, or respondent, conditioning, and the *R-S* deals with instrumental, or operant, conditioning. An understanding of these conditioning processes is vital to the study of learning and serves as a point of departure for understanding and modifying organizational behavior.

### Classical Conditioning

Pavlov's classical conditioning experiment using dogs as subjects is arguably the single most famous study ever conducted in the behavioral sciences. A simple surgical procedure permitted Pavlov to measure accurately the amount of saliva secreted by a dog. When he presented meat powder (unconditioned stimulus) to the dog in the experiment, Pavlov noticed a great deal of salivation (unconditioned response). On the other hand, when he merely rang a bell (neutral stimulus), the dog did not salivate. The next step taken by Pavlov was to accompany the meat with the ringing of the bell. After doing this a number of times, Pavlov rang the bell without presenting the meat. This time, the dog salivated to the bell alone. The dog had become classically conditioned to salivate (conditioned response) to the sound of the bell (conditioned stimulus). Thus, *classical conditioning* can be defined as a process in which a formerly neutral stimulus, when paired with an unconditioned stimulus, becomes a conditioned stimulus that elicits a conditioned response; in other words, the S-R (i.e., bell-saliva) connection is learned. The Pavlov experiment was a major break-through and has had a lasting impact on the understanding of learning.

Despite the theoretical possibility of the widespread applicability of classical conditioning and its continued refinement and application to areas such as modern marketing,[5] most contemporary learning theorists agree that it represents only a very small part of total human learning and behavior. Skinner in particular felt that classical conditioning explains only respondent (reflexive) behaviors. These are the involuntary responses that are elicited by a stimulus. Skinner felt that the more complex, but common, human behaviors cannot be explained by classical conditioning alone. When explaining why he was abandoning a stimulus-response psychology, Skinner noted, "The greater part of the behavior of an organism was under the control of stimuli which were effective only because they were correlated with reinforcing consequences."[6] Thus, Skinner, through his extensive research, posited that *behavior was a function of consequences,* not the classical conditioning eliciting stimuli. He felt that most human behavior affects, or operates on, the environment to receive a desirable consequence. This type of behavior is learned through operant conditioning.

### Operant Conditioning

*Operant conditioning* is concerned primarily with learning that occurs as a consequence of behavior, or R-S. It is not concerned with the eliciting causes of behavior, as classical, or respondent, conditioning is. The specific differences between classical and operant conditioning may be summarized as follows:

1. In classical conditioning, a change in the stimulus (unconditioned stimulus to conditioned stimulus) will elicit a particular response. In operant conditioning, one particular response out of many possible ones occurs in a given stimulus situation. The stimulus situation serves as a cue in operant conditioning. It does not elicit the response but serves as a cue for a person to emit the response. The critical aspect of operant conditioning is what happens as a consequence of the response. The strength and frequency of classically conditioned behaviors are determined mainly by the frequency of the eliciting stimulus (the environmental event that precedes the behavior). The strength and frequency of operantly conditioned behaviors are determined mainly by the consequences (the environmental event that follows the behavior).

2. During the classical conditioning process, the unconditioned stimulus, serving as a reward, is presented every time. In operant conditioning, the reward is presented only if the organism gives the correct response. The organism must operate on the environment (thus the term *operant conditioning*) in order to receive a reward. The response is

**TABLE 12.1**
**Examples of Classical and Operant Conditioning**

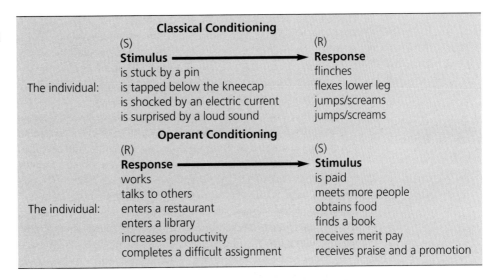

| | **Classical Conditioning** | |
|---|---|---|
| | (S) | (R) |
| | **Stimulus** ⟶ | **Response** |
| | is stuck by a pin | flinches |
| The individual: | is tapped below the kneecap | flexes lower leg |
| | is shocked by an electric current | jumps/screams |
| | is surprised by a loud sound | jumps/screams |
| | **Operant Conditioning** | |
| | (R) | (S) |
| | **Response** ⟶ | **Stimulus** |
| | works | is paid |
| | talks to others | meets more people |
| The individual: | enters a restaurant | obtains food |
| | enters a library | finds a book |
| | increases productivity | receives merit pay |
| | completes a difficult assignment | receives praise and a promotion |

instrumental in obtaining the reward. Table 12.1 gives some simple examples of classical (S-R) and operant (R-S) conditioning.

Operant conditioning has a much greater impact on human learning than classical conditioning. Today, even though Skinner died in 1990, he remains somewhat controversial[7] and his views are commonly misrepresented,[8] the operant theory is still being refined and expanded,[9] historical analyses recognize some limitations but also definite contributions,[10] and applications are being made in areas such as marketing[11] and performance management.[12] Operant conditioning also explains, at least in a very simple sense, much of organizational behavior. For example, it might be said that employees work eight hours a day, five days a week, in order to feed, clothe, and shelter themselves and their families. Working (conditioned response) is instrumental in obtaining the food, clothing, and shelter.

Some significant insights can be gained directly from operant analysis. The consequences of organizational behavior can change the environmental situation and greatly affect subsequent employee behaviors.[13] Managers can analyze the consequences of organizational behavior to help accomplish the goals of prediction and control. Some organizational behavior researchers are indeed using the operant framework to analyze specific areas such as escalation of commitment (where a tendency of decision makers is to "throw good money after bad")[14] as well as more generally the effectiveness of managers at work.[15] In addition, this theory serves as the framework for operationalizing much of behavioral performance management presented in this chapter.

## Cognitive Theories

As was covered in Chapter 1 for understanding organizational behavior in general, the cognitive theories can also be used to understand learning and, especially as an input into social and social cognitive theories, to better understand behavioral performance management.[16] Edward Tolman is widely recognized as a pioneering cognitive theorist. He felt that *cognitive learning* consists of a relationship between cognitive environmental cues and expectation. He developed and tested this theory through controlled experimentation. In fact, even though behaviorists are mostly associated with animal subjects in their research, Tolman was one of the first to extensively use the now-famous white rat in psychological experiments. He found that a rat could learn to run through an intricate maze, with purpose and direction, toward a goal (food). Tolman observed that at each choice point in the maze, expectations were established. In other words, the rat learned to expect that certain cognitive cues associated with the choice point might eventually lead to food. If the rat actually received the food, the association between the cue and the expectancy was strengthened, and learning occurred. In contrast to the S-R and R-S learning in the classical and operant approaches, Tolman's approach could be depicted as S-S (stimulus-stimulus), or learning the association between the cue and the expectancy.

In another early, classic study to demonstrate cognitive learning, Wolfgang Kohler used chimps presented with a problem of obtaining an out-of-reach suspended banana. At first the chimps attempted to jump for it, but soon gave up and seized a box that had been placed in another part of the room, dragged it under the object, mounted it, and took down the fruit. Kohler called this more complex learning "insight." The solution to the problem appeared as a whole, not as a series, gradual shaping of new responses as the operant approach would suggest. At the time (1927), famous social philosopher/critic Bertrand Russell concluded, "there are two ways of learning, one by experience, and the other by what Kohler calls 'insight.'"[17]

Besides being the forerunner of modern cognitive theory, Tolman's S-S connection and Kohler's insightful learning also had a great impact on the early human relations movement. Industrial training programs starting after World War II (and in many respects still today) drew heavily on their ideas. Programs were designed to strengthen the relationship between cognitive cues (supervisory, organizational, and job procedures) and worker expectations (incentive payments for good performance). The theory was that the worker would learn to be more productive by building an association between taking orders or following directions and expectancies of monetary reward for this effort. The same is true for the creativity, problem-solving groups that have been so popular over the years; they have drawn heavily from the notion of insightful learning.

Today, the cognitive sciences focus more on the structures and processes of human competence (for example, the role of memory and information processing) rather than on the acquisition and transition processes that have dominated learning theory explanations.[18] In organizational behavior, the cognitive approach has been applied mainly to motivation theories. Expectations, attributions and locus of control, and goal setting (which are in the forefront of modern work motivation) are all cognitive concepts and represent the purposefulness of organizational behavior. Many researchers are currently concerned about the relationship or connection between cognitions and organizational behavior.[19]

## Social Learning and Social Cognitive Theory

As brought out in Chapter 1, social learning theory served as the conceptual framework for the past several editions of this text. However, similar to the theory building in social psychology, primarily from the extensive work of widely recognized psychologist Albert Bandura,[20] this edition of the text and this overview of learning recognizes the evolution to the more comprehensive social cognition. After first recognizing social learning, the discussion turns to social cognition and its derivatives of modeling and self-efficacy.

### *Social Learning*

This theoretical approach to learning was the first to combine and integrate both behaviorist and cognitive concepts and emphasized the interactive, reciprocal nature of cognitive, behavioral, and environmental determinants. It is important to recognize that social learning theory recognizes and draws from the principles of classical and operant conditioning. But equally important is the fact that social learning theory went beyond classical and operant theory by recognizing that there is more to learning than direct learning via antecedent stimuli and contingent consequences. Social learning theory posits that learning can also take place via vicarious, or modeling, and self-control processes (see Chapter 1). Thus, social learning theory agrees with classical and operant conditioning processes, but says they are too limiting and adds vicarious, modeling, and self-control processes.

### Social Cognition

This theory has emerged in recent years to go beyond social learning theory. Social cognitive theory extends learning and/or modifying behavior by giving more attention to the self-regulatory mechanisms. Specifically, as was presented in Chapter 1, social cognitive theory identifies five capabilities that people use to initiate, regulate, and sustain their behavior: (1) symbolizing, (2) forethought, (3) vicarious/modeling learning, (4) self-regulation, and (5) self-reflection.[21] These human capabilities recognize cognitive processes, social learning, and self-efficacy. A closer look at social learning through the social cognitive derivatives of modeling and self-efficacy can lead to the better understanding of learning and contribute to the theoretical underpinning of behavioral performance management.

### Modeling Processes

The vicarious, or modeling, processes essentially involve observational learning. "Modeling in accordance with social learning theory can account for certain behavior acquisition phenomena that cannot be easily fitted into either operant or respondent conditioning."[22]

Many years ago, Miller and Dollard suggested that learning need not result from discrete stimulus-response or response-consequence connections. Instead, learning can take place through imitating (i.e., modeling) others. Bandura states:

> Although behavior can be shaped into new patterns to some extent by rewarding and punishing consequences, learning would be exceedingly laborious and hazardous if it proceeded solely on this basis. . . . [It] is difficult to imagine a socialization process in which the language, mores, vocational activities, familial customs and educational, religious and political practices of a culture are taught to each new member by selective reinforcement of fortuitous behavior, without benefit of models who exemplify the cultural patterns in their own behavior. Most of the behaviors that people display are learned either deliberately or inadvertently, through the influence of example.[23]

Bandura has done considerable research demonstrating that people can indeed learn from others.[24] This learning takes place in two steps. First, the person observes how others act and then acquires a mental picture of the act and its consequences (rewards and punishers). Second, the person acts out the acquired image, and if the consequences are positive, he or she will tend to do it again. If the consequences are negative, the person will tend not to do it again. These positive and negative consequences, of course, are where there is a tie-in with operant theory. But because there is cognitive, symbolic representation of the modeled activities instead of discrete response-consequence connections in the acquisition of new behavior or modifying existing behavior, modeling goes beyond the operant explanation. In particular, Bandura concludes that *modeling* involves interrelated subprocesses, such as attention, retention, and motoric reproduction, as well as reinforcement.

### Self-Efficacy

Although given detailed attention in Chapter 7 as a key positive construct in psychological capital, self-efficacy has also been recognized as a construct in behavioral performance management.[25] Bandura has defined *self-efficacy* as the "beliefs in one's capabilities to organize and execute the courses of action required to produce given attainments."[26] In particular, when faced with a specific task or job, an employee's efficacy will determine whether the necessary behavior will be initiated, how much effort will be expended and sustained, and how much persistence and resilience there will be when there are obstacles or even failure.[27] In other words, people who believe they can perform well on a task (high self-efficacy) do better than those who think they will fail (low self-efficacy). Importantly for the field of organizational behavior, a stream of research studies meta-analyzed has found a strong relationship between self-efficacy and work-related performance.[28] Also, those with high self-efficacy have the tendency to remain calm in a stressful situation.[29] In other words, there is considerable evidence that those employees with high self-efficacy tend to persevere and end up doing a good job without suffering stress or burnout. Unlike predisposed personality traits, efficacy is a state that can be trained and developed. As discussed in detail in Chapter 7, the input into efficacy is recognized to be mastery experiences, vicarious/modeling learning, social persuasion, and physiological/psychological arousal.[30] Both managers and their employees who experience success, are trained through modeling, and are encouraged and aroused on a given task or job, will have their efficacy enhanced and will perform well. There seems to be considerable practical implications for understanding and developing self-efficacy in managers and employees for performance improvement.[31]

# PRINCIPLES OF LEARNING: REINFORCEMENT AND PUNISHMENT

Reinforcement and punishment play a central role in the learning process and provide evidence-based principles for behavioral performance management. Most learning experts agree that reinforcement is more important than punishment and is the single most important concept and application principle. Yet there is still some controversy over its theoretical explanation. The first theoretical treatment given to reinforcement in learning and the framework that still dominates today is pioneering psychologist Edward Thorndike's classic law of effect.

## Laws of Behavior

In Thorndike's own words, the *law of effect* is simply stated as follows: "Of several responses made to the same situation, those which are accompanied or closely followed by satisfaction [reinforcement] . . . will be more likely to recur; those which are accompanied or closely followed by discomfort [punishment] . . . will be less likely to occur." From a strictly empirical standpoint, most behavioral scientists, even those with a strict cognitive orientation, generally accept the validity of this law. It has been demonstrated time after time in highly controlled learning experiments and is directly observable in everyday learning experiences. Sometimes called the laws of behavior, desirable, or reinforcing, consequences will increase the strength of the preceding behavior and increase its probability of being repeated in the future. Undesirable, or punishing, consequences will decrease the strength of the preceding behavior and decrease its probability of being repeated in the future. Sometimes a third law is added: If the behavior is followed by no consequence (neither a positive nor a negative contingent consequence) the behavior will extinguish over time (thus this is called the extinction principle or law).[32]

## Critique of Reinforcement Theory

Although there is wide acceptance of the laws of behavior, there may be some occasions when a person's cognitive rationalizations might neutralize them. For example, people with inaccurate self-efficacy beliefs may not be affected by the consequences of their actions. In the workplace, this is a real problem for managers. Those with inaccurate or false self-efficacy beliefs who experience performance failures time after time will not learn from their mistakes or respond to the manager's comments on how to correct the problem. They have high self-efficacy (they believe that their behaviors are appropriate to successfully accomplish the task), but they are wrong.[33] In addition to this type of cognitive processing that may neutralize the law of effect, there is some disagreement when it is carried a step further and used as an overall theory or an absolute requirement for learning.

Both Tolman's and Kohler's classic studies providing initial support for cognitive theories, presented earlier, discounted the need for incremental reinforcement as necessary for learning to occur. For example, Tolman conducted place learning, latent learning, and transposition experiments in an attempt to demonstrate that reinforcement was not a precondition for learning to occur. Specifically, in the place learning he trained a rat to turn right in a T maze in order to obtain the reward of food. Then he started the rat from the opposite part of the maze. According to operant theory, the rat should have turned right because of past conditioning. However, the rat turned toward where the food had been placed. Tolman concluded that the behavior was purposive; the rat had formed a cognitive map to figure out how to get to the food. Over time, the behaviorists were able to counteract Tolman's studies with more controlled (e.g., sterile mazes, etc.) experiments, and Kohler's conclusions about insight were also explained away by a reinforcement history alternative explanation.[34]

More recently, Deci[35] and Deci and Ryan,[36] through their cognitive evaluation theory and laboratory research studies, have posited that external consequences (i.e., rewards) have a negative impact on intrinsically motivated (see Chapter 6) behavior dealing with task persistence and creativity. These findings generated considerable follow-up research with mixed findings. One review of about 100 studies found some rewards may have a detrimental effect, but an equal number found no effect or a positive effect.[37] The conclusion from this extensive review was that (1) the detrimental effects of rewards occur under highly restricted, easily avoidable conditions; (2) mechanisms of classical and operant conditioning are basic for understanding incremental and detrimental effects of reward on task motivation; and (3) positive effects of rewards on performance are easily attainable using procedures derived from behavioral theory.[38]

Finally, a meta-analysis of 96 studies found that the only detrimental effect of rewards was the time spent carrying out laboratory activity following a performance-independent (i.e., a noncontingent) reward.[39] There is also systematic analysis that discounts cognitive evaluation theory when compared to operant theory explanations.[40] Yet, despite this considerable empirical and theoretical counterevidence, an unconvinced few such as popular author Alfie Kohn continue to write (not do research) with titles such as *Punished by Rewards* and "Why Incentive Plans Cannot Work."[41] Based on his own assumptions and the now-countered Deci and Ryan theory and research, and in stark contrast to the large body of reinforcement theory and research, he makes unequivocal statements such as: "The bottom line is that any approach that offers a reward for better performance is destined to be ineffective."[42]

Unfortunately, Kohn's largely unsupported statements do not fall on deaf ears in the real world. This is because practicing managers have indeed experienced some implementation problems with pay-for-performance programs.[43] For example, after an extensive review of the relevant literature, Lawler concluded that process/design problems, not the underlying theory of reinforcement or the supporting basic research, limit the effectiveness of pay for performance.[44] There is also a research study that found that highly dispersed reward systems (i.e., very large differences between highest and lowest payouts) may have a negative effect on both individual and organizational performace, especially when collaborative efforts (such as in teams) are important.[45] Yet, once again, it is not that the theory/research on reinforcement is wrong, but rather it is the implementation that can cause problems. As Bandura points out, "To say that [only] thought guides action is an abbreviated statement of convenience rather than a conferral of agency of thought,"[46] because "if people acted. . . on the basis of informative cues but remained unaffected by the results of their actions, they would be insensible to survive very long."[47] As a final summary statement, it can be said that the theory of reinforcement, like learning in general, is not perfect and still needs development. However, it can also be said that reinforcement does serve as an excellent theoretical foundation and evidence-based guiding principle, and the implementation issues need to be overcome by effective behavioral performance management.

## Reinforcement as Used in Behavioral Management

The terms *rewards* and *reinforcers* are often used interchangeably and loosely, but in behavioral performance management have very precise definitions and usage. An often cited circular definition of reinforcement says that it is anything the person finds rewarding. This definition is of little value because the words *reinforcing* and *rewarding* are used interchangeably, but neither one is operationally defined. A more operational definition can be arrived at by reverting to the laws of behavior. Specifically, *reinforcement* in behavioral management is defined as anything that both increases the strength and tends to induce repetitions of the behavior that preceded the reinforcement. A *reward,* on the other hand, is simply something that the person who presents it deems to be desirable.

Reinforcement is functionally defined. Something is reinforcing only if it strengthens the behavior preceding it and induces repetitions. For example, a manager may ostensibly reward an employee who found an error in a report by publicly praising the employee. Yet on examination it is found that the employee is embarrassed and chided by coworkers, and the error-finding behavior of this employee decreases in the future. In this example, the "reward" of public praise is not reinforcing. Besides clearing up differences between reinforcers and rewards, behavioral management also requires making the distinction between positive and negative reinforcers.

## Positive and Negative Reinforcers

There is much confusion surrounding the terms *positive reinforcement, negative reinforcement,* and *punishment.* First of all, it must be understood that reinforcement, positive *or* negative, strengthens the behavior and increases the probability of repetition. But positive and negative reinforcers accomplish this impact on behavior in completely different ways. *Positive reinforcement* strengthens and increases behavior by the *presentation* of a desirable consequence. *Negative reinforcement* strengthens and increases behavior by the threat of the use of an undesirable consequence or the *termination or withdrawal* of an undesirable consequence. Figure 12.1 briefly summarizes the differences between positive and

**FIGURE 12.1**
**Summary of the Operational Definitions of Positive and Negative Reinforcement and Punishment**

| Consequence of Contingent | Reward (something desirable) | Noxious stimuli (something aversive and undesirable) |
|---|---|---|
| Application | POSITIVE REINFORCEMENT Behavior increases | PUNISHMENT Behavior decreases |
| Withdrawal | PUNISHMENT Behavior decreases | NEGATIVE REINFORCEMENT Behavior increases |

negative reinforcement and punishment. Giving recognition and attention to an employee for the successful completion of a task could be an example of positive reinforcement (if this does in fact strengthen and subsequently increase this task behavior). On the other hand, a worker is negatively reinforced for getting busy when the supervisor walks through the area. Getting busy prevents or terminates being "chewed out" by the supervisor.

Negative reinforcement is more complex than positive reinforcement, but it should not be equated with punishment. In fact, they have opposite effects on behavior. Negative reinforcement strengthens and increases behavior, whereas punishment weakens and decreases behavior. However, both are considered to be forms of negative control of behavior. Negative reinforcement is really a form of social blackmail, because the person will behave in a certain way in order not to be punished. A clearer understanding of punishment will help further clarify how it differs from negative reinforcement.

## The Use of Punishment

Punishment is one of the most used but least understood and badly administered aspects of behavioral management. Whether in rearing children or dealing with employees in a complex organization, parents and supervisors or managers often revert to punishment instead of positive reinforcement in order to modify or control behavior. Punishment is commonly thought to be the reverse of reinforcement but equally effective in altering behavior. However, this simple analogy with reinforcement is not warranted. The reason is that punishment is a very complex phenomenon and must be carefully defined and used.[48]

### The Meaning of Punishment

*Punishment* is anything that weakens behavior and tends to decrease its subsequent frequency. Punishment usually consists of the application of an undesirable or noxious consequence, but as shown in Figure 12.1, it can also be defined as the withdrawal of a desirable consequence. Thus, taking away certain organizational privileges from a manager who has a poor performance record could be thought of as punishment.

Regardless of the distinction between punishment as the application of an undesirable consequence and as the withdrawal of a desirable consequence, in order for punishment to be effective, there must be a weakening of, and a decrease in, the behavior that preceded it. Just because a supervisor criticizes an associate and thinks this is a punishment, it is not necessarily the case unless the behavior that preceded the criticism weakens and decreases in subsequent frequency. In many situations when supervisors think they are punishing employees, they are in fact reinforcing them because they are giving attention, and attention tends to be very reinforcing. This explains the common complaint that supervisors often make: "I call Joe in, give him heck for goofing up, and he goes right back out and goofs up again." What is happening in this case is that the supervisor thinks Joe is being punished, when operationally, what is obviously happening is that the supervisor is reinforcing Joe's undesirable behavior by giving him attention and recognition. Punishment, like reinforcement, is defined and operationalized by its effects on behavior, not by what the person thinks is or should be punishment.

### Administering Punishment

Opinions on administering punishment range all the way from the one extreme of dire warnings never to use it to the other extreme that it is the only effective way to modify behavior. As yet, research has not been able to support either view completely. However, there is little doubt that the use of punishment tends to cause many undesirable side effects.[49] Neither children nor adults like to be punished. The punished behavior tends to be only temporarily suppressed rather than permanently changed, and the punished person

Holiday shopping, yearend deadlines, and emotional family dramas aren't the only stresses in December. 'Tis the season for companies to embark on that dreaded annual rite, the often bureaucratic and always time-consuming performance review. The process can be brutal: As many as one-third of U.S. corporations evaluate employees based on systems that pit them against their colleagues, and some even lead to the firing of low performers.

Fans say such "forced ranking" systems ensure that managers take a cold look at performance. But the practice increasingly is coming under fire. Following a string of discrimination lawsuits from employees who feel they were ranked and yanked based on age and not merely their performance, fewer companies are adopting the controversial management tool. Critics charge that it unfairly penalizes groups made up of stars and hinders collaboration and risk-taking, a growing concern for companies that are trying to innovate their way to growth. And a new study calls into question the long-term value of forced rankings. "It creates a zero-sum game, and so it tends to discourage cooperation," says Steve Kerr, a managing director at Goldman Sachs Group Inc., who heads the firm's leadership training program.

Even General Electric Co., the most famous proponent of the practice, is trying to inject more flexibility into its system. Former Chief Executive Jack Welch required managers to divide talent into three groups—a top 20%, a middle 70%, and a bottom 10%, many of whom were shown the door. Eighteen months ago, GE launched a proactive campaign to remind managers to use more common sense in assigning rankings.

A recent study lends hard data to that theory. Steve Scullen, an associate professor of management at Drake University in Des Moines, found that forced ranking, including the firing of the bottom 5% or 10%, results in an impressive 16% productivity improvement—but only over the first couple of years. After that, Scullen says, the gains drop off, from 6% climbs in the third and fourth years to basically zero by year 10. "It's a terrific idea for companies in trouble, done over one or two years, but to do it as a long-term solution is not going to work," says Dave Ulrich, a business professor at the University of Michigan at Ann Arbor. "Over time it gets people focused on competing with each other rather than collaborating."

Yahoo is looking for better dialogue and less demoralizing labels when it made substantial changes this year to its rating system, which compared employees' performance to an absolute standard rather than to each other. Libby Sartain, Yahoo's senior vice-president for human resources, knew that review discussions at the Sunnyvale (Calif.) tech leader frequently included the wink-wink "I wanted to put you here, but I was forced by human resources to do something different" comment that discredits so many appraisals. This year, Yahoo stripped away its performance labels, partly in hopes that reviews would center more on substance and less on explaining away a grade.

But that doesn't mean Yahoo went all Pollyanna on its employees. To do a better job of finding and showering top performers with the rewards necessary to keep them from jumping ship in talent-tight Silicon Valley, the company also instituted a "stack-ranking" system this year to determine how compensation increases are distributed. It asks managers to rank employees within each unit—a group of 20 people would be ranked 1 through 20, for example—with raises and bonuses distributed accordingly. During reviews, employees are told how their increases generally compare to those of others.

Some Yahoo managers are livid about the new system. "It's going to kill morale," laments one senior engineering manager who says he's getting a stronger message to cull his bottom performers. Yahoo says its new program doesn't automatically weed out a bottom group and was designed specifically to reward its stars.

Indeed, what Yahoo has introduced in place of its old system shows how hard it is for companies to find ways to foster merit-driven cultures that coddle standouts while staying tough on low performers. Whether a company calls it stack ranking, forced ranking, or differentiation, "there's no magic process," says Sartain. "We just want to make sure we're making our bets and that we're investing in the people we most want to keep. That's what this is all about."

tends to get anxious or uptight and resentful of the punisher. There is growing research evidence that punishment has unintended negative effects on employees. For example, one recent study found that those who received rude, punishing feedback hurt their performance on complex tasks requiring creativity, flexibility, and memory recall[50] and another study found that over 90 percent of employees reported a negative outcome associated with being punished.[51] Thus, the use of punishment as a strategy to control behavior is a lose-lose approach. Unless the punishment is severe, the behavior will reappear very quickly, but the more severe the punishment, the greater the side effects such as hate and revenge. As described in the accompanying OB in Action, "forced rankings" in annual performance appraisals can be interpreted as punishing, and have undesirable side-effects.

To minimize the problems with using punishment, persons administering it must always provide an acceptable alternative to the behavior that is being punished. If they do not, the undesirable behavior will tend to reappear and will cause fear and anxiety in the person being punished. The punishment must always be administered as close in time to the undesirable behavior as possible. Calling subordinates into the office to give them a reprimand for breaking a rule the week before is not effective. All the reprimand tends to do at this time is to punish them for getting caught. The punishment has little effect on the rule-breaking behavior. When punishment is administered, it should be remembered that there is also an effect on the relevant others who are observing the punishment. While managers often believe those watching a coworker being punished can learn what not to do, a recent survey found that nearly a third of the observers reported a loss of respect for the manager administering the punishment.[52]

### Guidelines for Discipline

A rule of thumb for effective behavioral management should be: always attempt to reinforce instead of punish in order to change behavior. Furthermore, the use of a reinforcement strategy is usually more effective in accelerating desirable behaviors than the use of punishment is for decelerating undesirable behaviors because no bad side effects accompany reinforcement. As one comprehensive analysis of punishment concluded: "In order to succeed, [punishment] must be used in an orderly, rational manner—not, as is too often the case, as a handy outlet for a manager's anger or frustration. If used with skill, and concern for human dignity, it can be useful."[53] In behavioral management, discipline should attempt to be a learning experience, never purely a coercive experience to prove mastery or control over others. Perhaps the best practical advice is the old red-hot-stove rule of discipline—like the stove, punishment should give advance warning (it is red) and be immediate, consistent, and impersonal (it burns everyone who touches it). In addition, most modern approaches stress that punishment should be situationally applied (a crew of nineteen-year-old high school dropouts should be treated differently from a team of $100,000-per-year professionals) and progressive. The progressive discipline may start off with a clarifying verbal discussion, then move to a written mutual agreement signed by the person being disciplined, next move to time off with or without pay, and then only as a last step end in termination. As a recent comprehensive analysis of discipline concluded, "Regardless of an employee's infraction, managers must strive to maintain a positive working relationship by remaining open to dialogue and ensuring that the worker understands why he's being reprimanded. It's no small task."[54]

# THE ROLE OF ORGANIZATIONAL REWARD SYSTEMS

Because positive reinforcement consequences are so important to employee behavior, organizational reward systems become critical to behavioral performance management. The organization may have the latest advanced information technology, well-thought-out strategic plans, detailed job descriptions, and comprehensive training programs, but unless the people are reinforced for their performance-related behaviors, the "up-front" variables (technology, plans, and so on) for the rules that govern[55] or the establishing operation (i.e., there is enough motivation)[56] of their behavior, there will be little impact. In other words, going back to Skinner's original conception, the antecedent cues (technology, plans, and the like) have power to control or provide rules and establishing operation for behavior only if there are reinforcing consequences. As one behavioral management consultant points out:

> A company is always perfectly designed to produce what it is producing. If it has quality problems, cost problems, productivity problems, then the behaviors associated with those undesirable outcomes are being reinforced. This is not conjecture. This is the hard, cold reality of human behavior.[57]

The challenge for performance management is to understand this behavioral reality, eliminate the reinforcers for the undesirable behaviors, and more importantly and effectively, reinforce the desirable behavior. Thus, organizational reward systems become a key, often-overlooked, factor in bringing about improved performance and success.

Chapter 4 is specifically devoted to reward systems that are a vital part of the organizational environment (along with structure and culture) in the social cognitive model for this text. As was pointed out, money (pay) dominates organizational reward systems. The following sections analyze both monetary and nonfinancial reinforcers that can be used in behavioral performance management.

## Analysis of Money as a Reinforcer

Unfortunately, about the only reinforcing function that traditional monetary reward systems (covered in Chapter 4) such as base-pay techniques provide is to reinforce employees for walking up to the pay window or for opening an envelope and seeing their paycheck or direct deposit stub every two weeks or every month. These traditional pay plans certainly have come up short of having the intended impact on improving employee performance at all levels.[58] Yet, despite the problems with traditional pay approaches, money is still a very important reward to employees at all levels. For example, former GE head and now with his wife giving advice to managers in an online column, Jack Welch recently quipped,

> You surely have seen how effective money is in lighting a motivational fire—even in employees who claim money doesn't matter to them. Plaques gather dust. Checks can be cashed. And employees know the difference in their bones.[59]

Recent analyses of the research studies also conclude that money contingently administered can have a positive effect on employee behavior.[60] However, there are even shortcomings with merit pay mainly due to implementation issues such as poor measurement of performance, lack of acceptance of supervisory feedback, limited desirability of merit increases that are too small, a lack of linkage between merit pay and performance, and potential unintended consequences such as focusing only on merit-related activities and behaviors[61] and lingering inequalities on merit pay for women and minorities.[62] Some compensation practitioners argue that merit pay only makes employees unhappy because they view it as an unfair way to reward for past performance instead of being geared to improved future performance.[63] Also, a laboratory study of merit pay led to the following conclusions:

1. Unless a merit raise is at least 6 to 7 percent of base pay, it will not produce the desired effects on employee behavior.
2. Beyond a certain point, increases in merit-raise size are unlikely to improve performance.
3. When merit raises are too small, employee morale will suffer.
4. Cost-of-living adjustments, seniority adjustments, and other nonmerit components of a raise should be clearly separated from the merit component.
5. Smaller percentage raises given to employees at the higher ends of base-pay ranges are demotivating.[64]

In other words, both the traditional base- and merit-pay plans have some problems.

The "New Pay" plans covered in Chapter 4 (e.g., pay for performance at both the individual and group levels, paying for customer and/or employee satisfaction, pay for knowledge, skill pay, competency pay, and broadbanding) have overcome many of the problems.[65] For example, a large study sponsored by the American Compensation Association was able to place a dollar value on the positive impact of pay-for-performance plans. The value of the performance improvement translates into a 134 percent net return on what is paid out to employees (excluding the costs associated with training, communications, and consulting), or, for every $1 of payout, a gain of $2.34 was attained.[66]

In terms of basic research, a field experiment conducted by Stajkovic and Luthans in the biggest credit card processing firm in the world found the following:

1. A traditionally administered pay-for-performance plan (i.e., announced through normal channels in terms of the amount of pay that would be received for various levels of performance) did increase performance by 11 percent; but

2. The same plan that was implemented through the behavioral performance management approach discussed next (i.e., specifying the critical performance behaviors that would lead to monetary consequences) had a significantly higher 32 percent increase in performance.[67]

In other words, because the performance behaviors strengthened and increased, the theory and principles of reinforcement explain that money can indeed be a powerful reinforcer. Importantly, money may not be a reinforcer when administered through the traditional pay plans, but when made contingent on identified performance behaviors as in behavioral performance management, money can be a powerful reinforcer.

The same could be said for the very expensive benefit plans in the organizational reward system (see Chapter 4). Flexible benefit plans and those that depend on performance may have better intended results.[68] Instead of benefits taking on an entitlement mentality, an increasing number of firms (18% according to an American Compensation Association survey) are making the amount and choice of benefits dependent on employee performance. For example, under Owens-Corning's "Rewards and Resources Program," workers get to clearly see how their work is reinforced with extra pay in the form of more benefit choices.[69]

## Nonfinancial Rewards

As Chapter 4 pointed out, money is the most obvious organizational reward, but the nonfinancial rewards are receiving increased attention. In fact, one comprehensive review of surveys that ask the value employees place on various rewards found that nonfinancial rewards were ranked much higher than financial ones.[70] For example, one study of 1,500 employees in a wide variety of work settings found personalized, instant recognition from managers as being the most important of the 65 types of rewards evaluated. However, more than half of these same employees reported that they seldom, if ever, received such personal recognition from their managers.[71] Also, a staffing company reported that the number-one reason employees give for leaving companies is the lack of praise and recognition.[72] Also in the same Stajkovic and Luthans research study cited previously, it was found that both social recognition (24%) and performance feedback (20%) had a significantly higher relative performance increase than did the traditionally administered pay for performance (11%).[73] Finally, in a recently conducted study in the fast-food industry, we (Peterson and Luthans) found that financial incentives initially had a bigger effect on profit, customer service, and employee retention outcomes, but, over time, except for employee retention, both financial and nonfinancial incentives had an equally significant impact.[74] In other words, there is little doubt that the nonfinancials can be very powerful, but are often overlooked as a reinforcer in behavioral performance management.

Table 12.2 summarizes some of the major categories of nonfinancial rewards. Notice that even though these are considered nonfinancial, they may still cost the organization.

**TABLE 12.2**  Categories of Nonfinancial Rewards

| Consumables | Manipulatables | Visual and Auditory | Job Design | Formal Recognition | Performance Feedback | Social Recognition and Attention |
|---|---|---|---|---|---|---|
| Coffee-break treats | Desk accessories | Office with a window | Jobs with more responsibility | Formal acknowledgment of achievement | Nonverbal performance information | Friendly greetings |
| Free lunches | Wall plaques | Piped-in music | Job rotation | Feature in house newsletter | Verbal performance information | Informal recognition |
| Food baskets | Company car | Internet and e-mail for personal use | Special assignments | Story in newspaper/TV | Written reports | Solicitation of suggestions |
| Easter hams | Watches | Redecoration of work environment | Cross training | Celebrations/banquets | Performance evaluations/appraisals (including 360 degree) | Solicitation of advice |
| Christmas turkeys | Trophies | Company literature | Knowledge training | Letters of commendation | Performance charts and graphs | Compliment of work progress |
| Dinners for the family on the company | Commendations | Private office | Authority to schedule own work | Acknowledgment/praise in front of others | Meters/counters or performance information | Pat on the back |
| Company picnics | Rings/tie pins | Popular speakers or lecturers | Flexible hours | | Self-information from performance or problem solutions | Smile |
| After-work wine and cheese parties | Appliances and furniture for the home | Book club discussions | Flexible breaks | | | Verbal or nonverbal recognition or praise |
| Time off | PC for the home/personal use | | Job sharing | | | |
| Trips | Home shop tools | | Participation in decisions | | | |
| Entertainment/Sports events | Garden tools | | Participation in teams | | | |
| Education classes | Clothing | | Self-managed teams | | | |
| | Club privileges | | | | | |
| | Use of company recreation facilities | | | | | |
| | Use of company convenience center | | | | | |
| | Use of company facilities for personal projects | | | | | |

This is true of the consumables, manipulatables, and visual and auditory rewards. The job design category is a special case and is usually not, but could be, considered as an organizational reward. Chapter 6 was devoted to these, and they are not included here as part of behavioral performance management. On the other hand, the social recognition and attention and performance feedback categories are relatively easy to apply in behavioral performance management, cost nothing (except perhaps for preparing some of the performance feedback), and may be even more powerful than the cost-based nonfinancial rewards. These two are major reinforcers and deserve special coverage.

### Social Recognition and Attention

Informally providing contingent recognition and attention (and praise, if genuine) tends to be a very powerful reinforcer for most people. In addition, few people become satiated or filled up with this; no one "suffers" from too much genuine recognition. However, similar to monetary reinforcers, social reinforcers should be administered on a contingent basis to have a positive effect on employee performance. For example, a pat on the back or verbal praise that is insincere or randomly given (as under the old human relations approach) may have no effect or even a punishing "boomerang" effect. But genuine social reinforcers, contingently administered for performance of the target behavior, can be a very effective positive reinforcer for most employees and improve their performance.[75] The added benefit of such a strategy, in contrast to the use of monetary rewards, is that the cost of social reinforcers to the organization is absolutely nothing.

Importantly, this informal *social* recognition based on a valued person's (e.g., boss, peer, subordinate, friend, spouse, etc.) attention and appreciation may have not only a bigger impact as a reinforcer in behavioral management than money, but also than formal recognition programs as detailed in Chapter 4. Unlike valued social recognition and attention, formal recognition programs, especially over time, can easily turn into being phoney, not valued by the recipient, or go against group and/or cultural norms. As Luthans and Stajkovic noted:

> A formal recognition award such as the "Golden Banana" at Hewlett-Packard or "Employee of the Month" given at many companies can initially be a reinforcer, but over time may cross the line and become an empty reward and be perceived even in a negative light. The first few Employee of the Month recipients may be very deserving instances that everyone would agree with, but over time selections become more and more controversial and subjective, usually resulting in selecting less-qualified or not-qualified employees. At this point company politics often come into play and those who truly deserved the recognition feel betrayed. In this case, the program would actually produce negative effects (e.g., "rewarding A while hoping for B"). Also, from a (collectivistic) cultural values and individual differences standpoint, although everyone may like to be recognized for their efforts and achievements, not everyone likes to be singled out in the public way that usually goes along with formal recognition.[76]

With the increasing use of teams, there is also recent evidence that they may be providing social reinforcement to their members that yields organizationally desirable outcomes. For example, in the American Compensation Association research study cited earlier, team suggestion plans, under the umbrella of an organizational performance reward plan or operating independently, were found to be particularly powerful contributors to organizational success. Importantly, the team suggestion plans, which typically used nonfinancial rewards, outperformed the individually based plans, which typically used financial rewards, by 4 to 1.[77] For example, the average value per idea adopted from team suggestion plans using nonfinancial rewards was an impressive $46,200 for a major airline, $14,500 for a manufacturer, $19,344 for a newspaper, and $19,266 for a bank.[78]

### Performance Feedback

There is little question that despite the tremendous amount of data being generated by today's advanced information systems, individuals still receive very little, if any, feedback about their performance. People generally have an intense desire to know how they are doing; they engage in feedback-seeking behavior.[79] Even though feedback has been found to be complex in research studies,[80] it is generally accepted that feedback enhances individual performance in behavioral management.[81] A comprehensive review (30 laboratory and 42 field experiments) concluded that performance feedback had a positive effect.[82] Also, as cited earlier, the Stajkovic and Luthans study found that, although not as high as contingently administered money and social recognition reinforcers, the performance feedback intervention still yielded a highly significant 20 percent performance improvement.[83] Importantly, this was significantly higher than the traditionally administered pay for performance (11 percent). As a general guideline for behavioral management, the performance feedback should be as *p*ositive, *i*mmediate, *g*raphic, and *s*pecific—thus, the acronym PIGS—as possible to be effective.[84]

Despite the recognized importance, there is still disagreement among scholars as to whether feedback per se is automatically reinforcing or too simplistic.[85] For example, after reviewing the existing research literature on feedback, one researcher concluded that its impact is contingent on factors such as the nature of the feedback information, the process of using feedback, individual differences among the recipients of the feedback, and the nature of the task.[86] One study, for instance, found that self-generated feedback with goal setting had a much more powerful effect on technical or engineering employees than externally generated feedback with goal setting.[87] Also, another study found subjects rated specific feedback more positively than they rated nonspecific feedback and preferred feedback that suggested an external cause of poor performance to feedback that suggested an internal cause.[88]

An argument can also be made that "actionable feedback" (feedback that leads to learning and appropriate results) is more effective than just critical, negative feedback.[89] And the source of the feedback seems important as well.[90] Not only are the amount and the frequency of feedback generated by a source important, but also the consistency and usefulness of the information generated, as a study found. Individuals viewed feedback from formal organizations least positively, from coworkers next, then from supervisors and tasks, with the best being self-generated feedback.[91] Feedback from multiple sources may be most effective,[92] and the 360-degree feedback systems (the individual is anonymously appraised not only by the boss but also by subordinates, peers, and sometimes customers) can be automated on a software system to provide more timely, objective, and less-costly feedback. Also, studies have found that choice of reward interacting with feedback had a positive impact on task performance in a laboratory exercise,[93] but workers in highly routine jobs who received positive feedback did not improve their performance.[94] Despite these qualifications and contingencies, a general guideline regarding performance feedback is that it can be a very effective reinforcer for behavioral performance management.

# BEHAVIORAL PERFORMANCE MANAGEMENT, OR O.B. MOD.

Behavioral performance management is based on behavioristic, social learning, and social cognitive theories, and especially the evidence-based principles of reinforcement as summarized above. Figure 12.2 graphically depicts the historical development and theory building up to the present influence of Bandura's social cognitive theory. The full-blown organizational behavior modification, or O.B. Mod. model, is shown in Figure 12.3. The

**FIGURE 12.2**
**Chronological Development of Conceptual Foundation for O.B. Mod.**

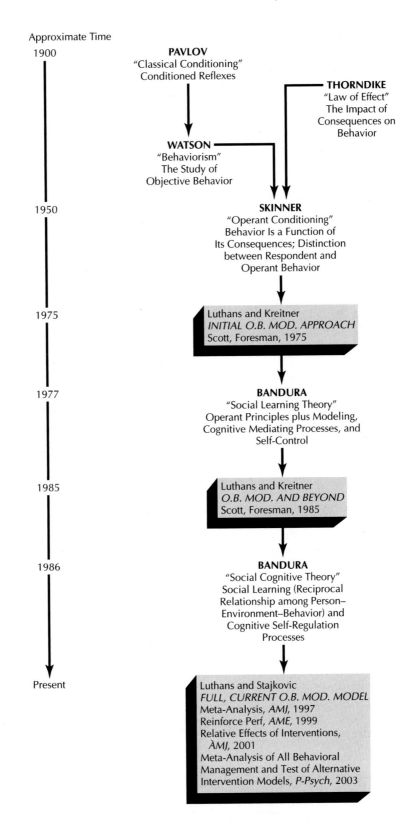

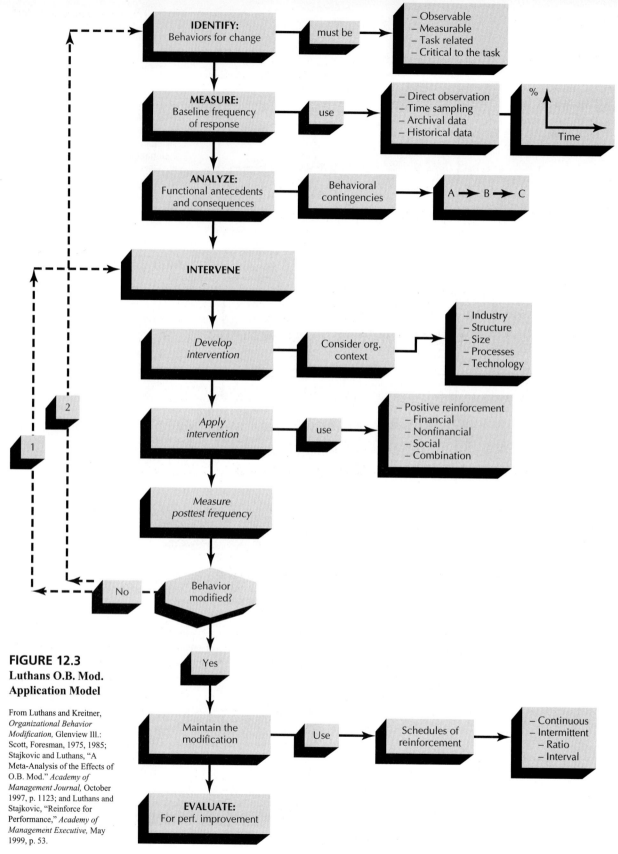

**FIGURE 12.3**
**Luthans O.B. Mod.**
**Application Model**

From Luthans and Kreitner,
*Organizational Behavior
Modification,* Glenview Ill.:
Scott, Foresman, 1975, 1985;
Stajkovic and Luthans, "A
Meta-Analysis of the Effects of
O.B. Mod." *Academy of
Management Journal,* October
1997, p. 1123; and Luthans and
Stajkovic, "Reinforce for
Performance," *Academy of
Management Executive,* May
1999, p. 53.

**396**

**FIGURE 12.4**
**Major Steps of Luthans O.B. Mod. Approach to Behavioral Performance Management**

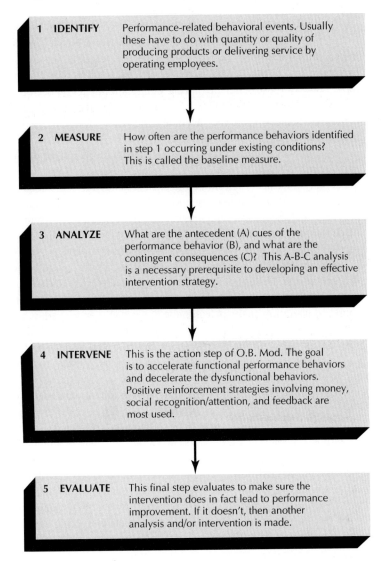

| 1 | IDENTIFY | Performance-related behavioral events. Usually these have to do with quantity or quality of producing products or delivering service by operating employees. |

| 2 | MEASURE | How often are the performance behaviors identified in step 1 occurring under existing conditions? This is called the baseline measure. |

| 3 | ANALYZE | What are the antecedent (A) cues of the performance behavior (B), and what are the contingent consequences (C)? This A-B-C analysis is a necessary prerequisite to developing an effective intervention strategy. |

| 4 | INTERVENE | This is the action step of O.B. Mod. The goal is to accelerate functional performance behaviors and decelerate the dysfunctional behaviors. Positive reinforcement strategies involving money, social recognition/attention, and feedback are most used. |

| 5 | EVALUATE | This final step evaluates to make sure the intervention does in fact lead to performance improvement. If it doesn't, then another analysis and/or intervention is made. |

simplified steps are depicted in Figure 12.4. There are also other systematic approaches to behavioral performance management based on academic work and consultants.[95] Our (Stajkovic and Luthans) most recent meta-analysis of all the available behavioral management studies (including those using O.B. Mod.) found 72 studies that met the inclusion criteria (use of reinforcement interventions, task performance measures, and statistical information necessary to calculate effect sizes). We found an average of 16 percent improvement in performance from these behavioral management approaches.[96] However, most relevant, consistent, and recognized in the organizational behavior field is the O.B. Mod. approach. In a meta-analysis on just O.B. Mod. studies (as generally followed in Figures 12.3 and 12.4), we identified 19 studies with 115 effect sizes, and a total sample size of 2,818 subjects met the O.B. Mod. inclusion criteria and found an average of 17 percent improvement in performance (see the meta-analytically based principles at the end of the chapter for details and complete results).[97] The following discussion summarizes the steps of applying the O.B. Mod. approach to behavioral performance management.

## Step 1: Identification of Performance Behaviors

In this first step the critical behaviors that make a significant impact on performance (making or selling a product or providing a service to clients or customers) are identified. In every organization, regardless of type or level, numerous behaviors are occurring all the time. Some of these behaviors have a significant impact on performance, and some do not. The goal of the first step of O.B. Mod. is to identify the critical behaviors—the 5 to 10 percent of the behaviors that may account for up to 70 or 80 percent of the performance in the area in question.

The process of identifying critical behaviors can be carried out in a couple of ways. One approach is to have the person closest to the job in question—the immediate supervisor or the actual jobholder—determine the critical behaviors. This goes hand in hand with using O.B. Mod. as a problem-solving approach for the individual manager or a team. Its advantages are that the person who knows the job best can most accurately identify the critical behaviors, and, because that person is participating, he or she may be more committed to carrying the O.B. Mod. process to its successful completion.

Another approach to identifying critical behaviors would be to conduct a systematic *behavioral audit*. The audit would use internal staff specialists and/or outside consultants. The audit would systematically analyze each job in question, in the manner that jobs are analyzed using job analysis techniques commonly employed in human resource management. The advantages of the personal approach (where the jobholder, immediate supervisor, and/or team makes a vital input into the audit) can be realized by the audit. In addition, the advantages of information from those closest to the action and consistency can be gained.

Regardless of the method used, there are certain guidelines that can be helpful in identifying critical behaviors. First, only direct performance behaviors are included. A team's lack of commitment and teamwork or someone's "goofing off" all the time is unacceptable. Only direct performance behaviors such as absenteeism or attendance, tardiness or promptness, or, most importantly, doing or not doing a particular task or procedure that leads to quantity and/or quality outcomes play the major role in O.B. Mod. Something like goofing off is not acceptable because it is not operationally measurable. It could be broken down into measurable behaviors such as not being at the workstation, being tardy when returning from breaks, spending time at the water cooler, disrupting coworkers, playing computer games or surfing for personal reasons, and even socializing with coworkers face-to-face or with others online. However, for a behavior to be identified as a critical behavior appropriate for O.B. Mod., there must be a positive answer to the questions: (1) Can it be directly measured? and (2) Does it have a significant impact on a performance outcome?

Most organizations do not have problems with their technology or the ability or training of their people, but they have many behaviorally related performance problems. Functional behaviors (those that contribute to performance goals) need to be strengthened and accelerated in frequency, and dysfunctional behaviors (those that detract from, or are detrimental to, performance goals) need to be weakened and decelerated in frequency. As in the initial step of any problem-solving process, these behaviors must be properly identified, or the subsequent steps of O.B. Mod. become meaningless for attaining the overall goal of performance improvement.

## Step 2: Measurement of the Behavior

After the performance behaviors have been identified in step 1, they are measured. A *baseline measure* is obtained by determining (either by observing and counting or by extracting from existing records) the number of times that the identified behavior is occurring under existing conditions. Often this baseline frequency is in and of itself very revealing. Sometimes it is discovered that the behavior identified in step 1 is occurring much less or much more frequently than anticipated. The baseline measure may indicate that the problem is much smaller or much bigger than was thought to be the case. In some instances, the baseline measure may cause the "problem" to be dropped because its low (or high) frequency is now deemed not to need change. For example, attendance may have been identified in step 1 as a critical behavior that needed to be improved. The supervisor reports that the people "never seem to be here." The baseline measure, however, reveals that on average there is 96 percent attendance, which is deemed to be acceptable. In this example, the baseline measure rules out attendance as being a problem. The reverse, of course, could also have occurred. Attendance may have been a much bigger problem than anticipated.

The purpose of the baseline measure is to provide objective frequency data on the critical behavior. A baseline frequency count is an operational definition of the strength of the behavior under existing conditions. Such precise measurement is the hallmark of any scientific endeavor, and it separates O.B. Mod. from more subjective human resource management approaches, such as participation. Although the baseline is established before the intervention to see what happens to the behavior as a result of the intervention, it is important to realize that measures are taken after the intervention as well. Busy managers may feel that they do not have time to record behavioral frequencies objectively, but, at least initially, they should record them in order to use the O.B. Mod. approach effectively. Most measures, however, can be taken from existing archival data (e.g., quality, sales, and productivity numbers) that are gathered for other purposes and can be easily obtained for this measurement step of O.B. Mod.

## Step 3: Functional Analysis of the Behavior

Once the performance behavior has been identified and a baseline measure has been obtained, a functional analysis is performed. A *functional analysis* identifies both the antecedents (A) and consequences (C) of the target behavior (B), or, simply stated, an A-B-C analysis is performed. As discussed under behavioristic learning theory and operant conditioning, both the antecedent and the consequent environments are vital to the understanding, prediction, and control of human behavior in organizations. Remember that in an operant approach, cognitive mediating processes do not play a role. Such an omission may detract from the comprehensive understanding of organizational behavior and the analysis of modeling and self-control processes, but for pragmatic application, an A-B-C functional analysis may be sufficient.[98] In the A-B-C functional analysis, A is the antecedent cue, B is the performance behavior identified in step 1, and C is the contingent consequence. Table 12.3 identifies some of the As, Bs, and Cs for attendance and absenteeism. A review of absenteeism found work unit size, worker responsibility, and organizational scheduling to be three potential antecedent influences that could be used to improve employee attendance, and feedback, rewards, and punishers to be effective attendance control procedures.[99]

This functional analysis step of O.B. Mod. brings out the problem-solving nature of the approach. Both the antecedent cues that emit the behavior, and sometimes control it, and the consequences that are currently maintaining the behavior must be identified and understood before an effective intervention strategy can be developed. In this step, the question may be asked as to whether the employee can do the identified performance behavior if his/her life depended on it. If the answer is "no," then there may be an "A" problem (i.e., equipment, training, even expectations) that must be attended to. However, this is usually not the case. The human resources of an organization can do the identified critical performance behavior if their lives depend on it, but they are not doing it. Then this becomes

**TABLE 12.3**

**An Example of Functional Analysis**

*Source:* Fred Luthans and Mark Martinko, "An Organizational Behavior Modification Analysis of Absenteeism," *Human Resources Management,* Fall 1976, p. 15. Used with permission.

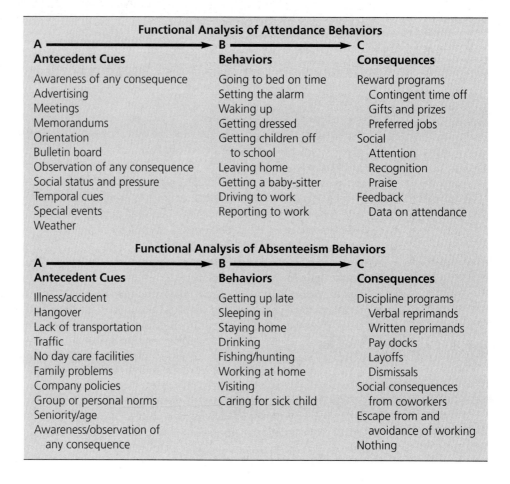

**Functional Analysis of Attendance Behaviors**

| A ──→ Antecedent Cues | B ──→ Behaviors | C ──→ Consequences |
|---|---|---|
| Awareness of any consequence | Going to bed on time | Reward programs |
| Advertising | Setting the alarm | Contingent time off |
| Meetings | Waking up | Gifts and prizes |
| Memorandums | Getting dressed | Preferred jobs |
| Orientation | Getting children off | Social |
| Bulletin board | to school | Attention |
| Observation of any consequence | Leaving home | Recognition |
| Social status and pressure | Getting a baby-sitter | Praise |
| Temporal cues | Driving to work | Feedback |
| Special events | Reporting to work | Data on attendance |
| Weather | | |

**Functional Analysis of Absenteeism Behaviors**

| A ──→ Antecedent Cues | B ──→ Behaviors | C ──→ Consequences |
|---|---|---|
| Illness/accident | Getting up late | Discipline programs |
| Hangover | Sleeping in | Verbal reprimands |
| Lack of transportation | Staying home | Written reprimands |
| Traffic | Drinking | Pay docks |
| No day care facilities | Fishing/hunting | Layoffs |
| Family problems | Working at home | Dismissals |
| Company policies | Visiting | Social consequences |
| Group or personal norms | Caring for sick child | from coworkers |
| Seniority/age | | Escape from and |
| Awareness/observation of | | avoidance of working |
| any consequence | | Nothing |

a "C" problem. They know how to do the desired performance behavior and there is all the necessary support to do it, but there are not reinforcing consequences and therefore the behavior is not occurring. This lack of reinforcing consequences is the major problem and challenge facing behavioral management. The accompanying Application Example: Functional Analysis in Action gives the functional analysis of a supervisor's problem of his workers' taking unscheduled breaks.

## Step 4: Development of an Intervention Strategy

The first three steps in an O.B. Mod. approach are preliminary to this action step, the intervention. The goal of the intervention is to strengthen and accelerate functional performance behaviors and/or weaken and decelerate dysfunctional behaviors. There are several strategies that can be used, but the main ones are positive reinforcement and punishment–positive reinforcement.

### A Positive Reinforcement Strategy

Positive, not negative, reinforcement is recommended as an effective intervention strategy for O.B. Mod. The reason is that positive reinforcement represents a form of *positive control of behavior,* whereas negative reinforcement represents a form of *negative control of behavior.* Traditionally, and to a large extent still today, organizations depend on negative control. People come to work in order not to be fired, and they look busy when the supervisor walks by in order not to be punished. Under positive control, the person behaves in a certain way in order to

In an actual case of an O.B. Mod. application, a production supervisor in a large manufacturing firm identified unscheduled breaks as a critical behavior affecting the performance of his department. It seemed that workers were frequently wandering off the job, and when they were not tending their machines, time—and irrecoverable production—was lost. When a baseline measure of this critical behavior was obtained, the supervisor was proved to be right. The data indicated that unscheduled breaks (defined as leaving the job for reasons other than to take a scheduled break or to obtain materials) were occurring in the department on a relatively frequent basis. The functional analysis was performed to determine the antecedent(s) and consequence(s) of the unscheduled-break behavior.

It was found that the clock served as the antecedent cue for the critical behavior. The workers in this department started work at 8 A.M., they had their first scheduled break at 10 A.M., and they had lunch at noon. They started again at 1 P.M., had a break at 3 P.M., and quit at 5 P.M. The functional analysis revealed that almost precisely at 9 A.M., 11 A.M., 2 P.M., and 4 P.M., a consistent number of workers were leaving their jobs and going to the rest room. In other words, the clock served as a cue for them to take an unscheduled break midway between starting time and the first scheduled break, between the first scheduled break and lunch, between lunch and the scheduled afternoon break, and between the afternoon break and quitting time. The clock did not cause the behavior; it served only as a cue to emit the behavior. On the other hand, the behavior was under stimulus control of the clock because the clock dictated when the behavior would occur. The consequence, however, was what was maintaining the behavior. The critical behavior was a function of its consequences. The functional analysis revealed that the consequence of the unscheduled-break behavior was escaping from a dull, boring task (that is, the unscheduled-break behavior was being negatively reinforced) and/or meeting with coworkers and friends to socialize and have a cigarette (that is, the unscheduled-break behavior was being positively reinforced). Through such a functional analysis, the antecedents and consequences are identified so that an effective intervention strategy can be developed.

receive the desired consequence. Under positive control, people come to work in order to be recognized for making a contribution to their department's goal of perfect attendance, or they keep busy whether the supervisor is around or not in order to receive incentive pay or because they get social recognition/attention and feedback for their good work. Positive control through a positive reinforcement intervention strategy is much more effective and longer lasting than negative control. It creates a much healthier and more productive organizational climate.

A positive reinforcer used as an O.B. Mod. intervention strategy could be anything, as long as it increases the performance behavior. Most often money is thought of as the logical, or sometimes the only, positive reinforcer available to managers using this approach. However, as the discussion of monetary reward systems in Chapter 4 and earlier in this chapter points out, money is potentially a very powerful reinforcer, but it often turns out to be ineffective because it is not contingently administered as a consequence of the behavior being managed. Besides money, positive reinforcers that are also very powerful, readily available to all behavioral managers, and cost nothing are the social reinforcers (attention and recognition) and performance feedback. These reinforcers (money, recognition, and feedback) can be and, as has been demonstrated through research,[100] have been used as an effective O.B. Mod. strategy to improve employee performance. In fact, the most comprehensive evidence shown in Figure 12.5 indicates that when these three reinforcers are used in combination in the intervention, they produce a stronger (synergistic) effect and probability of success than any of the reinforcers used by themselves, the sum of the individual effects, or the combination of any two of the interventions.[101]

### A Punishment–Positive Reinforcement Strategy

There is little debate that a positive reinforcement strategy is the most effective intervention for O.B. Mod. Yet realistically it is recognized that in some cases the use of punishment to weaken and decelerate undesirable behaviors cannot be avoided. This would be true in the

**FIGURE 12.5** Average Probability of Success from Interventions of Money, Social Recognition, and Feedback, and the Various Combinations

*Source:* Adapted from Alexander D. Stajkovic and Fred Luthans, "Behavioral Management and Task Performance in Organizations: Conceptual Background, Meta-Analysis, and Test of Alternative Models," *Personnel Psychology,* Vol. 56, 2003, p. 174. ($N$ = 72 studies and total sample of $N$ = 13,301).

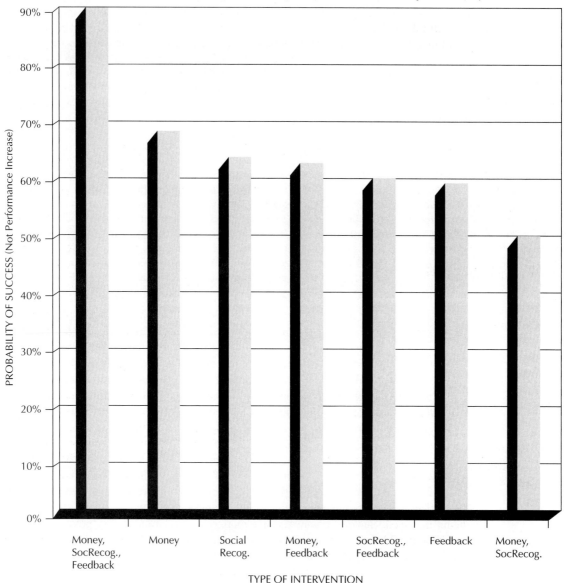

case of something like unsafe behaviors that need to be decreased immediately. However, as was pointed out earlier, so many negative side effects such as hate and revenge accompany the use of punishment that it should be avoided if at all possible. Punished behavior tends to be only temporarily suppressed; for example, if a supervisor reprimands an associate for some dysfunctional behavior, the behavior will decrease in the presence of the supervisor but will surface again when the supervisor is absent. In addition, a punished person becomes very anxious and uptight; reliance on punishment may have a disastrous impact on employee satisfaction and commitment and create unnecessary stress.

Perhaps the biggest problem with the use of punishment, however, is that it is very difficult for a supervisor to switch roles from punisher to positive reinforcer. Some supervisors and managers rely on a negative approach so much in dealing with their associates that it is almost impossible for them to administer positive reinforcement effectively. This is a bad situation for the management of human resources because the use of positive reinforcement is a much more effective way of changing employee behavior. If punishment is deemed necessary, the desirable alternative behavior (for example, safe behavior) should be positively reinforced at the first opportunity. Use of this combination strategy will cause the alternative desirable behavior to begin to replace the undesirable behavior in the person's behavioral repertoire. Punishment should never be used alone as an O.B. Mod. intervention. If punishment is absolutely necessary, it should only be used in combination with positive reinforcement of the desirable alternative behavior.

## Step 5: Evaluation to Ensure Performance Improvement

A glaring weakness of most human resource management programs is the absence of any systematic, built-in evaluation. A comprehensive analysis of the evaluation of human resources programs concluded that the traditional approach has been "to review a program with one or two vice presidents at the corporate office, various managers in the field, and perhaps a group of prospective trainees. It continues to be used until someone in a position of authority decides that the program has outlived its usefulness. All of this is done on the basis of opinion and judgment."[102] Such haphazard evaluations have resulted in the termination of some effective programs and the perpetuation of some ineffective ones. In either case, there are severe credibility problems, and today all programs dealing with people, whether they are government social service programs or human resource management programs, are under the pressure of evaluation and accountability. Human resource managers no longer have the luxury of just trying something new and different and hoping they can improve performance. Today there is pressure for everything that is tried to be proved to have value. As in the case of the validity of selection, training, and appraisal techniques, systematic evaluations of all human resource management techniques should have been done all along.

O.B. Mod. attempts to meet the credibility and accountability problems head on by including evaluation as an actual part of the process. In this last step of the approach, the need for Kirkpatrick's well-known four levels of evaluation (reaction, learning, behavioral change, and performance improvement) is stressed. The reaction level refers simply to whether the people using the approach and those having it used on them like it. If O.B. Mod. is well received and there is a positive reaction to it, there is a better chance of its being used effectively. In addition, reaction evaluations are helpful because (1) positive reactions help ensure organizational support, (2) they can provide information for planning future programs, (3) favorable reactions can enhance the other levels of evaluation (learning, behavioral change, and performance improvement), and (4) they can provide useful comparative data between units and across time.[103]

The second level of evaluation is learning, which is especially important when first implementing an O.B. Mod. approach. Do the people using the approach understand the theoretical background and underlying assumptions and the meaning of, and reasons for, the steps in the model? If they do not, the model will again tend to be used ineffectively. The third level is aimed at behavioral change. Are behaviors actually being changed? The charting of behaviors started in step 2 of the O.B. Mod. process gives objective data for this level of evaluation. The fourth and final level, performance improvement, is the most important. The major purpose of O.B. Mod. is not just to receive a favorable reaction, learn the concepts, and change behaviors. These dimensions are important mainly because they contribute to the overriding purpose, which is to improve performance. "Hard" measures (for example, data on quantity and quality, turnover, absenteeism, customer complaints, customer satisfaction, employee grievances, safety, length of patient stay, number of clients served, sales revenue, and rate of return on investment) and scientific methodology are used whenever possible to systematically evaluate the impact of O.B. Mod. on performance.

## Application of Behavioral Management

There is a considerable body of research that has evaluated the effectiveness of behavioral performance management in general and the five-step O.B. Mod. approach in particular. It has been widely applied in manufacturing as well as in nonmanufacturing, service-oriented organizations. In addition to the direct application of O.B. Mod. as described, considerable basic research has been conducted on operant and social learning and social cognitive variables in experimental psychology. For many years and in very recent times, a number of studies have assessed the application of the behavioral management approach to improving employee performance in a number of different areas. The following summarizes some of these areas:

1. *Employee productivity.* Most applications by far have focused on performance output. The considerable number of research studies clearly indicate that employee productivity or task completion is positively affected by behavioral management techniques. The performance improvement is for both quantity and quality of employee output and cuts across virtually all organizational settings and all intervention techniques.[104]

2. *Absenteeism and tardiness.* This is probably the second-biggest area of application. Studies that have examined this area have typically used small monetary incentives or lottery incentive systems for attendance or promptness and/or punishers for absenteeism or tardiness. One extensive search of this literature found very positive results.[105] The six most sound methodological studies reported an 18 to 50 percent reduction in the absence rate and a 90 percent reduction in the frequency of tardiness. One study found a positive, causal impact that an O.B. Mod. program had on the attendance of employees in a bank.[106]

3. *Safety and accident prevention.* Most organizations, especially manufacturing firms and others in which dangerous equipment is used, are very concerned about safety. However, because accidents occur at such a relatively low frequency, most studies have focused on reducing identifiable safety hazards or increasing safe behaviors (for example, wearing earplugs, which went from 35 to 95 percent compliance according to one study;[107] wearing hard hats; and keeping the safety guard in place on dangerous equipment). A review of the research indicates the considerable success that behavioral management techniques have had in these areas.[108] Some actual company examples are Boston Gas, where employees without accidents are eligible for lottery drawings; Virginia Power, where employees can win from $50 to $1,000 for safe work habits; Southern New England Telecommunications, which gives gift coupons to employees without accidents; and Turner Corporation, a New York–based engineering and construction firm, where employees can earn company stock if they meet safety goals. All these companies report lower accident rates through the use of a behavioral management approach. Southern Fineblanking, a 225-employee metal stamping plant in South Carolina, reported a 33 percent reduction in accidents after implementing a behavioral management program aimed at safety, and the average cost per injury decreased from $1,400 to $500.[109]

4. *Sales performance.* Sales managers and trainers have traditionally relied on internal motivation techniques to get their salespeople to improve their performance. For example, one behavioral performance management consultant tells about a company that gave its

sales personnel a typical high-powered, multimedia training program, which supposedly taught them effective selling skills. However, when the enthusiastic trainees finished the program and actually tried the things presented to them in the program, they received little, if any, feedback or reinforcement. Within a few weeks the enthusiasm began to wane, and, most important, actual sales performance began to decline.[110] In other words, even though these salespeople had probably acquired effective selling skills during their training, the environment did not support (reinforce) the use of these skills. A behavioral performance management approach, in which important selling behaviors such as customer approach, suggestive statements, and closing statements are identified, measured, analyzed, intervened in, and evaluated, would be an alternative to the motivation-skill-teaching approach. A comprehensive review of the behavioral approach to sales in restaurants, retail stores, wholesale establishments, and telephone operations found considerable success.[111] When a combination of antecedent and consequence intervention strategies was used, dramatic improvements were shown in areas such as wine and dessert sales, average customer transactions, customer assistance, sales forecasting, sales-call frequency, sales of telephone services, and airline reservations. A study of fast-food restaurants also found that antecedent prompts ("Can I get you some fries with that?") significantly increased consumer purchases,[112] and another more recent study in the same industry indicated a significant increase in customer service.[113] The successful application of O.B. Mod. to the selling, absent-from-the-workstation, and idle-time behaviors of clerks in a large retail store was also found.[114]

Although these results are not exhaustive and do not always reflect the exact O.B. Mod. model outlined in this chapter, they are representative of the very extensive application of the behavioral performance management approach. In addition, both comprehensive qualitative[115] and quantitative (meta-analytic)[116] reviews strongly support the findings.

## Manufacturing versus Service Applications

As cited throughout, the specific O.B. Mod. model has been directly tested by basic research and has been found to have positive performance results in both manufacturing[117] and service organizations (retail, restaurants, banking, and hospitals).[118] The O.B. Mod. approach has also "gone international" and has been shown to have a positive impact on the performance behaviors and output of Russian factory workers,[119] Russian retail clerks,[120] and most recently South Korean telecommunication employees.[121]

The two Stajkovic and Luthans meta-analyses mentioned earlier and, especially, the one that specifically reviewed O.B. Mod. studies (as opposed to the latest one on all behavioral management studies) and is utilized in the principles at the end of the chapter, examined the relationship between O.B. Mod. as defined here and task performance.[122] The overall result of the O.B. Mod. meta-analysis was, on average, an impressive 17 percent increase in task performance (as indicated, it was 16 percent for all behavioral management studies). Further analysis revealed that O.B. Mod. had a stronger average effect in manufacturing firms (33%) than in service organizations (13%), but the O.B. Mod. approach was highly significant in both. The difference in application effectiveness of O.B. Mod. between manufacturing and service organizations was explained as

> (1) the definition and accurate assessment of performance outcomes; and (2) the nature of the employee behaviors and work processes involved in the delivery of performance outcomes. The first point refers to the difference between the definition and measurement of the more vague and complex service organization performance outcomes (e.g., customer satisfaction, return business) versus tangible performance outcomes (e.g., productivity and quality) in manufacturing organizations. The second point refers to the difference between

specifying service delivery employee behaviors and processes that go into making a tangible product. Service performance behaviors and outcomes are more complex and less identifiable than those found in manufacturing organizations.[123]

So, although O.B. Mod. may be more difficult to apply in service than in manufacturing organizations, it still works in both, and the challenge is to make it even more effective in service applications. The overall implications of these findings from the meta-analyses are that behavioral management systematically applied through steps such as the O.B. Mod. model can help meet the performance improvement challenges facing today's and future organizations.

---

## Summary

Learning is a major psychological process, but it has not been as popular in the study of organizational behavior as constructs such as personality, attitudes, or motivation. Also, it has not been generally recognized that there are different types of learning and different theoretical explanations of learning (behavioristic, cognitive, and social). Despite the controversy surrounding learning theory, there are many evidence-based principles of learning that are derived largely from experimentation and the analysis of operant conditioning. Reinforcement is generally recognized as the single most important principle in the learning process and is most relevant to behavioral performance management. On the basis of the classic law of effect, or "Laws of Behavior," reinforcement can be operationally defined as anything that increases the strength of a behavior and that tends to induce repetitions of the behavior that preceded the reinforcement. Reinforcers may be positive (the application of a desirable consequence) or negative (prevention, termination, or withdrawal of an undesirable consequence), but both have the impact of strengthening the behavior and increasing its frequency. Punishment, on the other hand, decreases the strength and frequency of the behavior. There is also the special case of extinction (no consequence) that also will decrease the behavior over time.

The major direct application of learning theories and the reinforcement principle in particular is behavioral performance management. Both financial and nonfinancial (social attention/recognition and performance feedback) are important but somewhat complex reinforcers that must be carefully applied in behavioral performance management. Behavioral management can be effectively applied through the O.B. Mod. steps: identify the performance-related behavior; measure it to determine the baseline frequency; functionally analyze both the antecedents and the consequences of the behavior (A-B-C); intervene through a positive reinforcement strategy to accelerate the critical performance behaviors; and evaluate to make sure the intervention is, in fact, increasing performance. The behavioral management approach in general and O.B. Mod. in particular have been demonstrated to have a significant positive impact on employee performance in both manufacturing and nonmanufacturing service-oriented organizations.

## Ending with Meta-Analytic Research Findings
### OB PRINCIPLE FOR EVIDENCED-BASED PRACTICE

The use of organizational behavior modification (O.B. Mod.) increases employee performance.

### Meta-Analysis Results:

[*19 studies; 2,818 participants; d = .51*] *On average, there is a **64 percent probability** that utilizing the five-step O.B. Mod. model to systematically manage performance-related employee behavior will lead to higher performance than not using the O.B. Mod. approach.* Further analysis indicated that the effect of O.B. Mod. interventions on performance is moderated by the type of organization and contingent reinforcer used. The effect of O.B. Mod. was found to be greater in manufacturing over service organizations. There were no significant differences among monetary, feedback, and social recognition interventions in manufacturing, but certain combinations had a bigger impact in service organizations.

### Conclusion:

As you have learned in this chapter, the overriding premise of reinforcement theory is that behavior is a function of its contingent consequences. This is an external, behavioral paradigm as opposed to the internal, cognitive paradigm that served as the foundation for the topics of perception, attribution, personality, attitudes, and motivation. Whereas job design and goal setting are application techniques for the cognitive paradigm, O.B. Mod. represents an effective method of applying the behavioral paradigm to manage employee behavior for performance improvement. In particular, by training supervisors and managers in the five-step O.B. Mod. model of identifying, measuring, analyzing, intervening, and evaluating, there is a proven way to improve performance. Importantly, besides monetary reward interventions, no-cost performance feedback and social attention/recognition are found to be effective ways to improve employee performance using the O.B. Mod. approach to behavioral performance management.

**Source:** Adapted from Alexander D. Stajkovic and Fred Luthans, "A Meta-Analysis of the Effects of Organizational Behavior Modification on Task Performance," *Academy of Management Journal,* Vol. 40, No. 5, 1997, pp. 1122–1149.

## OB PRINCIPLE:

The use of nonfinancial interventions of feedback and social recognition administered in an O.B. Mod. approach improves employee performance.

### Meta-Analysis Results:

[*19 studies; 2,818 participants; (1) d = 1.48 for feedback in manufacturing; (2) d = 1.49 for feedback simultaneously applied with social recognition in manufacturing; (3) d = .19 for feedback in service organizations; (4) d = .53 for feedback simultaneously applied with social recognition in service organizations; and (5) d = .44 for social recognition in service organizations (there were no studies with social recognition only in manufacturing)*] *On average, there is a: (1) **85 percent probability** that employees receiving performance feedback only in manufacturing firms; (2) **85 percent probability** that employees receiving simultaneous feedback and social recognition in manufacturing; (3) **55 percent probability** that employees receiving feedback in service organizations; (4) **65 percent probability** that employees receiving simultaneous feedback and social recognition in service organizations; and (5) **62 percent probability** that employees receiving social recognition only in service organizations will perform better than those employees whose behavior is not contingently reinforced by performance feedback and/or social recognition.*

### Conclusion:

Providing contingently administered nonfinancial rewards of performance feedback and social attention/recognition are perhaps the most overlooked methods of effectively increasing employee performance. Although financial incentives, when administered contingently, can be powerful reinforcers, so can no-cost feedback and social attention/recognition. In fact, many employees, depending on the situation, respond more positively to the nonfinancial rewards than they do to money. In addition to performance, studies have shown that a major reason why employees leave organizations is due to a lack of feedback on how they are doing and recognition from their supervisors. All employees want to be informed of how they are doing, noticed, and given attention for their contributions. Thus, effective supervisors and managers are taking advantage of feedback and social attention/recognition as alternatives to costly and often poorly administered incentive pay and pay-for-performance plans.

**Source:** Adapted from Alexander D. Stajkovic and Fred Luthans, "A Meta-Analysis of the Effects of Organizational Behavior Modification on Task Performance," *Academy of Management Journal,* Vol. 40, No. 5, 1997, pp. 1122–1149.

## Questions for Discussion and Review

1. Do you agree with the statement that learning is involved in almost everything that everyone does? Explain.
2. What are the major dimensions of behavioristic, cognitive, social learning, and social congnitive theories of learning?
3. What is the difference between classical and operant conditioning?
4. What is the difference between positive and negative reinforcement? What is the difference between negative reinforcement and punishment? Provide some examples.
5. What could be done to make money more effective as a reinforcer for behavioral management?
6. What are some examples of nonfinancial reinforcers? How can these be used to improve employee performance?
7. What are the five steps of O.B. Mod.? Briefly summarize the critical dimensions of each step that will help improve employee performance.
8. In what areas has behavioral management been successfully applied?
9. Summarize the results of the meta-analysis on O.B. Mod. What recommendations would you make to the HRM department based on these findings?

## Internet Exercise: Applying Behavior Management Principles to Athletic Performance

The principles of reinforcement and behavior management can and should be found in all sports. Go to the Web sites of various sports and see how reinforcement does and should play a role in the performance of the athletes. For example, you might compare golfers (**http://www.pgatour.com**) with football (**http://www./nFl.com**) players.

1. What specific reinforcers drive the behavior and resulting performance of the athletes in the sport you chose?
2. How might the reinforcers be different for college versus professional athletes?
3. How could a coach effectively use behavioral management? Give some specific examples by sport.

---

## Real Case: *The Elite Circle of $1 CEOs*

Richard Kinder, chief executive of Houston energy transportation and storage company Kinder Morgan, is not a poor man. But since he founded the company with Bill Morgan in 1997, he has drawn a salary of $1 and left his cabinet clear of any bonuses, stock awards, or option grants. He doesn't use a corporate jet or chauffeured cars. He even cuts a personal check for his contribution to the health insurance plan.

To be sure, he lives more than comfortably off the dividends from his approximately 24 million shares in Kinder Morgan (KMI); annual payouts from his shares top $60 million. The value of the shares has also risen steadily in the last decade, closing on May 9 at $106.95. "I'm not saying I'll need to get on the welfare line," says Kinder. "But all my pay comes from the performance of the company. I'm opposed to guaranteed salary, stock, options, and the rest of it. The philosophy is that senior management does well when the company does well."

## An Exclusive Club

In an era of skyrocketing CEO pay and growing shareholder angst about it, a handful of chief executives are opting to draw a $1 paycheck or none at all. Among the most well-known are Steve Jobs of Apple and Eric Schmidt of Google. The others are James Rogers of Duke Energy, Richard Fairbank of Capital One Financial, and Terry Semel of Yahoo. The latest CEO to agree to a token base salary is John Mackey at Whole Foods Market. Jerrold Perenchio of Univision Communication and William Ford Jr. of Ford Motor also received no salary as CEO until 2006, when each stepped down to take the post of chairman.

The common characteristics among this varied cast of characters? A strong belief in personal responsibility, a passion for the business, a penchant for risk-taking—and a healthy dose of ego. "With this gesture the executive is calling him or herself an 'employee-in-chief,' and saying he or she will fall with the fate of the company," says Dr. Kerry Sulkowicz, founder of Boswell Group, a consulting firm that advises senior executives on psychological issues. "Of course, it can be a double-edged sword, since in doing so they're inevitably pointing to their own wealthy status—that effectively as far as pay is concerned they can take it or leave it."

## Taking One for the Team

The current crop of low-salaried CEOs isn't the first. Lee Iacocca set the precedent in 1978, when he was chairman of Chrysler. Realizing the automaker was in dire financial straits, Iacocca fired executives and pushed the United Auto Workers to accept salary and benefit cuts. In an effort to lead by example, Iacocca lowered his own salary to $1 a year. Five years later, with a helping hand from the government, the company has been restored to financial health.

## The Ultimate Pay for Performance?

But these days drawing a $1-or-less salary is more common at radically successful companies than at hobbling ones. Jobs at Apple and Schmidt at Google are the highest-profile examples. In this new context, the message of the $1 salary has changed. When Iacocca sliced his salary, he was telling Chrysler's line workers that they were all in the battle for survival together. Now CEOs like Jobs are sending the message to investors that they'll make money only if other shareholders do, too. Brothers in arms have become partners in profit. "The climate in the country for CEOs was different then," says Sulkowicz. "Now there's so much emphasis on CEO accountability and performance, and getting rid of your salary makes a strong statement."

The new message placates some groups, but not others. This year the AFL-CIO, an umbrella group of 54 labor unions, is taking issue with Jobs' compensation, despite his $1 salary. The unions' investment arm filed a proposal at Apple, as well as at several other companies, to require a nonbinding vote each year on the CEO's pay. Such initiatives are known as "say on pay" proposals.

The labor federation takes issue with the number of options Jobs has received, especially because the timing of those grants has been questioned. "The gesture looks all warm and fuzzy, but it's a facade," says Daniel Pedrotty, director of the AFL-CIO's office of investment. "It obscures the real number of what an executive gets and in that sense is an insult to investors' intelligence. In the case of Apple it's even more serious and allegations of options fraud."

## Varying Degrees of Success

Executive compensation expert and consultant Graef Crystal cays CEOs have different motivations for taking $1 or less, but that for some the gesture means little. "I don't feel sorry for the Richard Fairbanks of the world," he says, referring to Capital One's chief executive. "I wouldn't book a benefit concert for this guy." Shareholders brought a "say on pay" proposal to Capital One's shareholder meeting on April 26, garnering 37% support.

The most recent entrant to the $1-or-less club is John Mackey of Whole Foods. He announced that he's not doing it to tie pay to performance, but because he feels he's earned enough money. "I continue to work for Whole Foods not because of the money I can make but because of the pleasure I get from leading such a great company, and the ongoing passion I have to help make the world a better place," said Mackey in a statement. "I am now 53 years old, and I have reached a place in my life where I no longer want to work for money, but simply for the joy of the work itself and to better answer the call to service that I feel so clearly in my own heart."

1. What implications does the $1 pay have for the use of money as a reinforcer?

2. Why is taking a $1 salary called a "double-edged sword"?

3. What conditions would be necessary and how would you publicly explain if you ever would join the $1 Circle?

---

# Organizational Behavior Case: *Contrasting Styles*

Henry Adams has been a production supervisor for eight years. He came up through the ranks and is known as a tough but hardworking supervisor. Jane Wake has been a production supervisor for about the same length of time and also came up through the ranks. Jane is known as a nice, hardworking boss. Over the past several years these two supervisors' sections have been head and shoulders above the other six sections on hard measures of performance (number of units produced). This is true despite the almost opposite approaches the two have taken in handling their workers. Henry explained his approach as follows:

> The only way to handle workers is to come down hard on them whenever they make a mistake. In fact, I call them together every once in a while and give them heck whether they deserve it or not, just to keep them on their toes. If they are doing a good job, I tell them that's what they're getting paid for. By taking this approach, all I have to do is walk through my area, and people start working like mad.

Jane explained her approach as follows:

> I don't believe in that human relations stuff of being nice to workers. But I do believe that a worker deserves some recognition and attention from me if he or she does a good job. If people make a mistake, I don't jump on them. I feel that we are all entitled to make some errors. On the other hand, I always do point out what the mistake was and what they should have done, and as soon as they do it right, I let them know it. Obviously, I don't have time to give attention to everyone doing things right, but I deliberately try to get around to people doing a good job every once in a while.

Although Henry's section is still right at the top along with Jane's section in units produced, personnel records show that there has been three times more turnover in Henry's section than in Jane's section, and the quality control records show that Henry's section has met quality standards only twice in the last six years, while Jane has missed attaining quality standards only once in the last six years.

1. Both these supervisors have similar backgrounds. On the basis of learning theory, how can you explain their opposite approaches to handling people?

2. What are some of the examples of punishment, positive reinforcement, and negative reinforcement found in this case? If Jane is using a reinforcement approach, how do you explain this statement: "I don't believe in that human relations stuff of being nice to workers"?

3. How do you explain the performance, turnover, and quality results in these two sections of the production department?

---

# Organizational Behavior Case: *Volunteers Can't Be Punished*

Jenette Jackson is head of a volunteer agency in a large city, in charge of a volunteer staff of over 25 people. Weekly, she holds a meeting with this group in order to keep them informed and teach them the specifics of any new laws or changes in state and federal policies and procedures that might affect their work, and she discusses priorities and assignments for the group. This meeting is also a time when members can share some of the problems with and concerns for what they are personally doing and what the agency as a whole is doing.

The meeting is scheduled to begin at 9 A.M. sharp every Monday. Lately, the volunteers have been filtering in every five minutes or so until almost 10 A.M. Jenette has felt she has to delay the start of the meetings until all the people arrive. The last few weeks the meetings haven't started until 10 A.M. In fact, at 9 A.M, nobody has shown up. Jenette cannot understand what has happened. She feels it is important to start the meetings at 9 A.M so that they can be over before the whole morning is gone. However, she feels that her hands are tied because, after all, the people are volunteers and she can't push them or make them get to the meetings on time.

1. What advice would you give Jenette? In terms of reinforcement theory, explain what is happening here and what Jenette needs to do to get the meetings started on time.

2. What learning theories (operant, cognitive, and/or social) could be applied to Jenette's efforts to teach her volunteers the impact of new laws and changes in state and federal policies and procedures?

3. How could someone like Jenette use modeling to train her staff to do a more effective job?

# Organizational Behavior Case: *Up the Piece Rate*

Larry Ames has successfully completed a company training program in O.B. Mod. He likes the approach and has started using it on the workers in his department. Following the O.B. Mod. model, he has identified several performance behaviors, measured and analyzed them, and used a positive reinforcement intervention strategy. His evaluation has shown a significant improvement in the performance of his department. Over coffee one day he commented to one of the other supervisors, "This contingent reinforcement approach really works. Before, the goody-goody people up in human resources were always telling us to try to understand and be nice to our workers. Frankly, I couldn't buy that. In the first place, I don't think there is anybody who can really *understand* my people—I certainly can't. More important, though, is that under this approach I am only nice *contingently*—contingent on good performance. That makes a lot more sense, and my evaluation proves that it works." The other supervisor commented, "You are being reinforced for use of the reinforcement technique on your people." Larry said, "Sure I am. Just like the trainer said: 'Behavior that is reinforced will strengthen and repeat itself.' I'm so

reinforced that I am starting to use it on my wife and kids at home, and you know what? It works there, too."

The next week Larry was called into the department head's office and was told, "Larry, as you know, your department has shown a substantial increase in performance since you completed the O.B. Mod. program. I have sent our industrial engineer down there to analyze your standards. I have received her report, and it looks like we will have to adjust your rates upward by 10 percent. Otherwise, we are going to have to pay too much incentive pay. I'm sure you can use some of the things you learned in that O.B. Mod. program to break the news to your people. Good luck, and keep up the good work."

1. Do you think Larry's boss, the department head, attended the O.B. Mod. program? Analyze the department head's action in terms of O.B. Mod.

2. What do you think Larry's reaction will be now and in the future? How do you think Larry's people will react?

3. Given the 10 percent increase in standards, is there any way that Larry could still use the O.B. Mod. approach with his people? With his boss? How?

# Organizational Behavior Case: *A Tardiness Problem*

You have been getting a lot of complaints recently from your boss about the consistent tardiness of your department's sales associates at a large retail store. The time-sheet records indicate that your people's average start-up time is about 10 minutes late. Although you have never been concerned about the tardiness problem, your boss is really getting upset. He points out that the tardiness reduces the amount of time associates are providing assistance and replenishing items on display. You realize that the tardiness is a type of avoidance behavior—it delays the start of a very boring job. Your work group is very cohesive, and each of the members will follow what the group wants to do. One of the leaders of the group seems to spend a lot of time getting the group into trouble. You want the group to come in on time, but you don't really want a confrontation on the issue because, frankly, you don't think it is important enough to risk getting everyone upset with you. You decide to use an O.B. Mod. approach.

1. Trace through the five steps in the O.B. Mod. model to show how it could be applied to this tardiness problem. Make sure you are specific in identifying the critical performance behaviors and the antecedents and consequences of the functional analysis.

2. Do you think the approach you have suggested in your answer will really work? Why or why not?

# Chapter **Thirteen**

# Effective Leadership Processes

### Learning Objectives

- **Define** leadership.
- **Present** the background and classic studies of leadership.
- **Discuss** the traditional theories of leadership, including the trait, group and exchange, contingency, and path-goal approaches.
- **Identify** modern theoretical processes for leadership, such as charismatic, transformational, substitutes, and now authentic leadership.
- **Examine** leadership across cultures giving special attention to the GLOBE project.

This chapter on leadership processes and the next on great leaders' styles, activities, and skills are an appropriate conclusion to the study of organizational behavior. Leadership is the focus and conduit of most of the other areas of organizational behavior. The first half of this chapter deals with the definition and classical background. The last half then presents the major theoretical processes of leadership. Particular attention is devoted to both traditional and modern theories of leadership.

## WHAT IS LEADERSHIP?

Leadership has probably been written about, formally researched, and informally discussed more than any other single topic. The introduction to a recent article on leadership noted, "Professors and pupils, historians and psychologists, management gurus and motivational speakers, political hacks and statesmen—is there anybody who doesn't have an opinion on what constitutes a good leader?"[1] Despite all this attention given to leadership, there remains considerable controversy. For example, in one of his articles, leadership guru Warren Bennis gives the title "The End of Leadership" to make the point that effective leadership cannot exist without the full inclusion, initiatives, and the cooperation of employees. In other words, one cannot be a great leader without great followers.[2] Another leadership guru, Barry Posner, makes the following observations about the needed change in how business leadership is viewed:

> In the past, business believed that a leader was like the captain of a ship: cool, calm,
> collected. Now, we see that leaders need to be human. They need to be in touch, they need to
> be empathetic, and they need to be with people. Leaders need to be a part of what's going on,
> not apart from what's going on.[3]

413

Globalization has also changed the traditional view of an organizational leader as "the heroic individual, often charismatic, whose positional power, intellectual strength, and persuasive gifts motivate followers. But this is not necessarily the ideal in Asia, nor does it match the requirements in large global corporations, where forms of distributed and shared leadership are needed to address complex interlocking problems."[4]

There are also problems with the ways leaders have been traditionally developed, a multi-billion dollar effort. For example, we note on the opening page of our (Avolio and Luthans) book on authentic leadership development that "we are dismayed at how few leadership development programs actually can substantiate that even one leader has been developed as a consequence of most programs."[5] As a result, new paradigms of leadership development are beginning to emerge. For example, the director of Leadership at Google recently commented, "In the '90s at Pepsi, I taught leaders to develop leaders. Now I ask people within the company to name employees they respect and then give them training tasks."

In spite of the seeming discontent, at least with the traditional approaches to leadership theory, practice, and development, throughout history the difference between success and failure, whether in a war, a business, a protest movement, or a basketball game, has been attributed to leadership. A Gallup survey indicates that most employees believe that it is the leader, not the company, that guides the culture and creates situations where workers can be happy and successful.[6] As the opening statement of a recent cover story on leadership in *Fortune* declares, "Your competition can copy every advantage you've got—except one. That's why the best companies are realizing that no matter what business they're in, their real business is building leaders."[7]

Regardless of all the attention given to leadership and its recognized importance, it does remain pretty much of a "black box," or unexplainable concept. It is known to exist and to have a tremendous influence on human performance, but its inner workings and specific dimensions cannot be precisely spelled out. Despite these inherent difficulties, many attempts have been made over the years to define leadership.[8] Unfortunately, almost everyone who studies or writes about leadership defines it differently. About the only commonality is the role that influence plays in leadership.[9]

In recent years, many theorists and practitioners have emphasized the difference between managers and leaders. For example, as Bennis has noted: "To survive in the twenty-first century, we are going to need a new generation of leaders—leaders, not managers. The distinction is an important one. Leaders conquer the context—the volatile, turbulent, ambiguous surroundings that sometimes seem to conspire against us and will surely suffocate us if we let them—while managers surrender to it."[10] He then goes on to point out his thoughts on some specific differences between leaders and managers, as shown in Table 13.1. Obviously, these are not scientifically derived differences, but it is probably true that an individual can be a leader without being a manager and be a manager without being a leader.[11]

Although many specific definitions could be cited, most would depend on the theoretical orientation taken. Besides influence, leadership has been defined in terms of group processes, personality, compliance, particular behaviors, persuasion, power, goal achievement, interaction, role differentiation, initiation of structure, and combinations of two or more of these.[12] The extremely turbulent, adverse environment facing organizational leaders in recent years has led Bennis and Thomas to conclude:

> One of the most reliable indicators and predictors of true leadership is an individual's ability to find meaning in negative events and to learn from even the most trying circumstances. Put another way, the skills required to conquer adversity and emerge stronger and more committed than ever are the same ones that make for extraordinary leaders.[13]

**TABLE 13.1**
**Some Characteristics of Managers versus Leaders in the Twenty-First Century**

*Source:* Adapted from Warren G. Bennis, "Managing the Dream: Leadership in the 21st Century," *Journal of Organizational Change Management,* Vol. 2, No. 1, 1989, p. 7.

| Manager Characteristics | Leader Characteristics |
|---|---|
| Administers | Innovates |
| A copy | An original |
| Maintains | Develops |
| Focuses on systems and structure | Focuses on people |
| Relies on control | Inspires trust |
| Short-range view | Long-range perspective |
| Asks how and when | Asks what and why |
| Eye on the bottom line | Eye on the horizon |
| Imitates | Originates |
| Accepts the status quo | Challenges the status quo |
| Classic good soldier | Own person |
| Does things right | Does the right thing |

Most recently, Avolio, Luthans, and colleagues at the Leadership Institute at the University of Nebraska concentrate on *authentic leaders,* which means

> to know oneself, to be consistent with oneself, and to have a positive and strength-based orientation toward one's development and the development of others. Such leaders are transparent with their values and beliefs. They are honest with themselves and with others. They exhibit a higher level of moral reasoning capacity, allowing them to judge between gray and shades of gray.[14]

As the former head of successful medical technology firm Medtronic, and now author/lecturer, Bill George says, authentic leaders "bring people together around a shared mission and values and empower them to lead, in order to serve their customers while creating value for all their stakeholders."[15] This authentic leadership is considered a root construct that is considered necessary, but not sufficient, for other types of leadership covered in this chapter and the next.

Perhaps as good a simple definition of leadership as any comes from a *Fortune* article, which states: "When you boil it all down, contemporary leadership seems to be a matter of aligning people toward common goals and empowering them to take the actions needed to reach them."[16] An equally good definition of leadership is implied in hockey great Wayne Gretzky's famous quote: "I don't go where the puck is; I go to where the puck is going to be." But, as Bennis points out, "the issue is not just interpreting and envisioning the future, or knowing where the puck is going to be, but being able to create the kind of meaning for people, the values that make sense to them, where there's enough trust in the system so it's going to stick."[17] For the purpose of this chapter, the specific definition that is used is not important. What is important is to interpret leadership in terms of a specific theoretical process and to realize that leadership, however defined, does make a difference. The OB in Action: High Tech Leader (p. 417) indicates how this leader made a difference at her firm and gained the respect of all those around her.

# THE HISTORICALLY IMPORTANT STUDIES ON LEADERSHIP

Unlike many other topics in the field of organizational behavior, there are a number of studies and a considerable body of knowledge on leadership. A review of the better-known classic studies can help set the stage for the traditional and modern theories of leadership.

## The Iowa Leadership Studies

A series of pioneering leadership studies conducted in the late 1930s by Ronald Lippitt and Ralph K. White under the general direction of Kurt Lewin at the University of Iowa have had a lasting impact. Lewin is recognized as the father of group dynamics and as an important cognitive theorist. In the initial studies, hobby clubs for ten-year-old boys were formed. Each club was submitted to all three different styles of leadership—authoritarian, democratic, and laissez-faire. The authoritarian leader was very directive and allowed no participation. This leader tended to give individual attention when praising and criticizing, but tried to be friendly or impersonal rather than openly hostile. The democratic leader encouraged group discussion and decision making. This leader tried to be "objective" in giving praise or criticism and to be one of the group in spirit. The laissez-faire leader gave complete freedom to the group; this leader essentially provided no leadership.

Unfortunately, the effects that styles of leadership had on productivity were not directly examined. The experiments were designed primarily to examine patterns of aggressive behavior. However, an important by-product was the insight that was gained into the productive behavior of a group. For example, the researchers found that the boys subjected to the autocratic leaders reacted in one of two ways: either aggressively or apathetically. Both the aggressive and apathetic behaviors were deemed to be reactions to the frustration caused by the autocratic leader. The researchers also pointed out that the apathetic groups exhibited outbursts of aggression when the autocratic leader left the room or when a transition was made to a freer leadership atmosphere. The laissez-faire leadership climate actually produced the greatest number of aggressive acts from the group. The democratically led group fell between the one extremely aggressive group and the four apathetic groups under the autocratic leaders.

Sweeping generalizations on the basis of the Lippitt and White studies are dangerous. Preadolescent boys making masks and carving soap are a long way from adults working in a complex, modern organization. Furthermore, from the viewpoint of today's behavioral science research methodology, many of the variables were not controlled. Nevertheless, these leadership studies have important historical significance. They were the first attempts to determine, experimentally, what effects styles of leadership have on a group. Like the Hawthorne studies presented in Chapter 1, the Iowa studies are too often automatically discounted or at least marginalized because they are hard to generalize to modern organizational leadership. The value of the studies was that they were the first to analyze leadership from the standpoint of scientific methodology, and, more important, they showed that different styles of leadership can produce different, complex reactions from the same or similar groups.

## The Ohio State Leadership Studies

At the end of World War II, the Bureau of Business Research at Ohio State University initiated a series of studies on leadership. An interdisciplinary team of researchers from psychology, sociology, and economics developed and used the Leader Behavior Description Questionnaire (LBDQ) to analyze leadership in numerous types of groups and situations. Studies were made of Air Force commanders and members of bomber crews; officers, noncommissioned personnel, and civilian administrators in the Navy Department; manufacturing supervisors; executives of regional cooperatives; college administrators; teachers, principals, and school superintendents; and leaders of various student and civilian groups.

The Ohio State studies started with the premise that no satisfactory definition of leadership existed. They also recognized that previous work had too often assumed that

As a girl growing up on a farm in Alma, a Wisconsin town of 800, four decades ago, Carol A. Bartz had two career choices: nurse or teacher. With big feet for her age—they stopped growing at size 11—she jokes that being a nurse was out: "These boats coming down in white? Can you imagine?" So Bartz dreamed of being a math teacher, even though it was more the math part than the teacher part that appealed to her. "At the time, that was all you could do," she shrugs.

All Bartz wound up doing was becoming one of the most important women in tech. As head of Autodesk Inc., the world's leading supplier of design software with an $8.3 billion market cap, she turned an insular, narrowly focused company into a diversified player targeting industries ranging from automotive to entertainment. Autodesk, based in San Rafael, Calif., isn't a household name, but its software is behind a raft of everyday products, and is used to design buildings, cars, even movie icons like King Kong.

For a sense of how highly Bartz is regarded, listen to John Chambers, chief executive of Cisco Systems, where Bartz has had a board seat since 1994. Chambers ticks off her accomplishments—going from a couple hundred million in sales to $1.5 billion, a market capitalization that's risen much faster than the Standard & Poor's 500-stock index, a quality team.

Praise like that explains why shock and disappointment ran through techdom when Bartz, 57, announced that she would step down as CEO to become executive chairman. She leaves Autodesk in top form.

Neither Bartz's husband, Bill Marr, nor her CEO-in-waiting, Carl Bass, were sure she was serious about giving up the job until she actually told the board. "Until she really did it—until the moment—I didn't know," Bass says.

Over the holidays Bartz wrestled with whether it was time to leave. Fourteen years as CEO was a marathon stint in Silicon Valley. Her husband was retired, and her youngest child, Layne, would go to college soon. Before, Bartz could see her daughter between business trips; now she'd have to travel to see her. She knew that if the business stalled again there'd be no way she could back off from a challenge. Also, Bass was getting job offers, and Bartz didn't want to spend another five years grooming a successor.

Bartz, who's unabashed about her almost maternal love for Autodesk, "cried her eyes out" at the thought of leaving. She never felt she had to choose one "child" over the other, but as a working mom she had to strike a balance between her real and her metaphorical child every day.

Consider this recent morning. She's in back-to-back meetings at a Starbucks near her home, dressed in jeans and an orange sweater, wearing no makeup. Earlier that morning Layne, who's anxiously awaiting responses from colleges, crawled into bed with her, something she hasn't done since she was a child. "She's more stressed than I've ever seen her," Bartz says. "I knew something was wrong and so I just hung." All the while, she knew the clock was ticking on a breakfast meeting she had scheduled. She comforted her daughter, threw on clothes, and raced out, already late. "The concept of balance is perfection," she says, miming a seesaw motion. "And that's crazy."

Bartz may have cried about moving on, but she's no softie. She prides herself on running a "real" tech company, bristling when put in the same camp as eBay Inc.'s Meg Whitman, who some say runs a retailer. And she's blunt. "If she thinks you're stupid, she'll tell you," says Alfred S. Chuang, CEO of BEA Systems Inc., who worked under Bartz at Sun Microsystems Inc.

What's next? Bartz won't allow her staff to even use the word "retirement." She's booked solid with Autodesk duties and began teaching a Stanford Graduate School of Business class. Those close to her suspect her days as a CEO are not over. "If you told me that one day she'd be CEO of one of the largest tech companies, I wouldn't be surprised," says Chuang.

---

*leadership* was synonymous with *good leadership*. The Ohio State group was determined to study leadership, regardless of definition or whether it was effective or ineffective.

In the first step, the LBDQ was administered in a wide variety of situations. In order to examine how the leader was described, the answers to the questionnaire were then subjected to factor analysis. The outcome was amazingly consistent. The same two dimensions of leadership continually emerged from the questionnaire data. They were *consideration* and *initiating structure*. These two factors were found in a wide variety of studies encompassing many kinds of leadership positions and contexts. The researchers carefully emphasize that the studies show only *how* leaders carry out their leadership function. Initiating structure and consideration are very similar to the time-honored military commander's functions of mission and concern with the welfare of the troops. In simple terms, the Ohio State factors are task or goal orientation (initiating structure) and recognition of individual needs and relationships (consideration). The two dimensions are separate and distinct from each other.

The Ohio State studies certainly have value for the study of leadership. They were the first to point out and emphasize the importance of *both* task and human dimensions in assessing leadership. This two-dimensional approach lessened the gap between the strict task orientation of the scientific management movement and the human relations emphasis, which had been popular up to that time. Interestingly, when Colin Powell, usually considered one of the most-effective and most-admired leaders of recent years, speaks of his own leadership process, he uses this two-dimensional approach. Today leadership is recognized as both multidimensional, as first pointed out by the Ohio State studies, and multilevel (person, dyad, group, and collective/community).[18]

### The Early Michigan Leadership Studies

At about the same time that the Ohio State studies were being conducted, a group of researchers from the Survey Research Center at the University of Michigan began their studies of leadership. In the original study at the Prudential Insurance Company, 12 high-low productivity pairs of groups were selected for examination. Each pair represented a high-producing section and a low-producing section, with other variables such as type of work, conditions, and methods being the same in each pair. Nondirective interviews were conducted with the 24 section supervisors and 419 clerical workers. Results showed that supervisors of high-producing sections were significantly more likely to be general rather than close in their supervisory styles and be employee-centered (have a genuine concern for their people). The low-producing-section supervisors had essentially opposite characteristics and techniques. They were found to be close, production-centered supervisors. Another important, but sometimes overlooked, finding was that employee satisfaction was *not* directly related to productivity, the type of supervision was the key to their performance.

The general, employee-centered supervisor, described here, became the standard-bearer for the traditional human relations approach to leadership. The results of the Prudential studies were always cited when human relations advocates were challenged to prove their theories. The studies have been followed up with hundreds of similar studies in a wide variety of industrial, hospital, governmental, and other organizations. Thousands of employees, performing unskilled to highly professional and scientific tasks, have been analyzed. Rensis Likert, the one-time director of the Institute for Social Research of the University of Michigan, presented the results of the years of similar research in his books and became best known for his "System 4" (democratic) leadership style.

## TRADITIONAL THEORIES OF LEADERSHIP

The Iowa, Ohio State, and Michigan studies are three of the historically most important leadership studies for the field of organizational behavior. Unfortunately, leadership research has not surged ahead from this relatively auspicious beginning. Before analyzing the current status of leadership research, it is important also to examine the theoretical development that has occurred through the years.

There are several distinct theoretical bases for leadership. At first, leaders were felt to be born, not made. This so-called great person theory of leadership implied that some individuals are born with certain traits that allow them to emerge out of any situation or period of history to become leaders. Similar to research on personality, showing the impact of genetics and neurology/brain research (see Chapter 5), there is recent interest in the role that genetics and hardwiring may play in leadership. For example, one non-research-based analysis noted: "Our experience has led us to believe that much of leadership talent is hardwired in people before they reach their early or mid-twenties"[19] and researchers at the University of Minnesota using large samples of twins are investigating whether genetics predicts leadership. Although this research is ongoing, the findings so far do indicate that genetics may account for about 30 percent of the variance in leadership style and emergence in leadership roles, but the majority still comes from development.[20]

Perhaps the best way to view the born versus made issue is to recognize the interaction between the two. As noted by Avolio and Luthans:

> We already know that how a person's genetic makeup engages and is affected by its environment is not stable. Instead, the genetic–environment interaction is elastic (i.e., changes) over time. Specifically, as the "genetic program" unfolds, it is greatly affected by the context in which it unfolds.[21]

In other words, as was pointed out in the discussion of personality in Chapter 5, leadership is affected by both nature (genetics) *and* nurture (development).

Traditionally, however, the great person approach became associated with the *trait theory* of leadership. The trait approach is concerned mainly with identifying the personality traits of the leader. Dissatisfied with this trait approach, and stimulated by research such as the pioneering Ohio State studies, researchers next switched their emphasis from the individual leader's traits to the group being led. In the group approach, leadership is viewed more in terms of the leader's behavior and how such behavior affects and is affected by the group of followers. This role of the follower in leadership has received little attention over the years. As Avolio concluded in his summary of the leadership research literature, "unfortunately, most leadership research has considered the follower a passive or nonexistent element when examining what constitutes leadership."[22]

In addition to the leader's traits and the group, the situation then began to receive increased attention in leadership theory. The situational approach was initially called *Zeitgeist* (a German word meaning "spirit of the time"); the leader is viewed as a product of the times and the situation. The person with the particular qualities or traits that a situation requires will emerge as the leader. This view has much historical support as a theoretical basis for leadership and serves as the basis for situational—and then termed contingency and now contextual—theories of leadership. Fiedler's classic contingency theory, which suggests that leadership styles must fit or match the situation in order to be effective, is the best known. Another traditional situational, or contingency, theory took some of the expectancy concepts of motivation that are discussed in Chapter 6 and applied them to leadership and situations. Called the path-goal theory of leadership, it is an attempt to synthesize motivational and leadership processes. The following sections examine these traditionally recognized trait, group, contingency, and path-goal theories of leadership.

## Trait Theories of Leadership

The scientific analysis of leadership started off by concentrating on the trait approach to leadership. Attention was given to the search for universal traits possessed by leaders. The results of this voluminous early research effort were generally very disappointing. Only intelligence seemed to hold up with any degree of consistency. When these findings were combined with those of studies on physical traits, the conclusion seemed to be that leaders were bigger and brighter than those being led, but not too much so. For example, this line of research concluded that the leader was more intelligent than the average of the group being led, but, interestingly, was not the most intelligent of the group. Political analysts indicate that candidates should not come across as too intelligent to be electable, and the most intelligent member of a criminal gang is not the leader, but usually a lieutenant of the leader, the "brains" of the outfit.

When the trait approach was applied to organizational leadership, the result was even cloudier. One of the biggest problems is that all managers think they know what the qualities of a successful leader are. Obviously, almost any adjective can be used to describe a successful leader. However, it should be recognized that there are semantic limitations and historically, little supporting evidence on these observed descriptive traits and successful leadership. In recent years, however, with the emergence of the importance of the "Big Five" personality traits in organizational behavior (see Chapter 5), the trait approach to leadership effectiveness has resurfaced. For example, a recent qualitative and quantitative meta-analysis review found strong empirical support for the leader trait perspective when traits are organized according to the five-factor model.[23] Specifically, the personality trait of extraversion had the highest (.31) average correlation with leader emergence and leadership effectiveness, followed by conscientiousness (.28), openness to experience (.24), neuroticism (−.24), and nonsignificant agreeableness (.08).[24] These results and newly developed traitlike theoretical frameworks such as the motivation to lead (MTL), which has been demonstrated to predict leadership potential,[25] indicate that a dispositional, traitlike approach to leadership is still alive and may have potential for the future.

## From Traits to States and Skills Development

Picking up where the fixed, traitlike approach to leadership has left off are the newly emerging states and more-established skills for leadership development. Still in the tradition of concentrating on the great person approach, but moving away from a strict traits approach and serving as a bridge to the situational theories, are the newly emerging psychological states. As presented in Chapter 7, the statelike (situationally based capacities, those open to development and change, as opposed to the dispositional, relatively fixed traits) positive organizational behavior (POB) constructs have potential for understanding and developing leadership.[26] Specifically, both intuitive and beginning research evidence indicate that optimism,[27] hope,[28] resiliency,[29] emotional intelligence,[30] and especially self-efficacy[31] are related to effective leaders. Incorporating these POB variables of the leader—describing who they are—into newly emerging theories such as authentic leadership[32] (described in the introductory definitions and more fully later in the chapter) seems important for the development of leadership to meet today's challenges.

In addition to developing the POB states, another departure from the trait approach that still focuses on leaders themselves is their skill development. For example, a number of years ago, Katz identified the technical, conceptual, and human skills needed for effective management.[33] Yukl includes leadership skills such as creativity, organization, persuasiveness, diplomacy and tactfulness, knowledge of the task, and the ability to speak well.[34] These skills have become very important in the application of leadership theory and are also given specific attention in the next chapter.

Closely related to the skills approach is the study of leader "competencies." One stream of research has identified several such competencies that are related to leadership effectiveness both in the United States and other cultures:[35]

1. Drive, or the inner motivation to pursue goals
2. Leadership motivation, which is the use of socialized power to influence others to succeed
3. Integrity, which includes truthfulness and the will to translate words into deeds
4. Self-confidence that leads others to feel confidence, usually exhibited through various forms of impression management directed at employees
5. Intelligence, which is usually focused in the ability to process information, analyze alternatives, and discover opportunities
6. Knowledge of the business, so that ideas that are generated help the company to survive and thrive
7. Emotional intelligence, based on a self-monitoring personality, making quality leaders strong in situation sensitivity and the ability to adapt to circumstances as needed

Importantly, these competencies seem to hold in the current environment facing organizational leaders, but require further theory building and research.

## Group and Exchange Theories of Leadership

The group theories of leadership have their roots in social psychology. Classic exchange theory, in particular, serves as an important basis for this approach. Discussed in previous chapters, this means simply that the leader provides more benefits/rewards than burdens/costs for followers. There must be a positive exchange between the leaders and followers in order for group goals to be accomplished. Pioneering theorist Chester Barnard applied such an analysis to managers and subordinates in an organizational setting more than a half-century ago. More recently, this social exchange view of leadership has been summarized by Yammarino and Dansereau as follows:

> In work organizations, the key partners involved in exchange relationships of investments and returns are superiors and subordinates. Superiors make investments (e.g., salary, office space) in and receive returns (e.g., performance) from subordinates; subordinates make investments in and receive returns from superiors; and the investments and returns occur on a one-to-one basis in each superior-subordinate dyad.[36]

This quotation emphasizes that leadership is an exchange process between the leader and followers. Social psychological research can be used to support this notion of exchange. Table 13.2 compares and contrasts the theory and research on three domains of leadership. Importantly, although traditionally ignored, there is considerable evidence that followers affect leaders, and there is considerable theory and research on the relationship, or exchange-based, approach to leadership.

### *Followers' Impact on Leaders*

A growing number of research studies indicate that followers/associates may actually affect leaders as much as leaders affect followers/associates. For example, one study found that when associates were not performing very well, the leaders tended to emphasize the task or initiating structure, but when associates were doing a good job, leaders increased emphasis on their people or consideration.[37] In a laboratory study it was found that group productivity had a greater impact on leadership style than leadership style had on group productivity,[38] and in another study it was found that in newly formed groups, leaders may adjust their supportive behavior in response to the level of group cohesion and arousal already present.[39] In other words, such studies seem to indicate that followers affect leaders and their behaviors as much as leaders and their behaviors affect followers. Some practicing managers, such as the vice president of Saga Corporation, feel that

**TABLE 13.2**
**Summary of Three Domains of Leadership**

*Source:* Adapted from George B. Graen and Mary Uhl-Bien, "Development of Leader–Member Exchange (LMX) Theory of Leadership over 25 Years: Applying a Multi-Level Multi-Domain Perspective," *Leadership Quarterly,* Vol. 6, No. 2, 1995, p. 224.

| | Leader-Based | Follower-Based | Relationship-Based |
|---|---|---|---|
| What is leadership? | Appropriate behavior of the person in leader role | Ability and motivation to manage one's own performance | Trust, respect, and mutual obligation that generates influence between parties |
| What behaviors constitute leadership? | Establishing and communicating vision; inspiring, instilling pride | Empowering, coaching, facilitating, giving up control | Building strong relationships with followers; mutual learning and accommodation |
| Advantages | Leader as rallying point for organization; common understanding of mission and values; can initiate wholesale change | Makes the most of follower capabilities; frees up leaders for other responsibilities | Accommodates differing needs of subordinates; can elicit superior work from different types of people |
| Disadvantages | Highly dependent on leader; problems if leader changes or is pursuing inappropriate vision | Highly dependent on follower initiative and ability | Time consuming; relies on long-term relationship between specific leaders and members |
| When appropriate? | Fundamental change; charismatic leader in place; limited diversity among followers | Highly capable and task-committed followers | Continuous improvement of teamwork; substantial diversity and stability among followers; network building |
| Where most effective? | Structured tasks; strong leader position power; member acceptance of leader | Unstructured tasks; weak position power; member nonacceptance of leader | Situation favorability for leader between two extremes |

employees lack followership skills, and there is growing evidence that these skills are becoming increasingly important.[40] In other words, it is probably not wise to ignore followership. Most managers feel that their associates have an obligation to follow and support their leader and Kellerman argues that this arrangement is in the natural order of things (e.g., the "pecking order" of chickens in the barnyard or the dominant alpha male in the wolf pack). She concludes, "in order for large groups to govern themselves effectively, some must be willing to be leaders, others must be willing to be followers, and the majority must be willing to go along with this arrangement."[41] As the CEO of Commerce Union Corporation noted in a *Wall Street Journal* article: "Part of a subordinate's responsibility is to make the boss look good."

### The Leader-Member Exchange (LMX) Model

Relevant to the exchange view of leadership is the vertical dyad linkage (VDL) approach,[42] now commonly called leader-member exchange (LMX).[43] LMX theory says that leaders treat individual followers differently. In particular, leaders and their associates develop dyadic (two-person) relationships that affect the behavior of both. For example, associates who are committed and who expend a lot of effort for the unit are rewarded with more of the leader's positional resources (for example, information, confidence, and concern) than those who do not display these behaviors.

Over time, the leader will develop an "in-group" of associates and an "out-group" of associates and treat them accordingly. Thus, for the same leader, research has shown that in-group associates report fewer difficulties in dealing with the leader and perceive the leader as being more responsive to their needs than out-group associates do.[44] Also, leaders spend more time "leading" members of the in-group (that is, they do not depend on formal authority to influence them), and they tend to "supervise" those in the out-group (that is, they depend on formal roles and authority to influence them).[45] Finally, there is evidence that members of the in-group (those who report a high-quality relationship with their leader) assume greater job responsibility, contribute more to their units, and are rated as higher performers than those reporting a low-quality relationship.[46]

This exchange theory has been around for some time now, and although it is not without criticism,[47] in general, the research continues to be relatively supportive.[48] However, as traditionally presented, LMX seems to be more descriptive of the typical process of role making by leaders, rather than prescribing the pattern of downward exchange relations optimal for leadership effectiveness.[49] Research is also using more sophisticated methodologies[50] and suggests that there are a number of moderators in the LMX-performance relationship.[51]

Graen and Uhl-Bien have emphasized that LMX has evolved through various stages: (1) the discovery of differentiated dyads; (2) the investigation of characteristics of LMX relationships and their organizational implications/outcomes; (3) the description of dyadic partnership building; and (4) the aggregation of differentiated dyadic relations to group and network levels.[52] New insights into the manner in which leaders differentiate between employees in order to form in-groups and out-groups may in part be explained by social network analysis. Positive social networks and exchange processes assist leaders in selecting those who may become part of the inner circle of an organization.[53] Also, the fourth stage recognizes the new cross-functional or network emphasis in organizations and even external relations with customers, suppliers, and other organizational stakeholders. Research that identifies leader-follower relationships that are best suited to specific environmental contingencies is still needed.[54]

Finally, from the social cognitive perspective taken by this text, it should be remembered that leader-member exchanges are a reciprocal process. Evidence of this process of interaction suggests that leaders may be inclined to change follower self-concepts in the short term to achieve performance goals and more enduring changes. At the same time, followers reciprocally shape leaders' self-schemas through their responses, both as individuals and through collective or group reactions.[55] These and other elements of the continual negotiation between the leader and followers, which is also recognized by the psychological contract concept discussed at the end of Chapter 6, deserve additional consideration in the future.

## Contingency Theory of Leadership

After concentrating just on leaders themselves proved to fall short of being an adequate overall theory of leadership, attention turned not only to the group being led and the exchange relationship, but also to the situational or contextual aspects of leadership. Social psychologists began the search for situational variables that affect leadership roles, skills, behavior, and followers' performance and satisfaction. Numerous situational variables were identified, but no overall theory pulled it all together until Fred Fiedler proposed the now classic situation-based, or contingency, theory for leadership effectiveness.

### *Fiedler's Contingency Model of Leadership Effectiveness*

To test the hypotheses he had formulated from previous research findings, Fiedler developed what he called a *contingency model of leadership effectiveness.* This model contained the relationship between leadership style and the favorableness of the situation. Situational favorableness was described by Fiedler in terms of three empirically derived dimensions:

1. The *leader-member relationship,* which is the most critical variable in determining the situation's favorableness

2. The *degree of task structure,* which is the second most important input into the favorableness of the situation

3. The *leader's position power* obtained through formal authority, which is the third most critical dimension of the situation[56]

Situations are favorable to the leader if all three of these dimensions are high. In other words, if the leader is generally accepted and respected by followers (high first dimension), if the task is very structured and everything is "spelled out" (high second dimension), and if a great deal of authority and power are formally attributed to the leader's position (high third dimension), the situation is favorable. If the opposite exists (if the three dimensions are low), the situation will be very unfavorable for the leader. Fiedler concluded through his research that the favorableness of the situation in combination with the leadership style determines effectiveness.

Through the analysis of research findings from all types of situations, Fiedler was able to discover that under very favorable *and* very unfavorable situations, the task-directed, or hard-nosed and authoritarian, type of leader was most effective. However, when the situation was only moderately favorable or unfavorable (the intermediate range of favorableness), the human-oriented or democratic type of leader was most effective. Figure 13.1 summarizes this relationship between leadership style and the favorableness of the situation.

Why is the task-directed leader successful in very favorable situations? Fiedler offered the following explanation:

> In the very favorable conditions in which the leader has power, informal backing, and a relatively well-structured task, the group is ready to be directed, and the group expects to be told what to do. Consider the captain of an airliner in its final landing approach. We would hardly want him to turn to his crew for a discussion on how to land.[57]

**FIGURE 13.1**
**Fiedler's Contingency Model of Leadership**

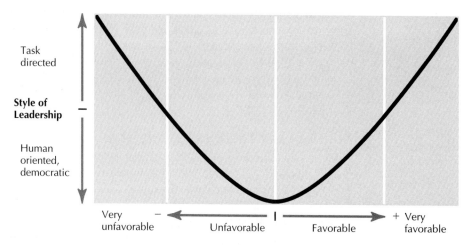

**Favorableness of the Situation**

As an example of why the task-oriented leader is successful in a highly unfavorable situation, Fiedler cited

> the disliked chairman of a volunteer committee which is asked to plan the office picnic on a beautiful Sunday. If the leader asks too many questions about what the group ought to do or how he should proceed, he is likely to be told that "we ought to go home."[58]

The leader who makes a wrong decision in this highly unfavorable type of situation is probably better off than the leader who makes no decision at all. In essence, what Fiedler's model suggests is that in highly unfavorable situations, the effective leader takes charge and makes the decisions that need to be made to accomplish the task without asking for input or trying to keep everyone happy.

Figure 13.1 shows that the human-oriented, democratic leader is effective in the intermediate range of favorableness. An example of such situations is the typical committee or unit. In these situations, the leader may not be wholly accepted by the other members of the group, the task may not be completely structured, and some authority and power may be granted to the leader. Under such a relatively but not extremely unfavorable situation, the model predicts that a human-oriented, democratic type of leader will be most effective. The same would be true of a moderately favorable situation. Such moderately unfavorable or favorable situations are most common for supervisors and managers. The implication is that in general the human-oriented, democratic style of leadership would be most effective in managing human resources in the large majority of organizational situations.

### Research Support for the Contingency Model

As is true of any widely publicized theoretical development, Fiedler's model has stimulated a great deal of research over the years. Not surprisingly, the results are mixed and a controversy has been generated. Fiedler and his students have provided almost all the support for the model over the years. For example, to defend the validity of his theory, he cited 30 studies in a wide variety of teams and organizations (Navy teams, chemical research teams, shop departments, supermarkets, heavy machinery plant departments, engineering groups, hospital wards, public health teams, and others) and concluded that "the theory is highly predictive and that the relations obtained in the validation studies are almost identical to those obtained in the original studies."[59] With one exception, which Fiedler explains away, he maintains that the model correctly predicted the correlations that should exist between the leader's style and performance in relation to the identified favorableness of the situation. As predicted, his studies showed that in very unfavorable and very favorable situations, the task-oriented leader performs best. In moderately favorable and moderately unfavorable situations, the human-oriented leader was more effective. Although Fiedler recognized that there was indeed criticism of his conclusions, he maintained that "methodologically sound validation studies have on the whole provided substantial support for the theory."[60] Meta-analytic investigations of the predictions of the model have yielded a whole range of support,[61] mixed results,[62] and nonsupport.[63]

### Fiedler's Contingency Theory in Perspective

Overall, few would argue that Fiedler provided one of the major breakthroughs for leadership theory, research, and practice. Although some of the criticism cannot be ignored, there are several reasons that Fiedler's model made a historically important contribution:

1. It was the first highly visible leadership theory to present the contingency approach, thus giving widespread attention to the important role that the situation or context plays in leadership.

2. It also emphasized the importance of the interaction between the situation and the leader's characteristics in determining leader effectiveness.

3. It stimulated a great deal of research, including tests of its predictions and attempts to improve on the model, and inspired the formulation of alternative contingency theories.[64]

## Path-Goal Leadership Theory

The other widely recognized theoretical development from a contingency approach is the path-goal theory derived from the expectancy framework of motivation theory (see Chapter 6). Although Georgopoulos and his colleagues at the University of Michigan's Institute for Social Research used path-goal concepts and terminology many years ago for analyzing the impact of leadership on performance, the recognized development is usually attributed to Martin Evans and Robert House, who at about the same time wrote separate papers on the subject.[65] In essence, the path-goal theory attempts to explain the impact that leader behavior has on associate motivation, satisfaction, and performance. The House version of the theory incorporates four major types, or styles, of leadership.[66] Briefly summarized, these are:

1. *Directive leadership.* This style is similar to that of the Lippitt and White authoritarian leader. Associates know exactly what is expected of them, and the leader gives specific directions. There is no participation by subordinates.

2. *Supportive leadership.* The leader is friendly and approachable and shows a genuine concern for associates.

3. *Participative leadership.* The leader asks for and uses suggestions from associates but still makes the decisions.

4. *Achievement-oriented leadership.* The leader sets challenging goals for associates and shows confidence that they will attain these goals and perform well.

This path-goal theory—and here is how it differs in one respect from Fiedler's contingency model—suggests that these various styles can be and actually are used by the same leader in different situations.[67] Two of the situational factors that have been identified are the personal characteristics of associates and the environmental pressures and demands facing associates. With respect to the first situational factor, the theory asserts:

> Leader behavior will be acceptable to subordinates to the extent that the subordinates see such behavior as either an immediate source of satisfaction or as instrumental to future satisfaction.[68]

And with respect to the second situational factor, the theory states:

> Leader behavior will be motivational (e.g., will increase subordinate effort) to the extent that (1) it makes satisfaction of subordinate needs contingent on effective performance, and (2) it complements the environment of subordinates by providing the coaching, guidance, support, and rewards which are necessary for effective performance and which may otherwise be lacking in subordinates or in their environment.[69]

Using one of the four styles contingent on the situational factors as outlined, the leader attempts to influence associates' perceptions and motivate them, which in turn leads to their role clarity, goal expectancies, satisfaction, and performance. This is specifically accomplished by the leader as follows:

1. Recognizing and/or arousing associates' needs for outcomes over which the leader has some control

2. Increasing personal payoffs to associates for work-goal attainment

3. Making the path to those payoffs easier to travel by coaching and direction

**FIGURE 13.2**
**A Summary of
Path-Goal
Relationships**

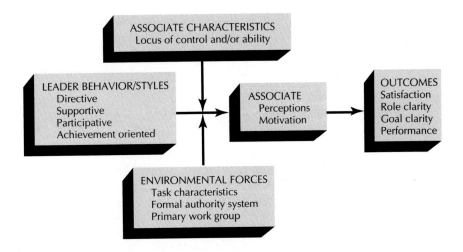

4. Helping associates clarify expectancies

5. Reducing frustrating barriers

6. Increasing the opportunities for personal satisfaction contingent on effective performance[70]

In other words, by doing the preceding, the leader attempts to make the path to associates' goals as smooth as possible. But to accomplish this path-goal facilitation, the leader must use the appropriate style contingent on the situational variables present. Figure 13.2 summarizes this path-goal approach.

As happened with the expectancy theory of motivation, there was a surge of research on the path-goal theory of leadership. However, the research concentrated only on parts of the theory rather than on the entire theory. A sampling of the research findings indicated the following:

1. Studies of seven organizations found that *leader directiveness* was (a) positively related to satisfactions and expectancies of associates engaged in ambiguous tasks and (b) negatively related to satisfactions and expectancies of associates engaged in clear tasks.

2. Studies involving 10 different samples of employees found that *supportive leadership* had its most positive effect on satisfaction for associates who work on stressful, frustrating, or dissatisfying tasks.

3. In a major study in a manufacturing organization, it was found that in nonrepetitive, ego-involving tasks, employees were more satisfied under *participative leaders* than under nonparticipative leaders.

4. In three separate organizations it was found that for employees performing ambiguous, nonrepetitive tasks, the higher the *achievement orientation of the leader,* the more associates were confident that their efforts would pay off in effective performance.[71]

Other reviews of the research on the path-goal theory are not as supportive as the preceding. For example, Schriesheim and DeNisi note that only a few hypotheses have really been drawn from the theory, which means that the theory may be incapable of generating meaningful predictions.[72] However, a comprehensive review of 48 studies demonstrated that the mixed results of the individual studies, when cumulated, were transformed into support for path-goal theory.[73]

Overall, the path-goal theory, like the other traditional theories presented in this section, provide a theoretical and research foundation for the better understanding of leadership.

One analysis concluded that leaders will be perceived most favorably by their associates, and succeed in exerting most influence over them, when they behave in ways that closely match (1) the needs and values of associates and (2) the requirements of a specific work situation.[74] In other words, the path-goal theory, like the expectancy theory in work motivation, can help in understanding the complexities of the leadership process.

# MODERN THEORETICAL PROCESSES OF LEADERSHIP

Despite a relative degree of acceptance of the traditional theories of leadership and the considerable (at least relative to other areas in organizational behavior) amount of research that has been conducted, few would disagree today that leadership still needs much more theory building and research. For example, a comprehensive review of the traditional theories concluded that many of the tests conducted to identify moderating effects were judged to be inappropriate and that most of the results reported in this domain have not been replicated.[75] There is a need to go beyond the traditional approaches with alternative theories, research methods, and applications for leadership studies.

Besides the established trait, group and exchange, contingency, and path-goal theories of leadership, a number of other widely recognized theories have emerged in recent years. These include the charismatic, transformational, substitutes, and authentic theories of leadership. An overview of each of these provides better understanding of the complex leadership process.

## Charismatic Leadership Theories

Charismatic leadership is a throwback to the old conception of leaders as being those who "by the force of their personal abilities are capable of having profound and extraordinary effects on followers."[76] Although the charismatic concept, or charisma, goes as far back as the ancient Greeks and is cited in the Bible, its modern development is often attributed to the work of Robert House.[77] On the basis of the analysis of political and religious leaders, House suggests that charismatic leaders are characterized by self-confidence and confidence in their associates, high expectations for associates, ideological vision, and the use of personal example. Followers of charismatic leaders identify with the leader and the mission of the leader, exhibit extreme loyalty to and confidence in the leader, emulate the leader's values and behavior, and derive self-esteem from their relationship with the leader.[78] Bass has extended the profile of charismatic leaders to include superior debating and persuasive skills as well as technical expertise and the fostering of attitudinal, behavioral, and emotional changes in their followers.[79] A *Fortune* article humorously describes a manager with charisma as follows:

> He attended some middling college. Doesn't have an MBA. But he has an aura. He persuades people—subordinates, peers, customers, even the S.O.B. you both work for—to do things they'd rather not. People charge over the hill for him. Run through fire. Walk barefoot on broken glass. He doesn't demand attention, he commands it.[80]

Because of the effects that charismatic leaders have on followers, the theory predicts that charismatic leaders will produce in followers performance beyond expectations as well as strong commitment to the leader and his or her mission. Research indicates that the impact of such charismatic leaders will be enhanced when the followers exhibit higher levels of self-awareness and self-monitoring, especially when observing the charismatic leaders' behaviors and activities[81] and when operating in a social network.[82] House and his colleagues provide some support for charismatic theory[83] and research finds a positive effect on desirable outcomes such as cooperation[84] and motivation,[85] and recent conceptualization

**TABLE 13.3**
**Ethical and Unethical Characteristics of Charismatic Leaders**

*Source:* Jane M. Howell and Bruce J. Avolio, "The Ethics of Charismatic Leadership: Submission or Liberation?" *Academy of Management Executive,* May 1992, p. 45. Used with permission.

| Ethical Charismatic Leader | Unethical Charismatic Leader |
|---|---|
| • Uses power to serve others | • Uses power only for personal gain or impact |
| • Aligns vision with followers' needs and aspirations | • Promotes own personal vision |
| • Considers and learns from criticism | • Censures critical or opposing views |
| • Stimulates followers to think independently and to question the leader's view | • Demands own decisions be accepted without question |
| • Open, two-way communication | • One-way communication |
| • Coaches, develops, and supports followers; shares recognition with others | • Insensitive to followers' needs |
| • Relies on internal moral standards to satisfy organizational and societal interests | • Relies on convenient, external moral standards to satisfy self-interests |

proposing that alternative forms (personalized versus socialized) are relevant to successful implementation of mergers and acquisitions.[86] However, as with the other leadership theories, complexities are found[87] and more research is needed. For example, one study that assessed charismatic leader behaviors, individual level correlates, and unit-level correlates (outcomes) in the military yielded only limited support for the theory's propositions and led the researchers to conclude that greater sensitivity to multiple constituencies of leaders is needed in theories and studies focused on charismatic leadership.[88] Also, extensions of the theory are being proposed. For example, Conger and Kanungo treat charisma as an attributional phenomenon and propose that it varies with the situation.[89] Leader traits that foster charismatic attributions include self-confidence, impression-management skills, social sensitivity, and empathy. Situations that promote charismatic leadership include a crisis requiring dramatic change[90] or followers who are very dissatisfied with the status quo. For example, a study in a university setting revealed a situation in which a charismatic leader was able to successfully implement a technical change, but at the same time suffered through major political turmoil, which appeared to be side effects of the technical change. This suggests that studies of charismatic leadership must be considered in the context in which the leader operates, and the nature of the task or work being performed should be included in the analysis.[91]

Included in the extensions of charismatic leadership is also the recognition of a dark side.[92] Charismatic leaders tend to be portrayed as wonderful heroes, but as Table 13.3 shows, there can also be unethical characteristics associated with charismatic leaders. With regard to meeting the challenge of being ethical, it has been noted that charismatic leaders

> deserve this label only if they create transformations in their organizations so that members are motivated to follow them and to seek organization objectives not simply because they are ordered to do so, and not merely because they calculate that such compliance is in their self-interest, but because they voluntarily identify with the organization, its standards of conduct and willingly seek to fulfill its purpose.[93]

This transformation idea is also picked up by Bass, who suggests that charismatic leadership is really just a component of the broader-based transformational leadership, covered next.[94]

**TABLE 13.4**
**Characteristics and Approaches of Transactional versus Transformational Leaders**

*Source:* Bernard M. Bass, "From Transactional to Transformational Leadership: Learning to Share the Vision," *Organizational Dynamics,* Winter 1990, p. 22. Used with permission.

**Transactional Leaders**

1. *Contingent reward:* Contracts the exchange of rewards for effort; promises rewards for good performance; recognizes accomplishments.
2. *Management by exception* (active): Watches and searches for deviations from rules and standards; takes corrective action.
3. *Management by exception* (passive): Intervenes only if standards are not met.
4. *Laissez-faire:* Abdicates responsibilities; avoids making decisions.

**Transformational Leaders**

1. *Charisma:* Provides vision and sense of mission; instills pride; gains respect and trust.
2. *Inspiration:* Communicates high expectations; uses symbols to focus efforts; expresses important purposes in simple ways.
3. *Intellectual stimulation:* Promotes intelligence; rationality; and careful problem solving.
4. *Individual consideration:* Gives personal attention; treats each employee individually; coaches; advises.

## Transformational Leadership Theory

Many years ago James MacGregor Burns identified two types of political leadership: transactional and transformational.[95] The more traditional transactional leadership involves an exchange relationship between leaders and followers, but transformational leadership is based more on leaders' shifting the values, beliefs, and needs of their followers. Table 13.4 summarizes the characteristics and approaches of transactional versus transformational leaders. More recently, the "charisma" characteristic of transformational leadership has been changed to "idealized influence." This was done to not confuse transformational with charismatic leadership, which Bass treats as different theories. Although there are a number of contrasts between the two theories, the major differentiators are how followers are treated. Key to transformational leaders is that they seek to empower and elevate followers (i.e., develop followers into leaders) while charismatic leaders may try to keep followers weak and dependent on them (i.e., instill personal loyalty to the leader rather than developing them to attain ideals).

In contrast to transactional leaders that behave in one of the ways shown in Table 13.4, Avolio notes that transformational leaders characterized by *idealized leadership, inspiring leadership, intellectual stimulation,* and *individualized consideration* represent a cluster of interrelated styles aimed at the following:

1. Changing situations for the better
2. Developing followers into leaders
3. Overhauling organizations to provide them with new strategic directions
4. Inspiring people by providing an energizing vision and high ideal for moral and ethical conduct[96]

On the basis of his research findings, Bass concludes that in many instances (such as relying on passive management by exception), transactional leadership is a prescription for mediocrity and that transformational leadership leads to superior performance in organizations facing demands for renewal and change. He suggests that fostering transformational leadership through policies of recruitment, selection, promotion, training, and development will pay off in the health, well-being, and effective performance of today's organizations.[97] A meta-analysis of 39 studies found that the transformational behaviors of charisma (idealized influence), individualized consideration, and intellectual stimulation were related to leadership effectiveness in most studies, but, except for the contingent reward behaviors, the transactional leadership styles did not enhance leadership effectiveness,[98] and this more positive impact of transformational over transactional leadership has held through the years. For example, a recent meta-analysis of 87 studies found transformational leadership related (.44) to the composite of desired outcomes (follower job satisfaction, follower leader satisfaction, follower motivation, leader job performance, group or organizational performance and rated leader effectiveness).[99] However, in this meta-analysis, contingent reward transactional leadership also related (.39) to the same composite of outcomes, and transformational leadership failed to significantly predict leader job performance.

Most of the research on transformational leadership to date has relied on Bass and Avolio's MLQ (Multifactor Leadership Questionnaire)[100] or qualitative research that simply describes leaders through interviews. Examples of the latter were the interviews with top executives of major companies conducted by Tichy and Devanna. They found that effective transformational leaders share the following characteristics:

1. They identify themselves as change agents.
2. They are courageous.
3. They believe in people.
4. They are value driven.
5. They are lifelong learners.
6. They have the ability to deal with complexity, ambiguity, and uncertainty.
7. They are visionaries.[101]

Increasing empirical research has supported the transformational leadership characteristics. For example, field studies have shown that transformational leaders more frequently employ legitimating tactics and engender higher levels of identification and internalization[102] (see Chapter 10), have better performance[103] and develop their followers.[104] Recent studies are refining these general findings. For example, in a study comparing male and female sales managers, females were inclined to form unique relationships with each of their individual subordinates that were independent of their group memberships, suggesting transformational and contingent reward patterns that were somewhat different from their male counterparts.[105] In other studies, transformational leadership mediated by leader-member exchange produced effects on followers' performance and organizational citizenship behaviors (OCBs).[106] Also, the relationship transformational leadership and OCBs were found to be moderated by perceptions of procedural justice and trust, and extraversion and agreeableness of the "Big Five" personality traits (see Chapter 5).[107] Another recent study found ones' emotion and personality contributed to transformational leadership behavior.[108] Also, transformational leadership exhibited more moral reasoning[109] and has implications for ethical concerns.[110] A recent study got back to refining the impact of transformational leadership on performance by finding that one's identification with the work unit, self-efficacy (Chapter 7) and means efficacy (confidence in the tools and other support needed to get the job done) were mediators.[111] Conceptual analysis also indicates that contextual factors may influence receptivity to transformational leadership tactics, and therefore they should be considered and accounted for when research is being conducted.[112] In addition, other theories gained attention to help explain the complex process of leadership.

## Substitutes for Leadership

Because of dissatisfaction with the progress of leadership theory and research in explaining and predicting the effects of leader behavior on performance outcomes, some of the basic assumptions about the importance of leadership per se have been challenged over the

**FIGURE 13.3**
**Kerr and Jermier's Substitutes and Neutralizers for Leadership**

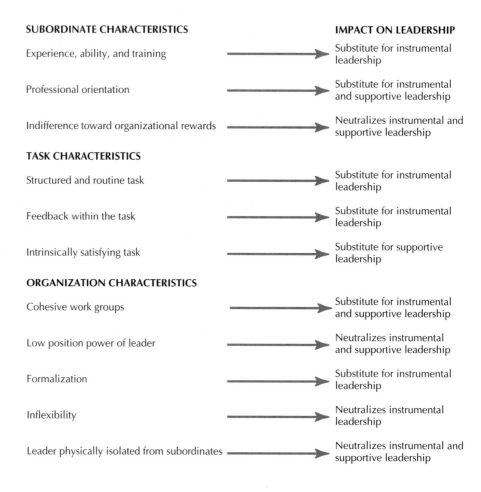

**SUBORDINATE CHARACTERISTICS**

Experience, ability, and training → Substitute for instrumental leadership

Professional orientation → Substitute for instrumental and supportive leadership

Indifference toward organizational rewards → Neutralizes instrumental and supportive leadership

**TASK CHARACTERISTICS**

Structured and routine task → Substitute for instrumental leadership

Feedback within the task → Substitute for instrumental leadership

Intrinsically satisfying task → Substitute for supportive leadership

**ORGANIZATION CHARACTERISTICS**

Cohesive work groups → Substitute for instrumental and supportive leadership

Low position power of leader → Neutralizes instrumental and supportive leadership

Formalization → Substitute for instrumental leadership

Inflexibility → Neutralizes instrumental leadership

Leader physically isolated from subordinates → Neutralizes instrumental and supportive leadership

**IMPACT ON LEADERSHIP**

years. One alternative approach that received attention proposed that there may be certain "substitutes" for leadership that make leader behavior unnecessary and redundant, and "neutralizers" that prevent the leader from behaving in a certain way or that counteract the behavior.[113] These substitutes or neutralizers can be found in subordinate, task, and organization characteristics. Figure 13.3 gives specific examples of possible substitutes and neutralizers according to supportive/relationship leadership and instrumental/task leadership.

As shown, employee experience, ability, and training may substitute for instrumental/task leadership. For example, craftspersons or professionals such as accountants or software engineers may have so much experience, ability, and training that they do not need instrumental/task leadership to perform well and be satisfied. Those employees who don't particularly care about organizational rewards (for example, professors or musicians) will neutralize both supportive/relationship and instrumental/task leadership attempts. Tasks that are highly structured and automatically provide feedback substitute for instrumental/task leadership, and those that are intrinsically satisfying (for example, teaching) do not need supportive/relationship leadership. There are also a number of organizational characteristics that substitute for or neutralize leadership.

There has been further analysis of the leader substitutes concept,[114] and Kerr and Jermier have provided some empirical support from field studies of police officers.[115] They found that substitutes such as feedback from the task being performed had more impact on certain job-related activities than leader behaviors did. Other studies have also been interpreted (post hoc) to support organizational characteristics such as formalization as leader substitutes.[116] More recent direct tests have yielded mixed results.[117] One study using hospital personnel with a wide variety of skills and backgrounds and in a wide variety of professions found several potential substitutes to predict subordinate satisfaction and commitment, but only one of the single substitutes (organizational formalization) rendered leadership impossible and/or unnecessary.[118] A follow-up study found that worker professionalism was an important moderator variable. It also found that professionals differed from nonprofessionals in that intrinsically satisfying work tasks and importance placed on organizational rewards were strong substitutes for leaders' support.[119]

The substitutes theory tries to point out that some things are beyond leaders' control; leaders do not have mystical powers over people. The situation or context plays a role. By the same token, recent research testing the substitutes for leadership theory was generally not supportive and demonstrated that leadership does matter.[120] In other words, the substitutes idea does not negate leadership; but it may put a more realistic boundary on what leadership is capable of achieving from followers. Some styles, behaviors, activities, and skills of leadership are more effective than others. The next chapter focuses on these effective approaches to the actual practice of leadership.

## Authentic Leadership

Although there are a number of newly emerging theories such as servant leadership,[121] political leadership,[122] contextual leadership,[123] e-leadership,[124] primal leadership,[125] relational leadership,[126] positive leadership,[127] shared leadership,[128] and responsible leadership,[129] in these times of unprecedented challenges facing organizational leaders, we (Avolio and Luthans and our colleagues working with the Leadership Institute at the University of Nebraska) believe that authentic leadership is a needed approach. Drawing from Luthans's work on positive organizational behavior[130] and psychological capital[131] (see Chapter 7), and Avolio's work on transformational[132] and full range leadership,[133] we have recently proposed a specific model of authentic leadership development.[134]

Authenticity has its roots in ancient Greek philosophy ("To thine own self be true") and descriptive words include genuine, transparent, reliable, trustworthy, real, and veritable. Positive psychologists refer to authenticity as both owning one's personal experiences (thoughts, emotions, or beliefs, "the real me inside") and acting in accord with the true self (behaving and expressing what you really think and believe).[135] We specifically define *authentic leadership* in organizations as:

> A process that draws from both positive psychological capacities and a highly developed organizational context, which results in both greater self-awareness and self-regulated positive behaviors on the part of leaders and associates, fostering positive self-development. The authentic leader is confident, hopeful, optimistic, resilient, transparent, moral/ethical, future-oriented, and gives priority to developing associates to be leaders.[136]

The concept of authentic leadership is more on a continuum, rather than just being dichotomous. Also, although we recognize authentic leaders draw from their genetic endowment and life experience, similar to positive organizational behavior (POB) capacities or psychological capital (see Chapter 7), authentic leadership is considered to be statelike and thus open to development and change. Historically important leaders such as Gandhi, Eleanor Roosevelt, and more recently Nelson Mandela would be considered authentic leaders by our definition, but so would day-to-day managers and leaders in all types and levels of organizations who know and are true to themselves and to their people, who do "the right thing," and who have sustainable effective performance in their area of responsibility, unit, and overall organization.

**FIGURE 13.4** **Authentic Leadership Development Model**

*Source:* Adapted from Fred Luthans and Bruce Avolio, "Authentic Leadership Development," in K. S. Cameron, S. E. Dutton, and R. E. Quinn (Eds.), *Positive Organizational Scholarship,* Berrett-Koehler, San Francisco, 2003, p. 251, and Bruce J. Avolio and Fred Luthans, *The High Impact Leader: Moments Matter in Accelerating Authentic Leadership Development,* McGraw-Hill, New York, 2006.

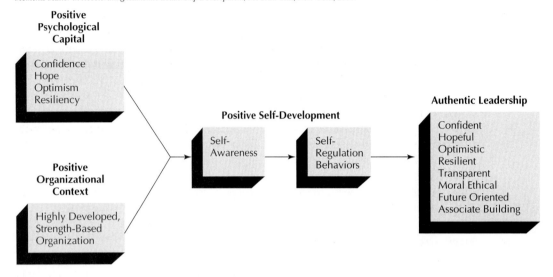

Although the term *authentic leadership* has been used in the practitioner-oriented popular literature,[137] this proposed theory is the first to treat leadership as both a developmental *process* and *product* centered on authenticity. Figure 13.4 depicts this authentic leadership development process and product. As shown, the authentic leadership process involves antecedent-positive psychological capacities and positive organizational context leading to positive self-development and the product of the authentic leader. In other words, this developmental approach to leadership focuses on the positive (both personal and contextual) in getting to know and regulate one's self. The outcomes of authentic leadership are positive psychological capital (confidence, hope, optimism, and resiliency) and transparency, moral/ethical behavior, future-orientation, and building associates.

Even though there is considerable indirect research support for this theoretical model of authentic leadership coming from positive organizational behavior (see Chapter 7) and transformational leadership (see previous section), the theory building and direct research testing the model is still emerging,[138] but a measure has recently been developed and validated.[139] Only time will tell; but this and other new leadership theories seem needed to help meet the daunting challenges facing organizational leaders now and in the future.

## Leadership across Cultures

Leadership takes on added significance in a global economy. As leadership guru Warren Bennis noted: "Given the nature and constancy of change and the transnational challenges facing American business leadership, the key to making the right choices will come from understanding and embodying the leadership qualities necessary to succeed in the volatile and mercurial global economy."[140] Research to date reveals both similarities and differences when leadership activities and styles are examined across cultures.

In their classic study, Haire, Ghiselli, and Porter studied managerial attitudes regarding different leadership styles in 14 countries. National groupings alone explained 28 percent of the variance in managerial attitudes.[141] Later research revealed that the degree of participation used by managers was different across eight countries.[142] In another study conducted by the author (Luthans) and colleagues, participative management techniques were actually ineffective in a Russian factory.[143] Further, results from the author's (Luthans) Real Managers Study, presented in detail in the next chapter,[144] were basically replicated in a Russian factory.[145] In a manner similar to U.S. managers studied (although the relative frequencies were a little different), the Russian managers were observed to perform, in order, traditional management, communication, human resources, and networking activities. Also, as was the case with the U.S. managers studied, the degree of networking activities conducted by Russian managers was related to their success levels within the organization. Still, the relationship between the activities of various Russian managers and their subsequent levels of effectiveness was similar, but less clear.[146] In other words, there are a number of factors that potentially contribute to differences in effective leader processes across cultures. Some that have been studied include personal values, the manager's background, and interpersonal skills.

### Personal Values

The personal values held by a manager shape his or her perception of a situation, influence the analysis of alternative solutions to a problem, and affect the ultimate decision made by the leader.[147] At the same time, the personal values of followers influence their leader, and these values are different across cultures. A study of similar U.S.-owned manufacturing plants located in five different cultures (Italian, Mexican, Spanish, United States, and British) revealed that the overall leadership approaches of the host-country nationals reflected the expectations of the local culture and workforce.[148]

### Backgrounds of the Managers

U.S. managers come from all economic backgrounds—lower, middle, and upper class. Although most are college educated, there is no guarantee that attending a given school will lead to success, as promotion is often based on performance. Whereas degrees from prestigious schools may offer a distinct advantage, U.S. managers come from a wide variety of colleges. The same may not be true in other countries. For example, in France managers are traditionally chosen from the graduates of the *grandes ecoles.*[149] In Japan, graduates of prestigious schools have much better chances to become top managers in the larger corporations, and in Korea many top business leaders are educated in the United States.

Besides educational background, class and family status also can have an influence. U.S. managers come from all classes, but the same is not true in other countries. Family name and class are important in France. In India, it is common to accept the authority of elders, and this is revealed through little delegation of authority in many companies. In Scandinavian countries, however, differing family patterns are reflected in participatory decision-making styles and the routine delegation of authority by leaders.

### Interpersonal Skills

There is considerable evidence that managers differ across cultures in their interpersonal styles and skills. Leaders vary in their views of rules and procedures, deference to authority, levels of dependence and independence, use of objectivity versus intuition, willingness to compromise, and other interpersonal tactics. A U.S. supervisor on an oil rig in Indonesia learned this lesson the hard way. In a moment of anger, he shouted at his timekeeper to take the next boat to shore. Immediately, a mob of outraged Indonesian coworkers grabbed fire axes and went after the supervisor. He escaped by barricading himself in his quarters. The leadership lesson this American learned was: never berate an Indonesian in public.[150] Even transformational and transactional tactics used by leaders may vary in their levels of success in differing cultures.[151]

As these research studies reviewed indicate, there is reason to believe that cultural issues in leadership should be studied to reveal both differences between cultures and specific within-country practices that will help expatriate leaders succeed. The accompanying OB in Action shows how communication will differ across cultures. Today's global leaders need to recognize such differences. The next step in the process is to systematize the study of leadership across cultures to build contingency models similar to what has been done with international human resource management.[152]

## Project GLOBE and the Future of International Leadership Studies

In recent years, a major international research project under the general direction of Robert House, called Global Leadership and Organizational Behavior Effectiveness, or GLOBE, started publishing its findings.[153] The meta-goal of the GLOBE program is to develop, over time, an empirically based theory to describe, understand, and predict the impact of cultural variables on leadership, organizational processes, and the effectiveness of the leader and the processes. For over a decade, 170 country-based coinvestigators (CCIs) gathered data from 18,000 managers from 62 countries. The CCIs were responsible for leading the study in the specific culture in which each had expertise.

A major goal of the GLOBE project was to develop societal and organizational measures of culture and leader attributes that were appropriate to use across all cultures. The GLOBE research indicated nine dimensions of cultures that differentiate societies and organizations. These identified cultural dimensions are:

1. *Power distance,* or the degree to which members of a collective expect power to be distributed equally
2. *Uncertainty avoidance,* which is the extent a society, organization, or groups rely on norms, rules, and procedures to alleviate the unpredictability of future events
3. *Humane orientation,* reflected in the degree to which a collective encourages and rewards individuals for being fair, altruistic, generous, caring, and kind to others
4. *Institutional Collectivism,* described as the degree to which organizational and societal institutional practices encourage and reward the collective distribution of resources and collective actions
5. *In-Group Collectivism,* which is the degree to which individuals express pride, loyalty, and cohesiveness in their organizations or families
6. *Assertiveness,* defined as the degree to which individuals are assertive, confrontational, and aggressive in their relationships with others
7. *Gender egalitarianism,* expressed as the degree a collective minimizes gender inequality
8. *Future orientation,* or the extent to which individuals engage in future-oriented behaviors such as delaying gratification, planning, and investing in the future
9. *Performance orientation,* suggested by the degree to which a collective encourages and rewards group members for performance improvement and excellence

The first six dimensions were originally defined by Hofstede.[154] One dimension Hofstede called "masculinity" has been relabeled as two constructs, assertiveness and gender egalitarianism, by the GLOBE researchers. Following the development and validation of the scale used to measure leader and cultural variables, studies were conducted to empirically assess the psychometric properties of the dimensions that had been established.

The second phase of the program was a further assessment of the leader and cultural scales. Unobtrusive measures were created to identify the latent constructs, manifest indicators,

One of the biggest challenges facing leaders doing business internationally is that the nationals of each country typically use their language and speech in a different way. In one culture people will lower their voice to indicate the seriousness of a situation, whereas in another culture they will speak very loudly to convey the same message. In one culture people will talk rapidly and be regarded as highly credible, whereas in another they will speak slowly and achieve the same result. The challenge in dealing with business leaders across cultures is to know how they use their language to communicate and what they are looking for from the other person. Here are some specific examples.

*British* The British tend to use a reserved tone in speaking and like to understate things. They also have a fondness for conceding points early to their opponents in order to take the steam out of the others' arguments. British business leaders are very good at being vague in order to maintain politeness and to avoid confrontation. When trying to influence them, use of humor and anecdotes and the offers of reasonable prices and good quality works best.

*Spaniards and Italians* Spaniards and Italians like to use a broad vocabulary and employ their hands, arms, and facial expressions when conveying their message. In particular, business leaders let others clearly understand how they feel about things. When trying to persuade others to a particular point of view, these business leaders appeal directly and strongly to good sense, a warm heart, and generosity. Additionally, these business leaders often insist that others make a decision right away.

*Germans* German business leaders rely on logic, but they also place strong importance on gathering a great deal of information to back up their positions. They like to present their points in a thorough and detailed way so that there is little opportunity for counterarguments, although effective negotiators find it very effective to work with German business leaders to find common ground and thus ward off a "win-lose" situation. German business leaders are influenced by technical information, good prices, high quality, and specific delivery dates.

*Scandinavians* Scandinavian business leaders like to list the pros and cons of a position before providing the other person with their decision on the matter. They are also very slow to give up on their position because they feel that they have more than ample support for it. They also like to forgo the niceties and get down to the business at hand. Quite often their presentations are factual, succinct, and well thought through. In persuading Scandinavian business leaders, it is important to emphasize quality, design, technical information, and delivery dates.

*Japanese* Japanese business leaders are extremely polite and almost never say no. On the other hand, the fact that they smile a great deal does not mean that they agree with the other person. Those who deal with Japanese business leaders on a regular basis find that they are greatly influenced by presentations that help them understand how something works or why it is a good idea or how it will be profitable for them. Two of the main things that outsiders need to focus on when dealing with Japanese business leaders are good price and politeness.

Finally, it is important to remember that business leaders from each culture have their own attention span, and if someone goes beyond this time period, they may find themselves losing out. For example, the British have a moderate time span, about 40 minutes. Scandinavians have a somewhat longer span, about 50 minutes. The Japanese typically give others about an hour before they begin losing interest. The Germans are the longest of all in this regard, tending to have attention spans of about 75 minutes. So when interacting with business leaders across cultures, attention must be given to both content and length, and communications must be adapted accordingly.

and qualitative indicators that could be used to assess the nine cultural dimensions, nine organizational practices, organizational contingencies including technology, the environment, and the size of the organization, plus societal culturally endorsed implicit leadership theories. In addition, hypotheses were developed regarding the relationships among various societal dimensions, organizational dimensions, and the culturally endorsed implicit theories that had been identified.

Phase three of the project was designed to study organizational cultures along with measures of leader and work-unit effectiveness, as well as individual cognitive, emotional, and evaluative responses to leader behaviors. The goal is to study leader behaviors within organizations and cultures longitudinally.

Phase four is based on phase three, in which universally perceived behaviors that impede or facilitate outstanding leadership were identified. Also, phase three is oriented toward identifying actual leader practices and universal organizational practices leading to positive or negative cognitive, affective, and performance consequences. Further, efforts were made to identify those perceived behaviors and practices that are culture specific. The researchers' goal in phase four was to answer the following questions:

1. Are there any universally effective leader behaviors?
2. What are the effects of violating strongly held culturally endorsed preferences for leader behaviors?
3. What types of consistent specific preferences for leader behaviors are present across cultures?

Some of the findings by the GLOBE team suggest 21 primary and then six leader attributes and behaviors that are viewed as contributing to leadership in various cultures. These six are summarized as follows:[155]

1. *Charismatic/Value-Base*—the ability to inspire, to motivate, and to expect high performance outcomes from others on the basis of core beliefs.
2. *Team-Oriented*—effective team building and implementation of a common purpose/goal among team members.
3. *Participative*—the degree to which managers/leaders involve others in making and implementing decisions.
4. *Humane-Oriented*—supportive, considerate, compassionate, and generous leadership.
5. *Autonomous*—independent and individualistic leadership.
6. *Self-Protective*—ensuring the safety and security of the individual, it tends to be an approach that is self-centered and face saving.

The GLOBE researchers found that these six leadership dimensions differed in terms of their desirability and effectiveness in various cultures. For example, the charismatic/value-based, team-oriented, and participative are generally reported to contribute to outstanding leadership, but each is found more often in specific cultures (e.g., charismatic in Anglo, team in Latin America, and participative in Germanic Europe). On the other hand, humane leadership is felt to be neutral in some cultures but moderately contribute to outstanding leadership in others; autonomous leadership is reported to range from impeding outstanding leadership to slightly facilitating it; and self-protective leadership is generally reported to impede outstanding leadership. Again, each of these types of leadership is found to different degrees in various cultures (e.g., humane in Southern Asia, autonomous in Eastern Europe, and self-protective in Southern Asia).

The general findings of the GLOBE project are that cultural dimensions do exist that can be identified and measured. Cultural differences can be studied through etic (across cultures) or emic (within cultures, or country-specific information) approaches. Cultural differences strongly influence the ways in which people think about their leaders as well as societal norms that exist concerning the status, influence, and the privileges granted to leaders. Although work remains to complete the project, the findings so far indicate a great deal of promise for furthering understanding of how leaders can effectively operate in various cultures.

Other smaller international research efforts have also been conducted. For example, Bass examined the nature of the transactional-transformational leadership paradigm across national boundaries.[156] Also, Church and Wacalawski investigated the relationship between leader style (transformational versus transactional) and subsequent organizational practices and outcomes, which supports the findings presented in the GLOBE report.[157] And finally, still another study suggests that there are indeed leadership concepts that are culturally endorsed, in which similar cultures share similar leadership concepts.[158] Clearly, the study of leadership across cultures is a growing and important body of knowledge for the leadership field.

---

## Summary

This chapter presents and analyzes the processes of leadership. The classic research studies on leadership set the stage for the theoretical development of leadership. The trait theories concentrate on the leaders themselves and through the years showed little promise for either the understanding of the leadership process or the relationship with effective leadership performance. Recently, however, there is renewed research interest indicating a significant relationship with the "Big Five" personality traits and effective leadership. There is also emerging interest in the statelike positive organizational behavior capacities (i.e., hope, optimism, resiliency, emotional intelligence, and, especially, self-efficacy) and effective leaders, and there is continuing concern with leader skills and competencies.

The group and exchange theories emphasize the importance of followers, and although the leader-member exchange (or LMX) model still generates considerable research, the group and exchange theories in general are recognized to be only partial theories. The traditionally recognized theories of leadership tend to be more situationally or contextually based. In particular, Fiedler's classic contingency model made a significant contribution to leadership theory and to the practice of human resource management. The path-goal approach also made an important contribution to leadership understanding. It incorporates expectancy motivation concepts.

All the traditional theories of leadership continue to provide understanding and a foundation for the practice of leadership in today's organizations. However, in recent years a number of alternative theories have emerged to supplement and, mostly, facilitate better understanding of the various processes of effective leadership. In particular, the charismatic and transformational, and to a much lesser extent, the substitutes approach have received attention. Charismatic leaders (characterized as having qualities beyond the usual appointed leader) get extraordinary commitment and performance from followers. The charismatic leaders, however, as a group are considered only a subsection of the larger group of transformational leaders characterized by idealized influence, inspirational motivation, intellectual stimulation, and individualized consideration. These transformational leaders are felt to be especially suited to today's organizations as they experience dramatic change. The substitutes approach recognizes that certain subordinate, task, and organizational characteristics may substitute for or neutralize the impact that leader behavior has on subordinate performance and satisfaction. All of these leadership theories continue to be researched to provide a better understanding of the complexities involved and to make the applications to practice more effective. Recently, to recognize the unprecedented challenges now facing organizational leaders, we have proposed authentic leadership theory. This approach draws from our positive organizational behavior and psychological capital approach (see Chapter 7) and Avolio's transformational/full-range leadership. The authentic leader is true to him- or herself and others and possesses considerable positive psychological capital, is transparent, moral/ethical, and future-oriented, and gives priority to developing associates to be leaders.

Finally, studies of international leadership indicate the importance of recognizing differences and similarities both across cultures and within cultures. The GLOBE project in particular is an example of a very comprehensive research program designed to discover the nature of leader effectiveness by identifying both universal and culture-specific dimensions that are associated with effective leadership processes.

# Ending with Meta-Analytic Research Findings

## OB PRINCIPLE FOR EVIDENCED-BASED PRACTICE

The leader's level of intelligence will influence others' perception of the leader's effectiveness.

### Meta-Analysis Results:

[13 studies; over 1,533 participants; $d = 1.21$] *On average, there is an **80 percent probability** that highly intelligent leaders will be perceived as more effective leaders than those of less intelligence.* Further analysis, although not as strong, also supported that the traits of dominance and masculinity/femininity are also significantly related to perceptions of leadership effectiveness.

### Conclusion:

Growing out of the "Great Person" theory of leadership, the trait approach suggests that certain dispositional, relatively fixed characteristics or traits of effective leaders can be identified. At first, physical attributes such as height, appearance, and age along with personality traits such as dominance and introversion/extroversion were all considered as potential leadership attributes. Although these lines of inquiry yielded some interesting findings, no generalizations, with the possible exception of intelligence as found in this meta-analysis, have emerged. However, in recent years attention to leaders themselves has resurfaced because the Big Five personality traits are found to relate to effective leaders and the statelike POB constructs (see Chapter 9) are beginning to show a relationship with effective leadership.

**Source:** Adapted from Robert G. Lord, Christy L. De Vader, and George M. Alliger, "A Meta-Analysis of the Relation between Personality Traits and Leadership Perceptions: An Application of Validity Generalization Procedures," *Journal of Applied Psychology,* Vol. 71, No. 3, 1986, pp. 402–410.

## OB PRINCIPLE FOR EVIDENCED-BASED PRACTICE

Leader–member exchange (LMX) is positively related to job performance, satisfaction, and commitment.

### Meta-Analysis Results:

[(1) 12 studies; 1,909 participants, $d = .91$ for performance ratings (leader LMX);(2) 30 studies; 4,218 participants; $d = .58$ for performance ratings (member LMX); (3) 8 studies; 982 participants; $d = .19$ for objective performance; (4) 27 studies; 5,302 participants; $d = 1.59$ for satisfaction with supervision; (5) 33 studies; 6,887 participants; $d = 1.03$ for overall satisfaction; and (6) 17 studies; 3,006 participants; $d = .75$ for organizational commitment.] *On average, there is a: (1) **74 percent probability** that the leader's perception of LMX will be more related to members' rated performance than for those leaders who do not perceive LMX; (2) **66 percent probability** that the members' perception of LMX will be more related to their rated performance than that of those who do not perceive LMX; (3) **55 percent probability** that perceived LMX will be more* *related to objective performance (e.g., quantity or quality of work) than if LMX is missing; (4) **87 percent probability** that perceived LMX will be more related to member satisfaction with supervision than if LMX is absent; (5) **77 percent probability** that perceived LMX will be more related to member overall satisfaction than if LMX is not perceived; and (6) **70 percent probability** that perceived LMX will be more related to member organizational commitment than if LMX is absent.* Further moderator analysis indicates that the strength of this relationship depends on the measurement used. When perceptions of LMX are measured from a leader's perspective, the relationship between LMX and performance ratings of members is stronger than when perceptions are measured from the member's point of view.

## Conclusion:

LMX perceptions of the leader's relationship with members and those in the in-group and out-group are important because of the linkages between leadership processes and outcomes of performance, satisfaction, and commitment. In particular, perceptions of a supervisor or leader regarding an employee's performance become criteria on which important decisions are made. A tendency for a supervisor to rate someone favorable as a result of being in the in-group can translate into favorable outcomes for in-group members and negative outcomes for out-group members. Furthermore, creating positive or negative expectations about an employee through the development of LMX perceptions may change the actual performance level of employees (i.e., become a self-fulfilling prophecy) and not just affect performance ratings. This LMX process highlights the importance of interpersonal relationships between leaders and their followers.

**Source:** Charlotte R. Gerstner and David V. Day, "Meta-Analytic Review of Leader-Member Exchange Theory: Correlates and Construct Issues," *Journal of Applied Psychology,* Vol. 82, No. 6, 1997, pp. 827–844.

**Questions for Discussion and Review**

1. Briefly summarize the findings of the three classic leadership studies.
2. Why do you think the "Big Five" personality traits have been recently found to relate to effective leaders whereas over the years personality traits in general have not?
3. How do the group theories differ from the trait theories of leadership?
4. Name and describe the main "competencies" that may be associated with a leader's effectiveness.
5. What are the three critical situational variables identified by Fiedler? If these are very favorable, what is the most effective style to use?
6. In simple terms, what is the path-goal theory of leadership? What is the leader's function in this conceptualization?
7. What are the major differences between transactional leaders and transformational leaders? Can you clarify these differences in how today's organizations are led?
8. What is meant by "substitutes for," and "neutralizers of," leadership? Give some subordinate, task, and organizational examples of these substitutes and neutralizers.
9. In your own words, describe what is meant by an authentic leader. How does this differ from previous theories, and why may it be so important now?
10. What is the GLOBE project? What cultural dimensions have been identified by the GLOBE researchers? What findings have been found by this GLOBE research effort in terms of the six major leadership dimensions found in various cultures?

**Internet Exercise: Leading in Times of Crisis**

Most organizations at one time or another face crisis situations in which leaders must make important choices to ensure the very survival of the organization. Visit **http://www.crisisexperts.com/** and **http://www.crisis-management-and-disaster-recovery.com/.** With the information from these Web sites, consider recent examples where an organization has been faced with a major crisis. Visit the company's Web site to see how the leaders are dealing with the situation(s). Consider the following questions:

1. What style is the leader using in order to solve the crisis? Does it seem effective? Why or why not? What would you have done differently if you were the leader in charge?
2. Frame the issue in the context of Fiedler's theory and specific contingency model of leadership (Figure 13.1). Does the leadership style in use fit the situation as defined by Fielder? If not, could this explain why the organization is not solving the problem?
3. Frame the issue in terms of your understanding of authentic leadership. Was it present? Should it be?

---

## Real Case: *No Organization Chart and an 80-Blank-Pages Policy Manual*

Ask Michael E. Marks about his company's procedures for making a big capital investment, and he is likely to refer you to the Flextronics International Corporate Policy Manual. It has 80 pages—all of them blank. Although Marks is Flextronics' chairman and CEO, he says he sometimes lets subordinates such as Humphrey W. Porter, the head of Flextronics' European operations, do multi-million-dollar acquisitions without showing him the paperwork. He disdains staff meetings at his San Jose (Calif.) headquarters, and he refuses to draw up an organization chart delineating his managers' responsibilities.

One might think Marks's style is too casual for a growing conglomerate. This is a giant that owns dozens of factories scattered over four continents and has big contracts with some of the most demanding corporate customers on earth, from Cisco Systems Inc. to Siemens. In recent years it has acquired manufacturing plants, design firms, and component makers in the United States, Europe, and Asia. It also has landed huge manufacturing contracts with Motorola Inc. and Microsoft Corp.

As Marks sees it, the business of global contract manufacturing is all about speed. The time it takes to get a prototype into mass production and onto retail shelves across the globe can determine whether a leading-edge digital gadget succeeds or flops. And with the Internet and corporate makeovers rapidly reconfiguring entire industries, Marks thinks it's a bigger sin to miss important opportunities than to make a mistake or two. So he doesn't want to tie down his top managers with bureaucracy. One of Marks's favorite dictums: "It's not the big who eat the small. It's the fast who eat the slow."

So far, Marks has managed to craft the right balance. A Harvard MBA who had run several small electronics makers, Marks helped engineer a takeover of Singapore-domiciled Flextronics in 1993, when it was nearly bankrupt. After turning the company around, he began to rebuild. Flextronics became a favored supplier to companies like Cisco, 3Com, and Palm. Flextronics is poised to become the world's second-largest contract manufacturer, after Milpitas (Calif.)-based Solectron Corp. Besides the industrial parks in Hungary, it also has huge manufacturing campuses in Mexico, China, and Brazil.

The basketball hoop hanging in Marks's modest, somewhat disheveled office seems to sum up his self-image. Marks is a passionate player—even though he stands all of 5 ft. 2 in. Likewise, in the business world, Marks seems determined to prove a point. One way or another, he's convinced he can retain the agile management style of a start-up, while making Flextronics a global enterprise that can play in the big leagues.

1. Based on your reading of the case, describe the leadership process used by Michael Marks. Do you think he is successful because of or in spite of his leadership approach?
2. What leadership theories covered in the chapter would best support Marks? Give specific examples.
3. How do you think Marks would do in another industry such as retail?

# Real Case:  *The Seven Secrets of Inspiring Leaders*

American business professionals are uninspired. Only 10 percent of employees look forward to going to work and most point to a lack of leadership as the reason why, according to a recent Maritz Research poll. But it doesn't have to be that way. All business leaders have the power to inspire, motivate, and positively influence the people in their professional lives.

For the past year, I have been interviewing renowned leaders, entrepreneurs, and educators who have an extraordinary ability to sell their vision, values, and themselves. I was researching their communications secrets for my new book, *Fire Them Up*. What I found were seven techniques that you can easily adopt in your own professional communications with your employees, clients, and investors.

1. **Demonstrate enthusiasm—constantly.** Inspiring leaders have an abundance of passion for what they do. You cannot inspire unless you're inspired yourself. Period. Passion is something I can't teach. You either have passion for your message or you don't. Once you discover your passion, make sure it's apparent to everyone within your professional circle. Richard Tait sketched an idea on a napkin during a cross-country flight, an idea to bring joyful moments to families and friends. His enthusiasm was so infectious that he convinced partners, employees, and investors to join him. He created a toy and game company called Cranium. Walk into its Seattle headquarters and you are hit with a wave of fun, excitement, and engagement the likes of which is rarely seen in corporate life. It all started with one man's passion.

2. **Articulate a compelling course of action.** Inspiring leaders craft and deliver a specific, consistent, and memorable vision. A goal such as "we intend to double our sales by this time next year" is not inspiring. Neither is a long, convoluted mission statement destined to be tucked away and forgotten in a desk somewhere. A vision is a short [usually 10 words or less], vivid description of what the world will look like if your product or service succeeds. Microsoft's (MSFT) Steve Ballmer once said that shortly after he joined the company, he was having second thoughts. Bill Gates and Gates' father took Ballmer out to dinner and said he had it all wrong. They said Ballmer saw his role as that of a bean counter for a start-up. They had a vision of putting a computer on every desk, in every home. That vision—a computer on every desk, in every home—remains consistent to this day. The power of a vision set everything in motion.

3. **Sell the benefit.** Always remember, it's not about you, it's about them. In my first class at Northwestern's Medill School of Journalism, I was taught to answer the question, "Why should my readers care?" That's the same thing you need to ask yourself constantly throughout a presentation, meeting, pitch, or any situation where persuasion takes place. Your listeners are asking themselves, what's in this for me? Answer it. Don't make them guess.

4. **Tell more stories.** Inspiring leaders tell memorable stories. Few business leaders appreciate the power of stories to connect with their audiences. A few weeks ago I was working with one of the largest producers of organic food in the country. I can't recall most, if any, of the data they used to prove organic is better. But I remember a story a farmer told. He said when he worked for a conventional grower, his kids could not hug him at the end of the day when he got home. His clothes had to be removed and disinfected. Now, his kids can hug him as soon as he walks off the field. No amount of data can replace that story. And now guess what I think about when I see the organic section in my local grocery store? You got it. The farmer's story. Stories connect with people on an emotional level. Tell more of them.

5. **Invite participation.** Inspiring leaders bring employees, customers, and colleagues into the process of building the company or service. This is especially important when trying to motivate young people. The command and control way of managing is over. Instead, today's managers solicit input, listen for feedback, and actively incorporate what they hear. Employees want more than a paycheck. They want to know that their work is adding up to something meaningful.

6. **Reinforce an optimistic outlook.** Inspiring leaders speak of a better future. Robert Noyce, the cofounder of Intel INTC, said, "Optimism is an essential ingredient of innovation. How else can the individual favor change over security?" Extraordinary leaders throughout history have been more optimistic than the average person. Winston Churchill exuded hope

and confidence in the darkest days of World War II. Colin Powell said that optimism was the secret behind Ronald Reagan's charisma. Powell also said that optimism is a force multiplier, meaning it has a ripple effect throughout an organization. Speak in positive, optimistic language. Be a beacon of hope.

7. **Encourage potential.** Inspiring leaders praise people and invest in them emotionally. Richard Branson has said that when you praise people they flourish; criticize them and they shrivel up. Praise is the easiest way to connect with people. When people receive genuine praise, their doubt diminishes and their spirits soar. Encourage people and they'll walk through walls for you.

By inspiring your listeners, you become the kind of person people want to be around. Customers will want to do business with you, employees will want to work with you, and investors will want to back you. It all starts with mastering the language of motivation.

1. How, if at all, do the theories presented in this chapter support such a list of secrets of effective leaders? Which theory would seem to provide the best explanation?

2. Which of these seven guidelines do you think can have the most impact?

3. In your own personal experience dealing/interacting with leaders, give examples of where you observed one or more of these.

# Chapter **Fourteen**

# Great Leaders: An Evidence-Based Approach

## Learning Objectives

- **Relate** the style implications from the classic and modern theories and supporting research evidence for effective leaders.
- **Present** the research findings on leadership roles and activities.
- **Examine** the evidence-based activities that relate to successful and effective leaders.
- **Identify** the skills that have been found to be needed for effective leaders of today's organizations.
- **Analyze** the various evidence-based approaches to leadership development.

The preceding chapter presented the evidence-based foundation for effective leadership: the traditional and modern theoretical processes and supporting research. This chapter serves as the follow-up application for evidence-based effective (great) leaders. There is empirical evidence that the demographics of organizational leaders are changing. A recent study of top level managers in *Fortune* 100 firms found that compared to 20 years ago "they are younger, more of them are female, and fewer of them were educated at elite institutions. They're making it to the top faster and taking fewer jobs along the way. They are increasingly moving from one company to another as their careers unfold."[1] There is also evidence that not only who leaders are is changing, but also what they do and how they behave is changing. Specifically, this chapter presents the evidence on the various styles, activities, and skills of great leaders/managers.

First, the style implications from the classic theories and research of the preceding chapter are examined. Then, the main part of the chapter presents and analyzes the widely recognized styles of leadership. This discussion is followed by an examination of what research says about leader roles and activities, with special attention given to successful and effective leaders/managers. The last part of the chapter focuses on the leadership skills that are increasingly being recognized and supported as necessary for today's dramatically changing organizations. Very simply, the differences among styles, activities, and skills express the *ways* leaders influence followers. Roles and activities are *what* leaders do, and skills are concerned with *how* leaders can be effective.

In this chapter the terms *leaders* and *managers* are used interchangeably, although the preceding chapter pointed out there may be differences between managers and leaders, and there is growing empirical evidence that there may be a difference.[2] Nevertheless, as one highly successful corporate leader noted: "In the business environment of the future, everyone will be in a leadership role."[3] Thus, this chapter on *leadership* styles, activities, and skills is also on *management* styles, activities, and skills. After first discussing the modern context for leadership, the chapter will give equal attention to evidence-based styles, activities, skills, and development of great leaders.

# LEADERSHIP IN THE NEW ENVIRONMENT

There is no question that leadership roles are changing in the extremely challenging overall environment and the organizational contexts outlined in the first part of the book. There is general agreement among all analyses of leadership that it is much more difficult to lead in difficult times, such as we have experienced in recent years, than in good times.[4] One analysis argues that five key leadership roles can help shape managerial successes (and failures) in the near future. They include: (1) a strategic vision to motivate and inspire, (2) empowering employees, (3) accumulating and sharing internal knowledge, (4) gathering and integrating external information, and (5) challenging the status quo and enabling creativity.[5] A recent observation is that organizational leaders now must have at least three "faces": (1) *manager* (disciplined, rational, organizing, controlling, intellect, strategic, decision maker); (2) *artist* (curious, independent, creative, emotional, innovator); and (3) *priest* (ethical, pure, empathetic, inspiring, comforting, transcendent).[6] In addition to this analogy is the view that great leaders must have energy, expertise, and integrity.[7] Especially in light of post-Enron and the financial crisis, the integrity component has taken on increased importance. As has recently been pointed out:

> Out of these three interacting gears of leadership, it is integrity that ensures that an organization is run in the right direction—with a view towards collective good rather than selfish motives. Therefore, it is the most nonnegotiable of the three elements. Henceforth, leaders ought not to be selected on the basis of the superficial qualities that have blinded us in the past. They must first pass the acid test of integrity.[8]

Although most of these observations are in reference to big corporations, others suggest that even the small-business leader faces a shifting role, moving from a local to a global focus, following the market, seeking innovation, being open, staying intent on the quality of the execution rather than the idea, remaining inquisitive and innovative, and being a networker rather than the lone ranger.[9] There are also pessimists that note a trend in which many young, capable new employees actively avoid the prospect of becoming a leader or manager, because the idea of managing itself is obsolete, exhausting, irrelevant, and an unfashionable career choice.[10] The same is true for what young people expect from their leaders. As the accompanying OB in Action indicates, the values and beliefs of the young Generation Xers are much different than those of the baby boomers in leadership positions.[11] In addition, Gallup recently asked about 10,000 followers of all ages in all types of jobs what they wanted from their organizational leaders. They clearly answered trust, compassion, stability, and hope.[12] In such a leadership environment, the understanding of effective styles, activities, and skills becomes an increasingly complex and challenging task.

Several new trends affect the study of leadership. As indicated, many jobs are now being performed away from the work site, at home, by telecommuters. These employees are not just operating out of their homes. For example, today about half of IBM's 320,000 employees are considered "mobile," meaning that they do not daily report to an IBM site. Although today's employees may not have regular face-to-face contact with coworkers and their

Leading human resources in the 21st century is a major challenge for every enterprise. In addition to the changes that are taking place in the environment in terms of technology and socioeconomic turbulence, organizations are finding that their incoming personnel are more demanding than ever before—and they can get away with it because if the company does not accede to their demands, they will go somewhere else. These young individuals, known as "Generation Xers," were born between 1965 and 1981. They have grown up during the computer revolution, the advent of MTV sound bites, and a business world that has gone haywire with corporate downsizing and massive layoffs. As a result, they have learned to expect change—and they are willing to deal with it.

Today there are approximately 44 million Generation Xers in the United States and many of them are being led by baby boomers, who are individuals born between 1945 and 1964. The values and beliefs of the two groups differ sharply. Although overgeneralizations and stereotypes can be wrong, it is generally agreed that baby boomers tend to be more loyal to their organizations and want to know what their bosses want done. Their attitude is one of "Thank you for the job opportunity. I'll try to please you." Generation Xers tend to have a different mind-set. Their attitude and approach may best be represented by the statement "Here's what I want to stay with the company and if I'm not happy and having fun, I'll take my skills elsewhere."

How can today's leaders deal effectively with Generation Xers? Experts who have studied the beliefs and attitudes of young GenX employees have found that there are a number of things that organizations can do in order to hire and retain them. These include:

1. Challenge them with assignments that let them use their entrepreneurial instincts and their strong pragmatism.

2. Create a team concept with a great deal of interaction with other employees so that they will enjoy their work.

3. Build their confidence by letting them use their problem-solving skills.

4. Explain to them what needs to be done and the outcomes in terms of pros and cons, so that they understand the trade-offs they are going to have to make.

5. Show them what they are doing is important to the organization and how their work relates to other areas.

6. Encourage them to participate in the planning process and to contribute their ideas and suggestions.

7. Explain the rationale behind instructions and directives so that they understand not only what needs to be done, but why it needs to be done.

8. Pair them up with older workers in a buddy system because they get along well with these people.

9. Help them understand the career paths that are available in the organization and offer them counseling and guidance so that they can make informed decisions regarding where they want to go and how they can get there.

10. Give them prompt feedback on their work: when they do a good job, praise them; when they make mistakes, show them how to avoid repeating them in the future.

Many of the management approaches that worked well a decade or two ago have limited value in leading the young GenX workforce today. As many managers are now discovering, with GenXers it's a whole new ball game!

managers, because of networked information technology, they may have more interactions with them and others. Forty years ago a study found that there were at most six degrees of separation between any two people in America (i.e., the chain of acquaintances between them never had more than six links). Recently, even with the great increase in population, this has become only 4.6 degrees of separation.[13] In other words, because of cell phones, e-mail, and texting, employees and managers may have less interaction in corridors and over coffee, but much more interactive communication.

Highly mobile, virtual employees do not have the same day-to-day personal contacts with leaders that more traditional employees experience. Motivational processes, incentives, and leadership tactics must be modified in telework. Further, the growing world of e-business has spawned an entirely new kind of leader: the e-boss, who focuses on speed, technology, high risk taking, and megaprofits in short periods of time. Jeff Bezos, CEO of Amazon.com, is a prime example of this new type of e-leader. He is a self-described "techie nerd" who takes high risks, but also generously rewards his people who have become very wealthy. At the same time, major swings in stock values, new competitors, governmental regulation, and other factors make the roles of e-leaders such as Bezos substantially different from those who are in more traditional settings.

More and more organizations are utilizing technology to e-manage their operations. In a manner similar to Kerr's view regarding substitutes for leadership (see Chapter 13), technology is being used to enhance the tactics used by traditional leaders. As an expert on applying cyber technology to leadership recently noted:

> Let's say you are looking for help with a specific topic, such as dealing with poor performers. In-person advice from a top coach or expert would likely be cost-prohibitive. But e-learning—downloading or playing a few short videos—can be a cost-effective way to get information from top thought leaders. E-learning ultimately can provide experts for any challenge that leaders may face.[14]

The same is true for leaders facing the new concern for ethics in the post-Enron, financial crisis era.[15] Leaders can no longer just give words to lofty, ethical values. Now they must "walk to talk."[16] Here is one observation of what happened at Enron:

> While the banners proclaimed the espoused values of the company, there is evidence that they did little to shape behaviors. According to an executive, they were ignored during the regular performance reviews. "I never heard a discussion about a person's teamwork or integrity or respect." Instead, he suggested, the one value the organization measured was revenue generation.[17]

A recent survey asked American workers to name the most important trait for a person to lead them. Clearly ranked highest was leading by example and second was strong ethics and morals. It was concluded from this evidence that "more than anything else, employees want leaders whose beliefs and actions line up."[18] Consequently, organizational behavior theory building and research is trying to better understand what makes a great leader in today's environment.

# LEADERSHIP STYLES

The classic leadership studies and the various leadership theories discussed in the preceding chapter all have direct implications for what style the effective manager or leader uses in human resource management. The word *style* is very vague. Yet it is widely used to describe effective leaders. For example, the leadership style of Steve Jobs, the founder of Apple Computer and given much credit for the iPod craze, was described as follows:

> Sometimes it's hard to tell whether Steve Jobs is a snake-oil salesman or a bona fide visionary, a promoter who got lucky or the epitome of the intrepid entrepreneur. What's indisputable is that he possesses consummate charm, infectious enthusiasm, and an overdose of charisma.[19]

This vivid description points out the difficulty of attaching a single style to a leader. Moreover, the problem with a "one best style" of effective leadership is also brought out by the contrast between two of the most successful coaches in the history of college basketball: Duke's beloved Coach K (Mike Krzyzewski) and the feared Bobby Knight:

> Coach K, whose leadership style relies on open communication and caring support, wrote a book called *Leading with the Heart.* Knight, on the other hand, has had a career marked by

controversies about his harshness, including allegations that he choked a player during practice. Despite his bullying, he inspires tremendous loyalty and even love.[20]

Besides these very contrasting styles leading to the same success in almost the same situations, it is also ironic that Krzyzewski played point-guard for Knight at West Point (while your author was teaching leadership there as a Captain in the Army in the mid-1960s and attended all the games to see first-hand Knight's harsh style and leadership and his best player's on-the-floor skills and leadership). It is interesting that Krzyzewski assumed almost an opposite leadership approach instead of modeling his mentor and leader. This complexity of style is also brought out in meta-analyses of gender and leadership that do not wholly support stereotypes of the styles and effectiveness of men and women leaders.[21] Styles also differ from one culture to another. As Avolio recently concluded, "The emerging field of cross-cultural leadership research has underscored the importance of examining how the inclusion of the context in models of leadership may alter how what constitutes effective or desirable leadership is operationally defined, measured, and interpreted."[22] The following sections describe how leadership styles have been studied and analyzed over the years.

## Style Implications of the Classic Studies and the Modern Theories

Chapter 1 discusses the major historical contributions to the study of organizational behavior. Most of this discussion has indirect or direct implications for leadership style. For example, the Hawthorne studies were interpreted in terms of their implications for supervisory style. Also relevant is the classic work done by Douglas McGregor, in which Theory X represents the traditional authoritarian style of leadership and Theory Y represents an enlightened, humanistic style. The studies discussed at the beginning of the preceding chapter are also directly concerned with style. The Iowa studies analyzed the impact of autocratic, democratic, and laissez-faire styles, and the studies conducted by the Michigan group found the employee-centered supervisor to be more effective than the production-centered supervisor. The Ohio State studies identified consideration (a supportive type of style) and initiating structure (a directive type of style) as being the major functions of leadership. The trait and group theories have indirect implications for style, and the human-oriented, democratic, and task-directed styles play an important role in Fiedler's classic contingency theory. The path-goal conceptualization also covered in detail in the last chapter depends heavily on directive, supportive, participative, and achievement-oriented styles of leadership.

The same is true of the more modern charismatic, transformational, and authentic leadership theories. They have an inspirational style with vision, and they "do the right thing" for their people. Table 14.1 summarizes the charismatic leader style according to three major types of behavior, with illustrative actions. An example of such a style would be Paul O'Neill of Alcoa. He espoused a clear vision for his firm, anchored on quality, safety, and innovation. He made his vision compelling and central to the company, set high expectations for his management team and employees throughout the organization, and provided continuous support and energy for his vision through meetings, task forces, videotapes, and extensive personal contact.[23] Another example of new leadership in action is Ricardo Semler, CEO of the innovative Brazilian firm Semco. He has no organization chart and allows his employees to choose who they want to work for: "We want people to follow their instincts and to choose as bosses people they respect—even if they don't like them."[24]

A rough approximation of the various styles derived from the studies and theories discussed so far can be incorporated into the continuum shown in Table 14.2. For ease of presentation, the styles listed may be substituted for the expressions "boss centered" and

**TABLE 14.1**
**Nadler and Tushman's Charismatic Leadership Styles**

| Types of Charismatic Leadership Styles | Meaning | Examples |
|---|---|---|
| Envisioning | Creating a picture of the future—or a desired future state—with which people can identify and that can generate excitement | Articulating a compelling vision<br>Setting high expectations |
| Energizing | Directing the generation of energy, the motivation to act, among members of the organization | Demonstrating personal excitement and confidence<br>Seeking, finding, and using success |
| Enabling | Psychologically helping people act or perform in the face of challenging goals | Expressing personal support<br>Empathizing |

"employee centered" used by Tannenbaum and Schmidt in their classic leadership continuum shown in Figure 14.1. The verbal descriptions and the relationship between authority and freedom found in Figure 14.1 give a rough representation of the characteristics of the various styles of leadership. Importantly, as shown in the contingency or contextual theories, both sides can be effective.[25] An example would be the well-known leadership style of Jack Welch when he headed the successful run of G.E. Jack admitted he was more involved in the day-to-day operations of his corporation than would even be the traditional boss-centered leader.[26] Although Welch was very successful, another admitted micromanager, the CEO of Rubicon Oil, recently revealed that his approach resulted in his employees not giving suggestions during meetings because they were afraid of getting "shot down."[27] Also, recent research indicates some effective leaders are perceived as caring and empathetic and others as intelligent and able to handle complex tasks.[28]

One thing is certain: leadership style can make a difference, both positively and negatively. For example, a survey found that senior executives view their companies' leadership styles as pragmatic rather than conceptual, and conservative rather than risk taking. These same executives felt that to meet their current and future challenges, the styles should be the other way around.[29] In contrast to the leaders in the classical bureaucracies, leaders of today's organizations, described in Chapter 3, "must be more entrepreneurial; more accountable; more customer-, process-, and results-focused; biased toward action; empowering; communicative; technologically sophisticated; on fire about innovation and continuous improvement; strong in the use of guidance, suggestion, and influence; and sparing in the

**TABLE 14.2**
**Summary Continuum of Leadership Styles Drawn from the Classic Studies and Theories of Leadership**

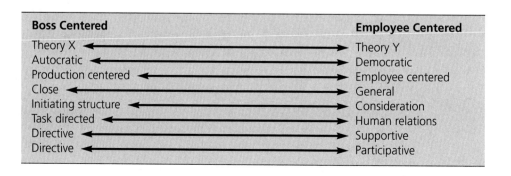

| Boss Centered | | Employee Centered |
|---|---|---|
| Theory X | ⟷ | Theory Y |
| Autocratic | ⟷ | Democratic |
| Production centered | ⟷ | Employee centered |
| Close | ⟷ | General |
| Initiating structure | ⟷ | Consideration |
| Task directed | ⟷ | Human relations |
| Directive | ⟷ | Supportive |
| Directive | ⟷ | Participative |

**FIGURE 14.1**
**The Tannenbaum and Schmidt Continuum of Leadership Behavior**

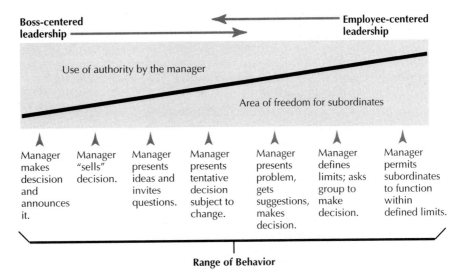

use of pure authority."[30] Obviously, other descriptive terms of effective leadership can be added to this comprehensive list, especially in times of an economic crisis[31] or in times where a more quiet, antihero approach is more effective. For example, as an alternative to the stereotyped self-heralding heroic style, one observation asserts that effective leaders are "quiet" and low profile, act with "modesty and restraint" and act "patiently, carefully, and incrementally."[32] Although "speak softly and carry a big stick" is still recommended,[33] abusive leadership is now recognized never to be appropriate. For example, one study of abusive leadership, characterized as a sustained display of hostile verbal and nonverbal behaviors, excluding physical contact, indicates a series of potential long-term undesirable outcomes, including employees with lower job and life satisfaction, lower normative and affective commitment, conflicts between work and family, and psychological distress.[34]

As a summary observation about style, Bennis notes: "Never before has American business faced so many challenges, and never before have there been so many choices in how to face those challenges. We must look now at what it is going to take not just to regain global leadership, but simply to stay a player in the game."[35] The following sections examine the widely recognized, evidence-based leadership styles available to today's managers to meet these challenges.

## Classic Styles

In addition to the Tannenbaum and Schmidt continuum shown in Figure 14.1, other historically important approaches to leadership styles include Hersey and Blanchard's *life-cycle* (later termed the *situational*) approach to leadership.[36] Following the original Ohio State studies, Hersey and Blanchard's approach[37] identifies two major styles:

1. *Task style.* The leader organizes and defines roles for members of the work group; the leader explains the tasks that group members are to do and when, where, and how they are to do them.
2. *Relationship style.* The leader has close, personal relationships with the members of the group, and there is open communication and psychological and emotional support.

Taking a contingency approach to recognize situational variables, Hersey and Blanchard incorporated the maturity of the followers into their model. The level of maturity is defined by three criteria:

1. Degree of achievement motivation
2. Willingness to take on responsibility
3. Amount of education and/or experience

Although they recognize that there may be other important situational variables, Hersey and Blanchard focus only on this maturity level of work group members in their model.

The key for leadership effectiveness in this model is to match up the situation with the appropriate style. The following summarizes the four basic styles:

1. *Telling style.*   This is a high-task, low-relationship style and is effective when followers are at a very low level of maturity.
2. *Selling style.*   This is a high-task, high-relationship style and is effective when followers are on the low side of maturity.
3. *Participating style.*   This is a low-task, high-relationship style and is effective when followers are on the high side of maturity.
4. *Delegating style.*   This is a low-task, low-relationship style and is effective when followers are at a very high level of maturity.

Hersey and Blanchard's approach includes a questionnaire instrument that presents 12 situations that generally depict the various levels of maturity of the group; respondents answer how they would handle each situation. These responses follow the four styles. How closely respondents match the situation with the appropriate style will determine their effectiveness score.

Even though this situational leadership model has some practical implications for the management of change,[38] the theoretical rationale is generally criticized as being "weak, because Hersey and Blanchard have neglected to provide a coherent, explicit rationale for the hypothesized relationships."[39] They also, by their own admission, highly oversimplify the situation by giving only surface recognition to follower maturity. Also, there is a noted absence of any empirical tests of the model. One review of all facets of the approach was particularly critical of the instrument that Hersey and Blanchard used to measure leader effectiveness,[40] and an empirical test did not find support for the underlying assumptions or predictions.[41] Overall, however, as is true of the other style approaches, this situational approach seems to be of some value in training and development work in that it can point out the need for flexibility and take into consideration the different variables affecting leaders. Yet, this popular approach lacks sufficient evidence to predict leader effectiveness.

## Leadership Styles in Perspective

Hersey and Blanchard's life cycle represent a popular, but not evidence-based, approach to leadership style. These and other traditional models such as the well-known managerial grid styles (that also use the same two dimensions of task and relationships as found in the Hersey and Blanchard life cycle model) are now largely gone as prescriptions for effective leader styles. In their place are other leadership style approaches found in the popular press. For example, Jim Collins, the author of recent best-selling books,[42] suggests that the key for companies transitioning from "good to great" is what he calls Level 5 leadership. Here is how he describes this style:

> The essence of Level 5 leadership is having an ambition for the cause of the work—the outcome, the company, the organization—above the self. And, at the same time, having the ferocious, frightening, terrifying willfulness to act on that ambition.[43]

Collins does have some empirically based investigations to support such leader styles as being effective. For example, Collins identified Level 5 leadership as a distinguishing factor in empirically derived great companies (outperforming the Standard & Poor's 500 by at least three to one for 15 years). However, he does not claim to have basic research supporting a causal relationship.[44] Yet, in the academic leadership field there has been considerable research on the modern theories discussed in the last chapter. For example, recent studies have found that transformational leadership had a significant, but indirect, effect on performance[45] and entrepreneurs who were perceived to be authentic leaders have associates with higher levels of job satisfaction, organizational commitment, and happiness.[46] Noted leadership researchers House and Podsakoff have summarized the behaviors and approaches of great leaders that they drew from modern theories (e.g., charismatic and transformational) and basic research findings as follows:[47]

1. *Vision.*  Great leaders articulate an ideological vision that is congruent with the deeply held values of followers, a vision that describes a better future to which the followers have a moral right.

2. *Passion and self-sacrifice.*  Great leaders display a passion for, and have a strong conviction of, the moral correctness of their vision. They engage in outstanding or extraordinary behavior and make extraordinary self-sacrifices in the interest of their vision and the mission.

3. *Confidence, determination, and persistence.*  Great leaders display a high degree of faith in themselves and in the attainment of the vision they articulate. Theoretically, such leaders need to have a very high degree of self-confidence and moral conviction because their mission usually challenges the status quo and, therefore, is likely to offend those who have a stake in preserving the established order.

4. *Image building.*  Great leaders are self-conscious about their own image. They recognize that they must be perceived by followers as competent, credible, and trustworthy.

5. *Role modeling.*  Leader image building sets the stage for effective role modeling because followers identify with the values of role models who are perceived positively.

6. *External representation.*  Great leaders act as the spokesperson for their organization and symbolically represent the organization to external constituencies.

7. *Expectations of and confidence in followers.*  Great leaders communicate high performance expectations to their followers and strong confidence in their followers' ability to meet such expectations.

8. *Selective motive arousal.*  Great leaders selectively arouse those motives of followers that are of special relevance to the successful accomplishment of the vision and mission.

9. *Frame alignment.*  To persuade followers to accept and implement change, great leaders engage in frame alignment. This refers to the linkage of individual and leader interpretive orientations such that some set of followers' interests, values, and beliefs, as well as the leader's activities, goals, and ideology, becomes congruent and complementary.

10. *Inspirational communication.*  Great leaders often, but not always, communicate their messages in an inspirational manner using vivid stories, slogans, symbols, and ceremonies.

These 10 leadership behaviors and approaches are not specific styles per se, but cumulatively they probably represent the best evidence-based list concerning the most effective style of today's leaders/managers. Moreover, there is clear evidence that a leader's style can make a difference. For example, studies have found that the leader's style is the key to the formulation and implementation of strategy[48] and even plays an important role in work group members' creativity,[49] team citizenship,[50] emotion,[51] and performance.[52] Even humor and fun may play a role in leader effectiveness.[53] There have been many anecdotal reports regarding the positive effects of humor at world-class companies such as Southwest Airlines, Ben & Jerry's Ice Cream, and Sun Microsystems. For example, recognized leader Scott McNealy of high-tech Sun Microsystems wears a Java "decoder" ring that has the motto "Kick butt and have fun." He also plays in an intramural squirt gun war with engineers. Recently retired founder Herb Kelleher of Southwest Airlines often showed up at meetings and on holidays in a variety of costumes, including the Easter Bunny, and arm wrestled an opponent in a trademark dispute in front of a big audience. Based on such an approach, one study of 115 Canadian financial managers and their 322 subordinates revealed a significant relationship between humor and individual performance as well as with work unit performance.[54] The note of caution in the study, however, was that humor and fun only meshed with a more active and involved leader style. In other words, there is little doubt that the *way* (style) leaders influence work group members can make a difference in their own and their people's performance.

## An Evidence-Based Positive, Authentic Leadership Style

Most recently, based on positive organizational behavior and psychological capital (see Chapter 7) and the authentic leadership theory covered in the last chapter, we have conducted a growing number of studies that provide evidence-based guidelines and implications for an effective leadership style. Here is a summary of some of this research on a positive, authentic leadership style:

1. A 16-item measure of authentic leadership consisting of self-awareness, relational transparency, internationalized moral perspective, and balanced processing has been validated. Combined, these stylelike components of authentic leadership were able to predict work-related attitudes and behaviors beyond more traditional ethical and transformational styles. Importantly, this measured authentic leadership style was found to be related to effective performance.[55]

2. A field experiment mentioned in Chapter 7 found that leaders' authentic style consisting of both positivity (as measured by the psychological capital questionnaire or PCQ[56]) and transparency significantly impacted followers' perceived trust and evaluations of leader effectiveness.[57] In other words, there is evidence that an effective authentic style would be very transparent (i.e., very open, honest, and trustworthy) and positive (i.e., exhibit high levels of psychological capital or PsyCap that involves confidence, hope, optimism, and resiliency).

3. In another field experiment utilizing high-tech engineers in a very large aerospace firm, a negative relationship was found between the problem complexity these engineers were facing and their level of psychological capital (PsyCap). In other words, the more complex the problem they were trying to solve, the lower their PsyCap (and vice versa). Importantly, another major finding was that leaders' style exhibiting a high level of PsyCap (i.e., they were seen as very confident, hopeful, optimistic, and resilient) related both to their followers' (the engineers) level of PsyCap and their followers' performance on both the quality and quantity of solutions to real problems.[58]

4. Although psychological capital and authentic leadership have a growing amount of research at the individual level of analysis, with the now recognized importance of groups and teams (see Chapter 11), a recent study examined the role that collective psychological capital and group trust may play in the relationship between authentic leadership and work groups' in a large bank desired outcomes. The results indicated a significant relationship between these groups' collective PsyCap and group trust with their performance and organizational citizenship behavior (see Chapter 5 on OCB). Also, to refine the leadership process, the groups' collective PsyCap and trust were

found to mediate the relationship between authentic leadership style and their performance and citizenship behaviors. In other words, authentic leadership style, psychological capital and trust all seem to play a positive role in the performance and desired behaviors of groups as well as individuals.[59]

This emerging research on a positive, authentic leadership style provides an evidence-based approach for effective leadership in these challenging times facing organizations. Besides the work being done on developing psychological capital given detailed attention in Chapter 7, Avolio and Luthans in their recent book provide specific guidelines such as the following in order for leaders to be authentic and effective:[60]

1. You must make sure that every follower fully understands the main message that guides the future direction you have chosen to pursue.
2. You must be consistent with your principles, beliefs, and values.
3. You need to provide appropriate reinforcing recognition for the contributions made by each follower.
4. Build ownership in the mission you are pursuing.
5. Build PsyCap (confidence, hope, optimism, and resiliency) in yourself and others.
6. Explore the future with others and help each other bring it to the present.

In recent years, in addition to the need for evidence-based styles of leadership, the importance of empirically derived roles and activities of leadership and the skills of effective leaders are also receiving attention. The rest of the chapter is concerned with this *what* (roles and activities) and *how* (skills) of effective leadership.

# THE ROLES AND ACTIVITIES OF LEADERSHIP

In answer to the question of what do leaders really do, separate observational studies by Henry Mintzberg and the author (Luthans) were conducted. These studies provide direct empirical evidence of the roles (Mintzberg) and activities (Luthans) of leaders/managers.

## Leader/Manager Roles

On the basis of his direct observational studies (as opposed to the questionnaire/interview studies so commonly used in leadership research), Mintzberg proposes the three types of managerial roles shown in Figure 14.2.[61] The *interpersonal roles* arise directly from formal authority and refer to the relationship between the manager and others. By virtue of the formal position, the manager has a *figurehead role* as a symbol of the organization. Most of the time spent as a figurehead is on ceremonial duties such as greeting a touring class of students or taking an important customer to lunch. The second interpersonal role is specifically called the *leader role*. In this role the manager uses his or her influence to motivate and encourage subordinates to accomplish organizational objectives. In the third type of interpersonal role the manager undertakes a *liaison role*. This role recognizes that managers often spend more time interacting with others outside their unit (with peers in other units or those completely outside the organization) than they do working with their own leaders and subordinates. The e-world, electronic transmissions and interaction with others, has greatly accelerated this role.

Besides the interpersonal roles flowing from formal authority, Figure 14.2 shows that managers also have important *informational roles*. Most observational studies find that managers spend a great deal of time giving and receiving information, again greatly

**FIGURE 14.2**
Mintzberg's
Managerial Roles

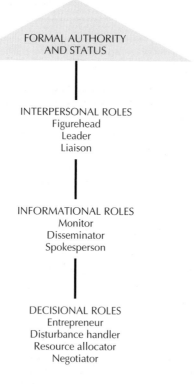

expanded by the e-environment. As *monitor,* the manager is continually scanning the environment and probing subordinates, bosses, and outside contacts and the Internet for information; as *disseminator,* the manager distributes information to key internal people; and as *spokesperson,* the manager provides information to outsiders.

In the *decisional role,* the manager acts upon the information. In the *entrepreneurial role* in Mintzberg's scheme, the manager initiates the development of a project and assembles the necessary resources. As *disturbance handler,* on the other hand, instead of being proactive like the entrepreneur, the manager is reactive to the problems and pressures of the situation. As disturbance handler, the manager has a crisis management type of role; for example, there is a cash flow problem, or a major subcontractor is threatening to pull out. As *resource allocator,* the manager decides who gets what in his or her department. Finally, as *negotiator,* the manager spends time at all levels in the give-and-take of negotiating with subordinates, bosses, and outsiders. For example, a finance manager may have to negotiate a bad debt settlement with a major customer, or a supervisor in a social services department may have to negotiate certain benefit payments that one of the counselors wants to give a client.

These informal managerial roles suggested by Mintzberg get much closer to describing what managers/leaders really do than the formally described and prescribed functions. Mintzberg's work has definitely shed some light on what leaders do, but as he stated in a retrospective commentary about the 10 roles: "We remain grossly ignorant about the fundamental content of the manager's job and have barely addressed the major issues and dilemmas in its practice."[62] A follow-up analysis of Mintzberg's various managerial roles concluded:

> Leaders today do indeed have interpersonal and informational responsibilities, though it may be argued that the informational responsibilities have moved to a position of primacy. And leaders indeed retain decisional responsibilities, but those responsibilities increasingly are

shared with various stakeholders and network partners. The nature of leadership, as defined by Mintzberg's work, may be similar today, but the networked economy places new demands on leaders at all levels.[63]

To go beyond Mintzberg's work, studies have used leadership roles such as vision setter, motivator, analyzer, and task master.[64] These roles were then tested concerning their relationships to three dimensions of firm performance. The results were that leaders with high behavioral complexity—the ability to play multiple, competing roles—produce the best performance, particularly with respect to business performance (growth and innovation) and organizational effectiveness.[65] Another study identified the roles of senior-level executives as mobilizer, ambassador, driver, auditor, and servant.[66] The results indicated that higher-level executives are rated more favorably than are their subordinates in all five roles and that there were no differences in the ratings of executives in public versus private organizations.[67]

## Activities of Successful and Effective Leaders: The Real Managers Study

Closely related to the study and identification of leader/manager roles are their day-to-day activities. Here is a recent description of managers' activities that are not found in the textbooks or academic journals:

> Jane, a senior vice president, and Mike, her CEO, have adjoining offices so they can communicate quickly, yet communication never seems to happen. "Whenever I go into Mike's office, his phone lights up, my cell phone goes off, someone knocks on the door, he suddenly turns to his screen and writes an e-mail, or he tells me about a new issue he wants me to address," Jane complains. "We're working flat out just to stay afloat, and we're not getting anything important accomplished. It's driving me crazy."[68]

The author (Luthans) and his colleagues conducted a comprehensive study to answer three major questions: (1) What do managers do? (2) What do successful managers do? and (3) What do effective managers do?[69] Answers to these questions can provide insights and specific descriptions of the daily activities of successful (those promoted relatively rapidly in their organizations) and effective (those with satisfied and committed subordinates and high-performing units) managers or leaders.

### What Do Managers Do?

The so-called Real Managers Study first used trained observers to freely observe and record for one varied hour per day over a two-week period the behaviors and activities of 44 managers from all levels and types of Midwest organizations. These included retail stores, hospitals, corporate headquarters, a railroad, government agencies, insurance companies, a newspaper office, financial institutions, and manufacturing plants. The voluminous data gathered from the free-observation logs were then reduced through the Delphi technique (a panel discussion with anonymous conclusions based on composite feedback from the group and several iterations) into 12 categories with observable behavioral descriptors, as shown in Table 14.3. These empirically derived behavioral descriptors were then conceptually collapsed into the four managerial activities shown in Figure 14.3. Briefly summarized, these activities are as follows:

1. *Communication.* This activity consists of exchanging routine information and processing paperwork. Its observed behaviors include answering procedural questions, receiving and disseminating requested information, conveying the results of meetings, giving or receiving routine information over the phone and e-mail, processing mail,

**TABLE 14.3** Managerial Activities and Behavioral Descriptors Derived from Free Observation of Luthans's Real Managers Study

**1. Planning/Coordinating**
  a. setting goals and objectives
  b. defining tasks needed to accomplish goals
  c. scheduling employees, timetables
  d. assigning tasks and providing routine instructions
  e. coordinating activities of each work group member to keep work running smoothly
  f. organizing the work

**2. Staffing**
  a. developing job descriptions for position openings
  b. reviewing applications
  c. interviewing applicants
  d. hiring
  e. contacting applicants to inform them of being hired or not
  f. "filling in" where needed

**3. Training/Developing**
  a. orienting employees, arranging for training seminars, etc.
  b. clarifying roles, duties, job descriptions
  c. coaching, mentoring, walking work group members through task
  d. helping work group members with personal development plans

**4. Decision Making/Problem Solving**
  a. defining problems
  b. choosing between two or more alternatives or strategies
  c. handling day-to-day operational crises as they arise
  d. weighing the trade-offs; cost-benefit analyses
  e. actually deciding what to do
  f. developing new procedures to increase efficiency

**5. Processing Paperwork**
  a. processing mail
  b. reading reports, in-box
  c. writing reports, memos, letters, etc.
  d. routine financial reporting and bookkeeping
  e. general desk work

**6. Exchanging Routine Information**
  a. answering routine procedural questions
  b. receiving and disseminating requested information
  c. conveying results of meetings
  d. giving or receiving routine information over the phone and e-mail
  e. staff meetings of an informational nature (status update, new company policies, etc.)

**7. Monitoring/Controlling Performance**
  a. inspecting work
  b. walking around and checking things out, touring
  c. monitoring performance data (e.g., computer printouts, product, financial reports)
  d. preventive maintenance

**8. Motivating/Reinforcing**
  a. allocating formal organizational rewards
  b. asking for input, participation
  c. conveying appreciation, compliments
  d. giving credit where due
  e. listening to suggestions
  f. giving positive performance feedback
  g. increasing job challenge
  h. delegating responsibility and authority
  i. letting work group members determine how to do their own work
  j. sticking up for the group to managers and others, backing a work group member

**9. Disciplining/Punishing**
  a. enforcing rules and policies
  b. nonverbal glaring, harassment
  c. demotion, firing, layoff
  d. any formal organizational reprimand or notice
  e. "chewing out" a work group member, criticizing
  f. giving negative performance feedback

**10. Interacting with Outsiders**
  a. public relations
  b. customers
  c. contacts with suppliers, vendors
  d. external meetings
  e. community service activities

**11. Managing Conflict**
  a. managing interpersonal conflict between work group members or others
  b. appealing to higher authority to resolve a dispute
  c. appealing to third-party negotiators
  d. trying to get cooperation or consensus between conflicting parties
  e. attempting to resolve conflicts between a work group member and self

**12. Socializing/Politicking**
  a. non-work-related chitchat (e.g., family or personal matters)
  b. informal "joking around," B.S.ing
  c. discussing rumors, hearsay, grapevine
  d. complaining, griping, putting others down
  e. politicking, gamesmanship

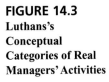

**FIGURE 14.3**
Luthans's
Conceptual
Categories of Real
Managers' Activities

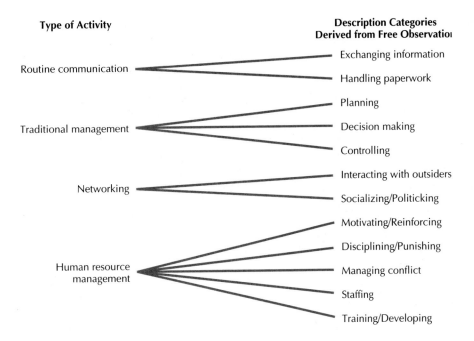

reading reports, writing reports/memos/letters, routine financial reporting and book-keeping, and general desk work.

2. *Traditional management.* This activity consists of planning, decision making, and controlling. Its observed behaviors include setting goals and objectives, defining tasks needed to accomplish goals, scheduling employees, assigning tasks, providing routine instructions, defining problems, handling day-to-day operational crises, deciding what to do, developing new procedures, inspecting work, walking around inspecting the work, monitoring performance data, and doing preventive maintenance.

3. *Human resource management.* This activity contains the most behavioral categories: motivating/reinforcing, disciplining/punishing, managing conflict, staffing, and training/developing. Because it was not generally permitted to be observed, the disciplining/punishing category was subsequently dropped from the analysis. The observed behaviors for this activity include allocating formal rewards, asking for input, conveying appreciation, giving credit where due, listening to suggestions, giving positive feedback, providing group support, resolving conflict between work group members, appealing to higher authorities or third parties to resolve a dispute, developing job descriptions, reviewing applications, interviewing applicants, filling in where needed, orienting employees, arranging for training, clarifying roles, coaching, mentoring, and walking work group members through a task.

4. *Networking.* This activity consists of socializing/politicking and interacting with outsiders. The observed behaviors associated with this activity include non-work-related chitchat; informal joking around; discussing rumors, hearsay, and the grapevine; complaining, griping, and putting others down; politicking and gamesmanship; dealing with customers, suppliers, and vendors; attending external meetings; and doing/attending community service events.

The preceding lists of activities empirically answer the question of what managers really do. The activities include some of the classic activities identified by pioneering theorists such as Henri Fayol[70] (the traditional activities), as well as more recent views by

**FIGURE 14.4**
**Relative Distribution of Managers' Activities**

*Source:* Fred Luthans, Richard M. Hodgetts, and Stuart A. Rosenkrantz, *Real Managers,* Ballinger, Cambridge, Mass., 1988, p. 27. Used with permission.

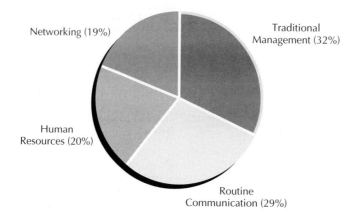

Networking (19%)

Traditional Management (32%)

Human Resources (20%)

Routine Communication (29%)

modern leadership theorists such as Henry Mintzberg[71] (the communication activities) and John Kotter[72] (the networking activities). The activities are also similar to how leaders are generally described in articles in recent years of the *Harvard Business Review,*[73] *Business Week,*[74] *Organizational Dynamics,*[75] and academic research.[76] As a whole, however, especially with the inclusion of human resource management activities, this study of real managers' activities is more comprehensive than previous studies of leader/manager activities.

After the nature of managerial activities was determined through the free observation of the 44 managers, the next phase of the study was to determine the relative frequency of these activities. Data on another sample of 248 real managers (not the 44 used in the initial portion of this study but from similar organizations) were gathered. Trained participant observers filled out a checklist based on the managerial activities shown in Table 14.3 at a random time, once every hour, over a two-week period (80 observation periods). As shown in Figure 14.4, the managers were found to spend about a third of their time and effort in routine communication activities, a third in traditional management activities, a fifth in human resource activities, and a fifth in networking activities. This relative-frequency analysis—based on observational data of a large sample from a broad cross-section of organizations—provides a fairly confident answer to the question of what real managers do. The environmental changes since this Real Managers Study was conducted have undoubtedly had an impact on managerial work.[77] However, although globalization has affected the scope and advanced information technology has affected the means and the speed of communication and other areas such as decision making, the identified activities themselves should remain relevant and valid. In fact, a more recent follow-up study specifically aimed at those in knowledge management/information technology found similar results.[78] Also, firms such as IBM are using software packages to map social networks. They are trying to exploit networking activities in order to "find and nurture their organizations' most in-the-know employees."[79]

### What Do Successful Managers Do?

Important though it is to get an empirical answer to the basic question of what leaders/ managers do, of even greater interest is determining what successful and effective leaders/ managers do. Success was defined in terms of the speed of promotion within an organization. A success index on the sample in the study was calculated by dividing the managers' levels in their respective organizations by their tenure (length of service) there. Thus, a manager at the fourth level of management who had been with the organization for five years would be rated more successful than a manager at the third level who had been at that level for 25 years. Obviously, there are some potential problems with such a measure of success, but for the large sample of managers, this was an objective and useful measure.

To answer the question of what successful managers do, several types of analyses were conducted. In all these analyses, the importance of networking in real managers' success was very apparent. Of the four major activities, only networking had a statistically significant relationship with success.[80] Overall, it was clear that networking made the biggest relative contribution to manager success and, interestingly, human resource management activities made the least relative contribution.

What does this mean? It means that in this study of real managers, using speed of promotion as the measure of success, it was found that successful managers spend relatively more time and effort socializing, politicking, and interacting with outsiders than did their less-successful counterparts. Perhaps equally important, the successful managers did not give relatively as much time or attention to the traditional management activities of planning, decision making, and controlling or to the human resource management activities of motivating/reinforcing, staffing, training/developing, and managing conflict. In other words, for the managers in this study, networking seems to be the key to success (as defined by rapid promotion). It should be noted that many managers aspire to success rather than being effective. One reason is that personal pride and mobility are at stake. Bedeian and Armenakis note what they call the "cesspool syndrome," in which organizations in decline lose their best employees first, leaving behind the "dreck," which then floats to the top.[81] Consequently, although being successful as opposed to effective may seem less desirable to the organization, from an individual manager's perspective, it may be part of an effective career strategy.

### *What Do Effective Managers Do?*

Although the operational measure of success used in the study was empirical and direct, the definition and measurement of effectiveness offers little agreement on criteria or measures. To overcome as many of the obstacles and disagreements as possible, for a sample of the managers, the study used a combined effectiveness index that represented the two major— and generally agreed upon—criteria of both leadership theory/research and practice: (1) getting the job done through high quantity and quality standards of performance, and (2) getting the job done through people, requiring their satisfaction and commitment.

In particular, a standardized organizational effectiveness questionnaire[82] that measures the unit's quality and quantity of performance, a standardized job satisfaction questionnaire,[83] and a standardized organizational commitment questionnaire[84] were used. This multiple-measures index was employed in the study to answer the most important question of what effective managers do. It was found that communication and human resource management activities made by far the largest relative contribution to the managers' effectiveness and that the traditional management activities, and especially the networking activities, made by far the least relative contribution.[85] In other words, if effectiveness is defined as the perceived quantity and quality of the performance of a manager's unit and his or her work group members' satisfaction and commitment, then the biggest relative contribution to leadership effectiveness comes from the human-oriented activities—communication and human resource management.

Another intriguing finding from this part of the study, alluded to earlier, was that the least-relative contribution to the managers' measured effectiveness came from the networking activity. This, of course, is in stark contrast to the results of the successful manager analysis. Networking activity had by far the strongest relative relationship to success, but the weakest to effectiveness. On the other hand, human resource management activities had a strong relationship to effectiveness (second only to human-oriented communication activities) but had the weakest relative relationship to success. In other words, the successful managers in this study did not perform the same activities as the effective managers (in fact, they did almost the opposite). These contrasting profiles may have significant implications (analyzed below) for understanding the performance problems facing today's organizations.

### *Implications across Cultures and for Entrepreneurs and Knowledge Managers*

The Real Managers Study is obviously bound by the definitions that were used, and, of course, one could question the generalizability of the findings and conclusions to all managers. As far as generalizability across cultures goes, a replication of this study that observed Russian managers in a large textile factory found very similar results.[86] This study provides evidence that the activities identified for the successful and effective U.S. managers may hold across cultures.

Besides holding across cultures, a follow-up study of the activities of U.S. entrepreneurs (those who started and sustained their own business for at least seven years) using the same methodology found basically the same results as the Real Managers Study.[87] The same is true of the previously mentioned latest follow-up study on knowledge managers. It was found that today's knowledge managers (defined in this study as both explicit knowledge managers, directly concerned with the generation, codification, and transfer of knowledge, and tacit knowledge managers, focused on providing necessary interaction between knowledge workers or experts) spend about the same amount of time on the traditional and networking activities as those in the Real Managers study.[88] However, even though the activities and their frequency of occurrence seem to hold both across cultures and for entrepreneurs as well as knowledge managers, more evidence is needed to draw any definitive conclusions about generalizability.

In the global arena, there are always confounding cultural variables. For example, there may be what has been called a "dark side" to leadership, which seems to be in evidence in many post-Communist countries.[89] This negative side of leadership includes power bases derived from the Communist era, which demanded loyalty at any cost. This form of leadership created an increasing escalation of commitment to various courses of action (e.g., the Russian armed conflicts with Chechnya) and takes advantage of a halo effect derived from leaders and a sense of nationalism ("Mother Russia" combined with the continued popularity of the Stalin legacy). Under this "dark" approach, opposition is quickly removed. Follower characteristics can also contribute to this dark side; they view change with suspicion and worry that unsuccessful attempts at free enterprise are indicative of weak and ineffective leadership. As a recent analysis noted, "The continued survival of transactional leadership has led to a resistance to organizational change that continues to hamper many Russian firms as they attempt to make the transition to a market economy."[90]

One analysis argues that the Russian economy must be rebuilt through a transformation in the leadership.[91] Centralized decision making must be curtailed, a culture of empowerment should be created, autocratic leader practices must be reduced, trust must be developed, accountability training needs to be introduced, and follower responses of learned helplessness must be eliminated and replaced with an entrepreneurial spirit. These needed changes in leadership called for "minishock therapy" for the entire Russian culture and economy.[92] However, at the national level, when Vladimir Putin became president, these needed economic reforms took a backseat to his appeal to national pride and the previous glory of "Mother Russia." As a recent detailed analysis of his now completed formal presidency concluded:

> Vladimir Putin changed the mood in Russia. Experts and opinion polls confirm that self-confidence has returned to the country and its population. After the chaotic Yeltsin years, the Russians welcomed Putin's nationalistic rhetoric, his strong stand when dealing with foreign

partners, his nostalgia for the old Soviet Union, and his determination to bring Russia back to greatness.[93]

Only time will tell what role Putin will play in Russian leadership now and in the future, but at the organizational level, challenges still remain. At both the national and organizational levels, knowing *what* leaders do, which was the purpose of the Real Managers Study, must be supplemented with *why* they are doing it.[94]

### *Implications of the Real Managers Study*

Despite some limitations, there seem to be a number of implications from the Real Managers Study for the application of leadership in today's organizations. Probably the major implication stems from the significant difference between the activities of successful and effective managers. The most obvious implication from this finding is that more attention may need to be given to formal reward systems (see Chapter 4) so that effective managers are promoted. Organizations need to tie formal rewards (especially promotions) to performance in order to move ahead and meet the challenges that lie ahead. This can be accomplished most pragmatically in the short run by performance-based appraisal and reward systems and in the long run by developing cultural values that support and reward effective performance, not just successful socializing and politicking. An important goal to meet the challenges of the years ahead might be as simple as making effective managers successful.

Besides the implications for performance-based appraisal and reward systems and organizational culture, much can be learned from the effective managers in the study. In particular, it is important to note the relative importance that they gave to the human-oriented activities of communication and human resource management. The effective managers' day-to-day activities revolved around their people—keeping them informed, answering questions, getting and giving information, processing information, giving feedback and recognition, resolving conflicts, and providing training and development. In other words, these effective managers provide some evidence-based answers to how to meet the challenges that lie ahead. Human-oriented leadership skills may be of considerable value in meeting the challenges of global competition, of information technology and knowledge management. The next section specifically focuses on these leadership skills.

## LEADERSHIP SKILLS

As the preceding chapter indicates, there is now recognition in both leadership theory and practice of the importance of skills—*how* leaders behave and perform effectively. Both styles and roles/activities covered so far in this chapter are closely related to skills and can be used as a point of departure for the discussion of skills. First, some of the commonly recognized leadership skills are identified; then, a number of techniques are suggested for enhancing the effectiveness of leadership.

### What Skills Do Leaders Need?

As mentioned in Chapter 13, the research on leader traits continues, but in recent years increasing attention is being given to identifying leader skills. There are many lists of such skills in the practitioner-oriented literature. For example, one such list of suggested leadership skills critical to success in the global economy includes the following:[95]

1. *Cultural flexibility.* In international assignments this skill refers to cultural awareness and sensitivity. In domestic organizations the same skill could be said to be critical for

success in light of increasing diversity. Leaders must have the skills not only to manage but also to recognize and celebrate the value of diversity in their organizations.

2. *Communication skills.* Effective leaders must be able to communicate—in written form, orally, and nonverbally.

3. *HRD skills.* Because human resources are so much a part of leadership effectiveness, leaders must have human resource development (HRD) skills of developing a learning climate, designing and conducting training programs, transmitting information and experience, assessing results, providing career counseling, creating organizational change, and adapting learning materials.

4. *Creativity.* Problem solving, innovation, and creativity provide the competitive advantage in today's global marketplace. Leaders must possess the skills to not only be creative themselves but also provide a climate that encourages creativity and assists their people to be creative.

5. *Self-management of learning.* This skill refers to the need for continuous learning of new knowledge and skills. In this time of dramatic change and global competitiveness, leaders must undergo continuous change themselves. They must be self-learners.

This list is up-to-date and is as good as any other; however, as an academic analysis recently noted: "The prevailing conceptualizations of skills required for successful managerial performance hinders our understanding of the phenomenon."[96] To get around this problem, Whetten and Cameron provide a more empirical derivation of effective leadership skills. On the basis of an interview study of more than 400 highly effective managers, the 10 skills most often identified were the following:[97]

1. Verbal communication (including listening)
2. Managing time and stress
3. Managing individual decisions
4. Recognizing, defining, and solving problems
5. Motivating and influencing others
6. Delegating
7. Setting goals and articulating a vision
8. Self-awareness
9. Team building
10. Managing conflict

Follow-up studies and related research have found skills similar to the 10 listed. Through statistical techniques, the results of the various research studies were combined into the following four categories of effective leadership skills:

1. Participative and human relations (for example, supportive communication and team building)
2. Competitiveness and control (for example, assertiveness, power, and influence)
3. Innovativeness and entrepreneurship (for example, creative problem solving)
4. Maintaining order and rationality (for example, managing time and rational decision making)[98]

Commenting on these various leadership skills identified through research, Whetten and Cameron note three characteristics:

1. The skills are behavioral. They are not traits or, importantly, styles. They consist of an identifiable set of actions that leaders perform and that result in certain outcomes.

**FIGURE 14.5**
**Whetten and Cameron Model of Personal Skills**

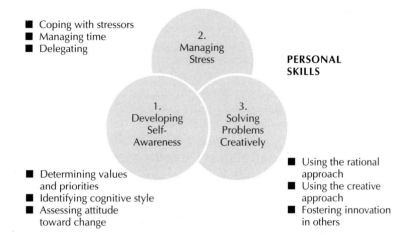

- Coping with stressors
- Managing time
- Delegating

**2. Managing Stress**

**PERSONAL SKILLS**

**1. Developing Self-Awareness**

**3. Solving Problems Creatively**

- Determining values and priorities
- Identifying cognitive style
- Assessing attitude toward change

- Using the rational approach
- Using the creative approach
- Fostering innovation in others

2. The skills, in several cases, seem contradictory or paradoxical. For example, they are neither all soft- nor all hard-driving, oriented neither toward teamwork and interpersonal relations exclusively nor toward individualism and entrepreneurship exclusively.

3. The skills are interrelated and overlapping. Effective leaders do not perform one skill or one set of skills independent of others. In other words, effective leaders are multi-skilled.[99]

On the basis of this background, Whetten and Cameron then develop models for both personal and interpersonal leadership skills. Figures 14.5 and 14.6 show these models.[100] As shown, the personal skills of developing self-awareness, managing stress, and solving problems creatively overlap with one another, and so do the interpersonal skills of communicating supportively, gaining power and influence, motivating others, and managing conflict. These models not only can be used to summarize what skills were found to be important in effective leaders but also can serve as guidelines for needed skill development in the future.

Besides the skills discussed so far that take a personal and interpersonal perspective, "career streams" should be recognized at the organization level. Among the keys from an

**FIGURE 14.6**
**Whetten and Cameron Model of Interpersonal Skills**

- Coaching
- Counseling
- Listening

- Gaining power
- Exercising influence
- Empowering others

**5. Gaining Power and Influence**

**INTERPERSONAL SKILLS**

**4. Communicating Supportively**

**6. Motivating Others**

**7. Managing Conflict**

- Identifying causes
- Selecting appropriate strategies
- Resolving confrontations

- Diagnosing poor performance
- Creating a motivating environment
- Rewarding accomplishments

organizational point of view are finding the right fit among the individual, the position, and the company's needs.[101] Also, firms developing leaders and seeking to retain them should be aware of what is called the "Pied Piper effect," where job hopping by an effective leader can lead to defections and attrition among the subordinates who were under the departed leader.[102] Leadership skills and career development programs may need to be extended to include recruitment, training, and even postcorporate career components (i.e., what to pursue after one's corporate career comes to an end).[103] Leadership skills and career development have become more critical than ever.

## Traditional Leadership Development Programs

One consistent need that has emerged in recent years is a foreboding lack of leadership talent under development. As an example, one survey indicates that the number of 35- to 44-year-old executives will fall by 15 percent in the near future, creating a major reduction in the leadership talent pool,[104] and a recent comprehensive Conference Board survey found only about one-third rated their company's leadership, or ability to meet business needs or respond to sudden changes, as "excellent" or "good."[105] One answer offered is to create options that extend the careers of current leaders while developing a means to attract and train those to replace them. However, as witnessed during the Clinton administration by the tragic plane crash in the Balkans that killed Secretary of Commerce Ron Brown and 16 corporate executives, there are always unexpected events that many companies are not prepared to handle. In the case of the fallen executives, most of the organizations that they represented were not able to fill the void and floundered for several years.[106]

Besides just gaining experience by being at the right place at the right time as depicted in the accompanying OB in Action, organizational behavior and human resource experts are now being asked to identify methods to train and develop leaders to help meet recent challenges. Zand suggests that the three primary areas to be developed are knowledge, trust, and power, which he refers to as the "leadership triad."[107] There is research support for the importance of these[108] and some other developable characteristics of effective leadership that are discussed throughout the chapter. However, there is also much dissatisfaction with leadership development programs. As Avolio and Hannah recently noted, "We find it rather curious that organizations in the United States recently spent approximately $12 billion on leadership development with little, if any, evidence to support the efficacy of these interventions."[109]

As was discussed in Chapter 1 on the need for an evidence-based approach, leadership development seems to be a case where there is a particularly noticeable gap between research and practice. As one summary of the current status of leadership development concluded, "With so much emphasis on the need for leadership, and the war for talent, the continuing disconnect between professional researchers and corporate practitioners is disappointing."[110] Like the rest of this text, the discussion of leadership development takes an evidenced-based perspective.

A recent panel of leadership experts agreed that leadership can be taught and learned.[111] For example, in answering this question, Jay Conger, well-known leadership researcher and author, noted:

> Work experiences, bosses, special projects, role models, education all play a role in leadership development. Using an analogy with sports, . . . not everyone can become an outstanding player despite coaching, yet most will benefit and improve their "game." A few will go on to become stars or outstanding leaders given coaching, extensive experiences, and personal drive.[112]

As indicated in the last chapter, behavioral genetics research using twins (identical twins have the same genetic endowment and thus differences between them can be

Unlike many chief executives who decided early in life what they wanted to be when they grew up, Larry C. Glasscock didn't have a clue. And when he was digging holes for a fence company to put himself through college, the idea that he would someday be a corporate titan and earn a titanic salary seemed pretty farfetched. At that point, he couldn't even imagine scraping together enough cash to buy the one thing he coveted, a Corvette. "I never had a notion that I would be a CEO," he says. "All I knew was I wanted to provide well for my family."

Glasscock, 57, who followed one of Corporate America's more winding career paths to the executive suite, eventually got the Corvette. Now, as chief executive officer of WellPoint Inc., the $45 billion-a-year health-care company that runs Blue Cross Blue Shield Assn. plans in 13 states, he certainly has no trouble providing for his family.

Glasscock's story is typical in one way: He managed to meet the right people and knew enough to follow their career advice. He was born in tiny Cullman, Ala., and was raised in a Cleveland suburb where his father had found a job in a battery factory. His mother was a waitress who later owned a small restaurant. The eldest of seven, Glasscock grew up in a two-bedroom house; his dad carved out extra rooms in the attic. "'Modest' would probably be a generous word," he says of family finances. In high school, Glasscock worked at a Ball Corp. factory, making rubber seals for containers. Of his later experience installing fences, he says: "I got paid by the foot. You learn about incentives early that way."

Genial and self-effacing, Glasscock also had a talent for networking. After he earned a bachelor's degree in business administration from Cleveland State University in 1970, one of the owners of the fence company introduced him to officials at the bank that became Ameritrust and is now part of KeyCorp. Glasscock started out in human resources and worked there four years before being promoted. During that time, a manager saw some potential and began pushing him: As an eager 24-year-old, Glasscock made presentations to the board. "He just never quit learning," recalls John H. Rogers, his first mentor.

Glasscock stayed at the bank for two decades, living comfortably, usually at home for dinner with his wife, Lee, whom he met in high school, and daughter and son. In 1987, Glasscock was recruited to serve on the board of a Blue Cross Blue Shield licensee in southern Ohio, an experience that piqued his interest in health care.

After a few detours, Glasscock was hired to revive a troubled Blue Cross Blue Shield operation in Washington, D.C., merging it in 1998 with a Maryland affiliate of the Blue network. He was then asked to return to the Midwest to help lead Anthem. Running a health insurer, he says, is much like running a bank: "They are customer-oriented businesses. The computer systems are extremely important. And the distribution systems—while different—have lots of similarities."

Even though Glasscock took the better-known WellPoint name after the deal, he isn't moving the company out of Indiana. He runs it from offices near Monument Circle in Indianapolis. No battling heavy traffic to get in at 6:30 a.m., and he hopes he'll soon be home for dinner more often.

---

attributed to development) indicates that about 30 percent of both male and female leader emergence can be attributed to heritability. Thus the vast majority of one's leadership is open to experience, learning, and development.[113] In other words, the research evidence on whether leaders are born versus made greatly favors that they are made, developed. Management/leadership education is certainly based on the preponderance of the role of development since about two-thirds of the 50 top-ranked business schools offer leadership courses and almost half have established executive leadership development programs.[114]

Besides business school education programs, there are a number of in-house leadership development programs,[115] and numerous techniques are being utilized. One method suggested is to develop an acceleration pool, in which key leadership competencies, the understanding of job challenges, and organizational knowledge bases are enhanced.[116] The acceleration pool utilizes information gained in assessment centers to identify potential new leaders along with the strengths and weaknesses individual candidates possess. From there it is possible to speed up the process by which they are trained to move into leadership positions.

There does seem to be merit in identifying key individual differences that are predictive of success. For example, a study of male cadets in a military college indicated that physical fitness, prior influence experiences, and great self-esteem were predictive of effectiveness in later leadership roles.[117] One study revealed that attitudes toward leadership and experience were related to leader emergence at a rate that was much stronger than the traditionally assumed prerequisite of masculine gender role characteristics[118] and another found that parental style and control were related to emergent charismatic leadership.[119] These studies are representative of the continuing body of research that will assist in leader training and development in the coming years.

Others believe an entire new development system should be used. Believing that most traditional leadership programs fail because they start with competencies and focus on individuals, one group of trainers recommends a different approach. Instead of individuals, the goal is to deliver leadership development by beginning with business results and working back to abilities.[120] In other words, it is more valuable to clarify the business purpose and desired outcomes first, and then move leader trainees toward methods of achieving these outcomes. What this and other new approaches indicate is that many companies are trying to make leader development programs more effective. One survey indicated that only 35 percent of the companies surveyed were satisfied with their investments in leadership development programs, leaving a great deal of room for improvement.[121]

## Contemporary Leadership Development Approaches

One modern approach to leadership development is centered on competencies. In this approach, there are three ways that competencies have been derived: (1) research based, (2) strategy based, and (3) values based. Research-based competencies are derived from behavioral data gathered from successful leaders. Strategy-based competency models derive information from key informants regarding strategic company issues and directions. The values-based model focuses on the company's cultural values, as interpreted by company leaders. Briscoe and Hall argue for the need to go beyond these three with what they call "metacompetancies."[122] Under this new approach, leaders would be trained utilizing a learning-based model. Continuous learning emphasizes flexibility and identity, so strong that the individual leader is able to "learn how to learn" and therefore adapt to continually changing circumstances as found in today's environment. Other competencies are not abandoned, but rather are augmented by this learning and knowledge-acquisition-based approach.

Most recently, Avolio and Luthans's authentic leadership approach, introduced in the last chapter and featured earlier in this chapter in the section on styles, gives considerable attention to how it can be developed. We start with the premise that very few leadership programs can demonstrate impact on development or performance. We emphasize that one's life course of events plays a big role in authentic leadership development (ALD), but also that life's both planned or unplanned "moments that matter" can be accelerated.[123] Avolio and Luthans define ALD as:

> The process that draws upon a leader's life course, psychological capital, moral perspective, and a "highly developed" supporting organizational climate to produce greater self-awareness and self-regulated positive behaviors, which in turn fosters continuous, positive self-development resulting in veritable, sustained performance.[124]

In other words, heredity, life events, and specific leadership experiences all affect one's ALD. However, it should be understood that this ALD process can be accelerated by both negative (e.g., painful life events such as being unjustly fired, loss of a loved one, or a heart attack) and positive (finding out what is really important such as helping a friend or traveling to a foreign country) moments. Also, the ALD process can be proactively accelerated by starting with a desired end-point, enhanced self-awareness (both understanding your actual self and your potential best self) and self-regulation. A key to ALD is bringing the future to the present.[125]

Another recently emerging method of leader development is coaching. When the relationship between a coach and a client is built on mutual trust, respect, and freedom of expression, the potential for heightened learning increases.[126] The goal of effective coaching is to move away from the concept that "managing equals controlling" and forward to the idea that "managing equals creating a context for coaching."[127] It is the partnership and the climate that are the keys to effective coaching development systems.

Tactics that support effective coaching include accessibility, attention, validation, empathy, support, compassion, and consistency. A supportive coach can reduce the loneliness of the CEO's role by creating bonds that help the leader renew energy levels and provide new challenges.[128] Also, effective coaches clarify boundaries and expectations for leaders, limiting leaders' efforts to definable targets and time frames for learning.[129] To obtain the greatest value from a coaching approach to leader development, some of the more important practices include a strategic focus for coaching efforts, integrating coaching into existing HR systems, building reliable "pools" of coaches, and systematically evaluating the results.[130]

This is an era in which CEO succession will become an even more vital concern for many organizations.[131] Indeed, many European firms that are family based have become targets for takeovers due to leadership succession problems.[132] In these environments, coaching systems can be effectively used to help identify and place the right new chief executive into the job (i.e., make the fit).

## Other Indirect Techniques for Developing Leadership Effectiveness

Besides the leadership skill development programs, other more indirect techniques involving training, job design, and behavioral management, discussed in previous chapters, can also be used. For example, leaders can undergo personal growth training that may involve a combination of psychological exercises and outdoor adventures. This approach is aimed at empowering participants to take greater responsibility for their own lives and ultimately their organizations.[133] As revealed in the following reflection of a personal growth training participant, these popular programs may be wrongly equating the thrills involved with effective leadership:

> I peer over the edge of the cliff, trying to be logical. The harness to which I am attached seems sturdy. I have just watched several other participants jump. Although they appeared anxious at first, they not only survived the leap—they seemed to enjoy it. I also trust the safety of the system because I trust that the training company does not want me to die. Okay, given that assessment, let's take the risk. It might even be fun. And somehow, I might become a better leader. So off the edge I go.[134]

Despite the potential for the "thrill" becoming an end in itself, there are arguments that personal training contributes to effective leadership. One recent professional book argues that bringing "peace, fulfillment, and awakening to all aspects of your life" are important components of transformational leadership,[135] and another suggests that too much attention may be paid to external aspects of leadership at the expense of internal matters. The argument is that for leaders, *who they are* is just as important as *what they do.*[136]

Although such personal growth training is controversial, there is no question that leaders need to use training techniques with their people. The Japanese, of course, have traditionally placed a high priority on training of all kinds. Recently, however, world-class United States corporations have also become committed to the importance of training. For example, all employees at the highly successful Quad/Graphics firm spend considerable time every week in training sessions—on their own time—to improve themselves and make their company more competitive. A major component of the Motorola "quality revolution" was that spending on employee training went to $100 million per year, with 40 percent directly devoted to the skills and procedures needed to produce a no-defect product or to provide timely, error-free, courteous service to internal and external customers. Old job-rotation training programs have also come to life following the adage that there is no training experience better than "walking a mile in the other person's shoes." The same goes for cross training and the newer "pay-for-knowledge" approaches (see Chapter 4) that an increasing number of U.S. firms are beginning to implement.

Besides training, job redesign is another important technique leaders can use effectively. Covered in Chapter 6, this approach attempts to manage the job rather than the extremely complex person who holds the job. From enriching the job by building in more responsibility, the more recent approach is to concentrate on the characteristics of identity, variety, significance, autonomy, and feedback identified by Hackman and his colleagues and covered in Chapter 6. There has been a stream of research to support the concept that when employees perceive these characteristics in their job, they do high-quality work. Leaders need to give special attention to the autonomy and feedback characteristics of their people's jobs. Autonomy involves empowering their subordinates to make decisions and solve their own problems, in other words, giving them more control over their own job. Feedback can be built into some jobs, but leaders also must provide specific, immediate performance feedback to their people.

The behavioral management approach, covered in Chapter 12, can also be effectively used by leaders to meet the challenges ahead. The organizational behavior modification (O.B. Mod.) techniques based on the principles of operant conditioning and social cognitive theory were shown in Chapter 12 to have excellent results on human performance in organizations. It is important to note that O.B. Mod. interventions have used mainly nonfinancial rewards—feedback systems and contingent recognition/attention—in both manufacturing and service organizations.

Besides drawing from the established job design and behavioral management approaches, the search for effective leadership practices has recently gone to some unusual sources for leadership wisdom.[137] Examples include: *Leadership Lessons from Star Trek, The Next Generation,* and even stranger sources such as *Goldilocks on Management* and *Beep! Beep! Competing in the Age of the Road Runner.* Also, the leadership style exhibited in the HBO TV hit *The Sopranos* has been examined, as well as an application of the principles of "Tough Love," which are ordinarily reserved for troubled and rebellious teenagers. Besides marketing books, these titles should remind researchers and practitioners of the wide variety of approaches to leadership development that have been underused or yet to be explored. One such example is the increasing use of so-called E-Tools that assist in leadership development online via the Internet.[138] For example, as indicated in Chapter 7, we were able to develop a broad cross-section of managers'/leaders' positive psychological capital, which is an important dimension of authentic leadership, in a short online training intervention.[139]

Leadership is clearly important in a wide variety of settings beyond business and industry. Recent studies indicate the importance of effective leadership in educational programs at the college and university level,[140] in urban renewal programs,[141] during the transformational process, from college students to those in military settings[142] and in the increasingly popular online multiplayer role-playing games. Researchers of the online games identified distinctive characteristics of leadership that, "as workplaces and overall business climate become more dynamic and gamelike, will be essential for tomorrow's leaders: speed, risk taking, and acceptance of leadership roles as temporary."[143] There are also many similarities between the capabilities of effective business leaders and political leaders, including the tendency to be a visionary with strong communications skills, even though there are also key differences.[144] The question remains, however, as to whether or not one set of skills (business) can be readily adapted to the political world.

The intent of this discussion is not to give an exhaustive list of leadership skills, techniques, and development approaches. All the styles, roles/activities, skills and development processes discussed in this chapter and the theories in the preceding chapter, plus the techniques discussed in the job design and behavioral management chapters, are relevant and have varying degrees of evidence that they can be effective. Obviously, there are others that exist and are emerging for the future. In total, how leaders apply their skills and techniques and become developed can and will make a difference in the daunting challenges that lie ahead.

## Summary

This chapter is concerned with leadership styles (the way leaders/managers influence followers/employees), activities (what leaders/managers do in their day-to-day jobs), skills (how leaders/managers can be effective), and development. Leadership styles have been studied the longest and are derived from both the classic and modern leadership theories and research. Examples of classic approaches to leadership styles include Hersey and Blanchard's situational, or life-cycle, model. Such approaches to style have been around for a long time and still have implications for the practice. For example, Hersey and Blanchard's approach shows how well managers can match the appropriate style with the maturity level of the group being led. However, such approaches to style lack the research backup to make sustainable contributions to effective evidence-based practice. By contrast, spurred on by recent ethical debacles and economic crisis, authentic leadership theory and positive, authentic styles, that involve self-awareness, transparency, trust, and psychological capital, are receiving attention. The emerging research on this approach shows promise of being able to contribute to a new evidence-based leadership style to help meet contemporary challenges.

The shift in focus from styles to roles and activities reflects a more direct empirical emphasis on what leaders really do. Through observational research methodology, Mintzberg identified interpersonal (figurehead, leader, liaison), informational (monitor, disseminator, spokesperson), and decisional (entrepreneur, disturbance handler, resource allocator, negotiator) roles. Closely related is the observational study of leader/manager activities. The author's (Luthans) Real Managers Study investigated the question of what leaders/managers do in their day-to-day activities and what successful and effective leaders/managers do. It was found that the managers spend about a third of their time and effort in communication activities, a third in traditional management activities, a fifth in human resource management activities, and a fifth in networking activities. The analysis of successful managers (those rapidly promoted) found that networking made the biggest relative contribution to their rise and human resource management activities the least. In contrast, however, the analysis of effective managers (those with satisfied and committed subordinates and high-performing units) found that communication and human resource management activities made the largest relative contribution, and networking, the least. This difference between successful and effective managers has considerable implications for how one gets ahead in an organization (networking that involves socializing/politicking and interacting with outsiders) and the reward systems of organizations (the effective managers may not be promoted as fast as the politically savvy ones).

The last part of the chapter is concerned with leadership skills—how leaders behave and perform effectively, and leadership development. Although there are many skills, such as cultural flexibility, communication, creativity, and self-management of learning, again the more evidence-based skills identified by Whetten and Cameron are the most effective and sustainable. Their personal skills model, involving developing self-awareness, managing stress, and solving problems creatively, and the interpersonal skills model, involving communicating supportively, gaining power and influence, motivating others, and managing conflict, are especially comprehensive and effective. Recently, leadership development, especially centered on competencies, authentic leadership development (ALD), and coaching, has been receiving increased attention in research and is being translated into evidence-based effective practice. Finally, the more widely recognized organizational behavior techniques found in other chapters (for example, training, job design, and behavioral management) can also provide evidence-based development techniques for effective leadership.

# Ending with Meta-Analytic Research Findings

## OB PRINCIPLE FOR EVIDENCE-BASED PRACTICE

Leaders with a charismatic style have high-performing followers and organizations.

### Meta-Analysis Results:

[32 studies; 4,611 participants; $d = 1.0$] *On average, there is a **76 percent probability** that leaders with a highly charismatic style will have better performing followers and organizations than leaders with a less-charismatic style.*

### Conclusion:

Charismatic leadership theory represents an attempt to define what types of characteristics and skills leaders possess that allow them to have profound effects on followers. Charismatic leadership results when leaders use their personal abilities and unique talents to increase levels of achievement and performance on the part of followers. Similar to trait theories of leadership, some say charisma is a natural born gift of chosen leaders. Others, however, suggest that charisma can be developed. Regardless, because of the great source of influence that a charismatic leadership style can have on followers, it is important that leaders do not use their charisma for their own self-interest. As this chapter points out, the "dark side" of leadership is a product of leaders who use their powerful influence in manipulative and potentially destructive ways. The key for this approach to leadership is to recognize the potential for good and bad. Because of the discontinuous change needed in today's environment, the vision provided, and the devotion of followers assured, the charismatic style of leadership is more important than ever.

**Source:** J. B. Fuller, C. E. P. Patterson, and D. Stringer, "A Quantitative Review of Research on Charismatic Leadership," *Psychological Reports,* Vol. 78, 1996, pp. 271–287.

## Questions for Discussion and Review

1. What are some styles of charismatic leadership? What do they mean? Give an example.
2. What is involved in a positive, authentic leadership style? How can such a leader cope with the challenges facing today's organizations?
3. What are the major categories of roles identified by Mintzberg? What are some of the subroles when leaders/managers give and receive information?
4. Use the Real Managers Study to briefly answer the following: What do managers do? What do successful managers do? What do effective managers do?
5. What are some of the needed skills for leaders/managers to be effective? What are the three major characteristics of these skills?

6. How can a competency, ALD, and coaching approach develop leaders and make them more effective?

**Internet Exercise: Leaders as Coaches**

The last few years have seen an increase in the popularity of viewing leaders as coaches. For practical information on coaching, visit **http://www.coachu.com/.** This is an organization that specializes in training coaches as managers. You also can look at the International Coaching Federation, at **http://www.coachfederation.com/.** Based on what you have found, answer the following questions.

1. Would you like to be led by a "coach" as these organizations define it? What would be some advantages and disadvantages of viewing leaders this way?

2. Based on your own leadership style, would you make a good coach? Why or why not?

3. Discuss a situation in which a coaching approach to leadership would be particularly effective. What would be a situation where a coaching approach would seem to be ineffective?

---

# Real Case: *Jeanne P. Jackson: A Retailing Leader*

When Jeanne P. Jackson, the merchant who transformed Banana Republic into a chic, urbane shopping destination, joined Walmart.com as CEO, some analysts considered it an odd mix of cultures. But while the world's biggest discounter is a far cry from upscale Banana, Jackson, 49, felt immediately at home when she attended a Saturday morning management meeting at Walmart Stores Inc. headquarters in Bentonville, Ark., before taking the job. To her amazement, then-CEO David D. Glass was sifting through store-by-store sales reports. "David Glass is concerned about how many lawn mowers were being sold in Poughkeepsie last week. I was blown away," says Jackson, who considers herself a fanatic about retail detail after 22 years in the business.

Up until that day, Jackson had rejected repeated overtures to lead Walmart.com, established by Walmart and venture capital firm Accel Partners. But Accel managing partner James W. Breyer says the companies persisted because Jackson "was absolutely our first choice."

No wonder. Jackson had established herself as a superstar since joining Gap Inc. in 1995. In one gutsy move, she persuaded Banana Republic's parent to open large, expensive flagship stores in key markets to sell the Banana Republic lifestyle. Banana Republic grew rapidly under her leadership, jumping from an estimated $750 million in sales to $1.5 billion in four years. That included reviving the chain's lapsed catalog. "She has taken [Banana Republic] from a niche brand to a megabrand," says Gap Executive Vice-President Ronald R. Beegle. In 1998, Jackson took over Gap's Direct division, which included managing its Internet sites.

The daughter of a Colorado architect, Jackson stumbled into retailing. While working her way through Harvard Business School, she caught the attention of a department store CEO who was attending an executive program. He frequented the campus pub, managed by Jackson and three male partners. Jackson was there first thing in the morning as the short-order cook, and she was back at night as the bartender. Anyone so tireless should be in retailing, he told her. Jackson was persuaded to give up her plan to go into packaged goods, and joined Federated's vaunted management training program. She later did stints at Saks Fifth Avenue, Walt Disney, and Victoria's Secret.

A mother of two who now travels to Arkansas almost every other week, Jackson hasn't changed much from those early days. She'll need that energy and quick mind as she attempts to extend the largest bricks-and-mortar brand onto the Web. Says Russell Stravitz, who hired her at Federated's Bullock's unit in Los Angeles: "The world is watching, and the pressure is on."

1. Why do you think this retailing leader made this move to Walmart?

2. How would you evaluate her background?

3. Evaluate her self-described "fanatic about retail detail." How would this and other details in the case fit into what you have learned in this chapter about what leaders really do?

# Real Case:  *For Leaders, Ignorance Isn't Bliss*

About two years before he died, Peter Drucker told an interviewer that among the things he regretted in the course of his long and productive career was not writing a book—it would have been his 40th—called *Managing Ignorance*. He added, tantalizingly, that it was bound to have been his best, but otherwise he didn't elaborate.

Most likely, it seems, Drucker was interested in figuring out how those running corporations and other institutions could get their arms around what they don't know [which, of course, tends to greatly outweigh what they do know]. "As significant as the problem of organizing knowledge was," noted John Flaherty in *Peter Drucker: Shaping the Managerial Mind*, "he considered the organization of ignorance an even more formidable challenge."

Possibly, too, Drucker was referring to the need for all of us, whether a top executive or an hourly employee, to engage in lifelong learning. As Drucker pointed out, with the world moving so fast, "today's advanced knowledge is tomorrow's ignorance." Or perhaps he would have taken the opportunity to underscore a lesson that one of his students, William Cohen, recalls in his new book, *A Class with Drucker:* "You must frequently approach problems with your ignorance—not what you think you know from past experience, because not infrequently, what you think you know is wrong."

And yet I keep coming back to another idea. Maybe, just maybe, Drucker would have zeroed in on a phenomenon that has brought down some of the biggest-name executives in Corporate America, and will undoubtedly bring down more: blind ignorance—the tendency, as one scholar has defined it, toward "ignorance of self-ignorance."

How else can anyone explain what happened to Zoe Cruz, whose sacking as co-president of Morgan Stanley (MS) made her the most recent high-profile casualty of the mortgage crisis on Wall Street? Ostensibly, Cruz's forced retirement was the result of the firm losing billions of dollars on subprime-related securities. But there is little question that her sudden fall, after 25 years at Morgan Stanley, stemmed as much from the way she mishandled colleagues—and evidently couldn't perceive the tremendous harm it was causing—as from the way she misjudged financial risk.

By all accounts, Cruz was polarizing. Her aggressiveness earned her the moniker "Cruz missile." And she had a propensity for playing politics. She shamelessly backed then-Chief Executive Philip Purcell while eight former Morgan Stanley executives were advocating his ouster in 2005—and then somehow not only survived but reached new heights under Purcell's replacement, current CEO John Mack.

"Many people at Morgan resented and mistrusted her because of her defense of Purcell," says Patricia Beard, whose *Blue Blood and Mutiny: The Fight for the Soul of Morgan Stanley* chronicles Purcell's tussle with the Group of Eight. "They were not sad to see her go."

Being disliked is not necessarily a problem in and of itself. "Popularity," Drucker wrote, "is not leadership; results are." Yet Cruz's flaws apparently went deeper. For instance, she is reported to have rebuked fellow employees for the mortgage losses while sidestepping responsibility for her own role in the debacle. If that's what she did, it was a huge mistake; nothing can undermine one's position of authority more quickly. "Effective leaders are rarely 'permissive,'" Drucker asserted. "But when things go wrong—and they always do—they do not blame others."

At the same time she was pointing fingers, Cruz is said to have discouraged dissent, another cardinal sin in Drucker's eyes. "Decisions of the kind the executive has to make are not made well by acclamation," he advised. "They are made well only if based on the clash of conflicting views, the dialogue between different points of view, the choice between different judgments. The first rule in decision making is that one does not make a decision unless there is disagreement."

What's fascinating to me is how someone as bright and accomplished as Cruz could behave in this manner. Surely she must have known that those around her believed her style to be terribly toxic and that, in the end, it might even prove her undoing. Then again, may be not. In September, an article in *Harvard Management Update* examined just how difficult it can be for the most talented employees, especially those at a senior level, to absorb honest feedback about their performance. It's not simply that they don't want to see their weaknesses; they've almost been preconditioned not to see them.

"Because they have rarely failed," the piece quotes Chris Argyris of Monitor Group as saying, "they have never learned how to learn from failure." Instead, they're apt to "screen out criticism and put the 'blame' on anyone and everyone but themselves. In short, their ability to learn shuts down precisely at the moment they need it most."

Beard recounts that in 2004, Cruz received a performance review from her then-boss, Vikram Pandit, which "included some negatives." Cruz, who resented Pandit, disputed the evaluation and even went so far as to protest the findings to a member of the board.

In the short term, it worked. Pandit left Morgan Stanley for Citigroup (C), and Cruz continued to rise through the ranks. Ignorance as bliss, however, can only last so long.

1. Summarize the famous management consultant and writer Peter Drucker's position on "ignorance." Do you agree?

2. Comment on the statement that Zoe Cruz's demise at Morgan Stanley was because of the way she mishandled colleagues as from the way she misjudged financial risk.

3. Do you agree with the Druckerism that "Popularity is not leadership; results are"?

4. Based on your reading of this chapter, how would you have coached Zoe Cruz to be a more effective leader?

---

# Organizational Behavior Case: *The Puppet*

Rex Justice is a long-term employee of the Carfax Corporation, and for the last several years he has been a supervisor in the financial section of the firm. He is very loyal to Carfax and works hard to follow the company policies and procedures and the orders of the managers above him. In fact, upper-level management think very highly of him; they can always count on Rex to meet any sort of demand that the company places on him. He is valued and well liked by all the top managers. His employees in the financial section have the opposite opinion of Rex. They feel that he is too concerned with pleasing the upper-level brass and not nearly concerned enough with the needs and concerns of the employees in his department. For example, they feel that Rex never really pushes hard enough for a more substantial slice of the budget. Relative to other departments in the company, they feel they are underpaid and overworked. Also, whenever one of them goes to Rex with a new idea or suggestion for improvement, he always seems to have five reasons why it can't be done. There is considerable dissatisfaction in the department, and everyone thinks that Rex is just a puppet for management. Performance has begun to suffer because of his style and leadership. Upper-level management seem to be oblivious to the situation in the finance section.

1. How would you explain Rex's leadership style in terms of one or more of the approaches discussed in the chapter?

2. What advice would you give Rex to improve his approach to leadership?

3. Could a leadership training program be set up to help Rex? What would it consist of?

# Experiential Exercises for Part Four

## EXERCISE:

Role Playing and O.B. Mod.[*]

## Goal:

To experience the application of the O.B. Mod. approach to human resource management.

## Implementation:

This role-playing situation involves two people: Casey, the supervisor of claims processing in a large insurance firm, and Pat, an employee in the department. One person will be selected to play the role of Casey, and another will play Pat. The information on and background for each of the participants follow. When the participants have carefully read their roles, the supervisor, Casey, will be asked to conduct a performance-related discussion with Pat. Those who are not playing one of the roles should carefully observe the conversation between Casey and Pat and provide the information requested below. The observers should not necessarily read the roles of Casey and Pat.

1. List those words, phrases, or sentences that Casey used that seem particularly reinforcing.
2. List any words, phrases, or sentences used by Casey that may have been punishing.
3. List any suggestions that you have for improving Casey's future conversations with employees.
4. Using the steps of O.B. Mod (identify, measure, analyze, intervene, and evaluate), how would you (or your group) improve the human performance in this claims department? Be as specific as you can for each step. You may have to fabricate some of the examples.

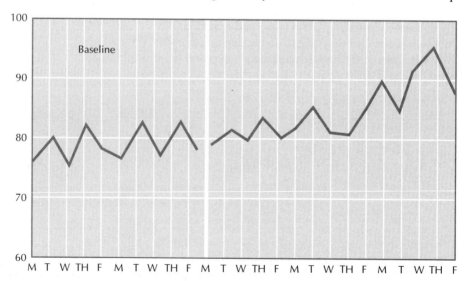

*Source: "Role Playing and O.B. Mod." is adapted from Fred Luthans and Mark J. Martinko, *The Power of Positive Reinforcement,* McGraw-Hill, New York, 1978, pp. 35–38.

### Role-Playing Situation for Casey:

After reading the following information, you are to conduct a performance-related discussion with Pat in order to reward increased productivity.

You are the supervisor of 20 people in the claims processing department of a large insurance company. Several weeks ago, you established standards for claims processing and measured each employee's work output. One employee, Pat Nelson, had particularly low output figures and averaged less than 80 percent of standard during the baseline data collection period. Your target for rewarding Pat was an 85 percent average for a one-week period. During the first two weeks, Pat failed to meet this goal. Now, in the third week after you have decided to use this approach, Pat has achieved the new goal. Pat's performance is illustrated in the graph on page 476.

### Role-Playing Situation for Pat:

After reading the following information, you are to be interviewed by your supervisor concerning your performance.

You are Pat Nelson, an employee in the claims processing department of a large insurance company. Recently your supervisor, Casey Parks, instituted a new system of measuring performance in the department. Most of the other employees have already discussed their performance with Casey, but for some reason Casey has not yet talked with you. Now this morning, Casey wants to have a talk about your performance. You are somewhat anxious about what Casey will have to say. You know that you are not the best employee in the department, but you do make your best effort. You hope that Casey will recognize this and not be too hard on you.

## EXERCISE:

Leadership Questionnaire[*]

## Goal:

To evaluate oneself in terms of the leadership dimensions of task orientation and people orientation.

## Implementation:

1. Without prior discussion, fill out the Leadership Questionnaire. Do *not* read the rest of this until you have completed the test.
2. In order to locate yourself on the Leadership Style Profile Sheet, you will score your own questionnaire on the dimensions of task orientation (T) and people orientation (P).

## Scoring:

The scoring is as follows:

1. Circle the item number for items 8, 12, 17, 18, 19, 30, 34, and 35.
2. Write the number 1 in front of a *circled item number* if you responded S (seldom) or N (never) to that item.
3. Also write a number 1 in front of *item numbers not circled* if you responded A (always) or F (frequently).

**\*Source:** Reprinted with permission from J. William Pfeiffer and John E. Jones (Eds.), *A Handbook of Structured Experiences for Human Relations Training.* Vol. 1. University Associates, San Diego, Calif., 1974. The questionnaire was adapted from Sergiovanni, Metzeus, and Burden's revision of the Leadership Behavior Description Questionnaire, *American Educational Research Journal,* Vol. 6, 1969, pp. 62–79.

4. Circle the number 1s that you have written in front of the following items: 3, 5, 8, 10, 15, 18, 19, 22, 24, 26, 28, 30, 32, 34, and 35.

5. *Count the circled number 1s.* This is your score for the level of your concern for people. Record the score in the blank following the letter P at the end of the questionnaire.

6. *Count the uncircled number 1s.* This is your score for your concern for the task. Record this number in the blank following the letter T.

7. Next, look at the Leadership Style Profile Sheet at the end of the exercise, and follow the directions.

## LEADERSHIP QUESTIONNAIRE

Name_____Group_____

*Directions:* The following items describe aspects of leadership behavior. Respond to each item according to the way you would most likely act if you were the leader of a work group. Circle whether you would most likely behave in the described way always (A), frequently (F), occasionally (O), seldom (S), or never (N). Once the test is completed, go back to number 2 under Implementation.

A  F  O  S  N   1. I would most likely act as the spokesperson of the group.
A  F  O  S  N   2. I would encourage overtime work.
A  F  O  S  N   3. I would allow members complete freedom in their work.
A  F  O  S  N   4. I would encourage the use of uniform procedures.
A  F  O  S  N   5. I would permit the members to use their own judgment in solving problems.
A  F  O  S  N   6. I would stress being ahead of competing groups.
A  F  O  S  N   7. I would speak as a representative of the group.
A  F  O  S  N   8. I would needle members for greater effort.
A  F  O  S  N   9. I would try out my ideas in the group.
A  F  O  S  N   10. I would let the members do their work the way they think best.
A  F  O  S  N   11. I would be working hard for a promotion.
A  F  O  S  N   12. I would tolerate postponement and uncertainty.
A  F  O  S  N   13. I would speak for the group if there were visitors present.
A  F  O  S  N   14. I would keep the work moving at a rapid pace.
A  F  O  S  N   15. I would turn the members loose on a job and let them go to it.
A  F  O  S  N   16. I would settle conflicts when they occur in the group.
A  F  O  S  N   17. I would get swamped by details.
A  F  O  S  N   18. I would represent the group at outside meetings.
A  F  O  S  N   19. I would be reluctant to allow the members any freedom of action.
A  F  O  S  N   20. I would decide what should be done and how it should be done.
A  F  O  S  N   21. I would push for increased production.
A  F  O  S  N   22. I would let some members have authority which I could keep.
A  F  O  S  N   23. Things would usually turn out as I had predicted.
A  F  O  S  N   24. I would allow the group a high degree of initiative.
A  F  O  S  N   25. I would assign group members to particular tasks.
A  F  O  S  N   26. I would be willing to make changes.
A  F  O  S  N   27. I would ask the members to work harder.
A  F  O  S  N   28. I would trust the group members to exercise good judgment.
A  F  O  S  N   29. I would schedule the work to be done.
A  F  O  S  N   30. I would refuse to explain my actions.
A  F  O  S  N   31. I would persuade others that my ideas are to their advantage.

| A F O S N | 32. I would permit the group to set its own pace. |
|---|---|
| A F O S N | 33. I would urge the group to beat its previous record. |
| A F O S N | 34. I would act without consulting the group. |
| A F O S N | 35. I would ask that group members follow standard rules and regulations. |

T_____                P_____

## Variations:

1. Participants can predict how they will appear on the profile prior to scoring the questionnaire.
2. Paired participants already acquainted can predict each other's scores. If they are not acquainted, they can discuss their reactions to the questionnaire items to find some bases for this prediction.
3. The leadership styles represented on the profile sheet can be illustrated through role playing. A relevant situation can be set up, and the "leaders" can be coached to demonstrate the styles being studied.
4. Subgroups can be formed of participants similarly situated on the shared leadership scale. These groups can be assigned identical tasks to perform. The work generated can be processed in terms of morale and productivity.

### T-P Leadership Style Profile Sheet

Name_____Group_____

*Directions:* To determine your style of leadership, mark your score on the concern for task dimension (T) on the left-hand arrow below. Next, move to the right-hand arrow and mark your score on the concern for people dimension (P). Draw a straight line that intersects the P and T scores. The point at which that line crosses the shared leadership arrow indicates your score on that dimension.

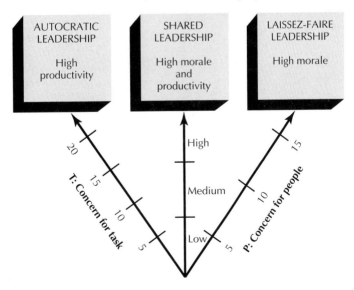

## EXERCISE:

Paper Plane Corporation

## Goals:

1. To work on an actual organizational task
2. To experience the dynamics of performance

## Implementation:

Unlimited groups of six participants each are used in this exercise. These groups may be directed simultaneously in the same room. Approximately a full class period is needed to complete the exercise. Each person should have assembly instructions and a summary sheet, which are shown below, and ample stacks of paper (8½ by 11 inches). The physical setting should be a room large enough so that the individual groups of six can work without interference from the other groups. A working space should be provided for each group.

1. The participants are doing an exercise in production methodology.
2. Each group must work independently of the other groups.
3. Each group will choose a manager and an inspector, and the remaining participants will be employees.
4. The objective is to make paper airplanes in the most profitable manner possible.
5. The facilitator will give the signal to start. This is a 10-minute, timed event utilizing competition among the groups.
6. After the first round, everyone should report his or her production and profits to the entire group. Each person also should note the effect, if any, of the manager in terms of the performance of the group.
7. This same procedure is followed for as many rounds as time allows.

## Paper Plane Corporation: Data Sheet

Your group is the complete workforce for Paper Plane Corporation. Established in 1943, Paper Plane has led the market in paper plane production. Presently under new management, the company is contracting to make aircraft for the U.S. Air Force. You must establish an efficient production plant to produce these aircraft. You must make your contract with the Air Force under the following conditions:

1. The Air Force will pay $20,000 per airplane.
2. The aircraft must pass a strict inspection made by the facilitator.
3. A penalty of $25,000 per airplane will be subtracted for failure to meet the production requirements.
4. Labor and other overhead will be computed at $300,000.
5. Cost of materials will be $3,000 per bid plane. If you bid for 10 but make only 8, you must pay the cost of materials for those that you failed to make or that did not pass inspection.

## Summary Sheet:

**Round 1:**

Bid: _____ Aircraft @ $20,000 per aircraft = _____

Results: _____ Aircraft @ $20,000 per aircraft = _____
Less: $300,000 overhead

_____ × $3,000 cost of raw materials
_____ × $25,000 penalty

Profit: _____

**Round 2:**
Bid: _____ Aircraft @ $20,000 per aircraft = _____
Results: _____ Aircraft @ $20,000 per aircraft = _____
Less: $300,000 overhead
_____ × $3,000 cost of raw materials
_____ × $25,000 penalty
Profit: _____

**Round 3:**
Bid: _____ Aircraft @ $20,000 per aircraft = _____
Results: _____ Aircraft @ $20,000 per aircraft = _____
Less $300,000 overhead
_____ × $3,000 cost of raw materials
_____ × $25,000 penalty
Profit: _____

### INSTRUCTIONS FOR AIRCRAFT ASSEMBLY

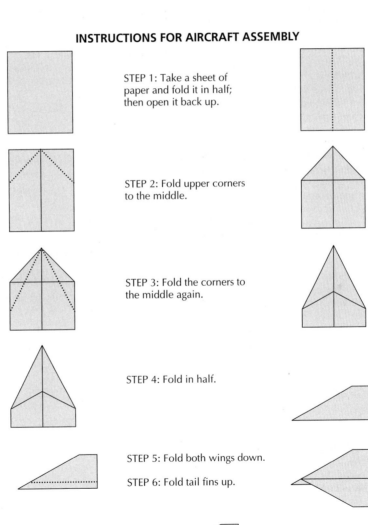

STEP 1: Take a sheet of paper and fold it in half; then open it back up.

STEP 2: Fold upper corners to the middle.

STEP 3: Fold the corners to the middle again.

STEP 4: Fold in half.

STEP 5: Fold both wings down.

STEP 6: Fold tail fins up.

**COMPLETED AIRCRAFT**

## Chapter 1 Footnote References and Supplemental Readings

1. Kamal Birdi et al., "The Impact of Human Resource and Operational Management Practices on Company Productivity: A Longitudinal Study," *Personnel Psychology*, Vol. 61, 2008, pp. 467–501. Also see Jeffrey Pfeffer, *The Human Equation*, Harvard Business School Press, Boston, 1998.

2. For example, see Jeffery A. Oxman, "The Hidden Leverage of Human Capital," *MIT Sloan Management Review*, Vol. 43, No. 4, 2002, pp. 79–83; Eilene Zimmerman, "What Are Employees Worth? Companies and Academics Are Working on Ways to Measure Human Capital," *Workforce*, February 2001, pp. 32–36; and Thomas O. Davenport, *Human Capital: What It Is and Why People Invest It*, Jossey-Bass, San Francisco, 1999.

3. Mahesh Subramony, Nicole Krause, Jacqueline Norton, and Gary Burns, "The Relationship between Human Resource Investments and Organizational Performance," *Journal of Applied Psychology*, Vol. 93, No. 4, 2008, pp. 778–788.

4. Paul S. Adler and Seok-Woo Kwon, "Social Capital: Prospects for a New Concept," *Academy of Management Review*, Vol. 27, No. 1, 2002, pp. 17–40; Michael A. Hitt and R. Duane Ireland, "The Essence of Strategic Leadership: Managing Human and Social Capital," *The Journal of Leadership and Organizational Studies*, Vol. 9, No. 1, 2002, pp. 3–14; and Rob Cross and Robert J. Thomas, *Driving Results Through Social Networks*, Jossey-Bass, San Francisco, 2009.

5. Fred Luthans, Kyle W. Luthans, and Brett C. Luthans, "Positive Psychological Capital: Beyond Human and Social Capital," *Business Horizons*, January–February 2004, pp. 45–50; Fred Luthans, Carolyn M. Youssef, and Bruce J. Avolio, *Psychological Capital*, Oxford, New York, 2007.

6. For example, see Fred Luthans, Bruce J. Avolio, James B. Avey, and Steven M. Norman, "Positive Psychological Capital: Measurement and Relationship with Performance and Satisfaction," *Personnel Psychology*, Vol. 60, 2007, pp. 541–572; and Fred Luthans, Steven M. Norman, Bruce J. Avolio, and James B. Avey, "The Mediating Role of Psychological Capital in the Supportive Organizational Climate-Employee Performance Relationship," *Journal of Organizational Behavior*, Vol. 29, 2008, pp. 219–238.

7. Geert Hofstede, "Problems Remain, but Theories Will Change: The Universal and the Specific in 21st-Century Global Management," *Organizational Dynamics*, Summer 1999, p. 34.

8. For example, see Jena McGregor and Steve Hamm, "Managing the Global Workplace," *BusinessWeek*, January 28, 2008, pp. 34–35; Rachael King, "Working from Home," *BusinessWeek*, February 12, 2007, p. 9; Amy Wrzesniewski, "It's Not Just a Job: Shifting Meanings of Work in the Wake of 9/11," *Journal of Management Inquiry*, Vol. 11, No. 3, 2002, pp. 230–234; and Daniel J. McAllister and Gregory A. Bigley, "Work Context and the Definition of Self," *Academy of Management Journal*, Vol. 45, No. 5, 2002, pp. 894–904.

9. Judith M. Bardwick, "The Psychological Recession," *The Conference Board Review*, May/June, 2008, pp. 47–53; Denise M. Rousseau, "Pieces of the Action: Ownership and the Changing Employment Relationship," *Academy of Management Review*, Vol. 46, 2003, pp. 553–571; Bharath Rajagopalan, Robert Peterson, and Stephen B. Watson, "The Rise of Free Agency: Is It Inevitable?" *Organizational Dynamics*, Vol. 32, No. 1, 2003, pp. 93–105; and Violet T. Ho, "Social Influence on Evaluations of Psychological Contract Fulfillment," *Academy of Management Review*, Vol. 30, No. 1, 2005, pp. 113–128.

10. Jeff Barbian, "Moving toward Diversity," *Training*, February 2003, pp. 45–47; Robert J. Grossman, "Race in the Workplace," *HR Magazine*, March 2000, pp. 41–45; and Karen Auby, "The Boomer's Guide to Communicating with GenX and GenY," *BusinessWeek*, August 28, 2008, p. 63.

11. Robert W. Gunn, "The Rewards of Rewarding Change," *Harvard Business Review*, April 2008, pp. 22–23.

12. Jennifer Reingold, "Meet Your New Leader," *Fortune*, November 24, 2008, pp. 145–146.

13. Ibid.

14. Bardwick, op. cit., p. 47.

15. Jim Clifton, "Global Migration Patterns and Job Creation," *Gallup World Poll*, Washington, DC, Gallup, 2007.

16. Ibid., p. 9.

17. See Reingold, op. cit., p. 145.

18. Thomas S. Kuhn, *The Structure of Scientific Revolutions*, 2nd ed., University of Chicago Press, Chicago, 1970. Kuhn discussed paradigms as far back as 1962.

19. Don Tapscott and Art Caston, *Paradigm Shift: The Promise of Information Technology*, McGraw-Hill, New York, 1993, p. xii; Elizabeth Goodrick, "From Management as a Vocation to Management as a Scientific Activity: An Institutional Account of a Paradigm Shift," *Journal of Management*, Vol. 28, No. 5, 2002, pp. 649–668; and Rodney L. Lowman, "Paradigm, Shift," *Psychologist-Manager Journal*, Vol. 4, No. 2, 2000, pp. 239–240.

20. Joel A. Barker, *Future Edge*, Morrow, New York, 1992, p. 32.

21. See Michelle Conlin, "How to Shine in Dark Times," *BusinessWeek*, November 3, 2008, pp. 52–53; and Jennifer Robinson, "What to Expect," *Gallup Management Journal*, January 12, 2009, pp. 1–3.

22. Patricia A. McLagan, "Portfolio Thinking," *Training & Development*, February 2000, p. 44. Also see Tamara Erickson, "Don't Treat Them Like Baby Boomers," *BusinessWeek*, August 25, 2008, p. 64 and "What Really Matters Most to Generation Y Employees?" *HR Focus*, August 2008, p. 5.

23. James Brian Quinn, "The Intelligent Enterprise a New Paradigm," *Academy of Management Executive*, Vol. 19, No. 4, 2005, pp. 109–121.

24. Norman Clark, "Similarities and Differences between Scientific and Technological Paradigms," *Futures*, February 1987, p. 28.

25. John D. Burdett, "Beyond Values—Exploring the Twenty-First Century Organization," *Journal of Management Development*, Vol. 17, No. 1, 1998, p. 28.

26. "The X and Y Factors," *The Economist*, January 21, 2006, p. 18.

27. Pfeffer, *The Human Equation*. op. cit. Also see Jeffrey Pfeffer, "Producing Sustainable Competitive Advantage Through the Effective Management of People," *Academy of Management Executive*, Vol. 19, No. 4, 2005, pp. 95–108; and Jeffrey Pfeffer, "What Ever Happened to Pragmatism?" *Journal of Management Inquiry*, Vol. 17, No. 1, 2008, pp. 57–60.

28. Jeffrey Pfeffer and Robert Sutton, *The Knowing-Doing Gap,* Harvard Business School Press, Boston, 2000. Also see Jeffrey Pfeffer, "Changing Mental Models: HR's Most Important Task," *Human Resource Management,* Vol. 44, No. 2, Summer 2005, pp. 123–128.

29. Pfeffer and Sutton, *The Knowing-Doing Gap.* op. cit.

30. Sara L. Rynes, Tamara L. Giluk, and Kenneth G. Brown, "The Very Separate Worlds of Academic and Practitioner Periodicals in Human Resource Management: Implications for Evidence-Based Management," *Academy of Management Journal,* Vol. 50, No. 5, 2007, p. 987.

31. See Wayne F. Cascio, "Evidence-Based Management and the Marketplace for Ideas," *Academy of Management Journal,* Vol. 50, No. 5, 2007, p. 1009.

32. Ibid.

33. See Debra J. Cohen, "The Very Separate Worlds of Academic and Practitioner Publications in Human Resource Management: Reasons for the Divide and Concrete Solutions for Bridging the Gap," *Academy of Management Journal,* Vol. 50, No. 5, 2007, p. 1015.

34. Denise M. Rousseau, "Is There Such a Thing as 'Evidence-Based Management'?" *Academy of Management Review,* Vol. 31, No. 2, p. 256. Also see Denise M. Rousseau and Sharon McCarthy, "Educating Managers from an Evidence-Based Perspective," *Academy of Management Learning and Education,* Vol. 6, No. 1, 2007, pp. 84–101.

35. Quoted in Gary P. Latham, "A Speculative Perspective on the Transfer of Behavioral Science Findings to the Workplace," *Academy of Management Journal,* Vol. 50, No. 5, 2007, pp. 1028–1029.

36. Rikki Abzug and Susan Phelps, "Everything Old Is New Again: Barnard's Legacy—Lessons for Participative Leaders," *Journal of Management Development,* Vol. 17, No. 3, 1998, p. 209.

37. Peter F. Drucker, "Toward the New Organization," *Leader to Leader,* Winter 1997, p. 8. Also see Drucker, "They're Not Employees, They're People," op. cit.

38. For example, see Lyle Yorks and David Whitsett, "Hawthorne, Topeka, and the Issue of Science versus Advocacy in Organizational Behavior," *Academy of Management Review,* January 1985, pp. 21–30.

39. Gary W. Yunker, "An Explanation of Positive and Negative Hawthorne Effects: Evidence from the Relay Assembly Test Room and Bank Wiring Observation Room Studies," *Academy of Management Best Papers Proceedings,* 1993, pp. 179–183.

40. H. McIlvaine Parsons, "Hawthorne: An Early OBM Experiment," *Journal of Organizational Behavior Management,* Vol. 12, No. 1, 1992, pp. 27–44.

41. C. E. Turner, "Test Room Studies in Employee Effectiveness," *American Journal of Public Health,* June 1933, p. 584.

42. See David Klahr and Herbert Simon, "Studies of Scientific Discovery: Complementary Approaches and Convergent Findings," *Psychological Bulletin,* Vol. 125, No. 5, 1999, pp. 524–543; Hayne W. Reese, "Some Recurrent Issues in the History of Behavioral Sciences," *The Behavior Analyst,* Vol. 24, No. 2, 2001, pp. 227–239; and J. R. Edwards, "To Prosper, Organizational Psychology Should . . . Overcome Methodological Barriers to

Progress," *Journal of Organizational Behavior,* Vol. 29, 2008, pp. 469–491

43. Chuck Williams, *Management,* South-Western College Publishing, Cincinnati, Ohio, 2000, pp. 5–6.

44. Katherine J. Klein and Sheldon Zedeck, "Theory in Applied Psychology: Lessons (Re)Learned," *Journal of Applied Psychology,* Vol. 89, No. 6, 2004, pp. 931–933.

45. See Katherine J. Klein, Henry Tosi, and Albert A. Cannella, Jr., "Multi-level Theory Building: Benefits, Barriers, and New Developments," *Academy of Management Review,* Vol. 24, No. 2, 1999, pp. 243–248.

46. Donald C. Hambrick, "Just How Bad Are Our Theories? A Response to Ghoshal," *Academy of Management Learning and Education,* Vol. 4, No. 1, 2005, p. 105.

47. Robert I. Sutton and Barry M. Staw, "What Theory Is Not," *Administrative Science Quarterly,* Vol. 40, 1995, p. 378.

48. Robert Folger and Carmelo J. Turillo, "Theorizing as the Thickness of Thin Abstraction," *Academy of Management Review,* Vol. 24, No. 4, 1999, p. 742. Also see Terence R. Mitchell and Lawrence R. James, "Building Better Theory: Time and the Specification of When Things Happen," *Academy of Management Review,* Vol. 26, No. 4, 2001, pp. 530–547.

49. Sumantra Ghoshal, "Bad Management Theories Are Destroying Good Management Practices," *Academy of Management Learning and Education,* Vol. 4, No. 1, 2005, p. 75.

50. Fabrizio Ferraro, Jeffrey Pfeffer, and Robert Sutton, "Economics Language and Assumptions: How Theories Can Become Self-Fulfilling," *Academy of Management Review,* Vol. 30, No. 1, 2005, p. 8.

51. Karl E. Weick, "Definition of Theory," in Nigel Nicholson (Ed.), *Blackwell Dictionary of Organizational Behavior,* Blackwell, Oxford, Engl., 1995. Also see Karl E. Weick, "What Theory Is Not, Theorizing Is," *Administrative Science Quarterly,* Vol. 40, 1995, pp. 385–390; Karl E. Weick, "That's Moving Theories That Matter," *Journal of Management Inquiry,* Vol. 8, No. 2, 1999, pp. 134–142; and Karl E. Weick, "Theory Construction as Disciplined Reflexivity: Tradeoffs in the 90s," *Academy of Management Review,* Vol. 24, No. 4, 1999, pp. 797–808.

52. J. Van Maanen, "Reclaiming Qualitative Methods for Organizational Research," *Administrative Science Quarterly,* Vol. 24, 1979, pp. 520–526.

53. Colin Eden, "On the Nature of Cognitive Maps," *Journal of Management Studies,* May 1992, p. 262. Also see C. Marlene Fiol and Anne Sigismund Huff, "Maps for Managers: Where Are We? Where Do We Go from Here?" *Journal of Management Studies,* May 1992, pp. 267–285.

54. An example arguing for cognition would be Robert Epstein, *Cognition, Creativity and Behavior,* Praeger, Westport, Conn., 1996 and for modern behaviorism Christina Lee, *Alternatives to Cognition: A New Look at Explaining Human Social Behavior,* Erlbaum, Mahwah, N.J., 1998 and Valentin Dragoi and J. E. R. Staddon, "The Dynamics of Operant Conditioning," *Psychological Review,* Vol. 106, No. 1, 1999, pp. 20–61. Also see John A. Bargh and Melissa J. Ferguson, "Beyond Behaviorism: On the Automaticity of Higher Mental Processes," *Psychological Bulletin,* Vol. 126, No. 6, 2000, pp. 925–945, and Cynthia M. Anderson, Robert P. Hawkins, Kurt A. Freeman, and Joseph R. Scotti, "Private Events: Do

They Belong in a Science of Human Behavior?" *The Behavior Analyst,* Vol. 23, No. 1, 2000, pp. 1–10.

55. Richard W. Robins, Samuel D. Gosling, and Kenneth H. Clark, "An Empirical Analysis of Trends in Psychology," *American Psychologist,* Vol. 54, No. 2, 1999, pp. 117–128.

56. Steven J. Haggbloom, et al., "The 100 Most Influential Psychologists of the 20th Century," *Review of General Psychology,* Vol. 6, No. 2, 2002, pp. 139–152.

57. For example, see Arthur W. Staats, "Psychological Behaviorism and Behaviorizing Psychology," *The Behavior Analyst,* Vol. 17, No. 1, 1994, pp. 93–112.

58. Richard J. DeGrandpre, "A Science of Meaning: Can Behaviorism Bring Meaning to Psychological Science?" *American Psychologist,* Vol. 55, No. 7, 2000, pp. 721–739.

59. See Tim R. V. Davis and Fred Luthans, "A Social Learning Approach to Organizational Behavior," *Academy of Management Review,* April 1980, pp. 281–290.

60. Robert Kreitner and Fred Luthans, "A Social Learning Approach to Behavior Management: Radical Behaviorists Mellowing Out," *Organizational Dynamics,* Autumn 1984, pp. 61–75 and Fred Luthans and Robert Kreitner, *Organizational Behavior Modification and Beyond,* Scott, Foresman, Glenview, Ill., 1985.

61. Albert Bandura, "Social Learning Theory," in J. T. Spence, R. C. Carson, and J. W. Thibaut (Eds.), *Behavioral Approaches to Therapy,* General Learning Press, Morristown, N.J., 1976; Albert Bandura, *Social Learning Theory,* Prentice Hall, Upper Saddle River, N.J., 1977; and Albert Bandura, "The Self System in Reciprocal Determinism," *American Psychologist,* April 1978, pp. 344–358.

62. Bandura, *Social Learning Theory,* op. cit. p. 9.

63. Albert Bandura, *Social Foundations of Thought and Action: A Social-Cognitive Theory,* Prentice Hall, Upper Saddle River, N.J., 1986; Albert Bandura, "Social Cognitive Theory: An Agentic Perspective," *Asian Journal of Social Psychology,* Vol. 2, 1999, pp. 21–41; and Deborah Smith, "The Theory Heard Round the World," *Monitor on Psychology,* Vol. 33, No. 9, 2002, pp. 30–32.

64. See Alexander D. Stajkovic and Fred Luthans, "Social Cognitive Theory and Self-Efficacy: Going beyond Traditional Motivational and Behavioral Approaches," *Organizational Dynamics,* Spring 1998, pp. 62–74.

65. Ibid., p. 63. Also see David R. Schwandt, "When Managers Become Philosophers: Integrating Learning with Sensemaking," *Academy of Management Learning and Education,* Vol. 4, No. 2, 2005, pp. 176–192.

## Chapter 2 Footnote References and Supplemental Readings

1. Thomas L. Friedman, *The World Is Flat,* Farrar, Straus and Giroux, New York, 2005.

2. Ibid., p. 174.

3. See Nancy J. Adler, *International Dimensions of Organizational Behavior,* 4th ed., South-Western, Cincinnati, Ohio, 2002.

4. Gregersen, Morrison, and Black, p. 22. Also see Morgan W. McCall, Jr., and George P. Hollenbeck, *Frequent Flyers: Developing Global Executives,* Harvard Business School Press, Boston, 2002.

5. Ibid.

6. For example, see Adler, op. cit., 2002, and Terence Jackson, "The Management of People across Cultures," *Human Resource Management,* Vol. 41, No. 4, 2002, pp. 455–475.

7. Aster Yong, "Cross-Cultural Comparisons of Managerial Perceptions on Profit," *Journal of Business Ethics,* Vol. 82, No. 4, 2008, pp. 775–791.

8. Dianne H. B. Welsh, Fred Luthans, and Steven M. Sommer, "Managing Russian Factory Workers: The Impact of U.S.-Based Behavioral and Participative Techniques," *Academy of Management Journal,* February 1993, pp. 58–79.

9. Lisa A. Mainiero, "Participation? Nyet: Rewards and Praise? Da!" *Academy of Management Executive,* August 1993, p. 87. Also see Snejina Michailova, "Contrasts in Culture: Russian and Western Perspectives on Organizational Change," *Academy of Management Executive,* Vol. 14, No. 4, 2000, pp. 99–112.

10. David G. Myers, *Social Psychology,* 3rd ed., McGraw-Hill, New York, 1990, pp. 226–227. Also see Moshe Banai and William D. Reisel, "The Influence of Supportive Leadership and Job Characteristics on Work Alienation: A Six Country Investigation," *Journal of World Business,* Vol. 42, No. 4, 2007, pp. 463–477.

11. Quoted in Nancy J. Adler, Robert Doktor, and S. Gordon Redding, "From the Atlantic to the Pacific Century: Cross-Cultural Management Reviewed," *Journal of Management,* Vol. 12, No. 2, 1986, p. 295.

12. Lucira Nardon and Richard M. Steers, "The New Global Manager: Learning Cultures on the Fly," *Organizational Dynamics,* Vol. 37, No. 1, 2007, p. 56.

13. For information on an online training tool for cultural differences see Steve Hamm, "Aperian: Helping Companies Bridge Cultures," *BusinessWeek,* September 8, 2008, p. 16.

14. Nardon and Steers, op. cit.

15. Michael A. Hitt, Mansour Javidan, and Richard M. Steers, "The Global Mindset: An Introduction," in Mansour Javidan, Richard M. Steers, and Michael A. Hitt (Eds.), *The Global Mindset,* Elsevier, Amsterdam, 2007, p. 3.

16. Rachel Clapp-Smith, Fred Luthans, and Bruce J. Avolio, "The Role of Psychological Capital in Global Mindset Development," in Mansour Javidan, Richard M. Steers, and Michael A. Hitt (Eds.), *The Global Mindset,* Elsevier, Amsterdam, 2007, p. 107.

17. Mark Foster, "The Global Talent Crises," *BusinessWeek,* September 22, 2008, p. 14.

18. "What Is Diversity?" *HR Focus,* May, 2008, p. 8.

19. Foster, op. cit.

20. "What Is Diversity?" op cit.

21. Ibid.

22. Douglas M. Branson, "Where Are the Women Directors?" *The Conference Board Review,* September/October, 2007, p. 53.

23. "Women's Weekly Pay Falls to 80.8% of Men's," *HR Focus,* January 2008, p. 12.

24. Branson, op. cit., p. 51.

25. Ibid., p. 53.

26. Gary Insch, Nancy McIntyre, and Nancy Napier, "The Expatriate Glass Ceiling: The Second Layer of Glass," *Journal of Business Ethics,* Vol. 83, No. 1, 2008, pp. 19–28.

27. "Diversity Boosts Performance," *HR Focus,* May 1999, p. 5.

28. See Joan Crockett, "Winning Competitive Advantage through a Diverse Workforce," *HR Focus,* May 1999, pp. 9–10.

29. Orlando C. Richard, "Racial Diversity, Business Strategy, and Firm Performance: A Resource-Based View," *Academy of Management Journal,* Vol. 43, No. 2, 2000, pp. 164–177.

30. Kevin Campbell and Antonio Minguez-Vera, "Gender Diversity in the Boardroom and Firm Financial Performance," *Journal of Business Ethics,* Vol. 83, No. 3, 2008, pp. 435–451.

31. Lisa Hope Pelled, Kathleen M. Eisenhardt, and Katherine R. Xin, "Exploring the Black Box: An Analysis of Work Group Diversity, Conflict, and Performance," *Administrative Science Quarterly,* Vol. 44, 1999, pp. 1–28; Dan Baugher, Andrew Varanelli, and Ellen Weisbord, "Gender and Culture Diversity Occurring in Self-Formed Work Groups," *Journal of Managerial Issues,* Vol. 12, No. 4, 2000, pp. 391–407; Luis L. Martins, Frances J. Milliken, Bata M. Wiesenfeld, and Sara R. Salgado, "Racioethnic Diversity and Group Members' Experiences," *Group and Organization Management,* Vol. 28, No. 1, 2003, pp. 75–106; and Samuel B. Bacharach, Peter A. Bamberger, and Dana Vashdi, "Diversity and Homophily at Work: Supportive Relations Among White and African-American Peers," *Academy of Management Journal,* Vol. 48, No. 4, 2005, pp. 619–644.

32. Patricia L. Nemetz and Sandra L. Christensen, "The Challenge of Cultural Diversity: Harnessing a Diversity of Views to Understand Multiculturalism," *Academy of Management Review,* April 1996, pp. 434–462.

33. Bailey W. Jackson, Frank LaFasto, Henry G. Schultz, and Don Kelly, "Diversity," *Human Resource Management,* Spring/Summer 1992, p. 22.

34. Ibid., pp. 22–24.

35. Susan Webber, "Fit vs. Fitness," *The Conference Board Review,* July/August, 2007, p. 19.

36. Joel Lefkowitz, "Race as a Factor in Job Placement: Serendipitous Findings of 'Ethnic Drift,'" *Personnel Psychology,* Vol. 47, No. 3, 1994, pp. 497–513.

37. Quoted in Richard S. Allen and Kendyl A. Montgomery, "Applying an Organizational Development Approach to Creating Diversity," *Organizational Dynamics,* Vol. 30, No. 2, 2001, p. 156. Also see J. T. (Ted) Childs, Jr., "Managing Workforce Diversity at IBM: A Global HR Topic that Has Arrived," *Human Resource Management,* Vol. 44, No. 1, Spring 2005, pp. 73–77.

38. Heather Golden and Steve Hinkle, "Reactions to Affirmative Action: Substance and Semantics," *Journal of Applied Social Psychology,* Vol. 31, No. 1, 2001, pp. 73–88, and Robert J. Grossman, "Is Diversity Working?" *HR Magazine,* March 2000, p. 49.

39. Carol T. Kulik, Molly B. Pepper, Loriann Roberson, and Sharon K. Parker, "The Rich Get Richer: Predicting Participation in Voluntary Diversity Training," *Journal of Organizational Behavior,* Vol. 28, No. 6, 2007, pp. 753–769.

40. Sara M. Freedman and Robert T. Keller, "The Handicapped in the Workforce," *Academy of Management Review,* July 1981, p. 453.

41. Maria Rotundo, Dung-Hanh Nguyen, and Paul R. Sackett, "A Meta-Analytic Review of Gender Differences in Perceptions of Sexual Harassment," *Journal of Applied Psychology,* Vol. 86, No. 5, 2001, pp. 914–922.

42. "What Constitutes 'Harassment,' and What HR Can Do About It," *HR Focus,* December 2008, pp. 4–5.

43. "Validate Hiring Tests to Withstand EEO Scrutiny," *HR Focus,* May 2008, pp. 8–9.

44. "Diversity Trends: Global Focus, Mainstream Training, Age Issues," *HR Focus,* March 2003, p. 8.

45. Sara Rynes and Benson Rosen, "A Field Survey of Factors Affecting the Adoption and Perceived Success of Diversity Training," *Personnel Psychology,* Vol. 48, 1995, p. 247.

46. Rynes and Rosen, op. cit., p. 247.

47. D. P. Frost, "Review Worst Diversity Practices to Learn from Others' Mistakes," *HR Focus,* April 1999, p. 12.

48. Louisa Wah, "Diversity: A Competitive Weapon at Allstate," *Management Review,* July-August 1999, pp. 24–30. Also see Jeff Barbian, "Moving toward Diversity," *Training,* February 2003, pp. 45–47.

49. Gwendolyn M. Combs and Fred Luthans, "Diversity Training: Analysis of the Impact of Self-Efficacy," *Human Resource Development Quarterly,* Vol. 18, No. 1, 2007, pp. 91–120.

50. Richard M. Hodgetts and K. Galen Kroeck, *Personnel and Human Resource Management,* Dryden, Fort Worth, Tex., 1992, p. 403, and Suzanne M. Crampton, "Women in Management," *Public Personnel Management,* Vol. 28, No. 1, Spring 1999, p. 92.

51. Branson, op. cit., p. 53.

52. Herminia Ibarra, "Race, Opportunity, and Diversity of Social Circles in Managerial Networks," *Academy of Management Journal,* June 1995, pp. 673–703.

53. Kimberly Palmer, "The New Mommy Track," *U.S. News & World Report,* September 3, 2007, p. 41.

54. See Cynthia Cunningham and Shelly Murray, "Two Executives, One Career," *Harvard Business Review,* February 2005, pp. 125–128.

55. Palmer, op. cit., p. 45.

56. Ibid., p. 42.

57. Stella E. Anderson, Betty S. Coffey, and Robin T. Byerly, "Formal Organizational Initiatives and Informal Workplace Practices: Links to Work-Family Conflict and Job-Related Outcomes," *Journal of Management,* Vol. 28, No. 6, 2002, pp. 787–810.

58. Marian N. Ruderman, Patricia J. Ohlott, Kate Panzer, and Sara N. King, "Benefits of Multiple Roles for Managerial Women," *Academy of Management Journal,* Vol. 45, No. 2, 2002, pp. 369–386; and Samuel Aryee, E. S. Srinivas, and Hwee Hoon Tan, "Rhythms of Life: Antecedents and Outcomes of Work-Family Balance in Employed Parents," *Journal of Applied Psychology,* Vol. 90, No. 1, 2005, pp. 132–146.

59. See Carol Sladek, "A Guide to Offering Work/Life Benefits," *Compensation and Benefits Review,* January–February 1995, pp. 43–44; and Leslie B. Hammer, Margaret B. Neal, Jason T. Newson, Krista J. Brockwood, and Cari L. Colton, "A Longitudinal Study of the Effects of Dual-Earner Couples' Utilization of Family-Friendly Workplace Supports on Work and Family Outcomes," *Journal of Applied Psychology,* Vol. 90, No. 4, 2005, pp. 799–810.

60. Ibid.

61. Linda Thiede Thomas and Daniel C. Ganster, "Impact of Family-Supportive Work Variables on Work-Family Conflict and Strain: A Control Perspective," *Journal of Applied Psychology,* Vol. 80, 1995, pp. 6–15.

62. Paul Osterman, "Work/Family Programs and the Employment Relationship," *Administrative Science Quarterly,* Vol. 40, 1995, pp. 681–700. Also see Dawn S. Carlson and K. Michele Kacmar, "Work-Family Conflict in Organizations," *Journal of Management,* Vol. 26, No. 5, 2000, pp. 1031–1054.

63. For example, see Dennis A. Gioia, "Business Education's Role in the Crisis of Corporate Confidence," *Academy of Management Executive,* Vol. 16, No. 3, 2002, pp. 142–144; Vikas Anand, Blake E. Ashforth, and Mahendra Joshi, "Business as Usual: The Acceptance and Perpetuation of Corruption in Organizations," *Academy of Management Executive,* Vol. 19, No. 4, 2005, pp. 9–23; and Min-Dong Lee, "A Review of the Theories of Corporate Social Responsibility: Its Evolutionary Path and the Road Ahead," *International Journal of Management Reviews,* Vol. 10, No. 1, 2008, pp. 53–73.

64. Jennifer Merritt, "Why Ethics Is Also B-School Business," *BusinessWeek,* January 27, 2003, p. 105.

65. "Why Appearance May Be Your Next Discrimination Law Challenge," *HR Focus,* August 2008, pp. 6–7.

66. Cynthia M. Marlowe, Sandra L. Schneider, and Carnot E. Nelson, "Gender and Attractiveness Biases in Hiring Decisions: Are More Experienced Managers Less Biased?" *Journal of Applied Psychology,* Vol. 81, No. 1, 1996, pp. 11–21.

67. David M. Bersoff, "Why Good People Sometimes Do Bad Things: Motivated Reasoning and Unethical Behavior," *Personality and Social Psychology Bulletin,* January 1999, pp. 28–39. Also see Andrew Molinsky and Joshua Margolis, "Necessary Evils and Interpersonal Sensitivity in Organizations," *Academy of Management Review,* Vol. 30, No. 2, 2005, pp. 245–268.

68. Rosabeth Moss Kanter, "What Theories Do Audiences Want? Exploring the Demand Side," *Academy of Management Learning and Education,* Vol. 4, No. 1, 2005, pp. 94–95. Also see Michael E. Brown, "Misconceptions of Ethical Leadership: How to Avoid Potential Pitfalls," *Organizational Dynamics,* Vol. 36, No. 2, 2007, pp. 140–155.

69. Linda Klebe Trevino and Bart Victor, "Peer Reporting of Unethical Behavior: A Social Context Perspective," *Academy of Management Journal,* March 1992, pp. 38–64.

70. For example, see Marshall Schminke, Deborah Wells, Joseph Peyrefitte, and Terrence C. Sebora, "Leadership and Ethics in Work Groups," *Group & Organization Management,* Vol. 27, No. 2, 2002, pp. 272–293.

71. G. Stephen Taylor and J. P. Shim, "A Comparative Examination of Attitudes toward Software Piracy among Business Professors and Executives," *Human Relations,* April 1993, pp. 419–433.

72. For example, see "Best Intentions vs. Bottom Lines: What Does It Take for Companies to Go Green?" *The Conference Board Review,* January/February 2008, pp. 55–59; B. L. Flannery and D. R. May, "Environmental Ethical Decision Making in the U.S. Metal-Finishing Industry," *Academy of Management Journal,* Vol. 43, 2000, pp. 642–662; and Ken Starkey and Andrew Crane, "Toward Green Narrative: Management and the Evolutionary Epic," *Academy of Management Review,* Vol. 28, No. 2, 2003, pp. 220–237.

73. For example, see K. D. Butterfield, L. K. Trevino, and G. R. Weaver, "Moral Awareness in Business Organizations: Influences of Issue-Related and Social Context Factors," *Human Relations,* Vol. 53, 2000, pp. 981–1018; J. S. Stevens, H. K. Steensma, D. A. Harrison, and P. L. Cochran, "Symbolic or Substantive Document? The Influence of Ethics Codes on Financial Executives' Decisions," *Strategic Management Journal,* Vol. 26, 2005, pp. 181–195; Jennifer Jordan, "A Social Cognition Framework for Examining Moral Awareness in Managers and Academics," *Journal of Business Ethics,* Vol. 84, No. 2, 2009, pp. 237–258; and Muel Kaptein, "Developing and Testing a Measure for the Ethical Culture of Organizations: The Corporate Ethical Virtues Model," *Journal of Organizational Behavior,* Vol. 29, No. 7, 2008, pp. 923–947.

74. For example, see Daniel J. McCarthy and Sheila M. Puffer, "Russia's Corporate Governance Scorecard in the Enron Era," *Organizational Dynamics,* Vol. 31, No. 1, 2002, pp. 19–34; Peter Rodriguez, Klaus Uhlenbruck, and Lorraine Eden, "Government Corruption and the Entry Strategies of Multinationals," *Academy of Management Review,* No. 30, No. 2, 2005, pp. 383–396; Wendy J. Bailey and Andrew Spicer, "When Does National Identity Matter? Convergence and Divergence in International Business Ethics," *Academy of Management Journal,* Vol. 50, No. 6, 2007, pp. 1462–1480; and Martin D. Kelly, John B. Cullen, Jean L. Johnson, and K. Praveen Parboteeah, "Deciding to Bribe: A Cross-Level Analysis of Firm and Home Country Influences on Bribery Activity," *Academy of Management Journal,* Vol. 50, No. 6, 2007, pp. 1401–1422.

75. Alexander D. Stajkovic and Fred Luthans, "Business Ethics across Cultures: A Social Cognitive Model," *Journal of World Business,* Spring 1997, pp. 17–34.

76. Simone Colle and Patricia H. Werhane, "Moral Motivation across Ethical Theories: What Can We Learn from Designing Corporate Ethics Programs?" *Journal of Business Ethics,* Vol. 81, No. 4, 2008, pp. 751–764; and Steven P. Feldman, "Moral Business Cultures," *Organizational Dynamics,* Vol. 36, No. 2, 2007, pp. 156–170.

77. Melissa A. Baucus and David A. Baucus, "Paying the Piper: An Empirical Examination of Longer-Term Financial Consequences of Illegal Corporate Behavior," *Academy of Management Journal,* February 1997, pp. 129–151.

78. Reported in "Ethics Linked to Financial Performance," *Management Review,* July-August 1999, p. 7.

79. Sandra A. Waddock and Samuel B. Graves, "The Corporate Social Performance-Financial Performance Link," *Strategic Management Journal,* April 1997, pp. 303–319; and Marc Orlitzky, Frank Schmidt, and Sara Rynes, "Corporate Social and Financial Performance: A Meta-Analysis," *Organization Studies,* Vol. 24, 2003, pp. 403–441.

80. William Roth, "Business Ethics—Grounded in Systems Thinking," *Journal of Organizational Excellence,* Summer 2002, pp. 3–16, and Dirk Matten and Andrew Crane, "Corporate Citizenship: Toward an Extended Theoretical Conceptualization," *Academy of Management Review,* Vol. 30, No. 1, 2005, pp. 166–179.

81. Dov Sidman, "From Success to Significance," *BusinessWeek,* September 8, 2008, p. 23.

82. Bernadette M. Ruf, Krishnamurty Muralidhar, and Karen Paul, "The Development of a Systematic, Aggregate Measure of Corporate Social Performance," *Journal of Management,* Vol. 24, No. 1, 1998, pp. 119–133.

83. See Ibid, and Abagail McWilliams and Donald Siegel, "Corporate Social Responsibility: A Theory of the Firm Perspective," *Academy of Management Review,* Vol. 26, No. 1, 2001, pp. 117–127.

84. Peter A. Heslin and Jenna D. Ochoa, "Understanding and Developing Strategic Corporate Social Responsibility," *Organizational Dynamics,* Vol. 37, No. 2, 2008, p. 126.

85. Gary R. Weaver, Linda Klebe Trevino, and Philip L. Cochran, "Corporate Ethics Programs as Control Systems," *Academy of Management Journal,* February 1999, pp. 41–57; James C. Wimbush, "The Effect of Cognitive Moral Development and Supervisory Influence on Subordinates' Ethical Behavior," *Journal of Business Ethics,* Vol. 18, 1999, pp. 383–395; and Sandra Waddock and Neil Smith, "Corporate Responsibility Audits," *Sloan Management Review,* Winter 2000, pp. 75–83.

86. See Fred Luthans and Bruce J. Avolio, "Authentic Leadership: A Positive Development Approach," in Kim S. Cameron, Jane E. Dutton, and Robert E. Quinn (Eds.), *Positive Organizational Scholarship,* Berrett-Koehler, San Francisco, 2003; and Douglas R. May, Adrian Chan, Timothy Hodges, and Bruce J. Avolio, "Developing the Moral Component of Authentic Leadership," *Organizational Dynamics,* Vol. 32, No. 3, 2003.

87. Jennifer J. Salopek, "Do the Right Thing," *Training & Development,* Vol. 55, No. 7, 2001, pp. 38–44.

## Chapter 3 Footnote References and Supplemental Readings

1. Robert Duncan, "What's the Right Organization Structure?" *Organizational Dynamics,* Winter 1979, p. 59.

2. Chester I. Barnard, *The Functions of the Executive,* Harvard University Press, Cambridge, Mass., 1938, p. 73.

3. See Philip M. Mirvis, "Historical Foundations of Organizational Learning," *Journal of Organizational Change Management,* Vol. 9, No. 1, 1996, pp. 13–31.

4. See Chris Argyris and Donald Schon, *Organizational Learning,* Addison-Wesley, Reading, Mass., 1978; Chris Argyris, *Overcoming Organizational Defenses,* Allyn & Bacon, Needham Heights, Mass., 1990; and Chris Argyris, "Double-Loop Learning, Teaching, and Research," *Academy of Management Learning and Education,* Vol. 1, No. 2, 2002, pp. 206–218.

5. For the historical background on the learning organization and the distinctions between single-loop and double-loop learning, see Dave Ulrich, Mary Ann Von Glinow, and Todd Jick, "High-Impact Learning," *Organizational Dynamics,* Autumn 1993, p. 53.

6. See Peter M. Senge, *The Fifth Discipline: The Art and Practice of the Learning Organization,* Doubleday, New York, 1991, and Peter M. Senge, "The Leader's New Work: Building Learning Organizations," *Sloan Management Review,* Fall 1990, pp. 7–23.

7. David A. Gavin, Amy C. Edmondson, and Francesca Gino, "Is Yours a Learning Organization?" *Harvard Business Review,* Vol. 86, No. 3, 2008, pp. 109–116.

8. Jerry W. Gilley, Peter Dean, and Laura Bierema, *Philosophy and Practice of Organizational Learning, Performance and Change,* Perseus, Cambridge, Mass., 2001; Barry Sugarman, "A Learning-Based Approach to Organizational Change," *Organizational Dynamics,* Vol. 30, No. 1, 2001, pp. 62–76; and Robert M. Price, "Infusing Innovation into Corporate Culture," *Organizational Dynamics,* Vol. 36, No. 3, 2007, pp. 320–328.

9. Fred Luthans, Michael J. Rubach, and Paul Marsnik, "Going beyond Total Quality: The Characteristics, Techniques, and Measures of Learning Organizations," *The International Journal of Organizational Analysis,* January 1995, pp. 24–44. Also see Constance R. James, "Designing Learning Organizations," *Organizational Dynamics,* Vol. 32, No. 1, 2002, pp. 46–61, and Raanan Lipshitz, Micha Popper, and Victor J. Friedman, "A Multi-Facet Model of Organizational Learning," *The Journal of Applied Behavioral Science,* Vol. 38, No. 1, 2002, pp. 78–98.

10. Gavin et al., op cit.

11. Tom Kramlinger, "Training's Role in a Learning Organization," *Training,* July 1992, p. 48. Also see Jim Harris, *The Learning Paradox: Gaining Success and Security in a World of Change,* John Wiley, New York, 2001.

12. David Lei, John W. Slocum, and Robert A. Pitts, "Designing Organizations for Competitive Advantage: The Power of Learning and Unlearning," *Organizational Dynamics,* Winter 1999, p. 25.

13. Quoted in "Think Horizontal," *The Conference Board Review,* November–December, 2008, p. 54.

14. Amy C. Edmondson, "The Local and Variegated Nature of Learning in Organizations: A Group-Level Perspective," *Organization Science,* Vol. 13, No. 2, 2002, pp. 128–148. Also see Jeffrey T. Polzer, "Making Diverse Teams Click," *Harvard Business Review,* July–August 2008, pp. 20–21; and John Mathieu, Maynard M. Travis, Tammy Rapp, and Lucy Gilson, "Team Effectiveness 1997–2007," *Journal of Management,* Vol. 34, No. 3, 2008, pp. 410–476.

15. Andrea D. Ellinger, Alexander E. Ellinger, Baiyin Yang, and Shelly W. Howton, "The Relationship between the Learning Organization Concept and Firms' Financial Performance: An Empirical Assessment," *Human Resource Development Quarterly,* Vol. 13, No. 1, 2002, pp. 5–15.

16. For example, see Joan Knutson, *Succeeding in Project-Driven Organizations,* Wiley, New York, 2001, and Leonard G. Love, Richard L. Priem, and G. T. Lumpkin, "Explicitly Articulated Strategy and Firm Performance under Alternative Levels of Centralization," *Journal of Management,* Vol. 28, No. 5, 2002, pp. 611–627.

17. David Lei and John W. Slocum, Jr., "Organization Designs to Renew Competitive Advantage," *Organizational Dynamics,* Vol. 31, No. 1, 2002, pp. 1–18.

18. N. Anand and Richard L. Daft, "What Is the Right Organization Design?" *Organizational Dynamics,* Vol. 36, No. 4, 2007, p. 331.

19. See John A. Byrne, "The Horizontal Corporation," *BusinessWeek,* December 20, 1993, pp. 78–79.

20. Dave Ulrich, Steve Kerr, and Ron Ashkenas, *The GE Work Out,* McGraw-Hill, New York, 2002.

21. Frank Ostroff, *The Horizontal Organization,* Oxford University Press, New York, 1999.

22. See Anand and Daft, op. cit. and Norman Jonas, "The Hollow Corporation," *BusinessWeek,* March 3, 1986, pp. 57–59.

23. See Anand and Daft, op. cit. and Shawn Tully and Tricia Welsh, "The Modular Corporation," *Fortune,* February 8, 1993, pp. 106–115.

24. Anand and Daft, op. cit., p. 335.

25. "Is the Practice of Offshoring Jobs Headed for an About Face?" *HR Focus,* December 2008, p. 3.

26. Anand and Daft, op. cit., p. 336.

27. Ibid., p. 337.

28. Rosalie L. Tung, "Building Effective Networks," *Journal of Management Inquiry,* Vol. 11, No. 2, 2002, p. 94.

29. Raymond E. Miles and Charles C. Snow, "Organizations: New Concepts for New Forms," *California Management Review,* Spring 1986, p. 62. Also see Raymond E. Miles and Charles C. Snow, "Causes of Failure in Network Organizations," *California Management Review,* Summer 1992, pp. 53–72. Also see Raymond E. Miles, Grant Miles, and Charles C. Snow, *Collaborative Entrepreneurship: How Groups of Networked Firms Use Continuous Innovation to Create Economic Wealth,* Stanford, CA: Stanford University Press, 2005.

30. Raymond E. Miles and Charles C. Snow, "The New Network Firm: A Spherical Structure Built on a Human Investment Philosophy," *Organizational Dynamics,* Spring 1995, pp. 5–18. Also see Michael Goold and Andrew Campbell, *Designing Effective Organizations: How to Create Structured Networks,* Jossey-Bass, San Francisco, 2002.

31. Keith G. Provan and Juliann G. Sebastian, "Networks within Networks: Service Link Overlaps, Organizational Cliques, and Network Effectiveness," *Academy of Management Journal,* Vol. 41, No. 4, 1998, pp. 453–463; Gillian Symon, "Information and Communication Technologies and the Network Organization," *Journal of Occupational and Organizational Psychology,* Vol. 73, 2000, pp. 389–414; Melissa A. Schilling and H. Kevin Steensma, "The Use of Modular Organizational Forms: An Industry-Level Analysis," *Academy of Management Journal,* Vol. 44, No. 6, 2001, pp. 1149–1168; and Andrew C. Inkpen and Eric W. K. Tsang, "Social Capital, Networks, and Knowledge Transfer," *Academy of Management Review,* Vol. 30, No. 1, 2005, pp. 146–165.

32. Tapscott and Caston, op. cit., p. 75. Also see Shawn Tully, "The Modular Corporation," *Fortune,* February 8, 1993, pp. 106–115.

33. Raymond E. Miles, Henry J. Coleman, Jr., and W. E. Douglas Creed, "Keys to Success in Corporate Redesign," *California Management Review,* Spring 1995, pp. 133–140.

34. Kevin Freiberg and Jackie Freiberg, *Nuts,* Bard Press, Austin, Tex., 1996, p. xix.

35. Ibid., p. 75.

36. "Flying the (Occasionally) Friendly Skies," *The Conference Board Review,* January–February 2008, p. 21.

37. Paul S. Adler, "Building Better Bureaucracies," *Academy of Management Executive,* Vol. 13, No. 4, 1999, pp. 40–41.

38. Anand and Daft, op. cit., p. 338.

39. See "The Virtual Corporation," *BusinessWeek,* February 8, 1993, pp. 98–102.

40. Marie-Claude Boudreau, Karen D. Loch, Daniel Robey, and Detmar Straud, "Going Global: Using Information Technology to Advance the Competitiveness of Virtual Transnational Organization," *Academy of Management Executive,* Vol. 12, No. 4, 1998, p. 122.

41. Bo Hedberg, Göran Dahlgren, Jörgen Hansson, and Nils Göran Olve, *Virtual Organizations and Beyond: Discovering Imaginary Systems,* Wiley, New York, 2001.

42. Quoted in Kate Flaim, "Going Native," *Fast Company,* November 2007, p. 46.

43. Quoted in Louisa Wah, "Making Knowledge Stick," *Management Review,* May 1999, p. 24.

44. Edgar H. Schein, *Organizational Culture and Leadership,* Jossey-Bass, San Francisco, 1985, p. 9.

45. Joanne Martin, *Cultures in Organizations,* Oxford University Press, New York, 1992, p. 3.

46. Ibid.

47. Elizabeth Wolfe Morrison, "Longitudinal Study of the Effects of Information Seeking on Newcomer Socialization," *Journal of Applied Psychology,* April 1993, pp. 173–183.

48. For example, see Benjamin Schneider, Amy Nicole Salvaggio, and Montse Subirats, "Climate Strength: A New Direction for Climate Research," *Journal of Applied Psychology,* Vol. 87, No. 2, 2002, pp. 220–229.

49. Genevieve Soter Capowski, "Designing a Corporate Identity," *Management Review,* June 1993, p. 37.

50. Jennifer Reese, "America's Most Admired Corporations," *Fortune,* February 8, 1993, p. 44.

51. Ibid.

52. Melvyn J. Stark, "Five Years of Insight into the World's Most Admired Companies," *Journal of Organizational Excellence,* Winter 2002, pp. 4–5.

53. See Keith McFarland, "How Curiosity Empowers Toyota," *BusinessWeek,* October 22, 2007, p. 18.

54. Jena McGregor, "The Org Chart that Really Counts: How Mapping Unofficial Job Links Pays Off," *BusinessWeek,* February 27, 2006, pp. 48–49.

55. Jeff Rosenthal and Mary Ann Masarech, "High-Performance Cultures: How Values Can Drive Business Results," *Journal of Organizational Excellence,* Spring 2003, pp. 3–18.

56. Nancy C. Morey and Fred Luthans, "Refining the Displacement of Culture and the Use of Scenes and Themes in Organizational Studies," *Academy of Management Review,* April 1985, p. 221.

57. Freiberg, op. cit., p. 151.

58. John Guaspari, "We Make People Happy," *Across the Board,* April 2000, p. 53.

59. Henry W. Head, "How Culture Helped Dow AgroSciences Succeed in Achieving Business Objectives of an Acquisition," *Journal of Organizational Excellence,* Winter 2001, pp. 17–24.

60. Avan R. Jassawalla and Hemant C. Sashittal, "Cultures That Support Product-Innovation Processes," *Academy of Management Executive,* Vol. 16, No. 3, 2002, pp. 42–54.

61. Laura Riolli-Saltzman and Fred Luthans, "After the Bubble Burst: How Small High-Tech Firms Can Keep in Front of

the Wave," *Academy of Management Executive,* Vol. 15, No. 3, 2001, pp. 114–124.

62. "General Electric," *Merrill Lynch & Co.,* May 25, 2000, pp. 10–11.

63. For example, see Frances Cairncross, "New Ways to Bind a Fragmented Workforce into a Cultural Community," *Journal of Organizational Excellence,* Summer 2002, pp. 31–42.

64. "GE Chief Has Electric Presence," *The Honolulu Advertiser,* April 17, 2000, p. B6.

65. "A Spanner in the Works," *The Economist,* October 23, 1993, p. 75.

66. Schein, op. cit., p. 210.

67. See John A. Byrne and Ben Elgin, "Cisco behind the Hype," *BusinessWeek,* January 21, 2002, pp. 54–61.

68. Andy Serwer, "There's Something about Cisco," *Fortune,* May 15, 2000, p. 118.

69. This process is described in Richard Pascale, "The Paradox of 'Corporate Culture': Reconciling Ourselves to Socialization," *California Management Review,* Winter 1985, pp. 29–38.

70. Annelies E. M. Van Vianen, "Person-Organization Fit: The Match between Newcomers' and Recruiters' Preferences for Organizational Cultures," *Personnel Psychology,* Vol. 53, 2000, p. 13.

71. See Gregory B. Northcraft and Margaret A. Neale, *Organizational Behavior,* Dryden, Chicago, 1990, pp. 460–461, for a review of this literature, and Robert Vandenberg and Vida Scarpello, "The Matching Model: An Examination of the Processes Underlying Realistic Job Previews," *Journal of Applied Psychology,* February 1990, pp. 60–67, for more research.

72. Peter Cappelli and Anne Crocker-Hefter, "Distinctive Human Resources Are Firms' Core Competencies," *Organizational Dynamics,* Winter 1996, p. 18.

73. Pascale, op. cit., p. 32.

74. James M. Higgins and Craig McAllaster, "Want Innovation? Then Use Cultural Artifacts That Support It," *Organizational Dynamics,* Vol. 31, No. 1, 2002, pp. 74–84.

75. Fred Luthans and Alexander D. Stajkovic, "Provide Recognition for Performance Improvement," in Edwin A. Locke (Ed.), *Handbook of Principles of Organizational Behavior,* 2nd ed. Blackwell, London, 2009, pp. 239–253, and Alexander D. Stajkovic and Fred Luthans, "Behavioral Management and Task Performance in Organizations: Conceptual Background, Meta-Analysis, and Test of Alternative Models," *Personnel Psychology,* Vol. 56, 2003, pp. 155–194.

76. Kenneth Thompson and Fred Luthans, "Organizational Culture: A Behavioral Perspective," in Benjamin Schneider (Ed.), *Organizational Climate and Culture,* Jossey-Bass, San Francisco, 1990, pp. 319–344. Also see David W. Schaal, "Applying a Selectionist Analysis of Culture: A Review of Cultural Contingencies," *The Behavior Analyst,* Vol. 25, No. 1, 2002, pp. 93–101.

77. Sarah Mahoney, "Managing Remotely (and Well)," *Fortune Small Business,* Vol. 17, No. 9, 2007, pp. 70–72.

78. Jennifer Reingold and Jia Yang, "What's Your OQ?" *Fortune,* Vol. 156, No. 2, 2007, pp. 98–106.

79. Robin Ely and Debra Meyerson, "Unmasking Manly Men," *Harvard Business Review,* July–August, 2008, p. 20.

80. Ibid.

81. Quoted in Sylvia DeVoge and Scott Spreier, "The Soft Realities of Mergers," *Across the Board,* November/December 1999, p. 27.

82. Mark N. Clemente and David S. Greenspan, "M&A's: Preventing Culture Clash," *HR Focus,* February 1999, p. 9.

83. Dapha Oyserman and Spike W. S. Lee, "Does Culture Influence What and How We Think?" *Psychological Bulletin,* Vol.134, No. 2, 2008, pp. 311–342.

84. Cyrus F. Freidheim, Jr., "The Battle of the Alliances," *Manage- ment Review,* September 1999, pp. 46–51.

85. Andrew Rosenbaum, "Testing Cultural Waters," *Management Review,* July–August 1999, p. 42.

86. Reported in Gail Dutton, "Building a Global Brain," *Management Review,* May 1999, p. 36.

87. Wayne F. Cascio and Peter Cappelli, "Lessons from the Financial Services Crisis," *HR Magazine,* January 2009, p. 49.

88. Quoted in Ibid., p. 50.

89. Quoted in Ibid., p. 50.

90. Robert Marshak and David Grout, "Organizational Discourse and New Organization Development Practices," *British Journal of Management,* Vol. 19, 2008, pp. S7–S19.

91. Patrick Flanagan, "The ABC's of Changing Corporate Cultural," *Management Review,* July 1995, p. 61. Also see John Kotter and Dan S. Cohen, "Creative Ways to Empower Action to Change the Organization: Cases in Point," *Journal of Organizational Excellence,* Winter 2002, pp. 73–82.

92. "Google: The Faces and Voices of the World's Most Innovative Company," *Fast Company,* March 2008, pp. 74–91.

## Chapter 4 Footnote References and Supplemental Readings

1. Albert Bandura, *Social Foundations of Thought and Action,* Prentice Hall, Upper Saddle River, N.J., 1986, p. 228.

2. Sandy J. Wayne, Lynn M. Shore, William H. Bommer, and Lois E. Tetrick, "The Role of Fair Treatment and Rewards in Perceptions of Organizational Support and Leader-Member Exchange," *Journal of Applied Psychology,* Vol. 87, No. 3, 2002, pp. 590–598.

3. Fred Luthans and Alexander D. Stajkovic, "Reinforce for Performance: The Need to Go beyond Pay and Even Rewards," *Academy of Management Executive,* Vol. 13, No. 2, 1999, pp. 49–57.

4. Thomas B. Wilson, *Rewards That Drive High Performance: Success Stories from Leading Organizations,* American Management Association, New York, 1999, and Eilene Zimmerman, "What Are Employees Worth?" *Workforce,* February 2001, pp. 32–36.

5. See Bob Nelson, *1001 Ways to Reward Employees,* Workman, New York, 1994, and Fred Luthans and Alexander Stajkovic, "Provide Recognition for Performance Improvement," in E. Locke (Ed.), *Handbook of Principles of Organizational Behavior,* Blackwell, Oxford, U.K., 2000, pp. 166–180.

6. Diann R. Newman and Richard M. Hodgetts, *Human Resource Management: A Customer-Oriented Approach,* Prentice Hall, Upper Saddle River, N.J., 1998, p. 227. Also see "Employee Job Satisfaction: The Latest Ratings," *HR Focus,* August 2008, p. 3.

7. Manfred Kets de Vries, "Money, Money, Money," *Organizational Dynamics*, Vol. 36, No. 3, 2007, pp. 231–243.

8. Stephen Kerr, "Organization Rewards, Practical, Cost-Neutral Alternatives That You May Know, but Don't Practice," *Organizational Dynamics*, Summer 1999, p. 68.

9. "Many Workers Would Take Pay Cut for Their Dream Job," *HR Focus*, July 2008, p. 9.

10. Patricia K. Zingheim and Jay R. Schuster, *Pay People Right! Breakthrough Reward Strategies to Create Great Companies*, Jossey-Bass Publishers, San Francisco, 2000.

11. Terence R. Mitchell and Amy E. Mickel, "The Meaning of Money: An Individual-Difference Perspective," *Academy of Management Review*, July 1999, p. 569.

12. Ibid.

13. The quote is in Kets de Vries, op. cit., p. 234.

14. Thomas J. Hackett and Donald G. McDermott, "Seven Steps to Successful Performance-Based Rewards," *HR Focus*, September 1999, pp. 11–12. Also see Sara L. Rynes and Barry Gerhart (Eds.), *Compensation in Organizations: Current Research and Practice*, Jossey-Bass, San Francisco, 2000.

15. The quote is in ibid., p. 232.

16. Matt Bloom and George T. Milkovich, "Relationships among Risk, Incentive Pay, and Organizational Performance," *Academy of Management Journal*, June 1998, pp. 283–297.

17. Wayne F. Cascio and Peter Cappelli, "Lessons from the Financial Services Crisis," *HR Magazine*, January 2009, pp. 47, 49–50.

18. Timothy Fogarty, Michel Magnan, Garen Markarian, and Serge Bohdjalian, "Inside Agency: The Rise and Fall of Nortel," *Journal of Business Ethics*, Vol. 85, No. 2, 2009, pp. 165–187.

19. Also see John R. Deckop, Robert Mangel, and Carol C. Cirka, "Getting More Than You Pay For: Organizational Citizenship Behavior and Pay-for-Performance Plans," *Academy of Management Journal*, August 1999, pp. 420–428.

20. A. Furnham and M. Argyle, *The Psychology of Money*, Routledge, London, 1998.

21. Edward E. Lawler, *Rewarding Excellence*, Jossey-Bass, San Francisco, 2000. Also see Jack Dolmar-Connell, "Developing a Reward Strategy That Delivers Shareholder and Employee Value," *Compensation and Benefits Review*, March–April 1999, pp. 46–53.

22. Nina Gupta and Jason D. Shaw, "Financial Incentives are Effective," *Compensation and Benefits Review*, March–April 1998, pp. 27–32; "Pay Preview," *The Economist*, August 29, 1998, pp. 59–60; and Harry G. Barkema and Luis R. Gomez-Mejia, "Managerial Compensation and Firm Performance," *Academy of Management Journal*, April 1998, pp. 135–145. Also see C. Bram Cadsby, Fei Song, and Francis Tapon, "Sorting and Incentive Effects of Pay for Performance," *Academy of Management Journal*, Vol. 50, No. 2, 2007, pp. 387–405.

23. Tara Kalwarski, "Extravagant Executive Pay Shows Signs of Moderation," *BusinessWeek*, August 25, 2008, p. 9.

24. John W. Miller, "Offshore Rig Workers Call the Shots," *The Wall Street Journal*, November 10, 2008, p. B-1.

25. Kerr, op. cit., p. 74. Also see Marta E. Elvira, "Pay Me Now or Pay Me Later," *Work and Occupations*, Vol. 28, No. 3, 2001, pp. 346–370.

26. "Cutting Pay Could Hurt Morale," *HR Focus*, December 1999, p. 5.

27. Donald L. Ferrin and Kurt T. Dirks, "The Use of Rewards to Increase and Decrease Trust: Mediating Processes and Differential Effects," *Organization Science*, Vol. 14, No. 1, 2003, pp. 18–31. Also see Kimberly Merriman, "Low-Trust Teams Prefer Individualized Pay," *Harvard Business Review*, November 2008, p. 32.

28. Phred Dvorak, "Slump Yields Employee Rewards," *The Wall Street Journal*, October 10, 2008, p. B2.

29. Mitchell and Mickel, op. cit., pp. 568–578. Also see Kristin L. Scott, Jason D. Shaw, and Michelle K. Duffy, "Merit Pay Raises and Organization-Based Self-Esteem," *Journal of Organizational Behavior*, Vol. 29, No. 7, 2008, pp. 967–980; and Evert Van de Vliert, Nico W. Van Yperen, and Henk Thierry, "Are Wages More Important for Employees in Poorer Countries with Harsher Climates?" *Journal of Organizational Behavior*, Vol. 29, No. 1, 2007, pp. 79–94.

30. Matt Bloom, "The Performance Effects of Pay Dispersion on Individuals and Organizations," *Academy of Management Journal*, March 1999, pp. 25–40.

31. For more on this see Christy Eidson, "A Lesson from the Ballpark," *Across the Board*, November/December 1999, p. 35.

32. Lawler quoted in Eidson, op. cit., p. 38.

33. For more on this see Phyllis Gail Doloff, "Missionary Zeal," *Across the Board*, April 2000, p. 30.

34. Eric Krell, "Getting a Grip on Executive Compensation," *Workforce*, February 2003, p. 30.

35. Alexander D. Stajkovic and Fred Luthans, "Behavioral Management and Task Performance in Organizations: Conceptual Background, Meta-Analysis, and Test of Alternative Models," *Personnel Psychology*, Vol. 56, 2003, pp. 155–194.

36. E. L. Deci, "The Effect of Contingent and Non-Contingent Rewards and Controls on Intrinsic Motivation," *Organizational Behavior and Human Performance*, Vol. 8, 1970, pp. 218–219, and E. L. Deci, *Intrinsic Motivation*, Plenum, New York, 1975. Also see A. Kohn, *Punished by Rewards*, Hought on Mifflin, Boston, 1993.

37. Judy Cameron and W. David Pierce, "Reinforcement, Reward, and Intrinsic Motivation: A Meta-Analysis," *Review of Educational Research*, Fall 1994, p. 363. Also see Judy Cameron, Katherine M. Banko, and W. David Pierce, "Pervasive Negative Effects of Rewards on Intrinsic Motivation: The Myth Continues," *The Behavior Analyst*, Vol. 24, No. 1, 2001, pp. 1–44.

38. Bob Filipczak, "Why No One Likes Your Incentive Program," *Training*, August 1993, pp. 19–25, and Yochi Cohen-Charash and Paul E. Spector, "The Role of Justice in Organizations: A Meta-Analysis," *Organizational Behavior and Human Decision Processes*, Vol. 86, No. 2, 2001, pp. 278–321.

39. Luthans and Stajkovic, "Reinforce for Performance: The Need to Go beyond Pay and Even Rewards," op. cit., and Alexander Stajkovic and Fred Luthans, "The Differential Effects of Incentive Motivators on Work Performance," *Academy of Management Journal*, Vol. 44, No. 1, 2001, pp. 580–590.

40. Kerr, op. cit., p. 61.

41. Steven Gross quoted in "Why Companies Are Shifting to Performance-Related Pay," *HR Focus*, December 2008, p. 7.

42. Michelle Conlin, "The Software Says You're Just Average," *BusinessWeek*, February 25, 2002, p. 126.

43. See, for example, Charles A. Wrege and Richard M. Hodgetts, "Frederick W. Taylor's 1899 Pig Iron Observations: Examining Fact, Fiction, and Lessons for the New Millennium," *Academy of Management Journal,* Vol. 43, No. 6, 2000, pp. 1283–1291.

44. Richard M. Hodgetts, "A Conversation with Donald Hastings of the Lincoln Electric Company," *Organizational Dynamics,* Winter 1997, pp. 68–74.

45. Calmetta Y. Coleman, "Conseco Package Has $45 Million for CEO Wendt," *The Wall Street Journal,* July 11, 2000, p. A4.

46. Charles Gasparino and Pui-Wing Tam, "Hot Broker Market Fuels Questions about Pay," *The Wall Street Journal,* March 28, 2000, pp. C1, C4.

47. Michelle Conlin, "A Little Less in the Envelope This Week," *BusinessWeek,* February 18, 2002, p. 64.

48. Sarah E. Needleman, "Pay Raises Seen Taking a Hit," *The Wall Street Journal,* December 16, 2008, p. D4.

49. See Pamela Brandes, Ravi Dharwadkar, and G. Victor Lemesis, "Effective Employee Stock Option Design," *Academy of Management Executive,* Vol. 17, No. 1, 2003, pp. 77–93, and W. Gerard Sanders, "Behavioral Responses of CEOs to Stock Ownership and Stock Option Pay," *Academy of Management Journal,* Vol. 44, No. 3, 2001, pp. 477–492.

50. John A. Byrne, "Executive Pay," *BusinessWeek,* April 15, 2002, p. 80.

51. Phred Dvorak, "Firms Jump to Salvage 'Underwater' Stock Options," *The Wall Street Journal,* December 22, 2008, pp. B1, B4.

52. John Gapper, "Comment on Sumantra Ghoshal's 'Bad Management Theories Are Destroying Good Management Practices'," *Academy of Management Learning and Education,* Vol. 4, No. 1, 2005, p. 101.

53. Gerard W. Sanders and Donald C. Hambrick, "Swinging for the Fences: The Effects of CEO Stock Options on Company Risk Taking and Performance," *Academy of Management Journal,* Vol. 50, No. 5, 2007, pp. 1055–1078.

54. Songjun Luo, "Does Your Sales Incentive Plan Pay for Performance?" *Compensation & Benefits Review,* January/February 2003, pp. 18–24.

55. Ben W. Heineman, Jr., "The Fatal Flaw in Pay for Performance," *Harvard Business Review,* June 2008, p. 31.

56. Dirk Johnson, "Teachers Reject Linking Job Performance to Bonuses," *New York Times,* July 6, 2000, p. A16.

57. Janet Wiscombe, "Can Pay for Performance Really Work?" *Workforce,* Vol. 80, No. 8, 2001, pp. 28–34.

58. See Ronald Piccolo, Christine L. Jackson, John E. Mathieu, and Jessica R. Saul, "A Meta-Analysis of Teamwork Processes: Tests of a Multidimensional Model and Relationships with Team Effectiveness Criteria," *Personnel Psychology,* Vol. 61, No. 2, 2008, pp. 273–307; John Mathieu, Travis M. Maynard, Tommy Rapp, and Lucy Gilson, "Team Effectiveness 1997–2007," *Journal of Management,* Vol. 34, No. 3, 2008, pp. 410–476; and Anne Delarue, Geert Van Hootegen, Stephen Procter, and Mark Burridge, "Team-working and Organizational Performance," *International Journal of Management Reviews,* Vol. 10, No. 2, 2008, pp. 127–148.

59. Judith A. Honeywell-Johnson and Alyce M. Dickinson, "Small Group Incentives: A Review of the Literature," *Journal of Organizational Behavior Management,* Vol. 9, No. 2, 1999, pp. 89–120.

60. Denis Collins, *Gainsharing and Power: Lessons from Six Scanlon Plans,* Cornell University Press, Ithaca, N.Y., 1998, and Dong-One Kim, "Determinants of the Survival of Gainsharing Programs," *Industrial and Labor Relations Review,* Vol. 53, No. 1, October 1999, pp. 21–42.

61. Jeffrey B. Arthur and Lynda Aiman-Smith, "Gainsharing and Organizational Learning: An Analysis of Employee Suggestions over Time," *Academy of Management Journal,* Vol. 44, No. 4, 2001, pp. 737–754, and Jeffrey A. Arthur and Christopher L. Huntley, "Ramping Up the Organizational Learning Curve: Assessing the Impact of Deliberate Learning on Organizational Performance Under Gainsharing," *Academy of Management Journal,* Vol. 48, No. 6, 2005, pp. 1159–1170.

62. Jacqueline Coyle-Shapiro, Paula C. Morrow, Ray Richardson, and Stephen R. Dunn, "Using Profit Sharing to Enhance Employee Attitudes," *Human Resource Management,* Vol. 41, No. 4, 2002, pp. 423–439.

63. Corey Rosen, John Case, and Martin Staubas, "Every Employee an Owner," *Harvard Business Review,* June, 2005, p. 123.

64. Ellen E. Schultz, "Tribune Filing Exposes Risks of ESOPs," *The Wall Street Journal,* December 10, 2008, p. B6.

65. See Patricia K. Zingheim and Jay R. Schuster, "Getting Ahead in the Reward Game," *Strategy and Leadership,* Vol. 29, No. 6, 2001, pp. 34–36.

66. Karl Fischer, Steven E. Gross, and Helen M. Friedman, "Marriott Makes the Business Case for an Innovative Total Rewards Strategy," *Journal of Organizational Excellence,* Spring 2003, pp. 19–24. Harry G. Barkema and Luis R. Gomez-Mejia, "Managerial Compensation and Firm Performance: A General Research Framework," *Academy of Management Journal,* April 1998, pp. 135–145.

67. Amy Borrus and Dean Foust, "A Battle Royal against Regal Paychecks," *BusinessWeek,* February 24, 2003, p. 127, and Paul Gavejian, "Compensation: Today and Tomorrow," *HR Focus,* November 1998, pp. 55–56.

68. Kathryn M. Bartol and Abhishek Srivastava, "Encouraging Knowledge Sharing: The Role of Organizational Reward Systems," *Journal of Leadership and Organization Studies,* Vol. 9, No. 1, 2002, pp. 64–76.

69. Calvin Reynolds (Ed.), *Guide to Global Compensation and Benefits,* Harcourt Professional Publishing, New York, 2001.

70. These techniques are drawn from Patricia K. Zingheim and Jay R. Schuster, "Introduction: How Are the New Pay Tools Being Deployed?" *Compensation and Benefits Review,* July–August 1995, pp. 10–11 and Fred Luthans and Alexander D. Stajkovic, "Reinforce for Performance: The Need to Go beyond Pay and Even Rewards," *Academy of Management Executive,* May 1999, pp. 49–57.

71. For additional insights into the effectiveness of these plans, see Brian Murray and Barry Gerhart, "An Empirical Analysis of a Skill-Based Pay Program and Plant Performance Outcomes," *Academy of Management Journal,* January 1998, pp. 68–78.

72. Susan Haslett, "Broadbanding: A Strategic Tool for Organizational Change," *Compensation and Benefits Review,* November–December 1995, p. 40.

73. Suzanne J. Peterson and Fred Luthans," The Impact of Financial and Nonfinancial Incentives on Business-Unit

Outcomes over Time," *Journal of Applied Psychology,* Vol. 91, No. 1, 2006, pp. 156–165; Alexander D. Stajkovic and Fred Luthans, "The Differential Effects of Incentive Motivators on Work Performance," *Academy of Management Journal,* Vol. 44, No. 3, 2001, pp. 580–590; Alexander Stajkovic and Fred Luthans, "A Meta-Analysis of the Effects of Organizational Behavior Modification on Task Performance, 1975-1995," *Academy of Management Journal,* Vol. 40, 1997, pp. 1122–1149; and Alexander D. Stajkovic and Fred Luthans, "Behavioral Management and Task Performance in Organizations," *Personnel Psychology,* Vol. 56, 2003, pp. 155–194.

74. Quoted in Andrea C. Poe, "Keeping Hotel Workers," *HR Magazine,* February 2003, p. 93.

75. Kerr, op. cit., p. 68.

76. Fred Luthans and Alexander D. Stajkovic, "Provide Recognition for Performance Improvement," in E. Locke (Ed.), *Handbook on Principles of Organizational Behavior,* 2nd ed. Blackwell, Oxford U.K., 2009, pp. 239–253.

77. "Employee Loyalty Hangs on Company Recognition That There Is Life beyond Work," *HR Focus,* August 1999, p. 5.

78. http://www.recognition.org/walker.htm. July 2000.

79. Richard Florida and Jim Goodnight, "Managing for Creativity," *Harvard Business Review,* July–August, 2005, p. 125.

80. "Companies Are Working to Improve Recognition Programs," *The Conference Board,* p. 7, and Paul A. Gilster, "Online Incentives Sizzle—and You Shine," *Workforce,* January 2001, pp. 44–47.

81. Stajkovic and Luthans, op. cit., 1997, 2003.

82. "Morale Maintenance," *Across the Board,* January 2000, p. 79.

83. These examples can be found in Bob Nelson, *1001 Ways to Reward Employees,* Workman Publishing, New York, 1994.

84. Alex C. Pacquariello, "Grant Makers," *Fast Company,* April 2007, p. 32.

85. K. Barron, "Praise and Poodles with That Order," *Forbes,* September 20, 1999, p. 153.

86. Kyle Luthans, "Recognition: A Powerful, but Often Overlooked Leadership Tool to Improve Employee Performance," *Journal of Leadership Studies,* Winter 2000, p. 36.

87. Quoted in Karen E. Klein, "Employee Benefits: Making It Easy," *Business Week,* September 20, 2007, p. 25.

88. Ibid.

89. "Most Employers Offer Health Insurance and Use Cost-Sharing," *HR Focus,* January 2008, p. 12.

90. Howard Gleckman and John Carey, "An Apple a Day—On the Boss," *BusinessWeek,* October 14, 2002, p. 122.

91. "Obesity Is Expensive but Wellness Programs Help," *HR Focus,* July 2008, p. 12.

92. Ibid.

93. Sarah E. Needleman, "Time Off for Good Behavior," *The Wall Street Journal,* December 2, 2008, p. R9.

94. M. P. McQuuen, "Workers Get Health Care at the Office," *The Wall Street Journal,* November 18, 2008, pp. D1–D2.

95. Michelle Conlin, "Glum Chums? Call in the Happiness Police," *BusinessWeek,* August 25, 2008, p. 34.

96. "More Flextime but Lower Paid Health Care Premiums," *HR Focus,* July 2008, p. 12.

97. Alison E. Barber, Randall B. Dunham, and R. A. Formisano, "The Impact of Flexible Benefits on Employee Satisfaction: A Field Study," *Personnel Psychology,* Vol. 45, 1992, pp. 55–57.

98. See Carolyn Hirschman, "Kinder, Simpler Cafeteria Rules," *HR Magazine,* January 2001, pp. 74–79.

99. Also see Melissa W. Barringer and George T. Milkovich, "A Theoretical Exploration of the Adoption and Design of Flexible Benefit Plans: A Case of Human Resource Innovation," *Academy of Management Review,* January 1998, pp. 305–324.

## Chapter 5 Footnote References and Supplemental Readings

1. Alan Feingold, "Gender Differences in Personality: A Meta Analysis," *Psychological Bulletin,* Vol. 116, No. 3, 1994, pp. 429–456.

2. See "What We Learn from Twins: The Mirror of Your Soul," *The Economist,* January 3, 1998, pp. 74–76.

3. Beth Azar, "Nature, Nurture: Not Mutually Exclusive," *APA Monitor,* May 1997, p. 1. Also see "Who Wants to Be a Genius," *The Economist,* January 13, 2001, pp. 77–78.

4. See John Cary, "Gene Tests: Behind the Hype," *BusinessWeek,* November 2, 2008, pp. 68–74.

5. Beth Azar, "Searching for Genes That Explain Our Personalities," *Monitor on Psychology,* Vol. 33, No. 8, 2002, p. 44.

6. Azar, "Nature, Nurture," op. cit., and William T. Dickens and James R. Flynn, "Heritability Estimates versus Large Environmental Effects: The IQ Paradox Resolved," *Psychological Review,* Vol. 108, No. 2, 2001, pp. 346–369. See also W. Andrew Collins, Eleanor E. Maccoby, Laurence Steinberg, E. Mavis Hetherington, and Marc H. Bornstein, "Contempory Research on Parenting: The Case for Nature and Nurture," *American Psychologist,* February 2000, pp. 218–232.

7. Nigel Nicholson, "How Hardwired Is Human Behavior?" *Harvard Business Review,* July–August 1998, p. 135. Also see Barbara Decker Pierce and Roderick White, "The Evolution of Social Structure: Why Biology Matters," *Academy of Management Review,* Vol. 24, No. 4, 1999, pp. 843–853; Elisabeth A. Lloyd, "Evolutionary Psychology: A View from Evolutionary Biology," *Psychological Inquiry,* Vol. 13, No. 2, 2002, pp. 150–156; and Annemie Ploeger, Han L. J. van der Maas, and Maartje Raijmakers, "Is Evolutionary Psychology a Metatheory for Psychology?" *Psychological Inquiry,* Vol. 19, No. 1, 2008, pp. 1–18.

8. "The Story of Man," *The Economist,* December 20, 2005, p. 11.

9. Mark Nichols, "Secrets of the Brain," *McClean's,* January 22, 1996, p. 44. Also see Marcus Buckingham and Donald O. Clifton, *Now, Discover Your Strengths,* The Free Press, New York, 2001, pp. 50–56.

10. M. Greengrass, "Emotion and Cognition Work Together in the Brain," *Monitor on Psychology,* Vol. 33, No. 6, 2002, p. 18, and Dominic T. Cheng, David C. Knight, Christine N. Smith, Elliot A. Stein, and Fred J. Helmstetter, "Functional MRI of Human Amygdala Activity during Pavlovian Fear Conditioning: Stimulus Processing versus Response Expression," *Behavioral Neuroscience,* Vol. 117, No. 1, 2003, pp. 3–10.

11. Curt Coffman and Gabriel Gonzalez-Molina, *Follow This Path,* AOL Time Warner, New York, 2002, pp. 22–23. Also see Joseph LeDoux, *The Emotional Brain,* Simon & Schuster, New York, 1996; Joseph LeDoux, *Synaptic Self,* Viking, New York, 2002; and Barbara L. Frederickson, "Why Positive Emotions Matter in Organizations," *Psychologist-Manager Journal,* Vol. 4, No. 2, 2000, pp. 131–142.

12. Reported in Jane Spencer, "Lessons from the Brain-Damaged Investor," *The Wall Street Journal,* July 21, 2005, pp. D-1, D-2.

13. D. Rock and J. Schwartz, "The Neuroscience of Leadership," *Strategy and Business,* Vol. 43, 2007, pp. 1–10.

14. Suzanne J. Peterson, Pierre A. Balthazard, David A. Waldman, and Robert W. Thatcher, "Neuroscientific Implications of Psychological Capital," *Organizational Dynamics,* Vol. 37, No. 4, 2008, pp. 342–353.

15. For example, see Steven F. Faux, "Cognitive Neuroscience from a Behavioral Perspective: A Critique of Chasing Ghosts with Geiger Counters," *Behavior Analyst,* Vol. 25, No. 2, 2002, pp. 161–173.

16. Murray R. Barrick and Michael K. Mount, "The Big Five Personality Dimensions and Job Performance: A Meta-Analysis," *Personnel Psychology,* Vol. 44, 1991, p. 1; Michael K. Mount and Murray R. Barrick, "Five Reasons Why the 'Big Five' Article Has Been Frequently Cited," *Personnel Psychology,* Vol. 51, 1998, pp. 849–857; and Joyce Hogan and Brent Holland, "Using Theory to Evaluate Personality and Job-Performance Relations: A Socioanalytic Perspective," *Journal of Applied Psychology,* Vol. 88, No. 1, 2003, pp. 100–112.

17. See P. G. Dodgson and J. V. Wood, "Self-Esteem and the Cognitive Accessibility of Strength and Weaknesses after Failure," *Journal of Personality and Social Psychology,* July 1998, pp. 178–197.

18. B. R. Schlenker, M. F. Weigeld, and J. R. Hallam, "Self-Serving Attributions in Social Context: Effects of Self-Esteem and Social Pressure," *Journal of Personality and Social Psychology,* May 1990, pp. 855–863.

19. For example, see R. F. Baumeister, L. Smart, and J. M. Boden, "Relation of Threatened Egotism to Violence and Aggression: The Dark Side of High Self-Esteem," *Psychological Review,* January 1996, pp. 5–33. Also see E. L. Kersten, "The Threat of Threatened Egotism," *The Conference Board Review,* January–February 2009, pp. 70–71.

20. Robert Kreitner and Angelo Kinicki, *Organizational Behavior,* 5th ed., McGraw-Hill, New York, 2001, p. 139. Also see Riël Vermunt, Daan van Knippenberg, Barbara van Knippenberg, and Eric Blaauw, "Self-Esteem and Outcome Fairness: Differential Importance of Procedural and Outcome Considerations," *Journal of Applied Psychology,* Vol. 86, No. 4, 2001, pp. 621–628.

21. J. L. Pierce, D. G. Gardner, L. L. Cummings, and R. B. Dunham, "Organization-Based Self-Esteem: Construct Definition, Measurement, and Validation," *Academy of Management Journal,* September 1989, p. 625.

22. Timothy A. Judge and Joyce E. Bono, "Relationship of Core Self-Evaluation Traits—Self-Esteem, Generalized Self-Efficacy, Locus of Control, and Emotional Stability—With Job Satisfaction and Job Performance: A Meta Analysis," *Journal of Applied Psychology,* Vol. 86, No. 1, 2001, pp. 80–92.

23. K. W. Mossholder, A. G. Bedeian, and A. A. Armenakis, "Role Perceptions, Satisfaction, and Performance: Moderating Effects of Self-Esteem and Organizational Level," *Organizational Behavior and Human Performance,* Vol. 28, 1981, pp. 224–234, and K. W. Mossholder, A. G. Bedeian, and A. A. Armenakis, "Group Process–Work Outcome Relationships: A Note on the Moderating Impact of Self-Esteem," *Academy of Management Journal,* Vol. 25, 1982, pp. 575–585.

24. Jon L. Pierce, Donald G. Gardner, Randall B. Dunham, and Larry L. Cummings, "Moderation by Organization-Based Self-Esteem of Role Condition–Employee Response Relationships," *Academy of Management Journal,* April 1993, pp. 271–288; Daniel C. Ganster and John Schaubroeck, "Work Stress and Employee Health," *Journal of Management,* Vol. 17, 1991, pp. 235–271; and Daniel C. Ganster and John Schaubroeck, "Role Stress and Worker Health: An Extension of the Plasticity Hypothesis of Self-Esteem," *Journal of Social Behavior and Personality,* Vol. 6, 1991, pp. 349–360.

25. Roy J. Blitzer, Colleen Petersen, and Linda Rogers, "How to Build Self-Esteem," *Training and Development,* February 1993, p. 59. However, for some of the measurement issues, see Richard W. Robins, Holly M. Hendin, and Kali H. Trzesniewski, "Measuring Global Self Esteem," *Personality and Social Psychology Bulletin,* Vol. 27, No. 2, 2001, pp. 151–161, and for conceptual issues, see Amir Erez and Timothy A. Judge, "Relationship of Core Self-Evaluations to Goal Setting, Motivation, and Performance," *Journal of Applied Psychology,* Vol. 86, No. 6, 2001, pp. 1270–1279.

26. Nathaniel Branden, *Self-Esteem at Work,* Jossey-Bass, San Francisco, 1998, quoted in Perry Pescarella, "It All Begins with Self-Esteem," *Management Review,* February 1999, p. 60.

27. David DeCremer, Barbara van Knippenberg, Daan van Knippenberg, Danny Mullenders, and Florence Stinglhamber, "Rewarding Leadership and Fair Procedures as Determinants of Self-Esteem," *Journal of Applied Psychology,* Vol. 90, No. 1, 2005, pp. 2–12.

28. Amy L. Kristof, "Person–Organization Fit: An Integrative Review of Its Conceptualizations, Measurement, and Implications," *Personnel Psychology,* Vol. 49, 1996, pp. 1–49.

29. Joseph P. Forgas, "Feeling and Doing: Affective Influences on Interpersonal Behavior," *Psychological Inquiry,* Vol. 13, No. 1, 2002, pp. 1–28.

30. Robert Eisenberger, Stephen Armeli, Barbara Rexwinkel, Patrick D. Lynch, and Linda Rhoades, "Reciprocation of Perceived Organizational Support," *Journal of Applied Psychology,* Vol. 86, No. 1, 2001, pp. 42–51.

31. Cheryl L. Adkins, "Previous Work Experience and Organizational Socialization: A Longitudinal Examination," *Academy of Management Journal,* June 1995, pp. 839–862.

32. Edgar H. Schein, "Organizational Socialization and the Profession of Management," in David Kolb, Irwin Rubin, and James McIntyre (Eds.), *Organizational Psychology: A Book of Readings,* Prentice Hall, Upper Saddle River, N.J., 1971, pp. 14–15.

33. Blake E. Ashforth and Alan M. Saks, "Socialization Tactics: Longitudinal Effects on Newcomer Adjustment," *Academy of Management Journal,* February 1996, pp. 146–178.

34. Ruth Kanfer, Connie R. Wanberg, and Tracy M. Kantrowitz, "Job Search and Employment: A Personality-Motivational Analysis and Meta-Analytic Review," *Journal of Applied Psychology,* Vol. 86, No. 5, 2001, pp. 837–855.

35. Phyllis Tharenou, "Going Up? Do Traits and Informal Social Processes Predict Advancing in Management?" *Academy of Management Journal,* Vol. 44, No. 5, 2001, pp. 1005–1017.

36. Schein, op. cit., p. 3.

37. Daniel C. Feldman and Hugh J. Arnold, *Managing Individual and Group Behavior in Organizations,* McGraw-Hill, New York, 1983, pp. 83–86.

38. Howard J. Klein and Natasha A. Weaver, "The Effectiveness of an Organization Level Orientation Training Program in the Socialization of New Hires," *Personnel Psychology,* Vol. 53, 2000, p. 47.

39. Tae-Yeol Kim, Daniel M. Cable, and Sang-Pyo Kim, "Socialization Tactics, Employee Proactivity, and Person-Organization Fit," *Journal of Applied Psychology,* Vol. 90, No. 2, 2005, pp. 232–241.

40. Clyde Kluckhohn and H. A. Murray, "Personality Formation: The Determinants," in C. Kluckhohn and H. A. Murray (Eds.), *Personality,* Knopf, New York, 1948, p. 35.

41. G. W. Allport and H. S. Odbert, "Trait Names: A Psychological Study," *Psychological Monographs,* Vol. 4, 1936, pp. 211–214.

42. See J. M. Digman, "Personality Structure: Emergence of the Five-Factor Model," *Annual Review of Psychology,* Vol. 41, 1990, pp. 417–440.

43. See Barrick and Mount, op. cit.; Mount and Barrick, op. cit.; R. J. Schneider and L. M. Hough, "Personality and Industrial/Organizational Psychology," *International Review of Industrial and Organizational Psychology,* Vol. 10, 1995, pp. 75–129; M. Zuckerman, D. M. Kuhlman, J. Joireman, P. Teta, and M. Kraft, "A Comparison of Three Structural Models for Personality: The Big Three, The Big Five, and The Alternative Five," *Journal of Personality and Social Psychology,* October 1993, pp. 757–768; and Gregory M. Hurtz and John J. Donovan, "Personality and Job Performance: The Big Five Revisited," *Journal of Applied Psychology,* Vol. 85, No. 6, 2000, pp. 869–879.

44. S. V. Paunonen et al., "The Structure of Personality in Six Cultures," *Journal of Cross-Cultural Psychology,* May 1996, pp. 339–353, and G. Saucier and F. Ostendorf, "Hierarchical Subcomponents of the Big Five Personality Factors: A Cross-Language Replication," *Journal of Personality and Social Psychology,* April 1999, pp. 613–627.

45. See Barrick and Mount, op. cit., and Mount and Barrick, op. cit. Also see J. F. Salgado, "The Five-Factor Model of Personality and Job Performance in the European Community," *Journal of Applied Psychology,* Vol. 82, 1997, pp. 30–45.

46. Timothy A. Judge and Remus Ilies, "Relationship of Personality to Performance Motivation: A Meta-Analytic Review," *Journal of Applied Psychology,* Vol. 87, No. 4, 2000, pp. 797–807.

47. Timothy A. Judge, Daniel Heller, and Michael K. Mount, "Five-Factor Model of Personality and Job Satisfaction: A Meta-Analysis," *Journal of Applied Psychology,* Vol. 87, No. 3, 2002, pp. 530–541.

48. Robert J. House, Scott A. Shane, and David M. Herold, "Rumors of the Death of Dispositional Research Are Vastly Exaggerated," *Academy of Management Review,* January 1996, p. 203.

49. Robert R. McCrae and Paul T. Costa, Jr., "The Stability of Personality: Observations and Evaluations," *Current Directions in Psychological Science,* December 1994, p. 173. Also see Martin P. Seligman, *What You Can Change . . . And What You Can't,* Fawcett Columbine, New York, 1993.

50. Marcus Buckingham and Curt Coffman, *First, Break All The Rules,* Simon and Schuster, New York, 1999, pp. 177–214, and S. B. Gustafson and M. D. Mumford, "Personal Style and Person-Environment Fit: A Pattern Approach," *Journal of Vocational Behavior,* April 1995, pp. 163–188.

51. Mount and Barrick, op. cit., p. 851.

52. T. A. Judge, J. J. Martocchio, and C. J. Thoresen, "Five-Factor Model of Personality and Employee Absence," *Journal of Applied Psychology,* Vol. 82, 1998, pp. 745–755.

53. Paula M. Caligiuri, "The Big Five Personality Characteristics as Predictors of Expatriate's Desire to Terminate the Assignment and Supervisor-Rated Performance," *Personnel Psychology,* Vol. 53, 2000, p. 67.

54. Ivan T. Robertson, Helen Baron, Patrick Gibbons, Rab MacIver, and Gill Nyfield, "Conscientiousness and Managerial Performance," *Journal of Occupational Psychology,* Vol. 73, 2000, pp. 171–180, and Maxine Dalton and Meena Wilson, "The Relationship of the Five-Factor Model of Personality to Job Performance for a Group of Middle Eastern Expatriate Managers," *Journal of Cross Cultural Psychology,* Vol. 31, No. 2, 2000, pp. 250–258.

55. Michael K. Mount, Murray R. Barrick, and J. Perkins Strauss, "The Joint Relationship of Conscientiousness and Ability with Performance: Test of the Interaction Hypothesis," *Journal of Management,* Vol. 25, No. 5, 1999, pp. 707–721.

56. Michael K. Mount, Amy E. Colbert, James K. Harter, and Murray R. Barrick, "Does Job Satisfaction Moderate the Relationship between Conscientiousness and Job Performance?" Paper presented at Academy of Management Annual Meeting, Toronto, Canada, August 2000.

57. H. John Bernardin, Donna K. Cooke, and Peter Villanova, "Conscientiousness and Agreeableness as Predictors of Rating Leniency," *Journal of Applied Psychology,* Vol. 85, No. 2, 2000, pp. 232–234.

58. L. A. Witt, "The Interactive Effects of Extraversion and Conscientiousness on Performance," *Journal of Management,* Vol. 28, No. 6, 2002, pp. 835–851.

59. L. A. Witt, Lisa A. Burke, Murray R. Barrick, and Michael K. Mount, "The Interactive Effects of Conscientiousness and Agreeableness on Job Performance," *Journal of Applied Psychology,* Vol. 87, No. 1, 2002, pp. 164–169.

60. Jennifer M. George and Jing Zhou, "When Openness to Experience and Conscientiousness Are Related to Creative Behavior: An Interactional Approach," *Journal of Applied Psychology,* Vol. 86, No. 3, 2001, pp. 513–524.

61. Murray R. Barrick, Greg L. Stewart, and Mike Piotrowski, "Personality and Job Performance: Test of the Mediating Effects of Motivation among Sales Representatives," *Journal of Applied Psychology,* Vol. 87, No. 1, 2002, pp. 43–51;

Bennett J. Tepper, Michelle K. Duffy, and Jason D. Shaw, "Personality Moderators of the Relationship between Abusive Supervision and Subordinates' Resistance," *Journal of Applied Psychology,* Vol. 86, No. 5, 2001, pp. 974–983; and Henry Moon, "The Two Faces of Conscientiousness: Duty and Achievement Striving in Escalation of Commitment Dilemmas," *Journal of Applied Psychology,* Vol. 86, No. 3, 2001, pp. 533–540.

62. Salgado, op. cit.

63. Judge, Martocchio, and Thoresen, op. cit.

64. See Salgado, op. cit., Barrick and Mount, op. cit., and Mount and Barrick, op. cit. For the decision-making simulation study showing the positive relationship with openness, see Jeffrey A. Lepine, Jason A. Colquitt, and Amir Erez, "Adaptability to Changing Task Contexts: Effects of General Cognitive Ability, Conscientiousness, and Openness to Experience," *Personnel Psychology,* Vol. 53, 2000, pp. 563–593.

65. Kenneth H. Craik, Aaron P. Ware, John Kamp, Charles O'Reilly III, Barry Staw, and Sheldon Zedeck, "Explorations of Construct Validity in a Combined Managerial and Personality Assessment Programme," *Journal of Occupational and Organizational Psychology,* Vol. 75, 2002, pp. 171–193.

66. M. R. Barrick, G. L. Stewart, M. J. Neubert, and M. K. Mount, "Relating Member Ability and Personality to Work-Team Processes and Team Effectiveness," *Journal of Applied Psychology,* Vol. 83, 1998, pp. 377–391.

67. For example, see W. L. Gardner and M. J. Martinko, "Using the Myers-Briggs Type Indicator to Study Managers: A Literature Review and Research Agenda," *Journal of Management,* Vol. 22, 1996, pp. 45–83, and R. Zemke, "Second Thoughts about the MBTI," *Training,* April 1992, pp. 42–47.

68. See Debra L. Nelson and James Campbell Quick, *Organizational Behavior,* 3rd ed., South-Western, Cincinnati, Ohio, 2000, pp. 88–92, for an extensive treatment of the MBTI. The discussion and Table 7.2 is adapted from this source.

69. See J. B. Murray, "Review of Research on the Myers-Briggs Type Indicator," *Perceptual and Motor Skills,* Vol. 70, 1990, pp. 1187–1202, and J. G. Carlson, "Recent Assessment of the Myers-Briggs Type Indicator," *Journal of Personality Assessment,* Vol. 49, 1985, pp. 356–365.

70. Gardner and Martinko, op. cit., and Zemke, op. cit.

71. Nelson and Quick, op. cit., p. 92.

72. Marcus Buckingham and Curt Coffman, *First Break All The Rules,* Simon and Schuster, New York, 1999, pp. 76, 78.

73. For example, see Joseph Weber, "Please Don't Promote Me," *BusinessWeek,* May 14, 2007, p. 13 and Kerry Sulkawicz, "Stressed for Success," *BusinessWeek,* May 21, 2007, p. 18.

74. The quote is found in Shannon Brownlee with Traci Watson, "The Senses," *U.S. News and World Report,* January 13, 1997, p. 52.

75. James M. Carroll and James A. Russell, "Do Facial Expressions Signal Specific Emotions? Judging Emotion from the Face in Context," *Journal of Personality and Social Psychology,* Vol. 70, No. 2, 1996, pp. 205–218.

76. Min-Sun Kim and John E. Hunter, "Attitude-Behavior Relations: A Meta-Analysis of Attitudinal Relevance and Topic," *Journal of Communication,* Winter 1993, pp. 101–142, and Min-Sun Kim and John E. Hunter, "Relationships among Attitudes, Behavioral Intentions, and Behavior," *Communication Research,* June 1993, pp. 331–364.

77. Sheldon S. Zalkind and Timothy W. Costello, "Perception: Some Recent Research and Implications for Administration," *Administrative Science Quarterly,* September 1962, pp. 227–229.

78. Fred Luthans and Bruce Avolio, "Authentic Leadership Development," in Kim Cameron, Jane Dutton, and Robert Quinn (Eds.), *Positive Organizational Scholarship,* Berrett Koehler, San Francisco, 2003, pp. 241–258.

79. Zalkind and Costello, op. cit., p. 230.

80. James O'Toole, "Hump? What Hump?" *Across the Board,* October 1999, p. 8.

81. See Claude M. Steele, "A Threat in the Air: How Stereotypes Shape Intellectual Identity and Performance," *American Psychologist,* June 1997, p. 617.

82. For example, see Linda A. Jackson, Linda A. Sullivan, and Carole N. Hodge, "Stereotype Effects on Attributions, Predictions, and Evaluations: No Two Social Judgments Are Quite Alike," *Journal of Personality and Social Psychology,* July 1993, pp. 69–84.

83. Angelo S. DeNisi and Ricky W. Griffin, *Human Resource Management,* Houghton Mifflin, Boston, 2001, p. 251.

84. J. John Bernardin and Peter Villanova, "Performance Appraisal," in Edwin A. Locke (Ed.), *Generalizing from Laboratory to Field Settings,* Lexington (Heath), Lexington, Mass., 1986, pp. 45, 53; and Alex C. Pacquariello, "Grant Makers," *Fast Company,* April 2007, p. 32.

85. Kevin R. Murphy, Robert A. Jako, and Rebecca L. Anhalt, "Nature and Consequences of Halo Error: A Critical Analysis," *Journal of Applied Psychology,* April 1993, p. 218.

86. Ibid., pp. 218–225.

87. Rick Jacobs and Steve W. J. Kozlowski, "A Closer Look at Halo Error in Performance Ratings," *Academy of Management Journal,* March 1985, pp. 201–212; and quoted in Karen E. Klein, "Employee Benefits: Making It Easy," *BusinessWeek,* September 20, 2007, p. 25.

88. Jennifer M. George, "Personality, Affect, and Behavior in Groups," *Journal of Applied Psychology,* Vol. 75, No. 2, 1990, p. 108.

89. Larry J. Williams, Mark B. Gavin, and Margaret L. Williams, "Measurement and Nonmeasurement Processes with Negative Affectivity and Employee Attitudes," *Journal of Applied Psychology,* Vol. 81, No. 1, 1996, pp. 88–101 and Thomas Begley and Cynthia Lee, "The Role of Negative Affectivity in Pay-at-Risk Reactions: A Longitudinal Study," *Journal of Applied Psychology,* Vol. 90, No. 2, 2005, pp. 382–388.

90. Karl Aquino, Steven L. Grover, Murray Bradfield, and David G. Allen, "The Effects of Negative Affectivity, Hierarchical Status, and Self-Determination on Workplace Victimization," *Academy of Management Journal,* Vol. 42, No. 3, 1999, pp. 260–272.

91. Simon S. K. Lam, Michelle S. M. Yik, and John Schaubroeck, "Responses to Formal Performance Appraisal Feedback: The Role of Negative Affectivity," *Journal of Applied Psychology,* Vol. 87, No. 1, 2002, pp. 192–201.

92. James A. Russell and James M. Carroll, "On the Bipolarity of Positive and Negative Affect," *Psychological Bulletin,* Vol. 125, No. 1, 1999, pp. 3–30.

93. B. M. Staw and S. G. Barsade, "Affect and Managerial Performance: A Test of the Sadder-but-Wiser vs. Happier-and-Smarter Hypotheses," *Administrative Science Quarterly,* Vol. 38, 1993, pp. 304–331.

94. J. M. George, "Mood and Absence," *Journal of Applied Psychology,* Vol. 74, 1989, pp. 287–324.

95. Jason D. Shaw, Michelle K. Duffy, G. Douglas Jenkins, Jr., and Nina Gupta, "Positive and Negative Affect, Signal Sensitivity, and Pay Satisfaction," *Journal of Management,* Vol. 25, No. 2, 1999, pp. 189–206, and Howard M. Weiss, Jeffrey P. Nicholas, and Catherine S. Daus, "An Examination of the Joint Effects of Affective Experiences and Job Beliefs on Job Satisfaction and Variations in Affective Experiences over Time," *Organizational Behavior and Human Decision Processes,* Vol. 78, No. 1, April 1999, pp. 1–24.

96. M. J. Burke, A. P. Brief, and J. M. George, "The Role of Negative Affectivity in Understanding Relations between Self-Reports of Stressors and Strains," *Journal of Applied Psychology,* Vol. 78, 1993, pp. 402–412.

97. J. M. George, "Personality, Affect, and Behavior in Groups," *Journal of Applied Psychology,* Vol. 75, 1990, pp. 107–116.

98. Brooks C. Holtom, Thomas W. Lee, and Simon T. Tidd, "The Relationship between Work Status Congruence and Work-Related Attitudes and Behaviors," *Journal of Applied Psychology,* Vol. 87, No. 5, 2002, pp. 903–915.

99. Nilly Mor and Jennifer Winquist, "Self-Focused Attention and Negative Affect: A Meta-Analysis," *Psychological Bulletin,* Vol. 128, No. 4, 2002, pp. 638–662.

100. Mark A. Griffin, "Dispositions and Work Reactions: A Multilevel Approach," *Journal of Applied Psychology,* Vol. 86, No. 6, 2001, pp. 1142–1151.

101. E. A. Locke, "The Nature and Cause of Job Satisfaction," in M. D. Dunnette (Ed.), *Handbook of Industrial and Organizational Psychology,* Rand McNally, Chicago, 1976, p. 1300.

102. Andrè Bussing, Thomas Bissls, Vera Fuchs, and Klaus M. Perrar, "A Dynamic Model of Work Satisfaction: Qualitative Approaches," *Human Relations,* Vol. 52, No. 8, 1999, p. 999.

103. P. C. Smith, L. M. Kendall, and C. L. Hulin, *The Measurement of Satisfaction in Work and Retirement,* Rand McNally, Chicago, 1969.

104. Angelo J. Kinicki, Chester A. Schriesheim, Frances M. McKee-Ryan, and Kenneth P. Carson, "Assessing the Construct Validity of the Job Descriptive Index: A Review and Meta-Analysis," *Journal of Applied Psychology,* Vol. 87, No. 1, 2002, pp. 14–32.

105. Mary Ann M. Fricko and Terry A. Beehr, "A Longitudinal Investigation of Interest Congruence and Gender Concentration as Predictors of Job Satisfaction," *Personnel Psychology,* September 1992, pp. 99–118.

106. Timothy A. Judge, Joyce E. Bono, and Edwin A. Locke, "Personality and Job Satisfaction: The Mediating Role of Job Characteristics," *Journal of Applied Psychology,* Vol. 85, No. 2, 2000, pp. 237–249.

107. Christina E. Shalley, Lucy L. Gilson, and Terry C. Blum, "Matching Creativity Requirements and the Work Environment: Effects on Satisfaction and Intentions to Leave," *Academy of Management Journal,* Vol. 43, No. 2, 2000, pp. 215–223.

108. "IT Workers Expect Career Development and Job Satisfaction," *HR Focus,* August 1999, p. 4.

109. David Guest, "Human Resource Management, Corporate Performance and Employee Wellbeing: Building the Worker into HRM," *The Journal of Industrial Relations,* Vol. 44, No. 3, 2002, pp. 335–358.

110. Elaine Leuchars, Shauna Harrington, and Carrie Erickson, "Putting People First: How VSP Achieves High Employee Satisfaction Year after Year," *Journal of Organizational Excellence,* Spring 2003, pp. 33–41.

111. Shawn M. Carraher and M. Ronald Buckley, "Cognitive Complexity and the Perceived Dimensionality of Pay Satisfaction," *Journal of Applied Psychology,* Vol. 81, No. 1, 1996, pp. 102–109, and A. Furnham and M. Argyle, *The Psychology of Money,* Routledge, London, 1998.

112. See Timothy A. Judge, "Validity of the Dimensions of the Pay Satisfaction Questionnaire: Evidence of Differential Prediction," *Personnel Psychology,* Summer 1993, pp. 331–355, and Terence R. Mitchell and Amy E. Mickel, "The Meaning of Money: An Individual Difference Perspective," *Academy of Management Review,* July 1999, pp. 568–578.

113. Brenda Major and Ellen Konar, "An Investigation of Sex Differences in Pay Expectations and Their Possible Causes," *Academy of Management Journal,* December 1984, pp. 777–792.

114. Alison E. Barber, Randall B. Dunham, and Roger A. Formisano, "The Impact of Flexible Benefits on Employee Satisfaction: A Field Study," *Personnel Psychology,* September 1992, pp. 55–76.

115. "Executives Heed Employee Priorities," *HR Focus,* August 1999, p. 4.

116. See Marcus Buckingham and Curt Coffman, *First, Break All the Rules,* Simon and Schuster, New York, 1999, p. 264.

117. Katharine I. Miller and Peter R. Monge, "Participation, Satisfaction, and Productivity: A Meta-Analytic Review," *Academy of Management Journal,* December 1986, p. 748.

118. Gerben S. Van der Vegt, Ben J. M. Emans, and Evert Vande Vliert, "Patterns of Interdependence in Work Teams: A Two-Level Investigation of the Relations with Job and Team Satisfaction," *Personnel Psychology,* Vol. 54, 2001, pp. 51–69.

119. Bradley L. Kirkman and Debra L. Shapiro, "The Impact of Cultural Values on Job Satisfaction and Organizational Commitment in Self-Managing Work Teams: The Mediating Role of Employee Resistance," *Academy of Management Journal,* Vol. 44, No. 3, 2001, pp. 557–569.

120. M. Tait, M.Y. Padgett, and T. T. Baldwin, "Job and Life Satisfaction: A Reevaluation of the Strength of the Relationship and Gender Effects as a Function of the Date of the Study," *Journal of Applied Psychology,* June 1989, pp. 502–507.

121. T. A. Judge and S. Watanabe, "Another Look at the Job Satisfaction-Life Satisfaction Relationship," *Journal of Applied Psychology,* Vol. 78, 1993, pp. 939–948.

122. M. T. Iffaldano and P. M. Muchinsky, "Job Satisfaction and Job Performance: A Meta-Analysis," *Psychological Bulletin,* Vol. 97, 1985, pp. 251–273.

123. For example, see T. A. Judge, K. A. Hanisch, and R. D. Drankoski, "Human Resources Management and Employee

Attitudes," in G. R. Ferris, S. D. Rosen, and D. T. Barnum (Eds.), *Handbook of Human Resources Management*, Blackwell Publishers, Oxford, England, 1995; C. L. Hulin, "Adaptation, Persistence, and Commitment in Organizations," in M. D. Dunnette and L. M. Hough (Eds.), *Handbook of Industrial and Organizational Psychology*, 2nd ed., Vol. 2, Consulting Psychologist Press, Palo Alto, Calif.; and M. M. Petty, G. W. McGee, and J. W. Cavender; "A Meta-Analysis of the Relationships between Individual Job Satisfaction and Individual Performance," *Academy of Management Review*, Vol. 9, 1984, pp. 712–721.

124. Timothy A. Judge, Carl J. Thoresen, Joyce E. Bono, and Gregory K. Patton, "The Job Satisfaction–Job Performance Relationship: A Qualitative and Quantitative Review," *Psychological Bulletin*, Vol. 127, No. 3, 2001, pp. 376–407.

125. Alexander D. Stajkovic and Fred Luthans, "Self-Efficacy and Work-Related Performance: A Meta-Analysis," *Psychological Bulletin*, Vol. 124, No. 2, 1998, pp. 240–261.

126. Daniel J. Koys, "The Effects of Employee Satisfaction, Organizational Citizenship Behavior, and Turnover on Organizational Effectiveness: A Unit-Level, Longitudinal Study," *Personnel Psychology*, Vol. 54, 2001, pp. 101–114. Also see Michael Riketta, "The Causal Relation Between Job Attitudes and Performance: A Meta-Analysis of Panel Studies," *Journal of Applied Psychology*, Vol. 93, No. 2, 2008, pp. 472–481.

127. P. M. Podsakoff and L. J. Williams, "The Relationship between Job Performance and Job Satisfaction," in E. A. Locke (Ed.), *Generalizing from Laboratory to Field Settings*, Lexington Books, Lexington, Mass., 1986.

128. Dennis J. Adsit, Manuel London, Steven Crom, and Dana Jones, "Relationships between Employee Attitudes, Customer Satisfaction and Departmental Performance," *Journal of Management Development*, Vol. 15, No. 1, 1996, pp. 62–75.

129. Cheri Ostroff, "The Relationship between Satisfaction, Attitudes, and Performance: An Organizational Level Analysis," *Journal of Applied Psychology*, December 1992, pp. 963–974.

130. James K. Harter, Frank L. Schmidt, and Theodore L. Hayes, "Business-Unit-Level Relationship between Employee Satisfaction, Employee Engagement, and Business Outcomes: A Meta-Analysis," *Journal of Applied Psychology*, Vol. 87, No. 2, 2002, pp. 268–279.

131. For an example of a study that verifies the relationship between satisfaction and turnover, see Thomas W. Lee and Richard T. Mowday, "Voluntarily Leaving an Organization: An Empirical Investigation of Steers and Mowday's Model of Turnover," *Academy of Management Journal*, December 1987, pp. 721–743. Also see Robert P. Tett and John P. Meyer, "Job Satisfaction, Organizational Commitment, Turnover Intention, and Turnover: Path Analyses Based on Meta-Analytic Findings," *Personnel Psychology*, Summer 1993, pp. 259–294; P. W. Hom and R. W. Griffith, *Employee Turnover*, South-Western, Cincinnati, 1995, pp. 35–50; and John D. Kammeyer-Mueller, Connie R. Wanberg, Theresa M. Glomb, and Dennis Ahlburg, "The Role of Temporal Shifts in Turnover Processes: It's About Time," *Journal of Applied Psychology*, Vol. 90, No. 4, 2005, pp. 644–658.

132. Peter W. Hom and Angelo J. Kinicki, "Toward a Greater Understanding of How Dissatisfaction Drives Employee Turnover," *Academy of Management Journal*, Vol. 44, No. 5, 2001, pp. 975–987; and Kammeyer-Mueller, et al., op. cit., 2005. Also see Barry Gerhart, Ingo Weller, and Charlie Trevor, "Understanding Voluntary Turnover: Path Specific Job Satisfaction Effects and the Importance of Unsolicited Job Offers," *Academy of Management Journal*, Vol. 51, No. 4, 2008, pp. 651–671.

133. R. D. Hackett, "Work Attitudes and Employee Absenteeism: A Synthesis of the Literature," *Journal of Occupational Psychology*, 1989, pp. 235–248.

134. C. W. Clegg, "Psychology of Employee Lateness, Absenteeism, and Turnover: A Methodological Critique and an Empirical Study," *Journal of Applied Psychology*, February 1983, pp. 88–101. Also see John P. Hausknecht, Nathan J. Hiller, and Robert J. Vance, "Work-Unit Absenteeism: Effects of Satisfaction, Commitment, Labor Market Conditions, and Time," *Academy of Management Journal*, Vol. 51, No. 6, pp. 1223–1245.

135. M. A. Blegen, "Nurses' Job Satisfaction: A Meta-Analysis of Related Variables," *Nursing Research*, January–February 1993, pp. 36–41.

136. These guidelines are structured and drawn from Jerald Greenberg and Robert A. Baron, *Behavior in Organizations*, 7th ed., Prentice Hall, Upper Saddle River, N.J., 2000, pp. 179–180.

137. Kevin Freiberg and Jackie Freiberg, *Nuts*, Bord Press, Austin, Tex., 1996, p. 151.

138. "Employee Job Satisfaction: The Latest Ratings," *HR Focus*, August 2008, p. 3.

139. Edwin A. Locke and Gary P. Latham, *A Theory of Goal Setting and Task Performance*, Prentice Hall, Upper Saddle River, N.J., 1990, pp. 249–250, and R. P. Tett and J. P. Meyer, "Job Satisfaction, Organizational Commitment, Turnover Intention, and Turnover: Path Analysis Based on Meta-Analytic Findings," *Personnel Psychology*, Summer 1993, pp. 259–293.

140. K. Carson, P. Carson, C. Roe, B. Birkenmeier, and J. Philips, "Four Commitment Profiles and Their Relationships to Empowerment, Service Recovery and Work Attitudes," *Public Personnel Management*, Vol. 28, No. 1, 1999, pp. 1–13.

141. ADL Associates, *Commitment: If You Build It . . . Results Will Come*, ADL Associates, Lewisville, Tex., 1998, p.6. Also see Adam Grant, "Giving Commitment: Employee Support Programs and the Prosocial Sensemaking Process," *Academy of Management Journal*, Vol. 51, No. 5, 2008, pp. 898–918.

142. See Thomas E. Becker, Donna M. Randall, and Carl D. Riegel, "The Multidimensional View of Commitment and the Theory of Reasoned Action: A Comparative Evaluation," *Journal of Management*, Vol. 21, No. 4, 1995, pp. 617–638.

143. R. T. Mowday, L. W. Porter, and R. M. Steers, *Employee–Organization Linkages*, Academic Press, New York, 1982.

144. For example, see Fred Luthans, Donald Baack, and Lew Taylor, "Organizational Commitment: Analysis of Antecedents," *Human Relations*, Vol. 40, No. 4, 1987, pp. 219–236; Joan E. Finegan, "The Impact of Person and Organizational Values on Organizational Commitment," *Journal of Occupational and Organizational Psychology*, Vol. 73, 2000, pp. 149–169;

Linda Rhodes, Robert Eisenberger, and Stephen Armeli, "Affective Commitment to the Organization: The Contribution of Perceived Organizational Support," *Journal of Applied Psychology,* Vol. 86, No. 5, 2001, pp. 825–836; Jack K. Ito and Celeste M. Brotheridge, "Does Supporting Employees' Career Adaptability Lead to Commitment, Turnover, or Both?" *Human Resource Management,* Vol. 44, No. 1, Spring 2005, pp. 5–19; Phyllis A. Siegel, Corinne Post, Joel Brockner, Ariel Y. Fishman, and Charlee Garden, "The Moderating Influence of Procedural Fairness on the Relationship between Work-Life Conflict and Organizational Commitment," *Journal of Applied Psychology,* Vol. 90, No. 1, 2005, pp. 13–24. "Hired, with Hard Feelings," *BusinessWeek,* November 10, 2008, p. 15.

145. Gregory B. Northcraft and Margaret A. Neale, *Organizational Behavior,* Dryden, Chicago, 1990, p. 472.

146. Eunmi Chang, "Career Commitment as a Complex Moderator of Organizational Commitment and Turnover Intention," *Human Relations,* Vol. 52, No. 10, 1999, p. 1257.

147. J. P. Meyer and N. J. Allen, "A Three-Component Conceptualization of Organizational Commitment," *Human Resource Management Review,* Vol. 1, 1991, pp. 61–89.

148. For some tests of the Meyer and Allen model, see Rich D. Hackett, Peter Bycio, and Peter Hausdoft, "Further Assessments of a Three-Component Model of Organizational Commitment," *Academy of Management Best Papers Proceedings,* 1992, pp. 212–216; Mark John Somers, "A Test of the Relationship between Affective and Continuance Commitment Using Non-Recursive Models," *Journal of Occupational and Organizational Psychology,* June 1993, pp. 185–192; and N. J. Allen and J. P. Meyer, "Affective Continuance and Normative Commitment to the Organization: An Examination of Construct Validity," *Journal of Vocational Behavior,* Vol. 49, 1996, pp. 252–276.

149. See Ed Snape and Tom Redman, "An Evaluation of a Three-Component Model of Occupational Commitment: Dimensionality and Consequences among United Kingdom Human Resource Management Specialists," *Journal of Applied Psychology,* Vol. 88, No. 1, 2003, pp. 152–159; J. Ko, J. L. Price, and C. W. Mueller, "Assessment of Meyer and Allen's Three Component Model of Organizational Commitment in South Korea," *Journal of Applied Psychology,* Vol. 82, 1997, pp. 961–973; and Abubakr M. Sulimand and Paul A. Iles, "The Multi-Dimensional Nature of Organisational Commitment in a Non-Western Context," *Journal of Management Development,* Vol. 19, No. 1, 2000, pp. 71–82.

150. R. T. Mowday, R. M. Steers, and L. W. Porter, "The Measurement of Organizational Commitment," *Journal of Vocational Behavior,* Vol. 14, 1979, pp. 224–247.

151. J. E. Mathieu and D. M. Zajac, "A Review and Meta-Analysis of the Antecedents, Correlates, and Consequences of Organizational Commitment," *Psychological Bulletin,* Vol. 108, 1990, pp. 171–199; J. P. Meyer and J. J. Allen, *Commitment in the Workplace: Theory, Research and Application,* Sage, Thousand Oaks, Calif., 1997; B. Benkhoff, "Ignoring Commitment Is Costly: New Approaches Establish the Missing Link between Commitment and Performance," *Human Relations,* Vol. 50, No. 6, 1997, pp. 701–726; M. J. Somers, "Organizational Commitment, Turnover and Absenteeism: An Examination of Direct and Interaction Effects," *Journal of Organizational*

*Behavior,* Vol. 16, 1995, pp. 49–58; and L. Lum, J. Kervin, K. Clark, F. Ried, and W. Sirola, "Explaining Nursing Turnover Intent: Job Satisfaction, Pay Satisfaction, or Organizational Commitment?" *Journal of Organizational Behavior,* Vol. 19, 1998, pp. 305–320.

152. Fred Luthans, La Vonne K. Wahl, and Carol S. Steinhaus, "The Importance of Social Support for Employee Commitment," *Organizational Development Journal,* Winter 1992, pp. 1–10.

153. See J. W. Bishop and K. D. Scott, "How Commitment Affects Team Performances," *HR Magazine,* February 1997, pp. 107–111.

154. For example, see Donna M. Randall, Donald B. Fedor, and Clinton O. Longenecker, "The Behavioral Expression of Organizational Commitment," *Journal of Vocational Behavior,* Vol. 36, 1990, pp. 210–224.

155. Joan F. Brett, William L. Cron, and John W. Slocum, Jr., "Economic Dependency on Work: A Moderator of the Relationship between Organizational Commitment and Performance," *Academy of Management Journal,* Vol. 38, No. 1, 1995, pp. 261–271.

156. Thomas A. Wright and Douglas G. Bonett, "The Moderating Effects of Employee Tenure on the Relation between Organizational Commitment and Job Performance: A Meta-Analysis," *Journal of Applied Psychology,* Vol. 87, No. 6, 2002, pp. 1183–1190.

157. Thomas E. Becker, Robert S. Billings, Daniel M. Eveleth, and Nicole L. Gilbert, "Foci and Bases of Employee Commitment: Implications for Job Performance," *Academy of Management Journal,* April 1996, pp. 464–482.

158. See Russell Cropanzano, Deborah E. Rupp, and Zinta S. Byrne, "The Relationship of Emotional Exhaustion to Work Attitudes, Job Performance, and Organizational Citizenship Behaviors," *Journal of Applied Psychology,* Vol. 88, No. 1, 2003, pp. 160–169; Larry W. Hunter and Sherry M. B. Thatcher, "Feeling the Heat: Effects of Stress, Commitment, and Job Experience on Job Performance," *Academy of Management Journal,* Vol. 50, No. 4, pp. 953–968.

159. Lynn McMarlane Shore, George C. Thornton, and Lucy A. Newton, "Job Satisfaction and Organizational Commitment as Predictors of Behavioral Intentions and Employee Behavior," *Academy of Management Proceedings,* 1989, pp. 229–333, and Locke and Latham, op. cit., p. 250.

160. Gary Dessler, "How to Earn Your Employees' Commitment," *Academy of Management Executive,* Vol. 13, No. 2, 1999, p. 65. Also see Quinn Price, "Failure to Commit," *HR Magazine,* November 2002, pp. 99–104.

161. Dessler, op. cit., p. 66.

162. D. W. Organ, *Organizational Citizenship Behavior: The Good Soldier Syndrome,* Lexington Books, Lexington, Mass., 1988, p. 4.

163. Sheila M. Rioux and Louis A. Penner, "The Causes of Organizational Citizenship Behavior: A Motivational Analysis," *Journal of Applied Psychology,* Vol. 86, No. 6, 2001, pp. 1306–1314 and John P. Meyer, Thomas E. Becker, and Christian Vandenberghe, "Employee Commitment and Motivation: A Conceptual Analysis and Integrative Model," *Journal of Applied Psychology,* Vol. 89, No. 6, 2004, pp. 991–1007.

164. D. W. Organ and K. Ryan, "A Meta-Analytic Review of Attitudinal and Dispositional Predictors of Organizational

Citizenship Behavior," *Personnel Psychology,* Winter 1995, pp. 775–802.

165. See C. O. Reilly and J. Chatman, "Organizational Commitment and Psychological Attachment: The Affective Compliance, Identification, and Internalization on Pro-Social Behavior," *Journal of Applied Psychology,* Vol. 71, 1986, p. 493, and Randall, Fedor, and Longenecker, op. cit.

166. For reviews of this literature, see L. VanDyne, L. L. Cummings, and J. McLean Parks, "Extra-Role Behaviors: In Pursuit of Construct and Definitional Clarity," in L. L. Cummings and B. M. Staw (Eds.), *Research in Organizational Behavior,* Vol. 17, JAI Press, Greenwich, Conn., 1995; Maureen L. Ambrose and Carol T. Kulick, "Old Friends, New Faces: Motivation Research in the 1990's," *Journal of Management,* Vol. 25, No. 3, 1999, p. 245; and Bennett J. Tepper and Edward C. Taylor, "Relationships among Supervisors' and Subordinates' Procedural Justice Perceptions and Organizational Citizenship Behaviors," *Academy of Management Journal,* Vol. 46, No. 1, 2003, pp. 97–105.

167. Robert H. Moorman, Gerald L. Blakely, and Brian P. Niehoff, "Does Perceived Organizational Support Mediate the Relationship between Procedural Justice and Organizational Citizenship Behavior?" *Academy of Management Journal,* Vol. 41, No. 3, 1998, pp. 351–357.

168. D. W. Organ, "Organizational Citizenship Behavior: It's Construct Clean-Up Time," *Human Performance,* Vol. 10, 1997, pp. 85–98.

169. See E. W. Morrison, "Role Definition and Organizational Citizenship Behavior: The Importance of Employee's Perspective," *Academy of Management Journal,* Vol. 37, 1994, pp. 1543–1567 and summarized by Greenberg and Baron, op. cit., pp. 372–373. Also see Jeffrey A. LePine, Amir Erex, and Diane E. Johnson, "The Nature and Dimensionality of Organizational Citizenship Behavior: A Critical Review and Meta-Analysis," *Journal of Applied Psychology,* Vol. 87, No. 1, 2002, pp. 52–65.

170. Gerald L. Blakely, Abhishek Srivastava, and Robert H. Moorman, "The Effects of Nationality, Work Role Centrality, and Work Locus of Control on Role Definitions of OCB," *Journal of Leadership and Organizational Studies,* Vol. 12, No. 1, 2005, pp. 103–117.

171. Theresa M. Glomb and Elizabeth T. Welsh, "Can Opposites Attract? Personality Heterogeneity in Supervisor-Subordinate Dyads as a Predictor of Subordinate Outcomes," *Journal of Applied Psychology,* Vol. 90, No. 4, 2005, pp. 749–757.

172. Lance A. Bettencourt, Kevin P. Gwinner, and Matthew L. Meuter, "A Comparison of Attitude, Personality, and Knowledge Predictors of Service-Oriented Organizational Citizenship Behaviors," *Journal of Applied Psychology,* Vol. 86, No. 1, 2001, pp. 29–41.

173. Randall P. Settoon and Kevin W. Mossholder, "Relationship Quality and Relationship Context as Antecedents of Person- and Task-Focused Interpersonal Citizenship Behavior," *Journal of Applied Psychology,* Vol. 87, No. 2, 2002, pp. 255–267.

174. T. D. Allen and M. C. Rush, "The Effects of Organizational Citizenship Behavior on Performance Judgments: A Field Study and a Laboratory Experiment," *Journal of Applied Psychology,* Vol. 83, 1998, pp. 247–260.

175. See P. M. Podsakoff and S. B. MacKenzie, "Organizational Citizenship Behaviors and Sales Unit Effectiveness," *Journal of Marketing Research,* Vol. 31, No. 3, 1994, pp. 351–363; Sandra M. Walz and Brian P. Niehoff, "Organizational Citizenship Behaviors and Their Effect on Organizational Effectiveness in Limited-Menu Restaurants," *Academy of Management Best Paper Proceedings,* 1996, pp. 307–311; P. M. Podsakoff, M. Ahearne, and S. B. MacKenzie, "Organizational Citizenship Behavior and the Quantity and Quality of Work Group Performance," *Journal of Applied Psychology,* April 1997, pp. 262–270; and Linn Van Dyne and Jeffrey A. LePine, "Helping and Voice Extra-Role Behaviors: Evidence of Construct and Predictive Validity," *Academy of Management Journal,* Vol. 41, No. 1, 1998, pp. 108–119.

176. See Mark C. Bolino, "Citizenship and Impression Management: Good Soldiers or Good Actors?" *Academy of Management Review,* Vol. 24, No. 1, 1999, pp. 82–98, and Linn Van Dyne and Soon Ang, "Organizational Citizenship Behavior of Contingent Workers in Singapore," *Academy of Management Journal,* Vol. 41, No. 6, 1998, pp. 692–703.

177. Koys, op. cit.

178. Deborah Kidder, "The Influence of Gender on the Performance of Organizational Citizenship Behaviors," *Journal of Management,* Vol. 28, No. 5, 2002, pp. 629–648.

179. Mark C. Bolino and William H. Turnley, "The Personal Costs of Citizenship Behavior: The Relationship between Individual Initiative and Role Overload, Job Stress, and Work-Family Conflict," *Journal of Applied Psychology,* Vol. 90. No. 4, 2005, pp. 740–748.

## Chapter 6 Footnote References and Supplemental Readings

1. John B. Miner, Bahman Ebrahimi, and Jeffrey M. Wachtel, "How Deficiencies in Motivation to Manage Contribute to the United States' Competitiveness Problem (and What Can Be Done about It)," *Human Resource Management,* Fall 1995, p. 363. Also see Tina Benitez, "Risky Business: As Corporate America Faces Criminal Charges and Economic Woes, Motivation Is More Important than Ever," *Incentive,* Vol. 176, No. 7, 2002, pp. 24–27, and Richard Boyatzis, Annie McKee, and Daniel Goleman, "Reawakening Your Passion for Work," *Harvard Business Review,* April 2002, pp. 87–94.

2. Martin G. Evans, "Organizational Behavior: The Central Role of Motivation," *Journal of Management,* Vol. 12, No. 2, 1986, p. 203.

3. The most frequently cited exception is the need for oxygen. A deficiency of oxygen in the body does not automatically set up a corresponding drive. This is a fear of high-altitude pilots. Unless their gauges show an oxygen leak or the increased intake of carbon dioxide sets up a drive, they may die of oxygen deficiency without a drive's ever being set up to correct the situation. The same is true of the relatively frequent deaths of teenagers parked in "lovers' lanes." Carbon monoxide leaks into the parked automobile, and they die from oxygen deficiency without its ever setting up a drive (to open the car door).

4. See Paul R. Lawrence and Nitin Nohria, *Driven: How Human Nature Shapes Our Choices,* Jossey-Bass, San Francisco, 2002.

5. Curt Coffman and Gabriel Gonzalez-Molina, *Follow This Path,* Warner Books, New York, 2002, p. 20.

6. For example, see Nitin Nohria and Boris Groysberg, "Employee Motivation," *Harvard Business Review,* July–August 2008, pp. 78–84.

7. Ronald E. Riggio, *Introduction to Industrial/Organizational Psychology,* Scott Foresman/Little, Brown, Glenview, Ill., 1990, p. 175.

8. "Morale Boosters for Tough Times—Or Any Time," *HR Focus,* September, 2008, p. 13.

9. For example, see Alexander D. Stajkovic and Fred Luthans, "Differential Effects of Incentive Motivators on Work Performance," *Academy of Management Journal,* Vol. 44, No. 3, 2001, pp. 580–590.

10. Erika A. Patall, Harris Cooper, and Jorgianne Civey Robinson, "The Effects of Choice on Intrinsic Motivation and Related Outcomes: A Meta-Analysis of Research Findings," *Psychological Bulletin,* Vol. 134, No. 2, 2008, pp. 270–300.

11. Adam M. Grant, "Does Intrinsic Motivation Fuel the Prosocial Fire: Motivational Synergy in Predicting Persistence, Performance and Productivity," *Journal of Applied Psychology,* Vol. 93, No. 1, 2008, pp. 48–58.

12. Lyman W. Porter, Edward E. Lawler, III, and J. R. Hackman, *Behavior in Organizations,* McGraw-Hill, New York, 1975.

13. Charles C. Manz and Christopher P. Neck, *Mastering Self-Leadership,* 3rd ed., Pearson-Prentice Hall, Upper Saddle River, N.J., 2004, p. 43. Also see Stanley Fawcett et al., "Spirituality and Organizational Culture: Cultivating the ABCs of an Inspiring Workplace," *International Journal of Public Administration,* Vol. 31, No. 4, 2008, pp. 420–438.

14. R. de Charms, *Personal Causation: The Internal Affective Determinants of Behavior,* Academic Press, New York, 1968. An example of recent measures of intrinsic and extrinsic motivation can be found in Frederic Guay, Robert J. Vallerand, and Celine Blanchard, "On the Assessment of Situational Intrinsic and Extrinsic Motivation: The Situational Motivation Scale (SIMS)," *Motivation and Emotion,* Vol. 24, No. 3, 2000, pp. 175–213.

15. P. C. Jordan, "Effects of an Extrinsic Reward on Intrinsic Motivation: A Field Experiment," *Academy of Management Journal,* 1986, pp. 405–412.

16. Also see Judy Cameron and W. David Pierce, "Reinforcement, Reward, and Intrinsic Motivation: A Meta Analysis," *Review of Educational Research,* Fall 1994, p. 363, and Judy Cameron, Katherine M. Banko, and W. David Pierce, "Pervasive Negative Effects of Rewards on Intrinsic Motivation: The Myth Continues," *The Behavior Analyst,* Vol. 24, No. 1, 2001, pp. 1–44.

17. Richard M. Ryan and Edward L. Deci, "Self-Determination Theory and the Facilitation of Intrinsic Motivation, Social Development, and Well-Being," *American Psychologist,* Vol. 55, 2000, pp. 68–78.

18. For example, see Daniel J. Bernstein, "Of Carrots and Sticks: A Review of Deci and Ryan's Intrinsic Motivation and Self-Determination in Human Behavior," *Journal of the Experimental Analysis of Behavior,* Vol. 54, 1990, pp. 323–332.

19. Terence R. Mitchell, "Motivation: New Directions for Theory, Research, and Practice," *Academy of Management Review,* January 1982, p. 86.

20. See Maureen L. Ambrose and Carol T. Kulik, "Old Friends, New Faces: Motivation Research in the 1990s," *Journal of Management,* Vol. 25, No. 3, 1999, pp. 231–292; E. A. Locke, "The Motivation to Work: What We Know," *Advances in Motivation and Achievement,* Vol. 10, 1997, pp. 375–412; and C. A. Pinder, *Work Motivation in Organizational Behavior,* Prentice Hall, Upper Saddle River, N.J., 1998.

21. Richard M. Steers, "Introduction of the Special Research Forum on the Future of Work Motivation Theory," *Academy of Management Review,* Vol. 27, 2002, p. 146.

22. A. H. Maslow, "A Theory of Human Motivation," *Psychological Review,* July 1943, pp. 370–396.

23. Robert A. Baron, *Behavior in Organizations,* 2nd ed., Allyn & Bacon, Boston, 1986, p. 78.

24. See Tom Rath, *Vital Friends,* Gallup Press, New York, 2006 and "You Schmooze, You Win," *Fast Company,* July/August 2006, p. 109.

25. For example, see Robert S. Kaplan, "Reaching Your Potential," *Harvard Business Review,* July–August 2008, pp. 45–49.

26. A. J. Kinicki, G. E. Prussia, and F. M. McKee-Ryan, "A Panel Study of Coping with Involuntary Job Loss," *Academy of Management Journal,* Vol. 43, No. 1, 2000, pp. 90–100.

27. Rebecca A. Clay, "A Renaissance for Humanistic Psychology," *Monitor on Psychology,* Vol. 33, No. 8, 2002, pp. 42–43.

28. David L. Stum, "Maslow Revisited: Building the Employee Commitment Pyramid," *Strategy and Leadership,* Vol. 29, No. 4, 2001, pp. 4–9.

29. Ambrose and Kulik, op. cit. Also see Kennon M. Sheldon, Andrew J. Elliot, Youngmee Kim, and Tim Kasser, "What Is Satisfying about Satisfying Events? Testing 10 Candidate Psychological Needs," *Journal of Personality and Social Psychology,* Vol. 80, No. 2, 2001, pp. 325–339.

30. For example, see S. Caudron, "Be Cool!" *Workforce,* April 1998, pp. 50–61. Also see Ross R. Reck, *The X-Factor: Getting Extraordinary Results from Ordinary People,* John Wiley, New York, 2001.

31. Some examples of research using Vroom's concepts include Mark E. Tubbs, Donna M. Boehne, and James G. Dahl, "Expectancy, Valence, and Motivational Force Functions in Goal-Setting Research: An Empirical Test," *Journal of Applied Psychology,* June 1993, pp. 361–373; N. T. Feather, "Expectancy-Value Theory and Unemployment Effects," *Journal of Occupational and Organizational Psychology,* December 1992.

32. Gary Blau, "Operationalizing Direction and Level of Effort and Testing Their Relationships to Individual Job Performance," *Organizational Behavior and Human Decision Processes,* June 1993, pp. 152–170.

33. Philip M. Podsakoff and Larry Williams, "The Relationship between Job Performance and Job Satisfaction," in Edwin Locke (Ed.), *Generalizing from Laboratory to Field Settings,* Lexington Books, Lexington, Mass., 1986, p. 244. Also see Edwin A. Locke and Gary P. Latham, *A Theory of Goal Setting and Task Performance,* Prentice Hall, Upper Saddle

River, N.J., 1990, pp. 265–267, and E. Brian Peach and Daniel A. Wren, "Pay for Performance from Antiquity to the 1950's," *Journal of Organizational Behavior Management,* Vol. 12, 1992, pp. 5–26.

34. Oren Harari, "The Missing Link in Performance," *Management Review,* March 1995, pp. 21–24.

35. Erik P. Thompson, Shelly Chaiken, and J. Douglas Hazlewood, "Need for Cognition and Desire for Control as Moderators of Extrinsic Reward Effects: A Person $\times$ Situation Approach to the Study of Intrinsic Motivation," *Journal of Personality and Social Psychology,* June 1993, pp. 987–999.

36. James N. Baron and Karen S. Cook, "Process and Outcome: Perspectives on the Distribution of Rewards in Organizations," *Administrative Science Quarterly.* Vol. 37, 1992, pp. 191–197.

37. James M. McFillen and Philip M. Podsakoff, "A Coordinated Approach to Motivation Can Increase Productivity," *Personnel Administrator,* July 1983, p. 46.

38. K. A. Karl, A. M. O'Leary-Kelly, and J. J. Martoccio, "The Impact of Feedback and Self-Efficacy on Performance in Training," *Journal of Organizational Behavior,* Vol. 14, 1993, pp. 379–394, and T. Janz, "Manipulating Subjective Expectancy through Feedback: A Laboratory Study of the Expectancy-Performance Relationship," *Journal of Applied Psychology,* Vol. 67, 1982, pp. 480–485.

39. Robert A. Baron, *Behavior in Organizations,* Allyn & Bacon, Boston, 1983, p. 137.

40. Mark C. Bolino and William H. Turnley, "Old Faces, New Places: Equity Theory in Cross-Cultural Contexts," *Journal of Organizational Behavior,* Vol. 29, No. 1, 2007, pp. 29–50.

41. Michael R. Carrell and John E. Dittrich, "Equity Theory: The Recent Literature, Methodological Considerations, and New Directions," *Academy of Management Review,* April 1978, pp. 202–210.

42. Robert G. Lord and Jeffrey A. Hohenfeld, "Longitudinal Field Assessment of Equity Effects on the Performance of Major League Baseball Players," *Journal of Applied Psychology,* February 1979, pp. 19–26.

43. Dennis Duchon and Arthur G. Jago, "Equity and Performance of Major League Baseball Players: An Extension of Lord and Hohenfeld," *Journal of Applied Psychology,* December 1981, pp. 728–732.

44. Ambrose and Kulik, op. cit.

45. Larry W. Howard and Janis L. Miller, "Fair Pay for Fair Play: Estimating Pay Equity in Professional Baseball with Data Envelopment Analysis," *Academy of Management Journal,* August 1993, pp. 882–894.

46. Robert D. Bretz, Jr., and Steven L. Thomas, "Perceived Equity, Motivation, and Final-Offer Arbitration in Major League Baseball," *Journal of Applied Psychology,* June 1993, pp. 280–287.

47. Joseph W. Harder, "Play for Pay: Effect of Inequity in a Pay-for-Performance Context," *Administrative Science Quarterly,* June 1992, pp. 321–335.

48. See Jerald Greenberg and Russell Cropanzano (Eds.), *Advances in Organizational Justice,* Stanford University Press, Palo Alto, Calif., 2001.

49. Jason A. Colquitt, Donald E. Conlon, Michael J. Wesson, Christopher O. L. H. Porter, and K. Yee Ng, "Justice at the Millennium: A Meta-Analytic Review of 25 Years of Organizational Justice Research," *Journal of Applied Psychology,* Vol. 86, No. 3, 2001, pp. 425–445, and Jason A. Colquitt, "On the Dimensionality of Organizational Justice: A Construct Validation of a Measure," *Journal of Applied Psychology,* Vol. 86, No. 3, 2001, pp. 386–400.

50. Ibid.

51. Ibid.

52. Yochi Cohen-Charash and Paul E. Spector, "The Role of Justice in Organizations: A Meta-Analysis," *Organizational Behavior and Human Decision Processes,* Vol. 86, No. 2, 2001, pp. 278–321.

53. M. Audrey Korsgaard, Harry J. Sapienza, and David M. Schweiger, "Beaten before Begun: The Role of Procedural Justice in Planning Change," *Journal of Management,* Vol. 28, No. 4, 2002, pp. 497–516, and Janice M. Paterson, Andrea Green, and Jane Cary, "The Measurement of Organizational Justice in Organizational Change Programmes: A Reliability, Validity and Context-Sensitivity Assessment," *Journal of Occupational and Organizational Psychology,* Vol. 75, 2002, pp. 393–408.

54. Onne Janssen, "Fairness Perceptions as a Moderator in the Curvilinear Relationships between Job Demands, and Job Performance and Job Satisfaction," *Academy of Management Journal,* Vol. 44, No. 5, 2001, pp. 1039–1050.

55. Russell Cropanzano, Cynthia A. Prehar, and Peter Y. Chen, "Using Social Exchange Theory to Distinguish Procedural from Interactional Justice," *Group & Organization Management,* Vol. 27, No. 3, 2002, pp. 324–351.

56. Dan Chiaburu and Lim Audrey, "Manager Trustworthiness or International Justice? Predicting Organizational Citizenship Behaviors," *Journal of Business Ethics,* Vol. 83, No. 3, 2008, pp. 453–467.

57. Derek R. Avery and Miguel A. Quiñones, "Disentangling the Effects of Voice: The Incremental Roles of Opportunity, Behavior, and Instrumentality in Predicting Procedural Fairness," *Journal of Applied Psychology,* Vol. 87, No. 1, 2002, pp. 81–86.

58. Jody Clay-Warner, "Perceiving Procedural Injustice: The Effects of Group Membership and Status," *Social Psychology Quarterly,* Vol. 64, No. 3, 2001, pp. 224–238.

59. Hui Liao and Deborah E. Rupp, "The Impact of Justice Climate and Justice Orientation on Work Outcomes: A Cross-Level Multifoci Framework," *Journal of Applied Psychology,* Vol. 90, No. 2, 2005, pp. 242–256.

60. See Jerald Greenberg and Robert A. Baron, *Behavior in Organizations,* 7th ed., Prentice-Hall, Upper Saddle River, N.J., 2000, pp. 142–148; A. Furnham, B. D. Kirkcaldy, and R. Lynn, "National Attitudes to Competitiveness, Money, and Work among Young People: First, Second, and Third World Differences," *Human Relations,* Vol. 47, 1994, pp. 119–132; J. Greenberg, *The Quest for Justice on the Job,* Sage, Thousand Oaks, Calif., 1997; and R. Cropanzano and J. Greenberg, "Progress in Organizational Justice: Tunneling through the Maze," in C. L. Cooper and I. T. Robertson (Eds.), *International Review of Industrial and Organizational Psychology,* Vol. 12, Wiley, New York, 1997.

61. Suzanne S. Masterson, "A Trickle-Down Model of Organizational Justice: Relating Employees' and Customer's

Perceptions of and Reactions to Fairness," *Journal of Applied Psychology,* Vol. 86, No. 4, 2001, pp. 594–604.

62. Donald L. McCabe and Jane E. Dutton, "Making Sense of the Environment: The Role of Perceived Effectiveness," *Human Relations,* May 1993, pp. 623–643.

63. Spencer A. Rathus, *Psychology,* 4th ed., Holt, Rinehart & Winston, Fort Worth, Tex., 1990, pp. 613–614.

64. For summaries of this literature, see Mark J. Martinko (Ed.), *Attribution Theory: An Organizational Perspective,* St. Lucie Press, Delray Beach, Fla., 1995, and for more practical application, see Mark J. Martinko, *Thinking Like a Winner,* Gulf Coast Publishing, Tallahassee, Fla., 2002. Also see new attributional analysis in areas such as workplace violence: Mark Martinko and Kelly Zellars, "Toward a Theory of Workplace Violence and Aggression: A Cognitive Appraisal Perspective," in R. W. Griffin, A. O'Leary-Kelly, and J. M. Collins (Eds.), *Dysfunctional Behavior in Organizations,* JAI Press, Stamford, Conn., 1998, and S. C. Douglas and Mark J. Martinko, "Exploring the Role of Individual Differences in the Prediction of Workplace Aggression, *Journal of Applied Psychology,* Vol. 86, No. 4, 2001, pp. 547–559; work exhaustion: Jo Ellen Moore, "Why Is This Happening? A Causal Attribution Approach to Work Exhaustion Consequences," *Academy of Management Review,* Vol. 25, No. 2, 2000, pp. 235–349; empowerment and learned helplessness: Constance R. Campbell and Mark J. Martinko, "An Integrative Attributional Perspective of Empowerment and Learned Helplessness: A Multimethod Field Study," *Journal of Management,* Vol. 24, No. 2, 1998, pp. 173–200; and across cultures: Incheol Choi, Richard E. Nisbett, and Ara Norenzayan, "Causal Attribution across Cultures: Variation and Universality," *Psychological Bulletin,* Vol. 125, No. 1, 1999, pp. 47–63, and Paul E. Spector, Cary L. Cooper, Juan I. Sanchez, Michael O'Driscoll, and Kate Sparks, "Locus of Control and Well-Being at Work: How Generalizable Are Western Findings?" *Academy of Management Journal,* Vol. 45, No. 2, 2002, pp. 453–466.

65. David G. Myers, *Social Psychology,* 2nd ed., McGraw-Hill, New York, 1990, p. 71. Also see David G. Myers, *Social Psychology,* 9th ed., McGraw-Hill, New York, 1999, Chapter 3.

66. Terence R. Mitchell, Charles M. Smyser, and Stan E. Weed, "Locus of Control: Supervision and Work Satisfaction," *Academy of Management Journal,* September 1975, pp. 623–631.

67. The higher performance of internally controlled managers was verified by the use of student subjects in a study by Carl R. Anderson and Craig Eric Schneier, "Locus of Control, Leader Behavior and Leader Performance among Management Students," *Academy of Management Journal,* December 1978, pp. 690–698. For a more recent study, see Gary Blau, "Testing the Relationships of Locus of Control to Different Performance Dimensions," *Journal of Occupational and Organizational Psychology,* June 1993, pp. 125–138.

68. Margaret W. Pryer and M. K. Distenfano, "Perceptions of Leadership, Job Satisfaction, and Internal–External Control across Three Nursing Levels," *Nursing Research,* November–December 1971, pp. 534–537.

69. Eli Glogow, "Research Note: Burnout and Locus of Control," *Public Personnel Management,* Spring 1986, p. 79.

70. Danny Miller, Manfred F. R. Kets DeVries, and Jean-Marie Toulouse, "Top Executive Locus of Control and Its Relationship to Strategy-Making, Structure, and Environment," *Academy of Management Journal,* June 1982, pp. 237–253.

71. Simon S. K. Lam and John Schaubroeck, "The Role of Locus of Control in Reactions to Being Promoted and to Being Passed Over," *Academy of Management Journal,* Vol. 43, No. 1, 2000, pp. 66–78.

72. Joanne Silvester, Fiona Mary Anderson-Gough, Neil R. Anderson, and Afandi R. Mohamed, "Locus of Control, Attributions and Impression Management in the Selection Interview," *Journal of Occupational and Organizational Psychology,* Vol. 75, 2002, pp. 59–76.

73. John A. Pearce and Angelo S. DeNisi, "Attribution Theory and Strategic Decision Making: An Application to Coalition Formation," *Academy of Management Journal,* March 1983, pp. 119–128.

74. Douglas E. Durand and Walter R. Nord, "Perceived Leader Behavior as a Function of Personality Characteristics of Supervisors and Subordinates," *Academy of Management Journal,* September 1976, pp. 427–428.

75. Dennis L. Dossett and Carl I. Greenberg, "Goal Setting and Performance Evaluation: An Attributional Analysis," *Academy of Management Journal,* December 1981, pp. 767–779.

76. Daniel G. Bachrach, Elliot Bendoly, and Philip M. Podsakoff, "Attributions of the 'Causes' of Group Performance as an Alternative Explanation of the Relationship between Organizational Citizenship Behavior and Organizational Performance," *Journal of Applied Psychology,* Vol. 86, No. 6, 2001, pp. 1285–1293, and Jeffrey A. Lepine and Linn Van Dyne, "Peer Responses to Low Performers: An Attributional Model of Helping in the Context of Groups," *Academy of Management Review,* Vol. 26, No. 1, 2001, pp. 67–84.

77. Bobby J. Calder, "An Attribution Theory of Leadership," in Barry Staw and Gerald Salancik (Eds.), *New Directions in Organizational Behavior,* St. Clare Press, Chicago, 1977, pp. 179–204; James C. McElroy, "A Typology of Attribution Leadership Research," *Academy of Management Review,* July 1982, pp. 413–417; Gregory Dobbins, "Effects of Gender on Leaders' Responses to Poor Performers: An Attributional Interpretation," *Academy of Management Journal,* September 1985, pp. 587–598; and James C. McElroy and Charles B. Shrader, "Attribution Theories of Leadership and Network Analysis," *Journal of Management,* Vol. 12, No. 3, 1986, pp. 351–362.

78. Terence R. Mitchell and Robert E. Wood, "Supervisors' Responses to Subordinate Poor Performance: A Test of an Attribution Model," *Organizational Behavior and Human Performance,* February 1980, pp. 123–138, and Jeffrey A. Lepine and Linn Van Dyne, "Peer Responses to Low Performers: An Attributional Model of Helping in the Context of Groups," *Academy of Management Review,* Vol. 26, No. 1, 2001, pp. 67–84.

79. Lisa H. Nishii, David P. LePak, and Benjamin Schneider, "Employee Attributions of the 'Why' of HR Practices: Their Effects on Employee Attitudes and Behaviors, and Customer Satisfaction," *Personnel Psychology,* Vol. 61, 2008, pp. 503–545.

80. C. Ward Struthers, Bernard Weiner, and Keith Allred, "Effects of Causal Attributions on Personnel Decisions: A Social Motivation Perspective," *Basic and Applied Social Psychology,* Vol. 20, No. 2, 1998, pp. 155–166.

81. Sherry E. Moss and Mark J. Martinko, "The Effects of Performance Attributions and Outcome Dependence on Leader Feedback following Poor Subordinate Performance," *Journal of Organizational Behavior,* Vol. 19, 1998, pp. 259–274.

82. Paul E. Spector, "Behavior in Organizations as a Function of Employees' Locus of Control," *Psychological Bulletin,* May 1982, pp. 482–497. Also see Leslie Kren, "The Moderating Effects of Locus of Control on Performance Incentives and Participation," *Human Relations,* September 1992, p. 991.

83. Peter J. Frost, "Special Issue on Organizational Symbolism," *Journal of Management,* Vol. 11, No. 2, 1985, pp. 5–9.

84. Farzad Moussavi and Dorla A. Evans, "Emergence of Organizational Attributions: The Role of Shared Cognitive Schema," *Journal of Management,* Spring 1993, pp. 79–95.

85. Suzyn Ornstein, "Organizational Symbols: A Study of Their Meanings and Influences on Perceived Psychological Climate," *Organizational Behavior and Human Decision Processes,* October 1986, pp. 207–229.

86. Bernard Weiner, *Theories of Motivation,* Rand McNally, Chicago, 1972, Chap. 5.

87. Harold H. Kelley, "The Process of Causal Attribution," *American Psychologist,* February 1973, pp. 107–128.

88. Robert Kreitner and Angelo Kinicki, *Organizational Behavior,* 6th ed., McGraw-Hill, New York, 2004, p. 243.

89. Mitchell and Wood, op. cit.

90. Bernard Weiner, "An Attribution Theory of Achievement Motivation and Emotion," *Psychological Review,* October 1985, pp. 548–573.

91. See Kreitner and Kinicki, op. cit., p. 150, for a summary of this research.

92. Myers, op. cit., pp. 74–77.

93. Ibid., p. 82.

94. B. Mullen and C. A. Riordan, "Self-Serving Attributions for Performance in Naturalistic Settings," *Journal of Applied Social Psychology,* Vol. 18, 1988, pp. 3–22.

95. Gary Johns, "A Multi-Level Theory of Self-Serving Behavior in and by Organizations," *Research in Organizational Behavior,* Vol. 21, 1999, pp. 1–38.

96. James L. Bowditch and Anthony F. Buono, *A Primer on Organizational Behavior,* 3rd ed., Wiley, New York, 1994, p. 90.

97. Mark J. Martinko, (Ed.), *Attribution Theory: An Organizational Perspective,* St. Lucie Press, Delray Beach, Fla., 1995.

98. See "Control in the Workplace and Its Health-Related Aspects," in S. L. Sauter, J. J. Hurrell, and C. L. Cooper (Eds.), *Job Control and Worker Health,* Wiley, Chichester, U.K., 1989, pp. 129–159; D. C. Ganster and M. R. Fusilier, "Control in the Workplace," in C. L. Cooper and I. T. Robertson (Eds.), *International Review of Industrial and Organizational Psychology,* Wiley, Chichester, U.K., 1989, pp. 235–280; and Marilyn L. Fox, Deborah J. Dwyer, and Daniel C. Ganster, "Effects of Stressful Job Demands and Control on Physiological and Attitudinal Outcomes in a Hospital Setting," *Academy of Management Journal,* April 1993, pp. 289–318.

99. D. J. Dwyer and D. C. Ganster, "The Effects of Job Demands and Control on Employee Attendance and Satisfaction," *Journal of Organizational Behavior,* Vol. 12, 1991, pp. 595–608.

100. For example, see Scott A. Snell, "Control Theory in Strategic Human Resource Management: The Mediating Effect of Administrative Information," *Academy of Management Journal,* June 1992, pp. 292–327.

101. Leisa D. Sargent and Deborah J. Terry, "The Effects of Work Control and Job Demands on Employee Adjustment and Work Performance," *Journal of Occupational and Organizational Psychology,* Vol. 71, 1998, pp. 219–236. Also see Jeffrey B. Vancouver, "The Depth of History and Explanation as Benefit and Bane for Psychological Control Theories," *Journal of Applied Psychology,* Vol. 90, No. 1, 2005, pp. 38–52.

102. For some of the original development of agency theory, see M. C. Jensen and W. H. Meckling, "Theory of the Firm, Managerial Behavior, Agency Costs, and Ownership Structure," *Journal of Financial Economics,* Vol. 3, 1976, pp. 305–360. For recent applications of agency theory to the management literature, see Charles W. L. Hill and Thomas M. Jones, "Stakeholder-Agency Theory," *Journal of Management Studies,* March 1992, pp. 131–154.

103. See H. L. Tosi and L. R. Gomez-Mejia, "The Decoupling of CEO Pay and Performance: An Agency Theory Perspective," *Administrative Science Quarterly,* Vol. 34, 1989, pp. 169–189, and Luis R. Gomez-Mejia and David B. Balkin, "Determinants of Faculty Pay: An Agency Theory Perspective," *Academy of Management Journal,* December 1992, pp. 921–955.

104. Judi McLean Parks and Edward J. Conlon, "Compensation Contracts: Do Agency Theory Assumptions Predict Negotiated Agreements?" *Academy of Management Journal,* June 1995, pp. 821–838.

105. Kendall Roth and Sharon O'Donnell, "Foreign Subsidiary Compensation Strategy: An Agency Theory Perspective," *Academy of Management Journal,* June 1996, pp. 678–703.

106. Linda K. Stroh, Jeanne M. Brett, Joseph P. Baumann, and Anne H. Reilly, "Agency Theory and Variable Pay Compensation Strategies," *Academy of Management Journal,* June 1996, pp. 751–767.

107. Dan R. Dalton, S. Trevis Certo, and Rungpen Roengpitya, "Meta-Analyses of Financial Performance and Equity: Fusion or Confusion?" *Academy of Management Journal,* Vol. 46, No. 1, 2003, pp. 13–26. Also see Michael H. Lubatkin, "Organization Theorist and Microeconomists: Working Together Apart," *Journal of Management Inquiry,* Vol. 14, No. 4, December 2005, pp. 407–408; and Thomas Lange, "A Theory of the Firm Only a Microeconomist Could Love? A Microeconomist's Reply to Lubatkin's Critique of Agency Theory," *Journal of Management Inquiry,* Vol. 14, No. 4, December 2005, pp. 404–406.

108. Donald C. Hambrick, "Just How Bad Are Our Theories? A Response to Ghoshal," *Academy of Management Learning and Education,* Vol. 4, No. 1, 2005, p. 106.

109. Chip Heath, "On the Social Psychology of Agency Relationships: Lay Theories of Motivation Overemphasis

on Extrinsic Incentives," *Organizational Behavior and Human Decision Processes,* Vol. 78, No. 1, April 1999, pp. 25–62.

110. W. Jack Duncan, "Stock Ownership and Work Motivation," *Organizational Dynamics,* Vol. 30, No. 1, 2001, pp. 1–11.

111. J. C. Combs and D. J. Ketchen, Jr., "Can Capital Scarcity Help Agency Theory Explain Franchising? Revisiting the Capital Scarcity Hypothesis," *Academy of Management Journal,* Vol. 42, No. 2, 1999, 196–207.

112. Anurag Sharma, "Professional as Agent: Knowledge Assymmetry in Agency Exchange," *Academy of Management Review,* Vol. 22, No. 3, 1997, pp. 758–798.

113. Michael A. Campion, Lisa Cheraskin, and Michael J. Stevens, "Career Related Antecedents and Outcomes of Job Rotation," *Academy of Management Journal,* December 1996, pp. 1512–1542.

114. Martha Frase-Blunt, "Ready, Set, Rotate!" *HR Magazine,* Vol. 46, No. 10, 2001, pp. 46–53.

115. John B. Miner, *Organizational Behavior,* Random House, New York, 1988, p. 201.

116. Michael A. Campion and Carol L. McClelland, "Follow-Up and Extension of the Interdisciplinary Costs and Benefits of Enlarged Jobs," *Journal of Applied Psychology,* June 1993, pp. 339–351.

117. Greg R. Oldham and Anne Cummings, "Employee Creativity: Personal and Contextual Factors at Work," *Academy of Management Journal,* June 1996, pp. 607–634.

118. For example, see Nico W. Van Yperen and Mariët Hagedoorn, "Do High Job Demands Increase Intrinsic Motivation or Fatigue or Both? The Role of Job Control and Job Social Support," *Academy of Management Journal,* Vol. 46, No. 2, 2003, pp. 339–348.

119. J. Richard Hackman and Greg R. Oldham, "Motivation through the Design of Work: Test of a Theory," *Organizational Behavior and Human Performance,* Vol. 16, 1976, pp. 250–279.

120. J. Richard Hackman, "Work Design," in J. Richard Hackman and J. Lloyd Suttle (Eds.), *Improving Life at Work,* Goodyear, Santa Monica, Calif., 1977, p. 129.

121. Ibid., p. 130.

122. Robert W. Renn and Robert J. Vandenberg, "The Critical Psychological States: An Underrepresented Component in Job Characteristics Model Research," *Journal of Management,* Vol. 21, No. 2, 1995, pp. 279–303. Also see Frederick P. Morgeson, Kelly Delaney-Klinger, and Monica A. Hemingway, "The Importance of Job Autonomy, Cognitive Ability, and Job-Related Skill for Predicting Role Breadth and Job Performance," *Journal of Applied Psychology,* Vol. 90, No. 2, 2005, pp. 399–406, and Claus W. Langfred and Meta A. Moye, "Effects of Task Autonomy on Performance: An Extended Model Considering Motivational, Informational, and Structural Mechanisms," *Journal of Applied Psychology,* Vol. 89, No. 6, 2004, pp. 934–945.

123. Fred Luthans, Barbara Kemmerer, Robert Paul, and Lew Taylor, "The Impact of a Job Redesign Intervention on Salespersons' Observed Performance Behaviors," *Group and Organization Studies,* March 1987, pp. 55–72.

124. Ibid.

125. Edwin A. Locke, "Toward a Theory of Task Motivation and Incentives," *Organizational Behavior and Human Performance,* May 1968, pp. 157–189.

126. Edwin A. Locke, "The Ubiquity of the Technique of Goal Setting in Theories and Approaches to Employee Motivation," *Academy of Management Review,* July 1978, p. 600.

127. Edwin A. Locke, "The Ideas of Frederick W. Taylor: An Evaluation," *Academy of Management Review,* January 1982, p. 16.

128. Edwin A. Locke, "Personal Attitudes and Motivation," *Annual Review of Psychology,* Vol. 26, 1975, pp. 457–480, 596–598.

129. For a sampling of this extensive research, see Locke, "Toward a Theory of Task Motivation and Incentives," summarizing the laboratory studies, and Gary P. Latham and Gary A. Yukl, "A Review of the Research on the Application of Goal Setting in Organizations," *Academy of Management Journal,* December 1975, pp. 824–845, summarizing the field studies. Comprehensive summaries of this research can be found in Edwin A. Locke, Karylle A. Shaw, Lise M. Saari, and Gary P. Latham, "Goal Setting and Task Performance: 1969–1980," *Psychological Bulletin,* July 1981, pp. 125–152; Gary P. Latham and Thomas W. Lee, "Goal Setting," in Edwin A. Locke (Ed.), *Generalizing from Laboratory to Field Settings,* Lexington Books, Lexington. Mass., 1986, pp. 101–117; Mark E. Tubbs, "Goal Setting: A Meta-Analytic Examination of the Empirical Evidence," *Journal of Applied Psychology,* Vol. 71, No. 3, 1986, pp. 474–483; and Faten M. Moussa, "Determinants, Process, and Consequences of Personal Goals and Performance," *Journal of Management,* Vol. 26, No. 6, 2000, pp. 1259–1285.

130. Edwin A. Locke and Gary P. Latham, "Building a Practically Useful Theory of Goal Setting and Task Motivation," *American Psychologist,* Vol. 57, No. 9, 2002, p. 714.

131. P. C. Earley, C. E. Shalley, and G. B. Northcraft, "I Think I Can, I Think I Can . . . Processing Time and Strategy Effects of Goal Acceptance/Rejection Decisions," *Organizational Behavior and Human Decision Processes,* Vol. 53, 1992, pp. 1–13.

132. D. J. Campbell and D. M. Furrer, "Goal Setting and Competition as Determinants of Task Performance," *Journal of Organizational Behavior,* Vol. 16, 1995, pp. 377–389; S. P. Allscheid and D. F. Cellar, "An Interactive Approach to Work Motivation: The Effects of Competition, Rewards, and Goal Difficulty on Task Performance," *Journal of Business and Psychology,* Vol. 11, 1996, pp. 219–237.

133. R. H. Rasch and Henry L. Tosi, "Factors Affecting Software Developers' Performance: An Integrated Approach," *MIS Quarterly,* Vol. 16, 1992, pp. 395–413.

134. For example, see Gary P. Latham and Gary A. Yukl, "The Effects of Assigned and Participative Goal Setting on Performance and Job Satisfaction," *Journal of Applied Psychology,* April 1976, pp. 166–171, and Katherine I. Miller and Peter Monge, "Participation, Satisfaction, and Productivity: A Meta-Analytic Review," *Academy of Management Journal,* December 1986, pp. 727–753.

135. Maureen L. Ambrose and Carol T. Kulik, "Old Friends, New Faces: Motivation Research in the 1990s," *Journal of Management,* Vol. 25, No. 3, 1999, pp. 231–292.

136. See Howard J. Klein, Michael J. Wesson, John R. Hollenbeck, Patrick M. Wright, and Richard P. DeShon, "The Assessment of Goal Commitment: A Measurement Model

Meta-Analysis," *Organizational Behavior and Human Decision Processes,* Vol. 85, No. 1, 2001, pp. 32–55.

137. J. C. Wofford, V. L Goodwin, and S. Premack, "Meta-analysis of the Antecedents and Consequences of Goal Commitment," *Journal of Management,* Vol. 18, 1992, pp. 595–615.

138. E. A. Locke and G. P. Latham, "Work Motivation and Satisfaction: Light at the End of the Tunnel," *Psychological Science,* Vol. 1, 1990, pp. 240–246.

139. T. W. Lee, E. A. Locke, and S. H. Phan, "Explaining the Assigned Goal-Incentive Interaction: The Role of Self-Efficacy and Personal Goals," *Journal of Management,* Vol. 23, 1997, pp. 541–559.

140. For example, see Poppy Lauretta McLeod, Jeffrey K. Liker, and Sharon A. Lobel, "Process Feedback in Task Groups: An Application of Goal Setting," *Journal of Applied Behavioral Science,* March 1992, pp. 15–41, and A. N. Kluger and Angelo DeNisi, "The Effects of Feedback Interventions on Performance," *Psychological Bulletin,* Vol. 119, 1996, pp. 254–284.

141. Leslie A. Wilk and William K. Redmon, "The Effects of Feedback and Goal Setting on the Productivity and Satisfaction of University Admissions Staff," *Journal of Organizational Behavior Management,* Vol. 18, No. 1, 1998, pp. 45–56.

142. Richard P. DeShon, Steve W. J. Kozlowski, Aaron M. Schmidt, Karen R. Milner, and Darin Wiechmann, "A Multiple-Goal, Multilevel Model of Feedback Effects on the Regulation of Individual and Team Performance," *Journal of Applied Psychology,* Vol. 89, No. 6, 2004, pp. 1035–1056.

143. David D. Van Fleet, Tim O. Peterson, and Ella W. Van Fleet, "Closing the Performance Feedback Gap with Expert Systems," *Academy of Management Executive,* Vol. 19, No. 3, 2005, pp. 38–53.

144. Donald J. Campbell, "Task Complexity: A Review and Analysis," *Academy of Management Review,* January 1988, pp. 40–52, and Rich P. DeShon and Ralph A. Alexander, "Goal Setting Effects on Implicit and Explicit Learning of Complex Tasks," *Organizational Behavior and Human Decision Processes,* January 1996, pp. 18–36.

145. Gary P. Latham and Lise M. Saari, "Importance of Supportive Relationships in Goal Setting," *Journal of Applied Psychology,* April 1979, pp. 151–156.

146. Howard Garland, "Goal Level and Task Performance: A Compelling Replication of Some Compelling Results," *Journal of Applied Psychology,* April 1982, pp. 245–248, and Thomas S. Bateman, Hugh O'Neill, and Amy Kenworthy-U'Ren, "A Hierarchical Taxonomy of Top Managers' Goals," *Journal of Applied Psychology,* Vol. 87, No. 6, 2002, pp. 1134–1148.

147. Howard J. Klein and Jay S. Kim, "A Field Study of the Influence of Situational Constraints, Leader-Member Exchange, and Goal Commitment on Performance," *Academy of Management Journal,* Vol. 41, No. 1, 1998, 88–95.

148. James T. Austin and Philip Bobko, "Goal Setting Theory: Unexplored Areas and Future Research Needs," *Journal of Occupational Psychology,* Vol. 58, No. 4, 1985, pp. 289–308.

149. Maureen L. Ambrose and Carol T. Kulik, "Old Friends, New Faces: Motivation Research in the 1990s," *Journal of Management,* Vol. 25, No. 3, 1999, pp. 231–292.

150. Barry M. Staw and R. D. Boettger, "Task Revision: A Neglected Form of Work Performance," *Academy of Management Journal,* Vol. 33, No. 4, 1990, pp. 534–559.

151. E. A. Locke and G. P. Latham, *Goal Setting: A Motivational Technique That Really Works,* Prentice Hall, Upper Saddle River, N.J., 1984, pp. 171–172. Also see D. Christopher Kayes, "The Destructive Pursuit of Idealized Goals," *Organizational Dynamics,* Vol. 34, No. 4, 2005, pp. 391–401.

152. Patrick M. Wright, Jennifer M. George, S. Regena Farnsworth, and Gary C. McMahan, "Productivity and Extra-Role Behavior: The Effects of Goals and Incentives on Spontaneous Helping," *Journal of Applied Psychology,* June 1993, pp. 374–381.

153. Locke and Latham, *Goal Setting: A Motivational Technique,* op. cit., pp. 171–172, and Gary P. Latham, "Motivate Employee Performance through Goal Setting," in Edwin Locke (Ed.), *Handbook of Principles of Organizational Behavior,* Blackwood, Oxford, U.K., 2000, pp. 107–119.

154. Ibid.

155. Gerard H. Seijts and Gary P. Latham, "Learning Versus Performance Goals: When Should Each Be Used?" *Academy of Management Executive,* Vol. 19, No. 1, 2005, pp. 124–131.

156. See Carol Dweck and Ellen Leggett, "A Social-Cognitive Approach to Motivation and Personality," *Psychological Review,* Vol. 20, 1998, pp. 256–273, and Carol Dweck, *Self-Theories: Their Role in Motivation, Personality, and Development,* Psychology Press, Philadelphia, 1999.

157. For example, see S. Button, J. Mathieu, and D. Zajac, "Goal Orientation in Organizational Behavior Research," *Organizational Behavior and Human Decision Processes,* Vol. 67, 1995, pp. 26–48; D. VandeWalle, S. Brown, W. Cron, and J. Slocum, "The Influence of Goal Orientation and Self-Regulation Tactics on Sales Performance," *Journal of Applied Psychology,* Vol. 84, 1999, pp. 249–259; Don VandeWalle, William L. Cron, and John W. Slocum, Jr., "The Role of Goal Orientation following Performance Feedback," *Journal of Applied Psychology,* Vol. 86, No. 4, 2001, pp. 629–640; and Nico W. Van Yperen and Onne Janssen, "Fatigued and Dissatisfied or Fatigued but Satisfied? Goal Orientations and Responses to High Job Demands," *Academy of Management Journal,* Vol. 45, No. 6, 2002, pp. 1161–1171.

158. Don VandeWalle, "Goal Orientation: Why Wanting to Look Successful Doesn't Always Lead to Success," *Organizational Dynamics,* Vol. 30, No. 2, 2001, pp. 162–171.

159. Ibid., p. 168.

160. Carol S. Dweck, *Mindset,* Ballantine Books, New York, 2006.

161. Ibid., pp. 132–133.

162. Kenneth R. Thompson, Wayne A. Hochwarter, and Nicholas J. Mathys, "Stretch Targets: What Makes Them Effective?" *Academy of Management Executive,* Vol. 11, No. 3, 1997, p. 48.

163. P. C. Earle, "Supervisors and Shop Stewards as Sources of Contextual Information in Goal Setting: A Comparison of the United States with England," *Journal of Applied Psychology,* Vol. 71, 1986, pp. 111–117.

164. Denise M. Rousseau, *Psychological Contracts in Organizations: Understanding Written and Unwritten Agreements,* Sage, Thousand Oaks, Calif., 1995, and Denise M. Rousseau

and Michael B. Arthur, "The Boundaryless Human Resource Function," *Organizational Dynamics,* Spring 1999, pp. 7–18.

165. For example, see Violet T. Ho, "Social Influence on Evaluations of Psychological Contract Fulfillment," *Academy of Management Review,* Vol. 30, No. 1, 2005, pp. 113–128.

166. Elizabeth Wolfe Morrison and Sandra L. Robinson, "When Employees Feel Betrayed: A Model of How Psychological Contract Violation Develops," *Academy of Management Review,* Vol. 22, No. 1, 1997, pp. 226–256. Also see Mark M. Suazo, William H. Turnley, and Renate R. Mai-Dalton, "The Role of Perceived Violation in Determining Employees' Reactions to Psychological Contract Breach," *Journal of Leadership and Organizational Studies,* Vol. 12, No. 1, 2005, pp. 24–36.

## Chapter 7 Footnote References and Supplemental Readings

1. Fred Luthans, "Positive Organizational Behavior: Developing and Managing Psychological Strengths," *Academy of Management Executive,* Vol. 16, 2002, p. 59.

2. See Barbara L. Fredrickson, *Positivity,* Crown Publishers, New York, 2009.

3. See Fred Luthans, Carolyn M. Youssef, and Bruce J. Avolio, *Psychological Capital,* Oxford, UK, Oxford University Press, 2007; Fred Luthans, "The Need for and Meaning of Positive Organizational Behavior," *Journal of Organizational Behavior,* Vol. 23, 2002, pp. 695–706; Luthans, op. cit.; and Fred Luthans, "Positive Organizational Behavior (POB): Implications for Leadership and HR Development and Motivation," in R. M. Steers, L. W. Porter, and G. A. Begley (Eds.), *Motivation and Leadership at Work,* New York, McGraw-Hill, 2003.

4. Kim S. Cameron, Jane E. Dutton, and Robert E. Quinn (Eds.), *Positive Organizational Scholarship,* San Francisco, Berrett-Koehler, 2003.

5. Christopher Peterson and Martin E. P. Seligman, *Character Strengths and Virtues,* Oxford, UK, Oxford University Press, 2004.

6. See Luthans, Youssef, and Avolio, op. cit.; Fred Luthans and Carolyn Youssef, "Emerging Positive Organizational Behavior," *Journal of Management,* Vol. 33, 2007, pp. 321–349; and Carolyn M. Youssef and Fred Luthans, "An Integrated Model of Psychological Capital in the Workplace," in Alex Linley (Ed.), *Handbook of Positive Psychology and Work,* Oxford University Press, New York, 2009.

7. See Fred Luthans, Bruce J. Avolio, James B. Avey, and Steven M. Norman, "Psychological Capital: Measurement and Relationship with Performance and Satisfaction," *Personnel Psychology,* Vol. 60, 2007, pp. 541–572 and James B. Avey, Fred Luthans, and Carolyn M. Youssef, "The Additive Value of Positive Psychological Capital in Predicting Work Attitudes and Behaviors," *Journal of Management,* Vol. 36, 2010, in press.

8. The term *psychological capital* consisting of the four dimensions of efficacy, hope, optimism, and resiliency was first used in two articles published in 2004: Fred Luthans and Carolyn M. Youssef, "Human, Social, and Now Positive Psychological Capital," *Organizational Dynamics,* Vol. 33, No. 2,

2004, pp. 143–160; and Fred Luthans, Kyle W. Luthans, and Brett C. Luthans, "Positive Psychological Capital: Going Beyond Human and Social Capital," *Business Horizons,* Vol. 47, No. 1, 2004, pp. 45–50; and was fully developed in the book Luthans, Youssef, and Avolio, op. cit.

9. Chapters 6 and 7 in the Luthans, Youssef, and Avolio op. cit. are devoted to evaluating several positive constructs for potential inclusion under the POB/PsyCap criteria.

10. For the original published pieces launching the positive psychology movement, see M. E. P. Seligman, "Positive Social Science," *APA Monitor,* April 1998, p. 2; M. E. P. Seligman, "What Is the 'Good Life'?" *APA Monitor,* October 1998, p. 2; M. E. P. Seligman, "The President's Address," *American Psychologist,* Vol. 54, 1999, pp. 559–562; and M. E. P. Seligman and M. Csikszentmihalyi, "Positive Psychology: An Introduction, *American Psychologist,* Vol. 55, 2000, pp. 5–14. For Seligman's retrospective history, see Martin E. Seligman, *Authentic Happiness,* Free Press, New York, 2002, preface and Chapters 1–2.

11. For example, see Kennon M. Sheldon and Laura King, "Why Positive Psychology Is Necessary," *American Psychologist,* Vol. 56, No. 3, 2001, pp. 216–217; Ed Diener, "Subjective Well-Being: The Science of Happiness, and a Proposal for a National Index," *American Psychologist,* Vol. 55, 2000, pp. 34–43; and Steen J. Sandage and Peter C. Hill, "The Virtues of Positive Psychology," *Journal of the Theory of Social Behavior,* Vol. 31, No. 3, 2001, pp. 241–260.

12. Martin E. P. Seligman and Mihaly Csikszentmihalyi, "Positive Psychology," *American Psychologist,* January 2000, p. 5.

13. See Sonja Lyubomirsky, Laura King, and Ed Diener, "The Benefits of Frequent Positive Affect: Does Happiness Lead to Success?" *Psychological Bulletin,* Vol. 131, 2005, pp. 805–855.

14. This depiction is mainly drawn from ibid. Luthans and colleagues currently have a large research program underway on the Health, Relationships, Work (H-R-W) model of well-being.

15. See Sonja Lyubomirsky, *The How of Happiness: A Scientific Approach to Getting the Life You Want,* The Penguin Press, New York, 2008.

16. Ibid., p. 53.

17. Ibid., pp. 41–42.

18. Ibid., p. 39.

19. Albert Bandura, *Social Foundations of Thought and Action,* Prentice Hall, Upple Saddle River, N.J., 1986. For the many accolades for this landmark book, see "Book Review Essays on Bandura's *Social Foundations of Thought and Action,*" *Psychological Inquiry,* Vol. 1, No. 1, 1990, pp. 86–100.

20. For a comprehensive summary of the body of knowledge, see Albert Bandura, *Self-Efficacy: The Exercise of Control,* W. H. Freeman, New York, 1997. Also see J. E. Maddux, *Self-Efficacy, Adaptation and Adjustment: Theory, Research, and Application,* Plenum Press, New York, 1995, and James E. Maddux, "Self-Efficacy," in C. R. Snyder and Shane J. Lopez (Eds.), *Handbook of Positive Psychology,* Oxford, Oxford, U.K., 2002, pp. 277–287.

21. For a summary of the various applications, see Bandura, *Self-Efficacy: The Exercise of Control,* op. cit., and especially for research on the workplace, see Alexander D. Stajkovic and Fred Luthans, "Self-Efficacy and Work-Related

Performance: A Meta-Analysis," *Psychological Bulletin,* Vol. 124, No. 2, 1998, pp. 240–261, and Albert Bandura, "Cultivate Self-Efficacy for Personal and Organizational Effectiveness," in Edwin A. Locke (Ed.), *The Blackwell Handbook of Principles of Organizational Behavior,* Blackwell, Oxford, U.K., 2000.

22. This vast literature is summarized in Albert Bandura and Edwin A. Locke, "Negative Self-Efficacy and Goal Effects Revisited," *Journal of Applied Psychology,* Vol. 88, No. 1, 2003, pp. 87–99.

23. For example, see Rosabeth M. Kanter, *Confidence,* New York, Crown Business, 2004.

24. See Bandura, *Self-Efficacy: The Exercise of Control,* op. cit., and specifically Albert Bandura, "Social Cognitive Theory: An Agentic Perspective," *Asian Journal of Social Psychology,* Vol. 2, 1999, p. 21.

25. Bandura, "Cultivate Self-Efficacy," op. cit., p. 120.

26. Albert Bandura, "Self-Efficacy Mechanism in Human Agency," *American Psychologist,* Vol. 37, 1982, p. 122.

27. Alexander D. Stajkovic and Fred Luthans, "Social Cognitive Theory and Self-Efficacy: Going beyond Traditional Motivational and Behavioral Approaches," *Organizational Dynamics,* Spring 1998, p. 66.

28. See Stajkovic and Luthans, "Self-Efficacy and Work-Related Performance," op. cit., p. 244, for a review of the relationship and status of specific versus general efficacy. The discussion in this section mainly draws from this source.

29. For example, see D. Eden and Y. Zuk, "Seasickness as a Self-Fulfilling Prophecy: Raising Self-Efficacy to Boost Performance at Sea," *Journal of Applied Psychology,* Vol. 80, 1995, pp. 628–635; M. Sherer, J. E. Maddux, B. Mercadante, S. Prentice-Dunn, B. Jacobs, and R. W. Rogers, "The Self-Efficacy Scale: Construction and Validation," *Psychological Reports,* Vol. 51, 1982, pp. 663–671; and Pamela L. Perrewé et al., "Are Work Stress Relationships Universal? A Nine-Region Examination of Role Stressors, General Self-Efficacy, and Burnout," *Journal of International Management,* Vol. 8, 2002, pp. 163–187.

30. Bandura, *Social Foundations of Thought and Action,* op. cit., and Bandura, *Self-Efficacy: The Exercise of Control,* op. cit. For a similar conceptual argument, see R. S. Lazarus, *Emotion and Adaptation,* Oxford University Press, New York, 1991, and R. S. Lazarus, "Vexing Research Problems Inherent in Cognitive Mediational Theories of Emotion—and Some Solutions," *Psychological Inquiry,* Vol. 6, 1995, pp. 183–196.

31. See Eden and Zuk, op. cit., p. 629, and Sherer et al., op. cit., p. 664.

32. Bandura, *Self-Efficacy: The Exercise of Control,* op. cit., p. 42.

33. See Bandura, *Self-Efficacy: The Exercise of Control,* op. cit., and D. Cervone, "Social-Cognitive Mechanisms and Personality Coherence: Self-Knowledge, Situational Beliefs, and Cross-Situational Coherence in Perceived Self-Efficacy," *Psychological Science,* Vol. 8, 1997, pp. 43–50.

34. See Stajkovic and Luthans, "Social Cognitive Theory and Self-Efficacy," op. cit., pp. 67–68, for a summary of the differences. This section's discussion is largely drawn from this source.

35. See Donald G. Gardner and Jon L. Pierce, "Self-Esteem and Self-Efficacy within the Organizational Context," *Group and Organization Management,* Vol. 23, No. 1, 1998, pp. 48–70.

36. See Stajkovic and Luthans, "Social Cognitive Theory and Self-Efficacy," op. cit., pp. 67–68.

37. Ibid., p. 68.

38. For example, see Steven P. Brown, Shankar Ganesan, and Goutam Challagalla, "Self-Efficacy as a Moderator of Information-Seeking Effectiveness," *Journal of Applied Psychology,* Vol. 86, No. 5, 2001, pp. 1043–1051.

39. This discussion draws from Bandura, *Self-Efficacy: The Exercise of Control,* op. cit.

40. See Robert F. Mager, "No Self-Efficacy, No Performance," *Training,* April 1992, pp. 32, 34, for a summary of the effectiveness of efficacy.

41. Bandura, "Cultivate Self-Efficacy for Personal and Organizational Effectiveness," op. cit., pp. 120–121.

42. Ibid., and E. A. Locke and G. P. Latham, *A Theory of Goal Setting and Task Performance,* Prentice Hall, Upper Saddle River, N.J., 1990.

43. For example, see Fred Luthans, Alexander Stajkovic, and Elina Ibrayeva, "Environmental and Psychological Challenges Facing Entrepreneurial Development in Transitional Economies," *Journal of World Business,* Vol. 35, No. 1, 2000, pp. 95–110.

44. Bandura, "Cultivate Self-Efficacy for Personal and Organizational Effectiveness," op. cit., p. 121.

45. Stajkovic and Luthans, "Self-Efficacy and Work-Related Performance," op. cit.

46. In addition to Bandura's seminal book, *Self-Efficacy: The Exercise of Control,* op. cit., which is based on several hundred studies and his article aimed at organizational performance, "Cultivate Self-Efficacy for Personal and Organizational Effectiveness," op. cit., see his most recent article, Albert Bandura and Edwin A. Locke, "Negative Self-Efficacy and Goal Effects Revisited," *Journal of Applied Psychology,* Vol. 88, No. 1, 2003, pp. 87–99, that summarizes meta-analyses and defends these overwhelming positive results against a couple of recent, somewhat critical studies, namely: Jefferey B. Vancouver, Charles M. Thompson, and Amy A. Williams, "The Changing Signs in the Relationships among Self-Efficacy, Personal Goals, and Performance," *Journal of Applied Psychology,* Vol. 86, No. 4, 2001, pp. 605–620, and Jefferey B. Vancouver, Charles M. Thompson, E. Casey Tischner, and Dan J. Putka, "Two Studies Examining the Negative Effect of Self-Efficacy on Performance," *Journal of Applied Psychology,* Vol. 87, No. 3, 2002, pp. 506–516. Some examples of the various meta-analyses showing the very positive impact of efficacy include G. Holden, "The Relationship of Self-Efficacy Appraisals to Subsequent Health Related Outcomes: A Meta-Analysis," *Social Work in Health Care,* Vol. 16, 1991, pp. 53–93; G. Holden, M. S. Moncher, S. P. Schinke, and K. M. Barker, "Self-Efficacy of Children and Adolescents: A Meta-Analysis," *Psychological Reports,* Vol. 66, 1990, pp. 1044–1060; K. D. Multon, S. D. Brown, and R. W. Lent, "Relation of Self-Efficacy Beliefs to Academic Outcomes: A Meta-Analytic Investigation," *Journal of Counseling Psychology,* Vol. 38, 1991, pp. 30–38; and Stajkovic and

Luthans, "Self-Efficacy and Work-Related Performance," op. cit.

47. Albert Bandura, "Social Cognitive Theory of Personality," in L. Pervin and O. John (Eds.), *Handbook of Personality,* 2nd ed., Guilford, New York, 1999, p. 181.

48. Bandura, "Cultivate Self-Efficacy for Personal and Organizational Effectiveness," op. cit., p. 126, and Christine M. Shea and Jane M. Howell, "Efficacy-Performance Spirals: An Empirical Test," *Journal of Management,* Vol. 26, No. 4, 2000, pp. 791–812.

49. Bandura, "Social Cognitive Theory of Personality," op. cit., p. 181.

50. Robert F. Mager, "No Self-Efficacy, No Performance," *Training,* April 1992, p. 36.

51. Albert Bandura, "Self-Efficacy: Toward a Unifying Theory of Behavioral Change," *Psychological Review,* Vol. 84, 1977, p. 193.

52. For the full review including references on all the applications, see Daniel Cervone, "Thinking about Self-Efficacy," *Behavior Modification,* Vol. 24, No. 1, 2000, p. 33. Also see Bandura, *Self-Efficacy: The Exercise of Control,* op. cit.

53. Stajkovic and Luthans, "Self-Efficacy and Work-Related Performance: A Meta-Analysis," op. cit.

54. Ibid., p. 252.

55. R. E. Wood, A. J. Mento, and E. A. Locke, "Task Complexity as a Moderator of Goal Effects: A Meta Analysis," *Journal of Applied Psychology,* Vol. 72, 1987, pp. 416–425.

56. A. N. Kluger and A. DeNisi, "The Effects of Feedback Interventions on Performance: A Historical Review, a Meta-Analysis, and a Preliminary Feedback Intervention Theory," *Psychological Bulletin,* Vol. 119, 1996, pp. 254–284.

57. Alexander D. Stajkovic and Fred Luthans, "A Meta-Analysis of the Effects of Organizational Behavior Modification on Task Performance," *Academy of Management Journal,* Vol. 40, 1997, pp. 1122–1149, and Alexander D. Stajkovic and Fred Luthans, "Behavioral Management and Task Performance in Organizations: Conceptual Background, Meta-Analysis, and Test of Alternative Models," *Personnel Psychology,* Vol. 56, 2003, pp. 155–194.

58. For the extensive review of the literature from which this conclusion is drawn, see Stajkovic and Luthans, "Self-Efficacy and Work-Related Performance: A Meta-Analysis," op. cit., p. 253; Timothy A. Judge and Joyce E. Bono, "Relationship of Core Self-Evaluation Traits—Self-Esteem, Generalized Self-Efficacy, Locus of Control, and Emotional Stability—With Job Satisfaction and Job Performance: A Meta-Analysis," *Journal of Applied Psychology,* Vol. 86, No. 1, 2001, pp. 80–92; and Timothy A. Judge, Carl J. Thoresen, Joyce E. Bono, and Gregory K. Patton, "The Job Satisfaction—Job Performance Relationship: A Qualitative and Quantitative Review," *Psychological Bulletin,* Vol. 127, No. 3, 2001, pp. 376–407.

59. See Luthans, Avolio, Avey, and Norman, op. cit.

60. Bandura, *Self-Efficacy: The Exercise of Control,* op. cit., Chapter 12.

61. Bandura, "Cultivate Self Efficacy for Personal and Organizational Effectiveness," op. cit.

62. See E. A. Locke, E. Frederick, C. Lee, and P. Bobko, "Effects of Self-Efficacy, Goals and Task Strategies on Task Performance," *Journal of Applied Psychology,* Vol. 69, 1984, pp. 241–251, and Stajkovic and Luthans, "Social Cognitive Theory and Self-Efficacy," op. cit., pp. 68–69.

63. C. Lee and P. Bobko, "Self-Efficacy Beliefs: Comparison of Five Measures," *Journal of Applied Psychology,* Vol. 79, 1994, pp. 364–369.

64. Bandura, *Self-Efficacy: The Exercise of Control,* op. cit., p. 45.

65. See Bandura, "Cultivate Self-Efficacy for Personal and Organizational Effectiveness," op. cit., pp. 126–133.

66. M. E. Gist, "The Influence of Training Method on Self-Efficacy and Idea Generation among Managers," *Personnel Psychology,* Vol. 42, 1989, pp. 787–805.

67. Bandura, "Cultivating Self-Efficacy for Personal and Organizational Effectiveness," op. cit., p. 132, and Locke and Latham, op. cit.

68. Paul J. Taylor, Darlene F. Russ-Eft, and Daniel W. L. Chan, "A Meta-Analytic Review of Behavior Modeling Training," *Journal of Applied Psychology,* Vol. 90, No. 4, 2005, pp. 692–709.

69. Ibid.; Gist, op. cit.; and M. E. Gist, A. G. Bavetta, and C. K. Stevens, "Transfer Training Method," *Personnel Psychology,* Vol. 43, 1990, pp. 501–523.

70. Gwendolyn M. Combs and Fred Luthans, "Diversity Training: Analysis of the Impact of Self-Efficacy," *Human Resource Development Quarterly,* Vol. 18, No. 1, 2007, pp. 91–120.

71. Fred Luthans, James B. Avey, and Jaime L. Patera, "Experimental Analysis of a Web-Based Training Intervention to Develop Positive Psychological Capital," *Academy of Management Learning & Education,* Vol. 7, No. 2, 2008, pp. 209–221.

72. Fred Luthans, James B. Avey, Bruce J. Avolio, Steven M. Norman, and Gwendolyn M. Combs, "Psychological Capital Development: Toward a Micro-Intervention," *Journal of Organizational Behavior,* Vol. 27, 2006, pp. 387–393.

73. For example, see S. M. Jex and P. D. Bliese, "Efficacy Beliefs as a Moderator of the Impact of Work-Related Stressors: A Multilevel Study," *Journal of Applied Psychology,* Vol. 84, 1999, pp. 349–361, and John Schaubroeck, Simon S. K. Lam, and Jia LinXie, "Collective Efficacy versus Self-Efficacy in Coping Responses to Stressors and Control," *Journal of Applied Psychology,* Vol. 85, No. 4, 2000, pp. 512–525.

74. Stanley M. Gully, Kara A. Incalcaterra, Aparna Joshi, and J. Matthew Beaubien, "A Meta-Analysis of Team-Efficacy, Potency, and Performance," *Journal of Applied Psychology,* Vol. 87, No. 5, 2002, pp. 819–832; Cristina B. Gibson, "Me and Us: Differential Relationships among Goal Setting Training, Efficacy and Effectiveness at the Individual and Team Level," *Journal of Organizational Behavior,* Vol. 22, 2001, pp. 789–808; and Steve Alper, Dean Tjosvold, and Kenneth S. Law, "Conflict Management, Efficacy, and Performance in Organizational Teams," *Personnel Psychology,* Vol. 53, 2000, pp. 625–642.

75. For example, see Christina B. Gibson, Amy E. Randel, and P. Christopher Earley, "Understanding Group Efficacy," *Group & Organization Management,* Vol. 25, No. 1, 2000, pp. 67–97; C. B. Gibson, "Do They Do What They Believe They Can? Group Efficacy and Group Effectiveness across Tasks and Cultures," *Academy of Management Journal,* Vol. 42,

1999, pp. 138–152; and Alexander D. Stajkovic and Dongseop Lee, "A Meta-Analysis of the Relationship between Collective Efficacy and Group Performance," Working Paper, University of Wisconsin, Department of Management, Madison, Wis., 2003.

76. S. K. Parker, "Enhancing Role Breadth Self-Efficacy: The Roles of Job Enrichment and Other Organizational Interventions," *Journal of Applied Psychology,* Vol. 83, 1998, pp. 835–852, and Carolyn M. Axtell and Sharon K. Parker, "Promoting Role Breadth Self-Efficacy through Involvement, Work Redesign and Training," *Human Relations,* Vol. 56, No. 1, 2003, pp. 113–131.

77. See P. C. Earley and T. R. Lituchy, "Delineating Goal and Efficacy Effects: A Test of Three Models," *Journal of Applied Psychology,* February 1991, pp. 81–98; Locke and Latham, op. cit.; and Bradford S. Bell and Steve W. J. Kozlowski, "Goal Orientation and Ability: Interactive Effects on Self-Efficacy, Performance, and Knowledge," *Journal of Applied Psychology,* Vol. 87, No. 3, 2002, pp. 497–505.

78. Pamela Tierney and Steven M. Farmer, "Creative Self-Efficacy: Its Potential Antecedents and Relationship to Creative Performance," *Academy of Management Journal,* Vol. 45, No. 6, 2002, pp. 1137–1148.

79. For a recent comprehensive review article, see Sean T. Hannah, Bruce J. Avolio, Fred Luthans, and Peter Harms, "Leadership Efficacy: Review and Future Directions," *The Leadership Quarterly,* Vol. 19, No. 6, 2008, pp. 669–692.

80. See House and Shamir, op. cit.

81. See Chemers, Watson, and May, op. cit.; Gilad Chen and Paul D. Bliese, "The Role of Different Levels of Leadership in Predicting Self- and Collective-Efficacy," *Journal of Applied Psychology,* Vol. 87, No. 3, 2002, pp. 549–556; Laura L. Paglis and Stephen G. Green, "Leadership Self-Efficacy and Managers' Motivation for Leading Change," *Journal of Organizational Behavior,* Vol. 23, 2002, pp. 215–235; and Michael J. McCormick, "Self-Efficacy and Leadership Effectiveness: Applying Social Cognitive Theory to Leadership," *The Journal of Leadership Studies,* Vol. 8, No. 1, 2001, pp. 22–33.

82. For example, see F. Luthans, K. W. Luthans, R. M. Hodgetts, and B. C. Luthans, "Positive Approach to Leadership (PAL): Implications for Today's Organizations," *Journal of Leadership Studies,* Vol. 8, 2002, pp. 3–20; Fred Luthans and Bruce J. Avolio, "Authentic Leadership Develop-ment," in Kim S. Cameron, Jane E. Dutton, and Robert E. Quinn (Eds.), *Positive Organizational Scholarship,* Berrett-Koehler, San Francisco, 2003, pp. 241–258; Bruce J. Avolio and Fred Luthans, *The High Impact Leader: Moments Matter in Accelerating Authentic Leadership Development,* McGraw-Hill, New York, 2006; Susan Jensen and Fred Luthans, "The Relationship Between Entrepreneurs' Psychological Capital and Authentic Leadership Dimensions," *Journal of Managerial Issues,* Vol. 18, No. 2, 2006, pp. 254–273; and Susan Jensen and Fred Luthans, "The Entrepreneur as an Authentic Leader: Impact on Associates' Work-Related Attitudes," *Leadership and Organization Development Journal,* Vol. 27, No. 8, 2006, pp. 646–666.

83. Susan Webber, "The Dark Side of Optimism," *The Conference Board Review,* January/February 2008, p. 30.

84. Daniel Goleman, *Emotional Intelligence,* Bantam Books, New York, 1995, p. 89.

85. Christopher Peterson, "The Future of Optimism," *American Psychologist,* January 2000, p. 45.

86. For example, see Lionel Tiger, *Optimism: The Biology of Hope,* Simon & Schuster, New York, 1979, and S. E. Taylor, *Positive Illusions,* Basic Books, New York, 1989.

87. C. S. Carver and M. S. Scheier, "Optimism," in C. R. Snyder and S. J. Lopez (Eds.), *Handbook of Positive Psychology,* Oxford University Press, Oxford, UK, 2002, p. 231.

88. Martin E. P. Seligman, *Learned Optimism,* Pocket Books, New York, 1998 (originally published in 1991).

89. Ibid.

90. Christopher Peterson, "Meaning and Measurement of Explanatory Style," *Psychological Inquiry,* Vol. 2, 1991, pp. 1–10.

91. Peterson, "The Future of Optimism," op. cit., p. 47.

92. See Martin E. P. Seligman, *Helplessness: On Depression, Development and Death,* Freeman, San Francisco, 1975; Seligman and Csikszentmihalyi, "Positive Psychology," op. cit.; and Seligman, *Learned Optimism,* op. cit.

93. Peterson, op. cit., pp. 49–52.

94. M. F. Scheier and C. S. Carver, "The Effects of Optimism on Psychological and Physical Well-Being," *Cognitive Theory and Research,* Vol. 16, 1992, pp. 201–228.

95. See Seligman, *Learned Optimism,* op. cit.

96. Peterson, op. cit., pp. 50–51.

97. See Sandra L. Schneider, "In Search of Realistic Optimism," *American Psychologist,* Vol. 56, 2001, pp. 250–263, and Fred Luthans, Kyle Luthans, Richard M. Hodgetts, and Brett C. Luthans, "Positive Approach to Leadership," *The Journal of Leadership Studies,* Vol. 8, No. 2, 2001, pp. 3–20.

98. Seligman, *Learned Optimism,* op. cit., p. 99.

99. Ibid., pp. 102–104.

100. See Richard Boyatzis, *The Competent Manager: A Model for Effective Performance,* Wiley, New York, 1982, and Lyle M. Spencer, Jr., and Signe M. Spencer, *Competence at Work: Models for Superior Performance,* Wiley, New York, 1993.

101. Carolyn M. Youssef and Fred Luthans, "Positive Organizational Behavior in the Workplace," *Journal of Management,* Vol. 33, No. 5, 2007, pp. 774–800.

102. Fred Luthans, Bruce J. Avolio, Fred O. Walumbwa, and Weixing Li, "The Psychological Capital of Chinese Workers: Exploring the Relationship with Performance," *Management and Organizational Review,* Vol. 1, No. 2, 2005, pp. 249–271.

103. For example, see R. J. House and B. Shamir, "Towards the Integration of Transformational, Charismatic, and Visionary Theories," in M. M. Chemers and R. Ayman (Eds.), *Leadership Theory and Research: Perspectives and Directions,* Academic Press, San Diego, Calif., 1993, pp. 81–108.

104. Martin M. Chemers, Carl B. Watson, and Stephen T. May, "Dispositional Affect and Leadership Effectiveness: A Comparison of Self Esteem, Optimism, and Efficacy," *Personality and Social Psychology Bulletin,* Vol. 26, No. 3, 2000, pp. 267–277.

105. L. J. Wunderley, W. P. Reddy, and W. N. Dember, "Optimism and Pessimism in Business Leaders," *Journal of Applied Social Psychology,* Vol. 28, 1998, pp. 751–760.

106. E. Ransdell, "They Sell Suits with Soul," *Fast Company,* October 1998, pp. 66–68.

107. Daniel Goleman, *Working with Emotional Intelligence,* Bantam Books, New York, 1998, p. 128. Also see P. Schulman, "Applying Learned Optimism to Increase Sales Productivity," *Journal of Personal Selling and Sales Management,* Vol. 19, 1999, pp. 31–37.

108. Fred Luthans, "The Need for and Meaning of Positive Organizational Behavior," *Journal of Organizational Behavior,* Vol. 23, 2002, pp. 695–706.

109. For example, see R. C. Erickson, R. Post, and A. Paige, "Hope as a Psychiatric Variable," *Journal of Clinical Psychology,* Vol. 31, 1975, pp. 324–329, and J. E. Frank, "The Role of Hope in Psychotherapy," *International Journal of Psychiatry,* Vol. 5, 1968, pp. 383–395.

110. C. R. Snyder, L. Irving, and J. R. Anderson, "Hope and Health: Measuring the Will and the Ways," in C. R. Snyder and D. R. Forsyth (Eds.), *Handbook of Social and Clinical Psychology,* Pergamon, New York, 1991, p. 287.

111. Reported in Alan Bavley, "Researcher: Hope Leads to Greater Success," *Lincoln Journal Star,* March 24, 2000, p. 1A, 8A, and drawn from L. A. Curry et al., "The Role of Hope in Student-Athlete Academic and Sport Achievement," *Journal of Personality and Social Psychology,* Vol. 73, 1997, pp. 1257–1267; A. J. Onwuegbuzie and C. R. Snyder, "Relations between Hope and Graduate Students' Coping Strategies for Studying and Examination Taking," *Psychological Reports,* Vol. 86, 2000, pp. 803–806; and B. L. Simmons and D. L. Nelson, "Eustress at Work: The Relationship between Hope and Health in Hospital Nurses," *Health Care Management Review,* Vol. 6, 2001, pp. 7–18.

112. Goleman, *Emotional Intelligence,* op. cit., p. 87.

113. Seligman, *Learned Optimism,* op. cit., p. 48.

114. For a comprehensive analysis of the construct validity of hope, see C. R. Snyder, "Hope Theory: Rainbows in the Mind," *Psychological Inquiry,* Vol. 13, No. 4, 2002, pp. 256–258. Also see C. R. Snyder (Ed.), *Handbook of Hope,* Academic Press, San Diego, 2000.

115. For example, see P. R. Magaletta and J. M. Oliver, "The Hope Construct, Will and Ways: Their Relative Relations with Self-Efficacy, Optimism, and General Well-Being," *Journal of Clinical Psychology,* Vol. 55, 1999, pp. 539–551; F. B. Bryant and J. A. Cvengros, "Distinguishing Hope and Optimism," *Journal of Social and Clinical Psychology,* Vol. 23, 2004, pp. 273–302; Fred Luthans, Bruce J. Avolio, James B. Avey, and Steven M. Norman, "Psychological Capital: Measurement and Relationship with Performance and Satisfaction," *Personnel Psychology,* Vol. 60, 2007, pp. 541–572; and James Carifio and Lauren Roades, "Construct Validities and Empirical Relationships between Optimism, Hope, Self-Efficacy, and Locus of Control," *Work,* Vol. 19, 2002, pp. 125–136.

116. For the "Hope Scale," see C. R. Snyder, S. C. Sympson, F. C. Ybasco, T. F. Borders, M. A. Babyak, and R. L. Higgins, "Development and Validation of the State Hope Scale," *Journal of Personality and Social Psychology,* Vol. 70, 1996, pp. 321–335.

117. For examples of studies see L. A. Curry, C. R. Snyder, D. L. Cook, B. C. Ruby, and M. Rehm, "Role of Hope in Academic and Sport Achievement," *Journal of Personality and Social Psychology,* Vol. 73, 1997, pp. 1257–1267.

118. Spencer and Spencer, op. cit.

119. S. Kirk and G. Koeske, "The Fate of Optimism: A Longitudinal Study of Case Managers' Hopefulness and Subsequent Morale," *Research in Social Work Practice,* January 1995. Also see S. Taylor and J. D. Brown, "Illusion and Well-Being: A Social Psychological Perspective on Mental Health," *Psychological Bulletin,* Vol. 103, 1988, 193–210.

120. V. H. Adams et al. "Hope in the Workplace," in R. Giacalone and C. Jurkiewicz (Eds.), *Workplace Spirituality and Organizational Performance,* Sharpe, New York, 2003.

121. Suzanne J. Peterson and Fred Luthans, "The Positive Impact and Development of Hopeful Leaders," *Leadership and Organizational Development,* Vol. 24, No. 1, 2003, pp. 26–31.

122. Youssef and Luthans, op. cit.

123. Luthans, Avolio, Walumbwa, and Li, op. cit.

124. Suzanne J. Peterson and Kristin Byron, "Exploring the Role of Hope in Job Performance: Results from Four Studies," *Journal of Organizational Behavior,* Vol. 28, 2007, pp. 785–803.

125. Susan Jensen and Fred Luthans, "The Impact of Hope in the Entrepreneurial Process: Exploratory Research Findings," Working Paper, University of Nebraska, Department of Management, Lincoln, Nebr., 2003.

126. Fred Luthans and Susan Jensen, "Hope: A New Positive Strength for Human Resource Development," *Human Resource Development Review,* Vol. 1, 2002, pp. 304–322.

127. A. S. Masten and M. J. Reed, "Resilience in Development," in C. R. Snyder and S. Lopez (Eds.), *Handbook of Positive Psychology,* Oxford University Press, Oxford, UK, 2002, p. 75.

128. F. Luthans, "The Need for and Meaning of Positive Organizational Behavior," *Journal of Organizational Behavior,* Vol. 23, 2002, pp. 695–706.

129. A. S. Masten, "Ordinary Magic: Resilience Processes in Development," *American Psychologist,* Vol. 56, 2001, p. 235.

130. B. Egeland, E. Carlson, and L. A. Sroufe, "Resilience as a Process," *Development and Psychopathology,* Vol. 5, 1993, pp. 517–528.

131. For example, see A. S. Masten, K. M. Best, and N. Garmezy, "Resilience and Development: Contributions from the Study of Children Who Overcome Adversity," *Development and Psychopathology,* Vol. 2, 1990, pp. 425–444; A. S. Masten and N. Garmezy, "Risk, Vulnerability, and Protective Factors in Developmental Psychotherapy," in B. B. Lahey and A. E. Kazdin (Eds.), *Advances in Clinical Child Psychology,* Plenum, New York, Vol. 8, 1985, pp. 1–51; A. S. Masten and M. O. D. Weight, "Cumulative Risk and Protection Models of Child Maltreatment," in B. B. R. Rossman and M. S. Rosenberg (Eds.), *Multiple Victimization of Children: Conceptual, Developmental, Research and Treatment Issues,* Haworth, Binghamton, N.Y., 1998, pp. 7–30; and M. Stewart, G. Reid, and C. Mangham, "Fostering Children's Resilience," *Journal of Pediatric Nursing,* Vol. 12, No. 1, 1997, pp. 21–31.

132. J. LaMarch, "The Resilient Worker: Employees Who Can Cope with Change," *Hospital Material Management Quarterly,* Vol. 19, No. 2, 1997, pp. 54–58.

133. S. J. Zunz, "Resiliency and Burnout: Protective Factors for Human Service Managers," *Administration in Social Work*, Vol. 22, No. 3, 1998, pp. 39–54.

134. J. F. Horne III and J. E. Orr, "Assessing Behaviors That Create Resilient Organizations," *Employment Relations Today*, Vol. 24, No. 4, 1998, pp. 29–39; S. Klarreich, "Resiliency: The Skills Needed to Move Forward in a Changing Environment," in S. Klarreich (Ed.), *Handbook of Organizational Health Psychology: Programs to Make the Workplace Healthier*, Psychosocial Press, Madison, Conn., 1998, pp. 219–238; L. Ortiz, "The Resilience of a Company-Level System of Industrial Relations: Union Responses to Teamwork in Renault's Spanish Subsidiary," *European Journal of Industrial Relations*, Vol. 8, No. 3 2002, pp. 277–299.

135. C. K. Fay and K. Nordhaug, "Why Are There Differences in the Resilience of Malaysia and Taiwan to Financial Crisis?" *The European Journal of Development Research*, Vol. 14, No. 1, 2002, pp. 77–100.

136. D. L. Coutu, "How Resilience Works," *Harvard Business Review*, Vol. 80, 2002, 46–55, and F. Luthans and B. Avolio, "Authentic Leadership Development," in K. S. Cameron, J. E. Dutton, and R. E. Quinn (Eds.), *Positive Organizational Scholarship*, Berrett-Koehler, San Francisco, 2003, pp. 241–258.

137. Fred Luthans, Gretchen R. Vogelgesang and Paul B. Lester, "Developing the Psychological Capital of Resiliency," *Human Resource Development Review*, Vol. 5, No. 1, pp. 25–44.

138. J. Block and A. M. Kremen, "IQ and Ego-Resiliency: Conceptual and Empirical Connections and Separateness," *Journal of Personality and Social Psychology*, Vol. 70, 1996, pp. 349–361.

139. A. S. Masten and M. J. Reed, "Resilience in Development," in C. R. Snyder and S. Lopez (Eds.), *Handbook of Positive Psychology*, Oxford University Press, Oxford, U.K., 2002, pp. 74–88.

140. P. A. Cowan, C. P. Cowan, and M. S. Schulz, "Thinking about Risk and Resilience in Families," in E. M. Hetherington and E. A. Blechman (Eds.), *Stress, Coping, and Resiliency in Children and Families*, L. Erlbaum Associates, Mahwah, N.J., 1996, pp. 1–38.

141. D. L. Coutu, "How Resilience Works," *Harvard Business Review*, Vol. 80, 2002, p. 48.

142. See Carol D. Ryff and Burton Singer, "Flourishing under Fire: Resilience as a Prototype of Challenged Thriving," in C. L. Keys and J. Haidt (Eds.), *Flourishing*, American Psychological Association, Washington, D.C., 2003, pp. 15–36.

143. Carolyn M. Youssef and Fred Luthans, "Resiliency Development of Organizations, Leaders, and Employees: Multi-Level Theory Building for Sustained Performance." In William L. Gardner, Bruce J. Avolio, and Fred O. Walumbwa (Eds.), *Authentic Leadership Theory and Practice*, Elsevier, Oxford, UK, 2005, pp. 303–344.

144. See K. Reivich and A. Shatte, "Resilience at Work," *The Resilience Factor*, Broadway Books, New York, 2002, pp. 282–304.

145. J. F. Horne III and J. E. Orr, "Assessing Behaviors That Create Resilient Organizations," *Employment Relations Today*, Vol. 24, No. 4, 1998, pp. 29–39.

146. K. E. Weick, "The Collapse of Sensemaking in Organizations: The Mann Gulch Disaster," *Administrative Science Quarterly*, Vol. 38, 1993, pp. 628–652.

147. For example, see Luthans, Avolio, Avey, and Norman, op. cit.; and Fred Luthans, Bruce J. Avolio, Fred O. Walumbwa, and Weixing Li, "The Psychological Capital of Chinese Workers: Exploring the Relationship with Performance," *Management and Organization Review*, Vol. 1, 2005, pp. 247–269. Kathleen M. Sutcliffe and Timothy J. Vogus, "Organizing for Resilience," in Cameron, Dutton, and Quinn, op. cit., pp. 94–110.

148. Fred Luthans, Carolyn M. Youssef and Bruce J. Avolio, *Psychological Capital*, Oxford University Press, Oxford, UK, 2007.

149. Luthans, Avolio, Avey, and Norman, op. cit.

150. Luthans, Youssef, and Avolio, op. cit., p. 3.

151. See Luthans, Luthans, and Luthans, op. cit., 2004 and Luthans and Youssef, 2004.

152. Mihaly Csikszentmihalyi, *Good Business*, Viking, New York, 2003.

153. See Luthans, Youssef, and Avolio, op. cit., and Luthans, Avolio, Avey, and Norman, op. cit., p. 550.

154. Fred Luthans and Bruce J. Avolio, "The 'Point' of Positive Organizational Behavior," *Journal of Organizational Behavior*, Vol. 30, 2009, pp. 291–307.

155. Fred Luthans, Bruce J. Avolio, James B. Avey, and Steven M. Norman, "Positive Psychological Capital: Measurement and Relationship with Performance and Satisfaction," *Personnel Psychology*, Vol. 60, 2007, pp. 541–572.

156. Ibid.

157. James B. Avey, Fred Luthans, and Carolyn M. Youssef, "The Additive Value of Positive Psychological Capital in Predicting Work Attitudes and Behaviors," *Journal of Management*, Vol. 36, 2010, in press.

158. Luthans, Avolio, Walumbwa, and Li, op. cit.

159. Fred Luthans, James B. Avey, Rachel Clapp-Smith, and Weixing Li, "More Evidence on the Value of Chinese Workers' Psychological Capital: A Potentially Unlimited Competitive Resource?" *The International Journal of Human Resource Management*, Vol. 19, No. 5, 2008, pp. 818–827.

160. James B. Avey, Fred Luthans, and Susan M. Jensen, "Psychological Capital: A Positive Resource for Combating Employee Stress and Turnover," *Human Resource Management*, Vol. 48, No. 5, 2009, pp. 677–693.

161. James B. Avey, Tara S. Wernsing, and Fred Luthans, "Can Positive Employees Help Positive Organizational Change?" *The Journal of Applied Behavioral Science*, Vol. 44, No. 1, 2008, pp. 48–70.

162. Fred Luthans, Steven M. Norman, Bruce J. Avolio, and James B. Avey, "The Mediating Role of Psychological Capital in the Supportive Organizational Climate-Employee Performance Relationship," *Journal of Organizational Behavior*, Vol. 29, 2008, pp. 219–238.

163. David Sweetman, Fred Luthans, James B. Avey, and Brett C. Luthans, "Relationship between Positive Psychological Capital and Creative Performance," under second review at journal, 2009.

164. James B. Avey, Fred Luthans, Ronda M. Smith, and Noel Palmer, "Impact of Positive Psychological Capital on

Employee Well-Being Over Time," *Journal of Occupational Health Psychology,* 2009, in press.

165. See Bruce J. Avolio and Fred Luthans, *The High Impact Leader: Moments Matter in Accelerating Authentic Leadership Development,* McGraw-Hill, New York, 2006; and Fred Luthans and Bruce J. Avolio, "Authentic Leadership Development," in Kim S. Cameron, Jane E. Dutton, and Robert E. Quinn (Eds.), *Positive Organizational Scholarship,* Berrett-Koehler, San Francisco, 2003, pp. 241–258.

166. Steven M. Norman, Bruce J. Avolio, and Fred Luthans, "The Impact of Positivity and Transparency on Trust in Leaders and Their Perceived Effectiveness," *The Leadership Quarterly,* in press.

167. James B. Avey, Bruce J. Avolio, and Fred Luthans, "Experimentally Analyzing the Process and Impact of Leader Positivity on Follower Performance," under second review at journal, 2009.

168. Sean T. Hannah and Fred Luthans, "A Cognitive Affective Processing Explanation of Positive Leadership: Toward Theoretical Understanding of the Role of Psychological Capital," in R. H. Humphrey (Ed.), *Affect and Emotion—New Directions in Management Theory and Research,* Information Age Publishing, Charlotte, NC, 2008, pp. 95–134.

169. Luthans, Avolio, Avey, and Norman, op. cit.

170. Fred Luthans, James B. Avey, and Jaime Patera, "Experimental Analysis of a Web-Based Training Intervention to Develop Positive Psychological Capital," *Academy of Management Learning and Education,* Vol. 7, No. 2, 2008, pp. 209–221; and Fred Luthans, James B. Avey, Bruce J. Avolio, and Suzanne J. Peterson, "Impact of a Micro-Training Intervention on Psychological Capital Development and Performance," under second review at journal, 2009.

171. Luthans, Avey, and Avolio, Ibid.

172. For example, see Wayne F. Cascio, *Costing Human Resources: The Financial Impact of Behavior in Organizations.* PWS-Kent, Boston, 1991 and D. Kravetz, *Measuring Human Capital, Converting Workplace Behavior into Dollars,* KAP, Mesa, AZ, 2004.

173. See Luthans, Youssef, and Avolio, op. cit., Chapter 8 and Fred Luthans, James B. Avey, Bruce J. Avolio, Steven M. Norman, and Gwendolyn M. Combs, "Psychological Capital Development: Toward a Micro-Intervention," *Journal of Organizational Behavior,* Vol. 27, 2006, pp. 387–393.

174. Ibid.

175. See James B. Avey, Fred Luthans, and Ketan H. Mhatre, "A Call for Longitudinal Research in Positive Organizational Behavior," *Journal of Organizational Behavior,* Vol. 29, No. 5, 2008, pp. 705–711.

176. Suzanne J. Peterson, Fred Luthans, Bruce J. Avolio, and Fred O. Walumbwa, "A Longitudinal Investigation of Positive Psychological Capital and Workplace Performance," under review in journal, 2009.

177. Fred O. Walumbwa, Fred Luthans, James B. Avey, and Adegoke Oke, "Authentically Leading Groups: The Mediating Role of Psychological Capital and Trust," *Journal of Organizational Behavior,* Vol. 30, 2009, pp. 1–21.

178. See Luthans, Youssef, and Avolio, op. cit., Chapters 6 and 7.

179. Seligman and Csikszentmihalyi, op. cit., p. 9.

180. Ed Diener, "Subjective Well-Being: The Science of Happiness and a Proposal for a National Index," *American Psychologist,* January 2000, p. 34.

181. See ibid., and Ed Diener, Eunkook M. Suh, Richard E. Lucas, and Heidi L. Smith, "Subjective Well-Being: Three Decades of Progress," *Psychological Bulletin,* Vol. 125, No. 2, 1999, pp. 276–302. The discussion in this section largely draws from these two articles.

182. See Diener, op. cit., p. 34, and E. Suh, E. Diener, S. Oishi, and H. Triandis, "The Shifting Basis of Life Satisfaction Judgments across Cultures: Emotions versus Norms," *Journal of Personality and Social Psychology,* Vol. 74, 1998, pp. 482–493.

183. Diener, op. cit., p. 40.

184. Ed Diener and Robert Biswas-Diener, *Happiness,* Blackwell Publishing, Malden, MA, 2008.

185. Ibid., p. 9.

186. Deborah D. Danner, D. A. Snowden, and W. Friesen, "Positive Emotions in Early Life and Longevity: Findings from the Nun Study," *Journal of Personality and Social Psychology,* Vol. 80, 2001, pp. 804–813.

187. Reported in Jeffrey Kluger, "The Biology of Belief," *Time,* February 23, 2009, p. 66.

188. Diener and Biswas-Diener, op. cit., p. 50.

189. M. Tait, M. Y. Padgett, and T. T. Baldwin, "Job Satisfaction and Life Satisfaction: A Reexamination of the Strength of the Relationship and Gender Effects as a Function of the Date of the Study," *Journal of Applied Psychology,* Vol. 74, 1989, pp. 502–507.

190. T. A. Judge and C. L. Hulin, "Job Satisfaction as a Reflection of Disposition: A Multiple Source Causal Analysis," *Organizational Behavior and Human Decision Processes,* Vol. 56, 1993, pp. 388–421, and T. A. Judge and S. Watanabe, "Another Look at the Job Satisfaction–Life Satisfaction Relationship," *Journal of Applied Psychology,* Vol. 78, 1993, pp. 939–948.

191. M. J. Stones and A. Kozma, "Happy Are They Who Are Happy: A Test between Two Causal Models of Happiness and Its Correlates," *Experimental Aging Research,* Vol. 12, 1986, pp. 23–29.

192. For example, see Thomas A. Wright and Barry M. Staw, "Affect and Favorable Work Outcomes: Two Longitudinal Tests of the Happy-Productive Worker Thesis," *Journal of Organizational Behavior,* Vol. 20, 1999, pp. 1–23 and Thomas A. Wright, Russell Cropanzano and Douglas G. Bonett, "The Moderating Role of Employee Positive Well-Being on the Relation between Job Satisfaction and Job Performance," *Journal of Occupational Health Psychology,* Vol. 12, 2007, pp. 93–104.

193. Diener and Biswas-Diener, op. cit., p. 85.

194. Sonja Lyubomirsky, *The How of Happiness,* Penguin Press, New York, 2008, p. 64.

195. See ibid., Part Two, pp. 83–256.

196. Lyubomirsky, King, and Diener, op. cit.

197. Lyubomirsky, *The How of Happiness,* op. cit., pp. 250–251.

198. See Luthans, Youssef, and Avolio, op. cit., pp. 183–186.

199. For example, see Kenneth S. Law, Chi-Sum Wong, and Lynda J. Song, "The Construct and Criterion Validity of Emotional Intelligence and Its Potential Utility for Management Studies," *Journal of Applied Psychology,* Vol. 89, No. 3,

2004, pp. 483–496; Chi-Sum Wong, Ping-Man Wong, and Kenneth S. Law, "Evidence of the Practical Utility of Wong's Emotional Intelligence Scale in Hong Kong and Mainland China," *Asia Pacific Journal of Management,* Vol. 24, 2007, pp. 43–60; and Thomas Sy, Susanna Tram, and Linda A. O'Hara, "Relation of Employee and Manager Emotional Intelligence to Job Satisfaction and Performance," *Journal of Vocational Behavior,* Vol. 68, 2006, pp. 461–473.

200. For example, see Neal M. Ashkanasy, Charmine E. J. Hartel, and Wilfred J. Zerbe (Eds.), *Emotions in the Workplace: Research, Theory and Practice,* Quorum, Westport, Conn., 2000; and Richard P. Bagozzi, "Positive and Negative Emotions in Organizations," in Cameron, Dutton, and Quinn, op. cit.

201. Stephen P. Robbins, *Organizational Behavior,* 9th ed., Prentice Hall, Upper Saddle River, N.J., 2001, p. 104. Also see N. H. Frijda, "Moods, Emotion Episodes and Emotion," in M. Lewis and J. M. Haviland (Eds.), *Handbook of Emotions,* Guliford Press, New York, 1993, pp. 381–403.

202. See Cheryl L. Rusting, "Personality, Mood, and Cognitive Processing of Emotional Information," *Psychological Bulletin,* Vol. 124, No. 2, 1998, pp. 165–196. Also see John A. Lambie and Anthony J. Marcel, "Consciousness and the Varieties of Emotion Experience: A Theoretical Framework," *Psychological Review,* Vol. 109, No. 2, 2002, pp. 219–259.

203. Ibid. Also see Janice R. Kelly and Sigal G. Barsade, "Mood and Emotions in Small Groups and Work Teams," *Organizational Behavior and Human Decision Processes,* Vol. 86, No. 1, 2001, pp. 99–130; and Laurie J. Barclay, Daniel P. Skarlicki, and S. Douglas Pugh, "Exploring the Role of Emotions in Injustice Perceptions and Retaliation," *Journal of Applied Psychology,* Vol. 90, No. 4, 2005, pp. 629–643; and Nina Keith and Michael Frese, "Self-Regulation in Error Management Training: Emotion Control and Metacognition as Mediators of Performance Effects," *Journal of Applied Psychology,* Vol. 90, No. 4, 2005, pp. 677–691.

204. See J. M. Kidd, "Emotion: An Absent Presence in Career Theory," *Journal of Vocational Behavior,* June 1998, pp. 275–288.

205. The classic analysis of the limits of rational models is found in Herbert A. Simon, *Administrative Behavior,* 2d ed., Macmillan, New York, 1957, and Herbert A. Simon, *The New Science of Management Decision,* Harper, New York, 1960.

206. Barbara L. Fredrickson, "The Role of Positive Emotions in Positive Psychology: The Broaden-and-Build Theory of Positive Emotions," *American Psychologist,* Vol. 56, No. 3, 2001, pp. 218–226.

207. Barbara L. Fredrickson, "Positive Emotions and Upward Spirals in Organizations," in Cameron, Dutton, and Quinn, op. cit., pp. 163–175.

208. See Barbara L. Fredrickson, "The Role of Positive Emotions in Positive Psychology: The Broaden-and-Build Theory of Positive Emotions," *American Psychologist,* Vol. 56, 2001, pp. 218–226; and Barbara L. Fredrickson, *Positivity,* Crown Publishers, New York, 2009, pp. 21–24.

209. See ibid. and the meta-analysis by Lyubomirsky, King, and Diener, op. cit.

210. See R. S. Lazarus, *Emotion and Adaptation,* Oxford University Press, New York, 1991, and J. A. Russell and L. F. Barrett, "Core Affect, Prototypical Emotional Episodes, and Other Things Called Emotion: Dissecting the Elephant," *Journal of Personality and Social Psychology,* May 1999, pp. 805–819.

211. R. D. Woodworth, *Experimental Psychology,* Holt, New York, 1938.

212. See J. A. Morris and D. C. Feldman, "The Dimensions, Antecedents, and Consequences of Emotional Labor," *Academy of Management Review,* Vol. 21, 1996, pp. 986–1010.

213. Michael W. Kramer and Jon A. Hess, "Communication Rules for the Display of Emotions in Organizational Settings," *Management Communication Quarterly,* Vol. 16, No. 1, 2002, pp. 66–80.

214. Karen Pugliese, "The Consequences of Emotional Labor: Effects on Work Stress, Job Satisfaction, and Well-Being," *Motivation and Emotion,* Vol. 23, No. 2, 1999, pp. 125–153.

215. Quoted in Kevin Friberg and Jackie Friberg, *Nuts!* Bard Press, Austin, Tex., 1996, p. 65.

216. For example, see Rusting, op. cit.; Joanne Martin, Kathleen Knopoff, and Christine Beckman, "An Alternative to Bureaucratic Impersonality and Emotional Labor: Bounded Emotionality at the Body Shop," *Administrative Science Quarterly,* Vol. 43, 1998, pp. 429–469; and Wei-Chi Tsai, "Determinants and Consequences of Employee Displayed Positive Emotions," *Journal of Management,* Vol. 27, 2001, pp. 497–512.

217. See B. E. Ashforth and R. R. Humphrey, "Emotion in the Workplace: A Reappraisal," *Human Relations,* Vol. 48, 1995, pp. 97–125.

218. See A. R. Hochschild, "Emotion Work, Feeling Rules, and Social Structure," *American Journal of Sociology,* November 1979, pp. 551–575, and L. A. King, "Ambivalence over Emotional Expression and Reading Emotions," *Journal of Personality and Social Psychology,* March 1998, pp. 753–762.

219. For a summary of this research, see Etienne Benson, "Breaking New Ground," *Monitor on Psychology,* Vol. 34, No. 2, 2003, pp. 52–54. The research on the relationship of genes and intelligence mostly comes from Robert Plomin and colleagues.

220. Ibid.

221. Ibid. The research on the effect of stereotypes on test performance comes from Claude Steele and colleagues.

222. Ibid. This study was conducted by Paul Davies and collaborators and was published in *Personality and Social Psychology Bulletin,* Vol. 28, No. 12, 2002.

223. For a summary of this research, see Etienne Benson, "Intelligence across Cultures," *Monitor on Psychology,* Vol. 34, No. 2, 2003, pp. 56–58. Also see Richard Nisbett, *The Geography of Thought,* Free Press, New York, 2003.

224. Ibid.

225. Howard Gardner, *Frames of Mind: The Theory of Multiple Intelligences,* Basic Books, New York, 1983. A 10th anniversary edition, with a new introduction published in 1993.

226. Howard Gardner, "Reflections on Multiple Intelligences: Myths and Messages," *Phi Delta Kappa,* November 1995, pp. 200–203, 206–209.

227. Howard Gardner, *Multiple Intelligences: The Theory in Practice,* Basic Books, New York, 1993.

228. Frank L. Schmidt and John E. Hunter, "The Validity and Utility of Selection Methods in Personnel Psychology: Practical and Theoretical Implications of 85 Years of Research Findings," *Psychological Bulletin,* Vol. 124, No. 2, 1998, pp. 262–274. Also see Frank L. Schmidt and John E. Hunter, "Select on Intelligence," in Edwin A. Locke (Ed.), *The Blackwell Handbook of Principles of Organizational Behavior,* Blackwell, Oxford, U.K., 2000, pp. 3–14.

229. Frank Landy, "Some Historical and Scientific Issues Related to Research on Emotional Intelligence," *Journal of Organizational Behavior,* Vol. 26, No. 4, 2005, pp. 411–426.

230. P. Slovey and J. D. Mayer, "Emotional Intelligence," *Imagination, Cognition and Personality,* Vol. 9, No. 3, 1990, p. 189.

231. Daniel Goleman, *Working with Emotional Intelligence,* Bantam Books, New York, 1998, p. 317.

232. For example, see Gerald Matthews, Moshe Zeidner, and Richard D. Roberts, *Emotional Intelligence: Science and Myth,* MIT Press, Boston, 2003; Landy, op. cit.; and Edwin A. Locke, "Why Emotional Intelligence Is an Invalid Concept," *Journal of Organizational Behavior,* Vol. 26, No. 4, 2005, pp. 425–431.

233. For example, see Joseph Ciarrochi, Joseph P. Forgas, and John D. Mayer (Eds.), *Emotional Intelligence in Everyday Life: A Scientific Inquiry,* The Psychology Press, Philadelphia, 2001 and Peter Salovey, John D. Mayer, and David Caruso, "The Positive Psychology of Emotional Intelligence," in C. R. Snyder and Shane L. Lopez (Eds.), *Handbook of Positive Psychology,* Oxford, Oxford, U.K., 2002, pp. 159–171.

234. For example, see Neal M. Ashkanasy and Catherine S. Daus, "Rumors of the Death of Emotional Intelligence in Organizational Behavior Are Vastly Exaggerated," *Journal of Organizational Behavior,* Vol. 26, No. 4, 2005, pp. 441–452; Law, Wong, and Song, op. cit., and Joseph C. Rode et al., "Emotional Intelligence and Individual Performance: Evidence of Direct and Moderated Effects," *Journal of Organizational Behavior,* Vol. 28, No. 4, 2007, pp. 399–421.

235. Benson, "Breaking New Ground," op. cit., p. 53.

236. See Jeffrey M. Conte, "A Review and Critique of Emotional Intelligence Measures," *Journal of Organizational Behavior,* Vol. 26, No. 4, 2005, pp. 433–440.

237. Sy, Tram, and O'Hara, op. cit., p. 461.

238. Nancy Gibbs, "The EQ Factor," *Time,* October 2, 1995, p. 61. An example of such research would be Peter J. Jordan, Neal M. Ashkanasy, and Charmine E. J. Hartel, "Emotional Intelligence as a Moderator of Emotional and Behavioral Reactions to Job Insecurity," *Academy of Management Review,* Vol. 27, No. 3, 2002, pp. 361–372.

239. Daniel Goleman, *Emotional Intelligence,* Bantam Books, New York, 1995, p. xiii.

240. Goleman, *Working with Emotional Intelligence,* op. cit., p. 7.

241. For examples of the criticism, see Bridget Murray, "Does Emotional Intelligence Matter in the Workplace," *The APA Monitor,* Vol. 29, No. 7, July 1998, pp. 1–3, and M. Davies, L. Stankov, and R. D. Roberts, "Emotional Intelligence: In Search of an Elusive Construct," *Journal of Personality and Social Psychology,* October 1998, pp. 989–1015.

242. Richard E. Boyatzis, Elizabeth C. Stubbs, and Scott N. Taylor, "Learning Cognitive and Emotional Intelligence Competencies through Graduate Management Education," *Academy of Management Learning and Education,* Vol. 1, No. 2, 2002, pp. 150–162. Also see "The Feel-good Factor," *The Economist,* February 17, 2001, p. 59.

243. Goleman, Working with Emotional Intelligence, op. cit., p. 7.

## Chapter 8 Footnote References and Supplemental Readings

1. Fred Luthans, Richard M. Hodgetts, and Stuart A. Rosenkrantz, *Real Managers,* Ballinger, Cambridge, Mass., 1988, p. 27 and Chap. 6.

2. Eric M. Eisenberg and Marsha G. Witten, "Reconsidering Openness in Organizational Communication," *Academy of Management Review,* July 1987, pp. 418–426. Also see Brenda Allen, "Translating Organizational Communication Scholarship into Practice," *Management Communication Quarterly,* Vol. 16, No. 1, 2002, pp. 101–105.

3. Fred Luthans and Janet K. Larsen, "How Managers Really Communicate," *Human Relations,* Vol. 39, No. 2, 1986, pp. 161–178.

4. Ibid.

5. Bernard J. Reilly and Joseph A. Di Angelo, Jr., "Communication: A Cultural System of Meaning and Value," *Human Relations,* February 1990, p. 129.

6. "What You Should Know About Using Web 2.0," *HR Focus,* April 2008, pp. 10–11.

7. John M. Ivancevich and Michael T. Matteson, *Organizational Behavior and Management,* 3rd ed., McGraw-Hill, New York, 1993, p. 633.

8. Raymond S. Nickerson, "How We Know—And Sometimes Misjudge—What Others Know: Imputing One's Own Knowledge to Others," *Psychological Review,* Vol. 125, No. 6, 1999, pp. 737–759.

9. Aubrey Fisher, *Small Group Decision Making,* McGraw-Hill, New York, 1974, p. 23.

10. See Andres McAfee and Erik Brynjolfsson, "Investing in the IT that Makes a Competitive Difference," *Harvard Business Review,* July–August 2008, pp. 98–107.

11. For summary of research see Luis Martins, Lucy Gilson, and Travis Maynard, "Virtual Teams: What Do We Know and Where Do We Go from Here," *Journal of Management,* Vol. 30, 2004, pp. 805–836. Also see Benson Rosen, Stacie Furst, and Richard Blackburn, "Overcoming Barriers to Knowledge Sharing in Virtual Teams," *Organizational Dynamics,* Vol. 36, No. 3, 2007, pp. 259–273.

12. Don Hellriegel, John W. Slocum, Jr., and Richard W. Woodman, *Organizational Behavior,* 4th ed., West, St. Paul, Minn., 1986, p. 221.

13. Paul Preston, *Communication for Managers,* Prentice Hall, Upper Saddle River, N.J., 1979, p. 161.

14. Martin G. Groder, "Incongruous Behavior: How to Read the Signals," *Bottom Line,* March 30, 1983, p. 13.

15. V. Hale Starr, quoted in "Expert: Non-Verbal Body Language Counts," *Omaha World Herald,* December 20, 1982, p. 2.

16. Daniel Goleman, *Emotional Intelligence,* Bantam, New York, 1995, and Nancy Gibbs, "The EQ Factor," *Time,* October 2, 1995, pp. 60–66.

17. See Robert S. Feldman, *Understanding Psychology,* 2nd ed., McGraw-Hill, New York, 1990, pp. 329–330.

18. For an account of the work done in Albania, see Fred Luthans and Sang M. Lee, "There Are Lessons to Be Learned as Albania Undergoes a Paradigm Shift," *International Journal of Organizational Analysis,* Vol. 2, No. 1, 1994, pp. 5–17, and Fred Luthans and Laura Riolli, "Albania and Bora," *Academy of Management Executive,* August 1997, pp. 61–72.

19. Joanne Yates and Wanda J. Orlikowski, "Genres of Organizational Communication: A Structural Approach to Studying Communication and Media," *Academy of Management Review,* April 1992, p. 299.

20. "Speaking to the Boss," *Training,* February 2000, p. 28.

21. Paul W. B. Atkins, Robert E. Wood, and Philip J. Rutgers, "The Effects of Feedback Format on Dynamic Decision Making," *Organizational Behavior and Human Decision Processes,* Vol. 88, 2002, pp. 587–604.

22. For example, see James W. Smither, Manuel London, Nicholas L. Vasilopoulos, Richard R. Reilly, Roger E. Millsap, and Nat Salvemini, "An Examination of the Effects of an Upward Feedback Program over Time," *Personal Psychology,* Vol. 48, 1995, p. 432; A. N. Kluger and A. DeNisi, "The Effects of Feedback Interventions on Performance," *Psychological Bulletin,* Vol. 119, 1996, pp. 254–284; and Todd J. Maurer and Jerry K. Palmer, "Management Development Intentions following Feedback," *The Journal of Management Development,* Vol. 18, No. 9, 1999, pp. 733–751.

23. Patricia Schiff Estess, "Open-Book Policy," *Entrepreneur,* March 2000, pp. 130–131.

24. K. Denise Bane, "Gaining Control by Losing It? The Dilemma of Entrepreneurial Information," *Academy of Management Executive,* Vol. 11, No. 2, 1997, pp. 80–81.

25. See Stephanie Armour, "Job Reviews Take on Added Significance in a Down Economy," *USA Today,* July 23, 2003, pp. 6A–6B.

26. See W. Tornow and M. London, *Maximizing the Value of 360-Degree Feedback: A Process for Successful Individual and Organizational Development,* Jossey-Bass, San Francisco, 1998, and Todd J. Maurer, Stephane Brutus, John Fleenor, and Manuel London, "Does 360-Degree Feedback Work in Different Industries?" *Journal of Management Development,* Vol. 17, No. 3, 1998, pp. 177–190.

27. Albert Bandura, *Social Foundations of Thought and Action,* Prentice Hall, Upper Saddle River, N.J., 1986; Alexander D. Stajkovic and Fred Luthans, "Social Cognitive Theory and Self-Efficacy," *Organizational Dynamics,* Vol. 26, No. 4, 1998, pp. 62–74; and Clive Fletcher and Caroline Baldry, "A Study of Individual Differences and Self-Awareness in the Context of Multi-Source Feedback," *Journal of Occupational and Organizational Psychology,* Vol. 73, 2000, pp. 303–319.

28. For example, see A. H. Church, "Managerial Self-Awareness in High Performing Individuals in Organizations," *Journal of Applied Psychology,* Vol. 82, 1997, pp. 281–292, and A. G. Walker and J. W. Smither, "A Five-Year Study of Upward Feedback: What Managers Do with Their Results Matters," *Personnel Psychology,* Vol. 56, 1999, pp. 393–428.

29. Fred Luthans and Suzanne J. Peterson, "360-Degree Feedback with Systematic Coaching," *Human Resource Management Journal,* Vol. 42, No. 3, 2003, pp. 243–256.

30. See the special issue on trust in *Academy of Management Review,* Vol. 23, No. 2, 1998. Also see Manuel Becerra and Anil K. Gupta, "Perceived Trustworthiness within the Organization: The Moderating Impact of Communication Frequency on Trustor and Trustee Effects," *Organization Science,* Vol. 14, No. 1, 2003, pp. 32–44.

31. Karen Auby, "A Boomer's Guide to Communicating with Gen X and Gen Y," *BusinessWeek,* August 25, 2008, p. 63.

32. Luthans and Larsen, op. cit., p. 168.

33. Fred Luthans, Stuart A. Rosenkrantz, and Harry W. Hennessey, "What Do Successful Managers Really Do? An Observational Study of Managerial Activities," *Journal of Applied Behavioral Science,* Vol. 21, No. 3, 1985, pp. 255–270.

34. J. Fulk and E. R. Wendler, "Dimensionality of Leader–Subordinate Interactions: A Path–Goal Investigation," *Organizational Behavior and Human Performance,* Vol. 30, 1982, pp. 241–264, and Larry E. Penley and Brian Hawkins, "Studying Interpersonal Communications in Organizations: A Leadership Application," *Academy of Management Journal,* June 1985, pp. 309–326.

35. For example, see Catherine Durnell Cramton, "Finding Common Ground in Dispersed Collaboration," *Organizational Dynamics,* Vol. 30, No. 4, 2002, pp. 356–367.

36. Daniel Katz and Robert Kahn, *The Social Psychology of Organizations,* 2nd ed. Wiley, New York, 1978, p. 445.

37. Luthans, Hodgetts, and Rosenkrantz, op. cit., Chap. 4.

38. Gerald M. Goldhaber, *Organizational Communication,* Wm. C. Brown, Dubuque, Iowa, 1974, p. 121.

39. Nancy M. Dixon, "The Hallways of Learning," *Organizational Dynamics,* Spring 1997, p. 23.

40. Chester I. Barnard, *The Functions of the Executive,* Harvard University Press, Cambridge, Mass., 1938, p. 14.

41. Herbert A. Simon, *The New Science of Management Decision,* Harper, New York, 1960, p. 2.

42. Henry Mintzberg, Duru Raisin-ghani, and André Theoret, "The Structure of 'Unstructured' Decision Processes," *Administrative Science Quarterly,* June 1976, pp. 246–275.

43. Richard L. Daft, *Organization Theory and Design,* West, St. Paul, Minn., 1983, pp. 357–358.

44. For example, see Kathleen M. Eisenhardt, "Strategy as Strategic Decision Making," *Sloan Management Review,* Spring 1999, pp. 65–72, and Mark McNeilly, "Gathering Information for Strategic Decisions, Routinely," *Strategy and Leadership,* Vol. 30, No. 5, 2002, pp. 29–32.

45. James W. Dean, Jr., and Mark P. Sharfman, "Does Decision Process Matter? A Study of Strategic Decision-Making Effectiveness," *Academy of Management Journal,* Vol. 39, No. 2, 1996, pp. 368–396; Barbara A. Mellers, "Choice and the Relative Pleasure of Consequences," *Psychological Bulletin,* Vol. 126, No. 6, 2000, pp. 910–924; and W. Jack Duncan, Kevin G. LaFrance, and Peter M. Ginter, "Leadership and Decision Making: A Retrospective Application and Assessment," *Journal of Leadership and Organizational Studies,* Vol. 9, No. 4, 2003, pp. 1–20.

46. See for example Paul C. Nutt, "Surprising but True: Half the Decisions in Organizations Fail," *Academy of Management Executive,* Vol. 13, No. 4, 1999, pp. 75–90, and Paul C. Nutt, *Why Decisions Fail: Avoiding the Blunders and Traps That Lead to Debacles,* Berrett-Koehler, San Francisco, 2002.

47. See Tom Bateman, "Leading for Results: Brief-but-Powerful Lessons from Katrina and Iraq," *Organizational Dynamics,* Vol. 37, No. 4, 2008, pp. 301–312; Mark Martinko, Denise M. Breaux, Arthur D. Martinez, James Summers, and Paul Harvey, "Hurricane Katrina and Attributions of Responsibility," *Organizational Dynamics,* Vol. 38, No. 1, 2009, pp. 52–63; and Wayne F. Cascio and Peter Cappelli, "Lessons from the Financial Services Crisis," *HR Magazine,* January 2009, pp. 47–50.

48. See Gary Klein and Karl E. Weick, "Decisions: Making the Right Ones, Learning from the Wrong Ones," *Across the Board,* June 2000, pp. 16–22.

49. See Max H. Bazerman, *Judgement in Managerial Decision Making,* Wiley, New York, 1994; David M. Messick, and Max H. Bazerman, "Ethical Leadership and the Psychology of Decision Making," *Sloan Management Review,* Winter 1996, pp. 9–22; J. Keith Murnighan and John C. Mowen, *The Art of High-Stakes Decision Making: Tough Calls in a Speed-Driven World,* Wiley, New York, 2002; and Myeong-Gu Seo and Lisa Feldman Barrett, "Being Emotional During Decision Making—Good or Bad?" *Academy of Management Journal,* Vol. 50, No. 4, 2007, pp. 923–940.

50. See Madan M. Pillutla and Xiao-Ping Chen, "Social Norms and Cooperation in Social Dilemmas: The Effects of Context and Feedback," *Organizational Behavior and Human Decision Processes,* May 1999, pp. 81–103; Gerry McNamara and Philip Bromiley, "Risk and Return in Organizational Decision Making," *Academy of Management Journal,* Vol. 42, No. 3, 1999, pp. 330–339; and Stan Davis and Christopher Meyer, "Laying Off Risk," *Across the Board,* April 2000, pp. 33–37.

51. Herbert A. Simon, *Administrative Behavior,* 2d ed., Macmillan, New York, 1957, p. 64.

52. Ibid., pp. 76–77.

53. Paul Gray, "The Assault on Freud," *Time,* November 29, 1993, pp. 47–51.

54. For example, see Rajagopal Raghunathan and Michel Tuan Pham, "All Negative Moods Are Not Equal: Motivational Influences of Anxiety and Sadness on Decision Making," *Organizational Behavior and Human Decision Processes,* July 1999, pp. 56–77.

55. Solomon E. Asch, "Opinions and Social Pressure," *Scientific American,* November 1955, pp. 31–35.

56. Barry M. Staw and Jerry Ross, "Understanding Behavior in Escalation Situations," *Science,* October 1989, pp. 216–220. For recent research, see Donald A. Hantula and Jennifer L. DeNicolis Bragger, "The Effects of Equivocality on Escalation of Commitment: An Empirical Investigation of Decision Dilemma Theory," *Journal of Applied Social Psychology,* Vol. 29, No. 2, 1999, pp. 424–444.

57. Henry Moon, "Looking Forward and Looking Back: Integrating Completion and Sunk-Cost Effects within an Escalation-of-Commitment Progress Decision," *Journal of Applied Psychology,* Vol. 86, No. 1, 2001, pp. 104–113.

58. For meta-analytic analyses of the complex impact of various human dynamics on decision making, see Jay J. J. Christensen-Szalanski and Cynthia Fobian Willham, "The Hindsight Bias: A Meta-Analysis," *Organizational Behavior and Human Decision Processes,* Vol. 48, 1991, pp. 147–168; Charles R. Schwenk, "Effects of Devil's Advocacy and Dialectical Inquiry on Decision Making: A Meta-Analysis," *Organizational Behavior and Human Decision Processes,* Vol. 47, 1990, pp. 161–176; and Robert L. Cross and Susan E. Brodt, "How Assumptions of Consensus Undermine Decision Making," *MIT Sloan Management Review,* Winter 2001, pp. 86–94.

59. Fred Luthans and Robert Koester, "The Impact of Computer-Generated Information on the Choice Activity of Decision Makers," *Academy of Management Journal,* June 1976, pp. 328–332, and Robert Koester and Fred Luthans, "The Impact of the Computer on the Choice Activity of Decision Makers: A Replication with Actual Users of Computerized MIS," *Academy of Management Journal,* June 1979, pp. 416–422.

60. Gary A. Williams and Robert B. Miller, "Change the Way You Persuade," *Harvard Business Review,* May 2002, pp. 66–67.

61. See A. J. Rowe and R. O. Mason, *Managing with Style: A Guide to Understanding, Assessing and Improving Decision Making,* Jossey-Bass, San Francisco, 1987.

62. M. J. Dolinger and W. Danis, "Preferred Decision-Making Styles: A Cross-Cultural Comparison," *Psychological Reports,* 1998, pp. 255–261.

63. For example, see W. H. Weiss, "Organizing for Quality, Productivity, and Job Satisfaction," *Supervision,* Vol. 63, No. 2, 2002, pp. 13–16.

64. For example, see Robert S. Dooley and Gerald E. Fryxell, "Attaining Decision Quality and Commitment from Dissent: The Moderating Effects of Loyalty and Competence in Strategic Decision-Making Teams," *Academy of Management Journal,* Vol. 42, No. 4, 1999, pp. 389–402.

65. See J. A. Wagner III, C. R. Lenna, E. A. Locke, and D. M. Schweiger, "Cognitive and Motivational Frameworks in U.S. Research on Participation: A Meta-Analysis of Primary Effects," *Journal of Organizational Behavior,* Vol. 18, 1997, pp. 49–65.

66. Nathaniel Foote, Eric Matson, Leigh Weiss, and Etienne Wenger, "Leveraging Group Knowledge for High-Performance Decision-Making," *Organizational Dynamics,* Vol. 31, No. 3, 2002, pp. 280–295.

67. Simon S. K. Lam, Xiao-Ping Chen, and John Schaubroeck, "Participative Decision Making and Employee Performance in Different Cultures: The Moderating Effects of Allocentrism/Idiocentrism and Efficacy," *Academy of Management Journal,* Vol. 45, No. 5, 2002, pp. 905–914.

68. David M. Schweiger and Carrie R. Leana, "Participation in Decision Making," in Edwin A. Locke (Ed.), *Generalizing from Laboratory to Field Settings,* Lexington Books, Lexington, Mass., 1986, p. 148; Steve Alper, Dean Tjosvold, and Kenneth S. Law, "Interdependence and Controversy in Group Decision Making: Antecedents to Effective Self-Managing Teams," *Organizational Behavior and Human Decision Processes,* April 1998, pp. 33–52; and David E. Drehmer, James A. Belohlav, and Ray W. Coye, "An Exploration of Employee Participation Using a Scaling Approach," *Group and Organization Management,* Vol. 25, No. 4, 2000, pp. 397–418.

69. Stewart Black and Newton Margulies, "An Ideological Perspective on Participation: A Case for Integration," *Journal of Organizational Change Management,* Vol. 2, No. 1, 1989,

pp. 13–34, and L. Alan Witt, "Exchange Ideology as a Moderator of the Relationships between Importance of Participation in Decision Making and Job Attitudes," *Human Relations*, Vol. 45, 1992, pp. 73–86.

70. Wagner et al., op. cit.

71. John L. Cotton, David A. Vollrath, Kirk L. Froggatt, Mark L. Lengnick-Hall, and Kenneth R. Jennings, "Employee Participation: Diverse Forms and Different Outcomes," *Academy of Management Review*, January 1988, pp. 8–22.

72. For example, see Jane Henry (Ed.), *Creative Management*, Sage, Thousand Oaks, Calif., 2001, and Amy Muller and Llisa Välikangas, "Extending the Boundary of Corporate Innovation," *Strategy & Leadership*, Vol. 30, No. 3, 2002, pp. 4–9.

73. Teresa M. Amabile and Regina Conti, "Changes in the Work Environment for Creativity during Downsizing," *Academy of Management Journal*, Vol. 42, No. 6, 1999, pp. 630–640.

74. Teresa M. Amabile, "How to Kill Creativity," *Harvard Business Review*, September–October 1998, p. 78.

75. Teresa M. Amabile, Constance N. Hadley, and Steven J. Kramer, "Creativity under the Gun," *Harvard Business Review*, May 2003, pp. 52–61.

76. For a summary see Filiz Tabak, "Employee Creative Performance: What Makes It Happen," *Academy of Management Executive*, Vol. 11, No. 1, 1997, pp. 119–120. For the original research, see Greg R. Oldham and Anne Cummings, "Employee Creativity: Personal and Contextual Factors at Work," *Academy of Management Journal*, Vol. 39, 1996, pp. 607–634.

77. Robert Root-Bernstein and Michele Root-Bernstein, *Sparks of Genius*, Houghton Mifflin, Boston, 2000.

78. Lisa A. Burke and Monica K. Miller, "Taking the Mystery Out of Intuitive Decision Making," *Academy of Management Executive*, Vol. 13, No. 4, 1999, pp. 91–99.

79. Eric Berggren and Thomas Nacher, "Why Good Ideas Go Bust," *Management Review*, February 2000, pp. 32–36.

80. Liz Simpson, "Basic Instinct," *Training*, January 2003, p. 56.

81. See E. M. Brockmann and W. P. Anthony, "The Influence of Tacit Knowledge and Collective Mind on Strategic Planning," *Journal of Managerial Issues*, Vol. 10, 1998, pp. 204–222, and D. Lenard and S. Sensiper, "The Role of Tacit Knowledge in Group Innovation," *California Management Review*, Vol. 40, 1998, pp. 112–132.

82. See Ian Mitroff, *Smart Thinking for Crazy Times*, Berrett-Koehler, San Francisco, 1998, and Cameron M. Ford and Dennis A. Gioia, "Factors Influencing Creativity in the Domain of Managerial Decision Making," *Journal of Management*, Vol. 26, No. 4, 2000, pp. 705–732.

83. See, for example Warren Bennis and Patricia Ward Biederman, *Organizing Genius: The Secrets of Creative Collaboration*, Addison Wesley, Reading, Mass., 1997; Ruth Palombo Weiss, "How to Foster Creativity at Work," *Training & Development*, February 2001, pp. 61–65; and Shari Caudron, "Become an Idea Agent," *Training and Development*, Vol. 55, No. 10, 2001, pp. 26–31.

84. Cheryl Comeau-Kirschner and Louisa Wah, "Who Has Time to Think?" *Management Review*, January 2000, pp. 16–23.

85. Suzy Wetlaufer, "Common Sense and Conflict: An Interview with Disney's Michael Eisner," *Harvard Business Review*, January–February 2000, p. 119.

86. Trish Hall, "When Budding MBAs Try to Save Kool-Aid. Original Ideas Are Scarce," *Wall Street Journal*, November 25, 1986, p. 31.

87. M. D. Mumford and S. B. Gustafson, "Creativity Syndrome: Integration, Application, and Innovation," *Psychological Bulletin*, Vol. 103, 1988, pp. 27–43.

88. This description is part of a study reported in W. C. Ward, N. Kogan, and E. Pankove, "Incentive Effects in Children's Creativity," *Child Development*, Vol. 43, 1972, pp. 669–676, and is found in Robert S. Feldman, *Understanding Psychology*, 2nd ed., McGraw-Hill, New York, 1990, p. 243.

89. Feldman, op. cit., pp. 242–243.

90. Weston H. Agor, "Use of Intuitive Intelligence to Increase Productivity," *HR Focus*, September 1993, p. 9.

91. Min Basadur, "Managing Creativity: A Japanese Model," *Academy of Management Executive*, May 1992, pp. 29–42.

92. Allen Ward, Jeffrey K. Liker, John J. Cristiano, and Durward K. Sobek II, "The Second Toyota Paradox: How Delaying Decisions Can Make Better Cars Faster," *Sloan Management Review*, Spring 1995, p. 43.

93. Dorothy Leonard and Jeffrey F. Rayport, "Spark Innovation through Empathic Design," *Harvard Business Review*, November–December 1997, pp. 102–103. Also see Stefan Thomke, "Enlightened Experimentation: The New Imperative for Innovation," *Harvard Business Review*, February 2001, pp. 67–75.

94. See, for example, Gary Hamel and C. K. Prahalad, *Competing for the Future*, Harvard Business School Press, Boston, 1994; the more recent Gary Hamel, *Leading the Revolution*, Harvard Business School Press, Boston, 2000; and George M. Scott, "Top Priority Management Concerns about New Product Development," *Academy of Management Executive*, Vol. 13, No. 3, 1999, pp. 77–84.

95. Paco Underhill, *Why We Buy: The Science of Shopping*, Simon & Schuster, New York, 1999.

96. For some recent research on the complexity of risky decision making, see Anton K&uuml;hberger, "The Influence of Framing on Risky Decisions: A Meta-Analysis," *Organizational Behavior and Human Decision Processes*, Vol. 75, No. 1, 1998, pp. 23–55; Sim B. Sitkin and Laurie R. Weingart, "Determinants of Risky Decision-Making Behavior: A Test of the Mediating Role of Risk Perceptions and Propensity," *Academy of Management Journal*, Vol. 38, No. 6, 1995, pp. 1573–1592; and Richard L. Priem, David A. Harrison, and Nan Kanoff Muir, "Structured Conflict and Consensus Outcomes in Group Decision Making," *Journal of Management*, Vol. 21, No. 4, 1995, pp. 691–710.

97. For a recent review of this research, see M. L. Ambrose and C. T. Kulik, "Old Friends, New Faces: Motivation Research in the 1990s," *Journal of Management*, Vol. 25, No. 3, 1999, pp. 267–268.

98. Spencer A. Rathus, *Psychology*, 4th ed., Holt, Rinehart & Winston, Fort Worth, Tex., 1990, pp. 634–635.

99. William S. Silver and Terence R. Mitchell, "The Status Quo Tendency in Decision Making," *Organizational Dynamics*, Spring 1990, pp. 45–46. Also see Paul B. Paulus and Huei-Chuan Yang, "Idea Generation in Groups: A Basis for Creativity in Organizations," *Organizational Behavior and Human Decision Processes*, Vol. 82, No. 1, 2000, pp. 76–87.

## Chapter 9 Footnote References and Supplemental Readings

1. See Marcie A. Cavanaugh, Wendy R. Boswell, Mark V. Roehling, and John W. Boudreau, "An Empirical Examination of Self-Reported Work Stress among U.S. Managers," *Journal of Applied Psychology,* Vol. 85, 2000, pp. 65–74.

2. Richard S. DeFrank, Robert Konopaske, and John M. Ivancevich, "Executive Travel Stress: Perils of the Road Warrior," *Academy of Management Executive,* Vol. 14, No. 2, 2000, pp. 58–71.

3. See Margaret L. Frank, "What's So Stressful about Job Relocation?" *Academy of Management Executive,* Vol. 14, No. 2, 2000, pp. 122–123; Josh Martin, "New Moves," *Management Review,* March 2000, pp. 35–38; Purnima Bhaskar-Shrinivas, David A. Harrison, Margaret A. Shaffer, and Dora M. Luk, "Input-Based and Time-Based Models of International Adjustment: Meta-Analytic Evidence and Theoretical Extensions," *Academy of Management Journal,* Vol. 48, No. 2, 2005, pp. 257–281; and Kerry Sulkowicz, "The New Me Nobody Knows," *BusinessWeek,* March 26, 2007, p. 18.

4. Reported in Bruce Weinstein, "Downsizing 102: When It Happens to You," *BusinessWeek,* September 29, 2008, p. 13.

5. "Leading Productivity Killers in Today's Market: Overwork, Stress," *HR Focus,* April 2008, p. 8.

6. Ibid.

7. "Beware the Dangers of Workaholism," *HR Focus,* January 2008, p. 9.

8. Ibid.

9. Reported in Will Dunham and Cynthia Osterman, "Many Americans Struggling in Life, Survey Finds," *Reuters,* April 29, 2008.

10. Cong Liu, Paul E. Spector, and Lin Shi, "Cross-National Job Stress," *Journal of Organizational Behavior,* Vol. 28, No. 2, 2007, pp. 209–239.

11. Jenna Goudreau, Gail Edmondson, Michelle Conlin, "Dispatches from the War on Stress," *BusinessWeek,* August 6, 2007, pp. 74–75.

12. Reported in *HR Focus,* April 1999, p. 4.

13. For background on hindrance and challenge see M. A. Cavanaugh, W. R. Bosell, M. V. Roehling, and J. W. Boudreau, "An Empirical Examination of Self-Reported Work Stress Among U.S. Managers," *Journal of Applied Psychology,* Vol. 85, 2000, pp. 65–74, and for the meta-analytic results see Jeffery A. Lepine, Nathan P. Podsakoff, and Marcie A. Lepine, "A Meta-Analytic Test of the Challenge Stressor-Hindrance Stressor Framework: An Explanation for Inconsistent Relationships Among Stressors and Performance," *Academy of Management Journal,* Vol. 48, No. 5, 2005, pp. 764–775.

14. Robert K. Cooper, "Excelling under Pressure," *Strategy & Leadership,* Vol. 29, No. 4, 2001, pp. 15–20.

15. "Leading Productivity Killers in Today's Market: Overwork, Stress," *HR Focus,* April 2008, p. 8.

16. John M. Ivancevich and Michael T. Matteson, *Organizational Behavior and Management,* Business Publications, Plano, Tex., 1987, p. 211.

17. See Terry A. Beehr, "The Current Debate about the Meaning of Job Stress," *Journal of Organizational Behavior*

*Management,* Fall/Winter 1986, pp. 5–18. For a more recent analysis of the complexity and meaning of stress, see Jeffrey R. Edwards, "An Examination of Competing Versions of the Person-Environment Fit Approach to Stress," *Academy of Management Journal,* April 1996, pp. 292–339.

18. John M. Ivancevich and Michael T. Matteson, *Organizational Behavior and Management,* 3rd ed., McGraw-Hill, New York, 1993, p. 244.

19. Richard S. DeFrank and J. M. Ivancevich, "Stress on the Job: An Executive Update," *Academy of Management Executive,* August 1998, pp. 55–66.

20. T. A. Beehr and J. E. Newman, "Job Stress, Employee Health, and Organizational Effectiveness: A Facet Analysis, Model, and Literature Review," *Personnel Psychology,* Winter 1978, pp. 665–699.

21. This summary is based on Hans Selye, *Stress without Distress,* Lippincott, Philadelphia, 1974, and James C. Quick and Jonathan D. Quick, *Organizational Stress and Preventative Management,* McGraw-Hill, New York, 1984, pp. 8–9. Also see Debra L. Nelson and James Campbell Quick, *Organizational Behavior,* 3rd ed., South-Western, Cincinnati, Ohio, 2000, Chapter 7.

22. Daniel C. Ganster and John Schaubroeck, "Work, Stress and Employee Health," *Journal of Management,* Vol. 17, 1991, pp. 235–271.

23. For example, see Gilbert Sand and Anthony D. Miyazaki, "The Impact of Social Support on Salesperson Burnout and Burnout Components," *Psychology and Marketing,* Vol. 17, No. 1, 2000, pp. 13–26.

24. Quoted in Lin Grensing-Popbal, "Commuting HR Eases the Pain," *HR Magazine,* March 1999, p. 84.

25. Ibid.

26. Reported in Joanne Cole, "An Ounce of Prevention Beats Burnout," *HR Focus,* June 1999, p. 1.

27. Reported in Todd Balf, "Are You Burned Out?" *Work Smarter, Not Harder,* Fast Company's Roadmap to Success, 2000, p. 25.

28. Phillip T. Potter, Bruce W. Smith, Kari R. Strobel, and Alex J. Zautra, "Interpersonal Workplace Stressors and Well-Being: A Multi-Wave Study of Employees with and without Arthritis," *Journal of Applied Psychology,* Vol. 87, No. 4, 2002, pp. 789–796.

29. Robert Kreitner, "Personal Wellness: It's Just Good Business," *Business Horizons,* May–June 1982, p. 28. Also see James Campbell Quick, Joanne H. Gavin, Cary L. Cooper, and Jonathan D. Quick, "Executive Health: Building Strength, Managing Risks," *Academy of Management Executive,* Vol. 14, No. 2, 2000, pp. 34–46.

30. See Hugh B. Price, "Age of Anxiety," *Leader to Leader,* Winter, 1997, pp. 15–17.

31. Joanne H. Gavin, James Campbell Quick, Cary L. Cooper, and Jonathan D. Quick, "A Spirit of Personal Integrity: The Role of Character in Executive Health," *Organizational Dynamics,* Vol. 32, No. 2, 2003, pp. 165–179.

32. See William Atkinson, "Employee Fatigue," *Management Review,* October 1999, pp. 56–60.

33. Dawn S. Carlson and Pamela L. Perrewé, "The Role of Social Support in the Stressor-Strain Relationship: An Examination of Work Family Conflict," *Journal of Management,* Vol. 25, No. 4, 1999, pp. 513–540.

34. Defrank and Ivancevich, op. cit., pp. 55–56.

35. Juan I. Sanchez, Paul E. Spector and Cary L. Cooper, "Adapting to a Boundaryless World: A Developmental Expatriate Model," *Academy of Management Executive,* Vol. 14, No. 2, 2000, pp. 96–106.

36. T. H. Holmes and R. H. Rahe, "Social Readjustment Rating Scale," *Journal of Psychosomatic Research,* Vol. 11, 1967, pp. 213–218.

37. *Wall Street Journal,* December 23, 1986, p. 1.

38. Defrank and Ivancevich, op. cit., pp. 55–56.

39. For example, see Lisa Hope Pelled, Kathleen M. Eisenhardt, and Katherine R. Xin, "Exploring the Black Box: An Analysis of Work Group Diversity, Conflict, and Performance," *Administrative Science Quarterly,* Vol. 44, 1999, pp. 1–28, and Sherry K. Schneider and Gregory B. Northcraft, "Three Social Dilemmas of Workforce Diversity in Organizations," *Human Relations,* Vol. 52, No. 11, 1999, p. 1445.

40. Nelson and Burke, op. cit., pp. 110–111.

41. Joseph J. Martocchio and Anne M. O'Leary, "Sex Differences in Occupational Stress: A Meta-Analytic Review," *Journal of Applied Psychology,* Vol. 74, No. 3, 1989, pp. 495–501.

42. Nelson and Burke, op. cit., and Wayne A. Hochwarter, Pamela L. Perrewé, and Mark C. Dawkins, "Gender Differences in Perceptions of Stress-Related Variables," *Journal of Managerial Issues,* Spring 1995, pp. 62–74.

43. R. Marens, "The Residential Environment," in A. Campbell, P. E. Converse, and W. L. Rodgers (Eds.), *The Quality of American Life,* Russell Sage, New York, 1976, and Gary W. Evans and Dana Johnson, "Stress and Open-Office Noise," *Journal of Applied Psychology,* Vol. 85, No. 5, 2000, pp. 779–783.

44. Michele J. Gelfand, Lisa H. Nishii, Karen M. Holcombe, Naomi Dyer, Ken-Ichi Ohbuchi, and Mitsuteru Fukuno, "Cultural Influences on Cognitive Representations of Conflict: Interpretations of Conflict Episodes in the United States and Japan," *Journal of Applied Psychology,* Vol. 86, No. 6, 2001, pp. 1059–1074.

45. Tim Kasser, Steve Cohn, Allen D. Kanner, and Richard M. Ryan, "Some Costs of American Corporate Capitalism: A Psychological Exploration of Value and Goal Conflict," *Psychological Inquiry,* Vol. 18, No. 1, 2007, pp. 1–22.

46. For example, see Ronda Roberts Callister and James A. Wall, Jr., "Conflict across Organizational Boundaries: Managed Care Organizations versus Health Care Providers," *Journal of Applied Psychology,* Vol. 86, No. 4, 2001, pp. 754–763; Ram Charan, "Stop Whining, Start Thinking," *BusinessWeek,* August 25, 2008, pp. 57–58.

47. Simona Gilboa, Arie Shirom, Yitzhak Fried, and Cary Cooper, "A Meta-Analysis of Work Demand Stressors and Job Performance," *Personnel Psychology,* Vol. 61, No. 2, 2008, pp. 227–271.

48. Patricia M. Buhler, "Managing in the New Millennium: The Manager's Role in Building an Innovative Organization," *Supervision,* Vol. 63, No. 8, 2002, pp. 20–22.

49. For example, see Patricia K. Zingheim and Jay R. Schuster, "In a Downturn Do You Cut Pay, Slash the Workforce or Protect Precious Talent?" *Strategy and Leadership,* Vol. 30, No. 1, 2002, pp. 23–28.

50. See Defrank and Ivancevich, op. cit., p. 57.

51. See Atkinson, op. cit.

52. John Schaubroeck and Daniel C. Ganster, "Chronic Demands and Responsivity to Challenge," *Journal of Applied Psychology,* February 1993, pp. 73–85.

53. Liz Ryan, "Addressing Deep-Rooted Conflicts," *BusinessWeek,* August 24, 2007, p. 14.

54. "Battling Bullying," *HR Focus,* June 2008, p. 10.

55. Michael R. Manning, Conrad N. Jackson, and Marcelline R. Fusilier, "Occupational Stress, Social Support, and the Costs of Health Care," *Academy of Management Journal,* June 1995, pp. 738–750.

56. Gerald R. Ferris, Dwight D. Frink, Maria Carmen Galang, Jing Zhou, K. Michele Kacmar, and Jack L. Howard, "Perceptions of Organizational Politics: Prediction, Stress-Related Implications, and Outcomes," *Human Relations,* Vol. 49, No. 2, 1996, pp. 233–266.

57. Christian Dormann and Dieter Zapf, "Social Stressors at Work, Irritation, and Depressive Symptoms: Accounting for Unmeasured Third Variables in a Multi-Wave Study," *Journal of Occupational and Organizational Psychology,* Vol. 75, 2002, pp. 33–58, Stephane Cote, "A Social Interaction Model of the Effects of Emotion Regulation on Work Strain," *Academy of Management Review,* Vol. 30, No. 3, 2005, pp. 509–530.

58. Arthur P. Brief, Randall S. Schuler, and Mary Van Sell, *Managing Job Stress,* Little, Brown, Boston, 1981, p. 94.

59. Meyer Friedman and Ray H. Rosenman, *Type A Behavior and Your Heart,* Knopf, New York, 1974.

60. John H. Howard, David A. Cunningham, and Peter A. Rechnitzer, "Health Patterns Associated with Type A Behavior: A Managerial Population," *Journal of Human Stress,* March 1976, pp. 24–31.

61. Friedman and Rosenman, op. cit.

62. Brief, Schuler, and Van Sell, op. cit., pp. 11–12.

63. Sarah Sherman and John Harris, "How to Get a Life and Do Your Job," *BusinessWeek,* August 28, 2008, pp. 36–39.

64. See Edward Dolnick, "Hotheads and Heart Attacks," *Health,* July/August 1995, pp. 58–64.

65. "Heart Disease, Anger Linked Research Shows," *Lincoln Journal,* January 17, 1989, p. 4.

66. "Some Workers Just Stress-Prone," *New York Times,* reported in *Lincoln Journal Star,* October 3, 1993, p. 3E.

67. See S. D. Bluen, J. Barling, and W. Burns, "Predicting Sales Performance, Job Satisfaction, and Depression by Using the Achievement Striving and Impatience-Irritability Dimensions of Type A Behavior," *Journal of Applied Psychology,* April 1990, pp. 212–216, and C. Lee, L. F. Jamison, and P. C. Earley, "Beliefs and Fears and Type A Behavior: Implications for Academic Performance and Psychiatric Health Disorder Symptoms," *Journal of Organizational Behavior,* March 1996, pp. 151–177.

68. Richard M. Steers, *Introduction to Organizational Behavior,* 2nd ed., Scott, Foresman, Glenview, Ill., 1984, p. 518, and Ellen Van Velsor and Jean Brittain Leslie, "Why Executives Derail: Perspectives across Time and Cultures," *Academy of Management Executive,* November 1995, pp. 62–72.

69. Ronald E. Riggio, *Introduction to Industrial/Organizational Psychology,* Scott, Foresman/Little, Brown, Glenview, Ill., 1990, p. 204.

70. S. E. Jackson, "Participation in Decision Making as a Strategy for Reducing Job Related Strain," *Journal of Applied Psychology,* Vol. 68, 1983, pp. 3–19.

71. "Jobs with Little Freedom Boost Heart Risk," *Lincoln Journal,* April 11, 1990, p. 1.

72. Marilyn L. Fox, Deborah J. Dwyer, and Daniel C. Ganster, "Effects of Stressful Job Demands and Control on Physiological and Attitudinal Outcomes in a Hospital Setting," *Academy of Management Journal,* April 1993, pp. 289–318.

73. Marko Elovainio, Mika Kivimäki, and Klaus Helkama, "Organizational Justice Evaluations, Job Control, and Occupational Strain," *Journal of Applied Psychology,* Vol. 86, No. 3, 2001, pp. 418–424.

74. M. E. P. Seligman, *Helplessness: On Depression, Development, and Death,* Freeman, San Francisco, 1975.

75. S. Mineka and R. W. Henderson, "Controllability and Predictability in Acquired Motivation," *Annual Review of Psychology,* Vol. 36, 1985, pp. 495–529.

76. See L. Y. Abrahamson, J. Garber, and M. E. P. Seligman, "Learned Helplessness in Humans: An Attributional Analysis," in J. Garber and M. E. P. Seligman (Eds.), *Human Helplessness: Theory and Applications,* Academic Press, New York, 1980, and summarized in Robert S. Feldman, *Understanding Psychology,* 2nd ed., McGraw-Hill, New York, 1990, p. 525. Also see Mark J. Martinko and William L. Gardner, "Learned Helplessness: An Alternative Explanation for Performance Deficits," *Academy of Management Review,* Vol. 7, 1982, pp. 413–417.

77. S. C. Kobasa, "Stressful Life Events, Personality, and Health: An Inquiry into Hardiness," *Journal of Personality and Social Psychology,* Vol. 37, 1979, pp. 1–11, and S. C. Kobasa, S. R. Maddi, and S. Kahn, "Hardiness and Health: A Perspective Study," *Journal of Personality and Social Psychology,* Vol. 42, 1982, pp. 168–177.

78. Brian O'Reilly, "Is Your Company Asking Too Much?" *Fortune,* March 12, 1990, p. 39.

79. Richard A. Dienstbier and Lisa M. Pytlik Zillig, "Toughness," in C. R. Snyder and Shane J. Lopez (Eds.), *Handbook of Positive Psychology,* Oxford University Press, New York, 2002, p. 524.

80. James B. Avey, Fred Luthans, and Susan M. Jensen, "Psychological Capital: A Positive Resource for Combating Employee Stress and Turnover," *Human Resource Management,* Vol. 48, No. 5, 2009, pp. 677–693.

81. Michael Orey, "Attacks by Colleagues Are Creeping Up," *BusinessWeek,* May 7, 2007, p. 14.

82. Sarah E. Needleman, "Businesses Say Theft by Their Workers Is Up," *The Wall Street Journal,* December 11, 2008, p. B8.

83. Scott C. Douglas and Mark J. Martinko, "Exploring the Role of Individual Differences in the Prediction of Workplace Aggression," *Journal of Applied Psychology,* Vol. 86, No. 4, 2001, pp. 547–559. Also see Manon Mireille LeBlanc and E. Kevin Kelloway, "Predictors and Outcomes of Workplace Violence and Aggression," *Journal of Applied Psychology,* Vol. 87, No. 3, 2002, pp. 444–453.

84. Michelle Inness, Julian Barling, and Nick Turner, "Understanding Supervisor-Targeted Aggression: A Within-Person, Between-Jobs Design," *Journal of Applied Psychology,* Vol. 90, No. 4, 2005, pp. 731–739. Also see Marie S. Mitchell and Maureen L. Ambrose, "Abusive Supervision and Workplace Deviance and the Moderating Effects of Negative Reciprocity Beliefs," *Journal of Applied Psychology,* Vol. 92, No. 4, 2007, pp. 1159–1168.

85. Victor Jockin, Richard D. Arvey, and Matt McGue, "Perceived Victimization Moderates Self-Reports of Workplace Aggression and Conflict," *Journal of Applied Psychology,* Vol. 86, No. 6, 2001, pp. 1262–1269.

86. I. M. Jawahar, "A Model of Organizational Justice and Workplace Aggression," *Journal of Management,* Vol. 28, No. 6, 2002, pp. 811–834.

87. Joerg Dietz, Sandra L. Robinson, Robert Folger, Robert A. Baron, and Martin Schulz, "The Impact of Community Violence and an Organization's Procedural Justice Climate of Workplace Aggression," *Academy of Management Journal,* Vol. 46, No. 3, 2003, pp. 317–326.

88. "The Most Effective Tool against Workplace Violence," *HR Focus,* February 2003, pp. 11–12.

89. Paul Eder and Robert Eisenberger, "Perceived Organizational Support: Reducing the Negative Influence of Coworker Withdrawal Behavior," *Journal of Management,* Vol. 34, No. 1, 2008, pp. 55–68.

90. Roderick D. Iverson and Stephen J. Deery, "Understanding the 'Personological' Basis of Employee Withdrawal: The Influence of Affective Disposition on Employee Tardiness, Early Departure, and Absenteeism," *Journal of Applied Psychology,* Vol. 86, No. 5, 2001, pp. 856–866.

91. Steve M. Jex, Paul D. Bliese, Sheri Buzzell, and Jessica Primeau, "The Impact of Self-Efficacy on Stressor-Strain Relations: Coping Style as an Explanatory Mechanism," *Journal of Applied Psychology,* Vol. 86, No. 3, 2001, pp. 401–409.

92. Steven P. Brown, Robert A. Westbrook, and Goutam Challagalla, "Good Cope, Bad Cope: Adaptive and Maladaptive Coping Strategies Following a Critical Negative Work Event," *Journal of Applied Psychology,* Vol. 90, No. 4, 2005, pp. 792–798.

93. John Huey, "Managing in the Midst of Chaos," *Fortune,* April 5, 1993, p. 38.

94. Cliff Cheng, "Multi-Level Gender Conflict Analysis and Organizational Change," *Journal of Organizational Change Management,* Vol. 8, No. 6, 1996, pp. 26–38, and Cheryl Aavon-Corbin, "The Multiple-Role Balancing Act," *Management Review,* October 1999, p. 62.

95. Isis H. Settles, Robert M. Sellers, and Alphonse Damas, Jr., "One Role or Two? The Function of Psychological Separation in Role Conflict," *Journal of Applied Psychology,* Vol. 87, No. 3, 2002, pp. 574–582.

96. Yitzhak et. al., "The Interactive Effect of Role Conflict and Role Ambiguity on Job Performance," *Journal of Occupational and Organizational Psychology,* Vol. 71, 1998, pp. 19–27, and Paul F. Buller, John J. Kohls, and Kenneth S. Anderson, "When Ethics Collide: Managing Conflicts across Cultures," *Organizational Dynamics,* Vol. 28, No. 4, 2000, pp. 52–66.

97. Yaping Gong, Oded Shenkar, Yadong Luo, and Mee-Kau Nyaw, "Role Conflict and Ambiguity of CEOs in International Joint Ventures: A Transaction Cost Perspective," *Journal of Applied Psychology,* Vol. 86, No. 4, 2001, pp. 764–773.

98. Brian O'Reilly, "Is Your Company Asking Too Much?" *Fortune,* March 12, 1990, p. 39.

99. Susan E. Jackson and Randall S. Schuler, "A Meta-Analysis and Conceptual Critique of Research on Role Ambiguity and Role Conflict in Work Settings," *Organizational Behavior and Human Decision Processes,* Vol. 36, 1985, pp. 16–78, and Cynthia D. Fisher and Richard Gitelson, "A Meta-Analysis of the Correlates of Role Conflict and Ambiguity," *Journal of Applied Psychology,* Vol. 68, No. 2, 1983, pp. 320–333.

100. Steven W. Floyd and Peter J. Lane, "Strategizing throughout the Organization: Managing Role Conflict in Strategic Renewal," *Academy of Management Review,* Vol. 25, No. 1, 2000, pp. 154–177.

101. David A. Whetten and Kim S. Cameron, *Developing Management Skills,* 2nd ed., HarperCollins, New York, 1991, pp. 397–399.

102. Ibid., p. 398.

103. Ibid., p. 399.

104. Ibid., pp. 400–402. These categories are based on some of the original work of Alan C. Filley, *Interpersonal Conflict Resolution,* Scott, Foresman. Glenview, Ill., 1975.

105. For example, see Amy E. Randel, "Identity Salience: A Moderator of the Relationship between Group Gender Composition and Work Group Conflict," *Journal of Organizational Behavior,* Vol. 23, 2002, pp. 749–766.

106. Karen A. Jehn and Elizabeth A. Mannix, "The Dynamic Nature of Conflict: A Longitudinal Study of Intragroup Conflict and Group Performance," *Academy of Management Journal,* Vol. 44, No. 2, 2001, pp. 238–251.

107. Jay W. Jackson, "Realistic Group Conflict Theory: A Review and Evaluation of the Theoretical and Empirical Literature," *The Psychological Record,* Summer 1993, p. 397.

108. See Gary Yukl, *Skills for Managers and Leaders,* Prentice Hall, Upper Saddle River, N.J., 1990, pp. 283–285.

109. Howard M. Guttman, "Conflict at the Top," *Management Review,* November 1999, pp. 49–50.

110. Tony L. Simons and Randall S. Peterson, "Task Conflict and Relationship Conflict in Top Management Teams: The Pivotal Role of Intragroup Trust," *Journal of Applied Psychology,* Vol. 85, No. 1, 2000, pp. 102–111.

111. Giuseppe Labianca, Daniel Brass, and Barbara Gray, "Social Networks and Perceptions of Intergroup Conflict: The Role of Negative Relationships and Third Parties," *Academy of Management Journal,* Vol. 41, No. 1, 1998, pp. 55–67.

112. Jeanne M. Brett, Stephen B. Goldberg, and William L. Ury, "Designing Systems for Resolving Disputes in Organizations," *American Psychologist,* February 1990, pp. 162–170. Also see Donald E. Conlon and Daniel P. Sullivan, "Examining the Actions of Organizations in Conflict," *Academy of Management Journal,* Vol. 42, No. 3, 1999, pp. 319–329.

113. Howard M. Weiss, Daniel R. Ilgen, and Michael E. Sharbaugh, "Effects of Life and Job Stress on Information Search Behaviors of Organizational Members," *Journal of Applied Psychology,* February 1982, pp. 60–62.

114. See Michael J. Burke, Arthur P. Brief, and Jennifer M. George, "The Role of Negative Affectivity in Understanding Relations between Self-Reports of Stressors and Strains: A Comment on the Applied Psychology Literature," *Journal of Applied Psychology,* June 1993, pp. 402–412; John Schaubroeck, Daniel C. Ganster, and Marilyn L. Fox, "Dispositional Affect and Work-Related Stress," *Journal of Applied Psychology,* Vol. 77, No. 3, 1992, pp. 322–335; and Paul E. Spector, Peter Y. Chen, and Brian J. O'Connell, "A Longitudinal Study of Relations between Job Stressors and Job Strains while Controlling for Prior Negative Affectivity and Strains," *Journal of Applied Psychology,* Vol. 85, No. 2, 2000, pp. 211–218.

115. Jenny Firth-Cozens, "Why Me? A Case Study of the Process of Perceived Occupational Stress," *Human Relations,* Vol. 45, No. 2, 1992, pp. 131–142.

116. Robert A. Baron, *Behavior in Organizations,* 2nd ed., Allyn & Bacon, Boston, 1986, p. 223. Also, see the recent comprehensive study by Cavanaugh et al., op. cit.

117. See Defrank and Ivancevich, op. cit., p. 58.

118. Vernon Silver, "Heart Attacks Are a Way of Life for Wall Street," *Lincoln Journal Star,* January 4, 1998, p. 2E.

119. John M. Ivancevich and Michael T. Matteson, *Stress and Work,* Scott, Foresman, Glenview, Ill., 1980, p. 92.

120. Peter Y. Chen and Paul E. Spector, "Relationships of Work Stressors with Aggression, Withdrawal, Theft and Substance Use: An Exploratory Study," *Journal of Occupational and Organizational Psychology,* September 1992, pp. 177–184. Also see Laurel R. Goulet, "Modeling Aggression in the Workplace: The Role of Role Models," *Academy of Management Executive,* Vol. 11, No. 2, 1997, pp. 84–85.

121. J. E. McGrath, "Stress and Behavior in Organizations," in M. D. Dunnette (Ed.), *Handbook of Industrial and Organizational Psychology,* Rand McNally, Chicago, 1976.

122. Beehr and Newman, op. cit.; A. A. McLean, *Work Stress,* Addison-Wesley, Reading, Mass., 1980; and Cary L. Cooper and Judi Marshall, "Occupational Sources of Stress," *Journal of Occupational Psychology,* March 1976, pp. 11–28.

123. "Job Stress Said a 'Substantial Health Problem,'" *Lincoln Journal,* October 6, 1986, p. 15.

124. Robert L. Brady, "Stress-Related Claims: What Can You Do about Them?" *HR Focus,* December 1995, pp. 19–20.

125. David S. Allen, "Less Stress, Less Litigation," *Personnel,* January 1990, p. 33.

126. "Employees' Behavioral Health Neglected," *Management Review,* November 1999, p. 10.

127. Ivancevich and Matteson, *Stress and Work,* p. 96.

128. "Firm Hopes Breath Meter Curbs Workers' Drinking," *Lincoln Journal,* June 11, 1983, p. 13.

129. Ibid.

130. For example, see A. J. Kinicki, F. M. McKee, and K. J. Wade, "Annual Review, 1991–1995: Occupational Health," *Journal of Vocational Behavior,* October 1996, pp. 190–220, and J. R. Edwards and N. P. Rothbard, "Work and Family Stress and Well-Being," *Organizational Behavior and Human Decision Processes,* February 1999, pp. 85–129.

131. Jeffrey R. Edwards, "A Cybernetic Theory of Stress, Coping, and Well-Being in Organizations," *Academy of Management Review,* April 1992, pp. 238–274. Also see Susan Oakland and Alistair Ostell, "Measuring Coping: A Review and Critique," *Human Relations,* Vol. 49, No. 2, 1996, pp. 133–155.

132. Kelly L. Zellars and Pamela L. Perrewé, "Affective Personality and the Content of Emotional Social Support: Coping in Organizations," *Journal of Applied Psychology*, Vol. 86, No. 3, 2001, pp. 459–467.

133. M. Audrey Korsgaard, Susan E. Brodt, and Ellen M. Whitener, "Trust in the Face of Conflict: The Role of Managerial Trustworthy Behavior and Organizational Context," *Journal of Applied Psychology*, Vol. 87, No. 2, 2002, pp. 312–319.

134. Sean M. Lyden, "Stress Case," *Business Start-Ups*, March 2000, p. 62. Also see Mitchell Lee Marks and Kenneth P. DeMuse, "Resizing the Organization: Maximizing the Gain While Minimizing the Pain of Layoffs, Divestitures, and Closing," *Organizational Dynamics*, Vol. 34, No. 1, 2005, pp. 19–35; and "Managing Stress: Tips on Staying Strong," *HR Focus*, December 2008, p. 15.

135. For example, see "Stress Management 101," *Management Review*, November 1999, p. 9; Kathleen McLaughlin, "The Lighter Side of Learning," *Training*, February 2001, pp. 48–52; J. E. Loehr, *Stress for Success*, Times Books, New York, 1998; Robert K. Cooper, "Excelling under Pressure," *Strategy & Leadership*, Vol. 29, No. 4, 2001, pp. 15–20; and Ben W. Heineman, Jr., "Can You Maintain Integrity Under Pressure? Stress Test," *The Conference Board Record*, September/October 2008, pp. 44–46.

136. Daniel C. Feldman and Hugh J. Arnold, *Managing Individual and Group Behavior in Organizations*, McGraw-Hill, New York, 1986, pp. 223–225. Also see Erik J. Van Slyke, "Resolve Conflict, Boost Creativity," *HR Magazine*, November 1999, pp. 132–137; and Steward D. Friedman, "Dial Down the Stress Level," *Harvard Business Review*, December 2008, pp. 28–29.

137. Mitzi M. Montoya-Weiss, Anne P. Massey, and Michael Song, "Getting It Together: Temporal Coordination and Conflict Management in Global Virtual Teams," *Academy of Management Journal*, Vol. 44, No. 6, 2001, pp. 1251–1262. Also see Dean Tjosvold, "The Conflict-Positive Organization: It Depends on Us," *Journal of Organizational Behavior*, Vol. 29, No. 1, 2007, pp. 19–28.

138. For example, see Kenneth Cloke and Joan Goldsmith, *Resolving Conflict at Work*, Jossey-Bass, San Francisco, 2000.

139. For example, see James Campbell Quick, Cary L. Cooper, Jonathan D. Quick, and Joanne H. Gavin, *The Financial Times Guide to Executive Health: Building Your Strengths, Managing Your Risks*, Pearson Education, London, 2002.

140. Christopher P. Neck and Kenneth H. Cooper, "The Fit Executive: Exercise and Diet Guidelines for Enhancing Performance," *Academy of Management Executive*, Vol. 14, No. 2, 2000, pp. 72–83.

141. J. M. Smyth, A. A. Stone, A. Hurewitz, and K. Kaell, "Effects of Writing about Stressful Experiences on Symptom Reduction in Patients with Asthma or Rheumatoid Arthritis," *Journal of the American Medical Association*, Vol. 281, 1999, pp. 1304–1329.

142. Robert K. Wallace and Herbert Benson, "The Physiology of Meditation," *Scientific American*, February 1972, pp. 84–90.

143. Terri Schultz, "What Science Is Discovering about the Potential Benefits of Meditation," *Today's Health*, April 1972, pp. 34–37.

144. Sonja Lyubomirsky, *The How of Happiness*, The Penguin Press, New York, 2008, p. 241.

145. Albert Bandura, *Social Foundations of Thought and Action*, Prentice Hall, Englewood Cliffs, N.J., 1986, and Albert Bandura, *Self-Efficacy*, Freeman, New York, 1997.

146. S. M. Jex and P. D. Bliese, "Efficacy Beliefs as a Moderator of the Impact of Work-Related Stressors: A Multilevel Study," *Journal of Applied Psychology*, Vol. 84, 1999, pp. 349–361.

147. Bandura, op. cit., 1997; Albert Bandura, "Cultivate Self-Efficacy for Personal and Organizational Effectiveness," in E. Locke (Ed.), *Handbook of Principles of Organizational Behavior*, Blackwell, Malden, Mass., 2000; and James E. Maddux, "Self-Efficacy," in C. R. Snyder and S. Lopez (Eds.), *Handbook of Positive Psychology*, Oxford, New York, 2002, pp. 282–284.

148. An example of a recent study would be Vivien K. G. Lim, "Job Insecurity and Its Outcomes: Moderating Effects of Work-Based and Nonwork-Based Social Support," *Human Relations*, Vol. 49, No. 2, 1996, pp. 171–194. Also see Benedict Carey, "Don't Face Stress Alone," *Health*, April 1997, pp. 74–76, 78.

149. For example, see Raymond T. Sparrowe, Robert C. Liden, Sandy J. Wayne, and Maria L. Kaimer, "Social Networks and the Performance of Individuals and Groups," *Academy of Management Journal*, Vol. 44, No. 2, 2001, pp. 316–325; Paul S. Adler and Seok-Woo Kwon, "Social Capital: Prospects for a New Concept," *Academy of Management Review*, Vol. 27, No. 1, 2002, pp. 17–40; and Fred Luthans, Kyle W. Luthans, and Brett C. Luthans, "Positive Psychological Capital: Beyond Human and Social Capital," *Business Horizons*, January–February 2004, pp. 45–50.

150. Anson Seers, Gail W. McGee, Timothy T. Serey, and George B. Graen, "The Interaction of Job Stress and Social Support: A Strong Inference Investigation," *Academy of Management Journal*, June 1983, pp. 273–284.

151. McLean, op. cit.

152. John Kotter, *The General Managers*, Free Press, New York, 1982, and Sparrowe et al., op. cit.

153. Fred Luthans, Stuart A. Rosenkrantz, and Harry W. Hennessey, "What Do Successful Managers Really Do? An Observation Study of Managerial Activities," *Journal of Applied Behavioral Science*, Vol. 21, No. 3, 1985, pp. 255–270; Scott E. Seibert, Maria L. Kraimer, and Robert C. Liden, "A Social Capital Theory of Career Success," *Academy of Management Journal*, Vol. 44, No. 2, 2001, pp. 219–237; and Wayne Baker, *Achieving Success through Social Capital*, Jossey-Bass, San Francisco, 2000.

154. Tiziano Casciaro and Miguel Sousa Lobo, "Competent Jerks, Lovable Fools, and the Formation of Social Networks," *Harvard Business Review*, June 2005, p. 92.

155. Gunter K. Stahl and Paula Caligiuri, "The Effectiveness of Expatriate Coping Strategies: The Moderating Role of Cultural Distance, Position Level, and Time on the International Assignment," *Journal of Applied Psychology*, Vol. 90, No. 4, 2005, pp. 603–615.

156. John C. Erfurt, Andrea Foote, and Max A. Heirich, "The Cost-Effectiveness of Worksite Wellness Programs for Hypertension Control, Weight Loss, Smoking Cessation, and Exercise," *Personnel Psychology*, Spring 1992, pp. 5–28;

Shirley Reynolds, Emma Taylor, and David A. Shapiro, "Session Impact in Stress Management Training," *Journal of Occupational and Organizational Psychology,* June 1993, pp. 99–113; and Richard S. Lazarus, "Toward Better Research on Stress and Coping," *American Psychologist,* June 2000, pp. 665–673.

157. Gary L. Wirt, "The ABCs of EAPs," *HR Focus,* November 1998, p. S12.

158. "EAP: Another Element of Support," *HR Focus,* February 1999, p. 8, and for basic research see Chester S. Spell and Terry C. Blum, "Adoption of Workplace Substance Abuse Prevention Programs: Strategic Choice and Institutional Perspectives," *Academy of Management Journal,* Vol. 48, No. 6, 2005, pp. 1125–1142.

159. Janina C. Latack, Angelo J. Kinicki, and Gregory E. Prussia, "An Integrative Process Model of Coping with Job Loss," *Academy of Management Review,* April 1995, pp. 311–342.

160. Nathan Bennett, Christopher L. Martin, Robert J. Bies, and Joel Brockner, "Coping with a Layoff: A Longitudinal Study of Victims," *Journal of Management,* Vol. 21, No. 6, 1995, pp. 1025–1040, and Frances M. McKee-Ryan, Zhaoli Song, and Connie R. Wanberg, "Psychological and Physical Well-Being During Unemployment: A Meta-Analytic Study," *Journal of Applied Psychology,* Vol. 90, No. 1, 2005, pp. 53–76.

161. Joel Brockner, Mary Konovsky, Rochelle Cooper-Schneider, Robert Folger, Christopher Martin, and Robert Bies, "Interactive Effects of Procedural Justice and Outcome Negativity on Victims and Survivors of Job Loss," *Academy of Management Journal,* April 1994, pp. 397–409.

162. Roland E. Kidwell, "Pink Slips without Tears," *Academy of Management Executive,* May 1995, pp. 69–70.

163. Caudron, op. cit., p. 39.

164. Ibid., pp. 40–48.

165. Margaret A. Neale and Max H. Bazerman, "Negotiating Rationally: The Power and Impact of the Negotiator's Frame," *Academy of Management Executive,* August 1992, p. 42.

166. Whetten and Cameron, op. cit., p. 402.

167. Kathleen M. O'Connor, Josh A. Arnold, and Ethan R. Burris, "Negotiators' Bargaining Histories and Their Effects on Future Negotiation Performance," *Journal of Applied Psychology,* Vol. 90, No. 2, 2005, pp. 350–362.

168. Neale and Bazerman, op. cit., p. 43. Also see Deborah B. Basler and Robert N. Stern, "Resistance and Cooperation: A Response to Conflict over Job Performance," *Human Relations,* Vol. 52, No. 8, 1999, p. 1029.

169. Leigh Thompson, Erika Peterson, and Susan E. Brodt, "Team Negotiation: An Examination of Integrative and Distributive Bargaining," *Journal of Personality and Social Psychology,* Vol. 70, No. 1, 1996, pp. 66–78.

170. Whetten and Cameron, op. cit., p. 404.

171. Roger Fisher and William Ury, *Getting to Yes,* Penguin, New York, 1983, p. 4.

172. Ibid., p. 9.

173. See Whetten and Cameron, op. cit., p. 404, and research such as Laurie R. Weingart, Rebecca J. Bennett, and Jeanne M. Brett, "The Impact of Consideration of Issues and Motivational Orientation on Group Negotiation Process and

Outcome," *Journal of Applied Psychology,* June 1993, pp. 504–517, and Kathleen L. McGinn and Angela T. Keros, "Improvisation and the Logic of Exchange in Socially Embedded Transactions," *Administrative Science Quarterly,* Vol. 47, 2002, pp. 442–473; and Peter H. Kim and Alison R. Fragale, "Choosing the Path to Bargaining Power: An Empirical Comparison of BATNAs and Contributions in Negotiation," *Journal of Applied Psychology,* Vol. 90, No. 2, 2005, pp. 373–381.

174. Whetten and Cameron, op. cit., p. 404.

175. Gregory B. Northcraft and Margaret A. Neale, *Organizational Behavior,* Dryden, Chicago, 1990, pp. 247–248.

176. Robert Adler, Benson Rosen, and Elliot Silverstein, "Thrust and Parry: The Art of Tough Negotiating," *Training and Development Journal,* March 1996, pp. 44–48.

177. Ibid., pp. 45–46. Also see Deborah M. Kolb and Judith Williams, "Breakthrough Bargaining" *Harvard Business Review,* February 2001, pp. 89–97.

178. Maurice E. Schweitzer and Jeffrey L. Kerr, "Bargaining under the Influence: The Role of Alcohol in Negotiations," *Academy of Management Executive,* Vol. 14, No. 2, 2000, p. 47.

179. For example, see Wendi L. Adair, Tetsushi Okumura, and Jeanne M. Brett, "Negotiation Behavior When Cultures Collide: The United States and Japan," *Journal of Applied Psychology,* Vol. 86, No. 3, 2001, pp. 371–385, and Catherine H. Tinsley, "How Negotiators Get to Yes: Predicting the Constellation of Strategies Used across Cultures to Negotiate Conflict," *Journal of Applied Psychology,* Vol. 86, No. 4, 2001, pp. 583–593.

180. Fisher and Ury, op. cit., p. 11.

181. Ibid., p. 13.

182. Ibid., p. 14.

## Chapter 10 Footnote References and Supplemental Readings

1. Rosabeth Moss Kanter, "Power Failure in Management Circuits," *Harvard Business Review,* July–August 1979, p. 65.

2. Lawrence G. Hrebiniak, *Making Strategy Work: Leading Effective Execution and Change,* Wharton Publishing, Philadelphia, PA, 2005.

3. Lawrence G. Hrebiniak, "Obstacles to Effective Strategy Implementation," *Organizational Dynamics,* Vol. 35, No. 1, 2006, pp. 12–31.

4. Ibid., p. 18.

5. Wesley Clark, "The Potency of Persuasion," *Fortune,* November 12, 2007, p. 48.

6. Max Weber, *The Theory of Social and Economic Organization,* A. M. Henderson and Talcott Parsons (trans. and Ed.), Free Press, New York, 1947, p. 152.

7. David Krackhardt, "Assessing the Political Landscape: Structure, Cognition, and Power in Organizations," *Administrative Science Quarterly,* Vol. 35, 1990, p. 343.

8. Jeffrey Pfeffer, *Managing with Power,* Harvard Business School Press, Boston, 1992, p. 30.

9. A. J. Grimes, "Authority, Power, Influence and Social Control: A Theoretical Synthesis," *Academy of Management Review,* October 1978, p. 725.

10. Jerald Greenberg and Robert A. Baron, *Behavior in Organizations: Understanding and Managing the Human Side of Work,* Prentice Hall, Upper Saddle River, N.J., 2000, p. 409.

11. Chester I. Barnard, *The Functions of the Executive,* Harvard University Press, Cambridge, Mass., 1938, p. 163.

12. Grimes, op. cit., p. 726.

13. Jennifer Reingold and Jia Lynn Yang, "What's Your OQ?" *Fortune,* July 23, 2007, p. 98.

14. John R. P. French, Jr., and Bertram Raven, "The Bases of Social Power," in D. Cartwright (Ed.), *Studies in Social Power,* University of Michigan, Institute for Social Research, Ann Arbor, 1959.

15. Timothy G. Pollock, Harald M. Fischer, and James B. Wade, "The Role of Power and Politics in the Repricing of Executive Options," *Academy of Management Journal,* Vol. 45, No. 6, 2002, pp. 1172–1182.

16. H. Joseph Reitz, *Behavior in Organizations,* 3rd ed., McGraw-Hill, New York, 1987, p. 435.

17. David G. Myers, *Social Psychology,* 3rd ed., McGraw-Hill, New York, 1990, p. 240. Also see Serena Chen, Annette Y. Lee-Chai, and John A. Bargh, "Relationship Orientation as a Moderator of the Effects of Social Power," *Journal of Personality and Social Psychology,* Vol. 80, No. 27, 2001, pp. 173–187.

18. Mitchell S. Nesler, Herman Aguinis, Brian M. Quigley, and James T. Tedeschi, "The Effect of Credibility on Perceived Power," *Journal of Applied Social Psychology,* Vol. 23, No. 17, 1993, pp. 1407–1425.

19. Roderick M. Kramer, "When Paranoia Makes Sense," *Harvard Business Review,* July 2002, p. 64.

20. Andrew S. Grove, "Breaking the Chains of Command," *Newsweek,* October 3, 1983, p. 23.

21. Kathryn M. Bartol and David C. Martin, "When Politics Pays: Factors Influencing Managerial Compensation Decisions," *Personnel Psychology,* Vol. 43, 1990, p. 599.

22. Herman Aguinis, Mitchell S. Nesler, Brian M. Quigley, Suk-Jae Lee, and James T. Tedeschi, "Power Bases of Faculty Supervisors and Educational Outcomes for Graduate Students," *Journal of Higher Education,* May-June 1996, pp. 267–297.

23. Steven L. McShane and Mary Ann Von Glinow, *Organizational Behavior,* McGraw-Hill, New York, 2000, and Gary Yukl and Celia M. Falbe, "Importance of Different Power Sources in Downward and Lateral Relations," *Journal of Applied Psychology,* 1991, Vol. 76, pp. 416–423.

24. Herman Aguinis, Mitchell S. Nesler, Brian M. Quigley, and James T. Tedeschi, "Perceptions of Power: A Cognitive Perspective," *Social Behavior and Personality,* Vol. 22, No. 4, 1994, pp. 377–384.

25. M. S. Nesler, H. Aguinis, B. M. Quigley, Suk-Jae Lee, and J. T. Tedeschi, "The Development and Validation of a Scale Measuring Global Social Power Based on French and Raven's Power Taxonomy," *Journal of Applied Social Psychology,* Vol. 20, No. 4, 1999, pp. 750–771.

26. K. W. Mossholder, N. Bennett, E. R. Kemery and M. A. Wesolowski, "Relationships between Bases of Power and Work Reactions: The Mediational Role of Procedural Justice," *Journal of Management,* Vol. 24, No. 4, 1998, pp. 533–552.

27. Pfeffer, op. cit., p. 69.

28. For example, see Herminia Ibarra and Steven B. Andrews, "Power, Social Influence, and Sense Making: Effects of Network Centrality and Proximity on Employee Perceptions," *Administrative Science Quarterly,* June 1993, pp. 277–303.

29. Stephen P. Robbins, *Organizational Behavior,* Prentice Hall, Upper Saddle River, N.J., 1979, p. 276.

30. Carol Stoak Saunders, "The Strategic Contingencies Theory of Power: Multiple Perspectives," *Journal of Management Studies,* January 1990, p. 4.

31. Daniel J. Brass and Marlene E. Burkhardt, "Potential Power and Power Use: An Investigation of Structure and Behavior," *Academy of Management Journal,* June 1993, pp. 441–470, and Chen et al., op. cit.

32. Adapted from Reitz, op. cit., pp. 441–443.

33. Ibid., pp. 442–443.

34. See Herbert C. Kelman, "Compliance, Identification, and Internalization: Three Processes of Attitude Change," *Journal of Conflict Resolution,* March 1958, pp. 51–60.

35. For a recent comprehensive analysis of identification in organizations, see Blake E. Ashforth, Spencer H. Harrison, and Kevin G. Corley, "Identification in Organizations: An Examination of Four Fundamental Questions," *Journal of Management,* Vol. 34, No. 3, 2008, pp. 325–374.

36. Robert J. Vandenberg, Robin M. Self, and Jai Hyun Seo, "A Critical Examination of the Internalization, Identification, and Compliance Commitment Measures," *Journal of Management,* Vol. 20, No. 1, 1994, pp. 123–140.

37. David C. McClelland, "The Two Faces of Power," *Journal of International Affairs,* Vol. 24, No. 1, 1970, p. 36.

38. Ibid., p. 41.

39. Eugene M. Fodor and Terry Smith, "The Power Motive as an Influence on Group Decision Making," *Journal of Personality and Social Psychology,* January 1982, pp. 178–185.

40. W. Alan Randolph, "Navigating the Journey to Empowerment," *Organizational Dynamics,* Spring 1995, p. 20.

41. Jena McGregor and Manjeet Kripalani, "The Employee Is Always Right," *BusinessWeek,* November 19, 2007, pp. 80–82.

42. Kyle Dover, "Avoiding Empowerment Traps," *Management Review,* January, 1999, pp. 51–55.

43. Ibid.

44. Jeffrey B. Arthur, "Effects of Human Resource Systems on Manufacturing Performance and Turnover," *Academy of Management Journal,* June 1994, pp. 670–687.

45. Gretchen M. Spreitzer, "Social Structural Characteristics of Psychological Empowerment," *Academy of Management Journal,* April 1996, pp. 483–504.

46. Jay Klagge, "The Empowerment Squeeze—Views from the Middle Management Position, *Journal of Management Development,* Vol. 17, No. 8, 1998, pp. 548–558. Also see W. Alan Randolph, "Rethinking Empowerment: Why Is It So Hard to Achieve?" *Organizational Dynamics,* Vol. 29, No. 2, 2000, pp. 94–107.

47. Pasquale Gagliardi, "Theories Empowering for Action," *Journal of Management Inquiry,* Vol. 8, No. 2, 1999, pp. 143–147.

48. Monica Lee, "The Lie of Power: Empowerment as Impotence," *Human Relations,* Vol. 52, No. 2, 1999, pp. 225–235.

49. Randolph, op. cit., p. 22.

50. Taylor and Ramsey, op. cit., pp. 71–76.

51. Charley Braun, "Organizational Infidelity: How Violations of Trust Affect the Employee-Employer Relationship," *Academy of Management Executive,* Vol. 11, No. 4, 1997, pp. 94–96.

52. A. C. Wicks, S. L. Berman, and T. M. Jones, "The Structure of Optimal Trust: Moral and Strategic Implications," *Academy of Management Review,* Vol. 24, No. 1, 1999, pp. 99–116.

53. Tom D'Aquanni and Gary Taylor, "Breaking the Political Stranglehold in the Executive Suite," *Management Review,* March 2000, pp. 42–46.

54. Oren Harari, "The Trust Factor," *Management Review,* January 1999, pp. 28–31.

55. Laura Tiffany, "Let the Games Begin," *Business Start-Ups,* March 2000, p. 90.

56. David E. Bowen and Edward E. Lawler, "The Empowerment of Service Workers: What, Why, How, and When," *Sloan Management Review,* Spring 1992, pp. 36–39. Also see David E. Bowen and Edward E. Lawler III, "Empowering Service Employees," *Sloan Management Review,* Summer 1995, p. 73.

57. Alvin Toffler, "Powership—In the Workplace," *Personnel,* June 1990, p. 21.

58. Clifford M. Koen, Jr., and Stephen M. Crow, "Human Relations and Political Skills," *HR Focus,* December 1995, pp. 10–12.

59. See James Rieley, *Gaining the System,* Financial Times/Prentice Hall, Upper Saddle River, N.J., 2001.

60. Douglas A. Schuler, Kathleen Rehbein, and Roxy D. Cramer, "Pursuing Strategic Advantage through Political Means: A Multivariate Approach," *Academy of Management Journal,* Vol. 45, No. 4, 2002, pp. 659–672, and Jean-Philippe Bonardi and Gerald D. Keim, "Corporate Political Strategies for Widely Salient Issues," *Academy of Management Review,* Vol. 30, No. 3, 2005, pp. 555–576.

61. Jeffrey Pfeffer, "Understanding Power in Organizations," *California Management Review,* Winter 1992, p. 29.

62. Walter Nord, "Dreams of Humanization and the Realities of Power," *Academy of Management Review,* July 1978, pp. 675–677.

63. Lawrence B. MacGregor Serven, *The End of Office Politics as Usual: A Complete Strategy for Creating a More Productive and Profitable Organization,* AMACOM, New York, 2002.

64. Gerald R. Ferris and K. Michele Kacmar, "Perceptions of Organizational Politics," *Journal of Management,* Vol. 18, No. 1, 1992, p. 93.

65. Marilyn Moats Kennedy, "The Death of Office Politics," *The Conference Board Review,* September/October 2008, p. 20.

66. Barbara Gray and Sonny S. Ariss, "Politics and Strategic Change across Organizational Life Cycles," *Academy of Management Review,* October 1985, p. 707.

67. Thomas B. Lawrence, Michael K. Mauws, Bruno Dyck, and Robert F. Kleysen, "The Politics of Organizational Learning: Integrating Power into the 4I Framework," *Academy of Management Review,* Vol. 30, No. 1, 2005, pp. 180–191.

68. Patricia M. Fandt and Gerald R. Ferris, "The Management of Information and Impressions: When Employees Behave Opportunistically," *Organizational Behavior and Human Decision Processes,* Vol. 45, 1990, p. 140. Also see Martin Gargiulo, "Two-Step Leverage: Managing Constraint in Organizational Politics," *Administrative Science Quarterly,* March 1993, pp. 1–19.

69. David Butcher and Martin Clarke, "Organizational Politics: The Cornerstone for Organizational Democracy," *Organizational Dynamics,* Vol. 31, No. 1, p. 2 (Executive Summaries).

70. Robert H. Miles, *Macro Organizational Behavior,* Goodyear, Santa Monica, Calif., 1980, pp. 182–184.

71. Ibid., p. 182.

72. Jone L. Pearce and Robert A. Page, Jr., "Palace Politics: Resource Allocation in Radically Innovative Firms," *The Journal of High Technology Management Research,* Vol. 1, 1990, pp. 193–205.

73. Graham Brown, Thomas B. Lawrence, and Sandra L. Robinson, "Territoriality in Organizations," *Academy of Management Review,* Vol. 30, No. 3, 2005, pp. 577–594.

74. Timothy A. Judge and Robert D. Bretz, Jr., "Political Influence Behavior and Career Success," *Journal of Management,* Vol. 20, No. 1, 1994, pp. 43–65. Also see Christopher P. Parker, Robert L. Dipboye, and Stacy L. Jackson, "Perceptions of Organizational Politics: An Investigation of Antecedents and Consequences," *Journal of Management,* Vol. 21, No. 5, 1995, pp. 891–912, and K. M. Kacmar, D. P. Bozemen, D. S. Carlson, and W. P. Anthony, "An Examination of the Preceptions of Organizational Politics Model: Replication and Extension," *Human Relations,* Vol. 52, No. 3, 1999 p. 383.

75. Amy J. Hillman and Michael A. Hitt, "Corporate Political Strategy Formulation: A Model of Approach, Participation, and Strategy Decisions," *Academy of Management Review,* Vol. 24, No. 4, 1999, pp. 825–842.

76. Also see Michael D. Lord, "Constituency Building as the Foundation for Corporate Political Strategy," *Academy of Management Executive,* Vol. 17, No. 1, 2003, pp. 112–124.

77. For example, see N. Anand and Jay A. Conger, "Capabilities of the Consummate Networker," *Organizational Dynamics,* Vol. 36, No. 1, 2007, pp. 13–37.

78. Gary Yukl and Cecilia M. Falbe, "Influence Tactics and Objectives in Upward, Downward, and Lateral Influence Attempts," *Journal of Applied Psychology,* Vol. 75, 1990, pp. 132–140.

79. Gary Yukl and J. Bruce Tracey, "Consequences of Influence Tactics Used with Subordinates, Peers, and the Boss," *Journal of Applied Psychology,* August 1992, pp. 525–535.

80. Jeffrey Pfeffer, "Power and Resource Allocation in Organizations," in Barry M. Staw and Gerald R. Salancik (Eds.), *New Directions in Organizational Behavior,* St. Clair, Chicago, 1977, pp. 255–260.

81. Andrew Kakabadse, "Organizational Politics," *Management Decision,* Vol. 25, No. 1, 1987, pp. 35–36. Also see Gerald R. Ferris, Pamela L. Perrewé, William P. Anthony, and David C. Gilmore, "Political Skill at Work," *Organizational Dynamics,* Vol. 28, No. 4, 2000, pp. 25–37.

82. Leonard Bierman, "Regulating Reindeer Games," *Academy of Management Executive,* Vol. 11, No. 4, 1997, p. 92.

83. These strategies are discussed fully in Andrew J. DuBrin, *Human Relations,* Reston, Reston, Va., 1978, pp. 113–122;

DuBrin, in turn, abstracted them from the existing literature on power and politics. Also see Andrew J. DuBrin, *Winning Office Politics,* Prentice Hall, Upper Saddle River, N.J., 1990, Chaps. 8 and 9.

84. Nancy C. Morey and Fred Luthans, "The Use of Dyadic Alliances in Informal Organization: An Ethnographic Study," *Human Relations,* Vol. 44, 1991, pp. 597–618.

85. Anthony Jay, *Management and Machiavelli,* Holt, New York, 1967, p. 6.

86. Fred Luthans, Richard M. Hodgetts, and Stuart A. Rosenkrantz, *Real Managers,* Ballinger, Cambridge, Mass., 1988.

87. Annette Simmons, *Territorial Games: Understanding & Ending Turf Wars at Work,* AMACOM, New York, 1998.

88. Christine M. Pearson and Judith A. Clair, "Reframing Crisis Management," *Academy of Management Review,* Vol. 23, No. 1, 1998, pp. 59–76.

89. John Whitney and Tina Packer, *Power Plays: Shakespeare's Lessons in Leadership and Management,* Simon & Schuster, New York, 2000, and Norma Augustine and Kenneth Adelman, *Shakespeare in Charge: The Bard's Guide to Leading and Succeeding on the Business Stage,* Hyperion, New York, 2000.

90. Exceptions would include studies such as Glenn R. Carroll and Albert C. Teo, "On the Social Networks of Managers," *Academy of Management Journal,* Vol. 39, No. 2, 1996, pp. 421–440, and Rahul Varman and Deepti Bhatnagar, "Power and Politics in Grievance Resolution: Managing Meaning of Due Process in an Organization," *Human Relations,* Vol. 52, No. 3, 1999, pp. 349–381.

91. Commerce Clearing House, SHRM/CCH Survey, Chicago, 1991.

92. M. Velasquez, D. J. Moberg, and G. F. Cavanaugh, "Organizational Statesmanship and Dirty Politics: Ethical Guidelines for the Organizational Politician," *Organizational Dynamics,* Vol. 11, 1982, pp. 65–79.

93. Gerald F. Cavanagh, Dennis J. Moberg, and Manuel Velasquez, "The Ethics of Organizational Politics," *Academy of Management Review,* July 1981, p. 372. Also see Jill Woodilla and Jeanie M. Forray, "Justice and the Political in Organizational Life," *Journal of Management Inquiry,* Vol. 17, No. 1, 2008, pp. 4–19.

94. Brian K. Miller and Kay McGlashan Nicols, "Politics and Justice: A Mediated Moderation Model," *Journal of Managerial Issues,* Vol. 20, No. 2, 2008, pp. 214–237.

95. Robert P. Vecchio, *Organizational Behavior,* Dryden, Chicago, 1988, p. 270.

96. Nina Gupta and G. Douglas Jenkins, Jr., "The Politics of Pay," *Compensation & Benefits Review,* March/April 1996, pp. 23–30.

97. Dennis Collins, "Death of a Gainsharing Plan: Power, Politics and Participatory Management," *Organizational Dynamics,* Summer 1995, pp. 23–37.

98. Luthans, Hodgetts, and Rosenkrantz, op. cit.

99. Fred Luthans, Dianne H. B. Welsh, and Stuart A. Rosenkrantz, "What Do Russian Managers Really Do?" *Journal of International Business Studies,* Fourth Quarter 1993, pp. 741–761.

100. See George B. Weathersby, "You've Got the Power," *Management Review,* January 1999, p. 5.

101. Kennedy, op. cit., p. 20.

102. See Marilyn Moats Kennedy, "Politics Lost," *Across the Board,* May 2000, p. 67.

103. For different views of what made Google so successful, see "Google: The Faces and Voices of the World's Most Innovative Company," *Fast Company,* March 2008, pp. 74–91.

## Chapter 11 Footnote References and Supplemental Readings

1. For example, see Marlene E. Turner (Ed.), *Groups at Work: Theory and Research,* Lawrence Erlbaum, Mahwah, N.J., 2001.

2. Claus W. Langfred, "The Downside of Self-Management: A Longitudinal Study of the Effects of Conflict on Trust, Autonomy, and Task Interdependence in Self-Managing Teams," *Academy of Management Journal,* Vol. 50, No. 4, 2007, p. 885.

3. Michael Hickins, "Duh! Gen Xers Are Cool with Teamwork," *Management Review,* March, 1999, p. 7. Also see Michael M. Beyerlein, Sue Freedman, Craig McGee, and Linda Moran, "The Ten Principles of Collaborative Organizations," *Journal of Organizational Excellence,* Spring 2003, pp. 51–63.

4. John M. Ivancevich and Michael T. Matteson, *Organizational Behavior and Management,* 3rd ed., McGraw-Hill, New York, 1993, p. 286.

5. Dorothy A. Leonard and Walter C. Swap, *When Sparks Fly: Igniting Creativity in Groups,* Harvard Business School Press, Boston, 1999. Also see Leigh Thompson, "Improving the Creativity of Organizational Work Groups," *Academy of Management Executive,* Vol. 17, No. 1, 2003, pp. 96–109.

6. George C. Homans, *The Human Group,* Harcourt, Brace & World, New York, 1950, pp. 43–44. For recent theory building and research based on this foundation, see Robert K. Shelly and Lisa Troyer, "Emergency and Completion of Structure in Initially Undefined and Partially Defined Groups," *Social Psychology Quarterly,* Vol. 64, No. 4, 2001, pp. 318–332.

7. Theodore M. Newcomb, *The Acquaintance Process,* Holt, New York, 1961.

8. John W. Thibaut and Harold H. Kelley, *The Social Psychology of Groups,* Wiley, New York, 1959.

9. See Bruce W. Tuckman, "Developmental Sequence in Small Groups," *Psychological Bulletin,* November 1965, pp. 384–399, and Bruce W. Tuckman and Mary Ann C. Jensen, "Stages of Small Group Development Revisited," *Group and Organization Studies,* December 1977, pp. 419–427.

10. Susan C. Hanlon, David C. Meyer, and Robert R. Taylor, "Consequences of Gainsharing: A Field Experiment Revisited," *Group and Organizational Management,* Vol. 19, No. 1, 1994, pp. 87–111, and Michael Arndt, "A New Partnership: Sharing the Rewards," *Chicago Tribune,* August 18, 1996, pp. C1–C2.

11. Raymond A. Friedman and Brooks Holtom, "The Effects of Network Groups on Minority Employee Turnover Intentions," *Human Resource Management,* Vol. 41, No. 4, 2002, pp. 405–421.

12. Gerben S. Van Det Vegt and J. Stuart Bunderson, "Learning and Performance in Multidisciplinary Teams: The Importance

of Collective Team Identification," *Academy of Management Journal,* Vol. 48, No. 3, 2005, pp. 532–547; Gerald R. Ferris, Pamela L. Perrewé, and Ceasar Douglas, "Social Effectiveness in Organizations: Construct Validity and Research Directions," *Journal of Leadership and Organizational Studies,* Vol. 9, No. 1, 2002, pp. 49–63; and Blake Ashforth, Spencer H. Harrison, and Kevin G. Corley, "Identification in Organizations: An Examination of Four Fundamental Questions," *Journal of Management,* Vol. 34, No. 3, 2008, pp. 325–374.

13. E. Romanelli and E. Tushman, "Organizational Transformation as Punctuated Equilibrium: An Empirical Test," *Academy of Management Journal,* Vol. 37, No. 4, 1994, pp. 1141–1166.

14. Dora C. Lau and J. Keith Murnighan, "Demographic Diversity and Faultlines: The Compositional Dynamics of Organizational Groups," *Academy of Management Review,* Vol. 23, No. 2, 1998, pp. 325–340.

15. Jennifer A. Chatman and Francis J. Flynn, "The Influence of Demographic Heterogeneity on the Emergence and Consequences of Cooperative Norms in Work Teams," *Academy of Management Journal,* Vol. 44, No. 5, 2001, pp. 956–974. Also see Astrid C. Homan, John R. Hollenbeck, Stephen E. Humphrey, Daan Van Knippenberg, Daniel R. Ilgen, and Gergen A. Van Kleef, "Facing Differences with an Open Mind: Openness to Experience, Salience of Intragroup Differences, and Performance of Diverse Work Groups," *Academy of Management Journal,* Vol. 51, No. 6, 2008, pp. 1204–1222.

16. Cristina B. Gibson, "Do They Do What They Believe They Can? Group Efficacy and Group Effectiveness across Tasks and Cultures," *Academy of Management Journal,* Vol. 42, No. 2, 1999, pp. 138–152.

17. Rocio Fernandez-Ballesteros, Juan Diez-Nicolas, G. V. Caparara, C. Barbaranelli, and Albert Bandura, "Determinants and Structural Relation of Personal Efficacy to Collective Efficacy," Working Paper, 2000; and Robert R. Hirschfeld and Jeremy B. Bernerth, "Mental Efficacy and Physical Efficacy at the Team Level," *Journal of Applied Psychology,* Vol. 93, No. 6, 2008, pp. 1429–1437.

18. Quote by Grant Reid in "Think Horizontal," *The Conference Board Review,* November/December 2008, p. 57.

19. Ranjay Gulati, "Social Structure and Alliance Formation Patterns: A Longitudinal Analysis," *Administrative Science Quarterly,* Vol. 40, 1995, pp. 619–652.

20. William B. Stevenson, Jone L. Pearce, and Lyman Porter, "The Concept of 'Coalition' in Organization Theory and Research," *Academy of Management Review,* April 1985, pp. 261–262.

21. Nancy C. Morey and Fred Luthans, "The Use of Dyadic Alliances in Informal Organization: An Ethnographic Study," *Human Relations,* Vol. 44, No. 6, 1991, pp. 597–618.

22. Morten Huse, Alessandro Minichilli, and Margrethe Schoning, "The Value of Process-Oriented Boardroom Dynamics," *Organizational Dynamics,* Vol. 34, No. 3, 2005, pp. 285–297.

23. Jiatao Li and Donald C. Hambrick, "Factional Groups: A New Vantage on Demographic Faultlines, Conflict, and Disintegration in Work Team," *Academy of Management Journal,* Vol. 48, No. 5, 2005, pp. 794–813.

24. Chris Clarke-Epstein, "Increase Your ROM (Return of Meetings)," *Training and Development,* Vol. 56, No. 4, 2002, pp. 65–67.

25. For recent reviews of basic research on work groups and teams, see Maureen L. Ambrose and Carol T. Kulik, "Old Friends, New Faces–Motivation Research in the 1990s," *Journal of Management,* Vol. 25, No. 1, 1999, pp. 269–273; and Jeffery A. Lepine, Ronald F. Piccolo, Christine Jackson, John E. Mathieu, and Jessica R. Saul, "A Meta-Analysis of Teamwork Processes: Tests of a Multidimensional Model and Relationships with Team Effectiveness Criteria," *Personnel Psychology,* Vol. 61, No. 2, 2008, pp. 273–307.

26. David A. Nadler, J. Richard Hackman, and Edward E. Lawler, *Managing Organizational Behavior,* Little, Brown, Boston, 1979, p. 102. Also see John Mathieu, M. Travis Maynard, Tammy Rapp, and Lucy Gilson, "Team Effectiveness 1997–2007: A Review of Recent Advancements and a Glimpse into the Future," *Journal of Management,* Vol. 34, No. 3, 2008, pp. 410–476.

27. Stanley Schachter, Norris Ellertson, Dorothy McBride, and Doris Gregory, "An Experimental Study of Cohesiveness and Productivity," *Human Relations,* August 1951, pp. 229–239. Also see Jeffrey Polzer, "Making Diverse Teams Click," *Harvard Business Review,* Vol. 86, No. 7/8, 2008, pp. 20–21.

28. Brian Mullen and Carolyn Copper, "The Relation between Group Cohesiveness and Performance: An Integration," *Psychology Bulletin,* Vol. 115, No. 2, 1994, pp. 210–232.

29. J. Richard Hackman, *Leading Teams: Setting the Stage for Great Performance,* Harvard Business School Press, Boston, 2002.

30. Ibid.

31. Nagaraj Sivasubramaniam, William D. Murry, Bruce J. Avolio, and Dong I. Jung, "A Longitudinal Model of the Effects of Team Leadership and Group Potency on Group Performance, *Group & Organization Management,* Vol. 27, No. 1, 2002, pp. 66–96; and Jay B. Carson, Paul E. Tesluk, and Jennifer A. Marrone, "Shared Leadership in Teams: An Investigation of Antecedent Conditions and Performance," *Academy of Management Journal,* Vol. 50, No. 5, 20007, pp. 1217–1234.

32. D. A. Harrison, K. H. Price, and M. P. Bell, "Beyond Relational Demography: Time and the Effects of Surface- and Deep-Level Diversity on Work Group Cohesion," *Academy of Management Journal,* Vol. 41, No. 1, 1998, pp. 96–107, and David A. Harrison, Kenneth H. Price, Joanne H. Gavin, and Anna T. Florey, "Time, Teams, and Task Performance: Changing Effects of Surface- and Deep-Level Diversity on Group Functioning, *Academy of Management Journal,* Vol. 45, No. 5, 2002, pp. 1029–1045, and Lucy L. Gilson, John E. Mathieu, Christina E. Shalley, and Thomas M. Ruddy, "Creativity and Standardization: Complementary or Conflicting Drivers of Team Effectiveness?" *Academy of Management Journal,* Vol. 48, No. 3, 2005, pp. 521–531.

33. Barry W. Staw, "Organizational Psychology and the Pursuit of the Happy/Productive Worker," *California Management Review,* Summer 1986, p. 49. Also see Frank LaFasto and Carl Larson, *When Teams Work Best: 6,000 Team Members and Leaders Tell What It Takes to Succeed,* Sage Publications, Thousand Oaks, Calif., 2001.

34. Gregory P. Shea and Richard A. Guzzo, "Group Effectiveness: What Really Matters?" *Sloan Management Review,* Spring 1987, p. 25; Gerben Van Der Vegt, Ben Emans, and Evert Van De Vilert, "Team Members' Affective Responses to Patterns of Intragroup Interdependence and Job Complexity," *Journal of Management,* Vol. 26, No. 4, 2000, pp. 633–655; Gerben S. Van Der Vegt, Ben J. M. Emans, and Evert Van De Vliert, "Patterns of Interdependence in Work Teams: A Two-Level Investigation of the Relations with Job and Team Satisfaction," *Personnel Psychology,* Vol. 54, 2001, pp. 51–69; Craig L. Pearce, Cynthia A. Gallagher, and Michael D. Ensley, "Confidence at the Group Level of Analysis: A Longitudinal Investigation of the Relationship between Potency and Team Effectiveness," *Journal of Occupational and Organizational Psychology,* Vol. 75, 2002, pp. 115–119; Scott W. Lester, Bruce M. Meglino, and M. Audrey Korsgaard, "The Antecedents and Consequences of Group Potency: A Longitudinal Investigation of Newly Formed Work Groups," *Academy of Management Journal,* Vol. 45, No. 2, 2002, pp. 352–368; and Anne Delarue, Geert Van Hootegen, Stephen Procter, and Mark Burridge, "Team-Working and Organizational Performance: A Review of Survey-Based Research," *International Journal of Management Reviews,* Vol. 10, No. 2, 2008, pp. 127–148.

35. Russ Forrester and Allan B. Drexler, "A Model for Team-Based Organization Performance," *Academy of Management Executive,* Vol 13, No. 3, 1999, p. 36.

36. Greg L. Steward and Murray R. Barrick, "Team Structure and Performance: Assessing the Mediating Role of Intrateam Process and the Moderating Role of Task Type," *Academy of Management Journal,* Vol. 43, No. 2, 2000, pp. 135–148.

37. Jane S. Prichard and Neville A. Stanton, "Testing Belbin's Team Role Theory of Effective Groups," *The Journal of Management Development,* Vol. 18, No. 8, 1999, pp. 652–665, and David Partington and Hilary Harris, "Team Role Balance and Team Performance: An Empirical Study," *The Journal of Management Development,* Vol. 18, No. 8, 1999, pp. 694–705.

38. Jeffrey A. LePine, "Team Adaptation and Postchange Performance: Effects of Team Composition in Terms of Members' Cognitive Ability and Personality," *Journal of Applied Psychology,* Vol. 88, No. 1, 2003, pp. 27–39. Also see Christophe Boone, Woody Van Olffen, and Arjen Van Witteloostuijn, "Team Locus-of-Control Composition, Leadership Structure, Information Acquisitions, and Financial Performance: A Business Simulation Study," *Academy of Management Journal,* Vol. 48, No. 5, 2005, pp. 889–909.

39. Warren Bennis, "The Secrets of Great Groups," *Executive Forum,* Winter 1997, pp. 29–32.

40. See Jean Lipman-Bluman and Harold J. Leavitt, "Hot Groups and the HR Manager," *HR Focus,* August 1999, pp. 11–12, and Jean Lipman-Bluman and Harold J. Leavitt, "Hot Groups 'with Attitude': A New Organizational State of Mind," *Organizational Dynamics,* Spring 1999, p. 63.

41. Stefani L. Yorges, "The Impact of Group Formation and Perceptions of Fairness on Organizational Citizenship Behaviors," *Journal of Applied Social Psychology,* Vol. 29, No. 7, 1999, pp. 1444–1471.

42. Mark G. Enrhart and Stefanie Naumann, "Organizational Citizenship Behavior in Work Groups: A Group Norms Approach," *Journal of Applied Psychology,* Vol. 89, No. 6, 2004, pp. 960–974.

43. Mary J. Waller, "The Timing of Adaptive Group Responses to Nonroutine Events," *Academy of Management Journal,* Vol. 42, No. 2, 1999, pp. 127–137.

44. Don Hellriegel, John W. Slocum, Jr., and Richard W. Woodman, *Organizational Behavior,* 5th ed., West, St. Paul, Minn., 1989, p. 216.

45. Leigh L. Thompson, *Making the Team,* 2nd ed., Pearson/Prentice Hall, Upper Saddle River, N.J., 2004, p. 215.

46. For example, see N. Anand and Jay A. Conger, "Capabilities of the Consummate Networker," *Organizational Dynamics,* Vol. 36, No. 1, 2007, pp. 13–27.

47. Keith Davis and John W. Newstrom, *Human Behavior at Work,* 7th ed., McGraw-Hill, New York, 1985, p. 311.

48. Louis B. Barnes and Mark P. Kriger, "The Hidden Side of Organizational Leadership," *Sloan Management Review,* Fall 1986, p. 15.

49. Sandra L. Robinson and Anne M. O'Leary-Kelly, "Monkey See, Monkey Do: The Influence of Work Groups on the Antisocial Behavior of Employees," *Academy of Management Journal,* Vol. 41, No. 6, 1998, pp. 658–672.

50. Irving L. Janis, *Victims of Groupthink,* Houghton Mifflin, Boston, 1972, p. 9.

51. Mark Maier, "Ten Years after a Major Malfunction . . . Reflections on 'The Challenger Syndrome,'" *Journal of Management Inquiry,* Vol. 11, No. 3, 2002, pp. 282–292.

52. Carrie R. Leana, "A Partial Test of Janis' Groupthink Model: Effects of Group Cohesiveness and Leader Behavior on Defective Decision Making," *Journal of Management,* Vol. 11, No. 1, 1985, pp. 5–17.

53. M. M. Scharff, "Understanding WorldCom's Accounting Fraud: Did Groupthink Play a Role?" *Journal of Leadership and Organizational Studies,* Vol. 11, No. 3, 2005, pp. 109–118.

54. See Sally Riggs Fuller and Ramon J. Aldag, "Organizational Tonypandy: Lessons from a Quarter Century of the Groupthink Phenomenon," *Organizational Behavior and Human Decision Processes,* Vol. 73, No. 2/3, 1998, pp. 163–184.

55. See ibid., and Marlene E. Turner and Anthony R. Pratkanis, "Twenty-Five Years of Groupthink Theory and Research: Lessons from the Evaluation of a Theory," *Organizational Behavior and Human Decision Processes,* Vol. 73, No. 2/3, 1998, pp. 105–115.

56. The original research on risky shift goes back to a master's thesis by J. A. F. Stoner, "A Comparison of Individual and Group Decisions Involving Risk," Massachusetts Institute of Technology, Sloan School of Industrial Management, Cambridge, Mass., 1961.

57. See Daniel J. Isenberg, "Group Polarization: A Critical Review and Meta-Analysis," *Journal of Personality and Social Psychology,* Vol. 50, No. 6, 1986, pp. 1141–1151.

58. For example, see Jana L. Raver and Michele J. Gelfand, "Beyond the Individual Victim: Linking Sexual Harassment, Team Processes, and Team Performance," *Academy of Management Journal,* Vol. 48, No. 3, 2005, pp. 387–400.

59. Howard Guttman quoted in "Think Horizontal," *The Conference Board Review,* November/December, 2008, p. 53.

60. Richard A. Cosier and Charles R. Schwenk, "Agreement and Thinking Alike: Ingredients for Poor Decisions," *Academy of Management Executive,* February 1990, p. 70.

61. Liz Ryan, "The Slacker Teammate," *BusinessWeek,* August 20, 2007, p. 7.

62. M. Erez and A. Somech, "Is Group Productivity Loss the Rule or the Exception? Effects of Culture and Group-Based Motivation," *Academy of Management Journal,* Vol. 39, No. 5, 1996, pp. 1513–1537.

63. T. A. Judge and T. D. Chandler, "Individual-Level Determinants of Employee Shirking," *Relations Industrielles,* Vol. 51, 1996, pp. 468–486.

64. Robal Johnson, "Effective Team Building," *HR Focus,* April 1996, p. 18. Also see Lynn R. Offermann and Rebecca K. Spiros, "The Science and Practice of Team Development: Improving the Link," *Academy of Management Journal,* Vol. 44, No. 2, 2001, pp. 376–392.

65. Jon R. Katzenback and Douglas K. Smith, "The Discipline of Teams," *Harvard Business Review,* March–April 1993, p. 112.

66. Ibid., p. 113.

67. David W. Mann, "Steelcase Learns How Teamwork Evolves Effectively under Lean Production," *Journal of Organizational Excellence,* Summer 2002, pp. 43–48.

68. David Chaudron, "How to Improve Cross-Functional Teams," *HR Focus,* August 1995, pp. 4–5.

69. J. Stuart Bunderson and Kathleen M. Sutcliffe, "Comparing Alternative Conceptualizations of Functional Diversity in Management Teams: Process and Performance Effects," *Academy of Management Journal,* Vol. 45, No. 5, 2002, pp. 875–893; Michelle A. Marks, Mark J. Sabella, C. Shawn Burke, and Stephen J. Zaccaro, "The Impact of Cross Training on Team Effectiveness," *Journal of Applied Psychology,* Vol. 87, No. 1, 2002, pp. 3–13; and Christina Scott-Young and Danny Samson, "Project Success and Project Team Management: Evidence from Capital Projects in the Process Industries," *Journal of Operations Management,* Vol. 26, No. 6, 2008, pp. 749–766.

70. Randy Emelo and Laura M. Francis, "Virtual Team Interaction," *Training and Development,* October 2002, p. 17.

71. Bradford S. Bell and Steve W. J. Kozlowski, "A Typology of Virtual Teams," *Group & Organization Management,* Vol. 27, No. 1, 2002, pp. 14–49, and Likoebe M. Maruping and Ritu Agarway, "Managing Team Interpersonal Processes through Technology: A Task-Technology Fit Perspective," *Journal of Applied Psychology,* Vol. 89, No. 6, 2004, pp. 975–990.

72. Bradley L. Kirkman, Benson Rosen, Cristina B. Gibson, Paul E. Teslik, and Simon O. McPherson, "Five Challenges to Virtual Team Success: Lessons from Sabre, Inc.," *Academy of Management Executive,* Vol. 16, No. 3, 2002, p. 67. They draw the definition and theory base from J. Lipnack and J. Stamps, *Virtual Teams,* 2nd ed., Wiley, New York, 2000, and D. L. Duarte and N. T. Snyder, *Mastering Virtual Teams,* 2nd ed., Jossey-Bass, San Francisco, 2001.

73. M. L. Maznevski and K. M. Chudoba, "Bridging Space over Time: Global Virtual-Team Dynamics and Effectiveness," *Organization Science,* Vol. 11, 2000, pp. 473–492.

74. See Duarte and Snyder, op. cit. Also see Yuhyung Shin, "Conflict Resolution in Virtual Teams," *Organizational Dynamics,* Vol. 34, No. 4, 2005, pp. 331–345.

75. K. Kiser, "Building A Virtual Team," *Training,* March 1999, p. 34.

76. K. A. Graetz, E. S. Boyle, C. E. Kimble, P. Thompson, and J. L. Garloch, "Information Sharing in Face-to-Face, Teleconferencing, and Electronic Chat Groups," *Small Group Research,* December 1998, pp. 714–743.

77. Dale E. Yeatts and Cloyd Hyten, *High-Performing Self-Managed Work Teams: A Comparison of Theory and Practice,* Sage, Thousand Oaks, Calif., 1998. Also see Fabiola Bertolotti, Diego Maria Macri, and Maria Rita Tagliaventi, "Spontaneous Self-Managing Practices in Groups: Evidence from the Field," *Journal of Management Inquiry,* Vol. 14, No. 4, December 2005, pp. 366–384.

78. See Stratford Sherman, "Secrets of HP's 'Muddled' Team," *Fortune,* March 18, 1996, pp. 116–120, and Rich Teerlink and Lee Ozley, *More than a Motorcycle,* Harvard Business School Press, Boston, Mass., 2000.

79. See Yeatts and Hyten, op. cit., and Bradley L. Kirkman and Benson Rosen, "Beyond Self-Management: Antecedents and Consequences of Team Empowerment," *Academy of Management Journal,* Vol. 42, No. 1, 1999, pp. 58–74.

80. Joy H. Karriker, "Cyclical Group Development and Interaction-Based Leadership Emergence in Autonomous Teams: An Integrated Model," *Journal of Leadership and Organizational Studies,* Vol. 11, No. 4, 2005, pp. 54–64.

81. See Paul S. Goodman, Rukmini Devadas, and Terri L. Griffith Hughson, "Groups and Productivity: Analyzing the Effectiveness of Self-Managing Teams," in John P. Campbell, Richard J. Campbell, and Associates (Eds.), *Productivity in Organizations,* Jossey-Bass, San Francisco, 1988, pp. 295–327.

82. C. A. L. Pearson, "Autonomous Workgroups: An Evaluation at an Industrial Site," *Human Relations,* Vol. 45, No. 9, 1992, pp. 905–936.

83. "Work Teams Have Their Work Cut Out for Them," *HR Focus,* January 1993, p. 24.

84. Ibid.

85. Ibid., and John Beck and Neil Yeager, "Moving beyond Team Myths," *Training and Development,* March 1996, pp. S1–S5.

86. Joann S. Lublin, "My Colleague, My Boss," *The Wall Street Journal,* April 12, 1995, p. R4.

87. Kimberly Merriman, "Low-Trust Teams Prefer Individualized Pay," *Harvard Business Review,* Vol. 86, No. 11, 2008, p. 32.

88. Evelyn F. Rogers, William Metlay, Ira T. Kaplan, and Terri Shapiro, "Self-Managing Work Teams: Do They Really Work?" *Human Resource Planning,* Vol. 18, No. 2, 1996, pp. 53–57.

89. James W. Bishop, K. Dow Scott, and Susan H. Burroughs, "Support, Commitment, and Employee Outcomes in a Team Environment," *Journal of Management,* Vol. 26, No. 6, 2000, pp. 1113–1132, and P. Bordia, "Face-to-Face versus Computer-Mediated Communication: A Synthesis of the Experimental Literature," *Journal of Business Communication,* Vol. 34, January 1997, pp. 99–120. Also see V. K. Narayanan, Frank L. Douglas, Brock Guemsey, and John

Chames, "How Top Management Steers Fast Cycle Teams to Success," *Strategy and Leadership,* Vol. 30, No. 3, 2002, pp. 19–24, and Christopher O. L. H. Porter, "Goal Orientation: Effects on Backing Up Behavior, Performance, Efficacy, and Commitment in Teams," *Journal of Applied Psychology,* Vol. 90, No. 4, 2005, pp. 811–818.

90. B. Mullen and C. Copper, "The Relation between Group Cohesiveness and Group Performance: An Integration," *Psychological Bulletin,* Vol. 115, 1994, pp. 210–227, and Daan van Knippenberg, Carsten K. W. DeDreu, and Astrid C. Homan, "Work Group Diversity and Group Performance: An Integrative Model and Research Agenda," Vol. 89, No. 6, 2004, pp. 1008–1022.

91. Melville Cottrill, "Give Your Work Teams Time and Training," *Academy of Management Executive,* Vol. 11, No. 3, 1997, p. 87.

92. Ronald S. Landis, "A Note on the Stability of Team Performance," *Journal of Applied Psychology,* Vol. 86, No. 3, 2001, pp. 446–450.

93. Ted Bridis, "Hijacker Ordered Jet to Be Crashed Because of Passenger Uprising, FBI Says," *Lincoln Journal Star,* August 8, 2003, p. 6A.

94. D. Christopher Kayes, "Proximal Team Learning: Lessons from United Flight 93 on 9/11," *Organizational Dynamics,* Vol. 32, No. 1, 2003, pp. 80–92.

95. Carla Joinson, "Teams at Work," *HR Magazine,* May 1999, pp. 30–36.

96. Lea Soupata, "Engaging Employees in Company Success: The UPS Approach to a Winning Team," *Human Resource Management,* Vol. 44, No. 1, Spring 2005, pp. 95–98.

97. Richard F. Schubert, "The Power of Partnership," *Leader to Leader,* Winter 1997, pp. 9–10.

98. Svan Lembke and Marie G. Wilson, "Putting the 'Team' into Teamwork: Alternative Theoretical Contributions for Contemporary Management Practice," *Human Relations,* Vol. 51, No. 7, 1998, p. 927.

99. Kimball Fisher and Mareen Duncan Fisher, *The Distributed Mind,* AMACOM, New York, 1998.

100. Bradley L. Kirkman and Benson Rosen, "Powering Up Teams," *Organizational Dynamics,* Winter 2000, pp. 48–66.

101. Liz Ryan, "How to Keep Your Team Talking," *BusinessWeek,* February 5, 2007, p. 13.

102. Kambiz Maani and Campbell Benton, "Rapid Team Learning: Lessons from Team New Zealand's America's Cup Campaign," *Organizational Dynamics,* Spring 1999, pp. 48–62.

103. Kristina B. Dahlin, Laurie R. Weingart, and Pamela J. Hinds, " Team Diversity and Information Use," *Academy of Management Journal,* Vol. 48, No. 6, 2005, pp. 1107–1123.

104. Howard Prager, "Cooking Up Effective Team Building," *Training and Development,* December 1999, pp. 14–15.

105. Paul E. Brauchle and David W. Wright, "Training Work Teams," *Training and Development,* March 1993, p. 68.

106. Victoria A. Hovemeyer, "How Effective Is Your Team?" *Training and Development,* September 1993, pp. 67–68.

107. Ralph D. Ward, *21st Century Corporate Board,* Wiley, New York, 1997.

108. "Creating an Outstanding Leadership Team," *Management Review,* February 2000, p. 8.

109. Ram Charan, *Boards at Work: How Corporate Boards Create Competitive Advantage,* Jossey-Bass, San Francisco, 1998.

110. Henry L. Tosi, Wei Shen, and Richard J. Gentry, "Why Outsiders on Boards Can't Solve the Corporate Governance Problem," *Organizational Dynamics,* Vol. 32, No. 2, 2003, pp. 180–192.

111. Warren Bennis and Patricia Ward Biederman, *Organizing Genius: The Secrets of Creative Collaboration,* Addison-Wesley, Boston, 1997. Also see Cynthia Hardy, Thomas B. Lawrence, and David Grant, "Discourse and Collaboration: The Role of Conversations and Collective Identity," *Academy of Management Review,* Vol. 30, No. 1, 2005, pp. 58–77.

112. For background on open-sourcing, see Thomas L. Friedman, *The World Is Flat,* Farrar, Straus, and Giroux, New York, 2005, pp. 81–103.

113. Philip Evans and Bob World, "Collaboration Rules," *Harvard Business Review,* 2005, p. 96.

114. Avan R. Jasszwalla and Hemant C. Sashittal, "Building Collaborative Cross-Functional New Product Teams," *Academy of Management Executive,* Vol. 13, No. 3, 1999, p. 50. Also see Raymond E. Miles, Grant Miles, and Charles C. Snow, "Collaborative Entrepreneurship: A Business Model for Continuous Innovation," *Organizational Dynamics,* Vol. 35, No. 1, 2006, pp. 1–11.

115. Glenn Phelps, "The Relationship between Manager Talent and the Performance of the Teams They Lead," *GRS,* Winter/Spring 2000, p. 17.

116. "Do We Really Need Bosses?" *Omaha World Herald,* July 12, 1998, p. 1–G.

117. Jean M. Phillips, Elizabeth A. Douthitt, and MaryAnne M. Hyland, "The Role of Justice in Team Member Satisfaction with the Leader and Attachment to the Team," *Journal of Applied Psychology,* Vol. 86, No. 2, 2001, pp. 316–325.

118. J. A. Colquitt, R. A. Noe, and C. L. Jackson, "Justice in Teams: Antecedents and Consequences of Procedural Justice Climate," *Personnel Psychology,* Vol. 55, 2002, pp. 83–100. Also see Amy Colbert, Amy L. Kristof-Brown, Bret Bradley, and Murray Barrick, "CEO Transformational Leadership: The Role of Goal Importance Congruence in Top Management Teams," *Academy of Management Journal,* Vol. 51, No. 1, 2008, pp. 81–96.

119. J. Richard Hackman and Ruth Wageman, "A Theory of Team Coaching," *Academy of Management Review,* Vol. 30, No. 2, 2005, pp. 269–287.

120. Yochanan Altman and Paul Iles, "Learning, Leadership, Teams: Corporate Learning and Organisational Change," *Journal of Management Development,* Vol. 17, No. 1, 1998, pp. 44–55.

121. Sarah Heyward, "How I Taught My Team to Tango," *Across the Board,* July/August 2000, pp. 7–8.

122. K. T. Dirks, "Trust in Leadership and Team Performance: Evidence from NCAA Basketball," *Journal of Applied Psychology,* Vol. 85, 2000, pp. 1004–1012. Also see Manfred F. R. Kets de Vries, "Leadership Group Coaching in Action: The Zen of Creating High Performance Teams," *Academy of Management Executive,* Vol. 19, No. 1, 2005, pp. 61–76.

123. Thomas Sy, Stephane Cote, and Richard Saavedra, "The Contagious Leader: Impact of the Leader's Mood on the

Mood of Group Members, Group Affective Tone, and Group Processes," *Journal of Applied Psychology,* Vol. 90, No. 2, 2005, pp. 295–305. Also see Frank Walter and Heike Bruch, "The Positive Group Affect Spiral: A Dynamic Model of the Emergence of Positive Affective Similarity in Work Groups," *Journal of Organizational Behavior,* Vol. 29, No. 2, 2008, pp. 239–261.

124. Vijay Govindarajan and Anil K. Gupta, "Building an Effective Global Business Team," *MIT Sloan Management Review,* Vol. 42, No. 4, 2001, pp. 63–71.

125. Bradley L. Kirkman and Debra L. Shapiro, "The Impact of Cultural Values on Job Satisfaction and Organizational Commitment in Self-Managing Work Teams: The Mediating Role of Employee Resistance," *Academy of Management Journal,* Vol. 44, No. 3, 2001, pp. 557–569.

126. Ibid. and Bradley L. Kirkman and Debra L. Shapiro, "The Impact of Cultural Values on Employee Resistance to Teams: Toward a Model of Globalized Self-Managing Work Team Effectiveness," *Academy of Management Review,* Vol. 22, No. 3, 1997, pp. 730–757.

127. Chantell E. Nicholls, H. W. Lane, and M. B. Brechu, "Taking Self-Managed Teams to Mexico," *Academy of Management Executive.* Vol. 13, No. 3, 1999, p. 15.

128. Jane E. Salk and Mary Yoko Brannen, "National Culture, Networks, and Individual Influence in a Multinational Management Team," *Academy of Management Journal,* Vol. 43, No. 2, 2000, pp. 191–202.

129. See Nancy Katz, "Sports Teams as a Model for Workplace Teams: Lessons and Liabilities," *Academy of Management Executive,* Vol. 15, No. 3, 2001, pp. 56–67.

130. Christina B. Gibson and Mary E. Zellmer-Bruhn, "Minding Your Metaphors: Applying the Concept of Teamwork Metaphors to the Management of Teams in Multicultural Contexts," *Organizational Dynamics,* Vol. 31, No. 2, 2002, pp. 101–116.

131. P. Christopher Earley and Elaine Mosakowski, "Creating Hybrid Team Cultures: An Empirical Test of Transnational Team Functioning," *Academy of Management Journal,* Vol. 43, No. 1, 2000, pp. 26–49.

132. Bradley L. Kirkman, Christina B. Gibson, and Debra L. Shapiro, "'Exporting' Teams: Enhancing the Implementation and Effectiveness of Work Teams in Global Affiliates," *Organizational Dynamics,* Vol. 30, No. 1, 2001, pp. 12–29.

133. Yadong Luo, "How Important Are Shared Perceptions of Procedural Justice in Cooperative Alliances?" *Academy of Management Journal,* Vol. 48, No. 4, 2005, pp. 695–709.

134. Ambrose and Kulik, op. cit., pp. 269–271.

## Chapter 12 Footnote References and Supplemental Readings

1. Aubrey C. Daniels, *Bringing Out the Best in People,* McGraw-Hill, New York, 2000, p. xiv.

2. For a recent summary of various learning theories and how they contribute and complement sensemaking, see David R. Schwandt, "When Managers Become Philosophers: Integrating Learning with Sensemaking," *Academy of Management Learning and Education,* Vol. 4, No. 2, 2005, pp. 176–192.

3. For a comprehensive summary of behaviorism as applicable to organizational behavior, see Fred Luthans, Carolyn M. Youssef, and Brett C. Luthans, "Behaviorism," in N. Nicholson, P. Audia, and M. Pillutla (Eds.), *The Blackwell Encyclopedic Dictionary of Organizational Behavior,* 2nd ed., Blackwell, London, U.K., 2004.

4. See David C. Palmer, "On Skinner's Rejection of S–R Psychology," *The Behavior Analyst,* Vol. 21, 1998, pp. 93–96.

5. For example, see Brian D. Till and Randi Lynn Priluck, "Stimulus Generalization in Classical Conditioning: An Initial Investigation and Extension," *Psychology and Marketing,* Vol. 17, No. 1, 2000, pp. 55–72.

6. B. F. Skinner, *The Shaping of a Behaviorist,* Knopf, New York, 1979, p. 143.

7. For example, see David W. Schaal, "Skinner May Be Difficult, But . . ." *The Behavior Analyst,* Vol. 21, No. 1, 1998, pp. 97–101.

8. Roy A. Moxley, "Why Skinner Is Difficult," *The Behavior Analyst,* Vol. 21, No. 1, 1998, pp. 73–91, and Edward K. Morris, "Not So Disinterested or Objectivist: John A. Mills' Control: A History of Behavioral Psychology," *Behavior Analyst,* Vol. 25, 2002, pp. 238–240.

9. For example, see Valentin Dragoi and J. E. R. Staddon, "The Dynamics of Operant Conditioning," *Psychological Review,* Vol. 106, No. 1, 1999, pp. 20–61; Richard W. Malott, "Conceptual Behavior Analysis," *Journal of Organizational Behavior Management,* Vol. 19, No. 3, 1999, pp. 75–81; William M. Baum, "New Paradigm for Behavior Analysis," *The Behavior Analyst,* Vol. 20, No. 1, 1997, pp. 11–15; John A. Bargh and Melissa J. Ferguson, "Beyond Behaviorism: On the Automaticity of Higher Mental Processes," *Psychological Bulletin,* Vol. 126, No. 6, 2000, pp. 925–945; Cynthia M. Anderson and Kurt A. Freeman, "Positive Behavior Support: Expanding the Application of Applied Behavior Analysis," *Behavior Analyst,* Vol. 23, 2000, pp. 85–94; and Bryan Roche, Yvonne Barnes-Holmes, Dermot Barnes-Holmes, Ian Stewart, and Denis O'Hora, "Relational Frame Theory: A New Paradigm for the Analysis of Social Behavior," *Behavior Analyst,* Vol. 25, 2002, pp. 75–91.

10. See David J. Murry, Andrea R. Kilgour, and Louise Wasylkiw, "Conflicts and Missed Signals in Psychoanalysis, Behaviorism, and Gestalt Psychology," *American Psychologist,* April 2000, pp. 424–425, and Richard J. DeGrandpre, "A Science of Meaning: Can Behaviorism Bring Meaning to Psychological Science?" *American Psychologist,* July 2000, pp. 721–739.

11. See Gordon R. Foxall, "Radical Behaviorist Interpretation: Generating and Evaluating an Account of Consumer Behavior," *The Behavior Analyst,* Vol. 21, No. 2, 1998, pp. 321–354.

12. See Fred Luthans and Alexander D. Stajkovic, "Reinforce for Performance: The Need to Go beyond Pay and Even Rewards," *Academy of Management Executive,* Vol. 13, No. 2, 1999, pp. 49–57; Jeanne Bursch and Adrianne Von Strander, "Well-Structured Employee Reward/Recognition Programs Yield Positive Results," *HR Focus,* November 1999, pp. 1, 14–15; Paul L. Brown, "Communicating the Benefits of the Behavioral Approach to the Business Community,"

*Journal of Organizational Behavior Management,* Vol. 20, Nos. 3/4, 2000, pp. 59–72; and Thomas C. Mawhinney, "OBM Today and Tomorrow: Then and Now," *Journal of Organizational Behavior Management,* Vol. 20, Nos. 3/4, 2000, pp. 73–137.

13. See Judith A. Ouellette and Wendy Wood, "Habit and Intention in Everyday Life: The Multiple Processes by Which Past Behavior Predicts Future Behavior," *Psychological Bulletin,* Vol. 124, No. 1, 1998, pp. 54–74.

14. Sonia M. Goltz, "Escalation Research: Providing New Frontiers for Applying Behavior Analysis to Organizational Behavior," *Behavior Analyst,* Vol. 23, 2000, pp. 203–218.

15. For example, see Steven Kerr, "On the Folly of Rewarding A, while Hoping for B," *Academy of Management Executive,* February 1995, p. 7; Judith L. Komaki, "Toward Effective Supervision: An Operant Analysis and Comparison of Managers at Work," *Journal of Applied Psychology,* Vol. 71, No. 2, 1986, pp. 270–279; Fred Luthans and Robert Kreitner, *Organizational Behavior Modification,* Scott, Foresman, Glenview, Ill., 1975; Fred Luthans and Robert Kreitner, *Organizational Behavior Modification and Beyond,* Scott, Foresman, Glenview, Ill., 1985; W. E. Scott, Jr., and P. M. Podsakoff, *Behavioral Principles in the Practice of Management,* Wiley, New York, 1985; Daniels, op. cit.; and Beth Sulzer-Azaroff, "Of Eagles and Worms: Changing Behavior in a Complex World," *Journal of Organizational Behavior Management,* Vol. 20, Nos. 3/4, 2000, pp. 139–163.

16. For example, see Paul Chance, "Where Does Behavior Come From?" *The Behavior Analyst,* Vol. 22, No. 2, 1999, pp. 161–163, and R. Epstein (Ed.), *Cognition, Creativity, and Behavior: Selected Essays,* Praeger, Westport, Conn., 1996.

17. Bertrand Russell, *An Outline of Philosophy,* Meridian, New York, 1960. (Original work published in 1927.)

18. Robert Glaser, "The Reemergence of Learning Theory within Instructional Research," *American Psychologist,* January 1990, p. 29.

19. For example, see Dennis A. Gioia and Henry P. Sims, Jr., "Cognition–Behavior Connections: Attribution and Verbal Behavior in Leader–Subordinate Interactions," *Organizational Behavior and Human Decision Processes,* Vol. 37, 1986, pp. 197–229; Jeffrey L. Godwin, Christopher P. Neck, and Jeffery D. Houghton, "The Impact of Thought Self-Leadership on Individual Goal Performance: A Cognitive Perspective," *The Journal of Management Development,* Vol. 18, No. 2, 1999, pp. 153–169; Cheryl L. Rusting, "Personality, Mood, and Cognitive Processing of Emotional Information: Three Conceptual Frameworks," *Psychological Bulletin,* Vol. 124, No. 2, 1998, pp. 165–196; and Erika A. Patall, Harris Cooper, and Jorgianne Civey Robinson, "The Effects of Choice on Intrinsic Motivation and Related Outcomes: A Meta-Analysis of Research Findings," *Psychological Bulletin,* Vol. 134, No. 2, 2008, pp. 270–300.

20. Social learning and now social cognitive theory is mostly attributed to Albert Bandura, *Social Learning Theory,* Prentice Hall, Upper Saddle River, N.J., 1977; Albert Bandura, *Social Foundations of Thought and Action,* Prentice Hall, Upper Saddle River, N.J., 1986; and Albert Bandura, "Social Cognitive Theory: An Agentic Perspective," *Asian Journal of Social Psychology,* Vol. 2, 1999, pp. 21–41.

21. See Bandura, *Social Foundations* and "Social Cognitive Theory," op. cit., and Alexander D. Stajkovic and Fred Luthans, "Social Cognitive Theory and Self Efficacy," *Organizational Dynamics,* Spring 1998, pp. 62–74.

22. Thomas C. Mawhinney, "Learning," in Dennis W. Organ and Thomas Bateman, *Organizational Behavior,* 3rd ed., Business Publications, Plano, Tex., 1986, pp. 90–91.

23. Albert Bandura, "Social Learning Theory," in J. T. Spence, R. C. Carson, and J. W. Thibaut (Eds.), *Behavioral Approaches to Therapy,* General Learning, Morristown, N.J., 1976, p. 5.

24. For a summary of this research, see Albert Bandura, *Social Foundations of Thought and Action: A Social-Cognitive View,* Prentice Hall, Upper Saddle River, N.J., 1986.

25. See Stajkovic and Luthans, op. cit., and Fred Luthans and Alexander D. Stajkovic, "Provide Recognition for Performance Improvement," in Edwin A. Locke (Ed.), *Handbook of the Principles of Organizational Behavior,* Blackwell, Oxford, U.K., 2000, pp. 167–180.

26. Albert Bandura, *Self-Efficacy: The Exercise of Control,* W. H. Freeman, New York, 1997, p. 3.

27. Bandura, *Self-Efficacy: The Exercise of Control* and "Social Cognitive Theory: An Agentic Perspective," op. cit., and Stajkovic and Luthans, "Social Cognitive Theory and Self-Efficacy," op. cit.

28. Alexander D. Stajkovic and Fred Luthans, "Self-Efficacy and Work Related Performance: A Meta-Analysis," *Psychological Bulletin,* Vol. 24, No. 2, 1998, pp. 240–261.

29. A. Bandura, C. B. Taylor, S. C. Williams, I. N. Medford, and J. D. Barchas, "Catecholamine Secretion as a Function of Perceived Coping Self-Efficacy," *Journal of Consulting and Clinical Psychology,* Vol. 53, 1985, pp. 406–414.

30. Bandura, *Self-Efficacy: The Exercise of Control* and "Social Cognitive Theory: An Agentic Perspective," op. cit., and Stajkovic and Luthans, "Social Cognitive Theory and Self-Efficacy," op. cit.

31. For example, see Albert Bandura, "Cultivate Self-Efficacy for Personal and Organizational Effectiveness," in Edwin A. Locke (Ed.), *Handbook of Principles of Organizational Behavior,* Blackwell, Oxford, U.K., 2000, pp. 120–136; Stajkovic and Luthans, "Self-Efficacy and Work Related Performance," op. cit.; and Stajkovic and Luthans, "Social Cognitive Theory and Self-Efficacy," op. cit.

32. See Spencer A. Rathus, *Psychology,* 4th ed., Holt, Rinehart and Winston, Fort Worth, Tex., 1990, p. 201, for a more detailed discussion of the extinction process.

33. Gregory B. Northcraft and Margaret A. Neale, *Organizational Behavior,* Dryden, Chicago, 1990, p. 162.

34. See Chance, op. cit.

35. For example, see E. L. Deci, "The Effects of Contingent and Noncontingent Rewards and Controls on Intrinsic Motivation," *Organizational Behavior and Human Performance,* Vol. 8, 1972, pp. 217–229; E. L. Deci, *Intrinsic Motivation,* Plenum Press, New York, 1975; and E. L. Deci, "On the Nature and Functions of Motivation Theories," *Psychological Sciences,* Vol. 3, 1992, pp. 167–171.

36. See E. L. Deci and R. M. Ryan, *Intrinsic Motivation and Self Determination in Human Behavior,* Plenum Press, New York, 1985.

37. R. Eisenburger and J. Cameron, "Detrimental Effects of Reward: Reality or Myth?" *American Psychologist,* Vol. 51, 1996, p. 1157.

38. Ibid., p. 1153.

39. J. Cameron and W. D. Pierce, "Reinforcement, Reward and Intrinsic Motivation: A Meta-Analysis," *Review of Education Research,* Vol. 64, 1994, pp. 363–423.

40. John S. Carton, "The Differential Effects of Tangible Rewards and Praise on Intrinsic Motivation: A Comparison of Cognitive Evaluation Theory and Operant Theory," *The Behavior Analyst,* Vol. 19, 1996, pp. 237–255.

41. See Alfie Kohn, *Punished by Rewards,* Houghton Mifflin, Boston, 1993, and Alfie Kohn, "Why Incentive Plans Cannot Work," *Harvard Business Review,* September–October 1993, pp. 62–63.

42. Kohn, *Punished by Rewards,* op. cit., p. 119. For comprehensive critiques, see David Reitman, "Punished by Misunderstanding," *The Behavior Analyst,* Vol. 21, No. 1, 1998, pp. 143–157, and E. F. Montemayor, "Review of Punished by Rewards," *Personnel Psychology,* Vol. 48, 1995, pp. 941–945.

43. See Steve Kerr, "Practical, Cost-Neutral Alternatives that You May Know, but Don't Practice," *Organizational Dynamics,* Vol. 28, No. 1, 1999, pp. 61–70, and Jeffrey Pfeffer, *The Human Equation,* Harvard Business School Press, Boston, 1998.

44. Edward E. Lawler, *Strategic Pay,* Jossey-Bass, San Francisco, 1990.

45. See M. Bloom, "The Performance Effects of Pay Dispersion on Individuals and Organizations," *Academy of Management Journal,* March 1999, pp. 25–40, and Tim Gardner, "When Pay for Performance Works Too Well: The Negative Impact of Pay Dispersion," *Academy of Management Executive,* Vol. 13, No. 4, 1999, pp. 101–102.

46. Bandura, *Self-Efficacy: The Exercise of Control,* op. cit., p. 7.

47. Bandura, *Social Foundations,* op. cit., p. 228.

48. For a recent analysis, see Diana Baumrind, Robert E. Larzelere, and Philip A. Cowan, "Ordinary Physical Punishment: Is It Harmful? Comment on Gershaoff (2002)," *Psychological Bulletin,* Vol. 128, No. 4, 2002, pp. 580–589.

49. Christine M. Pearson and Christine L. Porath, "On the Nature, Consequence Remedies of Workplace Incivility: No Time for 'Nice'? Think Again," *Academic Management Executive,* Vol. 19, No. 1, 2005, pp. 7–18.

50. Christine Porath and Amir Erez, "Does Rudeness Matter?" *Academy of Management Journal,* Vol. 50, 2007, pp. 1181–1197.

51. Leanne E. Atwater, Joan F. Brett, and Atira Cherise Charles, "The Delivery of Workplace Discipline," *Organizational Dynamics,* Vol. 36, No. 4, 2007, pp. 392–403.

52. Ibid.

53. Robert A. Baron, *Behavior in Organizations,* Allyn & Bacon, Boston, 1986, p. 51.

54. Vadim Liberman, "The Perfect Punishment," *The Conference Board Review,* January/February 2009, p. 39.

55. Judy L. Agnew and William K. Redmon, "Contingency Specifying Stimuli: The Role of 'Rules' in Organizational Behavior Management," *Journal of Organizational Behavior Management,* Vol. 12, No. 2, 1992, pp. 67–76, and Richard W. Mallott, "A Theory of Rule-Governed Behavior," *Journal*

*of Organizational Behavior Management,* Vol. 12, No. 2, 1992, pp. 45–65.

56. See Judy L. Agnew, "The Establishing Operation in Organizational Behavior Management," *Journal of Organizational Behavior Management,* Vol. 18, No. 1, 1998, pp. 7–19, and J. Michael, "Establishing Operations," *The Behavior Analyst,* Vol. 16, No. 2, 1993, pp. 191–206. Establishing operation basically means there is enough motivation (e.g., the individual is not satiated) for the discriminative stimulus and the reinforcer to emit the behavior.

57. Aubrey Daniels, *Bringing Out the Best in People,* McGraw-Hill, New York, 1995, p. 27.

58. For example, see S. L. Rynes and B. Gerhart (Eds.), *Compensation in Organizations: Progress and Prospects,* New Lexington Press, San Francisco, 1999.

59. Jack Welch and Suzy Welch, "Keeping Your People Pumped," *BusinessWeek,* September 17, 2007, p. 28.

60. B. Gerhart, H. B. Minkoff, and R. N. Olson, "Employee Compensation: Theory, Practice and Evidence," in G. R. Ferris, S. D. Rosen, and D. T. Barnum (Eds.), *Handbook of Human Resource Management,* Blackwell, Cambridge, Mass., 1995; T. R. Mitchell and A. E. Mickel, "The Meaning of Money: An Individual Difference Perspective," *Academy of Management Review,* Vol. 24, 1999, pp. 568–578; and C. Bram Cadsby, Fei Song, and Francis Tapon, "Sorting and Incentive Effects of Pay for Performance: An Experimental Investigation," *Academy of Management Journal,* Vol. 50, No. 2, 2007, pp. 387–405.

61. Donald J. Campbell, Kathleen M. Campbell, and Ho-Beng Chia, "Merit Pay, Performance Appraisal, and Individual Motivation: An Analysis and Alternative," *Human Resource Management,* Summer 1998, pp. 131–146, and Jeffrey Pfeffer, "Six Dangerous Myths about Pay," *Harvard Business Review,* May–June 1998, pp. 109–119.

62. Reported in Jena McGregor, "Merit Pay? Not Exactly," *BusinessWeek,* September 22, 2008, p. 17.

63. Donald Brookes, "Merit Pay: Does It Help or Hinder Productivity?" *HR Focus,* January 1993, p. 13.

64. Atul Mitra, Nina Gupta, and G. Douglas Jenkins, Jr., "The Case of the Invisible Merit Raise: How People See Their Pay Raises," *Compensation and Benefits Review,* May–June 1995, pp. 75–76.

65. For a recent analysis of pay for performance, see Luthans and Stajkovic, "Reinforce for Performance," op. cit., pp. 49–57. For "New Pay," see Patricia K. Zingheim and Jay R. Schuster, "Introduction: How Are the New Pay Tools Being Deployed?" *Compensation and Benefits Review,* July–August, 1995, pp. 10–11, and Patricia K. Zingheim and Jay R. Schuster, *Pay People Right,* Jossey-Bass, San Francisco, 2000.

66. Virginia M. Gibson, "The New Employee Reward System," *Management Review,* February 1995, p. 18.

67. Alexander D. Stajkovic and Fred Luthans, "The Differential Effects of Incentive Motivators on Work Performance," *Academy of Management Journal,* Vol. 44, No. 3, 2001, pp. 580–590.

68. Melissa W. Barringer and George T. Milkovich, "A Theoretical Exploration of the Adoption and Design of Flexible Benefit Plans," *Academy of Management Review,* January 1998, pp. 305–324.

69. Jennifer Laabs, "Demand Performance for Benefits," *Workforce,* January 2000, pp. 45–46.

70. Bob Nelson, "Secrets of Successful Employee Recognition," *Quality Digest,* August 1996, p. 26.

71. This study was conducted by Gerald Graham and reported in ibid.

72. This is from Robert Half International and is reported in ibid.

73. Stajkovic and Luthans, "The Differential Effects," op. cit.

74. Suzanne J. Peterson and Fred Luthans, "The Impact of Financial and Non-Financial Incentives on Business Unit Outcomes Over Time," *Journal of Applied Psychology,* Vol. 91, No. 1, 2006, pp. 156–165.

75. See Peterson and Luthans, ibid. and Stajkovic and Luthans, "The Differential Effects," op. cit.

76. Luthans and Stajkovic, "Provide Recognition," op. cit., pp. 173–174.

77. Jerry L. McAdams, "Design, Implementation and Results: Employee Involvement and Performance Reward Plans," *Compensation and Benefits Review,* March–April 1995, p. 55.

78. Ibid., p. 54.

79. See S. J. Ashford and L. L. Cummings, "Feedback as an Individual Resource," *Organizational Behavior and Human Performance,* Vol. 32, 1983, pp. 370–398, and Mary F. Sully DeLuque and Steven Sommer, "The Impact of Culture on Feedback-Seeking Behavior," *Academy of Management Review,* Vol. 25, No. 4, 2000, pp. 829–849.

80. A. N. Kluger and Angelo DeNisi, "The Effects of Feedback Interventions on Performance: A Historical Review, a Meta-Analysis, and a Preliminary Feedback Intervention Theory," *Psychological Bulletin,* Vol. 119, 1996, pp. 254–248, and Angelo J. Kinicki, Gregory E. Prussia, Bin (Joshua) Wu, and Frances M. McKee-Ryan, "A Covariance Structure Analysis of Employees' Response to Performance Feedback," *Journal of Applied Psychology,* Vol. 89, No. 6, 2004, pp. 1057–1069.

81. D. M. Prue and J. A. Fairbank, "Performance Feedback in Organizational Behavior Management: A Review," *Journal of Organizational Behavior Management,* Spring 1981, pp. 1–16.

82. Richard E. Kopelman, "Objective Feedback," in Edwin A. Locke (Ed.), *Generalizing from Laboratory to Field Settings,* Lexington Books, Lexington, Mass., 1986, pp. 119–145.

83. Stajkovic and Luthans, "The Relative Effects," op. cit.

84. Fred Luthans, Richard M. Hodgetts, and Stuart A. Rosenkrantz, *Real Managers,* Ballinger, Cambridge, Mass., 1988, pp. 141–142.

85. Daniel R. Ilgen, Cynthia D. Fisher, and M. Susan Taylor, "Consequences of Individual Feedback on Behavior in Organizations," *Journal of Applied Psychology,* August 1979, pp. 349–371, and Locke and Latham, op. cit., pp. 185–189.

86. David A. Nadler, "The Effects of Feedback on Task Group Behavior: A Review of the Experimental Research," *Organizational Behavior and Human Performance,* June 1979, pp. 309–338.

87. John M. Ivancevich and J. Timothy McMahon, "The Effects of Goal Setting, External Feedback, and Self-Generated Feedback on Outcome Variables: A Field Experiment," *Academy of Management Journal,* June 1982, pp. 291–308.

88. Robert C. Liden and Terence R. Mitchell, "Reactions to Feedback: The Role of Attributions," *Academy of Management Journal,* June 1985, pp. 291–308.

89. Mark D. Cannon and Robert Witherspoon, "Actionable Feedback: Unlocking the Power of Learning and Performance Improvement," *Academy of Management Executive,* Vol. 19, No. 2, 2005, pp. 120–134.

90. Kenneth M. Nowack, "360-Degree Feedback: The Whole Story," *Training and Development,* January 1993, pp. 69–72.

91. David M. Herold, Robert C. Linden, and Marya L. Leatherwood, "Using Multiple Attributes to Assess Sources of Performance Feedback," *Academy of Management Journal,* December 1987, pp. 826–835.

92. For example, see Manuel London and James W. Smither, "Can Multisource Feedback Change Perceptions of Goal Accomplishment, Self-Evaluations, and Performance-Related Outcomes? Theory-Based Applications and Directions for Research," *Personnel Psychology,* Vol. 48, 1995, pp. 803–839, and Fred Luthans and Suzanne J. Peterson, "360-Degree Feedback with Systematic Coaching," *Human Resource Management Journal,* Vol. 42, No. 3, 2003, pp. 243–256.

93. Steve Williams and Fred Luthans, "The Impact of Choice of Rewards and Feedback on Task Performance," *Journal of Organizational Behavior,* Vol. 13, 1992, pp. 653–666.

94. Robert Waldersee and Fred Luthans, "The Impact of Positive and Corrective Feedback on Customer Service Performance," *Journal of Organizational Behavior,* Vol. 14, 1993, pp. 83–95.

95. For examples of academic models, see J. Komaki, "Toward Effective Supervision: An Operant Analysis and Comparison of Managers at Work," *Journal of Applied Psychology,* Vol. 71, 1986, pp. 270–279, and W. E. Scott, Jr. and P. M. Podsakoff, *Behavioral Principles in the Practice of Management,* Wiley, New York, 1985. For consulting models, see T. F. Gilbert, *Human Competence: Engineering Worthy Performance,* McGraw-Hill, New York, 1978; L. M. Miller, *Behavior Management: The New Science of Managing People at Work,* Wiley, New York, 1978; Daniels, op. cit.; and Victoria Williams, "Making Performance Management Relevant," *Compensation & Benefits Review,* Vol. 33, No. 4, 2001, pp. 47–51. For a comprehensive history, see Alyce M. Dickinson, "The Historical Roots of Organizational Behavior Management in the Private Sector," *Journal of Organizational Behavior Management,* Vol. 20, Nos. 3/4, 2000, pp. 9–58.

96. Alexander D. Stajkovic and Fred Luthans, "Behavioral Management and Task Performance in Organizations: Conceptual Background, Meta-Analysis, and Test of Alternative Models," *Personnel Psychology,* Vol. 56, 2003, pp. 155–194.

97. Alexander D. Stajkovic and Fred Luthans, "A Meta-Analysis of the Effects of Organizational Behavior Modification on Task Performance, 1975–95," *Academy of Management Journal,* Vol. 40, No. 5, 1997, pp. 1122–1149.

98. See Fred Luthans, "Resolved: Functional Analysis Is the Best Technique for Diagnostic Evaluation of Organizational Behavior," in Barbara Karmel (Ed.), *Point and Counterpoint in Organizational Behavior,* Dryden, Fort Worth, Tex., 1980, pp. 48–60.

99. V. Mark Daniel, "Employee Absenteeism: A Selective Review of Antecedents and Consequences," *Journal of*

*Organizational Behavior Management,* Spring/Summer 1985, p. 157.

100. Stajkovic and Luthans, "A Meta-Analysis," op. cit., and Stajkovic and Luthans, "The Relative Effects," op. cit.

101. Stajkovic and Luthans, "Behavioral Management and Task Performance in Organizations," op. cit.

102. Kenneth N. Wexley and Gary P. Latham, *Developing and Training Human Resources,* Scott, Foresman, Glenview, Ill., 1981, p. 78, and see Donna Goldwasser, "Beyond ROI," *Training,* January 2001, pp. 82–90.

103. Wexley and Latham, op. cit. Also see Greg G. Wang, Zhengxia Dou, and Ning Li, "Systems Approach to Measuring Return on Investment for HRD Interventions," *Human Resource Development Quarterly,* Vol. 13, No. 2, 2002, p. 203.

104. See Lee W. Frederiksen (Ed.), *Handbook of Organizational Behavior Management,* Interscience Wiley, New York, 1982, pp. 12–14; these findings are summarized in Luthans and Kreitner, *Organizational Behavior Modification and Beyond,* op. cit., Chap. 8; Stajkovic and Luthans, "A Meta-Analysis of the Effects of Organizational Behavior Modification on Task Performance," op. cit.; and Stajkovic and Luthans, "Behavioral Management and Task Performance in Organizations," op. cit.

105. R. W. Kempen, "Absenteeism and Tardiness," in Frederiksen, op. cit., p. 372.

106. Fred Luthans and Terry L. Maris, "Evaluating Personnel Programs through the Reversal Technique," *Personnel Journal,* October 1979, pp. 696–697.

107. Dov Zohar and Nahum Fussfeld, "A System Approach to Organizational Behavior Modification: Theoretical Considerations and Empirical Evidence," *International Review of Applied Psychology,* October 1981, pp. 491–505.

108. Beth Sulzer-Azaroff, "Behavioral Approaches to Occupational Health and Safety," in Frederiksen, op. cit., pp. 505–538. Also see Robert A. Reber, Jerry A. Wallin, and David L. Duhon, "Preventing Occupational Injuries through Performance Management," *Public Personnel Management,* Summer 1993, pp. 301–312.

109. See William Atkinson, "Behavior-Based Safety," *Management Review,* February 2000, pp. 41–45.

110. Thomas K. Connellan, *How to Improve Human Performance,* Harper & Row, New York, 1978, pp. 170–174.

111. Robert Mirman, "Performance Management in Sales Organizations," in Frederiksen, op. cit., pp. 427–475.

112. Mark J. Martinko, J. Dennis White, and Barbara Hassell, "An Operant Analysis of Prompting in a Sales Environment," *Journal of Organizational Behavior Management,* Vol. 10, No. 1, 1989, pp. 93–107.

113. Peterson and Luthans, op. cit.

114. Fred Luthans, Robert Paul, and Douglas Baker, "An Experimental Analysis of the Impact of Contingent Reinforcement on Salespersons Performance Behaviors," *Journal of Applied Psychology,* June 1981, pp. 314–323, and Fred Luthans, Robert Paul, and Lew Taylor, "The Impact of Contingent Reinforcement on Retail Salespersons' Performance Behaviors: A Replicated Field Experiment," *Journal of Organizational Behavior Management,* Spring/Summer 1985, pp. 25–35.

115. See Kirk O'Hara, C. Merle Johnson, and Terry A. Beehr, "Organizational Behavior Management in the Private Sector: A Review of Empirical Research and Recommendations for Further Investigation," *Academy of Management Review,* October 1985, pp. 848–864; Gerald A. Merwin, John A. Thompson, and Eleanor E. Sanford, "A Methodology and Content Review of Organizational Behavior Management in the Private Sector 1978–1986," *Journal of Organizational Behavior Management,* Vol. 10, No. 1, 1989, pp. 39–57; Frank Andrasik, "Organizational Behavior Modification in Business Settings: A Methodological and Content Review," *Journal of Organizational Behavior Management,* Vol. 10, No. 1, 1989, pp. 59–77; Timothy V. Nolan, Kimberly A. Jarema, and John Austin, "An Objective Review of the Journal of Organizational Behavior Management: 1987–1997," *Journal of Organizational Behavior Management,* Vol. 19, No. 3, 1999, pp. 83–114; and Maureen L. Ambrose and Carol T. Kulik, "Old Friends, New Faces: Motivation Research in the 1990s," *Journal of Management,* Vol. 25, No. 3, 1999, pp. 263–266.

116. Stajkovic and Luthans, "A Meta-Analysis of the Effects of Organizational Behavior Modification on Task Performance," op. cit., and Stajkovic and Luthans, "Behavioral Management and Task Performance in Organizations," op. cit.

117. For example, see Robert Ottemann and Fred Luthans, "An Experimental Analysis of the Effectiveness of an Organizational Behavior Modification Program in Industry," *Academy of Management Proceedings,* 1975, pp. 140–142; Fred Luthans and Jason Schweizer, "How Behavior Modification Techniques Can Improve Total Organizational Performance," *Management Review,* September 1979, pp. 43–50; Fred Luthans, Walter S. Maciag, and Stuart A. Rosenkrantz, "O.B. Mod.: Meeting the Productivity Challenge with Human Resource Management," *Personnel,* March–April 1983, pp. 28–36; and Alexander D. Stajkovic and Fred Luthans, "The Differential Effects of Incentive Motivators on Work Performance," *Academy of Management Journal,* Vol. 44, 2001, pp. 580–590.

118. For example, see Luthans, Paul, and Baker, op. cit.; Luthans, Paul and Taylor, op. cit.; Charles A. Snyder and Fred Luthans, "Using O.B. Mod. to Increase Hospital Productivity," *Personnel Administrator,* August 1982, pp. 67–73; and Peterson and Luthans, op. cit.

119. Dianne H. B. Welsh, Fred Luthans, and Steven M. Sommer, "Managing Russian Factory Workers: The Impact of U.S.-Based Behavioral and Participative Techniques," *Academy of Management Journal,* February 1993, pp. 58–79, and Dianne H. B. Welsh, Fred Luthans, and Steven M. Sommer, "Organizational Behavior Modification Goes to Russia: Replicating an Experimental Analysis across Cultures and Tasks," *Journal of Organizational Behavior Management,* Vol. 13, No. 2, 1993, pp. 15–35.

120. Dianne H. B. Welsh, Steven M. Sommer, and Nancy Birch, "Changing Performance among Russian Retail Workers: Effectively Transferring American Management Techniques," *Journal of Organizational Change Management,* Vol. 6, No. 2, 1993, pp. 34–50.

121. Fred Luthans, Shanggeun Rhee, Brett C. Luthans, and James B. Avey, "Impact of Behavioral Performance Management in a Korean Application," *Leadership and Organization Development Journal,* Vol. 29, No. 5, 2008, pp. 427–443.

122. Alexander D. Stajkovic and Fred Luthans, "A Meta-Analysis of the Effects of Organizational Behavior Modification on Task Performance: 1975–1995," *Academy of Management Journal,* Vol. 40, No. 5, 1997, pp. 1122–1149.

123. Luthans and Stajkovic, "Reinforce for Performance," op. cit., p. 55.

## Chapter 13 Footnote References and Supplemental Readings

1. "The 21st-Century Leader," *The Conference Board Review,* March/April 2007, p. 55.

2. Warren Bennis, "The End of Leadership," *Organizational Dynamics,* Summer 1999, pp. 71–80. Also see Warren Bennis,"Leading in Unnerving Times," *MIT Sloan Management Review,* Winter 2001, pp. 97–103. For more on the new concept of followership see: Barbara Kellerman, *Followership: How Followers Are Creating Change and Changing Leaders,* Harvard Business Press, Boston, 2008.

3. Quoted in Tricia Bisoux, "The Mind of a Leader," *Biz Ed,* September/October 2002, p. 26.

4. Philip Mirvis and Louis "Tex" Gunning, "Creating a Community of Leaders," *Organizational Dynamics,* Vol. 35, No. 1, 2005, p. 70.

5. Bruce J. Avolio and Fred Luthans, *The High Impact Leader: Moments Matter in Accelerating Authentic Leadership Development,* McGraw-Hill, New York, 2006, p. vii.

6. "It's the Manager, Stupid," *The Economist,* August 8, 1998, p. 54; and quoted in Mina Kimes, "How Do I Groom and Keep Talented Employees?" *Fortune* (International), November 10, 2008, p. 16.

7. Geoff Colvin, Telis Demos, Jenny Mero, John Elliott, and Jia Lynn Yang, "Leader Machines," *Fortune,* October 1, 2007, p. 98.

8. See Gary Yukl, Angela Gordon, and Tom Taber, "A Hierarchical Taxonomy of Leadership Behavior: Integrating a Half Century of Behavior Research," *Journal of Leadership and Organizational Studies,* Vol. 9, No. 1, 2002, pp. 15–32.

9. For some basic research on influence, see Herman Aguinis, Mitchell S. Nesler, Megumi Hosoda, and James T. Tedeschi, "The Use of Influence Tactics in Persuasion," *Journal of Social Psychology,* Vol. 124, No. 4, 1994, pp. 429–438.

10. Warren G. Bennis, "Managing the Dream: Leadership in the 21st Century," *Journal of Organizational Change Management,* Vol. 2, No. 1, 1989, p. 7. Also see W. Glenn Rowe, "Creating Wealth in Organizations: The Role of Strategic Leadership," *Academy of Management Executive,* Vol. 15, No. 1, 2001, pp. 81–94, and R. Duane Ireland and Michael A. Hitt, "Achieving and Maintaining Strategic Competitiveness in the 21st Century: The Role of Strategic Leadership," *Academy of Management Executive,* Vol. 19, No. 4, 2005, pp. 63–77.

11. Gary Yukl and Richard Lepsinger, "Why Integrating the Leading and Managing Roles Is Essential for Organizational Effectiveness," *Organizational Dynamics,* Vol. 34, No. 4, 2005, pp. 361–375.

12. Bernard M. Bass, *Bass and Stogdill's Handbook of Leadership,* 3rd ed., Free Press, New York, 1990, p. 11.

13. Warren G. Bennis and Robert J. Thomas, "Crucibles of Leadership," *Harvard Business Review,* September 2002, p. 39.

14. Bruce J. Avolio, *Leadership Development in Balance: Made/ Born,* Lawrence Erlbaum Associates, Mahwah, NJ, 2005, p. 194. Also see Fred Luthans, Steven Norman, and Larry Hughes, "Authentic Leadership: A New Approach for a New Time," in R. Burke and C. Cooper (Eds.), *Inspiring Leaders,* (pp. 84–104), Routledge, Taylor, and Francis, London, 2006.

15. Bill George, "Leadership in the 21st Century," Address at Westminster Town Hall Forum, Minneapolis, March 15, 2007, p. 9.

16. Stratford Sherman, "How Tomorrow's Best Leaders Are Learning Their Stuff," *Fortune,* November 27, 1995, p. 92.

17. Richard M. Hodgetts, "A Conversation with Warren Bennis on Leadership in the Midst of Downsizing," *Organizational Dynamics,* Summer 1996, p. 78.

18. Francis J. Yammarino, Fred Dansereau, and Christina J. Kennedy, "A Multi-Level Multidimensional Approach to Leadership: Viewing Leadership through an Elephant's Eye," *Organizational Dynamics,* Vol. 29, No. 3, 2001, pp. 149–163.

19. M. Sorcher and J. Brant, "Are You Picking the Right Leaders," *Harvard Business Review,* February 2002, p. 81.

20. Richard D. Arvey, et al., "The Determinants of Leadership Role Occupancy: Genetic and Personality Factors," *Leadership Quarterly,* Vol. 17, 2006, pp. 1–20.

21. Avolio and Luthans, *The High Impact Leader,* op. cit., p. 57.

22. Bruce J. Avolio, "Promoting More Integrative Strategies for Leadership Theory-Building," *American Psychologist,* Vol. 62, No. 1, 2007, p. 26.

23. Timothy A. Judge, Joyce E. Bono, Remus Ilies, and Megan W. Gerhardt, "Personality and Leadership: A Qualitative and Quantitative Review," *Journal of Applied Psychology,* Vol. 87, No. 4, 2002, pp. 765–780.

24. Ibid.

25. Kim-Yin Chan and Fritz Drasgow, "Toward a Theory of Individual Differences and Leadership: Understanding the Motivation to Lead," *Journal of Applied Psychology,* Vol. 86, No. 3, 2001, pp. 481–498.

26. For example, Fred Luthans, Kyle W. Luthans, Richard M. Hodgetts, and Brett C. Luthans, "Positive Approach to Leadership," *The Journal of Leadership Studies,* Vol. 8, No. 2, 2001, pp. 3–20; Fred Luthans and Bruce J. Avolio, "Authentic Leadership Development," in Kim S. Cameron, Jane E. Dutton, and Robert E. Quinn (Eds.), *Positive Organizational Scholarship,* Berrett-Koehler, San Francisco, 2003, pp. 241–258; and Francis J. Yammarino, Shelly D. Dionne, Chester A. Schriesheim, and Fred Danserau, "Authentic Leadership and Positive Organizational Behavior," *Leadership Quarterly,* Vol. 19, No. 6, 2008, pp. 693–707.

27. For example, see L. J. Wunderley, W. B. Reddy, and W. N. Dember, "Optimism and Pessimism in Business Leaders," *Journal of Applied Social Psychology,* Vol. 28, 1998, pp. 751–760, and Fred Luthans, Kyle W. Luthans, Richard M. Hodgetts, and Brett C. Luthans, "Positive Approach to Leadership (PAL): Implications for Today's Organizations," *Journal of Leadership Studies,* Vol. 8, No. 2, 2001, pp. 3–20.

28. For example, see Suzanne J. Peterson and Fred Luthans, "The Positive Impact and Development of Hopeful Leaders," *Leadership and Organizational Development Journal,*

Vol. 24, 2003, pp. 26–31; Luthans, Luthans, Hodgetts, and Luthans, op. cit.; and C. R. Snyder and H. Shorey, "Hope and Leadership," in K. Christensen (Ed.), *Encyclopedia of Leadership,* Berkshire Publishers, Harrison, N.Y., 2003.

29. At least for indirect support of resiliency for organizational leadership, see A. S. Masten and M. J. Reed, "Resiliency in Development," in C. R. Snyder and S. Lopez (Eds.), *Handbook of Positive Psychology,* Oxford University Press, Oxford, U.K., 2002, pp. 74–88; Kathleen M.Sutcliffe and Timothy J. Vogus, "Organizing for Resilience," in K. S. Cameron, J. E. Dutton, and R. E. Quinn (Eds.), *Positive Organizational Scholarship,* Berrett-Koehler, San Francisco, 2003, pp. 94–110; Fred Luthans, "The Need for and Meaning of Positive Organizational Behavior," *Journal of Organizational Behavior,* Vol. 23, 2002, pp. 695–706; C. R. Wanburg and J. T. Banas, "Predictors and Outcomes of Openness to Changes in a Reorganizing Workplace," *Journal of Applied Psychology,* Vol. 85, 2000, pp. 132–142; Carolyn M. Youssef and Fred Luthans, "Resiliency Development of Organizations, Leaders and Employees: Multi-Level Theory Building for Sustained Performance," in William Gardner, Bruce J. Avolio, and Fred Walumbwa (Eds.), *Authentic Leadership Theory and Practice,* Elsevier, Oxford, UK, 2005, pp. 303–344; and Carolyn M. Youssef and Fred Luthans, "Resiliency in Leadership," in J. Burns, G. Goethals, and G. Sorenson (Eds.), *Encyclopedia of Leadership,* Berkshire/Sage, Great Barrington, Mass., 2004, and Lynn Harland, Wayne Harrison, James R. Jones, and Roni Reiter-Palmon, "Leadership Behaviors and Subordinate Resilience," *Journal of Leadership and Organizational Studies,* Vol. 11, No. 2, 2005, pp. 2–14.

30. For example, see Daniel Goleman, "Leadership That Gets Results," *Harvard Business Review,* March/April 2000, pp. 79–90; Daniel Goleman, "What Makes a Leader?" *Harvard Business Review,* November/ December 1998, pp. 94–102; Daniel Goleman, Richard Boyatzis, and Annie McKee, *Primal Leadership,* Harvard Business School Press, Boston, 2002; and John Antonakis, Neal Ashkanasy, and Marie T. Dasborough, "Does Leadership Need Emotional Intelligence?" *Leadership Quarterly,* Vol. 20, No. 2, 2009, pp. 247–261.

31. Luthans, Luthans, Hodgetts, and Luthans, op. cit.; Michael J. McCormick, "Self-Efficacy and Leadership Effectiveness: Applying Social Cognitive Theory to Leadership," *The Journal of Leadership Studies,* Vol. 8, No. 1, 2001, pp. 22–33; Laura L. Paglis and Stephen G. Green, "Leadership Self-Efficacy and Managers' Motivation for Leading Change," *Journal of Organizational Behavior,* Vol. 23, 2002, pp. 215–235; Martin M. Chemers, Carl B. Watson, and Stephen T. May, "Dispositional Affect and Leadership Effectiveness: A Comparison of Self-Esteem, Optimism, and Efficacy," *Personality and Social Psychology Bulletin,* Vol. 26, No. 3, 2000, pp. 267–277; and Crystal L. Hoyt, "The Role of Leadership Efficacy and Stereotype Activation in Women's Identification with Leadership," *Journal of Leadership and Organizational Studies,* Vol. 11, No. 4, 2005, pp. 2–14; David W. Anderson, Henryk T. Krajewski, Richard Goffin, and Douglas N. Jackson, "A Leadership Self-Efficacy Taxonomy and Its Relation to Effective Leadership," *Leadership*

*Quarterly,* Vol. 19, No. 5, 2008, pp. 595–608; and Sean T. Hannah, Bruce J. Avolio, Fred Luthans, and Peter Harms, "Leadership Efficacy: Review and Future Directions," *Leadership Quarterly,* Vol. 19, No. 6, 2008, pp. 669–692.

32. Fred Luthans and Bruce Avolio, "Authentic Leadership Development," op. cit.; Avolio and Luthans, *The High Impact Leader,* op. cit.; Luthans, Norman, Hughes, op cit.; and William Gardner, Bruce Avolio, Fred Luthans, Douglas R. May, and Fred Walumbwa, "Can You See the Real Me? A Self-Based Model of Authentic Leader and Follower Development," *Leadership Quarterly,* Vol. 16, 2005, pp. 343–372.

33. Robert Katz, "Skills of an Effective Administrator," *Harvard Business Review,* September–October 1974, pp. 90–101. Also see David Finegold, George S. Benson, and Susan A. Mohrman, "Harvesting What They Grow: Can Firms Get a Return on Investments in General Skills?" *Organizational Dynamics,* Vol. 31, No. 2, 2002, pp. 151–164.

34. Gary A. Yukl, *Leadership in Organizations,* Prentice Hall, Upper Saddle River, N.J., 1981, p. 70.

35. See R. J. House and R. N. Aditya, "The Social Scientific Study of Leadership: Quo Vadis," *Journal of Management,* Vol. 23, 1997, pp. 409–473; H. G. Gregersen, A. J. Morrison, and J. S. Black, "Developing Leaders for the Global Frontier," *Sloan Management Review,* Vol. 40, Fall 1998, pp. 21–32; Karin Klenke, "Cinderella Stories of Women Leaders: Connecting Leadership Contexts and Compentencies," *Journal of Leadership and Organization Studies,* Vol. 9, No. 2, 2002, pp. 18–28; and S. A. Kirkpatrick and E. A. Locke, "Leadership: Do Traits Matter?" *Academy of Management Executive,* Vol. 5, May 1991, pp. 48–60.

36. Francis J. Yammarino and Fred Dansereau, "Individualized Leadership," *Journal of Leadership and Organizational Studies,* Vol. 9, No. 1, 2002, pp. 90–99.

37. Charles N. Greene, "The Reciprocal Nature of Influence between Leader and Subordinate," *Journal of Applied Psychology,* Vol. 60, 1975, pp. 187–193. Also see M. D. Mumford, F. Dansereau, and F. J. Yammarino, "Followers, Motivations, and Levels of Analysis," *Leadership Quarterly,* Vol. 11, 2000, pp. 313–340, and Gary Yukl, *Leadership in Organizations,* Prentice Hall, Upper Saddle River, N.J., 1998, pp. 161–167.

38. J. C. Barrow, "Worker Performance and Task Complexity as Casual Determinants of Leader Behavior Style and Flexibility," *Journal of Applied Psychology,* Vol. 61, 1976, pp. 433–440.

39. Charles N. Greene and Chester A. Schriesheim, "Leader-Group Interactions: A Longitudinal Field Investigation," *Journal of Applied Psychology,* February 1980, pp. 50–59.

40. Ronald Riggio, Ira Chaleff, and Jean Lipman-Blumen (Eds.), *The Art of Followership,* Jossey-Bass, San Francisco, 2008.

41. Barbara Kellerman, "Pecking Orders: Why Some Lead and Others Follow," *The Conference Board Review,* March/April 2008, p. 51.

42. F. Dansereau, Jr., G. Graen, and W. J. Haga, "A Vertical Dyad Linkage Approach to Leadership within Formal Organizations: A Longitudinal Investigation of the Role Making Process," *Organizational Behavior and Human Performance,* February 1975, pp. 46–78.

43. G. Graen, M. Novak, and P. Sommerkamp, "The Effects of Leader-Member Exchange and Job Design and Productivity

and Satisfaction: Testing a Dual Attachment Model," *Organizational Behavior and Human Performance,* Vol. 30, 1982, pp. 109–131.

44. Dansereau, Graen, and Haga, op. cit.

45. Fred Dansereau, Jr., Joseph A. Alutto, Steven E. Markham, and MacDonald Dumas, "Multi-Plexed Supervision and Leadership: An Application of Within and Between Analysis," in James G. Hunt, Uma Sekaran, and Chester A. Schriesheim (Eds.), *Leadership: Beyond Establishment Views,* Southern Illinois University Press, Carbondale, Ill., 1982, pp. 81–103.

46. Robert C. Liden and George Graen, "Generalizability of the Vertical Dyad Linkage Model of Leadership," *Academy of Management Journal,* September 1980, pp. 451–465, and Chester A Schriesheim, Linda L. Neider, and Terri A. Scandura, "Delegation and Leader-Member Exchange: Main Effects, Moderators, and Measurement Issues," *Academy of Management Journal,* Vol. 41, No. 3, 1998, pp. 298–318.

47. Robert P. Vecchio, "A Further Test of Leadership Effect due to Between-Group Variation and Within-Group Variation," *Journal of Applied Psychology,* April 1982, pp. 200–208, and Richard M. Dienesch and Robert C. Liden, "Leader-Member Exchange Model of Leadership: A Critique and Further Development," *Academy of Management Review,* July 1986, pp. 618–634.

48. For example, see John M. Maslyn and Mary Uhl-Bien, "Leader-Member Exchange and Its Dimensions: Effects of Self-Effort and Other's Effort on Relationship Quality," *Journal of Applied Psychology,* Vol. 86, No. 4, 2001, pp. 697–708.

49. Gary Yukl, "Managerial Leadership: A Review of Theory and Research," *Journal of Management,* Vol. 15, No. 2, 1989, p. 266.

50. Francis J. Yammarino and Alan J. Dubinsky, "Superior-Subordinate Relationships: A Multiple Levels of Analysis Approach," *Human Relations,* Vol. 45, No. 6, 1992, pp. 575–600, and F. Dansereau and F. J. Yammarino (Eds.), *Leadership: The Multiple-Level Approaches,* JAI Press, Stamford, Conn., 1998.

51. Kenneth J. Dunegan, Dennis Duchon, and Mary Uhl-Bien, "Examining the Link between Leader-Member Exchange and Subordinate Performance: The Role of Task Analyzability and Variety of Moderators," *Journal of Management,* Vol. 18, No. 1, 1992, pp. 59–76; David A. Hofmann, Frederick P. Morgeson, and Stephen J. Gerras, "Climate as a Moderator of the Relationship between Leader-Member Exchange and Content Specific Citizenship: Safety Climate as an Exemplar," *Journal of Applied Psychology,* Vol. 88, No. 1, 2003, pp. 170–178; Wing Lam, Xu Huang, and Ed Snape, "Feedback-Seeking Behavior and Leader-Member Exchange: Do Supervisor-Attributed Motives Matter?" *Academy of Management Journal,* Vol. 50, No. 2, 2007, pp. 348–363; and Robyn Brouer, Allison Duke, Darren Treadway, and Gerald Ferris, "The Moderating Effect of Political Skill on the Demographic Dissimilarity-Leader-Member Exchange Quality Relationship," *Leadership Quarterly,* Vol. 20, No. 2, 2009, pp. 61–69.

52. George B. Graen and Mary Uhl-Bien, "Development of Leader-Member Exchange (LMX) Theory of Leadership over 25 Years: Applying a Multi-Level Multi-Domain Perspective," *Leadership Quarterly,* Vol. 6, No. 2, 1995, p. 225.

53. Raymond T. Sparrowe and Rober C. Liden, "Process and Structure in Leader-Member Exchange," *Academy of Management Review,* Vol. 22, No. 2, 1997, pp. 522–552.

54. Patrick T. Gibbons, "Impacts of Organizational Evolution on Leadership Roles and Behaviors," *Human Relations,* Vol. 45, No. 1, 1992, pp. 1–18, and Janet Z. Burns and Fred L. Otte, "Implications of Leader-Member Exchange Theory and Research for Human Resource Development Research," *Human Resource Development Quarterly,* Vol. 10, No. 3, Fall 1999, pp. 225–247.

55. Robert G. Lord, Douglas J. Brown, and Steven J. Freiberg, "Understanding the Dynamics of Leadership: The Role of Follower Self-Concepts in the Leader/Follower Relationship," *Organizational Behavior and Human Decision Processes,* Vol. 78, No. 8, June 1999, pp. 167–203. Also see Kathryn M. Sherony and Stephen G. Green, "Coworker Exchange: Relationships between Coworkers, Leader-Member Exchange, and Work Attitudes," *Journal of Applied Psychology,* Vol. 87, No. 3, 2002, pp. 542–548.

56. Fred E. Fiedler, *A Theory of Leadership Effectiveness,* McGraw-Hill, New York, 1967, pp. 13–144.

57. Ibid., p. 147.

58. Ibid.

59. Fred Fiedler and Martin M. Chemers, *Leadership and Effective Management,* Scott, Foresman, Glenview, Ill., 1974, p. 83.

60. Fred E. Fiedler and Linda Mahar, "The Effectiveness of Contingency Model Training: A Review of the Validation of Leader Match," *Personnel Psychology,* Spring 1979, p. 46.

61. Michael J. Strube and Joseph E. Garcia, "A Meta-Analytic Investigation of Fiedler's Contingency Model of Leadership Effectiveness," *Psychological Bulletin,* September 1981, pp. 307–321, and Lawrence H. Peters, Darrell D. Hartke, and John T. Pohlman, "Fiedler's Contingency Theory of Leadership: An Application of the Meta-Analysis Procedures of Schmidt and Hunter," *Psychological Bulletin,* Vol. 97, No. 2, 1985, pp. 274–285.

62. Robert P. Vecchio, "Assessing the Validity of Fiedler's Contingency Model of Leadership Effectiveness: A Closer Look at Strube and Garcia," *Psychological Bulletin,* Vol. 93, No. 2, 1983, pp. 404–408.

63. Chester A. Schriesheim, Bennett J. Tepper, and Linda A. Tetrault, "Least Preferred Co-Worker Score, Situational Control, and Leadership Effectiveness: A Meta-Analysis of Contingency Model Performance Predictions," *Journal of Applied Psychology,* Vol. 79, No. 4, 1994, pp. 561–573.

64. Ronald E. Riggio, *Introduction to Industrial/Organizational Psychology,* Scott, Foresman/Little, Brown, Glenview, Ill., 1990, p. 293.

65. Basil S. Georgopoulos, Gerald M. Mahoney, and Nyle W. Jones, "A Path–Goal Approach to Productivity," *Journal of Applied Psychology,* December 1957, pp. 345–353; Martin G. Evans, "The Effect of Supervisory Behavior on the Path–Goal Relationship," *Organizational Behavior and Human Performance,* May 1970, pp. 277–298; and Robert J. House, "A Path–Goal Theory of Leader Effectiveness," *Administrative Science Quarterly,* September 1971, pp. 321–338.

66. Robert J. House and Terence R. Mitchell, "Path–Goal Theory of Leadership," *Journal of Contemporary Business,* Autumn 1974, pp. 81–97.

67. Ibid.

68. Ibid.

69. Alan C. Filley, Robert J. House, and Steven Kerr, *Managerial Process and Organizational Behavior,* 2nd ed., Scott, Foresman, Gleview, Ill., 1976, p. 254.

70. House and Mitchell, op. cit.

71. Filley, House, and Kerr, op. cit., pp. 256–260.

72. Chester A. Schriesheim and Angelo DeNisi, "Task Dimensions as Moderators of the Effects of Instrumental Leadership: A Two Sample Applicated Test of Path–Goal Leadership Theory," *Journal of Applied Psychology,* October 1981, pp. 589–597.

73. Julie Indvik, "Path–Goal Theory of Leadership: A Meta-Analysis," *Academy of Management Best Papers Proceedings,* 1986, pp. 189–192.

74. Robert A. Baron, *Behavior in Organizations,* 2nd ed., Allyn & Bacon, Boston, 1986, p. 292.

75. Philip M. Podsakoff, Scott B. MacKenzie, and Mike Ahearne, "Searching for a Needle in a Haystack: Trying to Identify the Illusive Moderators of Leadership Behaviors," *Journal of Management,* Vol. 21, No. 3, 1995, pp. 422–470.

76. R. J. House and J. L. Baetz, "Leadership: Some Empirical Generalizations and New Research Directions," in B. M. Staw (Ed.), *Research in Organizational Behavior,* Vol. 1, JAI Press, Greenwich, Conn., 1979, p. 399.

77. Robert J. House, "A 1976 Theory of Charismatic Leadership," in Hunt and Larson (Eds.), *Leadership: The Cutting Edge,* op. cit., pp. 189–207.

78. Ibid. Also see Jane M. Howell and Boas Shamir, "The Role of Followers in the Charismatic Leadership Process: Relationships and Their Consequences," *Academy of Management Review,* Vol. 30, No. 1, 2005, pp. 96–112.

79. Bernard M. Bass, *Leadership and Performance beyond Expectations,* Free Press, New York, 1985, pp. 54–61.

80. Patricia Sellers, "What Exactly Is Charisma?" *Fortune,* January 15, 1996, p. 68.

81. Stuart J. M. Weierter, "The Role of Self-Awareness and Self-Monitoring in Charismatic Relationships," *Journal of Applied Social Psychology,* Vol. 29, No. 6, 1999, pp. 1246–1262.

82. Juan-Carlos Pastor, James R. Meindl, and Margarita C. Mayo, "A Network Effects Model of Charisma Attributions," *Academy of Management Journal,* Vol. 45, No. 2, 2002, pp. 410–420.

83. R. J. House, J. Woycke, and E. M. Fodor, "Charismatic and Non Charismatic Leaders: Differences in Behavior and Effectiveness," in J. A. Conger and R. M. Kanungo (Eds.), *Charismatic Leadership: The Elusive Factor in Organizational Effectiveness,* Jossey-Bass, San Francisco, 1988, pp. 98–121, and Robert J. House, William D. Spangler, and James Woycke, "Personality and Charisma in the U.S. Presidency: A Psychological Theory of Leadership Effectiveness," *Academy of Management Best Papers Proceedings,* 1990, pp. 216–219.

84. David De Cremer and Daan van Knippenberg, "How Do Leaders Promote Cooperation? The Effects of Charisma and Procedural Fairness," *Journal of Applied Psychology,* Vol. 87, No. 5, 2002, pp. 858–866.

85. John E. Barbuto, Jr., "Motivation and Transactional, Charismatic, and Transformational Leadership: A Test of Antecedents," *Journal of Leadership and Organizational Studies,* Vol. 11, No. 4, 2005, pp. 26–40.

86. David A. Waldman and Mansour Javidan, "Alternative Forms of Charismatic Leadership in the Integration of Mergers and Acquisitions," *Leadership Quarterly,* Vol. 20, No. 2, 2009, pp. 130–142.

87. Shelly A. Kirkpatrick and Edwin A. Locke, "Direct and Indirect Effects of Three Core Charismatic Leadership Components of Performance and Attitudes," *Journal of Applied Psychology,* Vol. 81, No. 1, 1996, pp. 36–51.

88. Boas Shamir, Eliav Zakay, Esther Breinin, and Micha Popper, "Correlates of Charismatic Leader Behavior in Military Units: Subordinates' Attitudes, Unit Characteristics, and Superiors' Appraisals of Leader Performance," *Academy of Management Journal,* Vol. 41, No. 4, 1998, pp. 387–409.

89. J. A. Conger and R. Kanungo, "Toward a Behavioral Theory of Charismatic Leadership in Organizational Settings," *Academy of Management Review,* Vol. 12, 1987, pp. 637–647, and J. A. Conger and R. M. Kanungo, "Behavioral Dimensions of Charismatic Leadership," in Conger and Kanungo, *Charismatic Leadership,* op. cit., pp. 78–97.

90. Rajnandini Pillai, "Crisis and the Emergence of Charismatic Leadership in Groups: An Experimental Investigation," *Journal of Applied Social Psychology,* Vol. 26, No. 6, 1996, pp. 543–562.

91. Celia Romm and Nava Pliskin, "The Role of Charismatic Leadership in Diffusion and Implementation of E-mail." *The Journal of Management,* Vol. 18, No. 3, 1999, pp. 273–290.

92. Jane M. Howell and Bruce J. Avolio, "The Ethics of Charismatic Leadership: Submission or Liberation?" *Academy of Management Executive,* May 1992, pp. 43–54; Daniel Sankowsky, "The Charismatic Leader as Narcissist: Understanding the Abuse of Power," *Organizational Dynamics,* Spring 1995, pp. 57–71; and Fred Luthans, Suzanne Peterson, and Elina Ibrayeva, "The Potential for the 'Dark Side' of Leadership in Post–Communist Countries," *Journal of World Business,* Vol. 33, No. 2, 1998, pp. 185–201.

93. Howell and Avolio, op. cit., p. 52. Also see F. Bird and J. Gandz, *Good Management: Business Ethics in Action,* Prentice-Hall, Toronto, 1991, p. 166, and Y. Sankar, "Character Not Charisma Is the Critical Measure of Leadership Excellence," *Journal of Leadership and Organizational Studies,* Vol. 9, No. 4, 2003, pp. 45–55.

94. Bass, *Bass & Stogdill's Handbook,* op. cit., p. 221.

95. J. M. Burns, *Leadership,* Harper & Row, New York, 1978.

96. Bruce J. Avolio, *Leadership Development in Balance: Made/Born,* Lawrence Erlbaum Associates, Mahwah, NJ, 2005, p. 195.

97. Bernard M. Bass, "From Transactional to Transformational Leadership: Learning to Share the Vision," *Organizational Dynamics,* Winter 1990, pp. 19–31.

98. Kevin B. Low, K. G. Kroeck, and N. Sirasubramaniam, "Effectiveness of Correlates of Transformational and Transactional Leadership: A Meta-Analytic Review of the MLQ Literature," *The Leadership Quarterly,* Vol. 7, 1996, pp. 385–425.

99. Timothy A. Judge and Ronald F. Piccolo, "Transformational and Transactional Leadership: A Meta-Analytic Test of Their Relative Validity," *Journal of Applied Psychology*, Vol. 89, No. 5, 2004, pp. 755–768.

100. B. M. Bass and B. J. Avolio, *Full Range Leadership Development: Manual for the Multifactor Leadership Questionnaire*, Mindgarden, Palo Alto, Calif., 1997.

101. Noel M. Tichy and Mary Anne Devanna, *The Transformational Leader*, Wiley, New York, 1986, and Noel M. Tichy and Mary Anne Devanna, "The Transformational Leader," *Training and Development Journal*, July 1986, pp. 30–32.

102. Bennett J. Tepper, "Patterns of Downward Influence and Follower Conformity in Transactional and Transformational Leadership," *Academy of Management Best Papers Proceedings*, 1993, pp. 267–271.

103. Robert T. Keller, "Transformational Leadership and the Performance of Research and Development Project Groups," *Journal of Management*, Vol. 18, 1992, pp. 489–501; Bruce J. Avolio, *Full Leadership Development*, Sage, Thousand Oaks, Calif., 1999; and Kevin B. Lowe and William L. Gardner, "Ten Years of the 'Leadership Quarterly': Contributions and Challenges for the Future," *Leadership Quarterly*, Vol. 11, 2000, pp. 459–514.

104. Taly Dvir, Dov Eden, Bruce J. Avolio, and Boas Shamir, "Impact of Transformational Leadership on Follower Development and Performance: A Field Experiment," *Academy of Management Journal*, Vol. 45, No. 4, 2002, pp. 735–744. Also see Micha Popper and Ofra Mayseless, "Back to Basics: Applying a Parenting Perspective to Transformational Leadership," *Leadership Quarterly*, Vol. 14, 2003, pp. 41–65.

105. Francis J. Yammarino, Alan J. Dubinsky, Lucette B. Comer, and Marvin A. Jolson, "Women and Transformational and Contingent Reward Leadership: A Multiple-Levels-of-Analysis Perspective," *Academy of Management Journal*, Vol. 40, No. 1, 1997, pp. 205–222. Also see Kevin S. Groves, "Gender Differences in Social and Emotional Skills and Charismatic Leadership," *Journal of Leadership and Organizational Studies*, Vol. 11, No. 3, 2005, pp. 30–46.

106. Hui Wang, Kenneth S. Law, Rick D. Hackett, Duanxu Wang, and Zhen Xiong Chen, "Leader-Member Exchange as a Mediator of the Relationship Between Transformational Leadership and Followers' Performance and Organizational Citizenship Behavior," *Academy of Management Journal*, Vol. 48, No. 3, 2005, pp. 420–432.

107. Rajnandini Pillai, Chester A. Schriesheim, and Eric S. Williams, "Fairness Perceptions and Trust as Mediators for Transformational and Transactional Leadership: A Two-Sample Study," *Journal of Management*, Vol. 25, No. 6, 1999, pp. 897–933, and Timothy A. Judge and Joyce E. Bono, "Five Factor Model of Personality and Transformational Leadership," *Journal of Applied Psychology*, Vol. 85, No. 5, 2000, pp. 751–765.

108. Robert S. Rubin, David C. Munz, William H. Bommer, "Leading from Within: The Effects of Emotion Recognition and Personality on Transformational Leadership Behavior," *Academy of Management Journal*, Vol. 48, No. 5, 2005, pp. 845–858.

109. Nick Turner, Julian Barling, Olga Epitropaki, Vicky Butcher, and Caroline Milner, "Transformational Leadership and Moral Reasoning," *Journal of Applied Psychology*, Vol. 87, No. 2, 2002, pp. 304–311.

110. Terry L. Price, "The Ethics of Authentic Transformational Leadership," *Leadership Quarterly*, Vol. 14, 2003, pp. 67–81.

111. Fred O. Walumbwa, Bruce J. Avolio, and Weichun Zhu, "How Transformational Leadership Weaves Its Influence on Individual Job Performance: The Role of Identification and Efficacy Beliefs," *Personnel Psychology*, Vol. 61, 2008, pp. 793–825.

112. Badrinarayan Shankar Pawar and Kenneth K. Eastman, "The Nature and Implications of Contextual Influences on Transformational Leadership: A Conceptual Examination," *Academy of Management Review*, Vol. 22, No. 1, 1997, pp. 80–109. Also see Richard N. Osborn, James G. Hunt, and Lawrence R. Jauch, "Toward a Contextual Theory of Leadership," *Leadership Quarterly*, Vol. 13, 2002, pp. 797–837.

113. Steven Kerr and John M. Jermier, "Substitutes of Leadership: Their Meaning and Measurement," *Organizational Behavior and Human Performance*, December 1978, pp. 375–403. Also see Steven Kerr, "Substitutes for Leadership: Some Implications for Organizational Design," *Organization and Administrative Sciences*, Vol. 8, No. 1, 1977, p. 135, and Jon P. Howell, Peter Dorfman, and Steven Kerr, "Moderator Variables in Leadership Research," *Academy of Management Review*, Vol. 11, No. 1, 1986, pp. 88–102.

114. J. Jermier and L. Berkes, "Leader Behavior in a Police Command Bureaucracy: A Closer Look at the Quasi-Military Model," *Administrative Science Quarterly*, March 1979, pp. 1–23, and S. Kerr and J. W. Slocum, Jr., "Controlling the Performances of People in Organizations," in P. C. Nystrom and W. H. Starbuck (Eds.), *Handbook of Organizational Design*, Oxford, New York, 1981, pp. 116–134.

115. Kerr and Jermier, op. cit.

116. Robert H. Miles and M. M. Petty, "Leader Effectiveness in Small Bureaucracies," *Academy of Management Journal*, June 1977, pp. 238–250.

117. For example, see Robert House and Philip M. Podsakoff, "Leadership Effectiveness: Past Perspectives and Future Directions for Research," in Gerald Greenberg (Ed.), *Organizational Behavior: The State of the Science*, Erlbaum, Hillsdale, N.J., 1994, p. 53, and P. M. Podsakoff, B. P. Niehoff, S. B. MacKenzie, and M. L. Williams, "Do Substitutes for Leadership Really Substitute for Leadership? An Empirical Examination of Kerr and Jermier's Situational Leadership Model," *Organizational Behavior and Human Decision Processes*, Vol. 54, 1993, pp. 1–44.

118. Jon P. Howell and Peter W. Dorfman, "Substitutes for Leadership: Test of a Construct," *Academy of Management Journal*, December 1981, pp. 714–728.

119. Jon P. Howell and Peter W. Dorfman, "Leadership and Substitutes for Leadership among Professionals and Nonprofessional Workers," *Journal of Applied Behavioral Science*, Vol. 22, No. 1, 1986, pp. 29–46.

120. Shelley D. Dionne, Francis J. Yammarino, Leanne E. Atwater, and Lawrence R. James, "Neutralizing Substitutes for Leadership Theory: Leadership Effects and Common-Source Bias," *Journal of Applied Psychology*, Vol. 87, No. 3, 2002, pp. 454–464.

121. See R. K. Greenleaf, *Servant Leadership*, Paulist Press, Mahwah, N.J., 1977; J. W. Graham, "Servant Leadership in

Organizations," *Leadership Quarterly*, Vol. 2, No. 2, 1991, pp. 105–119; and Sen Sendjaya and James C. Sarros, "Servant Leadership: Its Origin, Development, and Application in Organizations," *Journal of Leadership and Organization Studies*, Vol. 9, No. 2, 2002, pp. 57–64.

122. Anthony P. Ammeter, Ceasar Douglas, William L. Gardner, Wayne A. Hochwarter, and Gerald R. Ferris, "Toward a Political Theory of Leadership," *Leadership Quarterly*, Vol. 13, 2002, pp. 751–796.

123. Osborn, Hunt, and Jauch, op. cit.

124. B. J. Avolio, S. Kahai, and G. Dodge, "E-Leadership and Its Implications for Theory, Research, and Practice," *Leadership Quarterly*, Vol. 11, 2000, pp. 615–670; Bruce J. Avolio and Surinder S. Kahai, "Adding the 'E' to E-Leadership," *Organizational Dynamics*, Vol. 31, No. 4, 2003, pp. 325–337; and Gary D. Kissler, "E-Leadership," *Organizational Dynamics*, Vol. 30, No. 2, 2001, pp. 121–133.

125. Goleman, Boyatzis and McKee, op. cit.

126. Mary Uhl-Bien, "Relational Leadership Theory: Exploring the Social Processes of Leadership and Organizing," *Leadership Quarterly*, Vol. 17, 2006, pp. 654–676.

127. Luthans, Luthans, Hodgetts, and Luthans, op. cit.; Sean T. Hannah, Robert L. Woolfolk, and Robert G. Lord, "Leader Self-Structure: A Framework for Positive Leadership," *Journal of Organizational Behavior*, Vol. 30, No. 2, 2009, pp. 269–290; and Sean T. Hannah and Fred Luthans, "A Cognitive Affective Processing Explanation of Positive Leadership: Toward a Theoretical Understanding of the Role of Psychological Capital," in R. H. Humphrey (Ed.), *Affect and Emotion—New Directions in Management Theory and Research, Vol. 7 of Research in Management*, Information Age Publishing, Greenwich, CT, 2008, pp. 97–136.

128. Craig L. Pearce, Jay A. Conger, and Edwin A. Locke, "Shared Leadership Theory," *Leadership Quarterly*, Vol. 19, No. 5, 2008, pp. 622–628.

129. David Waldman and Donald Siegel, "Defining the Socially Responsible Leader," *Leadership Quarterly*, Vol. 19, No. 1, 2008, pp. 117–131; and David Waldman and Benjamin M. Galvin, "Alternative Perspectives of Responsible Leadership," *Organizational Dynamics*, Vol. 37, No. 4, 2008, pp. 327–341.

130. Luthans, "The Need for and Meaning of Positive Organizational Behavior," op. cit.; Luthans, "Positive Organizational Behavior: Developing and Managing Psychological Strengths," op. cit.; Fred Luthans and Carolyn Youssef, "Emerging Positive Organizational Behavior," *Journal of Management*, Vol. 33, 2007, pp. 321–349; and Fred Luthans and Bruce J. Avolio, "The 'Point' of Positive Organizational Behavior," *Journal of Organizational Behavior*, Vol. 30, 2009, pp. 291–307.

131. Fred Luthans, Carolyn M. Youssef, and Bruce J. Avolio, *Psychological Capital*, Oxford University Press, Oxford, UK, 2007; and Fred Luthans, Bruce J. Avolio, James Avey, and Steven Norman, "Positive Psychological Capital: Measurement and Relationship with Performance and Satisfaction," *Personnel Psychology*, Vol. 60, 2007, pp. 541–572.

132. B. J. Avolio and T. C. Gibbons, "Developing Transformational Leaders: A Life Span Approach," in J. A. Conger and R. N. Kanungo et al. (Eds.), *Charismatic Leadership: The Elusive Factor in Organizational Effectiveness*, Jossey-Bass, San Francisco, 1998, pp. 276–308, and B. M. Bass and B. J. Avolio, *Improving Organizational Effectiveness through Transformational Leadership*, Sage, Thousand Oaks, Calif., 1994.

133. B. J. Avolio, *Full Leadership Development: Building the Vital Forces in Organizations*, Sage, Newbury Park, Calif., 1999, and B. J. Avolio, "Examining the Full Range Model of Leadership: Looking Back to Transform Forward," in D. Day and S. Zaccarro (Eds.), *Leadership Development for Transforming Organizations*, Erlbaum, Mahwah, N.J., 2003.

134. Fred Luthans and Bruce Avolio, "Authentic Leadership Development," in Kim S. Cameron, Jane E. Dutton, and Robert E. Quinn (Eds.), *Positive Organizational Scholarship*, Berrett-Koehler, San Francisco, 2003, pp. 241–259; Bruce J. Avolio and Fred Luthans, *The High Impact Leader: Moments Matter in Accelerating Authentic Leadership Development*, McGraw-Hill, New York, 2006; Bruce J. Avolio and William L. Gardner, "Authentic Leadership Development: Getting to the Root of Positive Forms of Leadership," *The Leadership Quarterly*, Vol. 16, 2005, pp. 315–338; and William L. Gardner, Bruce J. Avolio, Fred Luthans, Douglas R. May, and Fred Walumbwa, "Can You See the Real Me? A Self-Based Model of Authentic Leader and Follower Develop-ment," *The Leadership Quarterly*, Vol. 16, 2005, pp. 343–372.

135. S. Harter, "Authenticity," in C. R. Snyder and S. J. Lopez (Eds.), *Handbook of Positive Psychology*, Oxford University Press, Oxford, UK, 2002, and ibid., p. 242.

136. Luthans and Avolio, op. cit., p. 243.

137. For example, see Robert W. Terry, *Authentic Leadership: Courage in Action*, Jossey-Bass, San Francisco, 1993, and Bill George, *Authentic Leadership: Rediscovering the Secrets to Lasting Value*, John Wiley, New York, 2003.

138. Cecily D. Cooper, Terri A. Scandura, and Chester A. Schriesheim, "Looking Forward But Learning from Our Past: Potential Challenges to Developing Authentic Leadership Theory and Authentic Leaders," *The Leadership Quarterly*, Vol. 16, 2005, pp. 475–493; Steven J. Norman, Bruce J. Avolio, and Fred Luthans, "The Impact of Positivity and Transparency on Trust in Leaders and Their Perceived Effectiveness," *Leadership Quarterly*, in press; and Fred O. Walumbwa, P. Wang, H. Wang, John Schaubroeck, and Bruce J. Avolio, "Psychological Processes Linking Authentic Leadership to Follower Behaviors," *Leadership Quarterly*, in press.

139. Fred O. Walumbwa, Bruce J. Avolio, William L. Gardner, Tara S. Wernsing, and Suzanne J. Peterson, "Authentic Leadership: Development and Validation of a Theory-Based Measure," *Journal of Management*, Vol. 34, 2008, pp. 89–126.

140. Warren G. Bennis, "Managing the Dream: Leadership in the 21st Century," *Journal of Organizational Change Management*, Vol. 2, No. 1, 1989, p. 7. Also see Mark E. Mendenhall, Torsten M. Kuhlmann, and Gunter K. Stahl (Eds.), *Developing Global Business Leaders: Policies, Processes and Innovations*, Quorum, Westport, Conn., 2001, and Manfred Kets De Vries and Konstantin Korotov, "The Future of an Illusion: In Search of the New European Business Leader," *Organizational Dynamics*, Vol. 34, No. 3, 2005, pp. 218–230.

141. M. Haire, E. E. Ghiselli, and L. W. Porter, *Managerial Thinking: An International Study,* Wiley, New York, 1966.

142. F. A. Heller and B. Wilpert, *Competence and Power in Managerial Decision Making,* Wiley, London, 1981.

143. Dianne H. B. Welsh, Fred Luthans, and Steven M. Sommer, "Managing Russian Factory Workers: The Impact of U.S.–Based Behavioral and Participative Techniques," *Academy of Management Journal,* Vol. 36, No. 1, 1993, pp. 58–79.

144. Fred Luthans, Richard M. Hodgetts, and Stuart A. Rosenkrantz, *Real Managers,* Ballinger, Cambridge, Mass., 1988.

145. Fred Luthans, Dianne H. B. Welsh, and Stuart A. Rosenkrantz, "What Do Russian Managers Really Do? An Observational Study with Comparisons to U.S. Managers," *Journal of International Business Studies,* 4th Quarter, 1993, pp. 741–761.

146. Ibid. Also see Manfred F. R. Kets De Vries, "A Journey into the 'Wild East': Leadership Style and Organizational Practices in Russia," *Organizational Dynamics,* Vol. 28, No. 4, 2000, pp. 67–81.

147. Abbas J. Ali and Rachid Wahabit, "Managerial Value System in Morocco," *International Studies of Management and Organization,* Vol. 25, No. 3, 1995, pp. 87–96.

148. Cynthia Pavett and Tom Morris, "Management Styles within a Multinational Corporation: A Five Country Comparative Study," *Human Relations,* Vol. 48, No. 10, 1995, pp. 1171–1191.

149. Andrew Myers, Andrew Kakabadse, and Colin Gordon, "Effectiveness of French Management," *Journal of Management Development,* Vol. 14, No. 6, 1995, pp. 56–72.

150. Richard L. Daft, *Management,* 2nd ed., 1991, Dryden, Fort Worth, Tex., p. 625.

151. Dong I. Jung and Bruce J. Avolio, "Effects of Leadership Style of Followers' Cultural Orientation on Performance in Group and Individual Task Conditions," *Academy of Management Journal,* Vol. 42, No. 2, 1999, pp. 208–218, and Fred O. Walumbwa, John J. Lawler, Bruce J. Avolio, Peng Wang, and Kan Shi, "Transformational Leadership and Work-Related Attitudes: The Moderating Effects of Collective and Self-Efficacy Across Cultures," *Journal of Leadership and Organizational Studies,* Vol. 11, No. 3, 2005, pp. 2–16.

152. See Fred Luthans, Paul A. Marsnik, and Kyle W. Luthans, "A Contingency Matrix Approach to IHRM," *Human Resource Management,* Vol. 36, No. 2, 1997, pp. 183–199.

153. Project GLOBE, "Cultural Influences on Leadership and Organizations," *Advances in Global Leadership,* Vol. 1, 1999, JAI Press, Greenwich, Conn., pp. 171–233; Robert J. House, et al., *Culture, Leadership, and Organizations: The GLOBE Study of 62 Societies,* Sage, Thousand Oaks, CA, 2004; and Mansour Javidan, et al., "In the Eye of the Beholder: Cross Cultural Lessons in Leadership from Project GLOBE," *Academy of Management Perspective,* Vol. 20, No. 1, 2006, pp. 67–90.

154. G. Hofstede, *Culture's Consequences: International Differences in Work Related Values,* Sage, London, 1980 and for the new edition, see Geert Hofstede, *Cultures Consequences,* 2nd ed., Sage, Thousand Oaks, Calif., 2001.

155. See Javidan, et al., "In the Eye of the Beholder," op. cit., p. 73.

156. Bernard M. Bass, "Does the Transactional-Transformational Leadership Paradigm Transcend Organizational and National Boundaries?" *American Psychologist,* Vol. 52, No. 2, 1997, pp. 130–139.

157. Allan H. Church and Janine Waclawski, "The Impact of Leadership Style on Global Management Practices," *Journal of Applied Social Psychology,* Vol. 29, No. 7, 1999, pp. 1416–1443.

158. Felix C. Brodbeck et al., "Cultural Variation of Leadership Prototypes across 22 European Countries," *Journal of Occupational and Organizational Psychology,* Vol. 73, 2000, pp. 1–29, and Luke Pittaway, Olga Rivera, and Anne Murphy, "Social Identity and Leadership in the Basque Region: A Study of Leadership Development Programmes," *Journal of Leadership and Organizational Studies,* Vol. 11, No. 3, 2005, pp. 17–29.

## Chapter 14 Footnote References and Supplemental Readings

1. Peter Cappelli and Monika Hamori, "The New Road to the Top," *Harvard Business Review,* January 2005, p. 25.

2. Avis Johnson and Fred Luthans, "The Relationship between Leadership and Management: An Empirical Assessment," *Journal of Managerial Issues,* Spring 1990, pp. 13–25.

3. "Harley-Davidson: Going Whole Hog to Provide Stakeholder Satisfaction," *Management Review,* June 1993, p. 55. Also see Rich Teerlink and Lee Ozley, *More than a Motorcycle; The Leadership Journey at Harley-Davidson,* Harvard Business School Press, Boston, 2000.

4. For example, see Jane Dutton, Peter J. Frost, Monica C. Worline, Jacoba M. Lilius, and Jason M. Kanov, "Leading in Times of Trauma," *Harvard Business Review,* January 2002, pp. 55–61; Ronald A. Heifetz and Marty Linsky, "A Survival Guide for Leaders," *Harvard Business Review,* June 2002, pp. 65–74; and James M. Kouzes and Barry Z. Posner, "Leading in Cynical Times," *Journal of Management Inquiry,* Vol. 14, No. 4, 2005, pp. 357–364.

5. Gregory G. Dess and Joseph C. Picken, "Changing Roles: Leadership in the 21st Century," *Organizational Dynamics,* Winter 2000, pp. 18–33. Also see Rich Hughes, "Reflections on the State of Leadership and Leadership Development," *Human Resource Planning,* Vol. 25, No. 2, 2002, p. 4, and Tony Spaeth, "Brand-Name Leadership: A New Corporate Logo Says a Lot About the Company's CEO," *Across the Board,* March/April 2006, pp. 25–28.

6. Mary Jo Hatch, Monika Kostera, and Andrzej K. Kozminski, "The Three Faces of Leadership: Manager, Artist, Priest," *Organizational Dynamics,* Vol. 35, No. 1, 2006, pp. 49–68.

7. J. Singh, "Imposters Masquerading as Leaders: Can the Contagion Be Contained?" *Journal of Business Ethics,* Vol. 82, No. 3, 2008, pp. 733–745.

8. Ibid., p. 733.

9. *The State of Small Business,* 1997, pp. 50–56.

10. Marilyn Moats Kennedy, "The Decline of Management," *Across the Board,* July–August, 2000, pp. 57–58.

11. Raul O. Rodriguez, Mark T. Green, and Malcolm James Ree, "Leading Generation X: Do the Old Rules Apply?"

*Journal of Leadership and Organizational Studies,* Vol. 9, No. 4, 2003, pp. 67–75.

12. Reported in Tom Rath and Barry Conchie, *Strengths Based Leadership,* Gallup Press, New York, 2009.

13. "The New Organization," *The Economist,* January 21–27, 2006, p. 4.

14. Marshall Goldsmith, "E-Tools that Help Teach Leadership," *BusinessWeek,* September 3, 2008, p. 15.

15. For example, see Steven C. Currall and Marc J. Epstein, "The Fragility of Organizational Trust: Lessons from the Rise and Fall of Enron," *Organizational Dynamics,* Vol. 32, No. 2, 2003, pp. 193–206; and Wayne F. Cascio and Peter Cappelli, "Lessons from the Financial Services Crisis," *HR Magazine,* January 2009, pp. 47, 49–50.

16. See Douglas R. May, Adrian Y. L. Chan, Timothy D. Hodges, and Bruce Avolio, "Developing the Moral Component of Authentic Leadership," *Organizational Dynamics,* Vol. 32, No. 3, 2003, and Craig E. Johnson, *Meeting the Ethical Challenges of Leadership: Casting Light or Shadow,* Sage, Thousand Oaks, Calif., 2001.

17. Bert Spector, "HRM at Enron: The Unindicted Co-Conspirator," *Organizational Dynamics,* Vol. 32, No. 2, 2003, p. 215.

18. Reported in John C. Maxwell, "People Do What People See," *BusinessWeek,* November 20, 2007, p. 30.

19. Alan Deutschman, "Steve Jobs' Next Big Gamble," *Fortune,* February 8, 1993, p. 99.

20. Scott Snook, "Love and Fear and the Modern Boss," *Harvard Business Review,* Vol. 86, No. 1, 2008, p. 17.

21. Alice H. Eagly, Steven J. Karau, and Mona G. Makhijani, "Gender and the Effectiveness of Leaders: A Meta-Analysis," *Psychological Bulletin,* Vol. 117, No. 1, 1995, pp. 125–145; Alice H. Eagly, Mona G. Makhijani, and Bruce G. Klonsky, "Gender and the Evaluation of Leaders: A Meta-Analysis," *Psychological Bulletin,* Vol. 111, No. 1, 1992, pp. 3–22; Alice H. Eagly and Blair T. Johnson, "Gender and Leadership Style: A Meta-Analysis," *Psychological Bulletin,* Vol. 108, No. 2, 1993, pp. 233–256; and Robert P. Vecchio, "Leadership and Gender Advantage," *Leadership Quarterly,* Vol. 13, 2002, pp. 643–671.

22. Bruce J. Avolio, "Promoting More Integrative Strategies for Leadership Theory-Building," *American Psychologist,* Vol. 62, No. 1, 2007, pp. 25–33.

23. David A. Nadler and Michael L. Tushman, "Beyond the Charismatic Leader: Leadership and Organizational Change," *California Management Review,* Winter 1990, p. 83.

24. Sharon Shinn, "The Maverick CEO," *Biz Ed,* January–February, 2004, p. 18.

25. Jeffery D. Houghton and Steven K. Yoho, "Toward a Contingency Model of Leadership and Psychological Empowerment: When Should Self-Leadership Be Encouraged?" *Journal of Leadership and Organizational Studies,* Vol. 11, No. 4, 2005, pp. 65–83.

26. "GE Chief Has Electric Presence," from *Wall Street Journal* reprinted in *The Honolulu Advisor,* April 17, 2000, p. 1.

27. Cari Tuna, "Micromanagers Miss Bull's-Eye," *The Wall Street Journal,* November 3, 2008, p. B4.

28. Janet B. Kellett, Ronald H. Humphrey, and Randall G. Sleeth, "Empathy and Complex Task Performance: Two Routes to Leadership," *Leadership Quarterly,* Vol. 13, 2002, pp. 523–544.

29. "Changing Perspectives," *Wall Street Journal,* November 25, 1986, p. 1. Also see David A. Waldman, Gabriel G. Ramírez, Robert J. House, and Phanish Puranam, "Does Leadership Matter? CEO Leadership Attributes and Profitability under Conditions of Perceived Environmental Uncertainty," *Academy of Management Journal,* Vol. 44, No. 1, 2001, pp. 134–143.

30. B. Joseph White, "Developing Leaders for the High-Performance Workplace," *Human Resource Management,* Spring 1994, p. 163. Also see Manuel London, "Leadership and Advocacy: Dual Roles for Corporate Social Responsibility and Social Entrepreneurship," *Organizational Dynamics,* Vol. 37, No. 4, 2008, pp. 313–326.

31. For example, see Mark David, "Leadership during an Economic Slowdown," *Journal for Quality and Participation,* Vol. 24, No. 3, 2001, pp. 40–43; and Cascio and Cappelli, op. cit., 2009.

32. Joseph L. Badaracco, Jr., *Leading Quietly: An Unorthodox Guide to Doing the Right Thing,* Harvard Business School Press, Boston, 2002. Also see Robert J. Allio, "The Leader as Anti-Hero," *Strategy and Leadership,* Vol. 32, No. 2, 2002, pp. 45–46.

33. Jathan W. Janove, "Speak Softly and Carry a Big Stick," *HR Magazine,* January 2003, p. 73.

34. Bennett J. Teper, "Consequences of Abusive Supervision," *Academy of Management Journal,* Vol. 43, No. 2, 2000, pp. 178–190. Also see Martin Linsky and Ronald A. Heifetz, *Leadership on the Line: Staying Alive through the Dangers of Leading,* Harvard Business School Press, Boston, 2002; and Richard S. Tedlow, "Leaders in Denial," *Harvard Business Review,* Vol. 86, No. 7/8, 2008, pp. 18–19.

35. Warren G. Bennis, "Managing the Dream: Leadership in the 21st Century," *Journal of Organizational Change Management,* Vol. 2, No. 1, 1989, p. 6. Also see Warren Bennis, "Leading in Unnerving Times," *MIT Sloan Management Review,* Winter 2001, pp. 97–103.

36. Paul Hersey and Kenneth H. Blanchard, *Management of Organizational Behavior,* 4th ed., Prentice Hall, Upper Saddle River, N.J., 1982.

37. The discussion on the various styles and criteria of maturity is drawn from ibid.

38. For example, see Jim Holt, "Bring Big Blue Back: Lessons from the Turnaround of a Faltering Giant," *Management Review,* September 1999, p. 13, and Patricia Hunt Dirlam, "Taking CHARGE of Change," *Management Review,* September 1999, p. 61.

39. Gary A. Yukl, *Leadership in Organizations,* Prentice Hall, Upper Saddle River, N.J., 1981, pp. 143–144.

40. Claude L. Graeff, "The Situational Leadership Theory: A Critical View," *Academy of Management Review,* April 1983, pp. 285–291.

41. Warren Blank, John R. Weitzel, and Stephen G. Green, "A Test of the Situational Leadership Theory," *Personnel Psychology,* Vol. 43, 1990, pp. 579–597.

42. James Collins and Jerry Porras, *Built to Last: Successful Habits of Visionary Companies,* Harper Business, New York, 1994, and James Collins, *Good to Great,* Harper Business, New York, 2001.

43. Collins is quoted in William C. Finnie and Stanley C. Abraham, "Getting from Good to Great: A Conversation

with Jim Collins," *Strategy & Leadership,* Vol. 30, No. 5, 2002, p. 11.

44. Ibid.

45. Janet R. McColl-Kennedy and Ronald D. Anderson, "Impact of Leadership Style and Emotions on Subordinate Performance," *Leadership Quarterly,* Vol. 13, 2002, pp. 545–559.

46. Susan Jensen and Fred Luthans, "Entrepreneurs as Authentic Leaders: Impact on Employee's Attitudes," *Leadership and Organization Development Journal,* Vol. 27, No. 8, 2006, pp. 646–666.

47. Robert House and Philip M. Podsakoff, "Leadership Effectiveness: Past Perspectives and Future Directions for Research," in Jerald Greenberg (Ed.), *Organizational Behavior: The State of the Science,* Erlbaum, Hillsdale, N.J., 1994, pp. 58–64.

48. Afsaneh Nahavandi and Ali R. Malekzadeh, "Leader Style in Strategy and Organizational Performance: An Integrative Framework," *Journal of Management Studies,* May 1993, pp. 405–426. Also see W. Glen Rowe, "Creating Wealth in Organizations: The Role of Strategic Leadership," *Academy of Management Executive,* Vol. 15, No. 1, 2001, pp. 81–94, and William B. Werther, Jr., "Strategic Change and Leader-Follower Alignment," *Organizational Dynamics,* Vol. 32, No. 1, 2003, pp. 32–45.

49. Matthew R. Redmond and Michael D. Mumford, "Putting Creativity to Work: Effects of Leader Behavior on Subordinate Creativity," *Organizational Behavior and Human Decision Processes,* June 1993, pp. 120–151, and Michael D. Mumford, Ginamarie M. Scott, Blaine Gaddis, and Jill M. Strange, "Leading Creative People: Orchestrating Expertise and Relationships," *Leadership Quarterly,* Vol. 13, 2002, pp. 705–750.

50. Sabrina Salam, Jonathan Cox, and Henry P. Sims, Jr., "How to Make a Team Work: Mediating Effects of Job Satisfaction between Leadership and Team Citizenship," *Academy of Management Best Papers Proceedings,* 1996, p. 293.

51. Anthony T. Pescosolido, "Emergent Leaders as Managers of Group Emotion," *Leadership Quarterly,* Vol. 13, 2002, pp. 583–599.

52. Andrew Pirola-Merlo, Charmine Härtel, Leon Mann, and Giles Hirst, "How Leaders Influence the Impact of Affective Events on Team Climate and Performance in R&D Teams," *Leadership Quarterly,* Vol. 13, 2002, pp. 561–581.

53. See Richard M. Hodgetts, Fred Luthans, and John W. Slocum, Jr., "Strategies and HRM Initiatives for the 00's Environment," *Organizational Dynamics,* Autumn 1999, pp. 18–20.

54. Bruce Avolio, Jane M. Howell, and John J. Sosik, "A Funny Thing Happened on the Way to the Bottom Line: Humor as a Moderator of Leadership Style Effects," *Academy of Management Journal,* Vol. 42, No. 2, 1999, pp. 219–227.

55. Fred O. Walumbwa, Bruce J. Avolio, William L. Gardner, Tara S. Wernsing, and Suzanne J. Peterson, "Authentic Leadership: Development and Validation of a Theory-Based Measure," *Journal of Management,* Vol. 34, 2008, pp. 88–126.

56. See Fred Luthans, Carolyn M. Youssef, and Bruce J. Avolio, *Psychological Capital,* Oxford University Press, Oxford, UK,

2007; and Fred Luthans, Bruce J. Avolio, James B. Avey, and Steven M. Norman, "Positive Psychological Capital: Measurement and Relationship with Performance and Satisfaction," *Personnel Psychology,* Vol. 60, 2007, pp. 541–572.

57. Steven M. Norman, Bruce J. Avolio, and Fred Luthans, "The Impact of Positivity and Transparency on Trust in Leaders and Their Perceived Effectiveness," *Leadership Quarterly,* in press.

58. James B. Avey, Bruce J. Avolio, and Fred Luthans, "Experimentally Analyzing the Impact of Leader Psychological Capital on Follower Psychological Capital and Performance," under second review at a journal.

59. Fred O. Walumbwa, Fred Luthans, James B. Avey, and Adegoke Oke, "Authentically Leading Groups: The Mediating Role of Collective Psychological Capital and Trust," *Journal of Organizational Behavior,* Vol. 30, 2009, pp. 1–26.

60. Bruce J. Avolio and Fred Luthans, *The High Impact Leader,* McGraw-Hill, New York, 2006, pp. 242–243.

61. The figure and following discussion are based on Henry Mintzberg, "The Managers' Job: Folklore and Fact," *Harvard Business Review,* July–August 1975, pp. 49–61.

62. Henry Mintzberg, "Retrospective Commentary on 'The Manager's Job: Folklore and Fact,'" *Harvard Business Review,* March–April 1990, p. 170.

63. Albert A. Vicere, "Leadership and the Networked Economy," *Human Resource Planning,* Vol. 25, No. 2, 2002, p. 30. Also see Allen I. Kraut, Patricia R. Pedigo, D. Douglas McKenna, and Marvin D. Dunnette, "The Role of the Manager: What's Really Important in Different Management Jobs," *Academy of Management Executive,* Vol. 19, No. 1, 2005, pp. 122–129.

64. Stuart L. Hart and Robert E. Quinn, "Roles Executives Play: CEOs, Behavioral Complexity, and Firm Performance," *Human Relations,* May 1993, pp. 543–575.

65. Ibid.

66. Mansour Javidan and Ali Dastmalchian, "Assessing Senior Executives: The Impact of Context on Their Roles," *Journal of Applied Behavioral Science,* September 1993, pp. 328–342.

67. Ibid., p. 339.

68. Edward M. Hallowell, "Overloaded Circuits: Why Smart People Underperform," *Harvard Business Review,* January 2005, p. 55.

69. The following sections are drawn from Fred Luthans, Richard M. Hodgetts, and Stuart A. Rosenkrantz, *Real Managers,* Ballinger, Cambridge, Mass., 1988, and Fred Luthans, "Successful vs. Effective Real Managers," *Academy of Management Executive,* May 1988, pp. 127–132. The very extensive empirical (observational) study took place over a four-year period.

70. See Henri Fayol, *General and Industrial Management* (Constance Storrs, trans.), Pitman, London, 1949.

71. See Henry Mintzberg, *The Nature of Managerial Work,* Harper & Row, New York, 1973, and Henry Mintzberg, "The Manager's Job: Folklore and Fact," op. cit., pp. 49–61.

72. See John Kotter, *The General Managers,* Free Press, New York, 1982; John Kotter, "What Do Effective General Managers Really Do?" *Harvard Business Review,* November–December 1982, pp. 156–167; and John P. Kotter, "What Effective General Managers Really Do," *Harvard Business*

*Review,* March–April 1999, pp. 145–159. Also see Rob Cross and Robert J. Thomas, *Social Networks,* Jossey-Bass, San Francisco, 2009.

73. Daniel Goleman, *Harvard Business Review on What Makes a Leader,* Harvard Business School Press, Boston, 2001, and Andreas Priestland and Robert Hanig, "Developing First-Level Leaders," *Harvard Business Review,* June 2005, p. 113.

74. Nikos Mourkogiannis, "A Leader's Real Job Description," *BusinessWeek,* December 26, 2007, p. 34.

75. Peter A. Heslin, "Experiencing Career Success," *Organizational Dynamics,* Vol. 34, No. 4, 2005, pp. 376–390.

76. Gary Yukl, Angela Gordon, and Tom Taber, "A Hierarchical Taxonomy of Leadership Behavior: Integrating a Half Century of Behavior Research," *Journal of Leadership and Organizational Studies,* Vol. 9, No. 1, 2002, pp. 15–32.

77. See Gary Yukl, *Leadership in Organizations,* 4th ed., Prentice Hall, Upper Saddle River, N.J., 1998, pp. 32–33.

78. Arben Asllani and Fred Luthans, "What Knowledge Managers Really Do: An Empirical and Comparative Analysis," *Journal of Knowledge Management,* Vol. 7, No. 3, 2003, pp. 53–66.

79. Jena McGregor, "The Office Chart That Really Counts: How Mapping Unofficial Job Links Pays Off," *BusinessWeek,* February 27, 2006, p. 49.

80. Fred Luthans, Stuart Rosenkrantz, and Harry Hennessey, "What Do Successful Managers Really Do?" *Journal of Applied Behavioral Science,* August 1985, pp. 255–270.

81. Arthur G. Bedian and Achilles A. Armenakis, "The Cesspool Syndrome: How Dreck Floats to the Top of Declining Organizations," *Academy of Management Executive,* Vol. 12, No. 1, 1998, p. 58.

82. Paul E. Mott, *The Characteristics of Effective Organizations,* Harper & Row, New York, 1972.

83. P. C. Smith, L. M. Kendall, and C. L. Hulin, *The Measurement of Satisfaction in Work and Retirement,* Rand McNally, Chicago, 1969.

84. Richard T. Mowday, L. W. Porter, and Richard M. Steers, *Employee–Organizational Linkages: The Psychology of Commitment, Absenteeism, and Turnover,* Academic Press, New York, 1982.

85. Luthans, Hodgetts, and Rosenkrantz, op. cit., and Luthans, op. cit.

86. Fred Luthans, Dianne H. B. Welsh, and Stuart A. Rosenkrantz, "What Do Russian Managers Really Do? An Observational Study with Comparisons to U.S. Managers," *Journal of International Business Studies,* 4th Quarter 1993, pp. 741–761.

87. Brooke Envick and Fred Luthans, "Identifying the Activities of Entrepreneur-Managers: An Idiographic Study," Paper presented at the Academy of Entrepreneurship, Maui, Hawaii, October 10, 1996.

88. Asllani and Luthans, op. cit.

89. Fred Luthans, Suzanne J. Peterson, and Elina Ibrayeva, "The Potential for the 'Dark Side' of Leadership in Post-Communist Countries," *Journal of World Business,* Vol. 33, No. 2, 1998, pp. 185–201.

90. Daniel J. McCarthy, Sheila M. Puffer, Ruth C. May, Donna E. Ledgerwood, and Wayne H. Stewart, Jr., "Overcoming Resistance to Change in Russian Organizations: The Legacy of Transactional Leadership," *Organizational Dynamics,* Vol. 37, No. 3, 2008, p. 221.

91. Manfred F. R. Kets de Vries, "A Journey into the 'Wild East': Leadership Style and Organizational Practices in Russia," *Organizational Dynamics,* Vol. 28, No. 4, 2000, pp. 67–81.

92. Manfred Kets de Vries and Stanislav Shekshnia, "Vladimir Putin, CEO of Russia Inc.: The Legacy and the Future," *Organizational Dynamics,* Vol. 37, No. 3, 2008, p. 239.

93. David H. Gobeli, Krzysztof Pzybylowski, and William Rudelius, "Customizing Management Training in Central and Eastern Europe: Mini-Shock Therapy," *Business Horizons,* Vol. 41, No. 3, May–June 1998, pp. 61–72.

94. Manfred F. R. Kets de Vries, Danny Miller, and Alain Noel, "Understanding the Leader-Strategy Interface: Application of the Strategic Relationship Interview Method," *Human Relations,* January 1993, pp. 5–21.

95. Michael J. Marquart and Dean W. Engel, "HRD Competencies for a Shrinking World," *Training and Development,* May 1993, pp. 62–64. Also see Robert M. Fullmer, Philip A. Gibbs, and Marshall Goldsmith, "Developing Leaders: How Winning Companies Keep on Winning," *Sloan Management Review,* Fall 2000, pp. 49–59, and Warren Blank, *The 108 Skills of Natural Born Leaders,* AMACOM, New York, 2001.

96. Rabindra M. Kanungo and Sasi Misra, "Managerial Resourcefulness: A Reconceptualization of Management Skills," *Human Relations,* December 1992, pp. 1311–1332.

97. David A. Whetten and Kim S. Cameron, *Developing Management Skills,* HarperCollins, New York, 1991, p. 8.

98. Ibid., p. 11.

99. Ibid., pp. 8–11.

100. Ibid., pp. 16–17.

101. Hugh P. Gunz, R. Michael Jalland, and Martin G. Evans, "New Strategy, Wrong Managers? What You Need to Know about Career Streams," *Academy of Management Executive,* Vol. 12, No. 2, 1998, p. 21, and Charles H. Ferguson, "The Perfect CEO . . . Like Cinderella Is the Stuff of Fairy Tales. So Is Prince Charming," *Across the Board,* May 2000, pp. 34–39.

102. Bernard Wysocki, Jr., "Yet Another Hazard of the New Economy: The Pied Piper Effect," *The Wall Street Journal,* March 30, 2000, pp. A1, A6, and "Churning at the Top," *The Economist,* March 17, 2001, pp. 67–69.

103. Maury Peiperl and Yehuda Baruch, "Back to Square Zero: The Post-Corporate Career," *Organizational Dynamics,* Spring 1997, pp. 7–22.

104. "Of Executive Talent," *Management Review,* July–August 1999, pp. 17–22.

105. See Ann Barrett and John Beeson, *Developing Business Leaders for 2010,* Conference Board, New York, 2002, and Ayse Karaevli and Douglas T. Hall, "Growing Leaders for Turbulent Times," *Organizational Dynamics,* Vol. 31, No. 1, 2003, pp. 62–79.

106. Robert J. Grossman, "Heirs Apparent," *HR Magazine,* February 1999, pp. 36–44.

107. Dale E. Zand, *The Leadership Triad,* Oxford University Press, New York, 1997.

108. For example, see Kurt T. Dirks and Donald L. Ferrin, "Trust in Leadership: Meta-Analytic Findings and Implications for Research and Practice," *Journal of Applied*

*Psychology,* Vol. 87, No. 4, 2002, pp. 611–628, and Scott E. Bryant, "The Role of Transformational and Transactional Leadership in Creating, Sharing and Exploiting Organizational Knowledge," *Journal of Leadership and Organizational Studies,* Vol. 9, No. 4, 2003, pp. 32–44.

109. Bruce J. Avolio and Sean T. Hannah, "Developmental Readiness: Accelerating Leader Development," *Consulting Psychology Journal: Practice and Research,* Vol. 60, No. 4, 2008, p. 331.

110. Robert J. Kramer, "Have We Learned Anything about Leadership Development?" *The Conference Board Review,* May/June 2008, p. 29.

111. Jonathan P. Doh, "Can Leadership Be Taught? Perspectives from Management Educators," *Academy of Management Learning and Education,* Vol. 2, No. 1, 2003, pp. 54–67.

112. Conger is quoted in ibid., p. 59.

113. Richard D. Arvey, M. Rotundo, W. Johnson, Z. Zhang, and M. McGue, "The Determinants of Leadership Role Occupancy: Genetic and Personality Factors," *The Leadership Quarterly,* Vol. 17, 2006, pp. 1–20; and Richard D. Arvey, Z. Zhang, Bruce J. Avolio, and R. Kruger, "Understanding the Developmental and Genetic Determinants of Leadership among Females," *Journal of Applied Psychology,* Vol. 92, 2007, pp. 693–706.

114. Doh, op. cit., p. 61.

115. For example, see Robert M. Fulmer, "Johnson & Johnson: Frameworks for Leadership," *Organizational Dynamics,* Vol. 29, No. 3, 2001, pp. 211–220, and Kimberly Houston-Philpot, "Leadership Development Partnerships at Dow Corning Corporation," *Journal of Organizational Excellence,* Winter 2002, pp. 13–27.

116. William C. Byham, "How to Create a Reservoir of Ready-Made Leaders" *Training and Development,* March 2000, pp. 29–32. Also see William C. Byham, Audrey B. Smith, and Mathew J. Paese, *Grow Your Own Leaders: How to Identify, Develop, and Retain Leadership Talent,* Prentice Hall, Upper Saddle River, N.J., 2002.

117. Leanne E. Atwater, Shelly D. Dionne, Bruce Avolio, John F. Camobreco, and Alan W. Lau, "A Longitudinal Study of the Leadership Development Process: Individual Differences Predicting Leader Effectiveness," *Human Relations,* Vol. 52, No. 12, 1999, pp. 1543–1555.

118. Judity A. Kolb, "The Effect of Gender Role, Attitude toward Leadership, and Self-Confidence on Leader Emergence: Implications for Leadership Development," *Human Resource Development Quarterly,* Vol. 10, No. 4, Winter 1999, p. 305.

119. Annette Towler, "Charismatic Leadership Development: Role of Parental Attachment Style and Parental Psychological Control," *Journal of Leadership and Organizational Studies,* Vol. 11, No. 4, 2005, pp. 15–25.

120. Jack Zenger, Dave Ulrich, and Norm Smallwood, "The New Leadership Development," *Training and Development,* March 2000, pp. 22–27.

121. Roni Drew and Louisa Wah, "Making Leadership Development Effective," *Management Review,* October 1999, p. 8.

122. Jon P. Briscoe and Douglas T. Hall, "Using 'Competencies' to Groom and Pick Leaders: Are We on the Right Track?" *Organizational Dynamics,* Autumn 1999, pp. 37–52.

123. Also see Robert E. Quinn, "Moments of Greatness: Entering the Fundamental State of Leadership," *Harvard Business Review,* July–August, 2005, p. 75, and Daisy Wademan, "The Best Advice I Ever Got," *Harvard Business Review,* January 2005, p. 35.

124. Bruce J. Avolio and Fred Luthans, *The High Impact Leader: Moments Matter in Accelerating Authentic Leadership Development,* McGraw-Hill, New York, 2006, p. 2. Also see Bruce J. Avolio, William L. Gardner, Fred O. Walumbwa, Fred Luthans, and Douglas R. May, "Unlocking the Mask: A Look at the Process By Which Authentic Leaders Impact Follower Attitudes and Behaviors," *The Leadership Quarterly,* Vol. 15, 2004, pp. 801–823.

125. Avolio and Luthans, op. cit., pp. 74–78.

126. James Flaherty, *Coaching: Evoking Excellence In Others,* Butterworth, Heinemann, Boston, Mass., 1999.

127. Roger D. Evered and James C. Selman, "Coaching and the Art of Management," *Organizational Dynamics,* Autumn 1989, p. 16. Also see Jim Niemes, "Discovering the Value of Executive Coaching as a Business Transformation Tool," *Journal of Organizational Excellence,* Autumn 2002, pp. 61–69.

128. James P. Masciarelli, "Less Lonely at the Top," *Management Review,* April 1999, pp. 58–61.

129. Douglas T. Hall, Karen L. Otazo, and George P. Hollenbeck, "Behind Closed Doors: What Really Happens in Executive Coaching," *Organizational Dynamics,* Winter 1999, p. 39.

130. "Strategic Coaching: Five Ways to Get the Most Value," *HRFocus,* February 1999, p. S7.

131. Dennis C. Carey and Dayton Odgen, *CEO Succession,* Oxford University Press, New York, 2000; Kevin Cashman, "Succession Leadership: Is Your Organization Prepared?" *Strategy and Leadership,* Vol. 29, No. 4, 2001, pp. 32–33; and Yan Zhang and Nandini Rajagopalan, "Grooming for the Top Post and Ending the CEO Succession Crisis," *Organizational Dynamics,* Vol. 35, No. 1, 2006, pp. 96–105.

132. Anita Raghavan and Greg Steinmetz, "Bitter Sweets: Europe's Family Firms Become a Dying Breed amid Succession Woes," *Wall Street Journal,* March 3, 2000, pp. A1, A20.

133. Jay A. Conger, "Personal Growth Training: Snake Oil or Pathway to Leadership?" *Organizational Dynamics,* Summer 1993, pp. 19–30.

134. Ibid., p. 19.

135. Kevin Cashman, *Leadership from the Inside Out,* Executive Excellence Publishing, Provo, Utah, 1998. Also see Joseph E. Sanders III, Willie E. Hopkins, and Gary D. Geroy, "From Transactional to Transcendental: Toward an Integrated Theory of Leadership," *Journal of Leadership and Organizational Studies,* Vol. 9, No. 4, 2003, pp. 21–31.

136. William Q. Judge, *The Leader's Shadow: Exploring and Developing the Executive Character,* Sage, Thousand Oaks, Calif., 1999. Also see Frances Hesselbein, *Hesselbein on Leadership,* Jossey-Bass, San Francisco, 2002.

137. See, for example, Jeffrey A. Tannenbaum, "Goldilocks, Management Guru," *Wall Street Journal,* March 3, 2000, pp. B1, B6; James Krohe, "Leadership Books: Why Do We Buy Them?" *Across the Board,* January 2000, pp. 18–21; "You're Fired, Capisce?: Managing Tips—Sopranos Style," *Fortune,* May 1, 2000, p. 41; and Jerry Cole, "Tough Love

Supervision, *The American Management Association Journal,* March 1997, p. A.

138. Marshall Goldsmith, "E-Tools that Help Teach Leadership," *BusinessWeek,* September 3, 2008, p. 15.

139. Fred Luthans, James B. Avey, and Jaime Patera, "Experimental Analysis of a Web-Based Intervention to Develop Positive Psychological Capital," *Academy of Management Learning and Education,* Vol. 7, 2008, pp. 209–221.

140. Jianping Shen, Van E. Cooley, Connie D. Ruhl-Smith, and Nanette M. Keiser, "Quality and Impact of Educational Leadership Programs: A National Study," *The Journal of Leadership Studies,* Vol. 6, No. 1/2, 1999, pp. 1–16.

141. Deborah R. Rada, "Transformational Leadership and Urban Renewal," *The Journal of Leadership Studies,* Vol. 6, No. 3/4, 1999, pp. 18–33.

142. Randall H. Lucius and Karl Kuhnert, "Adult Development and Transformational Leader," *Journal of Leadership Studies,* Vol. 6, No. 1/2, 1999, pp. 73–85.

143. Byron Reeves, Thomas W. Malone, and Tony O'Driscoll, "Leadership's Online Labs," *Harvard Business Review,* Vol. 86, No. 5, 2008, p. 58.

144. See William G. Lee, "The Society Builders," *Management Review,* September 1999, pp. 52–57. Also see Ronald M. Peters, Jr., and Craig A. Williams, "The Demise of Newt Gingrich as a Transformational Leader: Does Organizational Leadership Theory Apply to Legislative Leaders," *Organizational Dynamics,* Vol. 30, No. 3, 2002, pp. 257–268.

# References for Application Boxes and Real Cases

## Chapter 1

**OB in Action: Good to Great Expectations.** Excerpted from Interview with Jim Collins, "Good to Great Expectations," *BusinessWeek,* August 25, 2008, pp. 32–33. Reprinted by special permission, copyright © 2008 by McGraw-Hill, Inc.

**OB in Action: Forget Going with Your Gut** Excerpted from Gena McGregor, "Forget Going with Your Gut," *BusinessWeek,* March 20, 2006, p. 112. Reprinted by special permission, copyright © 2006 by McGraw-Hill, Inc.

**Real Case: The Big Squeeze on Workers** Excerpted from Michelle Conlin, "The Big Squeeze on Workers," *BusinessWeek,* May 13, 2002, pp. 96–97. Reprinted by special permission, copyright © 2002 by McGraw-Hill, Inc.

## Chapter 2

**OB in Action: Managing the Global Workforce.** Excerpted from Jena McGregor, "Managing the Global Workforce," *BusinessWeek,* January 28, 2008, pp. 34–35. Reprinted by special permission, copyright © 2008 by McGraw-Hill, Inc.

**OB in Action: Cracks in a Particularly Thick Glass Ceiling.** Excerpted from Moon Ihlwan, "Cracks in a Particularly Thick Glass Ceiling," *BusinessWeek,* April 21, 2008, p. 58. Reprinted by special permission, copyright © 2008 by McGraw-Hill, Inc.

**OB in Action: After Enron: The Ideal Corporation** Excerpted from John A. Byrne, "After Enron: The Ideal Corporation," *BusinessWeek,* August 26, 2002, pp. 68, 70, 74. Reprinted by special permission, copyright © 2002 by McGraw-Hill, Inc.

**Real Case: Not Treating Everyone the Same** Sources: Michele Galen, Ann Therese Palmer, Alice Cuneo, and Mark Maremont, "Work and Family," *BusinessWeek,* June 28, 1993, pp. 80–88; Michelle Carpenter, "Aetna's Family-Friendly Executive," *BusinessWeek,* June 28, 1993, p. 83; Sharon Allred Decker, "We Had to Recognize That People Have Lives," *BusinessWeek,* June 28, 1993, p. 88; and Sue Shellenbarger, "Lessons from the Workplace: How Corporate Policies and Attitudes Lag behind Workers' Changing Needs," *Human Resource Management,* Fall 1992, pp. 157–169.

**Real Case: The Ethics of Downsizing.** Excerpted from Bruce Weinstein, "Downsizing 101," *BusinessWeek,* September 15, 2008, p. 11. Reprinted by special permission copyright © 2008 by McGraw-Hill, Inc.

## Chapter 3

**OB in Action: Breaking Out of the Box.** Excerpted from Martin Keohan (Ed.), "Breaking Out of the Box," *BusinessWeek,* August 25, 2008, pp. 54–56. Reprinted by special permission, copyright © 2008 by McGraw-Hill, Inc.

**OB in Action: One Size Doesn't Fit All** Sources: Yumiko Ono, "U.S. Superstores Find Japanese Are a Hard Sell," *Wall Street Journal,* February 14, 2000, pp. B1, 4; Andy Pasztor and Thomas Kamm, "Pardon My French, but It's English Only on the Flight Deck," *Wall Street Journal,* March 23, 2000, p. A1; and Robert Frank, "Big Boy's Adventures in Thailand," *Wall Street Journal,* April 12, 2000, pp. B1, 4.

**Real Case: Web-Based Organizations** Excerpted from Michael Mandel, "The Real Reasons You're Working So Hard," *BusinessWeek,* October 3, 2005, pp. 62, 64. Reprinted by special permission, copyright © 2005 by McGraw-Hill, Inc.

## Chapter 4

**OB in Action: Now It's Getting Personal** Excerpted from Michelle Conlin, "Now It's Getting Personal," *BusinessWeek,* December 16, 2002, pp. 90, 92. Reprinted by special permission, copyright © 2002 by McGraw-Hill, Inc.

**OB in Action: Some Easy Ways to Recognize Employees** Sources: Neil Ruffolo, "Don't Forget to Provide Incentives for Your Middle Performers," *Workforce,* January 2000, pp. 62–64; Stephen Kerr, "Organizational Rewards: Practical, Cost-Neutral Alternatives That You May Know, but Don't Practice," *Organizational Dynamics,* Summer 1999, pp. 61–70; and Jeanne Bursch and Adrianne Van Strander, "Well-Structured Employee Reward/ Recognition Programs Yield Positive Results," *HR Focus,* November 1999, pp. 1, 14.

**OB in Action: You Can't Make More Time.** Excerpted from "You Can't Make More Time" (with Randy Pausch, Jeffrey Zaslow, and Jessica Hodgins), *BusinessWeek,* August 25, 2008, p. 71. Reprinted by special permission, copyright © 2008 by McGraw-Hill, Inc.

**Real Case: CEOs Get Fewer Perks.** Excerpted from Jena McGregor, "CEOs Get Fewer Perks," *BusinessWeek,* August 29, 2008, p. 20. Reprinted by special permission, copyright © 2008 by McGraw-Hill, Inc.

**Real Case: Rewarding Teamwork in the Plains** Sources: Woodruff Imberman, "Gainsharing: A Lemon or Lemonade," *Business Horizons,* January–February 1996, pp. 36–40; Donald J. McNerney, "Case Study: Team Compensation," *Management Review,* February 1995, p. 16; and Donald J. McNerney, "Compensation Case Study: Rewarding Team Performance and Individual Skillbuilding," *HR Focus,* January 1995, pp. 1, 4–5.

**Real Case: Different Strokes for Different Folks** Sources: Many such examples of recognition are found in B. Nelson, *1001 Ways to Reward Employees,* Workman, New York, 1994; B. Nelson, "Secrets of Successful Employee Recognition," *Quality Digest,* August 1996, pp. 26–28; and Jeanne Bursch and Adrianne Van Stander, "Well-Structured Employee Reward/Recognition Programs Yield Positive Results," *HR Focus,* November 1999, pp. 1, 14.

## Chapter 5

**OB in Action: Using Information Technologies to Nurture Relationships** Excerpted from Christopher Farrell, "The Overworked, Networked Family," *BusinessWeek,* October 3, 2005, pp. 68–70. Reprinted by special permission, copyright © 2005 by McGraw-Hill, Inc.

**Real Case: It's All a Matter of Personality** Sources: "Working in Dilbert's World," *Newsweek,* August 12, 1996, p. 56; Andrew E. Serwer, "Huizenga's Third Act," *Fortune,* August 5, 1996, pp. 73–76; and Anne B. Fisher, "Corporate Reputations: Comebacks and Comeuppances," *Fortune,* March 6, 1996, pp. 90–98.

## Chapter 6

**OB in Action: Managing amid Economic Uncertainty.** Excerpted from Liz Ryan, "Managing amid Economic Uncertainty," *BusinessWeek,* September 22, 2008, p. 13. Reprinted by special permission, copyright © 2008 by McGraw-Hill, Inc.

**OB in Action: Nice Work If You Can Get It** Excerpted from Michael Arndt, "Nice Work If You Can Get It," *BusinessWeek,* January 9, 2006, pp. 56–57. Reprinted by special permission, copyright © 2006 by McGraw-Hill, Inc.

**OB in Action: Using Stretch Goals** Sources: Strat Sherman, "Stretch Goals: The Dark Side of Asking for Miracles," *Fortune,* November 13, 1995, pp. 231–232; Steven Kerr, "An Academy Classic: On the Folly of Rewarding A, While Hoping for B," *Academy of Management Executive,* February 1995, p. 7; Jerry L. McAdams, "Employee Involvement and Performance Reward Plans," *Compensation and Benefits Review,* March–April 1995, pp. 45–55; and Woodruff Imberman, "Gainsharing: A Lemon or Lemonade?" *Business Horizons,* January–February 1996, pp. 36–40.

**Real Case: At UPS Managers Learn to Empathize with Their Employees** Excerpted from Louis Lavelle, "From UPS Managers, A School of Hard Knocks," *BusinessWeek,* July 22, 2002, pp. 58–59. Reprinted by special permission, copyright © 2002 by McGraw-Hill, Inc.

**Real Case: Making It a Nice Place to Work** Sources: Joan O. C. Hamilton, Stephen Baker, and Bill Vlasic, "The New Workplace," *BusinessWeek,* April 29, 1996, pp. 107–117; Richard M. Hodgetts, *Implementing TQM in Small and Medium-Sized Organizations,* Amacom, New York, 1996, Chap. 7; and Barbara Ettorre, "When the Walls Come Tumbling Down," *Management Review,* November 1995, pp. 33–37.

## Chapter 7

**OB in Action: "Half-Empty" or "Half-Full"** Sources: Adapted from Salvatore E. Maddi and Suzanne C. Kobasa, *The Hardy Executive: Health under Stress,* McGraw-Hill, New York, 1984; Patricia Sellers, "So You Fail. Now Bounce Back," *Fortune,* May 1, 1995; and Daniel Goleman, *Working with Emotional Intelligence,* Bantam Books, New York, 1988, pp. 126–127.

**Real Case: High Tech–High Fear** Sources: Adapted from "The New Economy: Untangling E-Conomics," *Economist,* September 23, 2000, pp. 5–40; David J. Payne and William A. Minneman, "Apply a Human Solution to Electronic Fears," *HR Focus,* April 1999, pp. S1–S3; and T. McDonald and M. Siegall, "The Effects of Technological Self-Efficacy and Job Focus on Job Performance,

Attitudes, and Withdrawal Behaviors," *The Journal of Psychology,* Vol. 126, 1992, pp. 465–475.

## Chapter 8

**OB in Action: Go Ahead, Use Facebook** Excerpted from Rachael King, "Go Ahead, Use Facebook," *BusinessWeek,* August 25, 2008, p. 65. Reprinted by special permission, copyright © 2008, by McGraw-Hill, Inc.

**OB in Action: Nonverbal and Verbal Communication** Sources: Philip R. Harris and Robert T. Moran, *Managing Cultural Differences,* 3rd ed., Gulf Publishing, Houston, 1991, Chap. 16; Dara Khambata and Riad Ajami, *International Business: Theory and Practice,* Macmillan, New York, 1992, Chap. 13; Alan M. Rugman and Richard M. Hodgetts, *International Business,* McGraw-Hill, New York, 1995, Chap. 16; Karen Matthes, "Mind Your Manners When Doing Business in Europe," *Personnel,* January 1992, p. 19; and Roger E. Axtell, *Do's and Taboos around the World,* Wiley, New York, 1990.

**OB in Action: Creative Decision Making to Eliminate Downsizing** Sources: Nancy Wong, "Partners Awaken Cultural Change," *Workforce,* March 2000, pp. 72–78; Marlene Piturro, "Alternatives to Downsizing," *Management Review,* October 1999, pp. 37–41; Sharon Machrone and Linda Dini Jenkins, "Creating Cultural Infrastructure: The Third Leg of the Success Stool," *HR Focus,* September 1999, pp. 13–14; and Kevin Walker, "Meshing Cultures in a Consolidation," *Training & Development Journal,* May 1998, pp. 83–90.

**Real Case: Online Communication to Share Knowledge** Excerpted from Marcia Stepanek, "Spread the Knowledge," *BusinessWeek,* October 23, 2000, pp. EB52, 54, 56, Reprinted by special permission, copyright © 2000 by McGraw-Hill, Inc.

**Real Case: Putting a Human Face on Rational Decisions** Excerpted from Charles J. Whalen, "Putting a Human Face on Economics," *Business Week,* July 31, 2000, pp. 76–77. Reprinted by special permission, copyright © 2000 by McGraw-Hill, Inc.

## Chapter 9

**OB in Action: Dealing with Conflicting Goals** Sources: Alex Taylor III, "Speed! Power! Status! Mercedes and BMW Race Ahead," *Fortune,* June 10, 1996, pp. 46–58; Louis Kraar, "Daewoo's Daring Drive into Europe," *Fortune,* May 13, 1996, pp. 145–152; and Thomas A. Stewart, "The Nine Dilemmas Leaders Face," *Fortune,* March 18, 1996, pp. 112–113.

**OB in Action: Taking Time to Manage Time** Sources: "Ten Tricks to Keep Time Eaters Away!" *Working Woman,* August 1986, p. 71; "Don't Manage Time, Manage Yourself," *Work Smarter, Not Harder,* Fast Company's Roadmap to Success, 2000, pp. 6–9; and James Gleick, "How Much Time," *Across the Board,* November–December 1999, pp. 9–10.

**OB in Action: Making It Work By Not Doing It All** Excerpted from Nanette Byrnes, "Making It Work By Not Doing It All," *BusinessWeek,* March 20, 2006, pp. 84–85. Reprinted by special permission, copyright © 2006 by McGraw-Hill, Inc.

**Real Case: When Workers Just Can't Cope** Excerpted from Julie Forster, "When Workers Just Can't Cope," *BusinessWeek,* October 30, 2000, pp. 100, 102. Reprinted by special permission, copyright © 2000 by McGraw-Hill, Inc.

Real Case: Round-the-Clock Stress    Sources: Jaclyn Fierman, "It's 2 A.M., Let's Go to Work," *Fortune*, August 21, 1995, pp. 82–87; Sara Zeff Geber, "Pulling the Plug on Stress," *HR Focus*, April 1996, p. 12; and "Marriott Offers Hot Line for Low-Wage Employees," *Sunday Omaha World-Herald*, September 29, 1996, p. 18-G.

## Chapter 10

OB in Action: Empowerment and Trust    Sources: Thomas A. Stewart, "Whom Can You Trust? It's Not So Easy to Tell," *Fortune*, June 12, 2000, pp. 331–334; Amy Zipkin, "The Wisdom of Thoughtfulness," *New York Times*, May 31, 2000, pp. C1, 10; and "Global Leader of the Future," *Management Review*, October 1999, p. 9.

OB in Action: You Are Where You Sit.    Excerpted from Aili McConnon, "You Are Where You Sit," *BusinessWeek*, July 23, 2007, pp. 66–67. Reprinted by special permission, copyright © 2007 by McGraw-Hill, Inc.

Real Case: Fighting Back    Sources: Donald M. Spero, "Patent Protection or Piracy—a CEO Views Japan," *Harvard Business Review*, September–October 1990, pp. 58–67; Fred Luthans and Richard M. Hodgetts, *Business*, 2nd ed., Dryden, Fort Worth, Tex., 1993, pp. 640–641; and Donald F. Kuratko and Richard M. Hodgetts, *Entrepreneurship*, 2nd ed., Dryden, Fort Worth, Tex., 1992, pp. 357–361.

## Chapter 11

OB in Action: The Office Chart That Really Counts    Excerpted from Jena McGregor, "The Office Chart That Really Counts," *BusinessWeek*, February 27, 2006, pp. 48–49. Reprinted by special permission, copyright © 2006 by McGraw-Hill, Inc.

OB in Action: Greater Productivity through Cross-Functional Teams    Sources: David Chaudron, "How to Improve Cross-Functional Teams," *HR Focus*, August 1995, pp. 4–5; Stratford Sherman, "Secrets of HP's 'Muddled' Team," *Fortune*, March 18, 1996, pp. 116–120; and Kenneth Labich, "Elite Teams Get the Job Done," *Fortune*, February 19, 1996, pp. 90–99.

Real Case: There Are Teams, and There Are Teams    Sources: Howard W. French, "Japan Debates Culture of Covering Up," *New York Times*, May 2, 2000, p. A12; Yukimo Ono, "U.S. Superstores Find Japanese Are a Hard Sell," *Wall Street Journal*, February 14, 2000, pp. B1, 4; and Noboru Yoshimura and Philip Anderson, *Inside the Kaisa*, Harvard Business School Press, Boston, 1997.

## Chapter 12

OB in Action: The Struggle to Measure Performance    Excerpted from Gena McGregor, "The Struggle to Measure Performance,"

*BusinessWeek*, January 9, 2006, pp. 26, 28. Reprinted by special permission, copyright © 2006 by McGraw-Hill, Inc.

Real Case: The Elite Circle of $1 CEOs    Excerpted from Moira Herbst, "The Elite Circle of $1 CEOs," *BusinessWeek*, May 11, 2007, p. 11. Reprinted by special permission, copyright © 2007 by McGraw-Hill, Inc.

## Chapter 13

OB in Action: High Tech Leader    Excerpted from Sarah Lacy, "Just Don't Call It Retirement," *BusinessWeek*, March 6, 2006, pp. 66–68. Reprinted by special permission, copyright © 2006 by McGraw-Hill, Inc.

OB in Action: How Business Leaders Communicate across Cultures    Sources: Sheida Hodge, *Global Smarts*, John Wiley & Sons, New York, 2000; Richard M. Hodgetts and Fred Luthans, *International Management*, 4th ed., McGraw-Hill, New York, 2000, Chapters 5–6; and Richard D. Lewis, *When Cultures Collide*, Nicholas Brealey Publishing, London, 1999.

Real Case: No Organization Chart and an 80-Blank-Pages Policy Manual    Excerpted from Pete Engardio, "Flextronics: Few Rules, Fast Responses," *BusinessWeek*, October 23, 2000, p. 148F. Reprinted by special permission, copyright © 2000 by McGraw-Hill, Inc.

Real Case: The Seven Secrets of Inspiring Leaders.    Excerpted from Carmin Gallo, "The Seven Secrets of Inspiring Leaders," *BusinessWeek*, October 11, 2007, p. 20. Reprinted by special permission, copyright © 2007 by McGraw-Hill, Inc.

## Chapter 14

OB in Action: With GenXers, It's a Whole New Ball Game    Sources: Richard W. Oliver, "'My' Generation," *Management Review*, January 2000, pp. 12–13; Joanne Cole, "The Art of Wooing Gen Xers," *HR Focus*, November 1999, pp. 7–8; and "Gearing Up for Tomorrow's Workforce," *HR Focus*, February 1999, pp. 14–16.

OB in Action: Health Care Insurance Leader    Excerpted from Joseph Weber, "In the Pink of Health," *BusinessWeek*, May 23, 2005, pp. 72, 75. Reprinted by special permission, copyright © 2005 by McGraw-Hill, Inc.

Real Case: Jeanne P. Jackson: A Retailing Leader    Excerpted from Wendy Zellmer, "Why Banana Republic's Star Jumped to Wal-Mart," *BusinessWeek*, November 6, 2000, p. 112. Reprinted by special permission, copyright © 2000 by McGraw-Hill, Inc.

Real Case: For Leaders, Ignorance Isn't Bliss    Excerpted from Rick Wartzman, "For Managers, Ignorance Isn't Bliss," *Business Week*, December 10, 2007, p. 8. Reprinted by special permission, copyright © 2007 by McGraw-Hill, Inc.

# Name Index

# Subject Index